Weiss Ratings' Guide to Health Insurers

Weiss Ratings' Guide to Health Insurers

A Quarterly Compilation of Health
Insurance Company Ratings and Analyses

Spring 2021

GREY HOUSE PUBLISHING

Weiss Ratings
4400 Northcorp Parkway
Palm Beach Gardens, FL 33410
561-627-3300

Published by Grey House Publishing, Inc., located at 4919 Route 22, Amenia, NY 12501; telephone 518-789-8700. Grey House Publishing neither guarantees the accuracy of the data contained herein nor assumes any responsibility for errors, omissions or discrepancies. Grey House Publishing accepts no payment for listing; inclusion in the publication of any organization, agency, institution, publication, service or individual does not imply endorsement of the publisher.

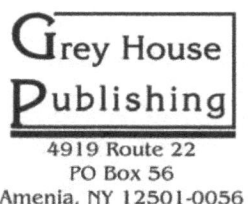

4919 Route 22
PO Box 56
Amenia, NY 12501-0056

Edition No. 104, Spring 2021

ISBN: 978-1-64265-877-4
ISSN: 2158-5938

Contents

Introduction

Appendix

Terms and Conditions

This document is prepared strictly for the confidential use of our customer(s). It has been provided to you at your specific request. It is not directed to, or intended for distribution to or use by, any person or entity who is a citizen or resident of or located in any locality, state, country or other jurisdiction where such distribution, publication, availability or use would be contrary to law or regulation or which would subject Weiss Ratings or its affiliates to any registration or licensing requirement within such jurisdiction.

No part of the analysts' compensation was, is, or will be, directly or indirectly, related to the specific recommendations or views expressed in this research report.

Message To Insurers
All data on insurers filing a Health financial statement received on or before June 18, 2021 has been considered or incorporated into this edition of the Directory. If there are particular circumstances which you believe could affect your rating, please use the online survey (http://weissratings.com/survey/) or e-mail Weiss Ratings (insurancesurvey@weissinc.com) with documentation to support your request. If warranted, we will make every effort to incorporate the changes in our next edition.

Welcome to Weiss Ratings'
Guide to Health Insurers

Most people automatically assume their insurance company will survive, year after year. However, prudent consumers and professionals realize that in this world of shifting risks, the solvency of insurance companies can't be taken for granted.

If you are looking for accurate, unbiased ratings and data to help you choose health insurance for yourself, your family, your company, or your clients, *Weiss Ratings Guide to Health Insurers* gives you precisely what you need.

In fact, it's the only source that currently provides ratings and analyses on over 1,000 health insurers.

Weiss Ratings' Mission Statement

Weiss Ratings' mission is to empower consumers, professionals, and institutions with high quality advisory information for selecting or monitoring a financial services company or financial investment.

In doing so, Weiss Ratings will adhere to the highest ethical standards by maintaining our independent, unbiased outlook and approach to advising our customers.

Why rely on Weiss Ratings?

Weiss Ratings provides fair, objective ratings to help professionals and consumers alike make educated purchasing decisions.

At Weiss Ratings, integrity is number one. Weiss Ratings never takes a penny from insurance companies for its ratings. And, we publish Weiss Safety Ratings without regard for insurers' preferences. However, other rating agencies like A.M. Best, Fitch, Moody's, and Standard & Poor's are paid by insurance companies for their ratings and may even suppress unfavorable ratings at an insurer's request.

Our ratings are more frequently reviewed and updated than any other ratings. You can be sure that the information you receive is accurate and current – providing you with advance warning of financial vulnerability early enough to do something about it.

Other rating agencies focus primarily on a company's current claims paying ability and consider only mild economic adversity. Weiss Ratings also considers these issues, but in addition, our analysis covers a company's ability to deal with severe economic adversity and a sharp increase in claims.

Our use of more rigorous standards stems from the viewpoint that an insurance company's obligations to its policyholders should not depend on favorable business conditions. An insurer must be able to honor its policy commitments in bad times as well as good.

Our rating scale, from A to F, is easy to understand. Only a few outstanding companies receive an A (Excellent) rating, although there are many to choose from within the B (Good) category. An even larger group falls into the broad average range which receives C (Fair) ratings. Companies that demonstrate marked vulnerabilities receive either D (Weak) or E (Very Weak) ratings.

How to Use This Guide

The purpose of the *Guide to Health Insurers* is to provide policyholders and prospective policy purchasers with a reliable source of insurance company ratings and analyses on a timely basis. We realize that the financial strength of an insurer is an important factor to consider when making the decision to purchase a policy or change companies. The ratings and analyses in this Guide can make that evaluation easier when you are considering:

- Medical reimbursement insurance
- Managed health care (PPOs and HMOs)
- Disability income
- Long-term care (nursing home) insurance

This Guide includes ratings for health insurers such as commercial for-profit insurers, mutual insurers, Blue Cross/Blue Shield plans, and for-profit and not-for-profit insurers. This is the only source of ratings on many of these companies.

In addition, many companies that offer health insurance also offer life, property or liability insurance. If you are shopping for any of those types of coverage, please refer to either our *Guide to Life and Annuity Insurers* or our *Guide to Property and Casualty Insurers.*

The rating for a particular company indicates our opinion regarding that company's ability to meet its commitments to the policyholder – not only under current economic conditions, but also during a declining economy or in the event of a sharp increase in claims. Such an increase in claims and related expenses may be triggered by any number of occurrences including rising medical costs, malpractice lawsuits, out-of-control administrative expenses, or the unexpected spread of a disease such as AIDS. The safest companies, however, should be prepared to deal with harsh and unforeseen circumstances.

To use this Guide most effectively, we recommend you follow the steps outlined below:

Step 1 To ensure you evaluate the correct company, verify the company's exact name and state of domicile as it was given to you or appears on your policy. Many companies have similar names but are not related to one another, so you want to make sure the company you look up is really the one you are interested in evaluating.

Step 2 Turn to Section I, the Index of Companies, and locate the company you are evaluating. This section contains all health insurance companies analyzed by Weiss Ratings including those that did not receive a Safety Rating. It is sorted alphabetically by the name of the company and shows the state of domicile following the name for additional verification.

Step 3 Once you have located your specific company, the first column after the state of domicile shows its Weiss Safety Rating. See *About Weiss Safety Ratings* for information about what this rating means. If the rating has changed since the last issue of this Guide, a downgrade will be indicated with a down triangle ▼ to the left of the company name; an upgrade will be indicated with an up triangle ▲.

Step 4   Following Weiss Safety Rating is some additional information about the company such as its type, size and capital level. Refer to the introduction of Section I, to see what each of these factors measures.

Step 5   Some insurers have a bullet ● following the domicile state in Section I. This means that more detailed information about the company is available in Section II.

If the company you are evaluating is identified with a bullet, turn to Section II, the Analysis of Largest Companies , and locate it there (otherwise skip to step 9). Section II contains all health insurers and Blue Cross/Blue Shield plans plus the largest property & casualty and life & annutiy insurers offering health insurance rated by Weiss, regardless of rating. It too is sorted alphabetically by the name of the company.

Step 6   Once you have identified your company in Section II, you will find its Safety Rating and a description of the rating immediately to the right of the company name. Then, below the company name is a description of the various rating factors that were considered in assigning the company's rating. These factors and the information below them are designed to give you a better feel for the company and its strengths and weaknesses. Refer to the introduction of Section II to get a better understanding of what each of these factors means.

Step 7   To the right, you will find a five-year summary of the company's Safety Rating, capitalization and income. Look for positive or negative trends in these data. Below the five-year summary, we have included a graphic illustration of the most crucial factor or factors impacting the company's rating. Again, the Section II introduction provides an overview of the content of each graph or table.

Step 8   If the company you are evaluating is a Medicare HMO, you can also look it up in Section VII to get some idea of the quality of service being offered. Here you can see the number of complaints against a company that have reached the federal review level based on the most recent data available.

Step 9   If you are interested in long-term care insurance, you can turn to Section V and get a listing of long-term care insurers. To compare long-term care policies see the Long-Term Care Insurance Planner within the Appendix.

Step 10   If the company you are evaluating is not highly rated and you want to find an insurer with a higher rating, turn to the page in Section IV that has your state's name at the top. This section contains those Recommended Companies (rating of A+, A, A- or B+) that are licensed to underwrite health insurance in your state, sorted by rating. From here you can select a company and then refer back to Sections I and II to analyze it.

Step 11   If you decide that you would like to contact one of Weiss Recommended Companies about obtaining a policy or for additional information, refer to Section III where you will find all of Weiss recommended companies listed alphabetically by name. Following each company's name is its address and phone number to assist you in making contact.

Step 12 Many consumers have reported to us the difficulties they have encountered in finding a Recommended Company that offers the best pricing and benefits. Therefore, when considering medical reimbursement or managed care coverage, you may want to consider other companies that have received a good (B or B-) rating even though they did not make Weiss Recommended List. However, for long-term policies such as nursing home care or disability income, we recommend sticking to companies with a rating of B+ or higher.

Step 13 In order to use Weiss Safety Ratings most effectively, we strongly recommend you consult the Important Warnings and Cautions. These are more than just "standard disclaimers." They are very important factors you should be aware of before using this Guide. If you have any questions regarding the precise meaning of specific terms used in the Guide, refer to the Glossary.

Step 14 Make sure you stay up to date with the latest information available since the publication of this Guide. For information on how to set up a rating change notification service, acquire follow-up reports, or receive a more in-depth analysis of an individual company, visit www.weissratings.com or call 1-877-934-7778.

Data Sources: Annual and quarterly statutory statements filed with state insurance commissioners and data provided by the insurance companies being rated. Medicare HMO complaint data were provided by the Centers for Medicare and Medicaid Services: The Center for Health Dispute Resolution, (formerly known as Health Care Financing Administration), and is reprinted here. The National Association of Insurance Commissioners has provided some of the raw data. Any analyses or conclusions are not provided or endorsed by the NAIC.

Date of data analyzed: June 30, 2020 unless otherwise noted

About Weiss Safety Ratings

The Weiss Ratings of insurers are based upon the annual and quarterly financial statements filed with state insurance commissioners. This data may be supplemented by information that we request from the insurance companies themselves. However, if a company chooses not to provide supplemental data, we reserve the right to rate the company based exclusively on publicly available data.

The Weiss Ratings are based on a complex analysis of hundreds of factors that are synthesized into a series of indexes: capitalization, investment safety (life, health and annuity companies only), reserve adequacy (property and casualty companies only), profitability, liquidity, and stability. These indexes are then used to arrive at a letter grade rating. A weak score on any one index can result in a low rating, as financial problems can be caused by any one of a number of factors, such as inadequate capital, unpredictable claims experience, poor liquidity, speculative investments, inadequate reserving, or consistent operating losses.

Our **Capital Index** gauges capital adequacy in terms of each insurer's ability to handle a variety of business and economic scenarios as they may impact investment performance, claims experience, persistency, and market position. The index combines two Risk-Adjusted Capital ratios as well as a leverage test that examines pricing risk.

Our **Investment Safety Index** measures the exposure of the company's investment portfolio to loss of principal and/or income due to default and market risks. Each investment area is rated by a factor that takes into consideration both quality and liquidity. (This factor is measured as a separate index only for life, health, and annuity insurers.)

Our **Reserve Adequacy Index** measures the adequacy of the company's reserves and its ability to accurately anticipate the level of claims it will receive. (This factor is measured as a separate index only for property and casualty insurers.)

Our **Profitability Index** measures the soundness of the company's operations and the contribution of profits to the company's financial strength. The profitability index is a composite of five sub-factors: 1) gain or loss on operations; 2) consistency of operating results; 3) impact of operating results on surplus; 4) adequacy of investment income as compared to the needs of policy reserves (life, health and annuity companies only); and 5) expenses in relation to industry norms for the types of policies that the company offers.

Our **Liquidity Index** evaluates a company's ability to raise the necessary cash to settle claims and honor cash withdrawal obligations. We model various cash flow scenarios, applying liquidity tests to determine how the company might fare in the event of an unexpected spike in claims and/or a run on policy surrenders.

Our **Stability Index** integrates a number of sub-factors that affect consistency (or lack thereof) in maintaining financial strength over time. These sub-factors will vary depending on the type of insurance company being evaluated but may include such things as 1) risk diversification in terms of company size, group size, number of policies in force, types of policies written, and use of reinsurance; 2) deterioration of operations as reported in critical asset, liability, income and expense items, such as surrender rates and premium volume; 3) years in operation; 4) former problem areas where, despite recent improvement, the company has yet to establish a record of stable performance over a suitable period of time; 5) a substantial shift in the company's operations; 6) potential instabilities such as reinsurance quality, asset/liability matching, and sources of capital; and 7) relationships with holding companies and affiliates.

In order to help guarantee our objectivity, we reserve the right to publish ratings expressing our opinion of a company's financial stability based exclusively on publicly available data and our own proprietary standards for safety.

Each of these indexes is measured according to the following range of values.

Critical Ranges In Our Indexes

STRONG	GOOD	FAIR	WEAK
10	7	5	3	0

What Our Ratings Mean

A   **Excellent.** The company offers excellent financial security. It has maintained a conservative stance in its investment strategies, business operations and underwriting commitments. While the financial position of any company is subject to change, we believe that this company has the resources necessary to deal with severe economic conditions.

B   **Good.** The company offers good financial security and has the resources to deal with a variety of adverse economic conditions. It comfortably exceeds the minimum levels for all of our rating criteria and is likely to remain healthy for the near future. However, in the event of a severe recession or major financial crisis, we feel that this assessment should be reviewed to make sure that the firm is still maintaining adequate financial strength.

C   **Fair.** The company offers fair financial security and is currently stable. But during an economic downturn or other financial pressures, we feel it may encounter difficulties in maintaining its financial stability.

D   **Weak.** The company currently demonstrates what, in our opinion, we consider to be significant weaknesses which could negatively impact policyholders. In an unfavorable economic environment, these weaknesses could be magnified.

E   **Very Weak.** The company currently demonstrates what we consider to be significant weaknesses and has also failed some of the basic tests that we use to identify fiscal stability. Therefore, even in a favorable economic environment, it is our opinion that policyholders could incur significant risks.

F   **Failed.** The company is deemed failed if it is either 1) under supervision of an insurance regulatory authority; 2) in the process of rehabilitation; 3) in the process of liquidation; or 4) voluntarily dissolved after disciplinary or other regulatory action by an insurance regulatory authority.

+   The **plus sign** is an indication that the company is in the upper third of the letter grade.

-   The **minus sign** is an indication that the company is in the lower third of the letter grade.

U   **Unrated.** The company is unrated for one or more of the following reasons: (1) total assets are less than $1 million; (2) premium income for the current year was less than $100,000; (3) the company functions almost exclusively as a holding company rather than as an underwriter; (4) in our opinion, we do not have enough information to reliably issue a rating.

How Our Ratings Differ From Those of Other Services

Weiss Safety Ratings are conservative and consumer oriented. We use tougher standards than other rating agencies because our system is specifically designed to inform risk-averse consumers about the financial strength of health insurers.

Our rating scale (A to F) is easy to understand by the general public. Users can intuitively understand that an A+ rating is at the top of the scale rather than in the middle like some of the other rating agencies.

Other rating agencies give top ratings more generously so that most companies receive excellent ratings.

More importantly, other rating agencies focus primarily on a company's *current* claims paying ability or consider only relatively mild economic adversity. We also consider these scenarios but extend our analysis to cover a company's ability to deal with severe economic adversity and potential liquidity problems. This stems from the viewpoint that an insurance company's obligations to its policyholders should not be contingent upon a healthy economy. The company must be capable of honoring its policy commitments in bad times as well.

Looking at the insurance industry as a whole, we note that several major rating firms have poor historical track records in identifying troubled companies. The 1980s saw a persistent decline in capital ratios, increased holdings of risky investments in the life and health industry as well as recurring long-term claims liabilities in the property and casualty industry. The insurance industry experienced similar issues before and during the Great Recession of 2007-2009. Despite these clear signs that insolvency risk was rising, other rating firms failed to downgrade at-risk insurance companies. Instead, they often rated companies by shades of excellence, understating the gravity of potential problems.

Other ratings agencies have not issued clear warnings that the ordinary consumer can understand. Few, if any, companies receive "weak" or "poor" ratings. Surely, weak companies do exist. However, the other rating agencies apparently do not view themselves as consumer advocates with the responsibility of warning the public about the risks involved in doing business with such companies.

Additionally, these firms will at times agree *not* to issue a rating if a company denies them permission to do so. In short, too often insurance rating agencies work hand-in-glove with the companies they rate.

At Weiss Ratings, although we seek to maintain good relationships with the firms, we owe our primary obligation to the consumer, not the industry. We reserve the right to rate companies based on publicly-available data and make the necessary conservative assumptions when companies choose not to provide additional data we might request.

Comparison of Insurance Company Rating Agency Scales				
Weiss Ratings [a]	**Best** [a]	**S&P**	**Moody's**	**Fitch**
A+, A, A-	A++, A+	AAA	Aaa	AAA
B+, B, B-	A, A-	AA+, AA AA-	Aa1, Aa2, Aa3	AA+, AA, AA-
C+, C, C-	B++, B+,	A+, A, A-, BBB+, BBB, BBB-	A1, A2, A3, Baa1, Baa2, Baa3	A+, A, A-, BBB+, BBB, BBB-
D+, D, D-	B, B- C++, C+, C, C-	BB+, BB, BB-, B+, B, B-	Ba1, Ba2, Ba3, B1, B2, B3	BB+, BB, BB-, B+, B, B-
E+, E, E- F	D E, F	CCC R	Caa, Ca, C	CCC+, CCC, CCC- DD

[a] Weiss Ratings and Best use additional symbols to designate that they recognize an insurer's existence but do not provide a rating. These symbols are not included in this table.

Rate of Insurance Company Failures

Weiss Ratings provides quarterly safety ratings for thousands of insurance companies each year. Weiss Ratings strives for fairness and objectivity in its ratings and analyses, ensuring that each company receives the rating that most accurately depicts its current financial status, and more importantly, its ability to deal with severe economic adversity and a sharp increase in claims. Weiss Ratings has every confidence that its safety ratings provide an accurate representation of a company's stability.

In order for these ratings to be of any true value, it is important that they prove accurate over time. One way to determine the accuracy of a rating is to examine those insurance companies that have failed, and their respective Safety Ratings. A high percentage of failed companies with "A" ratings would indicate that Weiss Ratings is not being conservative enough with its "secure" ratings, while conversely, a low percentage of failures with "vulnerable" ratings would show that Weiss Ratings is overly conservative.

Over the past 31 years (1989–2019) Weiss Ratings has rated 659 insurance companies, for all industries, that subsequently failed. The chart below shows the number of failed companies in each rating category, the average number of companies rated in each category per year, and the percentage of annual failures for each letter grade.

	Safety Rating	Number of Failed Companies	Average Number of Companies Rated per year	Percentage of Failed companies per year (by ratings category)*
Secure	A	1	150	0.02%
	B	9	1,116	0.03%
	C	76	1,614	0.15%
Vulnerable	D	284	729	1.26%
	E	289	216	4.36%

A=Excellent, B=Good, C=Fair, D=Weak, E=Very Weak

On average, only 0.10% of the companies Weiss rates as "secure" fail each year. On the other hand, an average of 1.96% of the companies Weiss rates as "vulnerable" fail annually. That means that a company rated by Weiss Ratings as "Vulnerable" is almost 20.4 times more likely to fail than a company rated as "Secure".

When considering a Weiss Safety Rating, one can be sure that they are getting the most fair, objective, and accurate financial rating available anywhere.

*Percentage of Failed companies per year = (Number of Failed Companies) / [(Average Number of Companies Rated per year) x (years in study)]

Data as of December 31, 2019 for Life and Annuity Insurers, Property & Casualty Insurers, and Health Insurers.

What Does Average Mean?

At Weiss Ratings, we consider the words average and fair to mean just that – average and fair. So when we assign our ratings to insurers, a large percentage of companies receive an average C rating. That way, you can be sure that a company receiving Weiss B or A rating is truly above average. Likewise, you can feel confident that companies with D or E ratings are truly below average.

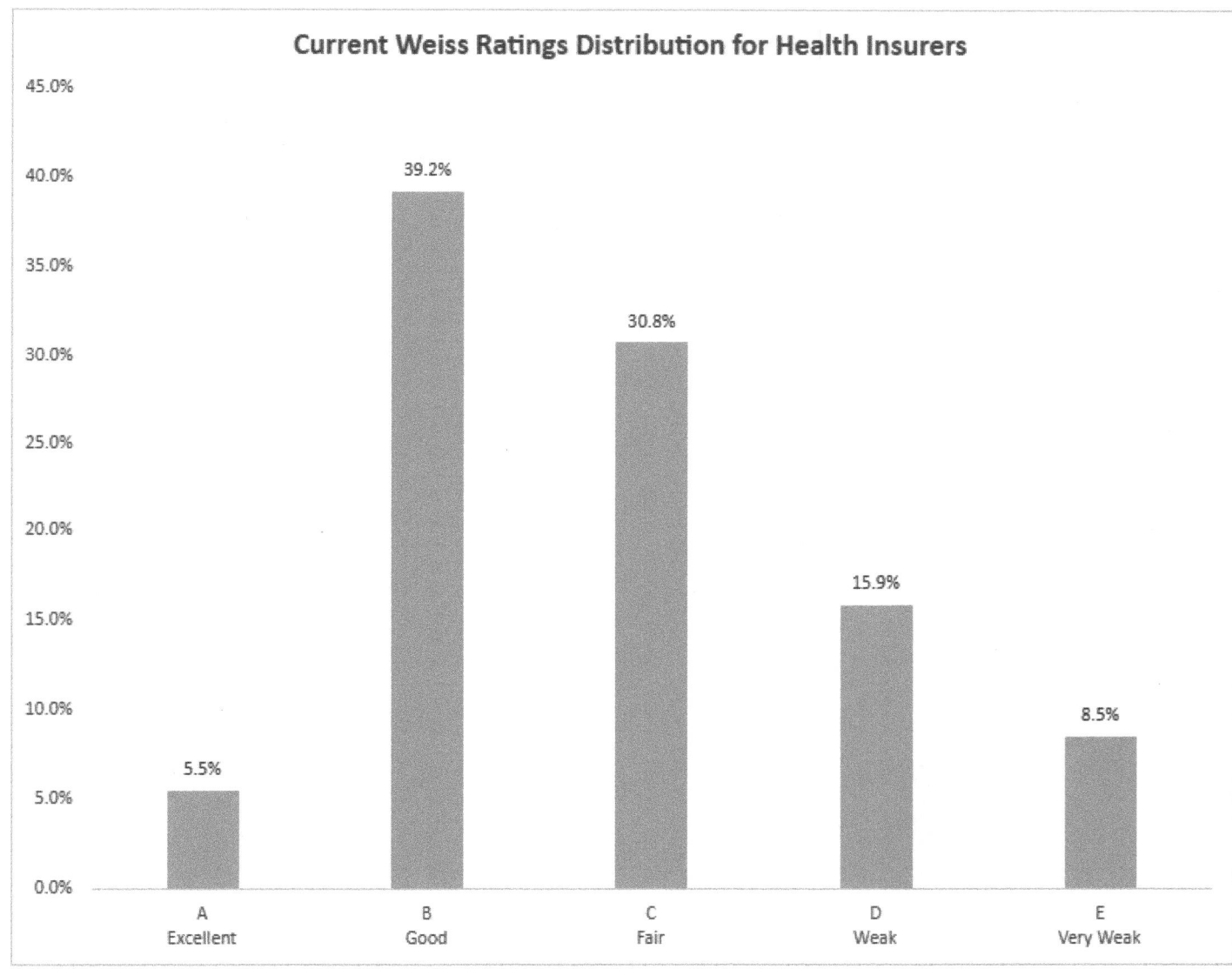

Important Warnings and Cautions

1. A rating alone cannot tell the whole story. Please read the explanatory information contained in this publication. It is provided in order to give you an understanding of our rating philosophy, as well as paint a more complete picture of how we arrive at our opinion of a company's strengths and weaknesses.

2. Weiss Safety Ratings represent our opinion of a company's insolvency risk. As such, a high rating means we feel that the company has less chance of running into financial difficulties. A high rating is not a guarantee of solvency nor is a low rating a prediction of insolvency. Weiss Safety Ratings are not deemed to be a recommendation concerning the purchase or sale of the securities of any insurance company that is publicly owned.

3. Company performance is only one factor in determining a rating. Conditions in the marketplace and overall economic conditions are additional factors that may affect the company's financial strength. Therefore, a rating upgrade or downgrade does not necessarily reflect changes in the company's profits, capital or other financial measures, but may be due to external factors. Likewise, changes in Weiss indexes may reflect changes in our risk assessment of business or economic conditions as well as changes in company performance.

4. All firms that have the same Safety Rating should be considered to be essentially equal in strength. This is true regardless of any differences in the underlying numbers which might appear to indicate greater strengths. Weiss Safety Rating already takes into account a number of lesser factors which, due to space limitations, cannot be included in this publication.

5. A good rating requires consistency. If a company is excellent on four indicators and fair on one, the company may receive a fair rating. This requirement is necessary due to the fact that fiscal problems can arise from any *one* of several causes including speculative investments, inadequate capital resources or operating losses.

6. We are an independent rating agency and do not depend on the cooperation of the companies we rate. Our data are derived from annual and quarterly financial statements that we obtain from federal regulators and filings with state insurance commissioners. The latter may be supplemented by information insurance companies voluntarily provide upon request. Although we seek to maintain an open line of communication with the companies, we do not grant them the right to stop or influence publication of the ratings. This policy stems from the fact that this publication is designed for the protection of the consumer.

7. Affiliated companies do not automatically receive the same rating. We recognize that a troubled company may expect financial support from its parent or affiliates. Weiss Safety Ratings reflect our opinion of the measure of support that may become available to a subsidiary , if the subsidiary were to experience serious financial difficulties. In the case of a strong parent and a weaker subsidiary, the affiliate relationship will generally result in a higher rating for the subsidiary than it would have on a stand-alone basis. Seldom, however, would the rating be brought up to the level of the parent. This treatment is appropriate because we do not assume the parent would have either the resources or the will to "bail out" a troubled subsidiary during a severe economic crisis. Even when there is a binding legal obligation for a parent corporation to honor the policy obligations of its subsidiaries, the possibility exists that the subsidiary could be sold and lose its parental support. Therefore, it is quite common for one affiliate to have a higher rating than another. This is another reason why it is especially important that you have the precise name of the company you are evaluating.

Section I

Index of Companies

An analysis of over 1,604 rated and unrated

U.S. Health Insurers

Companies are listed in alphabetical order.

Section I Contents

This section contains the information about company type, size and capital level for all rated and unrated health insurers analyzed by Weiss Ratings.

1. **Insurance Company Name**

    The legally-registered name, which can sometimes differ from the name that the company uses for advertising. If you cannot find the company you are interested in, or if you have any doubts regarding the precise name, verify the information with the company before looking the name up in this Guide. Also, determine the domicile state for confirmation. (See column 2.)

2. **Domicile State**

    The state which has primary regulatory responsibility for the company. It may differ from the location of the company's corporate headquarters. You do not have to be living in the domicile state to purchase insurance from this firm, provided it is licensed to do business in your state.

    Also use this column to confirm that you have located the correct company. It is possible for two unrelated companies to have the same name if they are domiciled in different states.

3. **Safety Rating**

    Our rating is measured on a scale from A to F and considers a wide range of factors. Please see *What Our Ratings Mean* for specific descriptions of each letter grade and the following pages for information on how our ratings differ from those of other rating agencies. Most important, when using this rating, please be sure to consider the Important Warnings and Cautions regarding the ratings' limitations and the underlying assumptions.

4. **Data Date**

    The latest quarter-end for which we have received the company's financial statement.

5. **Total Assets**

    All assets admitted by state insurance regulators in millions of dollars as of the most recent quarter end. This includes investments and current business assets such as receivables from agents, reinsurers and subscribers.

    The overall size is an important factor which affects the ability of a company to manage risk. Mortality, morbidity (sickness) and investment risks can be more effectively diversified by large companies. Because the insurance business is based on probability, the number of policies must be large enough so that actuarial statistics are valid. The larger the number of policyholders, the more reliable the actuarial projections will be. A large company with a correspondingly large policy base can spread its risk and minimize the effects of claims experience that exceeds actuarial expectations.

6. **Total Premiums**

    The amount of insurance premiums received from policyholders as of the most recent year end. If the company issues life insurance or property insurance, those premiums are included in this figure as well.

    Generally speaking, companies with large premium volume generally have more predictable claims experience.

7. Health Premiums

The amount of insurance premiums received from policyholders for health policies only as of the most recent year end.

Compare this figure with Total Premiums in the previous column to see how much of the company's business relates to health coverage.

8. Capital and Surplus

The company's statutory net worth in millions of dollars as of the most recent quarter end. Consumers may wish to limit the size of any policy so that the policyholder's maximum benefits do not exceed approximately 1% of the company's capital and surplus. For example, when buying a policy from a company with capital and surplus of $10,000,000, the 1% limit would be $100,000. (When performing this calculation, do not forget that figures in this column are expressed in millions of dollars.)

Critical Ranges In Our Ratios

Indicators	*Strong*	*Good*	*Fair*	*Weak*
Risk-Adjusted Capital Ratio #1	—	1.0 or more	0.75 - 0.99	0.74 or less
Risk-Adjusted Capital Ratio #2	1.0 or more	0.75 - 0.99	0.5 - 0.74	0.49 or less

---

9. Risk-Adjusted Capital Ratio #1

This ratio examines the adequacy of the company's capital base and whether the company has sufficient capital resources to cover potential losses which might occur in an average recession or other moderate loss scenario. Specifically, the figure cited in this column answers the question: For every dollar of capital that we feel would be needed, how many dollars in capital resources does the company actually have? (See the table above for the levels which we believe are critical.) You may find that some companies have unusually high levels of capital. This often reflects special circumstances related to the small size or unusual operations of the company.

10. Risk-Adjusted Capital Ratio #2

This is similar to item 9. But in this case, the question relates to whether the company has enough capital cushion to withstand a *severe* recession or other severe loss scenario. For more details on risk-adjusted capital, see the Appendix.

INSURANCE COMPANY NAME	DOM. STATE	RATING	DATA DATE	TOTAL ASSETS ($MIL)	TOTAL PREMIUMS ($MIL)	HEALTH PREMIUMS ($MIL)	CAPITAL & SURPLUS ($MIL)	RISK ADJUSTED CAPITAL RATIO 1	RATIO 2
MY CHOICE WISCONSIN HEALTH PLAN INC	WI	● B+	2q 2020	74.2	165.7	165.7	47.1	2.56	2.14
21ST CENTURY CENTENNIAL INS CO	PA	C	2q 2020	212.3	86.7	0.0	212.3	2.20	2.18
21ST CENTURY PREMIER INS CO	PA	C	2q 2020	103.3	0.7	0.1	101.2	6.44	6.30
4 EVER LIFE INS CO	IL	● B	2q 2020	179.4	159.0	151.7	80.8	7.38	4.69
AAA LIFE INS CO	MI	B	1q 2020	707.6	972.6	73.8	188.9	3.60	1.99
ABILITY INS CO	NE	D-	2q 2020	942.9	61.9	61.5	14.2	0.65	0.32
ABSOLUTE TOTAL CARE INC	SC	● B	2q 2020	198.8	649.3	649.3	93.4	1.84	1.53
ACCENDO INS CO	UT	U	--	--	--	--	--	--	--
ACCESS INS CO	TX	F	3q 2017	214.1	311.3	0.0	30.6	0.90	0.78
ACCESS SENIOR HEALTHCARE INC	CA	● E-	2q 2020	5.3	30.4	30.4	1.9	0.36	0.23
ACCESSCARE GENERAL WI INS INC	WI	U		--	--	--	--	--	--
ACE AMERICAN INS CO	PA	B-	2q 2020	24,352.6	5,475.0	591.3	5,007.6	1.90	1.32
ADVANCE INS CO OF KANSAS	KS	● B+	2q 2020	65.6	12.1	4.2	55.7	4.07	2.66
ADVENTIST HEALTH PLAN INC	CA	● D	2q 2020	7.6	29.6	29.6	1.7	0.48	0.30
ADVICARE CORP	SC	U		--	--	--	--	--	--
AEGIS SECURITY INS CO	PA	D+	2q 2020	193.8	227.9	12.0	64.7	0.52	0.38
AETNA BETTER HEALTH (AN OHIO CORP)	OH	● B	2q 2020	328.7	993.7	993.7	160.4	2.14	1.78
AETNA BETTER HEALTH INC	IL	● B-	2q 2020	112.0	203.9	203.9	75.4	4.41	3.68
AETNA BETTER HEALTH INC (A CT CORP)	CT	U		--	--	--	--	--	--
AETNA BETTER HEALTH INC (A LA CORP)	LA	● C	3q 2019	195.8	634.7	634.7	81.4	3.39	2.83
AETNA BETTER HEALTH INC (A NJ CORP)	NJ	● B	3q 2019	145.5	364.1	364.1	63.7	3.25	2.71
AETNA BETTER HEALTH INC (A PA CORP)	PA	● C	2q 2020	460.9	1,004.5	1,004.5	133.1	1.87	1.56
AETNA BETTER HEALTH OF CA INC	DE	● D+	2q 2020	105.5	73.7	73.7	42.7	4.45	3.00
AETNA BETTER HEALTH OF FLORIDA INC	FL	● D	2q 2020	315.0	561.6	561.6	155.5	4.11	3.43
AETNA BETTER HEALTH OF KS INC	KS	U		--	--	--	--	--	--
AETNA BETTER HEALTH OF MICHIGAN INC	MI	● B	2q 2020	135.4	318.0	318.0	50.2	2.11	1.76
AETNA BETTER HEALTH OF MISSOURI LLC	MO	● C	3q 2019	31.1	1.0	1.0	23.4	25.47	21.23
AETNA BETTER HEALTH OF NV INC	NV	U		--	--	--	--	--	--
AETNA BETTER HEALTH OF OKLAHOMA INC	OK	U		--	--	--	--	--	--
AETNA BETTER HEALTH OF TEXAS INC	TX	● B	3q 2019	81.6	314.5	314.5	36.2	2.57	2.14
AETNA BETTER HLTH OF KY INS CO	KY	● B+	3q 2019	536.6	1,121.8	1,121.8	365.4	6.30	5.25
AETNA BETTER HLTH OF NC INC	NC	U		--	--	--	--	--	--
AETNA BETTER HLTH OF WA INC	WA	U		--	--	--	--	--	--
AETNA HEALTH & LIFE INS CO	CT	● C-	2q 2020	432.1	442.8	442.8	156.0	1.51	1.34
AETNA HEALTH INC (A CT CORP)	CT	● B-	2q 2020	87.0	132.8	132.8	58.2	4.54	3.78
AETNA HEALTH INC (A FLORIDA CORP)	FL	● B	2q 2020	491.6	1,508.1	1,508.1	209.4	1.94	1.62
AETNA HEALTH INC (A GEORGIA CORP)	GA	● C	2q 2020	195.5	181.9	181.9	74.4	4.57	3.80
AETNA HEALTH INC (A MAINE CORP)	ME	● B	2q 2020	40.4	80.4	80.4	25.6	2.75	2.29
AETNA HEALTH INC (A NEW JERSEY CORP)	NJ	● C	2q 2020	260.4	739.3	739.3	135.6	1.94	1.62
AETNA HEALTH INC (A NEW YORK CORP)	NY	● D+	2q 2020	171.1	228.9	228.9	105.3	4.12	3.43
AETNA HEALTH INC (A PA CORP)	PA	● B	2q 2020	1,270.4	3,371.9	3,371.9	610.2	3.18	2.65
AETNA HEALTH INC (A TEXAS CORP)	TX	● C	2q 2020	160.6	495.3	495.3	89.0	1.96	1.63
AETNA HEALTH INC (LA)	LA	● B-	2q 2020	41.8	72.1	72.1	27.7	3.18	2.65
AETNA HEALTH INS CO	PA	● C-	2q 2020	73.4	60.6	60.6	36.8	5.64	4.70
AETNA HEALTH INS CO OF NY	NY	U		--	--	--	--	--	--
AETNA HEALTH OF CALIFORNIA INC	CA	● B	2q 2020	453.5	1,314.4	1,314.4	202.2	2.15	1.45
AETNA HEALTH OF IOWA INC	IA	● C	2q 2020	59.0	5.5	5.5	48.7	22.86	19.05
AETNA HEALTH OF UTAH INC	UT	● C	2q 2020	81.2	178.9	178.9	43.8	3.90	3.25
AETNA HEALTHASSURANCE PA INC	PA	● D	3q 2019	82.5	299.2	299.2	56.1	3.12	2.60
AETNA LIFE INS CO	CT	● B	2q 2020	24,024.6	34,640.6	33,852.7	5,608.3	1.60	1.24
AF&L INS CO	PA	D	2q 2020	117.0	12.6	12.6	20.9	1.49	0.96
AHF MCO OF GEORGIA INC	GA	● C-	3q 2019	4.5	0.2	0.2	4.0	152.27	126.89

Arrows denote recent upgrades ▲ or downgrades▼   ● Bullets denote a more detailed analysis is available in Section II.

INSURANCE COMPANY NAME	DOM. STATE	RATING	DATA DATE	TOTAL ASSETS ($MIL)	TOTAL PREMIUMS ($MIL)	HEALTH PREMIUMS ($MIL)	CAPITAL & SURPLUS ($MIL)	RISK ADJUSTED CAPITAL Ratio 1	Ratio 2
AIDS HEALTHCARE FOUNDATION MCO OF FL	FL	● D-	2q 2020	28.5	101.8	101.8	14.8	1.26	1.05
AIG INS CO - PR	PR	B	2q 2020	180.0	93.2	0.1	102.8	3.28	2.35
AIG SPECIALTY INS CO	IL	C+	2q 2020	119.1	712.6	0.8	51.6	6.84	6.16
AIOI NISSAY DOWA INS CO LTD	GU	D-	2q 2020	42.0	12.8	0.0	18.9	2.29	1.44
ALAMEDA ALLIANCE FOR HEALTH	CA	F	2q 2020	546.3	950.1	950.1	206.2	3.08	1.88
ALFA LIFE INS CORP	AL	B-	2q 2020	1,536.3	168.0	0.5	243.6	2.24	1.23
ALIGN SENIOR CARE FLORIDA INC	FL	U	--	--	--	--	--	--	--
ALIGN SENIOR CARE INC	VA	U		--	--	--	--	--	--
ALIGN SENIOR CARE MI LLC	MI	U		--	--	--	--	--	--
ALIGNMENT HEALTH PLAN	CA	● E	2q 2020	142.7	680.0	680.0	31.3	0.40	0.25
ALIGNMENT HLTH PLAN OF IL INC	IL	U		--	--	--	--	--	--
ALIGNMENT HLTH PLAN OF NC INC	NC	U		--	--	--	--	--	--
ALL SAVERS INS CO	IN	● C	4q 2019	606.2	723.9	723.9	375.7	4.26	3.40
ALLCARE CCO INC	OR	U		--	--	--	--	--	--
ALLCARE HEALTH PLAN INC	OR	● E	2q 2020	15.3	43.8	43.8	9.4	1.27	1.06
ALLEGIANCE L&H INS CO	MT	● C+	2q 2020	17.2	13.5	13.5	14.2	5.00	4.17
ALLIANCE HEALTH & LIFE INS CO	MI	● C-	2q 2020	163.7	317.5	317.5	62.3	2.08	1.73
ALLIANT HEALTH PLANS INC	GA	● D-	2q 2020	155.8	297.0	297.0	91.2	3.76	3.13
ALLIANZ GLOBAL RISKS US INS CO	IL	C	2q 2020	8,776.8	1,750.1	12.3	1,607.1	0.81	0.59
ALLIANZ LIFE INS CO OF NORTH AMERICA	MN	B-	2q 2020	158,080.0	13,295.9	171.6	7,157.9	3.05	1.63
ALLIANZ LIFE INS CO OF NY	NY	B+	2q 2020	3,829.8	376.1	3.3	201.5	4.93	3.59
ALLIED WORLD NATL ASR CO	NH	C	2q 2020	527.5	523.4	0.0	159.0	2.18	1.47
ALLINA HLTH & AETNA INS CO	MN	● C	3q 2019	28.4	0.2	0.2	11.2	6.28	5.23
ALLSTATE LIFE INS CO	IL	B	2q 2020	29,487.2	480.5	17.2	3,740.8	2.16	1.29
ALLSTATE LIFE INS CO OF NEW YORK	NY	B-	2q 2020	6,089.9	220.2	47.7	533.9	2.08	1.08
ALLWAYS HEALTH PARTNERS INS CO	MA	D	2q 2020	26.6	6.7	6.7	3.3	0.87	0.74
ALLWAYS HLTH PTNRS SELECT LLC	MA	U		--	--	--	--	--	--
ALOHACARE	HI	● C	2q 2020	127.2	343.9	343.9	55.8	1.19	0.99
ALTAMED HEALTH NETWORK INC		U		--	--	--	--	--	--
AMALGAMATED CASUALTY INS CO	DC	C	2q 2020	52.2	13.1	0.0	35.2	2.88	2.47
AMALGAMATED LIFE & HEALTH INS CO	IL	C	2q 2020	4.2	2.9	2.9	3.8	2.52	2.27
AMALGAMATED LIFE INS CO	NY	● A	2q 2020	154.2	78.6	41.1	78.8	4.20	3.17
AMBETTER OF MAGNOLIA INC	MS	● B	3q 2019	166.1	493.8	493.8	72.3	5.98	4.98
AMBETTER OF NORTH CAROLINA INC	NC	U		--	--	--	--	--	--
AMBETTER OF PEACH STATE INC	GA	● B	3q 2019	372.6	1,136.9	1,136.9	176.5	4.64	3.87
AMERICAN ALTERNATIVE INS CORP	DE	C	2q 2020	427.7	867.1	9.8	181.8	17.63	13.51
AMERICAN BANKERS INS CO OF FL	FL	B	2q 2020	2,361.9	5,225.9	147.7	614.9	2.30	1.44
AMERICAN BANKERS LIFE ASR CO OF FL	FL	● B	2q 2020	322.0	300.7	152.1	52.7	4.71	2.69
▲ AMERICAN BENEFIT LIFE INS CO	OK	B-	2q 2020	211.7	11.7	0.0	28.1	3.31	1.88
AMERICAN CASUALTY CO OF READING	PA	C	2q 2020	125.4	596.6	0.0	125.4	2.00	1.96
▲ AMERICAN CONTINENTAL INS CO	TN	● C+	2q 2020	336.1	485.4	441.7	146.0	2.38	1.77
AMERICAN FAMILY INS CO	WI	B	2q 2020	411.8	2,142.9	0.4	26.7	2.31	2.08
AMERICAN FAMILY LIFE ASR CO OF NY	NY	● A-	2q 2020	1,043.6	342.6	329.2	356.2	6.08	4.07
AMERICAN FAMILY MUTL INS CO SI	WI	B+	2q 2020	24,090.2	4,440.2	26.3	7,074.9	1.54	1.24
AMERICAN FEDERATED LIFE INS CO	MS	B-	2q 2020	27.0	18.2	9.1	10.6	2.39	2.15
AMERICAN FIDELITY ASR CO	OK	● B+	1q 2020	6,608.0	1,327.8	911.4	545.8	2.06	1.21
AMERICAN FINANCIAL SECURITY L I C	MO	D	2q 2020	25.9	30.0	29.9	11.0	1.73	1.39
AMERICAN GENERAL LIFE INS CO	TX	B	2q 2020	198,522.0	16,953.5	97.1	7,137.7	2.69	1.26
AMERICAN HEALTH & LIFE INS CO	TX	● B-	2q 2020	1,302.0	405.8	188.9	257.1	3.87	2.40
AMERICAN HEALTH PLAN INC	TN	U		--	--	--	--	--	--
AMERICAN HEALTH PLAN OF FL INC	FL	U		--	--	--	--	--	--
AMERICAN HERITAGE LIFE INS CO	FL	● C+	2q 2020	2,143.1	1,103.2	945.7	380.3	1.39	1.05

www.weissratings.com

Arrows denote recent upgrades ▲ or downgrades▼   ● Bullets denote a more detailed analysis is available in Section II.

INSURANCE COMPANY NAME	DOM. STATE	RATING	DATA DATE	TOTAL ASSETS ($MIL)	TOTAL PREMIUMS ($MIL)	HEALTH PREMIUMS ($MIL)	CAPITAL & SURPLUS ($MIL)	RISK ADJUSTED CAPITAL RATIO 1	RATIO 2
AMERICAN HLTH PLAN OF TX INC	TN	U		--	--	--	--	--	--
AMERICAN HOME ASR CO	NY	C+	2q 2020	23,199.7	507.5	13.3	6,160.2	2.47	1.60
AMERICAN HOME LIFE INS CO	KS	C-	2q 2020	270.4	27.3	0.0	19.9	1.79	0.93
AMERICAN INCOME LIFE INS CO	IN	B-	2q 2020	4,558.2	1,147.9	92.8	259.2	1.17	0.68
AMERICAN INDEPENDENT NETWORK INS CO	NY	E-	2q 2020	18.1	1.8	1.8	-33.2	-4.98	-3.64
AMERICAN INTEGRITY LIFE INS CO	AR	C-	2q 2020	4.6	0.4	0.1	3.5	4.88	4.39
AMERICAN LABOR LIFE INS CO	AZ	D	2q 2020	11.3	1.0	1.0	9.2	3.68	3.31
AMERICAN LIFE & SECURITY CORP	NE	D	2q 2020	345.7	165.8	0.0	25.8	2.35	1.03
AMERICAN LIFE INS CO	DE	• C	2q 2020	11,395.9	1,335.7	443.5	4,553.8	1.11	1.05
AMERICAN MEMORIAL LIFE INS CO	SD	B-	2q 2020	3,654.1	592.3	0.0	178.8	1.53	0.78
AMERICAN MODERN HOME INS CO	OH	C+	2q 2020	1,152.5	435.5	0.0	318.1	1.51	1.26
AMERICAN NATIONAL INS CO	TX	B	2q 2020	21,736.7	1,823.5	35.9	3,419.1	1.06	0.90
AMERICAN NATIONAL LIFE INS CO OF TX	TX	• B-	2q 2020	135.2	80.8	77.0	37.3	2.93	2.01
AMERICAN PROGRESSIVE L&H I C OF NY	NY	• C	2q 2020	333.4	677.8	669.4	142.6	1.25	1.01
AMERICAN PUBLIC LIFE INS CO	OK	• B	2q 2020	105.7	96.3	95.0	38.1	2.45	1.84
AMERICAN REPUBLIC CORP INS CO	IA	C	2q 2020	14.7	45.7	45.5	8.0	2.71	2.44
AMERICAN REPUBLIC INS CO	IA	• B-	2q 2020	1,193.0	115.4	104.1	536.9	3.63	2.70
AMERICAN RETIREMENT LIFE INS CO	OH	• C+	2q 2020	157.2	420.5	420.3	83.2	1.51	1.16
AMERICAN SECURITY INS CO	DE	B	2q 2020	1,492.7	1,165.1	2.1	580.6	1.79	1.39
AMERICAN SENTINEL INS CO	PA	C-	2q 2020	40.0	37.9	0.1	11.8	0.44	0.36
AMERICAN SPECIALTY HEALTH INS CO	IN	• B	2q 2020	9.4	2.9	2.9	9.3	34.89	29.08
AMERICAN SPECIALTY HEALTH ODS OF NJ	NJ	• B	4q 2019	4.3	14.0	14.0	2.6	1.10	0.92
AMERICAN STATES INS CO	IN	C+	2q 2020	49.7	314.1	0.1	41.9	20.69	18.62
AMERICAN UNITED LIFE INS CO	IN	B	2q 2020	31,433.3	4,356.8	171.4	1,006.3	2.20	1.09
AMERICAS 1ST CHOICE SOUTH CAROLINA	SC	• C+	3q 2019	5.6	7.3	7.3	2.1	2.45	2.04
AMERICASHEALTH PLAN INC	CA	• D	2q 2020	5.5	10.2	10.2	2.8	4.56	3.16
AMERICHOICE OF NEW JERSEY INC	NJ	• B-	2q 2020	778.1	2,649.8	2,649.8	420.5	1.92	1.60
AMERICO FINANCIAL LIFE & ANNUITY INS	TX	B-	2q 2020	5,055.6	662.5	32.3	550.7	2.15	1.19
AMERIGROUP COMMUNITY CARE NM	NM	• B-	2q 2020	22.5	14.7	14.7	18.3	7.96	6.64
AMERIGROUP DISTRICT	DC	• B-	3q 2019	138.1	220.1	220.1	100.1	12.27	10.22
AMERIGROUP INS CO	TX	• B+	2q 2020	322.8	1,041.5	1,041.5	149.8	1.64	1.37
AMERIGROUP IOWA INC	IA	• C	3q 2019	677.8	1,445.4	1,445.4	171.2	1.97	1.64
AMERIGROUP KANSAS INC	KS	U		--	--	--	--	--	--
AMERIGROUP MARYLAND INC	MD	• B-	2q 2020	495.8	1,188.6	1,188.6	196.8	2.21	1.84
AMERIGROUP MICHIGAN INC	MI	U		--	--	--	--	--	--
AMERIGROUP MISSISSIPPI INC	MS	U		--	--	--	--	--	--
AMERIGROUP NEW JERSEY INC	NJ	• A-	2q 2020	454.1	1,451.9	1,451.9	221.2	1.82	1.52
AMERIGROUP OHIO INC	OH	U		--	--	--	--	--	--
AMERIGROUP OKLAHOMA INC	OK	U		--	--	--	--	--	--
AMERIGROUP PENNSYLVANIA INC	PA	U		--	--	--	--	--	--
AMERIGROUP TENNESSEE INC	TN	• B-	2q 2020	650.1	1,805.2	1,805.2	265.7	1.97	1.64
AMERIGROUP TEXAS INC	TX	• B	2q 2020	1,228.2	5,055.1	5,055.1	531.2	1.59	1.32
AMERIGROUP WASHINGTON INC	WA	• A-	2q 2020	314.7	643.5	643.5	184.1	4.02	3.35
AMERIHEALTH ADMINISTRATORS	PA	U		--	--	--	--	--	--
AMERIHEALTH CARITAS NC INC	NC	U		--	--	--	--	--	--
AMERIHEALTH CARITAS NH INC	NH	U		--	--	--	--	--	--
AMERIHEALTH CARITAS NM INC	NM	U		--	--	--	--	--	--
AMERIHEALTH CARITAS OF LOUISIANA INC	LA	• C	2q 2020	296.2	1,149.1	1,149.1	98.4	1.42	1.18
AMERIHEALTH CARITAS TEXAS INC	TX	U		--	--	--	--	--	--
AMERIHEALTH DISTRICT OF COLUMBIA INC	DC	• C	2q 2020	192.2	578.2	578.2	88.4	1.74	1.45
AMERIHEALTH HMO INC	PA	• C+	2q 2020	158.6	7.3	7.3	26.7	9.23	7.70
AMERIHEALTH INSURANCE CO OF NJ	NJ	• B-	4q 2019	508.9	1,107.2	1,107.2	186.1	3.17	2.64

www.weissratings.com
Arrows denote recent upgrades ▲ or downgrades▼

25

• Bullets denote a more detailed analysis is available in Section II.

INSURANCE COMPANY NAME	DOM. STATE	RATING	DATA DATE	TOTAL ASSETS ($MIL)	TOTAL PREMIUMS ($MIL)	HEALTH PREMIUMS ($MIL)	CAPITAL & SURPLUS ($MIL)	RISK ADJUSTED CAPITAL RATIO 1	RATIO 2
AMERIHEALTH MICHIGAN INC	MI	● C	3q 2019	27.4	75.4	75.4	15.0	2.95	2.46
AMERIHEALTH NEBRASKA INC	NE	U	--	--	--	--	--	--	--
AMERITAS LIFE INS CORP	NE	● B	2q 2020	23,704.7	3,255.9	955.7	1,726.8	2.43	1.40
AMERITAS LIFE INS CORP OF NY	NY	● B-	2q 2020	1,697.8	182.3	45.6	106.7	2.03	1.06
AMEX ASSURANCE CO	IL	● B-	2q 2020	242.0	190.8	54.5	199.4	10.76	6.33
AMFIRST INS CO	OK	● B-	2q 2020	76.6	58.9	58.9	60.7	3.68	3.07
AMGP GEORGIA MANAGED CARE CO INC	GA	● A-	2q 2020	401.2	1,254.1	1,254.1	171.2	1.74	1.45
AMGUARD INS CO	PA	C	2q 2020	1,726.7	1,220.2	15.8	226.5	1.16	0.75
AMH HEALTH LLC	ME	U	--	--	--	--	--	--	--
ANTHEM BLUE CROSS LIFE & HEALTH INS	CA	● B-	2q 2020	2,396.4	2,182.8	2,182.8	1,475.0	8.64	7.20
ANTHEM HEALTH PLANS INC	CT	● B	2q 2020	788.2	1,803.4	1,803.4	321.2	2.09	1.74
ANTHEM HEALTH PLANS OF KENTUCKY INC	KY	● B-	2q 2020	927.8	2,099.1	2,099.1	374.5	2.70	2.25
ANTHEM HEALTH PLANS OF MAINE INC	ME	● B	2q 2020	683.6	1,169.0	1,169.0	220.0	3.75	3.12
ANTHEM HEALTH PLANS OF NEW HAMPSHIRE	NH	● B	2q 2020	538.2	934.6	934.6	277.8	2.68	2.24
ANTHEM HEALTH PLANS OF VIRGINIA	VA	● B	2q 2020	2,015.1	3,097.3	3,097.3	740.2	3.70	3.08
ANTHEM INS COMPANIES INC	IN	● B-	2q 2020	3,877.8	7,986.4	7,986.4	1,395.5	2.65	2.21
ANTHEM KENTUCKY MANAGED CARE PLAN	KY	● A-	2q 2020	314.7	758.5	758.5	182.2	2.75	2.29
ANTHEM LIFE & DISABILITY INS CO	NY	B	2q 2020	33.0	18.5	10.9	17.9	2.06	1.55
ANTHEM LIFE INS CO	IN	● B+	2q 2020	799.2	304.3	173.7	163.2	2.14	1.50
APC PASSE LLC	AR	U	--	--	--	--	--	--	--
APEX HEALTH INC	NC	U	--	--	--	--	--	--	--
AR HEALTH & WELLNESS HLTH PLAN	AR	● C-	3q 2019	73.2	42.6	42.6	44.6	10.62	8.85
ARCADIAN HEALTH PLAN INC	WA	● B	2q 2020	1,750.0	4,345.8	4,345.8	798.0	3.86	3.22
ARCH INS CO	MO	C	2q 2020	5,020.7	2,344.3	63.8	968.3	0.98	0.77
ARCH LIFE INS CO OF AM	KS	U	--	--	--	--	--	--	--
ARKANSAS ADVANCED CARE INC	AR	U	--	--	--	--	--	--	--
ARKANSAS BANKERS LIFE INS CO	AR	D+	2q 2020	2.5	0.7	0.1	1.6	1.90	1.71
ARKANSAS SUPERIOR SELECT INC	AR	● E	3q 2019	10.6	27.9	27.9	4.7	0.84	0.70
ARKANSAS TOTAL CARE INC	AR	U	--	--	--	--	--	--	--
ARROWOOD INDEMNITY CO	DE	E	2q 2020	916.0	-0.2	0.0	130.3	0.28	0.17
ASPEN AMERICAN INS CO	TX	C+	2q 2020	1,359.6	501.3	12.8	486.4	1.07	0.78
ASPIRE HEALTH PLAN	CA	● E-	2q 2020	14.2	45.8	45.8	-46.2	0.00	0.00
ASPIRUS ARISE HEALTH PLAN OF WISCONS	WI	● C	2q 2020	71.0	105.0	105.0	31.9	2.92	2.43
ASSURANCEAMERICA INS CO	NE	D+	2q 2020	106.5	191.9	1.7	24.8	0.90	0.81
ASSURITY LIFE INS CO	NE	● B+	2q 2020	2,670.3	275.8	124.6	351.7	2.59	1.49
ASSURITY LIFE INS CO OF NY	NY	B	2q 2020	8.1	0.6	0.5	7.0	3.35	3.01
ASURIS NORTHWEST HEALTH	WA	● B	2q 2020	127.7	155.7	155.7	86.2	6.13	5.11
ATHENE ANNUITY & LIFE ASR CO	DE	C	2q 2020	34,816.7	105.7	13.1	1,683.4	0.83	0.54
ATHENE ANNUITY & LIFE ASR CO OF NY	NY	C+	2q 2020	3,233.3	265.5	0.2	331.0	2.18	1.24
ATHENE ANNUITY & LIFE CO	IA	C	2q 2020	67,398.6	12,089.8	1.5	1,378.0	0.98	0.51
ATHENE LIFE INS CO OF NEW YORK	NY	C	2q 2020	928.6	40.5	0.5	73.8	2.44	1.18
ATLANTA LIFE INS CO	GA	D	2q 2020	22.1	1.0	0.0	6.9	1.04	0.67
ATLANTIC COAST LIFE INS CO	SC	C-	2q 2020	649.0	531.0	1.5	42.1	1.40	0.72
ATLANTIC SPECIALTY INS CO	NY	C	2q 2020	2,628.7	1,072.1	166.4	718.1	1.42	0.99
ATRIO HEALTH PLANS INC	OR	● D+	2q 2020	64.1	210.1	210.1	21.1	1.10	0.91
AULTCARE HEALTH INSURING CORP	OH	● B	3q 2019	117.6	242.6	242.6	99.0	2.18	1.81
AULTCARE INS CO	OH	● B+	2q 2020	106.6	266.0	266.0	54.0	1.56	1.30
AUTO CLUB LIFE INS CO	MI	C	2q 2020	919.4	7.0	0.5	79.1	0.89	0.64
AUTO-OWNERS LIFE INS CO	MI	B-	2q 2020	4,279.2	252.3	18.0	557.4	3.14	1.67
AUXILIO PLATINO INC	PR	U	--	--	--	--	--	--	--
AVALON INS CO	PA	● D+	2q 2020	42.8	55.5	55.5	19.9	1.66	1.38
AVEMCO INS CO	MD	C+	2q 2020	81.5	34.2	0.0	49.1	4.03	3.77

Arrows denote recent upgrades ▲ or downgrades▼   ● Bullets denote a more detailed analysis is available in Section II.

INSURANCE COMPANY NAME	DOM. STATE	RATING	DATA DATE	TOTAL ASSETS ($MIL)	TOTAL PREMIUMS ($MIL)	HEALTH PREMIUMS ($MIL)	CAPITAL & SURPLUS ($MIL)	RISK ADJUSTED CAPITAL RATIO 1	RATIO 2
AVERA HEALTH PLANS INC	SD	• B	2q 2020	118.6	260.5	260.5	69.2	2.31	1.92
AVMED INC	FL	• B-	2q 2020	281.4	699.8	699.8	115.8	1.84	1.53
AXIS INS CO	IL	B-	2q 2020	1,857.9	971.0	107.9	572.4	2.25	1.68
AXIS REINS CO	NY	C+	2q 2020	4,031.3	83.6	0.3	960.9	2.13	1.30
BALTIMORE LIFE INS CO	MD	B	2q 2020	1,297.8	121.4	0.6	89.1	1.77	0.91
BANKERS CONSECO LIFE INS CO	NY	D	2q 2020	528.4	65.8	12.0	60.6	3.49	1.78
BANKERS FIDELITY ASR CO	GA	C	2q 2020	11.5	45.2	45.2	8.7	3.46	2.28
BANKERS FIDELITY LIFE INS CO	GA	• C-	2q 2020	153.3	150.3	141.6	34.7	0.77	0.65
BANKERS LIFE & CAS CO	IL	• D+	2q 2020	16,460.6	2,480.9	726.7	1,234.6	1.76	0.98
BANKERS LIFE OF LOUISIANA	LA	C	2q 2020	19.8	35.3	22.9	8.3	2.41	2.17
BANKERS RESERVE LIFE INS CO OF WI	WI	• C+	2q 2020	569.0	2,157.2	2,157.2	286.6	1.77	1.48
BANNER HEALTH & AETNA HLTH INS	AZ	• B	3q 2019	134.5	233.3	233.3	81.1	5.26	4.38
BANNER HLTH & AETNA HLTH PLAN	AZ	• B	3q 2019	23.4	27.5	27.5	14.4	5.88	4.90
BANNER LIFE INS CO	MD	C	2q 2020	5,117.0	2,290.2	4.2	267.5	0.91	0.64
BAY AREA ACCOUNTABLE CARE	CA	• D	2q 2020	58.5	238.6	238.6	19.0	0.69	0.42
BAYCARE SELECT HEALTH PLANS	FL	• E-	2q 2020	27.3	34.9	34.9	6.5	0.66	0.55
BC&BS OF NEW MEXICO INS CO	NM	U		--	--	--	--	--	--
BCBSIL GP HMO NFP	IL	U		--	--	--	--	--	--
BCS INS CO	OH	• B-	2q 2020	356.0	442.2	167.2	149.9	9.03	5.40
BEACON HEALTH OPTIONS OF PA	PA	• C	2q 2020	30.1	12.9	12.9	20.4	8.61	7.17
BEAZLEY INS CO	CT	B-	2q 2020	917.7	428.1	23.2	219.5	1.89	1.24
BEHEALTHY FLORIDA INC	FL	• C-	3q 2019	34.6	108.2	108.2	21.8	4.16	3.47
BENCHMARK INS CO	KS	C+	2q 2020	552.5	390.6	7.7	141.1	3.53	2.70
BENEFICIAL LIFE INS CO	UT	B	2q 2020	2,041.9	56.3	0.0	200.6	3.25	1.73
BERKLEY INS CO	DE	B	2q 2020	19,851.1	658.6	27.6	5,544.8	1.29	1.09
BERKLEY LIFE & HEALTH INS CO	IA	• A	2q 2020	382.0	415.5	415.4	209.6	6.11	4.33
BERKSHIRE HATHAWAY SPECIALTY INS CO	NE	C	2q 2020	5,371.5	1,152.8	162.0	3,584.7	6.84	4.00
BERKSHIRE LIFE INS CO OF AMERICA	MA	• B	2q 2020	4,291.1	628.2	618.7	221.6	2.54	1.23
BEST CARE PARTNERS INC	FL	U		--	--	--	--	--	--
BEST LIFE & HEALTH INS CO	TX	B+	2q 2020	30.1	40.0	39.3	19.4	1.93	1.56
BEST MERIDIAN INS CO	FL	B-	2q 2020	381.7	61.6	10.9	63.7	1.61	1.07
BLUE ADVANTAGE PLUS OF KANSAS CITY	MO	• C	3q 2019	44.4	100.6	100.6	16.0	1.04	0.87
BLUE CARE NETWORK OF MICHIGAN	MI	• B+	2q 2020	2,936.0	4,252.4	4,252.4	1,922.2	7.65	6.38
BLUE CROSS & BLUE SHIELD MA HMO BLUE	MA	• B+	2q 2020	2,748.4	5,195.3	5,195.3	1,579.0	3.88	3.23
BLUE CROSS & BLUE SHIELD OF FLORIDA	FL	• B	2q 2020	7,561.3	11,259.2	11,259.2	2,412.8	4.41	3.68
BLUE CROSS BLUE SHIELD HEALTHCARE GA	GA	• A-	2q 2020	2,685.2	4,434.6	4,434.6	1,209.4	4.93	4.11
BLUE CROSS BLUE SHIELD OF ALABAMA	AL	• A-	2q 2020	4,861.0	6,108.0	6,108.0	2,446.9	6.31	5.26
BLUE CROSS BLUE SHIELD OF ARIZONA	AZ	• A+	2q 2020	2,830.5	2,297.5	2,297.5	1,470.9	4.60	3.84
BLUE CROSS BLUE SHIELD OF KANSAS INC	KS	• B	2q 2020	2,072.8	2,392.8	2,392.8	1,040.0	2.18	1.65
BLUE CROSS BLUE SHIELD OF KC	MO	• B	2q 2020	1,360.5	1,615.8	1,615.8	819.3	5.25	4.37
BLUE CROSS BLUE SHIELD OF MA	MA	• B-	2q 2020	2,583.3	3,164.9	3,164.9	872.0	2.66	2.21
BLUE CROSS BLUE SHIELD OF MICHIGAN	MI	• B-	2q 2020	10,124.9	9,237.2	9,237.2	5,629.4	4.33	3.61
BLUE CROSS BLUE SHIELD OF MINNESOTA	MN	• C	2q 2020	3,037.6	3,866.5	3,866.5	1,227.2	4.17	3.47
BLUE CROSS BLUE SHIELD OF MS, MUTUAL	MS	• A	2q 2020	1,156.0	1,403.0	1,403.0	737.2	8.51	7.09
BLUE CROSS BLUE SHIELD OF NC	NC	• B+	2q 2020	6,502.9	8,939.3	8,939.3	4,078.3	6.33	5.27
BLUE CROSS BLUE SHIELD OF ND	ND	• B	2q 2020	780.7	1,204.6	1,204.6	472.8	3.57	2.98
BLUE CROSS BLUE SHIELD OF NEBRASKA	NE	• B-	2q 2020	945.2	1,576.8	1,576.8	402.0	4.67	3.89
BLUE CROSS BLUE SHIELD OF RI	RI	• B	2q 2020	932.3	1,698.2	1,698.2	367.8	2.94	2.45
BLUE CROSS BLUE SHIELD OF SC INC	SC	• B	2q 2020	5,318.1	3,949.0	3,949.0	3,398.6	6.16	5.13
BLUE CROSS BLUE SHIELD OF VERMONT	VT	• B-	2q 2020	309.4	537.7	537.7	157.7	2.84	2.36
BLUE CROSS BLUE SHIELD OF WISCONSIN	WI	• B-	2q 2020	643.4	727.3	727.3	377.1	2.65	2.21
BLUE CROSS BLUE SHIELD OF WYOMING	WY	• B-	2q 2020	652.9	611.5	611.5	428.9	5.91	4.93

Arrows denote recent upgrades ▲ or downgrades▼   • Bullets denote a more detailed analysis is available in Section II.

INSURANCE COMPANY NAME	DOM. STATE	RATING	DATA DATE	TOTAL ASSETS ($MIL)	TOTAL PREMIUMS ($MIL)	HEALTH PREMIUMS ($MIL)	CAPITAL & SURPLUS ($MIL)	RISK ADJUSTED CAPITAL RATIO 1	RATIO 2
BLUE CROSS COMPLETE OF MICHIGAN	MI	● B+	2q 2020	355.7	818.9	818.9	147.6	2.47	2.06
BLUE CROSS OF CALIFORNIA	CA	● A+	2q 2020	7,804.6	16,500.9	16,500.9	3,444.9	3.58	2.27
BLUE CROSS OF IDAHO CARE PLUS INC	ID	● B	2q 2020	231.5	534.1	534.1	96.2	1.45	1.21
BLUE CROSS OF IDAHO HEALTH SERVICE	ID	● B+	2q 2020	1,144.5	1,290.3	1,290.3	688.2	6.07	5.06
BLUE RIDGE INDEMNITY CO	DE	C	2q 2020	21.1	6.3	0.0	15.8	8.98	4.80
BLUE SHIELD OF CALIFORNIA L&H INS CO	CA	● B	2q 2020	289.7	248.7	238.4	157.7	4.29	3.24
BLUEBONNET LIFE INS CO	MS	A-	2q 2020	69.5	5.0	0.0	65.4	8.70	7.83
BLUECHOICE HEALTHPLAN OF SC INC	SC	● B	2q 2020	472.2	666.1	666.1	279.2	5.32	4.43
BLUECROSS BLUESHIELD KANSAS SOLUTION	KS	U	--	--	--	--	--	--	--
BLUECROSS BLUESHIELD OF TENNESSEE	TN	● A-	2q 2020	5,279.4	5,130.7	5,130.7	3,718.9	6.97	5.81
▲ BOSTON MEDICAL CENTER HEALTH PLAN	MA	● B-	2q 2020	662.9	2,667.1	2,667.1	394.6	1.80	1.50
BOSTON MUTUAL LIFE INS CO	MA	B+	2q 2020	1,547.3	236.5	58.4	244.9	2.15	1.39
▲ BRAVO HEALTH MID-ATLANTIC INC	MD	● B	2q 2020	95.9	278.6	278.6	57.8	2.30	1.92
BRAVO HEALTH PENNSYLVANIA INC	PA	● B	2q 2020	227.2	710.3	710.3	119.6	2.29	1.91
BRIDGESPAN HEALTH CO	UT	● B	2q 2020	49.0	15.6	15.6	36.0	14.72	12.27
BRIDGEWAY HEALTH SOL OF AZ	AZ	● D+	2q 2020	53.1	111.8	111.8	15.0	1.32	1.10
BRIGHT HEALTH CO OF ARIZONA	AZ	● D	3q 2019	47.3	10.8	10.8	16.2	6.33	5.27
BRIGHT HEALTH CO OF GEORGIA	GA	U	--	--	--	--	--	--	--
BRIGHT HEALTH CO OF NC	NC	U	--	--	--	--	--	--	--
BRIGHT HEALTH INS CO	CO	● D	3q 2019	74.4	108.7	108.7	20.0	1.92	1.60
BRIGHT HEALTH INS CO OF FL	FL	U	--	--	--	--	--	--	--
BRIGHT HLTH CO OF SC INC	SC	U	--	--	--	--	--	--	--
BRIGHT HLTH INS CO OF NEW YORK	NY	U	--	--	--	--	--	--	--
BRIGHT HLTH INS CO OH	OH	U	--	--	--	--	--	--	--
BRIGHT HLTH INS CO TN	TN	U	--	--	--	--	--	--	--
BRIGHT HLTH INSURANCE CO OF IL	IL	U	--	--	--	--	--	--	--
▲ BRIGHTHOUSE LIFE INSURANCE CO	DE	D+	2q 2020	181,255.0	7,949.0	220.2	6,776.6	2.87	1.59
BROWN & TOLAND HEALTH SERVICES	CA	● D	2q 2020	60.7	146.4	146.4	29.4	2.56	1.59
BUCKEYE COMMUNITY HEALTH PLAN INC	OH	● B	2q 2020	724.5	2,732.0	2,732.0	300.6	1.67	1.39
BUCKEYE HEALTH PLAN COMMUNITY	OH	● C	3q 2019	8.5	9.2	9.2	3.9	2.87	2.39
BUPA INS CO	FL	● C+	2q 2020	308.9	313.7	313.7	129.9	3.29	2.74
▼ CALIFORNIA HEALTH & WELLNESS PLAN	CA	● E	2q 2020	241.7	722.6	722.6	34.6	0.46	0.31
CALIFORNIA PHYSICIANS SERVICE	CA	● A+	2q 2020	10,417.9	17,386.5	17,386.5	6,284.0	4.15	2.80
CANADA LIFE ASSURANCE CO-US BRANCH	MI	C	2q 2020	4,110.0	77.1	1.9	262.7	2.17	1.15
CANADA LIFE REINSURANCE COMPANY	PA	● C+	2q 2020	132.1	0.0	0.0	60.1	6.63	5.94
CAPITAL ADVANTAGE ASR CO	PA	● C	2q 2020	735.4	1,356.7	1,356.7	415.9	3.63	3.03
CAPITAL ADVANTAGE INS CO	PA	● C	2q 2020	692.8	287.2	287.2	482.9	2.74	2.28
CAPITAL BLUE CROSS	PA	● B-	2q 2020	1,298.6	345.4	345.4	749.5	3.54	2.95
CAPITAL DISTRICT PHYSICIANS HEALTH P	NY	● A-	2q 2020	660.1	1,599.7	1,599.7	431.8	2.91	2.42
CAPITAL HEALTH PLAN INC	FL	● A	2q 2020	666.5	900.7	900.7	517.2	6.95	5.79
CAPITOL INDEMNITY CORP	WI	C	2q 2020	775.7	81.9	0.0	276.8	1.92	1.43
CARE 1ST HEALTH PLAN INC	CA	● B	2q 2020	1,003.7	2,232.4	2,232.4	428.3	3.04	2.53
CARE IMPROVEMENT PLUS OF TEXAS INS	TX	● B-	2q 2020	759.2	1,937.7	1,937.7	386.5	2.44	2.03
CARE IMPROVEMENT PLUS SOUTH CENTRAL	AR	● B	2q 2020	930.2	1,972.7	1,972.7	593.6	5.11	4.26
CARE IMPROVEMENT PLUS WI INS	WI	● B	2q 2020	177.5	345.3	345.3	96.5	3.39	2.82
CARE N CARE INS CO	TX	● C	2q 2020	61.8	131.8	131.8	28.0	1.85	1.54
CARE N CARE INS CO OF NORTH CAROLINA	NC	● E-	3q 2019	45.3	128.7	128.7	13.2	0.51	0.43
CAREAMERICA LIFE INS CO	CA	U	--	--	--	--	--	--	--
CARECONNECT INS CO	NY	● E-	3q 2019	62.4	44.2	44.2	41.9	3.75	3.12
CARECORE NJ LLC	NJ	● D	4q 2019	33.9	125.4	125.4	6.7	3.66	3.05
CAREFIRST ADVANTAGE INC	MD	U	--	--	--	--	--	--	--
CAREFIRST BLUECHOICE INC	DC	● B-	2q 2020	1,715.5	3,465.2	3,465.2	945.6	4.96	4.13

Arrows denote recent upgrades ▲ or downgrades▼

www.weissratings.com

● Bullets denote a more detailed analysis is available in Section II.

INSURANCE COMPANY NAME	DOM. STATE	RATING	DATA DATE	TOTAL ASSETS ($MIL)	TOTAL PREMIUMS ($MIL)	HEALTH PREMIUMS ($MIL)	CAPITAL & SURPLUS ($MIL)	RISK ADJUSTED CAPITAL RATIO 1	RATIO 2
CAREFIRST BLUECROSS BLUESHIELD MEDIC	MD	● E-	2q 2020	35.0	90.7	90.7	18.0	1.47	1.22
CAREFIRST OF MARYLAND INC	MD	● B-	2q 2020	2,120.0	1,952.1	1,952.1	1,020.1	5.30	4.42
CAREMORE HEALTH PLAN	CA	● B	2q 2020	307.6	970.5	970.5	82.6	1.92	1.20
CAREPARTNERS OF CT INC	CT	● D	2q 2020	22.7	2.6	2.6	17.9	5.63	4.69
CAREPLUS HEALTH PLANS INC	FL	● B	2q 2020	797.6	2,138.3	2,138.3	212.2	2.32	1.93
CARESOURCE GEORGIA CO	GA	● C	3q 2019	152.2	659.7	659.7	74.6	0.98	0.82
CARESOURCE INDIANA INC	IN	● D+	3q 2019	297.0	782.1	782.1	129.4	2.37	1.97
CARESOURCE KENTUCKY CO	KY	● C	3q 2019	77.2	281.3	281.3	44.0	2.47	2.06
▲ CARESOURCE OHIO INC	OH	● B	2q 2020	2,038.5	8,701.3	8,701.3	954.2	1.92	1.60
CARESOURCE WEST VIRGINIA CO	WV	● C	3q 2019	26.1	49.4	49.4	13.0	2.07	1.72
CARIBBEAN AMERICAN LIFE ASR CO	PR	B	2q 2020	39.3	28.6	13.0	11.1	2.35	2.01
CARIBBEAN AMERICAN PROPERTY INS CO	PR	C	2q 2020	49.2	58.6	0.0	21.4	0.68	0.44
CARILION CLINIC MEDICARE RESOURCES	VA	U		--	--	--	--	--	--
CARITEN HEALTH PLAN INC	TN	● B	2q 2020	545.8	1,547.0	1,547.0	183.0	2.01	1.68
CAROLINA COMPLETE HEALTH INC	NC	U		--	--	--	--	--	--
CASCADE HEALTH ALLIANCE LLC	OR	U		--	--	--	--	--	--
CATHOLIC SPECIAL NEEDS PLAN LLC	NY	● C	2q 2020	16.7	55.1	55.1	7.1	0.82	0.69
CATLIN INS CO	TX	● C	2q 2020	257.8	85.9	33.0	34.7	0.44	0.27
CBHNP SERVICES INC	PA	U		--	--	--	--	--	--
CCHA LLC	CO	U		--	--	--	--	--	--
CDI GROUP INC	CA	● E-	2q 2020	3.0	17.4	17.4	1.0	0.44	0.44
CDPHP UNIVERSAL BENEFITS INC	NY	● B-	2q 2020	265.2	565.7	565.7	193.3	4.52	3.76
CELTIC INS CO	IL	● B-	2q 2020	3,180.7	3,081.8	3,081.8	439.8	1.72	1.43
CELTICARE HEALTH PLAN OF MA INC	MA	● C-	4q 2019	16.5	0.2	0.2	6.8	6.91	5.75
CENPATICO OF ARIZONA INC	AZ	U		--	--	--	--	--	--
CENTENE VENTURE CO AL HEALTH	AL	U		--	--	--	--	--	--
CENTENE VENTURE CO IN INC	IN	U		--	--	--	--	--	--
CENTENE VENTURE CO TENNESSEE	TN	U		--	--	--	--	--	--
CENTENE VENTURE CO FLORIDA	FL	U		--	--	--	--	--	--
CENTENE VENTURE CO ILLINOIS	IL	U		--	--	--	--	--	--
CENTENE VENTURE CO KANSAS	KS	U		--	--	--	--	--	--
CENTENE VENTURE CO MICHIGAN	MI	U		--	--	--	--	--	--
CENTENNIAL CASUALTY CO	AL	B-	2q 2020	133.6	22.2	3.1	94.3	3.38	2.00
CENTRAL HEALTH PLAN OF CALIFORNIA	CA	● E+	2q 2020	85.2	488.7	488.7	18.6	0.48	0.29
CENTRAL SECURITY LIFE INS CO	TX	C	2q 2020	84.2	2.3	0.1	6.3	0.77	0.69
CENTRAL STATES H & L CO OF OMAHA	NE	● B	2q 2020	372.6	64.8	26.8	154.5	3.65	2.72
CENTRAL STATES INDEMNITY CO OF OMAHA	NE	● C+	2q 2020	551.9	122.9	75.5	490.0	4.86	3.11
CENTRE LIFE INS CO	MA	● C	2q 2020	1,558.7	14.7	14.7	85.7	4.02	2.37
CENTURY INS CO GUAM LTD	GU	C	2q 2020	30.5	7.8	0.0	21.8	4.00	2.64
CHA HMO INC	KY	● B-	2q 2020	1,174.1	3,664.7	3,664.7	415.3	2.16	1.80
CHAMBER BUS SOLUTIONS TRUST	KY	U		--	--	--	--	--	--
CHEROKEE INS CO	MI	● B-	2q 2020	631.2	245.0	61.6	207.7	2.86	1.75
CHESAPEAKE LIFE INS CO	OK	● A+	2q 2020	253.5	265.3	225.4	147.7	3.31	2.64
CHILDRENS COMMUNITY HEALTH PLAN INC	WI	● B+	2q 2020	239.7	343.6	343.6	127.4	4.56	3.80
CHILDRENS MEDICAL CENTER HEALTH PLAN	TX	● E-	3q 2019	76.2	264.6	264.6	40.9	1.21	1.01
CHINESE COMMUNITY HEALTH PLAN	CA	● E-	2q 2020	76.2	137.5	137.5	10.5	0.62	0.41
CHOICE PHYSICIANS NETWORK	CA	● D+	2q 2020	45.6	151.0	151.0	10.6	0.81	0.49
CHRISTIAN FIDELITY LIFE INS CO	TX	● A-	2q 2020	58.3	23.7	22.1	29.6	4.11	2.95
CHRISTUS HEALTH PLAN	TX	● C-	2q 2020	130.7	150.6	150.6	43.6	1.71	1.42
CHRISTUS HEALTH PLAN LOUISIANA	LA	U		--	--	--	--	--	--
CHUBB CUSTOM INS CO	NJ	B-	2q 2020	280.8	159.6	0.0	238.7	40.99	36.89
CHUBB INS CO OF PR	PR	B-	2q 2020	206.5	143.1	14.6	73.7	2.27	1.68

www.weissratings.com

29

Arrows denote recent upgrades ▲ or downgrades▼   ● Bullets denote a more detailed analysis is available in Section II.

INSURANCE COMPANY NAME	DOM. STATE	RATING	DATA DATE	TOTAL ASSETS ($MIL)	TOTAL PREMIUMS ($MIL)	HEALTH PREMIUMS ($MIL)	CAPITAL & SURPLUS ($MIL)	RISK ADJUSTED CAPITAL RATIO 1	RATIO 2
CICA LIFE INS CO OF AMERICA	CO	C	2q 2020	150.3	4.8	0.7	27.9	1.15	0.99
CIGNA HEALTH & LIFE INS CO	CT	● B	2q 2020	12,993.2	19,057.0	19,056.8	5,746.5	2.23	1.69
CIGNA HEALTHCARE OF ARIZONA INC	AZ	● D+	2q 2020	178.2	617.6	617.6	61.4	0.91	0.76
CIGNA HEALTHCARE OF CALIFORNIA INC	CA	● C	2q 2020	180.4	952.9	952.9	72.7	1.74	1.07
CIGNA HEALTHCARE OF COLORADO INC	CO	● C	2q 2020	8.0	1.4	1.4	5.2	5.03	4.19
▼ CIGNA HEALTHCARE OF FLORIDA INC	FL	● C-	2q 2020	3.0	1.5	1.5	2.2	1.89	1.57
CIGNA HEALTHCARE OF GEORGIA INC	GA	● C	2q 2020	87.0	241.6	241.6	38.4	1.48	1.23
▼ CIGNA HEALTHCARE OF ILLINOIS INC	IL	● D	2q 2020	83.2	59.6	59.6	10.4	1.46	1.22
CIGNA HEALTHCARE OF INDIANA INC	IN	U		--	--	--	--	--	--
CIGNA HEALTHCARE OF NEW JERSEY INC	NJ	● E	2q 2020	14.5	2.2	2.2	13.8	13.49	11.24
CIGNA HEALTHCARE OF NORTH CAROLINA	NC	● D	2q 2020	56.5	104.3	104.3	28.6	2.40	2.00
CIGNA HEALTHCARE OF SOUTH CAROLINA	SC	● C	2q 2020	27.7	48.8	48.8	17.3	2.63	2.19
CIGNA HEALTHCARE OF ST LOUIS	MO	● C	2q 2020	15.4	14.0	14.0	7.4	2.60	2.17
CIGNA HEALTHCARE OF TENNESSEE INC	TN	● C-	2q 2020	11.4	19.0	19.0	7.8	2.28	1.90
CIGNA HEALTHCARE OF TEXAS INC	TX	● C-	2q 2020	43.9	64.7	64.7	33.2	5.05	4.21
CIGNA LIFE INS CO OF NEW YORK	NY	● A-	2q 2020	449.3	218.8	156.2	100.3	2.27	1.57
CIGNA NATIONAL HEALTH INS CO	OH	B	2q 2020	16.9	4.0	3.4	15.7	1.78	1.68
CIGNA WORLDWIDE INS CO	DE	B-	2q 2020	56.7	0.0	0.0	14.4	2.14	1.93
▲ CINCINNATI EQUITABLE LIFE INS CO	OH	B	2q 2020	176.3	37.2	0.0	8.0	1.00	0.68
CINCINNATI LIFE INS CO	OH	B-	2q 2020	4,721.5	384.6	6.2	207.6	1.16	0.61
CITIZENS NATIONAL LIFE INS CO	TX	C	2q 2020	11.8	0.9	0.0	1.6	2.89	2.60
CITIZENS SECURITY LIFE INS CO	KY	C	2q 2020	34.5	90.5	85.9	19.5	0.75	0.67
CLAREMONT BEHAVIORAL SVCS		● C-	2q 2020	2.4	5.4	5.4	1.2	2.17	1.75
CLEAR SPRING HEALTH (CO)	CO	U		--	--	--	--	--	--
CLEAR SPRING HEALTH (VA) INC	VA	U		--	--	--	--	--	--
CLEAR SPRING HEALTH INS CO	AZ	U		--	--	--	--	--	--
CLEAR SPRING HEALTH OF IL INC	IL	● D+	2q 2020	4.5	0.4	0.4	3.8	1.94	1.62
CLOISTER MUTL CAS INS CO	PA	C	2q 2020	10.1	0.0	0.0	10.0	13.45	6.11
CLOVER HMO NEW JERSEY INC	NJ	U		--	--	--	--	--	--
CLOVER INSURANCE COMPANY	NJ	● C	2q 2020	196.8	427.4	427.4	94.3	1.58	1.32
CMFG LIFE INS CO	IA	B-	2q 2020	21,989.7	2,978.3	589.8	2,247.0	1.52	1.16
CMNTY CARE HLTH PLAN INC (WI)	WI	● B	2q 2020	26.5	90.7	90.7	17.8	1.75	1.45
▲ CMNTY CARE HLTH PLAN OF LA INC	LA	● B	2q 2020	434.8	1,285.0	1,285.0	201.2	1.93	1.61
CMNTY CARE HLTH PLAN OF NV INC	NV	● A-	2q 2020	194.3	710.9	710.9	97.2	1.67	1.40
CMNTY HLTH NTWRK OF WA	WA	U		--	--	--	--	--	--
COLONIAL LIFE & ACCIDENT INS CO	SC	● C+	2q 2020	3,663.8	1,665.7	1,288.9	619.7	1.97	1.32
COLONIAL LIFE INS CO OF TX	TX	C-	2q 2020	17.0	0.7	0.2	15.4	5.07	2.97
COLONIAL PENN LIFE INS CO	PA	● D+	2q 2020	883.8	782.5	497.2	95.0	1.22	0.73
COLORADO ACCESS	CO	● D	2q 2020	77.2	357.8	357.8	33.6	N/A	N/A
COLUMBIA PACIFIC CCO LLC	OR	U		--	--	--	--	--	--
COLUMBIAN LIFE INS CO	IL	C	2q 2020	337.9	253.6	0.0	18.2	1.30	0.71
COLUMBIAN MUTUAL LIFE INS CO	NY	B	2q 2020	1,463.5	63.6	1.7	76.0	1.32	0.82
COLUMBUS LIFE INS CO	OH	C+	2q 2020	4,178.2	331.2	0.0	221.7	1.47	0.75
COMBINED INS CO OF AMERICA	IL	● C	2q 2020	2,501.6	1,119.7	990.0	273.9	1.18	0.87
COMBINED LIFE INS CO OF NEW YORK	NY	● C+	2q 2020	526.3	176.6	153.8	76.9	2.00	1.39
COMM TRAVELERS LIFE INS CO	NY	B	2q 2020	29.2	5.7	5.7	14.1	3.40	3.06
COMMENCEMENT BAY RISK MGMT INS	WA	● B	2q 2020	76.7	66.4	66.4	51.8	2.25	1.69
COMMON GROUND HEALTHCARE COOPERATIVE	WI	● C	2q 2020	346.0	468.7	468.7	214.8	4.53	3.78
COMMONWEALTH ANNUITY & LIFE INS CO	MA	C+	2q 2020	23,531.8	85.4	0.2	3,146.6	0.85	0.72
COMMUNITY CARE ALLIANCE OF ILLINOIS	IL	● D	2q 2020	27.2	59.1	59.1	14.2	1.27	1.05
COMMUNITY CARE BEHAVIORAL HEALTH	PA	● B+	2q 2020	611.0	1,105.6	1,105.6	265.5	3.11	2.59
COMMUNITY CARE HEALTH PLAN	CA	● C+	2q 2020	17.0	55.3	55.3	9.9	1.66	1.04

Arrows denote recent upgrades ▲ or downgrades▼   ● Bullets denote a more detailed analysis is available in Section II.

INSURANCE COMPANY NAME	DOM. STATE	RATING	DATA DATE	TOTAL ASSETS ($MIL)	TOTAL PREMIUMS ($MIL)	HEALTH PREMIUMS ($MIL)	CAPITAL & SURPLUS ($MIL)	RISK ADJUSTED CAPITAL RATIO 1	RATIO 2
COMMUNITY FIRST GROUP HOSPITAL SERVI	TX	U		--	--	--	--	--	--
COMMUNITY FIRST HEALTH PLANS INC	TX	● C	2q 2020	165.4	573.4	573.4	87.9	1.72	1.44
COMMUNITY HEALTH CHOICE INC	TX	● B-	2q 2020	211.1	742.3	742.3	75.8	1.18	0.98
COMMUNITY HEALTH CHOICE TX INC	TX	● C-	3q 2019	202.9	957.6	957.6	92.2	1.18	0.99
▼ COMMUNITY HEALTH GROUP	CA	● C-	2q 2020	101.0	1,045.5	1,045.5	43.0	0.54	0.33
COMMUNITY HEALTH PLAN OF WASHINGTON	WA	● B-	2q 2020	401.2	927.2	927.2	184.3	2.41	2.01
COMMUNITY INS CO	OH	● B-	2q 2020	2,163.0	5,951.5	5,951.5	941.9	2.62	2.18
COMMUNITYCARE GOVERNMENT PROGRAMS	OK	● D	3q 2019	8.8	26.3	26.3	2.9	0.83	0.69
COMMUNITYCARE HMO INC	OK	● C+	2q 2020	192.0	562.2	562.2	107.8	3.02	2.52
▼ COMMUNITYCARE L&H INS CO	OK	● D	2q 2020	19.5	42.0	42.0	9.3	1.70	1.41
COMPANION LIFE INS CO	NY	B-	2q 2020	1,107.2	139.5	0.0	43.2	1.37	0.73
COMPANION LIFE INS CO	SC	● B+	2q 2020	489.5	832.3	797.8	258.7	2.80	2.16
▲ COMPANION LIFE INS CO OF CA	CA	B+	2q 2020	29.6	28.0	28.0	12.2	2.89	2.60
COMPBENEFITS INS CO	TX	● B-	2q 2020	148.2	163.9	163.9	64.3	3.83	3.19
▲ COMPCARE HEALTH SERVICES INS CORP	WI	● A	2q 2020	535.2	1,248.8	1,248.8	235.9	2.47	2.06
COMPREHENSIVE MOBILE INS CO	AZ	● B	3q 2019	2.8	4.4	4.4	2.7	4.69	3.91
COMPREHENSIVE MOBILE PLAN UTAH INC	UT	U		--	--	--	--	--	--
CONNECTICARE BENEFITS INC	CT	● C	2q 2020	265.0	519.3	519.3	85.8	1.90	1.58
CONNECTICARE INC	CT	● C-	2q 2020	316.2	692.5	692.5	81.9	1.34	1.12
▲ CONNECTICARE INS CO	CT	● B-	2q 2020	303.1	565.7	565.7	143.0	1.57	1.30
CONNECTICARE OF MASSACHUSETTS INC	MA	● C	2q 2020	5.5	1.3	1.3	3.2	1.16	0.97
CONNECTICUT DENTAL PRACTICE	CT	U		--	--	--	--	--	--
CONNECTICUT GENERAL LIFE INS CO	CT	● B-	2q 2020	20,715.8	604.8	159.9	6,461.6	1.27	1.18
CONSTELLATION HEALTH LLC	PR	U		--	--	--	--	--	--
CONTINENTAL AMERICAN INS CO	SC	● B	2q 2020	874.4	657.7	632.0	274.5	3.91	2.92
CONTINENTAL CASUALTY CO	IL	B-	2q 2020	43,961.9	6,921.2	473.5	9,951.5	1.80	1.34
CONTINENTAL GENERAL INS CO	OH	● C+	2q 2020	4,371.2	238.3	224.3	321.0	2.21	1.17
CONTINENTAL LIFE INS CO OF BRENTWOOD	TN	● C+	2q 2020	431.0	576.5	573.0	234.0	1.11	0.97
CONTRA COSTA HEALTH PLAN	CA	● B	2q 2020	306.6	777.9	777.9	87.8	1.71	1.12
COOK CHILDRENS HEALTH PLAN	TX	● E+	2q 2020	151.0	566.6	566.6	86.9	1.62	1.35
COORDINATED CARE CORP	IN	● B	2q 2020	613.1	1,764.8	1,764.8	233.0	3.18	2.65
COORDINATED CARE OF WASHINGTON INC	WA	● C	3q 2019	251.3	596.6	596.6	82.5	2.46	2.05
COPIC INS CO	CO	B-	2q 2020	594.4	88.9	0.7	306.9	4.77	3.19
COUNTRY LIFE INS CO	IL	A+	2q 2020	10,112.1	551.7	113.3	1,258.8	2.22	1.40
COUNTY OF LOS ANGELES DEPT HEALTH	CA	U		--	--	--	--	--	--
COVENTRY HEALTH & LIFE INS CO	MO	● B-	2q 2020	1,238.2	2,047.3	2,047.3	867.3	5.03	4.19
▲ COVENTRY HEALTH CARE OF ILLINOIS INC	IL	● B	2q 2020	230.2	380.4	380.4	100.4	3.20	2.66
COVENTRY HEALTH CARE OF KANSAS INC	KS	● C	2q 2020	33.8	7.4	7.4	24.4	13.49	11.24
COVENTRY HEALTH CARE OF MISSOURI INC	MO	● B	2q 2020	356.7	865.2	865.2	163.6	2.79	2.32
COVENTRY HEALTH CARE OF NEBRASKA INC	NE	U		--	--	--	--	--	--
COVENTRY HEALTH CARE OF VIRGINIA INC	VA	● B-	2q 2020	555.2	1,362.6	1,362.6	212.6	1.98	1.65
COVENTRY HEALTH CARE OF WEST VA INC	WV	● B	2q 2020	287.4	604.7	604.7	116.3	2.48	2.07
COVENTRY HEALTH PLAN OF FLORIDA INC	FL	U		--	--	--	--	--	--
COVERYS SPECIALTY INS CO	NJ	B-	2q 2020	111.4	113.2	1.0	51.8	7.21	6.49
COX HEALTH SYSTEMS HMO INC	MO	U		--	--	--	--	--	--
COX HEALTH SYSTEMS INS CO	MO	● C-	2q 2020	52.8	132.6	132.6	22.5	1.07	0.89
CRESTPOINT HEALTH INS CO	TN	U		--	--	--	--	--	--
CSI LIFE INS CO	NE	B-	2q 2020	24.4	40.0	39.9	18.5	4.73	4.26
CYPRESS DENTAL INS CO OF CA	CA	U		--	--	--	--	--	--
DAILY UNDERWRITERS OF AMERICA	PA	C	2q 2020	60.1	18.7	0.0	41.2	2.91	2.17
▼ DAKOTA CAPITAL LIFE INS CO	ND	E+	2q 2020	10.3	2.1	0.1	1.5	0.68	0.61
▲ DAVITA HEALTHCARE PARTNERS PLAN INC	CA	● D	2q 2020	573.9	2,453.0	2,453.0	290.7	2.05	1.23

Arrows denote recent upgrades ▲ or downgrades▼ ● Bullets denote a more detailed analysis is available in Section II.

INSURANCE COMPANY NAME	DOM. STATE	RATING	DATA DATE	TOTAL ASSETS ($MIL)	TOTAL PREMIUMS ($MIL)	HEALTH PREMIUMS ($MIL)	CAPITAL & SURPLUS ($MIL)	RISK ADJUSTED CAPITAL RATIO 1	RATIO 2
DB INS CO LTD US GUAM BRANCH	GU	C	2q 2020	70.5	43.9	0.0	41.2	5.72	3.46
DC CHARTERED HEALTH PLAN INC	DC	F	4q 2018	5.2	0.0	0.0	-15.5	0.00	0.00
DEAN HEALTH INS INC	WI	U		--	--	--	--	--	--
DEAN HEALTH PLAN INC	WI	● A-	2q 2020	338.6	1,387.4	1,387.4	148.6	2.03	1.69
DEARBORN LIFE INS CO	IL	● B+	2q 2020	1,657.5	518.0	190.4	462.6	3.53	2.13
DEARBORN NATIONAL LIFE INS CO OF NY	NY	U		--	--	--	--	--	--
DELAWARE AMERICAN LIFE INS CO	DE	● B+	2q 2020	106.1	76.6	64.5	65.7	4.80	3.61
DELAWARE LIFE INS CO	DE	C	2q 2020	40,840.9	2,616.4	0.5	1,483.8	1.13	0.74
DELAWARE LIFE INS CO OF NEW YORK	NY	B-	2q 2020	2,193.7	28.7	0.0	400.3	10.40	4.93
DELSURE HEALTH INSURANCE INC	DE	U		--	--	--	--	--	--
DELTA LIFE INS CO	GA	E-	4q 2019	69.6	14.3	0.8	3.5	0.31	0.21
DENTAL NETWORK INC	MD	U		--	--	--	--	--	--
DENTAQUEST OF NEW JERSEY LLC	NJ	U		--	--	--	--	--	--
▲ DENVER HEALTH MEDICAL PLAN INC	CO	● B	2q 2020	86.0	385.7	385.7	36.3	1.06	0.88
DESERET MUTUAL INS CO	UT	U		--	--	--	--	--	--
DEVOTED HEALTH INSURANCE CO	FL	U		--	--	--	--	--	--
DEVOTED HEALTH PLAN OF FL INC	FL	● D-	2q 2020	44.6	45.2	45.2	16.4	1.59	1.32
DEVOTED HLTH PLAN OF OH INC	OH	U		--	--	--	--	--	--
DEVOTED HLTH PLAN OF TX INC	TX	U		--	--	--	--	--	--
DIGNITY CARE CORP	LA	U		--	--	--	--	--	--
DIGNITY HEALTH PROVIDER RESOURCES	CA	● E	2q 2020	9.9	178.6	178.6	6.3	0.44	0.27
DISTRICT COMMUNITY CARE INC	DC	U		--	--	--	--	--	--
DOCTORS HEALTHCARE PLANS INC	FL	● E	2q 2020	26.5	78.9	78.9	9.4	0.35	0.29
▲ DRISCOLL CHILDRENS HEALTH PLAN	TX	● C	2q 2020	224.2	709.3	709.3	140.4	2.14	1.78
EASTERN OR COORDINATED CARE	OR	U		--	--	--	--	--	--
EASY CHOICE HEALTH PLAN	CA	● C	2q 2020	160.1	455.0	455.0	40.0	1.28	0.80
▼ EL PASO FIRST HEALTH PLANS INC	TX	● B	2q 2020	57.1	203.6	203.6	36.0	1.79	1.49
ELAN INSURANCE USVI INC	VI	● E+	2q 2020	7.4	9.9	9.9	4.3	2.33	1.94
ELDERPLAN INC	NY	● C+	2q 2020	324.5	1,214.7	1,214.7	160.5	1.60	1.33
ELIPS LIFE INS CO	MO	● C	2q 2020	41.1	3.3	2.4	30.7	5.58	5.02
EMBLEMHEALTH INSURANCE COMPANY	NY	● D	2q 2020	48.4	29.8	29.8	37.1	7.78	6.48
EMC NATIONAL LIFE CO	IA	B	2q 2020	870.7	71.9	1.5	105.5	2.65	1.50
EMI HEALTH	UT	● A	2q 2020	198.8	72.0	72.0	128.1	3.88	3.23
EMPATHIA PACIFIC INC	CA	● C-	2q 2020	4.2	2.0	2.0	3.7	18.79	13.41
EMPHESYS INS CO	TX	U		--	--	--	--	--	--
EMPIRE FIRE & MARINE INS CO	IL	C+	2q 2020	51.7	358.3	6.6	38.1	13.56	12.20
EMPIRE HEALTHCHOICE ASSURANCE INC	NY	● B-	2q 2020	2,532.2	2,832.5	2,832.5	1,018.3	5.09	4.24
EMPIRE HEALTHCHOICE HMO INC	NY	● C	2q 2020	419.6	977.6	977.6	202.9	2.73	2.28
▼ EMPLOYERS PROTECTIVE INS CO	HI	B-	2q 2020	3.3	0.2	0.2	2.2	1.98	1.78
EMPOWER HLTHCR SOLUTIONS LLC	AR	U		--	--	--	--	--	--
ENTERPRISE LIFE INS CO	TX	● B+	2q 2020	148.0	0.5	0.5	115.3	1.32	1.16
ENVISION INS CO	OH	● C+	2q 2020	447.8	425.0	425.0	44.6	1.20	1.00
ENVOLVE DENTAL OF TEXAS INC	TX	U		--	--	--	--	--	--
EON HEALTH INC (GA)	GA	● C-	3q 2019	7.2	4.8	4.8	3.6	3.69	3.07
EPIC HEALTH PLAN	CA	● D	2q 2020	83.0	541.8	541.8	40.6	1.02	0.62
EQUITABLE FINL LIFE INS CO	NY	B	2q 2020	216,109.0	14,681.6	55.4	5,678.2	2.50	1.31
ERIE FAMILY LIFE INS CO	PA	B	2q 2020	2,756.7	245.0	1.7	307.7	2.93	1.60
ESSENCE HEALTHCARE INC	MO	● A-	2q 2020	260.9	783.0	783.0	121.3	2.01	1.67
EVEREST REINS CO	DE	C	2q 2020	13,642.5	387.6	85.0	4,045.6	1.00	0.71
EXCELLUS HEALTH PLAN INC	NY	● B	2q 2020	3,978.1	5,964.6	5,964.6	1,478.7	3.67	3.06
EXPERIENCE HEALTH INC	NC	U		--	--	--	--	--	--
EYEMED INSURANCE CO	AZ	U		--	--	--	--	--	--

Arrows denote recent upgrades ▲ or downgrades ▼   ● Bullets denote a more detailed analysis is available in Section II.

INSURANCE COMPANY NAME	DOM. STATE	RATING	DATA DATE	TOTAL ASSETS ($MIL)	TOTAL PREMIUMS ($MIL)	HEALTH PREMIUMS ($MIL)	CAPITAL & SURPLUS ($MIL)	RISK ADJUSTED CAPITAL RATIO 1	RATIO 2
FAIR AMERICAN INS & REINS CO	NY	● B	2q 2020	235.3	85.4	46.2	209.7	50.93	36.30
▲ FALLON COMMUNITY HEALTH PLAN	MA	● C+	2q 2020	514.8	1,569.2	1,569.2	171.3	1.35	1.12
FALLON HEALTH & LIFE ASR CO	MA	● D+	2q 2020	30.9	22.8	22.8	7.6	1.17	0.97
FAMILY BENEFIT LIFE INS CO	MO	D	2q 2020	245.2	91.2	0.0	8.6	0.62	0.37
FAMILY HERITAGE LIFE INS CO OF AMER	OH	● B-	2q 2020	1,375.1	301.7	298.0	107.8	1.52	0.90
FAMILY LIFE INS CO	TX	● C	2q 2020	142.2	64.6	43.4	27.0	2.94	2.21
FARM BUREAU LIFE INS CO	IA	B+	2q 2020	9,479.7	624.5	5.4	626.4	2.08	1.08
FARM BUREAU LIFE INS CO OF MISSOURI	MO	A-	2q 2020	639.5	47.5	0.1	74.7	1.61	1.08
FARM BUREAU MUTUAL INS CO OF AR	AR	B	2q 2020	442.5	249.0	0.1	257.7	5.52	4.76
FARM BUREAU MUTUAL INS CO OF MI	MI	B	2q 2020	856.6	173.3	0.1	413.8	4.54	3.04
FARM FAMILY LIFE INS CO	NY	B-	2q 2020	2,802.4	444.0	4.6	237.1	2.48	1.26
FARMERS MUTUAL HAIL INS CO OF IA	IA	B-	2q 2020	723.3	671.2	0.0	411.8	2.42	1.85
FARMERS NEW WORLD LIFE INS CO	WA	B-	2q 2020	5,274.1	1,068.3	19.9	431.9	2.16	1.14
FEDERAL INS CO	IN	C+	2q 2020	15,639.8	5,996.5	320.5	4,084.6	1.89	1.27
FEDERAL LIFE INS CO	IL	C-	2q 2020	253.6	19.1	0.1	20.3	2.40	1.28
FEDERATED LIFE INS CO	MN	A	2q 2020	2,189.3	224.7	31.9	482.8	4.89	2.58
FIDELITY LIFE ASSN A LEGAL RESERVE	IL	C+	2q 2020	421.6	155.4	0.9	104.5	10.45	5.08
FIDELITY SECURITY LIFE INS CO	MO	● A-	2q 2020	980.9	1,039.8	1,004.0	276.2	4.95	3.04
FIDELITY SECURITY LIFE INS CO OF NY	NY	B+	1q 2020	41.1	56.7	56.6	12.1	2.49	1.51
FIRST ALLMERICA FINANCIAL LIFE INS	MA	B	2q 2020	3,180.1	55.5	0.1	234.2	5.54	2.58
FIRST ASR LIFE OF AMERICA	LA	B	2q 2020	42.2	1.0	0.2	38.0	3.37	3.17
FIRST CARE INC	MD	● D	3q 2019	12.2	15.2	15.2	8.0	6.64	5.53
FIRST CHICAGO INS CO	IL	D	2q 2020	133.2	87.7	0.0	30.7	1.42	1.04
FIRST COMMUNITY HEALTH PLAN INC	AL	U		--	--	--	--	--	--
FIRST CONTINENTAL LIFE & ACC INS CO	TX	D-	2q 2020	6.2	27.4	27.4	3.7	0.96	0.85
FIRST HEALTH LIFE & HEALTH INS CO	TX	● C+	2q 2020	395.9	111.3	110.9	230.3	3.77	3.01
FIRST INS CO OF HI LTD	HI	C	2q 2020	671.4	89.9	0.0	271.1	4.49	3.05
FIRST MEDICAL HEALTH PLAN INC	PR	● D	2q 2020	258.0	1,050.3	1,050.3	83.7	1.00	0.83
FIRST NATIONAL LIFE INS CO	NE	C-	2q 2020	6.4	0.6	0.3	2.9	1.71	1.09
FIRST NET INS CO	GU	C	2q 2020	23.9	15.6	0.4	15.3	5.90	3.85
▼ FIRST PENN-PACIFIC LIFE INS CO	IN	B-	2q 2020	1,195.8	104.1	0.0	138.5	2.38	1.28
FIRST PRIORITY LIFE INS CO	PA	U		--	--	--	--	--	--
FIRST RELIANCE STANDARD LIFE INS CO	NY	● A-	2q 2020	237.6	102.0	71.6	76.8	5.41	3.59
FIRST SYMETRA NATL LIFE INS CO OF NY	NY	B	2q 2020	2,905.3	623.2	58.6	135.3	1.32	0.67
FIRST UNUM LIFE INS CO	NY	● C+	2q 2020	4,139.0	532.1	405.0	331.1	2.51	1.31
FIRSTCAROLINACARE INS CO	NC	● D	2q 2020	25.2	123.7	123.7	13.4	0.87	0.73
FIVE STAR LIFE INS CO	NE	C	2q 2020	316.6	138.5	0.2	30.5	2.08	1.27
FLORIDA BLUE MEDICARE INC	FL	U		--	--	--	--	--	--
▼ FLORIDA COMBINED LIFE INS CO INC	FL	C	2q 2020	32.8	140.2	122.8	15.5	3.37	3.04
FLORIDA HEALTH CARE PLAN INC	FL	● A	2q 2020	247.7	675.5	675.5	148.8	2.43	2.02
▲ FLORIDA MHS INC	FL	● C-	2q 2020	61.1	211.2	211.2	34.8	2.37	1.97
FLORIDA TRUE HEALTH INC	FL	● E-	2q 2020	110.1	330.5	330.5	46.8	1.61	1.34
FORETHOUGHT LIFE INS CO	IN	B	2q 2020	38,032.2	8,544.5	69.2	1,953.6	1.99	0.94
FOREVERCARE INC	AR	U		--	--	--	--	--	--
FOUNDATION LIFE INS CO OF AR	AR	C-	2q 2020	5.2	1.3	0.1	1.2	1.01	0.91
▼ FREEDOM HEALTH INC	FL	● B	2q 2020	374.0	1,149.6	1,149.6	83.4	1.13	0.94
FREEDOM LIFE INS CO OF AMERICA	TX	● B+	2q 2020	418.7	729.6	655.9	298.6	1.81	1.58
FREELANCERS INS CO	NY	U		--	--	--	--	--	--
FRESNO-KINGS-MADERA REGIONAL HEALTH	CA	● C+	2q 2020	296.4	1,162.2	1,162.2	109.4	1.94	1.18
FRIDAY HEALTH INSURANCE CO	TX	U		--	--	--	--	--	--
FRIDAY HEALTH PLANS OF CO INC	CO	● E-	2q 2020	34.5	70.7	70.7	12.1	0.75	0.63
GA CHAMBER FEDN BENEFIT PLAN	GA	U		--	--	--	--	--	--

INSURANCE COMPANY NAME	DOM. STATE	RATING	DATA DATE	TOTAL ASSETS ($MIL)	TOTAL PREMIUMS ($MIL)	HEALTH PREMIUMS ($MIL)	CAPITAL & SURPLUS ($MIL)	RISK ADJUSTED CAPITAL RATIO 1	RATIO 2
GA FARM BUREAU MEMBER HLTH	GA	U		--	--	--	--	--	--
GARDEN STATE LIFE INS CO	TX	A	2q 2020	147.1	22.1	0.0	91.6	9.89	8.90
GATEWAY HEALTH PLAN INC	PA	• B-	2q 2020	1,034.9	2,369.6	2,369.6	452.1	2.82	2.35
▼ GATEWAY HEALTH PLAN OF OHIO INC	OH	• C-	2q 2020	11.9	33.0	33.0	11.3	2.41	2.01
GEISINGER HEALTH PLAN	PA	• B+	2q 2020	665.0	2,493.6	2,493.6	292.7	1.49	1.24
GEISINGER INDEMNITY INS CO	PA	• C	2q 2020	91.3	241.0	241.0	35.9	0.86	0.72
GEISINGER QUALITY OPTIONS INC	PA	• C	2q 2020	91.2	318.0	318.0	34.5	0.96	0.80
GENESIS INS CO	DE	C	2q 2020	175.3	17.4	0.1	108.6	4.87	3.59
GENWORTH LIFE & ANNUITY INS CO	VA	C-	2q 2020	21,196.9	1,179.3	42.2	1,287.1	1.44	0.90
GENWORTH LIFE INS CO	DE	• C	2q 2020	41,599.5	2,789.8	2,508.3	2,116.7	0.95	0.66
GENWORTH LIFE INS CO OF NEW YORK	NY	• C	2q 2020	7,779.4	305.9	241.5	375.0	1.99	1.00
GEORGIA ASSURANCE INC	GA	U		--	--	--	--	--	--
GERBER LIFE INS CO	NY	• B+	2q 2020	4,677.1	1,042.7	531.0	505.3	2.36	1.34
GERMANIA LIFE INS CO	TX	B-	2q 2020	101.6	10.4	0.0	10.7	1.24	1.12
GHS HEALTH MAINTENANCE ORGANIZATION	OK	• C	2q 2020	65.9	27.8	27.8	30.8	6.13	5.11
GHS INS CO	OK	• E-	2q 2020	35.7	43.2	43.2	13.9	2.16	1.80
GLOBAL HEALTH PLAN INC	CA	U		--	--	--	--	--	--
▲ GLOBALHEALTH INC	OK	• D	2q 2020	84.7	267.9	267.9	38.7	1.40	1.17
GLOBE LIFE & ACCIDENT INS CO	NE	C+	2q 2020	4,902.0	853.8	39.2	274.8	0.92	0.58
GLOBE LIFE INSURANCE CO OF NY	NY	• B	2q 2020	256.1	70.9	42.3	43.6	2.38	1.47
GOLDEN RULE INS CO	IN	• B	2q 2020	716.8	1,492.2	1,468.0	352.3	1.74	1.38
▲ GOLDEN SECURITY INS CO	TN	• B+	2q 2020	69.3	73.1	73.1	48.1	1.54	1.29
GOLDEN STATE MEDICARE HEALTH PLAN	CA	• E-	2q 2020	16.0	58.6	58.6	2.4	0.31	0.19
GOOD HEALTH HMO INC	MO	• B-	2q 2020	81.8	148.5	148.5	59.1	4.36	3.63
GOOD SAMARITAN INS PLAN OF ND	ND	• D	3q 2019	2.0	1.2	1.2	1.1	1.41	1.18
GOOD SAMARITAN INS PLAN OF NE	NE	• D	3q 2019	4.2	3.1	3.1	1.0	1.30	1.08
GOOD SAMARITAN INS PLAN OF SD	SD	• E+	3q 2019	2.8	1.6	1.6	0.6	0.79	0.66
GOVERNMENT EMPLOYEES INS CO	MD	B	2q 2020	37,374.8	6,565.4	0.0	23,915.9	4.01	2.50
GOVERNMENT PERSONNEL MUTUAL L I C	TX	• B-	2q 2020	810.2	88.6	24.4	103.7	1.76	1.17
GPM HEALTH & LIFE INS CO	WA	B	2q 2020	145.1	62.3	59.1	20.7	2.31	1.89
GRANGE LIFE INS CO	OH	C+	2q 2020	456.3	92.7	0.1	40.3	2.09	1.22
GRANITE STATE HEALTH PLAN INC	NH	• C	2q 2020	93.7	410.3	410.3	31.0	0.92	0.77
GREAT AMERICAN INS CO	OH	B	2q 2020	8,900.0	2,443.2	53.8	2,206.8	1.86	1.35
GREAT AMERICAN LIFE INS CO	OH	B-	2q 2020	40,534.3	4,823.6	6.1	3,004.5	1.78	0.99
GREAT AMERICAN SPIRIT INS CO	OH	C	2q 2020	17.9	82.5	0.6	17.9	172.10	86.05
GREAT CENTRAL LIFE INS CO	LA	C+	4q 2019	27.0	1.7	0.1	10.4	1.63	1.08
GREAT MIDWEST INS CO	TX	• B-	2q 2020	186.6	144.4	110.2	117.6	3.12	2.31
GREAT NORTHERN INS CO	IN	B	2q 2020	581.7	1,323.8	0.8	400.2	42.80	35.68
GREAT PLAINS CASUALTY INC	IA	C	2q 2020	29.6	5.0	0.0	25.8	5.91	3.46
▼ GREAT SOUTHERN LIFE INS CO	TX	B-	2q 2020	202.4	53.1	6.4	48.7	5.35	3.21
GREAT-WEST LIFE & ANNUITY INS CO	CO	B-	2q 2020	50,134.3	4,868.3	62.1	1,335.7	1.75	0.95
GREAT-WEST LIFE & ANNUITY INS OF NY	NY	B-	2q 2020	1,688.9	303.0	0.0	115.4	4.21	2.20
GREATER GEORGIA LIFE INS CO	GA	B	2q 2020	70.9	47.3	21.2	20.7	1.08	0.80
GREENHOUSE LIFE INSURANCE CO	AZ	U		--	--	--	--	--	--
GREENVILLE CASUALTY INS CO INC	SC	C	2q 2020	11.1	8.8	1.3	8.0	2.79	2.58
GREENWICH INS CO	DE	C-	2q 2020	1,674.1	817.8	84.9	514.8	1.72	1.38
GROUP HEALTH COOP OF EAU CLAIRE	WI	• E+	2q 2020	65.7	148.5	148.5	30.9	2.09	1.74
GROUP HEALTH COOP OF S CENTRAL WI	WI	• C	2q 2020	89.5	408.1	408.1	40.1	1.13	0.94
GROUP HEALTH INCORPORATED	NY	• D+	2q 2020	648.0	773.9	773.9	243.6	1.86	1.55
GROUP HEALTH PLAN INC	MN	• E+	2q 2020	938.7	1,182.7	1,182.7	216.1	2.50	2.09
GROUP HOSP & MEDICAL SERVICES INC	DC	• B+	2q 2020	3,122.9	3,488.7	3,488.7	1,534.6	6.66	5.55
GUARANTEE TRUST LIFE INS CO	IL	• B	2q 2020	705.2	263.6	248.1	115.5	2.38	1.52

Arrows denote recent upgrades ▲ or downgrades▼

34

www.weissratings.com
• Bullets denote a more detailed analysis is available in Section II.

INSURANCE COMPANY NAME	DOM. STATE	RATING	DATA DATE	TOTAL ASSETS ($MIL)	TOTAL PREMIUMS ($MIL)	HEALTH PREMIUMS ($MIL)	CAPITAL & SURPLUS ($MIL)	RISK ADJUSTED CAPITAL RATIO 1	RATIO 2
GUARANTY ASSURANCE CO	LA	● E+	3q 2019	2.7	7.8	7.8	1.5	1.47	1.23
GUARANTY INCOME LIFE INS CO	IA	B	2q 2020	2,147.4	537.0	3.5	482.8	1.12	0.95
GUARDIAN INS CO	VI	C-	2q 2020	42.0	37.3	0.0	14.5	1.66	1.27
GUARDIAN LIFE INS CO OF AMERICA	NY	● A	2q 2020	65,189.0	8,624.0	3,454.6	8,085.2	2.82	1.81
GUGGENHEIM LIFE & ANNUITY CO	DE	B-	2q 2020	13,935.2	911.9	0.0	682.9	1.80	0.95
GULF GUARANTY LIFE INS CO	MS	C+	4q 2019	23.9	16.9	13.7	13.4	1.53	1.17
HALLMARK LIFE INSURANCE CO	AZ	● D	3q 2019	317.1	658.4	658.4	168.9	2.86	2.38
HAMASPIK INC	NY	U		--	--	--	--	--	--
▼ HAP EMPOWERED HEALTH PLAN INC	MI	● D+	2q 2020	70.0	142.0	142.0	22.8	1.89	1.58
HARKEN HEALTH INS CO	WI	● C+	2q 2020	111.8	58.1	58.1	81.7	10.41	8.68
HARLEYSVILLE LIFE INS CO	OH	B	2q 2020	404.2	30.0	0.0	56.1	3.58	1.88
HARMONY HEALTH PLAN INC	IL	● C-	2q 2020	422.6	1,007.0	1,007.0	148.2	2.68	2.23
HARTFORD FIRE INS CO	CT	B-	2q 2020	23,914.5	1,950.7	8.5	10,745.8	1.95	1.71
HARTFORD LIFE & ACCIDENT INS CO	CT	● B-	2q 2020	12,748.7	3,912.1	2,368.2	2,686.8	4.23	2.67
▲ HARVARD PILGRIM HC OF NEW ENGLAND	MA	● B	2q 2020	171.2	508.5	508.5	69.0	2.02	1.68
HARVESTPLAINS HEALTH OF IOWA	IA	U		--	--	--	--	--	--
HAWAII MANAGEMENT ALLIANCE ASSOC	HI	● C	2q 2020	56.1	169.3	169.3	27.6	1.21	1.01
HAWAII MEDICAL SERVICE ASSOCIATION	HI	● B	2q 2020	1,651.0	3,507.4	3,507.4	633.0	2.73	2.27
HCC LIFE INS CO	IN	● B	2q 2020	1,279.2	1,444.2	1,442.1	643.2	3.91	2.97
HCSC INS SERVICES CO	IL	● E-	2q 2020	1,063.8	460.2	460.2	166.3	2.56	2.13
HEALTH ALLIANCE CONNECT INC	IL	● B-	2q 2020	70.9	252.5	252.5	35.1	1.91	1.59
HEALTH ALLIANCE MEDICAL PLANS	IL	● B-	2q 2020	569.2	1,199.1	1,199.1	256.2	3.01	2.51
HEALTH ALLIANCE NORTHWEST HEALTH PL	WA	● B	2q 2020	23.8	99.1	99.1	17.1	2.13	1.78
HEALTH ALLIANCE PLAN OF MICHIGAN	MI	● C-	2q 2020	616.7	1,495.7	1,495.7	349.1	2.50	2.08
HEALTH ALLIANCE-MIDWEST INC	IL	● C	2q 2020	10.7	0.1	0.1	3.3	11.67	9.72
HEALTH CARE SVC CORP A MUT LEG RES	IL	● B+	2q 2020	33,429.9	38,553.6	38,553.6	20,200.9	8.03	6.69
HEALTH COLORADO INC	CO	● D-	2q 2020	22.0	96.5	96.5	4.9	N/A	N/A
HEALTH FIRST COMM PLANS INC	FL	● A-	2q 2020	104.0	237.4	237.4	58.1	2.53	2.11
HEALTH FIRST HEALTH PLANS INC	FL	● B	2q 2020	171.9	443.9	443.9	113.0	3.01	2.51
HEALTH FIRST INS INC	FL	● C+	2q 2020	5.1	0.1	0.1	5.0	2.70	2.25
HEALTH INS CO OF AM INC	NY	U		--	--	--	--	--	--
HEALTH INSURANCE PLAN OF GREATER NY	NY	● D+	2q 2020	1,390.9	5,029.6	5,029.6	364.4	0.63	0.52
HEALTH NET COMMUNITY SOLUTIONS INC	CA	● B	2q 2020	2,783.8	6,876.7	6,876.7	1,388.3	3.03	2.04
HEALTH NET COMMUNITY SOLUTIONS OF AR	AZ	● C	3q 2019	18.3	32.0	32.0	8.9	3.99	3.33
HEALTH NET HEALTH PLAN OF OREGON INC	OR	● D	2q 2020	135.0	487.0	487.0	54.4	1.05	0.88
HEALTH NET LIFE INS CO	CA	● C	2q 2020	624.8	1,389.0	1,388.0	395.5	3.39	2.68
HEALTH NET OF ARIZONA INC	AZ	● C+	2q 2020	343.0	670.2	670.2	137.6	9.89	8.24
HEALTH NET OF CALIFORNIA INC	CA	● B-	2q 2020	3,055.3	9,568.8	9,568.8	1,530.2	2.50	1.68
HEALTH NEW ENGLAND INC	MA	● B	2q 2020	243.2	729.1	729.1	109.8	1.51	1.26
HEALTH OPTIONS INC	FL	● A-	2q 2020	2,831.6	5,713.9	5,713.9	1,519.6	5.26	4.39
HEALTH PARTNERS PLANS INC	PA	● B	2q 2020	621.7	1,775.1	1,775.1	180.3	1.42	1.18
HEALTH PLAN OF CAREOREGON INC	OR	● C	2q 2020	83.7	185.1	185.1	44.0	2.32	1.94
HEALTH PLAN OF NEVADA INC	NV	● B+	2q 2020	754.1	2,045.0	2,045.0	395.8	3.06	2.55
▲ HEALTH PLAN OF WV INC	WV	● C	2q 2020	288.0	625.3	625.3	153.6	1.92	1.60
HEALTH POINTE OF NEW YORK LLC	NY	U		--	--	--	--	--	--
HEALTH SHARE OF OREGON	OR	U		--	--	--	--	--	--
HEALTH TRADITION HEALTH PLAN	WI	● C-	2q 2020	12.3	20.6	20.6	8.2	2.42	2.02
HEALTHASSURANCE PENNSYLVANIA INC	PA	● B-	2q 2020	292.3	765.9	765.9	137.9	2.48	2.07
HEALTHFIRST HEALTH PLAN INC	NY	● B+	2q 2020	961.8	3,031.3	3,031.3	379.7	1.57	1.31
HEALTHFIRST HEALTH PLAN NEW JERSEY	NJ	U		--	--	--	--	--	--
HEALTHFIRST INSURANCE CO	NY	● C+	3q 2019	41.7	34.2	34.2	14.8	3.63	3.03
HEALTHKEEPERS INC	VA	● B-	2q 2020	2,105.3	5,161.1	5,161.1	879.5	2.74	2.29

Arrows denote recent upgrades ▲ or downgrades▼   ● Bullets denote a more detailed analysis is available in Section II.

INSURANCE COMPANY NAME	DOM. STATE	RATING	DATA DATE	TOTAL ASSETS ($MIL)	TOTAL PREMIUMS ($MIL)	HEALTH PREMIUMS ($MIL)	CAPITAL & SURPLUS ($MIL)	RISK ADJUSTED CAPITAL RATIO 1	RATIO 2
HEALTHLINK HMO INC	MO	U	--	--	--	--	--	--	--
▲ HEALTHNOW NY INC	NY	● A	2q 2020	1,348.6	2,825.9	2,825.9	676.1	3.81	3.17
HEALTHPARTNERS	MN	● B	2q 2020	1,590.2	2,131.1	2,131.1	988.2	3.59	2.99
HEALTHPARTNERS INS CO	MN	● B+	2q 2020	475.5	1,085.0	1,085.0	238.3	2.25	1.87
HEALTHPARTNERS UNITYPOINT HLTH	IA	● D+	3q 2019	31.2	33.3	33.3	12.9	2.68	2.23
HEALTHPLEX OF NJ INC	NJ	U		--	--	--	--	--	--
HEALTHPLUS INS CO TRUST	MI	U		--	--	--	--	--	--
HEALTHSPAN INC	OH	U		--	--	--	--	--	--
HEALTHSPAN INTEGRATED CARE	OH	U		--	--	--	--	--	--
HEALTHSPRING L&H INS CO	TX	● B-	2q 2020	1,363.0	4,479.9	4,479.9	678.2	2.46	2.05
▲ HEALTHSPRING OF FLORIDA INC	FL	● B+	2q 2020	184.2	860.4	860.4	91.7	1.56	1.30
HEALTHSUN HEALTH PLANS INC	FL	● B+	2q 2020	299.0	1,091.2	1,091.2	146.1	2.59	2.16
HEALTHY ALLIANCE LIFE INS CO	MO	● B	2q 2020	1,098.8	2,271.2	2,271.2	462.3	2.95	2.46
HEARTLAND NATIONAL LIFE INS CO	IN	C	2q 2020	11.3	25.9	25.8	5.7	1.97	1.77
HEARTLANDPLAINS HEALTH	NE	U		--	--	--	--	--	--
HENNEPIN HEALTH	MN	● C+	2q 2020	68.1	213.8	213.8	35.7	1.52	1.27
HERITAGE PROVIDER NETWORK INC	CA	● D+	2q 2020	606.6	3,082.2	3,082.2	162.8	0.69	0.42
▲ HIGHMARK BCBSD INC	DE	● B+	2q 2020	745.7	757.3	757.3	413.9	7.55	6.29
HIGHMARK BENEFITS GROUP INC	PA	U		--	--	--	--	--	--
HIGHMARK CASUALTY INS CO	PA	● C	2q 2020	341.4	0.4	0.4	193.4	4.95	2.82
HIGHMARK CHOICE CO	PA	U		--	--	--	--	--	--
HIGHMARK COVERAGE ADVANTAGE INC	PA	U		--	--	--	--	--	--
▲ HIGHMARK INC	PA	● B	2q 2020	7,956.2	8,223.3	8,223.3	4,126.8	4.60	3.83
HIGHMARK SELECT RESOURCES INC	PA	U		--	--	--	--	--	--
HIGHMARK SENIOR HEALTH CO	PA	U		--	--	--	--	--	--
HIGHMARK SENIOR SOLUTIONS CO	WV	U		--	--	--	--	--	--
HIGHMARK WEST VIRGINIA INC	WV	● B	2q 2020	1,165.1	1,201.5	1,201.5	607.0	7.16	5.97
HILLTOP SPECIALTY INSURANCE CO	NY	D+	2q 2020	409.6	237.0	3.3	215.4	2.77	2.41
HM HEALTH INS CO	PA	U		--	--	--	--	--	--
HM LIFE INS CO	PA	● B	2q 2020	789.0	856.0	856.0	445.7	4.88	3.21
HM LIFE INS CO OF NEW YORK	NY	● B-	2q 2020	66.2	67.4	67.4	43.6	5.24	3.59
HMO COLORADO	CO	● B+	2q 2020	442.7	890.6	890.6	197.3	3.16	2.64
HMO LOUISIANA INC	LA	● A+	2q 2020	862.1	1,083.6	1,083.6	445.3	4.45	3.71
HMO MINNESOTA	MN	● B	2q 2020	1,153.1	2,315.7	2,315.7	639.1	3.80	3.16
HMO MISSOURI INC	MO	● C	2q 2020	73.1	106.3	106.3	28.7	3.61	3.01
HMO OF NORTHEASTERN PENNSYLVANIA INC	PA	U		--	--	--	--	--	--
HMO PARTNERS INC	AR	● A+	2q 2020	129.5	211.9	211.9	69.8	3.19	2.66
HN1 THERAPY NETWORK NEW JERSEY LLC	NJ	● C+	4q 2019	2.7	2.7	2.7	2.5	0.89	0.74
▼ HNE INS CO	MA	● B-	2q 2020	5.4	1.8	1.8	4.6	15.37	12.81
HNE OF CONNECTICUT INC	CT	U		--	--	--	--	--	--
HOME STATE HEALTH PLAN INC	MO	● C-	2q 2020	226.3	787.7	787.7	96.5	1.78	1.48
HOMELAND INS CO OF NY	NY	C	2q 2020	84.3	168.3	2.4	72.1	27.01	24.31
HOMETOWN HEALTH PLAN INC	NV	● D	2q 2020	108.3	248.1	248.1	59.8	2.13	1.78
▲ HOMETOWN HEALTH PROVIDERS INS CO	NV	● B-	2q 2020	85.6	184.2	184.2	43.5	2.12	1.77
▲ HOOSIER MOTOR MUTUAL INS CO	IN	● B	2q 2020	11.7	0.6	0.6	11.4	8.43	7.03
▼ HOPKINS HEALTH ADV INC	MD	● E	2q 2020	76.5	230.3	230.3	11.4	0.36	0.30
HORACE MANN INS CO	IL	B	2q 2020	517.5	249.3	0.0	175.0	2.86	1.93
HORACE MANN LIFE INS CO	IL	B	1q 2020	7,014.6	583.0	2.5	343.6	1.64	0.84
HORIZON HEALTHCARE OF NEW JERSEY INC	NJ	● C+	2q 2020	1,656.2	546.2	546.2	1,103.8	31.19	25.99
HORIZON HEALTHCARE SERVICES INC	NJ	● B	4q 2019	5,684.9	11,547.6	11,547.6	2,732.7	3.71	3.10
HORIZON INS CO	NJ	● C+	4q 2019	98.8	71.9	71.9	39.4	7.54	6.29
HOUSTON CASUALTY CO	TX	B-	2q 2020	3,802.2	599.6	23.8	1,897.0	1.37	1.20

Arrows denote recent upgrades ▲ or downgrades▼   www.weissratings.com

● Bullets denote a more detailed analysis is available in Section II.

INSURANCE COMPANY NAME	DOM. STATE	RATING	DATA DATE	TOTAL ASSETS ($MIL)	TOTAL PREMIUMS ($MIL)	HEALTH PREMIUMS ($MIL)	CAPITAL & SURPLUS ($MIL)	RISK ADJUSTED CAPITAL RATIO 1	RATIO 2
▲ HPHC INS CO	MA	• C	2q 2020	296.3	689.9	689.9	128.3	2.36	1.97
HUDSON INS CO	DE	C	2q 2020	1,571.1	1,278.4	3.4	457.1	1.93	1.66
HUMANA BENEFIT PLAN OF ILLINOIS	IL	• B+	2q 2020	1,104.8	2,581.5	2,581.5	505.1	3.24	2.70
HUMANA BENEFIT PLAN OF SC INC	SC	U		--	--	--	--	--	--
HUMANA EAP & WORK-LIFE SVCS	CA	• C-	2q 2020	2.6	0.3	0.3	2.5	194.60	194.51
HUMANA EMPLOYERS HEALTH PLAN OF GA	GA	• C	2q 2020	541.8	1,486.5	1,486.5	253.2	2.29	1.91
▲ HUMANA HEALTH BENEFIT PLAN LA	LA	• B	2q 2020	715.9	2,250.7	2,250.7	317.9	2.21	1.84
▼ HUMANA HEALTH CO OF NEW YORK INC	NY	• C-	2q 2020	184.9	315.7	315.7	59.2	1.87	1.56
HUMANA HEALTH INS CO OF FL INC	FL	• C-	2q 2020	104.5	93.0	93.0	63.1	2.58	2.15
▼ HUMANA HEALTH PLAN INC	KY	• D	2q 2020	701.8	1,124.0	1,124.0	257.0	3.36	2.80
HUMANA HEALTH PLAN OF CA INC	CA	• B-	2q 2020	31.7	57.5	57.5	13.2	2.71	2.25
HUMANA HEALTH PLAN OF CALIFORNIA INC	CA	U		--	--	--	--	--	--
HUMANA HEALTH PLAN OF OHIO INC	OH	• C	2q 2020	85.5	209.9	209.9	42.9	1.94	1.62
HUMANA HEALTH PLAN OF TEXAS INC	TX	• C	2q 2020	212.8	673.9	673.9	96.7	1.80	1.50
HUMANA HEALTH PLANS OF PUERTO RICO	PR	• E-	2q 2020	171.2	382.1	382.1	35.1	0.98	0.81
▲ HUMANA INS CO (WI)	WI	• A	2q 2020	10,594.3	26,445.9	26,445.9	4,705.3	2.73	2.28
HUMANA INS CO OF KENTUCKY	KY	• B-	2q 2020	213.7	161.7	148.9	156.1	3.19	2.48
HUMANA INS CO OF NY	NY	• B	2q 2020	234.1	371.9	371.9	112.4	3.80	3.17
HUMANA INS CO OF PUERTO RICO INC	PR	• C+	3q 2019	76.2	133.2	132.7	44.7	1.90	1.46
HUMANA MEDICAL PLAN INC	FL	• A-	2q 2020	3,307.4	10,549.7	10,549.7	1,056.8	2.47	2.06
HUMANA MEDICAL PLAN OF MICHIGAN INC	MI	• B-	2q 2020	84.0	153.0	153.0	34.0	2.47	2.06
HUMANA MEDICAL PLAN OF PENNSYLVANIA	PA	• B-	2q 2020	9.5	3.6	3.6	8.0	3.14	2.61
▼ HUMANA MEDICAL PLAN OF UTAH INC	UT	• D+	2q 2020	11.7	26.4	26.4	5.4	1.58	1.31
HUMANA REGIONAL HEALTH PLAN INC	AR	• C-	2q 2020	49.4	137.0	137.0	14.8	1.08	0.90
HUMANA WISCONSIN HEALTH ORGANIZATION	WI	• B+	2q 2020	1,259.4	3,362.9	3,362.9	417.9	2.23	1.86
▲ HUMANADENTAL INS CO	WI	• C+	2q 2020	216.5	384.3	384.3	102.8	3.51	2.92
IA AMERICAN LIFE INS CO	TX	C	2q 2020	165.7	29.9	0.3	58.2	0.85	0.80
IDEALIFE INS CO	CT	B-	2q 2020	22.8	1.3	0.5	14.6	3.76	3.39
IL BLUE CROSS BLUE SHIELD	IL	U		--	--	--	--	--	--
ILLINICARE HEALTH PLAN INC	IL	• C	2q 2020	688.0	2,319.1	2,319.1	163.7	0.90	0.75
ILLINOIS MUTUAL LIFE INS CO	IL	• B+	1q 2020	1,520.9	115.7	56.0	240.6	3.37	1.83
ILLINOIS UNION INS CO	IL	C	2q 2020	448.8	671.7	0.4	139.6	12.83	11.54
IMPERIAL HEALTH PLAN OF CALIFORNIA	CA	• D	2q 2020	30.4	62.8	62.8	5.0	0.71	0.44
IMPERIAL INSURANCE COS INC	TX	U		--	--	--	--	--	--
IN UNIVERSITY HLTH PLANS INS	IN	U		--	--	--	--	--	--
INDEMNITY INS CO OF NORTH AMERICA	PA	C	2q 2020	266.0	1,256.6	1.1	159.9	17.70	15.93
INDEPENDENCE AMERICAN INS CO	DE	• B-	2q 2020	146.8	156.5	105.3	88.7	2.23	1.64
INDEPENDENCE ASSURANCE CO	PA	U		--	--	--	--	--	--
INDEPENDENCE BLUE CROSS	PA	• C	2q 2020	281.8	356.2	356.2	40.4	2.13	1.77
INDEPENDENT CARE HEALTH PLAN	WI	• A-	2q 2020	107.2	305.7	305.7	45.3	1.86	1.55
▲ INDEPENDENT HEALTH ASSOC INC	NY	• B+	2q 2020	761.8	1,444.0	1,444.0	499.0	4.40	3.66
▲ INDEPENDENT HEALTH BENEFITS CORP	NY	• B	2q 2020	326.8	539.1	539.1	119.5	2.57	2.14
INDIANA UNIVERSITY HEALTH PLANS INC	IN	• E-	3q 2019	18.0	39.3	39.3	6.1	2.05	1.71
INDIANA UNIVERSITY HEALTH PLANS NFP	IN	• D	3q 2019	38.9	157.1	157.1	14.7	1.08	0.90
INDIVIDUAL ASR CO LIFE HEALTH & ACC	OK	D+	2q 2020	19.4	87.7	74.2	8.1	1.44	1.24
INLAND EMPIRE HEALTH PLAN	CA	• A	2q 2020	1,685.2	5,578.2	5,578.2	977.4	3.26	2.09
▲ INNOVATION HEALTH INS CO	VA	• C	2q 2020	152.1	162.8	162.8	118.3	5.32	4.44
INNOVATION HEALTH PLAN INC	VA	• C-	2q 2020	56.2	102.1	102.1	30.7	2.75	2.29
INS CO OF NORTH AMERICA	PA	• C	2q 2020	279.5	167.5	60.0	267.0	67.26	24.60
INS CO OF SCOTT & WHITE	TX	• D+	2q 2020	47.0	72.7	72.7	31.0	3.62	3.02
INS CO OF THE SOUTH	GA	C-	2q 2020	76.1	110.8	0.3	19.3	0.92	0.62
INS CO OF THE STATE OF PA	IL	C-	2q 2020	123.2	628.3	7.7	43.0	5.30	4.77

Arrows denote recent upgrades ▲ or downgrades▼   • Bullets denote a more detailed analysis is available in Section II.

INSURANCE COMPANY NAME	DOM. STATE	RATING	DATA DATE	TOTAL ASSETS ($MIL)	TOTAL PREMIUMS ($MIL)	HEALTH PREMIUMS ($MIL)	CAPITAL & SURPLUS ($MIL)	RISK ADJUSTED CAPITAL RATIO 1	RATIO 2
INSTIL HEALTH INS CO	SC	U		--	--	--	--	--	--
INSUREMAX INS CO	NE	D	2q 2020	21.2	15.4	0.2	3.9	1.04	0.86
INTEGON INDEMNITY CORP	NC	C	2q 2020	254.4	542.4	68.3	35.6	1.14	1.05
INTEGON NATIONAL INS CO	NC	B-	2q 2020	4,636.8	1,342.2	22.5	1,311.9	2.38	1.78
INTEGRAND ASR CO	PR	F	1q 2019	94.2	62.3	1.0	28.6	0.67	0.43
INTER-COUNTY HOSPITALIZATION PLAN	PA	U		--	--	--	--	--	--
INTERCOMMUNITY HLTH PLANS INC	OR	U		--	--	--	--	--	--
INTERVALLEY HEALTH PLAN	CA	• D+	2q 2020	36.5	282.8	282.8	18.5	0.70	0.44
INTRAMERICA LIFE INS CO	NY	B	2q 2020	34.2	0.2	0.0	10.6	2.15	1.93
INVESTORS HERITAGE LIFE INS CO	KY	C-	2q 2020	876.4	275.3	3.6	58.2	1.73	0.85
INVESTORS LIFE INS CO NORTH AMERICA	TX	B	2q 2020	516.2	15.7	0.0	25.6	2.03	1.05
IRONSHORE INDEMNITY INC	MN	• B-	2q 2020	224.1	322.0	107.6	99.7	11.02	9.92
ISLAND HOME INS CO	GU	C-	2q 2020	25.9	38.4	36.9	13.1	2.54	1.38
ISNP VENTURES LLC	MD	U		--	--	--	--	--	--
JACKSON COUNTY CCO LLC	OR	U		--	--	--	--	--	--
JACKSON NATIONAL LIFE INS CO	MI	B	2q 2020	253,984.0	19,422.5	40.1	7,849.2	2.84	1.55
JEFFERSON INS CO	NY	C-	2q 2020	511.5	830.0	29.2	364.6	2.93	2.55
JEFFERSON LIFE INS CO	TX	D	2q 2020	9.1	0.5	0.2	1.7	0.78	0.60
JEFFERSON NATIONAL LIFE INS CO	TX	C	2q 2020	7,619.8	1,040.9	1.4	67.3	1.08	0.73
JOHN ALDEN LIFE INS CO	WI	B-	2q 2020	189.6	16.2	9.3	19.1	4.59	4.13
JOHN HANCOCK LIFE & HEALTH INS CO	MA	• C	2q 2020	17,892.6	730.8	724.3	1,215.3	4.31	2.32
JOHN HANCOCK LIFE INS CO (USA)	MI	B-	2q 2020	254,625.0	20,649.2	1,472.5	9,585.5	1.83	1.15
JOHN HANCOCK LIFE INS CO OF NY	NY	B	2q 2020	18,484.3	1,112.5	2.2	1,474.9	4.21	2.18
JUNTOS HEALTH PLAN INC	TX	U		--	--	--	--	--	--
JUSTIFY HOLDINGS INC	KY	U		--	--	--	--	--	--
K S PLAN ADMINISTRATORS LLC	TX	• B	2q 2020	128.5	433.1	433.1	71.6	1.94	1.62
▼ KAISER FNDTN HLTH PLAN OF WA	WA	• C+	2q 2020	1,663.4	3,026.7	3,026.7	697.6	2.63	2.19
▼ KAISER FNDTN HLTH PLAN WA OPTN	WA	• C	2q 2020	347.1	945.7	945.7	98.8	1.45	1.21
KAISER FOUNDATION HEALTH PLAN INC	CA	• A+	2q 2020	82,017.8	79,932.4	79,932.4	38,683.7	4.34	3.10
KAISER FOUNDATION HP INC HI	HI	• C	2q 2020	916.8	1,648.4	1,648.4	248.8	3.55	2.96
KAISER FOUNDATION HP MID-ATL STATES	MD	• C	2q 2020	1,938.5	4,546.3	4,546.3	695.6	1.86	1.55
KAISER FOUNDATION HP NORTHWEST	OR	• B	2q 2020	1,223.0	4,307.7	4,307.7	578.4	3.44	2.87
KAISER FOUNDATION HP OF CO	CO	• B-	2q 2020	1,656.8	4,032.9	4,032.9	841.4	5.32	4.44
KAISER FOUNDATION HP OF GA	GA	• C	2q 2020	744.5	1,928.7	1,928.7	235.0	1.27	1.06
KAISER PERMANENTE INS CO	CA	• A	2q 2020	220.6	150.4	150.4	125.1	7.52	6.26
KANSAS CITY LIFE INS CO	MO	B	2q 2020	3,384.5	314.0	59.4	274.5	1.52	0.93
KANSAS SUPERIOR SELECT INC	KS	• D+	3q 2019	2.9	3.3	3.3	1.2	0.90	0.75
KELSEYCARE ADMINISTRATORS LLC	TX	U		--	--	--	--	--	--
KENTUCKY HOME LIFE INS CO	KY	C-	2q 2020	5.2	2.2	0.6	3.3	3.02	2.72
KENTUCKY SPIRIT HEALTH PLAN INC	KY	U		--	--	--	--	--	--
KERN HEALTH SYSTEMS	CA	• B+	2q 2020	699.5	767.4	767.4	221.7	4.46	2.74
KEYSTONE HEALTH PLAN CENTRAL INC	PA	• D	2q 2020	86.7	260.7	260.7	38.2	1.50	1.25
KEYSTONE HEALTH PLAN EAST INC	PA	• B+	2q 2020	1,526.3	3,143.3	3,143.3	580.5	2.97	2.47
KILPATRICK LIFE INS CO	LA	D-	2q 2020	232.4	14.9	0.2	14.1	1.50	1.04
LA HEALTH SERVICE & INDEMNITY CO	LA	• B	2q 2020	2,367.0	2,381.0	2,381.0	1,543.2	5.46	4.55
LAFAYETTE LIFE INS CO	OH	B	2q 2020	5,780.5	614.7	0.3	345.0	1.67	0.82
LANDCAR LIFE INS CO	UT	U		--	--	--	--	--	--
LASSO HEALTHCARE INSURANCE CO	TX	U		--	--	--	--	--	--
LEADERS LIFE INS CO	OK	B	2q 2020	8.2	12.3	0.8	3.9	1.84	1.65
LEGAL SERVICE PLANS OF VIRGINIA INC	VA	• C+	3q 2019	1.2	9.5	9.5	0.3	0.61	0.51
LEON HEALTH PLANS INC	FL	U		--	--	--	--	--	--
LIBERTY ADVANTAGE LLC	NC	• D	3q 2019	7.3	15.4	15.4	3.2	1.24	1.03

Arrows denote recent upgrades ▲ or downgrades▼   • Bullets denote a more detailed analysis is available in Section II.

INSURANCE COMPANY NAME	DOM. STATE	RATING	DATA DATE	TOTAL ASSETS ($MIL)	TOTAL PREMIUMS ($MIL)	HEALTH PREMIUMS ($MIL)	CAPITAL & SURPLUS ($MIL)	RISK ADJUSTED CAPITAL RATIO 1	RATIO 2
LIBERTY BANKERS LIFE INS CO	OK	C+	2q 2020	2,033.0	465.2	14.2	233.7	1.23	0.83
LIBERTY INS UNDERWRITERS INC	IL	C	2q 2020	225.8	3,589.7	120.7	129.9	14.73	13.26
LIBERTY MUTUAL INS CO	MA	B-	2q 2020	53,653.5	2,323.1	14.0	16,634.0	1.04	0.95
LIBERTY NATIONAL LIFE INS CO	NE	B	2q 2020	8,230.3	580.3	144.7	515.6	1.72	0.91
LIBERTY UNION LIFE ASR CO	MI	• C+	2q 2020	14.9	17.0	17.0	8.5	9.97	8.31
LIFE ASSURANCE CO INC	OK	C-	1q 2020	4.5	1.3	0.2	3.0	2.21	1.99
LIFE INS CO OF ALABAMA	AL	• C+	2q 2020	128.3	38.3	30.2	40.0	3.37	2.19
LIFE INS CO OF BOSTON & NEW YORK	NY	• A-	2q 2020	175.9	29.2	9.8	35.4	3.67	2.12
LIFE INS CO OF LOUISIANA	LA	D	4q 2019	10.8	0.3	0.0	4.6	2.25	1.55
LIFE INS CO OF NORTH AMERICA	PA	• B	2q 2020	9,027.0	3,875.9	2,370.8	2,155.9	2.90	1.89
LIFE INS CO OF THE SOUTHWEST	TX	B	2q 2020	23,392.3	2,995.9	0.0	1,353.1	1.97	0.97
LIFE OF AMERICA INS CO	TX	C	4q 2019	8.7	0.0	0.0	2.5	0.77	0.59
LIFE OF THE SOUTH INS CO	GA	• C	2q 2020	132.5	157.2	100.5	27.1	0.86	0.68
LIFEMAP ASR CO	OR	• B-	2q 2020	104.4	88.5	56.0	55.8	2.38	1.71
LIFESECURE INS CO	MI	• C-	2q 2020	494.3	62.0	57.0	49.6	2.45	1.55
LIFESHIELD NATIONAL INS CO	OK	C+	2q 2020	84.1	101.2	90.8	20.4	0.98	0.79
LIFEWISE ASR CO	WA	• A	4q 2019	249.5	176.1	176.1	178.2	7.47	5.52
LIFEWISE HEALTH PLAN OF OREGON	OR	U	--	--	--	--	--	--	--
LIFEWISE HEALTH PLAN OF WASHINGTON	WA	• B	2q 2020	166.7	121.0	121.0	98.6	10.13	8.44
LIFEWORKS ADVANTAGE, LLC	VA	• D+	3q 2019	5.3	17.8	17.8	2.1	0.64	0.53
LINCOLN BENEFIT LIFE CO	NE	C+	2q 2020	9,648.2	1,256.9	56.8	373.9	1.27	0.65
LINCOLN HERITAGE LIFE INS CO	IL	B-	2q 2020	1,123.2	578.4	2.5	95.4	2.18	1.18
LINCOLN LIFE & ANNUITY CO OF NY	NY	B	2q 2020	15,595.0	1,168.4	61.4	1,102.9	4.17	2.13
LINCOLN LIFE ASSR CO OF BOSTON	NH	• C+	2q 2020	4,396.3	2,436.4	1,370.4	316.8	2.50	1.14
LINCOLN NATIONAL LIFE INS CO	IN	B	2q 2020	269,889.0	27,581.2	1,350.2	8,155.4	1.11	0.81
LOCAL INITIATIVE HEALTH AUTH LA	CA	• C	2q 2020	4,319.6	8,095.8	8,095.8	1,035.6	3.22	1.97
LONGEVITY HLTH PLAN IL INC	IL	U		--	--	--	--	--	--
LONGEVITY HLTH PLAN MI INC	MI	U		--	--	--	--	--	--
LONGEVITY HLTH PLAN NEW JERSEY	NJ	U		--	--	--	--	--	--
LONGEVITY HLTH PLAN NY INC	NY	U		--	--	--	--	--	--
LONGEVITY HLTH PLAN OF CO INC	CO	U		--	--	--	--	--	--
LONGEVITY HLTH PLAN OF FL INC	FL	U		--	--	--	--	--	--
LONGEVITY HLTH PLAN OF NC INC	NC	U		--	--	--	--	--	--
LONGEVITY HLTH PLAN OK INC	OK	U		--	--	--	--	--	--
LOUISIANA FARM BUREAU MUTUAL INS CO	LA	B-	2q 2020	252.9	141.3	0.1	167.0	6.35	5.57
LOUISIANA HEALTHCARE CONNECTIONS INC	LA	• E+	2q 2020	559.9	2,406.6	2,406.6	178.4	1.32	1.10
LOYAL AMERICAN LIFE INS CO	OH	• B	2q 2020	395.6	306.1	298.4	159.5	1.30	1.11
LUMICO LIFE INSURANCE CO	MO	• C	2q 2020	144.8	73.1	22.4	96.7	10.48	9.43
LYNDON SOUTHERN INS CO	DE	C+	2q 2020	312.1	503.7	0.0	64.8	1.53	1.05
MA DELIVERY INNOVATIONS INC	IL	U		--	--	--	--	--	--
MADISON NATIONAL LIFE INS CO INC	WI	• C+	2q 2020	206.5	149.0	96.3	83.9	4.23	3.08
MAGELLAN BEHAVIORAL HEALTH OF NE	NE	U		--	--	--	--	--	--
MAGELLAN BEHAVIORAL HEALTH OF NJ LLC	NJ	U		--	--	--	--	--	--
MAGELLAN BEHAVIORAL HEALTH OF PA INC	PA	• B-	2q 2020	120.8	536.3	536.3	66.8	1.29	1.07
MAGELLAN COMPLETE CARE OF ARIZONA	AZ	• D+	3q 2019	26.1	5.7	5.7	6.2	2.89	2.41
MAGELLAN COMPLETE CARE OF LOUISIANA	LA	• C+	3q 2019	24.7	12.4	12.4	6.2	3.00	2.50
MAGELLAN COMPLETE CARE OF VA	VA	• D+	3q 2019	221.4	473.2	473.2	81.7	2.02	1.68
MAGELLAN LIFE INS CO	DE	• B-	2q 2020	12.0	39.6	39.6	9.9	1.31	1.09
MAGNA INS CO	MS	• D	3q 2019	5.1	12.6	12.6	2.9	0.54	0.45
MAGNOLIA GUARANTY LIFE INS CO	MS	C	2q 2020	10.6	1.6	0.0	1.4	0.62	0.56
MAGNOLIA HEALTH PLAN INC	MS	• D+	2q 2020	284.1	1,166.3	1,166.3	164.3	1.72	1.43
MAINE COMMUNITY HEALTH OPTIONS	ME	• D+	2q 2020	182.1	242.5	242.5	78.0	2.01	1.67

Arrows denote recent upgrades ▲ or downgrades▼   • Bullets denote a more detailed analysis is available in Section II.

INSURANCE COMPANY NAME	DOM. STATE	RATING	DATA DATE	TOTAL ASSETS ($MIL)	TOTAL PREMIUMS ($MIL)	HEALTH PREMIUMS ($MIL)	CAPITAL & SURPLUS ($MIL)	RISK ADJUSTED CAPITAL Ratio 1	RISK ADJUSTED CAPITAL Ratio 2
MAMSI L&H INS CO	MD	● C	2q 2020	63.4	151.8	151.8	29.6	2.11	1.76
MANHATTAN LIFE INS CO	NY	● B	2q 2020	657.2	233.8	162.5	65.7	1.50	1.03
MANHATTAN NATIONAL LIFE INS CO	OH	B-	2q 2020	140.0	13.4	0.1	9.3	1.11	1.00
MANHATTANLIFE ASSR CO OF AM	AR	● C+	2q 2020	750.4	205.9	181.5	193.4	0.98	0.86
MAPFRE PAN AMERICAN INS CO	PR	C	2q 2020	61.0	49.1	0.0	35.1	1.84	1.26
MAPFRE PRAICO INS CO	PR	B-	2q 2020	527.2	306.6	0.0	150.4	1.62	1.04
MARKEL INS CO	IL	B-	2q 2020	2,696.4	659.1	16.7	1,371.5	1.35	1.25
MARQUETTE INDEMNITY & LIFE INS CO	AZ	C	2q 2020	5.5	1.0	0.6	2.4	1.54	1.38
MARQUIS ADVANTAGE, INC.	OR	● D+	3q 2019	6.7	9.5	9.5	3.4	1.04	0.86
MARTINS POINT GENERATIONS ADVANTAGE	ME	● B	2q 2020	168.5	456.0	456.0	90.7	2.25	1.87
MARTINS POINT GENERATIONS LLC	ME	U	--	--	--	--	--	--	--
MARY WASHINGTON HEALTH PLAN	VA	U	--	--	--	--	--	--	--
MASSACHUSETTS MUTUAL LIFE INS CO	MA	B	2q 2020	298,464.0	25,378.6	761.8	23,016.3	1.82	1.30
MATTHEW THORNTON HEALTH PLAN	NH	● B	2q 2020	331.0	569.5	569.5	173.4	4.08	3.40
MCLAREN HEALTH PLAN COMMUNITY	MI	● B-	3q 2019	37.4	143.8	143.8	16.6	1.34	1.12
MCLAREN HEALTH PLAN INC	MI	● C+	2q 2020	324.0	785.6	785.6	177.6	2.33	1.94
MCNA INS CO	TX	● B-	2q 2020	358.8	694.8	694.8	126.3	1.93	1.61
MCS ADVANTAGE INC	PR	● E+	2q 2020	499.5	1,821.2	1,821.2	210.8	1.71	1.43
MD INDIVIDUAL PRACTICE ASSOC INC	MD	● C	2q 2020	89.0	246.8	246.8	56.1	9.12	7.60
MDWISE INC	IN	● B+	3q 2019	389.2	1,264.2	1,264.2	130.8	2.08	1.73
MDWISE MARKETPLACE INC	IN	U		--	--	--	--	--	--
MEDAMERICA INS CO	PA	● C	2q 2020	1,123.4	84.5	84.5	29.8	0.86	0.44
▼ MEDAMERICA INS CO OF FL	FL	C	2q 2020	65.6	4.0	4.0	6.6	0.93	0.84
▼ MEDAMERICA INS CO OF NEW YORK	NY	D+	2q 2020	1,004.8	49.6	49.6	18.9	0.52	0.30
MEDCO CONTAINMENT INS CO OF NY	NY	● C	2q 2020	84.8	127.3	127.3	40.9	2.93	2.44
▼ MEDCO CONTAINMENT LIFE INS CO	PA	● D+	2q 2020	645.6	896.8	896.8	248.7	2.44	2.03
MEDICA COMM HEALTH PLAN	WI	● C+	2q 2020	154.8	81.2	81.2	119.2	16.24	13.54
MEDICA HEALTH PLANS	MN	● C+	2q 2020	609.2	1,089.2	1,089.2	410.4	4.58	3.82
MEDICA HEALTH PLANS OF FLORIDA INC	FL	U		--	--	--	--	--	--
MEDICA HEALTHCARE PLANS INC	FL	● B	2q 2020	215.8	704.7	704.7	65.4	1.14	0.95
MEDICA INS CO	MN	● B	2q 2020	2,030.6	3,362.1	3,362.1	1,280.0	7.30	6.09
MEDICAL ASSOC CLINIC HEALTH PLAN	WI	● B-	3q 2019	4.6	26.1	26.1	3.4	1.44	1.20
▲ MEDICAL ASSOCIATES HEALTH PLAN INC	IA	● B	2q 2020	44.2	89.9	89.9	24.4	2.77	2.31
MEDICAL BENEFITS MUTUAL LIFE INS CO	OH	D+	2q 2020	14.9	0.8	0.6	10.9	2.23	1.79
MEDICAL HEALTH INS CORP OF OHIO	OH	● C	2q 2020	323.4	621.9	621.9	104.2	2.35	1.96
MEDICAL MUTUAL OF OHIO	OH	● A-	2q 2020	2,702.4	2,745.5	2,745.5	1,900.9	6.64	5.53
MEDICARE ADVANTAGE INS CO	NE	U		--	--	--	--	--	--
MEDICO CORP LIFE INS CO	NE	● B-	2q 2020	46.4	168.7	168.7	26.4	4.07	3.66
MEDICO INS CO	NE	● B-	2q 2020	57.3	135.8	134.6	34.6	5.07	4.56
MEDICO LIFE & HEALTH INS CO	IA	C	2q 2020	13.2	7.3	6.8	12.0	4.13	3.72
MEDISUN INC	AZ	● D	2q 2020	236.8	451.4	451.4	47.7	1.32	1.10
MEDMUTUAL LIFE INS CO	OH	B	2q 2020	48.1	32.3	6.8	35.1	2.49	1.91
▲ MEDSTAR FAMILY CHOICE INC	MD	● C	2q 2020	207.3	466.4	466.4	93.7	2.26	1.88
MEMBERS HEALTH INS CO	AZ	● C-	2q 2020	38.1	9.4	9.4	33.0	11.32	9.43
MEMBERS LIFE INS CO	IA	B	2q 2020	247.9	993.3	0.0	38.9	3.78	3.41
MEMORIAL HERMANN COMM HEALTH	TX	U		--	--	--	--	--	--
MEMORIAL HERMANN HEALTH INS CO	TX	● D	2q 2020	16.4	12.4	12.4	6.7	1.59	1.33
MEMORIAL HERMANN HEALTH PLAN INC	TX	● C-	3q 2019	37.8	78.9	78.9	13.1	1.34	1.11
MERCHANTS MUTUAL INS CO	NY	B-	2q 2020	648.5	253.6	0.0	245.5	2.65	2.19
MERCY HEALTH PLANS INC	MO	U		--	--	--	--	--	--
MERCY HEALTH PLANS OF MISSOURI, INC.	MO	U		--	--	--	--	--	--
MERCY MARICOPA INTEGRATED CARE	AZ	U		--	--	--	--	--	--

Arrows denote recent upgrades ▲ or downgrades ▼

● Bullets denote a more detailed analysis is available in Section II.

INSURANCE COMPANY NAME	DOM. STATE	RATING	DATA DATE	TOTAL ASSETS ($MIL)	TOTAL PREMIUMS ($MIL)	HEALTH PREMIUMS ($MIL)	CAPITAL & SURPLUS ($MIL)	RISK ADJUSTED CAPITAL RATIO 1	RATIO 2
MERCYCARE HMO	WI	• C	2q 2020	46.4	106.6	106.6	16.5	1.23	1.02
MERCYCARE INS CO	WI	• D+	2q 2020	25.6	0.4	0.4	22.5	1.66	1.39
MERIDIAN HEALTH PLAN OF ILLINOIS INC	IL	• C-	2q 2020	1,119.5	3,633.7	3,633.7	360.6	1.14	0.95
▲ MERIDIAN HEALTH PLAN OF MICHIGAN INC	MI	• C	2q 2020	742.7	2,026.0	2,026.0	292.2	1.76	1.47
MERIT HEALTH INS CO	IL	• C+	3q 2019	154.8	103.7	103.7	54.3	10.41	8.68
MERIT LIFE INS CO	TX	C	2q 2020	59.8	-8.7	0.0	22.9	3.29	2.72
METROPOLITAN LIFE INS CO	NY	• B-	2q 2020	408,407.0	29,928.9	8,422.6	13,691.2	2.49	1.28
METROPOLITAN P&C INS CO	RI	B-	2q 2020	6,761.9	1,574.7	46.0	2,095.2	1.91	1.48
METROPOLITAN TOWER LIFE INS CO	NE	B-	2q 2020	28,106.5	4,677.7	3.4	1,465.2	2.35	1.15
▲ MHS HEALTH WISCONSIN	WI	• B	2q 2020	105.9	228.9	228.9	67.7	3.32	2.76
MICHIGAN COMPLETE HEALTH INC	MO	• C-	2q 2020	36.0	67.0	67.0	20.5	3.47	2.89
▼ MID-WEST NATIONAL LIFE INS CO OF TN	TX	C+	2q 2020	49.9	15.4	6.0	16.8	2.32	2.08
MIDLAND NATIONAL LIFE INS CO	IA	B+	2q 2020	62,252.9	3,956.1	0.0	3,805.5	1.93	1.01
▼ MII LIFE INSURANCE INC	MN	• C-	2q 2020	1,528.1	41.1	41.1	32.9	1.45	1.21
MINNESOTA LIFE INS CO	MN	B	2q 2020	53,956.0	8,882.8	429.9	3,254.7	2.11	1.32
MISSISSIPPI TRUE	MS	U	--	--	--	--	--	--	--
▼ MISSOURI CARE INC	MO	• C	2q 2020	265.8	705.2	705.2	96.9	1.82	1.52
MISSOURI CHAMBER FEDN BENEFIT	MO	• C	3q 2019	23.2	2.5	2.5	2.4	5.05	4.21
MISSOURI MEDICARE SELECT LLC	MO	• D+	3q 2019	1.5	2.0	2.0	1.0	0.79	0.65
▲ MISSOURI VALLEY L&H INS CO	MO	• C+	2q 2020	85.6	72.9	72.9	50.9	1.89	1.58
MMM FLORIDA INC	FL	• D	2q 2020	17.1	30.4	30.4	11.6	1.51	1.26
MMM HEALTHCARE LLC	PR	• E-	2q 2020	689.6	2,696.9	2,696.9	200.5	1.01	0.84
MMM MULTI HEALTH LLC	PR	• D+	2q 2020	210.2	613.8	613.8	41.4	0.51	0.42
MODA ASSURANCE CO	AK	U	--	--	--	--	--	--	--
MODA HEALTH PLAN INC	OR	• E	2q 2020	334.0	640.9	640.9	98.2	1.15	0.96
MOLINA HEALTHCARE OF CALIFORNIA	CA	• C	2q 2020	758.0	2,334.5	2,334.5	141.4	1.16	0.72
▼ MOLINA HEALTHCARE OF FLORIDA INC	FL	• D	2q 2020	270.3	733.5	733.5	75.4	1.95	1.63
MOLINA HEALTHCARE OF ILLINOIS INC	IL	• C	2q 2020	332.2	1,076.2	1,076.2	141.7	1.80	1.50
MOLINA HEALTHCARE OF KY INC	KY	U	--	--	--	--	--	--	--
MOLINA HEALTHCARE OF MICHIGAN INC	MI	• B	2q 2020	597.3	1,692.5	1,692.5	265.9	2.23	1.86
MOLINA HEALTHCARE OF MS INC	MS	• D	3q 2019	102.6	22.8	22.8	31.4	9.34	7.78
MOLINA HEALTHCARE OF NEW MEXICO	NM	• C	2q 2020	97.2	169.2	169.2	35.5	4.51	3.76
MOLINA HEALTHCARE OF OHIO INC	OH	• B	2q 2020	769.0	2,727.7	2,727.7	306.6	1.76	1.46
MOLINA HEALTHCARE OF PUERTO RICO INC	PR	• C	2q 2020	174.4	473.5	473.5	71.7	1.92	1.60
MOLINA HEALTHCARE OF SOUTH CAROLINA	SC	• B	2q 2020	212.9	578.8	578.8	88.6	1.87	1.56
MOLINA HEALTHCARE OF TEXAS INC	TX	• B-	2q 2020	987.0	3,042.7	3,042.7	315.4	1.41	1.17
▼ MOLINA HEALTHCARE OF TEXAS INS CO	TX	C	2q 2020	10.1	32.9	32.9	9.4	4.07	3.67
MOLINA HEALTHCARE OF UTAH INC	UT	• B	2q 2020	236.3	403.5	403.5	83.5	2.61	2.18
MOLINA HEALTHCARE OF WASHINGTON INC	WA	• B	2q 2020	957.1	2,746.5	2,746.5	366.9	1.78	1.48
MOLINA HEALTHCARE OF WISCONSIN INC	WI	• C+	2q 2020	95.3	213.3	213.3	47.8	3.01	2.51
MONARCH HEALTH PLAN	CA	• E+	2q 2020	177.6	741.3	741.3	88.3	1.43	0.87
MONARCH LIFE INS CO	MA	F	4q 2019	615.4	8.8	7.9	3.8	0.36	0.22
MONITOR LIFE INS CO OF NEW YORK	NY	B-	2q 2020	16.1	4.7	3.9	12.4	4.02	3.62
MONTANA HEALTH COOPERATIVE	MT	• D	2q 2020	143.3	213.1	213.1	75.8	1.16	0.96
MONY LIFE INS CO	NY	B-	2q 2020	6,793.9	245.9	21.2	398.3	2.16	1.13
MONY LIFE INS CO OF AMERICA	AZ	C+	2q 2020	4,618.9	759.0	41.9	345.5	2.02	1.35
MOTIVHEALTH INSURANCE CO	UT	• C-	3q 2019	9.8	10.4	10.4	3.1	1.75	1.46
MOTORISTS COMMERCIAL MUTUAL INS CO	OH	B	2q 2020	646.0	216.4	0.0	164.8	2.83	1.92
MOUNT CARMEL HEALTH INS CO	OH	• C+	2q 2020	7.4	8.9	8.9	6.0	3.20	2.67
MOUNT CARMEL HEALTH PLAN INC	OH	• B+	2q 2020	407.5	557.3	557.3	306.1	6.42	5.35
MOUNT CARMEL HLTH PLAN OF ID	ID	U	--	--	--	--	--	--	--
MOUNT CARMEL HLTH PLAN OF NY	NY	U	--	--	--	--	--	--	--

INSURANCE COMPANY NAME	DOM. STATE	RATING	DATA DATE	TOTAL ASSETS ($MIL)	TOTAL PREMIUMS ($MIL)	HEALTH PREMIUMS ($MIL)	CAPITAL & SURPLUS ($MIL)	RISK ADJUSTED CAPITAL RATIO 1	RATIO 2
MOUNTAIN LIFE INS CO	TN	C-	2q 2020	5.2	2.6	0.6	3.5	2.16	1.95
MULTINATIONAL LIFE INS CO	PR	C-	3q 2019	122.6	56.9	34.4	23.4	2.43	1.36
MUTL OF OMAHA MEDICARE	NE	U		--	--	--	--	--	--
MUTUAL BENEFIT ASSN OF HAWAII	HI	U		--	--	--	--	--	--
MUTUAL OF AMERICA LIFE INS CO	NY	B	2q 2020	23,276.8	2,561.8	3.0	789.9	1.97	0.96
MUTUAL OF OMAHA INS CO	NE	• C+	2q 2020	8,980.8	1,494.2	1,494.2	3,494.3	0.93	0.87
MUTUAL SAVINGS LIFE INS CO	AL	B	2q 2020	480.6	37.3	3.8	54.7	2.96	1.78
MUTUAL TRUST LIFE INS CO	IL	B	2q 2020	2,153.5	211.0	0.2	164.1	2.18	1.08
MVP HEALTH INS CO	NY	• D	2q 2020	5.7	0.4	0.4	5.0	2.39	1.99
MVP HEALTH PLAN INC	NY	• B	2q 2020	792.4	2,672.5	2,672.5	424.0	2.14	1.78
▲ MVP HEALTH SERVICES CORP	NY	• B-	2q 2020	204.4	704.0	704.0	109.7	1.19	0.99
NASSAU LIFE INS CO OF KS	KS	D	2q 2020	70.8	16.9	13.3	17.4	2.34	2.10
NASSAU LIFE INS COMPANY OF TEXAS	TX	• D	2q 2020	396.2	74.3	62.4	48.2	3.03	1.51
NASSAU LIFE INSURANCE CO	NY	D-	2q 2020	11,538.7	354.3	0.5	420.9	1.48	0.74
NATIONAL BENEFIT LIFE INS CO	NY	A-	2q 2020	595.9	180.2	0.7	128.7	5.05	2.71
NATIONAL CASUALTY CO	OH	B	2q 2020	800.0	1,208.5	1.4	135.6	9.63	8.67
NATIONAL FAMILY CARE LIFE INS CO	TX	C	2q 2020	15.9	6.0	5.0	9.3	3.01	2.71
▲ NATIONAL FOUNDATION LIFE INS CO	TX	• A	2q 2020	87.8	95.3	88.2	61.0	2.71	2.13
NATIONAL GUARDIAN LIFE INS CO	WI	• B	1q 2020	4,372.4	933.8	375.5	394.1	1.62	1.05
NATIONAL HEALTH INS CO	TX	• C+	2q 2020	103.3	474.2	471.2	32.8	2.24	0.93
NATIONAL INCOME LIFE INS CO	NY	B+	2q 2020	319.9	92.3	6.9	31.4	1.93	1.12
NATIONAL INTEGRITY LIFE INS CO	NY	C+	2q 2020	4,443.3	211.0	0.0	388.2	3.92	1.85
NATIONAL INTERSTATE INS CO	OH	C+	2q 2020	1,423.9	536.9	0.0	293.2	1.33	1.09
NATIONAL LIABILITY & FIRE INS CO	CT	C+	2q 2020	2,957.4	685.7	0.0	1,081.4	2.51	1.56
NATIONAL LIFE INS CO	VT	B-	2q 2020	9,835.3	529.0	17.5	2,240.5	1.18	1.03
NATIONAL LLOYDS INS CO	TX	C	2q 2020	157.8	103.4	0.0	71.2	2.88	2.48
NATIONAL PROSPERITY L&H INS CO	TX	U		--	--	--	--	--	--
NATIONAL SECURITY INS CO	AL	B	2q 2020	59.9	5.9	1.8	17.1	2.45	1.92
NATIONAL SPECIALTY INS CO	TX	C	2q 2020	101.9	279.3	0.0	60.7	10.46	9.42
NATIONAL TEACHERS ASSOCIATES L I C	TX	• B-	2q 2020	586.9	130.5	127.2	55.6	1.94	1.22
NATIONAL UNION FIRE INS CO	PA	C+	2q 2020	23,207.0	5,032.6	379.1	5,834.8	2.23	1.44
NATIONAL WESTERN LIFE INS CO	CO	B-	2q 2020	10,616.4	548.5	3.0	1,489.9	2.41	1.57
NATIONWIDE LIFE & ANNUITY INS CO	OH	C	2q 2020	34,736.6	7,043.5	0.0	1,994.7	2.59	1.24
NATIONWIDE LIFE INS CO	OH	B-	2q 2020	152,728.0	11,252.7	443.6	8,764.7	2.32	1.63
NATIONWIDE MUTUAL INS CO	OH	B	2q 2020	37,112.7	2,896.8	24.3	14,332.8	1.48	1.34
NATL PREVENTIVE SOLUTIONS CORP	IL	U		--	--	--	--	--	--
NAVICENT HEALTHPLAN INC	GA	U		--	--	--	--	--	--
NAVIGATORS INS CO	NY	B-	2q 2020	3,970.9	790.4	0.9	983.0	1.39	1.03
NC PROVIDER OWNED PLANS INC	NC	U		--	--	--	--	--	--
NEBRASKA TOTAL CARE INC	NE	• C	3q 2019	111.8	444.8	444.8	46.0	1.99	1.66
▼ NEIGHBORHOOD HEALTH PARTNERSHIP INC	FL	• C+	2q 2020	268.7	840.5	840.5	57.2	0.77	0.64
NEIGHBORHOOD HEALTH PLAN	MA	• D	2q 2020	285.2	792.6	792.6	143.2	2.28	1.90
NEIGHBORHOOD HEALTH PLAN OF RI INC	RI	• C+	2q 2020	353.2	1,345.9	1,345.9	109.7	1.00	0.83
NETCARE LIFE & HEALTH INS CO	GU	E	2q 2020	36.5	19.5	13.6	3.4	0.58	0.53
▲ NETWORK HEALTH INS CORP	WI	• B	2q 2020	239.6	653.5	653.5	118.3	2.08	1.74
NETWORK HEALTH PLAN	WI	• B	2q 2020	138.8	377.5	377.5	72.0	2.20	1.84
▼ NEW ENGLAND LIFE INS CO	MA	D+	2q 2020	8,615.8	187.3	5.6	156.2	1.58	0.82
NEW ERA LIFE INS CO	TX	• C	1q 2020	555.1	180.6	93.4	98.4	0.93	0.75
NEW ERA LIFE INS CO OF THE MIDWEST	TX	C+	2q 2020	156.7	81.4	51.0	16.7	1.40	0.82
NEW HAMPSHIRE INS CO	IL	C+	2q 2020	125.5	1,084.6	3.5	46.9	5.83	5.25
NEW HEALTH VENTURES INC	CO	U		--	--	--	--	--	--
NEW MEXICO HEALTH CONNECTIONS	NM	• E-	2q 2020	28.4	20.9	20.9	2.3	0.22	0.18

Arrows denote recent upgrades ▲ or downgrades▼

42

• Bullets denote a more detailed analysis is available in Section II.

INSURANCE COMPANY NAME	DOM. STATE	RATING	DATA DATE	TOTAL ASSETS ($MIL)	TOTAL PREMIUMS ($MIL)	HEALTH PREMIUMS ($MIL)	CAPITAL & SURPLUS ($MIL)	RISK ADJUSTED CAPITAL RATIO 1	RATIO 2
NEW WEST HEALTH SERVICES	MT	U		--	--	--	--	--	--
NEW YORK LIFE INS CO	NY	A-	2q 2020	198,377.0	15,627.2	553.5	23,197.4	1.76	1.32
NEXTBLUE OF ND INSURANCE CO	ND	U		--	--	--	--	--	--
NEXTLEVEL HEALTH PARTNERS INC	IL	• E-	2q 2020	77.9	269.9	269.9	11.4	0.10	0.09
NHC ADVANTAGE LLC	MO	• C-	3q 2019	7.6	2.7	2.7	1.5	1.79	1.49
NIAGARA LIFE & HEALTH INS CO	NY	A-	2q 2020	17.2	34.2	33.3	10.8	3.22	2.83
NIPPON LIFE INS CO OF AMERICA	IA	• A-	2q 2020	246.1	362.5	359.8	148.5	3.40	2.67
NORTH AMERICAN CAPACITY INS CO	NH	C	2q 2020	196.3	417.7	0.1	69.9	7.57	6.81
NORTH AMERICAN CO FOR LIFE & H INS	IA	B	2q 2020	30,473.1	3,058.4	0.0	1,497.5	1.73	0.81
NORTH AMERICAN INS CO	WI	B+	2q 2020	19.2	9.9	9.9	14.2	4.35	3.25
NORTH CAROLINA FARM BU MUTUAL INS CO	NC	B	2q 2020	2,205.0	1,198.5	0.1	1,260.1	6.37	4.22
NORTH RIVER INS CO	NJ	C-	2q 2020	1,168.0	302.7	7.1	300.4	1.14	0.82
NORTHWESTERN LONG TERM CARE INS CO	WI	• B+	2q 2020	290.3	763.0	763.0	176.3	10.17	4.10
NORTHWESTERN MUTUAL LIFE INS CO	WI	B+	2q 2020	295,371.0	18,983.6	1,391.5	24,660.5	3.36	1.69
NTA LIFE INS CO OF NEW YORK	NY	B	2q 2020	8.9	1.8	1.8	7.2	3.36	3.03
OBI NATIONAL INS CO	PA	C	2q 2020	13.4	51.9	0.0	13.3	180.80	90.43
OCCIDENTAL LIFE INS CO OF NC	TX	C	2q 2020	269.2	74.3	0.1	31.2	3.02	1.73
OCEANVIEW LIFE AND ANNUITY CO	TX	C+	2q 2020	748.5	0.3	0.1	124.7	8.96	7.12
OH CHS SNP INC	OH	U		--	--	--	--	--	--
OHIO CASUALTY INS CO	NH	C	2q 2020	7,360.7	1,095.2	0.0	2,047.2	2.75	1.93
OHIO NATIONAL LIFE ASR CORP	OH	B	2q 2020	2,914.6	441.3	33.6	240.7	2.13	1.11
OHIO NATIONAL LIFE INS CO	OH	C+	2q 2020	26,621.8	975.8	11.7	981.6	1.37	0.89
▼ OHIO STATE LIFE INS CO	TX	E+	2q 2020	67.2	28.1	0.0	6.2	8.02	4.42
OKLAHOMA FARM BUREAU MUTUAL INS CO	OK	B-	2q 2020	338.6	213.4	0.0	137.7	2.71	2.20
OKLAHOMA SUPERIOR SELECT INC	OK	• E+	2q 2020	3.6	6.8	6.8	2.0	1.38	1.15
OLD AMERICAN INDEMNITY CO	KY	D	2q 2020	34.9	67.2	1.5	11.1	1.50	1.32
OLD AMERICAN INS CO	MO	B-	2q 2020	285.0	94.9	0.3	21.5	2.25	1.21
OLD REPUBLIC LIFE INS CO	IL	• B-	2q 2020	102.2	22.1	15.6	41.1	4.89	3.02
OLD SPARTAN LIFE INS CO INC	SC	C	2q 2020	24.3	4.6	3.7	19.0	2.44	1.51
OLD SURETY LIFE INS CO	OK	C	2q 2020	35.3	60.9	60.8	16.3	0.84	0.65
OLD UNITED LIFE INS CO	AZ	• B	2q 2020	99.7	6.6	3.4	70.4	6.70	4.07
OMAHA HEALTH INSURANCE CO	NE	U		--	--	--	--	--	--
OMAHA INS CO	NE	• B-	2q 2020	113.4	736.2	736.2	55.3	1.90	0.98
OMAHA SUPPLEMENTAL INS CO	NE	B	2q 2020	18.6	3.7	3.7	15.1	4.46	4.01
ON LOK SENIOR HEALTH SERVICES	CA	• B	2q 2020	181.1	174.4	174.4	142.8	3.86	2.81
OPTILEGRA INC	SD	U		--	--	--	--	--	--
OPTIMA FAMILY CARE OF NC INC	NC	U		--	--	--	--	--	--
OPTIMA HEALTH INS CO	VA	• D+	2q 2020	27.2	38.6	38.6	9.3	1.36	1.13
OPTIMA HEALTH PLAN	VA	• B	2q 2020	803.2	2,437.7	2,437.7	309.3	1.54	1.29
OPTIMA SEGUROS	PR	C-	2q 2020	99.6	60.0	0.1	32.2	1.44	0.93
OPTIMUM CHOICE INC	MD	• B+	2q 2020	119.3	275.9	275.9	38.6	2.53	2.11
OPTIMUM HEALTHCARE INC	FL	• B	2q 2020	228.5	737.2	737.2	59.1	1.23	1.02
OPTUM INS OF OH INC	OH	B	1q 2020	335.3	0.7	0.0	73.9	5.89	5.30
OPTUM NETWORKS OF NJ INC	DE	U		--	--	--	--	--	--
ORISKA INS CO	NY	E	2q 2020	41.6	9.3	0.2	10.7	0.19	0.15
OSCAR BUCKEYE STATE INS CORP	OH	U		--	--	--	--	--	--
OSCAR GARDEN STATE INSURANCE	NJ	• D	3q 2019	51.2	20.9	20.9	6.0	1.37	1.14
OSCAR HEALTH PLAN INC	AZ	U		--	--	--	--	--	--
OSCAR HEALTH PLAN OF CALIFORNIA	CA	• E-	2q 2020	305.2	49.6	49.6	-107.2	0.00	0.00
OSCAR HEALTH PLAN OF GEORGIA	GA	U		--	--	--	--	--	--
OSCAR HEALTH PLAN OF NY INC	NY	U		--	--	--	--	--	--
OSCAR HLTH PLAN PA INC	PA	U		--	--	--	--	--	--

www.weissratings.com
Arrows denote recent upgrades ▲ or downgrades▼

43

• Bullets denote a more detailed analysis is available in Section II.

INSURANCE COMPANY NAME	DOM. STATE	RATING	DATA DATE	TOTAL ASSETS ($MIL)	TOTAL PREMIUMS ($MIL)	HEALTH PREMIUMS ($MIL)	CAPITAL & SURPLUS ($MIL)	RISK ADJUSTED CAPITAL RATIO 1	RATIO 2
OSCAR INS CORP	NY	● E-	3q 2019	142.6	180.4	180.4	16.9	1.91	1.59
OSCAR INS CORP OF NEW JERSEY	NJ	● D	4q 2019	7.6	0.5	0.5	7.5	4.52	3.76
OSCAR INSURANCE CO FLORIDA	FL	U		--	--	--	--	--	--
OSCAR INSURANCE COMPANY	TX	● D-	3q 2019	255.4	359.8	359.8	32.2	0.95	0.79
OSCAR INSURANCE CORP OF OHIO	OH	● D	3q 2019	43.6	86.3	86.3	31.5	2.60	2.16
OXFORD HEALTH INS INC	NY	● B	2q 2020	3,058.9	8,535.0	8,535.0	1,455.2	3.11	2.59
OXFORD HEALTH PLANS (CT) INC	CT	● B+	2q 2020	586.6	1,768.4	1,768.4	233.2	1.76	1.47
OXFORD HEALTH PLANS (NJ) INC	NJ	● B	2q 2020	369.2	806.6	806.6	170.9	3.21	2.67
OXFORD HEALTH PLANS (NY) INC	NY	● B	2q 2020	487.6	780.5	780.5	315.8	5.14	4.29
OXFORD LIFE INS CO	AZ	B+	2q 2020	2,408.0	327.7	34.2	207.7	1.93	1.19
OZARK NATIONAL LIFE INS CO	MO	C+	2q 2020	802.0	83.3	0.2	69.8	2.53	1.42
PA HEALTH & WELLNESS INC	PA	● B-	3q 2019	359.8	483.4	483.4	177.4	5.42	4.52
PACIFIC CENTURY LIFE INS CORP	AZ	U		--	--	--	--	--	--
PACIFIC EMPLOYERS INS CO	PA	C	2q 2020	952.9	103.4	0.0	905.9	6.97	6.68
PACIFIC GUARDIAN LIFE INS CO LTD	HI	● B+	2q 2020	579.2	84.4	45.5	85.1	2.82	1.66
PACIFIC INDEMNITY CO	WI	B-	2q 2020	11,699.6	644.3	0.0	3,268.0	2.34	1.44
▼ PACIFICARE LIFE & HEALTH INS CO	IN	● B-	2q 2020	193.9	12.0	12.0	188.7	19.29	17.36
PACIFICARE LIFE ASR CO	CO	● C	2q 2020	26.1	29.7	29.7	11.7	2.33	1.95
PACIFICARE OF ARIZONA INC	AZ	U		--	--	--	--	--	--
PACIFICARE OF COLORADO INC	CO	● B	2q 2020	877.0	4,143.5	4,143.5	443.4	1.96	1.63
PACIFICARE OF NEVADA INC	NV	U		--	--	--	--	--	--
PACIFICSOURCE CMNTY SOLUTIONS	OR	U		--	--	--	--	--	--
PACIFICSOURCE COMMUNITY HEALTH PLANS	OR	● B	2q 2020	218.7	343.6	343.6	169.9	3.15	2.63
PACIFICSOURCE HEALTH PLANS	OR	● B-	2q 2020	519.0	919.6	919.6	349.6	2.65	2.20
PAN AMERICAN LIFE INS CO OF PR	PR	B	2q 2020	12.0	16.7	16.4	7.4	2.35	1.82
PAN-AMERICAN LIFE INS CO	LA	● B	2q 2020	1,279.8	307.2	265.5	255.8	2.50	1.59
PARAMOUNT ADVANTAGE	OH	● D	2q 2020	390.8	1,493.1	1,493.1	205.2	1.61	1.34
PARAMOUNT CARE OF MI INC	MI	● D+	2q 2020	10.3	24.3	24.3	6.7	1.37	1.14
PARAMOUNT HEALTH CARE	OH	● D	2q 2020	72.3	182.6	182.6	26.0	1.22	1.02
PARAMOUNT INS CO (OH)	OH	● C-	2q 2020	73.7	149.6	149.6	27.2	1.47	1.22
PARKLAND COMMUNITY HEALTH PLAN INC	TX	● C	2q 2020	154.2	569.7	569.7	88.8	1.99	1.65
PARTNERRE AMERICA INS CO	DE	● C+	2q 2020	288.6	103.3	66.9	99.6	2.40	1.90
▼ PARTNERSHIP HEALTHPLAN OF CALIFORNIA	CA	● C	2q 2020	1,228.1	2,790.9	2,790.9	576.7	4.67	2.86
PATRIOT INS CO	ME	C	2q 2020	153.9	54.2	0.0	59.1	5.40	3.81
PAUL REVERE LIFE INS CO	MA	● C+	2q 2020	3,129.3	217.5	203.6	194.9	1.60	1.00
▲ PAVONIA LIFE INS CO OF MICHIGAN	MI	D+	2q 2020	1,040.1	22.9	2.1	70.3	1.73	0.95
▲ PAVONIA LIFE INS CO OF NEW YORK	NY	C-	2q 2020	29.2	3.3	0.1	8.2	1.84	1.65
▲ PEACH STATE HEALTH PLAN INC	GA	● B	2q 2020	441.8	1,114.0	1,114.0	278.6	3.62	3.01
PEKIN LIFE INS CO	IL	B	2q 2020	1,572.4	196.0	41.8	124.2	1.84	1.03
PENN MUTUAL LIFE INS CO	PA	B	2q 2020	23,733.8	2,136.2	7.2	2,167.3	1.69	1.16
PEOPLES HEALTH INC	LA	● C	3q 2019	78.8	843.7	843.7	47.9	1.36	1.13
PERENNIAL ADVANTAGE OF CO INC	CO	U		--	--	--	--	--	--
PERENNIAL ADVANTAGE OF OH INC	OH	U		--	--	--	--	--	--
PHILADELPHIA AMERICAN LIFE INS CO	TX	● B	2q 2020	353.6	308.7	273.5	66.6	1.75	1.12
PHILADELPHIA INDEMNITY INS CO	PA	B-	2q 2020	9,621.2	3,459.4	27.3	2,404.8	2.16	1.62
PHP INS CO	MI	● C-	2q 2020	18.5	21.5	21.5	15.0	4.34	3.62
PHP INS CO OF IN INC	IN	● C+	3q 2019	3.6	0.6	0.6	2.5	8.04	6.70
PHP MEDICARE	MI	U		--	--	--	--	--	--
PHYSICIANS HEALTH CHOICE OF TEXAS	TX	● C	2q 2020	188.3	1,250.0	1,250.0	70.9	0.81	0.68
▲ PHYSICIANS HEALTH PLAN OF NO IN	IN	● B+	2q 2020	112.6	185.1	185.1	73.7	3.36	2.80
PHYSICIANS HP OF MID-MICHIGAN	MI	● C	2q 2020	91.3	178.7	178.7	56.8	2.17	1.81
PHYSICIANS LIFE INS CO	NE	A-	1q 2020	1,730.5	349.8	65.9	167.4	2.90	1.47

Arrows denote recent upgrades ▲ or downgrades ▼

www.weissratings.com
● Bullets denote a more detailed analysis is available in Section II.

INSURANCE COMPANY NAME	DOM. STATE	RATING	DATA DATE	TOTAL ASSETS ($MIL)	TOTAL PREMIUMS ($MIL)	HEALTH PREMIUMS ($MIL)	CAPITAL & SURPLUS ($MIL)	RISK ADJUSTED CAPITAL RATIO 1	RATIO 2
PHYSICIANS MUTUAL INS CO	NE	● A+	2q 2020	2,506.1	428.9	428.9	1,058.8	3.27	2.44
PICA HEALTH INC	PR	U		--	--	--	--	--	--
PIEDMONT COMMUNITY HEALTHCARE	VA	● D+	2q 2020	9.8	57.2	57.2	7.0	0.64	0.53
PIEDMONT COMMUNITY HEALTHCARE HMO	VA	● C	3q 2019	35.4	176.2	176.2	27.9	1.44	1.20
PIONEER EDUCATORS HEALTH TRUST	OR	● D-	4q 2019	2.8	2.8	2.8	2.7	N/A	N/A
PIONEER MUTUAL LIFE INS CO	ND	B	2q 2020	508.9	18.8	0.0	44.3	2.82	1.44
PL MEDICO SERV DE SALUD BELLA VISTA	PR	● B	2q 2020	4.6	7.3	7.3	2.2	1.27	1.06
PLAN DE SALUD MENONITA	PR	● D+	2q 2020	49.7	198.4	198.4	21.2	0.98	0.82
▲ PLATEAU INS CO	TN	B	2q 2020	29.3	47.2	27.5	18.6	3.73	2.78
PMC MEDICARE CHOICE LLC	PR	U		--	--	--	--	--	--
PREFERRED CARE PARTNERS INC	FL	● B+	2q 2020	706.7	2,584.8	2,584.8	235.6	1.43	1.19
PREFERREDONE COMMUNITY HEALTH PLAN	MN	● D+	2q 2020	3.6	2.3	2.3	3.1	3.17	2.64
▲ PREFERREDONE INS CO	MN	● C	2q 2020	127.4	269.9	269.9	58.6	1.44	1.20
PREMERA BLUE CROSS	WA	● B	2q 2020	3,687.2	3,925.1	3,925.1	1,946.5	5.91	4.93
PREMIER CHOICE DENTAL INC	AZ	U		--	--	--	--	--	--
PREMIER HEALTH PLAN SERVICES INC	CA	● D	2q 2020	46.3	93.8	93.8	22.1	2.78	1.74
PRESBYTERIAN HEALTH PLAN INC	NM	● B	2q 2020	936.5	3,064.0	3,064.0	328.8	1.53	1.27
PRESBYTERIAN INS CO	NM	● C	2q 2020	54.0	100.2	100.2	38.1	1.78	1.48
PRESIDENTIAL LIFE INS CO	NC	U		--	--	--	--	--	--
PRIMECARE MEDICAL NETWORK INC	CA	● B-	2q 2020	377.0	1,168.9	1,168.9	121.7	2.34	1.44
PRIMERICA LIFE INS CO	TN	B	2q 2020	1,587.6	2,329.4	0.4	627.4	1.27	1.10
PRINCIPAL LIFE INS CO	IA	B+	2q 2020	208,421.0	10,685.0	2,005.2	5,404.6	2.09	1.18
PRIORITY HEALTH	MI	● A	2q 2020	1,860.0	3,405.8	3,405.8	1,036.6	4.20	3.50
PRIORITY HEALTH CHOICE INC	MI	● B+	2q 2020	254.8	471.0	471.0	136.1	4.16	3.47
PRIORITY HEALTH INS CO	MI	● B	2q 2020	163.4	293.8	293.8	70.8	2.16	1.80
PROCARE ADVANTAGE LLC	TX	U		--	--	--	--	--	--
PROFESSIONAL INS CO	TX	● C	2q 2020	115.2	17.0	15.8	56.5	6.28	5.65
PROMINENCE HEALTHFIRST	NV	● D-	2q 2020	60.4	143.8	143.8	17.4	1.04	0.86
PROMINENCE HEALTHFIRST FL INC	FL	U		--	--	--	--	--	--
PROMINENCE HEALTHFIRST OF TEXAS INC	TX	● D-	2q 2020	7.2	12.6	12.6	3.1	1.80	1.50
PROMINENCE PREFERRED HEALTH INS CO	NV	● D-	2q 2020	9.5	14.5	14.5	4.0	1.99	1.66
PROSPECT HEALTH PLAN	CA	● E+	2q 2020	31.4	257.9	257.9	10.7	0.50	0.31
PROTEC INS CO	IL	C+	2q 2020	6.4	5.5	0.1	6.1	3.46	3.12
PROTECTIVE INS CO	IN	B-	2q 2020	1,046.6	507.3	21.2	338.8	1.24	0.91
PROTECTIVE LIFE & ANNUITY INS CO	AL	C+	2q 2020	6,134.1	359.6	0.0	356.4	1.81	0.94
PROTECTIVE LIFE INS CO	TN	B	2q 2020	70,691.9	3,525.9	17.5	5,490.0	1.66	1.13
PROVIDENCE HEALTH ASR	OR	● A-	2q 2020	586.5	868.4	868.4	327.9	4.18	3.48
PROVIDENCE HEALTH NETWORK	CA	● D-	2q 2020	44.5	156.7	156.7	16.8	1.16	0.70
PROVIDENCE HEALTH PLAN	OR	● B	2q 2020	1,064.2	1,278.8	1,278.8	652.0	4.29	3.57
PROVIDENT AMER LIFE & HEALTH INS CO	OH	B	2q 2020	9.4	6.6	6.1	8.4	1.82	1.66
PROVIDENT AMERICAN INS CO	TX	C	2q 2020	35.0	0.7	0.4	12.8	0.86	0.77
PROVIDENT LIFE & ACCIDENT INS CO	TN	● C+	2q 2020	7,994.3	1,011.9	707.1	660.2	2.65	1.32
PROVIDENT LIFE & CAS INS CO	TN	● B-	2q 2020	748.3	98.9	97.2	133.1	4.23	2.46
PROVIDER PARTNERS HEALTH PLAN INC	MD	● E	3q 2019	4.9	8.0	8.0	1.5	0.61	0.51
PROVIDER PARTNERS HEALTH PLAN OF PA	PA	● E-	3q 2019	5.0	12.9	12.9	1.8	0.71	0.59
PROVIDER PTNRS HLTH PLAN OF IL	IL	U		--	--	--	--	--	--
PROVIDER PTNRS HLTH PLAN OF MO	MO	U		--	--	--	--	--	--
PRUDENTIAL INS CO OF AMERICA	NJ	B	2q 2020	305,158.0	25,525.1	1,668.4	12,455.0	1.61	1.15
PRUITTHEALTH PREMIER INC	GA	● D+	3q 2019	13.5	39.9	39.9	3.0	0.54	0.45
PRUITTHEALTH PREMIER NC LLC	NC	U		--	--	--	--	--	--
PRVDR PTNRS HLTH PLAN OH INC	OH	U		--	--	--	--	--	--
PUPIL BENEFITS PLAN INC	NY	● C-	2q 2020	13.6	8.4	8.4	10.4	7.29	6.07

Arrows denote recent upgrades ▲ or downgrades▼   ● Bullets denote a more detailed analysis is available in Section II.

INSURANCE COMPANY NAME	DOM. STATE	RATING	DATA DATE	TOTAL ASSETS ($MIL)	TOTAL PREMIUMS ($MIL)	HEALTH PREMIUMS ($MIL)	CAPITAL & SURPLUS ($MIL)	RISK ADJUSTED CAPITAL RATIO 1	RATIO 2
PURITAN LIFE INS CO OF AMERICA	TX	C	2q 2020	218.2	101.9	31.1	21.1	2.67	1.58
QBE INS CORP	PA	• B	2q 2020	2,961.3	1,160.7	339.2	680.9	1.20	0.78
QBE SPECIALTY INS CO	ND	C+	2q 2020	429.0	810.1	14.1	121.5	1.58	1.01
QCA HEALTH PLAN INC	AR	• D	2q 2020	144.0	219.3	219.3	42.4	1.78	1.48
QCC INS CO	PA	• B-	2q 2020	1,499.1	2,091.6	2,091.6	567.1	3.27	2.72
QUALCHOICE ADVANTAGE INC	AR	U	--	--	--	--	--	--	--
QUALCHOICE L&H INS CO	AR	• D+	2q 2020	116.7	142.2	142.2	34.8	2.16	1.80
QUALITY HEALTH PLANS OF NEW YORK INC	NY	F	4q 2019	4.4	30.8	30.8	-30.2	0.00	0.00
QUARTZ HEALTH INS CORP	WI	• C-	2q 2020	117.3	3.9	3.9	115.6	1.54	1.28
QUARTZ HEALTH PLAN CORP	WI	• C-	2q 2020	66.1	251.3	251.3	19.7	1.03	0.86
▲ QUARTZ HEALTH PLAN MN CORP	MN	• C+	2q 2020	8.9	15.5	15.5	4.0	1.48	1.24
QUARTZ HLTH BENEFIT PLANS CORP	WI	• C	2q 2020	329.2	1,421.1	1,421.1	107.8	1.51	1.26
REGAL LIFE OF AMERICA INS CO	TX	D-	2q 2020	8.1	0.7	0.5	6.0	1.11	1.10
REGENCE BL CROSS BL SHIELD OREGON	OR	• A-	2q 2020	1,622.0	2,128.5	2,128.5	834.8	6.16	5.13
REGENCE BLUE CROSS BLUE SHIELD OF UT	UT	• B+	2q 2020	792.1	1,059.1	1,059.1	436.3	6.52	5.44
REGENCE BLUESHIELD	WA	• B	2q 2020	1,835.9	1,715.8	1,715.8	1,265.9	7.77	6.48
REGENCE BLUESHIELD OF IDAHO INC	ID	• B+	2q 2020	395.1	408.2	408.2	239.1	6.08	5.07
RELIABLE LIFE INS CO	MO	B-	2q 2020	32.5	116.8	8.9	13.3	2.18	1.09
RELIANCE HMO INC	MI	U	--	--	--	--	--	--	--
RELIANCE STANDARD LIFE INS CO	IL	• C+	2q 2020	16,728.5	2,671.5	815.1	1,580.4	1.29	0.76
RELIASTAR LIFE INS CO	MN	• B-	2q 2020	19,407.1	3,080.7	1,400.3	1,551.3	1.83	1.11
RELIASTAR LIFE INS CO OF NEW YORK	NY	B	2q 2020	2,850.1	255.7	54.2	277.9	3.33	1.77
▲ RENAISSANCE L&H INS CO OF AMERICA	DE	• B	2q 2020	101.0	152.5	149.6	58.6	1.65	1.22
▲ RENAISSANCE L&H INS CO OF NY	NY	C+	2q 2020	14.4	12.0	10.1	9.0	2.00	1.57
RESERVE NATIONAL INS CO	OK	• B-	2q 2020	149.2	173.6	159.0	45.8	1.49	1.14
RESPONSE INDEMNITY CO OF CA	CA	C-	2q 2020	37.3	58.1	0.0	6.3	1.33	1.20
RETAILERS INS CO	MI	C-	2q 2020	25.5	10.6	0.5	11.5	1.72	1.38
RGA REINSURANCE CO	MO	• B-	1q 2020	41,983.4	37.8	12.7	2,055.3	1.60	0.84
RIVERLINK HEALTH	OH	U		--	--	--	--	--	--
RIVERLINK HEALTH OF KENTUCKY INC	KY	U		--	--	--	--	--	--
▲ RIVERSOURCE LIFE INS CO	MN	B	2q 2020	110,337.0	5,282.5	324.4	3,968.2	2.41	1.49
RIVERSOURCE LIFE INS CO OF NY	NY	C	2q 2020	7,396.9	368.8	16.4	383.4	3.97	1.99
ROCKY MOUNTAIN HEALTH MAINT ORG	CO	• B-	2q 2020	189.1	443.9	443.9	87.4	2.55	2.13
ROCKY MOUNTAIN HEALTHCARE OPTIONS	CO	U		--	--	--	--	--	--
ROCKY MOUNTAIN HOSPITAL & MEDICAL	CO	• B	2q 2020	1,192.6	1,733.4	1,733.4	620.7	2.63	2.19
ROYAL STATE NATIONAL INS CO LTD	HI	U		--	--	--	--	--	--
ROYALTY CAPITAL LIFE INS CO	MO	D	2q 2020	3.7	0.3	0.0	3.5	3.23	2.91
RURAL MUTUAL INS CO	WI	B-	2q 2020	601.8	213.7	0.7	341.7	8.16	5.46
RYDER HEALTH PLAN INC	PR	• B	2q 2020	1.8	1.8	1.8	0.8	2.02	1.68
S USA LIFE INS CO INC	AZ	B-	2q 2020	275.8	84.3	15.5	31.8	4.01	1.90
SAGICOR LIFE INS CO	TX	D	2q 2020	2,046.0	451.9	0.0	108.2	0.61	0.31
▲ SAMARITAN HEALTH PLANS INC	OR	• B-	2q 2020	32.7	96.6	96.6	16.0	1.31	1.09
SAN FRANCISCO HEALTH AUTHORITY	CA	• B-	1q 2020	823.1	598.3	598.3	103.6	2.50	1.57
SAN JOAQUIN CNTY HEALTH	CA	• B+	2q 2020	880.8	1,088.6	1,088.6	342.1	5.42	3.30
SAN MATEO HEALTH COMMISSION	CA	• B	2q 2020	598.2	781.2	781.2	329.4	6.15	3.78
SANFORD HEALTH PLAN	SD	• C	2q 2020	338.5	946.3	946.3	156.3	1.69	1.41
SANFORD HEALTH PLAN OF MINNESOTA	MN	• D+	2q 2020	4.3	5.7	5.7	2.6	1.87	1.56
SANTA BARBARA SAN LUIS OBISPO REGION	CA	• B-	2q 2020	521.4	955.0	955.0	195.8	3.74	2.28
SANTA CLARA COUNTY HEALTH AUTHORITY	CA	• C	2q 2020	917.0	1,214.7	1,214.7	209.2	3.07	1.87
SANTA CLARA VALLEY	CA	• C	2q 2020	285.4	579.8	579.8	49.1	1.00	0.62
SANTA CRUZ-MONTEREY-MERCED MGD MED	CA	• C	2q 2020	733.6	1,221.4	1,221.4	419.0	6.85	4.23
SAPPHIRE EDGE INC	NE	U		--	--	--	--	--	--

www.weissratings.com

Arrows denote recent upgrades ▲ or downgrades▼   • Bullets denote a more detailed analysis is available in Section II.

INSURANCE COMPANY NAME	DOM. STATE	RATING	DATA DATE	TOTAL ASSETS ($MIL)	TOTAL PREMIUMS ($MIL)	HEALTH PREMIUMS ($MIL)	CAPITAL & SURPLUS ($MIL)	RISK ADJUSTED CAPITAL RATIO 1	RATIO 2
SATELLITE HEALTH PLAN INC	CA	U		--	--	--	--	--	--
SBLI USA MUT LIFE INS CO INC	NY	B-	2q 2020	1,851.0	213.2	7.0	107.7	1.45	0.80
SC FARM BUREAU MUTUAL INS CO	SC	C+	2q 2020	140.8	78.4	0.1	84.5	4.16	3.68
SCAN HEALTH PLAN	CA	• B+	2q 2020	758.9	3,081.3	3,081.3	484.8	3.26	2.02
SCOTT & WHITE CARE PLANS	TX	U		--	--	--	--	--	--
SCOTT & WHITE HEALTH PLAN	TX	• C+	2q 2020	502.3	574.6	574.6	303.4	2.05	1.71
SCRIPPS HEALTH PLAN SERVICES INC	CA	• C-	2q 2020	158.2	742.6	742.6	43.8	0.84	0.51
SD STATE MEDICAL HOLDING CO	SD	• D	2q 2020	18.3	30.8	30.8	12.2	1.02	0.85
SEASIDE HEALTH PLAN	CA	• E-	2q 2020	13.3	35.3	35.3	7.2	0.55	0.35
SECURIAN LIFE INS CO	MN	B	2q 2020	1,541.7	1,390.5	131.1	453.2	5.04	3.19
SECURITY HEALTH PLAN OF WI INC	WI	• B+	2q 2020	507.0	1,326.7	1,326.7	281.4	3.09	2.57
SECURITY LIFE OF DENVER INS CO	CO	B-	2q 2020	14,879.2	916.3	0.0	877.7	1.32	0.75
SECURITY MUTUAL LIFE INS CO OF NY	NY	C	2q 2020	2,860.9	392.1	6.5	187.9	1.85	0.98
SECURITY NATIONAL LIFE INS CO	UT	D	2q 2020	702.7	87.2	0.1	47.2	0.86	0.55
SECURITY PLAN LIFE INS CO	LA	D+	2q 2020	316.4	42.3	0.7	13.1	0.76	0.51
▼ SECURITYCARE OF TENNESSEE INC	TN	• C	2q 2020	7.5	0.2	0.2	7.4	2.56	2.14
SELECT HEALTH OF SOUTH CAROLINA INC	SC	• B	2q 2020	375.1	1,376.8	1,376.8	167.2	1.62	1.35
SELECTCARE HEALTH PLANS INC	TX	• B	2q 2020	15.4	23.2	23.2	9.0	2.38	1.98
SELECTCARE OF TEXAS INC	TX	• C-	2q 2020	277.2	920.1	920.1	74.0	1.31	1.09
SELECTHEALTH BENEFIT ASR CO INC	UT	• B	2q 2020	34.1	35.5	35.5	23.7	2.78	2.32
▲ SELECTHEALTH INC	UT	• B+	2q 2020	1,703.8	3,308.7	3,308.7	808.1	3.64	3.03
SELECTIVE INS CO OF AM	NJ	B	2q 2020	2,875.3	668.0	0.0	656.4	2.67	1.76
SENDERO HEALTH PLANS INC	TX	• E+	2q 2020	44.4	83.6	83.6	20.6	1.26	1.05
SENIOR LIFE INS CO	GA	D+	2q 2020	72.0	71.6	0.0	10.7	1.20	0.63
SENIOR WHOLE HEALTH OF NEW YORK INC	NY	• C+	2q 2020	257.1	838.1	838.1	114.1	1.65	1.37
SENTARA MEDICARE ADVANTAGE	NC	U		--	--	--	--	--	--
SENTINEL SECURITY LIFE INS CO	UT	D	2q 2020	759.6	505.2	42.1	56.3	1.11	0.54
SENTRY INS A MUTUAL CO	WI	B	2q 2020	9,682.2	550.7	1.3	5,973.2	3.04	2.46
SENTRY LIFE INS CO	WI	A	2q 2020	8,165.9	772.7	0.3	323.5	3.37	1.88
SENTRY LIFE INS CO OF NEW YORK	NY	B	2q 2020	134.3	9.4	0.0	10.1	1.11	1.00
SENTRY SELECT INS CO	WI	B	2q 2020	936.6	652.5	2.6	236.8	3.09	1.97
SEQUOIA HEALTH PLAN INC	CA	• E+	2q 2020	5.7	88.1	88.1	3.1	0.39	0.24
SERVICE LIFE & CAS INS CO	TX	U		--	--	--	--	--	--
SETON HEALTH PLAN INC	TX	• B	2q 2020	48.9	32.0	32.0	37.7	4.31	3.59
SETTLERS LIFE INS CO	WI	B	2q 2020	449.0	48.2	0.2	63.0	3.51	1.89
SHA LLC	TX	• D	2q 2020	162.7	535.5	535.5	90.2	1.71	1.42
SHARP HEALTH PLAN	CA	• B+	2q 2020	217.8	792.2	792.2	127.8	1.99	1.31
SHELTER LIFE INS CO	MO	B	2q 2020	1,334.7	154.8	14.2	250.8	3.78	2.25
SHELTERPOINT INS CO	FL	B	2q 2020	10.6	3.3	3.2	8.3	3.91	3.52
SHELTERPOINT LIFE INS CO	NY	• A	2q 2020	235.2	210.2	208.5	64.5	1.53	1.28
SHENANDOAH LIFE INS CO	VA	• B-	2q 2020	1,208.4	54.6	15.6	94.2	1.93	1.07
SHERIDAN LIFE INS CO	OK	U		--	--	--	--	--	--
SIDNEY HILLMAN HEALTH CENTRE	IL	U		--	--	--	--	--	--
SIERRA HEALTH AND LIFE INS CO INC	NV	• B	2q 2020	6,825.8	18,882.8	18,882.8	3,778.7	3.51	2.93
SIGNATURE ADVANTAGE LLC	KY	• D	3q 2019	2.2	4.7	4.7	1.0	0.42	0.35
SILAC INSURANCE CO	UT	D+	2q 2020	2,295.1	1,448.8	158.9	143.4	1.37	0.70
▲ SILVERSCRIPT INS CO	TN	• D+	2q 2020	3,694.8	2,578.0	2,578.0	1,053.4	8.01	6.68
SILVERSUMMIT HEALTHPLAN INC	NV	• C	3q 2019	158.0	372.0	372.0	90.2	6.34	5.28
SIMPLY HEALTHCARE PLANS INC	FL	• B	2q 2020	704.5	3,279.1	3,279.1	226.1	0.94	0.78
SIMPRA ADVANTAGE INC	AL	• C	3q 2019	23.4	40.7	40.7	8.0	1.24	1.04
SIRIUS AMERICA INS CO	NY	• C+	2q 2020	1,430.9	271.7	221.8	519.2	1.47	0.92
SISTEMAS MEDICOS NACIONALES SA DE CV	CA	• B-	2q 2020	93.3	105.4	105.4	51.5	3.59	2.37

Arrows denote recent upgrades ▲ or downgrades▼   • Bullets denote a more detailed analysis is available in Section II.

INSURANCE COMPANY NAME	DOM. STATE	RATING	DATA DATE	TOTAL ASSETS ($MIL)	TOTAL PREMIUMS ($MIL)	HEALTH PREMIUMS ($MIL)	CAPITAL & SURPLUS ($MIL)	RISK ADJUSTED CAPITAL RATIO 1	RATIO 2
SOLIS HEALTH PLANS INC	FL	• E+	2q 2020	12.3	11.2	11.2	4.3	0.49	0.41
SOLSTICE HEALTHPLANS AZ INC	AZ	U		--	--	--	--	--	--
SOLSTICE OF ILLINOIS INC	IL	U		--	--	--	--	--	--
SOUNDPATH HEALTH	WA	• D	2q 2020	45.0	0.2	0.2	44.0	12.16	10.13
SOUTHEASTERN INDIANA HEALTH ORG INC	IN	• B-	2q 2020	17.8	33.0	33.0	10.1	2.12	1.76
SOUTHERN FARM BUREAU LIFE INS CO	MS	A	2q 2020	14,723.1	946.4	29.1	2,684.4	4.09	2.18
SOUTHERN FINANCIAL LIFE INS CO	KY	C	2q 2020	14.3	15.2	9.1	4.3	1.52	1.36
SOUTHERN GUARANTY INS CO	WI	• C	2q 2020	33.3	19.2	19.2	30.6	7.93	4.28
SOUTHERN NATL LIFE INS CO INC	LA	B	2q 2020	20.3	3.5	0.0	16.3	2.90	2.28
SOUTHWEST L&H INS CO	TX	• D	2q 2020	8.7	8.0	8.0	6.6	2.42	2.02
SOUTHWEST SERVICE LIFE INS CO	TX	D-	2q 2020	12.0	11.5	10.1	5.2	0.97	0.84
SPARTAN PLAN NY INC	NY	• E-	3q 2019	2.0	0.5	0.5	0.5	0.75	0.62
SPARTAN PLAN VA INC	VA	• D+	3q 2019	2.9	0.4	0.4	2.0	0.93	0.77
SSM HEALTH INSURANCE CO	MO	U		--	--	--	--	--	--
SSM HEALTH PLAN	MO	U		--	--	--	--	--	--
STANDARD GUARANTY INS CO	DE	B-	2q 2020	336.4	352.3	0.0	155.6	2.77	2.15
STANDARD INS CO	OR	• B+	2q 2020	27,265.4	6,159.9	1,667.5	1,497.6	2.40	1.25
STANDARD LIFE & ACCIDENT INS CO	TX	• B	2q 2020	482.2	102.8	90.4	287.3	6.72	4.04
STANDARD LIFE & CAS INS CO	UT	D	2q 2020	38.7	15.3	4.4	5.4	1.01	0.68
STANDARD LIFE INS CO OF NY	NY	• A-	2q 2020	307.0	107.5	75.1	117.3	5.22	3.49
STANDARD SECURITY LIFE INS CO OF NY	NY	• B+	2q 2020	142.7	89.3	87.5	59.4	5.34	4.20
STANFORD HEALTH CARE ADVANTAGE	CA	• E-	2q 2020	15.0	43.6	43.6	4.7	0.70	0.44
STARMOUNT LIFE INS CO	ME	• C	2q 2020	140.7	254.5	247.7	75.4	2.05	1.60
STARNET INS CO	IA	C+	2q 2020	256.0	379.7	2.4	121.3	13.03	11.73
STARR INDEMNITY & LIABILITY CO	TX	B-	2q 2020	6,349.0	2,384.2	21.7	2,247.4	1.32	0.93
STARR SURPLUS LINES INS CO	TX	B-	2q 2020	751.3	874.1	0.0	181.3	1.33	0.92
STARSTONE NATIONAL INS CO	DE	C-	2q 2020	698.9	343.5	2.8	142.5	1.19	0.74
STATE AUTOMOBILE MUTUAL INS CO	OH	C+	2q 2020	2,349.6	464.5	0.0	729.7	1.17	1.08
STATE FARM FIRE & CAS CO	IL	B	2q 2020	45,191.7	19,905.5	0.0	21,302.0	3.51	2.26
STATE FARM MUTUAL AUTOMOBILE INS CO	IL	B	2q 2020	175,115.0	39,905.7	1,019.5	113,909.0	2.21	1.92
STATE LIFE INS CO	IN	B	2q 2020	9,746.4	1,095.8	20.0	560.1	1.76	0.89
STATE MUTUAL INS CO	GA	D	2q 2020	181.3	74.0	59.7	16.4	0.84	0.55
STATE NATIONAL INS CO	TX	C	2q 2020	612.3	847.3	0.3	484.9	1.54	1.50
STERLING DENTAL OF MO INC	MO	U		--	--	--	--	--	--
STERLING DENTAL OF NORTH AM	KS	U		--	--	--	--	--	--
STERLING INVESTORS LIFE INS CO	IN	C	2q 2020	93.3	27.6	6.7	10.6	1.30	1.08
STERLING LIFE INS CO	IL	B-	2q 2020	38.9	56.2	54.9	20.2	1.28	0.99
STERLING NATL LIFE INS CO	CT	D+	2q 2020	14.4	15.7	15.7	9.5	3.39	3.05
STEWARD HEALTH CHOICE INC	AZ	U		--	--	--	--	--	--
STEWARD HEALTH CHOICE UTAH INC	UT	• E-	2q 2020	50.3	67.8	67.8	15.8	1.65	1.37
STRYDEN INC	VA	U		--	--	--	--	--	--
SUMMA INS CO	OH	• C-	2q 2020	45.3	126.0	126.0	21.9	1.59	1.32
SUMMACARE INC	OH	• C	2q 2020	95.8	269.4	269.4	49.1	1.48	1.24
SUMMACARE OF MICHIGAN INC	MI	U		--	--	--	--	--	--
SUMMIT HEALTH PLAN INC	OR	U		--	--	--	--	--	--
SUN LIFE & HEALTH INS CO	MI	• D	2q 2020	971.7	219.3	151.3	113.9	2.36	1.39
SUN LIFE ASR CO OF CANADA	MI	• D+	2q 2020	20,100.8	3,688.4	2,603.6	887.6	0.66	0.37
SUNFLOWER STATE HEALTH PLAN INC	KS	• C	2q 2020	380.0	1,537.3	1,537.3	154.3	1.42	1.19
SUNSET LIFE INS CO OF AMERICA	MO	B-	2q 2020	293.9	14.3	0.0	24.9	2.66	1.38
▲ SUNSHINE HEALTH	FL	• C+	2q 2020	849.2	4,111.0	4,111.0	374.3	1.21	1.01
SUNSHINE HEALTH COMMUNITY SOLUTIONS	FL	• C-	3q 2019	15.7	21.7	21.7	6.5	2.38	1.98
SUPERIOR HEALTHPLAN COMMUNITY SOLUTI	TX	• C	3q 2019	10.4	10.3	10.3	4.9	3.57	2.98

www.weissratings.com

Arrows denote recent upgrades ▲ or downgrades▼   • Bullets denote a more detailed analysis is available in Section II.

INSURANCE COMPANY NAME	DOM. STATE	RATING	DATA DATE	TOTAL ASSETS ($MIL)	TOTAL PREMIUMS ($MIL)	HEALTH PREMIUMS ($MIL)	CAPITAL & SURPLUS ($MIL)	RISK ADJUSTED CAPITAL RATIO 1	RATIO 2
SUPERIOR HEALTHPLAN INC	TX	● B-	2q 2020	1,040.8	4,448.6	4,448.6	508.5	1.61	1.35
SUPERIOR VISION OF NEW JERSEY INC	NJ	● C	4q 2019	5.8	5.0	5.0	5.0	9.68	8.07
SURENCY LIFE & HEALTH INS CO	KS	C-	2q 2020	15.4	12.5	12.5	12.9	4.01	2.97
SURETY LIFE & CASUALTY INS CO	ND	C-	2q 2020	13.5	1.4	0.6	5.2	2.09	1.89
SURETY LIFE INS CO	NE	D	2q 2020	28.8	31.2	0.0	27.3	4.85	2.34
SUTTER HEALTH PLAN	CA	● C-	2q 2020	158.2	517.4	517.4	53.3	1.50	0.93
SWBC LIFE INS CO	TX	● A-	2q 2020	36.1	13.6	7.8	25.4	4.07	2.83
SWISS RE LIFE & HEALTH AMER INC	MO	● C+	2q 2020	13,054.3	0.3	0.3	1,568.7	2.07	1.33
SYMETRA LIFE INS CO	IA	B	2q 2020	43,094.3	4,749.9	959.1	1,989.0	1.81	0.96
TAKECARE INS CO	GU	● D-	2q 2020	30.8	91.3	91.3	8.5	0.31	0.26
TALCOTT RESOLUTION LIFE	CT	B-	2q 2020	32,554.7	929.9	0.3	1,201.2	3.15	1.59
TALCOTT RESOLUTION LIFE INS CO	CT	B-	2q 2020	88,639.9	1,743.0	32.5	3,788.5	2.27	1.58
TEACHERS INS & ANNUITY ASN OF AM	NY	A+	2q 2020	320,701.0	14,922.7	12.6	39,629.1	3.66	2.20
TECHNOLOGY INS CO	DE	D+	2q 2020	5,203.4	1,018.7	7.7	1,197.4	2.24	1.41
TEXAS CHILDRENS HEALTH PLAN INC	TX	● C	2q 2020	424.9	1,756.4	1,756.4	248.9	1.51	1.25
TEXAS FARM BUREAU MUTUAL INS CO	TX	B-	2q 2020	893.5	548.8	0.8	405.2	2.87	2.62
TEXAS HLTH + AETNA HLTH INS CO	TX	● C	3q 2019	159.4	278.7	278.7	90.7	4.81	4.00
TEXAS HLTH + AETNA HLTH PLAN	TX	● C	3q 2019	16.9	20.9	20.9	11.3	4.16	3.47
TEXAS LIFE INS CO	TX	C+	4q 2019	1,351.3	283.1	0.0	125.5	1.85	0.95
THE EPIC LIFE INSURANCE CO	WI	C	2q 2020	29.3	13.9	7.4	17.2	3.06	2.06
THE UNION LABOR LIFE INS CO	MD	● B	2q 2020	4,386.4	230.5	159.6	134.0	2.14	1.41
THP INS CO	WV	● C	2q 2020	69.1	108.2	108.2	38.6	1.86	1.55
TIAA-CREF LIFE INS CO	NY	B	2q 2020	14,710.6	727.9	6.9	554.8	1.94	1.00
TIG INS CO	CA	U	--	--	--	--	--	--	--
TIMBER PRODUCTS MANUFACTURERS TRUST	WA	● B	2q 2020	24.1	38.9	38.9	18.6	3.42	2.85
TIME INS CO	PR	E-	2q 2020	11.4	117.5	84.9	-1.9	0.67	0.33
TOTAL HEALTH CARE INC	MI	● C	2q 2020	100.9	180.7	180.7	46.2	1.43	1.19
TOTAL HEALTH CARE USA INC	MI	● B	2q 2020	91.2	181.2	181.2	37.2	2.42	2.02
TOWN & COUNTRY LIFE INS CO	UT	C-	2q 2020	8.3	4.7	4.7	5.5	2.75	2.47
TRANS CITY LIFE INS CO	AZ	C-	2q 2020	19.4	2.0	0.3	9.9	3.44	3.10
TRANS OCEANIC LIFE INS CO	PR	● B+	4q 2019	77.3	31.0	28.8	32.4	1.97	1.34
TRANSAMERICA CASUALTY INS CO	IA	C+	2q 2020	53.1	4.4	0.3	43.3	3.09	2.70
TRANSAMERICA FINANCIAL LIFE INS CO	NY	B	2q 2020	31,080.7	5,728.5	109.5	957.9	2.67	1.29
TRANSAMERICA LIFE INS CO	IA	C+	2q 2020	137,455.0	15,103.3	987.4	5,916.6	1.39	1.03
TRH HEALTH INS CO	TN	● B	2q 2020	144.2	282.3	282.3	115.1	4.59	3.83
TRILLIUM COMMUNITY HEALTH PLAN INC	OR	● C+	2q 2020	142.6	565.7	565.7	56.4	1.24	1.03
TRINITY LIFE INS CO	OK	D-	2q 2020	314.2	95.3	0.0	12.3	0.46	0.30
TRIPLE S VIDA INC	PR	● B-	3q 2019	696.4	188.3	68.2	55.4	1.08	0.70
TRIPLE-S ADVANTAGE INC	PR	● B	2q 2020	427.3	1,408.0	1,408.0	160.2	1.09	0.91
TRIPLE-S BLUE II	PR	D+	3q 2019	13.9	10.2	9.8	2.2	0.77	0.63
TRIPLE-S SALUD INC	PR	● B	2q 2020	884.5	1,581.5	1,581.5	351.0	1.55	1.29
TRITON INS CO	TX	B-	2q 2020	644.4	158.9	38.6	109.7	2.38	1.40
TROY HEALTH INC	NC	U		--	--	--	--	--	--
TRUE HEALTH NEW MEXICO INC	NM	● B	3q 2019	63.9	159.7	159.7	24.2	1.41	1.18
TRUSTED HEALTH PLAN INC	DC	● B	2q 2020	46.1	140.7	140.7	20.2	1.99	1.66
TRUSTMARK INS CO	IL	● B+	2q 2020	1,752.8	375.1	152.5	331.7	2.61	1.49
TRUSTMARK LIFE INS CO	IL	● B+	2q 2020	296.8	123.5	120.9	180.9	8.10	5.57
TSG GUARD INC	OH	● D+	2q 2020	3.3	6.7	6.7	1.9	1.22	1.01
TUFTS ASSOCIATED HEALTH MAINT ORG	MA	● C	2q 2020	1,269.3	2,698.4	2,698.4	666.6	3.03	2.53
TUFTS HEALTH FREEDOM INS CO	NH	● C-	2q 2020	49.3	114.9	114.9	18.2	1.34	1.12
TUFTS HEALTH PUBLIC PLANS INC	MA	● C	2q 2020	871.4	2,191.0	2,191.0	323.7	1.74	1.45
TUFTS INS CO	MA	● B-	2q 2020	137.2	312.5	312.5	71.8	2.48	2.07

Arrows denote recent upgrades ▲ or downgrades▼   ● Bullets denote a more detailed analysis is available in Section II.

INSURANCE COMPANY NAME	DOM. STATE	RATING	DATA DATE	TOTAL ASSETS ($MIL)	TOTAL PREMIUMS ($MIL)	HEALTH PREMIUMS ($MIL)	CAPITAL & SURPLUS ($MIL)	RISK ADJUSTED CAPITAL RATIO 1	RATIO 2
TX INDEPDCE HEALTH PLAN INC	TX	U		--	--	--	--	--	--
U S HEALTH & LIFE INS CO	MI	● B	2q 2020	30.7	24.3	24.3	16.8	2.04	1.70
UCARE HEALTH INC	WI	● C+	3q 2019	37.6	6.7	6.7	34.7	15.27	12.72
UCARE MINNESOTA	MN	● B	2q 2020	1,488.0	3,709.6	3,709.6	759.8	2.82	2.35
UHC OF CALIFORNIA INC	CA	● B	2q 2020	1,169.8	6,750.8	6,750.8	433.7	1.49	0.93
ULTIMATE HEALTH PLANS INC	FL	● E-	2q 2020	30.3	71.8	71.8	14.0	1.33	1.11
UMPQUA HEALTH ALLIANCE LLC	OR	U		--	--	--	--	--	--
UNDERWRITERS AT LLOYDS (KY)	KY	D-	2q 2020	153.5	44.2	0.1	33.4	0.32	0.21
UNDERWRITERS AT LLOYDS (VI)	VI	E+	2q 2020	262.1	98.3	0.3	100.0	0.77	0.52
▲ UNICARE HEALTH PLAN OF WEST VIRGINIA	WV	● A	2q 2020	186.1	490.0	490.0	116.7	2.83	2.36
▲ UNICARE LIFE & HEALTH INS CO	IN	B	2q 2020	695.4	200.6	40.7	232.5	3.74	2.56
UNIFIED LIFE INS CO	TX	B	2q 2020	217.7	51.3	44.2	24.9	1.64	1.00
▼ UNIMERICA INS CO	WI	● B-	2q 2020	441.8	398.7	389.2	226.3	4.47	3.50
UNIMERICA LIFE INS CO OF NY	NY	B-	2q 2020	34.4	6.6	3.5	23.2	4.57	4.11
UNION FIDELITY LIFE INS CO	KS	● E	1q 2020	20,412.2	22.3	13.1	637.6	1.39	0.70
UNION HEALTH SERVICE INC	IL	● C	2q 2020	30.0	84.6	84.6	17.9	1.10	0.92
UNION MEDICAL CENTER	IL	● C-	4q 2019	2.6	6.2	6.2	2.2	N/A	N/A
UNION NATIONAL LIFE INS CO	LA	B	2q 2020	27.7	84.4	6.2	17.1	4.85	2.42
UNION SECURITY INS CO	KS	● B	2q 2020	2,610.6	357.7	258.6	125.8	2.87	1.47
UNION SECURITY LIFE INS CO OF NY	NY	● C+	2q 2020	54.7	20.0	19.0	42.5	6.06	5.46
▲ UNITED AMERICAN INS CO	NE	● B	2q 2020	755.1	507.9	479.4	171.4	1.42	1.08
UNITED FARM FAMILY LIFE INS CO	IN	B+	2q 2020	2,442.0	143.8	0.5	347.4	3.33	1.99
UNITED FIDELITY LIFE INS CO	TX	C	2q 2020	822.0	5.6	0.1	571.2	0.80	0.79
UNITED HEALTHCARE INS CO	CT	● C	2q 2020	21,367.3	55,384.1	55,224.5	7,726.7	1.09	0.92
▲ UNITED HEALTHCARE INS CO OF IL	IL	● A-	2q 2020	453.6	1,200.4	1,200.4	164.1	1.74	1.45
UNITED HEALTHCARE INS CO OF NY	NY	● B	2q 2020	1,547.5	2,215.9	2,215.9	730.6	7.53	6.28
▼ UNITED HEALTHCARE OF ALABAMA INC	AL	● D	2q 2020	116.8	154.2	154.2	37.4	2.52	2.10
UNITED HEALTHCARE OF ARIZONA INC	AZ	● D+	2q 2020	47.7	106.6	106.6	17.3	1.72	1.44
UNITED HEALTHCARE OF ARKANSAS INC	AR	● B-	2q 2020	67.2	131.1	131.1	28.5	2.05	1.71
UNITED HEALTHCARE OF COLORADO INC	CO	● C	2q 2020	61.7	99.8	99.8	24.8	2.70	2.25
▼ UNITED HEALTHCARE OF FLORIDA INC	FL	● C+	2q 2020	440.3	2,070.6	2,070.6	158.4	1.05	0.87
UNITED HEALTHCARE OF GEORGIA INC	GA	● B	2q 2020	105.8	331.3	331.3	52.9	1.68	1.40
UNITED HEALTHCARE OF ILLINOIS INC	IL	● B	2q 2020	70.6	163.2	163.2	34.3	2.63	2.19
UNITED HEALTHCARE OF KENTUCKY LTD	KY	● B-	2q 2020	62.1	171.7	171.7	31.9	1.76	1.47
UNITED HEALTHCARE OF LOUISIANA INC	LA	● B	2q 2020	607.2	2,347.4	2,347.4	234.2	1.60	1.33
UNITED HEALTHCARE OF MID-ATLANTIC	MD	● B	2q 2020	633.4	1,794.0	1,794.0	267.2	2.01	1.68
UNITED HEALTHCARE OF MISSISSIPPI INC	MS	● B	2q 2020	303.6	993.4	993.4	198.9	2.35	1.96
UNITED HEALTHCARE OF NC INC	NC	● C	2q 2020	284.3	505.5	505.5	155.7	4.05	3.38
UNITED HEALTHCARE OF NEW ENGLAND INC	RI	● B	2q 2020	409.2	1,305.2	1,305.2	190.4	1.88	1.57
UNITED HEALTHCARE OF NY INC	NY	● B	2q 2020	1,500.1	5,192.5	5,192.5	593.3	1.66	1.38
UNITED HEALTHCARE OF OHIO INC	OH	● C	2q 2020	27.8	53.5	53.5	18.2	3.98	3.31
UNITED HEALTHCARE OF THE MIDLANDS	NE	● B+	2q 2020	1,032.6	3,569.9	3,569.9	476.5	1.93	1.61
UNITED HEALTHCARE OF THE MIDWEST INC	MO	● C	2q 2020	589.7	1,232.4	1,232.4	258.0	2.92	2.43
UNITED HEALTHCARE OF TX INC	TX	● B+	2q 2020	95.9	155.5	155.5	44.0	7.06	5.88
UNITED HEALTHCARE OF UTAH	UT	● B	2q 2020	166.8	905.1	905.1	86.6	1.24	1.03
UNITED HEALTHCARE OF WISCONSIN INC	WI	● B+	2q 2020	2,701.9	7,259.1	7,259.1	1,253.8	3.47	2.89
UNITED HERITAGE LIFE INS CO	ID	B	2q 2020	626.4	95.7	7.1	70.9	2.17	1.08
UNITED HOME LIFE INS CO	IN	B	2q 2020	107.9	54.6	0.0	22.2	2.58	2.32
UNITED INS CO OF AMERICA	IL	B-	2q 2020	4,416.6	169.1	7.5	446.4	1.44	0.87
UNITED LIFE INS CO	IA	B	2q 2020	1,850.8	244.0	1.1	159.9	2.32	1.11
UNITED NATIONAL LIFE INS CO OF AM	IL	B	2q 2020	41.6	20.0	18.9	13.8	1.89	1.36
UNITED OF OMAHA LIFE INS CO	NE	● B	2q 2020	26,836.2	5,587.6	1,839.0	1,916.2	2.15	1.21

www.weissratings.com

Arrows denote recent upgrades ▲ or downgrades▼   ● Bullets denote a more detailed analysis is available in Section II.

INSURANCE COMPANY NAME	DOM. STATE	RATING	DATA DATE	TOTAL ASSETS ($MIL)	TOTAL PREMIUMS ($MIL)	HEALTH PREMIUMS ($MIL)	CAPITAL & SURPLUS ($MIL)	RISK ADJUSTED CAPITAL RATIO 1	RATIO 2
UNITED OHIO INS CO	OH	B-	2q 2020	397.5	174.0	0.0	213.8	7.62	5.52
UNITED SECURITY ASR CO OF PA	PA	E+	2q 2020	42.8	28.6	28.4	11.7	2.08	1.87
UNITED SECURITY HEALTH & CASUALTY	IL	C	2q 2020	14.4	8.3	2.2	7.0	1.85	1.38
UNITED STATES LIFE INS CO IN NYC	NY	C+	2q 2020	30,169.3	2,045.9	38.7	1,720.8	2.26	1.07
UNITED SURETY & INDEMNITY CO	PR	C+	2q 2020	113.6	63.5	0.5	67.6	1.98	1.33
UNITED WORLD LIFE INS CO	NE	● B+	2q 2020	141.0	571.8	570.7	49.7	3.25	1.35
UNITEDHEALTHCARE BENEFITS OF TEXAS	TX	● B	2q 2020	663.6	4,108.0	4,108.0	300.9	1.27	1.06
UNITEDHEALTHCARE BENEFITS PLAN OF CA	CA	U		--	--	--	--	--	--
UNITEDHEALTHCARE COMMUNITY PLAN INC	MI	● B+	2q 2020	336.3	941.0	941.0	153.7	2.10	1.75
UNITEDHEALTHCARE COMMUNITY PLAN TX	TX	● B	2q 2020	627.5	2,799.5	2,799.5	304.7	1.34	1.11
UNITEDHEALTHCARE COMMUNITYPLAN OHIO	OH	● B+	2q 2020	739.4	2,638.5	2,638.5	393.9	2.03	1.69
UNITEDHEALTHCARE INS CO RIVER VALLEY	IL	● B	2q 2020	736.8	1,848.2	1,848.2	309.5	2.24	1.87
UNITEDHEALTHCARE INSURANCE COMPANY O	IL	● E+	2q 2020	362.3	479.8	479.8	189.1	5.04	4.20
UNITEDHEALTHCARE LIFE INS CO	WI	● C	4q 2019	239.3	474.3	474.2	136.6	2.42	1.93
UNITEDHEALTHCARE OF NEW MEXICO INC	NM	● C	2q 2020	162.9	52.0	52.0	143.0	48.03	40.02
UNITEDHEALTHCARE OF OKLAHOMA INC	OK	● B	2q 2020	186.8	524.8	524.8	92.9	2.75	2.29
UNITEDHEALTHCARE OF OREGON	OR	● B+	2q 2020	645.9	1,603.4	1,603.4	293.1	2.79	2.33
UNITEDHEALTHCARE OF PENNSYLVANIA INC	PA	● B	2q 2020	644.4	1,204.3	1,204.3	239.0	4.01	3.34
UNITEDHEALTHCARE OF SC INC	SC	U		--	--	--	--	--	--
UNITEDHEALTHCARE OF WASHINGTON INC	WA	● B	2q 2020	318.9	864.8	864.8	168.4	2.70	2.25
UNITEDHEALTHCARE PLAN RIVER VALLEY	IL	● B	2q 2020	1,216.8	4,701.0	4,701.0	652.9	2.16	1.80
UNIVERSAL CARE	CA	● E	2q 2020	119.8	500.2	500.2	25.1	0.66	0.42
UNIVERSAL FIDELITY LIFE INS CO	OK	B-	2q 2020	16.0	7.0	6.6	6.0	1.97	1.73
UNIVERSAL GUARANTY LIFE INS CO	OH	C+	2q 2020	347.3	7.8	0.0	69.6	2.28	1.32
UNIVERSAL LIFE INS CO	PR	B+	2q 2020	1,953.3	453.0	7.7	147.4	2.24	1.20
UNIVERSITY HEALTH ALLIANCE	HI	● B	2q 2020	200.4	333.5	333.5	125.4	3.21	2.67
UNIVERSITY HEALTH CARE INC	KY	● D-	2q 2020	16.2	1,943.3	1,943.3	8.8	0.13	0.11
UNIVERSITY OF UTAH HEALTH INS PLANS	UT	● B-	3q 2019	119.1	181.1	181.1	58.0	3.64	3.03
UNUM INS CO	ME	● C	2q 2020	75.2	23.7	21.5	48.1	4.91	3.03
UNUM LIFE INS CO OF AMERICA	ME	● C+	2q 2020	22,729.7	5,129.0	3,538.8	1,715.8	2.13	1.12
UPMC FOR YOU INC	PA	● B+	2q 2020	1,528.6	4,670.7	4,670.7	646.1	2.13	1.78
UPMC HEALTH BENEFITS INC	PA	● C	2q 2020	298.2	150.0	66.2	136.1	0.81	0.50
UPMC HEALTH COVERAGE INC	PA	● C+	2q 2020	25.1	30.2	30.2	19.8	4.05	3.38
UPMC HEALTH NETWORK INC	PA	● C+	2q 2020	60.6	112.8	112.8	48.9	1.76	1.47
UPMC HEALTH OPTIONS INC	PA	● B	2q 2020	638.4	2,387.6	2,387.6	348.6	1.73	1.44
UPMC HEALTH PLAN INC	PA	● C+	2q 2020	984.5	1,859.5	1,859.5	360.4	2.13	1.78
UPPER PENINSULA HEALTH PLAN INC	MI	● B	2q 2020	111.6	286.2	286.2	54.0	2.27	1.90
US ALLIANCE LIFE & SECURITY CO	KS	E+	2q 2020	83.9	5.6	0.3	4.5	0.46	0.32
US FIRE INS CO	DE	● C	2q 2020	4,499.8	1,267.1	454.8	1,397.1	1.24	0.98
US SPECIALTY INS CO	TX	C+	2q 2020	2,129.4	702.8	0.5	496.2	1.67	1.05
USA INS CO	MS	C-	2q 2020	4.8	0.3	0.2	3.6	2.68	2.41
USAA LIFE INS CO	TX	A	2q 2020	26,903.7	2,412.8	375.1	2,565.5	3.63	1.97
USABLE HMO INC	AR	U		--	--	--	--	--	--
USABLE LIFE	AR	● B+	2q 2020	496.4	237.2	122.7	246.1	2.91	2.13
USABLE MUTUAL INS CO	AR	● B+	2q 2020	1,921.0	2,395.0	2,395.0	955.9	4.49	3.74
USABLE PPO INSURANCE CO	AR	U		--	--	--	--	--	--
UTIC INS CO	AL	● B	2q 2020	129.7	11.7	11.7	31.7	3.36	2.02
UTMB HEALTH PLANS INC	TX	● B-	2q 2020	6.1	0.5	0.5	6.0	61.72	51.43
VALUEOPTIONS OF TEXAS INC	TX	U		--	--	--	--	--	--
VANTAGE HEALTH PLAN INC	LA	● C+	2q 2020	109.7	385.8	385.8	47.3	1.23	1.03
VANTAGE HLTH PLAN AR INC	AR	U		--	--	--	--	--	--
VANTIS LIFE INS CO	CT	C+	2q 2020	543.2	43.8	0.0	69.3	1.76	1.11

Arrows denote recent upgrades ▲ or downgrades▼

● Bullets denote a more detailed analysis is available in Section II.

INSURANCE COMPANY NAME	DOM. STATE	RATING	DATA DATE	TOTAL ASSETS ($MIL)	TOTAL PREMIUMS ($MIL)	HEALTH PREMIUMS ($MIL)	CAPITAL & SURPLUS ($MIL)	RISK ADJUSTED CAPITAL RATIO 1	RATIO 2
VENERABLE INS AND ANNTY CO	IA	B-	2q 2020	49,463.2	108.2	0.1	2,652.6	1.31	0.93
▲ VENTURA COUNTY HEALTH CARE PLAN	CA	• E+	2q 2020	17.8	80.4	80.4	6.5	0.66	0.42
VERMONT HEALTH PLAN LLC	VT	• C	2q 2020	38.6	33.3	33.3	32.9	6.88	5.74
VERSANT LIFE INS CO	MS	B-	2q 2020	6.2	0.1	0.0	5.3	3.00	2.70
VIBRA HEALTH PLAN INC	PA	• E-	3q 2019	7.0	12.6	12.6	3.4	2.00	1.67
VIGILANT INS CO	NY	B	2q 2020	446.1	433.2	0.2	345.4	22.08	18.21
VIRGINIA FARM BUREAU MUTUAL INS CO	VA	C+	2q 2020	462.6	139.6	0.0	266.6	2.64	2.16
VIRGINIA PREMIER HEALTH PLAN INC	VA	• C+	2q 2020	569.1	2,000.0	2,000.0	294.2	1.85	1.54
VISTA HEALTH PLAN INC	PA	• B+	3q 2019	1,350.1	5,009.8	5,009.8	408.1	2.50	2.08
VITALITY HEALTH PLAN OF CA INC		• E-	2q 2020	4.8	87.6	87.6	-32.4	0.00	0.00
VIVA HEALTH INC	AL	• A-	2q 2020	225.3	785.5	785.5	141.0	2.48	2.06
VOLUNTARY EMPLOYEES BENEFIT	HI	U		--	--	--	--	--	--
VOLUNTEER STATE HEALTH PLAN INC	TN	• A+	2q 2020	987.7	2,690.3	2,690.3	536.9	2.78	2.31
VOYA RETIREMENT INS & ANNUITY CO	CT	B+	2q 2020	110,637.0	12,627.1	0.1	1,926.3	2.01	0.98
WASHINGTON NATIONAL INS CO	IN	• D+	2q 2020	5,651.2	719.7	659.9	334.9	1.42	0.84
WEA INS CORP	WI	• C	2q 2020	746.9	589.3	589.1	203.0	1.64	1.17
WELLCALL INC	CA	• C-	2q 2020	4.5	1.2	1.2	3.7	2.40	1.56
▲ WELLCARE HEALTH INS OF ARIZONA INC	AZ	• B-	2q 2020	238.1	707.9	707.9	80.8	1.53	1.27
WELLCARE HEALTH INS OF KENTUCKY INC	KY	• C+	2q 2020	1,034.5	2,946.8	2,946.8	328.6	1.77	1.47
WELLCARE HEALTH INS OF NEW YORK INC	NY	• C+	3q 2019	6.9	0.5	0.5	6.2	4.10	3.42
WELLCARE HEALTH INS OF TN INC	TN	U		--	--	--	--	--	--
WELLCARE HEALTH PLANS OF KENTUCKY	KY	U		--	--	--	--	--	--
WELLCARE HEALTH PLANS OF NEW JERSEY	NJ	• B	2q 2020	247.9	886.3	886.3	102.3	1.59	1.33
WELLCARE HLTH INS CO OF LA	LA	U		--	--	--	--	--	--
WELLCARE HLTH INS CO AM	AR	U		--	--	--	--	--	--
WELLCARE HLTH INS CO OF NH INC	NH	U		--	--	--	--	--	--
WELLCARE HLTH INS CO OF OK	OK	U		--	--	--	--	--	--
WELLCARE HLTH INS CO OF WA INC	WA	U		--	--	--	--	--	--
WELLCARE HLTH INS CO OF WI INC	WI	U		--	--	--	--	--	--
WELLCARE HLTH INS OF CT INC	CT	U		--	--	--	--	--	--
WELLCARE HLTH INS OF NC INC	NC	U		--	--	--	--	--	--
WELLCARE HLTH INS OF THE SW	AZ	U		--	--	--	--	--	--
WELLCARE HLTH PLANS OF AZ INC	AZ	U		--	--	--	--	--	--
WELLCARE HLTH PLANS OF MO INC	MO	U		--	--	--	--	--	--
WELLCARE HLTH PLANS OF VT INC	VT	U		--	--	--	--	--	--
WELLCARE HLTH PLANS OF WI INC	WI	U		--	--	--	--	--	--
WELLCARE HLTH PLANS RI INC	RI	U		--	--	--	--	--	--
WELLCARE HLTH PLANS TN INC	TN	U		--	--	--	--	--	--
WELLCARE NATL HLTH INS CO	TX	U		--	--	--	--	--	--
WELLCARE OF ALABAMA INC	AL	U		--	--	--	--	--	--
WELLCARE OF ARKANSAS INC	AR	U		--	--	--	--	--	--
WELLCARE OF CONNECTICUT INC	CT	• C	2q 2020	52.7	117.4	117.4	29.0	2.51	2.10
WELLCARE OF FLORIDA INC	FL	• D+	2q 2020	1,805.3	6,745.2	6,745.2	444.4	0.99	0.83
▲ WELLCARE OF GEORGIA INC	GA	• B+	2q 2020	685.5	2,102.4	2,102.4	303.8	2.25	1.87
WELLCARE OF ILLINOIS INC	IL	U		--	--	--	--	--	--
WELLCARE OF MAINE INC	ME	U		--	--	--	--	--	--
WELLCARE OF MISSISSIPPI INC	MS	U		--	--	--	--	--	--
WELLCARE OF MO HLTH INS CO	MO	U		--	--	--	--	--	--
WELLCARE OF NEBRASKA INC	NE	• B-	3q 2019	171.2	341.3	341.3	58.4	3.91	3.26
WELLCARE OF NEVADA INC	NV	U		--	--	--	--	--	--
WELLCARE OF NEW HAMPSHIRE INC	NH	U		--	--	--	--	--	--
WELLCARE OF NORTH CAROLINA INC	NC	U		--	--	--	--	--	--

Arrows denote recent upgrades ▲ or downgrades▼

52

www.weissratings.com
• Bullets denote a more detailed analysis is available in Section II.

INSURANCE COMPANY NAME	DOM. STATE	RATING	DATA DATE	TOTAL ASSETS ($MIL)	TOTAL PREMIUMS ($MIL)	HEALTH PREMIUMS ($MIL)	CAPITAL & SURPLUS ($MIL)	RISK ADJUSTED CAPITAL RATIO 1	RATIO 2
WELLCARE OF OHIO INC	OH	U		--	--	--	--	--	--
WELLCARE OF OKLAHOMA INC	OK	U		--	--	--	--	--	--
▲ WELLCARE OF SOUTH CAROLINA INC	SC	• B	2q 2020	141.3	343.2	343.2	58.9	2.08	1.73
▲ WELLCARE OF TEXAS INC	TX	• A-	2q 2020	201.1	409.4	409.4	67.7	2.13	1.77
WELLCARE OF VIRGINIA INC	VA	U		--	--	--	--	--	--
WELLCARE OF WASHINGTON INC	WA	U		--	--	--	--	--	--
WELLCARE PRESCRIPTION INS INC	FL	• D	2q 2020	2,713.2	966.9	966.9	166.4	4.25	3.54
WELLCENTRIC HEALTH GROUP DC	DC	U		--	--	--	--	--	--
WELLFLEET INS CO	IN	• C-	2q 2020	129.2	112.6	110.7	62.1	10.36	9.32
WELLFLEET NEW YORK INS CO	NY	• C	2q 2020	84.2	116.3	105.4	28.4	2.52	1.80
WELLMARK HEALTH PLAN OF IOWA	IA	• B	2q 2020	433.3	490.6	490.6	253.6	5.55	4.62
WELLMARK INC	IA	• B-	2q 2020	3,078.5	2,560.2	2,560.2	1,995.1	6.84	5.70
WELLMARK OF SOUTH DAKOTA INC	SD	• B	2q 2020	566.8	762.9	762.9	339.9	5.93	4.94
WELLMARK SYNERGY HEALTH INC	IA	U		--	--	--	--	--	--
WELLMARK VALUE HEALTH PLAN INC	IA	• C+	3q 2019	23.7	1.2	1.2	15.3	11.61	9.67
WELLSTAR HEALTH PLANS INC	GA	U		--	--	--	--	--	--
WESCO INS CO	DE	C	2q 2020	1,899.9	2,105.4	63.9	429.0	1.52	1.00
WEST COAST LIFE INS CO	NE	B-	2q 2020	5,397.7	544.1	0.0	375.1	2.17	1.05
WEST VIRGINIA FAMILY HEALTH PLAN INC	WV	• B	2q 2020	44.1	181.2	181.2	40.9	3.19	2.66
WESTERN & SOUTHERN LIFE INS CO	OH	B	2q 2020	10,679.2	237.1	25.0	5,350.8	1.27	1.17
WESTERN AMERICAN LIFE INS CO	TX	C	2q 2020	25.7	2.1	0.0	2.0	0.51	0.46
WESTERN GROCERS EMPLOYEE BENEFITS	OR	• E-	2q 2020	2.3	22.9	22.9	1.5	N/A	N/A
WESTERN HEALTH ADVANTAGE	CA	• E	2q 2020	81.6	807.7	807.7	12.8	0.21	0.13
WESTERN OR ADVANCED HLTH LLC	OR	U		--	--	--	--	--	--
WESTERN SKY CMNTY CARE INC	NM	U		--	--	--	--	--	--
WESTERN UNITED LIFE ASR CO	WA	B-	2q 2020	1,208.6	251.9	33.6	82.9	1.67	0.80
WESTPORT INS CORP	MO	• C+	2q 2020	4,585.6	1,029.2	408.2	1,566.2	1.96	1.32
WICHITA NATIONAL LIFE INS CO	OK	C-	2q 2020	14.9	4.5	0.8	7.3	2.46	2.21
WILCAC LIFE INS CO	IL	C	2q 2020	2,945.1	33.6	0.5	84.7	2.86	1.35
WILLIAM PENN LIFE INS CO OF NEW YORK	NY	C	2q 2020	1,265.0	227.6	0.1	94.3	2.21	1.06
WILMINGTON INSURANCE CO	DE	C-	2q 2020	12.5	4.3	0.3	6.3	1.52	1.26
WILTON REASSURANCE LIFE CO OF NY	NY	C+	2q 2020	866.6	45.1	0.1	99.3	2.34	1.11
WINDSOR LIFE INS CO	TX	B-	2q 2020	3.2	0.5	0.5	3.0	2.91	2.62
WISCONSIN COLLABORATIVE INSURANCE CO	WI	• B-	3q 2019	32.4	43.7	43.7	23.5	4.36	3.63
WISCONSIN PHYSICIANS SERVICE INS	WI	• C	2q 2020	351.0	346.0	346.0	175.0	3.69	3.08
WMI MUTUAL INS CO	UT	• B	2q 2020	16.7	16.6	16.6	12.4	4.32	3.60
WPS HEALTH PLAN INC	WI	• C-	2q 2020	28.3	72.0	72.0	14.6	1.63	1.36
WV SENIOR ADVANTAGE INC	WV	• C	3q 2019	7.0	10.3	10.3	3.1	1.85	1.54
YAMHILL COUNTY CARE ORG INC	OR	U		--	--	--	--	--	--
ZING HEALTH INC	IL	U		--	--	--	--	--	--
ZING HEALTH OF MICHIGAN INC	MI	U		--	--	--	--	--	--
ZURICH AMERICAN INS CO	NY	C	2q 2020	32,012.8	6,353.1	198.2	7,282.3	2.37	1.63
ZURICH AMERICAN LIFE INS CO	IL	C-	2q 2020	15,280.1	960.1	46.6	129.5	2.90	1.67
ZURICH AMERICAN LIFE INS CO OF NY	NY	C	2q 2020	98.7	18.8	8.5	18.2	2.23	2.01

www.weissratings.com

Arrows denote recent upgrades ▲ or downgrades▼

53

• Bullets denote a more detailed analysis is available in Section II.

Section II

Analysis of Largest Companies

A summary analysis of all rated

U.S. Health Plans and Blue Cross Blue Shield Plans

plus other **U.S. Insurers**
with capital in excess of $25 million and health insurance
premiums equaling at least 25% of total premiums.

Companies are listed in alphabetical order.

Section II Contents

This section contains rating factors, historical data, and general information on all rated health insurers and Blue Cross/Blue Shield plans plus other insurers with capital in excess of $25 million and health insurance premiums equaling at least 25% of total premiums.

A number of the contents listed below will only apply to health insurers filing the NAIC Health insurance financial statement.

1. **Safety Rating**   The current Weiss rating appears to the right of the company name. Our ratings are designed to distinguish levels of insolvency risk and are measured on a scale from A (Excellent) to F (Failed). Highly rated companies are, in our opinion, less likely to experience financial difficulties than lower rated firms. See *About Weiss Safety Ratings* for more information.

2. **Major Rating Factors**   A synopsis of the key indexes and sub-factors that have most influenced the rating of a particular insurer. Items are presented in the approximate order of their importance to the rating. There may be additional factors which have influenced the rating but do not appear due to space limitations or confidentiality agreements with insurers.

3. **Other Rating Factors**   A summary of those Weiss Ratings indexes that were not included as Major Rating Factors, but nevertheless may have had some impact on the final grade.

4. **Principal Business**   The major types of policies written by an insurer along with the percentages for each line in relation to the entire book of business, including direct premium, reinsurance assumed and deposit funds. Lines of business for health insurers include comprehensive medical, medical only, medicare supplemental, administrative service contracts, point of service, dental, vision, stop-loss, long-term care, disability, Federal Employee Health Benefits (FEHB), medicare, and medicaid.

5. **Member Physicians**   The number of physicians who participated in the insurer's network of providers during the current and prior year.

6. **MLR (Medical Loss Ratio)**   The percentage of total premium income paid out as benefits to members.

7. **Administrative Expense Ratio**   The percentage of total premium income paid out for administrative expenses.

8. **Enrollment**   The total number of members (policyholders) as of the current quarter, current year end and prior year end. The letter Q followed by a number represents the quarter (first, second, or third) from which the enrollment numbers were last available.

9. Medical Expenses Per Member Per Month

The average dollar amount the insurer spends on a per member per month basis. Calculated as total medical expenses divided by the reported member months.

10. Principal Investments

The major investments in an insurer's portfolio. These include investment grade bonds, noninvestment grade bonds, collateralized mortgage obligations (CMOs) and other structured securities, which consist primarily of mortgage-backed bonds, real estate, mortgages in good standing, nonperforming mortgages, common and preferred stocks, contract loans and other investments.

11. Provider Compensation

The total annual amount the health insurer pays its providers (e.g., physicians, hospitals, etc.) and manner in which they are paid, including:

- fee-for-service (FFS) – amount paid for the services provided where the payment base is not fixed by contract

- contractual fees – amount paid for services whereby the amount is fixed by contract, e.g., hospital per diems, DRGs, etc.

- salary – amount paid providers who are direct employees of the HMO

- capitation – amount paid to providers on a per member basis as defined by contract

- other – amount paid under various contracts including bonus arrangements, stop-loss arrangements, etc.

12. Total Member Encounters

The number of contacts members of the health insurer who are not confined to a health care facility have with the providers during the current year.

13. Investments in Affiliates

The percentage of bonds, common and preferred stocks, and other financial instruments an insurer has invested with affiliated companies. This is not a subcategory of "Principal Investments."

14. Group Affiliation

The name of the group of companies to which a particular insurer belongs.

15. Licensed in

List of the states in which an insurer is licensed to conduct business.

16. Address

The address of an insurer's corporate headquarters. This location may differ from the company's state of domicile.

17. Phone

The telephone number of an insurer's corporate headquarters.

18. Domicile State

The state that has primary regulatory responsibility for this company. You do not have to live in the domicile state to do business with this firm, provided it is registered to do business in your state.

19. Commenced Business   The month and year the insurer started its operations

20. NAIC Code   The identification number assigned to an insurer by the National Association of Insurance Commissioners (NAIC).

21. Historical Data   Five years of background data for Weiss Safety Rating, risk-adjusted capital ratios (moderate and severe loss scenarios), total assets, capital (including capital stock and retained earnings), net premium, and net income. See the next page for more details on how to read the historical data table.

22. Customized Graph (or Table)   A graph or table depicting one of the company's major strengths or weaknesses.

How to Read the Historical Data Table

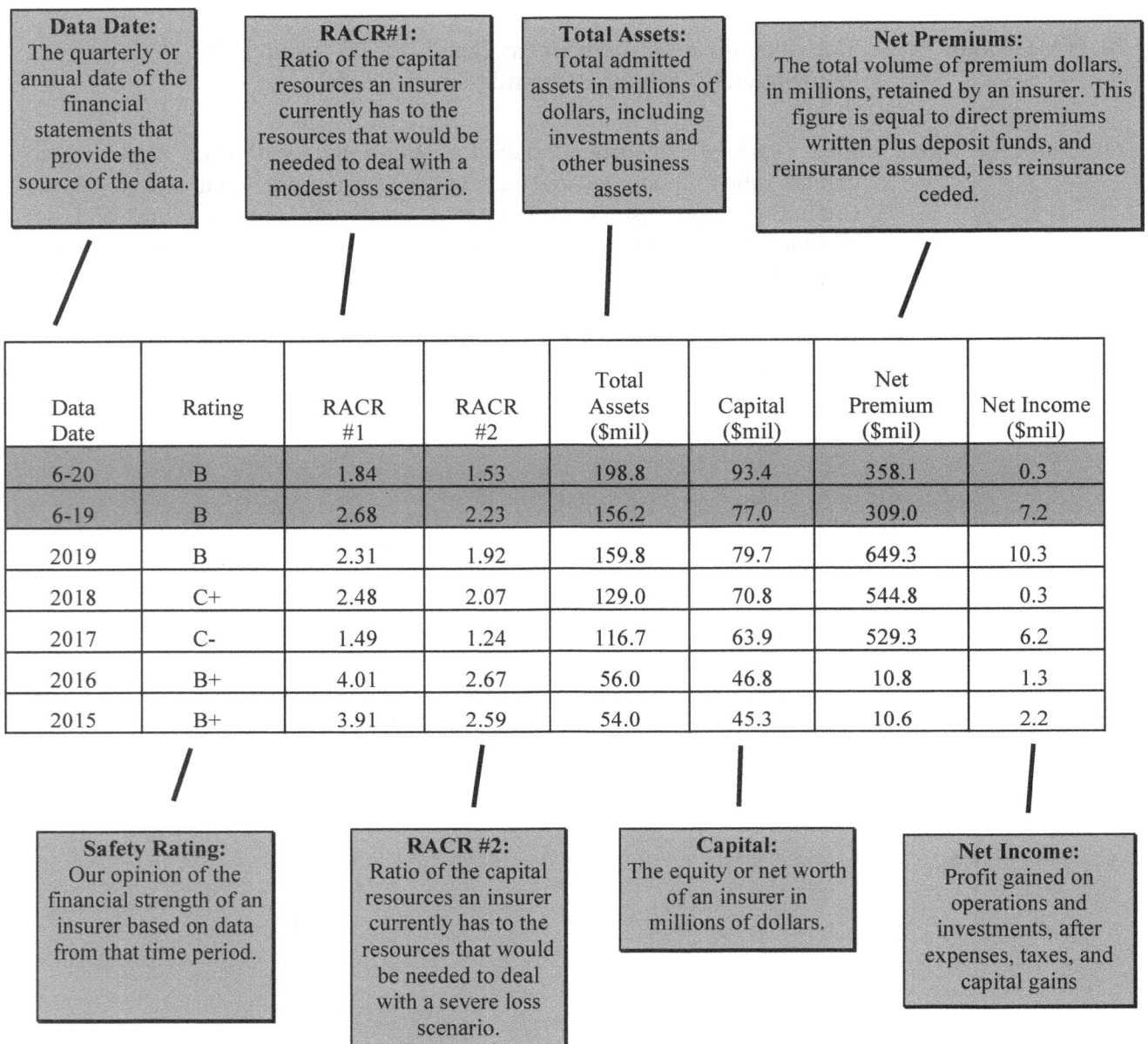

Data Date	Rating	RACR #1	RACR #2	Total Assets ($mil)	Capital ($mil)	Net Premium ($mil)	Net Income ($mil)
6-20	B	1.84	1.53	198.8	93.4	358.1	0.3
6-19	B	2.68	2.23	156.2	77.0	309.0	7.2
2019	B	2.31	1.92	159.8	79.7	649.3	10.3
2018	C+	2.48	2.07	129.0	70.8	544.8	0.3
2017	C-	1.49	1.24	116.7	63.9	529.3	6.2
2016	B+	4.01	2.67	56.0	46.8	10.8	1.3
2015	B+	3.91	2.59	54.0	45.3	10.6	2.2

Data Date: The quarterly or annual date of the financial statements that provide the source of the data.

RACR#1: Ratio of the capital resources an insurer currently has to the resources that would be needed to deal with a modest loss scenario.

Total Assets: Total admitted assets in millions of dollars, including investments and other business assets.

Net Premiums: The total volume of premium dollars, in millions, retained by an insurer. This figure is equal to direct premiums written plus deposit funds, and reinsurance assumed, less reinsurance ceded.

Safety Rating: Our opinion of the financial strength of an insurer based on data from that time period.

RACR #2: Ratio of the capital resources an insurer currently has to the resources that would be needed to deal with a severe loss scenario.

Capital: The equity or net worth of an insurer in millions of dollars.

Net Income: Profit gained on operations and investments, after expenses, taxes, and capital gains

Row Descriptions:

Row 1 contains the most recent quarterly data as filed with state regulators and is presented on a year-to-date basis. For example, the figure for third quarter premiums includes premiums received through the third quarter. **Row 2** consists of data from the same quarter of the prior year. Compare current quarterly results to those of a year ago.

Row 3 contains data from the most recent annual statutory filing. **Rows 4-7** includes data from year-end statements going back four years from the most recent annual filing. Compare current year-end results to those of the previous four years. With the exception of Total Assets and Capital, quarterly data are not comparable with annual data.

Customized Graphs

In the lower right-hand corner of each company section, a customized graph or text block highlights a key factor affecting that company's financial strength. One of twenty five types of information is found, identified by one of the following headings:

# of Months of Claims and Expenses in Capital illustrates the number of months' worth of medical and administrative expenses the company could cover by drawing solely on its current capital position.

Adverse Trends in Operations lists changes in key balance sheet and income statement items which may be leading indicators of deteriorating business performance.

Allocation of Premium Income shows what portion of the company's premium income is being spent on medical benefits and administrative expenses. Any income left after the payment of these two types of expense, is used to pay taxes and extraordinary expenditures; the remainder is profit.

Capital History plots the company's reported capital and surplus in millions of dollars over the last five years. Volatile changes in capital levels may indicate unstable operations.

Detail of Risk-Adjusted Capital Ratio provides a percentage breakdown of target capital components based on lines of business and investments in a moderate or severe loss scenario. Target capital is our opinion of the level of capital the company should have, based on the risk it assumes. For example, if the percentage of target capital for individual life is 33%, this means that 33% of the company's target capital relates to individual life. C2 refers to the pricing risk element of the risk-adjusted capital formula. C3 refers to disintermediation (interest rate) risk.

Enrollment Trend charts an insurer's year-end membership levels over the last five years.

Exposure to Withdrawals Without Penalty answers the question: For each dollar of capital and surplus, how much does the company have in annuity and deposit funds that can be withdrawn by policyholders with minimal or no penalty? The figures do not include the effects of reinsurance or funds subject to withdrawals from cash value life insurance policies.

Group Ratings shows the group name, a composite Weiss Safety Rating for the group, and a list of the largest members with their ratings. The composite Weiss Safety Rating is made up of the weighted average, by assets, of the individual ratings of each company in the group (including life/health companies, property/casualty companies, or HMOs) plus a factor for the financial strength of the holding company, where applicable.

High Risk Assets as a % of Capital answers the question: For each dollar of capital and surplus, how much does the company have in junk bonds, nonperforming mortgages and repossessed real estate? Accumulations in the Asset Valuation Reserve or AVR, which provide some protection against investment losses, have not been included in the figure for capital. These figures are based on year-end data.

Income Trends shows underwriting and net income results over the last five years.

Investment Income Compared to Needs of Reserves answers the question: Is the company earning enough investment income to meet the expectations of actuaries when they priced their policies and set reserve levels? According to state insurance regulators, it would be "unusual" if an insurer were to have less than $1.25 in actual investment income for each dollar of investment income that it projected in its actuarial forecasts. This provides an excess margin of at least 25 cents on the dollar to cover any unexpected decline in income or increase in claims. This graph shows whether or not the company is maintaining the appropriate 25% margin and is based on year-end data.

Junk Bonds as a % of Capital answers the question: For each dollar of capital and surplus, how much does the company have in junk bonds? In addition, it shows a breakdown of the junk bond portfolio by bond rating – BB, B, CCC or in default. Accumulations in the Asset Valuation Reserve or AVR, which provide some protection against investment losses, have not been included in the figure for capital. These figures are based on year-end data.

Largest Net Exposure Per Risk shows the ratio of the largest net aggregate amount insured in any one risk (excluding workers' compensation) as a percent of capital.

Liquidity Index evaluates a company's ability to raise the cash necessary to pay claims. Various cash flow scenarios are modeled to determine how the company might fare in the event of an unexpected spike in claims costs.

Net Income History plots operating gains and losses over the most recent five-year period.

Nonperforming Mortgages (plus repossessed real estate) as a % of Capital answers the question: For each dollar of capital and surplus, how much does the company have in nonperforming mortgages and repossessed real estate? Nonperforming mortgages include those overdue more than 90 days and mortgages currently in process of foreclosure. Accumulations in the Asset Valuation Reserve or AVR, which provide some protection against investment losses, have not been included in the figure for capital. These figures are based on year-end data.

Policy Leverage answers the question: To what degree is this insurer capable of handling an unexpected spike in claims? Low leverage indicates low exposure; high leverage is high exposure.

Target leverage represents the maximum exposure we feel would be appropriate for a top-rated company.

Premium Growth History depicts the change in the insurer's net premiums written. Such changes may be the result of issuing more policies or changes in reinsurance arrangements. In either case, growth rates above 20% per year are considered excessive. "Standard" growth is under 20%; "shrinkage" refers to net declines.

Rating Indexes illustrate the score and range – strong, good, fair, or weak – on each of Weiss indexes.

Reserve Deficiency shows whether the company has set aside sufficient funds to pay claims. A positive number indicates insufficient reserving and a negative number adequate reserving.

Reserves to Capital analyzes the relationship between loss and loss expense reserves to capital. Operating results and capital levels for companies with a high ratio are more susceptible to fluctuations than those with lower ratios.

Risk-Adjusted Capital Ratio #1 answers the question: In each of the past five years, does the insurer have sufficient capital to cover potential losses in its investments and business operations in a *moderate* loss scenario?

Risk-Adjusted Capital Ratio #2 answers the question: In each of the past five years, does the insurer have sufficient capital to cover potential losses in its investments and business operations in a *severe* loss scenario?

Risk-Adjusted Capital Ratios answers these questions for both a moderate loss scenario (RACR #1 shown by the dark bar), and a severe loss scenario (RACR #2, light bar).

4 EVER LIFE INS CO

B   **Good**

Major Rating Factors: Good overall results on stability tests (6.1 on a scale of 0 to 10). Stability strengths include excellent operational trends and good risk diversification. Good quality investment portfolio (6.7) despite mixed results such as: no exposure to mortgages and substantial holdings of BBB bonds but minimal holdings in junk bonds. Good liquidity (6.9).
Other Rating Factors: Fair profitability (4.9). Strong capitalization (10.0) based on excellent risk adjusted capital (severe loss scenario).
Principal Business: Group health insurance (54%), reinsurance (43%), and group life insurance (3%).
Principal Investments: NonCMO investment grade bonds (44%), CMOs and structured securities (26%), cash (8%), common & preferred stock (6%), and noninv. grade bonds (5%).
Investments in Affiliates: None
Group Affiliation: BCS Financial Corp
Licensed in: All states, the District of Columbia and Puerto Rico
Commenced Business: November 1949
Address: 2 Mid America Plaza Suite 200, Oakbrook Terrace, IL 60181
Phone: (630) 472-7700 **Domicile State:** IL **NAIC Code:** 80985

Data Date	Rating	RACR #1	RACR #2	Total Assets ($mil)	Capital ($mil)	Net Premium ($mil)	Net Income ($mil)
6-20	B	7.38	4.69	179.4	80.8	28.0	3.0
6-19	B	7.44	4.90	178.6	84.1	31.9	2.0
2019	B	6.33	4.12	176.9	78.6	64.3	4.0
2018	B	6.41	4.26	182.0	81.4	69.8	5.5
2017	B	5.81	3.83	212.5	85.0	76.8	5.1
2016	B	5.21	3.36	207.5	82.6	72.9	0.6
2015	A	5.63	3.67	200.0	93.1	86.9	5.5

Adverse Trends in Operations
Decrease in asset base during 2019 (3%)
Decrease in asset base during 2018 (14%)
Increase in policy surrenders from 2016 to 2017 (37%)
Decrease in capital during 2016 (11%)
Decrease in premium volume from 2015 to 2016 (16%)

ABSOLUTE TOTAL CARE INC

B   **Good**

Major Rating Factors: Good overall profitability index (5.8 on a scale of 0 to 10). Good liquidity (6.8) with sufficient resources (cash flows and marketable investments) to handle a spike in claims. Strong capitalization (7.6) based on excellent current risk-adjusted capital (severe loss scenario).
Other Rating Factors: High quality investment portfolio (7.7).
Principal Business: Medicaid (81%), Medicare (19%)
Mem Phys: 19: 16,276 **18:** 16,458 **19 MLR** 88.9% **/ 19 Admin Exp** N/A
Enroll(000): Q2 20: 149 **19:** 137 **18:** 122 **Med Exp PMPM:** $366
Principal Investments: Long-term bonds (73%), cash and equiv (26%)
Provider Compensation ($000): Contr fee ($509,818), salary ($37,087), capitation ($7,518), bonus arrang ($2,679)
Total Member Encounters: Phys (892,518), non-phys (876,866)
Group Affiliation: None
Licensed in: SC
Address: 1441 Main Street Suite 900, Columbia, SC 29201
Phone: (866) 433-6041 **Dom State:** SC **Commenced Bus:** N/A

Data Date	Rating	RACR #1	RACR #2	Total Assets ($mil)	Capital ($mil)	Net Premium ($mil)	Net Income ($mil)
6-20	B	1.84	1.53	198.8	93.4	358.1	0.3
6-19	B	2.68	2.23	156.2	77.0	309.0	7.2
2019	B	2.31	1.92	159.8	79.7	649.3	10.3
2018	C+	2.48	2.07	129.0	70.8	544.8	0.3
2017	C-	1.49	1.24	116.7	63.9	529.3	6.2
2016	C-	2.14	1.79	113.4	57.9	492.5	-1.7
2015	C-	2.09	1.74	107.9	50.1	435.7	-1.4

Rating Indexes

ACCESS SENIOR HEALTHCARE INC

E-   **Very Weak**

Major Rating Factors: Weak profitability index (0.8 on a scale of 0 to 10). Poor capitalization index (0.0) based on weak current risk-adjusted capital (severe loss scenario). Weak overall results on stability tests (2.8).
Other Rating Factors: Weak liquidity (2.8) as a spike in claims may stretch capacity.
Principal Business: Managed care (100%)
Mem Phys: 19: N/A **18:** N/A **19 MLR** 95.5% **/ 19 Admin Exp** N/A
Enroll(000): Q2 20: 2 **19:** 3 **18:** 3 **Med Exp PMPM:** $3,147
Principal Investments ($000): Cash and equiv ($4,867)
Provider Compensation ($000): None
Total Member Encounters: N/A
Group Affiliation: None
Licensed in: CA
Address: 21031 Ventura Blvd Suite 210, Woodland Hills, CA 91364
Phone: (818) 710-0315 **Dom State:** CA **Commenced Bus:** July 2013

Data Date	Rating	RACR #1	RACR #2	Total Assets ($mil)	Capital ($mil)	Net Premium ($mil)	Net Income ($mil)
6-20	E-	0.36	0.23	5.3	1.9	9.1	0.4
6-19	E-	0.31	0.19	5.7	1.5	16.0	0.1
2019	E-	0.29	0.18	6.7	1.5	30.4	-1.7
2018	E-	N/A	N/A	5.0	1.4	28.8	-1.8
2017	D	0.61	0.37	6.5	2.7	31.7	0.3
2016	N/A	N/A	N/A	N/A	N/A	N/A	N/A
2015	U	1.07	0.65	3.3	2.1	12.6	0.0

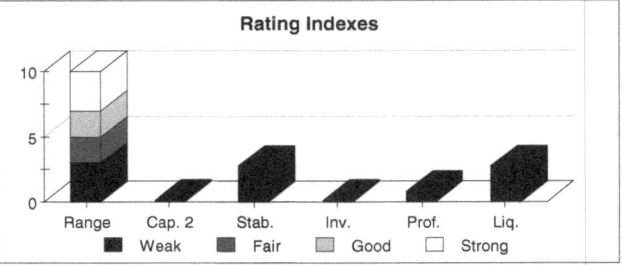

Rating Indexes

ADVANCE INS CO OF KANSAS *   B+   Good

Major Rating Factors: Good overall results on stability tests (6.7 on a scale of 0 to 10). Stability strengths include excellent operational trends and excellent risk diversification. Fair quality investment portfolio (4.4). Strong capitalization (9.5) based on excellent risk adjusted capital (severe loss scenario). Moreover, capital levels have been consistently high over the last five years.
Other Rating Factors: Excellent profitability (8.6) with operating gains in each of the last five years. Excellent liquidity (7.4).
Principal Business: Group life insurance (54%), group health insurance (35%), and individual life insurance (11%).
Principal Investments: Common & preferred stock (34%), CMOs and structured securities (34%), and nonCMO investment grade bonds (29%).
Investments in Affiliates: 3%
Group Affiliation: Blue Cross Blue Shield Kansas
Licensed in: KS
Commenced Business: July 2004
Address: 1133 SW Topeka Blvd, Topeka, KS 66629-0001
Phone: (785) 273-9804 **Domicile State:** KS **NAIC Code:** 12143

Data Date	Rating	RACR #1	RACR #2	Total Assets ($mil)	Capital ($mil)	Net Premium ($mil)	Net Income ($mil)
6-20	B+	4.07	2.66	65.6	55.7	5.7	0.8
6-19	B+	3.89	2.53	62.9	52.7	5.6	1.0
2019	B+	4.11	2.70	65.7	55.3	11.1	2.9
2018	B+	4.09	2.69	58.3	49.9	10.9	1.8
2017	B+	3.95	2.59	59.7	49.7	10.9	2.7
2016	B+	4.01	2.67	56.0	46.8	10.8	1.3
2015	B+	3.91	2.59	54.0	45.3	10.6	2.2

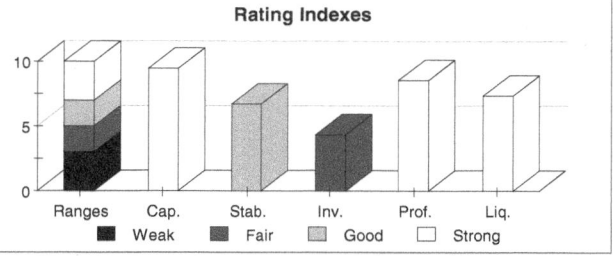

ADVENTIST HEALTH PLAN INC   D   Weak

Major Rating Factors: Weak profitability index (0.9 on a scale of 0 to 10). Poor capitalization index (2.8) based on weak current risk-adjusted capital (moderate loss scenario). Weak overall results on stability tests (2.0).
Other Rating Factors: Good liquidity (6.9) with sufficient resources (cash flows and marketable investments) to handle a spike in claims.
Principal Business: Managed care (100%)
Mem Phys: 19: N/A **18:** N/A **19 MLR** 102.8% **/ 19 Admin Exp** N/A
Enroll(000): Q2 20: 17 **19:** 17 **18:** 17 **Med Exp PMPM:** $147
Principal Investments ($000): Cash and equiv ($4,343)
Provider Compensation ($000): None
Total Member Encounters: N/A
Group Affiliation: None
Licensed in: CA
Address: 2100 Douglas Blvd, Roseville, CA 95661
Phone: (916) 789-4252 **Dom State:** CA **Commenced Bus:** N/A

Data Date	Rating	RACR #1	RACR #2	Total Assets ($mil)	Capital ($mil)	Net Premium ($mil)	Net Income ($mil)
6-20	D	0.48	0.30	7.6	1.7	14.6	0.1
6-19	D	0.96	0.61	6.7	3.2	14.9	0.5
2019	D	0.46	0.29	6.7	1.7	29.6	-1.0
2018	D	0.81	0.51	9.3	2.7	30.1	0.1
2017	D	0.83	0.53	5.0	2.6	28.1	0.8
2016	D	0.61	0.39	3.3	1.8	26.2	0.7
2015	E-	N/A	N/A	1.5	-1.9	N/A	-1.7

AETNA BETTER HEALTH (AN OHIO CORP)   B   Good

Major Rating Factors: Excellent overall profitability index (6.9 on a scale of 0 to 10). Strong capitalization (8.0) based on excellent current risk-adjusted capital (severe loss scenario). High quality investment portfolio (8.2).
Other Rating Factors: Excellent liquidity (6.9) with sufficient resources (cash flows and marketable investments) to handle a spike in claims.
Principal Business: Medicaid (63%), Medicare (37%).
Mem Phys: 19: 38,193 **18:** 23,790 **19 MLR** 81.8% **/ 19 Admin Exp** N/A
Enroll(000): Q2 20: 28 **19:** 26 **18:** 25 **Med Exp PMPM:** $2,583
Principal Investments: Long-term bonds (68%), cash and equiv (24%), mortgs (2%), other (6%)
Provider Compensation ($000): Contr fee ($617,269), FFS ($127,325), capitation ($19,134), bonus arrang ($1,206), other ($36,485)
Total Member Encounters: Phys (1,067,037), non-phys (3,577,318)
Group Affiliation: None
Licensed in: OH
Address: 7400 W CAMPUS ROAD, NEW ALBANY, OH 43054
Phone: (800) 872-3862 **Dom State:** OH **Commenced Bus:** N/A

Data Date	Rating	RACR #1	RACR #2	Total Assets ($mil)	Capital ($mil)	Net Premium ($mil)	Net Income ($mil)
6-20	B	2.14	1.78	328.7	160.4	505.9	19.1
6-19	B	3.52	2.94	339.5	163.7	498.2	31.0
2019	B	3.17	2.64	354.9	170.4	993.7	77.2
2018	B	4.02	3.35	331.7	189.5	960.8	102.5
2017	B	N/A	N/A	286.6	134.3	936.8	65.7
2016	C+	4.01	3.34	319.8	166.2	858.2	40.4
2015	C+	2.86	2.38	310.5	107.4	783.0	-10.1

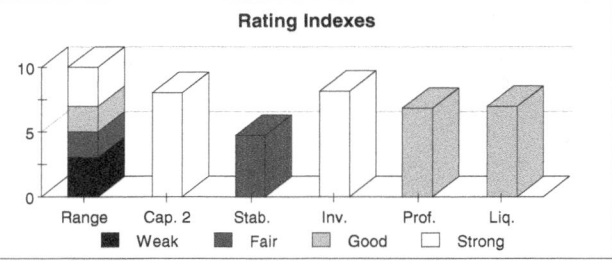

AETNA BETTER HEALTH INC   B-   Good

Major Rating Factors: Fair profitability index (4.8 on a scale of 0 to 10). Strong capitalization (10.0) based on excellent current risk-adjusted capital (severe loss scenario). High quality investment portfolio (8.2).
Other Rating Factors: Excellent liquidity (7.6) with ample operational cash flow and liquid investments.
Principal Business: Medicare (56%), Medicaid (44%)
Mem Phys: 19: 20,574 **18:** 18,171 **19 MLR** 71.0% **/ 19 Admin Exp** N/A
Enroll(000): Q2 20: 7 **19:** 8 **18:** 7 **Med Exp PMPM:** $1,650
Principal Investments: Long-term bonds (53%), cash and equiv (47%)
Provider Compensation ($000): Contr fee ($112,075), FFS ($43,153), capitation ($4,153), bonus arrang ($686), other ($10,096)
Total Member Encounters: Phys (253,620), non-phys (252,646)
Group Affiliation: None
Licensed in: IL
Address: 3200 HIGHLAND AVENUE F661, DOWNERS GROVE, IL 60515
Phone: (800) 872-3862 **Dom State:** IL **Commenced Bus:** N/A

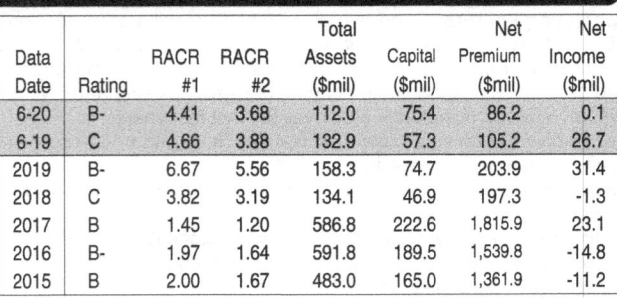

Data Date	Rating	RACR #1	RACR #2	Total Assets ($mil)	Capital ($mil)	Net Premium ($mil)	Net Income ($mil)
6-20	B-	4.41	3.68	112.0	75.4	86.2	0.1
6-19	C	4.66	3.88	132.9	57.3	105.2	26.7
2019	B-	6.67	5.56	158.3	74.7	203.9	31.4
2018	C	3.82	3.19	134.1	46.9	197.3	-1.3
2017	B	1.45	1.20	586.8	222.6	1,815.9	23.1
2016	B-	1.97	1.64	591.8	189.5	1,539.8	-14.8
2015	B	2.00	1.67	483.0	165.0	1,361.9	-11.2

Rating Indexes

Range   Cap. 2   Stab.   Inv.   Prof.   Liq.
■ Weak   ■ Fair   ▨ Good   □ Strong

AETNA BETTER HEALTH INC (A LA CORP)   C   Fair

Major Rating Factors: Weak profitability index (2.5 on a scale of 0 to 10). Good liquidity (6.8) with sufficient resources (cash flows and marketable investments) to handle a spike in claims. Strong capitalization (9.6) based on excellent current risk-adjusted capital (severe loss scenario).
Other Rating Factors: High quality investment portfolio (9.9).
Principal Business: Medicaid (100%)
Mem Phys: 18: 18,255 **17:** 16,045 **18 MLR** 84.9% **/ 18 Admin Exp** N/A
Enroll(000): Q3 19: 125 **18:** 119 **17:** 117 **Med Exp PMPM:** $379
Principal Investments: Long-term bonds (87%), cash and equiv (13%)
Provider Compensation ($000): Contr fee ($512,345), FFS ($28,825), capitation ($7,594), bonus arrang ($2,424)
Total Member Encounters: Phys (819,720), non-phys (741,061)
Group Affiliation: None
Licensed in: AL, LA, MS
Address: 2400 VETERANS MEMORIAL BOULEVA, KENNER, LA 70062
Phone: (504) 667-4461 **Dom State:** LA **Commenced Bus:** N/A

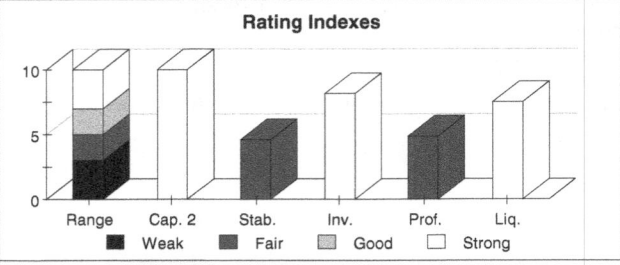

Data Date	Rating	RACR #1	RACR #2	Total Assets ($mil)	Capital ($mil)	Net Premium ($mil)	Net Income ($mil)
9-19	C	3.39	2.83	195.8	81.4	518.6	19.3
9-18	C+	N/A	N/A	234.8	83.9	466.8	-2.7
2018	C	2.85	2.38	219.5	64.5	634.7	-14.4
2017	C+	N/A	N/A	224.6	87.9	592.0	22.8
2016	C+	2.94	2.45	213.9	65.1	421.9	-7.9
2015	C+	1.67	1.39	89.4	24.5	180.7	-11.9
2014	N/A	N/A	N/A	3.0	3.0	N/A	N/A

Rating Indexes

Range   Cap. 2   Stab.   Inv.   Prof.   Liq.
■ Weak   ■ Fair   ▨ Good   □ Strong

AETNA BETTER HEALTH INC (A NJ CORP)   B   Good

Major Rating Factors: Good liquidity (6.6 on a scale of 0 to 10) with sufficient resources (cash flows and marketable investments) to handle a spike in claims. Excellent profitability (8.2). Strong capitalization (9.4) based on excellent current risk-adjusted capital (severe loss scenario).
Other Rating Factors: High quality investment portfolio (9.7).
Principal Business: Medicaid (100%)
Mem Phys: 18: 10,804 **17:** 10,563 **18 MLR** 84.4% **/ 18 Admin Exp** N/A
Enroll(000): Q3 19: 65 **18:** 58 **17:** 46 **Med Exp PMPM:** $460
Principal Investments: Long-term bonds (84%), cash and equiv (16%)
Provider Compensation ($000): Contr fee ($220,103), FFS ($75,047), bonus arrang ($1,586), capitation ($1,155)
Total Member Encounters: Phys (418,114), non-phys (729,608)
Group Affiliation: None
Licensed in: NJ
Address: 3 INDEPENDENCE WAY SUITE 400, PRINCETON, NJ 8540
Phone: (855) 232-3596 **Dom State:** NJ **Commenced Bus:** N/A

Data Date	Rating	RACR #1	RACR #2	Total Assets ($mil)	Capital ($mil)	Net Premium ($mil)	Net Income ($mil)
9-19	B	3.25	2.71	145.5	63.7	329.0	12.2
9-18	B+	N/A	N/A	172.8	45.9	268.1	9.8
2018	B	2.50	2.08	133.3	46.3	364.1	10.7
2017	B+	N/A	N/A	134.6	36.3	233.8	16.2
2016	B	7.41	6.18	119.6	35.3	138.0	16.1
2015	C+	1.92	1.60	50.0	12.3	68.4	-2.6
2014	N/A	N/A	N/A	5.0	5.0	N/A	N/A

Rating Indexes

Range   Cap. 2   Stab.   Inv.   Prof.   Liq.
■ Weak   ■ Fair   ▨ Good   □ Strong

AETNA BETTER HEALTH INC (A PA CORP)   C   Fair

Major Rating Factors: Fair quality investment portfolio (4.4 on a scale of 0 to 10). Good liquidity (6.6) with sufficient resources (cash flows and marketable investments) to handle a spike in claims. Excellent profitability (8.2).
Other Rating Factors: Strong capitalization (7.6) based on excellent current risk-adjusted capital (severe loss scenario).
Principal Business: Medicaid (100%)
Mem Phys: 19: 40,748 **18:** 39,650 **19 MLR** 86.1% **/ 19 Admin Exp** N/A
Enroll(000): Q2 20: 225 **19:** 201 **18:** 199 **Med Exp PMPM:** $359
Principal Investments: Long-term bonds (87%), cash and equiv (10%), mortgs (3%)
Provider Compensation ($000): Contr fee ($567,116), FFS ($44,879), capitation ($7,451), bonus arrang ($6,442), other ($203,212)
Total Member Encounters: Phys (913,231), non-phys (1,168,738)
Group Affiliation: None
Licensed in: PA
Address: 1425 UNION MEETING ROAD, BLUE BELL, PA 19422
Phone: (800) 872-3862 **Dom State:** PA **Commenced Bus:** N/A

Data Date	Rating	RACR #1	RACR #2	Total Assets ($mil)	Capital ($mil)	Net Premium ($mil)	Net Income ($mil)
6-20	C	1.87	1.56	460.9	133.1	558.9	19.6
6-19	C	2.56	2.13	430.7	109.6	498.9	5.1
2019	C	2.33	1.94	339.9	114.0	1,004.5	17.4
2018	C	2.97	2.47	353.8	131.6	1,013.9	56.1
2017	D-	2.41	2.01	480.5	141.2	936.5	63.0
2016	D-	3.76	3.13	574.8	141.3	867.8	58.2
2015	D-	2.57	2.14	419.0	111.4	818.5	32.7

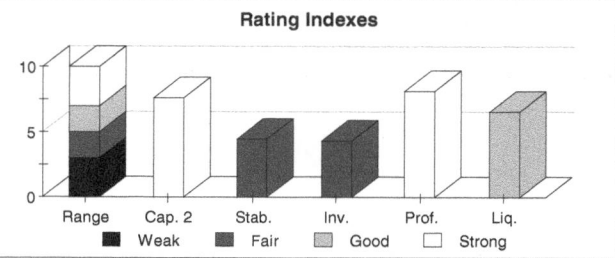

AETNA BETTER HEALTH OF CA INC   D+   Weak

Major Rating Factors: Weak profitability index (0.9 on a scale of 0 to 10). Good overall results on stability tests (5.9) based on healthy premium and capital growth during 2019. Strong capitalization index (9.8) based on excellent current risk-adjusted capital (severe loss scenario).
Other Rating Factors: Excellent liquidity (7.1) with ample operational cash flow and liquid investments.
Principal Business: Medicaid (100%)
Mem Phys: 19: N/A **18:** N/A **19 MLR** 88.6% **/ 19 Admin Exp** N/A
Enroll(000): Q2 20: 34 **19:** 11 **18:** 11 **Med Exp PMPM:** $865
Principal Investments ($000): Cash and equiv ($9,320)
Provider Compensation ($000): None
Total Member Encounters: N/A
Group Affiliation: Access Senior HealthCare Inc
Licensed in: (No states)
Address: , , CA 94598-2581
Phone: (Phone number **Dom State:** DE **Commenced Bus:** N/A

Data Date	Rating	RACR #1	RACR #2	Total Assets ($mil)	Capital ($mil)	Net Premium ($mil)	Net Income ($mil)
6-20	D+	4.45	3.00	105.5	42.7	109.4	-12.5
6-19	D+	2.64	1.82	43.8	13.4	33.7	-3.0
2019	D+	1.93	1.31	51.4	19.9	73.7	-1.6
2018	D+	5.41	3.40	27.0	16.3	21.2	8.1
2017	U	9.23	6.59	17.7	6.3	N/A	-8.7
2016	N/A	N/A	N/A	N/A	N/A	N/A	N/A
2015	N/A	N/A	N/A	N/A	N/A	N/A	N/A

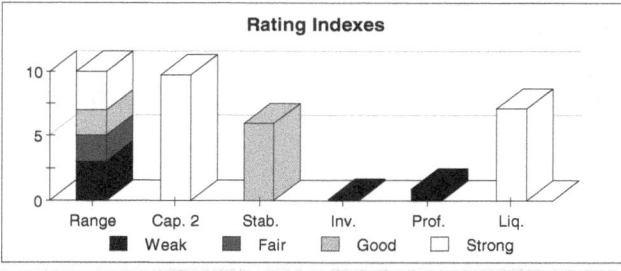

AETNA BETTER HEALTH OF FLORIDA INC   D   Weak

Major Rating Factors: Fair profitability index (3.7 on a scale of 0 to 10). Good overall results on stability tests (5.2) despite a decline in the number of member physicians during 2020. Good liquidity (5.1) with sufficient resources (cash flows and marketable investments) to handle a spike in claims.
Other Rating Factors: Strong capitalization index (10.0) based on excellent current risk-adjusted capital (severe loss scenario). High quality investment portfolio (9.0).
Principal Business: Medicaid (89%), comp med (11%)
Mem Phys: 19: 23,078 **18:** 41,044 **19 MLR** 74.9% **/ 19 Admin Exp** N/A
Enroll(000): Q2 20: 206 **19:** 146 **18:** 104 **Med Exp PMPM:** $247
Principal Investments: Long-term bonds (92%), cash and equiv (8%)
Provider Compensation ($000): Contr fee ($461,667), FFS ($62,954), capitation ($46,455)
Total Member Encounters: Phys (647,126), non-phys (944,709)
Group Affiliation: None
Licensed in: FL
Address: 1340 CONCORD TERRACE, SUNRISE,
Phone: (954) 693-2501 **Dom State:** FL **Commenced Bus:** N/A

Data Date	Rating	RACR #1	RACR #2	Total Assets ($mil)	Capital ($mil)	Net Premium ($mil)	Net Income ($mil)
6-20	D	4.11	3.43	315.0	155.5	338.0	4.0
6-19	D	3.07	2.56	400.1	130.5	274.4	58.1
2019	D	5.54	4.61	299.2	148.8	561.6	77.7
2018	D	1.67	1.39	346.0	73.2	493.7	-113.1
2017	C+	4.52	3.77	298.6	160.7	511.7	32.0
2016	C+	3.05	2.54	547.7	195.6	1,368.1	42.9
2015	C+	2.10	1.75	515.7	128.7	1,280.5	6.9

AETNA BETTER HEALTH OF MICHIGAN INC   B   Good

Major Rating Factors: Good overall profitability index (5.9 on a scale of 0 to 10). Strong capitalization (7.9) based on excellent current risk-adjusted capital (severe loss scenario). High quality investment portfolio (9.4).
Other Rating Factors: Excellent liquidity (7.1) with ample operational cash flow and liquid investments.
Principal Business: Medicare (50%), Medicaid (50%)
Mem Phys: 19: 44,797 **18:** 16,880 **19 MLR** 74.7% **/ 19 Admin Exp** N/A
Enroll(000): Q2 20: 53 **19:** 48 **18:** 45 **Med Exp PMPM:** $439
Principal Investments: Cash and equiv (83%), long-term bonds (17%)
Provider Compensation ($000): Contr fee ($164,052), FFS ($26,617), capitation ($7,305), bonus arrang ($1,122), other ($30,595)
Total Member Encounters: Phys (261,388), non-phys (273,416)
Group Affiliation: None
Licensed in: ID, MI, OR
Address: 1333 GRATIOT AVENUE SUITE 400, DETROIT, MI 48207
Phone: (800) 831-1166 **Dom State:** MI **Commenced Bus:** N/A

Data Date	Rating	RACR #1	RACR #2	Total Assets ($mil)	Capital ($mil)	Net Premium ($mil)	Net Income ($mil)
6-20	B	2.11	1.76	135.4	50.2	187.9	2.0
6-19	B	3.61	3.00	125.1	53.0	157.3	6.0
2019	B	3.86	3.22	131.3	57.9	318.0	15.0
2018	B	3.70	3.08	136.5	54.6	293.6	12.9
2017	B	1.51	1.26	121.5	41.5	349.5	3.2
2016	B	2.22	1.85	120.5	34.2	340.2	-3.5
2015	B+	3.04	2.53	110.4	36.9	282.1	5.6

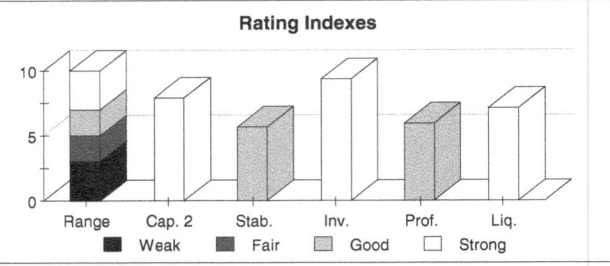

Rating Indexes

AETNA BETTER HEALTH OF MISSOURI LLC   C   Fair

Major Rating Factors: Weak overall results on stability tests (0.3 on a scale of 0 to 10) based on a steep decline in capital during 2018. Rating is significantly influenced by the good financial results of . Excellent profitability (7.3). Strong capitalization index (10.0) based on excellent current risk-adjusted capital (severe loss scenario).
Other Rating Factors: High quality investment portfolio (8.9). Excellent liquidity (10.0) with ample operational cash flow and liquid investments.
Principal Business: Medicaid (100%)
Mem Phys: 18: N/A **17:** N/A **18 MLR** -307.1% **/ 18 Admin Exp** N/A
Enroll(000): Q3 19: N/A **18:** N/A **17:** N/A **Med Exp PMPM:** N/A
Principal Investments: Long-term bonds (90%), cash and equiv (10%)
Provider Compensation ($000): Contr fee ($1,148)
Total Member Encounters: N/A
Group Affiliation: None
Licensed in: KS, MO
Address: 10 S BROADWAY SUITE 1200, ST. LOUIS,
Phone: (314) 241-5300 **Dom State:** MO **Commenced Bus:** N/A

Data Date	Rating	RACR #1	RACR #2	Total Assets ($mil)	Capital ($mil)	Net Premium ($mil)	Net Income ($mil)
9-19	C	25.47	21.23	31.1	23.4	0.3	0.1
9-18	C	3.99	3.33	43.6	40.9	1.2	1.4
2018	C	37.78	31.48	40.9	40.5	1.0	1.0
2017	C	6.59	5.49	129.2	117.6	258.9	7.9
2016	B	4.66	3.88	280.3	164.4	780.7	32.7
2015	B	4.29	3.58	252.9	135.4	707.0	20.1
2014	N/A	N/A	N/A	191.5	109.6	645.4	N/A

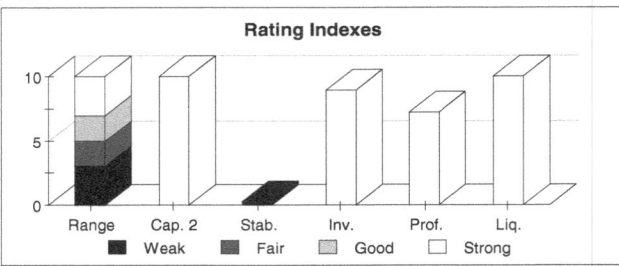

Rating Indexes

AETNA BETTER HEALTH OF TEXAS INC   B   Good

Major Rating Factors: Good liquidity (6.8 on a scale of 0 to 10) with sufficient resources (cash flows and marketable investments) to handle a spike in claims. Excellent profitability (8.2). Strong capitalization (8.5) based on excellent current risk-adjusted capital (severe loss scenario).
Other Rating Factors: High quality investment portfolio (9.9).
Principal Business: Medicaid (93%), comp med (7%)
Mem Phys: 18: 35,652 **17:** 31,056 **18 MLR** 80.7% **/ 18 Admin Exp** N/A
Enroll(000): Q3 19: 86 **18:** 88 **17:** 92 **Med Exp PMPM:** $234
Principal Investments: Long-term bonds (90%), cash and equiv (10%)
Provider Compensation ($000): Contr fee ($231,779), FFS ($18,215), capitation ($1,256), bonus arrang ($166)
Total Member Encounters: Phys (557,635), non-phys (522,121)
Group Affiliation: None
Licensed in: TX
Address: 2777 N STEMMONS FREEWAY SUIT, DALLAS, TX 75207-2265
Phone: (800) 872-3862 **Dom State:** TX **Commenced Bus:** N/A

Data Date	Rating	RACR #1	RACR #2	Total Assets ($mil)	Capital ($mil)	Net Premium ($mil)	Net Income ($mil)
9-19	B	2.57	2.14	81.6	36.2	231.8	3.6
9-18	B+	N/A	N/A	107.2	46.0	232.6	11.8
2018	B	3.36	2.80	103.5	50.2	314.5	16.6
2017	B+	N/A	N/A	119.5	53.3	284.3	19.1
2016	C+	3.55	2.96	102.1	48.8	251.1	15.4
2015	U	5.62	4.68	92.7	30.7	70.3	4.6
2014	N/A	N/A	N/A	N/A	N/A	N/A	N/A

Rating Indexes

AETNA BETTER HLTH OF KY INS CO *   B+   Good

Major Rating Factors: Good liquidity (6.7 on a scale of 0 to 10) with sufficient resources (cash flows and marketable investments) to handle a spike in claims. Excellent profitability (10.0). Strong capitalization (10.0) based on excellent current risk-adjusted capital (severe loss scenario).
Other Rating Factors: Fair quality investment portfolio (4.8).
Principal Business: Medicaid (97%), comp med (3%)
Mem Phys: 18: 30,303 **17:** 28,667 **18 MLR** 82.9% **/ 18 Admin Exp** N/A
Enroll(000): Q3 19: 212 **18:** 225 **17:** 243 **Med Exp PMPM:** $335
Principal Investments: Long-term bonds (93%), cash and equiv (4%), mortgs (3%)
Provider Compensation ($000): Contr fee ($909,602), FFS ($29,002), capitation ($11,496)
Total Member Encounters: Phys (1,654,807), non-phys (968,509)
Group Affiliation: None
Licensed in: KY
Address: 9900 CORPORATE CAMPUS DRIVE S, LOUISVILLE, KY 40223
Phone: (855) 300-5528 **Dom State:** KY **Commenced Bus:** N/A

Data Date	Rating	RACR #1	RACR #2	Total Assets ($mil)	Capital ($mil)	Net Premium ($mil)	Net Income ($mil)
9-19	B+	6.30	5.25	536.6	365.4	807.9	35.4
9-18	B+	N/A	N/A	524.0	298.8	833.0	25.7
2018	B+	5.67	4.72	496.0	326.5	1,121.8	59.1
2017	B+	N/A	N/A	526.8	261.9	1,124.5	55.7
2016	C+	3.29	2.74	563.5	213.4	1,111.9	122.2
2015	N/A	N/A	N/A	3.3	3.3	N/A	N/A
2014	N/A	N/A	N/A	N/A	N/A	N/A	N/A

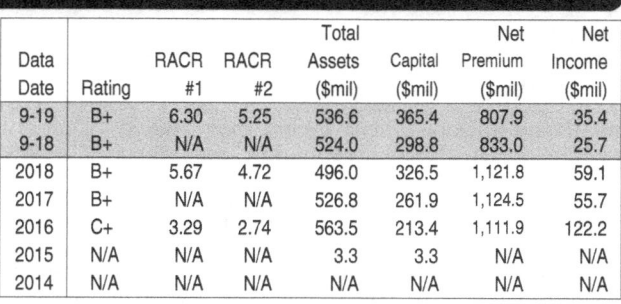

Rating Indexes

AETNA HEALTH & LIFE INS CO   C-   Fair

Major Rating Factors: Fair current capitalization (4.4 on a scale of 0 to 10) based on mixed results -- excessive policy leverage mitigated by excellent risk adjusted capital (severe loss scenario) reflecting significant improvement over results in 2019. Weak profitability (1.5). Excellent expense controls. Return on equity has been fair, averaging 8.7%. Weak liquidity (0.8).
Other Rating Factors: Weak overall results on stability tests (1.9) including weak results on operational trends and negative cash flow from operations for 2019. Good quality investment portfolio (6.6).
Principal Business: Individual health insurance (92%) and group health insurance (8%).
Principal Investments: NonCMO investment grade bonds (90%), CMOs and structured securities (14%), and noninv. grade bonds (7%).
Investments in Affiliates: None
Group Affiliation: Aetna Inc
Licensed in: All states except PR
Commenced Business: October 1971
Address: 151 FARMINGTON AVENUE, HARTFORD, CT 6156
Phone: (800) 872-3862 **Domicile State:** CT **NAIC Code:** 78700

Data Date	Rating	RACR #1	RACR #2	Total Assets ($mil)	Capital ($mil)	Net Premium ($mil)	Net Income ($mil)
6-20	C-	1.51	1.34	432.1	156.0	903.9	69.9
6-19	C	1.48	1.11	162.3	83.4	214.8	-34.0
2019	C-	0.95	0.73	134.5	53.0	442.8	-62.4
2018	C	2.11	1.59	185.2	106.5	374.0	-13.0
2017	C+	5.60	3.55	388.4	307.3	-1,183.1	418.9
2016	B+	2.14	1.33	2,388.6	282.5	804.5	9.5
2015	B+	2.59	1.58	2,290.6	299.9	655.8	76.8

Policy Leverage

Target Leverage — 100%
Actual Leverage — 276%

0%   100%   200%   300%

■ Recommended   □ Excess

AETNA HEALTH INC (A CT CORP)   B-   Good

Major Rating Factors: Fair profitability index (4.1 on a scale of 0 to 10). Fair overall results on stability tests (4.3) based on a significant 26% decrease in enrollment during the period. Good quality investment portfolio (6.4).
Other Rating Factors: Strong capitalization index (10.0) based on excellent current risk-adjusted capital (severe loss scenario). Excellent liquidity (7.0) with ample operational cash flow and liquid investments.
Principal Business: Medicare (99%)
Mem Phys: 19: 35,495 **18:** 33,909 **19 MLR** 83.0% **/ 19 Admin Exp** N/A
Enroll(000): Q2 20: 10 **19:** 11 **18:** 15 **Med Exp PMPM:** $786
Principal Investments: Long-term bonds (68%), cash and equiv (26%), mortgs (4%), other (1%)
Provider Compensation ($000): Contr fee ($105,978), FFS ($5,034), bonus arrang ($1,492), capitation ($428)
Total Member Encounters: Phys (362,720), non-phys (251,092)
Group Affiliation: None
Licensed in: CT
Address: 151 FARMINGTON AVENUE, HARTFORD,
Phone: (800) 872-3862 **Dom State:** CT **Commenced Bus:** N/A

Data Date	Rating	RACR #1	RACR #2	Total Assets ($mil)	Capital ($mil)	Net Premium ($mil)	Net Income ($mil)
6-20	B-	4.54	3.78	87.0	58.2	59.9	7.5
6-19	C	4.98	4.15	84.3	49.8	69.0	4.0
2019	B-	6.37	5.31	87.3	50.9	132.8	4.0
2018	C	4.59	3.83	86.9	45.5	156.1	-3.5
2017	C	3.47	2.89	112.7	74.5	254.1	11.3
2016	C	6.11	5.09	122.2	82.2	245.6	13.0
2015	C	5.02	4.18	103.2	68.2	225.4	1.5

Rating Indexes

AETNA HEALTH INC (A FLORIDA CORP)   B   Good

Major Rating Factors: Good overall profitability index (5.7 on a scale of 0 to 10). Good overall results on stability tests (4.9) based on a significant 20% decrease in enrollment during the period. Good liquidity (6.8) with sufficient resources (cash flows and marketable investments) to handle a spike in claims.
Other Rating Factors: Strong capitalization index (7.7) based on excellent current risk-adjusted capital (severe loss scenario). High quality investment portfolio (8.2).
Principal Business: Medicare (58%), comp med (42%)
Mem Phys: 19: 119,142 **18:** 78,135 **19 MLR** 84.6% **/ 19 Admin Exp** N/A
Enroll(000): Q2 20: 127 **19:** 152 **18:** 191 **Med Exp PMPM:** $643
Principal Investments: Long-term bonds (83%), cash and equiv (17%)
Provider Compensation ($000): Contr fee ($859,170), capitation ($120,337), FFS ($81,046), bonus arrang ($59,527), other ($188,886)
Total Member Encounters: Phys (1,881,767), non-phys (1,693,385)
Group Affiliation: None
Licensed in: FL, IA
Address: 4630 WOODLANDS CORPORATE BOULE, TAMPA,
Phone: (813) 775-0000 **Dom State:** FL **Commenced Bus:** N/A

Data Date	Rating	RACR #1	RACR #2	Total Assets ($mil)	Capital ($mil)	Net Premium ($mil)	Net Income ($mil)
6-20	B	1.94	1.62	491.6	209.4	707.5	31.6
6-19	B-	2.57	2.14	570.9	225.6	773.6	53.3
2019	B	2.41	2.01	503.7	186.5	1,508.1	51.2
2018	B-	2.05	1.71	499.9	174.5	1,673.8	-34.8
2017	B	1.64	1.37	431.4	200.9	1,843.4	52.5
2016	B+	2.58	2.15	541.2	249.8	1,982.9	69.6
2015	B	2.21	1.84	512.6	180.0	1,631.5	41.3

Rating Indexes

AETNA HEALTH INC (A GEORGIA CORP)   C   Fair

Major Rating Factors: Fair profitability index (4.1 on a scale of 0 to 10). Fair overall results on stability tests (3.2) based on a significant 32% decrease in enrollment during the period, a steep decline in premium revenue in 2019. Good liquidity (6.7) with sufficient resources (cash flows and marketable investments) to handle a spike in claims
Other Rating Factors: Strong capitalization index (10.0) based on excellent current risk-adjusted capital (severe loss scenario). High quality investment portfolio (9.9).
Principal Business: Comp med (52%), Medicare (39%), FEHB (8%), dental (2%)
Mem Phys: 19: 48,823 **18:** 31,276 **19 MLR** 86.5% **/ 19 Admin Exp** N/A
Enroll(000): Q2 20: 29 **19:** 34 **18:** 50 **Med Exp PMPM:** $362
Principal Investments: Long-term bonds (99%), cash and equiv (1%)
Provider Compensation ($000): Contr fee ($116,681), FFS ($5,004), capitation ($1,023), bonus arrang ($947), other ($38,522)
Total Member Encounters: Phys (436,598), non-phys (330,604)
Group Affiliation: None
Licensed in: GA
Address: 1100 ABERNATHY ROAD SUITE 375, ATLANTA,
Phone: (800) 872-3862 **Dom State:** GA **Commenced Bus:** N/A

Data Date	Rating	RACR #1	RACR #2	Total Assets ($mil)	Capital ($mil)	Net Premium ($mil)	Net Income ($mil)
6-20	C	4.57	3.80	195.5	74.4	73.3	2.3
6-19	C	5.24	4.37	209.6	72.3	94.1	6.9
2019	C	6.77	5.64	200.1	71.9	181.9	6.6
2018	C	4.75	3.96	193.5	65.1	255.1	4.9
2017	C+	4.37	3.64	235.8	105.3	317.8	10.2
2016	B	3.66	3.05	284.8	131.4	605.1	18.9
2015	B	3.01	2.51	298.3	116.0	642.9	-4.6

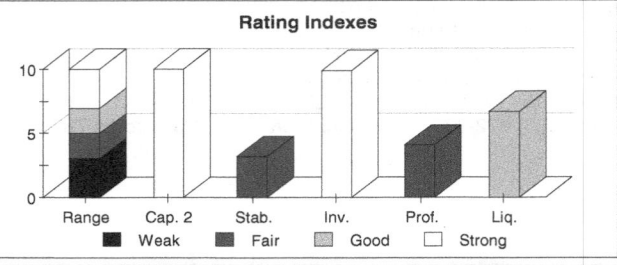

Rating Indexes

AETNA HEALTH INC (A MAINE CORP)   B   Good

Major Rating Factors: Good overall profitability index (6.2 on a scale of 0 to 10). Fair overall results on stability tests (4.3). Strong capitalization index (8.7) based on excellent current risk-adjusted capital (severe loss scenario).
Other Rating Factors: High quality investment portfolio (7.9). Excellent liquidity (7.0) with sufficient resources (cash flows and marketable investments) to handle a spike in claims.
Principal Business: Medicare (96%), comp med (4%)
Mem Phys: 19: 15,129 **18:** 14,925 **19 MLR** 84.9% **/ 19 Admin Exp** N/A
Enroll(000): Q2 20: 13 **19:** 10 **18:** 8 **Med Exp PMPM:** $609
Principal Investments: Long-term bonds (72%), cash and equiv (28%)
Provider Compensation ($000): Contr fee ($55,428), FFS ($3,065), bonus arrang ($1,044), capitation ($243), other ($7,179)
Total Member Encounters: Phys (267,801), non-phys (161,210)
Group Affiliation: None
Licensed in: ME
Address: 175 RUNNING HILL ROAD SUITE 30, SOUTH PORTLAND,
Phone: (800) 872-3862 **Dom State:** ME **Commenced Bus:** N/A

Data Date	Rating	RACR #1	RACR #2	Total Assets ($mil)	Capital ($mil)	Net Premium ($mil)	Net Income ($mil)
6-20	B	2.75	2.29	40.4	25.6	53.0	6.6
6-19	B	6.18	5.15	42.8	25.0	39.8	2.3
2019	B	3.61	3.01	36.9	19.1	80.4	1.4
2018	B	5.62	4.69	37.2	22.6	66.8	5.2
2017	B-	2.10	1.75	28.9	17.5	77.8	4.6
2016	B-	3.13	2.61	27.6	15.5	75.3	2.5
2015	B-	2.36	1.97	26.2	12.7	80.1	-1.2

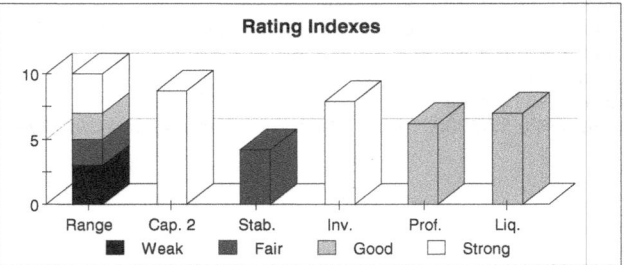

Rating Indexes

AETNA HEALTH INC (A NEW JERSEY CORP)   C   Fair

Major Rating Factors: Fair overall results on stability tests (3.0 on a scale of 0 to 10) based on a steep decline in capital during 2019. Weak profitability index (2.0). Good quality investment portfolio (5.0).

Other Rating Factors: Good liquidity (6.5) with sufficient resources (cash flows and marketable investments) to handle a spike in claims. Strong capitalization index (7.7) based on excellent current risk-adjusted capital (severe loss scenario).

Principal Business: Medicare (83%), comp med (13%), FEHB (4%)

Mem Phys: 19: 56,615 **18:** 51,944 **19 MLR** 95.5% **/ 19 Admin Exp** N/A

Enroll(000): Q2 20: 58 **19:** 67 **18:** 62 **Med Exp PMPM:** $870

Principal Investments: Long-term bonds (84%), cash and equiv (16%)

Provider Compensation ($000): Contr fee ($546,399), FFS ($32,536), capitation ($12,159), bonus arrang ($6,539), other ($95,650)

Total Member Encounters: Phys (1,992,446), non-phys (1,291,940)

Group Affiliation: None

Licensed in: NJ

Address: 9 ENTIN ROAD SUITE 203, PARSIPPANY,

Phone: (800) 872-3862 **Dom State:** NJ **Commenced Bus:** N/A

Data Date	Rating	RACR #1	RACR #2	Total Assets ($mil)	Capital ($mil)	Net Premium ($mil)	Net Income ($mil)
6-20	C	1.94	1.62	260.4	135.6	352.7	13.9
6-19	B-	4.15	3.46	318.6	158.5	374.8	-13.9
2019	C	2.50	2.08	263.2	122.7	739.3	-31.6
2018	B	4.43	3.70	301.1	170.5	699.4	2.5
2017	B	N/A	N/A	271.1	184.5	653.8	17.5
2016	B	3.87	3.22	302.9	187.8	887.0	17.7
2015	B	2.94	2.45	340.4	171.6	1,123.5	13.4

Rating Indexes

AETNA HEALTH INC (A NEW YORK CORP)   D+   Weak

Major Rating Factors: Weak profitability index (2.0 on a scale of 0 to 10). Weak overall results on stability tests (0.3) based on an excessive 116% enrollment growth during the period. Good liquidity (6.5) with sufficient resources (cash flows and marketable investments) to handle a spike in claims.

Other Rating Factors: Strong capitalization index (10.0) based on excellent current risk-adjusted capital (severe loss scenario). High quality investment portfolio (7.1).

Principal Business: Medicare (100%)

Mem Phys: 19: 106,211 **18:** 109,884 **19 MLR** 89.0% **/ 19 Admin Exp** N/A

Enroll(000): Q2 20: 24 **19:** 24 **18:** 11 **Med Exp PMPM:** $757

Principal Investments: Long-term bonds (60%), affiliate common stock (20%), cash and equiv (11%), mortgs (5%), other (5%)

Provider Compensation ($000): Contr fee ($178,868), FFS ($9,996), capitation ($3,115), bonus arrang ($577)

Total Member Encounters: Phys (672,150), non-phys (487,556)

Group Affiliation: None

Licensed in: NY

Address: 100 PARK AVENUE 12TH FLOOR, NEW YORK,

Phone: (800) 872-3862 **Dom State:** NY **Commenced Bus:** N/A

Data Date	Rating	RACR #1	RACR #2	Total Assets ($mil)	Capital ($mil)	Net Premium ($mil)	Net Income ($mil)
6-20	D+	4.12	3.43	171.1	105.3	122.9	10.6
6-19	B	17.56	14.63	310.7	225.3	112.6	8.8
2019	C	4.30	3.59	194.1	77.2	228.9	-11.8
2018	B-	17.28	14.40	289.7	221.7	117.4	-5.8
2017	C+	14.16	11.80	270.1	225.5	120.3	6.1
2016	C+	18.31	15.26	264.7	214.4	172.3	13.2
2015	C+	13.32	11.10	276.0	198.4	300.9	15.2

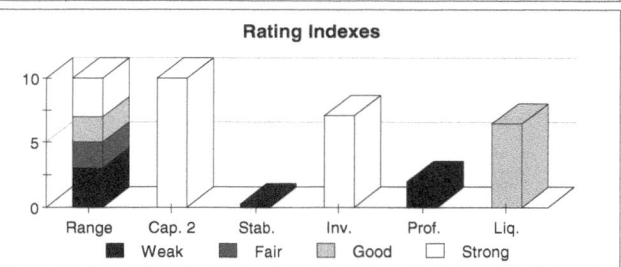

Rating Indexes

AETNA HEALTH INC (A PA CORP)   B   Good

Major Rating Factors: Good quality investment portfolio (6.7 on a scale of 0 to 10). Good overall results on stability tests (5.2). Good liquidity (6.6) with sufficient resources (cash flows and marketable investments) to handle a spike in claims.

Other Rating Factors: Excellent profitability (8.2). Strong capitalization index (9.3) based on excellent current risk-adjusted capital (severe loss scenario).

Principal Business: Medicare (60%), FEHB (20%), comp med (16%), Medicaid (3%)

Mem Phys: 19: 795,989 **18:** 554,080 **19 MLR** 87.7% **/ 19 Admin Exp** N/A

Enroll(000): Q2 20: 451 **19:** 482 **18:** 488 **Med Exp PMPM:** $511

Principal Investments: Long-term bonds (83%), affiliate common stock (8%), cash and equiv (7%), mortgs (2%), other (1%)

Provider Compensation ($000): Contr fee ($2,260,761), FFS ($109,536), capitation ($24,289), bonus arrang ($22,798), other ($519,176)

Total Member Encounters: Phys (6,750,760), non-phys (4,342,784)

Group Affiliation: None

Licensed in: AZ, CO, DC, DE, IL, IN, KS, KY, MD, MA, MO, NE, NV, NC, OH, OK, PA, SC, TN, VA, WA, WV

Address: 1425 UNION MEETING ROAD, BLUE BELL,

Phone: (800) 872-3862 **Dom State:** PA **Commenced Bus:** N/A

Data Date	Rating	RACR #1	RACR #2	Total Assets ($mil)	Capital ($mil)	Net Premium ($mil)	Net Income ($mil)
6-20	B	3.18	2.65	1,270.4	610.2	1,647.0	127.6
6-19	B	4.17	3.47	1,212.9	579.3	1,692.6	97.9
2019	B	3.17	2.64	1,190.3	510.0	3,371.9	127.0
2018	B	3.56	2.97	1,064.3	489.5	3,153.5	96.3
2017	B-	2.88	2.40	1,152.6	525.3	3,521.2	129.5
2016	C+	2.69	2.24	1,380.0	458.2	3,951.7	83.4
2015	B	4.17	3.47	1,479.3	672.3	4,192.9	113.8

Rating Indexes

AETNA HEALTH INC (A TEXAS CORP)   C   Fair

Major Rating Factors: Weak profitability index (1.3 on a scale of 0 to 10). Good overall results on stability tests (5.2). Good liquidity (6.7) with sufficient resources (cash flows and marketable investments) to handle a spike in claims. **Other Rating Factors:** Strong capitalization index (7.8) based on excellent current risk-adjusted capital (severe loss scenario). High quality investment portfolio (9.9).

Principal Business: Medicare (87%), comp med (13%)

Mem Phys: 19: 101,557 **18:** 66,203 **19 MLR** 92.8% **/ 19 Admin Exp** N/A

Enroll(000): Q2 20: 42 **19:** 51 **18:** 56 **Med Exp PMPM:** $731

Principal Investments: Long-term bonds (63%), cash and equiv (35%), other (2%)

Provider Compensation ($000): Contr fee ($344,552), FFS ($47,474), capitation ($5,131), bonus arrang ($1,479), other ($60,045)

Total Member Encounters: Phys (527,066), non-phys (380,841)

Group Affiliation: None

Licensed in: TX

Address: 2777 N STEMMONS FREEWAY SUITE, DALLAS,

Phone: (800) 872-3862 **Dom State:** TX **Commenced Bus:** N/A

Data Date	Rating	RACR #1	RACR #2	Total Assets ($mil)	Capital ($mil)	Net Premium ($mil)	Net Income ($mil)
6-20	C	1.96	1.63	160.6	89.0	211.3	19.4
6-19	C	1.89	1.58	181.5	56.9	255.8	-0.5
2019	C	1.99	1.66	175.8	59.1	495.3	-17.9
2018	C	1.93	1.61	170.2	58.1	472.3	-23.6
2017	C	1.83	1.53	128.4	68.0	407.9	-18.1
2016	C+	3.83	3.19	161.0	96.7	430.1	-7.6
2015	B	4.13	3.44	166.9	116.0	514.8	13.9

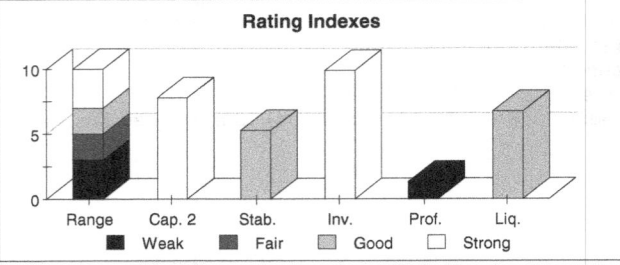

Rating Indexes

AETNA HEALTH INC (LA)   B-   Good

Major Rating Factors: Fair overall results on stability tests (4.5 on a scale of 0 to 10) based on a significant 27% decrease in enrollment during the period. Good overall profitability index (5.5). Strong capitalization index (9.3) based on excellent current risk-adjusted capital (severe loss scenario)

Other Rating Factors: High quality investment portfolio (9.6). Excellent liquidity (7.0) with ample operational cash flow and liquid investments.

Principal Business: Comp med (83%), Medicare (17%)

Mem Phys: 19: 11,997 **18:** 11,233 **19 MLR** 88.5% **/ 19 Admin Exp** N/A

Enroll(000): Q2 20: 9 **19:** 10 **18:** 13 **Med Exp PMPM:** $529

Principal Investments: Long-term bonds (59%), cash and equiv (41%)

Provider Compensation ($000): Contr fee ($59,403), FFS ($2,879), capitation ($2,265)

Total Member Encounters: Phys (168,003), non-phys (117,250)

Group Affiliation: None

Licensed in: LA

Address: 3838 N CAUSEWAY BLVD SUITE 335, METAIRIE,

Phone: (281) 986-8408 **Dom State:** LA **Commenced Bus:** N/A

Data Date	Rating	RACR #1	RACR #2	Total Assets ($mil)	Capital ($mil)	Net Premium ($mil)	Net Income ($mil)
6-20	B-	3.18	2.65	41.8	27.7	36.3	1.6
6-19	B-	4.56	3.80	37.8	26.1	37.0	0.9
2019	B-	5.17	4.31	37.4	26.2	72.1	0.9
2018	B-	4.43	3.69	35.2	25.3	95.5	5.1
2017	C+	2.15	1.79	33.7	20.3	102.0	8.8
2016	B-	4.51	3.76	43.7	24.4	111.1	6.1
2015	B-	2.29	1.91	45.9	17.6	139.7	-5.5

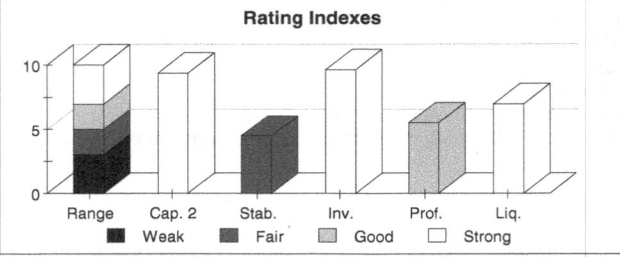

Rating Indexes

AETNA HEALTH INS CO   C-   Fair

Major Rating Factors: Weak profitability index (0.8 on a scale of 0 to 10). Strong capitalization (10.0) based on excellent current risk-adjusted capital (severe loss scenario). High quality investment portfolio (9.2).

Other Rating Factors: Excellent liquidity (7.2) with ample operational cash flow and liquid investments.

Principal Business: Med supp (94%), comp med (6%)

Mem Phys: 19: N/A **18:** N/A **19 MLR** 79.6% **/ 19 Admin Exp** N/A

Enroll(000): Q2 20: 169 **19:** 95 **18:** 70 **Med Exp PMPM:** $60

Principal Investments: Cash and equiv (78%), long-term bonds (22%)

Provider Compensation ($000): Contr fee ($42,409), other ($109)

Total Member Encounters: N/A

Group Affiliation: None

Licensed in: All states except CA, CT, MS, NY, PR

Address: 1425 UNION MEETING ROAD, BLUE BELL, PA 19422

Phone: (800) 872-3862 **Dom State:** PA **Commenced Bus:** N/A

Data Date	Rating	RACR #1	RACR #2	Total Assets ($mil)	Capital ($mil)	Net Premium ($mil)	Net Income ($mil)
6-20	C-	5.64	4.70	73.4	36.8	96.2	-4.2
6-19	C	4.06	3.38	19.1	9.3	21.8	-2.8
2019	C-	3.58	2.98	40.8	13.9	60.6	-8.2
2018	C	6.31	5.26	23.1	14.3	29.3	-2.4
2017	C	13.90	11.59	43.8	35.1	15.6	-0.2
2016	B-	9.96	8.30	43.1	34.8	34.8	0.6
2015	C+	6.42	5.35	59.0	32.3	33.8	-6.8

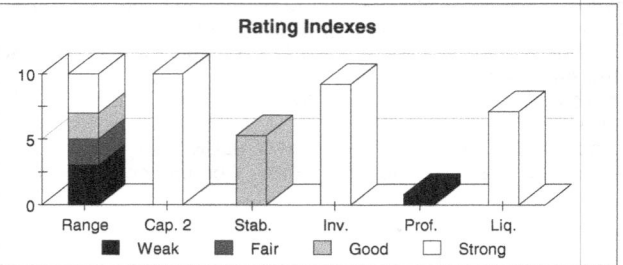

Rating Indexes

AETNA HEALTH OF CALIFORNIA INC   B   Good

Major Rating Factors: Good overall results on stability tests (6.0 on a scale of 0 to 10). Rating is significantly influenced by the good financial results of Aetna Inc. Excellent profitability (8.9). Strong capitalization index (7.5) based on excellent current risk-adjusted capital (severe loss scenario).
Other Rating Factors: Excellent liquidity (7.0) with ample operational cash flow and liquid investments.
Principal Business: Medicare (14%)
Mem Phys: 19: N/A **18:** N/A   **19 MLR** 83.6% **/ 19 Admin Exp** N/A
Enroll(000): Q2 20: 210   **19:** 224   **18:** 224   **Med Exp PMPM:** $389
Principal Investments ($000): Cash and equiv ($89,451)
Provider Compensation ($000): None
Total Member Encounters: N/A
Group Affiliation: Aetna Inc
Licensed in: CA
Address: 2850 Shadelands Drive, Walnut Creek, CA 94598
Phone: (925) 948-4207 **Dom State:** CA **Commenced Bus:** October 1981

Data Date	Rating	RACR #1	RACR #2	Total Assets ($mil)	Capital ($mil)	Net Premium ($mil)	Net Income ($mil)
6-20	B	2.15	1.45	453.5	202.2	643.9	44.7
6-19	B	2.32	1.57	444.6	219.3	662.3	37.1
2019	B	1.95	1.32	418.2	185.2	1,314.4	72.7
2018	B	1.90	1.29	406.7	176.6	1,389.2	70.8
2017	B	1.44	0.97	387.4	150.0	1,580.2	42.8
2016	C+	1.16	0.79	483.7	135.8	1,775.7	35.0
2015	C+	1.05	0.71	451.7	120.9	1,821.2	21.2

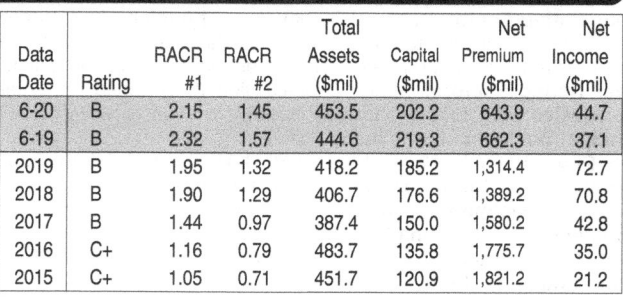

Rating Indexes

AETNA HEALTH OF IOWA INC   C   Fair

Major Rating Factors: Fair overall results on stability tests (3.6 on a scale of 0 to 10) based on a steep decline in premium revenue in 2019, a decline in the number of member physicians during 2020 and a significant 89% decrease in enrollment during the period. Good overall profitability index (5.4). Strong capitalization index (10.0) based on excellent current risk-adjusted capital (severe loss scenario).
Other Rating Factors: High quality investment portfolio (9.3). Excellent liquidity (9.7) with ample operational cash flow and liquid investments.
Principal Business: Comp med (101%)
Mem Phys: 19: 16,981 **18:** 33,791 **19 MLR** 47.2% **/ 19 Admin Exp** N/A
Enroll(000): Q2 20: 2 **19:** 0 **18:** 4 **Med Exp PMPM:** $221
Principal Investments: Long-term bonds (67%), cash and equiv (33%)
Provider Compensation ($000): Contr fee ($4,196), FFS ($129), bonus arrang ($94), other ($1,236)
Total Member Encounters: Phys (11,181), non-phys (8,901)
Group Affiliation: None
Licensed in: IA
Address: 15950 WEST DODGE ROAD, OMAHA,
Phone: (800) 471-0240 **Dom State:** IA **Commenced Bus:** N/A

Data Date	Rating	RACR #1	RACR #2	Total Assets ($mil)	Capital ($mil)	Net Premium ($mil)	Net Income ($mil)
6-20	C	22.86	19.05	59.0	48.7	12.8	6.1
6-19	C+	22.09	18.41	54.1	42.7	3.7	2.8
2019	C	32.87	27.39	52.5	42.6	5.5	2.8
2018	C+	20.69	17.24	54.0	39.9	31.8	2.0
2017	C+	1.90	1.59	97.0	37.5	209.6	8.3
2016	C+	1.92	1.60	87.5	29.4	240.4	-7.3
2015	B	2.13	1.78	96.9	39.1	311.4	-2.1

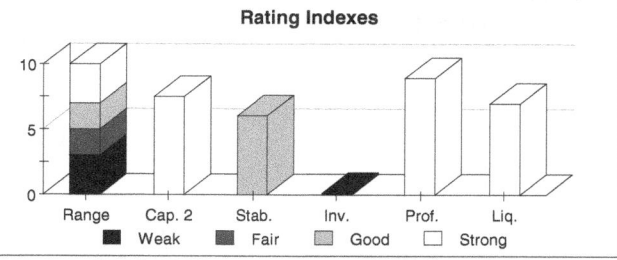

Rating Indexes

AETNA HEALTH OF UTAH INC   C   Fair

Major Rating Factors: Fair profitability index (4.7 on a scale of 0 to 10). Fair quality investment portfolio (3.8). Fair overall results on stability tests (4.2) based on a significant 31% decrease in enrollment during the period.
Other Rating Factors: Strong capitalization index (10.0) based on excellent current risk-adjusted capital (severe loss scenario). Excellent liquidity (7.1) with ample operational cash flow and liquid investments.
Principal Business: FEHB (53%), Medicare (36%), comp med (12%)
Mem Phys: 19: 13,139 **18:** 12,689 **19 MLR** 84.6% **/ 19 Admin Exp** N/A
Enroll(000): Q2 20: 22 **19:** 24 **18:** 35 **Med Exp PMPM:** $506
Principal Investments: Long-term bonds (52%), cash and equiv (48%)
Provider Compensation ($000): Contr fee ($109,572), FFS ($6,981), bonus arrang ($918), capitation ($185), other ($35,230)
Total Member Encounters: Phys (451,512), non-phys (304,869)
Group Affiliation: None
Licensed in: ID, NV, UT, WY
Address: 10150 S CENTENNIAL PARKWAY SUI, SANDY,
Phone: (801) 933-3500 **Dom State:** UT **Commenced Bus:** N/A

Data Date	Rating	RACR #1	RACR #2	Total Assets ($mil)	Capital ($mil)	Net Premium ($mil)	Net Income ($mil)
6-20	C	3.90	3.25	81.2	43.8	77.6	1.8
6-19	C	5.21	4.34	87.0	41.6	88.8	2.9
2019	C	6.20	5.17	84.6	42.0	178.9	7.0
2018	C	4.82	4.02	78.2	38.1	224.3	4.8
2017	C+	3.77	3.14	99.6	53.9	257.6	16.1
2016	B-	4.51	3.76	113.8	54.4	293.5	-2.7
2015	B	3.35	2.79	117.8	55.9	300.7	6.4

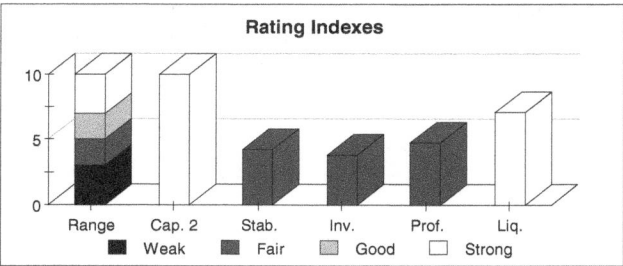

Rating Indexes

AETNA HEALTHASSURANCE PA INC

D **Weak**

Major Rating Factors: Fair quality investment portfolio (3.7 on a scale of 0 to 10). Good overall profitability index (5.5). Good liquidity (6.2) with sufficient resources (cash flows and marketable investments) to handle a spike in claims.
Other Rating Factors: Strong capitalization (9.2) based on excellent current risk-adjusted capital (severe loss scenario).
Principal Business: Comp med (100%)
Mem Phys: 18: N/A **17:** 43,426 **18 MLR** 84.6% **/ 18 Admin Exp** N/A
Enroll(000): Q3 19: 37 **18:** 45 **17:** 53 **Med Exp PMPM:** $444
Principal Investments: Long-term bonds (99%), cash and equiv (1%)
Provider Compensation ($000): Contr fee ($244,003), FFS ($6,384)
Total Member Encounters: Phys (502,169), non-phys (401,144)
Group Affiliation: None
Licensed in: PA
Address: 1425 UNION MEETING ROAD, BLUE BELL, PA 19422
Phone: (800) 872-3862 **Dom State:** PA **Commenced Bus:** N/A

Data Date	Rating	RACR #1	RACR #2	Total Assets ($mil)	Capital ($mil)	Net Premium ($mil)	Net Income ($mil)
9-19	D	3.12	2.60	82.5	56.1	181.8	6.7
9-18	D	N/A	N/A	97.4	48.4	227.0	-1.9
2018	D	2.87	2.39	84.4	51.5	299.2	1.9
2017	D	N/A	N/A	102.3	49.8	280.7	-6.4
2016	C+	1.90	1.58	26.9	9.9	71.6	4.9
2015	N/A	N/A	N/A	5.0	5.0	N/A	N/A
2014	N/A	N/A	N/A	N/A	N/A	N/A	N/A

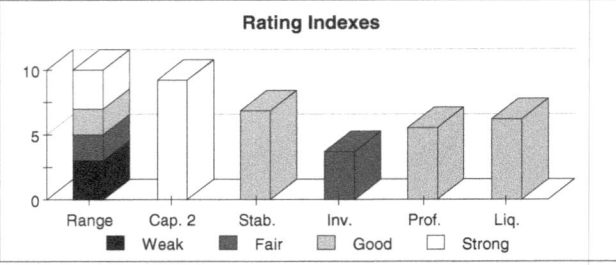

Rating Indexes

AETNA LIFE INS CO

B **Good**

Major Rating Factors: Good current capitalization (5.2 on a scale of 0 to 10) based on mixed results -- excessive policy leverage mitigated by excellent risk adjusted capital (severe loss scenario) reflecting improvement over results in 2017. Good quality investment portfolio (6.2) despite mixed results such as: minimal exposure to mortgages and large holdings of BBB rated bonds but small junk bond holdings. Fair overall results on stability tests (4.0).
Other Rating Factors: Weak liquidity (1.5). Excellent profitability (8.4) with operating gains in each of the last five years.
Principal Business: Individual health insurance (48%), group health insurance (46%), reinsurance (4%), and group life insurance (2%).
Principal Investments: NonCMO investment grade bonds (58%), CMOs and structured securities (13%), mortgages in good standing (9%), noninv. grade bonds (6%), and misc. investments (12%).
Investments in Affiliates: 5%
Group Affiliation: Aetna Inc
Licensed in: All states, the District of Columbia and Puerto Rico
Commenced Business: December 1850
Address: 151 FARMINGTON AVENUE, HARTFORD, CT 6156
Phone: (800) 872-3862 **Domicile State:** CT **NAIC Code:** 60054

Data Date	Rating	RACR #1	RACR #2	Total Assets ($mil)	Capital ($mil)	Net Premium ($mil)	Net Income ($mil)
6-20	B	1.60	1.24	24,024.6	5,608.3	12,222.6	1,950.4
6-19	B	1.31	1.00	21,694.6	4,037.6	11,704.2	1,309.2
2019	B	1.13	0.87	22,016.5	3,852.5	23,423.9	1,805.9
2018	B	1.28	0.97	20,230.7	3,697.1	19,837.6	1,933.0
2017	B	1.12	0.84	19,894.8	2,904.0	17,984.7	1,339.4
2016	B	1.34	1.00	22,376.2	3,479.2	18,556.4	1,251.7
2015	B	1.57	1.15	21,214.1	3,770.8	17,155.4	1,211.9

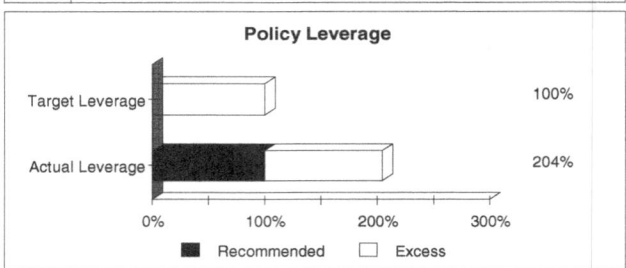

Policy Leverage

AHF MCO OF GEORGIA INC

C- **Fair**

Major Rating Factors: Weak profitability index (1.9 on a scale of 0 to 10). Strong capitalization (10.0) based on excellent current risk-adjusted capital (severe loss scenario). High quality investment portfolio (9.9).
Other Rating Factors: Excellent liquidity (10.0) with ample operational cash flow and liquid investments.
Principal Business: Medicare (100%)
Mem Phys: 18: N/A **17:** N/A **18 MLR** 91.1% **/ 18 Admin Exp** N/A
Enroll(000): Q3 19: 0 **18:** 0 **17:** N/A **Med Exp PMPM:** $3,271
Principal Investments: Cash and equiv (100%)
Provider Compensation ($000): FFS ($163)
Total Member Encounters: N/A
Group Affiliation: AIDS Healthcare Foundation
Licensed in: GA
Address: 735 Piedmont Ave NE, Atlanta, GA 30308
Phone: (323) 860-5200 **Dom State:** GA **Commenced Bus:** N/A

Data Date	Rating	RACR #1	RACR #2	Total Assets ($mil)	Capital ($mil)	Net Premium ($mil)	Net Income ($mil)
9-19	C-	152.27	126.89	4.5	4.0	0.6	-0.2
9-18	N/A	N/A	N/A	4.1	4.0	0.1	N/A
2018	D	150.80	125.70	4.2	4.0	0.2	0.0
2017	N/A	N/A	N/A	4.0	4.0	N/A	N/A
2016	N/A	N/A	N/A	N/A	N/A	N/A	N/A
2015	N/A	N/A	N/A	N/A	N/A	N/A	N/A
2014	N/A	N/A	N/A	N/A	N/A	N/A	N/A

Rating Indexes

AIDS HEALTHCARE FOUNDATION MCO OF FL — D- — Weak

Major Rating Factors: Weak profitability index (0.9 on a scale of 0 to 10). Good capitalization (6.9) based on excellent current risk-adjusted capital (severe loss scenario). Good liquidity (6.8) with sufficient resources (cash flows and marketable investments) to handle a spike in claims.
Other Rating Factors: High quality investment portfolio (9.3).
Principal Business: Medicare (93%), Medicaid (7%)
Mem Phys: 19: 4,246 **18:** 3,803 **19 MLR** 90.5% **/ 19 Admin Exp** N/A
Enroll(000): Q2 20: 2 **19:** 2 **18:** 3 **Med Exp PMPM:** $4,275
Principal Investments: Long-term bonds (56%), cash and equiv (26%), real estate (10%), nonaffiliate common stock (8%)
Provider Compensation ($000): Contr fee ($101,154)
Total Member Encounters: Phys (17,198), non-phys (13,109)
Group Affiliation: None
Licensed in: FL
Address: 700 SE 3rd Avenue 4th Floor, Ft Lauderdale, FL 33316
Phone: (323) 860-5200 **Dom State:** FL **Commenced Bus:** N/A

Data Date	Rating	RACR #1	RACR #2	Total Assets ($mil)	Capital ($mil)	Net Premium ($mil)	Net Income ($mil)
6-20	D-	1.26	1.05	28.5	14.8	48.3	-4.8
6-19	D-	0.62	0.52	28.5	12.3	53.8	-2.8
2019	D-	1.37	1.14	27.7	16.2	101.8	0.9
2018	E+	0.52	0.43	39.1	9.9	138.9	-14.5
2017	E-	0.91	0.76	51.4	14.5	135.9	1.0
2016	E+	0.41	0.34	37.9	7.1	121.8	-13.9
2015	E	0.17	0.14	18.9	2.8	111.2	-11.3

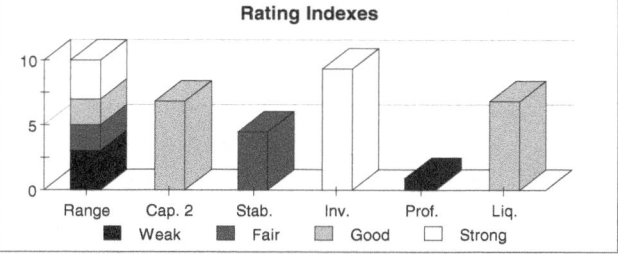

Rating Indexes

ALIGNMENT HEALTH PLAN — E — Very Weak

Major Rating Factors: Weak profitability index (1.4 on a scale of 0 to 10). Poor capitalization index (0.0) based on weak current risk-adjusted capital (severe loss scenario). Weak liquidity (0.0) as a spike in claims may stretch capacity.
Other Rating Factors: Good overall results on stability tests (5.5) based on healthy premium and capital growth during 2019 but fair risk diversification due to the company's size.
Principal Business: Medicare (100%)
Mem Phys: 19: N/A **18:** N/A **19 MLR** 86.6% **/ 19 Admin Exp** N/A
Enroll(000): Q2 20: 64 **19:** 40 **18:** 40 **Med Exp PMPM:** $1,268
Principal Investments ($000): Cash and equiv ($61,881)
Provider Compensation ($000): None
Total Member Encounters: N/A
Group Affiliation: Alignment Healthcare USA LLC
Licensed in: CA
Address: 1100 W Town & Country Rd #1600, Orange, CA 92868
Phone: (657) 218-7731 **Dom State:** CA **Commenced Bus:** May 2004

Data Date	Rating	RACR #1	RACR #2	Total Assets ($mil)	Capital ($mil)	Net Premium ($mil)	Net Income ($mil)
6-20	E	0.40	0.25	142.7	31.3	426.0	13.8
6-19	E	0.12	0.08	110.1	19.6	336.1	3.7
2019	E	0.15	0.10	119.3	16.4	680.0	-12.0
2018	E	N/A	N/A	72.5	13.9	449.2	-61.3
2017	E	N/A	N/A	66.8	13.7	361.4	-58.2
2016	E	N/A	N/A	46.4	10.0	227.8	-24.6
2015	E	0.24	0.15	52.2	11.6	205.6	-32.2

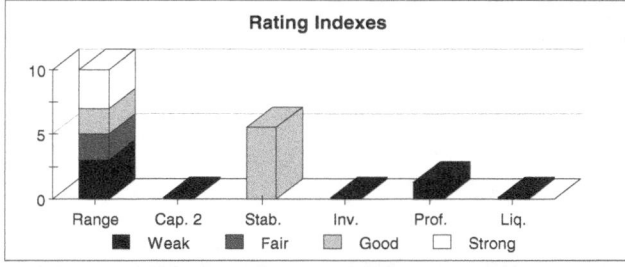

Rating Indexes

ALL SAVERS INS CO — C — Fair

Major Rating Factors: Fair overall results on stability tests (3.1 on a scale of 0 to 10) including excessive premium growth. Good liquidity (6.9) with sufficient resources to handle a spike in claims. Weak profitability (2.7). Excellent expense controls. Return on equity has been low, averaging -5.1%.
Other Rating Factors: Strong capitalization (10.0) based on excellent risk adjusted capital (severe loss scenario). High quality investment portfolio (8.1).
Principal Business: Group health insurance (100%).
Principal Investments: NonCMO investment grade bonds (54%), CMOs and structured securities (16%), and cash (1%).
Investments in Affiliates: None
Group Affiliation: UnitedHealth Group Inc
Licensed in: All states except CA, MA, MN, NJ, NY, PR
Commenced Business: February 1986
Address: 7440 WOODLAND DRIVE, INDIANAPOLIS, IN 46278-1719
Phone: (317) 715-7056 **Domicile State:** IN **NAIC Code:** 82406

Data Date	Rating	RACR #1	RACR #2	Total Assets ($mil)	Capital ($mil)	Net Premium ($mil)	Net Income ($mil)
2019	C	4.26	3.40	606.2	375.7	0.0	44.3
2018	C	9.17	6.84	733.4	579.7	493.8	57.6
2017	C	13.51	9.47	1,143.2	997.3	497.7	187.6
2016	C	5.31	3.99	1,551.5	1,054.2	1,603.1	-102.2
2015	C	5.60	4.41	1,067.5	600.8	891.4	-339.5

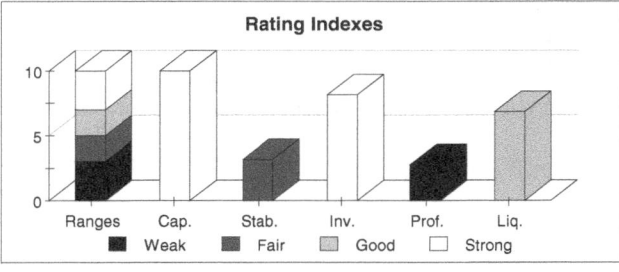

Rating Indexes

ALLCARE HEALTH PLAN INC | E | Very Weak

Major Rating Factors: Fair profitability index (4.5 on a scale of 0 to 10). Good capitalization (6.9) based on excellent current risk-adjusted capital (severe loss scenario). Good liquidity (6.8) with sufficient resources (cash flows and marketable investments) to handle a spike in claims.
Other Rating Factors: High quality investment portfolio (9.2).
Principal Business: Medicare (100%)
Mem Phys: 19: 1,925 **18:** 1,679 **19 MLR** 90.5% **/ 19 Admin Exp** N/A
Enroll(000): Q2 20: 4 **19:** 3 **18:** 3 **Med Exp PMPM:** $1,024
Principal Investments: Cash and equiv (47%), long-term bonds (43%), nonaffiliate common stock (10%)
Provider Compensation ($000): Contr fee ($37,879), FFS ($3,063)
Total Member Encounters: Phys (78,168), non-phys (29,357)
Group Affiliation: AllCare Health Inc
Licensed in: OR
Address: 1701 NE 7th Street, Grants Pass, OR 97526
Phone: (888) 460-0185 **Dom State:** OR **Commenced Bus:** N/A

Data Date	Rating	RACR #1	RACR #2	Total Assets ($mil)	Capital ($mil)	Net Premium ($mil)	Net Income ($mil)
6-20	E	1.27	1.06	15.3	9.4	25.4	2.2
6-19	N/A	N/A	N/A	N/A	N/A	N/A	N/A
2019	E	0.94	0.78	12.1	7.4	43.8	1.0
2018	E	0.77	0.64	11.2	5.6	33.1	-1.1
2017	E	0.99	0.82	12.7	6.9	35.8	0.4
2016	E	0.87	0.73	11.3	6.4	33.5	-0.8
2015	E	1.18	0.98	10.9	7.1	31.4	0.0

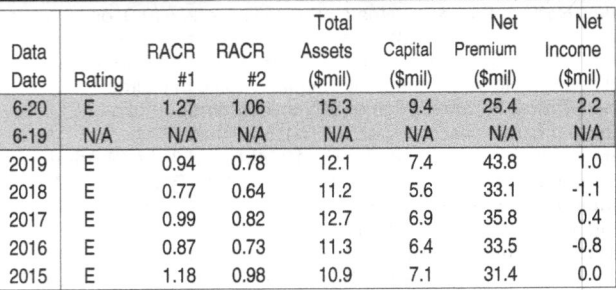

Rating Indexes

ALLEGIANCE L&H INS CO | C+ | Fair

Major Rating Factors: Excellent profitability (7.1 on a scale of 0 to 10). Strong capitalization (10.0) based on excellent current risk-adjusted capital (severe loss scenario). High quality investment portfolio (9.9).
Other Rating Factors: Excellent liquidity (7.9) with ample operational cash flow and liquid investments.
Principal Business: Comp med (100%)
Mem Phys: 19: N/A **18:** N/A **19 MLR** 92.6% **/ 19 Admin Exp** N/A
Enroll(000): Q2 20: 3 **19:** 3 **18:** 3 **Med Exp PMPM:** $375
Principal Investments: Cash and equiv (70%), long-term bonds (30%)
Provider Compensation ($000): FFS ($13,917)
Total Member Encounters: Phys (11,989), non-phys (43,425)
Group Affiliation: None
Licensed in: MT
Address: 2806 SOUTH GARFIELD STREET, MISSOULA, MT 59801
Phone: (406) 721-2222 **Dom State:** MT **Commenced Bus:** N/A

Data Date	Rating	RACR #1	RACR #2	Total Assets ($mil)	Capital ($mil)	Net Premium ($mil)	Net Income ($mil)
6-20	C+	5.00	4.17	17.2	14.2	7.2	0.6
6-19	C+	9.59	7.99	16.7	14.2	7.2	0.9
2019	C+	8.50	7.08	16.3	13.6	13.5	0.3
2018	C+	9.02	7.52	16.7	13.3	14.4	1.1
2017	C	5.19	4.32	14.6	12.2	13.3	0.8
2016	C	10.64	8.87	13.7	11.4	13.6	1.9
2015	C	4.13	3.44	12.5	9.5	22.9	1.3

Rating Indexes

ALLIANCE HEALTH & LIFE INS CO | C- | Fair

Major Rating Factors: Fair profitability index (2.9 on a scale of 0 to 10). Low quality investment portfolio (1.1). Strong capitalization (7.9) based on excellent current risk-adjusted capital (severe loss scenario).
Other Rating Factors: Excellent liquidity (7.2) with ample operational cash flow and liquid investments.
Principal Business: Comp med (70%), Medicare (18%), med supp (2%), other (10%)
Mem Phys: 19: 14,051 **18:** 12,553 **19 MLR** 73.8% **/ 19 Admin Exp** N/A
Enroll(000): Q2 20: 51 **19:** 53 **18:** 53 **Med Exp PMPM:** $367
Principal Investments: Cash and equiv (86%), long-term bonds (12%), nonaffiliate common stock (2%)
Provider Compensation ($000): Contr fee ($230,411), FFS ($3,133)
Total Member Encounters: Phys (318,449), non-phys (283,945)
Group Affiliation: None
Licensed in: MI
Address: 2850 West Grand Boulevard, Detroit, MI 48202
Phone: (313) 872-8100 **Dom State:** MI **Commenced Bus:** N/A

Data Date	Rating	RACR #1	RACR #2	Total Assets ($mil)	Capital ($mil)	Net Premium ($mil)	Net Income ($mil)
6-20	C-	2.08	1.73	163.7	62.3	150.3	1.3
6-19	C	2.17	1.81	145.1	59.4	164.2	5.9
2019	C-	2.47	2.06	139.6	61.2	317.5	6.6
2018	C	1.94	1.62	134.0	53.8	347.5	12.1
2017	C	1.10	0.92	135.1	42.2	367.8	-10.0
2016	C	1.19	0.99	111.2	36.2	399.0	-17.0
2015	C+	1.26	1.05	86.0	24.4	293.2	-2.1

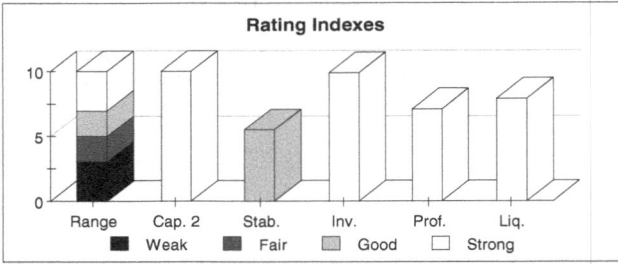

Rating Indexes

ALLIANT HEALTH PLANS INC — D- — Weak

Major Rating Factors: Fair overall results on stability tests (4.9 on a scale of 0 to 10) based on a significant 31% decrease in enrollment during the period. Excellent profitability (7.2). Strong capitalization index (10.0) based on excellent current risk-adjusted capital (severe loss scenario)

Other Rating Factors: High quality investment portfolio (9.8). Excellent liquidity (7.1) with ample operational cash flow and liquid investments.

Principal Business: Comp med (100%)

Mem Phys: 19: 18,397 **18:** 16,307 **19 MLR** 78.6% **/ 19 Admin Exp** N/A

Enroll(000): Q2 20: 35 **19:** 34 **18:** 49 **Med Exp PMPM:** $538

Principal Investments: Cash and equiv (52%), long-term bonds (48%)

Provider Compensation ($000): Contr fee ($249,636), capitation ($7,956)

Total Member Encounters: Phys (246,230), non-phys (82,861)

Group Affiliation: Health One Alliance LLC

Licensed in: GA

Address: 1503 N Tibbs Road, Dalton,

Phone: (706) 629-8848 **Dom State:** GA **Commenced Bus:** N/A

Data Date	Rating	RACR #1	RACR #2	Total Assets ($mil)	Capital ($mil)	Net Premium ($mil)	Net Income ($mil)
6-20	D-	3.76	3.13	155.8	91.2	115.5	1.4
6-19	N/A	N/A	N/A	N/A	N/A	N/A	N/A
2019	D-	3.62	3.01	140.4	88.4	297.0	18.8
2018	D-	1.86	1.55	156.1	71.1	481.8	55.7
2017	D-	0.61	0.51	54.2	15.2	253.2	3.6
2016	D-	1.08	0.90	33.4	12.8	114.3	-6.2
2015	C	1.19	0.99	36.0	15.2	129.8	-1.7

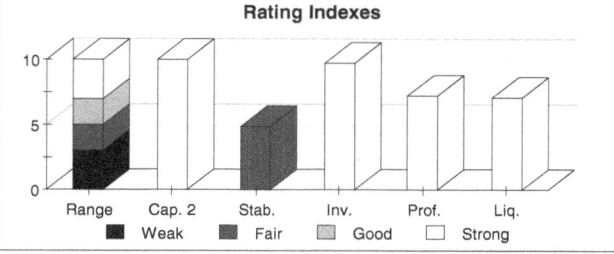

Rating Indexes

ALLINA HLTH & AETNA INS CO — C — Fair

Major Rating Factors: Weak profitability index (0.9 on a scale of 0 to 10). Good liquidity (6.6) with sufficient resources (cash flows and marketable investments) to handle a spike in claims. Strong capitalization (10.0) based on excellent current risk-adjusted capital (severe loss scenario).

Other Rating Factors: High quality investment portfolio (9.9).

Principal Business: Comp med (100%)

Mem Phys: 18: N/A **17:** N/A **18 MLR** 30.0% **/ 18 Admin Exp** N/A

Enroll(000): Q3 19: 9 **18:** 0 **17:** N/A **Med Exp PMPM:** $142

Principal Investments: Cash and equiv (90%), long-term bonds (10%)

Provider Compensation ($000): Contr fee ($58)

Total Member Encounters: Phys (202,199), non-phys (128,924)

Group Affiliation: Allina Health Aetna Insurance Holdin

Licensed in: MN

Address: 1550 UTICA AVENUE S SUITE 25, ST LOUIS PARK, MN 55416-5380

Phone: (800) 872-3862 **Dom State:** MN **Commenced Bus:** N/A

Data Date	Rating	RACR #1	RACR #2	Total Assets ($mil)	Capital ($mil)	Net Premium ($mil)	Net Income ($mil)
9-19	C	6.28	5.23	28.4	11.2	51.4	-13.9
9-18	N/A	N/A	N/A	6.3	5.1	N/A	-4.4
2018	C	2.60	2.17	5.5	4.7	0.2	-9.8
2017	N/A	N/A	N/A	4.6	2.7	N/A	-1.8
2016	N/A	N/A	N/A	N/A	N/A	N/A	N/A
2015	N/A	N/A	N/A	N/A	N/A	N/A	N/A
2014	N/A	N/A	N/A	N/A	N/A	N/A	N/A

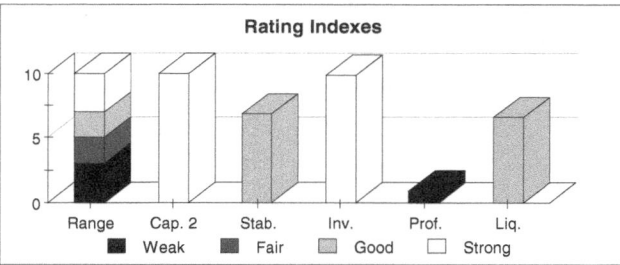

Rating Indexes

ALOHACARE — C — Fair

Major Rating Factors: Weak profitability index (1.1 on a scale of 0 to 10). Weak overall results on stability tests (2.1). Good capitalization index (6.7) based on good current risk-adjusted capital (severe loss scenario).

Other Rating Factors: Good liquidity (6.9) with sufficient resources (cash flows and marketable investments) to handle a spike in claims. High quality investment portfolio (9.9).

Principal Business: Medicaid (91%), Medicare (9%)

Mem Phys: 19: 6,601 **18:** 6,747 **19 MLR** 97.8% **/ 19 Admin Exp** N/A

Enroll(000): Q2 20: 69 **19:** 64 **18:** 66 **Med Exp PMPM:** $432

Principal Investments: Cash and equiv (60%), long-term bonds (30%), nonaffiliate common stock (10%)

Provider Compensation ($000): Contr fee ($240,662), FFS ($85,705), capitation ($3,149)

Total Member Encounters: Phys (367,060), non-phys (989,840)

Group Affiliation: None

Licensed in: HI

Address: 1357 Kapiolani Blvd Suite 1250, Honolulu,

Phone: (808) 973-1650 **Dom State:** HI **Commenced Bus:** N/A

Data Date	Rating	RACR #1	RACR #2	Total Assets ($mil)	Capital ($mil)	Net Premium ($mil)	Net Income ($mil)
6-20	C	1.19	0.99	127.2	55.8	191.7	-1.9
6-19	N/A	N/A	N/A	N/A	N/A	N/A	N/A
2019	C	1.18	0.98	147.2	55.5	343.9	-32.2
2018	B-	2.78	2.32	163.1	88.3	372.3	2.4
2017	C+	2.38	1.98	174.5	86.3	377.0	12.4
2016	C+	2.27	1.89	141.4	67.2	317.3	15.6
2015	N/A	N/A	N/A	113.8	51.6	271.0	-19.2

Rating Indexes

AMALGAMATED LIFE INS CO *

A   **Excellent**

Major Rating Factors: Good liquidity (6.3 on a scale of 0 to 10) with sufficient resources to handle a spike in claims. Strong capitalization (10.0) based on excellent risk adjusted capital (severe loss scenario). Furthermore, this high level of risk adjusted capital has been consistently maintained over the last five years. High quality investment portfolio (8.2).

Other Rating Factors: Excellent profitability (8.6) with operating gains in each of the last five years. Excellent overall results on stability tests (7.3) excellent operational trends and excellent risk diversification.

Principal Business: Group life insurance (34%), group health insurance (34%), reinsurance (27%), and individual health insurance (4%).

Principal Investments: NonCMO investment grade bonds (62%) and CMOs and structured securities (29%).

Investments in Affiliates: None

Group Affiliation: National Retirement Fund

Licensed in: All states except PR

Commenced Business: February 1944

Address: 333 WESTCHESTER AVENUE, WHITE PLAINS, NY 10604

Phone: (914) 367-5275 **Domicile State:** NY **NAIC Code:** 60216

Data Date	Rating	RACR #1	RACR #2	Total Assets ($mil)	Capital ($mil)	Net Premium ($mil)	Net Income ($mil)
6-20	A	4.20	3.17	154.2	78.8	59.6	2.8
6-19	A	4.00	3.02	145.1	68.1	50.0	2.5
2019	A	4.19	3.18	143.0	75.6	99.7	9.2
2018	A	3.96	3.00	146.5	66.8	96.5	4.9
2017	A	4.24	3.24	127.5	61.7	82.7	5.5
2016	A-	4.85	3.74	122.9	57.8	80.7	3.5
2015	A-	4.12	3.27	119.9	55.6	75.6	3.0

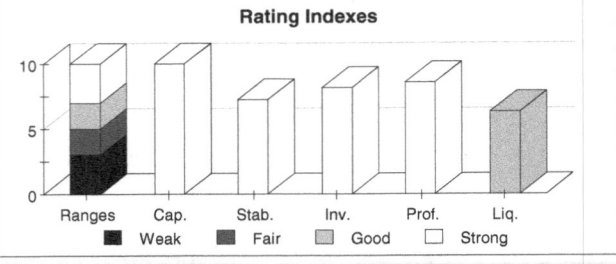

AMBETTER OF MAGNOLIA INC

B   **Good**

Major Rating Factors: Good quality investment portfolio (6.2 on a scale of 0 to 10). Excellent profitability (9.5). Strong capitalization (10.0) based on excellent current risk-adjusted capital (severe loss scenario).

Other Rating Factors: Excellent liquidity (7.2) with ample operational cash flow and liquid investments.

Principal Business: Comp med (100%)

Mem Phys: 18: 14,510 **17:** 11,245 **18 MLR** 66.5% **/ 18 Admin Exp** N/A

Enroll(000): Q3 19: 70 **18:** 59 **17:** 48 **Med Exp PMPM:** $418

Principal Investments: Cash and equiv (67%), long-term bonds (33%)

Provider Compensation ($000): Contr fee ($299,997), bonus arrang ($17,490), capitation ($934), salary ($834)

Total Member Encounters: Phys (309,287), non-phys (396,133)

Group Affiliation: None

Licensed in: MS

Address: 111 East Capitol Street Suite, Jackson, MS 39201

Phone: (314) 725-4477 **Dom State:** MS **Commenced Bus:** N/A

Data Date	Rating	RACR #1	RACR #2	Total Assets ($mil)	Capital ($mil)	Net Premium ($mil)	Net Income ($mil)
9-19	B	5.98	4.98	166.1	72.3	406.1	13.1
9-18	C+	N/A	N/A	137.2	55.6	377.3	37.1
2018	B-	4.87	4.06	136.9	58.8	493.8	40.3
2017	C+	N/A	N/A	62.1	17.6	298.4	9.2
2016	C-	1.35	1.12	49.7	8.4	126.1	0.1
2015	U	8.82	7.35	40.3	4.3	35.7	0.9
2014	N/A	N/A	N/A	N/A	N/A	N/A	N/A

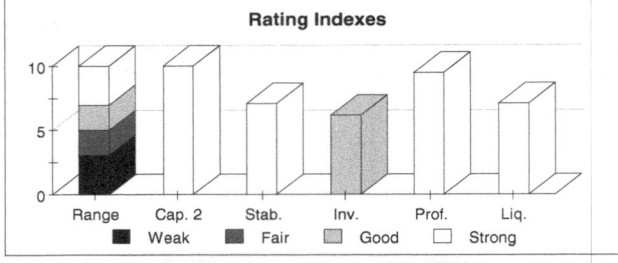

AMBETTER OF PEACH STATE INC

B   **Good**

Major Rating Factors: Excellent profitability (9.4 on a scale of 0 to 10). Strong capitalization (10.0) based on excellent current risk-adjusted capital (severe loss scenario). High quality investment portfolio (7.7).

Other Rating Factors: Excellent liquidity (7.0) with sufficient resources (cash flows and marketable investments) to handle a spike in claims.

Principal Business: Comp med (100%)

Mem Phys: 18: 19,961 **17:** 16,291 **18 MLR** 70.9% **/ 18 Admin Exp** N/A

Enroll(000): Q3 19: 209 **18:** 170 **17:** 116 **Med Exp PMPM:** $353

Principal Investments: Long-term bonds (50%), cash and equiv (50%)

Provider Compensation ($000): Contr fee ($650,989), bonus arrang ($120,991), capitation ($3,483), salary ($1,622)

Total Member Encounters: Phys (964,805), non-phys (836,830)

Group Affiliation: None

Licensed in: GA

Address: 1100 Circle 75 Parkway Ste 110, Atlanta, GA 30339

Phone: (314) 725-4477 **Dom State:** GA **Commenced Bus:** N/A

Data Date	Rating	RACR #1	RACR #2	Total Assets ($mil)	Capital ($mil)	Net Premium ($mil)	Net Income ($mil)
9-19	B	4.64	3.87	372.6	176.5	1,119.5	58.9
9-18	C+	N/A	N/A	338.4	105.7	860.9	73.6
2018	B-	3.07	2.56	328.7	116.7	1,136.9	84.6
2017	C+	N/A	N/A	198.8	33.4	489.4	17.7
2016	C-	2.91	2.42	165.8	17.9	197.2	13.6
2015	N/A	N/A	N/A	6.3	3.0	N/A	-0.2
2014	N/A	N/A	N/A	N/A	N/A	N/A	N/A

AMERICAN BANKERS LIFE ASR CO OF FL | B | Good

Major Rating Factors: Good overall results on stability tests (5.4 on a scale of 0 to 10). Stability strengths include good operational trends and excellent risk diversification. Good quality investment portfolio (6.3) despite mixed results such as: minimal exposure to mortgages and substantial holdings of BBB bonds but minimal holdings in junk bonds. Strong capitalization (9.5) based on excellent risk adjusted capital (severe loss scenario).

Other Rating Factors: Excellent profitability (7.8) with operating gains in each of the last five years. Excellent liquidity (8.4).

Principal Business: Credit life insurance (42%), credit health insurance (41%), reinsurance (12%), group health insurance (4%), and individual life insurance (2%).

Principal Investments: NonCMO investment grade bonds (54%), real estate (15%), cash (14%), CMOs and structured securities (7%), and misc. investments (5%).

Investments in Affiliates: None
Group Affiliation: Assurant Inc
Licensed in: All states except NY
Commenced Business: April 1952
Address: 11222 QUAIL ROOST DRIVE, MIAMI, FL 33157-6596
Phone: (305) 253-2244 **Domicile State:** FL **NAIC Code:** 60275

Data Date	Rating	RACR #1	RACR #2	Total Assets ($mil)	Capital ($mil)	Net Premium ($mil)	Net Income ($mil)
6-20	B	4.71	2.69	322.0	52.7	47.7	10.0
6-19	B-	4.51	2.59	347.4	46.8	52.4	6.1
2019	B	4.68	2.71	353.4	52.8	103.2	20.6
2018	C+	4.75	2.72	338.4	47.9	95.1	23.0
2017	C+	5.57	3.05	364.0	53.0	79.1	23.8
2016	C+	7.11	3.50	378.7	54.7	35.7	21.5
2015	C+	7.24	3.58	406.2	56.7	30.6	21.2

Adverse Trends in Operations

Decrease in capital during 2018 (10%)
Decrease in asset base during 2018 (7%)
Change in premium mix from 2016 to 2017 (7.2%)
Decrease in capital during 2016 (4%)
Decrease in asset base during 2016 (7%)

AMERICAN CONTINENTAL INS CO | C+ | Fair

Major Rating Factors: Fair profitability (4.3 on a scale of 0 to 10). Excellent expense controls. Return on equity has been low, averaging -7.1%. Fair overall results on stability tests (4.4). Good liquidity (5.9) with sufficient resources to handle a spike in claims.

Other Rating Factors: Strong capitalization (7.1) based on excellent risk adjusted capital (severe loss scenario). High quality investment portfolio (7.7).

Principal Business: Individual health insurance (91%) and individual life insurance (9%).

Principal Investments: NonCMO investment grade bonds (74%), CMOs and structured securities (30%), mortgages in good standing (2%), and policy loans (1%).

Investments in Affiliates: None
Group Affiliation: Aetna Inc
Licensed in: AL, AZ, AR, CO, FL, GA, IL, IN, IA, KS, KY, LA, MI, MN, MS, MO, MT, NE, NV, NM, NC, ND, OH, OK, PA, SC, SD, TN, TX, UT, VA, WV, WI, WY
Commenced Business: September 2005
Address: 800 CRESENT CENTRE DR STE 200, FRANKLIN, TN 37064
Phone: (800) 264-4000 **Domicile State:** TN **NAIC Code:** 12321

Data Date	Rating	RACR #1	RACR #2	Total Assets ($mil)	Capital ($mil)	Net Premium ($mil)	Net Income ($mil)
6-20	C+	2.38	1.77	336.1	146.0	232.9	20.0
6-19	C	1.77	1.33	284.4	111.5	245.4	-6.9
2019	C	2.02	1.51	299.3	124.8	485.4	0.0
2018	C	1.86	1.39	285.8	118.3	499.4	-5.1
2017	B-	1.82	1.37	276.9	115.2	506.3	-15.0
2016	B-	1.60	1.21	229.0	94.0	472.9	-17.7
2015	B-	1.49	1.14	203.1	79.7	430.1	-15.3

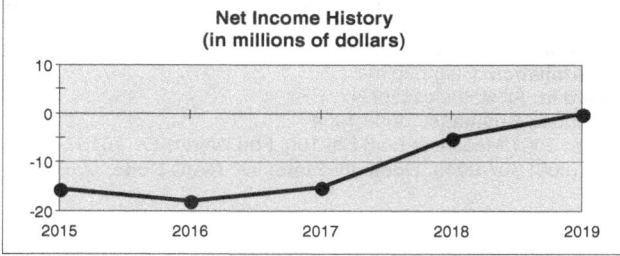

Net Income History
(in millions of dollars)

AMERICAN FAMILY LIFE ASR CO OF NY * | A- | Excellent

Major Rating Factors: Strong capitalization (10.0 on a scale of 0 to 10) based on excellent risk adjusted capital (severe loss scenario). Furthermore, this high level of risk adjusted capital has been consistently maintained over the last five years. High quality investment portfolio (7.9) despite no exposure to mortgages and large holdings of BBB rated bonds but minimal holdings in junk bonds. Excellent profitability (8.5) with operating gains in each of the last five years.

Other Rating Factors: Excellent liquidity (7.6). Excellent overall results on stability tests (7.3) excellent operational trends and excellent risk diversification.

Principal Business: Individual health insurance (94%), individual life insurance (4%), and group health insurance (2%).

Principal Investments: NonCMO investment grade bonds (93%), CMOs and structured securities (1%), and noninv. grade bonds (1%).

Investments in Affiliates: None
Group Affiliation: AFLAC Inc
Licensed in: CT, MA, NJ, NY, ND, VT
Commenced Business: December 1964
Address: 22 Corporate Woods Blvd Ste 2, Albany, NY 12211
Phone: (518) 438-0764 **Domicile State:** NY **NAIC Code:** 60526

Data Date	Rating	RACR #1	RACR #2	Total Assets ($mil)	Capital ($mil)	Net Premium ($mil)	Net Income ($mil)
6-20	A-	6.08	4.07	1,043.6	356.2	173.7	37.3
6-19	A-	5.13	3.45	990.5	283.4	170.9	39.0
2019	A-	5.57	3.76	982.9	319.5	342.5	75.1
2018	A-	5.55	3.65	965.2	310.1	335.4	66.6
2017	A-	5.60	3.74	915.6	300.6	326.8	58.9
2016	A-	5.91	3.97	870.1	304.3	315.9	51.6
2015	A-	6.11	4.20	817.9	298.5	304.2	47.4

Risk-Adjusted Capital Ratios
(Since 2015)

■ RACR #1   □ RACR #2

AMERICAN FIDELITY ASR CO *
B+   Good

Major Rating Factors: Good quality investment portfolio (6.4 on a scale of 0 to 10) despite significant exposure to mortgages . Mortgage default rate has been low. large holdings of BBB rated bonds in addition to minimal holdings in junk bonds. Good liquidity (6.6) with sufficient resources to handle a spike in claims as well as a significant increase in policy surrenders. Good overall results on stability tests (6.8) excellent operational trends and excellent risk diversification.

Other Rating Factors: Strong capitalization (7.3) based on excellent risk adjusted capital (severe loss scenario). Excellent profitability (8.5) with operating gains in each of the last five years.

Principal Business: Group health insurance (41%), individual health insurance (25%), individual annuities (16%), individual life insurance (13%), and other lines (5%).

Principal Investments: NonCMO investment grade bonds (64%), CMOs and structured securities (17%), mortgages in good standing (10%), cash (5%), and misc. investments (3%).

Investments in Affiliates: 1%

Group Affiliation: Cameron Associates Inc

Licensed in: All states except NY

Commenced Business: December 1960

Address: 9000 Cameron Parkway, Oklahoma City, OK 73114-3701

Phone: (405) 523-2000 **Domicile State:** OK **NAIC Code:** 60410

Data Date	Rating	RACR #1	RACR #2	Total Assets ($mil)	Capital ($mil)	Net Premium ($mil)	Net Income ($mil)
3-20	B+	2.06	1.21	6,608.0	545.8	327.6	33.5
3-19	B+	2.09	1.20	6,256.2	526.5	307.5	28.1
2019	B+	2.14	1.26	6,656.8	544.3	1,176.2	90.3
2018	B+	2.05	1.17	6,101.2	505.2	1,091.7	98.9
2017	B+	1.78	1.04	5,896.7	430.6	957.4	66.2
2016	B+	1.88	1.07	5,446.8	414.6	906.6	76.4
2015	B+	1.97	1.13	5,181.1	408.5	957.9	75.4

Adverse Trends in Operations

Increase in policy surrenders from 2018 to 2019 (40%)
Decrease in premium volume from 2015 to 2016 (5%)

AMERICAN HEALTH & LIFE INS CO
B-   Good

Major Rating Factors: Good overall results on stability tests (5.2 on a scale of 0 to 10) despite fair financial strength of affiliated Citigroup Inc. Other stability subfactors include good operational trends and excellent risk diversification. Good quality investment portfolio (6.3) despite mixed results such as: minimal exposure to mortgages and large holdings of BBB rated bonds but minimal holdings in junk bonds. Strong capitalization (9.1) based on excellent risk adjusted capital (severe loss scenario).

Other Rating Factors: Excellent profitability (7.9) with operating gains in each of the last five years. Excellent liquidity (9.0).

Principal Business: Credit health insurance (36%), credit life insurance (35%), reinsurance (17%), individual life insurance (8%), and other lines (4%).

Principal Investments: NonCMO investment grade bonds (71%), CMOs and structured securities (25%), noninv. grade bonds (2%), and common & preferred stock (1%).

Investments in Affiliates: None

Group Affiliation: Citigroup Inc

Licensed in: All states except NY, PR

Commenced Business: June 1954

Address: 3001 Meacham Blvd Ste 100, Fort Worth, TX 76137-4615

Phone: (800) 307-0048 **Domicile State:** TX **NAIC Code:** 60518

Data Date	Rating	RACR #1	RACR #2	Total Assets ($mil)	Capital ($mil)	Net Premium ($mil)	Net Income ($mil)
6-20	B-	3.87	2.40	1,302.0	257.1	106.7	61.9
6-19	B-	2.11	1.36	1,191.2	146.6	264.7	15.6
2019	B-	2.58	1.67	1,281.6	192.4	479.7	55.9
2018	A-	2.00	1.28	1,038.1	128.5	377.6	32.1
2017	A-	2.70	1.70	883.2	130.3	251.1	34.5
2016	A-	5.40	3.11	924.2	215.1	154.3	71.2
2015	A-	4.03	2.40	923.9	183.5	199.8	55.5

Citigroup Inc
Composite Group Rating: C

Largest Group Members	Assets ($mil)	Rating
ATHENE ANNUITY LIFE CO	65505	C
VENERABLE INS AND ANNTY CO	50252	B-
ATHENE ANNUITY LIFE ASR CO	28471	C
ATHENE ANNUITY LIFE ASR CO OF NY	3243	C+
AMERICAN HEALTH LIFE INS CO	1282	B-

AMERICAN HERITAGE LIFE INS CO
C+   Fair

Major Rating Factors: Fair overall results on stability tests (4.7 on a scale of 0 to 10). Good quality investment portfolio (5.4) despite mixed results such as: large holdings of BBB rated bonds but moderate junk bond exposure. Good overall profitability (6.7). Return on equity has been excellent over the last five years averaging 19.2%.

Other Rating Factors: Good liquidity (6.5). Strong capitalization (7.1) based on excellent risk adjusted capital (severe loss scenario).

Principal Business: Group health insurance (67%), individual health insurance (18%), individual life insurance (7%), group life insurance (7%), and reinsurance (1%).

Principal Investments: NonCMO investment grade bonds (50%), policy loans (16%), common & preferred stock (10%), mortgages in good standing (10%), and misc. investments (14%).

Investments in Affiliates: 7%

Group Affiliation: Allstate Group

Licensed in: All states except NY

Commenced Business: December 1956

Address: 1776 AMERICAN HERITAGE LIFE DR, JACKSONVILLE, FL 32224-6688

Phone: (904) 992-1776 **Domicile State:** FL **NAIC Code:** 60534

Data Date	Rating	RACR #1	RACR #2	Total Assets ($mil)	Capital ($mil)	Net Premium ($mil)	Net Income ($mil)
6-20	C+	1.39	1.05	2,143.1	380.3	476.0	26.0
6-19	B	1.39	1.06	2,073.3	384.1	480.2	49.1
2019	B	1.27	0.96	2,075.3	344.9	958.8	91.9
2018	B	1.18	0.91	2,003.1	323.9	952.5	101.8
2017	B	1.08	0.82	1,922.0	306.0	905.3	55.3
2016	B	1.22	0.97	1,885.6	344.3	861.4	63.1
2015	B	1.19	0.96	1,830.9	329.7	785.9	56.3

Rating Indexes

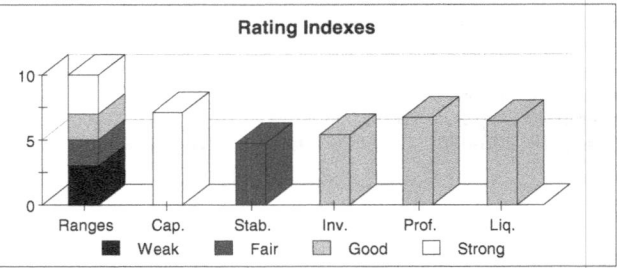

AMERICAN LIFE INS CO   C   Fair

Major Rating Factors: Fair quality investment portfolio (3.0 on a scale of 0 to 10). Fair overall results on stability tests (3.4). Good overall profitability (5.8) despite operating losses during the first six months of 2020. Return on equity has been excellent over the last five years averaging 24.2%.
Other Rating Factors: Strong capitalization (7.1) based on excellent risk adjusted capital (severe loss scenario). Excellent liquidity (9.0).
Principal Business: Individual life insurance (48%), reinsurance (22%), group health insurance (20%), individual health insurance (6%), and other lines (4%).
Principal Investments: Common & preferred stock (50%), noninv. grade bonds (18%), nonCMO investment grade bonds (18%), cash (9%), and misc. investments (5%).
Investments in Affiliates: 51%
Group Affiliation: MetLife Inc
Licensed in: DE
Commenced Business: August 1921
Address: 1209 Orange Street, Wilmington, DE 19801
Phone: (302) 594-2000 **Domicile State:** DE **NAIC Code:** 60690

Data Date	Rating	RACR #1	RACR #2	Total Assets ($mil)	Capital ($mil)	Net Premium ($mil)	Net Income ($mil)
6-20	C	1.11	1.05	11,395.9	4,553.8	651.5	-2.8
6-19	C	1.02	0.98	11,111.8	4,864.5	659.0	638.4
2019	C	1.11	1.06	11,623.1	4,970.1	1,309.9	1,386.0
2018	C	1.03	0.99	10,807.1	4,920.6	1,441.1	2,085.5
2017	C	1.21	1.17	11,986.6	6,547.6	1,389.6	3,076.8
2016	C	1.03	0.99	10,377.8	5,235.3	1,373.6	341.5
2015	C	1.02	0.99	11,097.5	6,115.1	1,204.5	334.6

Rating Indexes

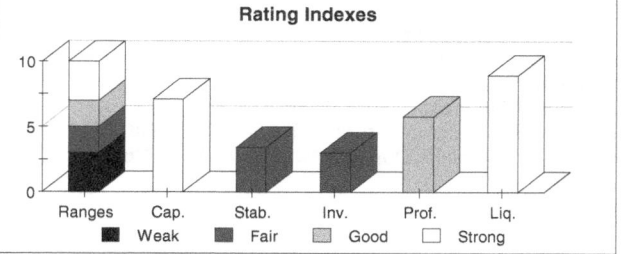

Ranges | Cap. | Stab. | Inv. | Prof. | Liq.
■ Weak   ■ Fair   ▨ Good   □ Strong

AMERICAN NATIONAL LIFE INS CO OF TX   B-   Good

Major Rating Factors: Good liquidity (6.2 on a scale of 0 to 10) with sufficient resources to handle a spike in claims. Good overall results on stability tests (5.0) despite excessive premium growth. Other stability subfactors include excellent operational trends and excellent risk diversification. Fair profitability (4.1). Return on equity has been low, averaging -3.0%.
Other Rating Factors: Strong capitalization (8.5) based on excellent risk adjusted capital (severe loss scenario). High quality investment portfolio (7.1).
Principal Business: Reinsurance (43%), group health insurance (32%), individual health insurance (22%), and individual life insurance (3%).
Principal Investments: NonCMO investment grade bonds (93%), noninv. grade bonds (3%), and policy loans (3%).
Investments in Affiliates: None
Group Affiliation: American National Group Inc
Licensed in: All states except ME, NJ, NY, VT, PR
Commenced Business: December 1954
Address: ONE MOODY PLAZA, GALVESTON, TX 77550
Phone: (409) 763-4661 **Domicile State:** TX **NAIC Code:** 71773

Data Date	Rating	RACR #1	RACR #2	Total Assets ($mil)	Capital ($mil)	Net Premium ($mil)	Net Income ($mil)
6-20	B-	2.93	2.01	135.2	37.3	31.4	1.2
6-19	B-	3.36	2.26	127.7	32.5	23.2	-0.1
2019	B-	3.00	2.06	131.6	35.4	52.0	1.8
2018	B-	3.59	2.39	127.7	33.0	39.2	-1.5
2017	B-	3.85	2.99	123.7	34.2	28.8	-0.5
2016	B-	3.95	3.48	122.5	35.2	26.8	-0.8
2015	B-	4.01	3.16	127.5	35.9	35.5	-5.3

Adverse Trends in Operations

Decrease in capital during 2018 (4%)
Decrease in asset base during 2016 (4%)
Decrease in capital during 2016 (2%)
Increase in policy surrenders from 2015 to 2016 (51%)
Decrease in premium volume from 2015 to 2016 (25%)

AMERICAN PROGRESSIVE L&H I C OF NY   C   Fair

Major Rating Factors: Fair overall results on stability tests (3.5 on a scale of 0 to 10). Good current capitalization (5.6) based on mixed results -- excessive policy leverage mitigated by excellent risk adjusted capital (severe loss scenario) reflecting improvement over results in 2019. Weak liquidity (1.5) as a spike in claims may stretch capacity.
Other Rating Factors: High quality investment portfolio (7.4). Excellent profitability (7.6) despite modest operating losses during 2015 and 2017.
Principal Business: Individual health insurance (97%), group health insurance (2%), and individual life insurance (1%).
Principal Investments: NonCMO investment grade bonds (89%), CMOs and structured securities (5%), cash (2%), common & preferred stock (1%), and noninv. grade bonds (1%).
Investments in Affiliates: None
Group Affiliation: WellCare Health Plans Inc
Licensed in: AL, AR, CO, CT, DC, DE, GA, HI, IL, IN, LA, ME, MD, MA, MN, MO, NH, NJ, NY, NC, OH, OK, OR, PA, RI, SC, TX, VT, VA, WV
Commenced Business: March 1946
Address: 44 South Broadway Suite 1200, New York, NY 10004
Phone: (314) 725-4477 **Domicile State:** NY **NAIC Code:** 80624

Data Date	Rating	RACR #1	RACR #2	Total Assets ($mil)	Capital ($mil)	Net Premium ($mil)	Net Income ($mil)
6-20	C	1.25	1.01	333.4	142.6	290.7	22.1
6-19	C	1.19	0.96	320.2	138.4	333.5	21.4
2019	C	1.04	0.84	301.2	126.1	656.9	26.3
2018	C	1.05	0.86	250.8	116.5	602.8	12.0
2017	C	1.04	0.84	222.9	102.1	535.7	-6.6
2016	C	1.25	1.02	215.0	109.3	463.9	10.0
2015	C	1.29	1.03	211.5	101.3	420.8	-13.0

Rating Indexes

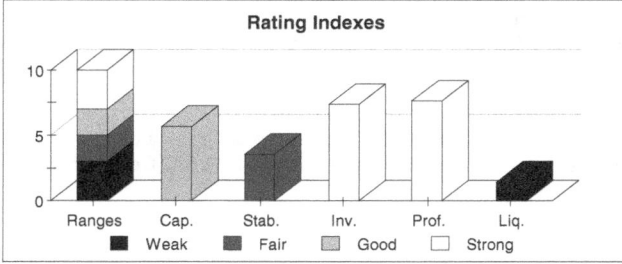

Ranges | Cap. | Stab. | Inv. | Prof. | Liq.
■ Weak   ■ Fair   ▨ Good   □ Strong

AMERICAN PUBLIC LIFE INS CO   B   Good

Major Rating Factors: Good liquidity (6.7 on a scale of 0 to 10) with sufficient resources to handle a spike in claims. Good overall results on stability tests (6.3) despite negative cash flow from operations for 2019. Other stability subfactors include excellent operational trends and excellent risk diversification. Strong capitalization (8.3) based on excellent risk adjusted capital (severe loss scenario).

Other Rating Factors: High quality investment portfolio (8.0). Excellent profitability (7.8) with operating gains in each of the last five years.

Principal Business: Group health insurance (86%), individual health insurance (11%), reinsurance (2%), and individual life insurance (1%).

Principal Investments: NonCMO investment grade bonds (50%), CMOs and structured securities (34%), mortgages in good standing (10%), cash (4%), and misc. investments (3%).

Investments in Affiliates: None

Group Affiliation: Cameron Associates Inc

Licensed in: All states except NY, PR

Commenced Business: March 1946

Address: 9000 Cameron Parkway, Oklahoma City, OK 73114

Phone: (601) 936-6600 **Domicile State:** OK **NAIC Code:** 60801

Data Date	Rating	RACR #1	RACR #2	Total Assets ($mil)	Capital ($mil)	Net Premium ($mil)	Net Income ($mil)
6-20	B	2.45	1.84	105.7	38.1	47.3	4.9
6-19	B	2.32	1.76	100.5	35.1	48.8	2.3
2019	B	2.18	1.65	99.2	33.8	96.5	7.1
2018	B	2.34	1.77	100.8	35.2	96.6	5.2
2017	B	2.11	1.59	99.5	30.8	90.9	5.5
2016	B	1.96	1.47	90.3	26.4	74.4	5.9
2015	B	1.95	1.44	86.7	23.6	61.4	5.0

Adverse Trends in Operations

Decrease in asset base during 2019 (2%)
Decrease in capital during 2019 (4%)

AMERICAN REPUBLIC INS CO   B-   Good

Major Rating Factors: Good quality investment portfolio (5.8 on a scale of 0 to 10) despite mixed results such as: minimal exposure to mortgages and large holdings of BBB rated bonds but minimal holdings in junk bonds. Good liquidity (6.9) with sufficient resources to handle a spike in claims as well as a significant increase in policy surrenders. Fair overall results on stability tests (4.9) including fair financial strength of affiliated American Enterprise Mutual Holding.

Other Rating Factors: Strong capitalization (9.6) based on excellent risk adjusted capital (severe loss scenario). Excellent profitability (9.0) with operating gains in each of the last five years.

Principal Business: Reinsurance (83%), individual health insurance (10%), group health insurance (5%), and individual life insurance (1%).

Principal Investments: NonCMO investment grade bonds (55%), CMOs and structured securities (22%), mortgages in good standing (8%), common & preferred stock (7%), and misc. investments (7%).

Investments in Affiliates: 6%

Group Affiliation: American Enterprise Mutual Holding

Licensed in: All states except NY, PR

Commenced Business: May 1929

Address: 601 Sixth Avenue, Des Moines, IA 50309

Phone: (800) 247-2190 **Domicile State:** IA **NAIC Code:** 60836

Data Date	Rating	RACR #1	RACR #2	Total Assets ($mil)	Capital ($mil)	Net Premium ($mil)	Net Income ($mil)
6-20	B-	3.63	2.70	1,193.0	536.9	279.1	19.0
6-19	B-	6.01	3.71	1,115.3	489.4	326.7	12.3
2019	B-	3.57	2.69	1,135.3	519.7	626.9	31.3
2018	B-	5.87	3.64	1,057.0	481.8	675.9	26.3
2017	A-	4.18	2.99	937.4	445.0	442.0	23.3
2016	A-	5.06	3.60	937.6	511.1	392.1	33.1
2015	A-	5.21	3.70	820.0	477.9	328.1	21.6

American Enterprise Mutual Holding
Composite Group Rating: C

Largest Group Members	Assets ($mil)	Rating
GREAT WESTERN INS CO	1370	C-
AMERICAN REPUBLIC INS CO	1135	B-
MEDICO INS CO	53	B-
MEDICO CORP LIFE INS CO	48	B-
AMERICAN REPUBLIC CORP INS CO	15	C

AMERICAN RETIREMENT LIFE INS CO   C+   Fair

Major Rating Factors: Fair overall results on stability tests (3.3 on a scale of 0 to 10) including negative cash flow from operations for 2019, fair risk adjusted capital in prior years. Good current capitalization (5.2) based on mixed results -- excessive policy leverage mitigated by excellent risk adjusted capital (severe loss scenario) reflecting significant improvement over results in 2016. Weak profitability (1.6).

Other Rating Factors: Weak liquidity (0.8). High quality investment portfolio (7.6).

Principal Business: Individual health insurance (100%).

Principal Investments: NonCMO investment grade bonds (110%) and noninv. grade bonds (1%).

Investments in Affiliates: None

Group Affiliation: CIGNA Corp

Licensed in: AL, AZ, AR, CA, CO, DE, FL, GA, IL, IN, IA, KS, KY, LA, MD, MN, MS, MO, MT, NE, NV, NH, NM, NC, ND, OH, OK, OR, PA, RI, SC, SD, TN, TX, UT, VA, WV, WI, WY

Commenced Business: November 1978

Address: 1300 East Ninth Street, Cleveland, OH 44114

Phone: (512) 451-2224 **Domicile State:** OH **NAIC Code:** 88366

Data Date	Rating	RACR #1	RACR #2	Total Assets ($mil)	Capital ($mil)	Net Premium ($mil)	Net Income ($mil)
6-20	C+	1.51	1.16	157.2	83.2	203.8	4.4
6-19	C+	1.30	1.00	133.1	71.2	209.0	-18.4
2019	C+	1.23	0.95	131.7	68.7	420.5	-27.4
2018	C+	1.17	0.91	123.9	63.1	401.2	-42.6
2017	C+	1.27	0.99	121.0	59.7	345.2	-38.1
2016	C+	0.91	0.71	76.9	40.7	255.5	-26.4
2015	C+	1.36	1.05	77.4	47.3	192.2	-22.1

Rating Indexes

AMERICAN SPECIALTY HEALTH INS CO   B   Good

Major Rating Factors: Good overall profitability index (6.7 on a scale of 0 to 10). Strong capitalization (10.0) based on excellent current risk-adjusted capital (severe loss scenario). High quality investment portfolio (9.9).
Other Rating Factors: Excellent liquidity (9.8) with ample operational cash flow and liquid investments.
Principal Business: Other (100%)
Mem Phys: 19: 25,653 **18:** 28,744 **19 MLR** 22.9% **/ 19 Admin Exp** N/A
Enroll(000): Q2 20: 111 **19:** 159 **18:** 189 **Med Exp PMPM:** $0
Principal Investments: Cash and equiv (98%), long-term bonds (2%)
Provider Compensation ($000): FFS ($653)
Total Member Encounters: Non-phys (25,504)
Group Affiliation: American Specialty Health Incorporat
Licensed in: All states except AK, CT, ME, NJ, NY, NC, RI, PR
Address: 12800 North Meridian Street, Carmel, IN 46032
Phone: (619) 578-2000 **Dom State:** IN **Commenced Bus:** N/A

Data Date	Rating	RACR #1	RACR #2	Total Assets ($mil)	Capital ($mil)	Net Premium ($mil)	Net Income ($mil)
6-20	B	34.89	29.08	9.4	9.3	0.8	0.2
6-19	B	47.01	39.18	9.2	8.9	2.0	0.5
2019	B	34.78	28.98	9.3	9.1	2.9	0.6
2018	B	44.41	37.01	9.6	8.4	1.1	0.0
2017	B-	41.93	34.94	8.8	8.4	1.4	0.1
2016	B-	34.50	28.75	9.5	8.4	1.8	0.2
2015	B	27.13	22.61	8.5	8.1	3.0	0.7

AMERICAN SPECIALTY HEALTH ODS OF NJ   B   Good

Major Rating Factors: Good overall profitability index (6.3 on a scale of 0 to 10). Good capitalization (6.2) based on good current risk-adjusted capital (severe loss scenario). High quality investment portfolio (9.9).
Other Rating Factors: Excellent liquidity (6.9) with sufficient resources (cash flows and marketable investments) to handle a spike in claims.
Principal Business: Other (100%)
Mem Phys: 19: 1,143 **18:** 1,018 **19 MLR** 78.3% **/ 19 Admin Exp** N/A
Enroll(000): **19:** 1,236 **18:** 1,253 **Med Exp PMPM:** $0
Principal Investments: Cash and equiv (100%)
Provider Compensation ($000): FFS ($10,800)
Total Member Encounters: Non-phys (274,414)
Group Affiliation: American Specialty Health, Incorpora
Licensed in: NJ
Address: 830 Bear Tavern Rd, Dayton,
Phone: (800) 848-3555 **Dom State:** NJ **Commenced Bus:** N/A

Data Date	Rating	RACR #1	RACR #2	Total Assets ($mil)	Capital ($mil)	Net Premium ($mil)	Net Income ($mil)
2019	B	1.10	0.92	4.3	2.6	14.0	-0.1
2018	B	1.14	0.95	3.8	2.3	11.4	0.0
2017	C+	1.11	0.93	3.7	2.2	10.4	0.1
2016	C	1.26	1.05	2.7	2.1	10.1	0.1
2015	U	1.32	1.10	0.9	0.6	3.0	0.1

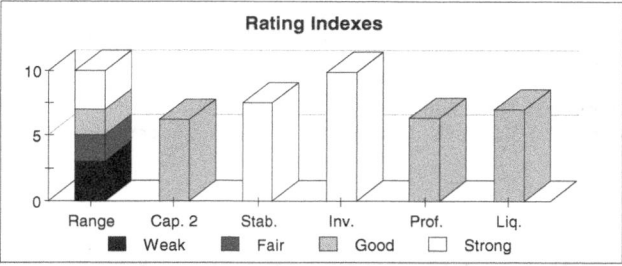

AMERICAS 1ST CHOICE SOUTH CAROLINA   C+   Fair

Major Rating Factors: Weak profitability index (0.9 on a scale of 0 to 10). Low quality investment portfolio (1.6). Strong capitalization (8.4) based on excellent current risk-adjusted capital (severe loss scenario).
Other Rating Factors: Excellent liquidity (7.0) with sufficient resources (cash flows and marketable investments) to handle a spike in claims.
Principal Business: Medicare (100%)
Mem Phys: 18: 310 **17:** 4,780 **18 MLR** 89.4% **/ 18 Admin Exp** N/A
Enroll(000): Q3 19: 1 **18:** 1 **17:** 1 **Med Exp PMPM:** $775
Principal Investments: Cash and equiv (100%)
Provider Compensation ($000): FFS ($7,035), capitation ($95), bonus arrang ($11)
Total Member Encounters: Phys (881), non-phys (601)
Group Affiliation: Anthem Inc
Licensed in: SC
Address: 250 BERRYHILL ROAD SUITE 311, COLUMBIA, SC 29210
Phone: (888) 563-3289 **Dom State:** SC **Commenced Bus:** N/A

Data Date	Rating	RACR #1	RACR #2	Total Assets ($mil)	Capital ($mil)	Net Premium ($mil)	Net Income ($mil)
9-19	C+	2.45	2.04	5.6	2.1	4.1	0.1
9-18	E-	N/A	N/A	4.0	2.1	5.2	-0.8
2018	C+	2.36	1.97	3.9	2.0	7.3	-0.9
2017	E-	N/A	N/A	3.1	1.2	7.6	-1.4
2016	D	4.32	3.60	2.3	1.8	1.9	0.1
2015	D-	3.77	3.14	2.2	1.7	1.2	0.1
2014	N/A	N/A	N/A	1.9	1.6	N/A	N/A

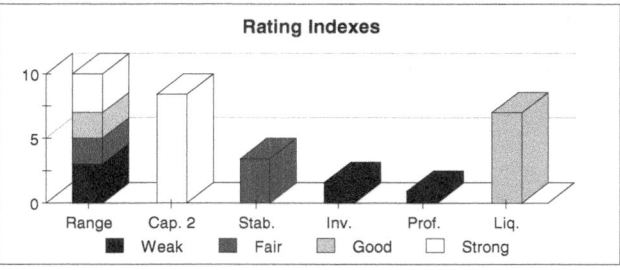

AMERICASHEALTH PLAN INC
D   **Weak**

Major Rating Factors: Weak overall results on stability tests (2.8 on a scale of 0 to 10) in spite of healthy premium and capital growth during 2019. Good overall profitability index (5.5). Strong capitalization index (10.0) based on excellent current risk-adjusted capital (severe loss scenario).

Other Rating Factors: Excellent liquidity (7.5) with ample operational cash flow and liquid investments.

Principal Business: Managed care (100%)

Mem Phys: 19: N/A **18:** N/A **19 MLR** 69.8% **/ 19 Admin Exp** N/A

Enroll(000): Q2 20: 2 **19:** 1 **18:** 1 **Med Exp PMPM:** $548

Principal Investments ($000): Cash and equiv ($4,626)

Provider Compensation ($000): None

Total Member Encounters: N/A

Group Affiliation: None

Licensed in: CA

Address: 200 South Wells Road Suite 200, Ventura, CA 93004

Phone: (615) 714-0232 **Dom State:** CA **Commenced Bus:** April 2013

Data Date	Rating	RACR #1	RACR #2	Total Assets ($mil)	Capital ($mil)	Net Premium ($mil)	Net Income ($mil)
6-20	D	4.56	3.16	5.5	2.8	7.5	0.8
6-19	D	4.29	3.03	5.2	2.2	5.9	0.7
2019	D	3.10	2.16	5.0	1.9	10.2	0.7
2018	D-	2.25	1.59	4.8	1.2	6.4	0.1
2017	E+	2.19	1.56	3.9	1.1	3.8	-0.6
2016	C-	14.90	9.82	2.3	1.7	0.9	-0.1
2015	N/A	N/A	N/A	1.4	1.4	N/A	N/A

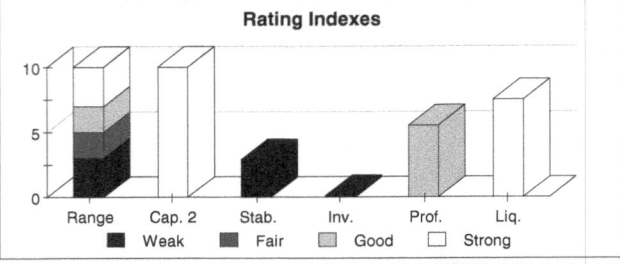

AMERICHOICE OF NEW JERSEY INC
B-   **Good**

Major Rating Factors: Fair profitability index (3.8 on a scale of 0 to 10). Good overall results on stability tests (6.5) despite a decline in enrollment during 2019. Good liquidity (6.8) with sufficient resources (cash flows and marketable investments) to handle a spike in claims.

Other Rating Factors: Strong capitalization index (7.7) based on excellent current risk-adjusted capital (severe loss scenario). High quality investment portfolio (9.9).

Principal Business: Medicaid (98%), comp med (2%)

Mem Phys: 19: 19,143 **18:** 17,377 **19 MLR** 91.1% **/ 19 Admin Exp** N/A

Enroll(000): Q2 20: 385 **19:** 419 **18:** 470 **Med Exp PMPM:** $454

Principal Investments: Long-term bonds (64%), cash and equiv (36%)

Provider Compensation ($000): Contr fee ($1,818,271), FFS ($567,786), capitation ($20,892), bonus arrang ($1,575)

Total Member Encounters: Phys (3,485,474), non-phys (2,676,097)

Group Affiliation: None

Licensed in: NJ

Address: 333 THORNALL STREET 9TH FLOOR, ISELIN,

Phone: (732) 623-1258 **Dom State:** NJ **Commenced Bus:** N/A

Data Date	Rating	RACR #1	RACR #2	Total Assets ($mil)	Capital ($mil)	Net Premium ($mil)	Net Income ($mil)
6-20	B-	1.92	1.60	778.1	420.5	1,193.3	66.7
6-19	C+	1.45	1.21	584.3	239.2	1,310.0	-101.2
2019	C+	2.07	1.73	728.1	354.7	2,649.8	-85.9
2018	B	1.70	1.42	587.7	283.3	2,714.5	-26.1
2017	B+	1.58	1.32	591.6	318.7	2,569.1	45.6
2016	B	2.05	1.71	547.6	272.9	2,549.2	87.7
2015	B	2.07	1.72	523.6	258.7	2,388.2	99.1

AMERIGROUP COMMUNITY CARE NM
B-   **Good**

Major Rating Factors: Good overall profitability index (5.8 on a scale of 0 to 10). Strong capitalization (10.0) based on excellent current risk-adjusted capital (severe loss scenario). High quality investment portfolio (9.9).

Other Rating Factors: Excellent liquidity (8.9) with ample operational cash flow and liquid investments.

Principal Business: Medicare (100%)

Mem Phys: 19: 6,762 **18:** 6,471 **19 MLR** 79.2% **/ 19 Admin Exp** N/A

Enroll(000): Q2 20: 2 **19:** 1 **18:** 2 **Med Exp PMPM:** $702

Principal Investments: Cash and equiv (98%), long-term bonds (2%)

Provider Compensation ($000): Contr fee ($9,374), FFS ($1,497), capitation ($894)

Total Member Encounters: Phys (13,506), non-phys (20,783)

Group Affiliation: Anthem Inc

Licensed in: NM

Address: 6565 AMERICAS PARKWAY NE SUI, ALBUQUERQUE, NM 87110

Phone: (317) 488-6000 **Dom State:** NM **Commenced Bus:** N/A

Data Date	Rating	RACR #1	RACR #2	Total Assets ($mil)	Capital ($mil)	Net Premium ($mil)	Net Income ($mil)
6-20	B-	7.96	6.64	22.5	18.3	10.9	0.8
6-19	B	48.70	40.59	74.5	70.9	7.5	1.6
2019	B-	13.66	11.38	20.3	17.8	14.7	3.4
2018	B	47.63	39.70	74.1	69.4	15.6	5.6
2017	B-	21.26	17.71	68.1	64.0	19.4	0.1
2016	B-	33.33	27.77	99.8	63.5	18.8	0.6
2015	B-	34.71	28.93	68.2	62.9	20.2	2.4

AMERIGROUP DISTRICT · B- · Good

Major Rating Factors: Excellent profitability (8.1 on a scale of 0 to 10). Strong capitalization (10.0) based on excellent current risk-adjusted capital (severe loss scenario). High quality investment portfolio (9.9).
Other Rating Factors: Excellent liquidity (8.3) with ample operational cash flow and liquid investments.
Principal Business: Medicaid (96%), comp med (4%)
Mem Phys: 18: 3,115 **17:** 3,008 **18 MLR** 56.3% **/ 18 Admin Exp** N/A
Enroll(000): Q3 19: 46 **18:** 47 **17:** 52 **Med Exp PMPM:** $212
Principal Investments: Cash and equiv (100%)
Provider Compensation ($000): Bonus arrang ($51,443), contr fee ($49,178), FFS ($31,942), capitation ($2,445)
Total Member Encounters: Phys (102,083), non-phys (146,163)
Group Affiliation: Anthem Inc
Licensed in: DC
Address: 609 H STREET NE STE 200, WASHINGTON, DC 20002
Phone: (757) 490-6900 **Dom State:** DC **Commenced Bus:** N/A

Data Date	Rating	RACR #1	RACR #2	Total Assets ($mil)	Capital ($mil)	Net Premium ($mil)	Net Income ($mil)
9-19	B-	12.27	10.22	138.1	100.1	144.8	19.4
9-18	N/A	N/A	N/A	115.9	65.6	167.5	35.4
2018	B-	10.23	8.53	124.8	80.6	220.1	50.7
2017	N/A	N/A	N/A	52.9	11.8	63.2	-4.5
2016	N/A	N/A	N/A	N/A	N/A	N/A	N/A
2015	N/A	N/A	N/A	N/A	N/A	N/A	N/A
2014	N/A	N/A	N/A	N/A	N/A	N/A	N/A

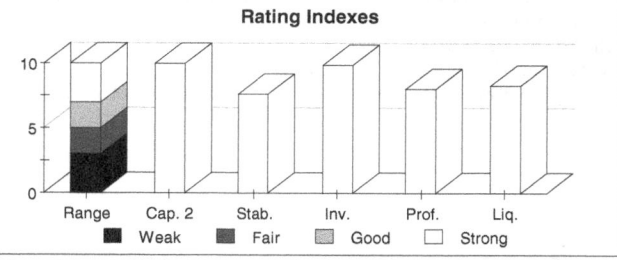

Rating Indexes

AMERIGROUP INS CO * · B+ · Good

Major Rating Factors: Good quality investment portfolio (6.3 on a scale of 0 to 10). Good liquidity (5.4) with sufficient resources (cash flows and marketable investments) to handle a spike in claims. Strong capitalization (7.4) based on excellent current risk-adjusted capital (severe loss scenario).
Other Rating Factors: Fair profitability index (4.1).
Principal Business: Medicaid (100%)
Mem Phys: 19: 27,424 **18:** 30,546 **19 MLR** 92.3% **/ 19 Admin Exp** N/A
Enroll(000): Q2 20: 168 **19:** 153 **18:** 152 **Med Exp PMPM:** $529
Principal Investments: Long-term bonds (94%), cash and equiv (6%)
Provider Compensation ($000): Bonus arrang ($556,501), contr fee ($208,568), FFS ($154,568), capitation ($2,054)
Total Member Encounters: Phys (689,961), non-phys (2,231,190)
Group Affiliation: Anthem Inc
Licensed in: AL, AZ, AR, DE, IA, LA, MD, MI, MS, NE, NM, ND, OR, PA, SD, TN, TX, UT, WA, WV, WY
Address: 3800 BUFFALO SPEEDWAY SUITE 4, HOUSTON, TX 77098
Phone: (757) 490-6900 **Dom State:** TX **Commenced Bus:** N/A

Data Date	Rating	RACR #1	RACR #2	Total Assets ($mil)	Capital ($mil)	Net Premium ($mil)	Net Income ($mil)
6-20	B+	1.64	1.37	322.8	149.8	564.5	9.4
6-19	B+	2.88	2.40	286.0	156.9	512.6	10.4
2019	B+	2.20	1.83	297.3	142.5	1,041.5	-17.2
2018	B	2.70	2.25	267.6	146.3	1,014.4	27.0
2017	B-	1.99	1.66	382.6	143.4	963.6	28.3
2016	B-	2.86	2.39	209.3	99.2	624.2	6.0
2015	B-	3.52	2.93	167.5	93.6	491.8	-0.1

Rating Indexes

AMERIGROUP IOWA INC · C · Fair

Major Rating Factors: Weak profitability index (1.9 on a scale of 0 to 10). Low quality investment portfolio (0.0). Strong capitalization (7.8) based on excellent current risk-adjusted capital (severe loss scenario).
Other Rating Factors: Excellent liquidity (7.0) with ample operational cash flow and liquid investments.
Principal Business: Medicaid (99%), comp med (1%)
Mem Phys: 18: 35,218 **17:** 32,435 **18 MLR** 92.0% **/ 18 Admin Exp** N/A
Enroll(000): Q3 19: 385 **18:** 202 **17:** 190 **Med Exp PMPM:** $576
Principal Investments: Cash and equiv (100%)
Provider Compensation ($000): Bonus arrang ($637,108), contr fee ($631,260), FFS ($71,375), capitation ($8,350)
Total Member Encounters: Phys (1,686,096), non-phys (5,551,330)
Group Affiliation: Anthem Inc
Licensed in: IA
Address: 4800 WESTOWN PARKWAY BLDG 3, WEST DES MOINES, IA 50266
Phone: (757) 490-6900 **Dom State:** IA **Commenced Bus:** N/A

Data Date	Rating	RACR #1	RACR #2	Total Assets ($mil)	Capital ($mil)	Net Premium ($mil)	Net Income ($mil)
9-19	C	1.97	1.64	677.8	171.2	1,560.9	-1.0
9-18	C	N/A	N/A	306.3	155.9	1,052.9	-12.4
2018	C	1.95	1.63	317.9	169.4	1,445.4	4.3
2017	C	N/A	N/A	309.7	149.1	1,231.2	-38.1
2016	B-	1.74	1.45	316.6	132.4	788.0	-133.3
2015	N/A	N/A	N/A	74.0	19.1	N/A	-50.5
2014	N/A	N/A	N/A	N/A	N/A	N/A	N/A

Rating Indexes

AMERIGROUP MARYLAND INC — B- — Good

Major Rating Factors: Fair quality investment portfolio (3.6 on a scale of 0 to 10). Excellent profitability (10.0). Strong capitalization (8.1) based on excellent current risk-adjusted capital (severe loss scenario).
Other Rating Factors: Excellent liquidity (7.0) with sufficient resources (cash flows and marketable investments) to handle a spike in claims.
Principal Business: Medicaid (94%), comp med (6%)
Mem Phys: 19: 22,218 **18:** 20,621 **19 MLR** 77.9% **/ 19 Admin Exp** N/A
Enroll(000): Q2 20: 287 **19:** 276 **18:** 275 **Med Exp PMPM:** $281
Principal Investments: Long-term bonds (89%), cash and equiv (9%), other (2%)
Provider Compensation ($000): Bonus arrang ($588,855), contr fee ($230,434), FFS ($91,142), capitation ($10,685)
Total Member Encounters: Phys (1,390,137), non-phys (1,093,745)
Group Affiliation: Anthem Inc
Licensed in: AL, MD, RI
Address: 7550 TEAGUE ROAD SUITE 500, HANOVER, MD 21076
Phone: (757) 490-6900 **Dom State:** MD **Commenced Bus:** N/A

Data Date	Rating	RACR #1	RACR #2	Total Assets ($mil)	Capital ($mil)	Net Premium ($mil)	Net Income ($mil)
6-20	B-	2.21	1.84	495.8	196.8	584.1	16.0
6-19	B-	3.87	3.22	485.5	238.1	618.5	75.9
2019	B-	2.81	2.34	417.4	180.2	1,188.6	103.3
2018	B-	2.66	2.22	448.6	162.1	1,113.1	82.7
2017	B	1.80	1.50	385.4	154.0	1,095.9	68.2
2016	B	2.14	1.78	346.3	128.7	1,088.1	54.3
2015	B	1.88	1.57	276.2	98.2	946.1	3.9

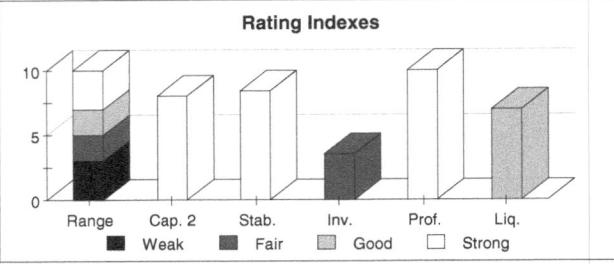

AMERIGROUP NEW JERSEY INC * — A- — Excellent

Major Rating Factors: Excellent profitability (8.7 on a scale of 0 to 10). Strong capitalization index (7.6) based on excellent current risk-adjusted capital (severe loss scenario). High quality investment portfolio (9.2).
Other Rating Factors: Excellent overall results on stability tests (7.5). Good liquidity (6.6) with sufficient resources (cash flows and marketable investments) to handle a spike in claims.
Principal Business: Medicaid (75%), Medicare (23%), comp med (2%)
Mem Phys: 19: 19,861 **18:** 17,706 **19 MLR** 88.4% **/ 19 Admin Exp** N/A
Enroll(000): Q2 20: 223 **19:** 193 **18:** 178 **Med Exp PMPM:** $569
Principal Investments: Long-term bonds (78%), cash and equiv (22%)
Provider Compensation ($000): Bonus arrang ($668,571), contr fee ($385,940), FFS ($165,806), capitation ($38,711)
Total Member Encounters: Phys (1,397,310), non-phys (3,293,116)
Group Affiliation: Anthem Inc
Licensed in: NJ
Address: 101 WOOD AVENUE SOUTH 8TH FLOO, ISELIN,
Phone: (757) 490-6900 **Dom State:** NJ **Commenced Bus:** N/A

Data Date	Rating	RACR #1	RACR #2	Total Assets ($mil)	Capital ($mil)	Net Premium ($mil)	Net Income ($mil)
6-20	A-	1.82	1.52	454.1	221.2	811.4	41.5
6-19	A-	2.21	1.85	350.2	172.3	691.9	10.7
2019	A-	2.07	1.73	357.3	182.4	1,451.9	18.9
2018	A-	2.11	1.76	359.0	163.8	1,381.2	41.6
2017	B+	1.54	1.28	313.5	161.5	1,365.9	41.1
2016	A-	2.52	2.10	318.0	168.8	1,304.3	65.2
2015	B	2.54	2.12	386.5	154.3	1,208.2	59.1

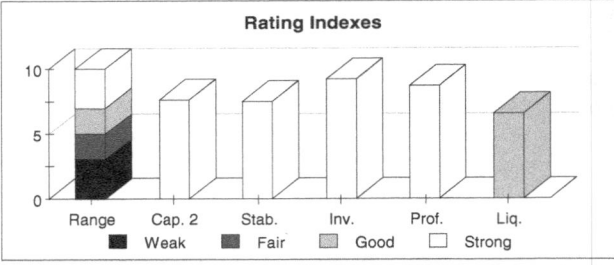

AMERIGROUP TENNESSEE INC — B- — Good

Major Rating Factors: Fair quality investment portfolio (3.7 on a scale of 0 to 10). Good liquidity (6.5) with sufficient resources (cash flows and marketable investments) to handle a spike in claims. Excellent profitability (7.7).
Other Rating Factors: Strong capitalization (7.8) based on excellent current risk-adjusted capital (severe loss scenario).
Principal Business: Medicaid (100%)
Mem Phys: 19: 30,422 **18:** 27,529 **19 MLR** 84.0% **/ 19 Admin Exp** N/A
Enroll(000): Q2 20: 421 **19:** 405 **18:** 381 **Med Exp PMPM:** $312
Principal Investments: Long-term bonds (85%), nonaffiliate common stock (10%), cash and equiv (3%), other (2%)
Provider Compensation ($000): Bonus arrang ($857,097), contr fee ($545,322), capitation ($47,512), FFS ($39,696)
Total Member Encounters: Phys (1,702,688), non-phys (3,835,552)
Group Affiliation: Anthem Inc
Licensed in: TN
Address: 22 CENTURY BOULEVARD SUITE 22, NASHVILLE, TN 37214
Phone: (757) 490-6900 **Dom State:** TN **Commenced Bus:** N/A

Data Date	Rating	RACR #1	RACR #2	Total Assets ($mil)	Capital ($mil)	Net Premium ($mil)	Net Income ($mil)
6-20	B-	1.97	1.64	650.1	265.7	999.7	36.7
6-19	B-	1.94	1.62	540.0	176.5	845.2	-16.7
2019	B-	2.34	1.95	623.0	231.6	1,805.2	38.1
2018	B-	2.05	1.71	515.5	187.2	1,739.0	14.8
2017	B-	1.90	1.58	488.9	233.2	1,777.3	56.2
2016	B-	1.76	1.47	531.9	178.2	1,905.9	13.4
2015	B	2.02	1.68	591.6	169.6	1,688.4	22.7

AMERIGROUP TEXAS INC　　　　　　　　　　B　　　Good

Major Rating Factors: Good quality investment portfolio (5.1 on a scale of 0 to 10). Good liquidity (6.1) with sufficient resources (cash flows and marketable investments) to handle a spike in claims. Excellent profitability (8.2).
Other Rating Factors: Strong capitalization index (7.3) based on excellent current risk-adjusted capital (severe loss scenario). Excellent overall results on stability tests (7.0) based on healthy premium and capital growth during 2019 but a decline in the number of member physicians during 2020.
Principal Business: Medicaid (64%), Medicare (34%), comp med (2%)
Mem Phys: 19: 61,126　**18:** 84,085　**19 MLR** 88.4%　**/ 19 Admin Exp** N/A
Enroll(000): Q2 20: 756　**19:** 698　**18:** 668　**Med Exp PMPM:** $533
Principal Investments: Long-term bonds (80%), other (21%)
Provider Compensation ($000): Bonus arrang ($2,071,796), contr fee ($1,341,884), FFS ($518,134), capitation ($462,500)
Total Member Encounters: Phys (4,692,387), non-phys (9,514,850)
Group Affiliation: Anthem Inc
Licensed in: TX
Address: 3800 BUFFALO SPEEDWAY SUITE 40, HOUSTON,
Phone: (757) 490-6900　**Dom State:** TX　**Commenced Bus:** N/A

Data Date	Rating	RACR #1	RACR #2	Total Assets ($mil)	Capital ($mil)	Net Premium ($mil)	Net Income ($mil)
6-20	B	1.59	1.32	1,228.2	531.2	2,845.3	21.4
6-19	A-	2.16	1.80	1,012.9	492.9	2,460.9	52.2
2019	A-	1.96	1.63	1,071.7	536.4	5,055.1	77.8
2018	A-	1.97	1.64	946.1	443.8	4,245.1	47.5
2017	A-	1.65	1.38	923.3	409.2	3,838.7	87.5
2016	A-	2.06	1.72	912.7	400.5	3,861.6	87.0
2015	B	1.86	1.55	874.5	352.8	3,610.8	54.3

AMERIGROUP WASHINGTON INC *　　　　A-　　　Excellent

Major Rating Factors: Excellent profitability (9.4 on a scale of 0 to 10). Strong capitalization (10.0) based on excellent current risk-adjusted capital (severe loss scenario). Good quality investment portfolio (6.7).
Other Rating Factors: Good liquidity (6.9) with sufficient resources (cash flows and marketable investments) to handle a spike in claims.
Principal Business: Medicaid (96%), Medicare (3%), comp med (1%)
Mem Phys: 19: 39,570　**18:** 29,993　**19 MLR** 82.0%　**/ 19 Admin Exp** N/A
Enroll(000): Q2 20: 196　**19:** 173　**18:** 153　**Med Exp PMPM:** $259
Principal Investments: Long-term bonds (85%), cash and equiv (15%)
Provider Compensation ($000): Bonus arrang ($385,125), capitation ($77,952), contr fee ($49,905), FFS ($2,103)
Total Member Encounters: Phys (661,086), non-phys (904,217)
Group Affiliation: Anthem Inc
Licensed in: WA
Address: 705 FIFTH AVENUE SOUTH SUITE, SEATTLE, WA 98104
Phone: (757) 490-6900　**Dom State:** WA　**Commenced Bus:** N/A

Data Date	Rating	RACR #1	RACR #2	Total Assets ($mil)	Capital ($mil)	Net Premium ($mil)	Net Income ($mil)
6-20	A-	4.02	3.35	314.7	184.1	406.8	13.2
6-19	A-	5.98	4.99	272.5	163.5	315.9	12.9
2019	A-	5.30	4.42	319.1	174.5	643.5	36.4
2018	A-	5.57	4.64	280.5	151.5	491.1	22.6
2017	A-	3.13	2.61	261.5	146.7	602.5	28.7
2016	A-	4.36	3.63	259.0	134.1	570.7	24.8
2015	B	4.33	3.60	240.5	120.9	509.6	18.7

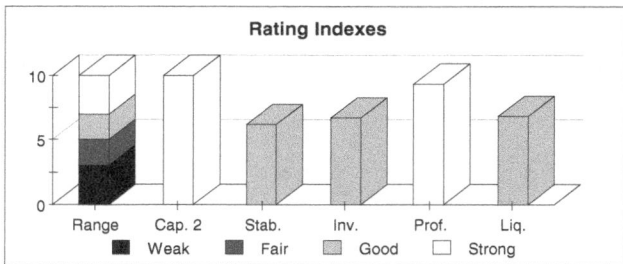

AMERIHEALTH CARITAS IOWA INC　　　　C　　　Fair

Major Rating Factors: Weak profitability index (1.9 on a scale of 0 to 10). Strong capitalization (10.0) based on excellent current risk-adjusted capital (severe loss scenario). High quality investment portfolio (9.9).
Other Rating Factors: Excellent liquidity (10.0) with ample operational cash flow and liquid investments.
Principal Business: Medicaid (100%)
Mem Phys: 18: N/A　**17:** 48,093　**18 MLR** -597.7%　**/ 18 Admin Exp** N/A
Enroll(000): Q3 19: N/A　**18:** N/A　**17:** N/A　**Med Exp PMPM:** N/A
Principal Investments: Cash and equiv (90%), long-term bonds (10%)
Provider Compensation ($000): Contr fee ($74,023), capitation ($1,104)
Total Member Encounters: N/A
Group Affiliation: Independence Health Group Inc
Licensed in: IA
Address: 601 Locust St Ste 900, Philadelphia,
Phone: (215) 937-8000　**Dom State:** IA　**Commenced Bus:** N/A

Data Date	Rating	RACR #1	RACR #2	Total Assets ($mil)	Capital ($mil)	Net Premium ($mil)	Net Income ($mil)
9-19	C	36.53	30.44	30.7	30.1	5.7	2.5
9-18	C	1.59	1.32	185.8	171.7	-2.6	22.3
2018	C	104.70	87.21	136.4	131.6	2.8	31.1
2017	C-	0.99	0.82	255.4	146.6	1,748.3	-169.3
2016	C-	1.18	0.99	453.6	140.1	1,398.0	-293.1
2015	N/A	N/A	N/A	41.2	8.2	N/A	-33.0
2014	N/A	N/A	N/A	N/A	N/A	N/A	N/A

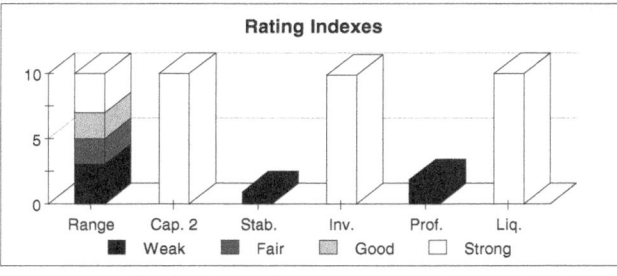

AMERIHEALTH CARITAS OF LOUISIANA INC

C   **Fair**

Major Rating Factors: Weak profitability index (2.6 on a scale of 0 to 10). Strong capitalization (7.1) based on excellent current risk-adjusted capital (severe loss scenario). High quality investment portfolio (9.9).
Other Rating Factors: Excellent liquidity (6.9) with sufficient resources (cash flows and marketable investments) to handle a spike in claims.
Principal Business: Medicaid (100%)
Mem Phys: 19: 24,929 **18:** 29,788 **19 MLR** 89.7% **/ 19 Admin Exp** N/A
Enroll(000): Q2 20: 212 **19:** 204 **18:** 209 **Med Exp PMPM:** $410
Principal Investments: Cash and equiv (91%), long-term bonds (9%)
Provider Compensation ($000): Contr fee ($801,914), capitation ($197,387), bonus arrang ($2,520)
Total Member Encounters: Phys (1,086,934), non-phys (876,785)
Group Affiliation: Independence Health Group Inc
Licensed in: LA
Address: 10000 Perkins Rowe Block G Ste, Baton Rouge, LA 70810
Phone: (215) 937-8000 **Dom State:** LA **Commenced Bus:** N/A

Data Date	Rating	RACR #1	RACR #2	Total Assets ($mil)	Capital ($mil)	Net Premium ($mil)	Net Income ($mil)
6-20	C	1.42	1.18	296.2	98.4	658.6	1.1
6-19	B	1.92	1.60	237.9	79.9	551.5	-4.1
2019	B-	2.06	1.72	303.4	100.0	1,149.1	-35.2
2018	B	2.06	1.72	261.7	87.0	1,100.2	2.6
2017	C+	1.43	1.20	268.2	94.2	1,020.3	27.3
2016	C	1.56	1.30	276.8	67.9	908.3	6.2
2015	C	1.96	1.63	155.6	59.8	622.8	9.7

Rating Indexes

AMERIHEALTH DISTRICT OF COLUMBIA INC

C   **Fair**

Major Rating Factors: Weak profitability index (1.6 on a scale of 0 to 10). Good liquidity (6.9) with sufficient resources (cash flows and marketable investments) to handle a spike in claims. Strong capitalization (7.5) based on excellent current risk-adjusted capital (severe loss scenario).
Other Rating Factors: High quality investment portfolio (9.9).
Principal Business: Medicaid (92%), comp med (8%)
Mem Phys: 19: 6,816 **18:** 6,505 **19 MLR** 94.0% **/ 19 Admin Exp** N/A
Enroll(000): Q2 20: 124 **19:** 125 **18:** 123 **Med Exp PMPM:** $362
Principal Investments: Cash and equiv (93%), long-term bonds (7%)
Provider Compensation ($000): Contr fee ($526,375), capitation ($7,691)
Total Member Encounters: Phys (861,972), non-phys (88,781)
Group Affiliation: Independence Health Group Inc
Licensed in: DC
Address: 1250 Maryland Avenue S W Su, Washington, DC 20024
Phone: (215) 937-8000 **Dom State:** DC **Commenced Bus:** N/A

Data Date	Rating	RACR #1	RACR #2	Total Assets ($mil)	Capital ($mil)	Net Premium ($mil)	Net Income ($mil)
6-20	C	1.74	1.45	192.2	88.4	310.2	13.8
6-19	C+	1.68	1.40	137.2	47.4	277.2	-18.8
2019	C+	2.17	1.81	166.4	73.3	578.2	-44.8
2018	C+	1.59	1.32	127.3	44.1	563.5	-15.2
2017	B-	N/A	N/A	145.2	59.9	507.2	21.1
2016	B-	2.95	2.46	155.1	72.2	493.9	19.2
2015	B	2.28	1.90	142.9	56.2	477.3	9.5

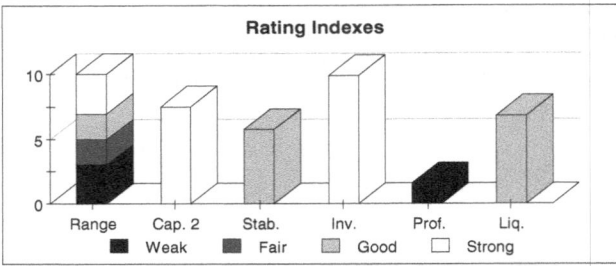

Rating Indexes

AMERIHEALTH HMO INC

C+   **Fair**

Major Rating Factors: Good overall results on stability tests (4.9 on a scale of 0 to 10). Weak liquidity (2.9) as a spike in claims may stretch capacity. Excellent profitability (7.1).
Other Rating Factors: Strong capitalization index (10.0) based on excellent current risk-adjusted capital (severe loss scenario). High quality investment portfolio (9.0).
Principal Business: Comp med (100%)
Mem Phys: 19: 65,996 **18:** 59,134 **19 MLR** 1933.0% **/ 19 Admin Exp** N/A
Enroll(000): Q2 20: 26 **19:** 27 **18:** 27 **Med Exp PMPM:** $419
Principal Investments: Long-term bonds (67%), cash and equiv (33%)
Provider Compensation ($000): Contr fee ($131,591), FFS ($8,572), capitation ($1,599), bonus arrang ($628)
Total Member Encounters: Phys (364,815), non-phys (49,509)
Group Affiliation: Independence Health Group Inc
Licensed in: DE, NJ, PA
Address: 1901 Market Street, Philadelphia,
Phone: (215) 241-2400 **Dom State:** PA **Commenced Bus:** N/A

Data Date	Rating	RACR #1	RACR #2	Total Assets ($mil)	Capital ($mil)	Net Premium ($mil)	Net Income ($mil)
6-20	C+	9.23	7.70	158.6	26.7	3.5	1.5
6-19	C+	14.37	11.98	121.1	24.5	3.6	1.4
2019	C+	14.92	12.44	109.8	25.1	7.3	2.7
2018	C+	13.73	11.44	107.8	23.3	7.7	1.0
2017	C	8.39	6.99	105.6	21.1	12.1	1.0
2016	C	9.04	7.53	162.0	18.6	14.9	1.9
2015	C	7.89	6.58	259.5	19.3	17.2	0.9

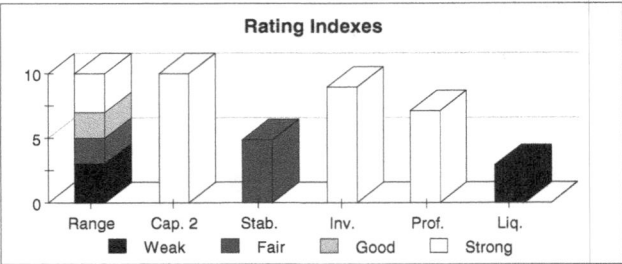

Rating Indexes

AMERIHEALTH INSURANCE CO OF NJ — B- — Good

Major Rating Factors: Fair profitability index (3.8 on a scale of 0 to 10). Strong capitalization (9.3) based on excellent current risk-adjusted capital (severe loss scenario). High quality investment portfolio (7.6).
Other Rating Factors: Excellent liquidity (7.0) with sufficient resources (cash flows and marketable investments) to handle a spike in claims.
Principal Business: Comp med (98%), med supp (2%)
Mem Phys: 19: 67,091 **18:** 60,337 **19 MLR** 75.3% **/ 19 Admin Exp** N/A
Enroll(000): 19: 164 **18:** 160 **Med Exp PMPM:** $403
Principal Investments: Long-term bonds (72%), cash and equiv (28%)
Provider Compensation ($000): Contr fee ($718,962), FFS ($104,830), capitation ($3,567), bonus arrang ($2,690)
Total Member Encounters: Phys (3,664,637), non-phys (366,095)
Group Affiliation: Independence Health Group, Inc.
Licensed in: NJ
Address: 8000 Midlantic Dr Ste 333, Cranbury,
Phone: (609) 662-2400 **Dom State:** NJ **Commenced Bus:** N/A

Data Date	Rating	RACR #1	RACR #2	Total Assets ($mil)	Capital ($mil)	Net Premium ($mil)	Net Income ($mil)
2019	B-	3.17	2.64	508.9	186.1	1,107.2	35.0
2018	C	3.68	3.07	551.5	209.6	1,095.4	51.0
2017	C-	2.07	1.73	396.8	168.1	1,072.2	17.3
2016	C-	1.59	1.32	421.3	126.6	1,356.1	-63.5
2015	C-	2.41	2.01	492.6	173.8	1,241.3	-46.9

Rating Indexes

AMERIHEALTH MICHIGAN INC — C — Fair

Major Rating Factors: Weak profitability index (0.9 on a scale of 0 to 10). Good liquidity (6.9) with sufficient resources (cash flows and marketable investments) to handle a spike in claims. Strong capitalization (9.0) based on excellent current risk-adjusted capital (severe loss scenario).
Other Rating Factors: High quality investment portfolio (9.9).
Principal Business: Medicare (100%)
Mem Phys: 18: 8,567 **17:** 9,400 **18 MLR** 94.9% **/ 18 Admin Exp** N/A
Enroll(000): Q3 19: 3 **18:** 3 **17:** 3 **Med Exp PMPM:** $1,866
Principal Investments: Cash and equiv (89%), long-term bonds (11%)
Provider Compensation ($000): Contr fee ($70,567), capitation ($936)
Total Member Encounters: Phys (57,944), non-phys (10,077)
Group Affiliation: Independence Health Group Inc
Licensed in: MI
Address: 4000 Town Center Suite 1300, Southfield, MI 48075
Phone: (215) 937-8000 **Dom State:** MI **Commenced Bus:** N/A

Data Date	Rating	RACR #1	RACR #2	Total Assets ($mil)	Capital ($mil)	Net Premium ($mil)	Net Income ($mil)
9-19	C	2.95	2.46	27.4	15.0	49.0	-4.9
9-18	C-	N/A	N/A	21.0	6.7	58.3	-6.9
2018	C	2.23	1.86	26.0	10.7	75.4	-10.7
2017	C-	N/A	N/A	25.5	12.9	73.2	-2.9
2016	C-	2.03	1.69	28.4	11.9	78.1	-10.7
2015	U	1.96	1.63	27.5	8.7	40.1	-13.5
2014	N/A	N/A	N/A	2.1	2.0	N/A	N/A

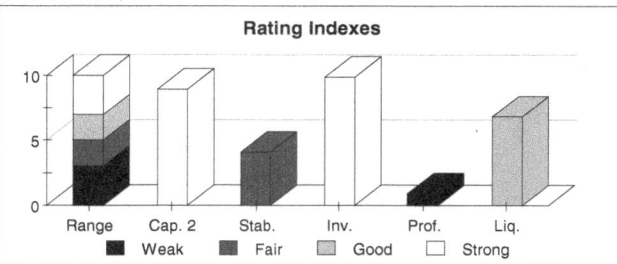

Rating Indexes

AMERITAS LIFE INS CORP — B — Good

Major Rating Factors: Good overall profitability (6.5 on a scale of 0 to 10). Return on equity has been low, averaging 2.4%. Good liquidity (6.1) with sufficient resources to handle a spike in claims as well as a significant increase in policy surrenders. Good overall results on stability tests (5.8). Stability strengths include good operational trends and excellent risk diversification.
Other Rating Factors: Fair quality investment portfolio (4.9). Strong capitalization (7.6) based on excellent risk adjusted capital (severe loss scenario).
Principal Business: Group retirement contracts (29%), individual annuities (22%), group health insurance (21%), individual life insurance (17%), and other lines (11%).
Principal Investments: NonCMO investment grade bonds (50%), mortgages in good standing (16%), CMOs and structured securities (16%), policy loans (4%), and misc. investments (11%).
Investments in Affiliates: 1%
Group Affiliation: Ameritas Mutual Holding Co
Licensed in: All states except NY, PR
Commenced Business: May 1887
Address: 5900 O Street, Lincoln, NE 68510-2234
Phone: (402) 467-1122 **Domicile State:** NE **NAIC Code:** 61301

Data Date	Rating	RACR #1	RACR #2	Total Assets ($mil)	Capital ($mil)	Net Premium ($mil)	Net Income ($mil)
6-20	B	2.43	1.40	23,704.7	1,726.8	1,510.3	57.3
6-19	B	2.31	1.35	23,210.4	1,584.8	1,567.3	-9.2
2019	B	2.44	1.43	24,057.1	1,693.3	3,113.1	91.2
2018	B	2.27	1.33	21,734.8	1,510.6	2,781.7	71.3
2017	B	2.25	1.34	20,076.5	1,555.6	2,724.5	106.3
2016	B	2.22	1.34	18,696.6	1,484.1	4,421.9	-4.8
2015	B	2.40	1.45	18,148.8	1,511.5	3,359.6	-9.5

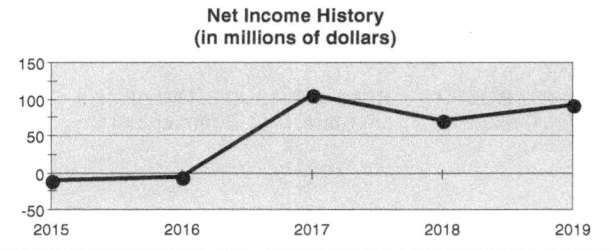

Net Income History
(in millions of dollars)

AMERITAS LIFE INS CORP OF NY

B-   **Good**

Major Rating Factors: Good quality investment portfolio (5.2 on a scale of 0 to 10) despite large holdings of BBB rated bonds in addition to moderate junk bond exposure. Exposure to mortgages is significant, but the mortgage default rate has been low. Fair profitability (3.0) with investment income below regulatory standards in relation to interest assumptions of reserves. Fair liquidity (4.5).

Other Rating Factors: Fair overall results on stability tests (4.9) including negative cash flow from operations for 2019. Strong capitalization (7.1) based on excellent risk adjusted capital (severe loss scenario).

Principal Business: Individual life insurance (35%), group retirement contracts (30%), group health insurance (18%), reinsurance (14%), and individual health insurance (4%).

Principal Investments: NonCMO investment grade bonds (57%), mortgages in good standing (18%), CMOs and structured securities (14%), policy loans (2%), and noninv. grade bonds (2%).

Investments in Affiliates: None

Group Affiliation: Ameritas Mutual Holding Co

Licensed in: NY

Commenced Business: May 1994

Address: 1350 Broadway Suite 2201, New York, NY 10018-7722

Phone: (402) 467-1122 **Domicile State:** NY **NAIC Code:** 60033

Data Date	Rating	RACR #1	RACR #2	Total Assets ($mil)	Capital ($mil)	Net Premium ($mil)	Net Income ($mil)
6-20	B-	2.03	1.06	1,697.8	106.7	62.3	1.3
6-19	B-	1.73	0.93	1,686.8	90.2	97.2	-3.8
2019	B-	2.06	1.10	1,746.7	108.2	185.6	-15.8
2018	B-	1.82	0.97	1,648.4	92.5	129.2	-11.8
2017	B-	2.29	1.22	1,275.7	106.4	154.8	0.0
2016	B-	2.18	1.18	1,204.4	97.2	131.7	20.1
2015	B-	1.60	0.87	1,149.7	65.8	100.8	-17.1

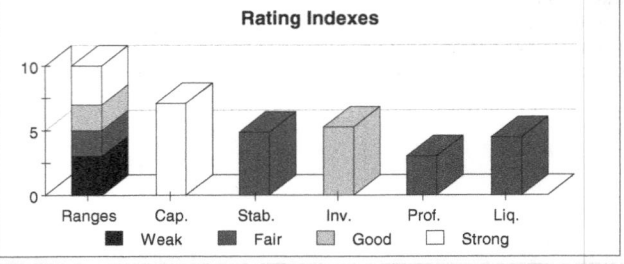

Rating Indexes

AMEX ASSURANCE CO

B-   **Good**

Major Rating Factors: Fair overall results on stability tests (3.5 on a scale of 0 to 10). History of adequate reserve strength (6.6) as reserves have been consistently at an acceptable level.

Other Rating Factors: Strong long-term capitalization index (10.0) based on excellent current risk adjusted capital (severe and moderate loss scenarios), despite some fluctuation in capital levels. Excellent profitability (7.1) with operating gains in each of the last five years. Return on equity has been excellent over the last five years averaging 31.6%. Excellent liquidity (7.6) with ample operational cash flow and liquid investments.

Principal Business: (Not applicable due to unusual reinsurance transactions.)

Principal Investments: Investment grade bonds (92%), cash (6%), and misc. investments (2%).

Investments in Affiliates: None

Group Affiliation: American Express Company

Licensed in: All states, the District of Columbia and Puerto Rico

Commenced Business: February 1973

Address: 2 Pierce Place Suite 900, Itasca, IL 60143

Phone: (602) 537-6511 **Domicile State:** IL **NAIC Code:** 27928

Data Date	Rating	RACR #1	RACR #2	Loss Ratio %	Total Assets ($mil)	Capital ($mil)	Net Premium ($mil)	Net Income ($mil)
6-20	B-	10.76	6.33	N/A	242.0	199.4	49.2	12.2
6-19	B-	10.32	6.07	N/A	273.8	226.9	97.3	34.7
2019	B	8.36	4.96	49.8	235.9	187.2	188.4	64.3
2018	B	9.32	5.47	44.2	237.8	192.2	185.6	69.4
2017	B	9.14	5.34	46.0	218.2	175.8	176.5	53.4
2016	B	10.58	6.07	39.0	227.8	181.4	177.4	59.7
2015	B	9.75	5.62	36.6	256.3	184.3	188.2	62.5

Rating Indexes

AMFIRST INS CO

B-   **Good**

Major Rating Factors: Fair quality investment portfolio (3.8 on a scale of 0 to 10). Excellent profitability (7.2). Strong capitalization (10.0) based on excellent current risk-adjusted capital (severe loss scenario).

Other Rating Factors: Excellent liquidity (7.3) with ample operational cash flow and liquid investments.

Principal Business: Dental (48%), other (46%)

Mem Phys: 19: N/A **18:** N/A **19 MLR** 24.5% **/ 19 Admin Exp** N/A

Enroll(000): Q2 20: 65 **19:** 56 **18:** 56 **Med Exp PMPM:** $23

Principal Investments: Affiliate common stock (41%), long-term bonds (39%), cash and equiv (9%), pref stock (5%), real estate (3%), nonaffiliate common stock (2%), other (1%)

Provider Compensation ($000): FFS ($14,985)

Total Member Encounters: Phys (49,480), non-phys (136,127)

Group Affiliation: Wheaton Management LLC

Licensed in: AL, AZ, AR, CA, CO, FL, GA, HI, IL, IN, IA, KY, LA, MD, MI, MS, MO, NJ, NC, OH, OK, PA, SC, TN, TX, VA, WV

Address: 201 ROBERT S KERR AVE SUITE, OKLAHOMA CITY, OK 73102

Phone: (601) 956-2028 **Dom State:** OK **Commenced Bus:** N/A

Data Date	Rating	RACR #1	RACR #2	Total Assets ($mil)	Capital ($mil)	Net Premium ($mil)	Net Income ($mil)
6-20	B-	3.68	3.07	76.6	60.7	38.3	7.2
6-19	B	3.38	2.81	70.5	62.5	35.0	5.7
2019	B	3.86	3.21	74.6	60.7	62.9	10.5
2018	B	2.97	2.48	81.1	55.9	78.9	6.5
2017	B+	N/A	N/A	58.8	50.8	61.9	4.4
2016	B	3.24	2.70	52.5	45.3	53.3	2.8
2015	B	2.84	2.37	47.4	41.3	52.4	5.8

Rating Indexes

AMGP GEORGIA MANAGED CARE CO INC *   A-   Excellent

Major Rating Factors: Excellent profitability (7.9 on a scale of 0 to 10). Strong capitalization (7.5) based on excellent current risk-adjusted capital (severe loss scenario). Good quality investment portfolio (6.4).
Other Rating Factors: Good liquidity (6.8) with sufficient resources (cash flows and marketable investments) to handle a spike in claims.
Principal Business: Medicaid (94%), comp med (6%)
Mem Phys: 19: 47,065 **18:** 42,695 **19 MLR** 83.0% **/ 19 Admin Exp** N/A
Enroll(000): Q2 20: 441 **19:** 394 **18:** 385 **Med Exp PMPM:** $219
Principal Investments: Long-term bonds (104%)
Provider Compensation ($000): Bonus arrang ($551,432), contr fee ($382,963), FFS ($91,145), capitation ($12,073)
Total Member Encounters: Phys (1,726,434), non-phys (2,184,345)
Group Affiliation: Anthem Inc
Licensed in: GA
Address: 4170 ASHFORD DUNWOODY ROAD SU, ATLANTA, GA 30319
Phone: (678) 587-4840 **Dom State:** GA **Commenced Bus:** N/A

Data Date	Rating	RACR #1	RACR #2	Total Assets ($mil)	Capital ($mil)	Net Premium ($mil)	Net Income ($mil)
6-20	A-	1.74	1.45	401.2	171.2	636.2	11.3
6-19	A-	2.28	1.90	312.3	147.0	600.1	-7.2
2019	A-	2.24	1.86	362.1	157.4	1,254.1	24.0
2018	A-	2.37	1.97	321.5	153.1	1,233.6	30.5
2017	A-	1.67	1.39	291.5	145.3	1,174.4	16.4
2016	A-	2.37	1.97	296.4	147.4	1,228.3	16.0
2015	A-	2.55	2.13	291.7	150.7	1,202.7	26.1

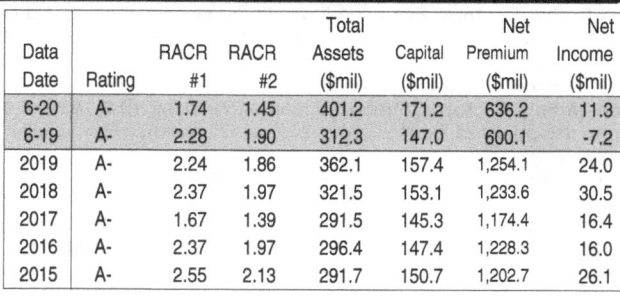

Rating Indexes

ANTHEM BLUE CROSS LIFE & HEALTH INS   B-   Good

Major Rating Factors: Fair quality investment portfolio (3.6 on a scale of 0 to 10). Excellent profitability (8.7). Strong capitalization (10.0) based on excellent current risk-adjusted capital (severe loss scenario).
Other Rating Factors: Excellent liquidity (7.1) with ample operational cash flow and liquid investments.
Principal Business: Comp med (45%), Medicaid (18%), dental (11%), Medicare (8%), vision (2%), other (17%)
Mem Phys: 19: 69,145 **18:** 66,674 **19 MLR** 68.4% **/ 19 Admin Exp** N/A
Enroll(000): Q2 20: 2,395 **19:** 2,386 **18:** 2,320 **Med Exp PMPM:** $51
Principal Investments: Long-term bonds (88%), other (12%)
Provider Compensation ($000): Contr fee ($622,630), bonus arrang ($438,445), FFS ($257,422), capitation ($4,980), other ($154,978)
Total Member Encounters: Phys (1,332,629), non-phys (1,502,743)
Group Affiliation: Anthem Inc
Licensed in: CA
Address: 4553 LA TIENDA DRIVE, THOUSAND OAKS, CA 91362
Phone: (818) 234-2345 **Dom State:** CA **Commenced Bus:** N/A

Data Date	Rating	RACR #1	RACR #2	Total Assets ($mil)	Capital ($mil)	Net Premium ($mil)	Net Income ($mil)
6-20	B-	8.64	7.20	2,396.4	1,475.0	1,060.5	123.8
6-19	B-	8.47	7.06	2,491.1	1,377.3	932.5	120.4
2019	B-	8.02	6.69	2,421.8	1,369.6	2,182.8	267.7
2018	B-	7.79	6.49	2,423.9	1,264.8	1,817.7	181.6
2017	B-	N/A	N/A	2,288.8	1,216.8	1,933.2	158.3
2016	B-	7.49	6.25	2,682.8	1,340.8	2,289.5	281.4
2015	B	5.69	4.75	2,521.6	1,274.7	3,631.5	243.6

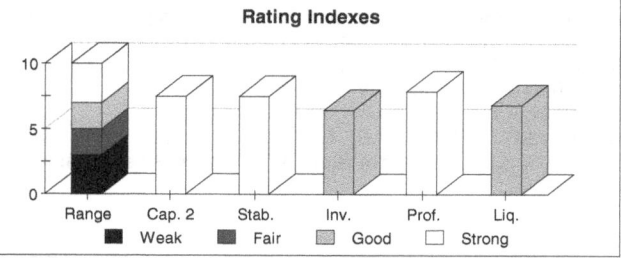

Rating Indexes

ANTHEM HEALTH PLANS INC   B   Good

Major Rating Factors: Good quality investment portfolio (6.5 on a scale of 0 to 10). Good liquidity (6.9) with sufficient resources (cash flows and marketable investments) to handle a spike in claims. Excellent profitability (8.2).
Other Rating Factors: Strong capitalization (7.9) based on excellent current risk-adjusted capital (severe loss scenario).
Principal Business: Comp med (46%), Medicare (21%), FEHB (17%), med supp (8%), dental (2%), other (5%)
Mem Phys: 19: 30,358 **18:** 31,777 **19 MLR** 85.0% **/ 19 Admin Exp** N/A
Enroll(000): Q2 20: 615 **19:** 614 **18:** 609 **Med Exp PMPM:** $207
Principal Investments: Long-term bonds (51%), nonaffiliate common stock (1%), other (52%)
Provider Compensation ($000): Bonus arrang ($1,052,713), contr fee ($299,397), FFS ($86,556), capitation ($22,463), other ($73,433)
Total Member Encounters: Phys (2,490,463), non-phys (1,992,991)
Group Affiliation: Anthem Inc
Licensed in: CT
Address: 108 LEIGUS ROAD, WALLINGFORD, CT 06492-2518
Phone: (203) 677-4000 **Dom State:** CT **Commenced Bus:** N/A

Data Date	Rating	RACR #1	RACR #2	Total Assets ($mil)	Capital ($mil)	Net Premium ($mil)	Net Income ($mil)
6-20	B	2.09	1.74	788.2	321.2	909.9	72.8
6-19	B	3.10	2.58	770.4	403.1	905.8	61.3
2019	B	2.78	2.32	706.6	322.8	1,803.4	99.1
2018	B	2.79	2.32	770.2	360.3	1,996.1	79.8
2017	B	1.84	1.53	765.8	293.7	1,979.1	42.4
2016	B-	2.44	2.03	800.4	232.2	1,663.8	22.5
2015	B-	3.49	2.91	697.2	284.1	1,570.9	91.9

Rating Indexes

ANTHEM HEALTH PLANS OF KENTUCKY INC — B- — Good

Major Rating Factors: Fair overall results on stability tests (3.7 on a scale of 0 to 10) based on a steep decline in capital during 2019. Good liquidity (5.9) with sufficient resources (cash flows and marketable investments) to handle a spike in claims. Excellent profitability (8.6).

Other Rating Factors: Strong capitalization index (8.7) based on excellent current risk-adjusted capital (severe loss scenario). High quality investment portfolio (7.9).

Principal Business: Comp med (73%), FEHB (16%), med supp (9%), dental (2%)

Mem Phys: 19: 31,344 **18:** 33,463 **19 MLR** 88.8% **/ 19 Admin Exp** N/A

Enroll(000): Q2 20: 937 **19:** 890 **18:** 772 **Med Exp PMPM:** $174

Principal Investments: Long-term bonds (102%), real estate (4%), affiliate common stock (1%), other (2%)

Provider Compensation ($000): Bonus arrang ($1,071,748), contr fee ($644,623), FFS ($130,696), capitation ($40), other ($1,126)

Total Member Encounters: Phys (3,132,762), non-phys (3,182,370)

Group Affiliation: Anthem Inc

Licensed in: KY

Address: 13550 TRITON PARK BLVD, LOUISVILLE,

Phone: (800) 331-1476 **Dom State:** KY **Commenced Bus:** N/A

Data Date	Rating	RACR #1	RACR #2	Total Assets ($mil)	Capital ($mil)	Net Premium ($mil)	Net Income ($mil)
6-20	B-	2.70	2.25	927.8	374.5	1,046.7	117.1
6-19	B	4.17	3.47	943.9	415.9	1,062.2	106.3
2019	B	2.39	1.99	822.4	248.9	2,099.1	131.6
2018	B	3.20	2.66	838.0	314.2	2,036.8	145.0
2017	B+	2.18	1.81	927.8	332.8	2,372.9	136.8
2016	B+	2.69	2.24	1,069.4	313.6	2,285.7	112.0
2015	B	2.85	2.38	866.8	299.3	2,161.2	101.8

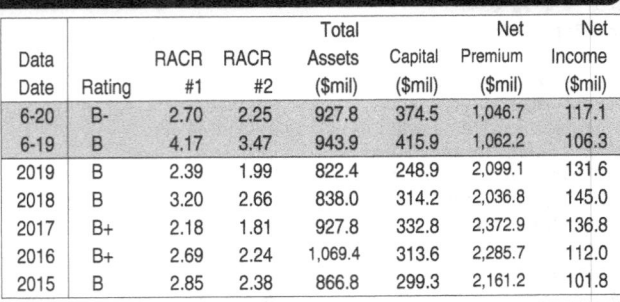

ANTHEM HEALTH PLANS OF MAINE INC — B — Good

Major Rating Factors: Good liquidity (6.9 on a scale of 0 to 10) with sufficient resources (cash flows and marketable investments) to handle a spike in claims. Excellent profitability (8.2). Strong capitalization (10.0) based on excellent current risk-adjusted capital (severe loss scenario).

Other Rating Factors: High quality investment portfolio (8.5).

Principal Business: Comp med (74%), FEHB (19%), med supp (4%)

Mem Phys: 19: 14,075 **18:** 7,792 **19 MLR** 86.3% **/ 19 Admin Exp** N/A

Enroll(000): Q2 20: 397 **19:** 394 **18:** 362 **Med Exp PMPM:** $215

Principal Investments: Long-term bonds (97%), cash and equiv (2%), other (2%)

Provider Compensation ($000): Bonus arrang ($864,488), contr fee ($71,539), FFS ($49,204), capitation ($36), other ($6,858)

Total Member Encounters: Phys (1,443,508), non-phys (1,044,118)

Group Affiliation: Anthem Inc

Licensed in: ME

Address: 2 GANNETT DRIVE, SOUTH PORTLAND, ME 04106-6911

Phone: (866) 583-6182 **Dom State:** ME **Commenced Bus:** N/A

Data Date	Rating	RACR #1	RACR #2	Total Assets ($mil)	Capital ($mil)	Net Premium ($mil)	Net Income ($mil)
6-20	B	3.75	3.12	683.6	220.0	558.1	38.7
6-19	B	5.58	4.65	498.5	202.1	597.8	47.9
2019	B	4.22	3.52	499.7	178.7	1,169.0	72.0
2018	B	3.41	2.84	493.9	120.1	991.7	58.6
2017	A-	2.57	2.14	498.0	165.4	1,139.5	37.7
2016	B	3.12	2.60	408.4	150.4	1,062.9	19.1
2015	B-	3.40	2.84	397.9	154.0	1,034.5	22.2

ANTHEM HEALTH PLANS OF NEW HAMPSHIRE — B — Good

Major Rating Factors: Good liquidity (6.8 on a scale of 0 to 10) with sufficient resources (cash flows and marketable investments) to handle a spike in claims. Fair quality investment portfolio (4.8). Excellent profitability (7.6).

Other Rating Factors: Strong capitalization (8.7) based on excellent current risk-adjusted capital (severe loss scenario).

Principal Business: Medicare (42%), FEHB (33%), comp med (14%), med supp (9%), other (1%)

Mem Phys: 19: 17,674 **18:** 22,509 **19 MLR** 89.8% **/ 19 Admin Exp** N/A

Enroll(000): Q2 20: 197 **19:** 198 **18:** 170 **Med Exp PMPM:** $366

Principal Investments: Long-term bonds (56%), affiliate common stock (42%), cash and equiv (2%)

Provider Compensation ($000): Bonus arrang ($573,063), contr fee ($164,627), FFS ($47,620), capitation ($6,867), other ($16,260)

Total Member Encounters: Phys (1,326,751), non-phys (1,439,671)

Group Affiliation: Anthem Inc

Licensed in: GA, KY, NH

Address: 1155 ELM STREET, MANCHESTER, NH 3101

Phone: (603) 541-2000 **Dom State:** NH **Commenced Bus:** N/A

Data Date	Rating	RACR #1	RACR #2	Total Assets ($mil)	Capital ($mil)	Net Premium ($mil)	Net Income ($mil)
6-20	B	2.68	2.24	538.2	277.8	446.1	28.6
6-19	B	3.58	2.99	460.1	241.9	458.3	7.5
2019	B	2.70	2.25	432.3	207.2	934.6	58.8
2018	B	3.00	2.50	398.9	202.3	738.6	58.5
2017	B	2.26	1.88	322.7	155.3	515.8	43.9
2016	B	2.96	2.46	316.0	142.7	488.2	35.2
2015	B+	3.68	3.06	339.9	162.9	466.9	41.7

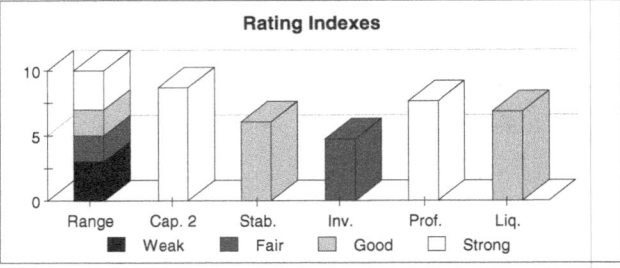

ANTHEM HEALTH PLANS OF VIRGINIA — B — Good

Major Rating Factors: Good quality investment portfolio (6.6 on a scale of 0 to 10). Good liquidity (5.9) with sufficient resources (cash flows and marketable investments) to handle a spike in claims. Excellent profitability (9.0).
Other Rating Factors: Strong capitalization (10.0) based on excellent current risk-adjusted capital (severe loss scenario).
Principal Business: FEHB (44%), comp med (37%), med supp (10%), dental (3%), other (5%)
Mem Phys: 19: 39,326 **18:** 35,955 **19 MLR** 101.4% **/ 19 Admin Exp** N/A
Enroll(000): Q2 20: 1,599 **19:** 1,551 **18:** 1,484 **Med Exp PMPM:** $156
Principal Investments: Long-term bonds (55%), affiliate common stock (3%), real estate (3%), nonaffiliate common stock (1%), other (39%)
Provider Compensation ($000): Bonus arrang ($2,292,420), contr fee ($542,422), FFS ($183,295), other ($99,676)
Total Member Encounters: Phys (5,891,855), non-phys (4,257,716)
Group Affiliation: Anthem Inc
Licensed in: VA
Address: 2015 STAPLES MILL ROAD, RICHMOND, VA 23230
Phone: (804) 354-7000 **Dom State:** VA **Commenced Bus:** N/A

Data Date	Rating	RACR #1	RACR #2	Total Assets ($mil)	Capital ($mil)	Net Premium ($mil)	Net Income ($mil)
6-20	B	3.70	3.08	2,015.1	740.2	1,532.2	118.5
6-19	B	4.80	4.00	1,945.2	835.0	1,539.6	161.8
2019	B	3.56	2.96	1,800.7	629.5	3,097.3	305.8
2018	B	3.84	3.20	1,799.8	661.7	3,210.7	293.6
2017	B-	3.55	2.96	2,271.8	698.2	3,658.1	241.0
2016	B-	3.52	2.93	1,941.2	655.3	3,825.9	230.2
2015	B-	3.09	2.58	1,991.9	594.2	3,740.6	216.1

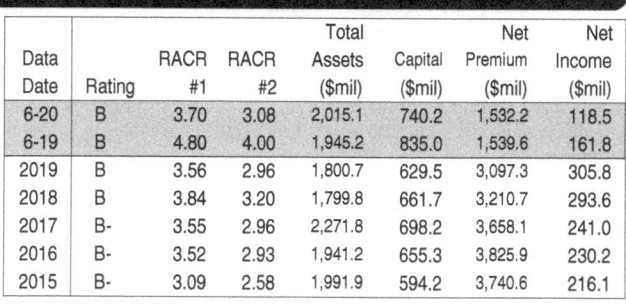

Rating Indexes

ANTHEM INS COMPANIES INC — B- — Good

Major Rating Factors: Fair quality investment portfolio (3.7 on a scale of 0 to 10). Good liquidity (6.8) with sufficient resources (cash flows and marketable investments) to handle a spike in claims. Excellent profitability (9.5).
Other Rating Factors: Strong capitalization (8.6) based on excellent current risk-adjusted capital (severe loss scenario).
Principal Business: Medicaid (37%), Medicare (30%), comp med (18%), FEHB (6%), med supp (2%), other (7%)
Mem Phys: 19: 42,470 **18:** 43,911 **19 MLR** 90.2% **/ 19 Admin Exp** N/A
Enroll(000): Q2 20: 3,141 **19:** 2,889 **18:** 2,770 **Med Exp PMPM:** $209
Principal Investments: Long-term bonds (75%), nonaffiliate common stock (4%), cash and equiv (1%), affiliate common stock (1%), other (20%)
Provider Compensation ($000): Bonus arrang ($3,977,775), contr fee ($2,040,559), FFS ($652,751), capitation ($100,781), other ($272,063)
Total Member Encounters: Phys (9,504,473), non-phys (9,987,920)
Group Affiliation: Anthem Inc
Licensed in: AL, AZ, AR, CA, CO, CT, GA, ID, IL, IN, IA, KS, KY, LA, ME, MS, MO, MT, NE, NV, NH, NM, NY, NC, ND, OH, OK, OR, SC, SD, TN, TX, UT, VA, WA, WI, WY
Address: 220 VIRGINIA AVENUE, INDIANAPOLIS, IN 46204-3709
Phone: (317) 488-6000 **Dom State:** IN **Commenced Bus:** N/A

Data Date	Rating	RACR #1	RACR #2	Total Assets ($mil)	Capital ($mil)	Net Premium ($mil)	Net Income ($mil)
6-20	B-	2.65	2.21	3,877.8	1,395.5	4,335.6	548.7
6-19	B-	2.42	2.02	3,693.3	1,113.5	3,985.6	348.8
2019	B-	2.29	1.91	3,818.1	1,196.4	7,986.4	392.5
2018	B-	2.56	2.14	3,480.9	1,180.3	7,116.0	498.9
2017	B-	2.67	2.22	3,337.6	1,186.4	6,933.8	420.0
2016	B-	2.42	2.02	2,947.5	968.6	6,126.1	431.0
2015	B-	2.36	1.97	2,853.0	816.5	5,320.0	405.5

Rating Indexes

ANTHEM KENTUCKY MANAGED CARE PLAN * — A- — Excellent

Major Rating Factors: Excellent profitability (7.5 on a scale of 0 to 10). Strong capitalization (8.7) based on excellent current risk-adjusted capital (severe loss scenario). High quality investment portfolio (7.5).
Other Rating Factors: Good liquidity (6.7) with sufficient resources (cash flows and marketable investments) to handle a spike in claims.
Principal Business: Medicaid (99%)
Mem Phys: 19: 36,208 **18:** 33,632 **19 MLR** 91.6% **/ 19 Admin Exp** N/A
Enroll(000): Q2 20: 143 **19:** 132 **18:** 131 **Med Exp PMPM:** $438
Principal Investments: Long-term bonds (95%), cash and equiv (5%)
Provider Compensation ($000): Bonus arrang ($343,304), contr fee ($236,295), FFS ($115,977)
Total Member Encounters: Phys (961,964), non-phys (1,367,792)
Group Affiliation: Anthem Inc
Licensed in: KY
Address: 13550 TRITON PARK BLVD, LOUISVILLE, KY 40223
Phone: (888) 641-5224 **Dom State:** KY **Commenced Bus:** N/A

Data Date	Rating	RACR #1	RACR #2	Total Assets ($mil)	Capital ($mil)	Net Premium ($mil)	Net Income ($mil)
6-20	A-	2.75	2.29	314.7	182.2	412.6	15.1
6-19	A-	3.62	3.02	246.0	156.4	377.1	-9.8
2019	A-	3.53	2.94	292.6	167.4	758.5	2.9
2018	A-	3.80	3.17	250.8	164.6	746.4	13.6
2017	A-	N/A	N/A	246.9	152.8	665.6	30.3
2016	A-	3.62	3.02	216.1	122.0	588.9	18.7
2015	B+	4.23	3.53	190.8	104.3	490.4	61.9

Rating Indexes

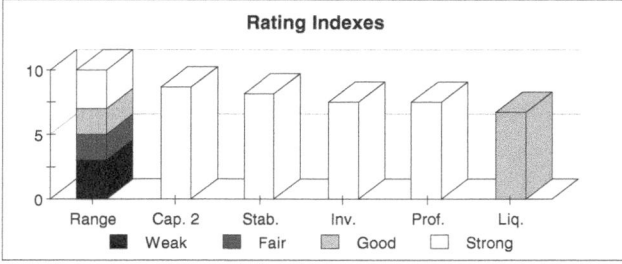

ANTHEM LIFE INS CO *

B+ **Good**

Major Rating Factors: Good liquidity (6.3 on a scale of 0 to 10) with sufficient resources to handle a spike in claims. Good overall results on stability tests (6.8). Stability strengths include excellent operational trends and excellent risk diversification. Strong capitalization (7.8) based on excellent risk adjusted capital (severe loss scenario). Capital levels have been relatively consistent over the last five years.

Other Rating Factors: High quality investment portfolio (7.4). Excellent profitability (7.9) with operating gains in each of the last five years.

Principal Business: Reinsurance (42%), group health insurance (33%), and group life insurance (25%).

Principal Investments: NonCMO investment grade bonds (53%), CMOs and structured securities (35%), cash (5%), and common & preferred stock (1%).

Investments in Affiliates: None

Group Affiliation: Anthem Inc

Licensed in: All states except NY, RI, VT, PR

Commenced Business: June 1956

Address: 120 MONUMENT CIRCLE, INDIANAPOLIS, IN 46204

Phone: (614) 433-8800 **Domicile State:** IN **NAIC Code:** 61069

Data Date	Rating	RACR #1	RACR #2	Total Assets ($mil)	Capital ($mil)	Net Premium ($mil)	Net Income ($mil)
6-20	B+	2.14	1.50	799.2	163.2	306.5	9.1
6-19	B+	2.61	1.82	774.4	172.1	257.9	17.1
2019	B+	2.30	1.62	761.7	180.6	508.0	23.2
2018	B	2.11	1.46	732.3	148.9	430.8	21.9
2017	B-	1.98	1.37	674.7	125.1	412.0	12.3
2016	A-	1.85	1.28	623.3	108.9	362.3	28.3
2015	A-	1.64	1.16	633.7	95.9	368.9	18.2

Adverse Trends in Operations

Increase in policy surrenders from 2016 to 2017 (3256%)
Decrease in asset base during 2016 (2%)
Decrease in premium volume from 2015 to 2016 (2%)

AR HEALTH & WELLNESS HLTH PLAN

C- **Fair**

Major Rating Factors: Weak profitability index (0.9 on a scale of 0 to 10). Low quality investment portfolio (2.8). Strong capitalization (10.0) based on excellent current risk-adjusted capital (severe loss scenario).

Other Rating Factors: Excellent liquidity (7.0) with sufficient resources (cash flows and marketable investments) to handle a spike in claims.

Principal Business: Medicare (100%)

Mem Phys: 18: 19,565 **17:** N/A **18 MLR** 101.6% **/ 18 Admin Exp** N/A

Enroll(000): Q3 19: 15 **18:** 5 **17:** N/A **Med Exp PMPM:** $773

Principal Investments: Cash and equiv (62%), long-term bonds (3%), other (35%)

Provider Compensation ($000): Contr fee ($33,875), salary ($776), capitation ($588), bonus arrang ($168)

Total Member Encounters: Phys (327,306), non-phys (65,482)

Group Affiliation: None

Licensed in: AR

Address: 1 Allied Drive Suite 2520, Little Rock, AR 72202

Phone: (314) 725-4477 **Dom State:** AR **Commenced Bus:** N/A

Data Date	Rating	RACR #1	RACR #2	Total Assets ($mil)	Capital ($mil)	Net Premium ($mil)	Net Income ($mil)
9-19	C-	10.62	8.85	73.2	44.6	102.2	-7.4
9-18	N/A	N/A	N/A	12.8	3.7	30.4	-2.4
2018	C-	1.77	1.48	21.8	7.4	42.6	-9.1
2017	N/A	N/A	N/A	5.5	5.2	N/A	N/A
2016	N/A	N/A	N/A	N/A	N/A	N/A	N/A
2015	N/A	N/A	N/A	N/A	N/A	N/A	N/A
2014	N/A	N/A	N/A	N/A	N/A	N/A	N/A

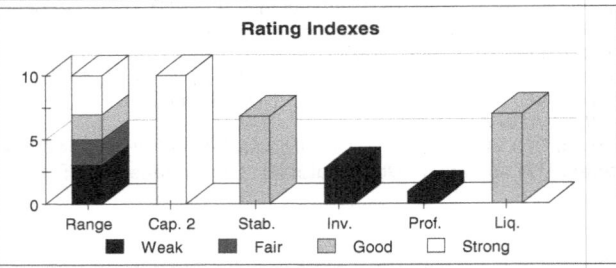

Rating Indexes

ARCADIAN HEALTH PLAN INC

B **Good**

Major Rating Factors: Good overall profitability index (5.3 on a scale of 0 to 10). Good quality investment portfolio (6.7). Good liquidity (6.8) with sufficient resources (cash flows and marketable investments) to handle a spike in claims.

Other Rating Factors: Strong capitalization (10.0) based on excellent current risk-adjusted capital (severe loss scenario).

Principal Business: Medicare (100%)

Mem Phys: 19: 186,866 **18:** 172,688 **19 MLR** 84.4% **/ 19 Admin Exp** N/A

Enroll(000): Q2 20: 429 **19:** 385 **18:** 323 **Med Exp PMPM:** $822

Principal Investments: Long-term bonds (75%), cash and equiv (25%)

Provider Compensation ($000): Contr fee ($1,766,124), capitation ($1,633,288), salary ($123,750), FFS ($21,833)

Total Member Encounters: Phys (7,378,910), non-phys (3,939,062)

Group Affiliation: None

Licensed in: AL, AZ, AR, CA, ID, IN, KY, ME, MO, NE, NH, OK, SC, TX, VA, WA, WV

Address: 300 DESCHUTES WAY SW SUITE 30, TUMWATER, WA 98501

Phone: (502) 580-1000 **Dom State:** WA **Commenced Bus:** N/A

Data Date	Rating	RACR #1	RACR #2	Total Assets ($mil)	Capital ($mil)	Net Premium ($mil)	Net Income ($mil)
6-20	B	3.86	3.22	1,750.0	798.0	2,728.3	70.2
6-19	B-	4.43	3.69	1,151.8	662.0	2,145.0	93.0
2019	B	3.80	3.17	1,246.9	716.8	4,345.8	134.5
2018	B-	3.42	2.85	834.3	511.5	3,417.7	59.7
2017	B-	5.62	4.68	305.9	237.5	803.6	29.0
2016	B-	4.86	4.05	275.8	171.0	812.9	-41.2
2015	C+	7.23	6.02	77.7	35.0	71.1	-32.7

Rating Indexes

ARKANSAS SUPERIOR SELECT INC   E   Very Weak

Major Rating Factors: Weak profitability index (0.6 on a scale of 0 to 10). Weak liquidity (0.3) as a spike in claims may stretch capacity. Fair capitalization (4.4) based on fair current risk-adjusted capital (moderate loss scenario).
Other Rating Factors: High quality investment portfolio (9.5).
Principal Business: Medicare (99%)
Mem Phys: 18: 2,611   **17:** 3,669   **18 MLR** 94.5%   / **18 Admin Exp** N/A
Enroll(000): Q3 19: 3   **18:** 3   **17:** 1   **Med Exp PMPM:** $1,067
Principal Investments: Cash and equiv (91%), other (9%)
Provider Compensation ($000): Contr fee ($18,947), capitation ($1,760)
Total Member Encounters: Phys (12,865), non-phys (90,056)
Group Affiliation: Select Founders LLC
Licensed in: AR
Address: 1 Riverfront Place Suite 615, North Little Rock, AR 72114
Phone: (501) 372-1922   **Dom State:** AR   **Commenced Bus:** N/A

Data Date	Rating	RACR #1	RACR #2	Total Assets ($mil)	Capital ($mil)	Net Premium ($mil)	Net Income ($mil)
9-19	E	0.84	0.70	10.6	4.7	22.3	-1.1
9-18	E	N/A	N/A	11.6	4.0	19.9	-1.5
2018	E	0.91	0.75	14.9	5.0	27.9	-4.2
2017	E	N/A	N/A	8.7	3.1	11.6	-4.5
2016	E	1.25	1.04	4.6	1.3	5.1	-3.5
2015	E	0.69	0.57	3.6	1.0	1.7	-4.1
2014	N/A	N/A	N/A	2.4	2.4	N/A	N/A

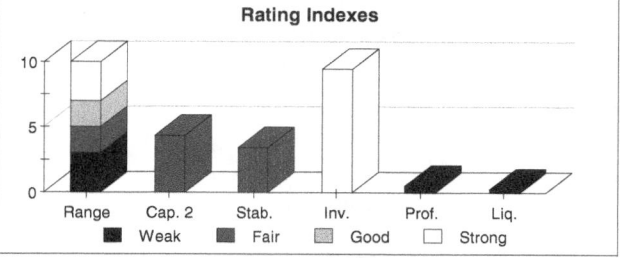

Rating Indexes

ASPIRE HEALTH PLAN   E-   Very Weak

Major Rating Factors: Weak profitability index (0.0 on a scale of 0 to 10). Poor capitalization index (0.0) based on weak current risk-adjusted capital (severe loss scenario). Weak overall results on stability tests (0.7) based on a steep decline in capital during 2019.
Other Rating Factors: Weak liquidity (0.1) as a spike in claims may stretch capacity.
Principal Business: Medicare (100%)
Mem Phys: 19: N/A   **18:** N/A   **19 MLR** 98.2%   / **19 Admin Exp** N/A
Enroll(000): Q2 20: 5   **19:** 3   **18:** 3   **Med Exp PMPM:** $1,131
Principal Investments ($000): Cash and equiv ($1,535)
Provider Compensation ($000): None
Total Member Encounters: N/A
Group Affiliation: None
Licensed in: CA
Address: 23625 Holman Highway, Monterey, CA 93940
Phone: (831) 625-4965   **Dom State:** CA   **Commenced Bus:** April 2013

Data Date	Rating	RACR #1	RACR #2	Total Assets ($mil)	Capital ($mil)	Net Premium ($mil)	Net Income ($mil)
6-20	E-	N/A	N/A	14.2	-46.2	32.3	-2.4
6-19	E-	N/A	N/A	8.2	-36.8	22.1	-4.0
2019	E-	N/A	N/A	13.6	-43.8	45.8	-11.2
2018	E-	N/A	N/A	6.5	-32.8	34.1	-10.0
2017	E-	N/A	N/A	4.9	-22.7	23.4	-7.3
2016	E-	N/A	N/A	8.5	-15.2	13.7	1.6
2015	E-	N/A	N/A	3.8	-1.6	7.8	-6.0

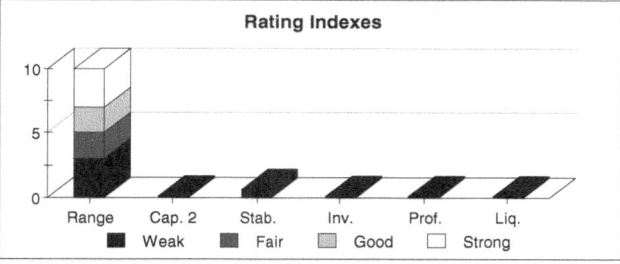

Rating Indexes

ASPIRUS ARISE HEALTH PLAN OF WISCONS   C   Fair

Major Rating Factors: Fair profitability index (4.5 on a scale of 0 to 10). Low quality investment portfolio (1.6). Strong capitalization (9.0) based on excellent current risk-adjusted capital (severe loss scenario).
Other Rating Factors: Excellent liquidity (7.5) with ample operational cash flow and liquid investments.
Principal Business: Comp med (100%)
Mem Phys: 19: 14,957   **18:** 6,209   **19 MLR** 85.5%   / **19 Admin Exp** N/A
Enroll(000): Q2 20: 12   **19:** 13   **18:** 14   **Med Exp PMPM:** $551
Principal Investments: Cash and equiv (75%), long-term bonds (25%)
Provider Compensation ($000): Contr fee ($80,206), FFS ($8,429)
Total Member Encounters: Phys (75,044), non-phys (32,983)
Group Affiliation: Aspirus Inc
Licensed in: WI
Address: 3000 WESTHILL DRIVE SUITE 303, WAUSAU, WI 54401
Phone: (715) 843-1387   **Dom State:** WI   **Commenced Bus:** N/A

Data Date	Rating	RACR #1	RACR #2	Total Assets ($mil)	Capital ($mil)	Net Premium ($mil)	Net Income ($mil)
6-20	C	2.92	2.43	71.0	31.9	47.1	5.0
6-19	N/A	N/A	N/A	N/A	N/A	N/A	N/A
2019	C	2.40	2.00	47.4	26.4	105.0	10.4
2018	C	1.34	1.11	43.2	15.9	92.5	-3.0
2017	U	1.10	0.92	30.8	12.9	65.1	-6.2
2016	N/A	N/A	N/A	2.4	1.1	N/A	-0.4
2015	N/A	N/A	N/A	N/A	N/A	N/A	N/A

Rating Indexes

ASSURITY LIFE INS CO *

| | | | B+ | | Good |

Major Rating Factors: Good quality investment portfolio (5.5 on a scale of 0 to 10) despite significant exposure to mortgages . Mortgage default rate has been low. large holdings of BBB rated bonds in addition to small junk bond holdings. Good overall profitability (5.8) although investment income, in comparison to reserve requirements, is below regulatory standards. Good liquidity (5.6).

Other Rating Factors: Good overall results on stability tests (6.6) despite negative cash flow from operations for 2019 excellent operational trends and excellent risk diversification. Strong capitalization (7.7) based on excellent risk adjusted capital (severe loss scenario).

Principal Business: Individual life insurance (47%), individual health insurance (26%), group health insurance (18%), group life insurance (4%), and other lines (5%).

Principal Investments: NonCMO investment grade bonds (54%), mortgages in good standing (18%), CMOs and structured securities (12%), common & preferred stock (6%), and misc. investments (11%).

Investments in Affiliates: 1%

Group Affiliation: Assurity Security Group Inc

Licensed in: All states except NY, PR

Commenced Business: March 1964

Address: 2000 Q STREET, LINCOLN, NE 68503

Phone: (402) 476-6500 **Domicile State:** NE **NAIC Code:** 71439

Data Date	Rating	RACR #1	RACR #2	Total Assets ($mil)	Capital ($mil)	Net Premium ($mil)	Net Income ($mil)
6-20	B+	2.59	1.49	2,670.3	351.7	102.4	9.0
6-19	B+	2.54	1.48	2,761.9	343.0	103.3	3.5
2019	B+	2.67	1.55	2,571.2	345.3	199.2	11.9
2018	B+	2.50	1.46	2,626.8	337.5	198.7	11.1
2017	B+	2.54	1.47	2,632.3	334.7	189.2	16.8
2016	B+	2.70	1.51	2,605.0	324.9	193.3	12.0
2015	B+	2.71	1.51	2,472.0	318.1	189.5	20.8

Rating Indexes

ASURIS NORTHWEST HEALTH

| | | | B | | Good |

Major Rating Factors: Excellent overall profitability index (7.0 on a scale of 0 to 10). Strong capitalization (10.0) based on excellent current risk-adjusted capital (severe loss scenario). High quality investment portfolio (9.6).

Other Rating Factors: Excellent liquidity (6.9) with sufficient resources (cash flows and marketable investments) to handle a spike in claims.

Principal Business: Comp med (79%), med supp (10%), Medicare (7%), other (3%)

Mem Phys: 19: 7,932 **18:** 7,273 **19 MLR** 77.8% **/ 19 Admin Exp** N/A

Enroll(000): Q2 20: 41 **19:** 43 **18:** 44 **Med Exp PMPM:** $239

Principal Investments: Long-term bonds (93%), cash and equiv (7%)

Provider Compensation ($000): Contr fee ($105,158), FFS ($16,053), capitation ($35), bonus arrang ($30)

Total Member Encounters: Phys (339,291), non-phys (478,030)

Group Affiliation: Cambia Health Solutions Inc

Licensed in: OR, WA

Address: 1800 NINTH AVENUE, SEATTLE, WA 98101

Phone: (206) 464-3600 **Dom State:** WA **Commenced Bus:** N/A

Data Date	Rating	RACR #1	RACR #2	Total Assets ($mil)	Capital ($mil)	Net Premium ($mil)	Net Income ($mil)
6-20	B	6.13	5.11	127.7	86.2	69.6	-4.0
6-19	B	8.69	7.24	123.6	87.9	77.7	5.7
2019	B	9.80	8.17	122.9	93.1	155.7	10.5
2018	B	8.14	6.78	112.3	82.2	168.7	11.0
2017	B-	3.46	2.89	98.7	68.5	185.4	2.2
2016	B-	6.94	5.79	92.1	65.8	141.6	0.8
2015	C+	6.94	5.78	91.7	64.5	145.4	5.1

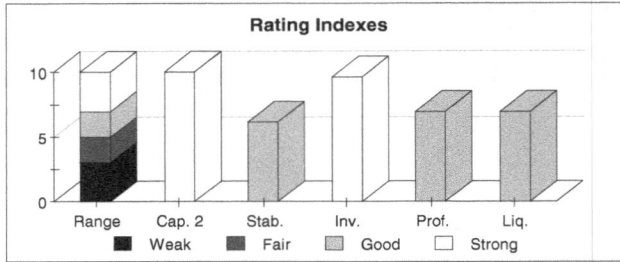

Rating Indexes

ATRIO HEALTH PLANS INC

| | | | D+ | | Weak |

Major Rating Factors: Low quality investment portfolio (0.0 on a scale of 0 to 10). Fair profitability index (3.7). Good capitalization (6.1) based on good current risk-adjusted capital (severe loss scenario).

Other Rating Factors: Excellent liquidity (7.0) with sufficient resources (cash flows and marketable investments) to handle a spike in claims.

Principal Business: Medicare (100%)

Mem Phys: 19: 5,201 **18:** 4,769 **19 MLR** 85.8% **/ 19 Admin Exp** N/A

Enroll(000): Q2 20: 19 **19:** 18 **18:** 20 **Med Exp PMPM:** $838

Principal Investments: Cash and equiv (58%), long-term bonds (35%), other (7%)

Provider Compensation ($000): Capitation ($175,073), FFS ($83)

Total Member Encounters: Phys (599,006), non-phys (263,957)

Group Affiliation: Chicago Pacific Founders Fund II LP

Licensed in: OR

Address: 2965 Ryan Drive SE, Salem, OR 97301

Phone: (541) 672-8620 **Dom State:** OR **Commenced Bus:** N/A

Data Date	Rating	RACR #1	RACR #2	Total Assets ($mil)	Capital ($mil)	Net Premium ($mil)	Net Income ($mil)
6-20	D+	1.10	0.91	64.1	21.1	110.4	0.7
6-19	N/A	N/A	N/A	N/A	N/A	N/A	N/A
2019	D+	1.08	0.90	69.9	20.8	210.1	4.5
2018	D	1.01	0.84	62.9	18.6	203.9	2.7
2017	D+	0.68	0.57	52.1	16.3	257.0	-9.4
2016	C-	1.68	1.40	50.4	25.5	203.3	-3.5
2015	C-	2.23	1.85	46.5	28.1	176.1	1.3

Rating Indexes

AULTCARE HEALTH INSURING CORP   B   Good

Major Rating Factors: Good quality investment portfolio (4.9 on a scale of 0 to 10). Good liquidity (6.8) with sufficient resources (cash flows and marketable investments) to handle a spike in claims. Fair profitability index (4.8).
Other Rating Factors: Strong capitalization (8.0) based on excellent current risk-adjusted capital (severe loss scenario).
Principal Business: Medicare (100%)
Mem Phys: 18: 3,564   **17:** 3,619   **18 MLR** 84.4%   / **18 Admin Exp** N/A
Enroll(000): Q3 19: 20   **18:** 20   **17:** 21   **Med Exp PMPM:** $850
Principal Investments: Affiliate common stock (49%), long-term bonds (28%), nonaffiliate common stock (9%), cash and equiv (2%), other (11%)
Provider Compensation ($000): Contr fee ($125,649), capitation ($61,305), FFS ($14,668)
Total Member Encounters: Phys (228,350), non-phys (477,720)
Group Affiliation: None
Licensed in: OH
Address: 2600 Sixth Street SW, Canton, OH 44710
Phone: (330) 363-4057   **Dom State:** OH   **Commenced Bus:** N/A

Data Date	Rating	RACR #1	RACR #2	Total Assets ($mil)	Capital ($mil)	Net Premium ($mil)	Net Income ($mil)
9-19	B	2.18	1.81	117.6	99.0	189.8	6.2
9-18	B	N/A	N/A	108.8	92.1	185.2	3.8
2018	B	1.91	1.59	105.8	87.1	242.6	7.1
2017	B	N/A	N/A	106.6	90.0	244.8	7.2
2016	B-	1.92	1.60	97.3	76.9	245.0	5.1
2015	C-	1.52	1.26	82.6	64.6	226.7	-3.9
2014	N/A	N/A	N/A	66.3	66.3	N/A	N/A

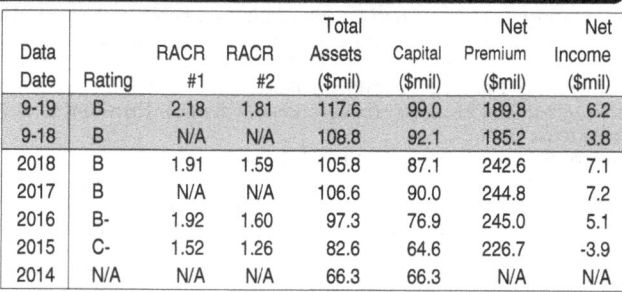

Rating Indexes

AULTCARE INS CO *   B+   Good

Major Rating Factors: Good liquidity (6.4 on a scale of 0 to 10) with sufficient resources (cash flows and marketable investments) to handle a spike in claims. Excellent profitability (7.6). Strong capitalization (7.3) based on excellent current risk-adjusted capital (severe loss scenario).
Other Rating Factors: High quality investment portfolio (8.3).
Principal Business: Comp med (83%), FEHB (5%), other (11%)
Mem Phys: 19: 3,589   **18:** 3,564   **19 MLR** 90.1%   / **19 Admin Exp** N/A
Enroll(000): Q2 20: 88   **19:** 91   **18:** 83   **Med Exp PMPM:** $218
Principal Investments: Long-term bonds (40%), cash and equiv (19%), nonaffiliate common stock (14%), other (27%)
Provider Compensation ($000): Contr fee ($158,797), FFS ($37,044), capitation ($31,014)
Total Member Encounters: Phys (131,097), non-phys (361,937)
Group Affiliation: None
Licensed in: OH
Address: 2600 Sixth Street SW, Canton, OH 44710
Phone: (330) 363-4057   **Dom State:** OH   **Commenced Bus:** N/A

Data Date	Rating	RACR #1	RACR #2	Total Assets ($mil)	Capital ($mil)	Net Premium ($mil)	Net Income ($mil)
6-20	B+	1.56	1.30	106.6	54.0	130.2	1.5
6-19	B	2.06	1.72	90.4	52.5	130.0	1.8
2019	B+	1.82	1.52	95.8	54.9	266.0	3.1
2018	B	1.90	1.58	94.5	48.3	277.1	3.8
2017	C+	1.93	1.61	95.6	49.2	254.7	6.5
2016	C	2.01	1.68	86.1	42.7	259.3	5.5
2015	C-	1.79	1.49	84.0	36.0	250.2	7.7

Rating Indexes

AVALON INS CO   D+   Weak

Major Rating Factors: Weak profitability index (0.8 on a scale of 0 to 10). Good liquidity (6.9) with sufficient resources (cash flows and marketable investments) to handle a spike in claims. Strong capitalization (7.4) based on excellent current risk-adjusted capital (severe loss scenario).
Other Rating Factors: High quality investment portfolio (7.8).
Principal Business: Med supp (2%), vision (1%), other (97%)
Mem Phys: 19: 800   **18:** 781   **19 MLR** 99.3%   / **19 Admin Exp** N/A
Enroll(000): Q2 20: 296   **19:** 277   **18:** 347   **Med Exp PMPM:** $16
Principal Investments: Cash and equiv (65%), long-term bonds (35%)
Provider Compensation ($000): Contr fee ($9,482), other ($51,781)
Total Member Encounters: Phys (11,677), non-phys (219,594)
Group Affiliation: Capital Blue Cross Inc
Licensed in: DC, DE, MD, PA, VA, WV
Address: 2500 Elmerton Avenue, Harrisburg, PA 17177-9799
Phone: (717) 541-7000   **Dom State:** PA   **Commenced Bus:** N/A

Data Date	Rating	RACR #1	RACR #2	Total Assets ($mil)	Capital ($mil)	Net Premium ($mil)	Net Income ($mil)
6-20	D+	1.66	1.38	42.8	19.9	30.7	-3.8
6-19	D+	1.69	1.41	34.6	13.9	29.2	-4.7
2019	D+	3.48	2.90	45.2	24.1	55.5	-13.3
2018	D+	2.24	1.86	42.9	18.6	63.7	-18.7
2017	C	2.18	1.82	39.7	19.7	62.9	-4.0
2016	C	2.05	1.70	38.3	15.5	63.8	-9.3
2015	C	2.81	2.35	41.4	18.4	62.4	-4.7

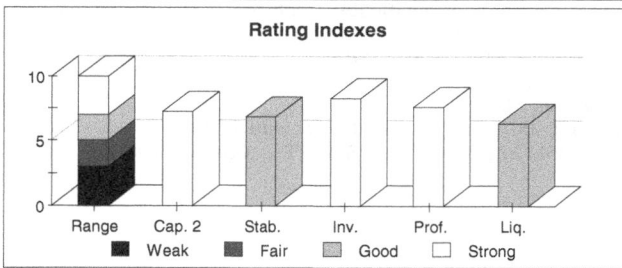

Rating Indexes

AVERA HEALTH PLANS INC

B   **Good**

Major Rating Factors: Good liquidity (6.8 on a scale of 0 to 10) with sufficient resources (cash flows and marketable investments) to handle a spike in claims. Fair quality investment portfolio (4.5). Excellent overall profitability index (7.0).
Other Rating Factors: Strong capitalization index (8.2) based on excellent current risk-adjusted capital (severe loss scenario). Excellent overall results on stability tests (7.7).
Principal Business: Comp med (92%), med supp (8%)
Mem Phys: 19: 7,383 **18:** 6,810 **19 MLR** 90.4% **/ 19 Admin Exp** N/A
Enroll(000): Q2 20: 55 **19:** 53 **18:** 50 **Med Exp PMPM:** $369
Principal Investments: Long-term bonds (42%), nonaffiliate common stock (39%), cash and equiv (19%)
Provider Compensation ($000): Contr fee ($118,598), FFS ($117,766)
Total Member Encounters: Phys (75,081), non-phys (49,670)
Group Affiliation: None
Licensed in: IA, NE, SD
Address: 3816 S Elmwood Ave Suite 100, Sioux Falls,
Phone: (605) 322-4545 **Dom State:** SD **Commenced Bus:** N/A

Data Date	Rating	RACR #1	RACR #2	Total Assets ($mil)	Capital ($mil)	Net Premium ($mil)	Net Income ($mil)
6-20	B	2.31	1.92	118.6	69.2	158.1	32.4
6-19	N/A	N/A	N/A	N/A	N/A	N/A	N/A
2019	B	1.65	1.37	94.8	51.2	260.6	11.7
2018	B	1.42	1.18	77.7	39.8	245.7	13.0
2017	C	1.09	0.90	77.1	31.8	249.8	8.2
2016	C-	0.91	0.76	56.6	22.2	191.6	0.6
2015	C-	1.19	0.99	47.7	22.1	123.5	-17.9

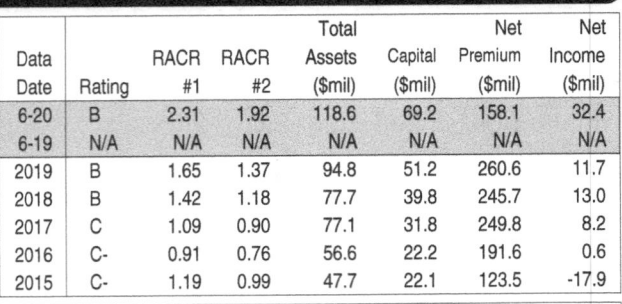

Rating Indexes

AVMED INC

B-   **Good**

Major Rating Factors: Fair profitability index (4.6 on a scale of 0 to 10). Fair overall results on stability tests (4.6) based on a significant 33% decrease in enrollment during the period. Good liquidity (6.2) with sufficient resources (cash flows and marketable investments) to handle a spike in claims.
Other Rating Factors: Strong capitalization index (7.6) based on excellent current risk-adjusted capital (severe loss scenario). High quality investment portfolio (7.6).
Principal Business: Medicare (51%), comp med (47%), FEHB (2%)
Mem Phys: 19: 42,045 **18:** 40,983 **19 MLR** 81.7% **/ 19 Admin Exp** N/A
Enroll(000): Q2 20: 69 **19:** 71 **18:** 105 **Med Exp PMPM:** $618
Principal Investments: Long-term bonds (61%), cash and equiv (18%), nonaffiliate common stock (17%), real estate (3%)
Provider Compensation ($000): Contr fee ($312,615), capitation ($146,669), FFS ($113,825), bonus arrang ($2,021)
Total Member Encounters: N/A
Group Affiliation: SantaFe HealthCare Inc
Licensed in: FL
Address: 9400 South Dadeland Boulevard, Miami,
Phone: (352) 372-8400 **Dom State:** FL **Commenced Bus:** N/A

Data Date	Rating	RACR #1	RACR #2	Total Assets ($mil)	Capital ($mil)	Net Premium ($mil)	Net Income ($mil)
6-20	B-	1.84	1.53	281.4	115.8	326.7	12.8
6-19	N/A	N/A	N/A	N/A	N/A	N/A	N/A
2019	B-	1.74	1.45	278.1	110.6	700.7	14.6
2018	C	1.03	0.86	251.8	94.0	923.8	14.9
2017	C	0.75	0.63	308.8	80.1	1,098.7	0.2
2016	C	0.99	0.83	281.1	81.7	967.8	-15.5
2015	B-	1.54	1.28	283.7	99.9	819.8	-6.0

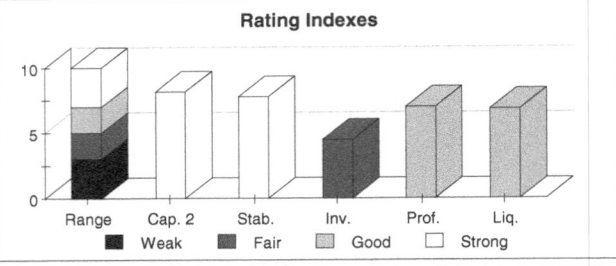

Rating Indexes

BANKERS FIDELITY LIFE INS CO

C-   **Fair**

Major Rating Factors: Fair current capitalization (4.2 on a scale of 0 to 10) based on fair risk adjusted capital (moderate loss scenario), although results have slipped from the good range over the last two years. Fair quality investment portfolio (4.8). Fair profitability (3.0). Excellent expense controls.
Other Rating Factors: Fair overall results on stability tests (3.3) including negative cash flow from operations for 2019, fair risk adjusted capital in prior years. Weak liquidity (2.1).
Principal Business: Individual health insurance (71%), reinsurance (23%), individual life insurance (4%), and group health insurance (1%).
Principal Investments: NonCMO investment grade bonds (71%), common & preferred stock (19%), noninv. grade bonds (2%), CMOs and structured securities (2%), and policy loans (1%).
Investments in Affiliates: 18%
Group Affiliation: Atlantic American Corp
Licensed in: All states except CA, CT, NY, VT, PR
Commenced Business: November 1955
Address: 4370 Peachtree Road NE, Atlanta, GA 30319
Phone: (800) 241-1439 **Domicile State:** GA **NAIC Code:** 61239

Data Date	Rating	RACR #1	RACR #2	Total Assets ($mil)	Capital ($mil)	Net Premium ($mil)	Net Income ($mil)
6-20	C-	0.77	0.65	153.3	34.7	61.7	2.6
6-19	C	0.97	0.77	147.4	30.5	62.2	-3.8
2019	C	0.85	0.72	159.1	35.5	123.3	-8.9
2018	C	1.09	0.87	152.5	34.2	119.0	-3.4
2017	B-	1.21	0.93	150.0	34.1	109.6	-2.9
2016	B	1.24	0.94	144.3	33.4	99.6	1.2
2015	B	1.28	0.96	143.9	35.3	96.1	4.0

Risk-Adjusted Capital Ratio #1
(Moderate Loss Scenario)

BANKERS LIFE & CAS CO

D+   **Weak**

Major Rating Factors: Weak overall results on stability tests (2.7 on a scale of 0 to 10). Fair quality investment portfolio (4.7) with large holdings of BBB rated bonds in addition to junk bond exposure equal to 54% of capital. Fair profitability (4.2). Excellent expense controls. Return on equity has been fair, averaging 9.6%.

Other Rating Factors: Good capitalization (6.8) based on good risk adjusted capital (severe loss scenario). Good liquidity (5.4).

Principal Business: Individual annuities (45%), individual health insurance (24%), individual life insurance (16%), reinsurance (14%), and group health insurance (1%).

Principal Investments: NonCMO investment grade bonds (50%), CMOs and structured securities (30%), mortgages in good standing (7%), noninv. grade bonds (4%), and common & preferred stock (2%).

Investments in Affiliates: 1%

Group Affiliation: CNO Financial Group Inc

Licensed in: All states except NY, PR

Commenced Business: January 1879

Address: 111 EAST WACKER DRIVE STE 2100, CHICAGO, IL 60601-4508

Phone: (312) 396-6000 **Domicile State:** IL **NAIC Code:** 61263

Data Date	Rating	RACR #1	RACR #2	Total Assets ($mil)	Capital ($mil)	Net Premium ($mil)	Net Income ($mil)
6-20	D+	1.76	0.98	16,460.6	1,234.6	1,210.1	236.6
6-19	D+	1.66	0.93	15,882.2	1,136.5	1,332.6	143.1
2019	D+	1.78	1.00	16,369.5	1,176.7	2,646.3	225.9
2018	D+	1.64	0.92	15,514.6	1,110.2	2,556.4	-299.9
2017	D+	2.10	1.11	18,273.9	1,336.8	2,581.5	249.3
2016	D+	2.32	1.20	17,602.0	1,300.3	2,535.9	171.2
2015	D+	2.23	1.16	16,905.4	1,238.6	2,385.0	188.7

Rating Indexes

BANKERS RESERVE LIFE INS CO OF WI

C+   **Fair**

Major Rating Factors: Fair profitability index (3.5 on a scale of 0 to 10). Strong capitalization (7.5) based on excellent current risk-adjusted capital (severe loss scenario). High quality investment portfolio (7.5).

Other Rating Factors: Excellent liquidity (7.0) with sufficient resources (cash flows and marketable investments) to handle a spike in claims.

Principal Business: Medicaid (94%), comp med (6%)

Mem Phys: 19: 57,651 18: 59,918 **19 MLR** 90.2% **/ 19 Admin Exp** N/A

Enroll(000): Q2 20: 498 19: 496 18: 512 **Med Exp PMPM:** $321

Principal Investments: Cash and equiv (73%), long-term bonds (22%), affiliate common stock (2%), other (3%)

Provider Compensation ($000): Contr fee ($1,250,808), bonus arrang ($604,738), salary ($95,309), capitation ($11,638)

Total Member Encounters: Phys (2,727,162), non-phys (9,870,150)

Group Affiliation: None

Licensed in: All states except AK, CA, CT, HI, MA, MN, NY, VT, PR

Address: 7700 Forsyth Blvd, St Louis, MO 63105

Phone: (314) 505-6341 **Dom State:** WI **Commenced Bus:** N/A

Data Date	Rating	RACR #1	RACR #2	Total Assets ($mil)	Capital ($mil)	Net Premium ($mil)	Net Income ($mil)
6-20	C+	1.77	1.48	569.0	286.6	1,137.3	42.8
6-19	C	2.23	1.86	459.8	252.3	1,060.0	16.3
2019	C	2.21	1.84	475.1	265.7	2,157.2	26.1
2018	C-	2.06	1.71	436.3	230.8	2,110.2	14.1
2017	C-	1.32	1.10	409.9	191.0	1,904.0	-65.9
2016	C-	2.14	1.78	410.4	223.7	1,958.6	-20.7
2015	C-	2.17	1.81	425.9	244.4	2,102.0	-21.7

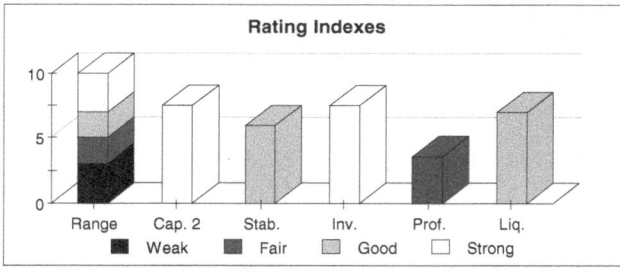

Rating Indexes

BANNER HEALTH & AETNA HLTH INS

B   **Good**

Major Rating Factors: Good overall profitability index (5.2 on a scale of 0 to 10). Good quality investment portfolio (6.8). Strong capitalization (10.0) based on excellent current risk-adjusted capital (severe loss scenario).

Other Rating Factors: Excellent liquidity (8.0) with ample operational cash flow and liquid investments.

Principal Business: Comp med (100%)

Mem Phys: 18: 14,484 17: N/A **18 MLR** 25.6% **/ 18 Admin Exp** N/A

Enroll(000): Q3 19: 36 18: 32 17: N/A **Med Exp PMPM:** $257

Principal Investments: Long-term bonds (52%), cash and equiv (34%), affiliate common stock (12%), nonaffiliate common stock (2%)

Provider Compensation ($000): Contr fee ($42,761), FFS ($5,820), bonus arrang ($4)

Total Member Encounters: Phys (398,177), non-phys (339,701)

Group Affiliation: None

Licensed in: AZ

Address: 4500 E COTTON CENTER BOULEVAR, PHOENIX, AZ 85040

Phone: (602) 659-1100 **Dom State:** AZ **Commenced Bus:** N/A

Data Date	Rating	RACR #1	RACR #2	Total Assets ($mil)	Capital ($mil)	Net Premium ($mil)	Net Income ($mil)
9-19	B	5.26	4.38	134.5	81.1	169.2	8.8
9-18	N/A	N/A	N/A	152.6	58.6	172.1	-1.9
2018	C	3.97	3.31	133.1	59.5	233.3	-7.6
2017	N/A	N/A	N/A	113.3	41.3	179.3	6.7
2016	N/A	N/A	N/A	N/A	N/A	N/A	N/A
2015	N/A	N/A	N/A	N/A	N/A	N/A	N/A
2014	N/A	N/A	N/A	N/A	N/A	N/A	N/A

Rating Indexes

BANNER HLTH & AETNA HLTH PLAN — B — Good

Major Rating Factors: Good overall profitability index (5.9 on a scale of 0 to 10). Strong capitalization (10.0) based on excellent current risk-adjusted capital (severe loss scenario). High quality investment portfolio (9.0).
Other Rating Factors: Excellent liquidity (7.0) with sufficient resources (cash flows and marketable investments) to handle a spike in claims.
Principal Business: Comp med (100%)
Mem Phys: 18: 14,484 **17:** N/A **18 MLR** 52.3% **/ 18 Admin Exp** N/A
Enroll(000): Q3 19: 4 **18:** 5 **17:** N/A **Med Exp PMPM:** $272
Principal Investments: Long-term bonds (61%), cash and equiv (37%), nonaffiliate common stock (2%)
Provider Compensation ($000): Contr fee ($9,981), FFS ($1,895), capitation ($6)
Total Member Encounters: Phys (43,652), non-phys (36,861)
Group Affiliation: None
Licensed in: AZ
Address: 4500 E COTTON CENTER BOULEVAR, PHOENIX, AZ 85040
Phone: (602) 659-1100 **Dom State:** AZ **Commenced Bus:** N/A

Data Date	Rating	RACR #1	RACR #2	Total Assets ($mil)	Capital ($mil)	Net Premium ($mil)	Net Income ($mil)
9-19	B	5.88	4.90	23.4	14.4	16.1	2.9
9-18	N/A	N/A	N/A	25.0	9.5	20.3	0.3
2018	C	4.22	3.51	25.9	9.8	27.5	-1.3
2017	N/A	N/A	N/A	14.8	6.5	16.6	1.6
2016	N/A	N/A	N/A	N/A	N/A	N/A	N/A
2015	N/A	N/A	N/A	N/A	N/A	N/A	N/A
2014	N/A	N/A	N/A	N/A	N/A	N/A	N/A

Rating Indexes

BAPTIST HEALTH PLAN INC — D — Weak

Major Rating Factors: Weak profitability index (0.2 on a scale of 0 to 10). Weak overall results on stability tests (2.0) based on a significant 100% decrease in enrollment during the period, a steep decline in capital during 2018. Fair capitalization index (2.9) based on good current risk-adjusted capital (moderate loss scenario
Other Rating Factors: Good quality investment portfolio (5.5). Good liquidity (5.4) with sufficient resources (cash flows and marketable investments) to handle a spike in claims.
Principal Business: Comp med (100%)
Mem Phys: 18: 44,773 **17:** 44,773 **18 MLR** 88.3% **/ 18 Admin Exp** N/A
Enroll(000): Q3 19: N/A **18:** N/A **17:** 22 **Med Exp PMPM:** N/A
Principal Investments: Long-term bonds (52%), nonaffiliate common stock (36%), cash and equiv (12%)
Provider Compensation ($000): Contr fee ($29,133), FFS ($704), capitation ($104)
Total Member Encounters: Phys (19,435), non-phys (4,852)
Group Affiliation: Baptist Healthcare System Inc
Licensed in: IL, IN, KY, OH, TN, WV
Address: 651 Perimeter Drive STE 300, Lexington,
Phone: (859) 269-4475 **Dom State:** KY **Commenced Bus:** N/A

Data Date	Rating	RACR #1	RACR #2	Total Assets ($mil)	Capital ($mil)	Net Premium ($mil)	Net Income ($mil)
9-19	D	1.27	1.05	13.8	9.0	-0.2	-0.9
9-18	E	0.35	0.29	19.0	11.4	16.4	-2.3
2018	D-	1.26	1.05	16.4	8.9	16.4	-4.2
2017	E	0.31	0.26	43.0	11.3	135.2	-11.8
2016	D+	0.63	0.53	76.2	19.1	153.1	-24.8
2015	C	2.71	2.26	68.0	34.9	129.8	-18.5
2014	N/A	N/A	N/A	100.6	71.7	145.8	N/A

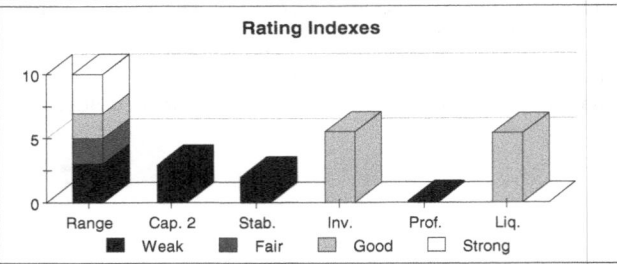

Rating Indexes

BAY AREA ACCOUNTABLE CARE — D — Weak

Major Rating Factors: Weak profitability index (0.9 on a scale of 0 to 10). Weak liquidity (0.4) as a spike in claims may stretch capacity. Fair capitalization index (4.3) based on weak current risk-adjusted capital (moderate loss scenario).
Other Rating Factors: Fair overall results on stability tests (4.3) in spite of healthy premium and capital growth during 2019.
Principal Business: Managed care (100%)
Mem Phys: 19: N/A **18:** N/A **19 MLR** 94.4% **/ 19 Admin Exp** N/A
Enroll(000): Q2 20: 44 **19:** 26 **18:** 26 **Med Exp PMPM:** $773
Principal Investments ($000): Cash and equiv ($37,753)
Provider Compensation ($000): None
Total Member Encounters: N/A
Group Affiliation: None
Licensed in: CA
Address: 6475 Christie Avenue Suite 360, Emeryville, CA 94608
Phone: (415) 299-7840 **Dom State:** CA **Commenced Bus:** N/A

Data Date	Rating	RACR #1	RACR #2	Total Assets ($mil)	Capital ($mil)	Net Premium ($mil)	Net Income ($mil)
6-20	D	0.69	0.42	58.5	19.0	130.9	-7.1
6-19	D	0.80	0.49	50.0	14.5	117.1	-6.6
2019	D	0.52	0.32	50.9	14.9	238.6	-10.9
2018	D-	0.46	0.28	33.1	9.4	126.7	-12.4
2017	D-	0.11	0.07	20.5	5.7	87.6	-4.1
2016	D+	2.43	1.53	18.1	9.7	31.5	-1.9
2015	N/A	N/A	N/A	N/A	N/A	N/A	N/A

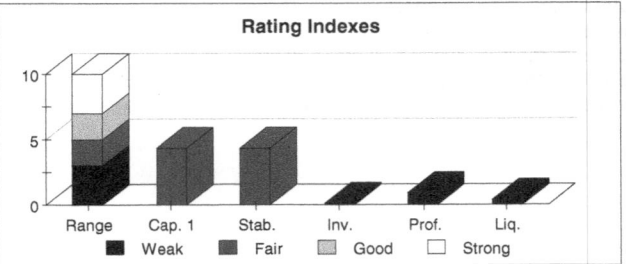

Rating Indexes

BAYCARE SELECT HEALTH PLANS   E-   Very Weak

Major Rating Factors: Weak profitability index (0.0 on a scale of 0 to 10). Weak liquidity (0.4) as a spike in claims may stretch capacity. Fair capitalization (3.2) based on weak current risk-adjusted capital (moderate loss scenario). Other Rating Factors: High quality investment portfolio (9.9).
Principal Business: Medicare (100%)
Mem Phys: 19: N/A **18:** N/A **19 MLR** 103.8% **/ 19 Admin Exp** N/A
Enroll(000): Q2 20: 8 **19:** 5 **18:** N/A **Med Exp PMPM:** $677
Principal Investments: Cash and equiv (100%)
Provider Compensation ($000): FFS ($30,688), capitation ($878), bonus arrang ($45)
Total Member Encounters: N/A
Group Affiliation: None
Licensed in: FL
Address: 300 Park Place Suite 170, Clearwater, FL 33759
Phone: (727) 519-1766 **Dom State:** FL **Commenced Bus:** N/A

Data Date	Rating	RACR #1	RACR #2	Total Assets ($mil)	Capital ($mil)	Net Premium ($mil)	Net Income ($mil)
6-20	E-	0.66	0.55	27.3	6.5	30.1	-6.2
6-19	N/A	N/A	N/A	N/A	N/A	N/A	N/A
2019	D-	1.10	0.91	29.3	10.1	34.9	-25.3
2018	N/A	N/A	N/A	22.4	21.7	N/A	N/A
2017	N/A	N/A	N/A	30.6	30.0	N/A	-3.9
2016	N/A	N/A	N/A	N/A	N/A	N/A	N/A
2015	N/A	N/A	N/A	N/A	N/A	N/A	N/A

BCS INS CO   B-   Good

Major Rating Factors: Fair overall results on stability tests (3.5 on a scale of 0 to 10). Good overall profitability index (5.4). Fair expense controls. Return on equity has been fair, averaging 8.2% over the past five years.
Other Rating Factors: Good liquidity (6.8) with sufficient resources (cash flows and marketable investments) to handle a spike in claims. Strong long-term capitalization index (10.0) based on excellent current risk adjusted capital (severe and moderate loss scenarios), despite some fluctuation in capital levels. Ample reserve history (8.7) that helps to protect the company against sharp claims increases.
Principal Business: Inland marine (45%), group accident & health (38%), other liability (8%), commercial multiple peril (7%), and aggregate write-ins for other lines of business (2%).
Principal Investments: Investment grade bonds (76%), misc. investments (14%), cash (9%), and non investment grade bonds (1%).
Investments in Affiliates: None
Group Affiliation: BCS Financial Corp
Licensed in: All states, the District of Columbia and Puerto Rico
Commenced Business: November 1952
Address: 6740 North High Street, Worthington, OH 43085
Phone: (630) 472-7700 **Domicile State:** OH **NAIC Code:** 38245

Data Date	Rating	RACR #1	RACR #2	Loss Ratio %	Total Assets ($mil)	Capital ($mil)	Net Premium ($mil)	Net Income ($mil)
6-20	B-	9.03	5.40	N/A	356.0	149.9	42.0	4.7
6-19	B-	10.56	6.04	N/A	343.6	158.3	48.0	8.5
2019	B	6.81	4.20	57.5	322.8	147.7	92.6	13.5
2018	B	9.94	5.66	58.1	336.6	141.9	97.6	11.3
2017	B	10.47	5.80	57.9	276.6	147.0	98.6	13.9
2016	B	8.93	5.13	64.9	269.4	155.2	101.8	11.4
2015	B	8.58	4.87	60.5	272.2	161.3	95.3	13.3

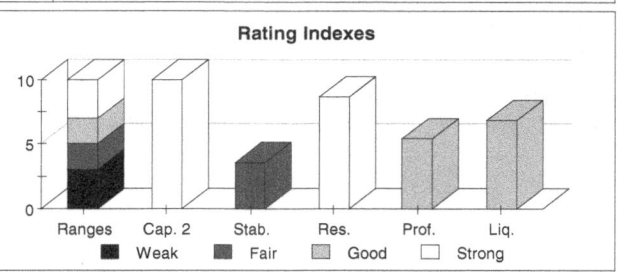

BEACON HEALTH OPTIONS OF PA   C   Fair

Major Rating Factors: Excellent profitability (8.9 on a scale of 0 to 10). Strong capitalization (10.0) based on excellent current risk-adjusted capital (severe loss scenario). High quality investment portfolio (9.9).
Other Rating Factors: Excellent liquidity (10.0) with ample operational cash flow and liquid investments.
Principal Business: Medicaid (100%)
Mem Phys: 19: 1,292 **18:** 1,245 **19 MLR** 67.7% **/ 19 Admin Exp** N/A
Enroll(000): Q2 20: 9 **19:** 9 **18:** 9 **Med Exp PMPM:** $82
Principal Investments: Cash and equiv (100%)
Provider Compensation ($000): Contr fee ($8,736)
Total Member Encounters: Phys (13,589), non-phys (518,282)
Group Affiliation: Anthem Inc
Licensed in: PA
Address: One Adams Place Suite 100 30, SEVEN FIELDS, PA 16046
Phone: (757) 459-5418 **Dom State:** PA **Commenced Bus:** N/A

Data Date	Rating	RACR #1	RACR #2	Total Assets ($mil)	Capital ($mil)	Net Premium ($mil)	Net Income ($mil)
6-20	C	8.61	7.17	30.1	20.4	6.2	4.5
6-19	E+	5.31	4.43	20.9	11.1	6.5	3.8
2019	C	12.15	10.13	22.5	16.2	12.9	8.8
2018	E	6.74	5.62	24.3	14.8	12.5	10.2
2017	E	4.71	3.93	34.0	18.2	28.7	8.6
2016	E	2.26	1.89	43.8	19.7	83.8	7.5
2015	E	1.87	1.56	46.5	19.1	105.2	7.4

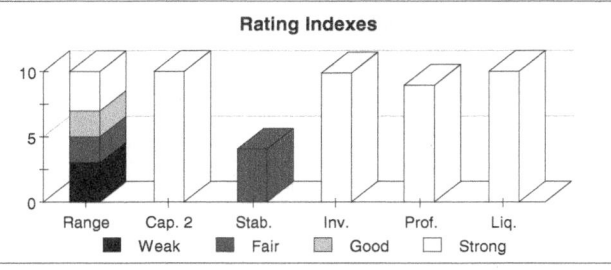

BEHEALTHY FLORIDA INC   C-   Fair

Major Rating Factors: Weak profitability index (1.9 on a scale of 0 to 10). Low quality investment portfolio (0.8). Strong capitalization (10.0) based on excellent current risk-adjusted capital (severe loss scenario).
Other Rating Factors: Excellent liquidity (7.7) with ample operational cash flow and liquid investments.
Principal Business: Medicare (100%)
Mem Phys: 18: N/A   **17:** N/A   **18 MLR** 87.4%   **/ 18 Admin Exp** N/A
Enroll(000): Q3 19: 6   **18:** 10   **17:** 9   **Med Exp PMPM:** $812
Principal Investments: Cash and equiv (100%)
Provider Compensation ($000): Capitation ($94,607)
Total Member Encounters: Phys (39,859), non-phys (11,930)
Group Affiliation: None
Licensed in: FL
Address: 4800 Deerwood Campus Parkway, Jacksonville, FL 32246
Phone: (904) 791-6111   **Dom State:** FL   **Commenced Bus:** N/A

Data Date	Rating	RACR #1	RACR #2	Total Assets ($mil)	Capital ($mil)	Net Premium ($mil)	Net Income ($mil)
9-19	C-	4.16	3.47	34.6	21.8	41.0	2.9
9-18	D+	N/A	N/A	43.6	16.9	80.6	-1.1
2018	C-	3.69	3.08	45.0	19.3	108.2	1.0
2017	D+	N/A	N/A	34.0	17.4	93.2	-0.8
2016	D	6.97	5.81	16.6	11.0	23.3	-1.5
2015	C-	5.23	4.36	8.8	5.3	7.0	-3.7
2014	N/A	N/A	N/A	3.6	2.2	5.1	N/A

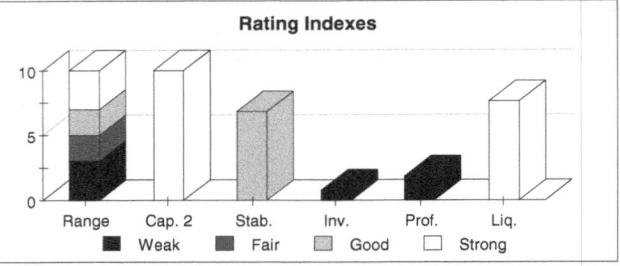

BERKLEY LIFE & HEALTH INS CO *   A   Excellent

Major Rating Factors: Excellent overall results on stability tests (7.8 on a scale of 0 to 10). Strengths that enhance stability include excellent operational trends and excellent risk diversification. Strong capitalization (10.0) based on excellent risk adjusted capital (severe loss scenario). Furthermore, this high level of risk adjusted capital has been consistently maintained over the last five years. High quality investment portfolio (7.7).
Other Rating Factors: Excellent profitability (8.7) with operating gains in each of the last five years. Excellent liquidity (7.1).
Principal Business: Group health insurance (99%) and reinsurance (1%).
Principal Investments: CMOs and structured securities (58%), nonCMO investment grade bonds (40%), and cash (1%).
Investments in Affiliates: None
Group Affiliation: W R Berkley Corp
Licensed in: All states except PR
Commenced Business: July 1963
Address: 11201 DOUGLAS AVE, URBANDALE, IA 50322
Phone: (609) 584-6990   **Domicile State:** IA   **NAIC Code:** 64890

Data Date	Rating	RACR #1	RACR #2	Total Assets ($mil)	Capital ($mil)	Net Premium ($mil)	Net Income ($mil)
6-20	A	6.11	4.33	382.0	209.6	107.7	17.9
6-19	A	4.99	3.62	353.6	181.4	131.5	14.8
2019	A	5.18	3.72	363.1	194.5	271.6	28.0
2018	A	4.59	3.35	324.2	166.6	268.0	16.5
2017	A	4.73	3.50	277.3	150.7	238.1	8.2
2016	B	4.60	3.45	267.7	143.7	237.9	14.1
2015	B-	5.35	4.11	223.9	129.2	187.3	23.1

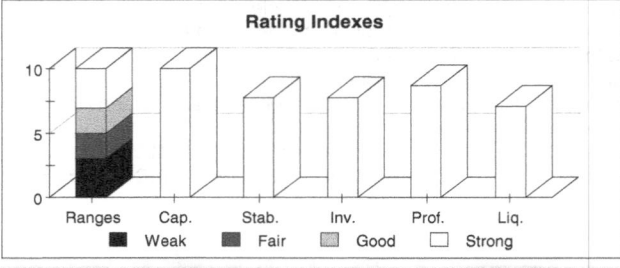

BERKSHIRE LIFE INS CO OF AMERICA   B   Good

Major Rating Factors: Good overall results on stability tests (6.2 on a scale of 0 to 10). Strengths include excellent financial support from affiliation with Guardian Group, excellent operational trends and excellent risk diversification. Fair quality investment portfolio (4.6). Strong capitalization (7.3) based on excellent risk adjusted capital (severe loss scenario).
Other Rating Factors: Excellent profitability (7.5). Excellent liquidity (8.0).
Principal Business: Individual health insurance (79%), reinsurance (20%), and individual life insurance (1%).
Principal Investments: NonCMO investment grade bonds (94%), mortgages in good standing (1%), and noninv. grade bonds (1%).
Investments in Affiliates: None
Group Affiliation: Guardian Group
Licensed in: All states except PR
Commenced Business: July 2001
Address: 700 SOUTH STREET, PITTSFIELD, MA 1201
Phone: (413) 499-4321   **Domicile State:** MA   **NAIC Code:** 71714

Data Date	Rating	RACR #1	RACR #2	Total Assets ($mil)	Capital ($mil)	Net Premium ($mil)	Net Income ($mil)
6-20	B	2.54	1.23	4,291.1	221.6	69.5	5.6
6-19	B	2.35	1.13	4,052.5	195.5	67.4	14.6
2019	B	2.85	1.40	4,181.5	219.9	135.3	83.6
2018	B	2.44	1.16	3,927.6	192.7	131.4	-13.3
2017	B	2.57	1.20	3,717.7	189.1	126.9	10.2
2016	B	2.97	1.36	3,526.7	201.6	123.3	17.8
2015	B	3.34	1.58	3,381.4	207.9	118.2	14.2

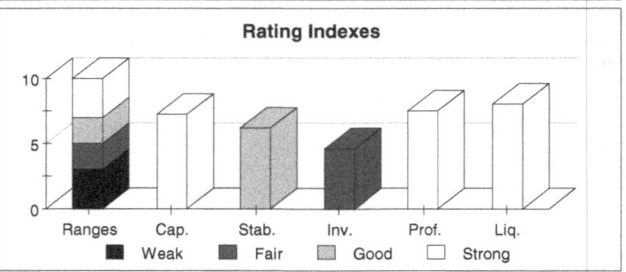

BLUE ADVANTAGE PLUS OF KANSAS CITY — C — Fair

Major Rating Factors: Fair capitalization (2.9 on a scale of 0 to 10) based on good current risk-adjusted capital (moderate loss scenario). Weak profitability index (0.5). Good liquidity (5.2) with sufficient resources (cash flows and marketable investments) to handle a spike in claims.
Other Rating Factors: High quality investment portfolio (8.7).
Principal Business: Medicare (100%)
Mem Phys: 18: 4,040 **17:** 3,059 **18 MLR** 93.1% **/ 18 Admin Exp** N/A
Enroll(000): Q3 19: 9 **18:** 10 **17:** 9 **Med Exp PMPM:** $779
Principal Investments: Long-term bonds (81%), cash and equiv (19%)
Provider Compensation ($000): Contr fee ($73,499), FFS ($18,374), capitation ($1,482)
Total Member Encounters: Phys (73,550), non-phys (20,132)
Group Affiliation: None
Licensed in: KS, MO
Address: 2301 Main Street, Kansas City, MO 64108-2428
Phone: (816) 395-2222 **Dom State:** MO **Commenced Bus:** N/A

Data Date	Rating	RACR #1	RACR #2	Total Assets ($mil)	Capital ($mil)	Net Premium ($mil)	Net Income ($mil)
9-19	C	1.04	0.87	44.4	16.0	67.9	-16.1
9-18	C	N/A	N/A	36.5	12.8	76.7	-3.2
2018	C	0.65	0.54	34.0	10.0	100.6	-9.1
2017	C	N/A	N/A	41.3	17.4	79.8	-16.7
2016	C	1.00	0.83	16.8	9.3	29.3	-5.9
2015	N/A	N/A	N/A	21.2	15.3	N/A	-8.7
2014	N/A	N/A	N/A	26.2	24.0	N/A	N/A

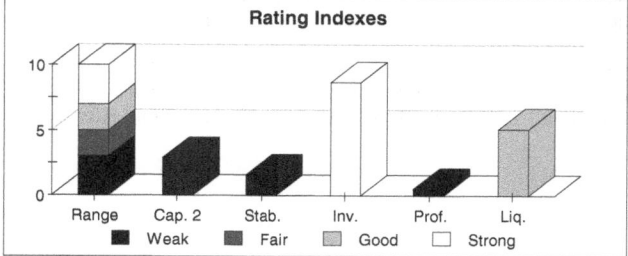

Rating Indexes

BLUE CARE NETWORK OF MICHIGAN * — B+ — Good

Major Rating Factors: Excellent profitability (7.3 on a scale of 0 to 10). Strong capitalization index (10.0) based on excellent current risk-adjusted capital (severe loss scenario). High quality investment portfolio (8.2).
Other Rating Factors: Excellent overall results on stability tests (8.4). Excellent liquidity (7.0) with sufficient resources (cash flows and marketable investments) to handle a spike in claims
Principal Business: Comp med (71%), Medicare (25%), FEHB (3%)
Mem Phys: 19: 63,008 **18:** 58,949 **19 MLR** 84.9% **/ 19 Admin Exp** N/A
Enroll(000): Q2 20: 726 **19:** 745 **18:** 739 **Med Exp PMPM:** $404
Principal Investments: Long-term bonds (63%), cash and equiv (25%), nonaffiliate common stock (9%), other (4%)
Provider Compensation ($000): Bonus arrang ($1,955,870), contr fee ($1,313,682), capitation ($240,160), FFS ($114,528)
Total Member Encounters: Phys (4,483,947), non-phys (2,392,113)
Group Affiliation: None
Licensed in: MI
Address: 20500 Civic Center Drive, Southfield,
Phone: (248) 799-6400 **Dom State:** MI **Commenced Bus:** N/A

Data Date	Rating	RACR #1	RACR #2	Total Assets ($mil)	Capital ($mil)	Net Premium ($mil)	Net Income ($mil)
6-20	B+	7.65	6.38	2,936.0	1,922.2	2,053.4	193.2
6-19	B+	7.40	6.17	2,661.9	1,745.1	2,142.2	108.7
2019	B+	6.87	5.73	2,649.2	1,728.9	4,252.4	74.7
2018	B	6.82	5.68	2,402.8	1,609.4	4,239.2	250.6
2017	A-	7.07	5.89	2,154.4	1,398.9	3,581.0	240.4
2016	B+	6.05	5.04	1,864.2	1,123.0	3,399.3	93.8
2015	B+	5.74	4.78	1,847.8	1,026.5	3,252.5	18.0

Rating Indexes

BLUE CROSS & BLUE SHIELD MA HMO BLUE * — B+ — Good

Major Rating Factors: Good overall profitability index (6.3 on a scale of 0 to 10). Good quality investment portfolio (5.3). Good liquidity (6.6) with sufficient resources (cash flows and marketable investments) to handle a spike in claims.
Other Rating Factors: Strong capitalization (10.0) based on excellent current risk-adjusted capital (severe loss scenario).
Principal Business: Comp med (88%), Medicare (11%)
Mem Phys: 19: 26,497 **18:** 25,340 **19 MLR** 88.0% **/ 19 Admin Exp** N/A
Enroll(000): Q2 20: 736 **19:** 776 **18:** 803 **Med Exp PMPM:** $492
Principal Investments: Long-term bonds (37%), nonaffiliate common stock (12%), cash and equiv (5%), real estate (4%), other (43%)
Provider Compensation ($000): Bonus arrang ($3,149,821), contr fee ($1,173,075), FFS ($207,260), capitation ($15,554)
Total Member Encounters: Phys (3,044,340), non-phys (3,077,760)
Group Affiliation: Blue Cross and Blue Shield of Massac
Licensed in: MA
Address: 101 HUNTINGTON AVENUE SUITE 1, BOSTON, MA 2199
Phone: (617) 246-5000 **Dom State:** MA **Commenced Bus:** N/A

Data Date	Rating	RACR #1	RACR #2	Total Assets ($mil)	Capital ($mil)	Net Premium ($mil)	Net Income ($mil)
6-20	B+	3.88	3.23	2,748.4	1,579.0	2,545.4	86.6
6-19	B+	4.11	3.42	2,380.4	1,566.2	2,603.0	80.5
2019	B+	4.01	3.34	2,551.5	1,630.9	5,195.3	111.6
2018	B+	3.72	3.10	2,266.5	1,413.8	5,096.3	94.0
2017	A-	3.87	3.22	2,411.7	1,383.7	4,817.4	121.4
2016	B+	3.89	3.24	2,098.2	1,207.7	4,596.5	74.2
2015	B	3.91	3.26	1,908.1	1,089.6	4,358.1	2.4

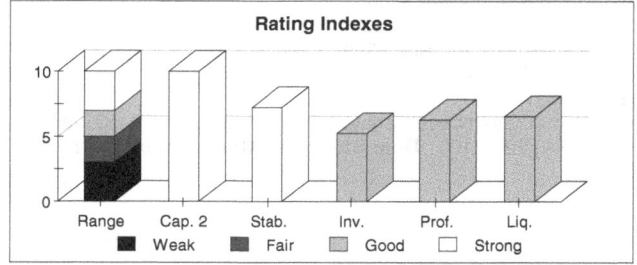

Rating Indexes

BLUE CROSS & BLUE SHIELD OF FLORIDA — B — Good

Major Rating Factors: Good quality investment portfolio (6.4 on a scale of 0 to 10). Excellent profitability (9.1). Strong capitalization (10.0) based on excellent current risk-adjusted capital (severe loss scenario).
Other Rating Factors: Excellent liquidity (7.0) with sufficient resources (cash flows and marketable investments) to handle a spike in claims.
Principal Business: Comp med (66%), FEHB (22%), Medicare (6%), med supp (4%), other (1%)
Mem Phys: 19: 33,122 **18:** 28,564 **19 MLR** 81.5% **/ 19 Admin Exp** N/A
Enroll(000): Q2 20: 1,975 **19:** 1,904 **18:** 1,861 **Med Exp PMPM:** $397
Principal Investments: Long-term bonds (65%), nonaffiliate common stock (14%), cash and equiv (11%), real estate (6%), other (4%)
Provider Compensation ($000): Contr fee ($7,998,764), FFS ($1,046,989), capitation ($48,185), bonus arrang ($44,894)
Total Member Encounters: Phys (15,359,641), non-phys (11,815,642)
Group Affiliation: None
Licensed in: FL, PA
Address: 4800 Deerwood Campus Parkway, Jacksonville, FL 32246
Phone: (904) 791-6111 **Dom State:** FL **Commenced Bus:** N/A

Data Date	Rating	RACR #1	RACR #2	Total Assets ($mil)	Capital ($mil)	Net Premium ($mil)	Net Income ($mil)
6-20	B	4.41	3.68	7,561.3	2,412.8	5,968.0	328.0
6-19	B	4.31	3.59	6,185.1	2,192.4	5,687.5	328.4
2019	B	4.08	3.40	6,210.2	2,225.2	11,266.7	775.3
2018	B	3.80	3.17	5,645.2	1,927.5	10,872.4	694.6
2017	B-	3.77	3.14	5,730.6	1,792.8	10,018.8	474.0
2016	B-	5.46	4.55	5,974.6	2,271.7	9,387.5	552.8
2015	C	4.69	3.91	5,612.2	1,842.1	8,789.8	327.5

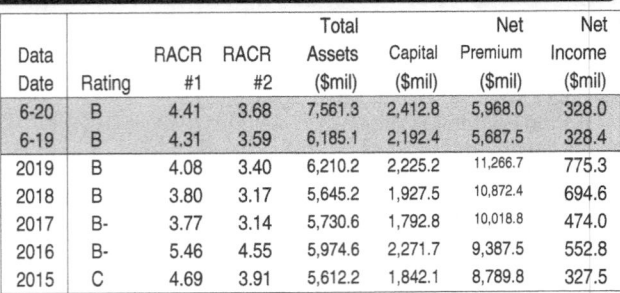

Rating Indexes

BLUE CROSS BLUE SHIELD HEALTHCARE GA * — A- — Excellent

Major Rating Factors: Excellent profitability (9.7 on a scale of 0 to 10). Strong capitalization index (10.0) based on excellent current risk-adjusted capital (severe loss scenario). High quality investment portfolio (7.7).
Other Rating Factors: Good overall results on stability tests (5.6). Good liquidity (6.9) with sufficient resources (cash flows and marketable investments) to handle a spike in claims.
Principal Business: Comp med (55%), FEHB (32%), med supp (3%), dental (2%), Medicare (1%), other (5%)
Mem Phys: 19: 23,198 **18:** 21,858 **19 MLR** 85.2% **/ 19 Admin Exp** N/A
Enroll(000): Q2 20: 1,969 **19:** 1,872 **18:** 1,821 **Med Exp PMPM:** $165
Principal Investments: Long-term bonds (89%), affiliate common stock (2%), other (9%)
Provider Compensation ($000): Bonus arrang ($2,099,883), contr fee ($1,202,102), FFS ($275,047), capitation ($6,109), other ($115,519)
Total Member Encounters: Phys (5,500,493), non-phys (3,576,072)
Group Affiliation: Anthem Inc
Licensed in: GA
Address: 3350 PEACHTREE ROAD NE, ATLANTA,
Phone: (404) 842-8000 **Dom State:** GA **Commenced Bus:** N/A

Data Date	Rating	RACR #1	RACR #2	Total Assets ($mil)	Capital ($mil)	Net Premium ($mil)	Net Income ($mil)
6-20	A-	4.93	4.11	2,685.2	1,209.4	2,118.9	185.4
6-19	A-	7.12	5.93	2,678.0	1,204.0	2,250.1	262.5
2019	A-	4.25	3.54	2,432.9	1,035.0	4,434.6	317.7
2018	A-	3.12	2.60	2,327.0	973.0	4,096.7	235.3
2017	A-	1.49	1.24	2,304.1	814.7	5,124.4	103.7
2016	A-	2.51	2.10	2,131.5	751.6	3,981.5	71.7
2015	A-	2.47	2.06	1,877.3	682.1	3,734.9	50.9

Rating Indexes

BLUE CROSS BLUE SHIELD OF ALABAMA * — A- — Excellent

Major Rating Factors: Strong capitalization (10.0 on a scale of 0 to 10) based on excellent current risk-adjusted capital (severe loss scenario). High quality investment portfolio (6.9). Excellent liquidity (7.1) with ample operational cash flow and liquid investments.
Other Rating Factors: Good overall profitability index (6.0).
Principal Business: Comp med (67%), FEHB (14%), Medicare (12%), med supp (4%), dental (2%)
Mem Phys: 19: 52,516 **18:** 47,650 **19 MLR** 89.9% **/ 19 Admin Exp** N/A
Enroll(000): Q2 20: 1,665 **19:** 1,642 **18:** 1,635 **Med Exp PMPM:** $277
Principal Investments: Long-term bonds (58%), nonaffiliate common stock (20%), cash and equiv (13%), affiliate common stock (3%), real estate (3%), other (4%)
Provider Compensation ($000): Contr fee ($5,443,902), capitation ($14,384), bonus arrang ($1,792), FFS ($990)
Total Member Encounters: Phys (24,073,520), non-phys (8,140,632)
Group Affiliation: None
Licensed in: AL
Address: 450 Riverchase Parkway East, Birmingham, AL 35244
Phone: (205) 220-2100 **Dom State:** AL **Commenced Bus:** N/A

Data Date	Rating	RACR #1	RACR #2	Total Assets ($mil)	Capital ($mil)	Net Premium ($mil)	Net Income ($mil)
6-20	A-	6.31	5.26	4,861.0	2,446.9	3,256.2	131.1
6-19	A-	7.16	5.97	4,462.9	2,455.0	3,081.3	354.0
2019	A-	6.08	5.06	4,567.2	2,356.5	6,108.0	403.1
2018	B+	5.84	4.87	3,960.0	2,001.7	6,027.4	403.2
2017	B	6.10	5.08	3,936.4	1,881.7	5,770.9	343.4
2016	B-	4.68	3.90	3,031.4	1,257.9	5,155.8	83.9
2015	B	4.55	3.79	2,840.7	1,142.2	4,864.7	-138.3

Rating Indexes

BLUE CROSS BLUE SHIELD OF ARIZONA *   A+   Excellent

Major Rating Factors: Excellent profitability (7.4 on a scale of 0 to 10). Strong capitalization (10.0) based on excellent current risk-adjusted capital (severe loss scenario). Excellent liquidity (7.2) with ample operational cash flow and liquid investments.
Other Rating Factors: Good quality investment portfolio (6.7).
Principal Business: Comp med (61%), FEHB (29%), med supp (5%), other (4%)
Mem Phys: 19: 35,452 **18:** 33,291 **19 MLR** 79.8% **/ 19 Admin Exp** N/A
Enroll(000): Q2 20: 1,679 **19:** 1,607 **18:** 1,529 **Med Exp PMPM:** $96
Principal Investments: Long-term bonds (34%), nonaffiliate common stock (13%), cash and equiv (7%), affiliate common stock (4%), real estate (3%), other (38%)
Provider Compensation ($000): Contr fee ($1,414,362), FFS ($387,672), bonus arrang ($4,618), capitation ($2,440)
Total Member Encounters: Phys (2,833,137), non-phys (1,997,363)
Group Affiliation: Blue Cross Blue Shield of Arizona In
Licensed in: AZ
Address: 2444 W LAS PALMARITAS DRIVE, PHOENIX, AZ 85021
Phone: (602) 864-4100 **Dom State:** AZ **Commenced Bus:** N/A

Data Date	Rating	RACR #1	RACR #2	Total Assets ($mil)	Capital ($mil)	Net Premium ($mil)	Net Income ($mil)
6-20	A+	4.60	3.84	2,830.5	1,470.9	1,198.8	75.1
6-19	N/A	N/A	N/A	N/A	N/A	N/A	N/A
2019	A+	4.49	3.75	2,741.5	1,436.0	2,297.5	186.8
2018	A+	7.19	5.99	2,268.1	1,504.8	2,207.4	158.7
2017	A+	7.05	5.87	2,104.4	1,335.3	2,106.9	196.7
2016	A+	6.02	5.02	1,782.4	1,084.4	2,048.1	61.0
2015	A+	5.92	4.94	1,627.1	1,004.2	1,975.8	2.6

Rating Indexes

BLUE CROSS BLUE SHIELD OF KANSAS INCORPORATED   B   Good

Major Rating Factors: Good liquidity (5.9 on a scale of 0 to 10) with sufficient resources to handle a spike in claims. Good overall results on stability tests (6.0). Stability strengths include excellent operational trends and excellent risk diversification. Fair quality investment portfolio (4.6).
Other Rating Factors: Strong capitalization (8.0) based on excellent risk adjusted capital (severe loss scenario). Excellent profitability (7.4) despite modest operating losses during 2015.
Principal Business: Group health insurance (67%) and individual health insurance (33%).
Principal Investments: NonCMO investment grade bonds (31%), common & preferred stock (23%), CMOs and structured securities (23%), noninv. grade bonds (2%), and real estate (2%).
Investments in Affiliates: 6%
Group Affiliation: Blue Cross Blue Shield Kansas
Licensed in: KS
Commenced Business: July 1942
Address: 1133 SW Topeka Boulevard, Topeka, KS 66629-0001
Phone: (785) 291-7000 **Domicile State:** KS **NAIC Code:** 70729

Data Date	Rating	RACR #1	RACR #2	Total Assets ($mil)	Capital ($mil)	Net Premium ($mil)	Net Income ($mil)
6-20	B	2.18	1.65	2,072.8	1,040.0	1,179.3	32.5
6-19	B	2.10	1.59	1,975.6	973.9	1,183.5	47.7
2019	B	2.10	1.60	1,929.4	976.6	2,367.7	65.5
2018	B	1.89	1.45	1,765.8	892.5	2,259.0	105.1
2017	B	2.06	1.54	1,730.4	791.6	1,775.0	3.4
2016	B	1.74	1.35	1,452.3	728.9	1,899.8	59.1
2015	B	1.84	1.39	1,404.1	686.7	1,854.4	-30.8

Adverse Trends in Operations

Decrease in premium volume from 2016 to 2017 (7%)

BLUE CROSS BLUE SHIELD OF KC   B   Good

Major Rating Factors: Good overall profitability index (6.7 on a scale of 0 to 10). Good quality investment portfolio (5.0). Good liquidity (6.8) with sufficient resources (cash flows and marketable investments) to handle a spike in claims.
Other Rating Factors: Strong capitalization (10.0) based on excellent current risk-adjusted capital (severe loss scenario).
Principal Business: Comp med (72%), FEHB (23%), med supp (4%), dental (1%)
Mem Phys: 19: 6,911 **18:** 6,712 **19 MLR** 82.4% **/ 19 Admin Exp** N/A
Enroll(000): Q2 20: 473 **19:** 499 **18:** 474 **Med Exp PMPM:** $227
Principal Investments: Long-term bonds (41%), nonaffiliate common stock (29%), affiliate common stock (10%), cash and equiv (3%), real estate (2%), other (16%)
Provider Compensation ($000): Contr fee ($1,118,077), FFS ($195,851), capitation ($17,515)
Total Member Encounters: Phys (1,072,976), non-phys (259,445)
Group Affiliation: None
Licensed in: KS, MO
Address: 2301 Main Street, Kansas City, MO 64108-2428
Phone: (816) 395-2222 **Dom State:** MO **Commenced Bus:** N/A

Data Date	Rating	RACR #1	RACR #2	Total Assets ($mil)	Capital ($mil)	Net Premium ($mil)	Net Income ($mil)
6-20	B	5.25	4.37	1,360.5	819.3	791.9	-6.4
6-19	C+	6.26	5.22	1,328.6	813.3	797.8	27.4
2019	B	5.81	4.84	1,353.0	861.2	1,615.8	49.4
2018	C+	5.67	4.72	1,246.0	758.1	1,590.0	66.6
2017	C+	4.94	4.12	1,265.9	706.6	1,834.0	106.1
2016	C	4.22	3.52	1,157.0	604.7	1,718.1	23.1
2015	C	4.05	3.38	1,108.9	562.2	1,484.8	-5.8

Rating Indexes

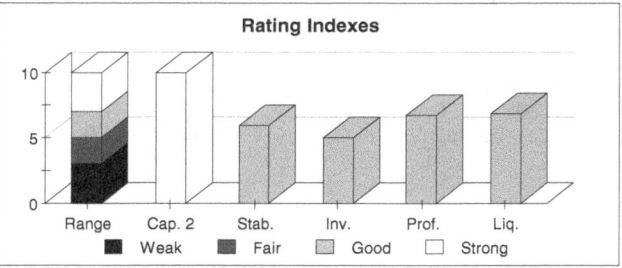

BLUE CROSS BLUE SHIELD OF MA — B- — Good

Major Rating Factors: Fair profitability index (3.8 on a scale of 0 to 10). Good quality investment portfolio (6.7). Good liquidity (6.8) with sufficient resources (cash flows and marketable investments) to handle a spike in claims.
Other Rating Factors: Strong capitalization (8.6) based on excellent current risk-adjusted capital (severe loss scenario).
Principal Business: Comp med (34%), FEHB (25%), med supp (17%), dental (11%), other (12%)
Mem Phys: 19: N/A **18:** 25,340 **19 MLR** 91.2% **/ 19 Admin Exp** N/A
Enroll(000): Q2 20: 1,501 **19:** 1,532 **18:** 1,480 **Med Exp PMPM:** $159
Principal Investments: Long-term bonds (44%), nonaffiliate common stock (10%), cash and equiv (9%), real estate (6%), other (31%)
Provider Compensation ($000): Contr fee ($1,673,058), FFS ($852,119), bonus arrang ($346,122), capitation ($2,501)
Total Member Encounters: Phys (3,628,811), non-phys (3,095,100)
Group Affiliation: Blue Cross and Blue Shield of Massac
Licensed in: MA
Address: 101 HUNTINGTON AVENUE SUITE 1, BOSTON, MA 2199
Phone: (617) 246-5000 **Dom State:** MA **Commenced Bus:** N/A

Data Date	Rating	RACR #1	RACR #2	Total Assets ($mil)	Capital ($mil)	Net Premium ($mil)	Net Income ($mil)
6-20	B-	2.66	2.21	2,583.3	872.0	1,555.1	127.3
6-19	C+	2.86	2.39	2,382.6	799.7	1,569.2	2.9
2019	C+	2.62	2.19	2,466.3	820.5	3,164.9	103.3
2018	C+	2.78	2.32	2,386.1	779.3	2,899.7	65.6
2017	C+	3.13	2.61	2,548.0	895.0	2,687.8	-128.4
2016	B	3.00	2.50	2,237.4	728.2	2,522.4	3.9
2015	B	3.14	2.61	2,005.4	618.7	2,439.3	12.6

Rating Indexes

BLUE CROSS BLUE SHIELD OF MICHIGAN — B- — Good

Major Rating Factors: Fair quality investment portfolio (3.1 on a scale of 0 to 10). Good overall profitability index (5.3). Strong capitalization (10.0) based on excellent current risk-adjusted capital (severe loss scenario).
Other Rating Factors: Excellent liquidity (6.9) with sufficient resources (cash flows and marketable investments) to handle a spike in claims.
Principal Business: Comp med (48%), Medicare (37%), FEHB (6%), med supp (5%), dental (1%), other (3%)
Mem Phys: 19: 66,178 **18:** 66,090 **19 MLR** 85.7% **/ 19 Admin Exp** N/A
Enroll(000): Q2 20: 3,300 **19:** 3,238 **18:** 1,322 **Med Exp PMPM:** $205
Principal Investments: Affiliate common stock (40%), long-term bonds (30%), nonaffiliate common stock (8%), cash and equiv (4%), real estate (1%), other (17%)
Provider Compensation ($000): Contr fee ($7,662,646), bonus arrang ($64,750), FFS ($23,562)
Total Member Encounters: N/A
Group Affiliation: None
Licensed in: MI
Address: 600 Lafayette East, DETROIT, MI 48226
Phone: (313) 225-9000 **Dom State:** MI **Commenced Bus:** N/A

Data Date	Rating	RACR #1	RACR #2	Total Assets ($mil)	Capital ($mil)	Net Premium ($mil)	Net Income ($mil)
6-20	B-	4.33	3.61	10,124.9	5,629.4	4,588.6	368.9
6-19	B	4.44	3.70	9,455.6	5,568.1	4,582.0	479.4
2019	B	4.10	3.42	8,997.8	5,332.1	9,237.2	905.3
2018	B-	3.93	3.28	8,990.4	4,933.2	9,086.6	559.5
2017	C	3.77	3.14	8,489.0	4,251.6	8,146.4	295.2
2016	C	3.17	2.64	7,543.7	3,432.5	7,899.3	-226.1
2015	C+	3.36	2.80	7,488.3	3,171.7	7,502.7	-344.3

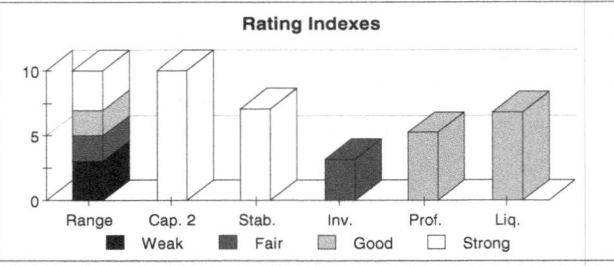

Rating Indexes

BLUE CROSS BLUE SHIELD OF MINNESOTA — C — Fair

Major Rating Factors: Fair profitability index (3.4 on a scale of 0 to 10). Fair quality investment portfolio (3.7). Good liquidity (6.8) with sufficient resources (cash flows and marketable investments) to handle a spike in claims.
Other Rating Factors: Strong capitalization (10.0) based on excellent current risk-adjusted capital (severe loss scenario).
Principal Business: Comp med (36%), Medicare (26%), FEHB (17%), med supp (12%), other (9%)
Mem Phys: 19: 54,719 **18:** 53,676 **19 MLR** 86.5% **/ 19 Admin Exp** N/A
Enroll(000): Q2 20: 778 **19:** 798 **18:** 812 **Med Exp PMPM:** $351
Principal Investments: Long-term bonds (48%), nonaffiliate common stock (17%), affiliate common stock (3%), cash and equiv (1%), other (32%)
Provider Compensation ($000): Contr fee ($1,669,567), bonus arrang ($1,254,073), FFS ($316,858), other ($80,636)
Total Member Encounters: Phys (4,645,095), non-phys (1,734,372)
Group Affiliation: Aware Integrated Inc
Licensed in: MN
Address: 3535 Blue Cross Road, Eagan, MN 55122
Phone: (651) 662-8000 **Dom State:** MN **Commenced Bus:** N/A

Data Date	Rating	RACR #1	RACR #2	Total Assets ($mil)	Capital ($mil)	Net Premium ($mil)	Net Income ($mil)
6-20	C	4.17	3.47	3,037.6	1,227.2	1,890.0	200.1
6-19	C+	3.95	3.29	2,856.9	1,182.3	1,920.3	90.0
2019	C	3.65	3.04	2,919.6	1,071.5	3,866.5	-77.0
2018	C	3.47	2.89	2,582.2	1,034.5	3,956.2	36.6
2017	C	3.97	3.31	2,454.4	1,043.9	3,655.8	-12.0
2016	C	2.58	2.15	2,544.3	990.5	3,938.7	-103.5
2015	C+	3.69	3.07	2,751.4	1,100.7	3,762.9	-178.4

Rating Indexes

BLUE CROSS BLUE SHIELD OF MS, MUTUAL *   A   Excellent

Major Rating Factors: Strong capitalization (10.0 on a scale of 0 to 10) based on excellent current risk-adjusted capital (severe loss scenario). High quality investment portfolio (7.2). Good overall profitability index (5.7).
Other Rating Factors: Good liquidity (6.8) with sufficient resources (cash flows and marketable investments) to handle a spike in claims.
Principal Business: Comp med (72%), FEHB (25%), med supp (2%)
Mem Phys: 19: 13,948 **18:** 13,297 **19 MLR** 90.0% **/ 19 Admin Exp** N/A
Enroll(000): Q2 20: 613 **19:** 625 **18:** 627 **Med Exp PMPM:** $168
Principal Investments: Long-term bonds (74%), cash and equiv (8%), affiliate common stock (7%), nonaffiliate common stock (6%), real estate (4%)
Provider Compensation ($000): Contr fee ($1,233,065), FFS ($24,394), bonus arrang ($673)
Total Member Encounters: Phys (2,150,374), non-phys (1,816,071)
Group Affiliation: Blue Cross & Blue Shield of Mississi
Licensed in: MS
Address: 3545 Lakeland Drive, Flowood, MS 39232
Phone: (601) 664-4590 **Dom State:** MS **Commenced Bus:** N/A

Data Date	Rating	RACR #1	RACR #2	Total Assets ($mil)	Capital ($mil)	Net Premium ($mil)	Net Income ($mil)
6-20	A	8.51	7.09	1,156.0	737.2	700.9	27.6
6-19	A	8.52	7.10	1,040.6	704.3	672.2	17.0
2019	A	8.25	6.87	1,064.4	704.8	1,403.0	20.1
2018	A	8.09	6.74	1,000.6	676.7	1,374.7	43.2
2017	A-	7.67	6.40	962.1	627.6	1,359.3	49.7
2016	B	7.35	6.12	899.1	597.3	1,334.1	23.6
2015	B+	7.65	6.38	877.5	583.6	1,287.2	13.6

Rating Indexes

BLUE CROSS BLUE SHIELD OF NC *   B+   Good

Major Rating Factors: Good quality investment portfolio (5.7 on a scale of 0 to 10). Good liquidity (6.7) with sufficient resources (cash flows and marketable investments) to handle a spike in claims. Excellent profitability (7.8).
Other Rating Factors: Strong capitalization (10.0) based on excellent current risk-adjusted capital (severe loss scenario).
Principal Business: Comp med (69%), FEHB (14%), Medicare (8%), med supp (4%), other (2%)
Mem Phys: 19: 68,307 **18:** 63,002 **19 MLR** 81.8% **/ 19 Admin Exp** N/A
Enroll(000): Q2 20: 1,701 **19:** 1,635 **18:** 1,580 **Med Exp PMPM:** $372
Principal Investments: Long-term bonds (63%), nonaffiliate common stock (15%), affiliate common stock (5%), pref stock (4%), other (13%)
Provider Compensation ($000): Contr fee ($4,921,694), FFS ($2,284,690), bonus arrang ($33,160), capitation ($32,256)
Total Member Encounters: Phys (8,278,566)
Group Affiliation: None
Licensed in: NC
Address: 4705 University Drive Buildin, Durham, NC 27707-3460
Phone: (919) 489-7431 **Dom State:** NC **Commenced Bus:** N/A

Data Date	Rating	RACR #1	RACR #2	Total Assets ($mil)	Capital ($mil)	Net Premium ($mil)	Net Income ($mil)
6-20	B+	6.33	5.27	6,502.9	4,078.3	4,429.3	364.5
6-19	B+	6.98	5.82	6,166.3	3,976.9	4,515.2	469.3
2019	B+	5.98	4.98	6,296.6	3,850.6	8,989.7	365.9
2018	B+	6.01	5.00	5,707.6	3,416.5	9,140.7	650.4
2017	B	5.45	4.54	5,210.5	2,954.5	8,732.1	699.6
2016	B-	4.85	4.04	4,110.2	2,210.5	7,189.0	272.0
2015	B-	4.16	3.47	4,102.7	2,067.1	7,457.1	-5.7

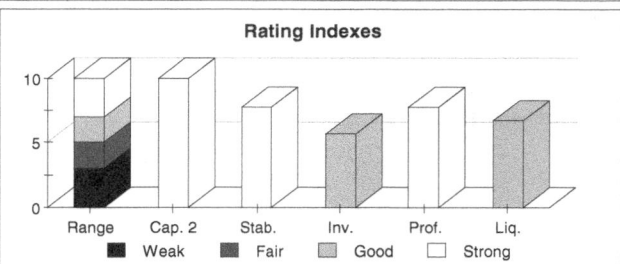

Rating Indexes

BLUE CROSS BLUE SHIELD OF ND   B   Good

Major Rating Factors: Good liquidity (6.8 on a scale of 0 to 10) with sufficient resources (cash flows and marketable investments) to handle a spike in claims. Fair profitability index (4.2). Fair quality investment portfolio (4.8).
Other Rating Factors: Strong capitalization (9.8) based on excellent current risk-adjusted capital (severe loss scenario).
Principal Business: Comp med (69%), FEHB (11%), med supp (8%), dental (2%), other (10%)
Mem Phys: 19: 8,608 **18:** 7,366 **19 MLR** 88.0% **/ 19 Admin Exp** N/A
Enroll(000): Q2 20: 287 **19:** 311 **18:** 323 **Med Exp PMPM:** $282
Principal Investments: Long-term bonds (58%), nonaffiliate common stock (14%), affiliate common stock (11%), cash and equiv (7%), real estate (3%), other (6%)
Provider Compensation ($000): FFS ($542,298), contr fee ($507,703), bonus arrang ($10,413)
Total Member Encounters: Phys (4,211,268), non-phys (2,134,569)
Group Affiliation: None
Licensed in: MN, ND, SD
Address: 4510 13th Ave S, Fargo, ND 58121
Phone: (701) 282-1523 **Dom State:** ND **Commenced Bus:** N/A

Data Date	Rating	RACR #1	RACR #2	Total Assets ($mil)	Capital ($mil)	Net Premium ($mil)	Net Income ($mil)
6-20	B	3.57	2.98	780.7	472.8	569.4	56.0
6-19	N/A	N/A	N/A	N/A	N/A	N/A	N/A
2019	B	3.33	2.78	765.8	444.8	1,204.6	6.1
2018	B	3.80	3.17	793.6	495.7	1,185.0	-30.5
2017	B	4.61	3.84	798.8	541.2	1,099.3	51.0
2016	B	3.66	3.05	640.5	399.2	1,080.4	70.3
2015	B	2.49	2.07	521.5	302.9	1,243.3	63.8

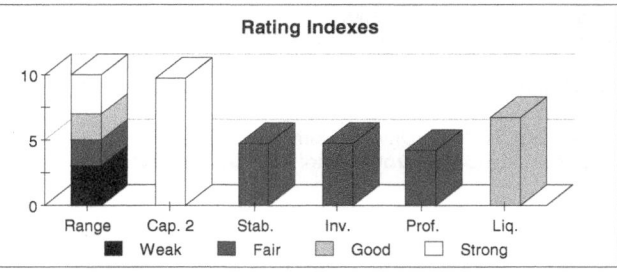

Rating Indexes

BLUE CROSS BLUE SHIELD OF NEBRASKA

B- **Good**

Major Rating Factors: Fair profitability index (4.0 on a scale of 0 to 10). Fair quality investment portfolio (4.8). Good liquidity (6.8) with sufficient resources (cash flows and marketable investments) to handle a spike in claims.
Other Rating Factors: Strong capitalization (10.0) based on excellent current risk-adjusted capital (severe loss scenario).
Principal Business: Comp med (67%), FEHB (17%), med supp (11%), other (5%)
Mem Phys: 19: N/A **18:** N/A **19 MLR** 83.3% **/ 19 Admin Exp** N/A
Enroll(000): Q2 20: 294 **19:** 307 **18:** 325 **Med Exp PMPM:** $352
Principal Investments: Long-term bonds (67%), nonaffiliate common stock (19%), affiliate common stock (4%), cash and equiv (1%), other (9%)
Provider Compensation ($000): Contr fee ($1,347,274), other ($18,297)
Total Member Encounters: Phys (1,447,280), non-phys (61,385)
Group Affiliation: GoodLife Partners Inc
Licensed in: NE
Address: 1919 Aksarben Drive, Omaha, NE 68180
Phone: (402) 982-7000 **Dom State:** NE **Commenced Bus:** N/A

Data Date	Rating	RACR #1	RACR #2	Total Assets ($mil)	Capital ($mil)	Net Premium ($mil)	Net Income ($mil)
6-20	B-	4.67	3.89	945.2	402.0	761.0	20.1
6-19	B-	5.12	4.26	924.6	429.1	751.6	22.0
2019	B-	4.67	3.89	908.9	401.7	1,576.8	0.9
2018	C	4.56	3.80	912.3	387.7	1,601.0	6.3
2017	C	4.28	3.57	943.4	406.5	1,676.9	46.9
2016	C	3.57	2.98	875.3	355.7	1,744.1	-21.6
2015	B-	4.80	4.00	880.3	391.9	1,648.2	-31.5

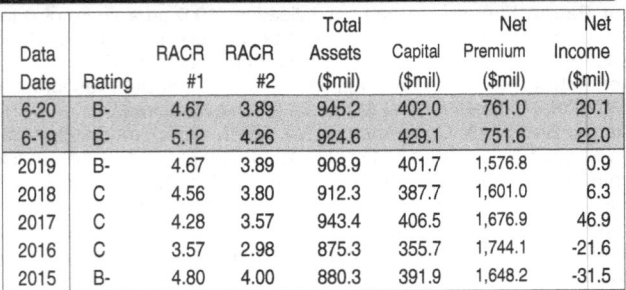

BLUE CROSS BLUE SHIELD OF RI

B **Good**

Major Rating Factors: Fair profitability index (4.1 on a scale of 0 to 10). Strong capitalization (9.0) based on excellent current risk-adjusted capital (severe loss scenario). High quality investment portfolio (7.2).
Other Rating Factors: Excellent liquidity (6.9) with sufficient resources (cash flows and marketable investments) to handle a spike in claims.
Principal Business: Comp med (51%), Medicare (36%), FEHB (7%), med supp (4%), dental (2%), other (1%)
Mem Phys: 19: 4,078 **18:** 4,346 **19 MLR** 84.5% **/ 19 Admin Exp** N/A
Enroll(000): Q2 20: 383 **19:** 384 **18:** 391 **Med Exp PMPM:** $311
Principal Investments: Long-term bonds (67%), nonaffiliate common stock (18%), real estate (7%), cash and equiv (6%), other (3%)
Provider Compensation ($000): Contr fee ($1,394,077), capitation ($1,046)
Total Member Encounters: Phys (1,710,701), non-phys (1,318,631)
Group Affiliation: None
Licensed in: RI
Address: 500 EXCHANGE STREET, PROVIDENCE, RI 2903
Phone: (401) 459-1000 **Dom State:** RI **Commenced Bus:** N/A

Data Date	Rating	RACR #1	RACR #2	Total Assets ($mil)	Capital ($mil)	Net Premium ($mil)	Net Income ($mil)
6-20	B	2.94	2.45	932.3	367.8	843.7	15.6
6-19	N/A	N/A	N/A	N/A	N/A	N/A	N/A
2019	B	2.97	2.47	751.0	371.6	1,698.2	68.8
2018	C	2.37	1.98	638.2	298.7	1,708.9	9.4
2017	C	2.23	1.86	627.2	293.0	1,719.4	22.6
2016	C	2.01	1.68	618.4	266.5	1,714.1	-34.5
2015	C	2.40	2.00	623.7	293.7	1,661.3	-125.9

BLUE CROSS BLUE SHIELD OF SC INC

B **Good**

Major Rating Factors: Fair quality investment portfolio (3.5 on a scale of 0 to 10). Excellent profitability (8.7). Strong capitalization (10.0) based on excellent current risk-adjusted capital (severe loss scenario).
Other Rating Factors: Excellent liquidity (7.1) with ample operational cash flow and liquid investments.
Principal Business: Comp med (74%), FEHB (15%), med supp (4%), dental (3%), Medicare (2%), other (1%)
Mem Phys: 19: 24,683 **18:** 23,112 **19 MLR** 75.9% **/ 19 Admin Exp** N/A
Enroll(000): Q2 20: 1,644 **19:** 1,542 **18:** 1,503 **Med Exp PMPM:** $162
Principal Investments: Long-term bonds (26%), affiliate common stock (20%), nonaffiliate common stock (19%), cash and equiv (11%), real estate (3%), other (20%)
Provider Compensation ($000): Contr fee ($2,728,436), FFS ($242,908), bonus arrang ($21,533), capitation ($1,432), other ($4,735)
Total Member Encounters: Phys (5,490,334), non-phys (2,115,283)
Group Affiliation: None
Licensed in: SC
Address: 2501 Faraway Drive, Columbia, SC 29219
Phone: (803) 788-3860 **Dom State:** SC **Commenced Bus:** N/A

Data Date	Rating	RACR #1	RACR #2	Total Assets ($mil)	Capital ($mil)	Net Premium ($mil)	Net Income ($mil)
6-20	B	6.16	5.13	5,318.1	3,398.6	1,940.8	61.7
6-19	B+	6.30	5.25	4,857.4	3,142.6	1,999.3	153.8
2019	B+	6.18	5.15	5,125.9	3,412.5	3,949.0	275.1
2018	B+	5.90	4.92	4,475.5	2,941.9	3,804.2	261.7
2017	B+	5.67	4.72	4,048.6	2,628.6	3,344.9	79.4
2016	A-	5.56	4.63	3,522.2	2,413.8	2,639.2	59.1
2015	A-	5.88	4.90	3,254.2	2,252.7	2,325.5	76.7

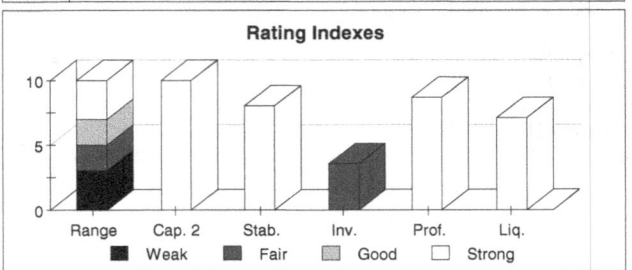

BLUE CROSS BLUE SHIELD OF VERMONT

B-   **Good**

Major Rating Factors: Fair profitability index (4.2 on a scale of 0 to 10). Good quality investment portfolio (5.0). Strong capitalization (8.8) based on excellent current risk-adjusted capital (severe loss scenario).
Other Rating Factors: Excellent liquidity (7.0) with ample operational cash flow and liquid investments.
Principal Business: Comp med (79%), FEHB (17%), med supp (2%), other (1%)
Mem Phys: 19: 8,421 **18:** 8,200 **19 MLR** 92.3% **/ 19 Admin Exp** N/A
Enroll(000): Q2 20: 185 **19:** 197 **18:** 198 **Med Exp PMPM:** $209
Principal Investments: Affiliate common stock (43%), long-term bonds (33%), cash and equiv (17%), real estate (4%), nonaffiliate common stock (3%)
Provider Compensation ($000): FFS ($214,643), contr fee ($181,467), capitation ($2,041), other ($92,762)
Total Member Encounters: Phys (216,730), non-phys (346,580)
Group Affiliation: None
Licensed in: VT
Address: 445 Industrial Lane, Berlin, VT 5602
Phone: (802) 223-6131 **Dom State:** VT **Commenced Bus:** N/A

Data Date	Rating	RACR #1	RACR #2	Total Assets ($mil)	Capital ($mil)	Net Premium ($mil)	Net Income ($mil)
6-20	B-	2.84	2.36	309.4	157.7	243.1	40.0
6-19	C+	2.29	1.91	289.2	119.1	275.8	11.5
2019	C+	2.43	2.02	294.6	133.5	537.7	13.4
2018	C+	2.12	1.77	257.6	110.2	517.4	-6.7
2017	B	2.36	1.96	288.3	134.1	578.3	7.6
2016	B	2.52	2.10	285.4	135.3	547.3	-9.7
2015	B+	2.81	2.34	266.6	148.4	539.9	12.2

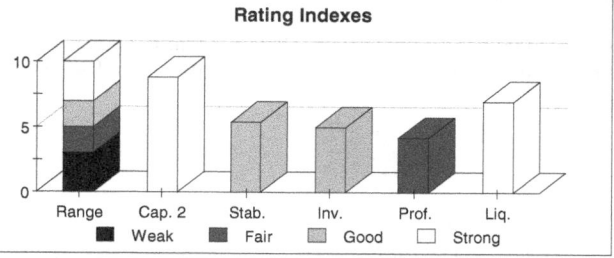

Rating Indexes

BLUE CROSS BLUE SHIELD OF WISCONSIN

B-   **Good**

Major Rating Factors: Fair quality investment portfolio (3.7 on a scale of 0 to 10). Good liquidity (6.5) with sufficient resources (cash flows and marketable investments) to handle a spike in claims. Excellent profitability (9.1).
Other Rating Factors: Strong capitalization (8.6) based on excellent current risk-adjusted capital (severe loss scenario).
Principal Business: FEHB (55%), comp med (26%), med supp (8%), dental (2%), other (8%)
Mem Phys: 19: 43,495 **18:** 44,905 **19 MLR** 112.1% **/ 19 Admin Exp** N/A
Enroll(000): Q2 20: 408 **19:** 400 **18:** 414 **Med Exp PMPM:** $169
Principal Investments: Affiliate common stock (55%), long-term bonds (46%), real estate (1%)
Provider Compensation ($000): Bonus arrang ($492,951), contr fee ($245,368), FFS ($31,993), other ($37,394)
Total Member Encounters: Phys (784,872), non-phys (808,386)
Group Affiliation: Anthem Inc
Licensed in: WI
Address: N17 W24340 RIVERWOOD DRIVE, WAUKESHA, WI 53188
Phone: (262) 523-4020 **Dom State:** WI **Commenced Bus:** N/A

Data Date	Rating	RACR #1	RACR #2	Total Assets ($mil)	Capital ($mil)	Net Premium ($mil)	Net Income ($mil)
6-20	B-	2.65	2.21	643.4	377.1	348.7	45.9
6-19	B-	4.35	3.63	638.6	382.0	358.8	51.8
2019	B-	2.65	2.21	560.4	289.3	727.3	112.2
2018	B-	3.47	2.89	565.5	302.8	726.9	123.0
2017	B-	2.58	2.15	576.6	276.7	769.1	92.8
2016	B-	3.01	2.50	544.6	260.5	758.6	81.2
2015	B-	2.56	2.13	463.8	206.4	735.1	78.6

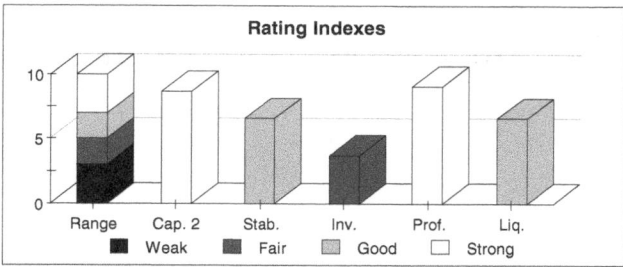

Rating Indexes

BLUE CROSS BLUE SHIELD OF WYOMING

B-   **Good**

Major Rating Factors: Fair quality investment portfolio (3.4 on a scale of 0 to 10). Good overall profitability index (6.0). Strong capitalization (10.0) based on excellent current risk-adjusted capital (severe loss scenario).
Other Rating Factors: Excellent liquidity (7.0) with sufficient resources (cash flows and marketable investments) to handle a spike in claims.
Principal Business: Comp med (76%), FEHB (19%), med supp (4%)
Mem Phys: 19: 5,042 **18:** 4,561 **19 MLR** 81.0% **/ 19 Admin Exp** N/A
Enroll(000): Q2 20: 89 **19:** 87 **18:** 89 **Med Exp PMPM:** $467
Principal Investments: Nonaffiliate common stock (44%), long-term bonds (39%), cash and equiv (7%), real estate (1%), other (9%)
Provider Compensation ($000): FFS ($462,430), contr fee ($33,134), bonus arrang ($50), other ($343)
Total Member Encounters: Phys (1,344,766), non-phys (1,045,222)
Group Affiliation: None
Licensed in: WY
Address: 4000 HOUSE AVENUE, CHEYENNE, WY 82001
Phone: (307) 634-1393 **Dom State:** WY **Commenced Bus:** N/A

Data Date	Rating	RACR #1	RACR #2	Total Assets ($mil)	Capital ($mil)	Net Premium ($mil)	Net Income ($mil)
6-20	B-	5.91	4.93	652.9	428.9	308.2	43.3
6-19	N/A	N/A	N/A	N/A	N/A	N/A	N/A
2019	B-	5.51	4.59	641.1	403.2	611.5	31.1
2018	B-	5.28	4.40	547.8	335.4	612.2	40.5
2017	B-	5.07	4.22	525.8	315.9	484.0	23.4
2016	B	4.91	4.09	481.1	276.4	467.8	-15.1
2015	B	6.13	5.11	437.3	275.1	369.1	20.1

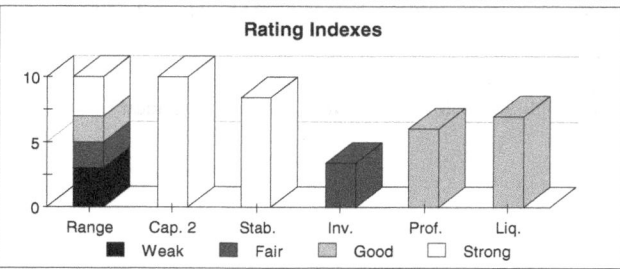

Rating Indexes

BLUE CROSS COMPLETE OF MICHIGAN *   B+   Good

Major Rating Factors: Excellent profitability (7.8 on a scale of 0 to 10). Strong capitalization (8.4) based on excellent current risk-adjusted capital (severe loss scenario). High quality investment portfolio (9.9).
Other Rating Factors: Excellent liquidity (7.3) with ample operational cash flow and liquid investments.
Principal Business: Medicaid (100%)
Mem Phys: 19: 40,382 **18:** 29,230 **19 MLR** 78.6% **/ 19 Admin Exp** N/A
Enroll(000): Q2 20: 250 **19:** 210 **18:** 210 **Med Exp PMPM:** $257
Principal Investments: Cash and equiv (91%), long-term bonds (9%)
Provider Compensation ($000): Contr fee ($615,546), capitation ($14,856), bonus arrang ($2,751)
Total Member Encounters: Phys (1,539,616), non-phys (273,798)
Group Affiliation: None
Licensed in: MI
Address: 4000 Town Center Suite 1300, Southfield, MI 48075
Phone: (215) 937-8000 **Dom State:** MI **Commenced Bus:** N/A

Data Date	Rating	RACR #1	RACR #2	Total Assets ($mil)	Capital ($mil)	Net Premium ($mil)	Net Income ($mil)
6-20	B+	2.47	2.06	355.7	147.6	445.6	24.1
6-19	B	3.08	2.56	293.4	120.8	406.4	13.6
2019	B+	2.93	2.44	306.3	123.1	819.1	19.7
2018	B	2.74	2.28	271.1	106.6	755.9	31.4
2017	E	1.12	0.93	229.9	74.9	884.8	17.1
2016	E	1.46	1.22	154.9	47.9	709.4	10.8
2015	E	1.95	1.63	115.5	37.9	418.5	-1.2

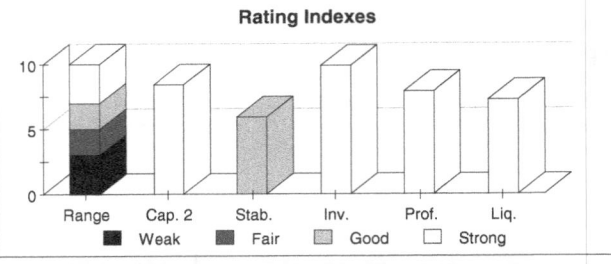

BLUE CROSS OF CALIFORNIA *   A+   Excellent

Major Rating Factors: Excellent profitability (9.1 on a scale of 0 to 10). Strong capitalization index (8.7) based on excellent current risk-adjusted capital (severe loss scenario). Excellent overall results on stability tests (7.8).
Other Rating Factors: Excellent liquidity (7.3) with ample operational cash flow and liquid investments.
Principal Business: Medicaid (22%), Medicare (11%)
Mem Phys: 19: N/A **18:** N/A **19 MLR** 84.2% **/ 19 Admin Exp** N/A
Enroll(000): Q2 20: 3,571 **19:** 3,552 **18:** 3,552 **Med Exp PMPM:** $327
Principal Investments ($000): Cash and equiv ($3,380,506)
Provider Compensation ($000): None
Total Member Encounters: N/A
Group Affiliation: Anthem Inc
Licensed in: CA
Address: 1 Wellpoint Way, Thousand Oaks, CA 91362
Phone: (916) 403-0526 **Dom State:** CA **Commenced Bus:** July 1982

Data Date	Rating	RACR #1	RACR #2	Total Assets ($mil)	Capital ($mil)	Net Premium ($mil)	Net Income ($mil)
6-20	A+	3.58	2.27	7,804.6	3,444.9	8,325.0	541.6
6-19	A+	3.79	2.41	7,704.6	3,302.7	8,208.3	550.8
2019	A+	3.44	2.18	7,473.0	3,268.3	16,500.9	853.9
2018	A+	3.52	2.24	7,154.9	3,043.0	15,774.6	773.4
2017	A+	3.18	2.02	7,871.8	2,819.6	16,792.3	993.3
2016	A+	2.62	1.65	7,350.6	2,109.1	16,650.0	710.4
2015	A+	2.49	1.57	6,611.5	1,801.2	14,977.4	502.0

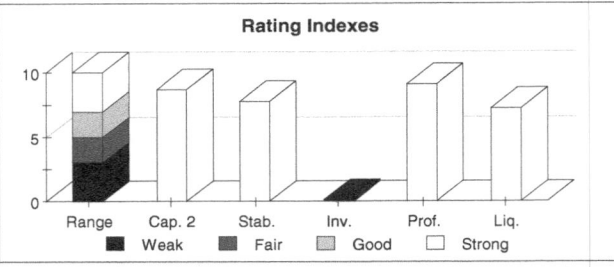

BLUE CROSS OF IDAHO CARE PLUS INC   B   Good

Major Rating Factors: Good overall profitability index (5.1 on a scale of 0 to 10). Good liquidity (6.2) with sufficient resources (cash flows and marketable investments) to handle a spike in claims. Strong capitalization (7.1) based on excellent current risk-adjusted capital (severe loss scenario).
Other Rating Factors: High quality investment portfolio (9.1).
Principal Business: Medicare (71%), Medicaid (28%), med supp (1%)
Mem Phys: 19: 8,355 **18:** 9,068 **19 MLR** 88.7% **/ 19 Admin Exp** N/A
Enroll(000): Q2 20: 51 **19:** 44 **18:** 29 **Med Exp PMPM:** $999
Principal Investments: Long-term bonds (71%), nonaffiliate common stock (17%), cash and equiv (8%), pref stock (1%), other (2%)
Provider Compensation ($000): Contr fee ($267,443), bonus arrang ($179,423), capitation ($497)
Total Member Encounters: Phys (428,855), non-phys (722,194)
Group Affiliation: Blue Cross of Idaho Health Service I
Licensed in: ID
Address: 3000 E Pine Ave, Meridian, ID 83642
Phone: (208) 345-4550 **Dom State:** ID **Commenced Bus:** N/A

Data Date	Rating	RACR #1	RACR #2	Total Assets ($mil)	Capital ($mil)	Net Premium ($mil)	Net Income ($mil)
6-20	B	1.45	1.21	231.5	96.2	351.1	27.1
6-19	C+	2.20	1.83	169.8	79.0	241.4	1.9
2019	B	1.25	1.05	181.8	73.3	534.1	-2.8
2018	C+	2.08	1.73	147.5	76.7	349.5	1.0
2017	C	N/A	N/A	144.9	78.0	305.7	17.5
2016	C	1.42	1.18	123.3	59.6	320.4	13.3
2015	C+	1.00	0.83	97.8	48.1	325.4	-5.7

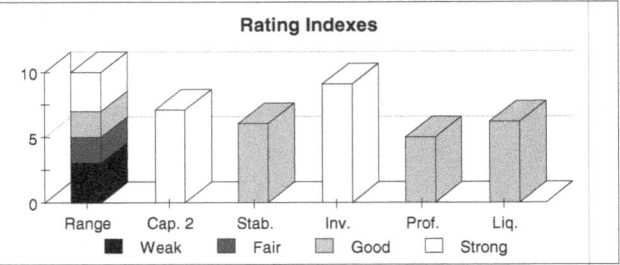

BLUE CROSS OF IDAHO HEALTH SERVICE *   B+   Good

Major Rating Factors: Good overall profitability index (6.1 on a scale of 0 to 10). Good quality investment portfolio (6.3). Good liquidity (6.8) with sufficient resources (cash flows and marketable investments) to handle a spike in claims. **Other Rating Factors:** Strong capitalization (10.0) based on excellent current risk-adjusted capital (severe loss scenario).
Principal Business: Comp med (79%), FEHB (15%), dental (3%), med supp (1%), other (3%)
Mem Phys: 19: 14,998 **18:** 15,349 **19 MLR** 86.1% **/ 19 Admin Exp** N/A
Enroll(000): Q2 20: 250 **19:** 260 **18:** 264 **Med Exp PMPM:** $353
Principal Investments: Long-term bonds (55%), nonaffiliate common stock (27%), cash and equiv (4%), real estate (3%), other (10%)
Provider Compensation ($000): Contr fee ($647,452), bonus arrang ($432,568), capitation ($6,300)
Total Member Encounters: Phys (1,551,852), non-phys (1,439,624)
Group Affiliation: Blue Cross of Idaho Health Service I
Licensed in: ID
Address: 3000 E Pine Ave, Meridian, ID 83642
Phone: (208) 345-4550 **Dom State:** ID **Commenced Bus:** N/A

Data Date	Rating	RACR #1	RACR #2	Total Assets ($mil)	Capital ($mil)	Net Premium ($mil)	Net Income ($mil)
6-20	B+	6.07	5.06	1,144.5	688.2	634.2	37.2
6-19	B	6.66	5.55	986.1	657.7	651.3	41.2
2019	B+	5.91	4.93	1,036.1	658.1	1,290.4	13.8
2018	B	6.34	5.28	937.4	632.9	1,244.2	48.5
2017	B	6.75	5.62	896.6	600.5	1,063.6	79.8
2016	B	5.47	4.56	770.1	486.6	1,173.6	11.0
2015	B	4.92	4.10	758.1	458.5	1,202.5	-3.1

Rating Indexes

BLUE SHIELD OF CALIFORNIA L&H INS CO   B   Good

Major Rating Factors: Good overall profitability (6.1 on a scale of 0 to 10). Excellent expense controls. Return on equity has been fair, averaging 8.7%. Good liquidity (6.7) with sufficient resources to handle a spike in claims. Fair overall results on stability tests (4.9).
Other Rating Factors: Strong capitalization (10.0) based on excellent risk adjusted capital (severe loss scenario). High quality investment portfolio (8.1).
Principal Business: Individual health insurance (55%), group health insurance (41%), and group life insurance (4%).
Principal Investments: CMOs and structured securities (53%), nonCMO investment grade bonds (38%), and cash (1%).
Investments in Affiliates: None
Group Affiliation: Blue Shield of California
Licensed in: CA
Commenced Business: July 1954
Address: 50 Beale Street, Oakland, CA 94607
Phone: (800) 642-5599 **Domicile State:** CA **NAIC Code:** 61557

Data Date	Rating	RACR #1	RACR #2	Total Assets ($mil)	Capital ($mil)	Net Premium ($mil)	Net Income ($mil)
6-20	B	4.29	3.24	289.7	157.7	123.0	21.8
6-19	B	3.69	2.72	322.1	139.9	123.4	12.9
2019	B	3.73	2.83	253.9	135.2	242.3	9.1
2018	B	5.09	3.75	303.2	191.1	242.3	12.4
2017	B	4.61	3.41	303.5	179.2	253.4	9.7
2016	B	5.28	4.03	463.6	323.0	310.2	22.9
2015	B	2.98	2.37	665.2	481.1	1,249.2	39.5

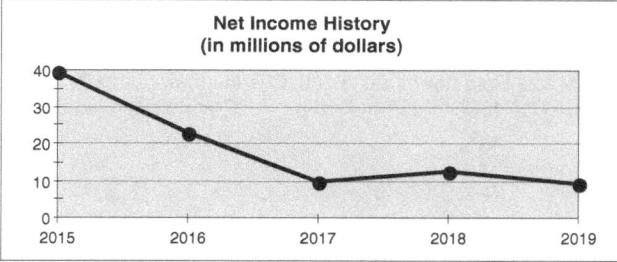

Net Income History
(in millions of dollars)

BLUECHOICE HEALTHPLAN OF SC INC   B   Good

Major Rating Factors: Good quality investment portfolio (6.6 on a scale of 0 to 10). Good overall results on stability tests (6.0). Good liquidity (6.1) with sufficient resources (cash flows and marketable investments) to handle a spike in claims.
Other Rating Factors: Fair profitability index (4.8). Strong capitalization index (10.0) based on excellent current risk-adjusted capital (severe loss scenario).
Principal Business: Comp med (65%), Medicaid (34%)
Mem Phys: 19: 26,891 **18:** 24,823 **19 MLR** 119.8% **/ 19 Admin Exp** N/A
Enroll(000): Q2 20: 222 **19:** 217 **18:** 188 **Med Exp PMPM:** $324
Principal Investments: Long-term bonds (61%), cash and equiv (21%), nonaffiliate common stock (13%), affiliate common stock (5%)
Provider Compensation ($000): Contr fee ($680,139), bonus arrang ($107,261), FFS ($2,171), capitation ($2,124)
Total Member Encounters: Phys (1,312,105), non-phys (631,273)
Group Affiliation: None
Licensed in: SC
Address: I-20 at Alpine Road, Columbia,
Phone: (803) 786-8466 **Dom State:** SC **Commenced Bus:** N/A

Data Date	Rating	RACR #1	RACR #2	Total Assets ($mil)	Capital ($mil)	Net Premium ($mil)	Net Income ($mil)
6-20	B	5.32	4.43	472.2	279.2	355.0	2.7
6-19	B	7.63	6.36	401.4	263.0	326.4	8.6
2019	B	7.26	6.05	425.0	284.1	666.1	27.0
2018	B	7.21	6.01	368.7	247.6	609.8	19.8
2017	B	5.62	4.69	352.6	231.4	562.6	29.6
2016	B	3.36	2.80	346.9	197.9	969.9	-23.4
2015	A	5.95	4.96	347.4	225.4	664.4	14.4

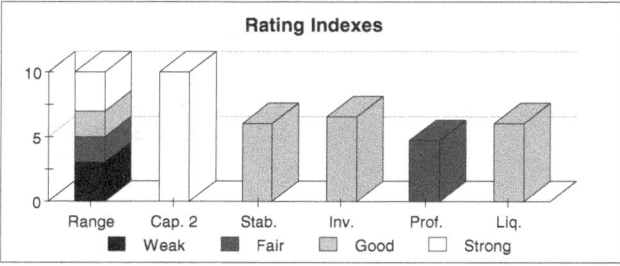

Rating Indexes

BLUECROSS BLUESHIELD OF TENNESSEE *

A-   Excellent

Major Rating Factors: Strong capitalization (10.0 on a scale of 0 to 10) based on excellent current risk-adjusted capital (severe loss scenario). Excellent liquidity (7.0) with ample operational cash flow and liquid investments. Good overall profitability index (6.7).
Other Rating Factors: Good quality investment portfolio (6.7).
Principal Business: Comp med (52%), Medicare (27%), FEHB (15%), dental (3%), med supp (3%)
Mem Phys: 19: 35,273 **18:** 33,337   **19 MLR** 84.1% **/ 19 Admin Exp** N/A
Enroll(000): Q2 20: 1,769 **19:** 1,771 **18:** 1,700 **Med Exp PMPM:** $204
Principal Investments: Long-term bonds (53%), nonaffiliate common stock (16%), affiliate common stock (14%), cash and equiv (10%), pref stock (2%), real estate (1%), other (5%)
Provider Compensation ($000): Contr fee ($3,351,521), FFS ($916,510), capitation ($19,546), bonus arrang ($7,948)
Total Member Encounters: Phys (10,493,099), non-phys (1,730,789)
Group Affiliation: BlueCross BlueShield of Tennessee In
Licensed in: TN
Address: 1 Cameron Hill Circle, Chattanooga, TN 37402-0001
Phone: (423) 535-5600 **Dom State:** TN **Commenced Bus:** N/A

Data Date	Rating	RACR #1	RACR #2	Total Assets ($mil)	Capital ($mil)	Net Premium ($mil)	Net Income ($mil)
6-20	A-	6.97	5.81	5,279.4	3,718.9	2,630.3	162.4
6-19	B+	7.34	6.12	4,534.2	3,528.8	2,590.0	218.6
2019	A-	6.80	5.66	4,674.1	3,628.1	5,130.7	227.5
2018	B+	6.54	5.45	3,995.9	3,139.3	5,411.3	679.2
2017	B	7.98	6.65	2,927.1	2,139.9	4,631.7	322.4
2016	B	6.32	5.27	2,556.7	1,733.5	4,739.9	2.4
2015	B+	6.19	5.16	2,465.5	1,678.6	4,525.2	-101.9

BOSTON MEDICAL CENTER HEALTH PLAN

B-   Good

Major Rating Factors: Fair profitability index (4.0 on a scale of 0 to 10). Good liquidity (6.9) with sufficient resources (cash flows and marketable investments) to handle a spike in claims. Strong capitalization (7.6) based on excellent current risk-adjusted capital (severe loss scenario).
Other Rating Factors: High quality investment portfolio (8.4).
Principal Business: Medicaid (85%), comp med (13%), Medicare (2%)
Mem Phys: 19: 54,170 **18:** 44,968 **19 MLR** 94.4% **/ 19 Admin Exp** N/A
Enroll(000): Q2 20: 405 **19:** 400 **18:** 395 **Med Exp PMPM:** $513
Principal Investments: Long-term bonds (53%), cash and equiv (33%), nonaffiliate common stock (14%)
Provider Compensation ($000): Contr fee ($2,237,902), capitation ($219,608), bonus arrang ($5,211)
Total Member Encounters: Phys (4,316,570), non-phys (9,513,583)
Group Affiliation: BMC Health System Inc
Licensed in: MA, NH
Address: 529 Main Street Suite 500, Charlestown, MA 2129
Phone: (617) 748-6000 **Dom State:** MA **Commenced Bus:** N/A

Data Date	Rating	RACR #1	RACR #2	Total Assets ($mil)	Capital ($mil)	Net Premium ($mil)	Net Income ($mil)
6-20	B-	1.80	1.50	662.9	394.6	1,340.8	73.7
6-19	N/A	N/A	N/A	N/A	N/A	N/A	N/A
2019	C	1.43	1.19	657.6	320.1	2,667.1	-6.4
2018	C	1.11	0.93	474.5	217.4	2,297.2	-17.5
2017	B-	N/A	N/A	463.5	233.2	1,618.5	-1.9
2016	B-	1.91	1.59	471.3	236.2	1,574.5	-4.5
2015	B-	2.12	1.77	459.4	253.6	1,564.1	47.8

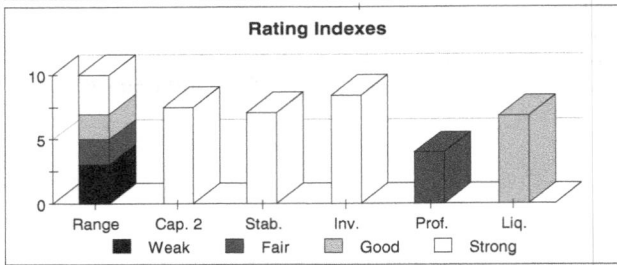

BRAVO HEALTH MID-ATLANTIC INC

B   Good

Major Rating Factors: Good overall profitability index (5.1 on a scale of 0 to 10). Good overall results on stability tests (5.3). Good liquidity (6.8) with sufficient resources (cash flows and marketable investments) to handle a spike in claims.
Other Rating Factors: Strong capitalization index (8.2) based on excellent current risk-adjusted capital (severe loss scenario). High quality investment portfolio (8.5).
Principal Business: Medicare (100%)
Mem Phys: 19: 12,190 **18:** 9,209 **19 MLR** 86.1% **/ 19 Admin Exp** N/A
Enroll(000): Q2 20: 15 **19:** 17 **18:** 18 **Med Exp PMPM:** $1,148
Principal Investments: Long-term bonds (69%), cash and equiv (31%)
Provider Compensation ($000): Contr fee ($191,962), capitation ($48,340), salary ($2,188), bonus arrang ($755), other ($4,702)
Total Member Encounters: Phys (172,763), non-phys (10,371)
Group Affiliation: None
Licensed in: DC, DE, MD
Address: 3601 ODONNELL STREET, BALTIMORE,
Phone: (800) 235-9188 **Dom State:** MD **Commenced Bus:** N/A

Data Date	Rating	RACR #1	RACR #2	Total Assets ($mil)	Capital ($mil)	Net Premium ($mil)	Net Income ($mil)
6-20	B	2.30	1.92	95.9	57.8	128.6	10.9
6-19	C	2.62	2.18	77.3	40.0	146.2	4.5
2019	B-	2.98	2.48	81.1	46.7	278.6	11.8
2018	C	1.86	1.55	73.0	27.9	259.1	7.9
2017	C	1.07	0.89	77.4	24.2	222.3	-18.4
2016	C+	2.19	1.82	80.6	35.6	279.3	-1.4
2015	B-	2.50	2.08	94.2	38.1	288.2	3.4

BRAVO HEALTH PENNSYLVANIA INC

B   Good

Major Rating Factors: Good overall profitability index (5.3 on a scale of 0 to 10). Good quality investment portfolio (6.7). Good liquidity (6.8) with sufficient resources (cash flows and marketable investments) to handle a spike in claims.
Other Rating Factors: Strong capitalization (8.2) based on excellent current risk-adjusted capital (severe loss scenario).
Principal Business: Medicare (100%)
Mem Phys: 19: 20,969 **18:** 19,494 **19 MLR** 84.1% **/ 19 Admin Exp** N/A
Enroll(000): Q2 20: 51 **19:** 46 **18:** 42 **Med Exp PMPM:** $1,095
Principal Investments: Long-term bonds (78%), cash and equiv (22%)
Provider Compensation ($000): Contr fee ($419,753), capitation ($134,124), bonus arrang ($2,566), salary ($2,315), other ($34,617)
Total Member Encounters: Phys (464,391), non-phys (24,142)
Group Affiliation: None
Licensed in: NJ, PA
Address: 1601 CHESTNUT STREET LP16L 2, PHILADELPHIA, PA 19192-4071
Phone: (800) 235-9188 **Dom State:** PA **Commenced Bus:** N/A

Data Date	Rating	RACR #1	RACR #2	Total Assets ($mil)	Capital ($mil)	Net Premium ($mil)	Net Income ($mil)
6-20	B	2.29	1.91	227.2	119.6	401.8	12.6
6-19	C+	3.73	3.11	197.6	116.1	359.8	9.1
2019	B	2.99	2.49	196.5	109.8	710.3	23.3
2018	C+	3.25	2.71	186.3	100.7	622.9	24.4
2017	B	3.33	2.78	236.9	149.8	596.7	9.8
2016	B	3.63	3.03	246.7	143.4	721.7	-4.8
2015	B	3.27	2.72	244.3	149.1	776.2	20.8

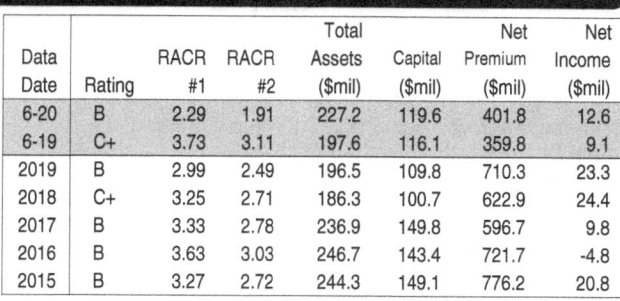

Rating Indexes

BRIDGESPAN HEALTH CO

B   Good

Major Rating Factors: Fair overall results on stability tests (4.6 on a scale of 0 to 10). Strong capitalization index (10.0) based on excellent current risk-adjusted capital (severe loss scenario). High quality investment portfolio (9.4).
Other Rating Factors: Excellent liquidity (7.9) with ample operational cash flow and liquid investments. Weak profitability index (2.3).
Principal Business: Comp med (97%), med supp (3%)
Mem Phys: 19: N/A **18:** N/A **19 MLR** 90.2% **/ 19 Admin Exp** N/A
Enroll(000): Q2 20: 5 **19:** 2 **18:** 2 **Med Exp PMPM:** $632
Principal Investments: Long-term bonds (85%), cash and equiv (15%)
Provider Compensation ($000): Contr fee ($8,586), bonus arrang ($2,630), FFS ($342)
Total Member Encounters: Phys (17,794), non-phys (23,159)
Group Affiliation: Cambia Health Solutions Inc
Licensed in: ID, OR, UT, WA
Address: 2890 EAST COTTONWOOD PARKWAY, SALT LAKE CITY,
Phone: (801) 333-2000 **Dom State:** UT **Commenced Bus:** N/A

Data Date	Rating	RACR #1	RACR #2	Total Assets ($mil)	Capital ($mil)	Net Premium ($mil)	Net Income ($mil)
6-20	B	14.72	12.27	49.0	36.0	14.8	-1.3
6-19	B	28.61	23.84	46.1	39.1	7.8	1.9
2019	B	26.05	21.71	44.8	38.0	15.6	1.0
2018	B	27.38	22.82	42.9	37.3	16.2	9.1
2017	E	1.33	1.11	68.0	27.3	183.8	-0.4
2016	E	5.71	4.76	50.1	23.9	61.3	3.5
2015	E	3.06	2.55	45.1	19.6	67.9	-18.7

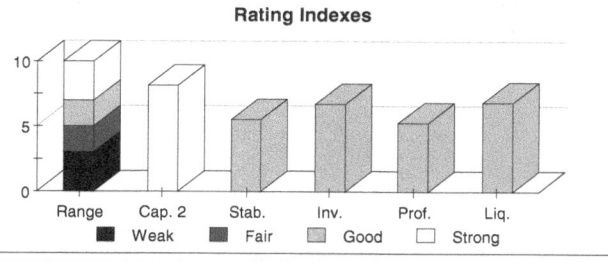

Rating Indexes

BRIDGEWAY HEALTH SOL OF AZ

D+   Weak

Major Rating Factors: Weak liquidity (0.0 on a scale of 0 to 10) as a spike in claims may stretch capacity. Excellent profitability (9.8). Strong capitalization (7.0) based on excellent current risk-adjusted capital (severe loss scenario).
Other Rating Factors: High quality investment portfolio (8.1).
Principal Business: Medicare (99%)
Mem Phys: 19: 49,092 **18:** 23,366 **19 MLR** 86.7% **/ 19 Admin Exp** N/A
Enroll(000): Q2 20: 12 **19:** 9 **18:** 1 **Med Exp PMPM:** $1,079
Principal Investments: Long-term bonds (53%), cash and equiv (47%)
Provider Compensation ($000): Contr fee ($67,731), capitation ($9,249), salary ($1,232)
Total Member Encounters: Phys (120,269), non-phys (30,486)
Group Affiliation: None
Licensed in: AZ
Address: 1870 West Rio Salado Parkway, Tempe, AZ 85281
Phone: (314) 725-4477 **Dom State:** AZ **Commenced Bus:** N/A

Data Date	Rating	RACR #1	RACR #2	Total Assets ($mil)	Capital ($mil)	Net Premium ($mil)	Net Income ($mil)
6-20	D+	1.32	1.10	53.1	15.0	80.4	0.8
6-19	C	13.94	11.62	30.0	12.8	47.4	3.5
2019	C	1.63	1.35	33.3	9.9	111.8	1.2
2018	C-	11.57	9.64	17.1	9.7	13.8	4.1
2017	N/A	N/A	N/A	N/A	N/A	N/A	N/A
2016	N/A	N/A	N/A	N/A	N/A	N/A	N/A
2015	N/A	N/A	N/A	N/A	N/A	N/A	N/A

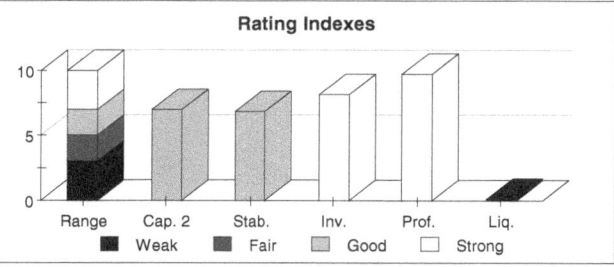

Rating Indexes

BRIGHT HEALTH CO OF ARIZONA   D   Weak

Major Rating Factors: Weak profitability index (0.9 on a scale of 0 to 10). Good liquidity (6.8) with sufficient resources (cash flows and marketable investments) to handle a spike in claims. Strong capitalization (10.0) based on excellent current risk-adjusted capital (severe loss scenario).
Other Rating Factors: High quality investment portfolio (9.8).
Principal Business: Medicare (100%)
Mem Phys: 18: 4,282 **17:** N/A **18 MLR** 84.6% **/ 18 Admin Exp** N/A
Enroll(000): Q3 19: 15 **18:** 1 **17:** N/A **Med Exp PMPM:** $614
Principal Investments: Cash and equiv (61%), long-term bonds (39%)
Provider Compensation ($000): Contr fee ($4,765), FFS ($1,782), capitation ($258)
Total Member Encounters: Phys (48,506), non-phys (13,640)
Group Affiliation: Bright Health Inc
Licensed in: AZ
Address: 4222 E THOMAS ROAD SUITE 402, PHOENIX, AZ 85018
Phone: (612) 238-1321 **Dom State:** AZ **Commenced Bus:** N/A

Data Date	Rating	RACR #1	RACR #2	Total Assets ($mil)	Capital ($mil)	Net Premium ($mil)	Net Income ($mil)
9-19	D	6.33	5.27	47.3	16.2	51.2	-11.1
9-18	N/A	N/A	N/A	9.0	4.1	7.9	-4.2
2018	D	3.74	3.12	16.9	10.1	10.8	-7.9
2017	N/A	N/A	N/A	7.4	7.4	N/A	N/A
2016	N/A	N/A	N/A	N/A	N/A	N/A	N/A
2015	N/A	N/A	N/A	N/A	N/A	N/A	N/A
2014	N/A	N/A	N/A	N/A	N/A	N/A	N/A

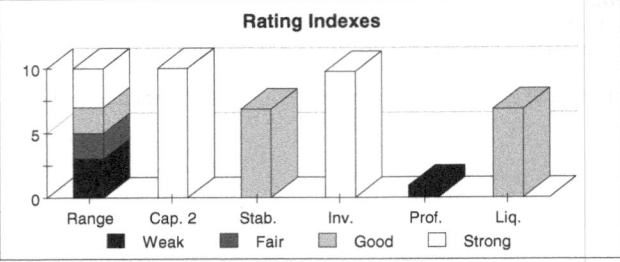

Rating Indexes

BRIGHT HEALTH INS CO   D   Weak

Major Rating Factors: Weak profitability index (0.9 on a scale of 0 to 10). Good liquidity (6.9) with sufficient resources (cash flows and marketable investments) to handle a spike in claims. Strong capitalization (7.7) based on excellent current risk-adjusted capital (severe loss scenario).
Other Rating Factors: High quality investment portfolio (9.9).
Principal Business: Comp med (95%), Medicare (5%)
Mem Phys: 18: 5,887 **17:** 5,804 **18 MLR** 75.4% **/ 18 Admin Exp** N/A
Enroll(000): Q3 19: 26 **18:** 22 **17:** 11 **Med Exp PMPM:** $300
Principal Investments: Long-term bonds (58%), cash and equiv (42%)
Provider Compensation ($000): Contr fee ($50,848), capitation ($13,808), FFS ($4,792)
Total Member Encounters: Phys (86,698), non-phys (23,081)
Group Affiliation: Bright Health Inc
Licensed in: AZ, CO, LA, NE, NC, OK, TX, WA, WI
Address: 10333 E DRY CREEK RD SUITE 15, MINNEAPOLIS, MN 55401
Phone: (612) 238-1321 **Dom State:** CO **Commenced Bus:** N/A

Data Date	Rating	RACR #1	RACR #2	Total Assets ($mil)	Capital ($mil)	Net Premium ($mil)	Net Income ($mil)
9-19	D	1.92	1.60	74.4	20.0	49.0	4.5
9-18	N/A	N/A	N/A	53.2	18.2	79.0	0.2
2018	E	1.62	1.35	62.6	17.7	108.7	-7.4
2017	N/A	N/A	N/A	33.5	13.7	36.2	-17.5
2016	N/A	N/A	N/A	17.0	14.3	N/A	-0.4
2015	N/A	N/A	N/A	N/A	N/A	N/A	N/A
2014	N/A	N/A	N/A	N/A	N/A	N/A	N/A

Rating Indexes

BROWN & TOLAND HEALTH SERVICES   D   Weak

Major Rating Factors: Weak profitability index (0.9 on a scale of 0 to 10). Good overall results on stability tests (5.5) based on healthy premium and capital growth during 2019. Strong capitalization index (7.7) based on excellent current risk-adjusted capital (severe loss scenario).
Other Rating Factors: Excellent liquidity (7.4) with ample operational cash flow and liquid investments.
Principal Business: Managed care (100%)
Mem Phys: 19: N/A **18:** N/A **19 MLR** 87.6% **/ 19 Admin Exp** N/A
Enroll(000): Q2 20: 18 **19:** 10 **18:** 10 **Med Exp PMPM:** $1,046
Principal Investments ($000): Cash and equiv ($29,576)
Provider Compensation ($000): None
Total Member Encounters: N/A
Group Affiliation: None
Licensed in: CA
Address: 1221 Broadway Street Suite 700, Oakland, CA 94612
Phone: (415) 322-9897 **Dom State:** CA **Commenced Bus:** April 2013

Data Date	Rating	RACR #1	RACR #2	Total Assets ($mil)	Capital ($mil)	Net Premium ($mil)	Net Income ($mil)
6-20	D	2.56	1.59	60.7	29.4	87.5	11.1
6-19	D-	1.07	0.65	44.6	9.1	69.8	3.6
2019	D	1.56	0.96	45.8	18.4	146.4	12.9
2018	E	0.60	0.37	27.5	5.5	99.2	4.3
2017	E-	0.13	0.08	22.2	1.1	93.9	4.2
2016	E-	N/A	N/A	24.1	-3.1	82.2	0.1
2015	E-	N/A	N/A	20.1	-3.3	85.3	-2.8

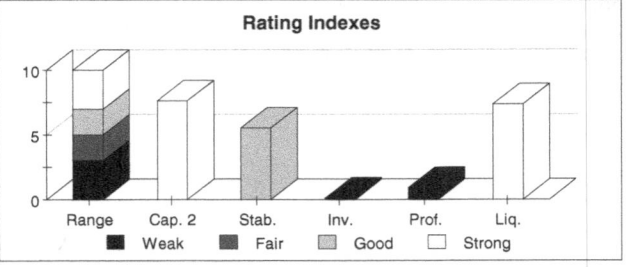

Rating Indexes

BUCKEYE COMMUNITY HEALTH PLAN INC　　　　　　B　　Good

Major Rating Factors: Good liquidity (6.8 on a scale of 0 to 10) with sufficient resources (cash flows and marketable investments) to handle a spike in claims. Excellent profitability (7.5). Strong capitalization (7.4) based on excellent current risk-adjusted capital (severe loss scenario).
Other Rating Factors: High quality investment portfolio (7.9).
Principal Business: Medicaid (81%), Medicare (12%), comp med (7%)
Mem Phys: 19: 47,959　**18:** 43,775　**19 MLR** 84.4%　**/ 19 Admin Exp** N/A
Enroll(000): Q2 20: 450　**19:** 380　**18:** 352　**Med Exp PMPM:** $525
Principal Investments: Long-term bonds (75%), cash and equiv (20%), affiliate common stock (1%), other (3%)
Provider Compensation ($000): Contr fee ($1,612,655), bonus arrang ($390,725), capitation ($164,286), salary ($60,499), other ($42,714)
Total Member Encounters: Phys (2,945,659), non-phys (6,798,402)
Group Affiliation: None
Licensed in: OH
Address: 4349 Easton Way Suite 200, Columbus, OH 43219
Phone: (314) 725-4477　**Dom State:** OH　**Commenced Bus:** N/A

Data Date	Rating	RACR #1	RACR #2	Total Assets ($mil)	Capital ($mil)	Net Premium ($mil)	Net Income ($mil)
6-20	B	1.67	1.39	724.5	300.6	1,599.5	-7.8
6-19	B	2.55	2.12	600.7	319.5	1,352.2	47.8
2019	B	2.49	2.07	645.3	339.3	2,732.0	71.7
2018	B	2.66	2.22	624.4	335.0	2,555.2	90.9
2017	B	1.78	1.48	473.3	253.5	2,207.3	44.2
2016	C+	2.26	1.88	429.4	211.0	2,048.4	22.8
2015	C+	1.96	1.63	454.5	178.3	1,981.9	25.9

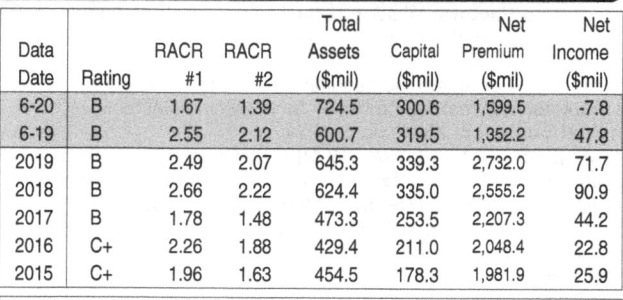

Rating Indexes

BUCKEYE HEALTH PLAN COMMUNITY　　　　　　　　C　　Fair

Major Rating Factors: Weak profitability index (0.9 on a scale of 0 to 10). Strong capitalization (8.9) based on excellent current risk-adjusted capital (severe loss scenario). High quality investment portfolio (9.9).
Other Rating Factors: Excellent liquidity (7.3) with ample operational cash flow and liquid investments.
Principal Business: Medicare (100%)
Mem Phys: 18: 43,775　**17:** N/A　**18 MLR** 104.9%　**/ 18 Admin Exp** N/A
Enroll(000): Q3 19: 2　**18:** 1　**17:** N/A　**Med Exp PMPM:** $865
Principal Investments: Cash and equiv (89%), long-term bonds (11%)
Provider Compensation ($000): Contr fee ($7,132), salary ($364), capitation ($21)
Total Member Encounters: Phys (34,727), non-phys (10,950)
Group Affiliation: None
Licensed in: OH
Address: 4349 Easton Way Suite 200, Columbus, OH 43219
Phone: (314) 725-4477　**Dom State:** OH　**Commenced Bus:** N/A

Data Date	Rating	RACR #1	RACR #2	Total Assets ($mil)	Capital ($mil)	Net Premium ($mil)	Net Income ($mil)
9-19	C	2.87	2.39	8.5	3.9	13.6	0.9
9-18	N/A	N/A	N/A	4.5	2.4	6.4	-0.4
2018	C-	2.21	1.84	7.2	3.0	9.2	-2.7
2017	N/A	N/A	N/A	1.7	1.7	N/A	N/A
2016	N/A	N/A	N/A	N/A	N/A	N/A	N/A
2015	N/A	N/A	N/A	N/A	N/A	N/A	N/A
2014	N/A	N/A	N/A	N/A	N/A	N/A	N/A

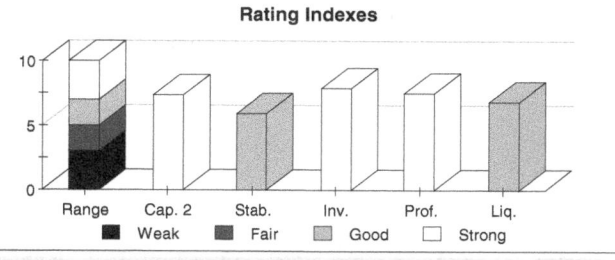

Rating Indexes

BUPA INS CO　　　　　　　　　　　　　　　　　　C+　　Fair

Major Rating Factors: Weak profitability index (2.2 on a scale of 0 to 10). Strong capitalization (9.4) based on excellent current risk-adjusted capital (severe loss scenario). High quality investment portfolio (9.9).
Other Rating Factors: Excellent liquidity (8.3) with ample operational cash flow and liquid investments.
Principal Business: Comp med (100%)
Mem Phys: 19: 10,405　**18:** 10,077　**19 MLR** 21.8%　**/ 19 Admin Exp** N/A
Enroll(000): Q2 20: 21　**19:** 22　**18:** 22　**Med Exp PMPM:** $258
Principal Investments: Long-term bonds (47%), cash and equiv (44%), affiliate common stock (4%), other (5%)
Provider Compensation ($000): FFS ($66,398)
Total Member Encounters: Phys (12,514), non-phys (5,218)
Group Affiliation: The British United Provident Associa
Licensed in: FL, PR
Address: 18001 Old Cutler Road Suite 30, Palmetto Bay, FL 33157
Phone: (305) 275-1400　**Dom State:** FL　**Commenced Bus:** N/A

Data Date	Rating	RACR #1	RACR #2	Total Assets ($mil)	Capital ($mil)	Net Premium ($mil)	Net Income ($mil)
6-20	C+	3.29	2.74	308.9	129.9	150.1	12.4
6-19	N/A	N/A	N/A	N/A	N/A	N/A	N/A
2019	C+	3.01	2.51	315.9	118.9	313.7	-7.9
2018	B	3.42	2.85	309.8	138.5	260.9	-5.9
2017	B	4.33	3.61	322.2	152.5	295.6	0.9
2016	B	3.63	3.02	320.0	153.0	315.4	12.7
2015	C	3.60	3.00	379.4	170.4	367.7	45.9

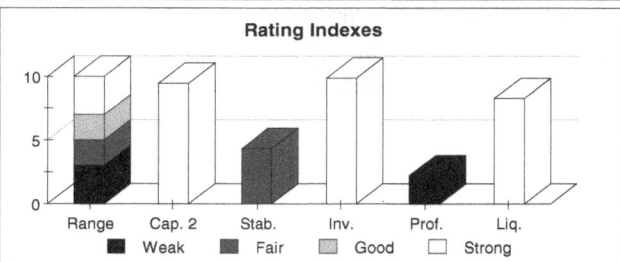

Rating Indexes

CALIFORNIA HEALTH & WELLNESS PLAN
E Very Weak

Major Rating Factors: Weak profitability index (0.2 on a scale of 0 to 10). Poor capitalization index (0.7) based on weak current risk-adjusted capital (moderate loss scenario). Weak overall results on stability tests (2.4).
Other Rating Factors: Good liquidity (6.7) with sufficient resources (cash flows and marketable investments) to handle a spike in claims.
Principal Business: Medicaid (100%)
Mem Phys: 19: N/A **18:** N/A **19 MLR** 92.6% **/ 19 Admin Exp** N/A
Enroll(000): Q2 20: 193 **19:** 195 **18:** 195 **Med Exp PMPM:** $284
Principal Investments ($000): Cash and equiv ($46,733)
Provider Compensation ($000): None
Total Member Encounters: N/A
Group Affiliation: None
Licensed in: CA
Address: 1740 Creekside Oaks Drive, Sacramento, CA 95833
Phone: (818) 676-8486 **Dom State:** CA **Commenced Bus:** October 2013

Data Date	Rating	RACR #1	RACR #2	Total Assets ($mil)	Capital ($mil)	Net Premium ($mil)	Net Income ($mil)
6-20	E	0.46	0.31	241.7	34.6	373.8	-28.7
6-19	D+	0.62	0.43	254.0	48.4	340.8	-25.7
2019	D+	0.79	0.54	255.2	58.3	722.6	-16.0
2018	D+	0.59	0.41	324.3	47.6	656.8	-32.2
2017	C	0.81	0.57	297.2	65.7	627.7	0.7
2016	C+	1.11	0.78	320.4	84.4	610.6	27.2
2015	C	0.85	0.59	274.8	57.5	581.5	15.0

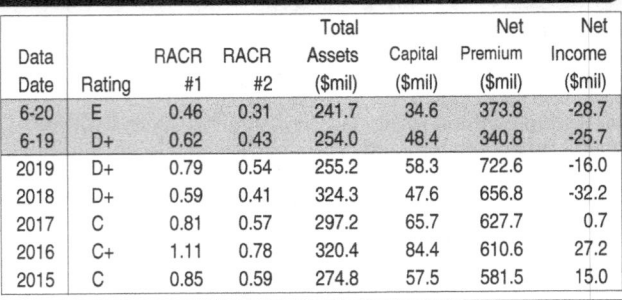

Rating Indexes
Range Cap. 2 Stab. Inv. Prof. Liq.
■ Weak ■ Fair ▨ Good □ Strong

CALIFORNIA PHYSICIANS SERVICE *
A+ Excellent

Major Rating Factors: Excellent profitability (7.8 on a scale of 0 to 10). Strong capitalization index (9.5) based on excellent current risk-adjusted capital (severe loss scenario). Excellent overall results on stability tests (8.3).
Other Rating Factors: Weak liquidity (0.1) as a spike in claims may stretch capacity.
Principal Business: Medicare (6%)
Mem Phys: 19: N/A **18:** N/A **19 MLR** 90.0% **/ 19 Admin Exp** N/A
Enroll(000): Q2 20: 3,556 **19:** 3,497 **18:** 3,497 **Med Exp PMPM:** $463
Principal Investments ($000): Cash and equiv ($2,170,731)
Provider Compensation ($000): None
Total Member Encounters: N/A
Group Affiliation: Blue Shield of California
Licensed in: CA
Address: 50 Beale Street 22nd Floor, San Francisco, CA 94105
Phone: (415) 229-5195 **Dom State:** CA **Commenced Bus:** February 1939

Data Date	Rating	RACR #1	RACR #2	Total Assets ($mil)	Capital ($mil)	Net Premium ($mil)	Net Income ($mil)
6-20	A+	4.15	2.80	10,417.9	6,284.0	8,870.6	658.4
6-19	A+	3.58	2.42	9,377.0	5,866.9	8,737.1	855.1
2019	A+	3.57	2.41	9,424.7	5,584.3	17,386.5	573.0
2018	A+	2.72	1.83	8,493.4	4,925.1	17,113.1	412.6
2017	A+	2.71	1.83	8,171.3	4,675.9	14,240.6	296.2
2016	A+	3.02	2.02	7,509.1	4,296.6	14,290.2	67.0
2015	A+	3.42	2.26	7,358.4	4,170.4	12,531.2	86.9

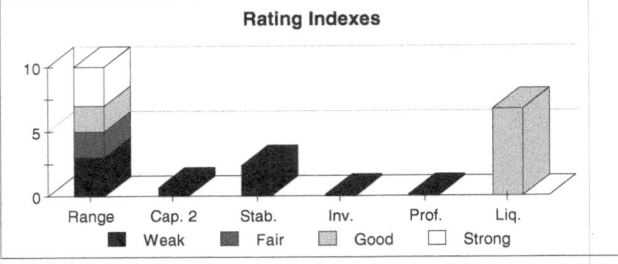

Rating Indexes
Range Cap. 2 Stab. Inv. Prof. Liq.
■ Weak ■ Fair ▨ Good □ Strong

CANADA LIFE REINSURANCE COMPANY
C+ Fair

Major Rating Factors: Fair overall results on stability tests (3.0 on a scale of 0 to 10) including weak results on operational trends, negative cash flow from operations for 2019. Good profitability (5.0). Excellent expense controls. Return on equity has been low, averaging 2.9%. Strong capitalization (10.0) based on excellent risk adjusted capital (severe loss scenario).
Other Rating Factors: High quality investment portfolio (8.0). Excellent liquidity (7.0).
Principal Business: Reinsurance (100%).
Principal Investments: NonCMO investment grade bonds (87%), CMOs and structured securities (7%), cash (4%), and noninv. grade bonds (1%).
Investments in Affiliates: None
Group Affiliation: Great West Life Asr
Licensed in: All states, the District of Columbia and Puerto Rico
Commenced Business: December 1969
Address: 1787 Sentry Pkwy W Bldg 16, Blue Bell, PA 19422-2240
Phone: (215) 542-7200 **Domicile State:** PA **NAIC Code:** 76694

Data Date	Rating	RACR #1	RACR #2	Total Assets ($mil)	Capital ($mil)	Net Premium ($mil)	Net Income ($mil)
6-20	C+	6.63	5.94	132.1	60.1	0.3	2.7
6-19	C+	6.73	6.05	148.6	61.3	0.5	0.9
2019	C+	6.37	5.62	144.1	59.4	2.3	-2.9
2018	C+	6.75	5.06	154.3	63.2	-55.6	4.7
2017	C+	5.97	3.66	204.0	58.3	1.1	0.9
2016	C+	5.58	3.21	289.3	58.5	1.5	2.3
2015	C+	5.43	2.91	301.3	57.4	1.9	2.1

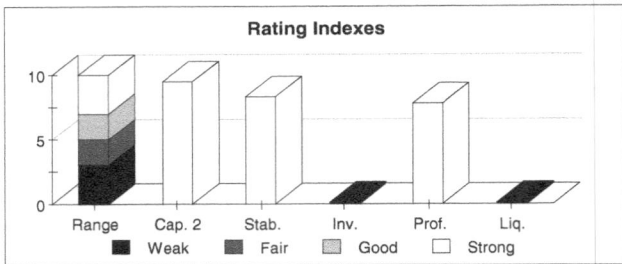

Adverse Trends in Operations

Decrease in asset base during 2018 (24%)
Decrease in premium volume from 2017 to 2018 (4967%)
Decrease in premium volume from 2016 to 2017 (25%)
Decrease in asset base during 2017 (29%)
Decrease in premium volume from 2015 to 2016 (18%)

CAPITAL ADVANTAGE ASR CO | C | Fair

Major Rating Factors: Good overall profitability index (5.7 on a scale of 0 to 10). Strong capitalization (10.0) based on excellent current risk-adjusted capital (severe loss scenario). High quality investment portfolio (7.7).
Other Rating Factors: Excellent liquidity (6.9) with sufficient resources (cash flows and marketable investments) to handle a spike in claims.
Principal Business: Comp med (82%), dental (2%), other (16%)
Mem Phys: 19: 34,805 **18:** 30,333 **19 MLR** 84.9% **/ 19 Admin Exp** N/A
Enroll(000): Q2 20: 153 **19:** 179 **18:** 175 **Med Exp PMPM:** $517
Principal Investments: Long-term bonds (90%), cash and equiv (10%)
Provider Compensation ($000): Contr fee ($1,136,222), capitation ($81)
Total Member Encounters: Phys (1,919,493), non-phys (2,754,710)
Group Affiliation: Capital Blue Cross Inc
Licensed in: PA
Address: 2500 Elmerton Avenue, Harrisburg, PA 17177-9799
Phone: (717) 541-7000 **Dom State:** PA **Commenced Bus:** N/A

Data Date	Rating	RACR #1	RACR #2	Total Assets ($mil)	Capital ($mil)	Net Premium ($mil)	Net Income ($mil)
6-20	C	3.63	3.03	735.4	415.9	580.4	38.9
6-19	C	4.70	3.92	650.2	386.6	695.1	31.5
2019	C	4.36	3.63	733.4	389.5	1,356.7	35.7
2018	C	4.24	3.53	667.4	347.6	1,380.5	88.6
2017	C-	N/A	N/A	588.5	257.3	1,533.3	22.3
2016	C-	2.82	2.35	529.1	231.6	1,218.0	-44.7
2015	C-	1.94	1.62	423.6	185.8	965.1	-28.4

Rating Indexes

CAPITAL ADVANTAGE INS CO | C | Fair

Major Rating Factors: Fair profitability index (4.2 on a scale of 0 to 10). Low quality investment portfolio (2.0). Good liquidity (6.9) with sufficient resources (cash flows and marketable investments) to handle a spike in claims.
Other Rating Factors: Strong capitalization (8.7) based on excellent current risk-adjusted capital (severe loss scenario).
Principal Business: Medicare (56%), med supp (15%), comp med (1%), other (27%)
Mem Phys: 19: 34,805 **18:** 30,333 **19 MLR** 95.5% **/ 19 Admin Exp** N/A
Enroll(000): Q2 20: 78 **19:** 79 **18:** 73 **Med Exp PMPM:** $285
Principal Investments: Affiliate common stock (94%), long-term bonds (9%), cash and equiv (3%)
Provider Compensation ($000): Contr fee ($169,206), capitation ($7,270), bonus arrang ($1,129), other ($32,244)
Total Member Encounters: Phys (1,154,752), non-phys (145,509)
Group Affiliation: Capital Blue Cross Inc
Licensed in: PA
Address: 2500 Elmerton Avenue, Harrisburg, PA 17177-9799
Phone: (717) 541-7000 **Dom State:** PA **Commenced Bus:** N/A

Data Date	Rating	RACR #1	RACR #2	Total Assets ($mil)	Capital ($mil)	Net Premium ($mil)	Net Income ($mil)
6-20	C	2.74	2.28	692.8	482.9	150.9	18.3
6-19	C	3.59	2.99	621.1	462.7	145.7	-3.6
2019	C	3.15	2.63	675.1	445.8	287.2	-14.3
2018	C	3.35	2.79	645.5	431.6	244.6	1.5
2017	C	2.06	1.72	579.5	367.6	233.4	-7.9
2016	C	2.73	2.27	464.2	349.0	219.2	4.2
2015	C	2.40	2.00	418.0	292.7	203.0	31.8

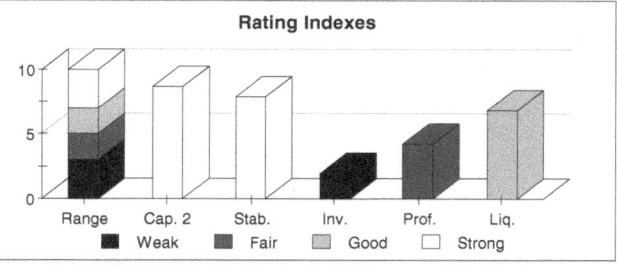

Rating Indexes

CAPITAL BLUE CROSS | B- | Good

Major Rating Factors: Fair profitability index (4.8 on a scale of 0 to 10). Strong capitalization (9.7) based on excellent current risk-adjusted capital (severe loss scenario). Excellent liquidity (7.3) with ample operational cash flow and liquid investments.
Other Rating Factors: Low quality investment portfolio (2.6).
Principal Business: FEHB (93%), med supp (5%), comp med (1%)
Mem Phys: 19: 800 **18:** 784 **19 MLR** 94.7% **/ 19 Admin Exp** N/A
Enroll(000): Q2 20: 103 **19:** 103 **18:** 89 **Med Exp PMPM:** $261
Principal Investments: Affiliate common stock (42%), long-term bonds (26%), nonaffiliate common stock (16%), cash and equiv (4%), real estate (3%), other (9%)
Provider Compensation ($000): Contr fee ($311,486)
Total Member Encounters: Non-phys (419,697)
Group Affiliation: Capital Blue Cross Inc
Licensed in: PA
Address: 2500 Elmerton Avenue, Harrisburg, PA 17177-9799
Phone: (717) 541-7000 **Dom State:** PA **Commenced Bus:** N/A

Data Date	Rating	RACR #1	RACR #2	Total Assets ($mil)	Capital ($mil)	Net Premium ($mil)	Net Income ($mil)
6-20	B-	3.54	2.95	1,298.6	749.5	159.6	0.4
6-19	B-	4.45	3.71	1,158.0	770.7	175.7	8.1
2019	B-	3.80	3.16	1,213.1	717.6	345.4	16.5
2018	B-	4.05	3.37	1,143.0	700.0	318.7	10.2
2017	B-	3.21	2.68	1,131.5	676.8	292.5	14.7
2016	B-	4.13	3.44	1,058.6	703.4	297.5	9.4
2015	B-	4.43	3.69	1,081.6	764.7	279.7	11.3

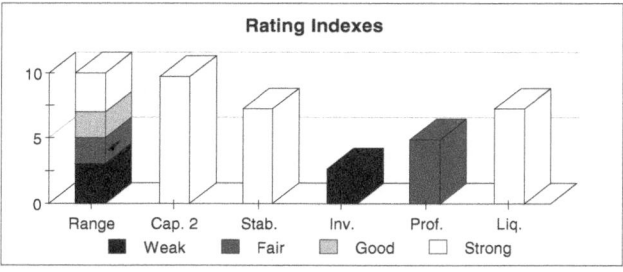

Rating Indexes

CAPITAL DISTRICT PHYSICIANS HEALTH P *   A-   Excellent

Major Rating Factors: Excellent profitability (7.9 on a scale of 0 to 10). Strong capitalization index (8.9) based on excellent current risk-adjusted capital (severe loss scenario). Excellent overall results on stability tests (7.9).
Other Rating Factors: Good quality investment portfolio (6.8). Good liquidity (6.8) with sufficient resources (cash flows and marketable investments) to handle a spike in claims.
Principal Business: Comp med (35%), Medicaid (33%), Medicare (32%).
Mem Phys: 19: 22,564 **18:** 20,898 **19 MLR** 88.3% **/ 19 Admin Exp** N/A
Enroll(000): Q2 20: 232 **19:** 217 **18:** 210 **Med Exp PMPM:** $548
Principal Investments: Long-term bonds (44%), cash and equiv (11%), affiliate common stock (11%), nonaffiliate common stock (8%), other (26%)
Provider Compensation ($000): Contr fee ($779,863), FFS ($503,459), bonus arrang ($72,932), capitation ($26,987), other ($22,897)
Total Member Encounters: Phys (1,948,018), non-phys (948,241)
Group Affiliation: Capital District Physicians Health P
Licensed in: CA, NY
Address: 500 Patroon Creek Boulevard, Albany,
Phone: (518) 641-3000 **Dom State:** NY **Commenced Bus:** N/A

Data Date	Rating	RACR #1	RACR #2	Total Assets ($mil)	Capital ($mil)	Net Premium ($mil)	Net Income ($mil)
6-20	A-	2.91	2.42	660.1	431.8	854.5	39.4
6-19	A	3.22	2.68	596.1	417.0	787.5	25.9
2019	A	2.69	2.24	616.7	385.1	1,599.7	17.8
2018	A	2.88	2.40	586.0	378.8	1,511.9	43.0
2017	B	2.53	2.10	523.8	334.3	1,442.0	19.4
2016	B	2.47	2.05	506.9	308.4	1,444.6	33.8
2015	B-	2.33	1.94	478.7	292.9	1,512.3	85.7

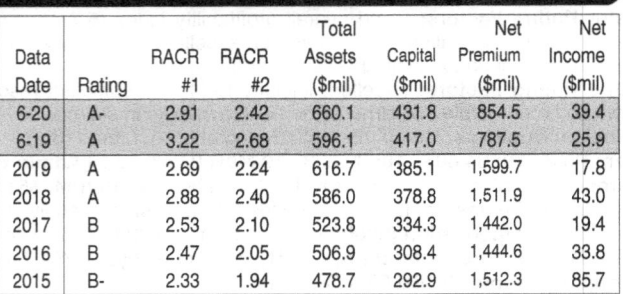

CAPITAL HEALTH PLAN INC *   A   Excellent

Major Rating Factors: Strong capitalization index (10.0 on a scale of 0 to 10) based on excellent current risk-adjusted capital (severe loss scenario). High quality investment portfolio (8.2). Excellent overall results on stability tests (8.2).
Other Rating Factors: Good overall profitability index (6.5). Good liquidity (6.8) with sufficient resources (cash flows and marketable investments) to handle a spike in claims.
Principal Business: Comp med (68%), Medicare (29%), FEHB (2%).
Mem Phys: 19: 623 **18:** 585 **19 MLR** 91.6% **/ 19 Admin Exp** N/A
Enroll(000): Q2 20: 132 **19:** 133 **18:** 134 **Med Exp PMPM:** $515
Principal Investments: Long-term bonds (72%), nonaffiliate common stock (19%), real estate (7%), cash and equiv (2%), other (1%)
Provider Compensation ($000): Contr fee ($462,933), FFS ($286,747), salary ($46,552), capitation ($31,510)
Total Member Encounters: N/A
Group Affiliation: None
Licensed in: FL
Address: 2140 Centerville Place, Tallahassee,
Phone: (850) 383-3333 **Dom State:** FL **Commenced Bus:** N/A

Data Date	Rating	RACR #1	RACR #2	Total Assets ($mil)	Capital ($mil)	Net Premium ($mil)	Net Income ($mil)
6-20	A	6.95	5.79	666.5	517.2	471.0	38.2
6-19	B+	7.91	6.60	589.9	458.0	454.9	25.5
2019	A	8.04	6.70	618.1	486.1	900.7	48.3
2018	B+	7.24	6.04	546.7	419.0	865.0	25.0
2017	B	5.95	4.95	532.7	405.4	808.1	20.6
2016	B	7.32	6.10	489.9	371.0	766.3	4.6
2015	B	7.76	6.46	467.8	364.1	716.9	8.8

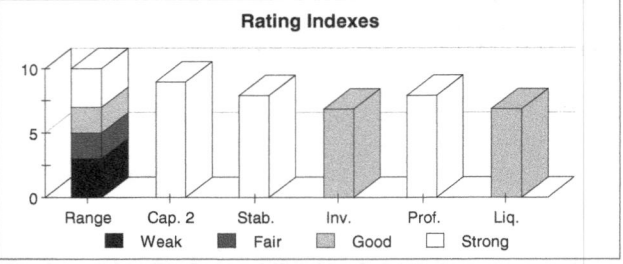

CARE 1ST HEALTH PLAN INC   B   Good

Major Rating Factors: Good liquidity (6.8 on a scale of 0 to 10) with sufficient resources (cash flows and marketable investments) to handle a spike in claims. Fair profitability index (3.0). Strong capitalization (9.1) based on excellent current risk-adjusted capital (severe loss scenario).
Other Rating Factors: High quality investment portfolio (9.2).
Principal Business: Medicaid (64%), Medicare (36%).
Mem Phys: 19: N/A **18:** N/A **19 MLR** 93.7% **/ 19 Admin Exp** N/A
Enroll(000): Q2 20: 462 **19:** 458 **18:** 493 **Med Exp PMPM:** $372
Principal Investments: Long-term bonds (76%), cash and equiv (21%), real estate (2%)
Provider Compensation ($000): Contr fee ($1,374,572), capitation ($710,511)
Total Member Encounters: Phys (2,211,121), non-phys (6,179,545)
Group Affiliation: None
Licensed in: CA, TX
Address: 601 POTRERO GRANDE DR, MONTEREY PARK, CA 91755
Phone: (323) 889-6638 **Dom State:** CA **Commenced Bus:** N/A

Data Date	Rating	RACR #1	RACR #2	Total Assets ($mil)	Capital ($mil)	Net Premium ($mil)	Net Income ($mil)
6-20	B	3.04	2.53	1,003.7	428.3	1,120.2	-34.1
6-19	A+	4.45	3.71	1,062.9	556.7	1,063.0	-1.5
2019	B+	3.41	2.84	1,138.9	451.9	2,232.4	-85.8
2018	A+	4.33	3.60	996.0	543.2	2,348.5	50.8
2017	A+	N/A	N/A	1,085.5	486.6	2,153.3	65.8
2016	B+	2.63	2.19	1,212.5	404.8	2,405.0	234.5
2015	C	0.68	0.57	742.6	190.3	1,870.4	16.9

CARE IMPROVEMENT PLUS OF TEXAS INS B- Good

Major Rating Factors: Fair liquidity (4.1 on a scale of 0 to 10) as cash resources may not be adequate to cover a spike in claims. Excellent profitability (8.3). Strong capitalization (8.4) based on excellent current risk-adjusted capital (severe loss scenario).
Other Rating Factors: High quality investment portfolio (8.6).
Principal Business: Medicare (100%)
Mem Phys: 19: 353,039 18: 257,761 **19 MLR** 87.6% / **19 Admin Exp** N/A
Enroll(000): Q2 20: 154 **19:** 131 **18:** 128 **Med Exp PMPM:** $1,113
Principal Investments: Long-term bonds (98%), cash and equiv (2%)
Provider Compensation ($000): Contr fee ($1,211,840), FFS ($416,657), capitation ($29,239), bonus arrang ($8,173)
Total Member Encounters: Phys (3,339,006), non-phys (1,773,494)
Group Affiliation: None
Licensed in: AL, CO, IL, IN, IA, NE, NM, NC, PA, SC, TN, TX, VA
Address: 4350 LOCKHILL-SELMA ROAD SUITE, SAN ANTONIO, TX 78249
Phone: (952) 936-1300 **Dom State:** TX **Commenced Bus:** N/A

Data Date	Rating	RACR #1	RACR #2	Total Assets ($mil)	Capital ($mil)	Net Premium ($mil)	Net Income ($mil)
6-20	B-	2.44	2.03	759.2	386.5	1,221.2	153.9
6-19	B	2.45	2.04	519.6	255.3	954.5	39.4
2019	B-	2.01	1.67	570.3	245.3	1,937.7	40.1
2018	B	2.15	1.79	557.5	223.6	1,701.8	48.9
2017	C+	1.94	1.62	497.8	189.9	1,376.9	59.2
2016	C	2.10	1.75	378.9	120.9	1,155.1	49.6
2015	B	2.17	1.81	377.0	140.5	1,297.7	34.6

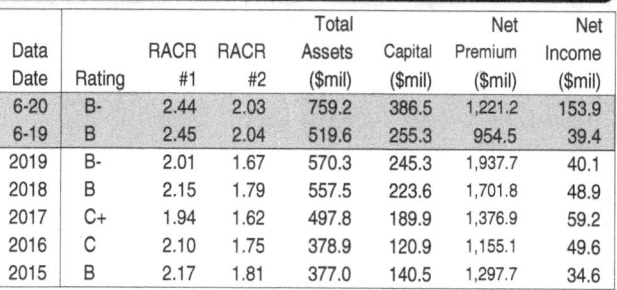

Rating Indexes — Range, Cap. 2, Stab., Inv., Prof., Liq. — Weak / Fair / Good / Strong

CARE IMPROVEMENT PLUS SOUTH CENTRAL B Good

Major Rating Factors: Good liquidity (6.8 on a scale of 0 to 10) with sufficient resources (cash flows and marketable investments) to handle a spike in claims. Excellent profitability (9.2). Strong capitalization (10.0) based on excellent current risk-adjusted capital (severe loss scenario).
Other Rating Factors: High quality investment portfolio (9.2).
Principal Business: Medicare (100%)
Mem Phys: 19: 953,350 18: 878,669 **19 MLR** 81.0% / **19 Admin Exp** N/A
Enroll(000): Q2 20: 113 **19:** 128 **18:** 121 **Med Exp PMPM:** $1,072
Principal Investments: Long-term bonds (91%), cash and equiv (9%)
Provider Compensation ($000): Contr fee ($1,080,869), FFS ($314,948), capitation ($173,738), bonus arrang ($13,942)
Total Member Encounters: Phys (3,034,374), non-phys (1,665,813)
Group Affiliation: None
Licensed in: All states except PR
Address: 1401 CAPITOL AVENUE 3RD FLOOR, LITTLE ROCK, AR 72205
Phone: (952) 936-1300 **Dom State:** AR **Commenced Bus:** N/A

Data Date	Rating	RACR #1	RACR #2	Total Assets ($mil)	Capital ($mil)	Net Premium ($mil)	Net Income ($mil)
6-20	B	5.11	4.26	930.2	593.6	1,007.8	121.1
6-19	B-	6.61	5.51	808.7	550.0	974.1	74.9
2019	B	5.13	4.27	772.4	497.7	1,972.7	144.8
2018	B-	5.70	4.75	727.7	473.0	1,673.8	125.9
2017	C	4.47	3.72	593.6	347.2	1,247.8	79.2
2016	C	2.17	1.81	1,029.5	423.1	3,705.3	241.4
2015	C	1.91	1.59	900.9	315.2	3,290.3	35.3

Rating Indexes — Range, Cap. 2, Stab., Inv., Prof., Liq. — Weak / Fair / Good / Strong

CARE IMPROVEMENT PLUS WI INS B Good

Major Rating Factors: Excellent profitability (7.7 on a scale of 0 to 10). Strong capitalization (9.5) based on excellent current risk-adjusted capital (severe loss scenario). High quality investment portfolio (9.9).
Other Rating Factors: Excellent liquidity (7.2) with ample operational cash flow and liquid investments.
Principal Business: Medicare (100%)
Mem Phys: 19: 29,873 18: 58,760 **19 MLR** 80.1% / **19 Admin Exp** N/A
Enroll(000): Q2 20: 42 **19:** 26 **18:** 20 **Med Exp PMPM:** $953
Principal Investments: Cash and equiv (100%)
Provider Compensation ($000): Contr fee ($213,315), FFS ($37,331), capitation ($15,410), bonus arrang ($2,121)
Total Member Encounters: Phys (573,818), non-phys (302,590)
Group Affiliation: None
Licensed in: MI, WI
Address: 10701 WEST RESEARCH DRIVE P O, WAUWATOSA, WI 53266-0649
Phone: (952) 936-1300 **Dom State:** WI **Commenced Bus:** N/A

Data Date	Rating	RACR #1	RACR #2	Total Assets ($mil)	Capital ($mil)	Net Premium ($mil)	Net Income ($mil)
6-20	B	3.39	2.82	177.5	96.5	276.1	31.6
6-19	B	4.08	3.40	101.0	56.7	167.1	10.0
2019	B	3.38	2.82	117.0	66.7	345.3	19.4
2018	B	3.39	2.83	78.2	47.1	242.8	18.2
2017	C+	1.82	1.52	50.5	25.2	131.0	5.3
2016	C	3.53	2.94	35.7	19.8	79.1	-0.9
2015	C	4.82	4.02	34.2	20.5	67.9	5.0

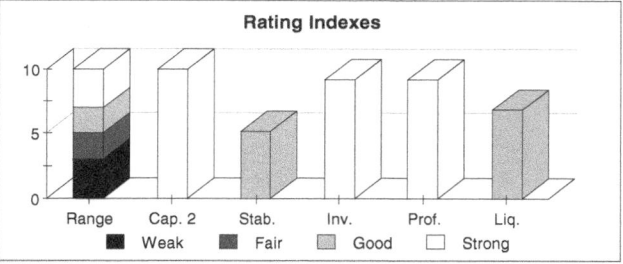

Rating Indexes — Range, Cap. 2, Stab., Inv., Prof., Liq. — Weak / Fair / Good / Strong

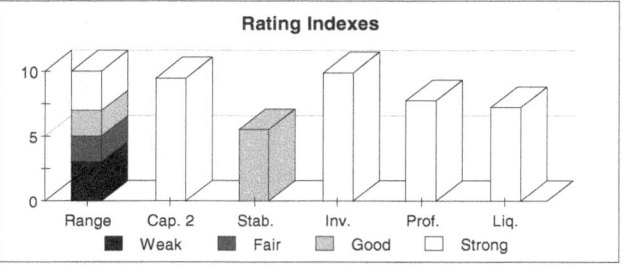

CARE N CARE INS CO

C   **Fair**

Major Rating Factors: Weak profitability index (2.2 on a scale of 0 to 10). Low quality investment portfolio (2.7). Good liquidity (6.8) with sufficient resources (cash flows and marketable investments) to handle a spike in claims.
Other Rating Factors: Strong capitalization (7.6) based on excellent current risk-adjusted capital (severe loss scenario).
Principal Business: Medicare (100%)
Mem Phys: 19: 3,352   **18:** 4,766   **19 MLR** 91.1%   **/ 19 Admin Exp** N/A
Enroll(000): Q2 20: 15   **19:** 13   **18:** 11   **Med Exp PMPM:** $777
Principal Investments: Cash and equiv (100%)
Provider Compensation ($000): Contr fee ($82,068), capitation ($23,576)
Total Member Encounters: Phys (14,676)
Group Affiliation: None
Licensed in: TX
Address: 1701 River Run Road Suite 402, Fort Worth, TX 76107
Phone: (817) 810-5213   **Dom State:** TX   **Commenced Bus:** N/A

Data Date	Rating	RACR #1	RACR #2	Total Assets ($mil)	Capital ($mil)	Net Premium ($mil)	Net Income ($mil)
6-20	C	1.85	1.54	61.8	28.0	77.5	3.4
6-19	N/A	N/A	N/A	N/A	N/A	N/A	N/A
2019	C	1.06	0.88	40.7	17.2	131.8	-8.7
2018	C	2.00	1.67	45.2	23.4	108.7	-0.8
2017	C	1.58	1.31	37.7	18.9	105.5	9.8
2016	C	1.16	0.97	30.0	14.4	113.8	-3.4
2015	C	1.31	1.09	30.3	16.6	101.6	-0.4

CARE N CARE INS CO OF NORTH CAROLINA

E-   **Very Weak**

Major Rating Factors: Weak profitability index (0.9 on a scale of 0 to 10). Poor capitalization (2.2) based on weak current risk-adjusted capital (moderate loss scenario). Weak liquidity (0.7) as a spike in claims may stretch capacity.
Other Rating Factors: High quality investment portfolio (9.9).
Principal Business: Medicare (100%)
Mem Phys: 18: 7,749   **17:** 3,412   **18 MLR** 91.0%   **/ 18 Admin Exp** N/A
Enroll(000): Q3 19: 15   **18:** 15   **17:** 13   **Med Exp PMPM:** $679
Principal Investments: Cash and equiv (83%), long-term bonds (17%)
Provider Compensation ($000): Contr fee ($107,591)
Total Member Encounters: Phys (133,249)
Group Affiliation: The Moses H Cone Memorial Hospital
Licensed in: NC
Address: 7800 McCloud Rd Suite 100, Greensboro, NC 27409
Phone: (336) 790-4386   **Dom State:** NC   **Commenced Bus:** N/A

Data Date	Rating	RACR #1	RACR #2	Total Assets ($mil)	Capital ($mil)	Net Premium ($mil)	Net Income ($mil)
9-19	E-	0.51	0.43	45.3	13.2	112.0	-15.6
9-18	D+	N/A	N/A	44.1	16.7	95.7	-1.2
2018	D+	0.69	0.58	37.6	16.1	128.7	-11.4
2017	D+	N/A	N/A	57.3	13.4	103.3	-18.5
2016	D+	0.89	0.74	21.0	8.1	56.8	-3.6
2015	N/A	N/A	N/A	4.6	4.1	N/A	-1.4
2014	N/A	N/A	N/A	N/A	N/A	N/A	N/A

CARECONNECT INS CO

E-   **Very Weak**

Major Rating Factors: Weak profitability index (0.2 on a scale of 0 to 10). Weak liquidity (0.7) as a spike in claims may stretch capacity. Strong capitalization (10.0) based on excellent current risk-adjusted capital (severe loss scenario).
Other Rating Factors: High quality investment portfolio (9.8).
Principal Business: Comp med (86%)
Mem Phys: 18: 28,015   **17:** 27,364   **18 MLR** 133.0%   **/ 18 Admin Exp** N/A
Enroll(000): Q3 19: N/A   **18:** N/A   **17:** 77   **Med Exp PMPM:** N/A
Principal Investments: Long-term bonds (96%), cash and equiv (4%)
Provider Compensation ($000): Contr fee ($62,702), capitation ($97), other ($1,148)
Total Member Encounters: N/A
Group Affiliation: Northwell Health Inc
Licensed in: NY
Address: 2200 Northern Blvd Suite 104, East Hills, NY 11548
Phone: (516) 401-5830   **Dom State:** NY   **Commenced Bus:** N/A

Data Date	Rating	RACR #1	RACR #2	Total Assets ($mil)	Capital ($mil)	Net Premium ($mil)	Net Income ($mil)
9-19	E-	3.75	3.12	62.4	41.9	0.1	N/A
9-18	E-	N/A	N/A	230.1	76.4	81.9	3.4
2018	E-	3.91	3.26	97.4	43.6	51.2	-29.3
2017	E-	N/A	N/A	326.7	73.5	555.6	-154.9
2016	E-	0.61	0.51	278.1	32.7	360.8	-156.2
2015	E	1.50	1.25	80.3	20.5	124.6	-29.8
2014	N/A	N/A	N/A	28.5	-1.8	44.4	N/A

CARECORE NJ LLC   D   Weak

Major Rating Factors: Fair profitability index (4.4 on a scale of 0 to 10). Good liquidity (6.8) with sufficient resources (cash flows and marketable investments) to handle a spike in claims. Strong capitalization (10.0) based on excellent current risk-adjusted capital (severe loss scenario).
Other Rating Factors: High quality investment portfolio (9.1).
Principal Business: Other (100%)
Mem Phys: 19: 1,128 **18:** 1,528 **19 MLR** 91.3% **/ 19 Admin Exp** N/A
Enroll(000): **19:** 1,093 **18:** 1,337 **Med Exp PMPM:** $8
Principal Investments: Cash and equiv (100%)
Provider Compensation ($000): Contr fee ($8,084), other ($106,501)
Total Member Encounters: N/A
Group Affiliation: Cigna Corporation
Licensed in: NJ
Address: 400 Buckwalter Place Blvd, Bluffton,
Phone: (800) 918-8924 **Dom State:** NJ **Commenced Bus:** N/A

Data Date	Rating	RACR #1	RACR #2	Total Assets ($mil)	Capital ($mil)	Net Premium ($mil)	Net Income ($mil)
2019	D	3.66	3.05	33.9	6.7	125.4	-1.2
2018	D	3.76	3.13	30.4	7.9	147.2	0.3
2017	D-	N/A	N/A	23.1	7.6	158.0	1.4
2016	D-	1.77	1.48	26.4	6.3	148.4	3.7
2015	U	9.43	7.86	21.0	12.5	140.6	18.3

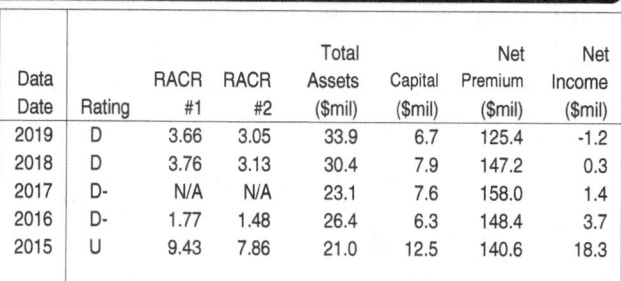
Rating Indexes

CAREFIRST BLUECHOICE INC   B-   Good

Major Rating Factors: Good profitability index (5.0 on a scale of 0 to 10). Good quality investment portfolio (4.9). Strong capitalization index (10.0) based on excellent current risk-adjusted capital (severe loss scenario).
Other Rating Factors: Excellent overall results on stability tests (7.0). Excellent liquidity (6.9) with sufficient resources (cash flows and marketable investments) to handle a spike in claims
Principal Business: Comp med (89%), FEHB (11%)
Mem Phys: 19: 51,191 **18:** 48,386 **19 MLR** 79.7% **/ 19 Admin Exp** N/A
Enroll(000): Q2 20: 650 **19:** 622 **18:** 630 **Med Exp PMPM:** $369
Principal Investments: Long-term bonds (46%), nonaffiliate common stock (16%), cash and equiv (3%), other (35%)
Provider Compensation ($000): Contr fee ($2,739,768), FFS ($16,047), capitation ($3,842)
Total Member Encounters: Phys (3,936,532), non-phys (3,219,505)
Group Affiliation: CareFirst Inc
Licensed in: DC, MD, VA
Address: 840 FIRST STREET NE, WASHINGTON,
Phone: (410) 581-3000 **Dom State:** DC **Commenced Bus:** N/A

Data Date	Rating	RACR #1	RACR #2	Total Assets ($mil)	Capital ($mil)	Net Premium ($mil)	Net Income ($mil)
6-20	B-	4.96	4.13	1,715.5	945.6	1,742.6	47.1
6-19	C+	4.10	3.41	1,337.7	796.4	1,720.5	86.3
2019	B-	4.93	4.11	1,434.1	916.8	3,465.2	183.6
2018	C+	3.72	3.10	1,213.8	721.1	3,620.5	63.9
2017	B	3.66	3.05	1,158.1	672.6	3,248.5	-27.8
2016	A-	4.72	3.93	1,145.5	697.5	3,102.9	-46.1
2015	A	5.30	4.42	1,177.0	741.1	2,986.5	-9.9

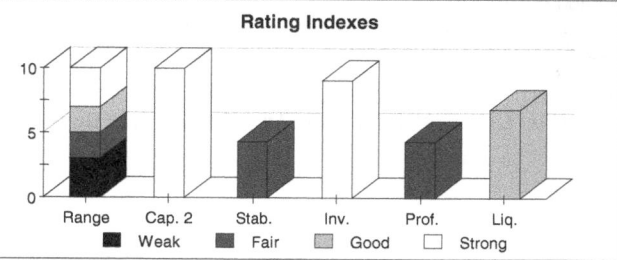
Rating Indexes

CAREFIRST BLUECROSS BLUESHIELD MEDIC   E-   Very Weak

Major Rating Factors: Weak profitability index (0.7 on a scale of 0 to 10). Good liquidity (6.3) with sufficient resources (cash flows and marketable investments) to handle a spike in claims. Strong capitalization (7.1) based on excellent current risk-adjusted capital (severe loss scenario).
Other Rating Factors: High quality investment portfolio (9.9).
Principal Business: Medicare (100%)
Mem Phys: 19: N/A **18:** N/A **19 MLR** 95.9% **/ 19 Admin Exp** N/A
Enroll(000): Q2 20: 6 **19:** 5 **18:** 11 **Med Exp PMPM:** $1,528
Principal Investments: Cash and equiv (99%), long-term bonds (1%)
Provider Compensation ($000): Contr fee ($108,770), FFS ($12,682)
Total Member Encounters: N/A
Group Affiliation: CareFirst Inc
Licensed in: MD
Address: 1966 Greenspring Drive Suite, Timonium, MD 21093
Phone: (410) 878-7709 **Dom State:** MD **Commenced Bus:** N/A

Data Date	Rating	RACR #1	RACR #2	Total Assets ($mil)	Capital ($mil)	Net Premium ($mil)	Net Income ($mil)
6-20	E-	1.47	1.22	35.0	18.0	55.9	9.2
6-19	E-	0.28	0.23	24.3	6.4	43.8	-1.7
2019	E-	0.53	0.45	17.7	6.8	90.7	-1.7
2018	E-	0.13	0.11	28.7	3.1	154.3	-32.4
2017	E-	N/A	N/A	23.4	8.4	91.0	-20.4
2016	D	0.49	0.41	15.9	5.1	41.6	-18.0
2015	N/A	N/A	N/A	N/A	N/A	N/A	N/A

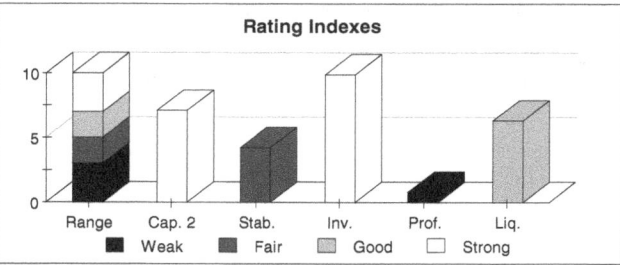
Rating Indexes

CAREFIRST OF MARYLAND INC   B-   Good

Major Rating Factors: Fair quality investment portfolio (4.6 on a scale of 0 to 10). Good overall profitability index (5.2). Strong capitalization (10.0) based on excellent current risk-adjusted capital (severe loss scenario).
Other Rating Factors: Excellent liquidity (7.3) with ample operational cash flow and liquid investments.
Principal Business: FEHB (72%), comp med (17%), med supp (7%), dental (4%)
Mem Phys: 19: 54,068 **18:** 52,141 **19 MLR** 87.4% **/ 19 Admin Exp** N/A
Enroll(000): Q2 20: 489 **19:** 494 **18:** 504 **Med Exp PMPM:** $291
Principal Investments: Long-term bonds (27%), cash and equiv (14%), nonaffiliate common stock (9%), other (49%)
Provider Compensation ($000): Contr fee ($1,665,539), FFS ($31,108), capitation ($4,791)
Total Member Encounters: Phys (3,337,958), non-phys (2,447,922)
Group Affiliation: CareFirst Inc
Licensed in: DC, MD
Address: 1501 SOUTH CLINTON STREET, BALTIMORE, MD 21224
Phone: (410) 581-3000 **Dom State:** MD **Commenced Bus:** N/A

Data Date	Rating	RACR #1	RACR #2	Total Assets ($mil)	Capital ($mil)	Net Premium ($mil)	Net Income ($mil)
6-20	B-	5.30	4.42	2,120.0	1,020.1	948.8	62.6
6-19	C+	4.35	3.63	1,877.6	832.9	979.8	56.6
2019	B-	4.89	4.08	2,070.9	940.0	1,952.1	90.9
2018	C+	3.79	3.16	1,803.8	724.5	1,966.4	110.1
2017	C+	3.35	2.79	1,535.1	642.8	1,889.8	-28.9
2016	C+	3.65	3.04	1,412.3	556.2	1,946.6	-21.1
2015	C+	3.88	3.24	1,406.7	553.5	1,914.6	-9.8

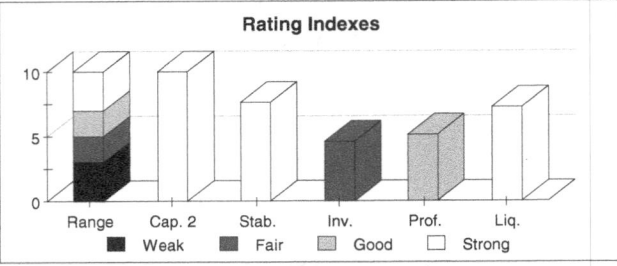

Rating Indexes

CAREMORE HEALTH PLAN   B   Good

Major Rating Factors: Good overall results on stability tests (5.8 on a scale of 0 to 10). Rating is significantly influenced by the good financial results of Anthem Inc. Excellent profitability (7.2). Strong capitalization index (7.1) based on excellent current risk-adjusted capital (severe loss scenario).
Other Rating Factors: Excellent liquidity (7.2) with ample operational cash flow and liquid investments.
Principal Business: Managed care (100%)
Mem Phys: 19: N/A **18:** N/A **19 MLR** 92.8% **/ 19 Admin Exp** N/A
Enroll(000): Q2 20: 54 **19:** 59 **18:** 59 **Med Exp PMPM:** $1,278
Principal Investments ($000): Cash and equiv ($189,881)
Provider Compensation ($000): None
Total Member Encounters: N/A
Group Affiliation: Anthem Inc
Licensed in: CA
Address: 12900 Park Plaza Dr Suite 150, Cerritos, CA 90703
Phone: (562) 677-2455 **Dom State:** CA **Commenced Bus:** November 2002

Data Date	Rating	RACR #1	RACR #2	Total Assets ($mil)	Capital ($mil)	Net Premium ($mil)	Net Income ($mil)
6-20	B	1.92	1.20	307.6	82.6	446.9	8.9
6-19	B-	1.98	1.24	274.2	73.8	487.9	14.5
2019	B	1.66	1.03	299.2	70.7	970.5	21.5
2018	B-	1.74	1.09	285.4	63.8	910.4	14.8
2017	B	2.58	1.60	254.6	81.9	977.3	49.7
2016	B-	3.05	1.91	299.6	91.3	949.8	58.1
2015	B+	2.78	1.75	263.4	84.4	928.2	34.6

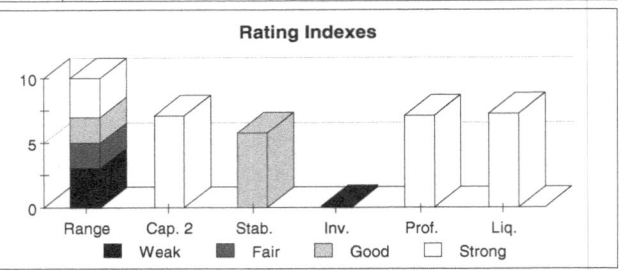

Rating Indexes

CAREPARTNERS OF CT INC   D   Weak

Major Rating Factors: Weak profitability index (0.1 on a scale of 0 to 10). Fair quality investment portfolio (4.1). Good liquidity (5.4) with sufficient resources (cash flows and marketable investments) to handle a spike in claims.
Other Rating Factors: Strong capitalization (10.0) based on excellent current risk-adjusted capital (severe loss scenario).
Principal Business: Medicare (100%)
Mem Phys: 19: 67,631 **18:** N/A **19 MLR** 89.0% **/ 19 Admin Exp** N/A
Enroll(000): Q2 20: 2 **19:** 0 **18:** N/A **Med Exp PMPM:** $590
Principal Investments: Long-term bonds (54%), cash and equiv (46%)
Provider Compensation ($000): Contr fee ($1,483), FFS ($344), capitation ($24)
Total Member Encounters: Phys (1,015), non-phys (302)
Group Affiliation: Health Plan Holdings Inc
Licensed in: (No states)
Address: 705 Mount Auburn Street, Watertown, MA 02472-1508
Phone: (617) 972-9400 **Dom State:** CT **Commenced Bus:** N/A

Data Date	Rating	RACR #1	RACR #2	Total Assets ($mil)	Capital ($mil)	Net Premium ($mil)	Net Income ($mil)
6-20	D	5.63	4.69	22.7	17.9	7.1	0.2
6-19	N/A	N/A	N/A	17.0	12.3	1.2	-0.7
2019	D	3.17	2.64	11.6	5.7	2.6	-7.1
2018	N/A	N/A	N/A	20.7	13.0	N/A	N/A
2017	N/A	N/A	N/A	N/A	N/A	N/A	N/A
2016	N/A	N/A	N/A	N/A	N/A	N/A	N/A
2015	N/A	N/A	N/A	N/A	N/A	N/A	N/A

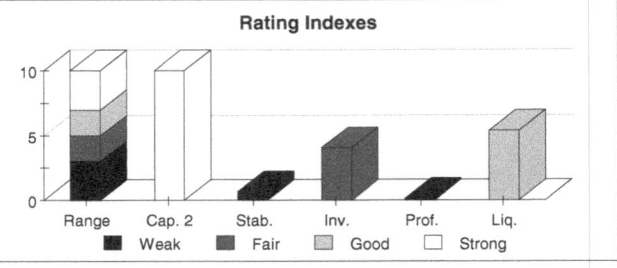

Rating Indexes

CAREPLUS HEALTH PLANS INC   B   Good

Major Rating Factors: Good overall results on stability tests (6.0 on a scale of 0 to 10). Good liquidity (6.8) with sufficient resources (cash flows and marketable investments) to handle a spike in claims. Excellent profitability (8.9).
Other Rating Factors: Strong capitalization index (8.2) based on excellent current risk-adjusted capital (severe loss scenario). High quality investment portfolio (8.9).
Principal Business: Medicare (100%)
Mem Phys: 19: 43,638 **18:** 29,075 **19 MLR** 85.0% **/ 19 Admin Exp** N/A
Enroll(000): Q2 20: 160 **19:** 151 **18:** 118 **Med Exp PMPM:** $1,102
Principal Investments: Long-term bonds (71%), cash and equiv (29%)
Provider Compensation ($000): Capitation ($1,035,199), contr fee ($403,610), salary ($312,233)
Total Member Encounters: Phys (2,937,355), non-phys (837,038)
Group Affiliation: None
Licensed in: FL
Address: 11430 NW 20TH STREET SUITE 300, MIAMI,
Phone: (305) 441-9400 **Dom State:** FL **Commenced Bus:** N/A

Data Date	Rating	RACR #1	RACR #2	Total Assets ($mil)	Capital ($mil)	Net Premium ($mil)	Net Income ($mil)
6-20	B	2.32	1.93	797.6	212.2	1,318.1	50.9
6-19	B-	2.54	2.12	465.8	111.3	1,054.4	45.0
2019	B	2.59	2.16	579.3	167.8	2,138.3	93.2
2018	B	3.37	2.81	461.8	158.2	1,771.3	109.6
2017	B-	2.18	1.82	425.4	150.6	1,688.5	95.9
2016	B-	3.25	2.71	405.6	154.7	1,721.4	96.8
2015	B	3.86	3.21	450.5	199.7	1,754.0	142.9

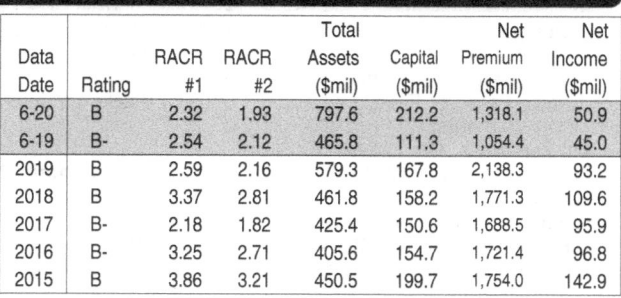

Rating Indexes

CARESOURCE GEORGIA CO   C   Fair

Major Rating Factors: Weak profitability index (2.1 on a scale of 0 to 10). Good capitalization (5.4) based on good current risk-adjusted capital (severe loss scenario). High quality investment portfolio (9.9).
Other Rating Factors: Excellent liquidity (6.9) with sufficient resources (cash flows and marketable investments) to handle a spike in claims.
Principal Business: Medicaid (100%)
Mem Phys: 18: 25,393 **17:** 24,049 **18 MLR** 93.4% **/ 18 Admin Exp** N/A
Enroll(000): Q3 19: 239 **18:** 216 **17:** 211 **Med Exp PMPM:** $237
Principal Investments: Cash and equiv (100%)
Provider Compensation ($000): Contr fee ($583,649), capitation ($1,387)
Total Member Encounters: Phys (1,652,557), non-phys (385,329)
Group Affiliation: None
Licensed in: GA
Address: 600 Galleria Parkway Suite 40, Atlanta, GA 30339
Phone: (678) 214-7500 **Dom State:** GA **Commenced Bus:** N/A

Data Date	Rating	RACR #1	RACR #2	Total Assets ($mil)	Capital ($mil)	Net Premium ($mil)	Net Income ($mil)
9-19	C	0.98	0.82	152.2	74.6	504.2	-4.2
9-18	N/A	N/A	N/A	136.1	60.8	493.4	17.0
2018	C-	1.06	0.88	184.0	79.2	659.7	-20.7
2017	N/A	N/A	N/A	119.6	45.1	313.9	15.5
2016	N/A	N/A	N/A	3.5	2.7	N/A	-1.3
2015	N/A	N/A	N/A	4.0	4.0	N/A	N/A
2014	N/A	N/A	N/A	N/A	N/A	N/A	N/A

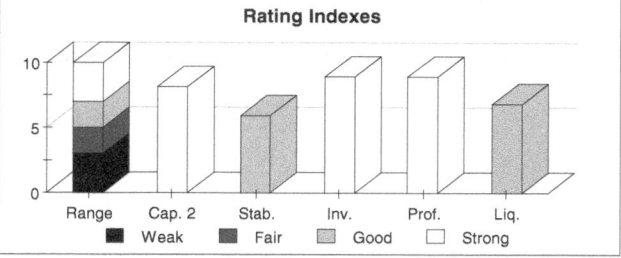

Rating Indexes

CARESOURCE INDIANA INC   D+   Weak

Major Rating Factors: Weak profitability index (2.5 on a scale of 0 to 10). Strong capitalization (8.3) based on excellent current risk-adjusted capital (severe loss scenario). High quality investment portfolio (9.8).
Other Rating Factors: Excellent liquidity (7.1) with ample operational cash flow and liquid investments.
Principal Business: Medicaid (51%), comp med (49%)
Mem Phys: 18: 26,398 **17:** 20,667 **18 MLR** 88.7% **/ 18 Admin Exp** N/A
Enroll(000): Q3 19: 131 **18:** 161 **17:** 126 **Med Exp PMPM:** $330
Principal Investments: Cash and equiv (83%), long-term bonds (17%)
Provider Compensation ($000): Contr fee ($732,400), capitation ($1,583)
Total Member Encounters: Phys (796,966), non-phys (675,973)
Group Affiliation: None
Licensed in: IN
Address: 135 N Pennsylvania Street Su, Indianapolis, IN 46204
Phone: (937) 531-3300 **Dom State:** IN **Commenced Bus:** N/A

Data Date	Rating	RACR #1	RACR #2	Total Assets ($mil)	Capital ($mil)	Net Premium ($mil)	Net Income ($mil)
9-19	D+	2.37	1.97	297.0	129.4	488.7	59.1
9-18	D+	N/A	N/A	303.8	93.6	584.2	49.6
2018	D+	1.20	1.00	302.1	73.4	782.1	9.7
2017	D+	N/A	N/A	201.3	39.1	350.5	5.7
2016	D+	2.15	1.79	64.6	15.9	92.4	-21.6
2015	B	2.05	1.71	49.8	8.6	55.6	-3.0
2014	N/A	N/A	N/A	3.0	2.2	N/A	N/A

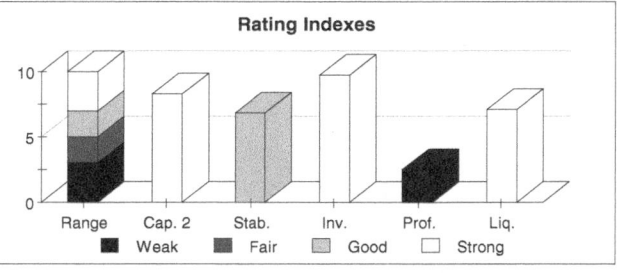

Rating Indexes

CARESOURCE KENTUCKY CO

C   **Fair**

Major Rating Factors: Weak profitability index (2.9 on a scale of 0 to 10). Strong capitalization (8.4) based on excellent current risk-adjusted capital (severe loss scenario). High quality investment portfolio (9.9).
Other Rating Factors: Excellent liquidity (7.0) with ample operational cash flow and liquid investments.
Principal Business: Comp med (100%)
Mem Phys: 18: 15,011 **17:** 12,207 **18 MLR** 85.2% **/ 18 Admin Exp** N/A
Enroll(000): Q3 19: 30 **18:** 45 **17:** 27 **Med Exp PMPM:** $414
Principal Investments: Cash and equiv (100%)
Provider Compensation ($000): Contr fee ($229,854), capitation ($454)
Total Member Encounters: Phys (205,861), non-phys (156,114)
Group Affiliation: None
Licensed in: KY
Address: 101 Enterprise Drive Suite A, Frankfort, KY 40601
Phone: (937) 531-3300 **Dom State:** KY **Commenced Bus:** N/A

Data Date	Rating	RACR #1	RACR #2	Total Assets ($mil)	Capital ($mil)	Net Premium ($mil)	Net Income ($mil)
9-19	C	2.47	2.06	77.2	44.0	184.1	28.6
9-18	C	N/A	N/A	78.6	29.6	213.4	11.5
2018	C	1.38	1.15	85.5	32.2	281.3	0.1
2017	C	N/A	N/A	58.3	19.4	103.0	-6.0
2016	C	2.26	1.88	30.2	8.9	31.3	-8.8
2015	B	5.02	4.18	12.4	5.8	10.0	-3.6
2014	N/A	N/A	N/A	3.8	3.7	N/A	N/A

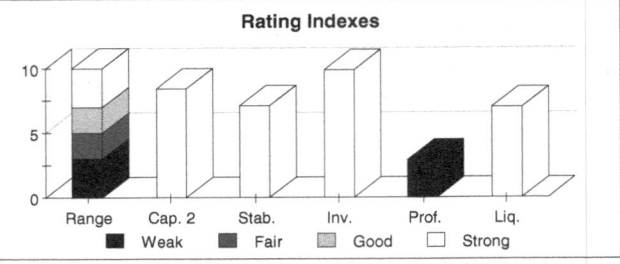

Rating Indexes

CARESOURCE OHIO INC

B   **Good**

Major Rating Factors: Good overall results on stability tests (5.9 on a scale of 0 to 10). Good liquidity (6.8) with sufficient resources (cash flows and marketable investments) to handle a spike in claims. Fair profitability index (4.1).
Other Rating Factors: Strong capitalization index (7.7) based on excellent current risk-adjusted capital (severe loss scenario). High quality investment portfolio (7.1).
Principal Business: Medicaid (91%), Medicare (5%), comp med (4%)
Mem Phys: 19: 45,737 **18:** 43,825 **19 MLR** 86.7% **/ 19 Admin Exp** N/A
Enroll(000): Q2 20: 1,360 **19:** 1,261 **18:** 1,322 **Med Exp PMPM:** $487
Principal Investments: Long-term bonds (52%), cash and equiv (41%), nonaffiliate common stock (8%)
Provider Compensation ($000): Contr fee ($6,894,131), capitation ($545,392)
Total Member Encounters: Phys (10,474,127), non-phys (16,890,869)
Group Affiliation: None
Licensed in: OH
Address: 230 North Main Street, Dayton,
Phone: (937) 531-3300 **Dom State:** OH **Commenced Bus:** N/A

Data Date	Rating	RACR #1	RACR #2	Total Assets ($mil)	Capital ($mil)	Net Premium ($mil)	Net Income ($mil)
6-20	B	1.92	1.60	2,038.5	954.2	4,816.2	107.6
6-19	B-	1.47	1.23	1,668.2	719.6	4,314.7	-43.4
2019	B-	1.73	1.44	1,898.0	842.0	8,701.3	55.7
2018	B-	1.53	1.28	1,655.8	753.0	8,334.8	76.1
2017	B-	1.74	1.45	1,721.0	804.0	7,784.4	28.1
2016	B	1.71	1.42	1,608.7	740.9	7,030.7	-186.2
2015	A-	2.32	1.93	1,762.0	929.2	6,723.9	191.0

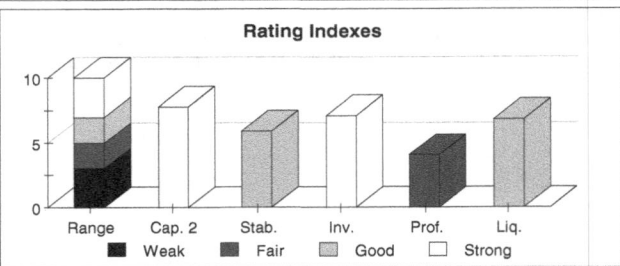

Rating Indexes

CARESOURCE WEST VIRGINIA CO

C   **Fair**

Major Rating Factors: Weak profitability index (2.6 on a scale of 0 to 10). Strong capitalization (7.9) based on excellent current risk-adjusted capital (severe loss scenario). High quality investment portfolio (9.9).
Other Rating Factors: Excellent liquidity (7.2) with ample operational cash flow and liquid investments.
Principal Business: Comp med (100%)
Mem Phys: 18: 6,663 **17:** 4,409 **18 MLR** 98.0% **/ 18 Admin Exp** N/A
Enroll(000): Q3 19: 6 **18:** 6 **17:** 5 **Med Exp PMPM:** $577
Principal Investments: Cash and equiv (100%)
Provider Compensation ($000): Contr fee ($48,699), capitation ($74)
Total Member Encounters: Phys (37,738), non-phys (24,951)
Group Affiliation: None
Licensed in: WV
Address: 230 North Main Street, Dayton, OH 45402
Phone: (937) 531-3300 **Dom State:** WV **Commenced Bus:** N/A

Data Date	Rating	RACR #1	RACR #2	Total Assets ($mil)	Capital ($mil)	Net Premium ($mil)	Net Income ($mil)
9-19	C	2.07	1.72	26.1	13.0	39.0	4.8
9-18	C	N/A	N/A	24.1	7.7	38.6	-1.0
2018	C	1.10	0.91	30.3	9.8	49.4	-6.0
2017	C	N/A	N/A	23.6	9.0	31.3	0.5
2016	C+	2.95	2.46	7.4	3.6	5.2	-0.5
2015	N/A	N/A	N/A	4.8	4.2	N/A	-0.3
2014	N/A	N/A	N/A	N/A	N/A	N/A	N/A

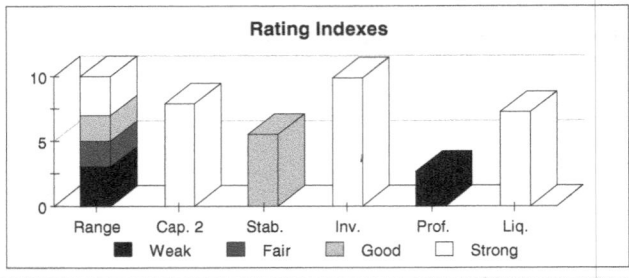

Rating Indexes

CARITEN HEALTH PLAN INC　　　　　　　　　　　　　　　B　　　　Good

Major Rating Factors: Good liquidity (6.9 on a scale of 0 to 10) with sufficient resources (cash flows and marketable investments) to handle a spike in claims. Fair overall results on stability tests (3.9). Excellent profitability (8.6).
Other Rating Factors: Strong capitalization index (7.8) based on excellent current risk-adjusted capital (severe loss scenario). High quality investment portfolio (8.3).
Principal Business: Medicare (100%)
Mem Phys: 19: 25,245　**18:** 24,893　**19 MLR** 79.8%　**/ 19 Admin Exp** N/A
Enroll(000): Q2 20: 123　**19:** 123　**18:** 118　**Med Exp PMPM:** $857
Principal Investments: Long-term bonds (81%), cash and equiv (19%)
Provider Compensation ($000): Contr fee ($691,131), capitation ($506,435), FFS ($4,270)
Total Member Encounters: Phys (2,851,910), non-phys (1,338,242)
Group Affiliation: None
Licensed in: AL, TN
Address: 2160 LAKESIDE CENTRE WAY, KNOXVILLE,
Phone: (865) 470-3993　**Dom State:** TN　**Commenced Bus:** N/A

Data Date	Rating	RACR #1	RACR #2	Total Assets ($mil)	Capital ($mil)	Net Premium ($mil)	Net Income ($mil)
6-20	B	2.01	1.68	545.8	183.0	861.3	66.0
6-19	B	2.82	2.35	433.0	168.3	771.6	62.3
2019	B	2.54	2.12	434.2	165.4	1,547.0	117.4
2018	B	3.39	2.82	454.6	203.6	1,403.1	100.2
2017	B	2.83	2.36	457.2	221.0	1,356.1	90.3
2016	B	3.03	2.53	300.4	174.0	1,283.3	44.7
2015	B-	2.59	2.16	243.2	144.6	1,173.7	12.7

Rating Indexes

CATHOLIC SPECIAL NEEDS PLAN LLC　　　　　　　　　C　　　　Fair

Major Rating Factors: Fair capitalization (4.3 on a scale of 0 to 10) based on fair current risk-adjusted capital (moderate loss scenario). Weak profitability index (2.5). High quality investment portfolio (9.9).
Other Rating Factors: Excellent liquidity (7.0) with ample operational cash flow and liquid investments.
Principal Business: Medicare (100%)
Mem Phys: 19: 28,879　**18:** N/A　**19 MLR** 87.9%　**/ 19 Admin Exp** N/A
Enroll(000): Q2 20: 1　**19:** 2　**18:** 2　**Med Exp PMPM:** $2,251
Principal Investments: Cash and equiv (100%)
Provider Compensation ($000): Contr fee ($33,427), capitation ($14,355), bonus arrang ($585)
Total Member Encounters: N/A
Group Affiliation: Providence Health Foundation Inc
Licensed in: NY
Address: 205 Lexington Avenue, New York, NY 10016
Phone: (855) 951-2273　**Dom State:** NY　**Commenced Bus:** N/A

Data Date	Rating	RACR #1	RACR #2	Total Assets ($mil)	Capital ($mil)	Net Premium ($mil)	Net Income ($mil)
6-20	C	0.82	0.69	16.7	7.1	25.4	0.0
6-19	N/A	N/A	N/A	N/A	N/A	N/A	N/A
2019	C	0.82	0.68	15.7	7.1	55.1	1.2
2018	C	0.69	0.58	14.3	5.9	47.3	-2.4
2017	C+	0.92	0.76	14.6	6.7	45.6	0.0
2016	C	0.83	0.69	15.1	6.3	48.3	0.4
2015	D+	0.71	0.59	14.9	5.8	46.1	0.8

Rating Indexes

CATLIN INS CO　　　　　　　　　　　　　　　　　　　　C　　　　Fair

Major Rating Factors: Weak overall results on stability tests (2.7 on a scale of 0 to 10) including weak risk adjusted capital in prior years and negative cash flow from operations for 2019. Strengths include potentially strong support from affiliation with XL Group Ltd. Poor long-term capitalization index (1.4) based on weak current risk adjusted capital (severe and moderate loss scenarios), although results have slipped from the good range over the last two years.
Other Rating Factors: A history of deficient reserves (2.2) that places pressure on both capital and profits. Deficiencies in the two year reserve development occurred in three of the previous five years and ranged between 18% and 37%. Weak profitability index (1.5) with operating losses during each of the last five years and the first six months of 2020. Average return on equity over the last five years has been poor at -10.9%. Good liquidity (6.5) with sufficient resources (cash flows and marketable investments) to handle a spike in claims.
Principal Business: Group accident & health (38%), homeowners multiple peril (23%), other liability (19%), fire (11%), inland marine (6%), products liability (1%), and boiler & machinery (1%).
Principal Investments: Investment grade bonds (84%) and cash (22%).
Investments in Affiliates: None
Group Affiliation: XL Group Ltd
Licensed in: All states, the District of Columbia and Puerto Rico
Commenced Business: April 1913
Address: 1999 Bryan Street, Dallas, TX 75201
Phone: (203) 964-5200　**Domicile State:** TX　**NAIC Code:** 19518

Data Date	Rating	RACR #1	RACR #2	Loss Ratio %	Total Assets ($mil)	Capital ($mil)	Net Premium ($mil)	Net Income ($mil)
6-20	C	0.44	0.27	N/A	257.8	34.7	28.7	-3.3
6-19	C	1.52	0.96	N/A	159.1	51.2	22.0	-0.9
2019	C	0.53	0.32	120.0	109.6	36.4	24.7	-7.2
2018	C+	1.45	0.92	85.3	209.7	50.8	46.9	-2.7
2017	C+	1.86	1.07	81.9	181.6	55.9	37.8	-7.6
2016	C	1.37	0.87	86.8	230.5	56.7	29.3	-0.9
2015	C	1.29	0.84	90.9	260.4	52.5	44.8	-5.3

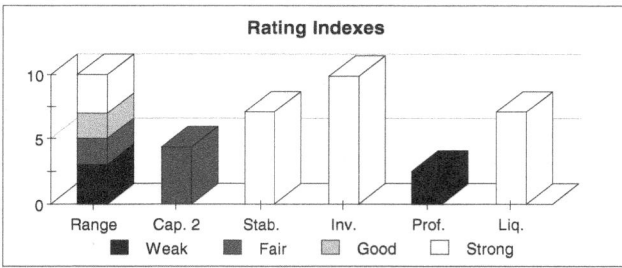

Capital

CDI GROUP INC   E-   Very Weak

Major Rating Factors: Poor capitalization index (2.3 on a scale of 0 to 10) based on weak current risk-adjusted capital (moderate loss scenario). Weak overall results on stability tests (2.7). Good overall profitability index (5.8).
Other Rating Factors: Excellent liquidity (7.2) with ample operational cash flow and liquid investments.
Principal Business: Managed care (100%)
Mem Phys: 19: N/A **18:** N/A **19 MLR** N/A **/ 19 Admin Exp** N/A
Enroll(000): Q2 20: 268 **19:** 170 **18:** 170 **Med Exp PMPM:** N/A
Principal Investments ($000): Cash and equiv ($1,206)
Provider Compensation ($000): None
Total Member Encounters: N/A
Group Affiliation: None
Licensed in: (No states)
Address: 601 Daily Dr Ste 215, Camarillo, CA 93010-5839
Phone: (800) 874-1986 **Dom State:** CA **Commenced Bus:** N/A

Data Date	Rating	RACR #1	RACR #2	Total Assets ($mil)	Capital ($mil)	Net Premium ($mil)	Net Income ($mil)
6-20	E-	0.44	0.44	3.0	1.0	7.6	0.5
6-19	E-	0.72	0.70	2.3	1.3	8.9	1.4
2019	E-	0.18	0.18	1.9	0.6	17.4	0.9
2018	E-	0.38	0.37	2.4	0.8	14.8	1.2
2017	E-	N/A	N/A	1.8	0.2	10.4	-0.6
2016	N/A	N/A	N/A	N/A	N/A	N/A	N/A
2015	N/A	N/A	N/A	N/A	N/A	N/A	N/A

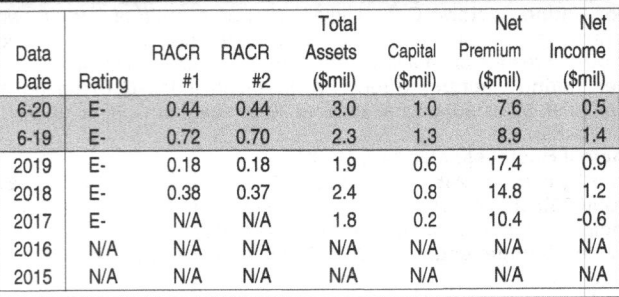

Rating Indexes

CDPHP UNIVERSAL BENEFITS INC   B-   Good

Major Rating Factors: Fair profitability index (3.3 on a scale of 0 to 10). Strong capitalization (10.0) based on excellent current risk-adjusted capital (severe loss scenario). High quality investment portfolio (9.3).
Other Rating Factors: Excellent liquidity (6.9) with sufficient resources (cash flows and marketable investments) to handle a spike in claims.
Principal Business: Comp med (76%), FEHB (15%), Medicare (8%)
Mem Phys: 19: 22,596 **18:** 20,930 **19 MLR** 88.7% **/ 19 Admin Exp** N/A
Enroll(000): Q2 20: 89 **19:** 89 **18:** 92 **Med Exp PMPM:** $461
Principal Investments: Long-term bonds (68%), cash and equiv (32%)
Provider Compensation ($000): Contr fee ($480,443), bonus arrang ($13,865), capitation ($2,645), other ($9,687)
Total Member Encounters: Phys (685,964), non-phys (266,703)
Group Affiliation: Capital District Physicians Health P
Licensed in: NY
Address: 500 Patroon Creek Blvd, Albany, NY 12206-1057
Phone: (518) 641-3000 **Dom State:** NY **Commenced Bus:** N/A

Data Date	Rating	RACR #1	RACR #2	Total Assets ($mil)	Capital ($mil)	Net Premium ($mil)	Net Income ($mil)
6-20	B-	4.52	3.76	265.2	193.3	292.7	15.3
6-19	B	4.01	3.34	201.3	145.1	280.9	10.8
2019	B	3.48	2.90	195.8	130.9	565.7	-2.7
2018	B	3.67	3.05	198.0	134.9	567.2	9.1
2017	E+	2.77	2.31	179.5	124.8	588.1	11.1
2016	E+	2.23	1.86	175.3	113.7	703.4	-17.5
2015	E	1.37	1.15	176.2	82.0	795.0	-45.6

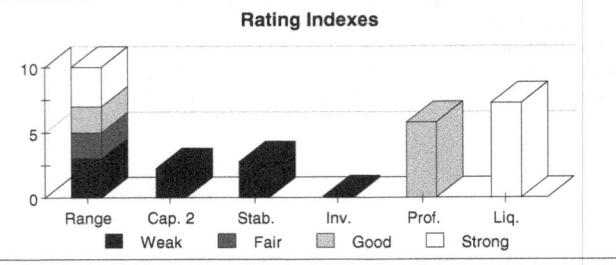

Rating Indexes

CELTIC INS CO   B-   Good

Major Rating Factors: Fair quality investment portfolio (3.9 on a scale of 0 to 10). Excellent profitability (8.4). Strong capitalization (7.5) based on excellent current risk-adjusted capital (severe loss scenario).
Other Rating Factors: Excellent liquidity (7.3) with ample operational cash flow and liquid investments.
Principal Business: Comp med (100%)
Mem Phys: 19: 183,267 **18:** 114,998 **19 MLR** 80.5% **/ 19 Admin Exp** N/A
Enroll(000): Q2 20: 1,228 **19:** 1,032 **18:** 751 **Med Exp PMPM:** $189
Principal Investments: Cash and equiv (50%), long-term bonds (39%), affiliate common stock (10%), other (1%)
Provider Compensation ($000): Contr fee ($1,709,390), bonus arrang ($740,670), salary ($22,882), capitation ($10,629)
Total Member Encounters: Phys (4,171,249), non-phys (3,495,449)
Group Affiliation: None
Licensed in: All states except NY, PR
Address: 200 East Randolph Street Suit, Chicago, IL 60601
Phone: (800) 714-4658 **Dom State:** IL **Commenced Bus:** N/A

Data Date	Rating	RACR #1	RACR #2	Total Assets ($mil)	Capital ($mil)	Net Premium ($mil)	Net Income ($mil)
6-20	B-	1.72	1.43	3,180.7	439.8	1,769.5	4.7
6-19	B	3.12	2.60	2,624.7	473.6	1,603.0	120.6
2019	B-	2.00	1.67	2,253.4	405.3	3,081.8	68.4
2018	B-	3.03	2.52	1,918.6	459.2	2,425.9	162.1
2017	C+	N/A	N/A	1,170.4	162.5	2,127.0	77.0
2016	C+	1.28	1.07	593.0	53.3	781.9	2.0
2015	C-	8.41	7.01	139.9	38.2	170.7	8.3

Rating Indexes

CELTICARE HEALTH PLAN OF MA INC — C- — Fair

Major Rating Factors: Excellent profitability (7.5 on a scale of 0 to 10). Strong capitalization (10.0) based on excellent current risk-adjusted capital (severe loss scenario). High quality investment portfolio (7.9).
Other Rating Factors: Excellent liquidity (10.0) with ample operational cash flow and liquid investments.
Principal Business: Comp med (97%), Medicaid (3%)
Mem Phys: 19: N/A **18:** N/A   **19 MLR** -8.1% **/ 19 Admin Exp** N/A
Enroll(000): **19:** N/A **18:** N/A   **Med Exp PMPM:** N/A
Principal Investments: Long-term bonds (66%), cash and equiv (34%)
Provider Compensation ($000): Capitation ($93)
Total Member Encounters: N/A
Group Affiliation: None
Licensed in: MA
Address: 200 West St Ste 250, Waltham,
Phone: (314) 725-4477   **Dom State:** MA   **Commenced Bus:** N/A

Data Date	Rating	RACR #1	RACR #2	Total Assets ($mil)	Capital ($mil)	Net Premium ($mil)	Net Income ($mil)
2019	C-	6.91	5.75	16.5	6.8	0.2	1.4
2018	C-	7.83	6.53	23.6	13.6	29.6	4.7
2017	C	2.17	1.81	69.3	33.9	173.9	2.4
2016	C+	4.70	3.92	80.7	46.4	174.2	5.6
2015	C+	6.11	5.09	99.6	55.7	220.1	26.6

Rating Indexes

CENTRAL HEALTH PLAN OF CALIFORNIA — E+ — Very Weak

Major Rating Factors: Poor capitalization index (2.8 on a scale of 0 to 10) based on weak current risk-adjusted capital (moderate loss scenario). Fair overall results on stability tests (4.7) based on fair risk diversification due to the company's size. Good overall profitability index (5.9).
Other Rating Factors: Excellent liquidity (6.9) with sufficient resources (cash flows and marketable investments) to handle a spike in claims.
Principal Business: Medicare (100%)
Mem Phys: 19: N/A **18:** N/A   **19 MLR** 89.3% **/ 19 Admin Exp** N/A
Enroll(000): Q2 20: 43 **19:** 41 **18:** 41   **Med Exp PMPM:** $918
Principal Investments ($000): Cash and equiv ($62,491)
Provider Compensation ($000): None
Total Member Encounters: N/A
Group Affiliation: AHMC Central Health LLC
Licensed in: CA
Address: 1540 Bridgegate Drive, Diamond Bar, CA 91765
Phone: (626) 388-2390   **Dom State:** CA   **Commenced Bus:** October 2004

Data Date	Rating	RACR #1	RACR #2	Total Assets ($mil)	Capital ($mil)	Net Premium ($mil)	Net Income ($mil)
6-20	E+	0.48	0.29	85.2	18.6	265.1	4.5
6-19	E+	0.38	0.24	61.1	13.2	237.5	0.2
2019	E+	0.36	0.22	83.1	14.1	488.7	1.1
2018	E+	0.38	0.23	51.1	13.0	408.2	-3.6
2017	E+	0.55	0.34	70.7	16.6	364.4	4.1
2016	E+	0.33	0.20	56.6	15.0	351.5	2.9
2015	E+	0.29	0.18	43.8	13.6	298.5	3.5

Rating Indexes

CENTRAL STATES H & L CO OF OMAHA — B — Good

Major Rating Factors: Good quality investment portfolio (5.8 on a scale of 0 to 10) despite mixed results such as: minimal exposure to mortgages and substantial holdings of BBB bonds but minimal holdings in junk bonds. Good liquidity (6.9) with sufficient resources to handle a spike in claims. Fair overall results on stability tests (4.9) including negative cash flow from operations for 2019.
Other Rating Factors: Strong capitalization (9.6) based on excellent risk adjusted capital (severe loss scenario). Excellent profitability (7.3) despite modest operating losses during 2018.
Principal Business: Reinsurance (56%), credit life insurance (25%), credit health insurance (11%), individual health insurance (6%), and other lines (2%).
Principal Investments: NonCMO investment grade bonds (36%), CMOs and structured securities (25%), common & preferred stock (14%), mortgages in good standing (5%), and misc. investments (19%).
Investments in Affiliates: 8%
Group Affiliation: Central States Group
Licensed in: All states except NY, PR
Commenced Business: June 1932
Address: 1212 North 96th Street, Omaha, NE 68114
Phone: (402) 397-1111 **Domicile State:** NE **NAIC Code:** 61751

Data Date	Rating	RACR #1	RACR #2	Total Assets ($mil)	Capital ($mil)	Net Premium ($mil)	Net Income ($mil)
6-20	B	3.65	2.72	372.6	154.5	54.6	5.5
6-19	B	3.55	2.64	378.0	142.2	54.4	3.8
2019	B	3.62	2.70	379.1	149.2	108.4	7.7
2018	B	3.45	2.58	383.8	137.1	111.3	-0.5
2017	A-	4.58	3.30	407.5	151.9	37.8	13.0
2016	A-	4.28	3.06	420.0	134.3	51.3	10.5
2015	A-	3.99	2.88	419.9	122.9	66.1	6.4

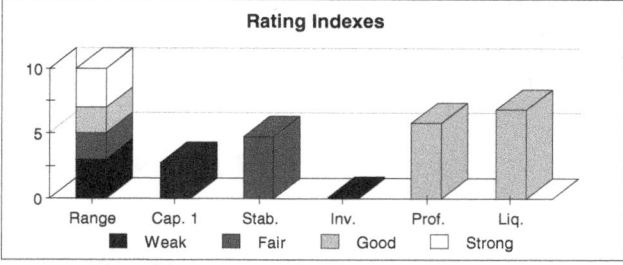

Rating Indexes

CENTRAL STATES INDEMNITY CO OF OMAHA — C+ — Fair

Major Rating Factors: Fair overall results on stability tests (3.6 on a scale of 0 to 10) including fair financial strength of affiliated Berkshire-Hathaway. History of adequate reserve strength (5.1) as reserves have been consistently at an acceptable level.

Other Rating Factors: Good overall profitability index (6.3). Weak expense controls. Return on equity has been low, averaging 4.8% over the past five years. Strong long-term capitalization index (9.4) based on excellent current risk adjusted capital (severe and moderate loss scenarios), despite some fluctuation in capital levels. Superior liquidity (10.0) with ample operational cash flow and liquid investments.

Principal Business: Other accident & health (59%), inland marine (32%), aggregate write-ins for other lines of business (4%), aircraft (2%), and credit accident & health (2%).

Principal Investments: Misc. investments (65%), investment grade bonds (33%), and cash (2%).

Investments in Affiliates: 3%

Group Affiliation: Berkshire-Hathaway

Licensed in: All states, the District of Columbia and Puerto Rico

Commenced Business: June 1977

Address: 1212 North 96th Street, Omaha, NE 68114

Phone: (402) 997-8000   **Domicile State:** NE   **NAIC Code:** 34274

Data Date	Rating	RACR #1	RACR #2	Loss Ratio %	Total Assets ($mil)	Capital ($mil)	Net Premium ($mil)	Net Income ($mil)
6-20	C+	4.86	3.11	N/A	551.9	490.0	4.5	1.3
6-19	C+	4.26	2.69	N/A	581.5	511.9	4.9	6.2
2019	C+	4.10	2.58	5.6	641.5	559.5	9.7	13.1
2018	C+	4.46	2.84	2.9	521.1	464.7	9.6	24.3
2017	C+	3.98	2.53	66.1	542.1	466.0	64.0	63.6
2016	C+	3.82	2.42	60.2	447.9	378.0	59.6	8.0
2015	C+	4.00	2.50	55.4	417.3	354.9	55.0	9.5

Berkshire-Hathaway Composite Group Rating: B- Largest Group Members	Assets ($mil)	Rating
NATIONAL INDEMNITY CO	285940	B-
GOVERNMENT EMPLOYEES INS CO	41582	B
COLUMBIA INS CO	30809	C+
BERKSHIRE HATHAWAY LIFE INS CO OF NE	20830	C+
GENERAL REINS CORP	18422	C+

CENTRE LIFE INS CO — C — Fair

Major Rating Factors: Fair overall results on stability tests (4.3 on a scale of 0 to 10) including fair financial strength of affiliated Zurich Financial Services Group and negative cash flow from operations for 2019. Good quality investment portfolio (6.5) with no exposure to mortgages and no exposure to junk bonds. Weak profitability (2.1) with operating losses during the first six months of 2020.

Other Rating Factors: Strong capitalization (9.1) based on excellent risk adjusted capital (severe loss scenario). Excellent liquidity (9.4).

Principal Business: Reinsurance (57%) and individual health insurance (43%).

Principal Investments: NonCMO investment grade bonds (80%) and CMOs and structured securities (19%).

Investments in Affiliates: None

Group Affiliation: Zurich Financial Services Group

Licensed in: All states except PR

Commenced Business: October 1927

Address: 1350 MAIN STREET SUITE 1600, SPRINGFIELD, MA 01103-1641

Phone: (212) 859-2640 **Domicile State:** MA **NAIC Code:** 80896

Data Date	Rating	RACR #1	RACR #2	Total Assets ($mil)	Capital ($mil)	Net Premium ($mil)	Net Income ($mil)
6-20	C	4.02	2.37	1,558.7	85.7	0.5	-1.4
6-19	B-	4.18	2.55	1,635.1	93.2	0.6	-1.0
2019	C	4.09	2.45	1,591.5	87.3	1.0	-6.5
2018	B-	4.22	2.46	1,680.2	93.9	1.3	0.5
2017	B-	4.04	2.40	1,790.7	93.6	1.4	-1.7
2016	B-	4.03	2.48	1,809.8	93.8	1.4	-0.5
2015	B-	3.94	2.57	1,884.1	94.5	1.9	-3.7

Zurich Financial Services Group Composite Group Rating: C Largest Group Members	Assets ($mil)	Rating
ZURICH AMERICAN INS CO	30416	C
ZURICH AMERICAN LIFE INS CO	15201	C-
FARMERS NEW WORLD LIFE INS CO	5261	B-
RURAL COMMUNITY INS CO	1955	B-
CENTRE LIFE INS CO	1591	C

CHA HMO INC — B- — Good

Major Rating Factors: Fair overall results on stability tests (4.4 on a scale of 0 to 10) in spite of healthy premium and capital growth during 2019 but an excessive 1460% enrollment growth during the period. Good overall profitability index (5.1). Good quality investment portfolio (6.8).

Other Rating Factors: Good liquidity (6.9) with sufficient resources (cash flows and marketable investments) to handle a spike in claims. Strong capitalization index (8.0) based on excellent current risk-adjusted capital (severe loss scenario).

Principal Business: Medicare (100%)

Mem Phys: 19: 204,828 **18:** 26,568 **19 MLR** 86.2% **/ 19 Admin Exp** N/A

Enroll(000): Q2 20: 351 **19:** 329 **18:** 21 **Med Exp PMPM:** $822

Principal Investments: Cash and equiv (55%), long-term bonds (45%)

Provider Compensation ($000): Contr fee ($1,304,461), capitation ($1,005,490), salary ($552,706), FFS ($20,253)

Total Member Encounters: Phys (6,023,230), non-phys (2,998,265)

Group Affiliation: None

Licensed in: HI, IN, IA, KY, NE, SD

Address: 500 WEST MAIN STREET, LOUISVILLE,

Phone: (502) 580-1000 **Dom State:** KY **Commenced Bus:** N/A

Data Date	Rating	RACR #1	RACR #2	Total Assets ($mil)	Capital ($mil)	Net Premium ($mil)	Net Income ($mil)
6-20	B-	2.16	1.80	1,174.1	415.3	2,227.4	61.8
6-19	C+	19.50	16.25	594.9	188.6	1,828.3	47.2
2019	B-	2.40	2.00	789.2	361.0	3,664.7	62.0
2018	C+	1.75	1.46	42.4	16.6	190.2	4.8
2017	C+	N/A	N/A	43.6	19.4	160.6	-4.5
2016	C+	3.79	3.16	33.0	23.3	128.3	0.0
2015	C+	6.07	5.06	32.6	24.0	77.6	-4.5

Rating Indexes

Legend: Weak / Fair / Good / Strong
Categories: Range, Cap. 2, Stab., Inv., Prof., Liq.

CHEROKEE INS CO   B-   Good

Major Rating Factors: Fair overall results on stability tests (3.5 on a scale of 0 to 10). History of adequate reserve strength (6.7) as reserves have been consistently at an acceptable level.

Other Rating Factors: Good liquidity (6.2) with sufficient resources (cash flows and marketable investments) to handle a spike in claims. Strong long-term capitalization index (8.1) based on excellent current risk adjusted capital (severe and moderate loss scenarios), despite some fluctuation in capital levels. Excellent profitability (7.2) with operating gains in each of the last five years. Excellent expense controls. Return on equity has been good over the last five years, averaging 10.6%.

Principal Business: Auto liability (48%), group accident & health (25%), workers compensation (12%), auto physical damage (11%), and other liability (3%).

Principal Investments: Misc. investments (48%), investment grade bonds (46%), cash (4%), and non investment grade bonds (2%).

Investments in Affiliates: None

Group Affiliation: Oakland Financial Corp

Licensed in: All states except AK, DC, HI, NH, PR

Commenced Business: October 1946

Address: 2700 HOWARD STREET, Port Huron, MI 48060

Phone: (800) 201-0450   **Domicile State:** MI   **NAIC Code:** 10642

Data Date	Rating	RACR #1	RACR #2	Loss Ratio %	Total Assets ($mil)	Capital ($mil)	Net Premium ($mil)	Net Income ($mil)
6-20	B-	2.86	1.75	N/A	631.2	207.7	109.0	13.6
6-19	B-	2.79	1.66	N/A	610.3	206.4	104.8	12.0
2019	B	3.02	1.84	87.6	627.4	227.1	219.9	26.4
2018	B	2.81	1.68	89.6	551.6	186.3	199.4	18.0
2017	B	3.01	1.77	93.7	541.6	197.8	186.4	25.5
2016	C+	2.52	1.46	91.5	498.5	180.7	190.3	13.6
2015	C	2.35	1.36	91.9	434.2	152.8	181.8	15.4

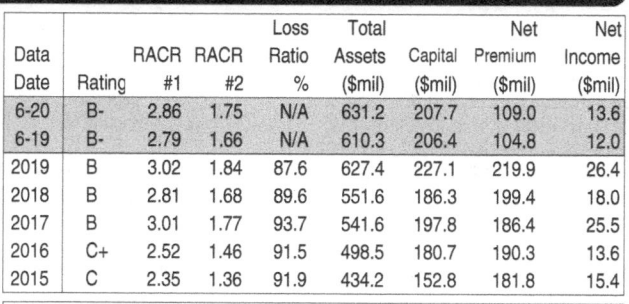

Rating Indexes

CHESAPEAKE LIFE INS CO *   A+   Excellent

Major Rating Factors: Good overall results on stability tests (5.8 on a scale of 0 to 10) despite fair financial strength of affiliated Blackstone Investor Group. Strengths that enhance stability include excellent risk diversification. Strong capitalization (9.5) based on excellent risk adjusted capital (severe loss scenario). Furthermore, this high level of risk adjusted capital has been consistently maintained over the last five years. High quality investment portfolio (8.8).

Other Rating Factors: Excellent profitability (8.6) despite modest operating losses during 2015. Excellent liquidity (7.9).

Principal Business: Individual health insurance (84%), individual life insurance (15%), and reinsurance (1%).

Principal Investments: NonCMO investment grade bonds (36%), CMOs and structured securities (3%), and cash (1%).

Investments in Affiliates: None

Group Affiliation: Blackstone Investor Group

Licensed in: All states except NJ, NY, VT, PR

Commenced Business: October 1956

Address: 1833 SOUTH MORGAN ROAD, OKLAHOMA CITY, OK 73128

Phone: (817) 255-3100   **Domicile State:** OK   **NAIC Code:** 61832

Data Date	Rating	RACR #1	RACR #2	Total Assets ($mil)	Capital ($mil)	Net Premium ($mil)	Net Income ($mil)
6-20	A+	3.31	2.64	253.5	147.7	122.2	16.8
6-19	A+	3.41	2.72	225.7	143.3	115.7	11.4
2019	A+	3.40	2.73	242.5	147.9	233.0	22.6
2018	A-	2.90	2.30	197.7	121.3	213.4	28.9
2017	B	2.21	1.76	158.7	86.7	200.8	16.6
2016	C+	1.85	1.47	133.3	69.7	184.3	11.6
2015	C+	1.38	1.11	99.8	46.8	159.6	-0.9

Blackstone Investor Group
Composite Group Rating: C
Largest Group Members

	Assets ($mil)	Rating
UNITED HEALTHCARE INS CO	20997	C
SIERRA HEALTH AND LIFE INS CO INC	5301	B
OXFORD HEALTH INS INC	2920	B
UNITED HEALTHCARE OF WISCONSIN INC	2069	B+
UNITED HEALTHCARE INS CO OF NY	1472	B

CHILDRENS COMMUNITY HEALTH PLAN INC *   B+   Good

Major Rating Factors: Excellent profitability (7.3 on a scale of 0 to 10). Strong capitalization (10.0) based on excellent current risk-adjusted capital (severe loss scenario). High quality investment portfolio (9.9).

Other Rating Factors: Excellent liquidity (7.5) with ample operational cash flow and liquid investments.

Principal Business: Medicaid (69%), comp med (31%)

Mem Phys: 19: 17,849   **18:** 16,676   **19 MLR** 84.5%   / **19 Admin Exp** N/A

Enroll(000): Q2 20: 146   **19:** 131   **18:** 146   **Med Exp PMPM:** $182

Principal Investments: Cash and equiv (85%), long-term bonds (15%)

Provider Compensation ($000): Contr fee ($279,925), FFS ($16,373), capitation ($1,218), bonus arrang ($714)

Total Member Encounters: Phys (334,767), non-phys (112,164)

Group Affiliation: Childrens Hospital and Health System

Licensed in: WI

Address: 9000 W Wisconsin Ave, Milwaukee, WI 53226

Phone: (800) 482-8010   **Dom State:** WI   **Commenced Bus:** N/A

Data Date	Rating	RACR #1	RACR #2	Total Assets ($mil)	Capital ($mil)	Net Premium ($mil)	Net Income ($mil)
6-20	B+	4.56	3.80	239.7	127.4	182.3	28.2
6-19	N/A	N/A	N/A	N/A	N/A	N/A	N/A
2019	B+	3.58	2.98	193.1	100.3	343.6	28.3
2018	B+	1.90	1.58	159.0	71.4	434.4	32.9
2017	B	1.54	1.28	92.9	40.2	258.4	-4.0
2016	B	1.95	1.63	85.3	44.1	235.8	4.2
2015	B	1.72	1.43	81.3	39.7	237.6	10.7

Rating Indexes

CHILDRENS MEDICAL CENTER HEALTH PLAN

E- **Very Weak**

Major Rating Factors: Weak profitability index (0.9 on a scale of 0 to 10). Good capitalization (6.8) based on excellent current risk-adjusted capital (severe loss scenario). High quality investment portfolio (9.9).
Other Rating Factors: Excellent liquidity (7.0) with sufficient resources (cash flows and marketable investments) to handle a spike in claims.
Principal Business: Medicaid (100%)
Mem Phys: 18: 7,614 **17:** 5,921 **18 MLR** 104.3% **/ 18 Admin Exp** N/A
Enroll(000): Q3 19: 8 **18:** 9 **17:** 10 **Med Exp PMPM:** $2,493
Principal Investments: Cash and equiv (100%)
Provider Compensation ($000): Contr fee ($263,896), capitation ($10,166)
Total Member Encounters: Phys (484,021), non-phys (74,865)
Group Affiliation: None
Licensed in: TX
Address: 1320 GREENWAY DR SUITE 1000, IRVING, TX 75038
Phone: (214) 456-7000 **Dom State:** TX **Commenced Bus:** N/A

Data Date	Rating	RACR #1	RACR #2	Total Assets ($mil)	Capital ($mil)	Net Premium ($mil)	Net Income ($mil)
9-19	E-	1.21	1.01	76.2	40.9	200.9	1.1
9-18	E-	N/A	N/A	76.3	12.2	196.4	-43.5
2018	E-	1.21	1.01	101.0	40.7	264.6	-53.7
2017	E-	N/A	N/A	85.4	31.9	242.9	-69.7
2016	D+	1.16	0.97	31.7	3.9	38.2	-13.4
2015	N/A	N/A	N/A	4.5	3.7	N/A	-4.6
2014	N/A	N/A	N/A	4.8	3.3	N/A	N/A

Rating Indexes

CHINESE COMMUNITY HEALTH PLAN

E- **Very Weak**

Major Rating Factors: Weak profitability index (2.3 on a scale of 0 to 10). Poor capitalization index (1.9) based on weak current risk-adjusted capital (moderate loss scenario). Weak overall results on stability tests (2.4) based on a steep decline in capital during 2019.
Other Rating Factors: Excellent liquidity (7.3) with ample operational cash flow and liquid investments.
Principal Business: Medicare (42%)
Mem Phys: 19: N/A **18:** N/A **19 MLR** 88.2% **/ 19 Admin Exp** N/A
Enroll(000): Q2 20: 15 **19:** 20 **18:** 20 **Med Exp PMPM:** $480
Principal Investments ($000): Cash and equiv ($20,079)
Provider Compensation ($000): None
Total Member Encounters: N/A
Group Affiliation: Chinese Hospital Association
Licensed in: CA
Address: 445 Grant Avenue Suite 700, San Francisco, CA 94108
Phone: (415) 955-8800 **Dom State:** CA **Commenced Bus:** August 1987

Data Date	Rating	RACR #1	RACR #2	Total Assets ($mil)	Capital ($mil)	Net Premium ($mil)	Net Income ($mil)
6-20	E-	0.62	0.41	76.2	10.5	66.4	6.5
6-19	E-	0.47	0.31	70.2	8.1	72.4	3.0
2019	E-	0.21	0.14	52.0	4.0	137.5	-2.0
2018	E-	0.28	0.18	55.7	5.1	133.7	-5.5
2017	E	0.77	0.51	65.0	12.7	136.1	-20.1
2016	N/A	N/A	N/A	N/A	N/A	N/A	N/A
2015	B	2.69	1.78	92.1	41.9	155.4	4.7

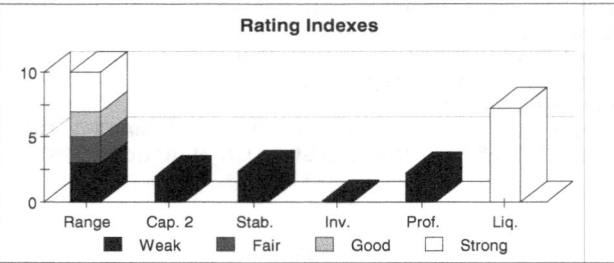

Rating Indexes

CHOICE PHYSICIANS NETWORK

D+ **Weak**

Major Rating Factors: Fair overall results on stability tests (3.6 on a scale of 0 to 10) in spite of healthy premium and capital growth during 2019. Good overall profitability index (5.1). Good capitalization index (5.3) based on fair current risk-adjusted capital (moderate loss scenario).
Other Rating Factors: Excellent liquidity (7.2) with ample operational cash flow and liquid investments.
Principal Business: Managed care (100%)
Mem Phys: 19: N/A **18:** N/A **19 MLR** 90.3% **/ 19 Admin Exp** N/A
Enroll(000): Q2 20: 14 **19:** 15 **18:** 15 **Med Exp PMPM:** $740
Principal Investments ($000): Cash and equiv ($33,362)
Provider Compensation ($000): None
Total Member Encounters: N/A
Group Affiliation: None
Licensed in: CA
Address: 18564 Hwy 18 Ste 105, Apple Valley, CA 92307
Phone: (626) 229-9828 **Dom State:** CA **Commenced Bus:** September 2009

Data Date	Rating	RACR #1	RACR #2	Total Assets ($mil)	Capital ($mil)	Net Premium ($mil)	Net Income ($mil)
6-20	D+	0.81	0.49	45.6	10.6	76.6	4.1
6-19	E+	0.89	0.54	35.9	11.3	78.8	10.8
2019	D+	0.84	0.51	39.5	10.9	151.0	13.0
2018	E	0.22	0.13	25.4	3.2	130.6	1.7
2017	N/A	N/A	N/A	N/A	N/A	N/A	N/A
2016	E+	0.34	0.21	17.3	4.3	105.6	-0.5
2015	D-	0.38	0.23	12.0	3.4	78.5	0.0

Rating Indexes

CHRISTIAN FIDELITY LIFE INS CO *   A-   Excellent

Major Rating Factors: Good overall results on stability tests (6.5 on a scale of 0 to 10). Strengths that enhance stability include good operational trends and good risk diversification. Strong capitalization (9.9) based on excellent risk adjusted capital (severe loss scenario). Furthermore, this high level of risk adjusted capital has been consistently maintained over the last five years. High quality investment portfolio (7.9).

Other Rating Factors: Excellent profitability (7.6) with operating gains in each of the last five years. Excellent liquidity (7.7).

Principal Business: Individual health insurance (85%), group health insurance (8%), and individual life insurance (7%).

Principal Investments: NonCMO investment grade bonds (85%), cash (8%), CMOs and structured securities (5%), policy loans (1%), and mortgages in good standing (1%).

Investments in Affiliates: None

Group Affiliation: Amerco Corp

Licensed in: AL, AZ, AR, CO, FL, GA, ID, IL, IN, KS, KY, LA, MS, MO, MT, NE, NV, NM, ND, OH, OK, OR, SC, SD, TN, TX, UT, VA, WA, WV, WY

Commenced Business: December 1935

Address: 1999 Bryan Street Suite 900, Dallas, TX 75201

Phone: (602) 263-6666 **Domicile State:** TX **NAIC Code:** 61859

Data Date	Rating	RACR #1	RACR #2	Total Assets ($mil)	Capital ($mil)	Net Premium ($mil)	Net Income ($mil)
6-20	A-	4.11	2.95	58.3	29.6	10.6	3.4
6-19	A-	3.80	2.72	61.3	30.8	12.2	3.7
2019	A-	3.54	2.56	55.3	26.3	23.7	8.0
2018	B+	3.28	2.39	58.2	27.2	26.9	8.7
2017	B	2.87	2.12	59.6	26.7	30.7	8.1
2016	B	2.75	2.03	63.9	28.0	34.5	8.1
2015	B	2.63	1.93	68.8	28.9	38.7	9.2

Adverse Trends in Operations

Decrease in asset base during 2019 (5%)
Decrease in premium volume from 2018 to 2019 (12%)
Decrease in premium volume from 2017 to 2018 (12%)
Decrease in premium volume from 2016 to 2017 (11%)
Decrease in premium volume from 2015 to 2016 (11%)

CHRISTUS HEALTH PLAN   C-   Fair

Major Rating Factors: Weak profitability index (0.9 on a scale of 0 to 10). Strong capitalization (7.4) based on excellent current risk-adjusted capital (severe loss scenario). High quality investment portfolio (9.4).

Other Rating Factors: Excellent liquidity (7.2) with ample operational cash flow and liquid investments.

Principal Business: Comp med (83%), Medicare (17%)

Mem Phys: 19: N/A **18:** N/A **19 MLR** 113.2% **/ 19 Admin Exp** N/A

Enroll(000): Q2 20: 33 **19:** 27 **18:** 29 **Med Exp PMPM:** $484

Principal Investments: Cash and equiv (100%)

Provider Compensation ($000): FFS ($117,292)

Total Member Encounters: N/A

Group Affiliation: None

Licensed in: NM, TX

Address: 919 Hidden Ridge Drive, Irving, TX 75038

Phone: (469) 282-2000 **Dom State:** TX **Commenced Bus:** N/A

Data Date	Rating	RACR #1	RACR #2	Total Assets ($mil)	Capital ($mil)	Net Premium ($mil)	Net Income ($mil)
6-20	C-	1.71	1.42	130.7	43.6	84.7	11.1
6-19	N/A	N/A	N/A	N/A	N/A	N/A	N/A
2019	C-	1.27	1.06	122.8	33.0	150.6	-64.6
2018	C-	2.06	1.72	84.3	36.5	168.5	16.8
2017	C-	1.19	0.99	51.6	19.7	135.9	-1.6
2016	C-	0.84	0.70	41.6	14.3	61.8	-11.4
2015	C-	1.44	1.20	10.7	7.6	21.2	-5.2

Rating Indexes

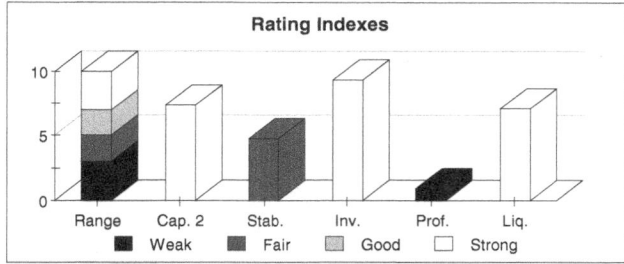

Range   Cap. 2   Stab.   Inv.   Prof.   Liq.

■ Weak   ■ Fair   ▨ Good   □ Strong

CIGNA HEALTH & LIFE INS CO   B   Good

Major Rating Factors: Good overall results on stability tests (5.6 on a scale of 0 to 10). Stability strengths include excellent operational trends and excellent risk diversification. Good liquidity (5.3) with sufficient resources to handle a spike in claims. Fair quality investment portfolio (3.7).

Other Rating Factors: Strong capitalization (7.9) based on excellent risk adjusted capital (severe loss scenario). Excellent profitability (9.8) with operating gains in each of the last five years.

Principal Business: Group health insurance (85%) and individual health insurance (15%).

Principal Investments: NonCMO investment grade bonds (53%), noninv. grade bonds (15%), mortgages in good standing (8%), common & preferred stock (5%), and misc. investments (19%).

Investments in Affiliates: 6%

Group Affiliation: CIGNA Corp

Licensed in: All states, the District of Columbia and Puerto Rico

Commenced Business: February 1964

Address: 900 COTTAGE GROVE ROAD, BLOOMFIELD, CT 6002

Phone: (860) 226-6000 **Domicile State:** CT **NAIC Code:** 67369

Data Date	Rating	RACR #1	RACR #2	Total Assets ($mil)	Capital ($mil)	Net Premium ($mil)	Net Income ($mil)
6-20	B	2.23	1.69	12,993.2	5,746.5	9,822.7	1,514.8
6-19	B	2.14	1.62	10,796.1	4,996.4	9,032.7	1,218.2
2019	B	2.06	1.57	11,675.8	5,207.4	18,363.8	2,184.5
2018	B	2.09	1.59	10,489.2	4,801.1	16,629.8	2,197.3
2017	B	1.86	1.42	9,002.2	3,680.6	13,779.7	1,569.1
2016	B	1.86	1.43	7,410.9	3,390.1	11,625.2	1,396.6
2015	B	1.66	1.31	6,559.9	3,008.9	11,457.7	1,187.2

Adverse Trends in Operations

Increase in policy surrenders from 2015 to 2016 (27%)

CIGNA HEALTHCARE OF ARIZONA INC
D+   Weak

Major Rating Factors: Weak profitability index (1.8 on a scale of 0 to 10). Weak overall results on stability tests (2.3) based on a decline in the number of member physicians during 2020. Weak liquidity (2.0) as a spike in claims may stretch capacity.

Other Rating Factors: Fair capitalization index (4.9) based on good current risk-adjusted capital (severe loss scenario). Good quality investment portfolio (5.5).

Principal Business: Medicare (100%), comp med (8%)

Mem Phys: 19: 23,920   **18:** 28,338   **19 MLR** 92.7%   **/ 19 Admin Exp** N/A

Enroll(000): Q2 20: 65   **19:** 56   **18:** 48   **Med Exp PMPM:** $868

Principal Investments: Long-term bonds (76%), real estate (18%), cash and equiv (6%)

Provider Compensation ($000): FFS ($257,954), contr fee ($171,000), capitation ($52,359), salary ($27,435), other ($49,712)

Total Member Encounters: Phys (168,428), non-phys (56,964)

Group Affiliation: None

Licensed in: AZ

Address: 25500 NNORTERRA DR, PHOENIX,

Phone: (860) 226-5076   **Dom State:** AZ   **Commenced Bus:** N/A

Data Date	Rating	RACR #1	RACR #2	Total Assets ($mil)	Capital ($mil)	Net Premium ($mil)	Net Income ($mil)
6-20	D+	0.91	0.76	178.2	61.4	382.5	13.7
6-19	C	2.30	1.91	165.8	74.8	323.4	6.1
2019	C	1.11	0.93	123.0	48.2	617.6	-3.5
2018	C	2.28	1.90	131.1	74.3	571.2	11.3
2017	E-	1.41	1.18	121.9	60.4	444.4	-16.9
2016	E-	2.05	1.71	130.3	66.6	566.0	-36.2
2015	C	1.46	1.21	94.6	39.0	536.7	-19.7

Rating Indexes

CIGNA HEALTHCARE OF CALIFORNIA INC
C   Fair

Major Rating Factors: Weak profitability index (2.2 on a scale of 0 to 10). Good overall results on stability tests (6.9). Rating is significantly influenced by the good financial results of CIGNA Corp. Strong capitalization index (6.9) based on excellent current risk-adjusted capital (severe loss scenario).

Other Rating Factors: Excellent liquidity (7.0) with ample operational cash flow and liquid investments.

Principal Business: Managed care (100%)

Mem Phys: 19: N/A   **18:** N/A   **19 MLR** 90.2%   **/ 19 Admin Exp** N/A

Enroll(000): Q2 20: 153   **19:** 151   **18:** 151   **Med Exp PMPM:** $1,929

Principal Investments ($000): Cash and equiv ($91,995)

Provider Compensation ($000): None

Total Member Encounters: N/A

Group Affiliation: CIGNA Corp

Licensed in: CA

Address: 400 N Brand Blvd Suite #400, Glendale, CA 91203

Phone: (818) 500-6276   **Dom State:** CA   **Commenced Bus:** November 1978

Data Date	Rating	RACR #1	RACR #2	Total Assets ($mil)	Capital ($mil)	Net Premium ($mil)	Net Income ($mil)
6-20	C	1.74	1.07	180.4	72.7	467.0	9.8
6-19	C	1.29	0.80	148.4	49.8	476.0	0.6
2019	C	1.42	0.87	142.0	58.9	952.9	9.2
2018	C	1.07	0.66	132.9	40.5	887.5	-14.6
2017	C	0.96	0.59	136.8	36.3	982.4	-20.4
2016	C	1.25	0.77	148.9	40.0	915.6	-16.5
2015	C	1.18	0.72	134.5	37.0	950.8	-18.6

Rating Indexes

CIGNA HEALTHCARE OF COLORADO INC
C   Fair

Major Rating Factors: Fair overall results on stability tests (3.9 on a scale of 0 to 10) based on a steep decline in premium revenue in 2019. Weak profitability index (1.9). Strong capitalization index (10.0) based on excellent current risk-adjusted capital (severe loss scenario).

Other Rating Factors: High quality investment portfolio (9.9). Excellent liquidity (9.0) with ample operational cash flow and liquid investments.

Principal Business: Comp med (100%)

Mem Phys: 19: 19,908   **18:** 17,257   **19 MLR** 89.3%   **/ 19 Admin Exp** N/A

Enroll(000): Q2 20: 1   **19:** 0   **18:** 0   **Med Exp PMPM:** $401

Principal Investments: Cash and equiv (61%), long-term bonds (39%)

Provider Compensation ($000): Contr fee ($1,002), FFS ($164), capitation ($41)

Total Member Encounters: Phys (909), non-phys (512)

Group Affiliation: None

Licensed in: CO

Address: 3900 EAST MEXICO AVENUE SUITE, DENVER,

Phone: (860) 226-6000   **Dom State:** CO   **Commenced Bus:** N/A

Data Date	Rating	RACR #1	RACR #2	Total Assets ($mil)	Capital ($mil)	Net Premium ($mil)	Net Income ($mil)
6-20	C	5.03	4.19	8.0	5.2	3.7	0.2
6-19	C	6.22	5.18	3.5	3.0	0.7	-0.1
2019	C	8.36	6.97	5.3	4.3	1.4	-0.8
2018	C	6.42	5.35	3.4	3.2	2.6	-0.5
2017	C	3.85	3.21	4.4	3.6	5.1	1.6
2016	C	3.99	3.32	4.3	2.0	4.8	-1.2
2015	C	3.88	3.24	4.1	2.3	7.1	-0.9

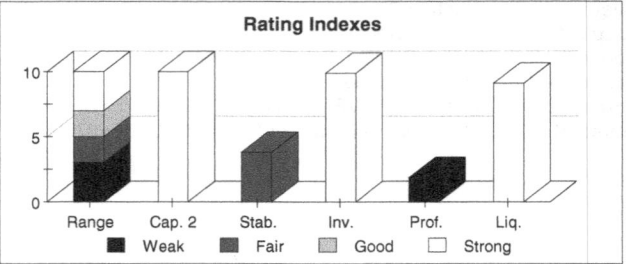

Rating Indexes

CIGNA HEALTHCARE OF FLORIDA INC   C-   Fair

Major Rating Factors: Fair overall results on stability tests (4.2 on a scale of 0 to 10) based on an excessive 60% enrollment growth during the period, a decline in the number of member physicians during 2020. Weak profitability index (0.7). Good liquidity (6.3) with sufficient resources (cash flows and marketable investments) to handle a spike in claims.

Other Rating Factors: Strong capitalization index (7.7) based on excellent current risk-adjusted capital (severe loss scenario). High quality investment portfolio (9.9).

Principal Business: Comp med (100%)

Mem Phys: 19: 56,277   **18:** 122,112   **19 MLR** 119.5%   **/ 19 Admin Exp** N/A

Enroll(000): Q2 20: 0   **19:** 0   **18:** 0   **Med Exp PMPM:** $523

Principal Investments: Long-term bonds (94%), cash and equiv (6%)

Provider Compensation ($000): Contr fee ($1,267), FFS ($250), capitation ($92)

Total Member Encounters: Phys (1,245), non-phys (440)

Group Affiliation: None

Licensed in: FL

Address: 2701 NORTH ROCKY POINT DRIVE S, TAMPA,

Phone: (860) 226-6000   **Dom State:** FL   **Commenced Bus:** N/A

Data Date	Rating	RACR #1	RACR #2	Total Assets ($mil)	Capital ($mil)	Net Premium ($mil)	Net Income ($mil)
6-20	C-	1.89	1.57	3.0	2.2	1.1	-0.3
6-19	C	5.14	4.29	3.2	3.0	0.7	0.0
2019	C	4.29	3.57	3.0	2.4	1.5	-0.4
2018	C	5.05	4.21	3.2	2.9	1.1	0.0
2017	C	2.54	2.12	3.3	2.9	1.5	0.1
2016	C	6.97	5.81	4.2	3.8	1.0	-0.1
2015	C	7.23	6.03	4.3	3.9	1.3	-0.1

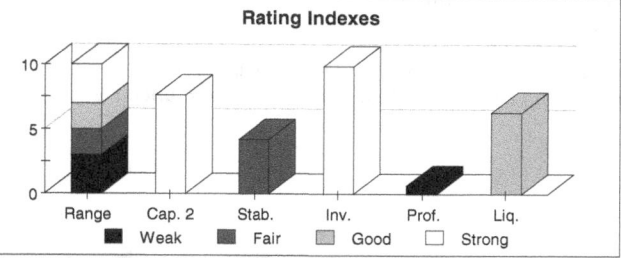

CIGNA HEALTHCARE OF GEORGIA INC   C   Fair

Major Rating Factors: Fair overall results on stability tests (3.6 on a scale of 0 to 10) based on a steep decline in capital during 2019, inconsistent enrollment growth in the past five years due to declines in 2017, 2018 and 2019 and a decline in the number of member physicians during 2020. Weak profitability index (0.9). Good quality investment portfolio (5.3).

Other Rating Factors: Good liquidity (6.5) with sufficient resources (cash flows and marketable investments) to handle a spike in claims. Strong capitalization index (7.2) based on excellent current risk-adjusted capital (severe loss scenario).

Principal Business: Medicare (98%), comp med (2%)

Mem Phys: 19: 19,534   **18:** 49,702   **19 MLR** 87.2%   **/ 19 Admin Exp** N/A

Enroll(000): Q2 20: 27   **19:** 21   **18:** 24   **Med Exp PMPM:** $828

Principal Investments: Long-term bonds (94%), cash and equiv (6%)

Provider Compensation ($000): FFS ($204,224), capitation ($8,662), contr fee ($2,927)

Total Member Encounters: Phys (499,653), non-phys (138,363)

Group Affiliation: None

Licensed in: GA

Address: TWO SECURITIES CENTRE 3500 PIE, ATLANTA,

Phone: (404) 443-8800   **Dom State:** GA   **Commenced Bus:** N/A

Data Date	Rating	RACR #1	RACR #2	Total Assets ($mil)	Capital ($mil)	Net Premium ($mil)	Net Income ($mil)
6-20	C	1.48	1.23	87.0	38.4	162.2	4.8
6-19	C	2.47	2.06	74.3	40.5	122.8	-4.7
2019	C	2.21	1.84	66.9	33.8	241.6	-10.8
2018	C	2.63	2.20	79.8	43.5	254.0	1.7
2017	E	1.49	1.24	93.9	43.7	269.6	-11.2
2016	E	1.85	1.54	111.7	54.5	383.6	-17.8
2015	E	1.50	1.25	78.8	20.8	173.7	-24.5

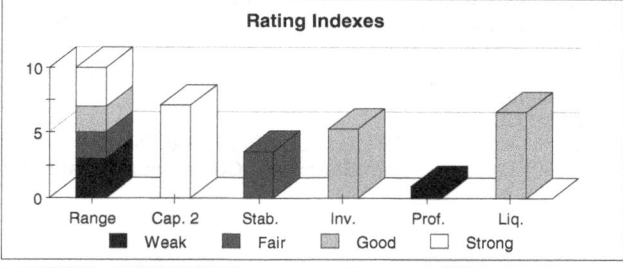

CIGNA HEALTHCARE OF ILLINOIS INC   D   Weak

Major Rating Factors: Weak profitability index (0.9 on a scale of 0 to 10). Weak overall results on stability tests (0.9) based on a decline in the number of member physicians during 2020, a significant 33% decrease in enrollment during the period. Strong capitalization index (7.1) based on excellent current risk-adjusted capital (severe loss scenario).

Other Rating Factors: High quality investment portfolio (9.8). Excellent liquidity (7.0) with sufficient resources (cash flows and marketable investments) to handle a spike in claims.

Principal Business: Comp med (100%)

Mem Phys: 19: 13,279   **18:** 61,398   **19 MLR** 69.5%   **/ 19 Admin Exp** N/A

Enroll(000): Q2 20: 14   **19:** 15   **18:** 22   **Med Exp PMPM:** $220

Principal Investments: Long-term bonds (75%), cash and equiv (25%)

Provider Compensation ($000): Contr fee ($35,427), FFS ($8,336), capitation ($18)

Total Member Encounters: Phys (210,525), non-phys (58,783)

Group Affiliation: None

Licensed in: IL, IN

Address: 525 WEST MONROE SUITE 1650, CHICAGO,

Phone: (860) 226-6000   **Dom State:** IL   **Commenced Bus:** N/A

Data Date	Rating	RACR #1	RACR #2	Total Assets ($mil)	Capital ($mil)	Net Premium ($mil)	Net Income ($mil)
6-20	D	1.46	1.22	83.2	10.4	26.5	-7.2
6-19	C	3.47	2.89	105.9	15.0	28.0	-3.5
2019	C	4.43	3.69	67.4	17.4	59.6	-2.9
2018	C	4.56	3.80	87.9	19.6	81.0	8.7
2017	C-	1.84	1.53	85.4	12.2	46.3	-10.9
2016	C	8.71	7.26	12.1	5.3	0.5	-4.1
2015	C	7.36	6.13	4.3	4.1	0.9	0.2

CIGNA HEALTHCARE OF NEW JERSEY INC   E   Very Weak

Major Rating Factors: Weak profitability index (2.1 on a scale of 0 to 10). Fair overall results on stability tests (4.5) based on a significant 43% decrease in enrollment during the period. Strong capitalization index (10.0) based on excellent current risk-adjusted capital (severe loss scenario).
Other Rating Factors: High quality investment portfolio (9.9). Excellent liquidity (10.0) with ample operational cash flow and liquid investments.
Principal Business: Comp med (100%)
Mem Phys: 19: 29,901 **18:** 30,756 **19 MLR** 4.3% **/ 19 Admin Exp** N/A
Enroll(000): Q2 20: 0 **19:** 0 **18:** 0 **Med Exp PMPM:** $98
Principal Investments: Cash and equiv (86%), long-term bonds (14%)
Provider Compensation ($000): Contr fee ($1,499), FFS ($118), capitation ($31)
Total Member Encounters: N/A
Group Affiliation: None
Licensed in: NJ
Address: 499 WASHINGTON BOULEVARD 5TH F, JERSEY CITY,
Phone: (860) 226-6000 **Dom State:** NJ **Commenced Bus:** N/A

Data Date	Rating	RACR #1	RACR #2	Total Assets ($mil)	Capital ($mil)	Net Premium ($mil)	Net Income ($mil)
6-20	E	13.49	11.24	14.5	13.8	0.2	0.0
6-19	E	15.85	13.21	15.2	13.7	2.0	3.6
2019	E	23.80	19.83	14.6	13.8	2.2	3.7
2018	E	11.71	9.76	13.9	10.0	4.8	-0.8
2017	E	N/A	N/A	7.5	2.1	4.4	-3.4
2016	E	12.91	10.76	10.3	7.2	3.9	1.4
2015	C	5.19	4.33	5.2	2.9	1.6	-2.7

Rating Indexes

CIGNA HEALTHCARE OF NORTH CAROLINA   D   Weak

Major Rating Factors: Fair overall results on stability tests (3.3 on a scale of 0 to 10) based on a steep decline in premium revenue in 2019, a steep decline in capital during 2019 and a decline in the number of member physicians during 2020. Good overall profitability index (5.9). Good quality investment portfolio (6.8).
Other Rating Factors: Good liquidity (6.9) with sufficient resources (cash flows and marketable investments) to handle a spike in claims. Strong capitalization index (8.3) based on excellent current risk-adjusted capital (severe loss scenario).
Principal Business: Medicare (63%), comp med (37%)
Mem Phys: 19: 33,293 **18:** 72,328 **19 MLR** 80.3% **/ 19 Admin Exp** N/A
Enroll(000): Q2 20: 16 **19:** 10 **18:** 21 **Med Exp PMPM:** $661
Principal Investments: Long-term bonds (96%), cash and equiv (4%)
Provider Compensation ($000): FFS ($60,857), contr fee ($28,171), capitation ($1,655)
Total Member Encounters: Phys (219,192), non-phys (84,595)
Group Affiliation: None
Licensed in: NC
Address: 701 CORPORATE CENTER DRIVE, RALEIGH,
Phone: (860) 226-6000 **Dom State:** NC **Commenced Bus:** N/A

Data Date	Rating	RACR #1	RACR #2	Total Assets ($mil)	Capital ($mil)	Net Premium ($mil)	Net Income ($mil)
6-20	D	2.40	2.00	56.5	28.6	86.6	0.9
6-19	D	3.85	3.21	76.3	38.9	54.8	4.3
2019	D	4.00	3.33	39.4	27.8	104.3	6.3
2018	D	3.66	3.05	82.9	37.0	170.7	15.6
2017	C	1.46	1.22	95.2	21.5	149.9	7.8
2016	C	1.86	1.55	27.2	13.5	88.9	-4.2
2015	C	1.31	1.09	18.2	7.7	74.9	0.6

Rating Indexes

CIGNA HEALTHCARE OF SOUTH CAROLINA   C   Fair

Major Rating Factors: Fair overall results on stability tests (4.1 on a scale of 0 to 10) based on a significant 16% decrease in enrollment during the period, a decline in the number of member physicians during 2020. Good overall profitability index (5.2). Good quality investment portfolio (6.2).
Other Rating Factors: Strong capitalization index (8.6) based on excellent current risk-adjusted capital (severe loss scenario). Excellent liquidity (6.9) with sufficient resources (cash flows and marketable investments) to handle a spike in claims.
Principal Business: Medicare (100%)
Mem Phys: 19: 16,476 **18:** 20,477 **19 MLR** 78.0% **/ 19 Admin Exp** N/A
Enroll(000): Q2 20: 6 **19:** 4 **18:** 5 **Med Exp PMPM:** $693
Principal Investments: Long-term bonds (99%), cash and equiv (1%)
Provider Compensation ($000): FFS ($38,569), capitation ($932), contr fee ($13)
Total Member Encounters: Phys (89,203), non-phys (26,620)
Group Affiliation: None
Licensed in: SC
Address: 4000 FABER PLACE DRIVE SUITE #, GREENVILLE,
Phone: (860) 226-6000 **Dom State:** SC **Commenced Bus:** N/A

Data Date	Rating	RACR #1	RACR #2	Total Assets ($mil)	Capital ($mil)	Net Premium ($mil)	Net Income ($mil)
6-20	C	2.63	2.19	27.7	17.3	36.1	0.7
6-19	C	4.88	4.07	28.7	21.4	25.0	1.4
2019	C	4.45	3.71	22.3	16.6	48.8	3.3
2018	C	4.57	3.81	27.7	19.9	56.1	2.0
2017	D-	2.18	1.81	28.1	17.9	62.3	2.1
2016	D-	2.09	1.74	29.6	15.7	95.4	-2.4
2015	D+	1.07	0.89	16.2	6.6	80.2	-1.2

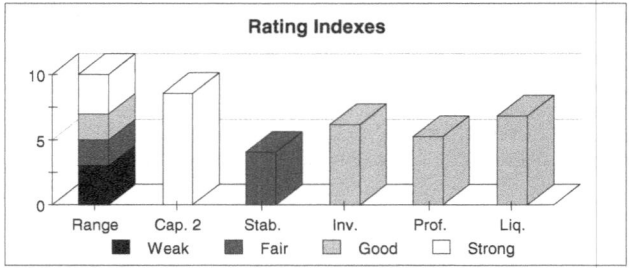

Rating Indexes

CIGNA HEALTHCARE OF ST LOUIS
C   Fair

Major Rating Factors: Fair overall results on stability tests (3.3 on a scale of 0 to 10) based on a steep decline in premium revenue in 2019, a significant 31% decrease in enrollment during the period. Weak profitability index (1.5). Strong capitalization index (8.6) based on excellent current risk-adjusted capital (severe loss scenario).
Other Rating Factors: High quality investment portfolio (9.5). Excellent liquidity (7.0) with ample operational cash flow and liquid investments.
Principal Business: Medicare (92%), comp med (8%)
Mem Phys: 19: 60,253 **18:** 60,253 **19 MLR** 86.3% **/ 19 Admin Exp** N/A
Enroll(000): Q2 20: 3 **19:** 2 **18:** 2 **Med Exp PMPM:** $637
Principal Investments: Long-term bonds (79%), cash and equiv (21%)
Provider Compensation ($000): FFS ($11,139), contr fee ($946), capitation ($506)
Total Member Encounters: Phys (26,775), non-phys (8,033)
Group Affiliation: None
Licensed in: IL, KS, MO
Address: 231 S BEMISTON, CLAYTON,
Phone: (860) 226-6000 **Dom State:** MO **Commenced Bus:** N/A

Data Date	Rating	RACR #1	RACR #2	Total Assets ($mil)	Capital ($mil)	Net Premium ($mil)	Net Income ($mil)
6-20	C	2.60	2.17	15.4	7.4	16.7	-1.3
6-19	C	5.30	4.41	14.4	9.7	7.0	0.4
2019	C	5.73	4.78	14.2	8.7	14.0	-0.6
2018	C	5.06	4.22	14.5	9.2	19.8	1.6
2017	D+	2.40	2.00	13.1	7.6	17.8	0.4
2016	D+	2.68	2.23	14.4	7.3	22.2	-1.4
2015	D+	15.69	13.07	13.3	8.9	6.3	0.0

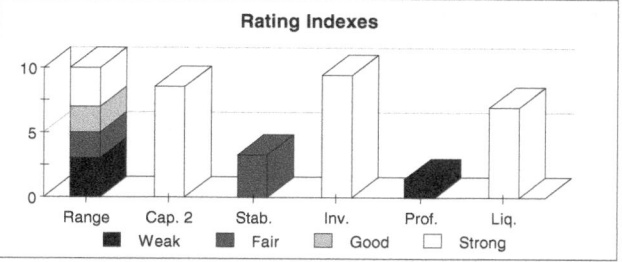

Rating Indexes

CIGNA HEALTHCARE OF TENNESSEE INC
C-   Fair

Major Rating Factors: Weak profitability index (1.7 on a scale of 0 to 10). Good overall results on stability tests (5.8) despite a decline in the number of member physicians during 2020. Strong capitalization index (8.2) based on excellent current risk-adjusted capital (severe loss scenario).
Other Rating Factors: High quality investment portfolio (9.9). Excellent liquidity (7.2) with ample operational cash flow and liquid investments.
Principal Business: Comp med (100%)
Mem Phys: 19: 25,562 **18:** 73,357 **19 MLR** 86.2% **/ 19 Admin Exp** N/A
Enroll(000): Q2 20: 3 **19:** 4 **18:** 4 **Med Exp PMPM:** $371
Principal Investments: Long-term bonds (54%), cash and equiv (46%)
Provider Compensation ($000): Contr fee ($11,828), FFS ($3,800), capitation ($1,313)
Total Member Encounters: Phys (13,039), non-phys (4,399)
Group Affiliation: None
Licensed in: MS, TN
Address: 1000 CORPORATE CENTRE DRIVE, FRANKLIN,
Phone: (860) 226-5634 **Dom State:** TN **Commenced Bus:** N/A

Data Date	Rating	RACR #1	RACR #2	Total Assets ($mil)	Capital ($mil)	Net Premium ($mil)	Net Income ($mil)
6-20	C-	2.28	1.90	11.4	7.8	7.0	0.6
6-19	C-	3.72	3.10	10.1	6.8	10.1	1.1
2019	C-	3.57	2.98	9.8	6.4	19.0	-0.5
2018	C-	3.15	2.62	8.7	5.7	21.3	-1.2
2017	C-	1.44	1.20	8.9	4.8	22.0	-1.1
2016	C	3.22	2.69	7.0	4.0	16.5	-1.2
2015	C	3.52	2.94	7.8	4.6	19.0	0.2

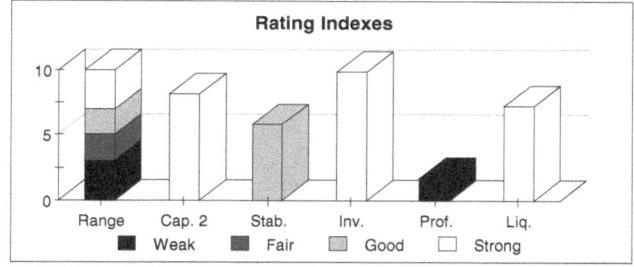

Rating Indexes

CIGNA HEALTHCARE OF TEXAS INC
C-   Fair

Major Rating Factors: Good overall profitability index (5.7 on a scale of 0 to 10). Good overall results on stability tests (5.1) despite a decline in enrollment during 2019, a decline in the number of member physicians during 2020. Strong capitalization index (10.0) based on excellent current risk-adjusted capital (severe loss scenario)
Other Rating Factors: High quality investment portfolio (9.2). Excellent liquidity (7.2) with ample operational cash flow and liquid investments.
Principal Business: Comp med (100%)
Mem Phys: 19: 58,691 **18:** 159,775 **19 MLR** 79.4% **/ 19 Admin Exp** N/A
Enroll(000): Q2 20: 7 **19:** 7 **18:** 9 **Med Exp PMPM:** $565
Principal Investments: Long-term bonds (70%), cash and equiv (30%)
Provider Compensation ($000): Contr fee ($31,441), FFS ($12,308), capitation ($8,881)
Total Member Encounters: Phys (18,806), non-phys (5,295)
Group Affiliation: None
Licensed in: TX
Address: 6600 EAST CAMPUS CIRCLE DRIVE, PLANO,
Phone: (860) 226-5634 **Dom State:** TX **Commenced Bus:** N/A

Data Date	Rating	RACR #1	RACR #2	Total Assets ($mil)	Capital ($mil)	Net Premium ($mil)	Net Income ($mil)
6-20	C-	5.05	4.21	43.9	33.2	30.9	2.6
6-19	C-	6.05	5.04	36.7	26.1	32.2	2.9
2019	C-	7.92	6.60	40.1	30.6	64.7	7.4
2018	C-	5.44	4.53	32.7	23.2	76.4	1.9
2017	C-	N/A	N/A	32.7	20.6	79.9	0.2
2016	C-	2.39	1.99	37.6	15.6	110.8	-7.5
2015	B	3.26	2.72	27.0	15.4	83.1	-0.6

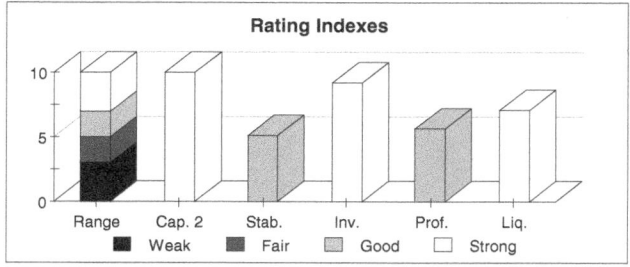

Rating Indexes

CIGNA LIFE INS CO OF NEW YORK *

A-   Excellent

Major Rating Factors: Good quality investment portfolio (5.6 on a scale of 0 to 10) despite mixed results such as: no exposure to mortgages and large holdings of BBB rated bonds but small junk bond holdings. Good overall profitability (6.9) despite operating losses during the first six months of 2020. Return on equity has been good over the last five years, averaging 13.4%. Excellent overall results on stability tests (7.0) excellent operational trends and excellent risk diversification.

Other Rating Factors: Strong capitalization (7.9) based on excellent risk adjusted capital (severe loss scenario). Excellent liquidity (7.1).

Principal Business: Group health insurance (71%) and group life insurance (29%).

Principal Investments: NonCMO investment grade bonds (95%), noninv. grade bonds (4%), and CMOs and structured securities (2%).

Investments in Affiliates: None

Group Affiliation: CIGNA Corp

Licensed in: AL, DC, MO, NY, PA, TN

Commenced Business: December 1965

Address: 140 EAST 45TH STREET, NEW YORK, NY 10017

Phone: (215) 761-1000   **Domicile State:** NY   **NAIC Code:** 64548

Data Date	Rating	RACR #1	RACR #2	Total Assets ($mil)	Capital ($mil)	Net Premium ($mil)	Net Income ($mil)
6-20	A-	2.27	1.57	449.3	100.3	121.6	-1.2
6-19	A-	2.44	1.62	422.0	107.3	111.6	1.7
2019	A-	2.38	1.66	424.4	104.9	217.1	15.1
2018	A-	2.49	1.65	408.7	108.8	202.0	17.8
2017	A-	2.71	1.77	403.7	109.0	178.7	22.9
2016	A-	2.41	1.58	383.4	92.0	164.4	5.1
2015	A-	2.69	1.78	364.4	97.4	150.3	18.9

Adverse Trends in Operations

Decrease in capital during 2019 (4%)
Decrease in capital during 2016 (5%)

CLAREMONT BEHAVIORAL SVCS

C-   Fair

Major Rating Factors: Fair overall results on stability tests (4.4 on a scale of 0 to 10) based on poor risk diversification due to the company's size. Excellent profitability (8.2). Strong capitalization index (7.9) based on excellent current risk-adjusted capital (severe loss scenario).

Other Rating Factors: Excellent liquidity (7.4) with ample operational cash flow and liquid investments.

Principal Business: Managed care (69%), indemnity (31%)

Mem Phys: 19: N/A   **18:** N/A   **19 MLR** 32.9%   **/ 19 Admin Exp** N/A

Enroll(000): Q2 20: 142   **19:** 129   **18:** 129   **Med Exp PMPM:** $13

Principal Investments ($000): Cash and equiv ($483)

Provider Compensation ($000): None

Total Member Encounters: N/A

Group Affiliation: Claremont Behavioral Services Inc

Licensed in: (No states)

Address: , , CA 94501-1075

Phone: (800) 834-3773   **Dom State:**   **Commenced Bus:** N/A

Data Date	Rating	RACR #1	RACR #2	Total Assets ($mil)	Capital ($mil)	Net Premium ($mil)	Net Income ($mil)
6-20	C-	2.17	1.75	2.4	1.2	2.9	0.1
6-19	C-	2.47	2.00	1.5	1.3	2.7	0.0
2019	C-	1.61	1.30	1.6	0.9	5.4	0.3
2018	C-	1.80	1.46	1.2	1.0	5.1	0.2
2017	N/A	N/A	N/A	N/A	N/A	N/A	N/A
2016	N/A	N/A	N/A	N/A	N/A	N/A	N/A
2015	N/A	N/A	N/A	N/A	N/A	N/A	N/A

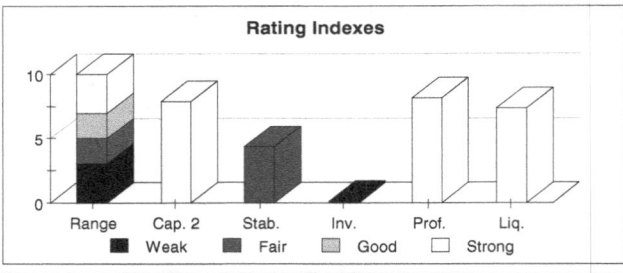

Rating Indexes

CLEAR SPRING HEALTH OF IL INC

D+   Weak

Major Rating Factors: Weak profitability index (0.9 on a scale of 0 to 10). Low quality investment portfolio (1.3). Strong capitalization (7.7) based on excellent current risk-adjusted capital (severe loss scenario).

Other Rating Factors: Excellent liquidity (7.2) with ample operational cash flow and liquid investments.

Principal Business: Medicare (100%)

Mem Phys: 19: 7,252   **18:** N/A   **19 MLR** 87.7%   **/ 19 Admin Exp** N/A

Enroll(000): Q2 20: 0   **19:** 0   **18:** N/A   **Med Exp PMPM:** $574

Principal Investments: Cash and equiv (92%), long-term bonds (8%)

Provider Compensation ($000): FFS ($228), bonus arrang ($81)

Total Member Encounters: Phys (535), non-phys (114)

Group Affiliation: Delaware Life Partners LLC

Licensed in: IL

Address: 208 South LaSalle Street Suit, Chicago, IL 60604

Phone: (847) 696-8521   **Dom State:** IL   **Commenced Bus:** N/A

Data Date	Rating	RACR #1	RACR #2	Total Assets ($mil)	Capital ($mil)	Net Premium ($mil)	Net Income ($mil)
6-20	D+	1.94	1.62	4.5	3.8	0.4	-0.1
6-19	N/A	N/A	N/A	6.2	2.3	0.2	N/A
2019	C-	4.07	3.40	4.8	4.0	0.4	1.1
2018	N/A	N/A	N/A	7.5	2.1	N/A	N/A
2017	N/A	N/A	N/A	2.0	2.0	N/A	N/A
2016	N/A	N/A	N/A	N/A	N/A	N/A	N/A
2015	N/A	N/A	N/A	N/A	N/A	N/A	N/A

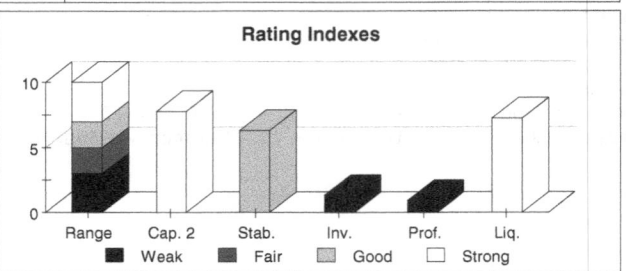

Rating Indexes

CLOVER INSURANCE COMPANY   C   Fair

Major Rating Factors: Weak profitability index (0.9 on a scale of 0 to 10). Good liquidity (5.5) with sufficient resources (cash flows and marketable investments) to handle a spike in claims. Strong capitalization (7.3) based on excellent current risk-adjusted capital (severe loss scenario).
Other Rating Factors: High quality investment portfolio (9.9).
Principal Business: Medicare (100%)
Mem Phys: 19: 30,225 **18:** 21,399 **19 MLR** 100.3% **/ 19 Admin Exp** N/A
Enroll(000): Q2 20: 52 **19:** 39 **18:** 32 **Med Exp PMPM:** $928
Principal Investments: Long-term bonds (53%), cash and equiv (47%)
Provider Compensation ($000): Contr fee ($413,035)
Total Member Encounters: Phys (1,224,412), non-phys (83,250)
Group Affiliation: NJ Healthcare Investments LLC
Licensed in: All states except MI, NH, NY, NC, VT, PR
Address: 30 Montgomery Street 15th Flo, Jersey City, NJ 7302
Phone: (201) 432-2133 **Dom State:** NJ **Commenced Bus:** N/A

Data Date	Rating	RACR #1	RACR #2	Total Assets ($mil)	Capital ($mil)	Net Premium ($mil)	Net Income ($mil)
6-20	C	1.58	1.32	196.8	94.3	307.6	33.7
6-19	C	0.46	0.39	113.3	35.1	221.9	-16.5
2019	C	0.65	0.54	145.3	55.6	427.4	-60.7
2018	C	0.46	0.38	107.7	35.1	290.1	-40.9
2017	C+	N/A	N/A	97.6	48.4	267.2	-21.5
2016	B-	6.41	5.34	189.0	67.9	46.0	-34.6
2015	N/A	N/A	N/A	35.5	10.2	52.5	N/A

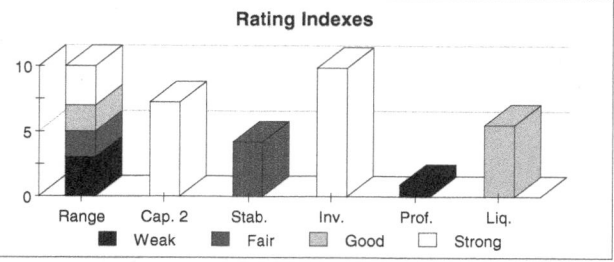

CMNTY CARE HLTH PLAN INC (WI)   B   Good

Major Rating Factors: Good overall profitability index (5.8 on a scale of 0 to 10). Strong capitalization (7.5) based on excellent current risk-adjusted capital (severe loss scenario). High quality investment portfolio (9.9).
Other Rating Factors: Excellent liquidity (7.0) with ample operational cash flow and liquid investments.
Principal Business: Medicaid (65%), Medicare (35%)
Mem Phys: 19: 16,531 **18:** N/A **19 MLR** 92.1% **/ 19 Admin Exp** N/A
Enroll(000): Q2 20: 2 **19:** 2 **18:** 2 **Med Exp PMPM:** $3,149
Principal Investments: Cash and equiv (74%), long-term bonds (26%)
Provider Compensation ($000): Contr fee ($60,977), salary ($15,712)
Total Member Encounters: Phys (29,235), non-phys (44,933)
Group Affiliation: Community Care Inc
Licensed in: WI
Address: 205 Bishops Way, Brookfield, WI 53005
Phone: (414) 385-6600 **Dom State:** WI **Commenced Bus:** N/A

Data Date	Rating	RACR #1	RACR #2	Total Assets ($mil)	Capital ($mil)	Net Premium ($mil)	Net Income ($mil)
6-20	B	1.75	1.45	26.5	17.8	49.3	3.0
6-19	N/A	N/A	N/A	N/A	N/A	N/A	N/A
2019	B	1.45	1.21	22.7	14.9	90.7	0.5
2018	B-	1.45	1.21	23.1	14.7	94.8	1.5
2017	C+	1.36	1.14	21.3	13.2	91.9	1.1
2016	C	1.31	1.09	20.3	12.5	94.6	3.2
2015	C-	0.87	0.73	16.8	8.8	96.2	-1.1

CMNTY CARE HLTH PLAN OF LA INC   B   Good

Major Rating Factors: Good overall profitability index (5.0 on a scale of 0 to 10). Good quality investment portfolio (5.3). Strong capitalization (7.7) based on excellent current risk-adjusted capital (severe loss scenario).
Other Rating Factors: Excellent liquidity (6.9) with sufficient resources (cash flows and marketable investments) to handle a spike in claims.
Principal Business: Medicaid (96%), comp med (4%)
Mem Phys: 19: 24,561 **18:** 18,617 **19 MLR** 86.9% **/ 19 Admin Exp** N/A
Enroll(000): Q2 20: 296 **19:** 268 **18:** 268 **Med Exp PMPM:** $373
Principal Investments: Long-term bonds (86%), cash and equiv (14%)
Provider Compensation ($000): Bonus arrang ($460,305), contr fee ($345,951), FFS ($283,611), capitation ($17,186)
Total Member Encounters: Phys (1,427,243), non-phys (2,237,042)
Group Affiliation: Anthem Inc
Licensed in: LA
Address: 10000 PERLOMS ROWE SOUTH G-51, BATON ROUGE, LA 70810
Phone: (757) 490-6900 **Dom State:** LA **Commenced Bus:** N/A

Data Date	Rating	RACR #1	RACR #2	Total Assets ($mil)	Capital ($mil)	Net Premium ($mil)	Net Income ($mil)
6-20	B	1.93	1.61	434.8	201.2	748.0	6.8
6-19	B-	3.04	2.54	360.8	193.1	629.5	24.1
2019	B-	2.55	2.13	417.7	192.5	1,285.0	26.2
2018	B-	2.77	2.31	394.5	174.5	1,138.8	-10.0
2017	B	1.76	1.47	333.7	124.0	947.5	12.5
2016	B-	1.61	1.34	282.8	68.9	785.3	-3.3
2015	B-	1.86	1.55	137.9	53.2	506.3	-3.9

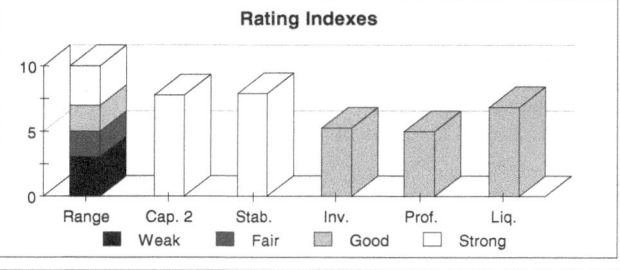

CMNTY CARE HLTH PLAN OF NV INC *   A-   Excellent

Major Rating Factors: Excellent profitability (7.1 on a scale of 0 to 10). Strong capitalization (7.4) based on excellent current risk-adjusted capital (severe loss scenario). High quality investment portfolio (8.0).
Other Rating Factors: Excellent liquidity (7.0) with sufficient resources (cash flows and marketable investments) to handle a spike in claims.
Principal Business: Medicaid (98%), comp med (2%)
Mem Phys: 19: 8,479 **18:** 7,640 **19 MLR** 82.9% **/ 19 Admin Exp** N/A
Enroll(000): Q2 20: 216 **19:** 194 **18:** 187 **Med Exp PMPM:** $260
Principal Investments: Long-term bonds (73%), cash and equiv (26%), other (1%)
Provider Compensation ($000): Bonus arrang ($397,167), FFS ($93,062), contr fee ($88,886), capitation ($4,179)
Total Member Encounters: Phys (1,059,188), non-phys (1,226,654)
Group Affiliation: Anthem Inc
Licensed in: NV
Address: 9133 W RUSSELL ROAD, LAS VEGAS, NV 89148
Phone: (757) 490-6900 **Dom State:** NV **Commenced Bus:** N/A

Data Date	Rating	RACR #1	RACR #2	Total Assets ($mil)	Capital ($mil)	Net Premium ($mil)	Net Income ($mil)
6-20	A-	1.67	1.40	194.3	97.2	362.1	-3.7
6-19	B	2.43	2.02	152.6	86.1	327.0	2.0
2019	A-	2.51	2.09	199.9	101.4	710.9	16.6
2018	B	2.33	1.94	189.1	82.2	652.4	9.8
2017	B	1.31	1.09	138.6	71.8	645.3	8.2
2016	B	1.91	1.59	122.1	64.7	635.1	4.9
2015	B	2.19	1.82	114.8	61.3	560.0	9.5

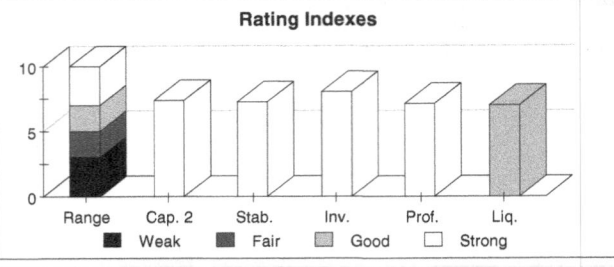

Rating Indexes — Range, Cap. 2, Stab., Inv., Prof., Liq. ■ Weak ■ Fair ▨ Good ▢ Strong

COLONIAL LIFE & ACCIDENT INS CO   C+   Fair

Major Rating Factors: Fair overall results on stability tests (4.9 on a scale of 0 to 10). Good quality investment portfolio (5.7) despite significant exposure to mortgages . Mortgage default rate has been low. large holdings of BBB rated bonds in addition to small junk bond holdings. Good liquidity (6.9) with sufficient resources to handle a spike in claims as well as a significant increase in policy surrenders.
Other Rating Factors: Strong capitalization (7.5) based on excellent risk adjusted capital (severe loss scenario). Excellent profitability (8.4) with operating gains in each of the last five years.
Principal Business: Individual health insurance (65%), individual life insurance (21%), group health insurance (13%), and group life insurance (2%).
Principal Investments: NonCMO investment grade bonds (79%), mortgages in good standing (12%), CMOs and structured securities (3%), policy loans (2%), and misc. investments (5%).
Investments in Affiliates: None
Group Affiliation: Unum Group
Licensed in: All states except NY
Commenced Business: September 1939
Address: 1200 COLONIAL LIFE BOULEVARD, COLUMBIA, SC 29210
Phone: (803) 798-7000 **Domicile State:** SC **NAIC Code:** 62049

Data Date	Rating	RACR #1	RACR #2	Total Assets ($mil)	Capital ($mil)	Net Premium ($mil)	Net Income ($mil)
6-20	C+	1.97	1.32	3,663.8	619.7	848.5	126.2
6-19	C+	2.45	1.56	3,464.4	595.0	816.3	102.3
2019	C+	2.00	1.35	3,525.2	610.9	1,612.7	233.4
2018	C+	2.20	1.40	3,421.9	528.0	1,589.6	200.4
2017	C+	2.14	1.35	3,220.0	490.4	1,503.0	157.9
2016	C+	2.53	1.57	3,143.9	562.1	1,414.5	151.5
2015	C+	2.65	1.64	3,018.8	566.0	1,333.8	157.8

Rating Indexes — Ranges, Cap., Stab., Inv., Prof., Liq. ■ Weak ■ Fair ▨ Good ▢ Strong

COLONIAL PENN LIFE INS CO   D+   Weak

Major Rating Factors: Weak overall results on stability tests (2.4 on a scale of 0 to 10) including weak financial strength of affiliated CNO Financial Group Inc. Weak profitability (1.8) with operating losses during the first six months of 2020. Weak liquidity (0.4) as a spike in claims or a run on policy withdrawals may stretch capacity.
Other Rating Factors: Fair quality investment portfolio (4.9). Good capitalization (5.3) based on good risk adjusted capital (moderate loss scenario).
Principal Business: Individual health insurance (63%), individual life insurance (24%), and group life insurance (13%).
Principal Investments: NonCMO investment grade bonds (73%), CMOs and structured securities (16%), policy loans (3%), noninv. grade bonds (2%), and misc. investments (6%).
Investments in Affiliates: None
Group Affiliation: CNO Financial Group Inc
Licensed in: All states except NY
Commenced Business: September 1959
Address: 399 MARKET STREET, PHILADELPHIA, PA 19181
Phone: (215) 928-8000 **Domicile State:** PA **NAIC Code:** 62065

Data Date	Rating	RACR #1	RACR #2	Total Assets ($mil)	Capital ($mil)	Net Premium ($mil)	Net Income ($mil)
6-20	D+	1.22	0.73	883.8	95.0	223.0	-9.6
6-19	D+	1.34	0.79	887.9	107.2	208.3	-3.7
2019	D+	1.13	0.67	835.7	82.2	390.6	-24.5
2018	D+	1.19	0.69	869.9	92.4	379.0	-21.1
2017	D+	1.28	0.73	868.5	99.7	366.4	-11.7
2016	D+	1.27	0.72	854.7	95.8	352.5	-1.9
2015	D+	1.13	0.66	816.0	79.3	330.3	-18.8

CNO Financial Group Inc Composite Group Rating: D+ Largest Group Members	Assets ($mil)	Rating
BANKERS LIFE CAS CO	16369	D+
WASHINGTON NATIONAL INS CO	5604	D+
COLONIAL PENN LIFE INS CO	836	D+
BANKERS CONSECO LIFE INS CO	523	D

COLORADO ACCESS | D | Weak

Major Rating Factors: Good overall profitability index (5.5 on a scale of 0 to 10). Good liquidity (6.9) with sufficient resources (cash flows and marketable investments) to handle a spike in claims. Strong capitalization index (10.0) based on weak current risk-adjusted capital (severe loss scenario).

Other Rating Factors: High quality investment portfolio (9.9). Excellent overall results on stability tests (7.0) based on healthy premium and capital growth during 2019 but a decline in the number of member physicians during 2020.

Principal Business: Medicaid (72%), other (28%)

Mem Phys: 19: 6,663 **18:** 13,957 **19 MLR** 93.4% / **19 Admin Exp** N/A

Enroll(000): Q2 20: 544 **19:** 513 **18:** 532 **Med Exp PMPM:** $53

Principal Investments: Cash and equiv (116%)

Provider Compensation ($000): Contr fee ($256,713), capitation ($67,276)

Total Member Encounters: Phys (357,820), non-phys (5,342)

Group Affiliation: None

Licensed in: CO

Address: 11100 E BETHANY DR, AURORA,

Phone: (720) 744-5100 **Dom State:** CO **Commenced Bus:** N/A

Data Date	Rating	RACR #1	RACR #2	Total Assets ($mil)	Capital ($mil)	Net Premium ($mil)	Net Income ($mil)
6-20	D	N/A	N/A	77.2	33.6	175.1	2.9
6-19	D	N/A	N/A	52.1	19.6	177.3	-2.8
2019	D	N/A	N/A	68.7	29.3	357.8	5.5
2018	D	N/A	N/A	63.0	23.1	295.9	5.8
2017	D-	N/A	N/A	53.8	20.0	273.9	12.0
2016	E	0.23	0.19	62.9	10.9	244.1	7.9
2015	N/A	N/A	N/A	42.8	0.3	258.7	-13.4

Rating Indexes

COMBINED INS CO OF AMERICA | C | Fair

Major Rating Factors: Fair overall results on stability tests (4.1 on a scale of 0 to 10) including fair risk adjusted capital in prior years. Good current capitalization (5.7) based on mixed results -- excessive policy leverage mitigated by good risk adjusted capital (severe loss scenario) reflecting some improvement over results in 2015. Good quality investment portfolio (6.6).

Other Rating Factors: Good liquidity (6.8). Weak profitability (2.0) with investment income below regulatory standards in relation to interest assumptions of reserves.

Principal Business: Individual health insurance (57%), group health insurance (30%), individual life insurance (6%), group life insurance (6%), and reinsurance (1%).

Principal Investments: NonCMO investment grade bonds (63%), CMOs and structured securities (24%), noninv. grade bonds (6%), common & preferred stock (3%), and misc. investments (2%).

Investments in Affiliates: 3%

Group Affiliation: Chubb Limited

Licensed in: All states except NY

Commenced Business: January 1922

Address: 111 E Wacker Drive, Chicago, IL 60601

Phone: (800) 225-4500 **Domicile State:** IL **NAIC Code:** 62146

Data Date	Rating	RACR #1	RACR #2	Total Assets ($mil)	Capital ($mil)	Net Premium ($mil)	Net Income ($mil)
6-20	C	1.18	0.87	2,501.6	273.9	514.0	32.4
6-19	C	1.01	0.73	2,361.8	197.7	546.9	-0.7
2019	C	0.97	0.72	2,417.9	218.7	1,076.4	16.8
2018	C	1.03	0.72	2,364.2	174.4	646.5	-158.7
2017	C+	1.37	0.97	1,495.7	178.7	480.2	33.4
2016	C+	1.15	0.80	1,432.1	131.5	447.5	30.7
2015	C	0.80	0.54	1,316.7	79.9	439.9	-14.1

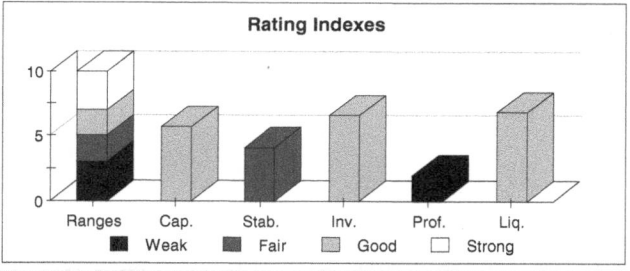

Rating Indexes

COMBINED LIFE INS CO OF NEW YORK | C+ | Fair

Major Rating Factors: Fair overall results on stability tests (4.5 on a scale of 0 to 10) including weak risk adjusted capital in prior years. Weak profitability (2.9) with investment income below regulatory standards in relation to interest assumptions of reserves. Strong current capitalization (7.6) based on excellent risk adjusted capital (severe loss scenario) reflecting significant improvement over results in 2015.

Other Rating Factors: High quality investment portfolio (7.6). Excellent liquidity (7.2).

Principal Business: Individual health insurance (80%), individual life insurance (11%), group health insurance (7%), and group life insurance (1%).

Principal Investments: NonCMO investment grade bonds (53%), CMOs and structured securities (45%), and policy loans (2%).

Investments in Affiliates: None

Group Affiliation: Chubb Limited

Licensed in: IL, NY

Commenced Business: June 1971

Address: 13 Cornell Road, Latham, NY 12110

Phone: (800) 951-6206 **Domicile State:** NY **NAIC Code:** 78697

Data Date	Rating	RACR #1	RACR #2	Total Assets ($mil)	Capital ($mil)	Net Premium ($mil)	Net Income ($mil)
6-20	C+	2.00	1.39	526.3	76.9	84.1	8.0
6-19	C+	1.61	1.15	485.8	61.1	87.2	6.9
2019	C+	1.78	1.25	502.8	69.1	176.4	13.8
2018	C+	1.42	1.01	472.3	52.7	167.2	7.8
2017	C+	1.21	0.86	441.6	44.3	163.4	10.0
2016	C+	0.95	0.67	420.3	33.4	155.2	7.6
2015	C	0.63	0.45	397.3	21.9	156.2	-9.7

Rating Indexes

COMMENCEMENT BAY RISK MGMT INS   B   Good

Major Rating Factors: Good quality investment portfolio (5.6 on a scale of 0 to 10) with no exposure to mortgages and no exposure to junk bonds. Good liquidity (6.8) with sufficient resources to handle a spike in claims. Fair overall results on stability tests (4.1) including excessive premium growth.
Other Rating Factors: Strong capitalization (8.0) based on excellent risk adjusted capital (severe loss scenario). Excellent profitability (9.3) with operating gains in each of the last five years.
Principal Business: Individual health insurance (100%).
Principal Investments: NonCMO investment grade bonds (38%), CMOs and structured securities (23%), common & preferred stock (19%), and cash (3%).
Investments in Affiliates: None
Group Affiliation: Regence Group
Licensed in: OR, UT, WA
Commenced Business: September 1992
Address: 1800 NINTH AVENUE, SEATTLE, WA 98101
Phone: (206) 464-3600 **Domicile State:** WA **NAIC Code:** 78879

Data Date	Rating	RACR #1	RACR #2	Total Assets ($mil)	Capital ($mil)	Net Premium ($mil)	Net Income ($mil)
6-20	B	2.25	1.69	76.7	51.8	37.6	8.0
6-19	A-	5.70	4.16	51.9	42.6	29.4	11.2
2019	B	2.08	1.56	65.7	44.3	65.8	7.8
2018	B-	6.54	5.89	32.0	31.4	1.6	1.4
2017	U	6.36	5.72	28.0	27.8	0.0	0.3
2016	U	3.75	3.38	7.7	7.5	0.0	0.2
2015	U	3.71	3.34	7.7	7.4	0.0	0.1

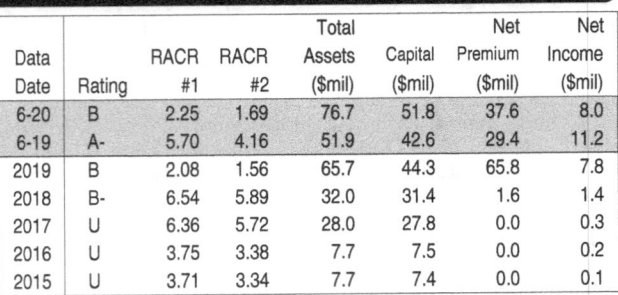

COMMON GROUND HEALTHCARE COOPERATIVE   C   Fair

Major Rating Factors: Good overall profitability index (5.5 on a scale of 0 to 10). Strong capitalization (10.0) based on excellent current risk-adjusted capital (severe loss scenario). High quality investment portfolio (9.4).
Other Rating Factors: Excellent liquidity (7.4) with ample operational cash flow and liquid investments.
Principal Business: Comp med (100%)
Mem Phys: 19: 8,972 **18:** 19,098 **19 MLR** 85.3% **/ 19 Admin Exp** N/A
Enroll(000): Q2 20: 53 **19:** 59 **18:** 52 **Med Exp PMPM:** $539
Principal Investments: Cash and equiv (63%), long-term bonds (37%)
Provider Compensation ($000): FFS ($314,793), contr fee ($82,929)
Total Member Encounters: N/A
Group Affiliation: None
Licensed in: WI
Address: 120 Bishops Way Suite 150, Brookfield, WI 53005-6271
Phone: (262) 754-9690 **Dom State:** WI **Commenced Bus:** N/A

Data Date	Rating	RACR #1	RACR #2	Total Assets ($mil)	Capital ($mil)	Net Premium ($mil)	Net Income ($mil)
6-20	C	4.53	3.78	346.0	214.8	165.0	4.6
6-19	N/A	N/A	N/A	N/A	N/A	N/A	N/A
2019	C	4.43	3.69	322.2	210.9	468.7	72.7
2018	D	2.40	2.00	217.9	144.8	557.5	135.5
2017	D	N/A	N/A	58.7	17.1	165.6	-11.1
2016	D	1.13	0.95	59.2	24.6	88.8	-36.0
2015	D	1.05	0.87	74.1	24.6	136.3	-28.2

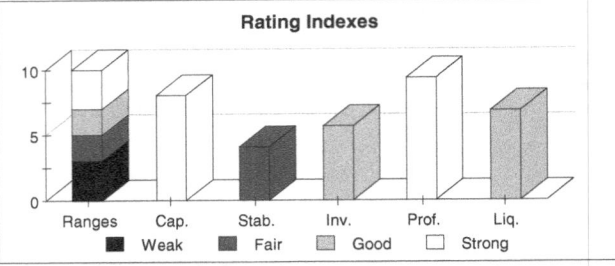

COMMUNITY CARE ALLIANCE OF ILLINOIS   D   Weak

Major Rating Factors: Weak profitability index (0.9 on a scale of 0 to 10). Low quality investment portfolio (1.0). Weak liquidity (2.0) as a spike in claims may stretch capacity.
Other Rating Factors: Good capitalization (6.9) based on excellent current risk-adjusted capital (severe loss scenario).
Principal Business: Medicare (100%)
Mem Phys: 19: 9,264 **18:** 9,889 **19 MLR** 92.0% **/ 19 Admin Exp** N/A
Enroll(000): Q2 20: 4 **19:** 5 **18:** 5 **Med Exp PMPM:** $967
Principal Investments: Cash and equiv (98%), long-term bonds (2%)
Provider Compensation ($000): FFS ($45,054), bonus arrang ($6,847)
Total Member Encounters: Phys (90,855), non-phys (18,917)
Group Affiliation: Delaware Life Partners LLC
Licensed in: IL
Address: 250 S Northwest Hwy Suite 3, Park Ridge, IL 60068
Phone: (847) 696-8520 **Dom State:** IL **Commenced Bus:** N/A

Data Date	Rating	RACR #1	RACR #2	Total Assets ($mil)	Capital ($mil)	Net Premium ($mil)	Net Income ($mil)
6-20	D	1.27	1.05	27.2	14.2	26.4	1.3
6-19	D	1.35	1.12	30.7	10.7	30.5	3.1
2019	D	2.04	1.70	26.4	13.1	59.1	2.6
2018	E-	N/A	N/A	6.8	-32.8	56.2	-39.3
2017	C-	N/A	N/A	13.5	4.2	62.5	-0.6
2016	D+	0.66	0.55	14.0	4.8	42.7	1.2
2015	D	0.29	0.24	8.6	2.7	19.6	0.1

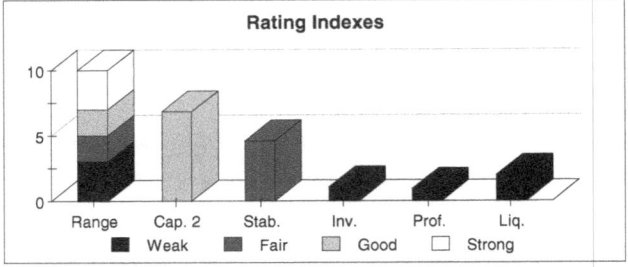

COMMUNITY CARE BEHAVIORAL HEALTH *   B+   Good

Major Rating Factors: Excellent profitability (8.3 on a scale of 0 to 10). Strong capitalization (9.2) based on excellent current risk-adjusted capital (severe loss scenario). Excellent liquidity (7.1) with ample operational cash flow and liquid investments.
Other Rating Factors: Fair quality investment portfolio (4.8).
Principal Business: Medicaid (90%), comp med (10%)
Mem Phys: 19: 5,464   **18:** 4,868   **19 MLR** 85.0%   **/ 19 Admin Exp** N/A
Enroll(000): Q2 20: 844   **19:** 771   **18:** 740   **Med Exp PMPM:** $100
Principal Investments: Long-term bonds (46%), cash and equiv (36%), nonaffiliate common stock (16%), other (2%)
Provider Compensation ($000): Contr fee ($926,209), capitation ($12,974)
Total Member Encounters: Phys (23,555,791), non-phys (198,158)
Group Affiliation: None
Licensed in: PA
Address: 339 Sixth Avenue Suite 1300, Pittsburgh, PA 15222
Phone: (412) 454-2120   **Dom State:** PA   **Commenced Bus:** N/A

Data Date	Rating	RACR #1	RACR #2	Total Assets ($mil)	Capital ($mil)	Net Premium ($mil)	Net Income ($mil)
6-20	B+	3.11	2.59	611.0	265.5	583.5	21.2
6-19	B+	4.56	3.80	431.1	259.1	564.8	27.5
2019	B+	4.04	3.37	431.4	254.7	1,106.2	32.1
2018	B+	4.03	3.36	347.1	227.7	970.5	18.6
2017	B	2.95	2.46	330.5	212.4	933.2	25.1
2016	C+	3.75	3.13	308.2	185.5	884.6	26.4
2015	C	3.10	2.59	244.5	156.9	811.3	4.5

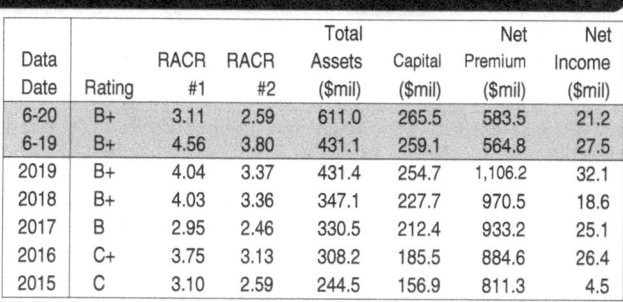

Rating Indexes

COMMUNITY CARE HEALTH PLAN   C+   Fair

Major Rating Factors: Fair overall results on stability tests (4.5 on a scale of 0 to 10) in spite of healthy premium and capital growth during 2019 but fair risk diversification due to the company's size. Good overall profitability index (5.8). Good capitalization index (6.9) based on excellent current risk-adjusted capital (severe loss scenario).
Other Rating Factors: Excellent liquidity (7.3) with ample operational cash flow and liquid investments.
Principal Business: Managed care (100%)
Mem Phys: 19: N/A   **18:** N/A   **19 MLR** 80.2%   **/ 19 Admin Exp** N/A
Enroll(000): Q2 20: 11   **19:** 10   **18:** 10   **Med Exp PMPM:** $410
Principal Investments ($000): Cash and equiv ($15,364)
Provider Compensation ($000): None
Total Member Encounters: N/A
Group Affiliation: Fresno Community Hosp & Med Center
Licensed in: CA
Address: 7370 N Palm Ave Ste 103, Fresno, CA 93711
Phone: (818) 458-2867   **Dom State:** CA   **Commenced Bus:** March 2013

Data Date	Rating	RACR #1	RACR #2	Total Assets ($mil)	Capital ($mil)	Net Premium ($mil)	Net Income ($mil)
6-20	C+	1.66	1.04	17.0	9.9	30.9	-0.6
6-19	C+	2.01	1.25	14.3	10.1	27.3	2.2
2019	C+	1.76	1.10	16.0	10.5	55.3	2.6
2018	C	1.50	0.93	12.2	7.9	46.4	2.8
2017	C-	1.42	0.89	8.7	5.1	30.3	1.2
2016	C-	1.79	1.14	6.9	4.7	20.8	0.1
2015	C-	1.91	1.21	7.5	4.6	19.2	0.3

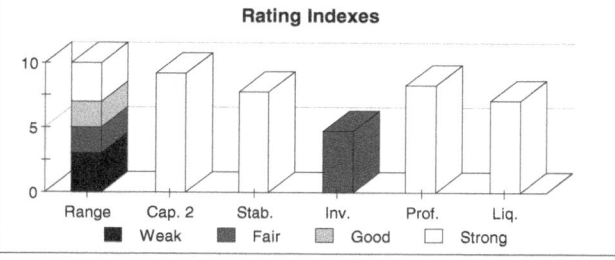

Rating Indexes

COMMUNITY FIRST HEALTH PLANS INC   C   Fair

Major Rating Factors: Fair profitability index (3.7 on a scale of 0 to 10). Fair quality investment portfolio (4.3). Good overall results on stability tests (6.0).
Other Rating Factors: Strong capitalization index (7.5) based on excellent current risk-adjusted capital (severe loss scenario). Excellent liquidity (7.0) with sufficient resources (cash flows and marketable investments) to handle a spike in claims.
Principal Business: Medicaid (91%), comp med (9%)
Mem Phys: 19: 7,673   **18:** 7,180   **19 MLR** 90.6%   **/ 19 Admin Exp** N/A
Enroll(000): Q2 20: 160   **19:** 154   **18:** 139   **Med Exp PMPM:** $281
Principal Investments: Cash and equiv (80%), long-term bonds (20%)
Provider Compensation ($000): Contr fee ($490,224), capitation ($22,114)
Total Member Encounters: Phys (678,763), non-phys (1,281,193)
Group Affiliation: None
Licensed in: TX
Address: 12238 Silicon Drive Ste 100, San Antonio,
Phone: (210) 227-2347   **Dom State:** TX   **Commenced Bus:** N/A

Data Date	Rating	RACR #1	RACR #2	Total Assets ($mil)	Capital ($mil)	Net Premium ($mil)	Net Income ($mil)
6-20	C	1.72	1.44	165.4	87.9	301.2	16.1
6-19	C+	1.47	1.23	137.7	73.7	281.6	1.2
2019	C	1.35	1.12	151.5	71.1	573.4	-0.6
2018	B-	1.43	1.19	142.7	71.7	537.4	-14.6
2017	A-	1.97	1.64	155.7	86.2	509.8	-3.6
2016	A	2.78	2.32	155.1	92.3	424.2	19.0
2015	A-	2.53	2.11	117.8	74.5	356.3	14.6

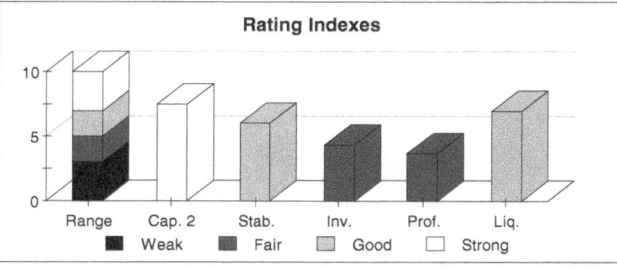

Rating Indexes

COMMUNITY HEALTH CHOICE INC

B- **Good**

Major Rating Factors: Fair overall results on stability tests (4.7 on a scale of 0 to 10) based on a significant 25% decrease in enrollment during the period. Good overall profitability index (5.7). Good capitalization index (6.6) based on good current risk-adjusted capital (severe loss scenario)
Other Rating Factors: High quality investment portfolio (9.9). Excellent liquidity (7.1) with ample operational cash flow and liquid investments.
Principal Business: Comp med (100%)
Mem Phys: 19: 16,131 **18:** 9,751 **19 MLR** 81.5% **/ 19 Admin Exp** N/A
Enroll(000): Q2 20: 94 **19:** 83 **18:** 111 **Med Exp PMPM:** $527
Principal Investments: Cash and equiv (100%)
Provider Compensation ($000): Contr fee ($587,430), capitation ($15,376)
Total Member Encounters: Phys (960,958), non-phys (235,347)
Group Affiliation: None
Licensed in: TX
Address: 2636 South Loop West Ste 700, Houston,
Phone: (713) 295-2200 **Dom State:** TX **Commenced Bus:** N/A

Data Date	Rating	RACR #1	RACR #2	Total Assets ($mil)	Capital ($mil)	Net Premium ($mil)	Net Income ($mil)
6-20	B-	1.18	0.98	211.1	75.8	344.5	10.1
6-19	C+	1.27	1.06	168.9	73.0	365.8	25.4
2019	B-	1.13	0.94	179.9	66.5	742.3	27.5
2018	C	0.98	0.82	175.1	57.3	706.2	35.4
2017	D	0.71	0.59	259.7	55.3	820.6	-24.9
2016	C+	0.84	0.70	305.1	81.5	1,126.9	-18.3
2015	B	1.47	1.23	239.9	101.6	850.6	5.4

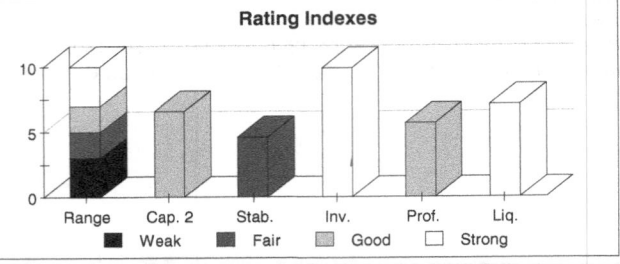

Rating Indexes

COMMUNITY HEALTH CHOICE TX INC

C- **Fair**

Major Rating Factors: Weak profitability index (1.8 on a scale of 0 to 10). Good capitalization (6.7) based on good current risk-adjusted capital (severe loss scenario). High quality investment portfolio (9.9).
Other Rating Factors: Excellent liquidity (6.9) with sufficient resources (cash flows and marketable investments) to handle a spike in claims.
Principal Business: Medicaid (92%), comp med (8%)
Mem Phys: 18: N/A **17:** 11,203 **18 MLR** 90.8% **/ 18 Admin Exp** N/A
Enroll(000): Q3 19: 270 **18:** 279 **17:** 290 **Med Exp PMPM:** $257
Principal Investments: Cash and equiv (91%), long-term bonds (9%)
Provider Compensation ($000): Contr fee ($863,960)
Total Member Encounters: Phys (2,712,789), non-phys (444,532)
Group Affiliation: Community Health Choice Texas Inc
Licensed in: TX
Address: 2636 SOUTH LOOP WEST SUITE 12, HOUSTON, TX 77054
Phone: (713) 295-2200 **Dom State:** TX **Commenced Bus:** N/A

Data Date	Rating	RACR #1	RACR #2	Total Assets ($mil)	Capital ($mil)	Net Premium ($mil)	Net Income ($mil)
9-19	C-	1.18	0.99	202.9	92.2	715.0	-6.4
9-18	N/A	N/A	N/A	152.9	46.0	712.3	-6.8
2018	C-	1.13	0.94	186.2	88.2	957.6	1.8
2017	N/A	N/A	N/A	143.6	51.0	688.3	-5.5
2016	N/A	N/A	N/A	N/A	N/A	N/A	N/A
2015	N/A	N/A	N/A	N/A	N/A	N/A	N/A
2014	N/A	N/A	N/A	N/A	N/A	N/A	N/A

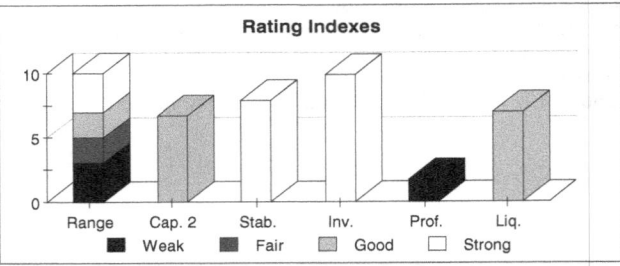

Rating Indexes

COMMUNITY HEALTH GROUP

C- **Fair**

Major Rating Factors: Fair profitability index (4.1 on a scale of 0 to 10). Fair capitalization index (3.1) based on weak current risk-adjusted capital (moderate loss scenario). Weak overall results on stability tests (1.4).
Other Rating Factors: Excellent liquidity (6.9) with sufficient resources (cash flows and marketable investments) to handle a spike in claims.
Principal Business: Medicaid (100%)
Mem Phys: 19: N/A **18:** N/A **19 MLR** 99.0% **/ 19 Admin Exp** N/A
Enroll(000): Q2 20: 6 **19:** 272 **18:** 272 **Med Exp PMPM:** $308
Principal Investments ($000): Cash and equiv ($494,077)
Provider Compensation ($000): None
Total Member Encounters: N/A
Group Affiliation: None
Licensed in: CA
Address: 2420 Fenton Street Suite 100, Chula Vista, CA 91914
Phone: (619) 498-6516 **Dom State:** CA **Commenced Bus:** N/A

Data Date	Rating	RACR #1	RACR #2	Total Assets ($mil)	Capital ($mil)	Net Premium ($mil)	Net Income ($mil)
6-20	C-	0.54	0.33	101.0	43.0	295.5	14.3
6-19	B-	7.00	4.25	744.0	482.3	524.4	-2.9
2019	B-	6.73	4.08	663.7	469.5	1,045.5	-15.7
2018	B-	7.04	4.28	754.2	485.2	950.4	-60.4
2017	A-	8.14	4.94	794.0	545.6	1,178.1	161.0
2016	B	5.72	3.46	776.0	384.5	1,184.5	197.3
2015	B-	3.02	1.83	529.4	187.3	1,038.5	113.7

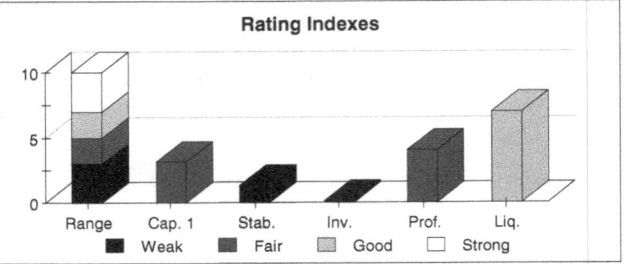

Rating Indexes

COMMUNITY HEALTH PLAN OF WASHINGTON   B-   Good

Major Rating Factors: Fair quality investment portfolio (3.9 on a scale of 0 to 10). Good overall profitability index (6.0). Good liquidity (6.8) with sufficient resources (cash flows and marketable investments) to handle a spike in claims.
Other Rating Factors: Strong capitalization (8.3) based on excellent current risk-adjusted capital (severe loss scenario).
Principal Business: Medicaid (85%), Medicare (13%), comp med (1%)
Mem Phys: 19: 27,720 **18:** 26,446 **19 MLR** 88.1% **/ 19 Admin Exp** N/A
Enroll(000): Q2 20: 240 **19:** 262 **18:** 265 **Med Exp PMPM:** $250
Principal Investments: Long-term bonds (48%), cash and equiv (33%), nonaffiliate common stock (19%)
Provider Compensation ($000): FFS ($629,139), capitation ($174,090)
Total Member Encounters: Phys (1,000,024), non-phys (800,917)
Group Affiliation: None
Licensed in: WA
Address: 1111 Third Avenue Suite 400, Seattle, WA 98101
Phone: (206) 521-8833 **Dom State:** WA **Commenced Bus:** N/A

Data Date	Rating	RACR #1	RACR #2	Total Assets ($mil)	Capital ($mil)	Net Premium ($mil)	Net Income ($mil)
6-20	B-	2.41	2.01	401.2	184.3	435.5	10.2
6-19	N/A	N/A	N/A	N/A	N/A	N/A	N/A
2019	B	2.54	2.12	459.3	195.0	927.2	11.1
2018	B	2.44	2.04	458.5	171.1	864.0	20.5
2017	B	2.17	1.81	458.1	188.8	1,087.3	24.2
2016	B	1.93	1.61	445.2	162.0	1,070.9	17.4
2015	B-	2.14	1.78	502.0	139.0	1,070.2	39.6

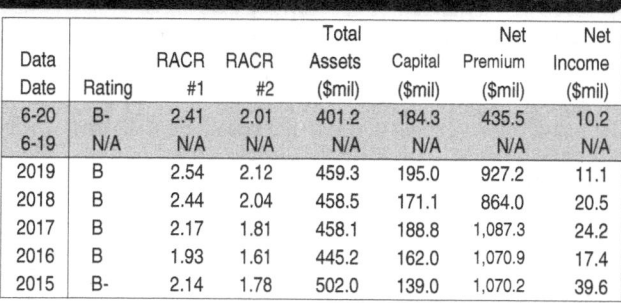

Rating Indexes

COMMUNITY INS CO   B-   Good

Major Rating Factors: Fair quality investment portfolio (3.7 on a scale of 0 to 10). Good liquidity (6.0) with sufficient resources (cash flows and marketable investments) to handle a spike in claims. Excellent profitability (9.0).
Other Rating Factors: Strong capitalization (8.6) based on excellent current risk-adjusted capital (severe loss scenario).
Principal Business: Comp med (38%), Medicare (37%), FEHB (14%), med supp (2%), other (7%)
Mem Phys: 19: 79,075 **18:** 76,561 **19 MLR** 90.4% **/ 19 Admin Exp** N/A
Enroll(000): Q2 20: 2,185 **19:** 2,066 **18:** 1,959 **Med Exp PMPM:** $217
Principal Investments: Long-term bonds (104%), nonaffiliate common stock (1%), other (9%)
Provider Compensation ($000): Bonus arrang ($3,625,472), contr fee ($1,003,120), FFS ($251,509), capitation ($133,088), other ($297,907)
Total Member Encounters: Phys (7,131,776), non-phys (6,584,134)
Group Affiliation: Anthem Inc
Licensed in: IN, OH
Address: 4361 IRWIN SIMPSON ROAD, MASON, OH 45040-9498
Phone: (513) 872-8100 **Dom State:** OH **Commenced Bus:** N/A

Data Date	Rating	RACR #1	RACR #2	Total Assets ($mil)	Capital ($mil)	Net Premium ($mil)	Net Income ($mil)
6-20	B-	2.62	2.18	2,163.0	941.9	3,242.2	277.7
6-19	B-	2.70	2.25	1,922.7	816.9	2,956.4	288.1
2019	B-	2.24	1.87	1,926.3	773.7	5,951.5	352.2
2018	B-	2.66	2.22	1,812.3	802.2	5,398.4	386.6
2017	B	2.45	2.04	1,990.4	830.0	5,714.2	348.6
2016	B+	2.64	2.20	2,138.7	807.8	5,297.0	319.1
2015	B+	2.56	2.13	2,091.4	754.1	5,255.4	266.3

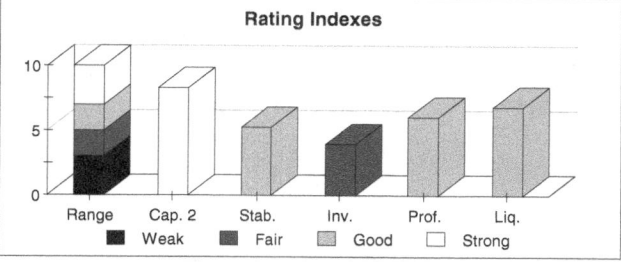

Rating Indexes

COMMUNITYCARE GOVERNMENT PROGRAMS   D   Weak

Major Rating Factors: Weak profitability index (0.9 on a scale of 0 to 10). Low quality investment portfolio (0.6). Fair capitalization (4.3) based on fair current risk-adjusted capital (moderate loss scenario).
Other Rating Factors: Excellent liquidity (7.1) with ample operational cash flow and liquid investments.
Principal Business: Medicare (100%)
Mem Phys: 18: 3,148 **17:** 3,833 **18 MLR** 91.8% **/ 18 Admin Exp** N/A
Enroll(000): Q3 19: 5 **18:** 3 **17:** 2 **Med Exp PMPM:** $651
Principal Investments: Cash and equiv (94%), long-term bonds (6%)
Provider Compensation ($000): Capitation ($14,317), contr fee ($5,786), FFS ($170)
Total Member Encounters: Phys (36,518), non-phys (42,904)
Group Affiliation: CommunityCare Government Programs In
Licensed in: OK
Address: Two West Second Street Suite, Tulsa, OK 74103
Phone: (918) 594-5202 **Dom State:** OK **Commenced Bus:** N/A

Data Date	Rating	RACR #1	RACR #2	Total Assets ($mil)	Capital ($mil)	Net Premium ($mil)	Net Income ($mil)
9-19	D	0.83	0.69	8.8	2.9	25.5	-0.2
9-18	D+	N/A	N/A	9.1	4.2	19.5	0.2
2018	D	1.28	1.06	9.0	4.4	26.3	0.2
2017	D+	N/A	N/A	6.5	4.4	13.8	0.6
2016	D+	1.16	0.96	3.6	2.9	5.6	-0.7
2015	N/A	N/A	N/A	1.8	1.7	N/A	-1.3
2014	N/A	N/A	N/A	N/A	N/A	N/A	N/A

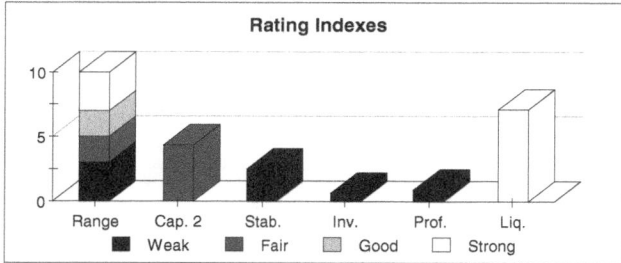

Rating Indexes

COMMUNITYCARE HMO INC
C+ — **Fair**

Major Rating Factors: Good overall profitability index (6.0 on a scale of 0 to 10). Good overall results on stability tests (5.7) despite a decline in enrollment during 2019. Low quality investment portfolio (1.4).
Other Rating Factors: Strong capitalization index (9.1) based on excellent current risk-adjusted capital (severe loss scenario). Excellent liquidity (7.2) with ample operational cash flow and liquid investments.
Principal Business: Medicare (52%), comp med (48%).
Mem Phys: 19: 9,883 **18:** 9,249 **19 MLR** 89.0% **/ 19 Admin Exp** N/A
Enroll(000): Q2 20: 47 **19:** 76 **18:** 85 **Med Exp PMPM:** $534
Principal Investments: Cash and equiv (86%), long-term bonds (14%)
Provider Compensation ($000): Contr fee ($288,465), capitation ($273,419), FFS ($1,394)
Total Member Encounters: Phys (585,503), non-phys (615,187)
Group Affiliation: CommunityCare Managed Healthcare Pla
Licensed in: OK
Address: 218 W 6th St, Tulsa,
Phone: (918) 594-5200 **Dom State:** OK **Commenced Bus:** N/A

Data Date	Rating	RACR #1	RACR #2	Total Assets ($mil)	Capital ($mil)	Net Premium ($mil)	Net Income ($mil)
6-20	C+	3.02	2.52	192.0	107.8	120.0	4.5
6-19	B	2.99	2.49	194.3	107.6	288.5	3.1
2019	B	2.86	2.38	178.4	101.4	562.2	4.1
2018	B	2.85	2.38	188.1	102.6	589.5	1.4
2017	B+	3.08	2.57	220.8	113.9	628.0	7.2
2016	B+	3.33	2.78	181.4	119.1	592.3	1.6
2015	A-	3.06	2.55	164.7	115.1	585.3	-0.1

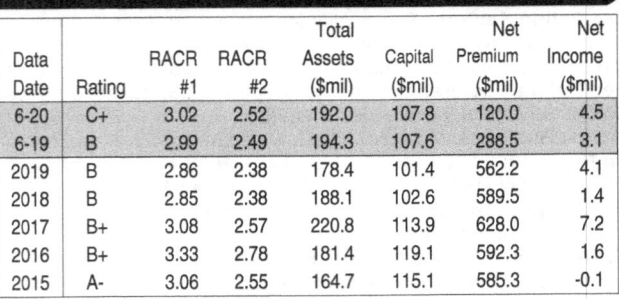

Rating Indexes

COMMUNITYCARE L&H INS CO
D — **Weak**

Major Rating Factors: Weak profitability index (1.7 on a scale of 0 to 10). Low quality investment portfolio (0.2). Strong capitalization (7.4) based on excellent current risk-adjusted capital (severe loss scenario).
Other Rating Factors: Excellent liquidity (7.2) with ample operational cash flow and liquid investments.
Principal Business: Comp med (97%), med supp (3%)
Mem Phys: 19: 12,942 **18:** 12,280 **19 MLR** 83.4% **/ 19 Admin Exp** N/A
Enroll(000): Q2 20: 5 **19:** 6 **18:** 10 **Med Exp PMPM:** $384
Principal Investments: Cash and equiv (91%), long-term bonds (9%)
Provider Compensation ($000): Contr fee ($35,191), FFS ($2,101)
Total Member Encounters: Phys (48,008), non-phys (36,003)
Group Affiliation: CommunityCare Managed Healthcare Pla
Licensed in: OK
Address: Two West 2nd Street Suite 100, Tulsa, OK 74103
Phone: (918) 594-5200 **Dom State:** OK **Commenced Bus:** N/A

Data Date	Rating	RACR #1	RACR #2	Total Assets ($mil)	Capital ($mil)	Net Premium ($mil)	Net Income ($mil)
6-20	D	1.70	1.41	19.5	9.3	15.2	-0.6
6-19	C	1.18	0.98	17.0	6.4	22.2	0.2
2019	C	2.27	1.89	21.1	9.9	42.0	1.4
2018	C	1.11	0.92	17.1	6.0	56.2	-2.3
2017	C	1.38	1.15	18.4	8.7	54.0	0.6
2016	B-	1.77	1.48	20.2	8.7	54.0	-1.3
2015	B-	1.68	1.40	20.0	10.1	66.0	-2.0

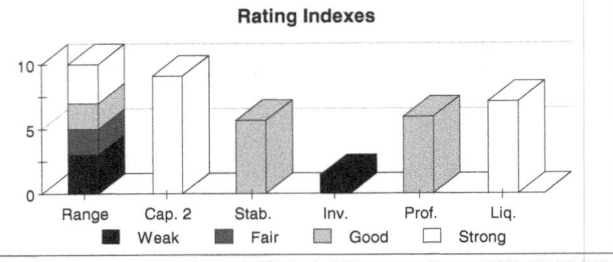

Rating Indexes

COMPANION LIFE INS CO *
B+ — **Good**

Major Rating Factors: Good liquidity (6.9 on a scale of 0 to 10) with sufficient resources to handle a spike in claims. Good overall results on stability tests (6.6). Stability strengths include excellent operational trends and excellent risk diversification. Fair quality investment portfolio (4.7).
Other Rating Factors: Strong capitalization (8.7) based on excellent risk adjusted capital (severe loss scenario). Excellent profitability (8.8) with operating gains in each of the last five years.
Principal Business: Group health insurance (76%), individual health insurance (12%), reinsurance (8%), and group life insurance (4%).
Principal Investments: NonCMO investment grade bonds (42%), common & preferred stock (33%), CMOs and structured securities (14%), and cash (4%).
Investments in Affiliates: 8%
Group Affiliation: Blue Cross Blue Shield of S Carolina
Licensed in: All states except CA, CT, HI, NJ, NY, PR
Commenced Business: July 1970
Address: 2501 Faraway Drive, Columbia, SC 29219
Phone: (800) 753-0404 **Domicile State:** SC **NAIC Code:** 77828

Data Date	Rating	RACR #1	RACR #2	Total Assets ($mil)	Capital ($mil)	Net Premium ($mil)	Net Income ($mil)
6-20	B+	2.80	2.16	489.5	258.7	164.2	7.8
6-19	B+	2.88	2.22	434.3	243.2	157.8	10.1
2019	B+	2.80	2.16	464.3	254.0	324.0	18.8
2018	B+	2.80	2.17	395.7	228.1	279.8	18.8
2017	B+	2.71	2.08	373.6	212.4	253.2	19.4
2016	B+	2.55	1.99	338.7	186.2	237.4	16.4
2015	A-	3.15	2.44	300.4	160.4	221.6	13.7

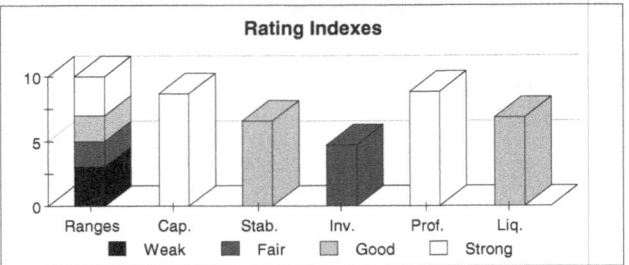

Rating Indexes

COMPBENEFITS INS CO   B-   Good

Major Rating Factors: Good overall profitability index (6.4 on a scale of 0 to 10). Strong capitalization (10.0) based on excellent current risk-adjusted capital (severe loss scenario). High quality investment portfolio (9.3).
Other Rating Factors: Excellent liquidity (7.0) with ample operational cash flow and liquid investments.
Principal Business: Medicare (95%), dental (5%)
Mem Phys: 19: 348,084 **18:** N/A **19 MLR** 82.1% **/ 19 Admin Exp** N/A
Enroll(000): Q2 20: 68 **19:** 53 **18:** 199 **Med Exp PMPM:** $206
Principal Investments: Long-term bonds (61%), cash and equiv (39%)
Provider Compensation ($000): Contr fee ($111,053), FFS ($10,818)
Total Member Encounters: Phys (260,140), non-phys (153,701)
Group Affiliation: None
Licensed in: AL, AZ, AR, CO, DC, FL, GA, ID, IL, IN, IA, KS, KY, LA, MD, MI, MS, MO, NE, NV, NM, NC, ND, OH, OK, OR, SC, TN, TX, UT, VA, WA, WV
Address: 2929 BRIARPARK SUITE 314, HOUSTON, TX 77042
Phone: (502) 580-1000 **Dom State:** TX **Commenced Bus:** N/A

Data Date	Rating	RACR #1	RACR #2	Total Assets ($mil)	Capital ($mil)	Net Premium ($mil)	Net Income ($mil)
6-20	B-	3.83	3.19	148.2	64.3	201.5	13.4
6-19	N/A	N/A	N/A	N/A	N/A	N/A	N/A
2019	B-	4.18	3.49	73.4	44.6	163.9	3.7
2018	N/A	N/A	N/A	29.8	21.5	38.8	N/A
2017	N/A	N/A	N/A	38.9	29.8	81.1	N/A
2016	N/A	N/A	N/A	37.9	30.7	94.4	N/A
2015	N/A	N/A	N/A	42.3	30.5	98.2	N/A

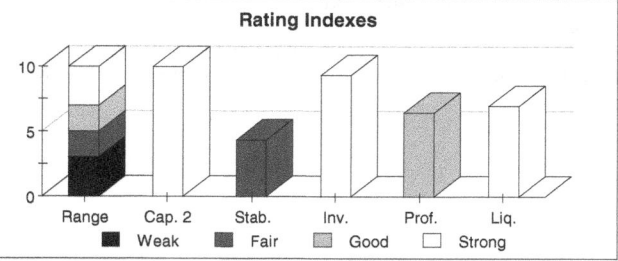

COMPCARE HEALTH SERVICES INS CORP *   A   Excellent

Major Rating Factors: Excellent profitability (9.8 on a scale of 0 to 10). Strong capitalization index (8.4) based on excellent current risk-adjusted capital (severe loss scenario). High quality investment portfolio (8.2).
Other Rating Factors: Excellent overall results on stability tests (8.4). Good liquidity (6.8) with sufficient resources (cash flows and marketable investments) to handle a spike in claims.
Principal Business: Medicare (43%), comp med (37%), Medicaid (19%)
Mem Phys: 19: 16,478 **18:** 15,733 **19 MLR** 82.8% **/ 19 Admin Exp** N/A
Enroll(000): Q2 20: 272 **19:** 242 **18:** 212 **Med Exp PMPM:** $365
Principal Investments: Long-term bonds (94%), cash and equiv (5%), other (1%)
Provider Compensation ($000): Contr fee ($490,924), bonus arrang ($429,078), FFS ($52,871), capitation ($29,006), other ($210)
Total Member Encounters: Phys (1,682,563), non-phys (2,012,475)
Group Affiliation: Anthem Inc
Licensed in: WI
Address: N17 W24340 RIVERWOOD DRIVE, WAUKESHA,
Phone: (262) 523-4020 **Dom State:** WI **Commenced Bus:** N/A

Data Date	Rating	RACR #1	RACR #2	Total Assets ($mil)	Capital ($mil)	Net Premium ($mil)	Net Income ($mil)
6-20	A	2.47	2.06	535.2	235.9	806.9	48.2
6-19	A-	3.82	3.18	421.6	195.9	585.0	32.4
2019	A-	2.76	2.30	426.1	191.8	1,248.8	69.0
2018	A-	3.29	2.74	329.3	167.9	914.3	59.1
2017	A-	2.44	2.04	308.5	152.9	798.4	41.5
2016	A-	3.11	2.60	265.3	135.4	769.1	45.8
2015	A-	2.50	2.09	233.6	100.7	681.2	6.8

COMPREHENSIVE MOBILE INS CO   B   Good

Major Rating Factors: Excellent profitability (7.1 on a scale of 0 to 10). Strong capitalization (10.0) based on excellent current risk-adjusted capital (severe loss scenario). High quality investment portfolio (9.9).
Other Rating Factors: Excellent liquidity (7.7) with ample operational cash flow and liquid investments.
Principal Business: Other (100%)
Mem Phys: 18: 74 **17:** 45 **18 MLR** 47.2% **/ 18 Admin Exp** N/A
Enroll(000): Q3 19: 3 **18:** 2 **17:** 2 **Med Exp PMPM:** $87
Principal Investments: Cash and equiv (57%), long-term bonds (35%), nonaffiliate common stock (9%)
Provider Compensation ($000): FFS ($2,092)
Total Member Encounters: Non-phys (5,383)
Group Affiliation: None
Licensed in: AZ, NM, TX, UT
Address: 19820 N 7TH STREET SUITE 290, PHOENIX, AZ 85024
Phone: (877) 929-0030 **Dom State:** AZ **Commenced Bus:** N/A

Data Date	Rating	RACR #1	RACR #2	Total Assets ($mil)	Capital ($mil)	Net Premium ($mil)	Net Income ($mil)
9-19	B	4.69	3.91	2.8	2.7	3.7	0.4
9-18	B	N/A	N/A	2.3	2.3	3.3	0.2
2018	B	4.14	3.45	2.5	2.4	4.4	0.4
2017	B	N/A	N/A	2.6	2.1	4.0	0.2
2016	B	2.71	2.26	1.4	1.0	2.9	0.2
2015	C-	7.29	6.08	1.2	0.9	1.1	0.2
2014	N/A	N/A	N/A	0.7	0.7	0.1	N/A

CONNECTICARE BENEFITS INC   C   Fair

Major Rating Factors: Good overall profitability index (6.3 on a scale of 0 to 10). Good liquidity (6.9) with sufficient resources (cash flows and marketable investments) to handle a spike in claims. Strong capitalization (7.7) based on excellent current risk-adjusted capital (severe loss scenario).
Other Rating Factors: High quality investment portfolio (8.7).
Principal Business: Comp med (100%)
Mem Phys: 19: 27,823 **18:** 26,611 **19 MLR** 81.3% **/ 19 Admin Exp** N/A
Enroll(000): Q2 20: 80 **19:** 70 **18:** 68 **Med Exp PMPM:** $467
Principal Investments: Long-term bonds (88%), cash and equiv (12%)
Provider Compensation ($000): Contr fee ($324,332), FFS ($80,536), capitation ($16,311)
Total Member Encounters: Phys (322,172), non-phys (278,637)
Group Affiliation: EmblemHealth Inc
Licensed in: CT
Address: 175 Scott Swamp Road, Farmington, CT 06032-3124
Phone: (860) 674-5700 **Dom State:** CT **Commenced Bus:** N/A

Data Date	Rating	RACR #1	RACR #2	Total Assets ($mil)	Capital ($mil)	Net Premium ($mil)	Net Income ($mil)
6-20	C	1.90	1.58	265.0	85.8	313.8	40.4
6-19	C	2.43	2.03	189.4	69.5	274.1	22.9
2019	C	1.50	1.25	180.2	46.1	519.3	9.6
2018	C	1.64	1.37	173.7	46.7	566.4	56.6
2017	D+	N/A	N/A	121.7	40.5	390.7	1.3
2016	D+	1.78	1.49	84.1	27.2	272.1	-17.5
2015	C	4.80	4.00	81.5	42.4	198.8	13.6

CONNECTICARE INC   C-   Fair

Major Rating Factors: Weak profitability index (2.0 on a scale of 0 to 10). Good overall results on stability tests (5.0). Strong capitalization index (7.0) based on excellent current risk-adjusted capital (severe loss scenario).
Other Rating Factors: High quality investment portfolio (9.5). Excellent liquidity (6.9) with sufficient resources (cash flows and marketable investments) to handle a spike in claims.
Principal Business: Medicare (74%), comp med (26%)
Mem Phys: 19: 27,823 **18:** 26,611 **19 MLR** 87.1% **/ 19 Admin Exp** N/A
Enroll(000): Q2 20: 64 **19:** 72 **18:** 77 **Med Exp PMPM:** $688
Principal Investments: Long-term bonds (81%), cash and equiv (19%)
Provider Compensation ($000): Contr fee ($471,435), FFS ($67,001), capitation ($60,271)
Total Member Encounters: Phys (607,193), non-phys (692,860)
Group Affiliation: EmblemHealth Inc
Licensed in: CT
Address: 175 Scott Swamp Road, Farmington,
Phone: (860) 674-5700 **Dom State:** CT **Commenced Bus:** N/A

Data Date	Rating	RACR #1	RACR #2	Total Assets ($mil)	Capital ($mil)	Net Premium ($mil)	Net Income ($mil)
6-20	C-	1.34	1.12	316.2	81.9	327.0	22.5
6-19	C-	1.59	1.32	192.9	62.7	350.9	-3.8
2019	C-	1.58	1.32	237.2	64.6	692.5	-14.8
2018	C-	1.67	1.39	216.5	66.8	679.9	-49.0
2017	C+	1.49	1.24	200.5	88.5	714.7	4.2
2016	C	2.19	1.82	209.2	94.5	793.8	7.1
2015	C+	2.51	2.09	214.0	108.9	835.4	5.1

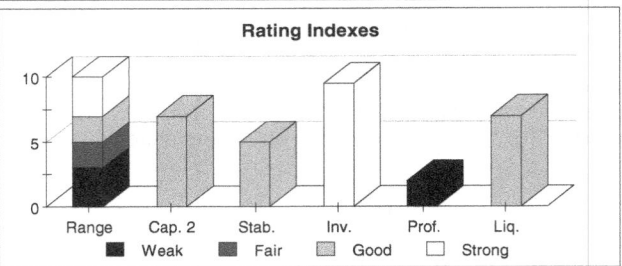

CONNECTICARE INS CO   B-   Good

Major Rating Factors: Fair profitability index (3.8 on a scale of 0 to 10). Good liquidity (6.9) with sufficient resources (cash flows and marketable investments) to handle a spike in claims. Strong capitalization (7.3) based on excellent current risk-adjusted capital (severe loss scenario).
Other Rating Factors: High quality investment portfolio (7.0).
Principal Business: Comp med (99%)
Mem Phys: 19: 27,823 **18:** 26,611 **19 MLR** 83.1% **/ 19 Admin Exp** N/A
Enroll(000): Q2 20: 76 **19:** 75 **18:** 87 **Med Exp PMPM:** $498
Principal Investments: Long-term bonds (62%), affiliate common stock (30%), cash and equiv (8%)
Provider Compensation ($000): Contr fee ($379,890), FFS ($81,200), capitation ($17,034)
Total Member Encounters: Phys (340,816), non-phys (322,566)
Group Affiliation: EmblemHealth Inc
Licensed in: CT
Address: 175 Scott Swamp Road, Farmington, CT 06032-3124
Phone: (860) 674-5700 **Dom State:** CT **Commenced Bus:** N/A

Data Date	Rating	RACR #1	RACR #2	Total Assets ($mil)	Capital ($mil)	Net Premium ($mil)	Net Income ($mil)
6-20	B-	1.57	1.30	303.1	143.0	265.8	-10.3
6-19	C	2.17	1.81	240.3	136.9	288.8	6.1
2019	C+	1.72	1.43	223.9	113.6	565.7	16.1
2018	C	1.71	1.42	245.1	108.4	591.2	54.8
2017	C	1.05	0.88	224.4	96.4	674.4	-3.1
2016	C	1.28	1.06	249.3	86.3	765.3	-49.8
2015	C	1.19	0.99	210.8	66.5	714.4	-19.7

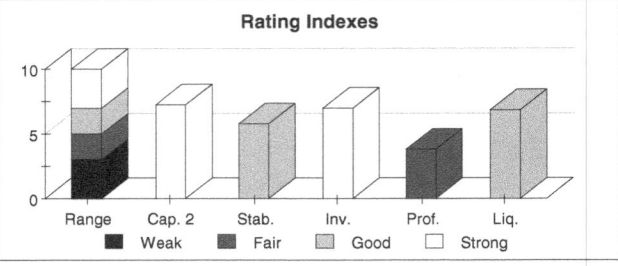

CONNECTICARE OF MASSACHUSETTS INC — C — Fair

Major Rating Factors: Fair overall results on stability tests (3.7 on a scale of 0 to 10) based on a steep decline in premium revenue in 2019, a significant 27% decrease in enrollment during the period. Good overall profitability index (5.3). Good capitalization index (6.6) based on good current risk-adjusted capital (severe loss scenario).

Other Rating Factors: High quality investment portfolio (8.4). Excellent liquidity (9.1) with ample operational cash flow and liquid investments.

Principal Business: Comp med (100%)

Mem Phys: 19: 27,823 **18:** 26,611 **19 MLR** 89.7% **/ 19 Admin Exp** N/A

Enroll(000): Q2 20: 0 **19:** 0 **18:** 0 **Med Exp PMPM:** $378

Principal Investments: Long-term bonds (51%), cash and equiv (49%)

Provider Compensation ($000): Contr fee ($918), FFS ($295), capitation ($51)

Total Member Encounters: Phys (1,028), non-phys (1,015)

Group Affiliation: EmblemHealth Inc

Licensed in: MA

Address: c/o Leboeuf Lamb Greene & McRa, Boston,

Phone: (860) 674-5700 **Dom State:** MA **Commenced Bus:** N/A

Data Date	Rating	RACR #1	RACR #2	Total Assets ($mil)	Capital ($mil)	Net Premium ($mil)	Net Income ($mil)
6-20	C	1.16	0.97	5.5	3.2	0.9	0.4
6-19	C	2.53	2.11	4.4	3.4	1.4	0.7
2019	C	2.07	1.73	4.4	2.8	1.3	0.1
2018	C	2.03	1.69	3.8	2.7	3.2	0.7
2017	E-	0.73	0.61	2.7	1.9	4.6	0.5
2016	E-	1.20	1.00	2.6	1.5	4.8	-0.7
2015	E-	1.74	1.45	3.7	2.1	8.3	-0.9

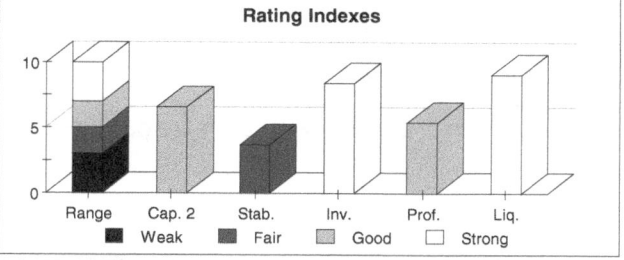

Rating Indexes

CONNECTICUT GENERAL LIFE INS CO — B- — Good

Major Rating Factors: Good overall results on stability tests (5.3 on a scale of 0 to 10). Stability strengths include excellent operational trends and excellent risk diversification. Fair quality investment portfolio (4.4). Strong capitalization (7.3) based on excellent risk adjusted capital (severe loss scenario). Moreover, capital has steadily grown over the last five years.

Other Rating Factors: Excellent profitability (9.4) with operating gains in each of the last five years. Excellent liquidity (7.4).

Principal Business: Group life insurance (37%), individual life insurance (33%), individual health insurance (24%), reinsurance (5%), and group health insurance (1%).

Principal Investments: Common & preferred stock (49%), nonCMO investment grade bonds (29%), policy loans (12%), mortgages in good standing (2%), and misc. investments (8%).

Investments in Affiliates: 50%

Group Affiliation: CIGNA Corp

Licensed in: All states, the District of Columbia and Puerto Rico

Commenced Business: October 1865

Address: 900 COTTAGE GROVE ROAD, BLOOMFIELD, CT 6002

Phone: (860) 226-6000 **Domicile State:** CT **NAIC Code:** 62308

Data Date	Rating	RACR #1	RACR #2	Total Assets ($mil)	Capital ($mil)	Net Premium ($mil)	Net Income ($mil)
6-20	B-	1.27	1.18	20,715.8	6,461.6	183.0	837.1
6-19	B-	1.25	1.17	19,556.1	5,712.3	162.0	1,087.6
2019	B-	1.23	1.17	19,753.4	5,934.0	310.7	1,881.7
2018	B-	1.25	1.17	19,056.7	5,494.5	333.7	1,239.4
2017	B-	1.32	1.22	18,137.2	4,412.2	346.3	1,013.8
2016	B-	1.32	1.20	17,646.3	4,074.4	402.2	1,180.4
2015	B-	1.33	1.19	17,374.4	3,631.0	490.7	916.2

Adverse Trends in Operations

Decrease in premium volume from 2018 to 2019 (7%)
Decrease in premium volume from 2017 to 2018 (4%)
Decrease in premium volume from 2016 to 2017 (14%)
Change in premium mix from 2015 to 2016 (4.3%)
Decrease in premium volume from 2015 to 2016 (17%)

CONTINENTAL AMERICAN INS CO — B — Good

Major Rating Factors: Good liquidity (6.5 on a scale of 0 to 10) with sufficient resources to handle a spike in claims. Fair overall results on stability tests (4.4). Weak profitability (1.9). Return on equity has been low, averaging 4.7%.

Other Rating Factors: Strong capitalization (8.7) based on excellent risk adjusted capital (severe loss scenario). High quality investment portfolio (7.5).

Principal Business: Group health insurance (95%), group life insurance (4%), and reinsurance (1%).

Principal Investments: NonCMO investment grade bonds (88%), noninv. grade bonds (1%), and policy loans (1%).

Investments in Affiliates: None

Group Affiliation: AFLAC Inc

Licensed in: All states except NY, PR

Commenced Business: January 1969

Address: 1600 Williams Street, Omaha, NE 68114-3743

Phone: (888) 730-2244 **Domicile State:** SC **NAIC Code:** 71730

Data Date	Rating	RACR #1	RACR #2	Total Assets ($mil)	Capital ($mil)	Net Premium ($mil)	Net Income ($mil)
6-20	B	3.91	2.92	874.4	274.5	254.6	0.4
6-19	B	1.94	1.45	677.1	159.2	217.7	1.7
2019	B	1.74	1.30	674.3	127.8	434.5	-16.3
2018	B	1.70	1.28	665.1	157.3	587.6	5.9
2017	B	1.79	1.33	673.3	153.4	524.7	-21.7
2016	B	1.98	1.44	607.0	174.4	536.1	46.8
2015	B	1.84	1.37	512.3	138.0	436.8	26.2

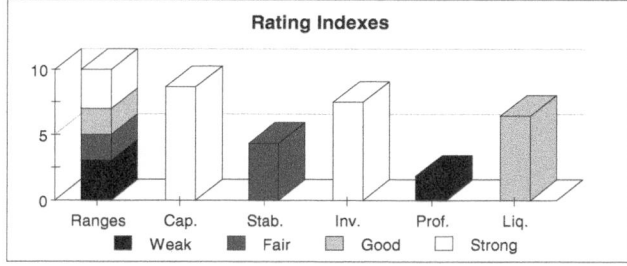

Rating Indexes

CONTINENTAL GENERAL INS CO

C+ **Fair**

Major Rating Factors: Fair quality investment portfolio (3.9 on a scale of 0 to 10) with large holdings of BBB rated bonds in addition to junk bond exposure equal to 54% of capital. Fair profitability (4.5). Excellent expense controls. Fair overall results on stability tests (3.8) including fair risk adjusted capital in prior years.

Other Rating Factors: Strong capitalization (7.3) based on excellent risk adjusted capital (severe loss scenario). Excellent liquidity (7.2).

Principal Business: Individual health insurance (84%), group health insurance (7%), individual life insurance (5%), reinsurance (3%), and group retirement contracts (1%).

Principal Investments: NonCMO investment grade bonds (66%), CMOs and structured securities (17%), noninv. grade bonds (4%), common & preferred stock (4%), and misc. investments (5%).

Investments in Affiliates: 2%

Group Affiliation: HC2 Holdings Inc

Licensed in: All states except NY, PR

Commenced Business: July 1961

Address: 11001 Lakeline Blvd Ste 120, Austin, TX 78717

Phone: (866) 830-0607 **Domicile State:** OH **NAIC Code:** 71404

Data Date	Rating	RACR #1	RACR #2	Total Assets ($mil)	Capital ($mil)	Net Premium ($mil)	Net Income ($mil)
6-20	C+	2.21	1.17	4,371.2	321.0	59.7	40.2
6-19	C+	1.94	1.06	4,286.4	294.4	60.8	52.5
2019	C+	2.10	1.14	4,297.3	300.5	119.9	64.6
2018	C+	1.78	0.96	4,206.9	255.5	126.2	-99.8
2017	C+	1.12	0.68	1,385.8	74.7	82.7	-0.1
2016	C+	1.10	0.72	1,344.1	76.9	82.2	-15.3
2015	C+	1.28	0.89	249.3	18.5	13.3	32.6

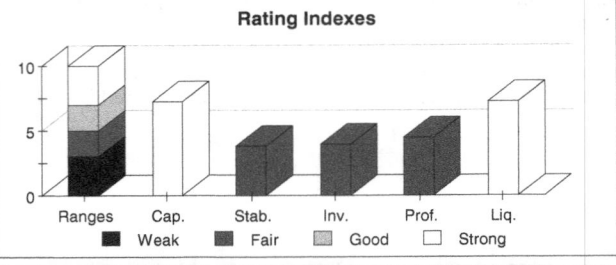

Rating Indexes

CONTINENTAL LIFE INS CO OF BRENTWOOD

C+ **Fair**

Major Rating Factors: Fair profitability (3.1 on a scale of 0 to 10). Excellent expense controls. Return on equity has been low, averaging -4.2%. Fair overall results on stability tests (4.5) including negative cash flow from operations for 2019. Good capitalization (6.8) based on good risk adjusted capital (severe loss scenario). Capital levels have been relatively consistent over the last five years.

Other Rating Factors: Good quality investment portfolio (5.4). Good liquidity (6.0).

Principal Business: Individual health insurance (99%), group health insurance (1%), and individual life insurance (1%).

Principal Investments: NonCMO investment grade bonds (45%), common & preferred stock (34%), CMOs and structured securities (23%), and mortgages in good standing (2%).

Investments in Affiliates: 34%

Group Affiliation: Aetna Inc

Licensed in: All states except AK, DC, HI, ME, NY, PR

Commenced Business: December 1983

Address: 800 CRESCENT CENTRE DR STE 200, FRANKLIN, TN 37064

Phone: (800) 264-4000 **Domicile State:** TN **NAIC Code:** 68500

Data Date	Rating	RACR #1	RACR #2	Total Assets ($mil)	Capital ($mil)	Net Premium ($mil)	Net Income ($mil)
6-20	C+	1.11	0.97	431.0	234.0	320.2	16.6
6-19	C+	0.97	0.87	346.7	181.7	279.6	-13.6
2019	C+	0.98	0.88	377.3	195.1	575.9	-26.9
2018	C+	1.10	0.99	366.7	204.0	508.5	-13.5
2017	C+	1.10	0.99	345.6	194.4	468.0	-9.5
2016	B	1.16	1.03	307.1	173.8	427.2	-7.8
2015	B	1.11	0.99	274.0	144.3	380.6	-1.2

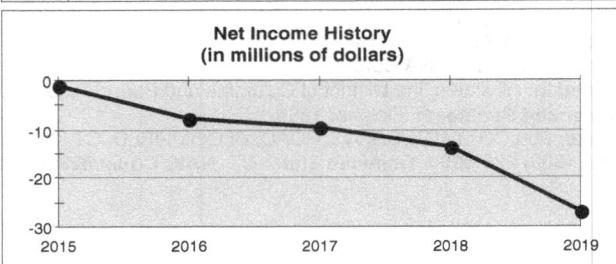

Net Income History
(in millions of dollars)

CONTRA COSTA HEALTH PLAN

B **Good**

Major Rating Factors: Excellent profitability (7.8 on a scale of 0 to 10). Strong capitalization index (7.0) based on excellent current risk-adjusted capital (severe loss scenario). Excellent overall results on stability tests (7.1).

Other Rating Factors: Excellent liquidity (7.2) with ample operational cash flow and liquid investments.

Principal Business: Medicaid (92%)

Mem Phys: 19: N/A **18:** N/A **19 MLR** 114.4% **/ 19 Admin Exp** N/A

Enroll(000): Q2 20: 187 **19:** 188 **18:** 188 **Med Exp PMPM:** $390

Principal Investments ($000): Cash and equiv ($99,078)

Provider Compensation ($000): None

Total Member Encounters: N/A

Group Affiliation: None

Licensed in: CA

Address: 595 Center Avenue Suite 100, Martinez, CA 94553

Phone: (925) 313-6004 **Dom State:** CA **Commenced Bus:** November 1973

Data Date	Rating	RACR #1	RACR #2	Total Assets ($mil)	Capital ($mil)	Net Premium ($mil)	Net Income ($mil)
6-20	B	1.71	1.12	306.6	87.8	344.2	8.1
6-19	B	1.84	1.16	276.3	82.4	397.7	4.1
2019	B	1.52	0.99	301.9	79.7	777.9	3.3
2018	B-	1.73	1.09	181.2	78.3	773.8	20.6
2017	C	0.94	0.63	392.9	53.7	743.6	6.9
2016	C	0.98	0.62	281.7	45.3	692.0	12.1
2015	C	1.16	0.74	206.2	45.5	622.6	24.6

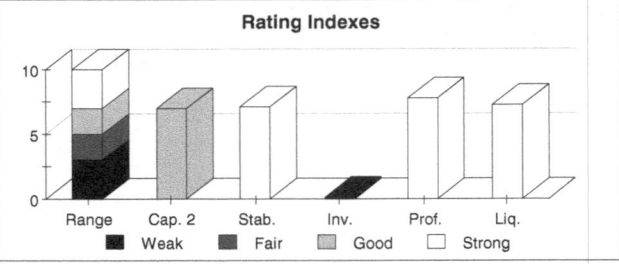

Rating Indexes

COOK CHILDRENS HEALTH PLAN   E+   Very Weak

Major Rating Factors: Fair profitability index (4.2 on a scale of 0 to 10). Fair overall results on stability tests (4.3). Good liquidity (6.9) with sufficient resources (cash flows and marketable investments) to handle a spike in claims. **Other Rating Factors:** Strong capitalization index (7.3) based on excellent current risk-adjusted capital (severe loss scenario). High quality investment portfolio (9.9).

Principal Business: Medicaid (93%), comp med (7%)

Mem Phys: 19: 11,044 **18:** 12,048 **19 MLR** 91.0% **/ 19 Admin Exp** N/A

Enroll(000): Q2 20: 142 **19:** 133 **18:** 138 **Med Exp PMPM:** $321

Principal Investments: Cash and equiv (59%), long-term bonds (41%)

Provider Compensation ($000): Contr fee ($524,145), bonus arrang ($1,140)

Total Member Encounters: Phys (4,106,208), non-phys (391,313)

Group Affiliation: W I Cook Foundation

Licensed in: TX

Address: 801 Seventh Avenue, Fort Worth,

Phone: (682) 885-2149 **Dom State:** TX **Commenced Bus:** N/A

Data Date	Rating	RACR #1	RACR #2	Total Assets ($mil)	Capital ($mil)	Net Premium ($mil)	Net Income ($mil)
6-20	E+	1.62	1.35	151.0	86.9	304.1	19.7
6-19	N/A	N/A	N/A	N/A	N/A	N/A	N/A
2019	E+	1.29	1.07	142.0	71.7	566.6	-9.4
2018	E+	1.71	1.42	155.3	84.6	549.9	11.0
2017	E+	1.53	1.28	131.1	71.9	506.9	-4.0
2016	E+	2.71	2.25	129.7	75.9	345.7	18.5
2015	E+	2.35	1.96	118.7	63.9	297.1	11.3

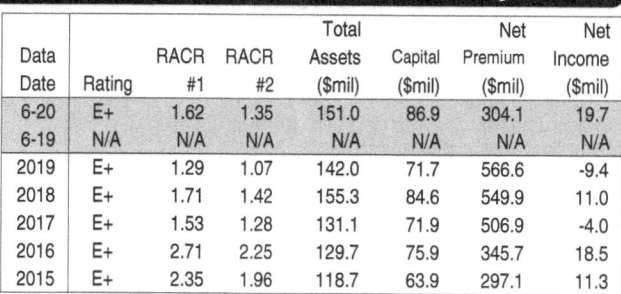

COORDINATED CARE CORP   B   Good

Major Rating Factors: Good quality investment portfolio (6.0 on a scale of 0 to 10). Excellent profitability (8.6). Strong capitalization index (9.3) based on excellent current risk-adjusted capital (severe loss scenario). **Other Rating Factors:** Excellent overall results on stability tests (8.2). Excellent liquidity (7.0) with sufficient resources (cash flows and marketable investments) to handle a spike in claims

Principal Business: Medicaid (83%), comp med (17%)

Mem Phys: 19: 34,829 **18:** 27,626 **19 MLR** 87.5% **/ 19 Admin Exp** N/A

Enroll(000): Q2 20: 318 **19:** 292 **18:** 294 **Med Exp PMPM:** $431

Principal Investments: Cash and equiv (55%), long-term bonds (38%), affiliate common stock (3%), other (4%)

Provider Compensation ($000): Contr fee ($1,438,384), bonus arrang ($47,935), salary ($21,536), capitation ($19,545)

Total Member Encounters: Phys (1,832,043), non-phys (2,038,155)

Group Affiliation: None

Licensed in: IN, WA

Address: 1099 N Meridian Street Suite 4, Indianapolis,

Phone: (314) 725-4477 **Dom State:** IN **Commenced Bus:** N/A

Data Date	Rating	RACR #1	RACR #2	Total Assets ($mil)	Capital ($mil)	Net Premium ($mil)	Net Income ($mil)
6-20	B	3.18	2.65	613.1	233.0	924.8	24.2
6-19	B-	2.78	2.31	535.0	206.7	887.6	23.1
2019	B	3.88	3.23	504.8	205.9	1,764.8	22.5
2018	C+	2.74	2.28	460.3	203.6	1,723.8	37.4
2017	C+	1.59	1.32	408.1	148.3	1,457.6	10.8
2016	C+	2.30	1.92	330.6	111.8	1,091.2	6.7
2015	C+	2.28	1.90	306.6	83.7	811.8	15.3

COORDINATED CARE OF WASHINGTON INC   C   Fair

Major Rating Factors: Weak profitability index (0.9 on a scale of 0 to 10). Good liquidity (6.0) with sufficient resources (cash flows and marketable investments) to handle a spike in claims. Strong capitalization (8.4) based on excellent current risk-adjusted capital (severe loss scenario). **Other Rating Factors:** High quality investment portfolio (7.4).

Principal Business: Medicaid (99%), comp med (1%)

Mem Phys: 18: 23,065 **17:** 25,488 **18 MLR** 94.5% **/ 18 Admin Exp** N/A

Enroll(000): Q3 19: 200 **18:** 191 **17:** 202 **Med Exp PMPM:** $234

Principal Investments: Long-term bonds (75%), cash and equiv (25%)

Provider Compensation ($000): Contr fee ($481,444), capitation ($31,542), bonus arrang ($21,282), salary ($14,008)

Total Member Encounters: Phys (716,873), non-phys (1,420,687)

Group Affiliation: None

Licensed in: WA

Address: 1145 Broadway Suite 300, Tacoma, WA 98402

Phone: (314) 725-4477 **Dom State:** WA **Commenced Bus:** N/A

Data Date	Rating	RACR #1	RACR #2	Total Assets ($mil)	Capital ($mil)	Net Premium ($mil)	Net Income ($mil)
9-19	C	2.46	2.05	251.3	82.5	490.5	-14.2
9-18	D+	N/A	N/A	242.3	93.0	463.5	-12.7
2018	C-	2.51	2.09	229.9	84.5	596.6	-19.9
2017	D+	N/A	N/A	237.4	88.0	697.7	-11.2
2016	D+	1.90	1.59	247.2	60.6	680.3	-38.4
2015	D+	2.88	2.40	231.0	84.6	558.5	-8.6
2014	N/A	N/A	N/A	167.6	86.6	N/A	N/A

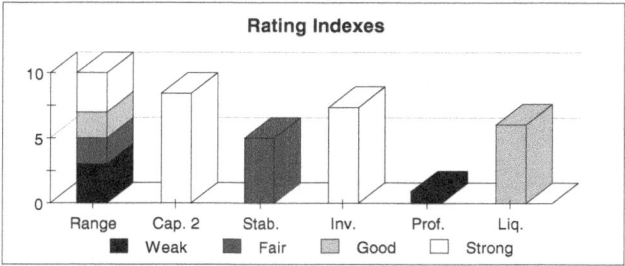

COVENTRY HEALTH & LIFE INS CO

B-   **Good**

Major Rating Factors: Good overall profitability index (6.3 on a scale of 0 to 10). Good quality investment portfolio (6.4). Good liquidity (6.8) with sufficient resources (cash flows and marketable investments) to handle a spike in claims. **Other Rating Factors:** Strong capitalization (10.0) based on excellent current risk-adjusted capital (severe loss scenario).
Principal Business: Medicare (100%)
Mem Phys: 19: N/A **18:** N/A **19 MLR** 84.3% **/ 19 Admin Exp** N/A
Enroll(000): Q2 20: 193 **19:** 200 **18:** 180 **Med Exp PMPM:** $739
Principal Investments: Long-term bonds (54%), affiliate common stock (36%), cash and equiv (6%), mortgs (2%), other (3%)
Provider Compensation ($000): Contr fee ($1,435,655), FFS ($143,028), capitation ($28,159), bonus arrang ($4,608), other ($99,275)
Total Member Encounters: Phys (2,183,057), non-phys (714,628)
Group Affiliation: None
Licensed in: All states except NY, PR
Address: 1285 FERN RIDGE PARKWAY SUITE, ST LOUIS, MO 63141
Phone: (800) 843-7421 **Dom State:** MO **Commenced Bus:** N/A

Data Date	Rating	RACR #1	RACR #2	Total Assets ($mil)	Capital ($mil)	Net Premium ($mil)	Net Income ($mil)
6-20	B-	5.03	4.19	1,238.2	867.3	1,002.7	65.5
6-19	B-	7.14	5.95	1,324.3	1,052.1	1,022.9	70.2
2019	B-	5.42	4.52	1,200.0	881.5	2,047.3	64.5
2018	B-	6.61	5.51	1,251.2	963.9	1,728.0	47.6
2017	B	8.10	6.75	1,354.3	1,108.4	1,673.5	114.9
2016	B	7.51	6.26	1,512.5	1,145.3	2,484.5	77.6
2015	B	4.82	4.01	1,699.7	949.3	4,066.1	260.2

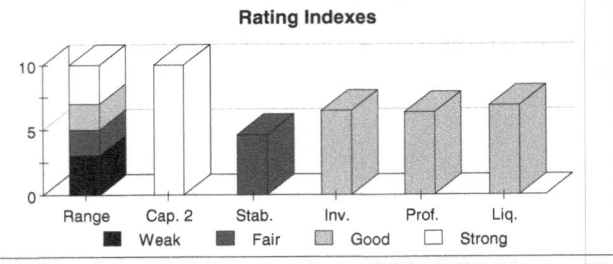

COVENTRY HEALTH CARE OF ILLINOIS INC

B   **Good**

Major Rating Factors: Good quality investment portfolio (6.7 on a scale of 0 to 10). Excellent overall profitability index (6.9). Strong capitalization (9.3) based on excellent current risk-adjusted capital (severe loss scenario).
Other Rating Factors: Excellent liquidity (7.4) with ample operational cash flow and liquid investments.
Principal Business: Medicare (99%), comp med (1%)
Mem Phys: 19: 40,312 **18:** 39,556 **19 MLR** 58.9% **/ 19 Admin Exp** N/A
Enroll(000): Q2 20: 36 **19:** 28 **18:** 25 **Med Exp PMPM:** $687
Principal Investments: Long-term bonds (61%), cash and equiv (37%), other (2%)
Provider Compensation ($000): Contr fee ($153,923), FFS ($23,000), bonus arrang ($9,282), capitation ($876), other ($29,607)
Total Member Encounters: Phys (842,327), non-phys (580,142)
Group Affiliation: None
Licensed in: IL
Address: 2110 FOX DRIVE, CHAMPAIGN, IL 61820
Phone: (847) 258-0800 **Dom State:** IL **Commenced Bus:** N/A

Data Date	Rating	RACR #1	RACR #2	Total Assets ($mil)	Capital ($mil)	Net Premium ($mil)	Net Income ($mil)
6-20	B	3.20	2.66	230.2	100.4	177.4	16.3
6-19	C	4.29	3.58	179.9	82.8	198.1	25.9
2019	B-	3.65	3.04	174.5	79.9	380.4	25.2
2018	C	3.45	2.87	138.9	66.1	321.6	5.2
2017	C	3.75	3.12	135.5	92.3	308.3	14.0
2016	C	3.32	2.77	177.9	88.2	481.2	1.1
2015	B-	2.84	2.37	131.4	47.6	351.9	7.8

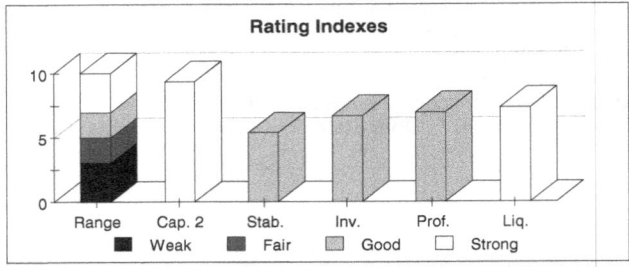

COVENTRY HEALTH CARE OF KANSAS INC

C   **Fair**

Major Rating Factors: Fair quality investment portfolio (3.8 on a scale of 0 to 10). Weak overall results on stability tests (2.8) based on a decline in the number of member physicians during 2020, a significant 52% decrease in enrollment during the period. Good overall profitability index (6.8).
Other Rating Factors: Strong capitalization index (10.0) based on excellent current risk-adjusted capital (severe loss scenario). Excellent liquidity (9.1) with ample operational cash flow and liquid investments.
Principal Business: Medicare (89%), FEHB (8%), comp med (4%)
Mem Phys: 19: 27,241 **18:** 32,064 **19 MLR** 54.0% **/ 19 Admin Exp** N/A
Enroll(000): Q2 20: 3 **19:** 1 **18:** 1 **Med Exp PMPM:** $877
Principal Investments: Long-term bonds (57%), cash and equiv (43%)
Provider Compensation ($000): Contr fee ($3,280), FFS ($237), capitation ($170), other ($292)
Total Member Encounters: Phys (5,402), non-phys (1,432)
Group Affiliation: None
Licensed in: AR, KS, MO, OK
Address: 8535 E 21ST STREET N, WICHITA,
Phone: (913) 202-5400 **Dom State:** KS **Commenced Bus:** N/A

Data Date	Rating	RACR #1	RACR #2	Total Assets ($mil)	Capital ($mil)	Net Premium ($mil)	Net Income ($mil)
6-20	C	13.49	11.24	33.8	24.4	25.1	6.5
6-19	C	18.19	15.16	21.4	14.9	3.0	1.5
2019	C	18.02	15.02	21.6	17.0	7.4	3.0
2018	C	17.31	14.43	21.7	13.7	6.0	3.0
2017	C-	27.26	22.72	61.9	51.8	13.1	5.0
2016	C+	4.28	3.57	116.0	73.8	367.9	25.7
2015	C+	3.43	2.86	211.3	93.1	573.7	28.2

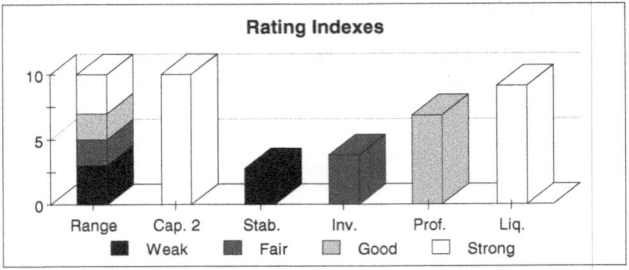

COVENTRY HEALTH CARE OF MISSOURI INC   B   Good

Major Rating Factors: Good quality investment portfolio (6.4 on a scale of 0 to 10). Good overall results on stability tests (5.5). Good liquidity (6.6) with sufficient resources (cash flows and marketable investments) to handle a spike in claims.
Other Rating Factors: Excellent profitability (8.1). Strong capitalization index (8.8) based on excellent current risk-adjusted capital (severe loss scenario).
Principal Business: Medicare (100%)
Mem Phys: 19: 17,146 **18:** 16,383 **19 MLR** 90.8% **/ 19 Admin Exp** N/A
Enroll(000): Q2 20: 72 **19:** 81 **18:** 83 **Med Exp PMPM:** $799
Principal Investments: Long-term bonds (81%), cash and equiv (16%), mortgs (3%), other (1%)
Provider Compensation ($000): Contr fee ($440,969), capitation ($195,359), bonus arrang ($76,208), FFS ($28,446), other ($45,444)
Total Member Encounters: Phys (933,376), non-phys (257,201)
Group Affiliation: None
Licensed in: AR, IL, KS, MO, OK
Address: 550 MARYVILLE CENTRE DRIVE, ST. LOUIS,
Phone: (314) 506-1700 **Dom State:** MO **Commenced Bus:** N/A

Data Date	Rating	RACR #1	RACR #2	Total Assets ($mil)	Capital ($mil)	Net Premium ($mil)	Net Income ($mil)
6-20	B	2.79	2.32	356.7	163.6	419.7	38.2
6-19	C+	3.67	3.06	295.9	148.3	442.1	29.2
2019	B	3.06	2.55	273.1	126.8	865.2	38.1
2018	C+	2.96	2.47	279.2	118.0	808.3	6.2
2017	B	2.91	2.43	309.5	163.8	883.6	61.9
2016	C+	5.72	4.76	323.0	154.4	588.3	37.1
2015	C+	4.55	3.79	236.3	116.9	563.5	32.4

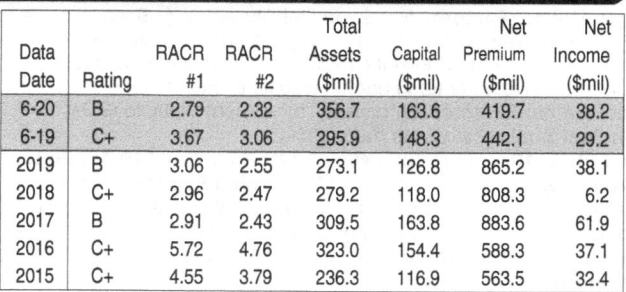

Rating Indexes

COVENTRY HEALTH CARE OF VIRGINIA INC   B-   Good

Major Rating Factors: Fair profitability index (4.6 on a scale of 0 to 10). Fair overall results on stability tests (4.6) based on an excessive 76% enrollment growth during the period. Good quality investment portfolio (6.8).
Other Rating Factors: Good liquidity (6.8) with sufficient resources (cash flows and marketable investments) to handle a spike in claims. Strong capitalization index (7.8) based on excellent current risk-adjusted capital (severe loss scenario).
Principal Business: Medicaid (97%), Medicare (3%)
Mem Phys: 19: 32,837 **18:** 6,735 **19 MLR** 89.2% **/ 19 Admin Exp** N/A
Enroll(000): Q2 20: 195 **19:** 164 **18:** 93 **Med Exp PMPM:** $691
Principal Investments: Long-term bonds (76%), cash and equiv (23%), mortgs (1%), real estate (1%)
Provider Compensation ($000): Contr fee ($812,877), FFS ($148,596), capitation ($5,519), other ($188,162)
Total Member Encounters: Phys (2,098,005), non-phys (1,559,951)
Group Affiliation: None
Licensed in: VA
Address: 9881 MAYLAND DRIVE, RICHMOND,
Phone: (804) 747-3700 **Dom State:** VA **Commenced Bus:** N/A

Data Date	Rating	RACR #1	RACR #2	Total Assets ($mil)	Capital ($mil)	Net Premium ($mil)	Net Income ($mil)
6-20	B-	1.98	1.65	555.2	212.6	825.1	35.6
6-19	B-	2.20	1.83	333.1	101.4	631.4	-3.8
2019	B-	2.30	1.92	422.6	177.3	1,362.6	8.6
2018	B-	1.73	1.45	231.7	78.7	731.9	-10.3
2017	C+	2.21	1.84	127.2	53.3	277.5	15.4
2016	C+	1.88	1.57	109.5	40.1	348.4	-4.3
2015	B+	2.52	2.10	126.0	60.7	463.0	14.9

Rating Indexes

COVENTRY HEALTH CARE OF WEST VA INC   B   Good

Major Rating Factors: Good quality investment portfolio (5.7 on a scale of 0 to 10). Good overall results on stability tests (6.6). Good liquidity (6.5) with sufficient resources (cash flows and marketable investments) to handle a spike in claims.
Other Rating Factors: Excellent profitability (7.1). Strong capitalization index (8.4) based on excellent current risk-adjusted capital (severe loss scenario).
Principal Business: Medicaid (89%), Medicare (11%)
Mem Phys: 19: 5,967 **18:** 5,207 **19 MLR** 92.6% **/ 19 Admin Exp** N/A
Enroll(000): Q2 20: 174 **19:** 144 **18:** 126 **Med Exp PMPM:** $347
Principal Investments: Long-term bonds (65%), cash and equiv (35%), other (1%)
Provider Compensation ($000): Contr fee ($464,569), FFS ($30,232), capitation ($20,045), bonus arrang ($9,558), other ($11,808)
Total Member Encounters: Phys (987,178), non-phys (309,356)
Group Affiliation: None
Licensed in: WV
Address: 500 VIRGINIA STREET EAST SUITE, CHARLESTON,
Phone: (804) 747-3700 **Dom State:** WV **Commenced Bus:** N/A

Data Date	Rating	RACR #1	RACR #2	Total Assets ($mil)	Capital ($mil)	Net Premium ($mil)	Net Income ($mil)
6-20	B	2.48	2.07	287.4	116.3	418.8	22.9
6-19	B	3.13	2.61	208.1	89.5	277.5	-1.4
2019	B	2.88	2.40	241.4	93.9	604.7	3.8
2018	B	3.14	2.61	208.3	89.7	632.8	22.5
2017	B	1.49	1.24	148.7	68.2	555.9	12.6
2016	B+	2.41	2.01	171.0	72.5	546.4	22.6
2015	B+	3.56	2.97	120.5	64.5	342.8	18.6

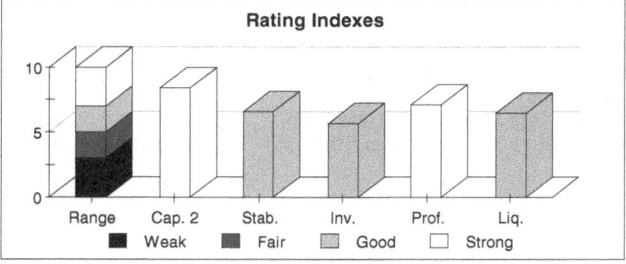

Rating Indexes

COX HEALTH SYSTEMS INS CO — C- Fair

Major Rating Factors: Weak profitability index (1.9 on a scale of 0 to 10). Good capitalization (5.9) based on good current risk-adjusted capital (severe loss scenario). Good liquidity (6.3) with sufficient resources (cash flows and marketable investments) to handle a spike in claims.
Other Rating Factors: High quality investment portfolio (9.9).
Principal Business: Comp med (99%)
Mem Phys: 19: 4,009 **18:** 3,495 **19 MLR** 89.7% **/ 19 Admin Exp** N/A
Enroll(000): Q2 20: 29 **19:** 27 **18:** 34 **Med Exp PMPM:** $355
Principal Investments: Long-term bonds (53%), cash and equiv (47%)
Provider Compensation ($000): Contr fee ($115,392), FFS ($3,590)
Total Member Encounters: Phys (180,151), non-phys (30,079)
Group Affiliation: None
Licensed in: MO
Address: 3200 South National Building, Springfield, MO 65801-5750
Phone: (417) 269-6762 **Dom State:** MO **Commenced Bus:** N/A

Data Date	Rating	RACR #1	RACR #2	Total Assets ($mil)	Capital ($mil)	Net Premium ($mil)	Net Income ($mil)
6-20	C-	1.07	0.89	52.8	22.5	68.9	2.3
6-19	D+	0.83	0.69	50.4	20.3	65.3	2.0
2019	C-	0.95	0.79	48.1	20.6	132.6	0.4
2018	D+	0.74	0.62	53.8	18.7	153.5	-5.0
2017	D+	0.75	0.63	49.3	18.1	141.7	-14.6
2016	C	1.03	0.86	41.5	14.7	131.8	-3.7
2015	C+	1.15	0.96	38.3	17.5	120.5	-0.1

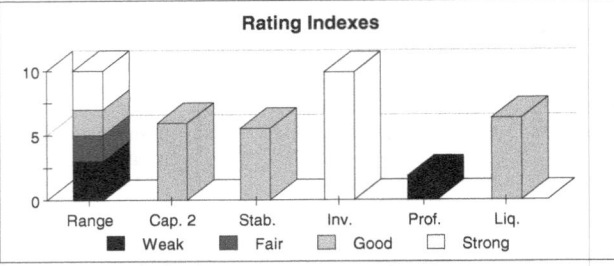

Rating Indexes

DAVITA HEALTHCARE PARTNERS PLAN INC — D Weak

Major Rating Factors: Good overall profitability index (6.2 on a scale of 0 to 10). Good overall results on stability tests (5.1). Good liquidity (6.8) with sufficient resources (cash flows and marketable investments) to handle a spike in claims.
Other Rating Factors: Strong capitalization index (7.2) based on excellent current risk-adjusted capital (severe loss scenario).
Principal Business: Managed care (94%)
Mem Phys: 19: N/A **18:** N/A **19 MLR** 93.5% **/ 19 Admin Exp** N/A
Enroll(000): Q2 20: 470 **19:** 477 **18:** 477 **Med Exp PMPM:** $396
Principal Investments ($000): Cash and equiv ($274,380)
Provider Compensation ($000): None
Total Member Encounters: N/A
Group Affiliation: HealthCare Partners Holdings LLC
Licensed in: CA
Address: 2220 E Gonzales Road Suite 210, Oxnard, CA 93036
Phone: (805) 981-5006 **Dom State:** CA **Commenced Bus:** January 2014

Data Date	Rating	RACR #1	RACR #2	Total Assets ($mil)	Capital ($mil)	Net Premium ($mil)	Net Income ($mil)
6-20	D	2.05	1.23	573.9	290.7	1,421.1	165.5
6-19	D-	0.68	0.41	289.8	95.1	1,250.9	56.7
2019	D-	0.83	0.50	314.6	125.2	2,453.0	86.8
2018	E+	0.24	0.14	183.8	38.4	2,125.6	-9.0
2017	D	0.33	0.20	187.4	47.4	1,947.3	-6.0
2016	D+	0.63	0.38	98.4	53.4	1,462.1	39.7
2015	D	0.51	0.31	79.0	43.6	1,458.0	40.8

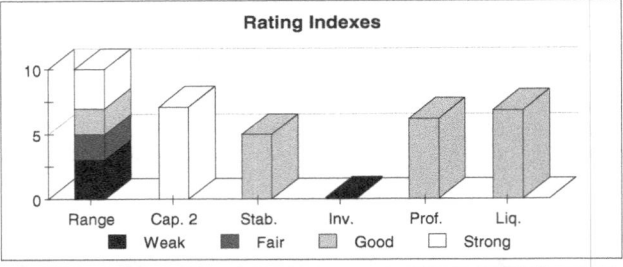

Rating Indexes

DEAN HEALTH PLAN INC * — A- Excellent

Major Rating Factors: Strong capitalization index (7.8 on a scale of 0 to 10) based on excellent current risk-adjusted capital (severe loss scenario). High quality investment portfolio (8.7). Excellent overall results on stability tests (6.9).
Other Rating Factors: Excellent liquidity (6.9) with sufficient resources (cash flows and marketable investments) to handle a spike in claims. Good overall profitability index (6.5).
Principal Business: Comp med (80%), Medicare (10%), Medicaid (5%), med supp (2%), FEHB (2%)
Mem Phys: 19: 5,158 **18:** 4,591 **19 MLR** 91.5% **/ 19 Admin Exp** N/A
Enroll(000): Q2 20: 258 **19:** 265 **18:** 264 **Med Exp PMPM:** $394
Principal Investments: Cash and equiv (50%), long-term bonds (23%), nonaffiliate common stock (19%), real estate (8%)
Provider Compensation ($000): Capitation ($1,172,794), FFS ($72,416), contr fee ($29,328)
Total Member Encounters: Phys (872,735), non-phys (833,287)
Group Affiliation: None
Licensed in: WI
Address: 1277 Deming Way, Madison,
Phone: (608) 836-1400 **Dom State:** WI **Commenced Bus:** N/A

Data Date	Rating	RACR #1	RACR #2	Total Assets ($mil)	Capital ($mil)	Net Premium ($mil)	Net Income ($mil)
6-20	A-	2.03	1.69	338.6	148.6	676.4	-4.6
6-19	A	2.49	2.07	303.8	166.9	694.7	7.4
2019	A	2.08	1.73	262.6	151.9	1,387.4	10.2
2018	A	2.31	1.92	280.6	155.8	1,373.4	27.8
2017	B+	2.12	1.77	241.0	129.2	1,245.1	9.3
2016	B+	1.85	1.54	212.7	113.1	1,250.9	15.9
2015	B	1.60	1.33	209.0	95.9	1,220.6	5.3

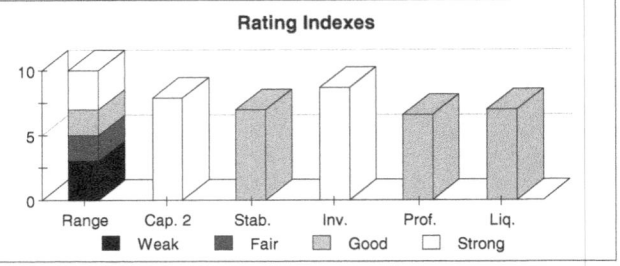

Rating Indexes

DEARBORN LIFE INS CO *   B+   Good

Major Rating Factors: Good quality investment portfolio (6.1 on a scale of 0 to 10) despite large holdings of BBB rated bonds in addition to moderate junk bond exposure. Exposure to mortgages is significant, but the mortgage default rate has been low. Good overall profitability (5.8). Return on equity has been fair, averaging 5.4%. Good liquidity (6.5).

Other Rating Factors: Good overall results on stability tests (6.5) despite negative cash flow from operations for 2019 excellent operational trends and excellent risk diversification. Strong capitalization (8.7) based on excellent risk adjusted capital (severe loss scenario).

Principal Business: Group life insurance (61%), group health insurance (37%), and individual life insurance (2%).

Principal Investments: NonCMO investment grade bonds (53%), CMOs and structured securities (20%), mortgages in good standing (12%), and noninv. grade bonds (9%).

Investments in Affiliates: None
Group Affiliation: HCSC Group
Licensed in: All states except NY
Commenced Business: April 1969
Address: 300 East Randolph Street, Chicago, IL 60601-5099
Phone: (800) 633-3696   **Domicile State:** IL   **NAIC Code:** 71129

Data Date	Rating	RACR #1	RACR #2	Total Assets ($mil)	Capital ($mil)	Net Premium ($mil)	Net Income ($mil)
6-20	B+	3.53	2.13	1,657.5	462.6	264.4	4.7
6-19	B+	3.35	2.09	1,669.1	459.4	246.6	9.8
2019	B+	3.59	2.18	1,660.0	461.7	491.4	17.6
2018	B+	3.33	2.06	1,676.5	453.0	462.0	25.7
2017	B+	3.40	2.09	1,785.1	474.3	437.9	34.0
2016	B+	3.36	2.11	1,872.5	497.0	408.0	19.7
2015	B+	3.63	2.25	1,990.5	522.1	382.5	59.1

Rating Indexes

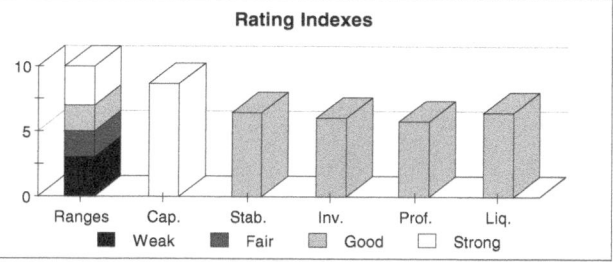

DELAWARE AMERICAN LIFE INS CO *   B+   Good

Major Rating Factors: Good overall results on stability tests (5.1 on a scale of 0 to 10). Stability strengths include good operational trends and excellent risk diversification. Good overall profitability (6.1). Return on equity has been good over the last five years, averaging 13.4%. Strong capitalization (10.0) based on excellent risk adjusted capital (severe loss scenario).

Other Rating Factors: High quality investment portfolio (7.6). Excellent liquidity (7.2).

Principal Business: Group health insurance (70%), reinsurance (17%), group life insurance (12%), and individual life insurance (1%).

Principal Investments: NonCMO investment grade bonds (56%), CMOs and structured securities (27%), cash (16%), and noninv. grade bonds (1%).

Investments in Affiliates: None
Group Affiliation: MetLife Inc
Licensed in: All states except PR
Commenced Business: August 1966
Address: 1209 Orange Street, Wilmington, DE 19801
Phone: (302) 594-2000   **Domicile State:** DE   **NAIC Code:** 62634

Data Date	Rating	RACR #1	RACR #2	Total Assets ($mil)	Capital ($mil)	Net Premium ($mil)	Net Income ($mil)
6-20	B+	4.80	3.61	106.1	65.7	41.5	3.5
6-19	B+	4.31	3.22	119.8	68.8	46.8	5.7
2019	B+	4.50	3.39	115.1	61.8	89.0	8.8
2018	B+	4.07	3.02	117.0	65.1	93.0	12.5
2017	B+	3.36	2.53	120.2	61.8	96.4	7.2
2016	B+	4.56	3.33	132.8	72.5	89.9	15.2
2015	A-	3.53	2.60	136.6	63.5	108.7	1.8

Adverse Trends in Operations

Decrease in asset base during 2018 (3%)
Decrease in capital during 2017 (15%)
Decrease in asset base during 2016 (3%)
Change in premium mix from 2015 to 2016 (6.7%)
Decrease in premium volume from 2015 to 2016 (17%)

DENVER HEALTH MEDICAL PLAN INC   B   Good

Major Rating Factors: Good capitalization index (5.8 on a scale of 0 to 10) based on good current risk-adjusted capital (severe loss scenario). Good quality investment portfolio (5.8). Good overall results on stability tests (5.9).

Other Rating Factors: Fair profitability index (4.9). Excellent liquidity (8.0) with ample operational cash flow and liquid investments.

Principal Business: Medicaid (53%), comp med (30%), Medicare (16%)

Mem Phys: 19: 26,649   18: 20,921   **19 MLR** 41.4%   **/ 19 Admin Exp** N/A

Enroll(000): Q2 20: 115   **19:** 24   **18:** 24   **Med Exp PMPM:** $559

Principal Investments: Long-term bonds (102%)

Provider Compensation ($000): FFS ($82,894), contr fee ($56,263), capitation ($24,700)

Total Member Encounters: Phys (196,327), non-phys (79,754)

Group Affiliation: None
Licensed in: CO
Address: 777 Bannock Street MC 6000, Denver,
Phone: (303) 602-2100   **Dom State:** CO   **Commenced Bus:** N/A

Data Date	Rating	RACR #1	RACR #2	Total Assets ($mil)	Capital ($mil)	Net Premium ($mil)	Net Income ($mil)
6-20	B	1.06	0.88	86.0	36.3	203.3	5.6
6-19	N/A	N/A	N/A	N/A	N/A	N/A	N/A
2019	B-	0.94	0.78	75.9	32.2	385.7	4.1
2018	B-	1.08	0.90	66.5	28.9	244.4	-0.7
2017	B-	1.76	1.46	56.8	30.7	157.1	-1.1
2016	B	2.29	1.91	52.1	32.0	137.6	6.1
2015	B	2.50	2.08	48.5	31.0	119.3	1.2

Rating Indexes

DEVOTED HEALTH PLAN OF FL INC   D-   Weak

Major Rating Factors: Weak profitability index (0.9 on a scale of 0 to 10). Low quality investment portfolio (0.0). Strong capitalization (7.3) based on excellent current risk-adjusted capital (severe loss scenario).
Other Rating Factors: Excellent liquidity (7.6) with ample operational cash flow and liquid investments.
Principal Business: Medicare (100%)
Mem Phys: 19: 17,723   **18:** N/A   **19 MLR** 113.5%   / **19 Admin Exp** N/A
Enroll(000): Q2 20: 13   **19:** 4   **18:** N/A   **Med Exp PMPM:** $1,274
Principal Investments: Cash and equiv (100%)
Provider Compensation ($000): FFS ($33,974), capitation ($5,648), other ($2,820)
Total Member Encounters: N/A
Group Affiliation: Devoted Health Inc
Licensed in: (No states)
Address: 2801 SW 149th Ave Suite 100, Miramar, FL 33027
Phone: (617) 958-1611   **Dom State:** FL   **Commenced Bus:** N/A

Data Date	Rating	RACR #1	RACR #2	Total Assets ($mil)	Capital ($mil)	Net Premium ($mil)	Net Income ($mil)
6-20	D-	1.59	1.32	44.6	16.4	75.8	-5.9
6-19	N/A	N/A	N/A	14.5	4.2	18.6	-4.9
2019	D-	1.33	1.11	41.7	13.9	45.2	-24.4
2018	N/A	N/A	N/A	7.5	4.1	N/A	-1.0
2017	N/A	N/A	N/A	N/A	N/A	N/A	N/A
2016	N/A	N/A	N/A	N/A	N/A	N/A	N/A
2015	N/A	N/A	N/A	N/A	N/A	N/A	N/A

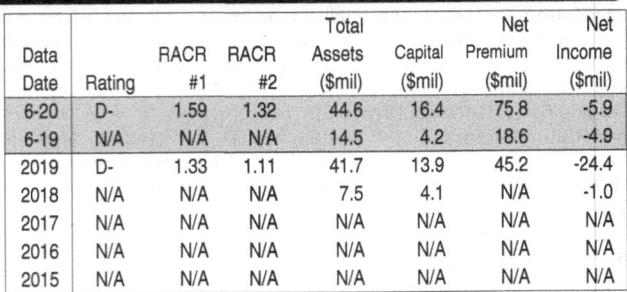

Rating Indexes

DIGNITY HEALTH PROVIDER RESOURCES   E   Very Weak

Major Rating Factors: Poor capitalization index (2.3 on a scale of 0 to 10) based on weak current risk-adjusted capital (moderate loss scenario). Fair profitability index (4.2). Good overall results on stability tests (5.3) based on healthy premium and capital growth during 2019.
Other Rating Factors: Good liquidity (6.9) with sufficient resources (cash flows and marketable investments) to handle a spike in claims.
Principal Business: Managed care (100%)
Mem Phys: 19: N/A   **18:** N/A   **19 MLR** 99.7%   / **19 Admin Exp** N/A
Enroll(000): Q2 20: 32   **19:** 32   **18:** 32   **Med Exp PMPM:** $455
Principal Investments ($000): Cash and equiv ($7,142)
Provider Compensation ($000): None
Total Member Encounters: N/A
Group Affiliation: None
Licensed in: CA
Address: 2175 Park Place, El Segundo, CA 90245
Phone: (310) 252-8834   **Dom State:** CA   **Commenced Bus:** N/A

Data Date	Rating	RACR #1	RACR #2	Total Assets ($mil)	Capital ($mil)	Net Premium ($mil)	Net Income ($mil)
6-20	E	0.44	0.27	9.9	6.3	95.5	1.6
6-19	E	0.31	0.19	11.1	4.1	91.3	-0.1
2019	E	0.33	0.20	7.4	4.9	178.6	-0.7
2018	E	0.32	0.19	5.3	4.2	152.9	-0.5
2017	E	0.40	0.24	5.5	4.7	136.7	-0.7
2016	N/A	N/A	N/A	1.6	1.5	N/A	-0.3
2015	N/A	N/A	N/A	N/A	N/A	N/A	N/A

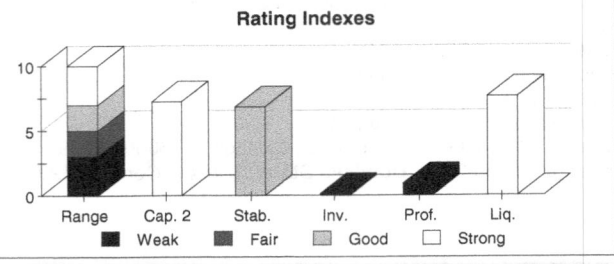

Rating Indexes

DOCTORS HEALTHCARE PLANS INC   E   Very Weak

Major Rating Factors: Weak profitability index (0.8 on a scale of 0 to 10). Poor capitalization (0.5) based on weak current risk-adjusted capital (moderate loss scenario). Weak liquidity (0.0) as a spike in claims may stretch capacity.
Other Rating Factors: High quality investment portfolio (9.9).
Principal Business: Medicare (100%)
Mem Phys: 19: 4,600   **18:** N/A   **19 MLR** 108.0%   / **19 Admin Exp** N/A
Enroll(000): Q2 20: 10   **19:** 6   **18:** N/A   **Med Exp PMPM:** $1,439
Principal Investments: Cash and equiv (100%)
Provider Compensation ($000): Contr fee ($60,180), capitation ($11,844), other ($6,200)
Total Member Encounters: N/A
Group Affiliation: Doctors Healthcare Plans Inc
Licensed in: FL
Address: 2020 Ponce de Leon Blvd PH-1, Coral Gables, FL 33134
Phone: (786) 460-3427   **Dom State:** FL   **Commenced Bus:** N/A

Data Date	Rating	RACR #1	RACR #2	Total Assets ($mil)	Capital ($mil)	Net Premium ($mil)	Net Income ($mil)
6-20	E	0.35	0.29	26.5	9.4	80.2	0.3
6-19	N/A	N/A	N/A	N/A	N/A	N/A	N/A
2019	E	0.32	0.27	21.0	8.7	78.9	-23.3
2018	N/A	N/A	N/A	10.8	9.2	N/A	-5.6
2017	N/A	N/A	N/A	18.1	18.0	N/A	-1.0
2016	N/A	N/A	N/A	N/A	N/A	N/A	N/A
2015	N/A	N/A	N/A	N/A	N/A	N/A	N/A

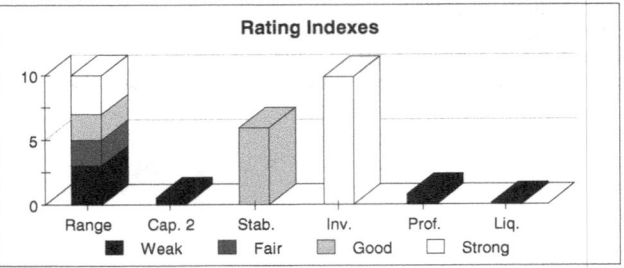

Rating Indexes

DRISCOLL CHILDRENS HEALTH PLAN   C   Fair

Major Rating Factors: Fair profitability index (3.1 on a scale of 0 to 10). Good overall results on stability tests (6.3) based on steady enrollment growth, averaging 5% over the past five years. Good liquidity (6.7) with sufficient resources (cash flows and marketable investments) to handle a spike in claims.
Other Rating Factors: Strong capitalization index (8.0) based on excellent current risk-adjusted capital (severe loss scenario). High quality investment portfolio (8.8).
Principal Business: Medicaid (98%), other (2%)
Mem Phys: 19: 3,378 **18:** 3,378 **19 MLR** 95.7% **/ 19 Admin Exp** N/A
Enroll(000): Q2 20: 192 **19:** 176 **18:** 173 **Med Exp PMPM:** $323
Principal Investments: Cash and equiv (57%), long-term bonds (43%)
Provider Compensation ($000): Contr fee ($652,217), capitation ($20,380), bonus arrang ($6,919)
Total Member Encounters: N/A
Group Affiliation: Driscoll Childrens Hospital Inc
Licensed in: TX
Address: Corpus Christi, Corpus Christi,
Phone: (361) 694-6432 **Dom State:** TX **Commenced Bus:** N/A

Data Date	Rating	RACR #1	RACR #2	Total Assets ($mil)	Capital ($mil)	Net Premium ($mil)	Net Income ($mil)
6-20	C	2.14	1.78	224.2	140.4	380.4	50.2
6-19	N/A	N/A	N/A	N/A	N/A	N/A	N/A
2019	C-	0.93	0.77	171.8	65.6	709.3	-61.4
2018	C-	0.86	0.71	142.7	67.2	667.7	-21.7
2017	C+	1.25	1.04	141.9	76.6	660.3	25.6
2016	C-	0.99	0.82	116.9	51.5	522.6	6.4
2015	C-	0.61	0.51	81.2	30.2	435.6	-15.6

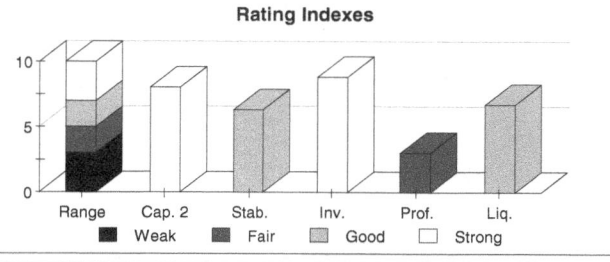

Rating Indexes

EASY CHOICE HEALTH PLAN   C   Fair

Major Rating Factors: Fair overall results on stability tests (4.2 on a scale of 0 to 10). Good overall profitability index (6.7). Strong capitalization index (7.2) based on good current risk-adjusted capital (moderate loss scenario).
Other Rating Factors: Excellent liquidity (7.1) with ample operational cash flow and liquid investments.
Principal Business: Medicare (100%)
Mem Phys: 19: N/A **18:** N/A **19 MLR** 84.6% **/ 19 Admin Exp** N/A
Enroll(000): Q2 20: 0 **19:** 31 **18:** 31 **Med Exp PMPM:** $1,082
Principal Investments ($000): Cash and equiv ($86,116)
Provider Compensation ($000): None
Total Member Encounters: N/A
Group Affiliation: None
Licensed in: CA
Address: 4550 California Ave Suite 100, Bakersfield, CA 93309
Phone: (310) 228-3745 **Dom State:** CA **Commenced Bus:** September 2006

Data Date	Rating	RACR #1	RACR #2	Total Assets ($mil)	Capital ($mil)	Net Premium ($mil)	Net Income ($mil)
6-20	C	1.28	0.80	160.1	40.0	292.9	5.4
6-19	C	0.89	0.58	123.9	26.8	232.8	8.7
2019	C	1.02	0.65	117.7	34.5	455.0	16.3
2018	C	1.21	0.75	104.4	30.1	388.9	13.2
2017	C-	1.54	0.95	118.8	35.4	352.2	15.5
2016	D	0.68	0.42	100.4	20.1	382.1	0.8
2015	E	0.50	0.31	62.2	19.3	380.0	-13.0

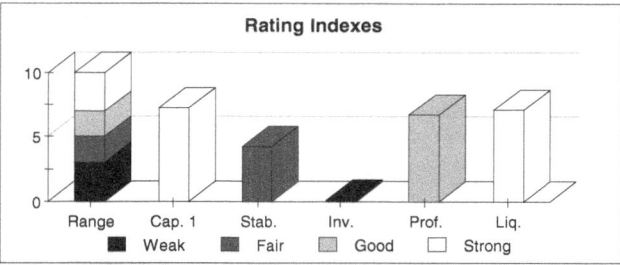

Rating Indexes

EL PASO FIRST HEALTH PLANS INC   B   Good

Major Rating Factors: Good overall profitability index (5.2 on a scale of 0 to 10). Fair overall results on stability tests (4.5). Strong capitalization index (7.5) based on excellent current risk-adjusted capital (severe loss scenario).
Other Rating Factors: High quality investment portfolio (9.5). Excellent liquidity (7.1) with ample operational cash flow and liquid investments.
Principal Business: Medicaid (93%), comp med (7%)
Mem Phys: 19: 1,945 **18:** 1,993 **19 MLR** 88.8% **/ 19 Admin Exp** N/A
Enroll(000): Q2 20: 76 **19:** 71 **18:** 74 **Med Exp PMPM:** $211
Principal Investments: Cash and equiv (86%), real estate (14%)
Provider Compensation ($000): Contr fee ($152,616), capitation ($19,242), FFS ($6,133), bonus arrang ($1,597)
Total Member Encounters: Phys (593,255), non-phys (142,482)
Group Affiliation: None
Licensed in: TX
Address: 1145 Westmoreland, El Paso,
Phone: (915) 298-7198 **Dom State:** TX **Commenced Bus:** N/A

Data Date	Rating	RACR #1	RACR #2	Total Assets ($mil)	Capital ($mil)	Net Premium ($mil)	Net Income ($mil)
6-20	B	1.79	1.49	57.1	36.0	105.7	7.0
6-19	N/A	N/A	N/A	N/A	N/A	N/A	N/A
2019	B+	2.27	1.90	64.4	44.8	205.0	0.5
2018	B+	2.42	2.02	61.7	45.4	196.2	0.1
2017	A-	2.55	2.12	60.5	45.6	190.3	8.5
2016	A-	2.20	1.83	60.3	42.5	201.0	8.6
2015	B	1.69	1.41	51.2	33.5	192.0	2.6

Rating Indexes

ELAN INSURANCE USVI INC

E+   **Very Weak**

Major Rating Factors: Good overall profitability index (6.1 on a scale of 0 to 10). Strong capitalization (8.2) based on excellent current risk-adjusted capital (severe loss scenario). High quality investment portfolio (9.6).
Other Rating Factors: Excellent liquidity (7.6) with ample operational cash flow and liquid investments.
Principal Business: Comp med (99%)
Mem Phys: 19: 1,844 **18:** 861 **19 MLR** 71.2% **/ 19 Admin Exp** N/A
Enroll(000): Q2 20: 2 **19:** 2 **18:** 2 **Med Exp PMPM:** $290
Principal Investments: Cash and equiv (90%), nonaffiliate common stock (6%), long-term bonds (3%)
Provider Compensation ($000): FFS ($6,993)
Total Member Encounters: Phys (4,627), non-phys (686)
Group Affiliation: Elan Insurance Group Inc
Licensed in: (No states)
Address: 8168 Crown Bay Marina Suite 5, St Thomas, VI 00802-5819
Phone: (305) 890-1544 **Dom State:** VI **Commenced Bus:** N/A

Data Date	Rating	RACR #1	RACR #2	Total Assets ($mil)	Capital ($mil)	Net Premium ($mil)	Net Income ($mil)
6-20	E+	2.33	1.94	7.4	4.3	5.1	0.3
6-19	N/A	N/A	N/A	N/A	N/A	N/A	N/A
2019	E+	2.15	1.79	5.7	4.0	9.9	0.3
2018	B	2.26	1.88	4.1	2.7	6.7	0.0
2017	N/A	N/A	N/A	2.5	1.5	4.0	N/A
2016	N/A	N/A	N/A	2.3	0.7	1.9	N/A
2015	N/A	N/A	N/A	N/A	N/A	N/A	N/A

Rating Indexes

ELDERPLAN INC

C+   **Fair**

Major Rating Factors: Excellent profitability (7.1 on a scale of 0 to 10). Strong capitalization index (7.3) based on excellent current risk-adjusted capital (severe loss scenario). High quality investment portfolio (9.9).
Other Rating Factors: Excellent overall results on stability tests (7.7). Excellent liquidity (6.9) with sufficient resources (cash flows and marketable investments) to handle a spike in claims
Principal Business: Medicaid (83%), Medicare (17%)
Mem Phys: 19: 28,281 **18:** 29,743 **19 MLR** 84.9% **/ 19 Admin Exp** N/A
Enroll(000): Q2 20: 26 **19:** 27 **18:** 26 **Med Exp PMPM:** $3,263
Principal Investments: Long-term bonds (49%), cash and equiv (42%), nonaffiliate common stock (9%)
Provider Compensation ($000): FFS ($965,354), contr fee ($54,356), capitation ($20,641)
Total Member Encounters: Phys (155,311), non-phys (87,745)
Group Affiliation: Elderplan Inc
Licensed in: NY
Address: 6323 Seventh Ave, Brooklyn,
Phone: (718) 921-7990 **Dom State:** NY **Commenced Bus:** N/A

Data Date	Rating	RACR #1	RACR #2	Total Assets ($mil)	Capital ($mil)	Net Premium ($mil)	Net Income ($mil)
6-20	C+	1.60	1.33	324.5	160.5	631.4	22.8
6-19	N/A	N/A	N/A	N/A	N/A	N/A	N/A
2019	C+	1.39	1.16	279.6	139.1	1,214.7	34.9
2018	C	1.10	0.92	256.3	101.2	1,081.6	21.2
2017	C	0.90	0.75	224.6	80.5	968.3	20.2
2016	C-	0.73	0.60	189.7	56.6	843.5	5.6
2015	D+	0.58	0.48	170.4	43.8	811.9	-30.7

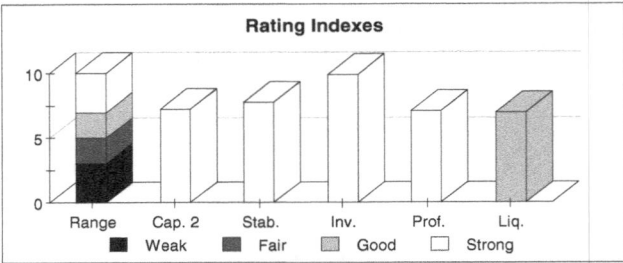

Rating Indexes

ELIPS LIFE INS CO

C   **Fair**

Major Rating Factors: Fair overall results on stability tests (3.7 on a scale of 0 to 10) including negative cash flow from operations for 2019. Weak profitability (1.9) with operating losses during the first six months of 2020. Return on equity has been low, averaging -8.7%. Strong capitalization (10.0) based on excellent risk adjusted capital (severe loss scenario).
Other Rating Factors: High quality investment portfolio (8.6). Excellent liquidity (9.0).
Principal Business: Group health insurance (73%), group life insurance (20%), individual life insurance (6%), and individual health insurance (1%).
Principal Investments: NonCMO investment grade bonds (97%) and cash (3%).
Investments in Affiliates: None
Group Affiliation: MAPFRE Ins Group
Licensed in: All states except NY, PR
Commenced Business: October 1975
Address: 116 WEST WATER STREET, JEFFERSON CITY, MO 65101
Phone: (847) 273-1261 **Domicile State:** MO **NAIC Code:** 85561

Data Date	Rating	RACR #1	RACR #2	Total Assets ($mil)	Capital ($mil)	Net Premium ($mil)	Net Income ($mil)
6-20	C	5.58	5.02	41.1	30.7	5.1	-3.3
6-19	C	5.93	5.33	36.0	33.9	0.0	-0.3
2019	C	6.08	5.47	38.5	33.4	1.6	-0.6
2018	C	5.99	5.39	40.5	34.3	0.1	-6.0
2017	C	5.39	4.85	22.6	20.4	-0.1	-1.7
2016	C	4.94	4.44	21.6	18.1	1.0	-1.0
2015	C-	5.30	4.77	23.5	20.6	0.0	-1.0

Rating Indexes

EMBLEMHEALTH INSURANCE COMPANY   D   Weak

Major Rating Factors: Weak profitability index (2.1 on a scale of 0 to 10). Strong capitalization (10.0) based on excellent current risk-adjusted capital (severe loss scenario). High quality investment portfolio (8.7).
Other Rating Factors: Excellent liquidity (7.0) with ample operational cash flow and liquid investments.
Principal Business: Comp med (100%)
Mem Phys: 19: 67,127 **18:** 63,923 **19 MLR** 89.1% / **19 Admin Exp** N/A
Enroll(000): Q2 20: 10 **19:** 8 **18:** 6 **Med Exp PMPM:** $291
Principal Investments: Long-term bonds (79%), cash and equiv (21%)
Provider Compensation ($000): Contr fee ($13,256), FFS ($9,535), capitation ($2,636)
Total Member Encounters: Phys (33,795), non-phys (15,770)
Group Affiliation: EmblemHealth Inc
Licensed in: NY
Address: 55 Water Street, New York, NY 10041-8190
Phone: (646) 447-5000 **Dom State:** NY **Commenced Bus:** N/A

Data Date	Rating	RACR #1	RACR #2	Total Assets ($mil)	Capital ($mil)	Net Premium ($mil)	Net Income ($mil)
6-20	D	7.78	6.48	48.4	37.1	36.6	1.4
6-19	D	32.42	27.02	45.8	41.7	12.0	2.4
2019	D	12.82	10.68	52.5	37.0	29.8	-2.3
2018	D	31.61	26.35	49.1	41.0	8.4	0.2
2017	D-	20.47	17.05	53.4	39.7	9.2	-0.9
2016	D-	38.10	31.75	53.7	41.6	8.3	1.2
2015	D-	28.95	24.12	51.6	42.5	20.1	4.4

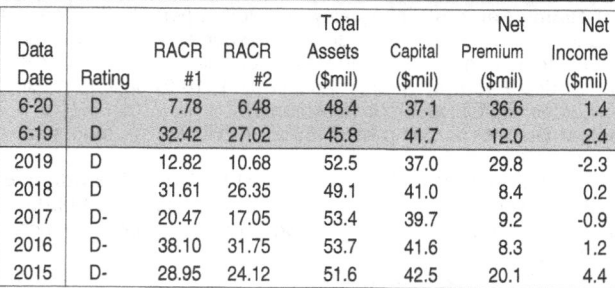

EMI HEALTH *   A   Excellent

Major Rating Factors: Excellent profitability (9.2 on a scale of 0 to 10). Strong capitalization (10.0) based on excellent current risk-adjusted capital (severe loss scenario). Excellent liquidity (8.5) with ample operational cash flow and liquid investments.
Other Rating Factors: Good quality investment portfolio (5.8).
Principal Business: Dental (6%), comp med (5%), med supp (3%), other (85%)
Mem Phys: 19: 20,532 **18:** 19,257 **19 MLR** 38.2% / **19 Admin Exp** N/A
Enroll(000): Q2 20: 63 **19:** 63 **18:** 58 **Med Exp PMPM:** $39
Principal Investments: Long-term bonds (38%), affiliate common stock (31%), real estate (16%), cash and equiv (14%), nonaffiliate common stock (1%)
Provider Compensation ($000): Contr fee ($20,578), FFS ($5,249)
Total Member Encounters: Phys (406,706), non-phys (252,025)
Group Affiliation: None
Licensed in: ID, UT
Address: 5101 S Commerce Dr, Murray, UT 84107
Phone: (801) 262-7476 **Dom State:** UT **Commenced Bus:** N/A

Data Date	Rating	RACR #1	RACR #2	Total Assets ($mil)	Capital ($mil)	Net Premium ($mil)	Net Income ($mil)
6-20	A	3.88	3.23	198.8	128.1	38.8	3.4
6-19	A	3.13	2.61	158.6	103.8	37.2	4.7
2019	A	3.67	3.06	170.5	121.5	72.4	14.1
2018	A	3.00	2.50	159.3	99.7	74.9	10.8
2017	A	N/A	N/A	118.7	84.9	30.6	7.9
2016	A	4.81	4.01	104.1	78.1	32.1	9.3
2015	A-	4.74	3.95	91.7	65.0	31.8	3.7

EMPATHIA PACIFIC INC   C-   Fair

Major Rating Factors: Good overall results on stability tests (4.9 on a scale of 0 to 10) in spite of healthy premium and capital growth during 2019. Excellent profitability (9.6). Strong capitalization index (10.0) based on excellent current risk-adjusted capital (severe loss scenario).
Other Rating Factors: Excellent liquidity (9.3) with ample operational cash flow and liquid investments.
Principal Business: Managed care (94%), indemnity (6%)
Mem Phys: 19: N/A **18:** N/A **19 MLR** 59.0% / **19 Admin Exp** N/A
Enroll(000): Q2 20: 153 **19:** 119 **18:** 119 **Med Exp PMPM:** $0
Principal Investments ($000): Cash and equiv ($3,008)
Provider Compensation ($000): None
Total Member Encounters: N/A
Group Affiliation: None
Licensed in: (No states)
Address: 5234 Chesebro Rd Ste 201, Agoura Hills, CA 91301-2268
Phone: (800) 634-6433 **Dom State:** CA **Commenced Bus:** N/A

Data Date	Rating	RACR #1	RACR #2	Total Assets ($mil)	Capital ($mil)	Net Premium ($mil)	Net Income ($mil)
6-20	C-	18.79	13.41	4.2	3.7	1.1	0.5
6-19	C-	24.44	17.32	3.3	2.8	0.9	0.3
2019	C-	26.26	17.85	3.7	3.3	2.0	0.8
2018	C-	20.97	14.76	2.8	2.4	1.5	0.3
2017	C-	18.05	13.01	2.4	2.1	1.5	0.3
2016	N/A	N/A	N/A	N/A	N/A	N/A	N/A
2015	N/A	N/A	N/A	N/A	N/A	N/A	N/A

EMPIRE HEALTHCHOICE ASSURANCE INC — B- — Good

Major Rating Factors: Fair quality investment portfolio (3.6 on a scale of 0 to 10). Good liquidity (6.5) with sufficient resources (cash flows and marketable investments) to handle a spike in claims. Excellent profitability (7.8).
Other Rating Factors: Strong capitalization (10.0) based on excellent current risk-adjusted capital (severe loss scenario).
Principal Business: Comp med (55%), FEHB (37%), med supp (3%), dental (2%), other (3%)
Mem Phys: 19: 99,512 **18:** 90,836 **19 MLR** 88.9% **/ 19 Admin Exp** N/A
Enroll(000): Q2 20: 1,108 **19:** 1,071 **18:** 906 **Med Exp PMPM:** $204
Principal Investments: Long-term bonds (89%), affiliate common stock (15%), other (13%)
Provider Compensation ($000): Bonus arrang ($1,755,666), contr fee ($513,433), FFS ($171,330), capitation ($2,370), other ($61,384)
Total Member Encounters: Phys (3,084,283), non-phys (1,952,908)
Group Affiliation: Anthem Inc
Licensed in: NY
Address: 9 PINE STREET 14TH FLOOR, NEW YORK, NY 10005
Phone: (212) 563-5570 **Dom State:** NY **Commenced Bus:** N/A

Data Date	Rating	RACR #1	RACR #2	Total Assets ($mil)	Capital ($mil)	Net Premium ($mil)	Net Income ($mil)
6-20	B-	5.09	4.24	2,532.2	1,018.3	1,390.3	98.4
6-19	B-	5.00	4.17	2,236.5	941.8	1,380.6	115.8
2019	B-	4.51	3.75	1,982.1	897.7	2,832.5	206.4
2018	B-	4.39	3.66	1,982.6	821.0	2,634.3	164.7
2017	B-	4.85	4.04	2,177.0	963.8	2,104.0	106.1
2016	B-	4.54	3.78	2,501.0	877.4	2,228.7	193.0
2015	B-	4.23	3.52	2,378.9	928.5	2,598.2	145.1

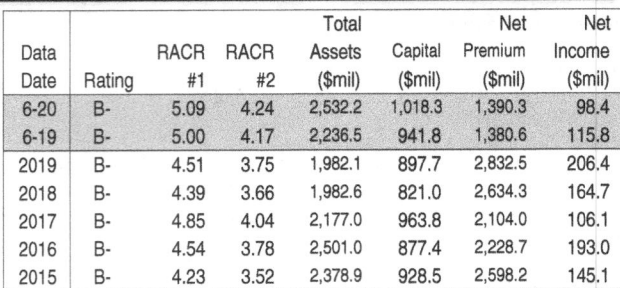

Rating Indexes (Range, Cap. 2, Stab., Inv., Prof., Liq. — Weak, Fair, Good, Strong)

EMPIRE HEALTHCHOICE HMO INC — C — Fair

Major Rating Factors: Fair overall results on stability tests (4.2 on a scale of 0 to 10). Weak profitability index (2.1). Good liquidity (6.5) with sufficient resources (cash flows and marketable investments) to handle a spike in claims.
Other Rating Factors: Strong capitalization index (8.7) based on excellent current risk-adjusted capital (severe loss scenario). High quality investment portfolio (8.0).
Principal Business: Medicare (89%), comp med (11%)
Mem Phys: 19: 98,503 **18:** 89,941 **19 MLR** 89.6% **/ 19 Admin Exp** N/A
Enroll(000): Q2 20: 74 **19:** 82 **18:** 86 **Med Exp PMPM:** $882
Principal Investments: Long-term bonds (96%), cash and equiv (3%), other (1%)
Provider Compensation ($000): Bonus arrang ($439,182), contr fee ($310,887), capitation ($74,045), FFS ($50,776)
Total Member Encounters: Phys (1,288,255), non-phys (832,314)
Group Affiliation: Anthem Inc
Licensed in: NY
Address: 1 LIBERTY PLAZA 165 BROADWAY, NEW YORK,
Phone: (212) 563-5570 **Dom State:** NY **Commenced Bus:** N/A

Data Date	Rating	RACR #1	RACR #2	Total Assets ($mil)	Capital ($mil)	Net Premium ($mil)	Net Income ($mil)
6-20	C	2.73	2.28	419.6	202.9	492.5	36.0
6-19	B-	3.65	3.04	433.4	203.0	493.5	13.9
2019	B-	3.01	2.51	408.7	157.2	977.6	-41.1
2018	B-	3.39	2.82	434.6	187.0	992.1	-15.8
2017	C	1.98	1.65	525.2	203.6	1,284.6	-38.4
2016	C+	2.96	2.47	616.1	223.9	1,381.4	-8.0
2015	B	3.53	2.94	615.5	241.8	1,248.0	-36.6

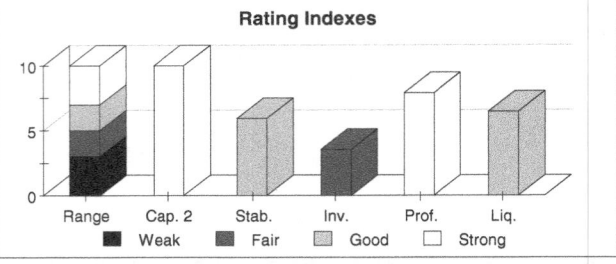

Rating Indexes (Range, Cap. 2, Stab., Inv., Prof., Liq. — Weak, Fair, Good, Strong)

ENTERPRISE LIFE INS CO * — B+ — Good

Major Rating Factors: Good quality investment portfolio (5.7 on a scale of 0 to 10) with no exposure to mortgages and no exposure to junk bonds. Good overall results on stability tests (6.4) despite fair risk adjusted capital in prior years. Other stability subfactors include excellent operational trends and excellent risk diversification. Strong capitalization (7.2) based on excellent risk adjusted capital (severe loss scenario).
Other Rating Factors: Excellent profitability (9.5) with operating gains in each of the last five years. Excellent liquidity (7.4).
Principal Business: Reinsurance (100%).
Principal Investments: Common & preferred stock (43%), nonCMO investment grade bonds (20%), CMOs and structured securities (10%), and cash (5%).
Investments in Affiliates: 43%
Group Affiliation: Credit Suisse Group
Licensed in: AZ, AR, IL, KS, LA, MS, NE, NM, OK, OR, TX, WI
Commenced Business: September 1978
Address: 300 Burnett Street Suite 200, Fort Worth, TX 76102-2734
Phone: (817) 878-3300 **Domicile State:** TX **NAIC Code:** 89087

Data Date	Rating	RACR #1	RACR #2	Total Assets ($mil)	Capital ($mil)	Net Premium ($mil)	Net Income ($mil)
6-20	B+	1.32	1.16	148.0	115.3	105.9	17.0
6-19	B	1.19	1.06	96.0	69.7	87.2	13.6
2019	B+	1.07	0.98	110.3	84.0	181.3	21.1
2018	B	0.84	0.74	73.5	49.1	145.8	15.2
2017	C+	0.77	0.69	47.9	29.6	103.3	7.4
2016	B-	0.84	0.75	34.9	23.5	62.7	0.1
2015	C	0.88	0.79	28.2	19.9	38.9	0.0

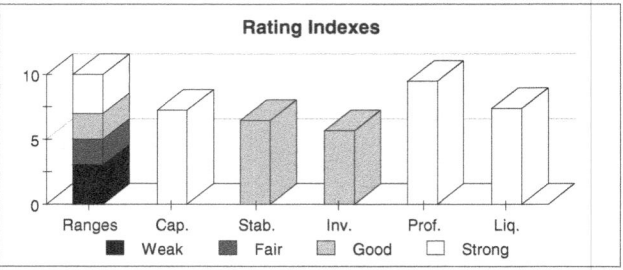

Rating Indexes (Ranges, Cap., Stab., Inv., Prof., Liq. — Weak, Fair, Good, Strong)

ENVISION INS CO   C+   Fair

Major Rating Factors: Good capitalization (6.8 on a scale of 0 to 10) based on excellent current risk-adjusted capital (severe loss scenario). Weak profitability index (2.7). High quality investment portfolio (9.9).

Other Rating Factors: Excellent liquidity (7.0) with ample operational cash flow and liquid investments.

Principal Business: Other (100%)

Mem Phys: 19: 61,211   **18:** 60,938   **19 MLR** 95.0%   **/ 19 Admin Exp** N/A

Enroll(000): Q2 20: 913   **19:** 722   **18:** 598   **Med Exp PMPM:** $50

Principal Investments: Cash and equiv (95%), long-term bonds (5%)

Provider Compensation ($000): Other ($352,828)

Total Member Encounters: N/A

Group Affiliation: None

Licensed in: (No states)

Address: 2181 East Aurora Road, Twinsburg, OH 44087

Phone: (330) 405-8089   **Dom State:** OH   **Commenced Bus:** N/A

Data Date	Rating	RACR #1	RACR #2	Total Assets ($mil)	Capital ($mil)	Net Premium ($mil)	Net Income ($mil)
6-20	C+	1.20	1.00	447.8	44.6	258.2	-4.4
6-19	N/A	N/A	N/A	N/A	N/A	N/A	N/A
2019	C+	1.52	1.27	704.3	54.8	425.0	6.3
2018	C	1.95	1.63	496.7	51.8	393.7	1.6
2017	C-	2.22	1.85	428.9	47.5	170.3	-2.6
2016	C-	1.77	1.48	309.9	49.6	235.9	-3.4
2015	C-	1.67	1.39	332.8	51.1	237.3	-6.8

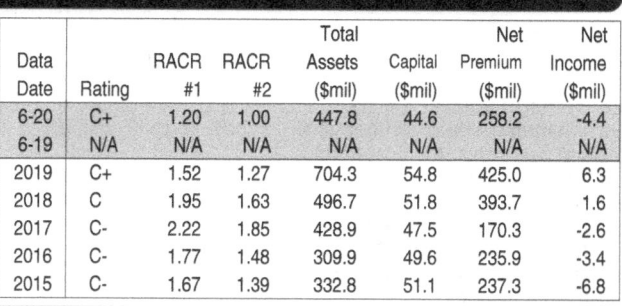

Rating Indexes

EON HEALTH INC (GA)   C-   Fair

Major Rating Factors: Weak profitability index (0.0 on a scale of 0 to 10). Good liquidity (6.9) with sufficient resources (cash flows and marketable investments) to handle a spike in claims. Strong capitalization (10.0) based on excellent current risk-adjusted capital (severe loss scenario).

Other Rating Factors: High quality investment portfolio (9.9).

Principal Business: Medicare (100%)

Mem Phys: 18: 3,194   **17:** 4,566   **18 MLR** 92.2%   **/ 18 Admin Exp** N/A

Enroll(000): Q3 19: 1   **18:** 1   **17:** 0   **Med Exp PMPM:** $707

Principal Investments: Long-term bonds (98%), cash and equiv (2%)

Provider Compensation ($000): FFS ($4,444)

Total Member Encounters: Phys (1,956), non-phys (269)

Group Affiliation: Delaware Life Partners LLC

Licensed in: GA

Address: 289 S Culver Street, Lawrenceville, GA 30046

Phone: (847) 696-8521   **Dom State:** GA   **Commenced Bus:** N/A

Data Date	Rating	RACR #1	RACR #2	Total Assets ($mil)	Capital ($mil)	Net Premium ($mil)	Net Income ($mil)
9-19	C-	3.69	3.07	7.2	3.6	3.4	0.1
9-18	N/A	N/A	N/A	6.0	3.2	3.7	0.1
2018	C-	3.41	2.84	9.6	3.3	4.8	-3.9
2017	N/A	N/A	N/A	5.7	1.0	4.7	-6.8
2016	N/A	N/A	N/A	8.1	8.1	N/A	N/A
2015	N/A	N/A	N/A	N/A	N/A	N/A	N/A
2014	N/A	N/A	N/A	N/A	N/A	N/A	N/A

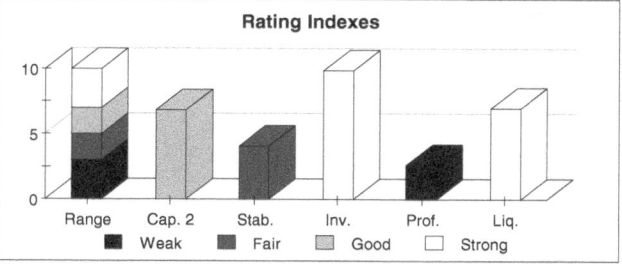

Rating Indexes

EPIC HEALTH PLAN   D   Weak

Major Rating Factors: Weak liquidity (0.0 on a scale of 0 to 10) as a spike in claims may stretch capacity. Good capitalization index (6.8) based on good current risk-adjusted capital (moderate loss scenario). Excellent profitability (8.8).

Other Rating Factors: Excellent overall results on stability tests (7.0).

Principal Business: Managed care (100%)

Mem Phys: 19: N/A   **18:** N/A   **19 MLR** 94.9%   **/ 19 Admin Exp** N/A

Enroll(000): Q2 20: 70   **19:** 72   **18:** 72   **Med Exp PMPM:** $600

Principal Investments ($000): Cash and equiv ($76,402)

Provider Compensation ($000): None

Total Member Encounters: N/A

Group Affiliation: None

Licensed in: CA

Address: 10803 Hope St Ste B, Cypress, CA 90630

Phone: (813) 206-7668   **Dom State:** CA   **Commenced Bus:** October 2010

Data Date	Rating	RACR #1	RACR #2	Total Assets ($mil)	Capital ($mil)	Net Premium ($mil)	Net Income ($mil)
6-20	D	1.02	0.62	83.0	40.6	272.1	5.0
6-19	D-	0.39	0.24	74.9	32.4	277.2	4.6
2019	D	0.88	0.54	81.5	35.7	541.8	7.2
2018	D-	0.25	0.15	65.0	27.8	477.3	14.1
2017	D-	N/A	N/A	35.1	13.7	388.4	2.9
2016	D-	N/A	N/A	28.9	10.7	343.1	2.2
2015	D-	0.06	0.04	29.3	8.5	348.2	2.4

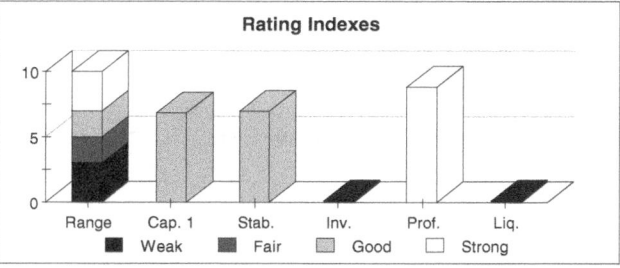

Rating Indexes

ESSENCE HEALTHCARE INC *   A-   Excellent

Major Rating Factors: Excellent profitability (9.2 on a scale of 0 to 10). Strong capitalization (7.8) based on excellent current risk-adjusted capital (severe loss scenario). High quality investment portfolio (9.3).
Other Rating Factors: Excellent liquidity (6.9) with sufficient resources (cash flows and marketable investments) to handle a spike in claims.
Principal Business: Medicare (100%)
Mem Phys: 19: 1,590 **18:** 1,514 **19 MLR** 84.5% **/ 19 Admin Exp** N/A
Enroll(000): Q2 20: 64 **19:** 63 **18:** 65 **Med Exp PMPM:** $871
Principal Investments: Long-term bonds (65%), cash and equiv (35%)
Provider Compensation ($000): Contr fee ($531,940), capitation ($126,420)
Total Member Encounters: Phys (534,143), non-phys (147,003)
Group Affiliation: None
Licensed in: IL, MO, TX, WA
Address: 13900 Riverport Drive, St Louis, MO 63043
Phone: (314) 209-2780 **Dom State:** MO **Commenced Bus:** N/A

Data Date	Rating	RACR #1	RACR #2	Total Assets ($mil)	Capital ($mil)	Net Premium ($mil)	Net Income ($mil)
6-20	A-	2.01	1.67	260.9	121.3	434.5	19.7
6-19	N/A	N/A	N/A	N/A	N/A	N/A	N/A
2019	A-	1.64	1.37	240.0	101.0	783.0	17.6
2018	A-	1.42	1.18	212.7	86.8	738.8	10.8
2017	B+	1.54	1.28	225.4	86.3	694.6	21.1
2016	B+	1.53	1.27	193.0	81.4	657.2	22.9
2015	B+	1.36	1.13	132.6	65.3	552.5	11.4

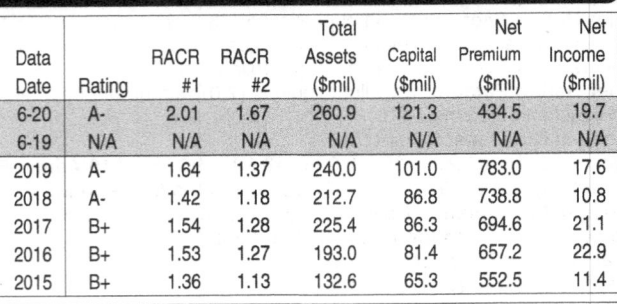
Rating Indexes

EXCELLUS HEALTH PLAN INC   B   Good

Major Rating Factors: Good quality investment portfolio (5.4 on a scale of 0 to 10). Good liquidity (6.8) with sufficient resources (cash flows and marketable investments) to handle a spike in claims. Excellent profitability (7.4).
Other Rating Factors: Strong capitalization (10.0) based on excellent current risk-adjusted capital (severe loss scenario).
Principal Business: Comp med (50%), Medicare (27%), Medicaid (17%), FEHB (3%), dental (1%), other (1%)
Mem Phys: 19: 30,829 **18:** 28,403 **19 MLR** 88.2% **/ 19 Admin Exp** N/A
Enroll(000): Q2 20: 1,096 **19:** 1,096 **18:** 1,083 **Med Exp PMPM:** $399
Principal Investments: Long-term bonds (63%), nonaffiliate common stock (20%), cash and equiv (8%), affiliate common stock (5%), real estate (1%), pref stock (1%), other (3%)
Provider Compensation ($000): Contr fee ($4,990,669), FFS ($116,260), capitation ($55,310), bonus arrang ($5,670), other ($64,005)
Total Member Encounters: Phys (9,779,919), non-phys (2,357,854)
Group Affiliation: Lifetime Healthcare Inc
Licensed in: NY
Address: 165 Court Street, Rochester, NY 14647
Phone: (585) 399-6652 **Dom State:** NY **Commenced Bus:** N/A

Data Date	Rating	RACR #1	RACR #2	Total Assets ($mil)	Capital ($mil)	Net Premium ($mil)	Net Income ($mil)
6-20	B	3.67	3.06	3,978.1	1,478.7	3,070.8	194.5
6-19	B	3.63	3.02	3,449.0	1,371.6	3,001.6	148.7
2019	B	3.53	2.94	3,727.7	1,417.4	5,964.6	170.8
2018	B	3.04	2.54	3,385.4	1,137.5	5,746.6	150.1
2017	B+	4.07	3.39	3,348.9	1,438.1	5,617.8	182.3
2016	B+	3.29	2.74	3,086.3	1,210.7	5,983.7	99.5
2015	A-	2.99	2.50	3,026.5	1,059.4	5,923.2	57.9

Rating Indexes

FAIR AMERICAN INS & REINS CO   B   Good

Major Rating Factors: Good overall profitability index (6.3 on a scale of 0 to 10). Fair expense controls. Return on equity has been low, averaging 2.8% over the past five years. Fair overall results on stability tests (4.4).
Other Rating Factors: Strong long-term capitalization index (10.0) based on excellent current risk adjusted capital (severe and moderate loss scenarios), despite some fluctuation in capital levels. Ample reserve history (7.2) that can protect against increases in claims costs. Excellent liquidity (7.0) with ample operational cash flow and liquid investments.
Principal Business: Group accident & health (54%), medical malpractice (43%), and surety (2%).
Principal Investments: Investment grade bonds (91%), misc. investments (6%), and cash (3%).
Investments in Affiliates: None
Group Affiliation: Alleghany Corp Group
Licensed in: All states except PR
Commenced Business: September 1985
Address: ONE LIBERTY PLAZA 165 BROADWAY, New York, NY 10006
Phone: (212) 365-2200 **Domicile State:** NY **NAIC Code:** 35157

Data Date	Rating	RACR #1	RACR #2	Loss Ratio %	Total Assets ($mil)	Capital ($mil)	Net Premium ($mil)	Net Income ($mil)
6-20	B	50.93	36.30	N/A	235.3	209.7	4.5	3.3
6-19	B	53.61	35.99	N/A	218.3	203.3	4.2	4.0
2019	B	53.32	36.10	67.0	225.2	206.5	8.4	7.1
2018	B	43.21	35.19	72.3	229.7	199.4	7.8	5.5
2017	B-	55.78	37.50	50.7	211.3	193.9	4.0	3.8
2016	B-	56.35	38.56	52.3	205.6	187.7	3.9	5.7
2015	B	81.08	49.01	52.8	256.9	241.8	3.5	6.0

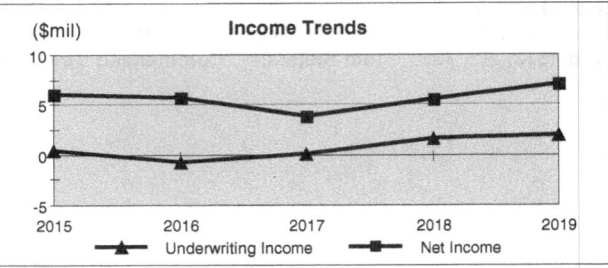
Income Trends

FALLON COMMUNITY HEALTH PLAN   C+   Fair

Major Rating Factors: Fair profitability index (3.4 on a scale of 0 to 10). Fair overall results on stability tests (4.9). Good liquidity (5.1) with sufficient resources (cash flows and marketable investments) to handle a spike in claims.
Other Rating Factors: Strong capitalization index (7.0) based on excellent current risk-adjusted capital (severe loss scenario). High quality investment portfolio (8.2).
Principal Business: Comp med (51%), Medicaid (40%), Medicare (10%)
Mem Phys: 19: 67,624 **18:** 64,400 **19 MLR** 94.4% **/ 19 Admin Exp** N/A
Enroll(000): Q2 20: 169 **19:** 166 **18:** 170 **Med Exp PMPM:** $740
Principal Investments: Long-term bonds (67%), nonaffiliate common stock (22%), cash and equiv (7%), affiliate common stock (2%), other (2%)
Provider Compensation ($000): Contr fee ($1,118,915), capitation ($326,413), salary ($24,369), bonus arrang ($2,850)
Total Member Encounters: Phys (674,884), non-phys (1,024,625)
Group Affiliation: Fallon Community Health Plan Inc
Licensed in: MA
Address: 10 Chestnut Street, Worcester,
Phone: (508) 799-2100 **Dom State:** MA **Commenced Bus:** N/A

Data Date	Rating	RACR #1	RACR #2	Total Assets ($mil)	Capital ($mil)	Net Premium ($mil)	Net Income ($mil)
6-20	C+	1.35	1.12	514.8	171.3	831.0	32.9
6-19	B-	1.56	1.30	445.0	180.6	769.9	8.3
2019	C	1.13	0.95	431.7	144.6	1,569.2	-19.1
2018	B-	1.38	1.15	401.2	160.3	1,514.4	8.8
2017	B-	1.63	1.36	383.6	163.1	1,242.2	17.9
2016	B-	1.59	1.33	347.2	145.8	1,149.0	-21.3
2015	B	1.82	1.52	368.4	151.3	1,095.9	8.8

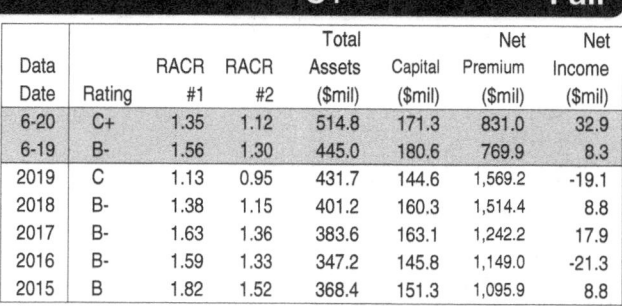

Rating Indexes

FALLON HEALTH & LIFE ASR CO   D+   Weak

Major Rating Factors: Weak profitability index (0.9 on a scale of 0 to 10). Good capitalization (6.6) based on good current risk-adjusted capital (severe loss scenario). High quality investment portfolio (9.9).
Other Rating Factors: Excellent liquidity (7.1) with ample operational cash flow and liquid investments.
Principal Business: Comp med (64%), med supp (36%)
Mem Phys: 19: 67,624 **18:** 64,400 **19 MLR** 132.5% **/ 19 Admin Exp** N/A
Enroll(000): Q2 20: 5 **19:** 5 **18:** 5 **Med Exp PMPM:** $533
Principal Investments: Cash and equiv (100%), affiliate common stock (39%)
Provider Compensation ($000): Contr fee ($29,429), capitation ($52), bonus arrang ($42)
Total Member Encounters: Phys (23,358), non-phys (9,234)
Group Affiliation: Fallon Community Health Plan Inc
Licensed in: MA
Address: 10 Chestnut Street, Worcester, MA 01608-2810
Phone: (508) 799-2100 **Dom State:** MA **Commenced Bus:** N/A

Data Date	Rating	RACR #1	RACR #2	Total Assets ($mil)	Capital ($mil)	Net Premium ($mil)	Net Income ($mil)
6-20	D+	1.17	0.97	30.9	7.6	11.5	-4.5
6-19	C	1.20	1.00	15.0	5.2	11.3	-3.4
2019	C-	1.26	1.05	25.3	6.0	22.8	-12.7
2018	C	1.57	1.31	18.8	6.8	23.6	-5.5
2017	E	1.05	0.88	24.0	6.5	28.7	-6.1
2016	E	2.02	1.68	25.9	8.4	30.1	1.8
2015	E	0.97	0.81	31.6	5.7	37.3	-11.0

Rating Indexes

FAMILY HERITAGE LIFE INS CO OF AMER   B-   Good

Major Rating Factors: Good current capitalization (6.2 on a scale of 0 to 10) based on good risk adjusted capital (severe loss scenario), although results have slipped from the excellent range during the last year. Good overall profitability (5.8) although investment income, in comparison to reserve requirements, is below regulatory standards. Fair quality investment portfolio (4.5).
Other Rating Factors: Fair overall results on stability tests (3.7). Excellent liquidity (8.1).
Principal Business: Individual health insurance (94%), group health insurance (5%), and individual life insurance (1%).
Principal Investments: NonCMO investment grade bonds (92%), CMOs and structured securities (2%), noninv. grade bonds (2%), and mortgages in good standing (1%).
Investments in Affiliates: None
Group Affiliation: Torchmark Corp
Licensed in: All states except NY
Commenced Business: November 1989
Address: 6001 East Royalton Rd Ste 200, Cleveland, OH 44147-3529
Phone: (440) 922-5252 **Domicile State:** OH **NAIC Code:** 77968

Data Date	Rating	RACR #1	RACR #2	Total Assets ($mil)	Capital ($mil)	Net Premium ($mil)	Net Income ($mil)
6-20	B-	1.52	0.90	1,375.1	107.8	157.2	17.8
6-19	B-	1.52	0.96	1,247.2	118.1	146.8	15.0
2019	B-	1.65	1.00	1,287.3	109.7	298.7	32.0
2018	B-	2.04	1.25	1,196.8	125.4	170.0	31.5
2017	B+	1.65	1.01	1,290.4	100.3	284.3	23.0
2016	B+	1.96	1.25	1,108.8	104.2	264.6	23.8
2015	A-	1.92	1.27	921.0	78.3	254.1	19.1

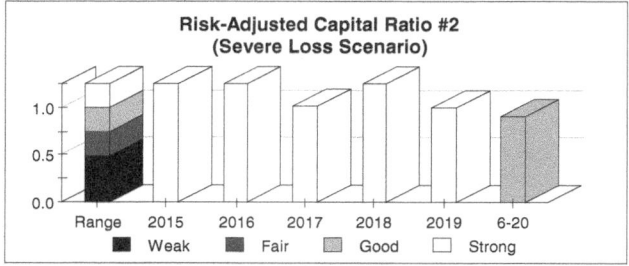

Risk-Adjusted Capital Ratio #2
(Severe Loss Scenario)

FAMILY LIFE INS CO   C   Fair

Major Rating Factors: Fair profitability (3.0 on a scale of 0 to 10) with investment income below regulatory standards in relation to interest assumptions of reserves. Fair overall results on stability tests (4.2). Good liquidity (5.9) with sufficient resources to handle a spike in claims as well as a significant increase in policy surrenders.

Other Rating Factors: Strong capitalization (8.8) based on excellent risk adjusted capital (severe loss scenario). High quality investment portfolio (8.1).

Principal Business: Individual health insurance (67%) and individual life insurance (33%).

Principal Investments: NonCMO investment grade bonds (72%), policy loans (9%), mortgages in good standing (3%), cash (2%), and misc. investments (3%).

Investments in Affiliates: None

Group Affiliation: Manhattan Life Group Inc

Licensed in: All states except NY, PR

Commenced Business: June 1949

Address: 10777 Northwest Freeway, Houston, TX 77092

Phone: (713) 529-0045 **Domicile State:** TX **NAIC Code:** 63053

Data Date	Rating	RACR #1	RACR #2	Total Assets ($mil)	Capital ($mil)	Net Premium ($mil)	Net Income ($mil)
6-20	C	2.94	2.21	142.2	27.0	13.4	0.6
6-19	C	3.05	2.38	143.1	28.2	13.3	0.4
2019	C	2.89	2.18	141.2	26.6	26.5	1.8
2018	C	3.06	2.40	146.8	28.4	25.6	1.6
2017	C	3.33	2.72	150.8	31.1	25.6	2.7
2016	C	3.61	3.03	155.8	34.0	26.0	1.0
2015	C	3.79	3.13	158.7	35.8	26.5	2.7

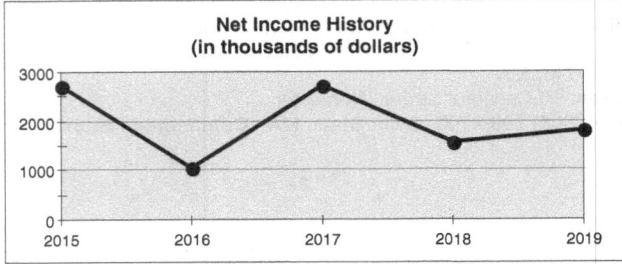

Net Income History
(in thousands of dollars)

FIDELITY SECURITY LIFE INS CO *   A-   Excellent

Major Rating Factors: Good quality investment portfolio (6.7 on a scale of 0 to 10) despite mixed results such as: minimal exposure to mortgages and large holdings of BBB rated bonds but minimal holdings in junk bonds. Good overall results on stability tests (6.9). Strengths that enhance stability include good operational trends and excellent risk diversification. Strong capitalization (10.0) based on excellent risk adjusted capital (severe loss scenario).

Other Rating Factors: Excellent profitability (7.7) with operating gains in each of the last five years. Excellent liquidity (7.0).

Principal Business: Group health insurance (88%), reinsurance (7%), individual health insurance (2%), individual life insurance (1%), and other lines (2%).

Principal Investments: NonCMO investment grade bonds (44%), CMOs and structured securities (36%), cash (3%), common & preferred stock (2%), and misc. investments (4%).

Investments in Affiliates: 1%

Group Affiliation: Fidelity Security Group

Licensed in: All states except PR

Commenced Business: July 1969

Address: 3130 Broadway, Kansas City, MO 64111-2452

Phone: (816) 750-1060 **Domicile State:** MO **NAIC Code:** 71870

Data Date	Rating	RACR #1	RACR #2	Total Assets ($mil)	Capital ($mil)	Net Premium ($mil)	Net Income ($mil)
6-20	A-	4.95	3.04	980.9	276.2	66.2	10.8
6-19	A-	4.71	2.85	921.3	254.3	63.8	11.7
2019	A-	4.93	3.04	952.3	266.6	126.8	25.5
2018	A-	4.60	2.81	999.4	242.3	119.4	39.2
2017	B	3.87	2.36	949.5	204.4	115.0	22.8
2016	B	3.46	2.07	875.1	186.8	121.6	17.5
2015	B	2.02	1.44	864.2	169.0	420.4	18.1

Adverse Trends in Operations

Decrease in asset base during 2019 (5%)
Decrease in premium volume from 2016 to 2017 (5%)
Change in premium mix from 2015 to 2016 (5.8%)
Decrease in premium volume from 2015 to 2016 (71%)

FIRST CARE INC   D   Weak

Major Rating Factors: Weak profitability index (0.0 on a scale of 0 to 10). Fair liquidity (4.5) as cash resources may not be adequate to cover a spike in claims. Strong capitalization (10.0) based on excellent current risk-adjusted capital (severe loss scenario).

Other Rating Factors: High quality investment portfolio (9.9).

Principal Business: Med supp (100%)

Mem Phys: 18: 46,809 **17:** 46,349 **18 MLR** 88.0% **/ 18 Admin Exp** N/A

Enroll(000): Q3 19: 14 **18:** 10 **17:** 6 **Med Exp PMPM:** $130

Principal Investments: Long-term bonds (81%), cash and equiv (19%)

Provider Compensation ($000): Contr fee ($11,906), FFS ($737)

Total Member Encounters: Phys (165,931), non-phys (75,351)

Group Affiliation: CareFirst Inc

Licensed in: AZ, DC, FL, ID, KY, LA, MD, MT, OK, OR, RI, TX, UT, VT, VA, WV, WI, WY

Address: 1501 SOUTH CLINTON STREET, BALTIMORE, MD 21224

Phone: (410) 581-3000 **Dom State:** MD **Commenced Bus:** N/A

Data Date	Rating	RACR #1	RACR #2	Total Assets ($mil)	Capital ($mil)	Net Premium ($mil)	Net Income ($mil)
9-19	D	6.64	5.53	12.2	8.0	17.2	-6.5
9-18	C+	N/A	N/A	6.6	3.9	10.8	-8.1
2018	C	12.07	10.06	17.6	14.5	15.2	-12.5
2017	C+	N/A	N/A	6.3	4.5	7.5	-3.1
2016	C	106.20	88.46	14.0	6.2	0.6	0.0
2015	N/A	N/A	N/A	13.2	5.9	N/A	0.1
2014	N/A	N/A	N/A	11.1	5.2	N/A	N/A

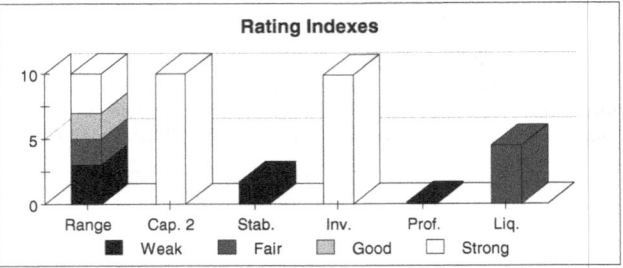

Rating Indexes

Range   Cap. 2   Stab.   Inv.   Prof.   Liq.

■ Weak   ■ Fair   ▨ Good   □ Strong

FIRST HEALTH LIFE & HEALTH INS CO — C+ — Fair

Major Rating Factors: Fair overall results on stability tests (4.4 on a scale of 0 to 10). Good quality investment portfolio (6.4) with no exposure to mortgages and minimal holdings in junk bonds. Strong capitalization (10.0) based on excellent risk adjusted capital (severe loss scenario).
Other Rating Factors: Excellent profitability (7.1) despite modest operating losses during 2016. Excellent liquidity (7.1).
Principal Business: Reinsurance (80%), individual health insurance (17%), and group health insurance (3%).
Principal Investments: NonCMO investment grade bonds (62%), cash (22%), CMOs and structured securities (10%), common & preferred stock (1%), and noninv. grade bonds (1%).
Investments in Affiliates: None
Group Affiliation: Aetna Inc
Licensed in: All states except PR
Commenced Business: June 1979
Address: DOWNERS GROVE, IL 60515
Phone: (630) 737-7900 **Domicile State:** TX **NAIC Code:** 90328

Data Date	Rating	RACR #1	RACR #2	Total Assets ($mil)	Capital ($mil)	Net Premium ($mil)	Net Income ($mil)
6-20	C+	3.77	3.01	395.9	230.3	76.5	8.5
6-19	C+	1.82	1.49	464.2	165.2	292.3	-0.7
2019	C+	2.26	1.85	391.7	220.5	550.6	55.3
2018	C+	1.86	1.53	371.1	192.8	559.3	53.3
2017	B-	1.70	1.39	400.7	227.8	761.1	16.5
2016	B-	1.50	1.24	454.9	211.1	798.3	-1.7
2015	B-	2.24	1.85	581.8	289.2	700.0	16.1

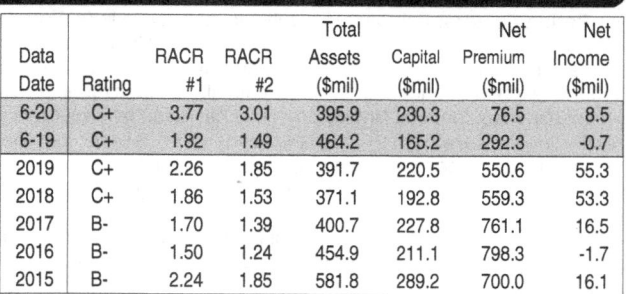

Rating Indexes — Ranges, Cap., Stab., Inv., Prof., Liq. — ■ Weak ■ Fair ▨ Good ☐ Strong

FIRST MEDICAL HEALTH PLAN INC — D — Weak

Major Rating Factors: Good overall profitability index (6.1 on a scale of 0 to 10). Good capitalization index (5.4) based on good current risk-adjusted capital (severe loss scenario). High quality investment portfolio (9.0).
Other Rating Factors: Excellent overall results on stability tests (7.7). Excellent liquidity (7.0) with sufficient resources (cash flows and marketable investments) to handle a spike in claims
Principal Business: Medicaid (54%), comp med (46%)
Mem Phys: 19: N/A **18:** N/A **19 MLR** 90.1% **/ 19 Admin Exp** N/A
Enroll(000): Q2 20: 527 **19:** 520 **18:** 508 **Med Exp PMPM:** $150
Principal Investments: Cash and equiv (100%)
Provider Compensation ($000): Capitation ($521,422), contr fee ($446,119)
Total Member Encounters: N/A
Group Affiliation: First Medical Health Plan Inc
Licensed in: PR
Address: 530 Marginal Buchanan, Guaynabo,
Phone: (787) 474-3999 **Dom State:** PR **Commenced Bus:** N/A

Data Date	Rating	RACR #1	RACR #2	Total Assets ($mil)	Capital ($mil)	Net Premium ($mil)	Net Income ($mil)
6-20	D	1.00	0.83	258.0	83.7	585.1	21.7
6-19	N/A	N/A	N/A	N/A	N/A	N/A	N/A
2019	D	0.74	0.62	218.1	67.1	1,050.3	11.6
2018	D-	0.59	0.49	217.8	57.3	1,080.5	6.9
2017	E	0.51	0.42	205.9	49.4	1,074.2	16.2
2016	E-	0.28	0.23	183.5	32.8	1,048.9	10.6
2015	E-	0.12	0.10	191.9	21.5	882.7	-12.5

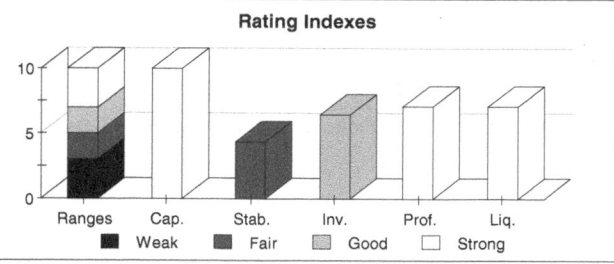

Rating Indexes — Range, Cap. 2, Stab., Inv., Prof., Liq. — ■ Weak ■ Fair ▨ Good ☐ Strong

FIRST RELIANCE STANDARD LIFE INS CO * — A- — Excellent

Major Rating Factors: Good overall results on stability tests (5.9 on a scale of 0 to 10) despite fair financial strength of affiliated Tokio Marine Holdings Inc. Strengths that enhance stability include excellent operational trends and excellent risk diversification. Good overall profitability (6.1). Return on equity has been fair, averaging 6.4%. Strong capitalization (10.0) based on excellent risk adjusted capital (severe loss scenario).
Other Rating Factors: High quality investment portfolio (7.7). Excellent liquidity (7.3).
Principal Business: Group health insurance (70%) and group life insurance (30%).
Principal Investments: NonCMO investment grade bonds (75%), CMOs and structured securities (15%), and noninv. grade bonds (3%).
Investments in Affiliates: None
Group Affiliation: Tokio Marine Holdings Inc
Licensed in: DC, DE
Commenced Business: October 1984
Address: 590 Madison Avenue 29th Floor, New York, NY 10022
Phone: (215) 787-4000 **Domicile State:** NY **NAIC Code:** 71005

Data Date	Rating	RACR #1	RACR #2	Total Assets ($mil)	Capital ($mil)	Net Premium ($mil)	Net Income ($mil)
6-20	A-	5.41	3.59	237.6	76.8	42.8	6.6
6-19	A-	4.91	3.27	220.6	65.1	41.7	3.8
2019	A-	5.04	3.32	227.3	70.0	83.1	8.8
2018	A-	4.81	3.19	212.1	61.0	74.7	-0.5
2017	A	5.19	3.33	199.1	61.2	61.8	-5.8
2016	A	6.14	4.05	188.9	68.3	63.0	9.5
2015	A	5.72	3.61	184.0	65.5	57.9	6.5

Tokio Marine Holdings Inc Composite Group Rating: C+ Largest Group Members	Assets ($mil)	Rating
RELIANCE STANDARD LIFE INS CO	15903	C+
PHILADELPHIA INDEMNITY INS CO	9437	B-
SAFETY NATIONAL CASUALTY CORP	9057	B
HOUSTON CASUALTY CO	3715	B-
US SPECIALTY INS CO	2131	C+

FIRST UNUM LIFE INS CO

C+ **Fair**

Major Rating Factors: Fair overall results on stability tests (4.8 on a scale of 0 to 10) including fair financial strength of affiliated Unum Group. Fair quality investment portfolio (4.4) with large holdings of BBB rated bonds in addition to junk bond exposure equal to 60% of capital. Good overall profitability (5.9). Excellent expense controls. Return on equity has been fair, averaging 9.9%.

Other Rating Factors: Strong capitalization (7.5) based on excellent risk adjusted capital (severe loss scenario). Excellent liquidity (7.4).

Principal Business: Group health insurance (57%), group life insurance (22%), individual health insurance (19%), and individual life insurance (2%).

Principal Investments: NonCMO investment grade bonds (83%), mortgages in good standing (7%), noninv. grade bonds (5%), and CMOs and structured securities (4%).

Investments in Affiliates: None

Group Affiliation: Unum Group

Licensed in: NY

Commenced Business: January 1960

Address: 666 THIRD AVENUE SUITE 301, NEW YORK, NY 10017

Phone: (212) 328-8830 **Domicile State:** NY **NAIC Code:** 64297

Data Date	Rating	RACR #1	RACR #2	Total Assets ($mil)	Capital ($mil)	Net Premium ($mil)	Net Income ($mil)
6-20	C+	2.51	1.31	4,139.0	331.1	248.9	19.5
6-19	C+	2.31	1.19	3,867.6	280.3	233.3	6.5
2019	C+	2.47	1.30	4,068.5	307.9	469.2	21.9
2018	C+	2.33	1.21	3,760.8	274.4	453.9	-13.6
2017	C+	2.66	1.36	3,457.4	299.1	392.7	27.4
2016	C+	2.63	1.32	3,260.8	282.4	375.7	82.4
2015	C+	2.54	1.27	3,130.4	263.5	363.2	26.5

Unum Group
Composite Group Rating: C+
Largest Group Members

Largest Group Members	Assets ($mil)	Rating
UNUM LIFE INS CO OF AMERICA	22430	C+
PROVIDENT LIFE ACCIDENT INS CO	7893	C+
FIRST UNUM LIFE INS CO	4069	C+
COLONIAL LIFE ACCIDENT INS CO	3525	C+
PAUL REVERE LIFE INS CO	3214	C+

FIRSTCAROLINACARE INS CO

D **Weak**

Major Rating Factors: Weak profitability index (0.7 on a scale of 0 to 10). Fair capitalization (4.6) based on fair current risk-adjusted capital (moderate loss scenario). Good liquidity (5.8) with sufficient resources (cash flows and marketable investments) to handle a spike in claims.

Other Rating Factors: High quality investment portfolio (7.8).

Principal Business: Medicare (62%), comp med (38%)

Mem Phys: 19: 3,300 **18:** 3,250 **19 MLR** 91.4% **/ 19 Admin Exp** N/A

Enroll(000): Q2 20: 14 **19:** 15 **18:** 16 **Med Exp PMPM:** $645

Principal Investments: Long-term bonds (61%), cash and equiv (23%), nonaffiliate common stock (16%)

Provider Compensation ($000): Contr fee ($100,781), capitation ($7,849), FFS ($5,070)

Total Member Encounters: Phys (61,847), non-phys (7,477)

Group Affiliation: None

Licensed in: NC, SC

Address: 42 MEMORIAL DRIVE, PINEHURST, NC 28374

Phone: (910) 715-8100 **Dom State:** NC **Commenced Bus:** N/A

Data Date	Rating	RACR #1	RACR #2	Total Assets ($mil)	Capital ($mil)	Net Premium ($mil)	Net Income ($mil)
6-20	D	0.87	0.73	25.2	13.4	58.6	-1.7
6-19	N/A	N/A	N/A	N/A	N/A	N/A	N/A
2019	D	1.00	0.84	28.8	15.3	123.7	-5.7
2018	D	0.77	0.64	26.9	12.1	132.2	-5.0
2017	D	1.00	0.83	34.1	17.0	134.4	-9.7
2016	D	0.47	0.39	25.9	7.9	117.7	-17.6
2015	B-	1.11	0.92	30.1	13.7	98.0	-12.7

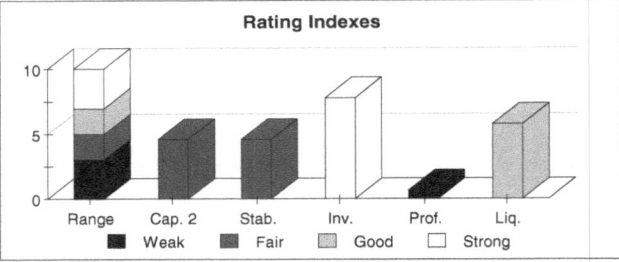

Rating Indexes

FLORIDA HEALTH CARE PLAN INC *

A **Excellent**

Major Rating Factors: Excellent profitability (9.3 on a scale of 0 to 10). Strong capitalization (8.3) based on excellent current risk-adjusted capital (severe loss scenario). High quality investment portfolio (9.4).

Other Rating Factors: Excellent liquidity (7.0) with ample operational cash flow and liquid investments.

Principal Business: Comp med (71%), other (29%)

Mem Phys: 19: 1,102 **18:** 1,072 **19 MLR** 80.9% **/ 19 Admin Exp** N/A

Enroll(000): Q2 20: 70 **19:** 70 **18:** 84 **Med Exp PMPM:** $618

Principal Investments: Cash and equiv (46%), long-term bonds (44%), real estate (10%)

Provider Compensation ($000): Contr fee ($329,355), salary ($64,641), FFS ($61,568), capitation ($16,676), bonus arrang ($1,786), other ($76,349)

Total Member Encounters: Phys (347,593), non-phys (125,328)

Group Affiliation: None

Licensed in: FL

Address: 1340 Ridgewood Avenue, Holly Hill, FL 32117

Phone: (386) 676-7100 **Dom State:** FL **Commenced Bus:** N/A

Data Date	Rating	RACR #1	RACR #2	Total Assets ($mil)	Capital ($mil)	Net Premium ($mil)	Net Income ($mil)
6-20	A	2.43	2.02	247.7	148.8	341.9	24.8
6-19	A-	4.18	3.48	231.2	132.4	337.1	29.8
2019	A	3.10	2.58	223.7	134.8	675.5	48.7
2018	A-	3.30	2.75	202.4	103.8	611.9	25.6
2017	B+	2.57	2.15	192.6	87.8	501.7	16.4
2016	B-	5.50	4.58	166.4	87.4	428.0	12.0
2015	N/A	N/A	N/A	115.8	75.5	358.1	7.5

Rating Indexes

FLORIDA MHS INC   C-   Fair

Major Rating Factors: Weak profitability index (2.7 on a scale of 0 to 10). Strong capitalization (8.3) based on excellent current risk-adjusted capital (severe loss scenario). High quality investment portfolio (9.9).
Other Rating Factors: Excellent liquidity (7.2) with ample operational cash flow and liquid investments.
Principal Business: Medicaid (100%)
Mem Phys: 19: 11,777   **18:** 35,675   **19 MLR** 88.2%   **/ 19 Admin Exp** N/A
Enroll(000): Q2 20: 21   **19:** 20   **18:** 52   **Med Exp PMPM:** $630
Principal Investments: Cash and equiv (97%), long-term bonds (3%)
Provider Compensation ($000): Contr fee ($208,387), capitation ($4,820)
Total Member Encounters: Phys (210,033), non-phys (492,704)
Group Affiliation: Molina Healthcare Inc
Licensed in: FL
Address: 8621 Robert Fulton Drive, Columbia, MD 21046
Phone: (314) 387-5044   **Dom State:** FL   **Commenced Bus:** N/A

Data Date	Rating	RACR #1	RACR #2	Total Assets ($mil)	Capital ($mil)	Net Premium ($mil)	Net Income ($mil)
6-20	C-	2.37	1.97	61.1	34.8	84.0	-0.3
6-19	D	0.81	0.67	88.0	29.2	118.2	-2.1
2019	D+	2.13	1.78	73.7	28.3	211.2	-6.3
2018	D	0.83	0.69	104.3	31.1	618.1	23.6
2017	D	N/A	N/A	241.2	111.4	605.6	34.9
2016	D	1.81	1.51	177.5	76.1	549.1	38.5
2015	D	0.90	0.75	122.9	39.2	440.9	-21.5

FLORIDA TRUE HEALTH INC   E-   Very Weak

Major Rating Factors: Weak profitability index (0.7 on a scale of 0 to 10). Strong capitalization (7.3) based on excellent current risk-adjusted capital (severe loss scenario). High quality investment portfolio (9.8).
Other Rating Factors: Excellent liquidity (6.9) with sufficient resources (cash flows and marketable investments) to handle a spike in claims.
Principal Business: Medicaid (100%)
Mem Phys: 19: 11,972   **18:** 38,510   **19 MLR** 97.1%   **/ 19 Admin Exp** N/A
Enroll(000): Q2 20: 86   **19:** 76   **18:** 321   **Med Exp PMPM:** $308
Principal Investments: Cash and equiv (100%)
Provider Compensation ($000): Contr fee ($348,641), capitation ($42,070)
Total Member Encounters: Phys (870,314), non-phys (293,479)
Group Affiliation: Independence Health Group Inc
Licensed in: FL
Address: 11631 Kew Gardens Ave Suite 2, Palm Beach Gardens, FL 33410
Phone: (215) 937-8000   **Dom State:** FL   **Commenced Bus:** N/A

Data Date	Rating	RACR #1	RACR #2	Total Assets ($mil)	Capital ($mil)	Net Premium ($mil)	Net Income ($mil)
6-20	E-	1.61	1.34	110.1	46.8	152.3	5.7
6-19	E-	0.42	0.35	61.6	17.4	177.2	-29.5
2019	E-	2.41	2.00	82.5	41.6	330.5	-34.0
2018	C	0.77	0.64	166.1	42.6	1,211.4	-241.0
2017	E	1.09	0.91	229.9	99.8	1,227.9	6.5
2016	E	1.68	1.40	219.2	95.2	1,104.9	18.3
2015	E	1.31	1.09	247.0	78.4	942.3	-152.5

FREEDOM HEALTH INC   B   Good

Major Rating Factors: Good capitalization (6.3 on a scale of 0 to 10) based on good current risk-adjusted capital (severe loss scenario). Good liquidity (6.1) with sufficient resources (cash flows and marketable investments) to handle a spike in claims. Excellent profitability (8.0).
Other Rating Factors: High quality investment portfolio (8.0).
Principal Business: Medicare (100%)
Mem Phys: 19: 12,518   **18:** 19,350   **19 MLR** 85.2%   **/ 19 Admin Exp** N/A
Enroll(000): Q2 20: 77   **19:** 75   **18:** 79   **Med Exp PMPM:** $1,062
Principal Investments: Long-term bonds (100%), other (3%)
Provider Compensation ($000): Capitation ($718,100), contr fee ($255,193), FFS ($5,794)
Total Member Encounters: Phys (62,779), non-phys (67,713)
Group Affiliation: Anthem Inc
Licensed in: FL
Address: 5600 MARINER STREET SUITE 227, INDIANAPOLIS, IN 46204
Phone: (813) 506-6000   **Dom State:** FL   **Commenced Bus:** N/A

Data Date	Rating	RACR #1	RACR #2	Total Assets ($mil)	Capital ($mil)	Net Premium ($mil)	Net Income ($mil)
6-20	B	1.13	0.94	374.0	83.4	656.9	23.0
6-19	B	1.68	1.40	267.8	84.2	587.0	39.4
2019	B+	2.05	1.71	270.0	101.7	1,149.6	61.5
2018	B	0.95	0.80	196.8	49.5	1,093.3	6.7
2017	D-	0.47	0.39	182.7	38.3	938.8	15.3
2016	E	0.32	0.27	165.5	32.2	871.2	3.4
2015	E	0.40	0.33	135.0	33.7	770.8	10.4

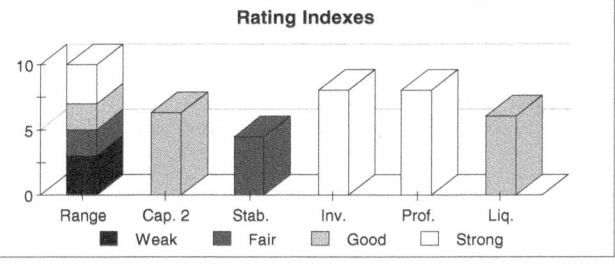

FREEDOM LIFE INS CO OF AMERICA *

B+   **Good**

Major Rating Factors: Good quality investment portfolio (6.4 on a scale of 0 to 10) with no exposure to mortgages and no exposure to junk bonds. Good overall results on stability tests (6.1) despite fair risk adjusted capital in prior years. Other stability subfactors include good operational trends and excellent risk diversification. Strong capitalization (7.9) based on excellent risk adjusted capital (severe loss scenario).

Other Rating Factors: Excellent profitability (8.6) with operating gains in each of the last five years. Excellent liquidity (7.4).

Principal Business: Group health insurance (66%), individual health insurance (24%), and individual life insurance (10%).

Principal Investments: Common & preferred stock (27%), nonCMO investment grade bonds (27%), and CMOs and structured securities (14%).

Investments in Affiliates: 27%

Group Affiliation: Credit Suisse Group

Licensed in: AL, AZ, AR, CO, DE, FL, GA, IL, IN, IA, KS, KY, LA, MD, MI, MN, MS, MO, NE, NV, NM, NC, OH, OK, OR, PA, SC, SD, TN, TX, UT, VA, WA, WV, WY

Commenced Business: June 1956

Address: 300 Burnett Street Suite 200, Fort Worth, TX 76102-2734

Phone: (817) 878-3300 **Domicile State:** TX **NAIC Code:** 62324

Data Date	Rating	RACR #1	RACR #2	Total Assets ($mil)	Capital ($mil)	Net Premium ($mil)	Net Income ($mil)
6-20	B+	1.81	1.58	418.7	298.6	306.8	45.6
6-19	B+	1.57	1.33	265.9	180.9	254.9	37.0
2019	B+	1.48	1.33	321.1	221.8	533.7	62.8
2018	B+	1.18	1.03	211.5	122.8	422.3	37.6
2017	C+	1.11	0.96	148.3	76.4	282.2	19.4
2016	C+	0.83	0.71	100.2	51.1	196.9	12.0
2015	C+	0.75	0.65	77.3	37.0	140.1	14.9

Adverse Trends in Operations

Change in asset mix during 2019 (6%)
Change in asset mix during 2017 (5.5%)

FRESNO-KINGS-MADERA REGIONAL HEALTH

C+   **Fair**

Major Rating Factors: Excellent profitability (9.5 on a scale of 0 to 10). Strong capitalization index (7.1) based on excellent current risk-adjusted capital (severe loss scenario). Excellent overall results on stability tests (7.4).

Other Rating Factors: Excellent liquidity (7.1) with ample operational cash flow and liquid investments.

Principal Business: Medicaid (100%)

Mem Phys: 19: N/A **18:** N/A **19 MLR** 89.9% **/ 19 Admin Exp** N/A

Enroll(000): Q2 20: 358 **19:** 356 **18:** 356 **Med Exp PMPM:** $243

Principal Investments ($000): Cash and equiv ($153,298)

Provider Compensation ($000): None

Total Member Encounters: N/A

Group Affiliation: None

Licensed in: CA

Address: 1615 Orange Tree Lane, Redlands, CA 92374

Phone: (909) 786-0702 **Dom State:** CA **Commenced Bus:** March 2011

Data Date	Rating	RACR #1	RACR #2	Total Assets ($mil)	Capital ($mil)	Net Premium ($mil)	Net Income ($mil)
6-20	C+	1.94	1.18	296.4	109.4	741.0	33.8
6-19	C+	1.14	0.69	202.2	70.3	587.0	5.9
2019	C+	1.25	0.76	260.0	75.6	1,162.2	11.2
2018	C+	1.03	0.63	283.8	64.4	1,178.2	9.1
2017	C	0.93	0.57	167.7	55.4	1,089.3	10.4
2016	E+	0.58	0.35	151.4	38.4	1,092.6	11.5
2015	E+	0.43	0.26	124.8	26.8	1,010.4	13.3

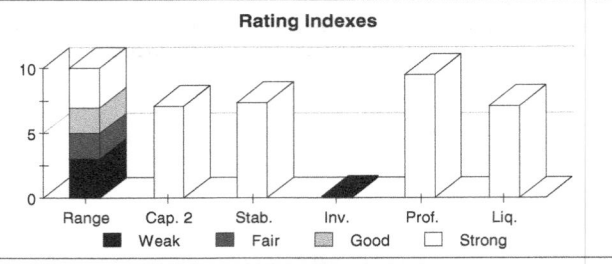

Rating Indexes

Range · Cap. 2 · Stab. · Inv. · Prof. · Liq.
■ Weak ■ Fair ▨ Good ☐ Strong

FRIDAY HEALTH PLANS OF CO INC

E-   **Very Weak**

Major Rating Factors: Weak profitability index (0.9 on a scale of 0 to 10). Weak overall results on stability tests (0.7) based on an inordinate decline in premium revenue in 2019. Weak liquidity (0.3) as a spike in claims may stretch capacity.

Other Rating Factors: Fair capitalization index (3.8) based on fair current risk-adjusted capital (moderate loss scenario). High quality investment portfolio (8.4).

Principal Business: Comp med (92%), Medicaid (6%), Medicare (2%)

Mem Phys: 19: 13,620 **18:** 13,450 **19 MLR** 78.1% **/ 19 Admin Exp** N/A

Enroll(000): Q2 20: 14 **19:** 10 **18:** 12 **Med Exp PMPM:** $429

Principal Investments: Long-term bonds (67%), cash and equiv (26%), real estate (7%)

Provider Compensation ($000): Contr fee ($43,110), FFS ($129)

Total Member Encounters: N/A

Group Affiliation: Friday Health Plans Inc

Licensed in: CO

Address: 700 Main Street Suite 100, Alamosa,

Phone: (719) 589-3696 **Dom State:** CO **Commenced Bus:** N/A

Data Date	Rating	RACR #1	RACR #2	Total Assets ($mil)	Capital ($mil)	Net Premium ($mil)	Net Income ($mil)
6-20	E-	0.75	0.63	34.5	12.1	60.7	-5.2
6-19	N/A	N/A	N/A	N/A	N/A	N/A	N/A
2019	E-	0.28	0.24	32.7	3.2	70.7	-5.5
2018	E	0.93	0.77	19.9	6.8	80.6	2.3
2017	E-	0.18	0.15	22.6	4.0	96.3	-2.1
2016	E-	0.07	0.06	24.3	1.6	92.5	-4.8
2015	C	0.68	0.57	22.2	5.1	49.5	-1.9

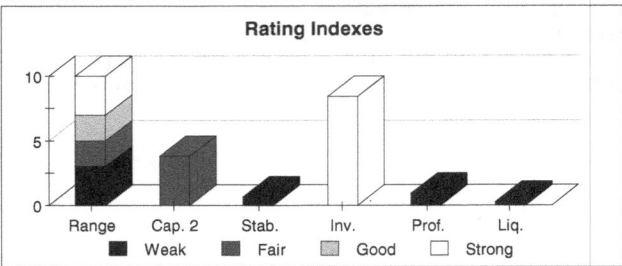

Rating Indexes

Range · Cap. 2 · Stab. · Inv. · Prof. · Liq.
■ Weak ■ Fair ▨ Good ☐ Strong

GATEWAY HEALTH PLAN INC   B-   Good

Major Rating Factors: Fair quality investment portfolio (3.7 on a scale of 0 to 10). Good liquidity (6.9) with sufficient resources (cash flows and marketable investments) to handle a spike in claims. Excellent profitability (7.9).
Other Rating Factors: Strong capitalization index (8.8) based on excellent current risk-adjusted capital (severe loss scenario). Excellent overall results on stability tests (6.9).
Principal Business: Medicaid (67%), Medicare (33%)
Mem Phys: 19: 27,975 **18:** 27,374 **19 MLR** 86.4% **/ 19 Admin Exp** N/A
Enroll(000): Q2 20: 335 **19:** 321 **18:** 336 **Med Exp PMPM:** $520
Principal Investments: Long-term bonds (45%), nonaffiliate common stock (38%), cash and equiv (17%)
Provider Compensation ($000): Contr fee ($1,923,326), capitation ($95,744)
Total Member Encounters: Phys (1,343,993), non-phys (306,492)
Group Affiliation: None
Licensed in: PA
Address: 4 Gateway Center 444 Liberty, Pittsburgh,
Phone: (412) 255-4640 **Dom State:** PA **Commenced Bus:** N/A

Data Date	Rating	RACR #1	RACR #2	Total Assets ($mil)	Capital ($mil)	Net Premium ($mil)	Net Income ($mil)
6-20	B-	2.82	2.35	1,034.9	452.1	1,227.5	51.9
6-19	B-	3.26	2.72	961.4	397.4	1,207.0	32.8
2019	B-	3.30	2.75	746.4	417.3	2,369.6	47.8
2018	B-	3.30	2.75	702.4	403.0	2,357.3	85.1
2017	B-	2.09	1.74	652.6	331.5	2,329.6	75.9
2016	B-	2.34	1.95	754.7	299.6	2,380.6	57.9
2015	B-	1.91	1.59	581.7	236.2	2,168.8	10.9

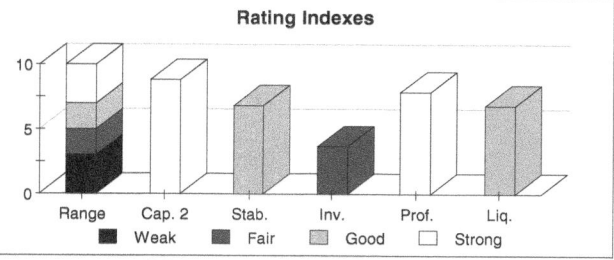

GATEWAY HEALTH PLAN OF OHIO INC   C-   Fair

Major Rating Factors: Weak profitability index (1.2 on a scale of 0 to 10). Low quality investment portfolio (1.2). Strong capitalization (8.3) based on excellent current risk-adjusted capital (severe loss scenario).
Other Rating Factors: Excellent liquidity (7.1) with ample operational cash flow and liquid investments.
Principal Business: Medicare (100%)
Mem Phys: 19: 40,691 **18:** 50,967 **19 MLR** 88.5% **/ 19 Admin Exp** N/A
Enroll(000): Q2 20: N/A **19:** 2 **18:** 10 **Med Exp PMPM:** $1,112
Principal Investments: Cash and equiv (91%), long-term bonds (9%)
Provider Compensation ($000): Contr fee ($36,981), capitation ($513)
Total Member Encounters: Phys (27,578), non-phys (19,760)
Group Affiliation: None
Licensed in: KY, NC, OH
Address: Four Gateway Center 444 Liber, Pittsburgh, PA 15222-1222
Phone: (412) 255-4640 **Dom State:** OH **Commenced Bus:** N/A

Data Date	Rating	RACR #1	RACR #2	Total Assets ($mil)	Capital ($mil)	Net Premium ($mil)	Net Income ($mil)
6-20	C-	2.41	2.01	11.9	11.3	0.0	1.5
6-19	C	1.76	1.46	19.0	11.1	19.1	-3.0
2019	C	4.00	3.33	14.6	10.4	33.0	-3.8
2018	C	2.14	1.78	29.0	14.0	109.2	-1.5
2017	C	N/A	N/A	37.5	16.2	106.5	-4.0
2016	C	2.69	2.24	29.6	12.7	78.5	0.8
2015	C	1.78	1.48	26.0	8.2	59.9	-1.0

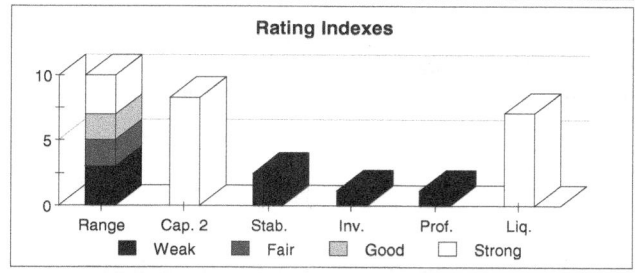

GEISINGER HEALTH PLAN *   B+   Good

Major Rating Factors: Good overall profitability index (6.6 on a scale of 0 to 10). Good liquidity (6.9) with sufficient resources (cash flows and marketable investments) to handle a spike in claims. Strong capitalization index (7.2) based on excellent current risk-adjusted capital (severe loss scenario).
Other Rating Factors: High quality investment portfolio (8.2). Excellent overall results on stability tests (7.4).
Principal Business: Medicaid (41%), Medicare (36%), comp med (22%)
Mem Phys: 19: 52,214 **18:** 47,329 **19 MLR** 88.2% **/ 19 Admin Exp** N/A
Enroll(000): Q2 20: 332 **19:** 332 **18:** 364 **Med Exp PMPM:** $541
Principal Investments: Long-term bonds (41%), cash and equiv (35%), nonaffiliate common stock (21%), real estate (3%)
Provider Compensation ($000): Contr fee ($1,857,103), FFS ($157,386), capitation ($134,303), bonus arrang ($41,899)
Total Member Encounters: Phys (2,560,778), non-phys (532,749)
Group Affiliation: None
Licensed in: NJ, PA
Address: 100 North Academy Avenue, Danville,
Phone: (570) 271-8777 **Dom State:** PA **Commenced Bus:** N/A

Data Date	Rating	RACR #1	RACR #2	Total Assets ($mil)	Capital ($mil)	Net Premium ($mil)	Net Income ($mil)
6-20	B+	1.49	1.24	665.0	292.7	1,284.3	6.7
6-19	B+	1.69	1.41	691.1	338.5	1,250.7	53.7
2019	B+	1.50	1.25	610.5	286.0	2,493.6	35.2
2018	B+	1.40	1.17	635.2	286.4	2,671.9	100.3
2017	B+	1.35	1.12	535.2	251.3	2,375.4	86.5
2016	B	1.33	1.11	545.3	216.5	2,132.4	50.3
2015	B	1.32	1.10	465.4	195.5	1,884.8	16.3

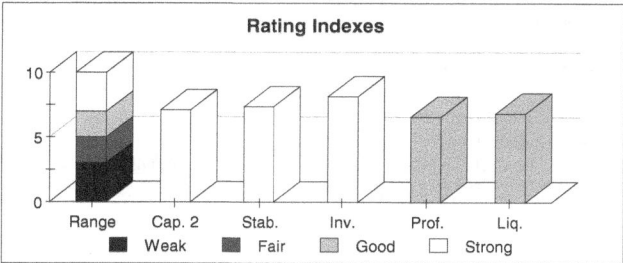

GEISINGER INDEMNITY INS CO | C | Fair

Major Rating Factors: Fair capitalization (4.6 on a scale of 0 to 10) based on fair current risk-adjusted capital (moderate loss scenario). Weak profitability index (0.9). Weak liquidity (0.0) as a spike in claims may stretch capacity.
Other Rating Factors: High quality investment portfolio (9.8).
Principal Business: Medicare (97%), med supp (1%), other (2%)
Mem Phys: 19: 52,377 **18:** 48,255 **19 MLR** 91.6% **/ 19 Admin Exp** N/A
Enroll(000): Q2 20: 30 **19:** 31 **18:** 31 **Med Exp PMPM:** $589
Principal Investments: Long-term bonds (52%), cash and equiv (48%)
Provider Compensation ($000): Contr fee ($201,739), FFS ($9,642), bonus arrang ($2,513), capitation ($2,062)
Total Member Encounters: Phys (325,008), non-phys (67,975)
Group Affiliation: None
Licensed in: PA, WV
Address: 100 North Academy Avenue MC 3, Danville, PA 17822
Phone: (570) 271-8777 **Dom State:** PA **Commenced Bus:** N/A

Data Date	Rating	RACR #1	RACR #2	Total Assets ($mil)	Capital ($mil)	Net Premium ($mil)	Net Income ($mil)
6-20	C	0.86	0.72	91.3	35.9	117.3	-0.8
6-19	B-	1.22	1.02	78.4	32.8	127.8	0.7
2019	B-	1.20	1.00	85.4	38.0	241.0	-12.0
2018	B-	1.23	1.03	78.7	33.6	241.3	-13.2
2017	C-	1.38	1.15	77.1	38.1	205.5	-2.1
2016	C	1.13	0.94	58.3	19.6	138.8	-8.1
2015	C	1.07	0.89	44.8	14.6	128.3	7.7

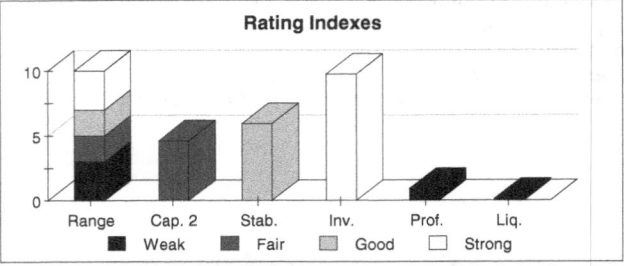

Rating Indexes
Range, Cap. 2, Stab., Inv., Prof., Liq.
Weak ■ Fair ■ Good □ Strong

GEISINGER QUALITY OPTIONS INC | C | Fair

Major Rating Factors: Weak profitability index (1.3 on a scale of 0 to 10). Good capitalization (5.2) based on good current risk-adjusted capital (severe loss scenario). Good liquidity (6.8) with sufficient resources (cash flows and marketable investments) to handle a spike in claims.
Other Rating Factors: High quality investment portfolio (9.5).
Principal Business: Comp med (100%)
Mem Phys: 19: 50,021 **18:** 45,328 **19 MLR** 87.4% **/ 19 Admin Exp** N/A
Enroll(000): Q2 20: 48 **19:** 55 **18:** 43 **Med Exp PMPM:** $451
Principal Investments: Long-term bonds (93%), cash and equiv (7%)
Provider Compensation ($000): Contr fee ($207,544), FFS ($66,907), capitation ($5,041), bonus arrang ($4,053)
Total Member Encounters: Phys (261,444), non-phys (33,514)
Group Affiliation: None
Licensed in: NJ, PA
Address: 100 North Academy Avenue MC 3, Danville, PA 17822
Phone: (570) 271-8777 **Dom State:** PA **Commenced Bus:** N/A

Data Date	Rating	RACR #1	RACR #2	Total Assets ($mil)	Capital ($mil)	Net Premium ($mil)	Net Income ($mil)
6-20	C	0.96	0.80	91.2	34.5	159.8	-7.8
6-19	B-	1.81	1.51	103.1	41.3	162.8	7.8
2019	B-	1.54	1.29	84.0	42.6	318.0	5.1
2018	B-	1.41	1.18	66.2	32.8	264.1	-2.4
2017	C+	1.25	1.04	72.1	37.5	284.4	6.1
2016	C	1.30	1.08	83.7	31.9	265.0	-6.2
2015	C	1.53	1.28	68.6	30.5	231.1	0.4

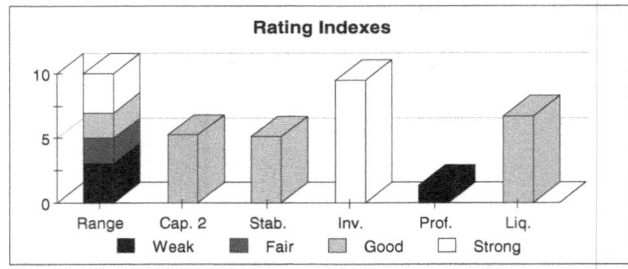

Rating Indexes
Range, Cap. 2, Stab., Inv., Prof., Liq.
Weak ■ Fair ■ Good □ Strong

GENWORTH LIFE INS CO | C | Fair

Major Rating Factors: Fair capitalization (4.6 on a scale of 0 to 10) based on fair risk adjusted capital (moderate loss scenario). Fair quality investment portfolio (3.9) with large holdings of BBB rated bonds in addition to junk bond exposure equal to 87% of capital. Exposure to mortgages is significant, but the mortgage default rate has been low. Fair overall results on stability tests (3.5) including fair risk adjusted capital in prior years.
Other Rating Factors: Good liquidity (6.7). Weak profitability (2.0) with investment income below regulatory standards in relation to interest assumptions of reserves.
Principal Business: Individual health insurance (71%), reinsurance (10%), group health insurance (10%), and individual life insurance (9%).
Principal Investments: NonCMO investment grade bonds (63%), mortgages in good standing (11%), CMOs and structured securities (9%), noninv. grade bonds (5%), and misc. investments (11%).
Investments in Affiliates: 4%
Group Affiliation: Genworth Financial
Licensed in: All states except NY
Commenced Business: October 1956
Address: 2711 CENTERVILLE ROAD STE 400, WILMINGTON, DE 19808
Phone: (800) 255-7836 **Domicile State:** DE **NAIC Code:** 70025

Data Date	Rating	RACR #1	RACR #2	Total Assets ($mil)	Capital ($mil)	Net Premium ($mil)	Net Income ($mil)
6-20	C	0.95	0.66	41,599.5	2,116.7	1,187.1	12.8
6-19	C	0.93	0.64	40,420.0	1,890.1	1,137.2	-103.2
2019	C	0.98	0.70	40,635.1	2,179.8	2,323.1	89.0
2018	C	0.94	0.65	39,995.4	1,871.0	2,287.8	-625.0
2017	C+	1.20	0.86	40,012.0	2,727.7	2,308.7	-39.1
2016	C+	1.17	0.87	40,225.8	3,152.9	2,084.8	-39.1
2015	B-	1.02	0.78	38,504.3	2,740.7	1,587.2	35.2

Risk-Adjusted Capital Ratio #1 (Moderate Loss Scenario)
Range, 2015, 2016, 2017, 2018, 2019, 6-20
Weak ■ Fair ■ Good □

GENWORTH LIFE INS CO OF NEW YORK   C   Fair

Major Rating Factors: Fair overall results on stability tests (3.7 on a scale of 0 to 10) including fair financial strength of affiliated Genworth Financial and negative cash flow from operations for 2019, fair risk adjusted capital in prior years. Fair quality investment portfolio (4.7) with large holdings of BBB rated bonds in addition to moderate junk bond exposure. Fair profitability (3.1).

Other Rating Factors: Good liquidity (5.8). Strong capitalization (7.0) based on excellent risk adjusted capital (severe loss scenario).

Principal Business: Individual health insurance (62%), reinsurance (17%), individual life insurance (17%), group health insurance (3%), and individual annuities (1%).

Principal Investments: NonCMO investment grade bonds (63%), CMOs and structured securities (21%), mortgages in good standing (9%), noninv. grade bonds (2%), and common & preferred stock (1%).

Investments in Affiliates: None

Group Affiliation: Genworth Financial

Licensed in: CT, DC, DE, FL, IL, NJ, NY, RI, VA

Commenced Business: October 1988

Address: 600 THIRD AVENUE SUITE 2400, NEW YORK, NY 10016

Phone: (800) 357-1066 **Domicile State:** NY **NAIC Code:** 72990

Data Date	Rating	RACR #1	RACR #2	Total Assets ($mil)	Capital ($mil)	Net Premium ($mil)	Net Income ($mil)
6-20	C	1.99	1.00	7,779.4	375.0	120.4	67.4
6-19	C	1.41	0.72	7,725.4	269.8	123.1	36.6
2019	C	1.73	0.89	7,604.8	316.6	247.6	82.0
2018	C	1.26	0.64	7,664.4	233.8	251.8	-56.0
2017	C	1.41	0.72	7,985.9	288.4	260.0	-168.1
2016	C	2.20	1.12	8,495.5	481.2	276.9	-20.0
2015	C+	2.22	1.12	8,372.2	494.8	356.1	-39.8

Genworth Financial Composite Group Rating: C Largest Group Members	Assets ($mil)	Rating
GENWORTH LIFE INS CO	40635	C
GENWORTH LIFE ANNUITY INS CO	21575	C-
GENWORTH LIFE INS CO OF NEW YORK	7605	C
GENWORTH MORTGAGE INS CORP	4278	C
JAMESTOWN LIFE INS CO	131	C+

GERBER LIFE INS CO *   B+   Good

Major Rating Factors: Good overall results on stability tests (6.4 on a scale of 0 to 10). Stability strengths include excellent operational trends and excellent risk diversification. Good quality investment portfolio (5.9) despite mixed results such as: large holdings of BBB rated bonds but moderate junk bond exposure. Good liquidity (5.3).

Other Rating Factors: Fair profitability (4.2) with operating losses during the first six months of 2020. Strong capitalization (7.5) based on excellent risk adjusted capital (severe loss scenario).

Principal Business: Individual life insurance (46%), group health insurance (40%), individual health insurance (8%), and reinsurance (5%).

Principal Investments: NonCMO investment grade bonds (68%), CMOs and structured securities (19%), policy loans (5%), noninv. grade bonds (5%), and misc. investments (3%).

Investments in Affiliates: None

Group Affiliation: Nestle SA

Licensed in: All states, the District of Columbia and Puerto Rico

Commenced Business: September 1968

Address: 1311 Mamaroneck Avenue, White Plains, NY 10605

Phone: (914) 272-4000 **Domicile State:** NY **NAIC Code:** 70939

Data Date	Rating	RACR #1	RACR #2	Total Assets ($mil)	Capital ($mil)	Net Premium ($mil)	Net Income ($mil)
6-20	B+	2.36	1.34	4,677.1	505.3	462.2	-11.2
6-19	B+	2.38	1.37	4,250.2	401.0	425.9	0.1
2019	B+	2.47	1.42	4,509.0	512.1	817.9	4.5
2018	B+	1.81	1.05	3,992.2	311.7	745.1	-1.1
2017	B+	1.83	1.07	3,703.2	300.7	727.1	-2.7
2016	B+	1.78	1.06	3,397.6	307.0	690.0	15.3
2015	B+	1.90	1.14	3,088.3	295.8	604.2	18.5

Adverse Trends in Operations
Decrease in capital during 2017 (2%)

GHS HEALTH MAINTENANCE ORGANIZATION   C   Fair

Major Rating Factors: Fair overall results on stability tests (3.9 on a scale of 0 to 10) based on an excessive 395% enrollment growth during the period. Weak profitability index (0.9). Weak liquidity (2.3) as a spike in claims may stretch capacity.

Other Rating Factors: Strong capitalization index (10.0) based on excellent current risk-adjusted capital (severe loss scenario). High quality investment portfolio (9.4).

Principal Business: Medicare (100%)

Mem Phys: 19: 15,769 **18:** 13,575 **19 MLR** 419.9% **/ 19 Admin Exp** N/A

Enroll(000): Q2 20: 32 **19:** 22 **18:** 4 **Med Exp PMPM:** $484

Principal Investments: Long-term bonds (66%), cash and equiv (34%)

Provider Compensation ($000): Contr fee ($82,433), FFS ($23,498), bonus arrang ($579), capitation ($222)

Total Member Encounters: Phys (167,113), non-phys (52,565)

Group Affiliation: Health Care Service Corporation a Mu

Licensed in: OK

Address: 1400 South Boston, Tulsa,

Phone: (312) 653-6000 **Dom State:** OK **Commenced Bus:** N/A

Data Date	Rating	RACR #1	RACR #2	Total Assets ($mil)	Capital ($mil)	Net Premium ($mil)	Net Income ($mil)
6-20	C	6.13	5.11	65.9	30.8	12.1	1.1
6-19	B	8.41	7.01	43.5	26.5	13.9	-0.6
2019	B	9.86	8.21	51.3	28.9	27.8	2.5
2018	B-	8.56	7.13	50.1	27.0	36.7	-23.3
2017	B-	N/A	N/A	70.8	26.2	65.1	-10.5
2016	C+	3.57	2.97	43.5	28.5	38.7	-3.8
2015	B-	4.10	3.42	42.2	29.8	27.6	-15.5

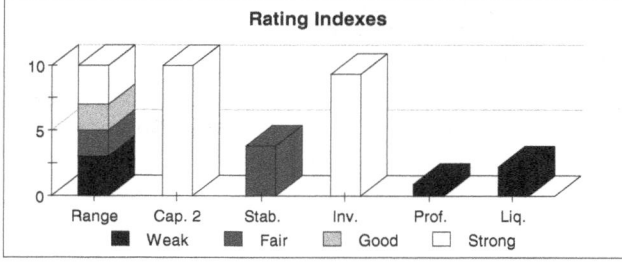

Rating Indexes

Range   Cap. 2   Stab.   Inv.   Prof.   Liq.

■ Weak   ■ Fair   ▨ Good   ☐ Strong

GHS INS CO
E-   Very Weak

Major Rating Factors: Weak profitability index (0.9 on a scale of 0 to 10). Strong capitalization (8.0) based on excellent current risk-adjusted capital (severe loss scenario). High quality investment portfolio (8.3).
Other Rating Factors: Excellent liquidity (7.0) with sufficient resources (cash flows and marketable investments) to handle a spike in claims.
Principal Business: Medicare (100%)
Mem Phys: 19: 36,736 **18:** 27,955 **19 MLR** 100.2% **/ 19 Admin Exp** N/A
Enroll(000): Q2 20: 5 **19:** 4 **18:** 6 **Med Exp PMPM:** $834
Principal Investments: Cash and equiv (52%), long-term bonds (48%)
Provider Compensation ($000): Contr fee ($33,397), capitation ($8,429), FFS ($2,596), bonus arrang ($260)
Total Member Encounters: Phys (34,179), non-phys (13,501)
Group Affiliation: Health Care Service Corporation a Mu
Licensed in: AR, CO, IL, IN, KS, NM, OK, TX
Address: 3817 Northwest Expressway Suit, Oklahoma City, OK 73112
Phone: (312) 653-6000 **Dom State:** OK **Commenced Bus:** N/A

Data Date	Rating	RACR #1	RACR #2	Total Assets ($mil)	Capital ($mil)	Net Premium ($mil)	Net Income ($mil)
6-20	E-	2.16	1.80	35.7	13.9	24.7	-0.2
6-19	E-	3.17	2.64	37.2	13.0	22.2	-1.1
2019	E-	3.46	2.89	38.8	12.5	43.2	-4.6
2018	E-	3.47	2.89	39.5	14.3	53.5	-14.2
2017	E-	N/A	N/A	34.6	13.6	45.4	5.7
2016	E	4.46	3.71	30.9	8.5	27.4	1.7
2015	E	4.59	3.83	24.6	4.4	6.8	-13.6

Rating Indexes

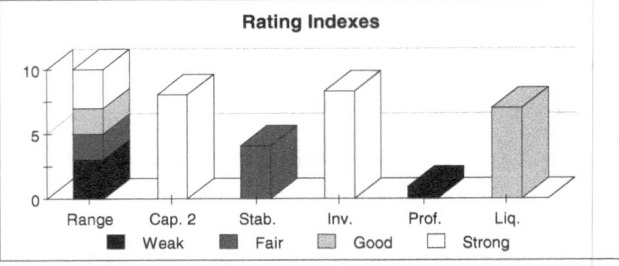

GLOBALHEALTH INC
D   Weak

Major Rating Factors: Weak profitability index (0.8 on a scale of 0 to 10). Weak liquidity (1.0) as a spike in claims may stretch capacity. Fair quality investment portfolio (3.1).
Other Rating Factors: Strong capitalization (7.1) based on excellent current risk-adjusted capital (severe loss scenario).
Principal Business: Medicare (57%), comp med (38%), FEHB (5%)
Mem Phys: 19: 4,291 **18:** 3,998 **19 MLR** 89.4% **/ 19 Admin Exp** N/A
Enroll(000): Q2 20: 22 **19:** 29 **18:** 44 **Med Exp PMPM:** $676
Principal Investments: Affiliate common stock (57%), cash and equiv (13%), long-term bonds (3%), other (27%)
Provider Compensation ($000): Contr fee ($189,408), capitation ($19,794), FFS ($16,746)
Total Member Encounters: Phys (360,291), non-phys (104,075)
Group Affiliation: MHH Healthcare LLC
Licensed in: OK
Address: 210 PARK AVE SUITE 2800, OKLAHOMA CITY, OK 73102
Phone: (405) 280-5656 **Dom State:** OK **Commenced Bus:** N/A

Data Date	Rating	RACR #1	RACR #2	Total Assets ($mil)	Capital ($mil)	Net Premium ($mil)	Net Income ($mil)
6-20	D	1.40	1.17	84.7	38.7	126.3	4.6
6-19	N/A	N/A	N/A	N/A	N/A	N/A	N/A
2019	D	0.40	0.33	60.2	10.5	267.9	-21.6
2018	D	0.49	0.41	58.8	7.0	326.0	0.3
2017	D	0.88	0.73	45.8	19.1	283.9	-6.4
2016	D	1.04	0.87	35.3	18.5	256.4	-1.4
2015	D	1.02	0.85	36.7	20.4	245.4	-5.9

Rating Indexes

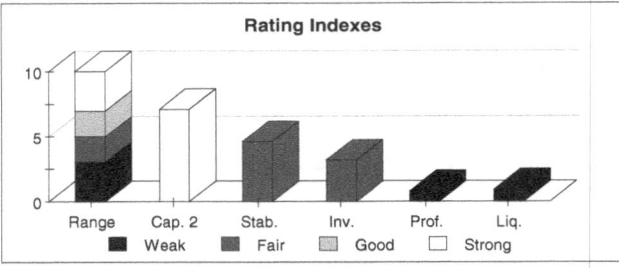

GLOBE LIFE INSURANCE CO OF NY
B   Good

Major Rating Factors: Good overall results on stability tests (5.9 on a scale of 0 to 10). Stability strengths include excellent operational trends and excellent risk diversification. Good quality investment portfolio (5.1) despite mixed results such as: no exposure to mortgages and large holdings of BBB rated bonds but small junk bond holdings. Good liquidity (5.3).
Other Rating Factors: Strong capitalization (7.7) based on excellent risk adjusted capital (severe loss scenario). Excellent profitability (7.5) with operating gains in each of the last five years.
Principal Business: Individual health insurance (58%), individual life insurance (39%), group health insurance (2%), and individual annuities (2%).
Principal Investments: NonCMO investment grade bonds (87%), CMOs and structured securities (4%), policy loans (4%), and noninv. grade bonds (3%).
Investments in Affiliates: None
Group Affiliation: Torchmark Corp
Licensed in: NY
Commenced Business: December 1984
Address: 1020 SEVENTH NORTH ST STE 130, LIVERPOOL, NY 13212
Phone: (315) 451-2544 **Domicile State:** NY **NAIC Code:** 74101

Data Date	Rating	RACR #1	RACR #2	Total Assets ($mil)	Capital ($mil)	Net Premium ($mil)	Net Income ($mil)
6-20	B	2.38	1.47	256.1	43.6	38.2	4.1
6-19	B-	2.26	1.41	246.4	39.7	37.4	10.9
2019	B-	2.38	1.48	250.2	41.8	70.9	13.3
2018	B	1.75	1.08	246.4	29.3	70.2	1.9
2017	B	1.87	1.16	238.8	30.3	68.6	0.2
2016	B+	2.25	1.41	229.1	39.0	76.7	6.2
2015	B+	2.26	1.43	209.7	35.6	72.9	3.0

Adverse Trends in Operations

Decrease in capital during 2018 (3%)
Decrease in premium volume from 2016 to 2017 (11%)
Increase in policy surrenders from 2016 to 2017 (27%)
Decrease in capital during 2017 (22%)

GOLDEN RULE INS CO   B   Good

Major Rating Factors: Good overall results on stability tests (5.3 on a scale of 0 to 10) despite fair financial strength of affiliated UnitedHealth Group Inc. Other stability subfactors include excellent operational trends and excellent risk diversification. Good current capitalization (5.5) based on mixed results -- excessive policy leverage mitigated by excellent risk adjusted capital (severe loss scenario) reflecting improvement over results in 2016. High quality investment portfolio (8.0).

Other Rating Factors: Excellent profitability (8.9) with operating gains in each of the last five years. Excellent liquidity (7.0).
Principal Business: Group health insurance (70%), individual health insurance (29%), and individual life insurance (1%).
Principal Investments: NonCMO investment grade bonds (73%) and CMOs and structured securities (25%).
Investments in Affiliates: None
Group Affiliation: UnitedHealth Group Inc
Licensed in: All states except NY, PR
Commenced Business: June 1961
Address: 7440 WOODLAND DRIVE, INDIANAPOLIS, IN 46278
Phone: (317) 290-8100 **Domicile State:** IN **NAIC Code:** 62286

Data Date	Rating	RACR #1	RACR #2	Total Assets ($mil)	Capital ($mil)	Net Premium ($mil)	Net Income ($mil)
6-20	B	1.74	1.38	716.8	352.3	780.9	125.4
6-19	B	1.95	1.52	638.5	355.3	712.2	114.8
2019	B	1.32	1.04	594.3	259.0	1,470.0	156.6
2018	B	1.44	1.12	522.6	242.0	1,264.0	130.6
2017	B	1.14	0.89	499.2	198.6	1,338.1	82.6
2016	B	0.99	0.78	529.5	170.1	1,354.2	65.2
2015	B	1.37	1.07	635.6	268.0	1,501.3	106.8

UnitedHealth Group Inc
Composite Group Rating: C
Largest Group Members

Largest Group Members	Assets ($mil)	Rating
UNITED HEALTHCARE INS CO	20997	C
SIERRA HEALTH AND LIFE INS CO INC	5301	B
OXFORD HEALTH INS INC	2920	B
UNITED HEALTHCARE OF WISCONSIN INC	2069	B+
UNITED HEALTHCARE INS CO OF NY	1472	B

GOLDEN SECURITY INS CO *   B+   Good

Major Rating Factors: Good liquidity (6.9 on a scale of 0 to 10) with sufficient resources (cash flows and marketable investments) to handle a spike in claims. Excellent profitability (9.2). Strong capitalization (7.2) based on excellent current risk-adjusted capital (severe loss scenario).

Other Rating Factors: High quality investment portfolio (6.9).
Principal Business: Other (100%)
Mem Phys: 19: N/A **18:** N/A   **19 MLR** 75.3% / **19 Admin Exp** N/A
Enroll(000): Q2 20: 210   **19:** 265   **18:** 272   **Med Exp PMPM:** $16
Principal Investments: Long-term bonds (79%), cash and equiv (11%), nonaffiliate common stock (10%)
Provider Compensation ($000): Other ($54,224)
Total Member Encounters: N/A
Group Affiliation: BlueCross BlueShield of Tennessee In
Licensed in: AR, MS, TN
Address: 1 Cameron Hill Circle, Chattanooga, TN 37402-0001
Phone: (423) 535-5600 **Dom State:** TN **Commenced Bus:** N/A

Data Date	Rating	RACR #1	RACR #2	Total Assets ($mil)	Capital ($mil)	Net Premium ($mil)	Net Income ($mil)
6-20	B+	1.54	1.29	69.3	48.1	33.6	3.7
6-19	B	2.48	2.06	61.5	43.0	36.7	4.6
2019	B	2.36	1.97	60.5	45.0	73.1	6.2
2018	B	1.92	1.60	49.2	33.3	67.9	2.0
2017	B	1.25	1.04	43.1	31.9	60.0	3.4
2016	B	2.38	1.98	43.0	28.3	56.6	5.2
2015	B	2.18	1.82	34.2	22.9	51.3	5.6

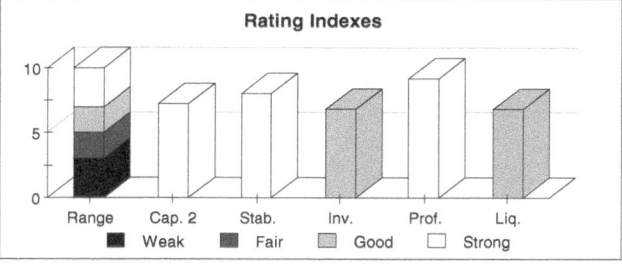

Rating Indexes

GOLDEN STATE MEDICARE HEALTH PLAN   E-   Very Weak

Major Rating Factors: Weak profitability index (0.9 on a scale of 0 to 10). Poor capitalization index (0.0) based on weak current risk-adjusted capital (severe loss scenario). Weak overall results on stability tests (0.4) based on a steep decline in capital during 2019.

Other Rating Factors: Weak liquidity (0.0) as a spike in claims may stretch capacity.
Principal Business: Medicare (100%)
Mem Phys: 19: N/A **18:** N/A   **19 MLR** 103.1% / **19 Admin Exp** N/A
Enroll(000): Q2 20: 8   **19:** 10   **18:** 10   **Med Exp PMPM:** $516
Principal Investments ($000): Cash and equiv ($5,441)
Provider Compensation ($000): None
Total Member Encounters: N/A
Group Affiliation: None
Licensed in: CA
Address: 3030 Old Ranch Pkwy Suite 155, Seal Beach, CA 90740
Phone: (608) 347-4897 **Dom State:** CA **Commenced Bus:** May 2009

Data Date	Rating	RACR #1	RACR #2	Total Assets ($mil)	Capital ($mil)	Net Premium ($mil)	Net Income ($mil)
6-20	E-	0.31	0.19	16.0	2.4	36.2	-6.9
6-19	E+	0.34	0.21	9.8	4.1	30.1	-1.7
2019	E-	0.33	0.20	9.2	2.6	58.6	-8.3
2018	D-	0.60	0.37	24.2	6.8	81.7	-14.5
2017	E+	0.20	0.12	9.8	1.6	68.2	-4.3
2016	D-	0.50	0.31	8.3	3.4	66.0	-0.4
2015	D+	1.55	0.96	7.6	6.4	33.4	-1.0

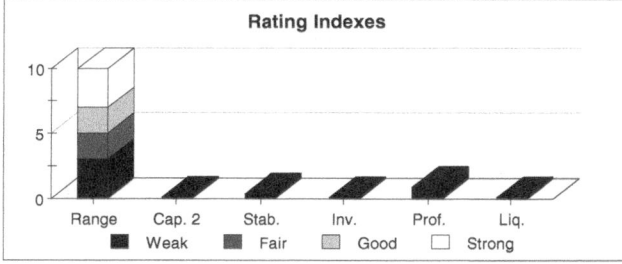

Rating Indexes

GOOD HEALTH HMO INC   B-   Good

Major Rating Factors: Good quality investment portfolio (6.6 on a scale of 0 to 10). Good overall results on stability tests (5.5) despite inconsistent enrollment growth in the past five years due to declines in 2017, 2018 and 2019. Good liquidity (6.9) with sufficient resources (cash flows and marketable investments) to handle a spike in claims.

Other Rating Factors: Strong capitalization index (10.0) based on excellent current risk-adjusted capital (severe loss scenario). Weak profitability index (2.7).

Principal Business: Comp med (100%)

Mem Phys: 19: 5,850 **18:** 5,645 **19 MLR** 84.5% **/ 19 Admin Exp** N/A

Enroll(000): Q2 20: 29 **19:** 35 **18:** 39 **Med Exp PMPM:** $295

Principal Investments: Long-term bonds (89%), cash and equiv (11%)

Provider Compensation ($000): Contr fee ($113,941), FFS ($11,268), capitation ($3,588)

Total Member Encounters: Phys (94,039), non-phys (59,331)

Group Affiliation: None

Licensed in: KS, MO

Address: 2301 Main Street, Kansas City,

Phone: (816) 395-2222 **Dom State:** MO **Commenced Bus:** N/A

Data Date	Rating	RACR #1	RACR #2	Total Assets ($mil)	Capital ($mil)	Net Premium ($mil)	Net Income ($mil)
6-20	B-	4.36	3.63	81.8	59.1	70.8	-3.4
6-19	C	5.90	4.92	81.0	63.6	75.4	4.9
2019	B-	7.00	5.83	78.1	61.5	148.5	3.9
2018	C	5.29	4.41	75.1	58.7	163.5	1.7
2017	C	2.90	2.42	80.8	56.4	187.7	-0.8
2016	C	4.13	3.44	86.7	57.7	189.5	-3.8
2015	C	5.86	4.88	73.9	56.0	138.0	0.5

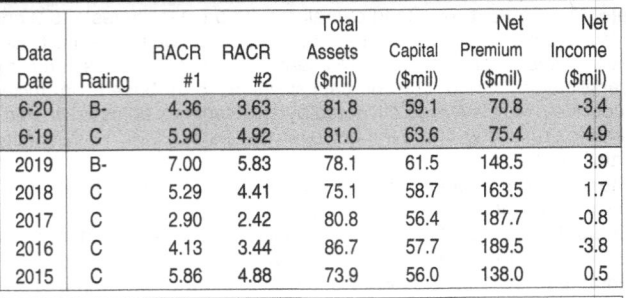

Rating Indexes

GOOD SAMARITAN INS PLAN OF ND   D   Weak

Major Rating Factors: Weak profitability index (0.5 on a scale of 0 to 10). Weak liquidity (2.2) as a spike in claims may stretch capacity. Strong capitalization (7.1) based on excellent current risk-adjusted capital (severe loss scenario).

Other Rating Factors: High quality investment portfolio (9.9).

Principal Business: Medicare (100%)

Mem Phys: 18: 8,906 **17:** N/A **18 MLR** 241.9% **/ 18 Admin Exp** N/A

Enroll(000): Q3 19: 0 **18:** 0 **17:** N/A **Med Exp PMPM:** $1,586

Principal Investments: Cash and equiv (80%), long-term bonds (20%)

Provider Compensation ($000): Capitation ($1,252), contr fee ($515)

Total Member Encounters: Phys (3,468), non-phys (6,909)

Group Affiliation: None

Licensed in: ND

Address: 301 Lorrain Dr, Bismarck, ND 58503-0311

Phone: (804) 396-6412 **Dom State:** ND **Commenced Bus:** N/A

Data Date	Rating	RACR #1	RACR #2	Total Assets ($mil)	Capital ($mil)	Net Premium ($mil)	Net Income ($mil)
9-19	D	1.41	1.18	2.0	1.1	3.3	-0.3
9-18	N/A	N/A	N/A	1.4	1.0	0.9	-0.2
2018	D	1.41	1.18	1.7	1.1	1.2	-0.2
2017	N/A	N/A	N/A	1.1	1.1	N/A	-0.8
2016	N/A	N/A	N/A	N/A	N/A	N/A	N/A
2015	N/A	N/A	N/A	N/A	N/A	N/A	N/A
2014	N/A	N/A	N/A	N/A	N/A	N/A	N/A

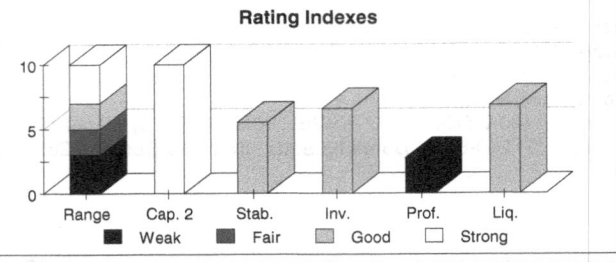

Rating Indexes

GOOD SAMARITAN INS PLAN OF NE   D   Weak

Major Rating Factors: Weak profitability index (0.0 on a scale of 0 to 10). Weak liquidity (1.4) as a spike in claims may stretch capacity. Strong capitalization (6.9) based on excellent current risk-adjusted capital (severe loss scenario).

Other Rating Factors: High quality investment portfolio (9.9).

Principal Business: Medicare (100%)

Mem Phys: 18: 8,959 **17:** N/A **18 MLR** 262.2% **/ 18 Admin Exp** N/A

Enroll(000): Q3 19: 1 **18:** 0 **17:** N/A **Med Exp PMPM:** $1,609

Principal Investments: Cash and equiv (81%), long-term bonds (19%)

Provider Compensation ($000): Capitation ($3,553), contr fee ($2,433)

Total Member Encounters: Phys (6,266), non-phys (22,396)

Group Affiliation: None

Licensed in: NE

Address: 12856 Deauville Drive, Omaha, NE 68137-3204

Phone: (804) 396-6412 **Dom State:** NE **Commenced Bus:** N/A

Data Date	Rating	RACR #1	RACR #2	Total Assets ($mil)	Capital ($mil)	Net Premium ($mil)	Net Income ($mil)
9-19	D	1.30	1.08	4.2	1.0	9.0	-0.7
9-18	N/A	N/A	N/A	2.0	1.1	2.3	-1.0
2018	D	1.43	1.19	2.3	1.1	3.1	-1.2
2017	N/A	N/A	N/A	2.1	2.1	N/A	-0.9
2016	N/A	N/A	N/A	N/A	N/A	N/A	N/A
2015	N/A	N/A	N/A	N/A	N/A	N/A	N/A
2014	N/A	N/A	N/A	N/A	N/A	N/A	N/A

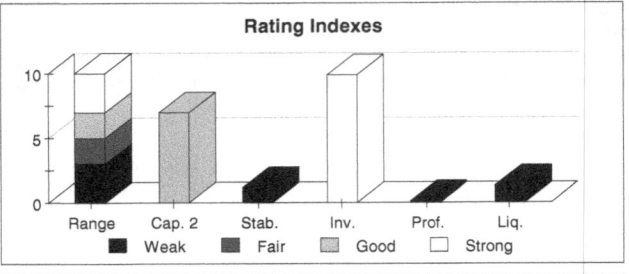

Rating Indexes

GOOD SAMARITAN INS PLAN OF SD — E+ — Very Weak

Major Rating Factors: Weak profitability index (0.2 on a scale of 0 to 10). Weak liquidity (2.2) as a spike in claims may stretch capacity. Fair capitalization (4.1) based on fair current risk-adjusted capital (moderate loss scenario). **Other Rating Factors:** High quality investment portfolio (9.9).
Principal Business: Medicare (100%)
Mem Phys: 18: 8,918 **17:** N/A **18 MLR** 238.9% **/ 18 Admin Exp** N/A
Enroll(000): Q3 19: 0 **18:** 0 **17:** N/A **Med Exp PMPM:** $1,373
Principal Investments: Cash and equiv (89%), long-term bonds (11%)
Provider Compensation ($000): Capitation ($1,748), contr fee ($710)
Total Member Encounters: Phys (2,465), non-phys (11,053)
Group Affiliation: None
Licensed in: SD
Address: 4800 W 57th Street, Sioux Falls, SD 57108
Phone: (804) 396-6412 **Dom State:** SD **Commenced Bus:** N/A

Data Date	Rating	RACR #1	RACR #2	Total Assets ($mil)	Capital ($mil)	Net Premium ($mil)	Net Income ($mil)
9-19	E+	0.79	0.66	2.8	0.6	4.6	-0.5
9-18	N/A	N/A	N/A	1.3	0.5	1.2	-0.4
2018	D+	1.54	1.28	2.2	1.2	1.6	-0.4
2017	N/A	N/A	N/A	0.6	0.6	N/A	-0.8
2016	N/A	N/A	N/A	N/A	N/A	N/A	N/A
2015	N/A	N/A	N/A	N/A	N/A	N/A	N/A
2014	N/A	N/A	N/A	N/A	N/A	N/A	N/A

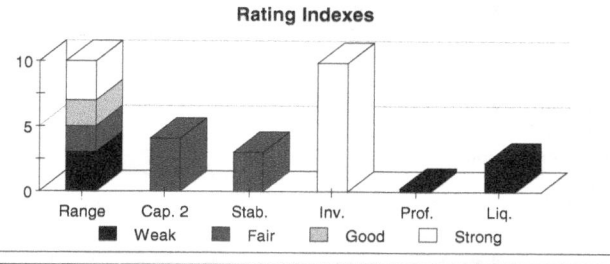

Rating Indexes

GOVERNMENT PERSONNEL MUTUAL L I C — B- — Good

Major Rating Factors: Good quality investment portfolio (5.8 on a scale of 0 to 10) despite significant exposure to mortgages . Mortgage default rate has been low. large holdings of BBB rated bonds in addition to small junk bond holdings. Good liquidity (6.4) with sufficient resources to handle a spike in claims as well as a significant increase in policy surrenders. Fair overall results on stability tests (4.9) including negative cash flow from operations for 2019.
Other Rating Factors: Weak profitability (2.8) with operating losses during the first six months of 2020. Strong capitalization (7.3) based on excellent risk adjusted capital (severe loss scenario).
Principal Business: Individual life insurance (72%) and individual health insurance (27%).
Principal Investments: NonCMO investment grade bonds (59%), mortgages in good standing (15%), policy loans (8%), cash (4%), and misc. investments (10%).
Investments in Affiliates: 3%
Group Affiliation: GPM Life Group
Licensed in: All states except NJ, NY, PR
Commenced Business: October 1934
Address: 2211 NE Loop 410, San Antonio, TX 78217
Phone: (800) 938-9765 **Domicile State:** TX **NAIC Code:** 63967

Data Date	Rating	RACR #1	RACR #2	Total Assets ($mil)	Capital ($mil)	Net Premium ($mil)	Net Income ($mil)
6-20	B-	1.76	1.17	810.2	103.7	30.2	-2.1
6-19	B	2.60	1.66	816.8	110.5	26.5	-0.9
2019	B-	1.86	1.24	812.1	105.5	51.9	-5.9
2018	B	2.68	1.70	820.2	114.8	46.1	-0.9
2017	B+	2.64	1.69	825.7	116.8	44.2	5.3
2016	B+	2.51	1.62	835.1	120.9	44.9	4.0
2015	B+	2.81	1.76	836.1	116.2	46.3	2.6

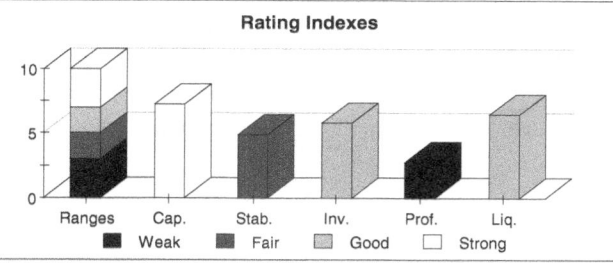

Rating Indexes

GRANITE STATE HEALTH PLAN INC — C — Fair

Major Rating Factors: Weak profitability index (1.4 on a scale of 0 to 10). Good capitalization (5.0) based on good current risk-adjusted capital (severe loss scenario). High quality investment portfolio (9.9).
Other Rating Factors: Excellent liquidity (7.0) with sufficient resources (cash flows and marketable investments) to handle a spike in claims.
Principal Business: Medicaid (100%)
Mem Phys: 19: 10,031 **18:** 4,810 **19 MLR** 89.4% **/ 19 Admin Exp** N/A
Enroll(000): Q2 20: 79 **19:** 77 **18:** 60 **Med Exp PMPM:** $382
Principal Investments: Cash and equiv (100%)
Provider Compensation ($000): Contr fee ($204,643), bonus arrang ($101,096), capitation ($50,549), salary ($9,104)
Total Member Encounters: Phys (451,795), non-phys (1,331,369)
Group Affiliation: None
Licensed in: NH
Address: 2 Executive Park Drive, Bedford, NH 3110
Phone: (314) 725-4477 **Dom State:** NH **Commenced Bus:** N/A

Data Date	Rating	RACR #1	RACR #2	Total Assets ($mil)	Capital ($mil)	Net Premium ($mil)	Net Income ($mil)
6-20	C	0.92	0.77	93.7	31.0	206.3	-11.3
6-19	C	2.02	1.68	72.7	26.0	201.3	-5.9
2019	C	1.62	1.35	79.7	32.1	410.3	-6.6
2018	C-	2.28	1.90	70.6	29.9	289.5	-6.5
2017	D+	N/A	N/A	94.9	24.2	276.1	-16.8
2016	D+	6.52	5.43	82.4	22.7	280.8	-15.7
2015	D+	4.31	3.59	91.1	25.1	325.8	-16.7

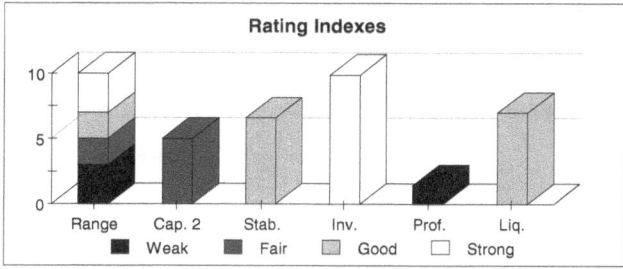

Rating Indexes

GREAT MIDWEST INS CO

B-   **Good**

Major Rating Factors: Fair reserve development (3.8 on a scale of 0 to 10) as reserves have generally been sufficient to cover claims. In 2017, the two year reserve development was 16% deficient. Fair profitability index (3.3) with operating losses during 2016, 2017 and the first six months of 2020. Average return on equity over the last five years has been poor at -4.4%.

Other Rating Factors: Fair overall results on stability tests (3.9) including negative cash flow from operations for 2019. Strong long-term capitalization index (7.9) based on excellent current risk adjusted capital (severe and moderate loss scenarios), despite some fluctuation in capital levels. Excellent liquidity (7.1) with ample operational cash flow and liquid investments.

Principal Business: Group accident & health (76%), other liability (13%), workers compensation (4%), surety (3%), auto liability (1%), inland marine (1%), and auto physical damage (1%).

Principal Investments: Investment grade bonds (88%) and misc. investments (26%).

Investments in Affiliates: 16%

Group Affiliation: Houston International Ins Group Ltd

Licensed in: All states except PR

Commenced Business: November 1985

Address: 800 Gessner Suite 600, Houston, TX 77024

Phone: (713) 935-0226   **Domicile State:** TX   **NAIC Code:** 18694

Data Date	Rating	RACR #1	RACR #2	Loss Ratio %	Total Assets ($mil)	Capital ($mil)	Net Premium ($mil)	Net Income ($mil)
6-20	B-	3.12	2.31	N/A	186.6	117.6	5.8	-14.7
6-19	B-	2.61	1.80	N/A	215.2	129.1	37.8	0.5
2019	B-	2.63	1.84	85.1	208.6	129.4	67.2	0.4
2018	B-	2.72	1.89	74.6	220.5	129.2	67.4	3.5
2017	B	2.62	1.69	75.8	215.3	107.0	73.0	-1.0
2016	B	2.29	1.51	94.5	215.8	104.8	86.2	-20.2
2015	B	2.42	1.50	63.8	211.1	107.6	93.5	6.1

Reserve Deficiency (as % of capital)

2015   2016   2017   2018   2019

* Adequate & redundant reserves show as negatives

■ 1 Yr Dev   □ 2 Yr Dev

GROUP HEALTH COOP OF EAU CLAIRE

E+   **Very Weak**

Major Rating Factors: Fair profitability index (4.5 on a scale of 0 to 10). Good overall results on stability tests (5.3) despite a decline in the number of member physicians during 2020. Good liquidity (6.8) with sufficient resources (cash flows and marketable investments) to handle a spike in claims.

Other Rating Factors: Strong capitalization index (7.9) based on excellent current risk-adjusted capital (severe loss scenario). High quality investment portfolio (7.3).

Principal Business: Medicaid (76%), comp med (24%)

Mem Phys: 19: 9,212   **18:** 10,268   **19 MLR** 82.8%   **/ 19 Admin Exp** N/A

Enroll(000): Q2 20: 57   **19:** 52   **18:** 56   **Med Exp PMPM:** $192

Principal Investments: Long-term bonds (87%), cash and equiv (13%)

Provider Compensation ($000): Contr fee ($91,521), FFS ($33,360), bonus arrang ($1,568), capitation ($594)

Total Member Encounters: Phys (312,182), non-phys (283,456)

Group Affiliation: None

Licensed in: WI

Address: 2503 N Hillcrest Parkway, Altoona,

Phone: (715) 552-4300   **Dom State:** WI   **Commenced Bus:** N/A

Data Date	Rating	RACR #1	RACR #2	Total Assets ($mil)	Capital ($mil)	Net Premium ($mil)	Net Income ($mil)
6-20	E+	2.09	1.74	65.7	30.9	75.2	0.9
6-19	N/A	N/A	N/A	N/A	N/A	N/A	N/A
2019	E+	2.10	1.75	53.3	31.1	148.6	8.4
2018	E+	1.30	1.08	52.0	22.7	163.8	0.4
2017	E+	1.20	1.00	51.2	22.4	176.9	-5.6
2016	E+	1.46	1.22	56.5	28.0	174.1	-2.9
2015	E+	1.81	1.51	58.2	31.0	163.7	6.5

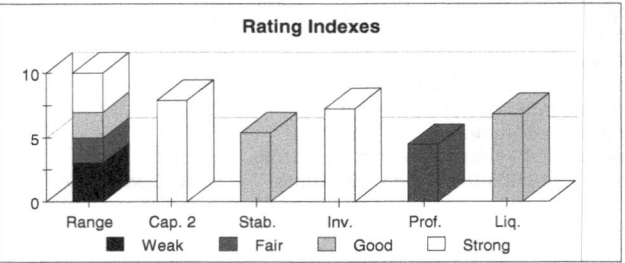

Rating Indexes

Range   Cap. 2   Stab.   Inv.   Prof.   Liq.

■ Weak   ■ Fair   ▨ Good   □ Strong

GROUP HEALTH COOP OF S CENTRAL WI

C   **Fair**

Major Rating Factors: Fair quality investment portfolio (4.0 on a scale of 0 to 10). Fair overall results on stability tests (4.7). Weak profitability index (2.3).

Other Rating Factors: Good capitalization index (6.3) based on good current risk-adjusted capital (severe loss scenario). Good liquidity (6.2) with sufficient resources (cash flows and marketable investments) to handle a spike in claims.

Principal Business: Comp med (88%), FEHB (8%), Medicaid (3%)

Mem Phys: 19: 3,485   **18:** 3,502   **19 MLR** 93.4%   **/ 19 Admin Exp** N/A

Enroll(000): Q2 20: 76   **19:** 79   **18:** 77   **Med Exp PMPM:** $399

Principal Investments: Long-term bonds (40%), real estate (21%), nonaffiliate common stock (20%), cash and equiv (19%)

Provider Compensation ($000): FFS ($155,309), contr fee ($89,507), salary ($75,181), capitation ($59,777)

Total Member Encounters: Phys (352,051), non-phys (201,586)

Group Affiliation: None

Licensed in: WI

Address: 1265 JOHN Q HAMMONS DRIVE, MADISON,

Phone: (608) 251-4156   **Dom State:** WI   **Commenced Bus:** N/A

Data Date	Rating	RACR #1	RACR #2	Total Assets ($mil)	Capital ($mil)	Net Premium ($mil)	Net Income ($mil)
6-20	C	1.13	0.94	89.5	40.1	204.7	2.9
6-19	N/A	N/A	N/A	N/A	N/A	N/A	N/A
2019	C	1.13	0.95	94.8	40.1	408.1	-7.7
2018	C	1.37	1.14	95.0	45.1	395.7	2.6
2017	D+	1.64	1.36	88.1	46.0	363.1	5.5
2016	D	1.25	1.04	86.0	39.6	364.9	0.9
2015	D	1.17	0.97	84.3	39.2	383.6	0.2

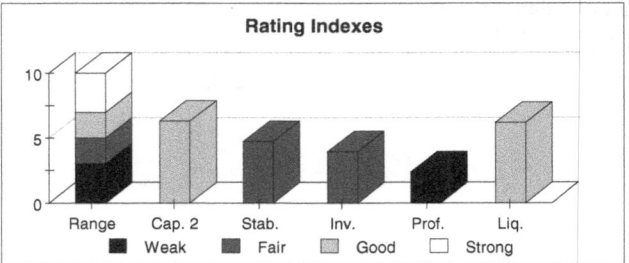

Rating Indexes

Range   Cap. 2   Stab.   Inv.   Prof.   Liq.

■ Weak   ■ Fair   ▨ Good   □ Strong

GROUP HEALTH INCORPORATED D+ Weak

Major Rating Factors: Fair profitability index (4.1 on a scale of 0 to 10). Strong capitalization (7.6) based on excellent current risk-adjusted capital (severe loss scenario). High quality investment portfolio (7.6).
Other Rating Factors: Excellent liquidity (7.0) with sufficient resources (cash flows and marketable investments) to handle a spike in claims.
Principal Business: Comp med (39%), dental (24%), FEHB (15%), other (22%)
Mem Phys: 19: 108,335 **18:** 104,191 **19 MLR** 81.0% **/ 19 Admin Exp** N/A
Enroll(000): Q2 20: 1,755 **19:** 1,771 **18:** 1,724 **Med Exp PMPM:** $29
Principal Investments: Long-term bonds (80%), cash and equiv (20%)
Provider Compensation ($000): FFS ($330,999), contr fee ($190,174), other ($93,539)
Total Member Encounters: N/A
Group Affiliation: EmblemHealth Inc
Licensed in: NY
Address: 55 Water Street, New York, NY 10041-8190
Phone: (646) 447-5000 **Dom State:** NY **Commenced Bus:** N/A

Data Date	Rating	RACR #1	RACR #2	Total Assets ($mil)	Capital ($mil)	Net Premium ($mil)	Net Income ($mil)
6-20	D+	1.86	1.55	648.0	243.6	377.7	6.0
6-19	D+	4.57	3.81	709.6	344.6	382.4	-15.5
2019	D+	3.71	3.09	661.6	328.6	773.9	29.9
2018	D+	4.15	3.45	706.5	365.1	808.1	-17.8
2017	E	4.15	3.46	723.1	336.1	774.1	34.1
2016	E	3.65	3.04	672.2	260.8	908.8	260.3
2015	E	2.86	2.39	602.4	213.8	912.7	30.2

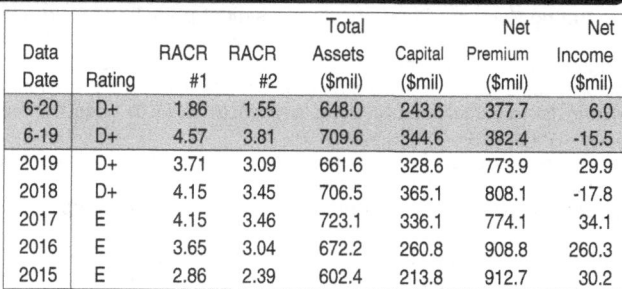

Rating Indexes

GROUP HEALTH PLAN INC E+ Very Weak

Major Rating Factors: Weak profitability index (0.9 on a scale of 0 to 10). Low quality investment portfolio (0.9). Good overall results on stability tests (5.3).
Other Rating Factors: Good liquidity (5.4) with sufficient resources (cash flows and marketable investments) to handle a spike in claims. Strong capitalization index (8.4) based on excellent current risk-adjusted capital (severe loss scenario).
Principal Business: Comp med (89%), FEHB (4%), dental (4%), Medicare (3%)
Mem Phys: 19: 85,336 **18:** 74,128 **19 MLR** 107.2% **/ 19 Admin Exp** N/A
Enroll(000): Q2 20: 62 **19:** 64 **18:** 122 **Med Exp PMPM:** $1,578
Principal Investments: Nonaffiliate common stock (38%), long-term bonds (36%), real estate (35%), affiliate common stock (2%), other (1%)
Provider Compensation ($000): Bonus arrang ($290,891), contr fee ($20,750)
Total Member Encounters: Phys (536,520), non-phys (73,899)
Group Affiliation: HealthPartners Inc
Licensed in: MN
Address: 8170 33RD AVENUE SOUTH POBOX 1, MINNEAPOLIS,
Phone: (952) 883-6000 **Dom State:** MN **Commenced Bus:** N/A

Data Date	Rating	RACR #1	RACR #2	Total Assets ($mil)	Capital ($mil)	Net Premium ($mil)	Net Income ($mil)
6-20	E+	2.50	2.09	938.7	216.1	490.1	-50.0
6-19	D	0.55	0.46	805.1	37.7	573.8	-64.7
2019	D	2.66	2.22	752.5	166.5	1,182.7	-105.4
2018	B	1.44	1.20	837.8	105.9	1,554.9	-21.5
2017	A-	1.74	1.45	831.3	163.7	1,424.9	27.2
2016	A-	2.84	2.37	822.2	168.2	1,262.9	-13.9
2015	A+	4.68	3.90	882.2	206.8	1,130.3	12.1

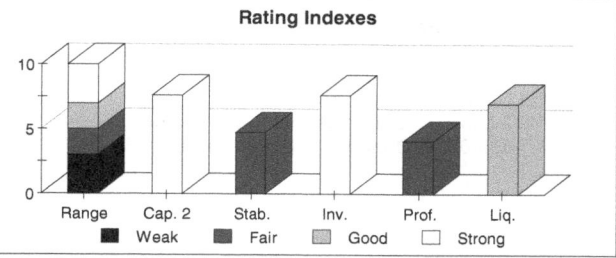

Rating Indexes

GROUP HOSP & MEDICAL SERVICES INC * B+ Good

Major Rating Factors: Good overall profitability index (6.9 on a scale of 0 to 10). Good quality investment portfolio (5.5). Strong capitalization (10.0) based on excellent current risk-adjusted capital (severe loss scenario).
Other Rating Factors: Excellent liquidity (7.1) with ample operational cash flow and liquid investments.
Principal Business: FEHB (66%), comp med (29%), dental (2%)
Mem Phys: 19: 54,068 **18:** 52,141 **19 MLR** 89.5% **/ 19 Admin Exp** N/A
Enroll(000): Q2 20: 586 **19:** 587 **18:** 565 **Med Exp PMPM:** $444
Principal Investments: Long-term bonds (33%), cash and equiv (18%), nonaffiliate common stock (11%), other (37%)
Provider Compensation ($000): Contr fee ($3,008,836), FFS ($96,087), capitation ($7,011)
Total Member Encounters: Phys (4,562,143), non-phys (2,914,052)
Group Affiliation: CareFirst Inc
Licensed in: DC, MD, VA
Address: 840 FIRST STREET NE, WASHINGTON, DC 20065
Phone: (410) 581-3000 **Dom State:** DC **Commenced Bus:** N/A

Data Date	Rating	RACR #1	RACR #2	Total Assets ($mil)	Capital ($mil)	Net Premium ($mil)	Net Income ($mil)
6-20	B+	6.66	5.55	3,122.9	1,534.6	1,675.8	82.4
6-19	B	5.79	4.83	2,875.9	1,311.8	1,722.9	59.2
2019	B+	6.25	5.21	3,047.8	1,440.1	3,507.7	98.8
2018	B	5.30	4.42	2,761.6	1,200.1	3,463.1	100.2
2017	B	5.84	4.86	2,550.3	1,161.2	3,352.0	34.5
2016	B-	4.89	4.07	2,284.1	963.2	3,502.0	-9.5
2015	B-	5.06	4.22	2,292.7	960.2	3,465.3	35.0

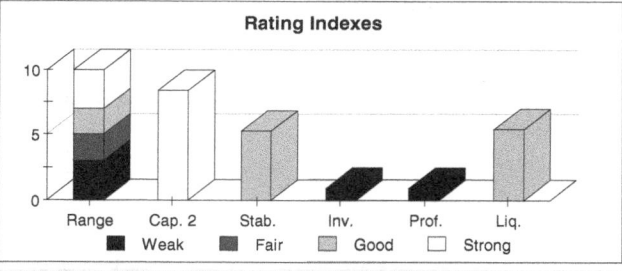

Rating Indexes

GUARANTEE TRUST LIFE INS CO | B | Good

Major Rating Factors: Good quality investment portfolio (6.5 on a scale of 0 to 10) despite mixed results such as: minimal exposure to mortgages and large holdings of BBB rated bonds but small junk bond holdings. Good overall results on stability tests (5.6). Stability strengths include excellent operational trends and excellent risk diversification. Strong capitalization (7.8) based on excellent risk adjusted capital (severe loss scenario).

Other Rating Factors: Excellent profitability (7.4) with operating gains in each of the last five years. Excellent liquidity (7.0).

Principal Business: Individual health insurance (77%), group health insurance (16%), individual life insurance (6%), and reinsurance (1%).

Principal Investments: NonCMO investment grade bonds (49%), CMOs and structured securities (34%), mortgages in good standing (10%), noninv. grade bonds (2%), and common & preferred stock (1%).

Investments in Affiliates: 1%
Group Affiliation: Guarantee Trust
Licensed in: All states except NY
Commenced Business: June 1936
Address: 1275 Milwaukee Avenue, Glenview, IL 60025
Phone: (847) 699-0600 **Domicile State:** IL **NAIC Code:** 64211

Data Date	Rating	RACR #1	RACR #2	Total Assets ($mil)	Capital ($mil)	Net Premium ($mil)	Net Income ($mil)
6-20	B	2.38	1.52	705.2	115.5	110.2	9.2
6-19	B	2.19	1.41	652.2	101.2	108.9	8.8
2019	B	2.22	1.45	679.9	106.3	232.4	16.0
2018	B	2.01	1.32	638.9	92.3	229.6	20.3
2017	B	1.84	1.21	594.8	79.2	218.7	12.4
2016	B	1.85	1.23	550.7	77.0	219.2	9.1
2015	B	1.75	1.18	495.8	70.0	221.4	8.7

Adverse Trends in Operations

Increase in policy surrenders from 2016 to 2017 (32%)
Increase in policy surrenders from 2015 to 2016 (46%)

GUARANTY ASSURANCE CO | E+ | Very Weak

Major Rating Factors: Weak profitability index (0.4 on a scale of 0 to 10). Weak liquidity (0.3) as a spike in claims may stretch capacity. Strong capitalization (7.2) based on excellent current risk-adjusted capital (severe loss scenario).

Other Rating Factors: High quality investment portfolio (8.0).

Principal Business: Dental (100%)
Mem Phys: 18: N/A **17:** N/A **18 MLR** 198.7% **/ 18 Admin Exp** N/A
Enroll(000): Q3 19: 33 **18:** 38 **17:** 39 **Med Exp PMPM:** $32
Principal Investments: Cash and equiv (37%), real estate (35%), long-term bonds (28%)
Provider Compensation ($000): FFS ($9,172), contr fee ($5,607), capitation ($214)
Total Member Encounters: N/A
Group Affiliation: Dental Economics Holdings Inc
Licensed in: LA
Address: 11969 Bricksome Ave Ste A, Baton Rouge, LA 70816
Phone: (281) 313-7150 **Dom State:** LA **Commenced Bus:** N/A

Data Date	Rating	RACR #1	RACR #2	Total Assets ($mil)	Capital ($mil)	Net Premium ($mil)	Net Income ($mil)
9-19	E+	1.47	1.23	2.7	1.5	11.3	0.3
9-18	U	N/A	N/A	0.8	0.4	5.8	-0.3
2018	U	0.12	0.10	0.8	0.1	7.8	-0.6
2017	U	N/A	N/A	1.2	0.6	4.1	-0.8
2016	D+	2.87	2.39	1.8	1.2	3.1	0.1
2015	D+	17.09	14.24	1.4	1.1	0.6	-0.3
2014	N/A	N/A	N/A	1.7	1.4	3.0	N/A

Rating Indexes

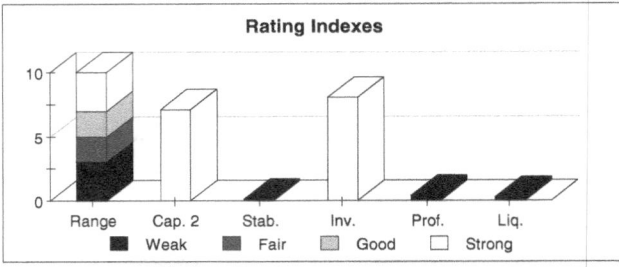

Range | Cap. 2 | Stab. | Inv. | Prof. | Liq.
■ Weak ■ Fair □ Good □ Strong

GUARDIAN LIFE INS CO OF AMERICA * | A | Excellent

Major Rating Factors: Good quality investment portfolio (6.6 on a scale of 0 to 10) despite mixed results such as: large holdings of BBB rated bonds but moderate junk bond exposure. Good liquidity (5.9) with sufficient resources to handle a spike in claims as well as a significant increase in policy surrenders. Strong capitalization (8.2) based on excellent risk adjusted capital (severe loss scenario).

Other Rating Factors: Excellent profitability (7.1) with operating gains in each of the last five years. Excellent overall results on stability tests (7.5) excellent operational trends and excellent risk diversification.

Principal Business: Individual life insurance (49%), group health insurance (36%), group life insurance (7%), reinsurance (6%), and individual health insurance (2%).

Principal Investments: NonCMO investment grade bonds (65%), mortgages in good standing (9%), policy loans (7%), CMOs and structured securities (7%), and misc. investments (13%).

Investments in Affiliates: 4%
Group Affiliation: Guardian Group
Licensed in: All states except PR
Commenced Business: July 1860
Address: 7 HANOVER SQUARE, NEW YORK, NY 10001
Phone: (212) 598-8000 **Domicile State:** NY **NAIC Code:** 64246

Data Date	Rating	RACR #1	RACR #2	Total Assets ($mil)	Capital ($mil)	Net Premium ($mil)	Net Income ($mil)
6-20	A	2.82	1.81	65,189.0	8,085.2	4,604.9	51.8
6-19	A	2.77	1.78	60,569.9	7,401.7	4,413.8	152.5
2019	A	2.83	1.84	62,204.0	7,615.6	8,742.0	548.5
2018	A	2.77	1.80	58,488.7	7,171.8	8,387.5	310.4
2017	A	2.84	1.83	55,568.8	6,683.7	8,116.1	423.1
2016	A	2.77	1.79	51,883.7	6,172.5	7,772.7	367.7
2015	A	2.55	1.66	48,120.9	6,089.7	7,337.7	433.1

Rating Indexes

Ranges | Cap. | Stab. | Inv. | Prof. | Liq.
■ Weak ■ Fair □ Good □ Strong

HALLMARK LIFE INSURANCE CO   D   Weak

Major Rating Factors: Weak profitability index (0.9 on a scale of 0 to 10). Low quality investment portfolio (2.7). Strong capitalization (8.9) based on excellent current risk-adjusted capital (severe loss scenario).
Other Rating Factors: Excellent liquidity (7.4) with ample operational cash flow and liquid investments.
Principal Business: Medicare (65%), comp med (35%)
Mem Phys: 18: N/A **17:** N/A **18 MLR** 91.6% **/ 18 Admin Exp** N/A
Enroll(000): Q3 19: 50 **18:** 172 **17:** N/A **Med Exp PMPM:** $576
Principal Investments: Cash and equiv (100%)
Provider Compensation ($000): Contr fee ($405,716), salary ($4,127), capitation ($143)
Total Member Encounters: Phys (939,436), non-phys (170,501)
Group Affiliation: None
Licensed in: AZ, NY
Address: 2394 East Camelback Road, Phoenix, AZ 85016
Phone: (Phone number   **Dom State:** AZ   **Commenced Bus:** N/A

Data Date	Rating	RACR #1	RACR #2	Total Assets ($mil)	Capital ($mil)	Net Premium ($mil)	Net Income ($mil)
9-19	D	2.86	2.38	317.1	168.9	498.0	43.2
9-18	N/A	N/A	N/A	N/A	N/A	N/A	N/A
2018	D	1.71	1.43	494.5	103.2	658.4	-51.9
2017	N/A	N/A	N/A	4.3	4.2	N/A	N/A
2016	N/A	N/A	N/A	17.9	11.9	14.1	N/A
2015	N/A	N/A	N/A	19.7	11.3	14.5	N/A
2014	N/A	N/A	N/A	23.7	16.2	9.4	N/A

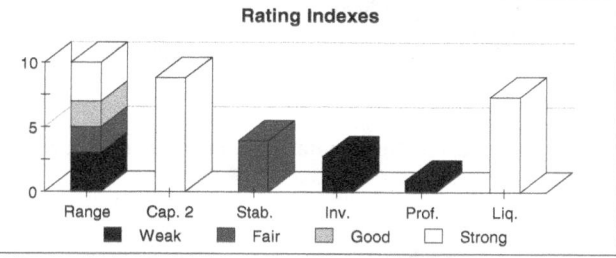

Rating Indexes

HAP EMPOWERED HEALTH PLAN INC   D+   Weak

Major Rating Factors: Weak profitability index (1.1 on a scale of 0 to 10). Low quality investment portfolio (1.5). Fair overall results on stability tests (4.5).
Other Rating Factors: Strong capitalization index (7.7) based on excellent current risk-adjusted capital (severe loss scenario). Excellent liquidity (7.0) with ample operational cash flow and liquid investments.
Principal Business: Medicare (71%), Medicaid (29%)
Mem Phys: 19: 7,362 **18:** N/A **19 MLR** 80.4% **/ 19 Admin Exp** N/A
Enroll(000): Q2 20: 62 **19:** 18 **18:** 16 **Med Exp PMPM:** $573
Principal Investments: Cash and equiv (100%)
Provider Compensation ($000): Contr fee ($95,427), FFS ($9,947), capitation ($7,199)
Total Member Encounters: N/A
Group Affiliation: None
Licensed in: MI
Address: 2850 West Grand Blvd, Detroit,
Phone: (888) 654-2200   **Dom State:** MI   **Commenced Bus:** N/A

Data Date	Rating	RACR #1	RACR #2	Total Assets ($mil)	Capital ($mil)	Net Premium ($mil)	Net Income ($mil)
6-20	D+	1.89	1.58	70.0	22.8	77.1	-5.8
6-19	C-	2.69	2.24	48.3	21.6	56.0	0.6
2019	C-	3.04	2.53	73.9	28.6	142.0	2.1
2018	C-	2.59	2.16	68.5	25.8	142.5	-5.4
2017	C-	2.53	2.11	54.8	26.5	115.4	1.8
2016	C	2.73	2.28	85.4	24.3	122.4	23.0
2015	B	1.91	1.59	180.6	57.4	501.9	27.5

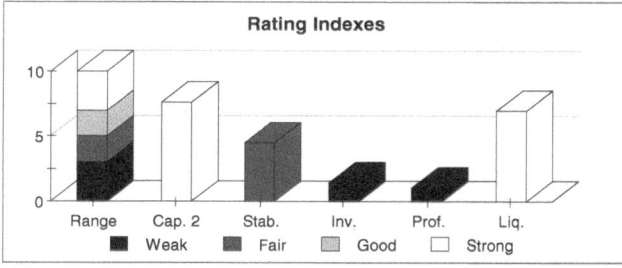

Rating Indexes

HARKEN HEALTH INS CO   C+   Fair

Major Rating Factors: Weak profitability index (0.0 on a scale of 0 to 10). Strong capitalization (10.0) based on excellent current risk-adjusted capital (severe loss scenario). High quality investment portfolio (9.9).
Other Rating Factors: Excellent liquidity (7.2) with ample operational cash flow and liquid investments.
Principal Business: Medicare (102%)
Mem Phys: 19: 103,693 **18:** 83,436 **19 MLR** 88.8% **/ 19 Admin Exp** N/A
Enroll(000): Q2 20: 28 **19:** 6 **18:** N/A **Med Exp PMPM:** $794
Principal Investments: Cash and equiv (93%), long-term bonds (7%)
Provider Compensation ($000): Contr fee ($35,855), FFS ($9,424), bonus arrang ($57), capitation ($30)
Total Member Encounters: Phys (127,388), non-phys (48,583)
Group Affiliation: None
Licensed in: FL, GA, IL, IN, IA, MI, NE, OH, SD, TX, WI
Address: 2700 MIDWEST DRIVE, ONALASKA, WI 54650-8764
Phone: (800) 797-9921   **Dom State:** WI   **Commenced Bus:** N/A

Data Date	Rating	RACR #1	RACR #2	Total Assets ($mil)	Capital ($mil)	Net Premium ($mil)	Net Income ($mil)
6-20	C+	10.41	8.68	111.8	81.7	151.6	11.5
6-19	U	348.70	290.60	32.5	23.5	25.9	-0.1
2019	C+	3.58	2.98	31.7	15.8	58.1	-5.0
2018	U	353.00	294.20	25.2	23.8	-0.1	0.6
2017	C-	12.89	10.74	46.1	42.1	16.7	0.3
2016	C	2.01	1.68	112.5	40.7	147.2	-63.7
2015	N/A	N/A	N/A	58.1	10.3	N/A	N/A

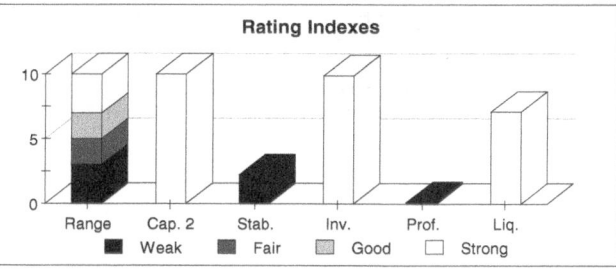

Rating Indexes

HARMONY HEALTH PLAN INC   C-   Fair

Major Rating Factors: Weak overall results on stability tests (2.1 on a scale of 0 to 10) based on a steep decline in premium revenue in 2019, a steep decline in capital during 2019 and a significant 74% decrease in enrollment during the period. Good overall profitability index (5.5). Strong capitalization index (8.7) based on excellent current risk-adjusted capital (severe loss scenario).
Other Rating Factors: High quality investment portfolio (9.5). Excellent liquidity (7.0) with sufficient resources (cash flows and marketable investments) to handle a spike in claims.
Principal Business: Medicare (100%)
Mem Phys: 19: 74,300 **18:** 70,800 **19 MLR** 71.2% **/ 19 Admin Exp** N/A
Enroll(000): Q2 20: 78 **19:** 80 **18:** 309 **Med Exp PMPM:** $734
Principal Investments: Long-term bonds (77%), cash and equiv (23%)
Provider Compensation ($000): Contr fee ($758,669), capitation ($56,824), bonus arrang ($33,814)
Total Member Encounters: Phys (973,757), non-phys (463,787)
Group Affiliation: None
Licensed in: AL, AR, IL, IN, MS, MO, MT, OK, SC, TN, VA
Address: 29 North Wacker Drive Suite 30, Chicago,
Phone: (813) 206-6200 **Dom State:** IL **Commenced Bus:** N/A

Data Date	Rating	RACR #1	RACR #2	Total Assets ($mil)	Capital ($mil)	Net Premium ($mil)	Net Income ($mil)
6-20	C-	2.68	2.23	422.6	148.2	509.0	26.5
6-19	C	1.90	1.58	448.4	147.7	512.2	82.2
2019	C	3.33	2.78	361.2	127.0	1,007.0	119.9
2018	C	2.52	2.10	595.2	203.2	1,654.1	88.8
2017	C	1.56	1.30	468.6	133.8	1,209.6	-57.2
2016	C	3.07	2.56	384.3	151.7	1,069.7	16.6
2015	C	3.78	3.15	334.1	180.9	968.2	30.4

Rating Indexes

HARTFORD LIFE & ACCIDENT INS CO   B-   Good

Major Rating Factors: Good overall profitability (5.3 on a scale of 0 to 10). Return on equity has been low, averaging 2.8%. Good liquidity (6.9) with sufficient resources to handle a spike in claims as well as a significant increase in policy surrenders. Fair overall results on stability tests (4.9).
Other Rating Factors: Strong capitalization (9.5) based on excellent risk adjusted capital (severe loss scenario). High quality investment portfolio (7.0).
Principal Business: Group health insurance (43%), reinsurance (29%), and group life insurance (28%).
Principal Investments: NonCMO investment grade bonds (61%), CMOs and structured securities (21%), mortgages in good standing (11%), noninv. grade bonds (2%), and common & preferred stock (1%).
Investments in Affiliates: None
Group Affiliation: Hartford Financial Services Inc
Licensed in: All states, the District of Columbia and Puerto Rico
Commenced Business: February 1967
Address: One Hartford Plaza, Hartford, CT 06155-0001
Phone: (860) 547-5000 **Domicile State:** CT **NAIC Code:** 70815

Data Date	Rating	RACR #1	RACR #2	Total Assets ($mil)	Capital ($mil)	Net Premium ($mil)	Net Income ($mil)
6-20	B-	4.23	2.67	12,748.7	2,686.8	2,076.1	250.5
6-19	C	3.95	2.54	12,911.3	2,532.7	2,018.6	261.5
2019	B-	4.24	2.69	12,877.7	2,643.9	4,083.1	514.7
2018	C	3.70	2.40	12,909.5	2,407.4	4,130.8	398.1
2017	C	3.42	2.19	12,935.8	2,028.5	5,777.5	-1,065.7
2016	B-	4.15	2.61	8,785.9	1,623.8	2,241.9	208.3
2015	C	3.96	2.47	8,992.2	1,651.4	2,296.5	168.1

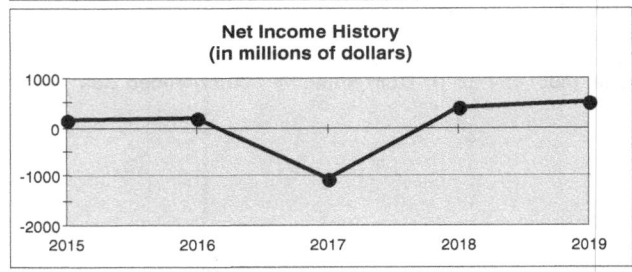

Net Income History
(in millions of dollars)

HARVARD PILGRIM HC OF NEW ENGLAND   B   Good

Major Rating Factors: Good overall results on stability tests (6.6 on a scale of 0 to 10). Good liquidity (6.8) with sufficient resources (cash flows and marketable investments) to handle a spike in claims. Fair profitability index (4.2).
Other Rating Factors: Strong capitalization index (7.8) based on excellent current risk-adjusted capital (severe loss scenario). High quality investment portfolio (7.8).
Principal Business: Comp med (86%), Medicare (14%)
Mem Phys: 19: 88,907 **18:** 83,960 **19 MLR** 82.7% **/ 19 Admin Exp** N/A
Enroll(000): Q2 20: 77 **19:** 72 **18:** 77 **Med Exp PMPM:** $493
Principal Investments: Long-term bonds (91%), cash and equiv (9%)
Provider Compensation ($000): Capitation ($169,084), contr fee ($159,270), bonus arrang ($90,280), FFS ($19,076), other ($1,398)
Total Member Encounters: Phys (293,421), non-phys (273,202)
Group Affiliation: Health Plan Holdings Inc
Licensed in: MA, NH
Address: 93 WORCESTER STREET, WELLESLEY,
Phone: (781) 263-6000 **Dom State:** MA **Commenced Bus:** N/A

Data Date	Rating	RACR #1	RACR #2	Total Assets ($mil)	Capital ($mil)	Net Premium ($mil)	Net Income ($mil)
6-20	B	2.02	1.68	171.2	69.0	263.8	3.3
6-19	B-	2.94	2.45	155.7	71.3	253.9	17.6
2019	B-	2.94	2.45	147.9	69.0	508.5	11.1
2018	C	2.38	1.98	154.5	58.9	552.2	2.5
2017	C	1.57	1.31	142.0	56.0	563.0	-2.9
2016	C	2.59	2.15	151.3	60.1	482.2	-7.7
2015	B	2.94	2.45	127.9	68.0	374.6	18.4

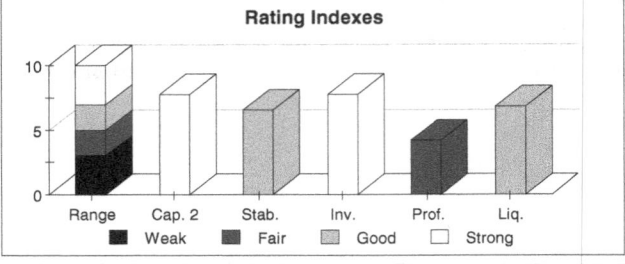

Rating Indexes

HAWAII MANAGEMENT ALLIANCE ASSOC   C   Fair

Major Rating Factors: Weak liquidity (2.7 on a scale of 0 to 10) as a spike in claims may stretch capacity. Good capitalization (6.8) based on excellent current risk-adjusted capital (severe loss scenario). Excellent profitability (8.0).
Other Rating Factors: High quality investment portfolio (9.2).
Principal Business: Comp med (81%), dental (3%), other (16%)
Mem Phys: 19: 7,354 **18:** N/A **19 MLR** 105.6% **/ 19 Admin Exp** N/A
Enroll(000): Q2 20: 34 **19:** 41 **18:** 43 **Med Exp PMPM:** $358
Principal Investments: Cash and equiv (62%), long-term bonds (33%), nonaffiliate common stock (5%)
Provider Compensation ($000): Contr fee ($174,119), FFS ($3,553), bonus arrang ($722)
Total Member Encounters: Phys (3,345), non-phys (4,316)
Group Affiliation: None
Licensed in: HI
Address: 500 Ala Moana Boulevard Suite, Honolulu, HI 96813-4018
Phone: (808) 791-7550 **Dom State:** HI **Commenced Bus:** N/A

Data Date	Rating	RACR #1	RACR #2	Total Assets ($mil)	Capital ($mil)	Net Premium ($mil)	Net Income ($mil)
6-20	C	1.21	1.01	56.1	27.6	84.1	7.1
6-19	N/A	N/A	N/A	N/A	N/A	N/A	N/A
2019	C	0.87	0.72	47.4	20.6	169.3	0.8
2018	C	0.86	0.72	45.8	19.5	161.1	0.7
2017	C	0.87	0.73	42.7	18.7	150.3	3.8
2016	C-	0.84	0.70	36.2	15.1	131.3	1.0
2015	C-	0.79	0.66	38.2	13.7	127.0	0.2

Rating Indexes

Range Cap. 2 Stab. Inv. Prof. Liq.
■ Weak ■ Fair ▨ Good □ Strong

HAWAII MEDICAL SERVICE ASSOCIATION   B   Good

Major Rating Factors: Good overall profitability index (6.4 on a scale of 0 to 10). Fair quality investment portfolio (4.4). Strong capitalization (8.7) based on excellent current risk-adjusted capital (severe loss scenario).
Other Rating Factors: Excellent liquidity (7.0) with ample operational cash flow and liquid investments.
Principal Business: Comp med (55%), Medicaid (20%), Medicare (13%), FEHB (11%)
Mem Phys: 19: 8,433 **18:** 7,942 **19 MLR** 90.5% **/ 19 Admin Exp** N/A
Enroll(000): Q2 20: 704 **19:** 698 **18:** 715 **Med Exp PMPM:** $376
Principal Investments: Cash and equiv (47%), nonaffiliate common stock (19%), long-term bonds (17%), real estate (9%), affiliate common stock (5%), other (3%)
Provider Compensation ($000): Contr fee ($2,553,379), bonus arrang ($256,323), capitation ($184,252), salary ($147,875)
Total Member Encounters: Phys (5,594,644)
Group Affiliation: None
Licensed in: HI
Address: 818 Keeaumoku Street, Honolulu, HI 96814
Phone: (808) 948-5145 **Dom State:** HI **Commenced Bus:** N/A

Data Date	Rating	RACR #1	RACR #2	Total Assets ($mil)	Capital ($mil)	Net Premium ($mil)	Net Income ($mil)
6-20	B	2.73	2.27	1,651.0	633.0	1,754.9	52.2
6-19	N/A	N/A	N/A	N/A	N/A	N/A	N/A
2019	B	2.85	2.38	1,416.3	656.7	3,507.4	62.7
2018	B-	2.40	2.00	1,295.2	562.4	3,539.8	68.9
2017	B-	2.08	1.73	1,173.6	478.0	3,332.7	58.0
2016	C+	1.92	1.60	1,004.0	417.6	3,158.0	28.5
2015	C	1.70	1.42	972.6	371.9	2,978.7	7.6

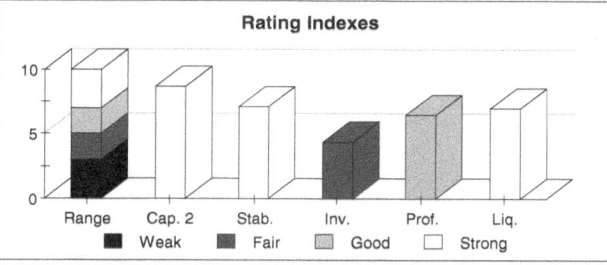

Rating Indexes

Range Cap. 2 Stab. Inv. Prof. Liq.
■ Weak ■ Fair ▨ Good □ Strong

HCC LIFE INS CO   B   Good

Major Rating Factors: Good overall results on stability tests (5.9 on a scale of 0 to 10) despite fair financial strength of affiliated HCC Ins Holdings Inc. Other stability subfactors include excellent operational trends and excellent risk diversification. Good liquidity (6.7) with sufficient resources to handle a spike in claims. Strong capitalization (10.0) based on excellent risk adjusted capital (severe loss scenario).
Other Rating Factors: High quality investment portfolio (7.8). Excellent profitability (8.2) with operating gains in each of the last five years.
Principal Business: Group health insurance (94%), individual health insurance (4%), and reinsurance (2%).
Principal Investments: NonCMO investment grade bonds (51%), CMOs and structured securities (45%), and cash (4%).
Investments in Affiliates: None
Group Affiliation: HCC Ins Holdings Inc
Licensed in: All states except PR
Commenced Business: March 1981
Address: 150 West Market Street Ste 800, Indianapolis, IN 46204
Phone: (770) 973-9851 **Domicile State:** IN **NAIC Code:** 92711

Data Date	Rating	RACR #1	RACR #2	Total Assets ($mil)	Capital ($mil)	Net Premium ($mil)	Net Income ($mil)
6-20	B	3.91	2.97	1,279.2	643.2	711.5	63.4
6-19	B	3.87	2.96	1,096.2	613.4	618.5	58.1
2019	B	4.14	3.15	1,182.6	644.8	1,248.7	85.9
2018	B	3.35	2.56	1,097.0	561.5	1,365.8	121.4
2017	B	3.06	2.40	994.8	406.2	1,095.5	90.9
2016	B	4.81	3.71	981.6	601.8	987.7	104.8
2015	B	4.44	3.40	921.5	552.7	973.3	112.1

HCC Ins Holdings Inc Composite Group Rating: C+ Largest Group Members	Assets ($mil)	Rating
RELIANCE STANDARD LIFE INS CO	15903	C+
PHILADELPHIA INDEMNITY INS CO	9437	B-
SAFETY NATIONAL CASUALTY CORP	9057	B
HOUSTON CASUALTY CO	3715	B-
US SPECIALTY INS CO	2131	C+

HCSC INS SERVICES CO   E-   Very Weak

Major Rating Factors: Weak profitability index (0.8 on a scale of 0 to 10). Weak liquidity (1.9) as a spike in claims may stretch capacity. Strong capitalization (8.5) based on excellent current risk-adjusted capital (severe loss scenario).
Other Rating Factors: High quality investment portfolio (8.9).
Principal Business: Medicare (32%), Medicaid (5%), other (63%)
Mem Phys: 19: 71,299 **18:** 61,714 **19 MLR** 393.7% **/ 19 Admin Exp** N/A
Enroll(000): Q2 20: 532 **19:** 544 **18:** 540 **Med Exp PMPM:** $277
Principal Investments: Long-term bonds (92%), cash and equiv (8%)
Provider Compensation ($000): Contr fee ($1,271,284), FFS ($229,293), capitation ($25,074), bonus arrang ($4), other ($235,407)
Total Member Encounters: Phys (1,321,763), non-phys (2,289,590)
Group Affiliation: Health Care Service Corporation a Mu
Licensed in: All states except CT, HI, ME, NH, NJ, NY, VT, PR
Address: 300 East Randolph Street, Chicago, IL 60601-5099
Phone: (312) 653-6000 **Dom State:** IL **Commenced Bus:** N/A

Data Date	Rating	RACR #1	RACR #2	Total Assets ($mil)	Capital ($mil)	Net Premium ($mil)	Net Income ($mil)
6-20	E-	2.56	2.13	1,063.8	166.3	284.8	-97.8
6-19	D-	1.67	1.39	821.0	193.5	284.1	-61.9
2019	D-	5.06	4.22	897.9	236.4	460.2	-101.2
2018	D-	2.12	1.77	1,043.9	247.8	1,523.2	-156.3
2017	D-	1.74	1.45	900.7	259.5	1,393.5	-114.3
2016	D	2.19	1.83	581.5	189.8	1,391.7	-37.3
2015	D	2.79	2.33	560.2	225.0	1,306.9	-122.1

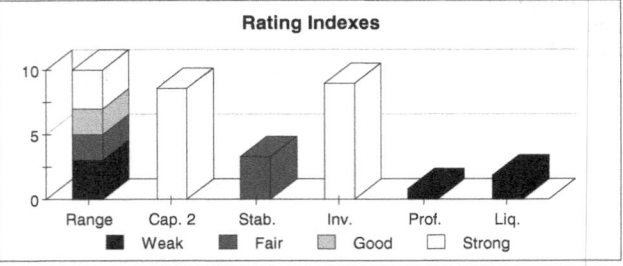
Rating Indexes

HEALTH ALLIANCE CONNECT INC   B-   Good

Major Rating Factors: Good overall profitability index (5.4 on a scale of 0 to 10). Good liquidity (6.9) with sufficient resources (cash flows and marketable investments) to handle a spike in claims. Strong capitalization (7.7) based on excellent current risk-adjusted capital (severe loss scenario).
Other Rating Factors: High quality investment portfolio (9.4).
Principal Business: Medicare (100%)
Mem Phys: 19: 48,150 **18:** 41,526 **19 MLR** 87.7% **/ 19 Admin Exp** N/A
Enroll(000): Q2 20: 25 **19:** 23 **18:** 21 **Med Exp PMPM:** $814
Principal Investments: Cash and equiv (52%), long-term bonds (48%)
Provider Compensation ($000): Contr fee ($109,639), capitation ($104,642), FFS ($5,991)
Total Member Encounters: Phys (134,825), non-phys (571,076)
Group Affiliation: None
Licensed in: IL, IN, IA, OH
Address: 3310 Fields South Drive, Champaign, IL 61822
Phone: (800) 851-3379 **Dom State:** IL **Commenced Bus:** N/A

Data Date	Rating	RACR #1	RACR #2	Total Assets ($mil)	Capital ($mil)	Net Premium ($mil)	Net Income ($mil)
6-20	B-	1.91	1.59	70.9	35.1	145.3	7.2
6-19	C	1.92	1.60	58.3	26.5	130.3	2.2
2019	B-	2.13	1.77	60.1	30.4	252.5	2.8
2018	C	1.81	1.51	54.4	25.1	227.5	6.6
2017	C	N/A	N/A	70.8	32.7	206.4	1.7
2016	C	0.96	0.80	166.1	72.3	647.4	4.9
2015	N/A	N/A	N/A	183.0	58.9	547.3	N/A

Rating Indexes

HEALTH ALLIANCE MEDICAL PLANS   B-   Good

Major Rating Factors: Fair quality investment portfolio (4.4 on a scale of 0 to 10). Good overall profitability index (6.3). Strong capitalization (9.1) based on excellent current risk-adjusted capital (severe loss scenario).
Other Rating Factors: Excellent liquidity (7.1) with ample operational cash flow and liquid investments.
Principal Business: Comp med (94%), Medicare (3%), FEHB (1%)
Mem Phys: 19: 57,359 **18:** 50,222 **19 MLR** 84.6% **/ 19 Admin Exp** N/A
Enroll(000): Q2 20: 143 **19:** 142 **18:** 156 **Med Exp PMPM:** $586
Principal Investments: Nonaffiliate common stock (50%), long-term bonds (45%), cash and equiv (4%), affiliate common stock (1%)
Provider Compensation ($000): Contr fee ($650,329), capitation ($360,781), FFS ($12,409)
Total Member Encounters: Phys (409,211), non-phys (1,495,351)
Group Affiliation: None
Licensed in: IL, MO
Address: 3310 Fields South Drive, Champaign, IL 61822
Phone: (800) 851-3379 **Dom State:** IL **Commenced Bus:** N/A

Data Date	Rating	RACR #1	RACR #2	Total Assets ($mil)	Capital ($mil)	Net Premium ($mil)	Net Income ($mil)
6-20	B-	3.01	2.51	569.2	256.2	17.6	14.6
6-19	B-	2.96	2.47	516.4	248.5	601.7	13.1
2019	B-	2.91	2.42	529.2	243.5	1,199.1	16.6
2018	B-	2.61	2.18	507.9	220.6	1,226.3	17.1
2017	B-	2.61	2.18	641.0	223.0	1,229.8	16.6
2016	B-	2.52	2.10	505.1	195.7	1,133.1	2.2
2015	N/A	N/A	N/A	526.3	184.5	1,156.4	N/A

Rating Indexes

HEALTH ALLIANCE NORTHWEST HEALTH PL — B — Good

Major Rating Factors: Good overall profitability index (6.2 on a scale of 0 to 10). Good liquidity (6.9) with sufficient resources (cash flows and marketable investments) to handle a spike in claims. Strong capitalization (8.0) based on excellent current risk-adjusted capital (severe loss scenario).
Other Rating Factors: High quality investment portfolio (8.9).
Principal Business: Medicare (100%)
Mem Phys: 19: 15,317 **18:** 11,200 **19 MLR** 88.2% **/ 19 Admin Exp** N/A
Enroll(000): Q2 20: 12 **19:** 11 **18:** 8 **Med Exp PMPM:** $670
Principal Investments: Long-term bonds (72%), cash and equiv (28%)
Provider Compensation ($000): Capitation ($68,101), contr fee ($16,679), FFS ($1,405)
Total Member Encounters: Phys (24,940), non-phys (252,867)
Group Affiliation: None
Licensed in: WA
Address: 411 N Chelan Ave, Wenatchee, WA 98801
Phone: (800) 851-3379 **Dom State:** WA **Commenced Bus:** N/A

Data Date	Rating	RACR #1	RACR #2	Total Assets ($mil)	Capital ($mil)	Net Premium ($mil)	Net Income ($mil)
6-20	B	2.13	1.78	23.8	17.1	50.8	1.4
6-19	B	3.55	2.96	20.9	15.5	50.0	0.5
2019	B	2.82	2.35	22.8	17.1	99.1	0.7
2018	B	2.60	2.16	15.6	11.5	64.7	0.8
2017	B-	N/A	N/A	16.8	10.8	57.2	1.3
2016	C+	3.39	2.82	16.0	9.5	44.5	0.5
2015	C	3.79	3.16	16.5	9.1	30.1	-0.2

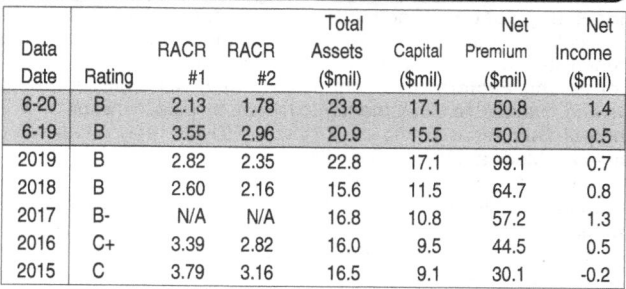

HEALTH ALLIANCE PLAN OF MICHIGAN — C- — Fair

Major Rating Factors: Fair profitability index (4.9 on a scale of 0 to 10). Low quality investment portfolio (1.6). Good overall results on stability tests (5.3).
Other Rating Factors: Strong capitalization index (8.4) based on excellent current risk-adjusted capital (severe loss scenario). Excellent liquidity (6.9) with sufficient resources (cash flows and marketable investments) to handle a spike in claims.
Principal Business: Medicare (50%), comp med (43%), FEHB (7%)
Mem Phys: 19: 12,989 **18:** 12,080 **19 MLR** 89.0% **/ 19 Admin Exp** N/A
Enroll(000): Q2 20: 179 **19:** 179 **18:** 181 **Med Exp PMPM:** $613
Principal Investments: Cash and equiv (40%), affiliate common stock (30%), long-term bonds (25%), nonaffiliate common stock (3%), other (1%)
Provider Compensation ($000): Contr fee ($982,603), capitation ($323,014), bonus arrang ($36,313), FFS ($4,559)
Total Member Encounters: Phys (1,309,014), non-phys (1,522,244)
Group Affiliation: None
Licensed in: MI
Address: 2850 West Grand Boulevard, Detroit,
Phone: (313) 872-8100 **Dom State:** MI **Commenced Bus:** N/A

Data Date	Rating	RACR #1	RACR #2	Total Assets ($mil)	Capital ($mil)	Net Premium ($mil)	Net Income ($mil)
6-20	C-	2.50	2.08	616.7	349.1	763.7	69.5
6-19	C-	2.02	1.68	548.5	284.5	754.3	15.2
2019	C-	2.01	1.68	494.4	278.8	1,495.7	26.1
2018	C-	1.78	1.49	515.8	254.7	1,468.0	3.5
2017	C	1.32	1.10	562.2	229.3	1,827.5	8.7
2016	C+	1.20	1.00	515.5	204.4	1,924.3	38.4
2015	C+	1.31	1.09	530.9	206.5	2,069.8	-33.1

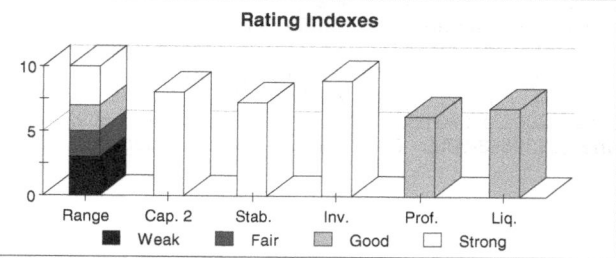

HEALTH ALLIANCE-MIDWEST INC — C — Fair

Major Rating Factors: Fair liquidity (3.0 on a scale of 0 to 10) as cash resources may not be adequate to cover a spike in claims. Weak profitability index (2.6). Good overall results on stability tests (4.9).
Other Rating Factors: Strong capitalization index (10.0) based on excellent current risk-adjusted capital (severe loss scenario). High quality investment portfolio (9.5).
Principal Business: FEHB (100%)
Mem Phys: 19: 59,174 **18:** 52,263 **19 MLR** 8778.7% **/ 19 Admin Exp** N/A
Enroll(000): Q2 20: 2 **19:** 2 **18:** 2 **Med Exp PMPM:** $620
Principal Investments: Cash and equiv (59%), long-term bonds (41%)
Provider Compensation ($000): Contr fee ($9,876), capitation ($2,550), FFS ($225)
Total Member Encounters: Phys (7,545), non-phys (26,664)
Group Affiliation: None
Licensed in: IL, IA, NE
Address: 301 S Vine, Urbana,
Phone: (800) 851-3379 **Dom State:** IL **Commenced Bus:** N/A

Data Date	Rating	RACR #1	RACR #2	Total Assets ($mil)	Capital ($mil)	Net Premium ($mil)	Net Income ($mil)
6-20	C	11.67	9.72	10.7	3.3	0.1	0.1
6-19	U	N/A	N/A	9.6	3.2	0.1	0.1
2019	C	17.95	14.96	9.3	3.3	0.1	0.1
2018	U	13.14	10.95	8.4	3.3	0.1	-0.4
2017	U	12.38	10.31	22.4	7.6	0.1	0.8
2016	E	2.01	1.67	10.2	6.8	18.8	-1.1
2015	E	1.42	1.18	8.2	4.0	17.1	-1.1

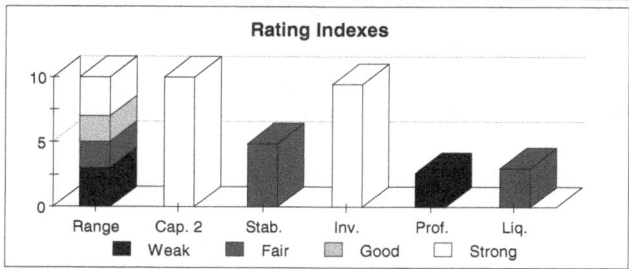

HEALTH CARE SVC CORP A MUT LEG RES *   B+   Good

Major Rating Factors: Good quality investment portfolio (6.5 on a scale of 0 to 10). Excellent profitability (7.2). Strong capitalization (10.0) based on excellent current risk-adjusted capital (severe loss scenario).
Other Rating Factors: Excellent liquidity (6.9) with sufficient resources (cash flows and marketable investments) to handle a spike in claims.
Principal Business: Comp med (63%), FEHB (14%), Medicaid (12%), med supp (4%), Medicare (3%), other (3%)
Mem Phys: 19: 264,336 **18:** 251,046 **19 MLR** 82.2% **/ 19 Admin Exp** N/A
Enroll(000): Q2 20: 10,033 **19:** 9,617 **18:** 8,817 **Med Exp PMPM:** $277
Principal Investments: Long-term bonds (84%), nonaffiliate common stock (7%), affiliate common stock (6%), real estate (5%), other (1%)
Provider Compensation ($000): Contr fee ($22,549,128), FFS ($6,988,769), capitation ($1,172,879), bonus arrang ($341,124), other ($795,219)
Total Member Encounters: Phys (53,344,903), non-phys (23,016,292)
Group Affiliation: Health Care Service Corporation a Mu
Licensed in: AK, AZ, AR, CO, CT, DC, DE, FL, GA, ID, IL, IN, KY, ME, MD, MA, MI, MN, MO, MT, NE, NJ, NM, OH, OK, OR, PA, SC, TX, UT, VA, WV, WI
Address: 300 East Randolph Street, Chicago, IL 60601-5099
Phone: (312) 653-6000 **Dom State:** IL **Commenced Bus:** N/A

Data Date	Rating	RACR #1	RACR #2	Total Assets ($mil)	Capital ($mil)	Net Premium ($mil)	Net Income ($mil)
6-20	B+	8.03	6.69	33,429.9	20,200.9	21,017.8	2,695.1
6-19	B+	8.47	7.06	28,760.1	19,139.8	19,340.3	2,332.4
2019	B+	7.38	6.15	29,355.7	18,526.2	38,553.6	2,270.2
2018	B	7.47	6.23	26,725.6	16,859.3	35,927.2	4,114.7
2017	B	5.85	4.87	22,028.2	12,049.0	32,603.5	1,262.6
2016	B	4.74	3.95	18,036.1	9,535.9	30,335.8	106.3
2015	B	4.47	3.72	17,661.1	9,445.0	31,185.3	-65.9

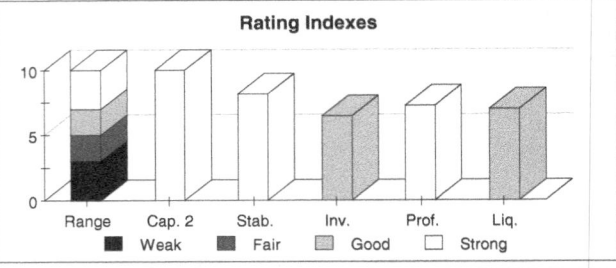

Rating Indexes

HEALTH COLORADO INC   D-   Weak

Major Rating Factors: Weak profitability index (1.1 on a scale of 0 to 10). Strong capitalization index (10.0) based on weak current risk-adjusted capital (severe loss scenario). High quality investment portfolio (9.9).
Other Rating Factors: Excellent liquidity (6.9) with sufficient resources (cash flows and marketable investments) to handle a spike in claims.
Principal Business: Medicaid (100%)
Mem Phys: 19: 1,252 **18:** 90 **19 MLR** 89.0% **/ 19 Admin Exp** N/A
Enroll(000): Q2 20: 125 **19:** 120 **18:** 133 **Med Exp PMPM:** $57
Principal Investments: Cash and equiv (100%)
Provider Compensation ($000): Contr fee ($67,416), other ($19,575)
Total Member Encounters: Non-phys (731,542)
Group Affiliation: Health Colorado Inc
Licensed in: CO
Address: 1740 Eagleridge Blvd Suite 1, PUEBLO, CO 81008
Phone: (Phone number **Dom State:** CO **Commenced Bus:** N/A

Data Date	Rating	RACR #1	RACR #2	Total Assets ($mil)	Capital ($mil)	Net Premium ($mil)	Net Income ($mil)
6-20	D-	N/A	N/A	22.0	4.9	46.9	0.2
6-19	N/A	N/A	N/A	N/A	N/A	N/A	N/A
2019	C-	N/A	N/A	11.3	4.2	96.5	-2.4
2018	C	0.79	0.66	11.6	5.8	45.4	1.1
2017	N/A	N/A	N/A	N/A	N/A	N/A	N/A
2016	N/A	N/A	N/A	N/A	N/A	N/A	N/A
2015	N/A	N/A	N/A	N/A	N/A	N/A	N/A

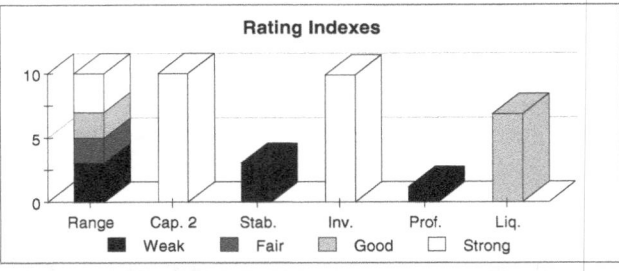

Rating Indexes

HEALTH FIRST COMM PLANS INC *   A-   Excellent

Major Rating Factors: Excellent profitability (8.2 on a scale of 0 to 10). Strong capitalization (8.5) based on excellent current risk-adjusted capital (severe loss scenario). High quality investment portfolio (9.1).
Other Rating Factors: Excellent liquidity (7.0) with sufficient resources (cash flows and marketable investments) to handle a spike in claims.
Principal Business: Comp med (100%)
Mem Phys: 19: 4,750 **18:** 1,947 **19 MLR** 80.8% **/ 19 Admin Exp** N/A
Enroll(000): Q2 20: 39 **19:** 35 **18:** 40 **Med Exp PMPM:** $444
Principal Investments: Long-term bonds (53%), cash and equiv (39%), nonaffiliate common stock (7%)
Provider Compensation ($000): Contr fee ($133,036), FFS ($57,123), capitation ($897)
Total Member Encounters: Phys (254,679), non-phys (97,339)
Group Affiliation: Health First Shared Services Inc
Licensed in: FL
Address: 6450 US HIGHWAY 1, ROCKLEDGE, FL 32955
Phone: (321) 434-5600 **Dom State:** FL **Commenced Bus:** N/A

Data Date	Rating	RACR #1	RACR #2	Total Assets ($mil)	Capital ($mil)	Net Premium ($mil)	Net Income ($mil)
6-20	A-	2.53	2.11	104.0	58.1	126.3	0.7
6-19	B	2.54	2.12	101.2	53.6	119.9	3.0
2019	A-	3.00	2.50	97.9	60.0	237.4	8.7
2018	C	2.23	1.86	87.1	47.0	259.8	12.6
2017	N/A	N/A	N/A	2.0	2.0	N/A	N/A
2016	N/A	N/A	N/A	N/A	N/A	N/A	N/A
2015	N/A	N/A	N/A	N/A	N/A	N/A	N/A

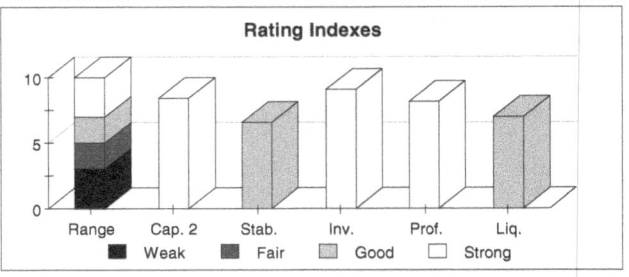

Rating Indexes

HEALTH FIRST HEALTH PLANS INC

B   **Good**

Major Rating Factors: Excellent profitability (7.2 on a scale of 0 to 10). Strong capitalization (9.1) based on excellent current risk-adjusted capital (severe loss scenario). High quality investment portfolio (8.7).
Other Rating Factors: Excellent liquidity (7.0) with ample operational cash flow and liquid investments.
Principal Business: Medicare (100%)
Mem Phys: 19: 4,974   **18:** 5,217   **19 MLR** 81.5%   **/ 19 Admin Exp** N/A
Enroll(000): Q2 20: 38   **19:** 38   **18:** 38   **Med Exp PMPM:** $784
Principal Investments: Long-term bonds (45%), cash and equiv (43%), nonaffiliate common stock (12%)
Provider Compensation ($000): Contr fee ($278,282), FFS ($77,188), capitation ($4,642)
Total Member Encounters: Phys (721,490), non-phys (362,777)
Group Affiliation: Health First Shared Services Inc
Licensed in: FL
Address: 6450 US HIGHWAY 1, ROCKLEDGE, FL 32955
Phone: (321) 434-5600   **Dom State:** FL   **Commenced Bus:** N/A

Data Date	Rating	RACR #1	RACR #2	Total Assets ($mil)	Capital ($mil)	Net Premium ($mil)	Net Income ($mil)
6-20	B	3.01	2.51	171.9	113.0	237.9	7.3
6-19	B	3.07	2.56	165.3	106.9	222.3	12.9
2019	B	2.95	2.46	158.2	108.5	443.9	13.4
2018	B	2.66	2.21	143.9	93.0	408.1	17.9
2017	B	1.94	1.61	120.6	65.8	373.5	17.2
2016	C-	2.01	1.68	130.8	70.6	443.3	22.5
2015	N/A	N/A	N/A	1.8	1.8	N/A	N/A

Rating Indexes

HEALTH FIRST INS INC

C+   **Fair**

Major Rating Factors: Weak profitability index (2.5 on a scale of 0 to 10). Strong capitalization (8.7) based on excellent current risk-adjusted capital (severe loss scenario). High quality investment portfolio (9.9).
Other Rating Factors: Excellent liquidity (10.0) with ample operational cash flow and liquid investments.
Principal Business: Med supp (52%), comp med (48%)
Mem Phys: 19: 4,681   **18:** 1,734   **19 MLR** 145.1%   **/ 19 Admin Exp** N/A
Enroll(000): Q2 20: 0   **19:** 0   **18:** 0   **Med Exp PMPM:** $668
Principal Investments: Cash and equiv (100%)
Provider Compensation ($000): FFS ($105), contr fee ($11)
Total Member Encounters: Phys (552), non-phys (295)
Group Affiliation: Health First Shared Services Inc
Licensed in: FL
Address: 6450 US HIGHWAY 1, ROCKLEDGE, FL 32955
Phone: (321) 434-5600   **Dom State:** FL   **Commenced Bus:** N/A

Data Date	Rating	RACR #1	RACR #2	Total Assets ($mil)	Capital ($mil)	Net Premium ($mil)	Net Income ($mil)
6-20	C+	2.70	2.25	5.1	5.0	0.0	0.0
6-19	C+	3.82	3.18	5.1	4.9	0.1	0.0
2019	B-	3.84	3.20	5.1	5.0	0.1	-0.1
2018	C	3.82	3.19	5.3	4.9	1.4	0.2
2017	D	1.96	1.64	4.4	3.5	3.5	0.2
2016	E	4.06	3.38	6.0	4.7	5.3	0.3
2015	E-	1.58	1.32	6.4	3.6	10.4	-2.0

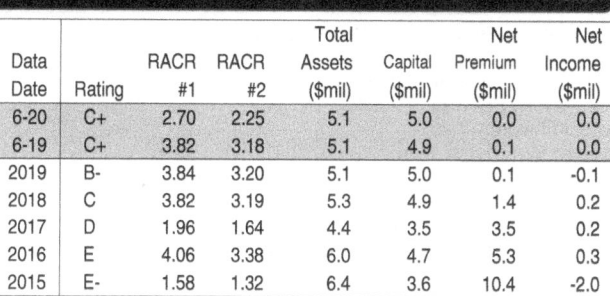

Rating Indexes

HEALTH INSURANCE PLAN OF GREATER NY

D+   **Weak**

Major Rating Factors: Weak profitability index (0.8 on a scale of 0 to 10). Fair capitalization (3.0) based on weak current risk-adjusted capital (moderate loss scenario). Fair quality investment portfolio (4.1).
Other Rating Factors: Good liquidity (6.2) with sufficient resources (cash flows and marketable investments) to handle a spike in claims.
Principal Business: Comp med (46%), Medicare (32%), Medicaid (21%), FEHB (1%)
Mem Phys: 19: 131,286   **18:** 110,096   **19 MLR** 88.1%   **/ 19 Admin Exp** N/A
Enroll(000): Q2 20: 594   **19:** 578   **18:** 604   **Med Exp PMPM:** $640
Principal Investments: Affiliate common stock (42%), cash and equiv (36%), real estate (6%), long-term bonds (1%), other (16%)
Provider Compensation ($000): Capitation ($1,668,177), FFS ($1,446,297), contr fee ($1,338,891), bonus arrang ($4,949)
Total Member Encounters: Phys (8,109,589), non-phys (2,881,430)
Group Affiliation: EmblemHealth Inc
Licensed in: NY
Address: 55 Water Street, New York, NY 10041-8190
Phone: (646) 447-5000   **Dom State:** NY   **Commenced Bus:** N/A

Data Date	Rating	RACR #1	RACR #2	Total Assets ($mil)	Capital ($mil)	Net Premium ($mil)	Net Income ($mil)
6-20	D+	0.63	0.52	1,390.9	364.4	2,607.9	-39.4
6-19	C-	0.82	0.68	1,197.3	341.0	2,495.3	-10.8
2019	C-	0.73	0.61	1,352.5	325.1	5,029.6	-11.7
2018	C-	0.87	0.72	1,220.8	360.7	5,008.6	-48.8
2017	C-	0.81	0.68	1,252.9	391.8	4,754.2	-199.5
2016	C-	1.15	0.96	1,424.4	469.9	4,855.3	-239.2
2015	C-	1.70	1.42	1,644.4	684.1	5,065.0	-143.2

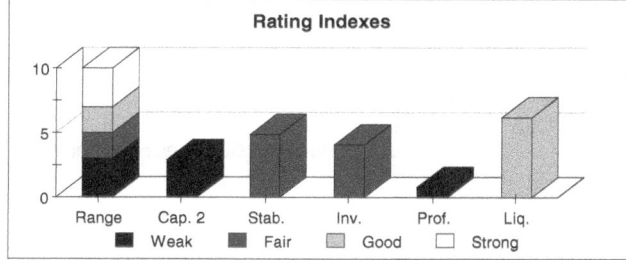

Rating Indexes

HEALTH NET COMMUNITY SOLUTIONS INC   B   Good

Major Rating Factors: Fair overall results on stability tests (4.7 on a scale of 0 to 10). Excellent profitability (8.4). Strong capitalization index (8.4) based on excellent current risk-adjusted capital (severe loss scenario).
Other Rating Factors: Excellent liquidity (7.1) with ample operational cash flow and liquid investments.
Principal Business: Medicaid (79%), Medicare (5%)
Mem Phys: 19: N/A **18:** N/A   **19 MLR** 86.3% **/ 19 Admin Exp** N/A
Enroll(000): Q2 20: 1,752   **19:** 1,792   **18:** 1,792   **Med Exp PMPM:** $266
Principal Investments ($000): Cash and equiv ($128,121)
Provider Compensation ($000): None
Total Member Encounters: N/A
Group Affiliation: Health Net Inc
Licensed in: CA
Address: 11971 Foundation Place, Rancho Cordova, CA 95670
Phone: (818) 676-8394 **Dom State:** CA **Commenced Bus:** June 2005

Data Date	Rating	RACR #1	RACR #2	Total Assets ($mil)	Capital ($mil)	Net Premium ($mil)	Net Income ($mil)
6-20	B	3.03	2.04	2,783.8	1,388.3	3,461.3	190.2
6-19	B	3.18	2.14	2,415.8	1,341.9	3,203.0	209.6
2019	B	2.81	1.89	2,400.6	1,292.0	6,876.7	454.1
2018	B	2.59	1.74	2,394.5	1,107.7	6,244.4	493.9
2017	B+	2.19	1.47	3,107.0	1,029.0	7,518.8	433.2
2016	B	1.62	1.09	3,043.0	737.2	7,482.8	541.9
2015	B	2.03	1.26	2,321.8	549.1	6,467.1	533.2

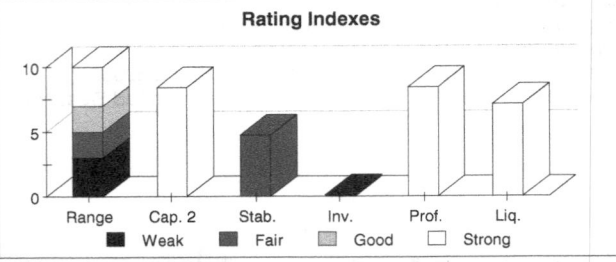

Rating Indexes

HEALTH NET COMMUNITY SOLUTIONS OF AR   C   Fair

Major Rating Factors: Weak profitability index (2.3 on a scale of 0 to 10). Strong capitalization (10.0) based on excellent current risk-adjusted capital (severe loss scenario). High quality investment portfolio (9.9).
Other Rating Factors: Excellent liquidity (7.2) with ample operational cash flow and liquid investments.
Principal Business: Medicare (100%)
Mem Phys: 18: 23,660   **17:** 19,324   **18 MLR** 77.5% **/ 18 Admin Exp** N/A
Enroll(000): Q3 19: 3   **18:** 36   **17:** 2   **Med Exp PMPM:** $683
Principal Investments: Cash and equiv (58%), long-term bonds (42%)
Provider Compensation ($000): Contr fee ($22,627), capitation ($431), salary ($256)
Total Member Encounters: Phys (32,113), non-phys (1,983)
Group Affiliation: None
Licensed in: AZ
Address: 1870 West Rio Salado Pkwy, Tempe, AZ 85281-1245
Phone: (314) 725-4477 **Dom State:** AZ **Commenced Bus:** N/A

Data Date	Rating	RACR #1	RACR #2	Total Assets ($mil)	Capital ($mil)	Net Premium ($mil)	Net Income ($mil)
9-19	C	3.99	3.33	18.3	8.9	22.5	1.0
9-18	N/A	N/A	N/A	15.1	4.5	23.9	1.3
2018	C-	3.69	3.07	15.0	8.1	32.0	4.6
2017	N/A	N/A	N/A	9.7	3.8	17.8	-3.5
2016	N/A	N/A	N/A	1.6	1.6	N/A	N/A
2015	N/A	N/A	N/A	N/A	N/A	N/A	N/A
2014	N/A	N/A	N/A	N/A	N/A	N/A	N/A

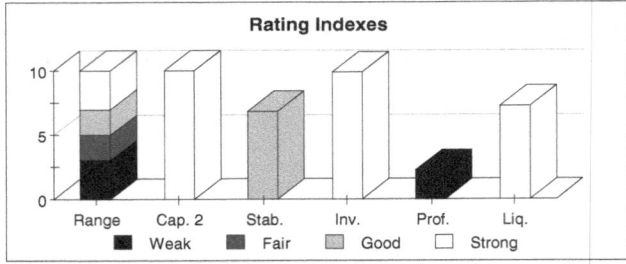

Rating Indexes

HEALTH NET HEALTH PLAN OF OREGON INC   D   Weak

Major Rating Factors: Weak profitability index (0.6 on a scale of 0 to 10). Fair overall results on stability tests (3.4) based on a steep decline in capital during 2019, a decline in the number of member physicians during 2020. Good capitalization index (5.8) based on good current risk-adjusted capital (severe loss scenario).
Other Rating Factors: Good liquidity (5.7) with sufficient resources (cash flows and marketable investments) to handle a spike in claims. High quality investment portfolio (9.0).
Principal Business: Medicare (74%), comp med (26%)
Mem Phys: 19: 14,161   **18:** 66,617   **19 MLR** 94.0% **/ 19 Admin Exp** N/A
Enroll(000): Q2 20: 42   **19:** 59   **18:** 66   **Med Exp PMPM:** $620
Principal Investments: Long-term bonds (90%), cash and equiv (10%)
Provider Compensation ($000): Contr fee ($419,860), capitation ($16,291), salary ($8,739), bonus arrang ($2,570)
Total Member Encounters: Phys (777,356), non-phys (254,276)
Group Affiliation: None
Licensed in: OR, WA
Address: 13221 SW 68th Parkway Suite 20, Tigard,
Phone: (314) 724-4477 **Dom State:** OR **Commenced Bus:** N/A

Data Date	Rating	RACR #1	RACR #2	Total Assets ($mil)	Capital ($mil)	Net Premium ($mil)	Net Income ($mil)
6-20	D	1.05	0.88	135.0	54.4	180.7	0.2
6-19	D	1.83	1.53	142.8	58.1	241.5	-5.3
2019	D	1.74	1.45	144.0	55.8	487.0	-23.4
2018	D	2.33	1.94	155.6	73.7	499.0	-0.1
2017	F	1.42	1.18	182.9	73.1	526.5	-23.5
2016	E-	2.53	2.11	181.6	99.7	506.2	-31.8
2015	E+	1.68	1.40	152.1	68.1	418.8	-25.4

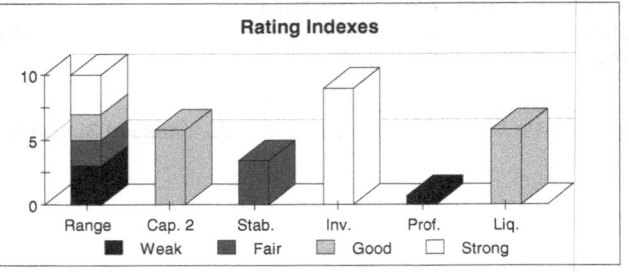

Rating Indexes

HEALTH NET LIFE INS CO

C   **Fair**

Major Rating Factors: Fair overall results on stability tests (3.9 on a scale of 0 to 10). Good liquidity (6.6) with sufficient resources to handle a spike in claims. Weak profitability (2.7). Excellent expense controls. Return on equity has been low, averaging -11.9%.

Other Rating Factors: Strong capitalization (9.5) based on excellent risk adjusted capital (severe loss scenario). High quality investment portfolio (8.1).

Principal Business: Individual health insurance (63%) and group health insurance (37%).

Principal Investments: NonCMO investment grade bonds (68%), CMOs and structured securities (27%), and cash (3%).

Investments in Affiliates: None

Group Affiliation: Centene Corporation

Licensed in: All states except MI, NY, PR

Commenced Business: January 1987

Address: 21281 Burbank Boulevard B3, Woodland Hills, CA 91367

Phone: (314) 725-4477 **Domicile State:** CA **NAIC Code:** 66141

Data Date	Rating	RACR #1	RACR #2	Total Assets ($mil)	Capital ($mil)	Net Premium ($mil)	Net Income ($mil)
6-20	C	3.39	2.68	624.8	395.5	329.9	21.8
6-19	C	2.99	2.37	659.7	372.3	392.8	55.1
2019	C	3.06	2.42	606.1	375.6	739.9	66.6
2018	C	2.98	2.36	704.7	363.0	752.6	-53.1
2017	C	3.44	2.79	691.4	399.9	763.3	-16.4
2016	C	3.59	2.94	727.2	410.0	809.8	-171.8
2015	C	1.84	1.52	618.5	331.3	1,181.3	-93.2

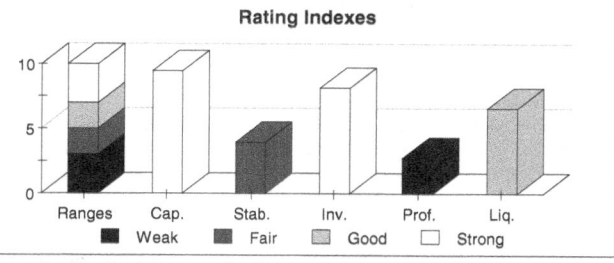

Rating Indexes

HEALTH NET OF ARIZONA INC

C+   **Fair**

Major Rating Factors: Fair profitability index (4.7 on a scale of 0 to 10). Fair overall results on stability tests (4.3) based on a significant 32% decrease in enrollment during the period. Good liquidity (6.8) with sufficient resources (cash flows and marketable investments) to handle a spike in claims.

Other Rating Factors: Strong capitalization index (10.0) based on excellent current risk-adjusted capital (severe loss scenario). High quality investment portfolio (8.0).

Principal Business: Comp med (79%), Medicare (22%)

Mem Phys: 19: 49,593 **18:** 12,471 **19 MLR** 75.5% **/ 19 Admin Exp** N/A

Enroll(000): Q2 20: 78 **19:** 83 **18:** 122 **Med Exp PMPM:** $466

Principal Investments: Long-term bonds (95%), cash and equiv (5%)

Provider Compensation ($000): Contr fee ($379,447), capitation ($21,077), salary ($10,546)

Total Member Encounters: Phys (751,795), non-phys (360,544)

Group Affiliation: None

Licensed in: AZ

Address: 1230 West Washington St Suite, Tempe,

Phone: (314) 725-4477 **Dom State:** AZ **Commenced Bus:** N/A

Data Date	Rating	RACR #1	RACR #2	Total Assets ($mil)	Capital ($mil)	Net Premium ($mil)	Net Income ($mil)
6-20	C+	9.89	8.24	343.0	137.6	283.9	-5.6
6-19	C	6.34	5.29	371.2	141.5	318.2	50.0
2019	C+	14.15	11.79	368.2	139.5	670.2	51.0
2018	C	7.37	6.14	419.8	163.9	932.6	43.0
2017	C	2.66	2.22	344.1	146.9	1,005.6	40.3
2016	C	2.63	2.19	455.4	130.5	360.9	-54.8
2015	C	1.39	1.16	451.0	65.8	684.2	-55.2

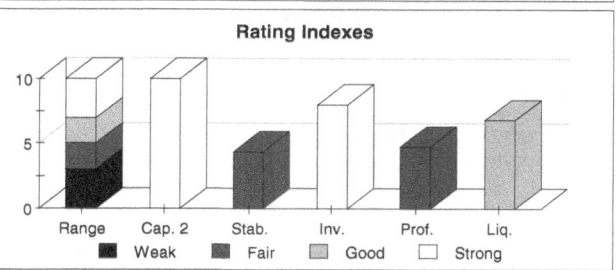

Rating Indexes

HEALTH NET OF CALIFORNIA INC

B-   **Good**

Major Rating Factors: Fair profitability index (3.6 on a scale of 0 to 10). Strong capitalization index (7.8) based on excellent current risk-adjusted capital (severe loss scenario). Excellent overall results on stability tests (7.0).

Other Rating Factors: Excellent liquidity (7.0) with sufficient resources (cash flows and marketable investments) to handle a spike in claims.

Principal Business: Medicare (21%)

Mem Phys: 19: N/A **18:** N/A **19 MLR** 82.1% **/ 19 Admin Exp** N/A

Enroll(000): Q2 20: 972 **19:** 960 **18:** 960 **Med Exp PMPM:** $653

Principal Investments ($000): Cash and equiv ($347,611)

Provider Compensation ($000): None

Total Member Encounters: N/A

Group Affiliation: Health Net Inc

Licensed in: CA

Address: 21281 Burbank Blvd, Woodland Hills, CA 91367

Phone: (818) 676-8394 **Dom State:** CA **Commenced Bus:** March 1979

Data Date	Rating	RACR #1	RACR #2	Total Assets ($mil)	Capital ($mil)	Net Premium ($mil)	Net Income ($mil)
6-20	B-	2.50	1.68	3,055.3	1,530.2	4,927.9	52.7
6-19	B-	2.47	1.69	2,903.3	1,473.9	4,944.1	223.3
2019	B-	2.35	1.59	2,755.8	1,464.5	9,568.8	202.8
2018	C	2.08	1.41	2,620.3	1,218.6	8,784.6	94.3
2017	C	2.05	1.39	2,048.7	949.7	6,300.2	-59.8
2016	C	1.88	1.25	2,280.5	1,001.6	6,751.6	-459.2
2015	C+	2.42	1.51	2,592.5	1,045.0	7,591.8	-189.6

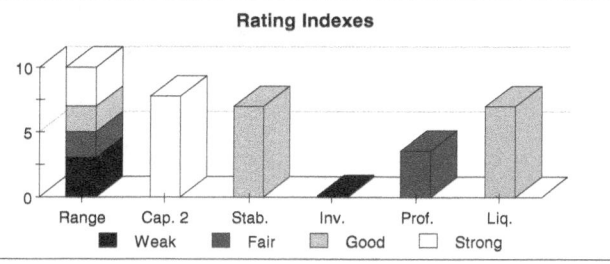

Rating Indexes

HEALTH NEW ENGLAND INC   B   Good

Major Rating Factors: Good overall profitability index (5.1 on a scale of 0 to 10). Good overall results on stability tests (5.2). Good liquidity (6.7) with sufficient resources (cash flows and marketable investments) to handle a spike in claims.
Other Rating Factors: Strong capitalization index (7.2) based on excellent current risk-adjusted capital (severe loss scenario). High quality investment portfolio (9.0).
Principal Business: Comp med (50%), Medicaid (37%), Medicare (13%)
Mem Phys: 19: 11,080 **18:** 11,353 **19 MLR** 90.5% **/ 19 Admin Exp** N/A
Enroll(000): Q2 20: 114 **19:** 110 **18:** 106 **Med Exp PMPM:** $507
Principal Investments: Long-term bonds (64%), cash and equiv (19%), nonaffiliate common stock (11%), affiliate common stock (3%), other (3%)
Provider Compensation ($000): Contr fee ($433,891), FFS ($205,662), bonus arrang ($45,948), capitation ($5,042)
Total Member Encounters: Phys (679,250), non-phys (152,204)
Group Affiliation: Baystate Health Inc
Licensed in: MA
Address: One Monarch Place Suite 1500, Springfield,
Phone: (413) 787-4000 **Dom State:** MA **Commenced Bus:** N/A

Data Date	Rating	RACR #1	RACR #2	Total Assets ($mil)	Capital ($mil)	Net Premium ($mil)	Net Income ($mil)
6-20	B	1.51	1.26	243.2	109.8	389.8	22.0
6-19	B	1.26	1.05	216.9	94.6	359.9	0.1
2019	B	1.15	0.96	227.8	87.0	729.1	2.5
2018	B-	1.04	0.87	185.7	80.9	771.1	6.5
2017	C	0.88	0.74	224.9	83.9	898.0	20.9
2016	D	0.53	0.44	185.2	57.5	936.9	18.1
2015	D	0.36	0.30	165.5	40.1	898.5	-20.5

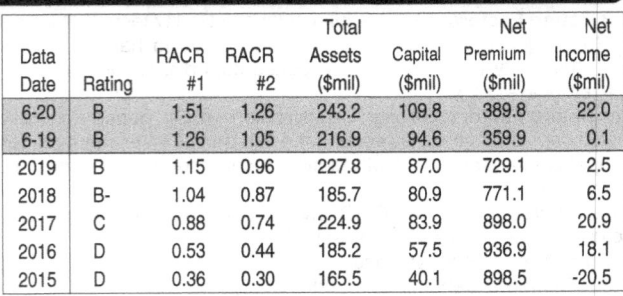

Rating Indexes

HEALTH OPTIONS INC *   A-   Excellent

Major Rating Factors: Excellent profitability (10.0 on a scale of 0 to 10). Strong capitalization index (10.0) based on excellent current risk-adjusted capital (severe loss scenario). Excellent overall results on stability tests (7.6) despite a decline in enrollment during 2019.
Other Rating Factors: Excellent liquidity (7.0) with sufficient resources (cash flows and marketable investments) to handle a spike in claims. Good quality investment portfolio (5.6).
Principal Business: Comp med (87%), Medicare (13%)
Mem Phys: 19: N/A **18:** N/A **19 MLR** 74.6% **/ 19 Admin Exp** N/A
Enroll(000): Q2 20: 834 **19:** 831 **18:** 899 **Med Exp PMPM:** $415
Principal Investments: Long-term bonds (57%), nonaffiliate common stock (27%), cash and equiv (12%), other (4%)
Provider Compensation ($000): Contr fee ($3,757,382), capitation ($401,568), bonus arrang ($89,068), FFS ($51,238)
Total Member Encounters: Phys (5,894,704), non-phys (4,417,273)
Group Affiliation: None
Licensed in: FL
Address: 4800 Deerwood Campus Parkway, Jacksonville,
Phone: (904) 791-6111 **Dom State:** FL **Commenced Bus:** N/A

Data Date	Rating	RACR #1	RACR #2	Total Assets ($mil)	Capital ($mil)	Net Premium ($mil)	Net Income ($mil)
6-20	A-	5.26	4.39	2,831.6	1,519.6	2,627.0	261.2
6-19	A-	4.72	3.93	2,595.2	1,312.5	2,941.6	292.9
2019	A-	4.54	3.78	2,227.3	1,308.6	5,713.9	540.6
2018	A-	3.58	2.98	2,077.4	992.9	5,477.0	415.3
2017	B+	2.51	2.09	1,337.0	591.5	3,768.2	171.6
2016	C	3.15	2.63	879.8	412.0	2,585.6	101.0
2015	U	3.01	2.50	689.5	326.9	2,014.2	24.6

Rating Indexes

HEALTH PARTNERS PLANS INC   B   Good

Major Rating Factors: Good overall profitability index (6.4 on a scale of 0 to 10). Strong capitalization index (7.1) based on excellent current risk-adjusted capital (severe loss scenario). High quality investment portfolio (9.9).
Other Rating Factors: Excellent overall results on stability tests (6.9). Excellent liquidity (7.2) with ample operational cash flow and liquid investments
Principal Business: Medicaid (84%), Medicare (15%), comp med (1%)
Mem Phys: 19: 10,092 **18:** 8,482 **19 MLR** 78.2% **/ 19 Admin Exp** N/A
Enroll(000): Q2 20: 264 **19:** 254 **18:** 275 **Med Exp PMPM:** $443
Principal Investments: Cash and equiv (77%), long-term bonds (23%)
Provider Compensation ($000): Contr fee ($1,264,042), capitation ($62,519)
Total Member Encounters: Phys (2,014,800), non-phys (416,069)
Group Affiliation: Health Partners Plans Inc
Licensed in: PA
Address: 901 MARKET STREET SUITE 500, PHILADELPHIA,
Phone: (215) 849-9606 **Dom State:** PA **Commenced Bus:** N/A

Data Date	Rating	RACR #1	RACR #2	Total Assets ($mil)	Capital ($mil)	Net Premium ($mil)	Net Income ($mil)
6-20	B	1.42	1.18	621.7	180.3	882.3	-0.6
6-19	N/A	N/A	N/A	N/A	N/A	N/A	N/A
2019	B	1.43	1.19	640.3	182.3	1,775.1	23.5
2018	B	1.03	0.86	556.7	159.3	1,956.2	20.2
2017	B-	0.93	0.77	579.2	138.8	1,943.5	11.0
2016	B-	0.90	0.75	620.7	126.8	1,917.0	27.3
2015	B-	0.83	0.69	469.9	96.9	1,502.9	N/A

Rating Indexes

HEALTH PLAN OF CAREOREGON INC | C | Fair

Major Rating Factors: Fair profitability index (3.3 on a scale of 0 to 10). Good liquidity (6.6) with sufficient resources (cash flows and marketable investments) to handle a spike in claims. Strong capitalization (8.2) based on excellent current risk-adjusted capital (severe loss scenario).
Other Rating Factors: High quality investment portfolio (9.4).
Principal Business: Medicare (100%)
Mem Phys: 19: 1,474 **18:** 1,472 **19 MLR** 82.1% **/ 19 Admin Exp** N/A
Enroll(000): Q2 20: 13 **19:** 12 **18:** 13 **Med Exp PMPM:** $1,106
Principal Investments: Long-term bonds (95%), cash and equiv (5%)
Provider Compensation ($000): Contr fee ($114,989), FFS ($37,252)
Total Member Encounters: Phys (77,635), non-phys (58,482)
Group Affiliation: CareOregon Inc
Licensed in: OR
Address: 315 SW FIFTH AVE, PORTLAND, OR 97204-1753
Phone: (503) 416-4100 **Dom State:** OR **Commenced Bus:** N/A

Data Date	Rating	RACR #1	RACR #2	Total Assets ($mil)	Capital ($mil)	Net Premium ($mil)	Net Income ($mil)
6-20	C	2.32	1.94	83.7	44.0	94.2	5.4
6-19	N/A	N/A	N/A	N/A	N/A	N/A	N/A
2019	C	2.17	1.81	71.6	41.3	185.1	9.0
2018	C	1.56	1.30	67.2	32.4	187.4	-1.5
2017	C	1.50	1.25	65.8	30.3	178.1	-15.6
2016	C	1.59	1.32	60.5	30.4	163.3	-8.6
2015	C	2.27	1.89	69.9	40.5	145.3	-16.2

HEALTH PLAN OF NEVADA INC * | B+ | Good

Major Rating Factors: Good overall results on stability tests (5.4 on a scale of 0 to 10). Good liquidity (6.8) with sufficient resources (cash flows and marketable investments) to handle a spike in claims. Excellent profitability (9.1).
Other Rating Factors: Strong capitalization index (9.1) based on excellent current risk-adjusted capital (severe loss scenario). High quality investment portfolio (7.2).
Principal Business: Comp med (56%), Medicaid (43%), FEHB (1%)
Mem Phys: 19: 12,991 **18:** 9,364 **19 MLR** 80.4% **/ 19 Admin Exp** N/A
Enroll(000): Q2 20: 518 **19:** 495 **18:** 581 **Med Exp PMPM:** $273
Principal Investments: Long-term bonds (81%), cash and equiv (16%), real estate (3%), pref stock (1%)
Provider Compensation ($000): Contr fee ($993,297), capitation ($352,337), FFS ($341,466), bonus arrang ($2,923)
Total Member Encounters: Phys (3,179,234), non-phys (1,136,419)
Group Affiliation: None
Licensed in: NV
Address: 2720 NORTH TENAYA WAY, LAS VEGAS,
Phone: (702) 242-7732 **Dom State:** NV **Commenced Bus:** N/A

Data Date	Rating	RACR #1	RACR #2	Total Assets ($mil)	Capital ($mil)	Net Premium ($mil)	Net Income ($mil)
6-20	B+	3.06	2.55	754.1	395.8	1,023.3	47.5
6-19	B+	2.96	2.47	695.5	388.0	1,034.5	89.3
2019	B+	3.55	2.96	629.4	353.9	2,045.0	132.2
2018	B+	2.67	2.22	672.4	348.1	2,943.4	201.1
2017	B+	1.80	1.50	621.9	291.3	2,763.9	155.2
2016	B	1.94	1.62	524.4	216.4	2,569.9	78.0
2015	B	2.43	2.02	505.6	226.5	2,345.0	99.5

HEALTH PLAN OF WV INC | C | Fair

Major Rating Factors: Fair quality investment portfolio (4.7 on a scale of 0 to 10). Weak profitability index (2.4). Good overall results on stability tests (5.9).
Other Rating Factors: Good liquidity (5.7) with sufficient resources (cash flows and marketable investments) to handle a spike in claims. Strong capitalization index (7.7) based on excellent current risk-adjusted capital (severe loss scenario).
Principal Business: Medicaid (52%), Medicare (30%), comp med (18%)
Mem Phys: 19: 27,102 **18:** 22,982 **19 MLR** 94.3% **/ 19 Admin Exp** N/A
Enroll(000): Q2 20: 136 **19:** 133 **18:** 116 **Med Exp PMPM:** $398
Principal Investments: Long-term bonds (44%), nonaffiliate common stock (30%), affiliate common stock (16%), cash and equiv (8%), real estate (2%)
Provider Compensation ($000): Contr fee ($565,614), capitation ($4,059)
Total Member Encounters: Phys (1,857,629), non-phys (590,887)
Group Affiliation: The Health Plan of West Virginia Inc
Licensed in: OH, WV
Address: 52160 National Road E, Wheeling,
Phone: (740) 695-3585 **Dom State:** WV **Commenced Bus:** N/A

Data Date	Rating	RACR #1	RACR #2	Total Assets ($mil)	Capital ($mil)	Net Premium ($mil)	Net Income ($mil)
6-20	C	1.92	1.60	288.0	153.6	352.0	24.5
6-19	C-	1.48	1.24	249.6	105.6	300.0	-32.5
2019	C-	1.60	1.33	259.9	127.2	625.6	-21.0
2018	C	1.77	1.48	232.4	126.0	575.1	-14.9
2017	C	2.38	1.98	257.3	161.4	608.9	-4.2
2016	C	2.37	1.98	265.2	149.7	567.1	-18.0
2015	B	3.81	3.17	274.0	171.0	407.7	-8.4

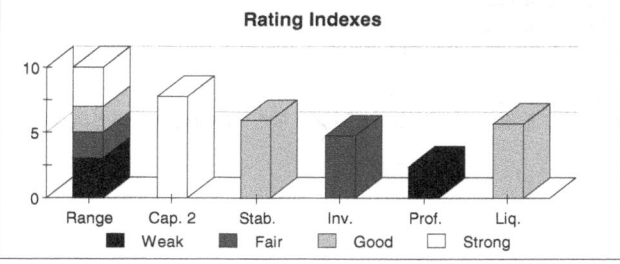

HEALTH TRADITION HEALTH PLAN   C-   Fair

Major Rating Factors: Fair overall results on stability tests (3.5 on a scale of 0 to 10) based on a significant 28% decrease in enrollment during the period, a steep decline in premium revenue in 2019. Weak profitability index (0.8). Strong capitalization index (8.3) based on excellent current risk-adjusted capital (severe loss scenario).
Other Rating Factors: High quality investment portfolio (9.9). Excellent liquidity (7.8) with ample operational cash flow and liquid investments.
Principal Business: Comp med (79%), med supp (21%)
Mem Phys: 19: 21,192 **18:** 2,036 **19 MLR** 78.9% **/ 19 Admin Exp** N/A
Enroll(000): Q2 20: 4 **19:** 4 **18:** 5 **Med Exp PMPM:** $313
Principal Investments: Cash and equiv (100%)
Provider Compensation ($000): FFS ($16,560)
Total Member Encounters: Phys (46,184), non-phys (743)
Group Affiliation: None
Licensed in: WI
Address: 1808 East Main Street, Onalaska,
Phone: (608) 276-4000 **Dom State:** WI **Commenced Bus:** N/A

Data Date	Rating	RACR #1	RACR #2	Total Assets ($mil)	Capital ($mil)	Net Premium ($mil)	Net Income ($mil)
6-20	C-	2.42	2.02	12.3	8.2	10.0	-0.3
6-19	C-	1.69	1.41	14.9	9.0	10.1	-0.7
2019	C-	3.20	2.67	12.4	8.2	20.6	-1.5
2018	C-	1.43	1.19	17.2	9.8	33.2	-3.9
2017	C+	0.98	0.81	54.3	10.1	150.1	-1.3
2016	B	1.20	1.00	40.6	12.1	142.2	0.0
2015	B	1.27	1.06	30.1	12.1	142.3	-0.3

Rating Indexes

HEALTHASSURANCE PENNSYLVANIA INC   B-   Good

Major Rating Factors: Fair overall results on stability tests (4.4 on a scale of 0 to 10). Good quality investment portfolio (5.5). Good liquidity (6.8) with sufficient resources (cash flows and marketable investments) to handle a spike in claims.
Other Rating Factors: Excellent profitability (7.7). Strong capitalization index (8.4) based on excellent current risk-adjusted capital (severe loss scenario).
Principal Business: Medicare (100%)
Mem Phys: 19: 59,627 **18:** 61,931 **19 MLR** 81.6% **/ 19 Admin Exp** N/A
Enroll(000): Q2 20: 74 **19:** 73 **18:** 71 **Med Exp PMPM:** $731
Principal Investments: Long-term bonds (95%), cash and equiv (3%), mortgs (2%)
Provider Compensation ($000): Contr fee ($555,747), FFS ($24,243), bonus arrang ($16,763), capitation ($8,921), other ($30,704)
Total Member Encounters: Phys (861,695), non-phys (217,312)
Group Affiliation: None
Licensed in: PA
Address: 3721 TECPORT DRIVE PO BOX 6710, HARRISBURG,
Phone: (800) 788-6445 **Dom State:** PA **Commenced Bus:** N/A

Data Date	Rating	RACR #1	RACR #2	Total Assets ($mil)	Capital ($mil)	Net Premium ($mil)	Net Income ($mil)
6-20	B-	2.48	2.07	292.3	137.9	396.4	36.3
6-19	C	3.10	2.58	246.2	120.1	389.9	18.9
2019	B-	2.69	2.24	214.8	102.1	765.9	32.6
2018	C	2.65	2.21	239.2	100.0	792.4	31.1
2017	B-	3.25	2.71	315.2	179.1	791.0	43.6
2016	B-	3.56	2.97	323.3	180.7	1,015.7	43.3
2015	B-	2.56	2.13	335.6	162.4	1,243.3	25.6

Rating Indexes

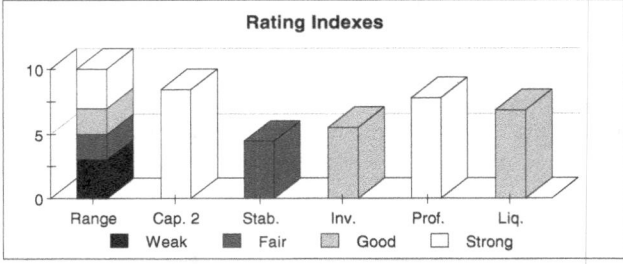

HEALTHFIRST HEALTH PLAN INC *   B+   Good

Major Rating Factors: Good overall profitability index (6.1 on a scale of 0 to 10). Good liquidity (6.1) with sufficient resources (cash flows and marketable investments) to handle a spike in claims. Strong capitalization index (7.3) based on excellent current risk-adjusted capital (severe loss scenario).
Other Rating Factors: High quality investment portfolio (7.9). Excellent overall results on stability tests (8.0).
Principal Business: Medicare (100%)
Mem Phys: 19: 50,086 **18:** 39,287 **19 MLR** 86.0% **/ 19 Admin Exp** N/A
Enroll(000): Q2 20: 196 **19:** 173 **18:** 158 **Med Exp PMPM:** $1,298
Principal Investments: Long-term bonds (82%), cash and equiv (10%), nonaffiliate common stock (7%), affiliate common stock (1%)
Provider Compensation ($000): Contr fee ($2,431,373), FFS ($83,327), capitation ($49,680)
Total Member Encounters: Phys (5,588,826), non-phys (8,102,000)
Group Affiliation: HealthFirst Inc
Licensed in: NY
Address: 100 Church St, New York,
Phone: (212) 801-6000 **Dom State:** NY **Commenced Bus:** N/A

Data Date	Rating	RACR #1	RACR #2	Total Assets ($mil)	Capital ($mil)	Net Premium ($mil)	Net Income ($mil)
6-20	B+	1.57	1.31	961.8	379.7	1,697.3	21.2
6-19	B	1.78	1.49	869.1	365.2	1,481.1	20.9
2019	B+	1.52	1.27	873.2	367.9	3,031.3	25.4
2018	B	1.64	1.36	775.9	339.0	2,620.6	28.7
2017	C+	1.56	1.30	751.4	299.0	2,283.8	-3.6
2016	B-	1.38	1.15	782.8	262.5	2,238.2	6.5
2015	B-	1.45	1.21	614.3	241.5	2,022.5	5.8

Rating Indexes

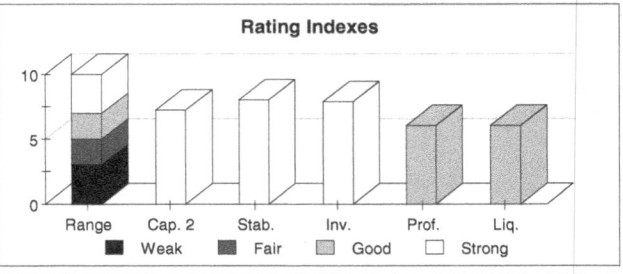

HEALTHFIRST INSURANCE CO

C+   Fair

Major Rating Factors: Fair quality investment portfolio (4.4 on a scale of 0 to 10). Weak profitability index (0.0). Strong capitalization (10.0) based on excellent current risk-adjusted capital (severe loss scenario).
Other Rating Factors: Excellent liquidity (8.1) with ample operational cash flow and liquid investments.
Principal Business: Comp med (100%)
Mem Phys: 18: N/A **17:** N/A **18 MLR** 87.2% **/ 18 Admin Exp** N/A
Enroll(000): Q3 19: 8 **18:** 9 **17:** 4 **Med Exp PMPM:** $353
Principal Investments: Cash and equiv (99%), long-term bonds (1%)
Provider Compensation ($000): Contr fee ($22,875), FFS ($2,350), capitation ($435)
Total Member Encounters: Phys (30,293), non-phys (40,221)
Group Affiliation: HealthFirst Inc
Licensed in: NY
Address: 100 Church St, New York, NY 10007
Phone: (212) 801-6000 **Dom State:** NY **Commenced Bus:** N/A

Data Date	Rating	RACR #1	RACR #2	Total Assets ($mil)	Capital ($mil)	Net Premium ($mil)	Net Income ($mil)
9-19	C+	3.63	3.03	41.7	14.8	39.9	-1.5
9-18	N/A	N/A	N/A	36.5	16.5	26.0	-3.0
2018	C+	3.62	3.01	40.1	14.8	34.2	-5.3
2017	N/A	N/A	N/A	24.5	19.6	1.4	-5.4
2016	N/A	N/A	N/A	25.1	25.0	N/A	N/A
2015	N/A	N/A	N/A	N/A	N/A	N/A	N/A
2014	N/A	N/A	N/A	N/A	N/A	N/A	N/A

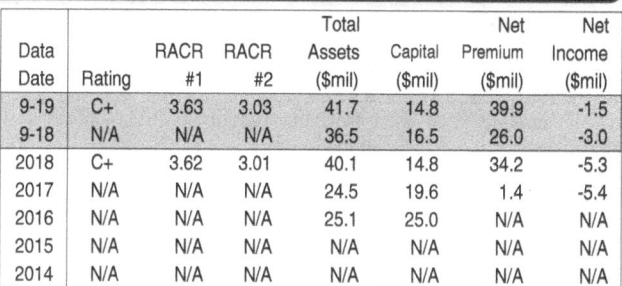

Rating Indexes

HEALTHKEEPERS INC

B-   Good

Major Rating Factors: Fair quality investment portfolio (3.1 on a scale of 0 to 10). Excellent profitability (9.3). Strong capitalization index (8.7) based on excellent current risk-adjusted capital (severe loss scenario).
Other Rating Factors: Excellent overall results on stability tests (7.0) based on healthy premium and capital growth during 2019. Excellent liquidity (7.0) with ample operational cash flow and liquid investments.
Principal Business: Medicaid (51%), comp med (33%), Medicare (16%)
Mem Phys: 19: 33,561 **18:** 29,248 **19 MLR** 81.3% **/ 19 Admin Exp** N/A
Enroll(000): Q2 20: 806 **19:** 708 **18:** 533 **Med Exp PMPM:** $506
Principal Investments: Long-term bonds (38%), cash and equiv (20%), nonaffiliate common stock (15%), other (28%)
Provider Compensation ($000): Bonus arrang ($2,319,272), contr fee ($1,202,492), FFS ($404,325), capitation ($138,768)
Total Member Encounters: Phys (5,442,273), non-phys (7,812,096)
Group Affiliation: Anthem Inc
Licensed in: VA
Address: 2015 STAPLES MILL ROAD, RICHMOND,
Phone: (804) 354-7000 **Dom State:** VA **Commenced Bus:** N/A

Data Date	Rating	RACR #1	RACR #2	Total Assets ($mil)	Capital ($mil)	Net Premium ($mil)	Net Income ($mil)
6-20	B-	2.74	2.29	2,105.3	879.5	2,937.6	204.2
6-19	B	3.45	2.87	1,841.4	778.6	2,532.3	212.5
2019	B	2.98	2.48	1,906.7	904.3	5,161.1	395.5
2018	B	2.57	2.15	1,234.6	566.9	3,484.9	146.8
2017	B	2.43	2.02	1,188.2	595.1	3,460.7	183.9
2016	B+	2.46	2.05	1,132.9	442.7	3,120.5	123.8
2015	A-	2.17	1.81	896.5	340.7	2,806.1	46.2

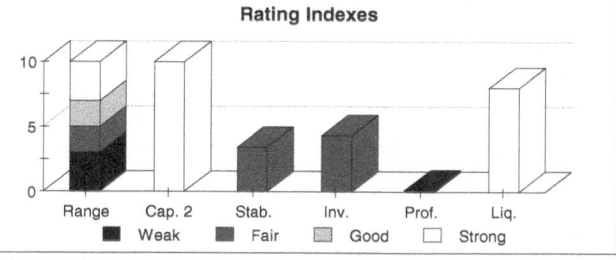

Rating Indexes

HEALTHNOW NY INC *

A   Excellent

Major Rating Factors: Strong capitalization (10.0 on a scale of 0 to 10) based on excellent current risk-adjusted capital (severe loss scenario). High quality investment portfolio (7.4). Excellent liquidity (6.9) with sufficient resources (cash flows and marketable investments) to handle a spike in claims.
Other Rating Factors: Good overall profitability index (6.0).
Principal Business: Comp med (58%), Medicare (30%), Medicaid (8%), FEHB (3%)
Mem Phys: 19: 25,747 **18:** 25,306 **19 MLR** 85.6% **/ 19 Admin Exp** N/A
Enroll(000): Q2 20: 419 **19:** 417 **18:** 402 **Med Exp PMPM:** $488
Principal Investments: Long-term bonds (72%), nonaffiliate common stock (20%), cash and equiv (6%), pref stock (1%), other (2%)
Provider Compensation ($000): Contr fee ($2,163,357), capitation ($244,071), bonus arrang ($14,916)
Total Member Encounters: Phys (3,164,905), non-phys (1,362,148)
Group Affiliation: Highmark Health
Licensed in: NY
Address: 257 West Genesee Street, Buffalo, NY 14202
Phone: (716) 887-6900 **Dom State:** NY **Commenced Bus:** N/A

Data Date	Rating	RACR #1	RACR #2	Total Assets ($mil)	Capital ($mil)	Net Premium ($mil)	Net Income ($mil)
6-20	A	3.81	3.17	1,348.6	676.1	1,423.2	25.0
6-19	N/A	N/A	N/A	N/A	N/A	N/A	N/A
2019	A-	3.99	3.33	1,238.1	702.1	2,825.9	55.1
2018	B-	3.71	3.09	1,113.3	624.6	2,647.1	47.0
2017	B-	3.78	3.15	1,072.5	611.7	2,484.3	54.9
2016	C+	3.37	2.81	1,062.3	541.5	2,311.2	4.2
2015	C+	3.53	2.94	1,037.8	544.4	2,242.3	63.8

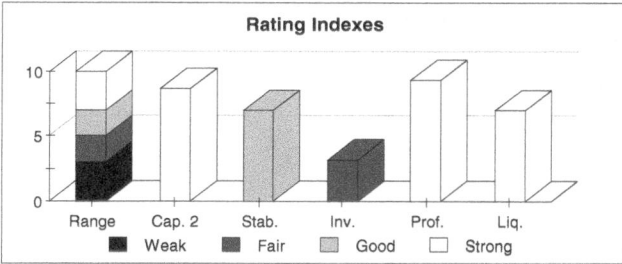

Rating Indexes

HEALTHPARTNERS

B   **Good**

Major Rating Factors: Fair profitability index (4.5 on a scale of 0 to 10). Fair quality investment portfolio (4.8). Strong capitalization index (9.8) based on excellent current risk-adjusted capital (severe loss scenario).
Other Rating Factors: Excellent overall results on stability tests (7.2). Excellent liquidity (7.0) with sufficient resources (cash flows and marketable investments) to handle a spike in claims
Principal Business: Medicaid (50%), comp med (34%), Medicare (13%), dental (3%)
Mem Phys: 19: 85,336 **18:** 74,128 **19 MLR** 91.2% **/ 19 Admin Exp** N/A
Enroll(000): Q2 20: 319 **19:** 319 **18:** 305 **Med Exp PMPM:** $500
Principal Investments: Affiliate common stock (45%), long-term bonds (23%), cash and equiv (19%), nonaffiliate common stock (8%), other (6%)
Provider Compensation ($000): Bonus arrang ($1,647,614), contr fee ($247,254)
Total Member Encounters: Phys (3,137,593), non-phys (424,630)
Group Affiliation: HealthPartners Inc
Licensed in: MN
Address: 8170 33RD AVENUE SOUTH, MINNEAPOLIS,
Phone: (952) 883-6000 **Dom State:** MN **Commenced Bus:** N/A

Data Date	Rating	RACR #1	RACR #2	Total Assets ($mil)	Capital ($mil)	Net Premium ($mil)	Net Income ($mil)
6-20	B	3.59	2.99	1,590.2	988.2	1,048.1	95.1
6-19	B+	3.46	2.88	1,287.0	956.1	1,039.2	35.2
2019	B	3.34	2.79	1,272.5	914.0	2,131.1	19.3
2018	B+	3.42	2.85	1,358.7	944.8	1,950.3	57.6
2017	B+	3.07	2.56	1,300.1	940.1	1,696.6	-36.4
2016	A+	3.40	2.83	1,179.5	911.4	1,371.7	22.2
2015	A+	3.89	3.24	1,247.4	938.1	1,425.0	76.8

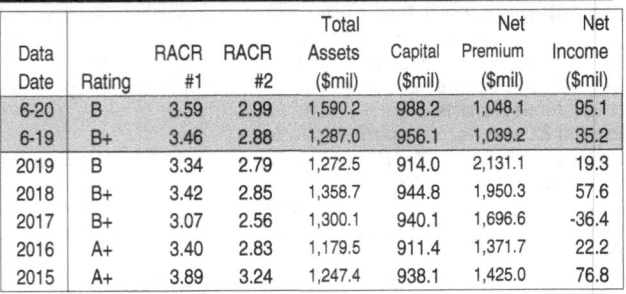

Rating Indexes

HEALTHPARTNERS INS CO *

B+   **Good**

Major Rating Factors: Good overall profitability index (5.9 on a scale of 0 to 10). Strong capitalization (8.1) based on excellent current risk-adjusted capital (severe loss scenario). High quality investment portfolio (9.9).
Other Rating Factors: Excellent liquidity (6.9) with sufficient resources (cash flows and marketable investments) to handle a spike in claims.
Principal Business: Comp med (89%), other (10%)
Mem Phys: 19: 85,336 **18:** 74,128 **19 MLR** 86.4% **/ 19 Admin Exp** N/A
Enroll(000): Q2 20: 653 **19:** 672 **18:** 682 **Med Exp PMPM:** $114
Principal Investments: Long-term bonds (55%), cash and equiv (33%), nonaffiliate common stock (12%)
Provider Compensation ($000): Bonus arrang ($626,468), contr fee ($302,037)
Total Member Encounters: Phys (1,336,747), non-phys (174,019)
Group Affiliation: HealthPartners Inc
Licensed in: IA, MN, NE, ND, SD, WI
Address: 8170 33RD AVENUE SOUTH, MINNEAPOLIS, MN 55440-1309
Phone: (952) 883-6000 **Dom State:** MN **Commenced Bus:** N/A

Data Date	Rating	RACR #1	RACR #2	Total Assets ($mil)	Capital ($mil)	Net Premium ($mil)	Net Income ($mil)
6-20	B+	2.25	1.87	475.5	238.3	533.9	58.3
6-19	B+	3.90	3.25	423.8	270.1	535.9	29.1
2019	B	3.62	3.02	434.8	283.9	1,085.0	41.2
2018	B+	3.39	2.83	375.8	233.2	992.7	31.8
2017	B	2.03	1.69	381.7	202.0	1,075.2	38.6
2016	B	2.33	1.94	372.7	159.1	1,053.8	-11.8
2015	B+	2.35	1.96	331.1	148.8	1,014.0	-10.5

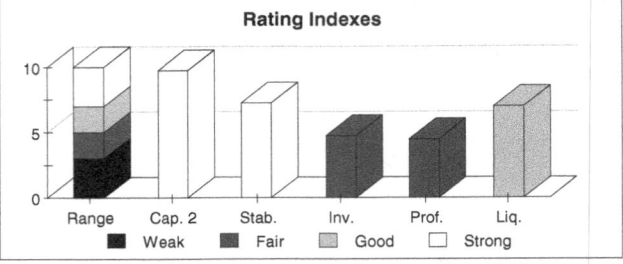

Rating Indexes

HEALTHPARTNERS UNITYPOINT HLTH

D+   **Weak**

Major Rating Factors: Weak profitability index (0.9 on a scale of 0 to 10). Low quality investment portfolio (0.0). Good liquidity (6.3) with sufficient resources (cash flows and marketable investments) to handle a spike in claims.
Other Rating Factors: Strong capitalization (8.7) based on excellent current risk-adjusted capital (severe loss scenario).
Principal Business: Comp med (57%), Medicare (17%)
Mem Phys: 18: 74,128 **17:** 64,829 **18 MLR** 77.5% **/ 18 Admin Exp** N/A
Enroll(000): Q3 19: 58 **18:** 8 **17:** 1 **Med Exp PMPM:** $461
Principal Investments: Cash and equiv (100%)
Provider Compensation ($000): Contr fee ($29,489), bonus arrang ($1,038)
Total Member Encounters: Phys (98,007), non-phys (17,223)
Group Affiliation: HealthPartners UnityPoint Health Inc
Licensed in: IL, IA
Address: 3737 WOODLAND AVE SUITE 310, WEST DES MOINES, IA 50266
Phone: (515) 695-3801 **Dom State:** IA **Commenced Bus:** N/A

Data Date	Rating	RACR #1	RACR #2	Total Assets ($mil)	Capital ($mil)	Net Premium ($mil)	Net Income ($mil)
9-19	D+	2.68	2.23	31.2	12.9	47.5	-6.5
9-18	N/A	N/A	N/A	26.4	15.9	22.0	-3.0
2018	U	2.12	1.77	22.7	13.4	45.1	-5.6
2017	N/A	N/A	N/A	21.7	15.0	15.1	-3.4
2016	N/A	N/A	N/A	19.2	18.4	N/A	-2.5
2015	N/A	N/A	N/A	7.0	7.0	N/A	N/A
2014	N/A	N/A	N/A	N/A	N/A	N/A	N/A

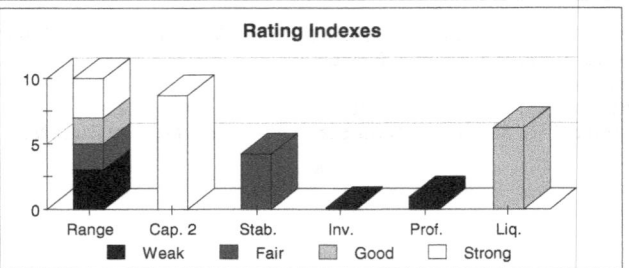

Rating Indexes

HEALTHSPRING L&H INS CO   B-   Good

Major Rating Factors: Fair quality investment portfolio (3.9 on a scale of 0 to 10). Good overall profitability index (5.9). Good liquidity (6.9) with sufficient resources (cash flows and marketable investments) to handle a spike in claims.
Other Rating Factors: Strong capitalization (8.4) based on excellent current risk-adjusted capital (severe loss scenario).
Principal Business: Medicare (78%), Medicaid (22%)
Mem Phys: 19: 70,052 **18:** 57,688 **19 MLR** 82.1% **/ 19 Admin Exp** N/A
Enroll(000): Q2 20: 331 **19:** 301 **18:** 299 **Med Exp PMPM:** $1,020
Principal Investments: Long-term bonds (93%), cash and equiv (7%)
Provider Compensation ($000): FFS ($2,655,446), capitation ($1,138,572)
Total Member Encounters: Phys (11,525,799), non-phys (2,567,235)
Group Affiliation: None
Licensed in: All states except CA, PR
Address: 2800 NORTH LOOP WEST SUITE 50, HOUSTON, TX 77092
Phone: (615) 291-7000 **Dom State:** TX **Commenced Bus:** N/A

Data Date	Rating	RACR #1	RACR #2	Total Assets ($mil)	Capital ($mil)	Net Premium ($mil)	Net Income ($mil)
6-20	B-	2.46	2.05	1,363.0	678.2	2,566.2	85.7
6-19	B-	2.91	2.43	1,131.6	643.5	2,269.3	84.4
2019	B-	2.54	2.11	1,096.6	601.4	4,479.9	148.4
2018	B-	2.56	2.14	1,060.3	562.7	4,142.2	90.3
2017	C+	1.66	1.39	1,047.7	550.7	4,087.0	-21.7
2016	B	2.16	1.80	602.8	280.2	2,367.0	-50.8
2015	B	2.78	2.32	614.0	327.4	2,213.5	46.1

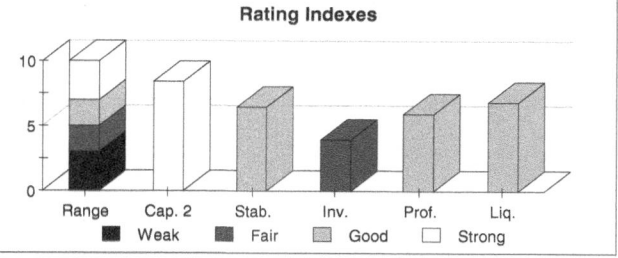

Rating Indexes

HEALTHSPRING OF FLORIDA INC *   B+   Good

Major Rating Factors: Good liquidity (6.8 on a scale of 0 to 10) with sufficient resources (cash flows and marketable investments) to handle a spike in claims. Excellent profitability (8.1). Strong capitalization (7.3) based on excellent current risk-adjusted capital (severe loss scenario).
Other Rating Factors: High quality investment portfolio (7.9).
Principal Business: Medicare (100%)
Mem Phys: 19: 2,006 **18:** 1,822 **19 MLR** 86.3% **/ 19 Admin Exp** N/A
Enroll(000): Q2 20: 55 **19:** 50 **18:** 47 **Med Exp PMPM:** $1,285
Principal Investments: Long-term bonds (93%), cash and equiv (7%)
Provider Compensation ($000): Capitation ($398,819), contr fee ($214,469), FFS ($139,313)
Total Member Encounters: Phys (1,093,697), non-phys (451,205)
Group Affiliation: None
Licensed in: FL
Address: 8600 NW 41ST STREET SUITE 201, DORAL, FL 33166
Phone: (305) 229-7461 **Dom State:** FL **Commenced Bus:** N/A

Data Date	Rating	RACR #1	RACR #2	Total Assets ($mil)	Capital ($mil)	Net Premium ($mil)	Net Income ($mil)
6-20	B+	1.56	1.30	184.2	91.7	495.1	10.9
6-19	B	2.59	2.16	162.5	96.2	430.3	12.8
2019	B	2.02	1.69	132.4	81.4	860.4	22.3
2018	B	2.31	1.92	153.3	85.5	826.4	26.2
2017	B+	1.86	1.55	169.2	95.9	776.1	6.6
2016	B+	2.42	2.02	157.0	89.5	866.7	26.9
2015	B	1.62	1.35	144.1	62.3	886.0	9.2

Rating Indexes

HEALTHSUN HEALTH PLANS INC *   B+   Good

Major Rating Factors: Good liquidity (6.8 on a scale of 0 to 10) with sufficient resources (cash flows and marketable investments) to handle a spike in claims. Excellent profitability (7.6). Strong capitalization (8.5) based on excellent current risk-adjusted capital (severe loss scenario).
Other Rating Factors: High quality investment portfolio (7.7).
Principal Business: Medicare (100%)
Mem Phys: 19: 2,971 **18:** 1,716 **19 MLR** 86.4% **/ 19 Admin Exp** N/A
Enroll(000): Q2 20: 52 **19:** 51 **18:** 47 **Med Exp PMPM:** $1,620
Principal Investments: Long-term bonds (97%), cash and equiv (3%)
Provider Compensation ($000): Capitation ($923,462)
Total Member Encounters: Phys (1,217,206), non-phys (893,084)
Group Affiliation: Anthem Inc
Licensed in: FL
Address: 3250 MARY STREET SUITE 400, COCONUT GROVE, FL 33133
Phone: (305) 448-8100 **Dom State:** FL **Commenced Bus:** N/A

Data Date	Rating	RACR #1	RACR #2	Total Assets ($mil)	Capital ($mil)	Net Premium ($mil)	Net Income ($mil)
6-20	B+	2.59	2.16	299.0	146.1	611.4	14.2
6-19	B-	2.91	2.42	195.9	93.2	545.3	11.3
2019	B	3.34	2.79	242.6	134.0	1,091.2	82.1
2018	B-	2.97	2.48	249.6	95.3	897.0	44.0
2017	C-	N/A	N/A	186.0	71.5	796.7	18.7
2016	N/A	N/A	N/A	134.8	29.9	709.0	N/A
2015	C-	0.62	0.51	130.1	30.8	695.7	23.5

Rating Indexes

HEALTHY ALLIANCE LIFE INS CO — B — Good

Major Rating Factors: Good quality investment portfolio (4.9 on a scale of 0 to 10). Good liquidity (6.9) with sufficient resources (cash flows and marketable investments) to handle a spike in claims. Excellent profitability (8.5).
Other Rating Factors: Strong capitalization (9.0) based on excellent current risk-adjusted capital (severe loss scenario).
Principal Business: Comp med (70%), FEHB (19%), med supp (4%), dental (1%), other (5%)
Mem Phys: 19: 25,164 **18:** 23,445 **19 MLR** 82.3% **/ 19 Admin Exp** N/A
Enroll(000): Q2 20: 636 **19:** 683 **18:** 706 **Med Exp PMPM:** $226
Principal Investments: Long-term bonds (101%), other (12%)
Provider Compensation ($000): Bonus arrang ($1,250,835), contr fee ($453,091), FFS ($101,048), other ($70,463)
Total Member Encounters: Phys (2,246,846), non-phys (2,259,925)
Group Affiliation: Anthem Inc
Licensed in: KS, MO
Address: 1831 CHESTNUT STREET, ST LOUIS, MO 63103-2275
Phone: (314) 923-4444 **Dom State:** MO **Commenced Bus:** N/A

Data Date	Rating	RACR #1	RACR #2	Total Assets ($mil)	Capital ($mil)	Net Premium ($mil)	Net Income ($mil)
6-20	B	2.95	2.46	1,098.8	462.3	982.9	121.5
6-19	B	4.40	3.66	1,060.4	485.3	1,138.6	119.5
2019	B	2.60	2.17	835.2	319.9	2,271.2	183.6
2018	B	3.35	2.79	985.6	365.8	2,303.2	198.6
2017	A	3.23	2.69	1,087.1	489.4	2,566.9	194.3
2016	A-	4.13	3.44	890.1	420.4	1,942.0	142.8
2015	A-	4.25	3.54	829.4	379.6	1,811.5	106.3

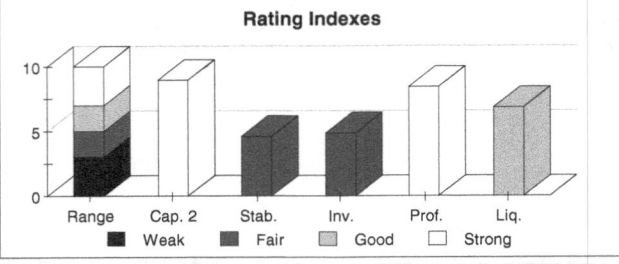

Rating Indexes

HENNEPIN HEALTH — C+ — Fair

Major Rating Factors: Weak profitability index (2.2 on a scale of 0 to 10). Weak overall results on stability tests (2.7). Strong capitalization index (7.2) based on excellent current risk-adjusted capital (severe loss scenario).
Other Rating Factors: High quality investment portfolio (8.4). Excellent liquidity (7.0) with ample operational cash flow and liquid investments.
Principal Business: Medicaid (96%), other (4%)
Mem Phys: 19: 1,737 **18:** 1,628 **19 MLR** 92.3% **/ 19 Admin Exp** N/A
Enroll(000): Q2 20: 28 **19:** 25 **18:** 26 **Med Exp PMPM:** $668
Principal Investments: Cash and equiv (98%), real estate (2%)
Provider Compensation ($000): Contr fee ($210,629), bonus arrang ($344)
Total Member Encounters: Phys (141,594), non-phys (108,213)
Group Affiliation: None
Licensed in: MN
Address: 400 South 4th Street Suite 201, Minneapolis,
Phone: (612) 596-1036 **Dom State:** MN **Commenced Bus:** N/A

Data Date	Rating	RACR #1	RACR #2	Total Assets ($mil)	Capital ($mil)	Net Premium ($mil)	Net Income ($mil)
6-20	C+	1.52	1.27	68.1	35.7	117.1	3.6
6-19	N/A	N/A	N/A	N/A	N/A	N/A	N/A
2019	C+	1.37	1.14	60.7	32.3	213.8	-14.5
2018	B-	2.00	1.66	100.0	46.8	235.0	6.5
2017	C	1.71	1.42	105.6	39.8	231.5	4.8
2016	C-	2.60	2.17	72.1	34.6	127.0	0.6
2015	C-	2.57	2.14	93.0	34.1	143.6	-3.4

Rating Indexes

HERITAGE PROVIDER NETWORK INC — D+ — Weak

Major Rating Factors: Fair capitalization index (4.3 on a scale of 0 to 10) based on weak current risk-adjusted capital (moderate loss scenario). Good overall profitability index (6.1). Good overall results on stability tests (6.7).
Other Rating Factors: Good liquidity (6.9) with sufficient resources (cash flows and marketable investments) to handle a spike in claims.
Principal Business: Managed care (100%)
Mem Phys: 19: N/A **18:** N/A **19 MLR** 94.0% **/ 19 Admin Exp** N/A
Enroll(000): Q2 20: 668 **19:** 697 **18:** 697 **Med Exp PMPM:** $351
Principal Investments ($000): Cash and equiv ($384,745)
Provider Compensation ($000): None
Total Member Encounters: N/A
Group Affiliation: Heritage California Medical Groups
Licensed in: CA
Address: 1 Park Plaza Suite 450, Irvine, CA 92614
Phone: (502) 580-1575 **Dom State:** CA **Commenced Bus:** May 1996

Data Date	Rating	RACR #1	RACR #2	Total Assets ($mil)	Capital ($mil)	Net Premium ($mil)	Net Income ($mil)
6-20	D+	0.69	0.42	606.6	162.8	1,633.3	1.8
6-19	D+	0.74	0.46	582.8	162.8	1,511.0	1.4
2019	D+	0.68	0.42	593.4	161.7	3,082.2	1.9
2018	D	0.70	0.43	623.5	155.7	2,866.4	4.1
2017	D	0.54	0.33	528.0	120.3	2,734.4	2.5
2016	D	0.66	0.41	575.3	127.8	2,432.2	2.3
2015	D	0.69	0.42	661.8	131.5	2,380.8	14.5

Rating Indexes

HIGHMARK BCBSD INC *   B+   Good

Major Rating Factors: Good quality investment portfolio (6.6 on a scale of 0 to 10). Excellent profitability (7.6). Strong capitalization (10.0) based on excellent current risk-adjusted capital (severe loss scenario).
Other Rating Factors: Excellent liquidity (7.1) with ample operational cash flow and liquid investments.
Principal Business: Comp med (76%), FEHB (20%), med supp (3%)
Mem Phys: 19: 18,516   **18:** 15,418   **19 MLR** 76.2%   **/ 19 Admin Exp** N/A
Enroll(000): Q2 20: 100   **19:** 99   **18:** 106   **Med Exp PMPM:** $465
Principal Investments: Long-term bonds (68%), nonaffiliate common stock (25%), cash and equiv (7%), other (1%)
Provider Compensation ($000): Contr fee ($555,140), FFS ($17,337), capitation ($1,759), bonus arrang ($1,066)
Total Member Encounters: Phys (765,556), non-phys (615,936)
Group Affiliation: None
Licensed in: DE
Address: 800 Delaware Avenue, Wilmington, DE 19801
Phone: (302) 421-3000   **Dom State:** DE   **Commenced Bus:** N/A

Data Date	Rating	RACR #1	RACR #2	Total Assets ($mil)	Capital ($mil)	Net Premium ($mil)	Net Income ($mil)
6-20	B+	7.55	6.29	745.7	413.9	331.5	14.7
6-19	B	9.01	7.51	617.0	374.5	387.2	69.4
2019	B	9.58	7.98	641.6	410.4	757.3	98.1
2018	B	7.34	6.12	543.8	304.2	724.5	85.2
2017	B	5.23	4.36	442.7	253.9	634.6	58.4
2016	B-	3.61	3.01	363.0	149.6	705.8	19.1
2015	B-	3.13	2.61	336.9	120.8	638.8	-26.5

Rating Indexes
Range / Cap. 2 / Stab. / Inv. / Prof. / Liq.
■ Weak ■ Fair ▨ Good □ Strong

HIGHMARK CASUALTY INS CO   C   Fair

Major Rating Factors: Fair overall results on stability tests (3.1 on a scale of 0 to 10) including fair financial strength of affiliated Highmark Inc. History of adequate reserve strength (6.8) as reserves have been consistently at an acceptable level.
Other Rating Factors: Good overall profitability index (6.7). Good expense controls. Return on equity has been fair, averaging 5.2% over the past five years. Good liquidity (5.1) with sufficient resources (cash flows and marketable investments) to handle a spike in claims. Strong long-term capitalization index (9.9) based on excellent current risk adjusted capital (severe and moderate loss scenarios), despite some fluctuation in capital levels.
Principal Business: Group accident & health (100%).
Principal Investments: Investment grade bonds (66%), misc. investments (25%), and non investment grade bonds (9%).
Investments in Affiliates: None
Group Affiliation: Highmark Inc
Licensed in: AL, FL, GA, ID, IL, IN, KS, KY, MD, MI, MS, MO, NV, NJ, NM, NC, OR, PA, SC, TX, UT, VA, WA, WV
Commenced Business: February 1978
Address: Fifth Ave Place 120 Fifth Ave, Pittsburgh, PA 15222-3099
Phone: (800) 328-5433   **Domicile State:** PA   **NAIC Code:** 35599

Data Date	Rating	RACR #1	RACR #2	Loss Ratio %	Total Assets ($mil)	Capital ($mil)	Net Premium ($mil)	Net Income ($mil)
6-20	C	4.95	2.82	N/A	341.4	193.4	136.1	7.4
6-19	C	5.08	2.93	N/A	314.1	196.2	138.7	4.8
2019	C	5.33	3.02	71.2	293.4	187.3	277.7	15.4
2018	C	5.92	3.40	69.1	293.1	189.3	244.9	15.5
2017	C	7.00	3.98	78.9	268.1	185.3	185.7	6.1
2016	C	4.28	2.84	74.5	274.7	179.2	218.0	1.9
2015	C	2.56	1.77	76.6	457.2	173.1	282.9	7.2

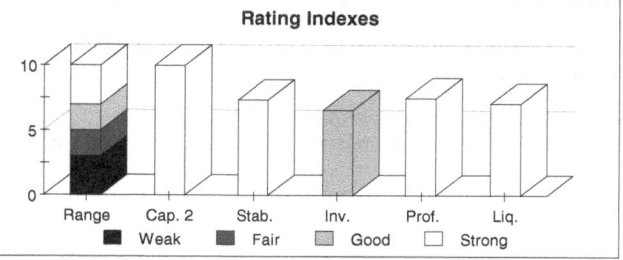

Rating Indexes
Ranges / Cap. 2 / Stab. / Res. / Prof. / Liq.
■ Weak ■ Fair ▨ Good □ Strong

HIGHMARK INC   B   Good

Major Rating Factors: Good quality investment portfolio (6.8 on a scale of 0 to 10). Fair profitability index (4.3). Strong capitalization (10.0) based on excellent current risk-adjusted capital (severe loss scenario).
Other Rating Factors: Excellent liquidity (8.1) with ample operational cash flow and liquid investments.
Principal Business: Comp med (40%), Medicare (35%), FEHB (12%), Medicaid (8%), med supp (3%), other (1%)
Mem Phys: 19: 104,889   **18:** 99,130   **19 MLR** 39.9%   **/ 19 Admin Exp** N/A
Enroll(000): Q2 20: 823   **19:** 819   **18:** 820   **Med Exp PMPM:** $333
Principal Investments: Long-term bonds (41%), nonaffiliate common stock (22%), affiliate common stock (7%), cash and equiv (3%), real estate (1%), mortgs (1%), other (25%)
Provider Compensation ($000): Contr fee ($2,932,777), FFS ($284,273), bonus arrang ($25,218), capitation ($281)
Total Member Encounters: Phys (6,600,946), non-phys (4,552,193)
Group Affiliation: None
Licensed in: PA
Address: 1800 Center Street, Camp Hill, PA 17011
Phone: (412) 544-7000   **Dom State:** PA   **Commenced Bus:** N/A

Data Date	Rating	RACR #1	RACR #2	Total Assets ($mil)	Capital ($mil)	Net Premium ($mil)	Net Income ($mil)
6-20	B	4.60	3.83	7,956.2	4,126.8	4,689.3	425.9
6-19	C	4.11	3.42	7,028.3	3,897.5	3,814.8	132.2
2019	C+	4.11	3.43	7,159.1	3,676.4	8,223.3	34.0
2018	C	3.91	3.26	6,954.8	3,704.4	7,988.7	163.3
2017	C	3.99	3.32	6,923.1	3,799.4	7,962.6	660.1
2016	C	3.24	2.70	7,526.6	3,886.3	8,742.8	-73.9
2015	C	3.18	2.65	7,565.3	3,860.6	8,745.5	-405.2

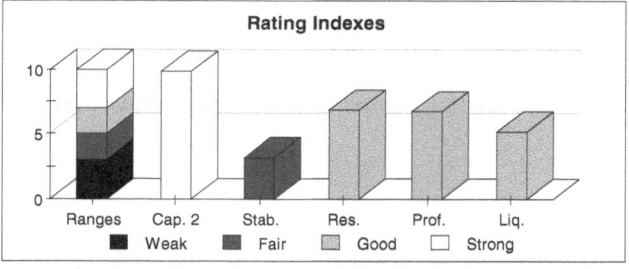

Rating Indexes
Range / Cap. 2 / Stab. / Inv. / Prof. / Liq.
■ Weak ■ Fair ▨ Good □ Strong

HIGHMARK WEST VIRGINIA INC
B   **Good**

Major Rating Factors: Good overall profitability index (6.8 on a scale of 0 to 10). Good quality investment portfolio (6.7). Strong capitalization (10.0) based on excellent current risk-adjusted capital (severe loss scenario).
Other Rating Factors: Excellent liquidity (7.0) with sufficient resources (cash flows and marketable investments) to handle a spike in claims.
Principal Business: Comp med (60%), FEHB (34%), Medicare (2%), med supp (2%), other (2%)
Mem Phys: 19: 27,021   **18:** 23,227   **19 MLR** 82.2%   **/ 19 Admin Exp** N/A
Enroll(000): Q2 20: 160   **19:** 161   **18:** 164   **Med Exp PMPM:** $506
Principal Investments: Long-term bonds (75%), nonaffiliate common stock (7%), cash and equiv (5%), affiliate common stock (3%), real estate (2%), other (8%)
Provider Compensation ($000): Contr fee ($960,960), FFS ($16,550), bonus arrang ($8,093), capitation ($215)
Total Member Encounters: Phys (1,144,944), non-phys (1,032,576)
Group Affiliation: None
Licensed in: PA, WV
Address: 614 Market Street, Parkersburg, WV 26101
Phone: (304) 424-7700   **Dom State:** WV   **Commenced Bus:** N/A

Data Date	Rating	RACR #1	RACR #2	Total Assets ($mil)	Capital ($mil)	Net Premium ($mil)	Net Income ($mil)
6-20	B	7.16	5.97	1,165.1	607.0	602.1	44.2
6-19	B	7.11	5.92	912.0	546.8	603.9	42.4
2019	B	7.87	6.56	1,046.1	560.7	1,201.5	50.0
2018	B	6.17	5.15	837.0	473.3	1,197.8	95.0
2017	B	5.49	4.57	762.5	421.9	1,171.1	72.3
2016	B	4.62	3.85	677.2	314.2	1,192.5	-4.2
2015	B	4.59	3.82	617.5	290.2	1,121.8	-12.6

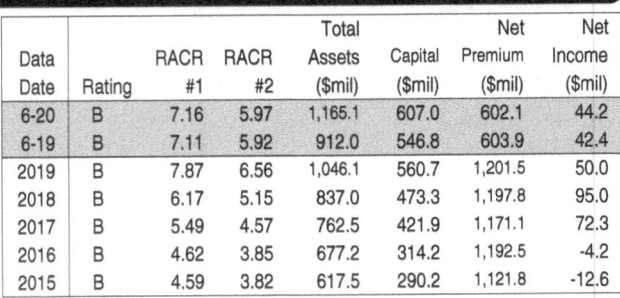

Rating Indexes

HM LIFE INS CO
B   **Good**

Major Rating Factors: Good quality investment portfolio (5.0 on a scale of 0 to 10) with no exposure to mortgages and small junk bond holdings. Good overall profitability (6.7). Return on equity has been fair, averaging 6.6%. Good liquidity (6.9) with sufficient resources to handle a spike in claims.
Other Rating Factors: Good overall results on stability tests (5.9) good operational trends and excellent risk diversification. Strong capitalization (10.0) based on excellent risk adjusted capital (severe loss scenario).
Principal Business: Group health insurance (96%) and reinsurance (4%).
Principal Investments: NonCMO investment grade bonds (42%), common & preferred stock (20%), CMOs and structured securities (18%), and noninv. grade bonds (9%).
Investments in Affiliates: None
Group Affiliation: Highmark Inc
Licensed in: All states except NY, PR
Commenced Business: May 1981
Address: Fifth AvePlace 120 Fifth Ave, Pittsburgh, PA 15222-3099
Phone: (800) 328-5433   **Domicile State:** PA   **NAIC Code:** 93440

Data Date	Rating	RACR #1	RACR #2	Total Assets ($mil)	Capital ($mil)	Net Premium ($mil)	Net Income ($mil)
6-20	B	4.88	3.21	789.0	445.7	195.9	15.8
6-19	B	4.66	3.08	752.7	417.3	200.4	22.1
2019	B	4.74	3.11	727.2	431.5	398.3	44.4
2018	B	4.28	2.84	677.8	391.3	421.9	56.1
2017	B-	3.20	2.29	674.0	360.1	720.9	-23.8
2016	B-	3.39	2.43	643.3	360.7	673.4	17.8
2015	B	3.73	2.73	620.8	348.6	640.3	37.3

Rating Indexes

HM LIFE INS CO OF NEW YORK
B-   **Good**

Major Rating Factors: Good overall results on stability tests (5.0 on a scale of 0 to 10) despite negative cash flow from operations for 2019. Other stability subfactors include good operational trends and excellent risk diversification. Good liquidity (6.7) with sufficient resources to handle a spike in claims. Fair profitability (3.1).
Other Rating Factors: Strong capitalization (10.0) based on excellent risk adjusted capital (severe loss scenario). High quality investment portfolio (8.3).
Principal Business: N/A
Principal Investments: NonCMO investment grade bonds (54%) and CMOs and structured securities (36%).
Investments in Affiliates: None
Group Affiliation: Highmark Inc
Licensed in: DC, NY, RI
Commenced Business: March 1997
Address: 420 Fifth Avenue 3rd Floor, New York, NY 10119
Phone: (800) 328-5433   **Domicile State:** NY   **NAIC Code:** 60213

Data Date	Rating	RACR #1	RACR #2	Total Assets ($mil)	Capital ($mil)	Net Premium ($mil)	Net Income ($mil)
6-20	B-	5.24	3.59	66.2	43.6	19.0	2.4
6-19	B	5.05	3.46	61.1	39.5	19.4	-4.5
2019	B-	4.95	3.43	61.0	41.2	39.2	-2.8
2018	B	5.77	3.94	66.2	43.8	36.2	-1.1
2017	B	3.64	2.90	67.3	45.1	72.8	5.1
2016	B	3.23	2.57	67.0	40.2	72.4	1.7
2015	B	3.33	2.64	65.7	38.9	66.2	-1.1

Adverse Trends in Operations

Decrease in capital during 2019 (6%)
Decrease in asset base during 2018 (2%)
Decrease in capital during 2018 (3%)
Change in asset mix during 2018 (4%)
Decrease in premium volume from 2017 to 2018 (50%)

HMO COLORADO *

B+ **Good**

Major Rating Factors: Good overall results on stability tests (6.2 on a scale of 0 to 10). Excellent profitability (7.4). Strong capitalization index (9.3) based on excellent current risk-adjusted capital (severe loss scenario).
Other Rating Factors: High quality investment portfolio (9.0). Excellent liquidity (7.0) with ample operational cash flow and liquid investments.
Principal Business: Comp med (81%), Medicare (19%)
Mem Phys: 19: 21,890 **18:** 21,963 **19 MLR** 80.4% **/ 19 Admin Exp** N/A
Enroll(000): Q2 20: 123 **19:** 99 **18:** 89 **Med Exp PMPM:** $596
Principal Investments: Long-term bonds (88%), cash and equiv (6%), real estate (2%), other (4%)
Provider Compensation ($000): Bonus arrang ($457,558), capitation ($145,890), contr fee ($52,159), FFS ($41,507)
Total Member Encounters: Phys (609,582), non-phys (431,349)
Group Affiliation: Anthem Inc
Licensed in: CO, NV
Address: 700 BROADWAY, DENVER,
Phone: (303) 831-2131 **Dom State:** CO **Commenced Bus:** N/A

Data Date	Rating	RACR #1	RACR #2	Total Assets ($mil)	Capital ($mil)	Net Premium ($mil)	Net Income ($mil)
6-20	B+	3.16	2.64	442.7	197.3	430.7	45.1
6-19	B	5.57	4.64	393.4	220.6	448.4	60.8
2019	B+	3.41	2.84	347.0	153.1	890.6	72.2
2018	B	4.08	3.40	285.3	160.6	820.6	96.8
2017	B-	1.19	0.99	185.4	71.0	651.2	18.2
2016	B-	2.85	2.38	153.5	51.4	285.2	2.3
2015	C+	2.53	2.11	102.1	37.0	240.4	-4.1

Rating Indexes

HMO LOUISIANA INC *

A+ **Excellent**

Major Rating Factors: Strong capitalization index (10.0 on a scale of 0 to 10) based on excellent current risk-adjusted capital (severe loss scenario). Excellent overall results on stability tests (7.4). Excellent liquidity (6.9) with sufficient resources (cash flows and marketable investments) to handle a spike in claims.
Other Rating Factors: Good quality investment portfolio (6.2). Fair profitability index (3.9).
Principal Business: Comp med (91%), Medicare (9%)
Mem Phys: 19: 36,695 **18:** 33,837 **19 MLR** 87.0% **/ 19 Admin Exp** N/A
Enroll(000): Q2 20: 181 **19:** 176 **18:** 175 **Med Exp PMPM:** $438
Principal Investments: Long-term bonds (61%), nonaffiliate common stock (35%), cash and equiv (3%), other (1%)
Provider Compensation ($000): FFS ($551,459), contr fee ($396,224), capitation ($2,123)
Total Member Encounters: Phys (1,921,357), non-phys (1,231,546)
Group Affiliation: None
Licensed in: LA
Address: 5525 Reitz Avenue, Baton Rouge,
Phone: (225) 295-3307 **Dom State:** LA **Commenced Bus:** N/A

Data Date	Rating	RACR #1	RACR #2	Total Assets ($mil)	Capital ($mil)	Net Premium ($mil)	Net Income ($mil)
6-20	A+	4.45	3.71	862.1	445.3	597.9	42.4
6-19	A+	6.80	5.66	819.2	452.3	554.3	25.1
2019	A+	5.36	4.47	781.7	424.2	1,083.6	-6.1
2018	A+	6.28	5.23	762.3	417.7	1,141.4	53.9
2017	A+	4.98	4.15	699.4	383.9	940.5	18.1
2016	A+	7.53	6.27	570.5	347.5	719.2	10.3
2015	A+	8.70	7.25	513.2	334.4	584.5	-28.8

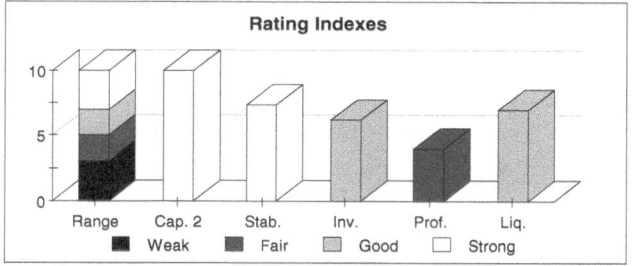

Rating Indexes

HMO MINNESOTA

B **Good**

Major Rating Factors: Good quality investment portfolio (6.8 on a scale of 0 to 10). Good liquidity (6.8) with sufficient resources (cash flows and marketable investments) to handle a spike in claims. Fair profitability index (4.0).
Other Rating Factors: Fair overall results on stability tests (4.9). Strong capitalization index (10.0) based on excellent current risk-adjusted capital (severe loss scenario).
Principal Business: Medicaid (93%), comp med (7%)
Mem Phys: 19: 41,922 **18:** 32,563 **19 MLR** 90.6% **/ 19 Admin Exp** N/A
Enroll(000): Q2 20: 408 **19:** 375 **18:** 385 **Med Exp PMPM:** $464
Principal Investments: Long-term bonds (59%), cash and equiv (27%), nonaffiliate common stock (14%)
Provider Compensation ($000): Contr fee ($1,233,738), bonus arrang ($747,503), FFS ($191,025)
Total Member Encounters: Phys (2,375,803), non-phys (2,894,108)
Group Affiliation: Aware Integrated Inc
Licensed in: MN
Address: 3535 Blue Cross Road, Eagan,
Phone: (651) 662-8000 **Dom State:** MN **Commenced Bus:** N/A

Data Date	Rating	RACR #1	RACR #2	Total Assets ($mil)	Capital ($mil)	Net Premium ($mil)	Net Income ($mil)
6-20	B	3.80	3.16	1,153.1	639.1	1,219.3	33.7
6-19	C+	4.22	3.52	1,295.2	627.5	1,149.4	19.9
2019	B	4.33	3.61	1,137.8	621.0	2,315.7	7.1
2018	C+	3.96	3.30	1,103.2	587.4	2,445.3	141.0
2017	C	2.57	2.14	1,011.3	473.0	2,406.5	32.2
2016	C	3.46	2.88	858.3	426.8	1,816.2	-156.7
2015	B-	9.49	7.91	825.1	570.2	895.0	52.0

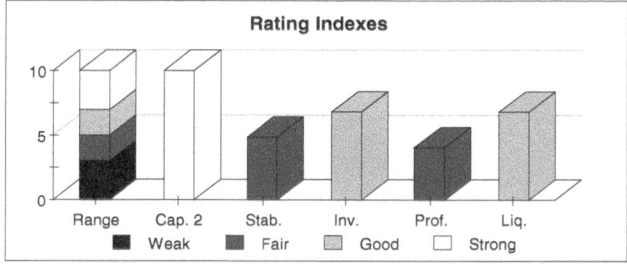

Rating Indexes

HMO MISSOURI INC   C   Fair

Major Rating Factors: Weak overall results on stability tests (2.7 on a scale of 0 to 10) based on a significant 41% decrease in enrollment during the period, a steep decline in capital during 2019. Excellent profitability (7.7). Strong capitalization index (10.0) based on excellent current risk-adjusted capital (severe loss scenario).

Other Rating Factors: High quality investment portfolio (9.3). Excellent liquidity (7.4) with ample operational cash flow and liquid investments.

Principal Business: FEHB (55%), comp med (44%), Medicare (1%)

Mem Phys: 19: 20,298 **18:** 19,000 **19 MLR** 88.3% **/ 19 Admin Exp** N/A

Enroll(000): Q2 20: 16 **19:** 17 **18:** 29 **Med Exp PMPM:** $454

Principal Investments: Long-term bonds (58%), cash and equiv (41%), other (1%)

Provider Compensation ($000): Bonus arrang ($72,833), contr fee ($22,771), FFS ($7,043), capitation ($63)

Total Member Encounters: Phys (89,581), non-phys (92,072)

Group Affiliation: Anthem Inc

Licensed in: IL, MO

Address: 1831 CHESTNUT STREET, ST. LOUIS,

Phone: (314) 923-4444 **Dom State:** MO **Commenced Bus:** N/A

Data Date	Rating	RACR #1	RACR #2	Total Assets ($mil)	Capital ($mil)	Net Premium ($mil)	Net Income ($mil)
6-20	C	3.61	3.01	73.1	28.7	48.3	3.5
6-19	B	3.74	3.12	88.5	37.0	53.6	1.3
2019	B-	5.26	4.39	84.7	24.6	106.3	6.8
2018	B	3.60	3.00	88.2	35.6	207.1	5.8
2017	C+	1.88	1.57	79.0	29.7	182.1	8.8
2016	B	6.74	5.61	75.1	45.2	149.5	8.8
2015	B-	7.08	5.90	68.9	38.3	134.8	9.9

Rating Indexes

HMO PARTNERS INC *   A+   Excellent

Major Rating Factors: Strong capitalization index (9.3 on a scale of 0 to 10) based on excellent current risk-adjusted capital (severe loss scenario). High quality investment portfolio (9.5). Excellent overall results on stability tests (7.1) despite a decline in enrollment during 2019.

Other Rating Factors: Good overall profitability index (5.1). Fair liquidity (4.2) as cash resources may not be adequate to cover a spike in claims.

Principal Business: Comp med (90%), Medicare (10%)

Mem Phys: 19: 18,783 **18:** 17,795 **19 MLR** 121.2% **/ 19 Admin Exp** N/A

Enroll(000): Q2 20: 54 **19:** 59 **18:** 69 **Med Exp PMPM:** $345

Principal Investments: Long-term bonds (47%), cash and equiv (37%), nonaffiliate common stock (6%), other (10%)

Provider Compensation ($000): Bonus arrang ($176,429), contr fee ($78,110), FFS ($2,092)

Total Member Encounters: Phys (58,735), non-phys (73,890)

Group Affiliation: HMO Partners Inc

Licensed in: AR

Address: 320 West Capitol, Little Rock,

Phone: (501) 221-1800 **Dom State:** AR **Commenced Bus:** N/A

Data Date	Rating	RACR #1	RACR #2	Total Assets ($mil)	Capital ($mil)	Net Premium ($mil)	Net Income ($mil)
6-20	A+	3.19	2.66	129.5	69.8	95.4	6.4
6-19	A+	5.10	4.25	138.8	74.9	106.8	6.2
2019	A+	4.86	4.05	149.5	68.5	211.9	-0.9
2018	A+	4.64	3.87	128.3	68.1	226.8	6.4
2017	A+	N/A	N/A	129.6	67.5	206.7	6.7
2016	A+	4.93	4.11	114.1	58.3	191.1	0.7
2015	A+	5.38	4.48	113.7	56.7	177.3	4.8

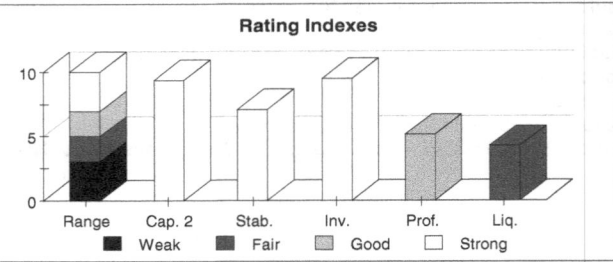

Rating Indexes

HN1 THERAPY NETWORK NEW JERSEY LLC   C+   Fair

Major Rating Factors: Fair capitalization (4.7 on a scale of 0 to 10) based on fair current risk-adjusted capital (moderate loss scenario). Excellent profitability (7.9). High quality investment portfolio (9.9).

Other Rating Factors: Excellent liquidity (8.8) with ample operational cash flow and liquid investments.

Principal Business: Medicaid (94%), Medicare (6%)

Mem Phys: 19: 429 **18:** 362 **19 MLR** 55.6% **/ 19 Admin Exp** N/A

Enroll(000): **19:** 191 **18:** 182 **Med Exp PMPM:** $0

Principal Investments: Cash and equiv (100%)

Provider Compensation ($000): FFS ($1,340), bonus arrang ($99)

Total Member Encounters: N/A

Group Affiliation: HN1 Therapy Network, LLC

Licensed in: NJ

Address: 801 E Hallandale Beach Blv 200, Fort Lauderdale,

Phone: (305) 614-0109 **Dom State:** NJ **Commenced Bus:** N/A

Data Date	Rating	RACR #1	RACR #2	Total Assets ($mil)	Capital ($mil)	Net Premium ($mil)	Net Income ($mil)
2019	C+	0.89	0.74	2.7	2.5	2.7	0.1
2018	C	0.83	0.69	2.6	2.3	2.7	0.5
2017	C-	N/A	N/A	2.8	2.5	2.9	0.9
2016	C-	0.86	0.71	2.8	2.3	3.0	0.9
2015	N/A	N/A	N/A	3.7	3.0	3.7	1.6

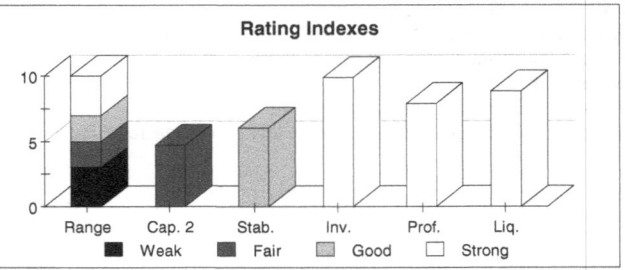

Rating Indexes

HNE INS CO   B-   Good

Major Rating Factors: Strong capitalization (10.0 on a scale of 0 to 10) based on excellent current risk-adjusted capital (severe loss scenario). High quality investment portfolio (9.9). Excellent liquidity (8.5) with ample operational cash flow and liquid investments.
Other Rating Factors: Weak profitability index (1.9).
Principal Business: Med supp (100%)
Mem Phys: 19: 5,768 **18:** 5,660 **19 MLR** 88.1% **/ 19 Admin Exp** N/A
Enroll(000): Q2 20: 1 **19:** 1 **18:** 1 **Med Exp PMPM:** $152
Principal Investments: Cash and equiv (100%)
Provider Compensation ($000): Bonus arrang ($1,440)
Total Member Encounters: Phys (7,606), non-phys (936)
Group Affiliation: Baystate Health Inc
Licensed in: MA
Address: 1 Monarch Place Suite 1500, Springfield MA, MA 1144
Phone: (413) 787-4000 **Dom State:** MA **Commenced Bus:** N/A

Data Date	Rating	RACR #1	RACR #2	Total Assets ($mil)	Capital ($mil)	Net Premium ($mil)	Net Income ($mil)
6-20	B-	15.37	12.81	5.4	4.6	1.4	-0.4
6-19	B	29.99	24.99	5.5	5.2	0.8	0.1
2019	B	23.09	19.24	5.7	5.1	1.8	0.0
2018	B-	28.44	23.70	5.4	5.1	1.4	0.1
2017	C	N/A	N/A	5.1	5.0	0.7	0.1
2016	D+	68.24	56.87	5.0	4.9	0.5	0.1
2015	D+	65.74	54.79	5.0	4.9	0.4	0.0

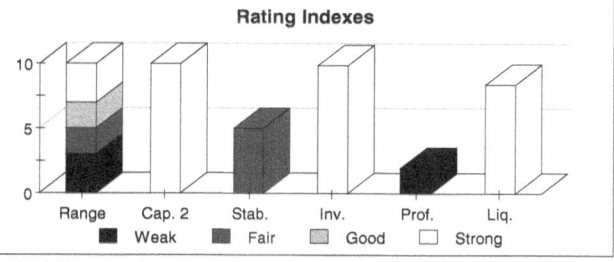

HOME STATE HEALTH PLAN INC   C-   Fair

Major Rating Factors: Fair liquidity (3.9 on a scale of 0 to 10) as cash resources may not be adequate to cover a spike in claims. Weak profitability index (1.1). Strong capitalization (7.5) based on excellent current risk-adjusted capital (severe loss scenario).
Other Rating Factors: High quality investment portfolio (8.4).
Principal Business: Medicaid (99%)
Mem Phys: 19: 27,032 **18:** 16,281 **19 MLR** 98.8% **/ 19 Admin Exp** N/A
Enroll(000): Q2 20: 225 **19:** 204 **18:** 235 **Med Exp PMPM:** $300
Principal Investments: Long-term bonds (78%), cash and equiv (18%), affiliate common stock (5%)
Provider Compensation ($000): Contr fee ($559,797), salary ($161,708), bonus arrang ($35,419), capitation ($17,416)
Total Member Encounters: Phys (171,804), non-phys (255,151)
Group Affiliation: None
Licensed in: MO
Address: 11720 Borman Drive, St Louis, MO 63146
Phone: (314) 725-4477 **Dom State:** MO **Commenced Bus:** N/A

Data Date	Rating	RACR #1	RACR #2	Total Assets ($mil)	Capital ($mil)	Net Premium ($mil)	Net Income ($mil)
6-20	C-	1.78	1.48	226.3	96.5	417.9	29.2
6-19	C-	2.29	1.91	193.5	91.7	390.6	-18.4
2019	C-	1.87	1.56	203.1	68.7	787.7	-50.2
2018	C-	2.68	2.23	227.3	108.4	914.1	1.0
2017	C-	1.31	1.10	195.5	76.4	729.3	-34.9
2016	C-	2.21	1.84	102.3	43.4	344.4	-12.9
2015	C-	2.35	1.96	86.4	34.3	266.6	-15.6

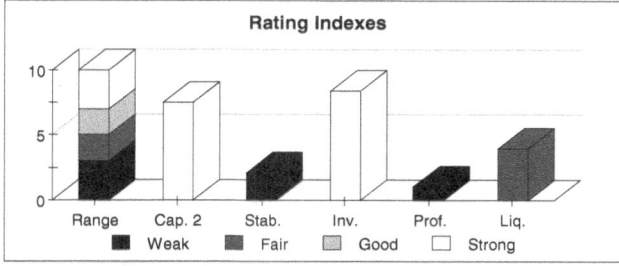

HOMETOWN HEALTH PLAN INC   D   Weak

Major Rating Factors: Fair profitability index (4.8 on a scale of 0 to 10). Good overall results on stability tests (5.2). Strong capitalization index (8.0) based on excellent current risk-adjusted capital (severe loss scenario).
Other Rating Factors: High quality investment portfolio (9.7). Excellent liquidity (7.1) with ample operational cash flow and liquid investments.
Principal Business: Medicare (89%), comp med (11%)
Mem Phys: 19: 4,045 **18:** 3,894 **19 MLR** 86.2% **/ 19 Admin Exp** N/A
Enroll(000): Q2 20: 24 **19:** 27 **18:** 27 **Med Exp PMPM:** $669
Principal Investments: Cash and equiv (59%), long-term bonds (30%), real estate (10%)
Provider Compensation ($000): FFS ($207,864), capitation ($11,069)
Total Member Encounters: Phys (343,158), non-phys (248,417)
Group Affiliation: None
Licensed in: NV
Address: 830 Harvard Way, Reno,
Phone: (775) 982-3100 **Dom State:** NV **Commenced Bus:** N/A

Data Date	Rating	RACR #1	RACR #2	Total Assets ($mil)	Capital ($mil)	Net Premium ($mil)	Net Income ($mil)
6-20	D	2.13	1.78	108.3	59.8	105.4	3.8
6-19	D	1.65	1.37	107.6	49.8	126.3	14.1
2019	D	2.25	1.87	104.2	56.7	248.1	19.7
2018	D	1.13	0.94	91.8	35.9	259.5	-16.0
2017	C	1.29	1.07	94.6	41.3	275.3	12.7
2016	C-	1.01	0.84	86.1	30.6	266.5	-7.5
2015	C-	1.29	1.07	79.0	38.9	271.5	2.7

HOMETOWN HEALTH PROVIDERS INS CO

B-   **Good**

Major Rating Factors: Good overall profitability index (6.7 on a scale of 0 to 10). Strong capitalization (8.0) based on excellent current risk-adjusted capital (severe loss scenario). High quality investment portfolio (9.2).
Other Rating Factors: Excellent liquidity (7.0) with ample operational cash flow and liquid investments.
Principal Business: Comp med (100%)
Mem Phys: 19: 4,053   **18:** 3,899   **19 MLR** 77.3%   **/ 19 Admin Exp** N/A
Enroll(000): Q2 20: 30   **19:** 33   **18:** 39   **Med Exp PMPM:** $370
Principal Investments: Cash and equiv (51%), long-term bonds (37%), real estate (13%)
Provider Compensation ($000): FFS ($143,503), capitation ($969)
Total Member Encounters: Phys (219,157), non-phys (105,227)
Group Affiliation: None
Licensed in: NV
Address: 10315 Professional Circle, RENO, NV 89521
Phone: (775) 982-3100   **Dom State:** NV   **Commenced Bus:** N/A

Data Date	Rating	RACR #1	RACR #2	Total Assets ($mil)	Capital ($mil)	Net Premium ($mil)	Net Income ($mil)
6-20	B-	2.12	1.77	85.6	43.5	87.2	1.2
6-19	C+	2.21	1.84	79.8	40.4	89.7	7.7
2019	C+	2.45	2.04	78.2	43.4	184.2	10.5
2018	C+	1.73	1.44	68.5	33.3	180.5	4.9
2017	B-	1.79	1.49	60.0	28.8	133.3	-0.5
2016	B-	2.75	2.29	50.3	30.9	97.4	0.2
2015	B-	3.48	2.90	45.6	30.9	72.4	0.8

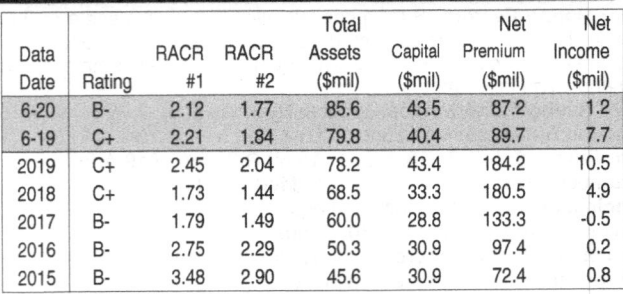

Rating Indexes

HOOSIER MOTOR MUTUAL INS CO

B   **Good**

Major Rating Factors: Good profitability index (4.9 on a scale of 0 to 10). Good quality investment portfolio (5.5). Strong capitalization (10.0) based on excellent current risk-adjusted capital (severe loss scenario).
Other Rating Factors: Excellent liquidity (10.0) with ample operational cash flow and liquid investments.
Principal Business: Medicare (100%)
Mem Phys: 19: N/A   **18:** N/A   **19 MLR** -0.0%   **/ 19 Admin Exp** N/A
Enroll(000): Q2 20: 431   **19:** 453   **18:** 446   **Med Exp PMPM:** N/A
Principal Investments: Long-term bonds (42%), nonaffiliate common stock (42%), real estate (11%), cash and equiv (5%)
Provider Compensation ($000): None
Total Member Encounters: N/A
Group Affiliation: None
Licensed in: IN
Address: 3750 Guion Road, Indianapolis, IN 46240-2587
Phone: (317) 923-1500   **Dom State:** IN   **Commenced Bus:** N/A

Data Date	Rating	RACR #1	RACR #2	Total Assets ($mil)	Capital ($mil)	Net Premium ($mil)	Net Income ($mil)
6-20	B	8.43	7.03	11.7	11.4	0.3	1.3
6-19	N/A	N/A	N/A	N/A	N/A	N/A	N/A
2019	C+	7.60	6.33	10.7	10.3	0.6	-0.3
2018	C+	7.98	6.65	10.5	10.0	0.6	-0.4
2017	B-	7.96	6.64	11.4	10.8	0.6	0.0
2016	C+	10.33	8.61	11.4	10.7	0.6	-0.3
2015	C-	10.58	8.81	11.2	10.8	0.6	-0.2

Rating Indexes

HOPKINS HEALTH ADV INC

E   **Very Weak**

Major Rating Factors: Weak profitability index (0.4 on a scale of 0 to 10). Poor capitalization (0.6) based on weak current risk-adjusted capital (moderate loss scenario). Good liquidity (5.9) with sufficient resources (cash flows and marketable investments) to handle a spike in claims.
Other Rating Factors: High quality investment portfolio (9.9).
Principal Business: Medicare (100%)
Mem Phys: 19: N/A   **18:** N/A   **19 MLR** 108.6%   **/ 19 Admin Exp** N/A
Enroll(000): Q2 20: 22   **19:** 20   **18:** 13   **Med Exp PMPM:** $1,077
Principal Investments: Cash and equiv (99%), other (1%)
Provider Compensation ($000): Contr fee ($233,015), capitation ($2,140)
Total Member Encounters: N/A
Group Affiliation: None
Licensed in: MD
Address: 7231 Parkway Drive, Hanover, MD 21076
Phone: (410) 424-4718   **Dom State:** MD   **Commenced Bus:** N/A

Data Date	Rating	RACR #1	RACR #2	Total Assets ($mil)	Capital ($mil)	Net Premium ($mil)	Net Income ($mil)
6-20	E	0.36	0.30	76.5	11.4	151.1	-9.2
6-19	N/A	N/A	N/A	N/A	N/A	N/A	N/A
2019	D	0.71	0.59	80.8	22.5	230.3	-36.9
2018	E+	0.84	0.70	61.5	16.5	137.8	-32.1
2017	E	N/A	N/A	38.5	8.7	85.2	-23.8
2016	D+	0.69	0.57	22.4	6.1	42.4	-19.7
2015	N/A	N/A	N/A	1.9	1.9	N/A	N/A

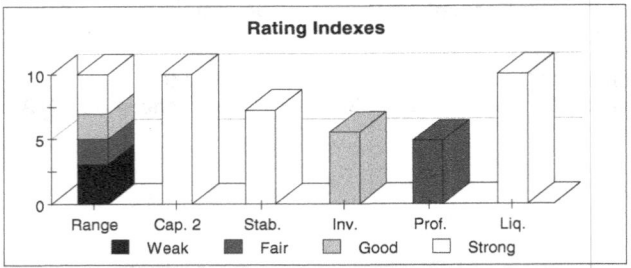

Rating Indexes

HORIZON HEALTHCARE OF NEW JERSEY INC   C+   Fair

Major Rating Factors: Good overall profitability index (5.4 on a scale of 0 to 10). Good overall results on stability tests (5.9). Weak liquidity (2.1) as a spike in claims may stretch capacity.
Other Rating Factors: Strong capitalization index (10.0) based on excellent current risk-adjusted capital (severe loss scenario). High quality investment portfolio (9.7).
Principal Business: Medicaid (94%), Medicare (5%)
Mem Phys: 19: 24,307 **18:** 22,908 **19 MLR** 897.8% **/ 19 Admin Exp** N/A
Enroll(000): Q2 20: 926 **19:** 845 **18:** 866 **Med Exp PMPM:** $478
Principal Investments: Long-term bonds (94%), nonaffiliate common stock (4%), cash and equiv (2%), other (1%)
Provider Compensation ($000): Contr fee ($4,327,785), FFS ($355,890), capitation ($152,553)
Total Member Encounters: Phys (12,662,624), non-phys (2,916,123)
Group Affiliation: Horizon Healthcare Services Inc
Licensed in: NJ
Address: 3 Penn Plz E Ste PP-15D, Newark,
Phone: (973) 466-5607 **Dom State:** NJ **Commenced Bus:** N/A

Data Date	Rating	RACR #1	RACR #2	Total Assets ($mil)	Capital ($mil)	Net Premium ($mil)	Net Income ($mil)
6-20	C+	31.19	25.99	1,656.2	1,103.8	283.5	-3.5
6-19	C+	26.78	22.32	1,213.4	1,078.0	266.8	35.9
2019	C+	31.48	26.24	1,342.5	1,115.1	546.2	51.3
2018	C+	26.28	21.90	1,228.0	1,055.9	539.7	26.3
2017	B	19.71	16.42	1,354.7	1,044.6	506.2	44.2
2016	A-	3.58	2.99	1,601.5	998.0	4,868.0	151.2
2015	A-	3.24	2.70	1,439.4	850.1	4,561.5	72.0

HORIZON HEALTHCARE SERVICES INC   B   Good

Major Rating Factors: Good quality investment portfolio (6.4 on a scale of 0 to 10). Fair profitability index (4.0). Strong capitalization (10.0) based on excellent current risk-adjusted capital (severe loss scenario).
Other Rating Factors: Excellent liquidity (7.1) with ample operational cash flow and liquid investments.
Principal Business: Comp med (44%), Medicaid (40%), FEHB (8%), Medicare (4%), med supp (2%), dental (1%)
Mem Phys: 19: 101,986 **18:** 95,620 **19 MLR** 46.8% **/ 19 Admin Exp** N/A
Enroll(000): 19: 1,239 **18:** 1,256 **Med Exp PMPM:** $362
Principal Investments: Long-term bonds (61%), affiliate common stock (37%), nonaffiliate common stock (8%)
Provider Compensation ($000): Contr fee ($5,134,710), capitation ($137,324), FFS ($68,174)
Total Member Encounters: Phys (11,641,038), non-phys (9,777,874)
Group Affiliation: Horizon Healthcare Services, Inc.
Licensed in: NJ
Address: 3 Penn Plaza East, PP-15D, Newark,
Phone: (973) 466-5607 **Dom State:** NJ **Commenced Bus:** N/A

Data Date	Rating	RACR #1	RACR #2	Total Assets ($mil)	Capital ($mil)	Net Premium ($mil)	Net Income ($mil)
2019	B	3.71	3.10	5,684.9	2,732.7	11,547.6	1.2
2018	B	3.79	3.16	5,527.8	2,985.3	12,456.5	336.1
2017	B	3.58	2.98	5,437.9	2,772.2	12,222.8	56.7
2016	B	3.59	3.00	4,257.6	2,385.9	6,692.7	-83.0
2015	B+	3.79	3.16	4,089.2	2,305.9	6,123.6	20.6

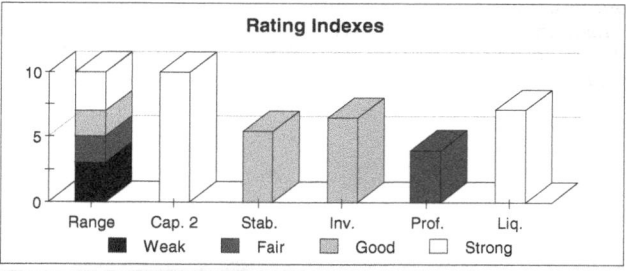

HORIZON INS CO   C+   Fair

Major Rating Factors: Good overall profitability index (5.0 on a scale of 0 to 10). Weak liquidity (2.0) as a spike in claims may stretch capacity. Strong capitalization (10.0) based on excellent current risk-adjusted capital (severe loss scenario).
Other Rating Factors: High quality investment portfolio (9.2).
Principal Business: Medicare (39%), med supp (37%), vision (15%), other (10%)
Mem Phys: 19: 49,912 **18:** 46,637 **19 MLR** 693.3% **/ 19 Admin Exp** N/A
Enroll(000): 19: 321 **18:** 365 **Med Exp PMPM:** $129
Principal Investments: Long-term bonds (98%), cash and equiv (2%)
Provider Compensation ($000): Contr fee ($511,773), FFS ($30,629), capitation ($17,727)
Total Member Encounters: Phys (2,749,388), non-phys (1,565,099)
Group Affiliation: Horizon Healthcare Services, Inc.
Licensed in: NJ
Address: 3 Penn Plaza East PP-15D, Newark,
Phone: (973) 466-5607 **Dom State:** NJ **Commenced Bus:** N/A

Data Date	Rating	RACR #1	RACR #2	Total Assets ($mil)	Capital ($mil)	Net Premium ($mil)	Net Income ($mil)
2019	C+	7.54	6.29	98.8	39.4	71.9	10.0
2018	C+	3.03	2.52	155.7	29.9	149.5	-1.6
2017	B-	N/A	N/A	201.4	31.2	139.9	4.0
2016	B-	8.75	7.29	123.8	27.3	64.1	3.2
2015	B	3.79	3.16	141.4	25.5	220.3	9.1

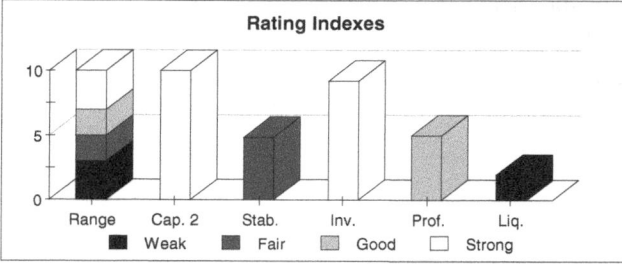

HPHC INS CO — C — Fair

Major Rating Factors: Fair profitability index (4.0 on a scale of 0 to 10). Good liquidity (6.6) with sufficient resources (cash flows and marketable investments) to handle a spike in claims. Strong capitalization (8.3) based on excellent current risk-adjusted capital (severe loss scenario).
Other Rating Factors: High quality investment portfolio (7.1).
Principal Business: Comp med (76%), med supp (22%), other (2%)
Mem Phys: 19: 88,907 **18:** 83,960 **19 MLR** 83.7% **/ 19 Admin Exp** N/A
Enroll(000): Q2 20: 138 **19:** 146 **18:** 154 **Med Exp PMPM:** $326
Principal Investments: Long-term bonds (100%), other (1%)
Provider Compensation ($000): Contr fee ($503,554), capitation ($42,344), FFS ($15,563), bonus arrang ($789), other ($22,115)
Total Member Encounters: Phys (1,002,057), non-phys (774,662)
Group Affiliation: Health Plan Holdings Inc
Licensed in: CT, ME, MA, NH
Address: 93 WORCESTER STREET, WELLESLEY, MA 02481-9181
Phone: (781) 263-6000 **Dom State:** MA **Commenced Bus:** N/A

Data Date	Rating	RACR #1	RACR #2	Total Assets ($mil)	Capital ($mil)	Net Premium ($mil)	Net Income ($mil)
6-20	C	2.36	1.97	296.3	128.3	321.7	15.4
6-19	D+	2.31	1.92	250.6	100.4	343.0	2.5
2019	C-	2.91	2.42	256.5	118.5	689.9	13.3
2018	D+	2.23	1.85	255.6	100.8	752.7	29.5
2017	D-	1.02	0.85	249.2	70.4	810.2	-0.1
2016	D-	1.43	1.19	268.9	70.6	774.5	-57.8
2015	C	1.23	1.02	226.3	51.8	665.4	-37.3

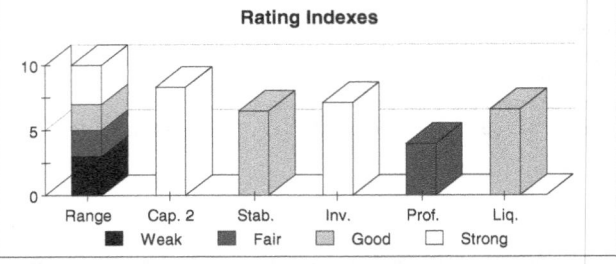

Rating Indexes

HUMANA BENEFIT PLAN OF ILLINOIS * — B+ — Good

Major Rating Factors: Good quality investment portfolio (6.7 on a scale of 0 to 10). Good liquidity (6.8) with sufficient resources (cash flows and marketable investments) to handle a spike in claims. Excellent profitability (8.8).
Other Rating Factors: Strong capitalization (9.4) based on excellent current risk-adjusted capital (severe loss scenario).
Principal Business: Medicare (99%), med supp (1%)
Mem Phys: 19: 446,869 **18:** 397,770 **19 MLR** 85.6% **/ 19 Admin Exp** N/A
Enroll(000): Q2 20: 303 **19:** 256 **18:** 178 **Med Exp PMPM:** $773
Principal Investments: Long-term bonds (84%), cash and equiv (16%)
Provider Compensation ($000): Contr fee ($1,361,422), capitation ($673,906), salary ($59,621), FFS ($33,966)
Total Member Encounters: Phys (4,784,566), non-phys (2,486,498)
Group Affiliation: None
Licensed in: All states except NY, PR
Address: 4501 NORTH STERLING AVE 2ND, PEORIA, IL 61615
Phone: (502) 580-1000 **Dom State:** IL **Commenced Bus:** N/A

Data Date	Rating	RACR #1	RACR #2	Total Assets ($mil)	Capital ($mil)	Net Premium ($mil)	Net Income ($mil)
6-20	B+	3.24	2.70	1,104.8	505.1	1,663.4	74.1
6-19	B+	4.17	3.47	724.7	374.5	1,269.5	46.8
2019	B+	3.31	2.76	757.1	416.0	2,581.5	63.2
2018	B+	3.66	3.05	551.0	328.5	1,906.1	40.2
2017	A-	2.85	2.38	367.0	208.9	1,016.5	51.8
2016	A-	3.13	2.61	248.6	161.8	969.5	32.1
2015	B	3.29	2.74	197.6	130.4	700.1	-0.9

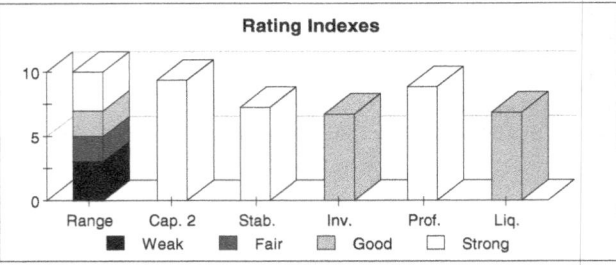

Rating Indexes

HUMANA EAP & WORK-LIFE SVCS — C- — Fair

Major Rating Factors: Fair profitability index (3.4 on a scale of 0 to 10). Fair overall results on stability tests (3.2) based on poor risk diversification due to the company's size. Strong capitalization index (10.0) based on excellent current risk-adjusted capital (severe loss scenario).
Other Rating Factors: Excellent liquidity (10.0) with ample operational cash flow and liquid investments.
Principal Business: Managed care (100%)
Mem Phys: 19: N/A **18:** N/A **19 MLR** 17.4% **/ 19 Admin Exp** N/A
Enroll(000): Q2 20: 31 **19:** 6 **18:** 6 **Med Exp PMPM:** N/A
Principal Investments ($000): Cash and equiv ($2,291)
Provider Compensation ($000): None
Total Member Encounters: N/A
Group Affiliation: Access Senior HealthCare Inc
Licensed in: (No states)
Address: , , CA 94598-2581
Phone: (Phone number **Dom State:** CA **Commenced Bus:** N/A

Data Date	Rating	RACR #1	RACR #2	Total Assets ($mil)	Capital ($mil)	Net Premium ($mil)	Net Income ($mil)
6-20	C-	194.60	194.51	2.6	2.5	0.2	0.0
6-19	U	444.20	443.50	2.5	2.4	0.1	0.0
2019	C-	192.40	192.30	2.5	2.5	0.3	0.1
2018	U	434.70	434.00	2.4	2.4	0.0	0.0
2017	U	77727.00	51267.00	2.5	2.4	N/A	-0.1
2016	N/A	N/A	N/A	N/A	N/A	N/A	N/A
2015	N/A	N/A	N/A	N/A	N/A	N/A	N/A

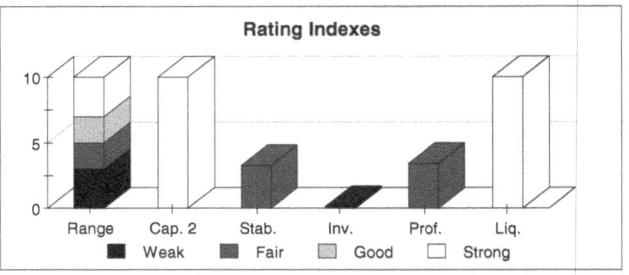

Rating Indexes

HUMANA EMPLOYERS HEALTH PLAN OF GA — C — Fair

Major Rating Factors: Weak profitability index (1.0 on a scale of 0 to 10). Weak overall results on stability tests (2.8) based on a steep decline in capital during 2019. Good quality investment portfolio (6.5).
Other Rating Factors: Good liquidity (6.0) with sufficient resources (cash flows and marketable investments) to handle a spike in claims. Strong capitalization index (8.2) based on excellent current risk-adjusted capital (severe loss scenario).
Principal Business: Comp med (50%), Medicare (48%), FEHB (1%)
Mem Phys: 19: 56,355 **18:** 53,096 **19 MLR** 87.2% **/ 19 Admin Exp** N/A
Enroll(000): Q2 20: 220 **19:** 232 **18:** 249 **Med Exp PMPM:** $452
Principal Investments: Long-term bonds (100%)
Provider Compensation ($000): Contr fee ($812,392), capitation ($229,669), FFS ($191,835), salary ($20,410)
Total Member Encounters: Phys (2,263,932), non-phys (981,382)
Group Affiliation: None
Licensed in: GA
Address: 1200 ASHWOOD PKWY STE 250, ATLANTA,
Phone: (770) 393-9226 **Dom State:** GA **Commenced Bus:** N/A

Data Date	Rating	RACR #1	RACR #2	Total Assets ($mil)	Capital ($mil)	Net Premium ($mil)	Net Income ($mil)
6-20	C	2.29	1.91	541.8	253.2	816.6	-1.0
6-19	C+	4.03	3.35	555.3	285.8	741.3	18.8
2019	C+	3.16	2.63	455.6	257.1	1,486.5	-10.2
2018	C+	5.15	4.29	533.3	367.0	1,323.8	16.2
2017	C	6.74	5.62	694.3	510.7	1,198.2	17.1
2016	C	4.23	3.52	862.2	557.2	1,903.8	-118.4
2015	C-	2.17	1.81	985.9	300.8	2,273.5	-205.7

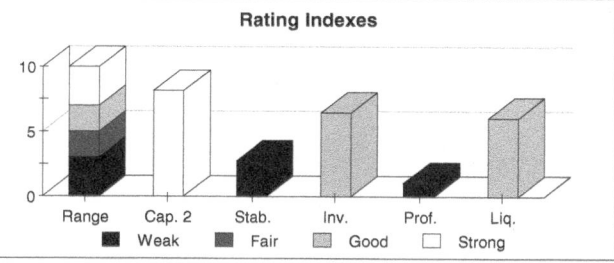

Rating Indexes

HUMANA HEALTH BENEFIT PLAN LA — B — Good

Major Rating Factors: Good overall results on stability tests (6.1 on a scale of 0 to 10). Good liquidity (6.7) with sufficient resources (cash flows and marketable investments) to handle a spike in claims. Excellent profitability (8.5).
Other Rating Factors: Strong capitalization index (8.1) based on excellent current risk-adjusted capital (severe loss scenario). High quality investment portfolio (8.5).
Principal Business: Medicare (84%), comp med (13%), other (1%)
Mem Phys: 19: 38,828 **18:** 36,720 **19 MLR** 83.9% **/ 19 Admin Exp** N/A
Enroll(000): Q2 20: 410 **19:** 401 **18:** 371 **Med Exp PMPM:** $404
Principal Investments: Long-term bonds (94%), cash and equiv (6%)
Provider Compensation ($000): Contr fee ($1,077,473), capitation ($662,263), FFS ($97,897), salary ($17,345)
Total Member Encounters: Phys (3,995,221), non-phys (2,167,676)
Group Affiliation: None
Licensed in: LA
Address: ONE GALLERIA BLVD SUITE 1200, METAIRIE,
Phone: (504) 219-6600 **Dom State:** LA **Commenced Bus:** N/A

Data Date	Rating	RACR #1	RACR #2	Total Assets ($mil)	Capital ($mil)	Net Premium ($mil)	Net Income ($mil)
6-20	B	2.21	1.84	715.9	317.9	1,290.0	71.6
6-19	C+	2.55	2.12	515.2	241.7	1,113.8	41.4
2019	B-	2.60	2.16	531.0	279.6	2,250.7	74.6
2018	C+	2.66	2.21	504.3	252.9	2,000.0	45.2
2017	B	2.36	1.96	595.6	294.3	2,080.3	81.9
2016	B	2.65	2.21	495.5	244.2	2,031.7	60.2
2015	B-	2.09	1.75	396.4	179.7	1,837.4	36.6

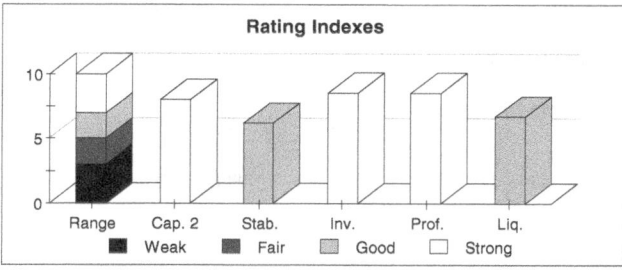

Rating Indexes

HUMANA HEALTH CO OF NEW YORK INC — C- — Fair

Major Rating Factors: Fair quality investment portfolio (4.2 on a scale of 0 to 10). Weak profitability index (0.9). Strong capitalization (7.6) based on excellent current risk-adjusted capital (severe loss scenario).
Other Rating Factors: Excellent liquidity (7.1) with ample operational cash flow and liquid investments.
Principal Business: Medicare (100%)
Mem Phys: 19: 38,827 **18:** 30,078 **19 MLR** 98.2% **/ 19 Admin Exp** N/A
Enroll(000): Q2 20: 36 **19:** 32 **18:** 21 **Med Exp PMPM:** $861
Principal Investments: Cash and equiv (100%)
Provider Compensation ($000): Contr fee ($238,699), capitation ($58,616), FFS ($5,842)
Total Member Encounters: Phys (644,797), non-phys (300,429)
Group Affiliation: None
Licensed in: NY
Address: 515 MADISON AVENUE 9TH FLOOR, NEW YORK, NY 10022
Phone: (800) 201-3687 **Dom State:** NY **Commenced Bus:** N/A

Data Date	Rating	RACR #1	RACR #2	Total Assets ($mil)	Capital ($mil)	Net Premium ($mil)	Net Income ($mil)
6-20	C-	1.87	1.56	184.9	59.2	207.8	-18.0
6-19	C+	4.63	3.86	124.8	60.7	153.8	-14.7
2019	C+	2.51	2.09	134.4	49.6	315.7	-47.2
2018	C+	2.85	2.37	95.4	36.9	197.4	-32.8
2017	D-	1.45	1.21	56.9	20.4	128.1	-20.3
2016	D-	3.10	2.58	40.1	21.3	108.1	-12.1
2015	D-	6.33	5.27	27.9	22.5	42.6	-1.0

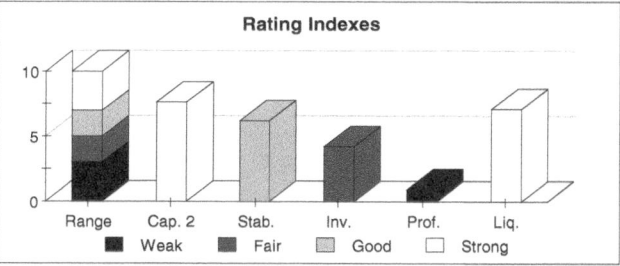

Rating Indexes

HUMANA HEALTH INS CO OF FL INC   C-   Fair

Major Rating Factors: Fair profitability index (3.1 on a scale of 0 to 10). Good quality investment portfolio (6.4). Strong capitalization (8.5) based on excellent current risk-adjusted capital (severe loss scenario).
Other Rating Factors: Excellent liquidity (7.2) with ample operational cash flow and liquid investments.
Principal Business: Comp med (23%), Medicare (16%), med supp (14%), other (48%)
Mem Phys: 19: 95,883 **18:** 77,529 **19 MLR** 88.3% **/ 19 Admin Exp** N/A
Enroll(000): Q2 20: 76 **19:** 67 **18:** 41 **Med Exp PMPM:** $114
Principal Investments: Long-term bonds (78%), cash and equiv (22%)
Provider Compensation ($000): Contr fee ($70,247), FFS ($8,566)
Total Member Encounters: Phys (221,888), non-phys (66,997)
Group Affiliation: None
Licensed in: AL, FL, GA, KY, NC, SC, VA
Address: 3501 SW 160TH AVENUE, MIRAMAR, FL 33027
Phone: (305) 626-5616 **Dom State:** FL **Commenced Bus:** N/A

Data Date	Rating	RACR #1	RACR #2	Total Assets ($mil)	Capital ($mil)	Net Premium ($mil)	Net Income ($mil)
6-20	C-	2.58	2.15	104.5	63.1	73.1	7.8
6-19	B-	9.79	8.16	119.5	47.7	37.2	-5.9
2019	B-	3.58	2.98	121.1	55.4	93.0	1.1
2018	B-	25.12	20.93	212.5	127.4	41.0	13.8
2017	B-	N/A	N/A	277.9	116.2	976.3	-10.5
2016	B-	4.03	3.36	107.3	52.6	206.8	8.0
2015	C+	4.43	3.69	133.5	72.5	265.6	12.8

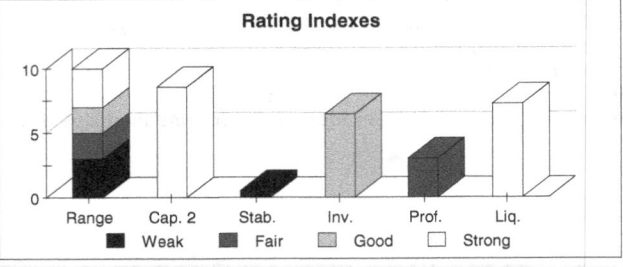

Rating Indexes

HUMANA HEALTH PLAN INC   D   Weak

Major Rating Factors: Weak overall results on stability tests (0.3 on a scale of 0 to 10) based on a steep decline in capital during 2019, a significant 46% decrease in enrollment during the period. Weak liquidity (2.1) as a spike in claims may stretch capacity. Fair profitability index (3.7).
Other Rating Factors: Strong capitalization index (9.5) based on excellent current risk-adjusted capital (severe loss scenario). High quality investment portfolio (8.1).
Principal Business: Comp med (72%), Medicare (14%), FEHB (8%), Medicaid (6%)
Mem Phys: 19: 557,834 **18:** 472,557 **19 MLR** 159.9% **/ 19 Admin Exp** N/A
Enroll(000): Q2 20: 334 **19:** 338 **18:** 622 **Med Exp PMPM:** $436
Principal Investments: Long-term bonds (72%), cash and equiv (22%), mortgs (6%)
Provider Compensation ($000): Contr fee ($1,720,650), FFS ($228,481), capitation ($75,160)
Total Member Encounters: Phys (3,919,586), non-phys (1,807,335)
Group Affiliation: None
Licensed in: AL, AZ, AR, CO, ID, IL, IN, KS, KY, MO, NE, NV, NM, OH, SC, TN, TX, VA, WA, WV
Address: 321 WEST MAIN STREET - 12TH FL, LOUISVILLE,
Phone: (502) 580-1000 **Dom State:** KY **Commenced Bus:** N/A

Data Date	Rating	RACR #1	RACR #2	Total Assets ($mil)	Capital ($mil)	Net Premium ($mil)	Net Income ($mil)
6-20	D	3.36	2.80	701.8	257.0	1,021.6	-4.4
6-19	C+	3.40	2.83	1,099.0	654.2	547.6	19.1
2019	C+	4.45	3.71	641.0	250.8	1,124.0	44.3
2018	C+	3.92	3.27	1,430.7	757.9	3,931.9	125.7
2017	B	3.08	2.56	2,029.1	998.9	7,259.6	117.2
2016	B-	2.65	2.21	1,678.6	866.7	7,278.9	37.0
2015	C+	2.15	1.79	1,385.6	601.3	5,790.9	-102.9

Rating Indexes

HUMANA HEALTH PLAN OF CA INC   B-   Good

Major Rating Factors: Good quality investment portfolio (6.0 on a scale of 0 to 10). Strong capitalization (8.7) based on excellent current risk-adjusted capital (severe loss scenario). Excellent liquidity (6.9) with sufficient resources (cash flows and marketable investments) to handle a spike in claims.
Other Rating Factors: Weak profitability index (2.6).
Principal Business: Medicare (100%)
Mem Phys: 19: 68,070 **18:** N/A **19 MLR** 88.3% **/ 19 Admin Exp** N/A
Enroll(000): Q2 20: 8 **19:** 6 **18:** N/A **Med Exp PMPM:** $871
Principal Investments: Long-term bonds (59%), cash and equiv (41%)
Provider Compensation ($000): Capitation ($40,359), contr fee ($10,882), salary ($1,071), FFS ($21)
Total Member Encounters: Phys (72,550), non-phys (32,470)
Group Affiliation: None
Licensed in: CA, KS, KY, MO, WA
Address: 1 PARK PLAZA SUITE 450, IRVINE, CA 92614
Phone: (800) 448-6262 **Dom State:** CA **Commenced Bus:** N/A

Data Date	Rating	RACR #1	RACR #2	Total Assets ($mil)	Capital ($mil)	Net Premium ($mil)	Net Income ($mil)
6-20	B-	2.71	2.25	31.7	13.2	48.7	-0.2
6-19	U	10.40	8.66	28.3	14.2	26.4	1.0
2019	B-	5.06	4.22	26.1	14.0	57.5	0.2
2018	U	10.03	8.36	24.9	13.7	-1.2	-0.5
2017	N/A	N/A	N/A	N/A	N/A	N/A	N/A
2016	N/A	N/A	N/A	N/A	N/A	N/A	N/A
2015	N/A	N/A	N/A	N/A	N/A	N/A	N/A

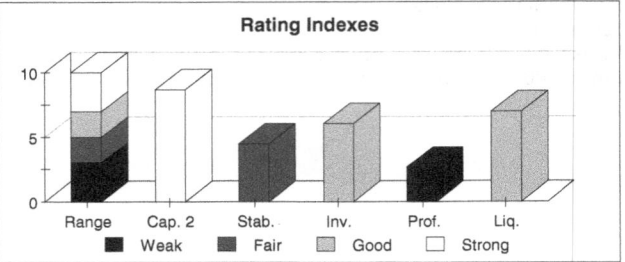

Rating Indexes

HUMANA HEALTH PLAN OF OHIO INC — C — Fair

Major Rating Factors: Weak profitability index (1.9 on a scale of 0 to 10). Weak overall results on stability tests (1.1) based on a steep decline in capital during 2019, a significant 15% decrease in enrollment during the period. Good liquidity (6.3) with sufficient resources (cash flows and marketable investments) to handle a spike in claims.

Other Rating Factors: Strong capitalization index (7.7) based on excellent current risk-adjusted capital (severe loss scenario). High quality investment portfolio (9.2).

Principal Business: Comp med (74%), Medicare (25%), FEHB (1%)

Mem Phys: 19: 49,651 **18:** 47,103 **19 MLR** 91.6% **/ 19 Admin Exp** N/A

Enroll(000): Q2 20: 35 **19:** 37 **18:** 44 **Med Exp PMPM:** $419

Principal Investments: Long-term bonds (84%), cash and equiv (16%), other (1%)

Provider Compensation ($000): Contr fee ($120,462), FFS ($44,540), capitation ($24,605)

Total Member Encounters: Phys (321,723), non-phys (139,398)

Group Affiliation: None

Licensed in: IN, KY, OH

Address: 640 EDEN PARK DRIVE, CINCINNATI,

Phone: (513) 784-5320 **Dom State:** OH **Commenced Bus:** N/A

Data Date	Rating	RACR #1	RACR #2	Total Assets ($mil)	Capital ($mil)	Net Premium ($mil)	Net Income ($mil)
6-20	C	1.94	1.62	85.5	42.9	117.1	5.3
6-19	C+	3.19	2.66	77.5	42.2	110.2	-1.6
2019	C+	2.49	2.07	65.5	32.8	209.9	-11.8
2018	C+	4.60	3.83	91.6	61.8	225.3	5.4
2017	C	6.15	5.12	160.9	113.2	230.8	8.8
2016	B-	2.68	2.23	180.5	102.5	728.8	8.4
2015	C+	2.32	1.93	176.8	77.3	591.0	-27.3

Rating Indexes

HUMANA HEALTH PLAN OF TEXAS INC — C — Fair

Major Rating Factors: Weak profitability index (1.0 on a scale of 0 to 10). Weak overall results on stability tests (2.8) based on a significant 16% decrease in enrollment during the period, an inordinate decline in premium revenue in 2019 and a steep decline in capital during 2019. Good liquidity (6.8) with sufficient resources (cash flows and marketable investments) to handle a spike in claims.

Other Rating Factors: Strong capitalization index (7.6) based on excellent current risk-adjusted capital (severe loss scenario). High quality investment portfolio (8.4).

Principal Business: Comp med (85%), FEHB (8%), Medicare (7%)

Mem Phys: 19: 68,529 **18:** 75,176 **19 MLR** 85.4% **/ 19 Admin Exp** N/A

Enroll(000): Q2 20: 112 **19:** 126 **18:** 150 **Med Exp PMPM:** $359

Principal Investments: Long-term bonds (84%), cash and equiv (11%), real estate (5%)

Provider Compensation ($000): Contr fee ($398,962), FFS ($161,496), capitation ($15,601)

Total Member Encounters: Phys (921,745), non-phys (238,830)

Group Affiliation: None

Licensed in: TX

Address: 1221 S MO PAC EXPY SUITE 200, AUSTIN,

Phone: (502) 580-1000 **Dom State:** TX **Commenced Bus:** N/A

Data Date	Rating	RACR #1	RACR #2	Total Assets ($mil)	Capital ($mil)	Net Premium ($mil)	Net Income ($mil)
6-20	C	1.80	1.50	212.8	96.7	312.7	5.6
6-19	C+	2.76	2.30	214.8	106.4	346.0	14.0
2019	C+	2.05	1.71	189.7	74.7	673.9	-18.3
2018	C+	2.48	2.07	206.2	94.6	749.9	-6.6
2017	C-	2.13	1.77	244.5	116.8	775.4	15.1
2016	C	4.65	3.87	404.6	233.9	805.9	-69.0
2015	C	2.28	1.90	584.5	199.6	2,044.9	-86.4

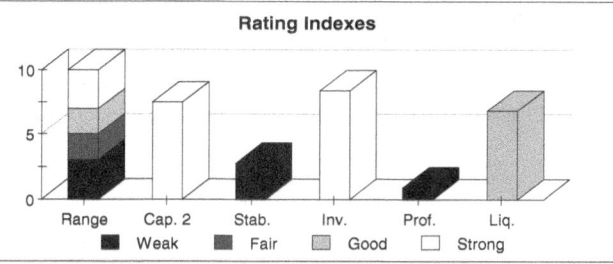

Rating Indexes

HUMANA HEALTH PLANS OF PUERTO RICO — E- — Very Weak

Major Rating Factors: Weak profitability index (0.7 on a scale of 0 to 10). Fair overall results on stability tests (4.4). Good capitalization index (5.3) based on good current risk-adjusted capital (severe loss scenario).

Other Rating Factors: Good liquidity (6.5) with sufficient resources (cash flows and marketable investments) to handle a spike in claims. High quality investment portfolio (9.2).

Principal Business: Medicare (92%), FEHB (6%), comp med (2%)

Mem Phys: 19: 23,051 **18:** 22,871 **19 MLR** 89.4% **/ 19 Admin Exp** N/A

Enroll(000): Q2 20: 38 **19:** 47 **18:** 43 **Med Exp PMPM:** $618

Principal Investments: Long-term bonds (63%), cash and equiv (37%)

Provider Compensation ($000): Contr fee ($163,089), capitation ($162,924), FFS ($2,427)

Total Member Encounters: N/A

Group Affiliation: None

Licensed in: PR

Address: 383 FD ROOSEVELT AVENUE, SAN JUAN,

Phone: (787) 282-7900 **Dom State:** PR **Commenced Bus:** N/A

Data Date	Rating	RACR #1	RACR #2	Total Assets ($mil)	Capital ($mil)	Net Premium ($mil)	Net Income ($mil)
6-20	E-	0.98	0.81	171.2	35.1	185.6	10.5
6-19	E-	0.39	0.32	145.4	9.6	189.0	-10.7
2019	E-	1.10	0.91	154.6	25.2	382.1	-24.7
2018	D	1.12	0.93	128.5	23.1	324.6	-23.6
2017	C	1.55	1.29	124.1	33.0	304.2	-12.9
2016	C+	3.21	2.67	114.7	42.8	312.2	-32.2
2015	C+	4.97	4.14	140.8	75.6	417.7	7.7

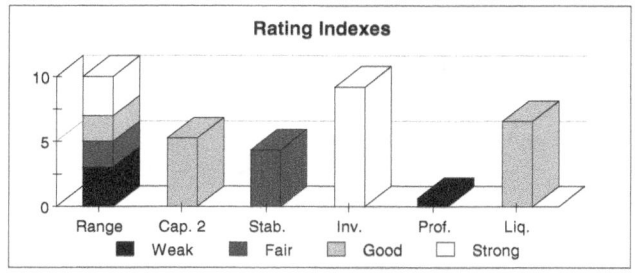

Rating Indexes

HUMANA INS CO (WI) * A Excellent

Major Rating Factors: Excellent profitability (8.6 on a scale of 0 to 10). Strong capitalization (8.7) based on excellent current risk-adjusted capital (severe loss scenario). High quality investment portfolio (8.5).
Other Rating Factors: Excellent liquidity (6.9) with sufficient resources (cash flows and marketable investments) to handle a spike in claims.
Principal Business: Medicare (78%), comp med (5%), med supp (2%), dental (2%), other (13%)
Mem Phys: 19: 1,519,823 **18:** 1,455,033 **19 MLR** 83.0% **/ 19 Admin Exp** N/A
Enroll(000): Q2 20: 10,147 **19:** 10,521 **18:** 10,813 **Med Exp PMPM:** $174
Principal Investments: Long-term bonds (61%), cash and equiv (27%), affiliate common stock (12%)
Provider Compensation ($000): Contr fee ($18,514,014), capitation ($2,356,860), FFS ($866,019)
Total Member Encounters: Phys (44,409,355), non-phys (24,908,655)
Group Affiliation: None
Licensed in: All states except NY
Address: 1100 EMPLOYERS BOULEVARD, DEPERE, WI 54115
Phone: (920) 336-1100 **Dom State:** WI **Commenced Bus:** N/A

Data Date	Rating	RACR #1	RACR #2	Total Assets ($mil)	Capital ($mil)	Net Premium ($mil)	Net Income ($mil)
6-20	A	2.73	2.28	10,594.3	4,705.3	14,642.5	916.2
6-19	B	2.42	2.02	7,860.6	3,722.4	13,350.1	778.8
2019	B+	2.41	2.01	7,990.5	4,129.4	26,445.9	1,184.7
2018	B	2.42	2.02	7,233.4	3,720.7	24,820.0	1,140.0
2017	A	3.09	2.57	8,716.6	4,184.5	22,921.2	891.7
2016	A-	2.88	2.40	6,870.6	4,224.7	22,960.9	506.1
2015	B+	2.47	2.06	6,583.3	3,642.1	23,141.9	421.8

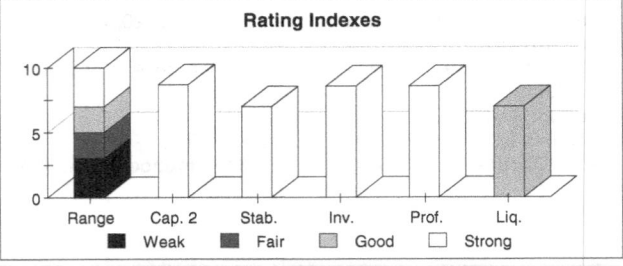

Rating Indexes

HUMANA INS CO OF KENTUCKY B- Good

Major Rating Factors: Good overall profitability (6.0 on a scale of 0 to 10). Excellent expense controls. Return on equity has been good over the last five years, averaging 10.5%. Good liquidity (6.9) with sufficient resources to handle a spike in claims. Fair overall results on stability tests (3.9) including excessive premium growth.
Other Rating Factors: Strong capitalization (9.2) based on excellent risk adjusted capital (severe loss scenario). High quality investment portfolio (7.3).
Principal Business: Individual health insurance (70%), reinsurance (24%), and group life insurance (6%).
Principal Investments: NonCMO investment grade bonds (61%), CMOs and structured securities (32%), noninv. grade bonds (3%), and cash (1%).
Investments in Affiliates: None
Group Affiliation: Humana Inc
Licensed in: CA, CO, KY, OR, TX, UT, WA
Commenced Business: January 2001
Address: 500 WEST MAIN STREET, LOUISVILLE, KY 40202
Phone: (502) 580-1000 **Domicile State:** KY **NAIC Code:** 60219

Data Date	Rating	RACR #1	RACR #2	Total Assets ($mil)	Capital ($mil)	Net Premium ($mil)	Net Income ($mil)
6-20	B-	3.19	2.48	213.7	156.1	156.9	18.1
6-19	B+	4.84	3.64	176.6	144.2	102.2	10.2
2019	B-	3.29	2.54	182.6	139.2	212.2	2.6
2018	B+	6.78	4.98	216.7	185.0	135.4	20.9
2017	B-	6.34	4.65	215.3	164.9	126.5	17.3
2016	C	6.43	4.69	204.5	149.9	90.9	37.4
2015	C	2.61	1.95	432.9	122.2	269.9	-2.8

Net Income History
(in millions of dollars)

HUMANA INS CO OF NY B Good

Major Rating Factors: Good liquidity (6.8 on a scale of 0 to 10) with sufficient resources (cash flows and marketable investments) to handle a spike in claims. Fair profitability index (4.3). Strong capitalization (10.0) based on excellent current risk-adjusted capital (severe loss scenario).
Other Rating Factors: High quality investment portfolio (7.8).
Principal Business: Medicare (58%), med supp (4%), other (37%)
Mem Phys: 19: 59,233 **18:** 36,744 **19 MLR** 84.1% **/ 19 Admin Exp** N/A
Enroll(000): Q2 20: 185 **19:** 175 **18:** 173 **Med Exp PMPM:** $150
Principal Investments: Long-term bonds (96%), cash and equiv (4%)
Provider Compensation ($000): Contr fee ($282,860), capitation ($14,875), FFS ($3,238)
Total Member Encounters: Phys (611,937), non-phys (270,660)
Group Affiliation: None
Licensed in: NY
Address: 515 MADISON AVENUE 9TH FLOOR, NEW YORK, NY 10022
Phone: (800) 201-3687 **Dom State:** NY **Commenced Bus:** N/A

Data Date	Rating	RACR #1	RACR #2	Total Assets ($mil)	Capital ($mil)	Net Premium ($mil)	Net Income ($mil)
6-20	B	3.80	3.17	234.1	112.4	314.6	-0.5
6-19	B-	5.69	4.74	147.9	77.5	179.0	-0.7
2019	B	3.92	3.27	142.1	81.8	371.9	1.8
2018	B-	5.91	4.92	134.0	80.4	270.9	8.9
2017	B-	3.26	2.72	154.4	71.9	277.2	4.0
2016	B-	4.49	3.74	105.5	68.1	291.8	-3.4
2015	C+	4.40	3.66	106.4	56.6	253.4	-4.9

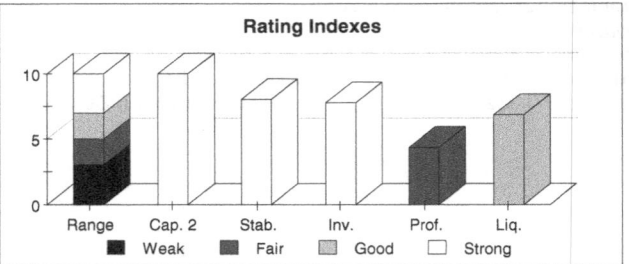

Rating Indexes

HUMANA INS CO OF PUERTO RICO INC   C+   Fair

Major Rating Factors: Fair overall results on stability tests (4.7 on a scale of 0 to 10) including negative cash flow from operations for 2018. Good quality investment portfolio (6.8) despite mixed results such as: no exposure to mortgages and substantial holdings of BBB bonds but minimal holdings in junk bonds. Good liquidity (5.5) with sufficient resources to handle a spike in claims.
Other Rating Factors: Weak profitability (2.2) with operating losses during the first nine months of 2019. Strong capitalization (7.7) based on excellent risk adjusted capital (severe loss scenario).
Principal Business: Group health insurance (90%) and individual health insurance (10%).
Principal Investments: NonCMO investment grade bonds (38%), CMOs and structured securities (27%), and noninv. grade bonds (1%).
Investments in Affiliates: None
Group Affiliation: Humana Inc
Licensed in: PR
Commenced Business: September 1971
Address: 383 FD ROOSEVELT AVENUE, SAN JUAN, PR 00918-2131
Phone: (787) 282-7900 **Domicile State:** PR **NAIC Code:** 84603

Data Date	Rating	RACR #1	RACR #2	Total Assets ($mil)	Capital ($mil)	Net Premium ($mil)	Net Income ($mil)
9-19	C+	1.90	1.46	76.2	44.7	104.8	-4.4
9-18	C+	2.12	1.70	77.8	46.1	98.5	-4.4
2018	C+	2.06	1.58	0.0	0.0	0.0	0.0
2017	B-	2.18	1.74	0.0	0.0	0.0	0.0
2016	C+	2.29	1.84	0.0	0.0	0.0	0.0
2015	B-	2.85	2.28	0.0	0.0	0.0	0.0
2014	B-	2.80	2.22	0.0	0.0	0.0	0.0

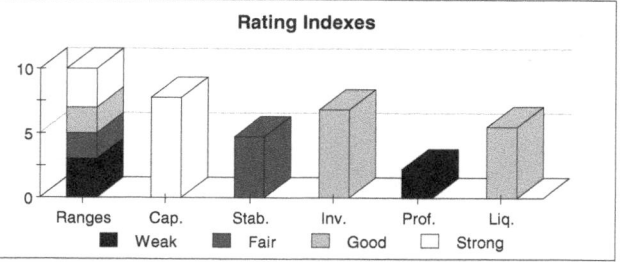

Rating Indexes

HUMANA MEDICAL PLAN INC *   A-   Excellent

Major Rating Factors: Excellent profitability (8.6 on a scale of 0 to 10). Strong capitalization index (8.4) based on excellent current risk-adjusted capital (severe loss scenario). High quality investment portfolio (9.1).
Other Rating Factors: Good overall results on stability tests (6.8). Good liquidity (6.4) with sufficient resources (cash flows and marketable investments) to handle a spike in claims.
Principal Business: Medicare (67%), Medicaid (25%), comp med (7%)
Mem Phys: 19: 185,919 **18:** 141,455 **19 MLR** 87.0% **/ 19 Admin Exp** N/A
Enroll(000): Q2 20: 1,179 **19:** 1,108 **18:** 935 **Med Exp PMPM:** $704
Principal Investments: Long-term bonds (79%), cash and equiv (21%)
Provider Compensation ($000): Capitation ($3,794,540), contr fee ($3,442,738), salary ($1,297,516), FFS ($317,295)
Total Member Encounters: Phys (17,278,537), non-phys (12,972,689)
Group Affiliation: None
Licensed in: FL, KY, MS, NC, OR, VA
Address: 3501 SW 160TH AVENUE, MIRAMAR,
Phone: (305) 626-5616 **Dom State:** FL **Commenced Bus:** N/A

Data Date	Rating	RACR #1	RACR #2	Total Assets ($mil)	Capital ($mil)	Net Premium ($mil)	Net Income ($mil)
6-20	A-	2.47	2.06	3,307.4	1,056.8	5,942.3	243.9
6-19	A-	2.24	1.87	2,258.4	739.5	5,252.8	145.6
2019	A-	1.95	1.62	2,306.0	827.2	10,549.7	228.1
2018	B+	2.61	2.17	2,108.1	867.4	8,928.2	281.6
2017	B+	2.68	2.23	2,037.6	900.2	8,736.0	252.0
2016	B	2.32	1.93	1,939.0	768.5	9,065.9	153.3
2015	B	2.21	1.84	2,013.8	683.1	8,867.8	328.3

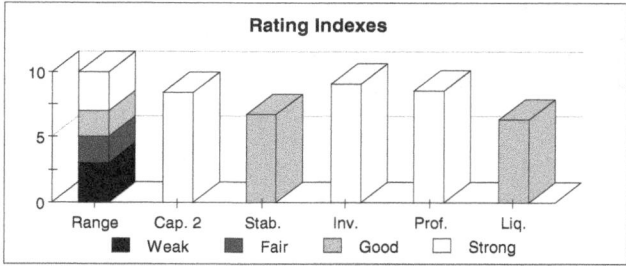

Rating Indexes

HUMANA MEDICAL PLAN OF MICHIGAN INC   B-   Good

Major Rating Factors: Fair profitability index (4.3 on a scale of 0 to 10). Strong capitalization (8.4) based on excellent current risk-adjusted capital (severe loss scenario). High quality investment portfolio (6.9).
Other Rating Factors: Excellent liquidity (7.0) with ample operational cash flow and liquid investments.
Principal Business: Medicare (100%)
Mem Phys: 19: 34,201 **18:** 33,333 **19 MLR** 84.4% **/ 19 Admin Exp** N/A
Enroll(000): Q2 20: 21 **19:** 15 **18:** 10 **Med Exp PMPM:** $826
Principal Investments: Cash and equiv (56%), long-term bonds (44%)
Provider Compensation ($000): Contr fee ($87,950), capitation ($37,361), FFS ($173)
Total Member Encounters: Phys (282,735), non-phys (154,418)
Group Affiliation: None
Licensed in: MI, OH
Address: 18610 FENKELL STREET, DETROIT, MI 48223-2378
Phone: (502) 580-1000 **Dom State:** MI **Commenced Bus:** N/A

Data Date	Rating	RACR #1	RACR #2	Total Assets ($mil)	Capital ($mil)	Net Premium ($mil)	Net Income ($mil)
6-20	B-	2.47	2.06	84.0	34.0	133.2	2.1
6-19	C+	6.20	5.16	53.3	33.2	71.0	5.2
2019	B-	3.80	3.16	56.8	30.9	153.0	4.8
2018	C+	5.50	4.58	41.3	29.3	88.7	3.7
2017	C+	N/A	N/A	39.8	24.3	77.3	-2.0
2016	C+	4.26	3.55	70.0	31.1	115.1	-8.0
2015	C+	4.10	3.41	56.6	21.0	80.1	1.3

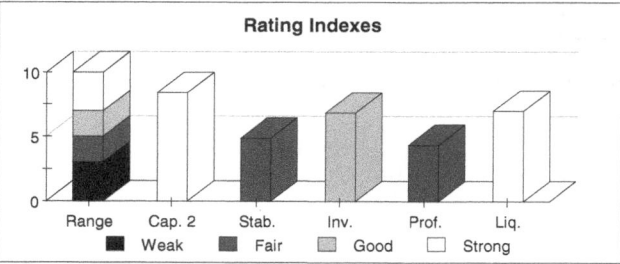

Rating Indexes

HUMANA MEDICAL PLAN OF PENNSYLVANIA   B-   Good

Major Rating Factors: Fair profitability index (3.5 on a scale of 0 to 10). Strong capitalization (9.2) based on excellent current risk-adjusted capital (severe loss scenario). High quality investment portfolio (7.4).
Other Rating Factors: Excellent liquidity (9.5) with ample operational cash flow and liquid investments.
Principal Business: Medicare (100%)
Mem Phys: 19: 21,983 **18:** N/A   **19 MLR** 72.7% **/ 19 Admin Exp** N/A
Enroll(000): Q2 20: 0 **19:** 0   **18:** N/A   **Med Exp PMPM:** $1,121
Principal Investments: Cash and equiv (83%), long-term bonds (17%)
Provider Compensation ($000): Contr fee ($2,938), FFS ($12)
Total Member Encounters: Phys (7,074), non-phys (4,708)
Group Affiliation: None
Licensed in: NC, PA, SC, VA
Address: 5000 RITTER ROAD SUITE 101, MECHANICSBURG, PA 17055
Phone: (502) 580-1000 **Dom State:** PA **Commenced Bus:** N/A

Data Date	Rating	RACR #1	RACR #2	Total Assets ($mil)	Capital ($mil)	Net Premium ($mil)	Net Income ($mil)
6-20	B-	3.14	2.61	9.5	8.0	2.4	-0.1
6-19	U	8.08	6.74	13.9	11.0	1.5	-1.0
2019	B-	9.18	7.65	13.7	12.6	3.6	0.5
2018	U	16.13	13.44	24.8	22.0	-0.2	-0.5
2017	B	N/A	N/A	36.0	22.7	97.9	1.0
2016	B	5.59	4.66	28.6	21.5	56.1	-1.1
2015	B	8.66	7.22	26.2	22.6	35.2	0.1

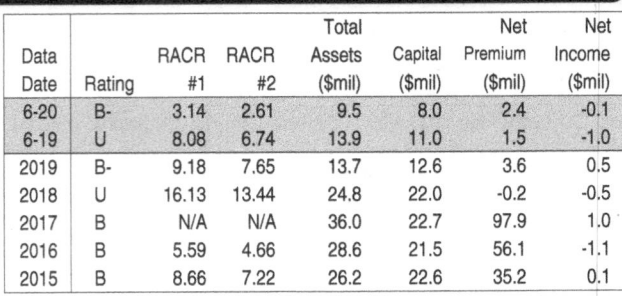

Rating Indexes

HUMANA MEDICAL PLAN OF UTAH INC   D+   Weak

Major Rating Factors: Fair profitability index (3.7 on a scale of 0 to 10). Good quality investment portfolio (5.6). Strong capitalization (7.3) based on excellent current risk-adjusted capital (severe loss scenario).
Other Rating Factors: Excellent liquidity (7.1) with ample operational cash flow and liquid investments.
Principal Business: Medicare (100%)
Mem Phys: 19: 10,922 **18:** 10,969   **19 MLR** 76.7% **/ 19 Admin Exp** N/A
Enroll(000): Q2 20: 3 **19:** 3 **18:** 4 **Med Exp PMPM:** $535
Principal Investments: Long-term bonds (51%), cash and equiv (49%)
Provider Compensation ($000): Contr fee ($15,045), capitation ($5,669), FFS ($29)
Total Member Encounters: Phys (42,682), non-phys (23,025)
Group Affiliation: None
Licensed in: UT
Address: 9815 SOUTH MONROE STREET SUIT, SANDY, UT 84070
Phone: (801) 256-6200 **Dom State:** UT **Commenced Bus:** N/A

Data Date	Rating	RACR #1	RACR #2	Total Assets ($mil)	Capital ($mil)	Net Premium ($mil)	Net Income ($mil)
6-20	D+	1.58	1.31	11.7	5.4	13.2	1.0
6-19	C+	3.50	2.92	10.9	5.8	12.9	1.4
2019	C+	3.47	2.89	10.9	6.2	26.4	1.7
2018	C+	6.74	5.62	17.4	12.0	29.8	2.0
2017	C	4.74	3.95	27.1	20.1	39.9	2.6
2016	C+	4.44	3.70	31.8	17.2	46.0	-10.9
2015	C-	4.47	3.73	43.4	19.2	68.6	-8.3

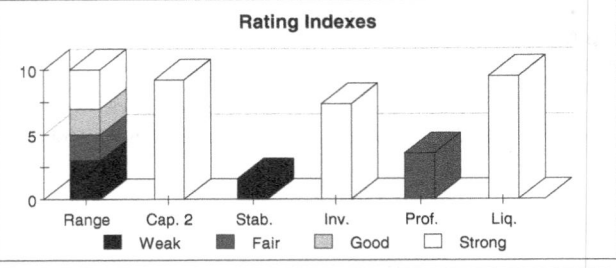

Rating Indexes

HUMANA REGIONAL HEALTH PLAN INC   C-   Fair

Major Rating Factors: Weak profitability index (1.0 on a scale of 0 to 10). Good capitalization (6.0) based on good current risk-adjusted capital (severe loss scenario). High quality investment portfolio (9.9).
Other Rating Factors: Excellent liquidity (7.0) with ample operational cash flow and liquid investments.
Principal Business: Medicare (100%)
Mem Phys: 19: 23,116 **18:** N/A   **19 MLR** 85.6% **/ 19 Admin Exp** N/A
Enroll(000): Q2 20: 16 **19:** 14 **18:** N/A **Med Exp PMPM:** $725
Principal Investments: Cash and equiv (92%), long-term bonds (8%)
Provider Compensation ($000): Contr fee ($76,627), capitation ($29,497), FFS ($1,500)
Total Member Encounters: Phys (231,460), non-phys (141,427)
Group Affiliation: None
Licensed in: AL, AR, IL, KS, MS, MO, OK, TX
Address: C/OCSC300 SPRING BLDG STE 900, LITTLE ROCK, AR 72201
Phone: (502) 580-1000 **Dom State:** AR **Commenced Bus:** N/A

Data Date	Rating	RACR #1	RACR #2	Total Assets ($mil)	Capital ($mil)	Net Premium ($mil)	Net Income ($mil)
6-20	C-	1.08	0.90	49.4	14.8	84.6	-3.5
6-19	U	522.00	435.00	32.7	15.4	66.8	2.0
2019	B-	2.48	2.06	37.3	19.3	137.0	-1.3
2018	U	491.60	409.70	16.8	14.5	-0.2	0.5
2017	C+	3.71	3.09	19.7	15.2	34.5	2.4
2016	B-	5.69	4.74	16.4	12.8	30.6	0.3
2015	C+	6.48	5.40	14.9	12.6	22.0	-1.1

Rating Indexes

HUMANA WISCONSIN HEALTH ORGANIZATION *

B+   **Good**

Major Rating Factors: Good quality investment portfolio (6.5 on a scale of 0 to 10). Good liquidity (6.3) with sufficient resources (cash flows and marketable investments) to handle a spike in claims. Excellent profitability (7.0).
Other Rating Factors: Strong capitalization index (8.1) based on excellent current risk-adjusted capital (severe loss scenario). Excellent overall results on stability tests (7.1) based on healthy premium and capital growth during 2019.
Principal Business: Medicare (97%), comp med (3%)
Mem Phys: 19: 225,634   **18:** 218,700   **19 MLR** 86.2%   **/ 19 Admin Exp** N/A
Enroll(000): Q2 20: 348   **19:** 302   **18:** 246   **Med Exp PMPM:** $828
Principal Investments: Long-term bonds (90%), cash and equiv (10%)
Provider Compensation ($000): Capitation ($1,427,693), contr fee ($1,295,450), salary ($49,877), FFS ($42,339)
Total Member Encounters: Phys (5,586,567), non-phys (3,104,464)
Group Affiliation: None
Licensed in: DE, KY, MT, NJ, OH, RI, VA, WI
Address: N19W24133 RIVERWOOD DR SUITE 3, WAUKESHA,
Phone: (262) 408-4300   **Dom State:** WI   **Commenced Bus:** N/A

Data Date	Rating	RACR #1	RACR #2	Total Assets ($mil)	Capital ($mil)	Net Premium ($mil)	Net Income ($mil)
6-20	B+	2.23	1.86	1,259.4	417.9	2,151.0	84.9
6-19	B+	3.13	2.61	811.5	347.6	1,668.1	59.3
2019	B+	2.35	1.96	875.5	344.7	3,362.9	88.7
2018	B	2.67	2.23	679.6	296.4	2,572.1	11.5
2017	B-	1.74	1.45	334.7	150.6	1,302.3	25.4
2016	B-	3.27	2.73	200.3	113.2	614.4	2.7
2015	C+	2.43	2.02	179.4	87.4	592.9	-17.6

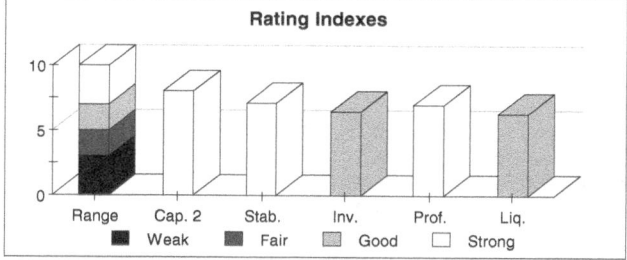

Rating Indexes

HUMANADENTAL INS CO

C+   **Fair**

Major Rating Factors: Fair profitability index (4.2 on a scale of 0 to 10). Good liquidity (6.9) with sufficient resources (cash flows and marketable investments) to handle a spike in claims. Strong capitalization (9.7) based on excellent current risk-adjusted capital (severe loss scenario).
Other Rating Factors: High quality investment portfolio (8.5).
Principal Business: Medicare (44%), dental (32%), med supp (17%), FEHB (7%)
Mem Phys: 19: 1,032,085   **18:** N/A   **19 MLR** 78.7%   **/ 19 Admin Exp** N/A
Enroll(000): Q2 20: 474   **19:** 476   **18:** 495   **Med Exp PMPM:** $51
Principal Investments: Long-term bonds (58%), cash and equiv (42%)
Provider Compensation ($000): Contr fee ($230,195), FFS ($50,248)
Total Member Encounters: Phys (907,026), non-phys (428,214)
Group Affiliation: None
Licensed in: All states except NY, PR
Address: 1100 EMPLOYERS BOULEVARD, DEPERE, WI 54115
Phone: (920) 336-1100   **Dom State:** WI   **Commenced Bus:** N/A

Data Date	Rating	RACR #1	RACR #2	Total Assets ($mil)	Capital ($mil)	Net Premium ($mil)	Net Income ($mil)
6-20	C+	3.51	2.92	216.5	102.8	300.1	20.3
6-19	N/A	N/A	N/A	N/A	N/A	N/A	N/A
2019	B-	3.69	3.08	142.3	75.6	384.3	-11.1
2018	N/A	N/A	N/A	101.0	55.6	205.5	N/A
2017	N/A	N/A	N/A	98.5	62.3	252.4	N/A
2016	N/A	N/A	N/A	111.1	69.8	318.8	N/A
2015	N/A	N/A	N/A	136.4	84.6	395.8	N/A

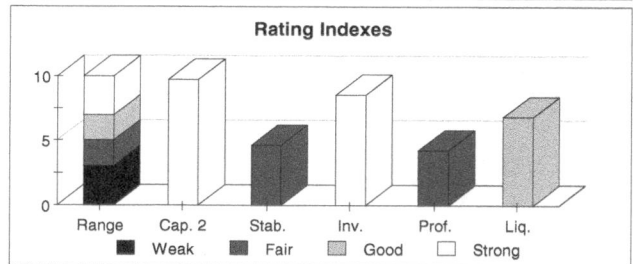

Rating Indexes

ILLINICARE HEALTH PLAN INC

C   **Fair**

Major Rating Factors: Fair capitalization (4.8 on a scale of 0 to 10) based on good current risk-adjusted capital (severe loss scenario). Weak profitability index (0.9). High quality investment portfolio (9.2).
Other Rating Factors: Excellent liquidity (7.0) with sufficient resources (cash flows and marketable investments) to handle a spike in claims.
Principal Business: Medicaid (94%), Medicare (6%)
Mem Phys: 19: 22,997   **18:** 24,949   **19 MLR** 91.8%   **/ 19 Admin Exp** N/A
Enroll(000): Q2 20: 360   **19:** 357   **18:** 360   **Med Exp PMPM:** $496
Principal Investments: Cash and equiv (189%)
Provider Compensation ($000): Contr fee ($1,944,748), salary ($65,007), capitation ($36,690), bonus arrang ($2,764), other ($21,109)
Total Member Encounters: Phys (1,919,152), non-phys (3,071,509)
Group Affiliation: None
Licensed in: IL
Address: 1333 BURR RIDGE PARKWAY, BURR RIDGE, IL 60527
Phone: (314) 725-4477   **Dom State:** IL   **Commenced Bus:** N/A

Data Date	Rating	RACR #1	RACR #2	Total Assets ($mil)	Capital ($mil)	Net Premium ($mil)	Net Income ($mil)
6-20	C	0.90	0.75	688.0	163.7	1,307.4	-197.9
6-19	C	1.83	1.53	458.8	166.1	1,054.1	7.0
2019	C	1.27	1.06	678.1	165.1	2,319.1	-3.0
2018	C-	1.83	1.52	450.0	165.3	1,830.8	30.2
2017	C-	1.30	1.08	352.6	128.8	1,367.1	4.4
2016	C-	1.85	1.54	360.9	123.9	1,201.2	-73.7
2015	C-	1.69	1.41	295.8	95.0	1,078.8	-33.4

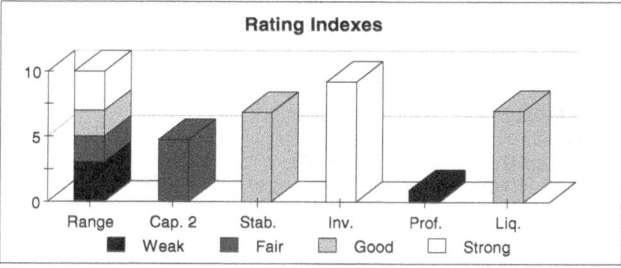

Rating Indexes

ILLINOIS MUTUAL LIFE INS CO *   B+   Good

Major Rating Factors: Good quality investment portfolio (6.0 on a scale of 0 to 10) despite mixed results such as: large holdings of BBB rated bonds but moderate junk bond exposure. Good overall profitability (6.1) despite operating losses during the first three months of 2020. Good liquidity (6.5) with sufficient resources to handle a spike in claims as well as a significant increase in policy surrenders.

Other Rating Factors: Good overall results on stability tests (6.7) despite negative cash flow from operations for 2019 excellent operational trends and excellent risk diversification. Strong capitalization (8.2) based on excellent risk adjusted capital (severe loss scenario).

Principal Business: Individual life insurance (51%), individual health insurance (45%), group health insurance (3%), and individual annuities (1%).

Principal Investments: NonCMO investment grade bonds (57%), CMOs and structured securities (24%), noninv. grade bonds (5%), common & preferred stock (5%), and misc. investments (7%).

Investments in Affiliates: None

Group Affiliation: None

Licensed in: All states except AK, DC, HI, NY, PR

Commenced Business: July 1912

Address: 300 SW Adams Street, Peoria, IL 61634

Phone: (309) 674-8255 **Domicile State:** IL **NAIC Code:** 64580

Data Date	Rating	RACR #1	RACR #2	Total Assets ($mil)	Capital ($mil)	Net Premium ($mil)	Net Income ($mil)
3-20	B+	3.37	1.83	1,520.9	240.6	24.7	-2.5
3-19	B+	3.69	2.06	1,507.2	241.5	24.7	-1.8
2019	B+	3.75	2.05	1,530.7	255.4	100.9	0.5
2018	B+	3.75	2.09	1,460.5	240.1	101.5	27.4
2017	B	3.74	2.12	1,442.3	229.8	105.4	12.7
2016	B	3.70	2.08	1,434.3	226.0	102.8	9.4
2015	A-	3.53	1.99	1,388.9	211.7	100.3	14.8

Rating Indexes

Ranges, Cap., Stab., Inv., Prof., Liq. — Weak, Fair, Good, Strong

IMPERIAL HEALTH PLAN OF CALIFORNIA   D   Weak

Major Rating Factors: Fair capitalization index (4.5 on a scale of 0 to 10) based on weak current risk-adjusted capital (moderate loss scenario). Fair overall results on stability tests (3.4) in spite of healthy premium and capital growth during 2019. Excellent profitability (8.7).

Other Rating Factors: Excellent liquidity (6.9) with sufficient resources (cash flows and marketable investments) to handle a spike in claims.

Principal Business: Medicare (7%)

Mem Phys: 19: N/A **18:** N/A **19 MLR** 80.7% **/ 19 Admin Exp** N/A

Enroll(000): Q2 20: 15 **19:** 2 **18:** 2 **Med Exp PMPM:** $1,362

Principal Investments ($000): Cash and equiv ($18,070)

Provider Compensation ($000): None

Total Member Encounters: N/A

Group Affiliation: None

Licensed in: CA

Address: 10801 6th Street Suite 120, Rancho Cucamonga, CA 91730

Phone: (951) 335-3987 **Dom State:** CA **Commenced Bus:** N/A

Data Date	Rating	RACR #1	RACR #2	Total Assets ($mil)	Capital ($mil)	Net Premium ($mil)	Net Income ($mil)
6-20	D	0.71	0.44	30.4	5.0	68.8	0.3
6-19	C-	0.97	0.64	14.5	3.7	25.2	1.3
2019	D+	0.66	0.41	19.7	4.7	62.8	2.3
2018	D+	0.60	0.40	9.5	2.4	24.9	1.1
2017	C-	0.71	0.47	3.3	1.3	15.6	0.0
2016	C-	2.38	1.57	3.0	1.3	5.1	0.1
2015	N/A	N/A	N/A	N/A	N/A	N/A	N/A

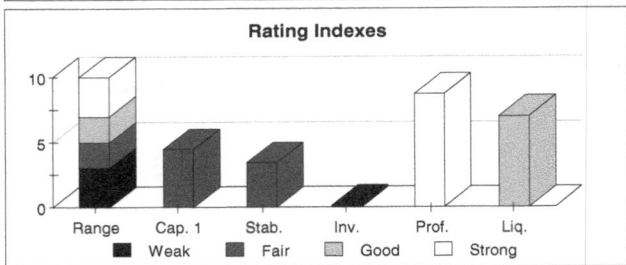

Rating Indexes

Range, Cap. 1, Stab., Inv., Prof., Liq. — Weak, Fair, Good, Strong

INDEPENDENCE AMERICAN INS CO   B-   Good

Major Rating Factors: Fair overall results on stability tests (3.7 on a scale of 0 to 10). History of adequate reserve strength (6.6) as reserves have been consistently at an acceptable level.

Other Rating Factors: Good liquidity (5.6) with sufficient resources (cash flows and marketable investments) to handle a spike in claims. Strong long-term capitalization index (8.0) based on excellent current risk adjusted capital (severe and moderate loss scenarios). Moreover, capital levels have been consistent in recent years. Excellent profitability (8.7) with operating gains in each of the last five years. Return on equity has been good over the last five years, averaging 13.1%.

Principal Business: Group accident & health (36%), other accident & health (31%), inland marine (26%), and aggregate write-ins for other lines of business (6%).

Principal Investments: Investment grade bonds (78%), misc. investments (19%), and cash (3%).

Investments in Affiliates: None

Group Affiliation: Geneve Holdings Inc

Licensed in: All states except PR

Commenced Business: March 1973

Address: 1209 Orange Street, Wilmington, DE 19801

Phone: (212) 355-4141 **Domicile State:** DE **NAIC Code:** 26581

Data Date	Rating	RACR #1	RACR #2	Loss Ratio %	Total Assets ($mil)	Capital ($mil)	Net Premium ($mil)	Net Income ($mil)
6-20	B-	2.23	1.64	N/A	146.8	88.7	83.3	4.5
6-19	B-	2.15	1.65	N/A	144.4	93.3	78.2	9.8
2019	B-	2.21	1.63	43.7	136.0	84.5	158.8	19.0
2018	B-	2.16	1.66	35.3	126.5	83.0	137.4	18.0
2017	B-	2.53	1.79	47.0	112.9	72.1	110.8	8.7
2016	B-	4.41	2.55	62.5	114.4	66.8	91.2	4.0
2015	C+	2.35	1.39	66.8	115.9	63.4	149.8	3.0

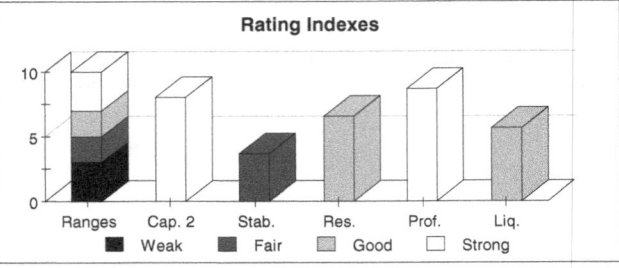

Rating Indexes

Ranges, Cap. 2, Stab., Res., Prof., Liq. — Weak, Fair, Good, Strong

INDEPENDENCE BLUE CROSS   C   Fair

Major Rating Factors: Weak profitability index (0.7 on a scale of 0 to 10). Good quality investment portfolio (6.3). Strong capitalization (8.0) based on excellent current risk-adjusted capital (severe loss scenario).
Other Rating Factors: Excellent liquidity (7.2) with ample operational cash flow and liquid investments.
Principal Business: FEHB (84%), med supp (13%), comp med (2%)
Mem Phys: 19: 864 **18:** 814 **19 MLR** 93.1% **/ 19 Admin Exp** N/A
Enroll(000): Q2 20: 111 **19:** 113 **18:** 117 **Med Exp PMPM:** $241
Principal Investments: Long-term bonds (60%), nonaffiliate common stock (13%), cash and equiv (10%), other (17%)
Provider Compensation ($000): Contr fee ($299,657), FFS ($33,590), bonus arrang ($3,376), other ($4,789)
Total Member Encounters: Non-phys (742,703)
Group Affiliation: Independence Health Group Inc
Licensed in: PA
Address: 1901 Market Street, Philadelphia, PA 19103-1480
Phone: (215) 241-2400 **Dom State:** PA **Commenced Bus:** N/A

Data Date	Rating	RACR #1	RACR #2	Total Assets ($mil)	Capital ($mil)	Net Premium ($mil)	Net Income ($mil)
6-20	C	2.13	1.77	281.8	40.4	159.9	-0.1
6-19	C+	3.36	2.80	275.0	33.4	181.7	-4.5
2019	C+	3.65	3.04	278.0	42.0	356.2	2.8
2018	C	3.32	2.77	272.3	32.9	351.4	-27.8
2017	C-	4.15	3.46	299.6	64.3	365.6	-9.1
2016	C-	6.74	5.62	285.0	68.7	391.8	7.0
2015	C-	5.44	4.53	303.9	56.0	358.8	-24.4

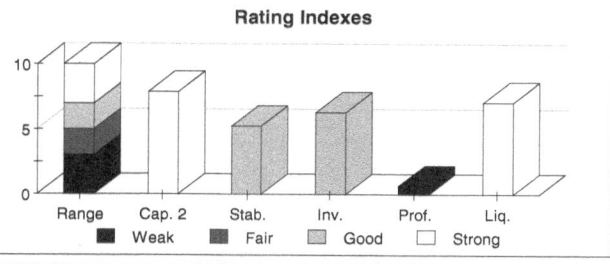

INDEPENDENT CARE HEALTH PLAN *   A-   Excellent

Major Rating Factors: Excellent profitability (8.8 on a scale of 0 to 10). Strong capitalization (7.6) based on excellent current risk-adjusted capital (severe loss scenario). High quality investment portfolio (9.9).
Other Rating Factors: Good liquidity (6.6) with sufficient resources (cash flows and marketable investments) to handle a spike in claims.
Principal Business: Medicare (50%), Medicaid (50%)
Mem Phys: 19: 6,479 **18:** 5,603 **19 MLR** 83.0% **/ 19 Admin Exp** N/A
Enroll(000): Q2 20: 41 **19:** 36 **18:** 35 **Med Exp PMPM:** $591
Principal Investments: Long-term bonds (78%), cash and equiv (22%)
Provider Compensation ($000): Contr fee ($256,533), capitation ($2,676)
Total Member Encounters: Phys (369,974), non-phys (333,486)
Group Affiliation: Humana Inc
Licensed in: IL, IN, MO, WI
Address: 1555 N RiverCenter Drive Sui, Milwaukee, WI 53212
Phone: (414) 223-4847 **Dom State:** WI **Commenced Bus:** N/A

Data Date	Rating	RACR #1	RACR #2	Total Assets ($mil)	Capital ($mil)	Net Premium ($mil)	Net Income ($mil)
6-20	A-	1.86	1.55	107.2	45.3	170.6	8.8
6-19	B+	2.52	2.10	86.4	31.0	152.0	0.3
2019	A-	2.58	2.15	81.5	36.3	305.7	6.9
2018	B+	2.61	2.18	87.3	32.5	285.1	4.6
2017	A-	1.64	1.37	78.5	29.3	228.0	2.8
2016	A-	2.68	2.23	71.2	27.4	215.1	-0.5
2015	B+	2.92	2.43	68.2	27.5	210.9	5.3

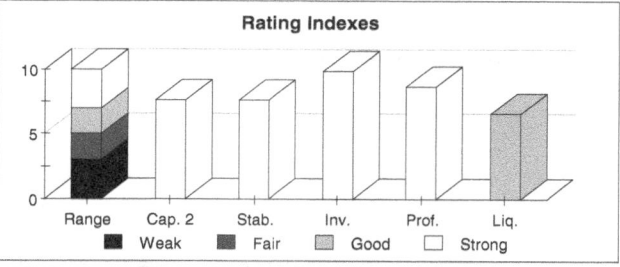

INDEPENDENT HEALTH ASSOC INC *   B+   Good

Major Rating Factors: Good overall profitability index (5.1 on a scale of 0 to 10). Strong capitalization index (10.0) based on excellent current risk-adjusted capital (severe loss scenario). High quality investment portfolio (8.0).
Other Rating Factors: Excellent overall results on stability tests (7.3). Excellent liquidity (7.0) with sufficient resources (cash flows and marketable investments) to handle a spike in claims
Principal Business: Medicare (57%), Medicaid (27%), comp med (15%)
Mem Phys: 19: 4,351 **18:** 4,278 **19 MLR** 86.6% **/ 19 Admin Exp** N/A
Enroll(000): Q2 20: 162 **19:** 159 **18:** 163 **Med Exp PMPM:** $651
Principal Investments: Long-term bonds (58%), nonaffiliate common stock (11%), cash and equiv (5%), real estate (4%), affiliate common stock (3%), other (19%)
Provider Compensation ($000): Capitation ($912,625), FFS ($308,335), other ($17,717)
Total Member Encounters: Phys (410,565), non-phys (295,006)
Group Affiliation: Independent Health Association Inc
Licensed in: NY
Address: 511 Farber Lakes Drive, Buffalo,
Phone: (716) 631-3001 **Dom State:** NY **Commenced Bus:** N/A

Data Date	Rating	RACR #1	RACR #2	Total Assets ($mil)	Capital ($mil)	Net Premium ($mil)	Net Income ($mil)
6-20	B+	4.40	3.66	761.8	499.0	715.3	27.5
6-19	B-	4.19	3.49	751.2	437.0	722.3	26.2
2019	B	3.98	3.32	774.9	442.4	1,444.0	37.0
2018	B-	3.63	3.02	688.8	387.1	1,403.3	26.5
2017	B-	3.37	2.81	722.0	367.5	1,386.1	23.7
2016	B-	3.23	2.69	710.1	367.1	1,511.3	26.1
2015	B-	2.99	2.49	764.7	337.3	1,507.7	-43.9

INDEPENDENT HEALTH BENEFITS CORP — B — Good

Major Rating Factors: Good overall profitability index (5.1 on a scale of 0 to 10). Strong capitalization (8.5) based on excellent current risk-adjusted capital (severe loss scenario). High quality investment portfolio (9.1).
Other Rating Factors: Excellent liquidity (7.5) with ample operational cash flow and liquid investments.
Principal Business: Comp med (72%), FEHB (15%), Medicare (13%)
Mem Phys: 19: 4,353 **18:** 4,270 **19 MLR** 84.5% **/ 19 Admin Exp** N/A
Enroll(000): Q2 20: 71 **19:** 74 **18:** 100 **Med Exp PMPM:** $467
Principal Investments: Long-term bonds (80%), cash and equiv (20%)
Provider Compensation ($000): FFS ($440,595), capitation ($788), other ($14,116)
Total Member Encounters: Phys (1,470,557), non-phys (3,212,999)
Group Affiliation: Independent Health Association Inc
Licensed in: NY
Address: 511 Farber Lakes Drive, Buffalo, NY 14221
Phone: (716) 631-3001 **Dom State:** NY **Commenced Bus:** N/A

Data Date	Rating	RACR #1	RACR #2	Total Assets ($mil)	Capital ($mil)	Net Premium ($mil)	Net Income ($mil)
6-20	B	2.57	2.14	326.8	119.5	251.5	14.1
6-19	C+	2.24	1.87	295.7	109.8	278.1	15.2
2019	B-	2.75	2.29	303.6	108.8	539.1	17.7
2018	C	1.93	1.61	247.3	96.4	632.6	2.2
2017	C	1.58	1.32	290.8	92.5	637.9	-1.3
2016	C	1.75	1.46	238.3	96.0	606.8	-13.1
2015	B-	2.48	2.07	270.2	107.0	584.3	-0.1

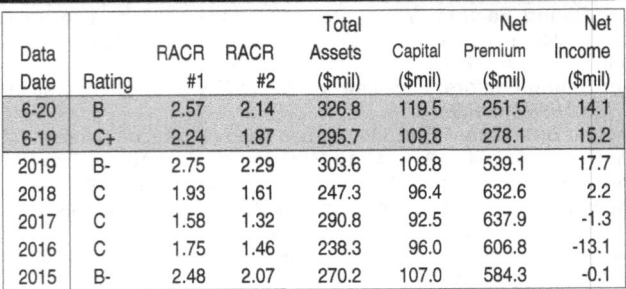

INDIANA UNIVERSITY HEALTH PLANS INC — E- — Very Weak

Major Rating Factors: Weak profitability index (0.6 on a scale of 0 to 10). Low quality investment portfolio (0.2). Strong capitalization (7.9) based on excellent current risk-adjusted capital (severe loss scenario).
Other Rating Factors: Excellent liquidity (7.3) with ample operational cash flow and liquid investments.
Principal Business: Comp med (100%)
Mem Phys: 18: 14,275 **17:** 13,843 **18 MLR** 84.9% **/ 18 Admin Exp** N/A
Enroll(000): Q3 19: 9 **18:** 8 **17:** 13 **Med Exp PMPM:** $374
Principal Investments: Cash and equiv (100%)
Provider Compensation ($000): Capitation ($33,399)
Total Member Encounters: N/A
Group Affiliation: Indiana University Health Inc
Licensed in: IN
Address: 950 N MERIDIAN STREET SUITE, INDIANAPOLIS, IN 46204
Phone: (317) 963-4822 **Dom State:** IN **Commenced Bus:** N/A

Data Date	Rating	RACR #1	RACR #2	Total Assets ($mil)	Capital ($mil)	Net Premium ($mil)	Net Income ($mil)
9-19	E-	2.05	1.71	18.0	6.1	40.4	-1.3
9-18	E-	N/A	N/A	18.8	5.4	29.8	-2.1
2018	E-	1.19	0.99	14.3	3.6	39.3	-3.4
2017	E-	N/A	N/A	36.3	7.2	60.9	-7.8
2016	E-	1.88	1.57	41.7	7.8	73.9	-19.7
2015	D	1.92	1.60	22.2	14.2	141.9	-3.7
2014	N/A	N/A	N/A	13.2	10.0	134.8	N/A

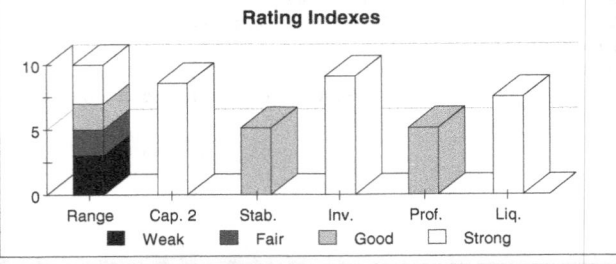

INDIANA UNIVERSITY HEALTH PLANS NFP — D — Weak

Major Rating Factors: Weak profitability index (0.9 on a scale of 0 to 10). Low quality investment portfolio (0.1). Good capitalization (6.0) based on good current risk-adjusted capital (severe loss scenario).
Other Rating Factors: Excellent liquidity (7.2) with ample operational cash flow and liquid investments.
Principal Business: Medicare (100%)
Mem Phys: 18: 15,533 **17:** 14,231 **18 MLR** 88.7% **/ 18 Admin Exp** N/A
Enroll(000): Q3 19: 14 **18:** 14 **17:** 15 **Med Exp PMPM:** $812
Principal Investments: Cash and equiv (100%)
Provider Compensation ($000): Capitation ($128,498), FFS ($13,936)
Total Member Encounters: N/A
Group Affiliation: Indiana University Health Inc
Licensed in: IN
Address: 950 N MERIDIAN STREET SUITE, INDIANAPOLIS, IN 46204
Phone: (317) 963-4822 **Dom State:** IN **Commenced Bus:** N/A

Data Date	Rating	RACR #1	RACR #2	Total Assets ($mil)	Capital ($mil)	Net Premium ($mil)	Net Income ($mil)
9-19	D	1.08	0.90	38.9	14.7	105.1	-4.6
9-18	C+	N/A	N/A	33.1	9.2	118.1	-3.9
2018	C-	0.96	0.80	38.1	13.5	157.1	-4.3
2017	C+	N/A	N/A	33.1	13.0	162.3	-4.4
2016	C	1.46	1.21	19.1	15.2	180.0	0.6
2015	N/A	N/A	N/A	1.5	1.5	N/A	N/A
2014	N/A	N/A	N/A	1.5	1.5	N/A	N/A

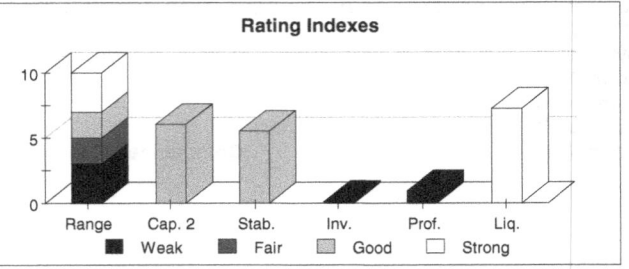

INLAND EMPIRE HEALTH PLAN *   A   Excellent

Major Rating Factors: Excellent profitability (8.6 on a scale of 0 to 10). Strong capitalization index (8.4) based on excellent current risk-adjusted capital (severe loss scenario). Excellent overall results on stability tests (8.0).
Other Rating Factors: Excellent liquidity (7.1) with ample operational cash flow and liquid investments.
Principal Business: Medicaid (92%), Medicare (8%)
Mem Phys: 19: N/A **18:** N/A **19 MLR** 92.7% / **19 Admin Exp** N/A
Enroll(000): Q2 20: 1,249 **19:** 1,245 **18:** 1,245 **Med Exp PMPM:** $345
Principal Investments ($000): Cash and equiv ($527,786)
Provider Compensation ($000): None
Total Member Encounters: N/A
Group Affiliation: None
Licensed in: CA
Address: 300 S Park Avenue, Pomona, CA 91769
Phone: (909) 623-6333 **Dom State:** CA **Commenced Bus:** September 1996

Data Date	Rating	RACR #1	RACR #2	Total Assets ($mil)	Capital ($mil)	Net Premium ($mil)	Net Income ($mil)
6-20	A	3.26	2.09	1,685.2	977.4	2,416.0	45.1
6-19	B+	3.35	2.14	1,454.6	868.5	2,572.5	-26.6
2019	A	3.05	1.96	1,884.8	932.3	5,578.2	37.3
2018	A	3.50	2.24	1,402.6	895.0	4,845.7	47.8
2017	A	3.32	2.10	1,381.7	847.3	5,099.5	68.0
2016	A	3.02	1.95	1,782.2	688.7	4,298.5	216.7
2015	B+	2.31	1.46	1,402.3	472.0	3,887.3	317.3

INNOVATION HEALTH INS CO   C   Fair

Major Rating Factors: Fair profitability index (3.7 on a scale of 0 to 10). Good quality investment portfolio (6.8). Strong capitalization (10.0) based on excellent current risk-adjusted capital (severe loss scenario).
Other Rating Factors: Excellent liquidity (8.3) with ample operational cash flow and liquid investments.
Principal Business: Medicare (63%), comp med (35%), other (2%)
Mem Phys: 19: 27,160 **18:** 76,024 **19 MLR** 30.4% / **19 Admin Exp** N/A
Enroll(000): Q2 20: 10 **19:** 11 **18:** 11 **Med Exp PMPM:** $371
Principal Investments: Long-term bonds (55%), affiliate common stock (30%), cash and equiv (15%)
Provider Compensation ($000): Contr fee ($49,875), FFS ($1,664), capitation ($12)
Total Member Encounters: Phys (178,845), non-phys (122,712)
Group Affiliation: Innovation Health Holdings LLC
Licensed in: DC, MD, VA
Address: 3190 FAIRVIEW PARK DRIVE SUIT, FALLS CHURCH, VA 22042
Phone: (703) 914-2925 **Dom State:** VA **Commenced Bus:** N/A

Data Date	Rating	RACR #1	RACR #2	Total Assets ($mil)	Capital ($mil)	Net Premium ($mil)	Net Income ($mil)
6-20	C	5.32	4.44	152.1	118.3	92.6	13.1
6-19	C-	6.04	5.03	145.3	96.5	83.2	8.8
2019	C-	6.50	5.41	131.8	100.1	162.8	16.2
2018	C-	5.25	4.37	119.3	82.7	163.2	12.4
2017	C-	N/A	N/A	198.7	62.5	315.8	-30.0
2016	C+	1.97	1.64	157.4	44.2	244.0	-26.0
2015	C+	3.52	2.93	120.4	63.2	204.6	3.1

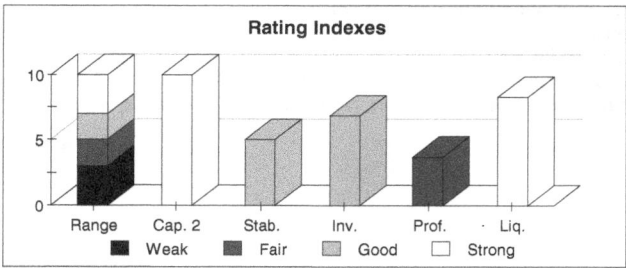

INNOVATION HEALTH PLAN INC   C-   Fair

Major Rating Factors: Fair profitability index (4.6 on a scale of 0 to 10). Good liquidity (6.9) with sufficient resources (cash flows and marketable investments) to handle a spike in claims. Strong capitalization (8.7) based on excellent current risk-adjusted capital (severe loss scenario).
Other Rating Factors: High quality investment portfolio (9.7).
Principal Business: Comp med (55%), Medicare (45%)
Mem Phys: 19: 27,160 **18:** 84,706 **19 MLR** 72.7% / **19 Admin Exp** N/A
Enroll(000): Q2 20: 17 **19:** 15 **18:** 15 **Med Exp PMPM:** $429
Principal Investments: Long-term bonds (94%), cash and equiv (6%)
Provider Compensation ($000): Contr fee ($70,429), FFS ($2,584), capitation ($251)
Total Member Encounters: Phys (233,917), non-phys (170,022)
Group Affiliation: Innovation Health Holdings LLC
Licensed in: DC, MD, VA
Address: 3190 FAIRVIEW PARK DRIVE SUIT, FALLS CHURCH, VA 22042
Phone: (703) 914-2925 **Dom State:** VA **Commenced Bus:** N/A

Data Date	Rating	RACR #1	RACR #2	Total Assets ($mil)	Capital ($mil)	Net Premium ($mil)	Net Income ($mil)
6-20	C-	2.75	2.29	56.2	30.7	58.7	3.4
6-19	C-	4.16	3.47	59.4	29.5	51.9	2.2
2019	C-	4.15	3.46	53.5	27.0	102.1	-1.6
2018	C-	3.82	3.18	53.1	26.9	112.2	3.3
2017	C-	N/A	N/A	46.0	22.5	104.7	0.3
2016	C-	2.74	2.28	44.1	18.4	95.7	-4.9
2015	C+	3.85	3.21	30.7	17.6	79.6	3.4

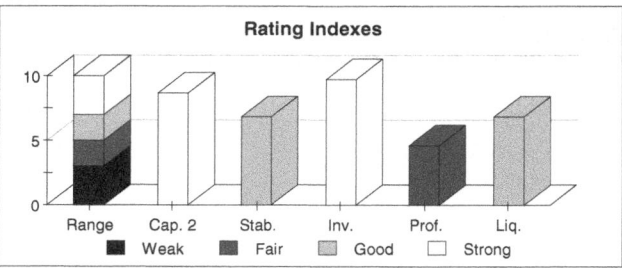

INS CO OF NORTH AMERICA — C — Fair

Major Rating Factors: Fair overall results on stability tests (3.5) including fair financial strength of affiliated Chubb Limited.

Other Rating Factors: Good overall profitability index (5.8) despite modest operating losses during 2019. Return on equity has been low, averaging 2.8% over the past five years. Strong long-term capitalization index (10.0) based on excellent current risk adjusted capital (severe and moderate loss scenarios), despite some fluctuation in capital levels. Excellent liquidity (7.4) with ample operational cash flow and liquid investments.

Principal Business: Other accident & health (28%), other liability (28%), fire (17%), group accident & health (8%), international (8%), products liability (4%), and other lines (8%).

Principal Investments: Investment grade bonds (100%) and real estate (9%).

Investments in Affiliates: None

Group Affiliation: Chubb Limited

Licensed in: All states, the District of Columbia and Puerto Rico

Commenced Business: January 1792

Address: 436 WALNUT STREET, Philadelphia, PA 19106

Phone: (215) 640-1000   **Domicile State:** PA   **NAIC Code:** 22713

Data Date	Rating	RACR #1	RACR #2	Loss Ratio %	Total Assets ($mil)	Capital ($mil)	Net Premium ($mil)	Net Income ($mil)
6-20	C	67.26	24.60	N/A	279.5	267.0	0.0	5.1
6-19	C	80.99	29.75	N/A	365.7	339.7	0.0	0.9
2019	C	65.62	23.93	0.0	271.8	263.0	0.0	-1.0
2018	C	119.30	37.10	0.0	357.3	343.1	-86.9	4.7
2017	C	2.20	1.45	83.9	999.4	251.2	270.6	6.0
2016	C	2.29	1.53	76.5	944.2	250.2	249.8	16.5
2015	C	2.08	1.40	72.8	883.8	233.6	237.9	8.6

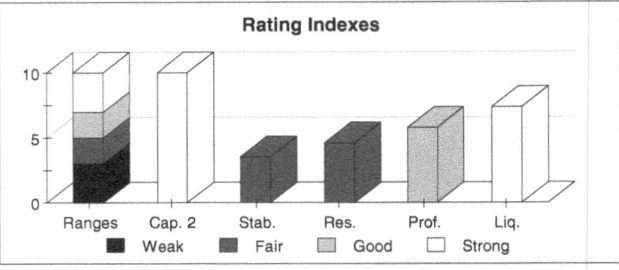

Rating Indexes

INS CO OF SCOTT & WHITE — D+ — Weak

Major Rating Factors: Weak profitability index (0.7 on a scale of 0 to 10). Strong capitalization (10.0) based on excellent current risk-adjusted capital (severe loss scenario). High quality investment portfolio (7.6).

Other Rating Factors: Excellent liquidity (7.5) with ample operational cash flow and liquid investments.

Principal Business: Comp med (64%), Medicare (36%)

Mem Phys: 19: 17,291 **18:** 15,215 **19 MLR** 75.3% **/ 19 Admin Exp** N/A

Enroll(000): Q2 20: 8 **19:** 8 **18:** 13 **Med Exp PMPM:** $518

Principal Investments: Cash and equiv (35%), nonaffiliate common stock (34%), long-term bonds (31%)

Provider Compensation ($000): Contr fee ($57,264), FFS ($2,508), capitation ($96), bonus arrang ($7)

Total Member Encounters: Phys (27,287), non-phys (16,046)

Group Affiliation: None

Licensed in: TX

Address: 1206 WEST CAMPUS DRIVE, TEMPLE, TX 76502

Phone: (254) 298-3000 **Dom State:** TX **Commenced Bus:** N/A

Data Date	Rating	RACR #1	RACR #2	Total Assets ($mil)	Capital ($mil)	Net Premium ($mil)	Net Income ($mil)
6-20	D+	3.62	3.02	47.0	31.0	32.9	7.5
6-19	D+	1.71	1.43	29.9	18.2	29.9	1.8
2019	D+	3.55	2.96	40.3	23.4	72.7	6.9
2018	D	1.39	1.16	31.9	15.5	87.1	-4.4
2017	E-	1.14	0.95	49.8	19.2	125.3	-7.2
2016	E-	0.82	0.68	155.1	70.1	293.8	-128.8
2015	E	1.36	1.13	17.5	6.8	40.5	-5.3

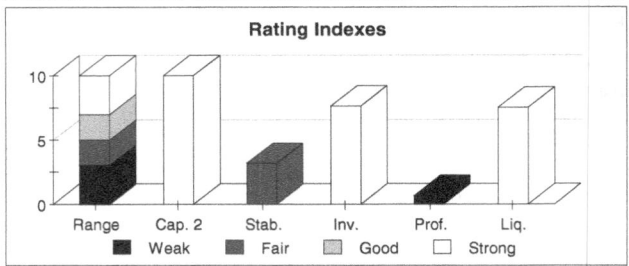

Rating Indexes

INTERVALLEY HEALTH PLAN — D+ — Weak

Major Rating Factors: Weak profitability index (1.5 on a scale of 0 to 10). Fair capitalization index (4.4) based on weak current risk-adjusted capital (moderate loss scenario). Fair overall results on stability tests (3.5).

Other Rating Factors: Excellent liquidity (7.0) with sufficient resources (cash flows and marketable investments) to handle a spike in claims.

Principal Business: Medicare (100%)

Mem Phys: 19: N/A **18:** N/A **19 MLR** 91.8% **/ 19 Admin Exp** N/A

Enroll(000): Q2 20: 19 **19:** 22 **18:** 22 **Med Exp PMPM:** $971

Principal Investments ($000): Cash and equiv ($19,590)

Provider Compensation ($000): None

Total Member Encounters: N/A

Group Affiliation: None

Licensed in: CA

Address: 1800 Harrison Street 20th Fl, Oakland, CA 94612

Phone: (510) 393-6574 **Dom State:** CA **Commenced Bus:** July 1979

Data Date	Rating	RACR #1	RACR #2	Total Assets ($mil)	Capital ($mil)	Net Premium ($mil)	Net Income ($mil)
6-20	D+	0.70	0.44	36.5	18.5	143.2	-1.6
6-19	D+	0.74	0.46	37.8	19.9	143.5	1.8
2019	D+	0.76	0.48	34.1	20.1	282.8	0.3
2018	D	0.70	0.44	33.7	18.9	293.7	-0.1
2017	D	0.72	0.45	36.8	19.1	287.3	-6.1
2016	D	1.00	0.63	41.6	26.0	289.7	2.8
2015	D	1.01	0.64	38.6	23.2	262.5	2.4

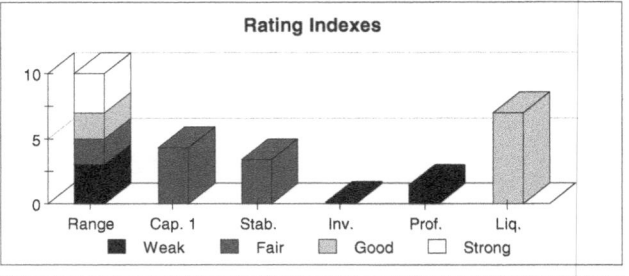

Rating Indexes

IRONSHORE INDEMNITY INC   B-   Good

Major Rating Factors: Fair overall results on stability tests (3.6) including negative cash flow from operations for 2019.

Other Rating Factors: Good liquidity (6.8) with sufficient resources (cash flows and marketable investments) to handle a spike in claims. Strong long-term capitalization index (10.0) based on excellent current risk adjusted capital (severe and moderate loss scenarios), despite some fluctuation in capital levels. Weak profitability index (2.9) with operating losses during 2015 and 2017. Return on equity has been low, averaging 1.9% over the past five years.

Principal Business: Other liability (44%), group accident & health (33%), inland marine (7%), homeowners multiple peril (5%), auto physical damage (5%), medical malpractice (1%), and other lines (3%).

Principal Investments: Investment grade bonds (73%), misc. investments (26%), and cash (1%).

Investments in Affiliates: None

Group Affiliation: Ironshore Holdings Inc

Licensed in: All states, the District of Columbia and Puerto Rico

Commenced Business: October 1919

Address: 100 SOUTH 5TH STREET, Saint Paul, MN 55117

Phone: (617) 357-9500   **Domicile State:** MN   **NAIC Code:** 23647

Data Date	Rating	RACR #1	RACR #2	Loss Ratio %	Total Assets ($mil)	Capital ($mil)	Net Premium ($mil)	Net Income ($mil)
6-20	B-	11.02	9.92	N/A	224.1	99.7	0.0	10.9
6-19	B-	8.92	8.03	N/A	336.0	90.9	0.0	2.4
2019	B-	10.10	9.09	0.0	191.2	89.2	0.0	4.5
2018	B-	9.50	8.55	0.0	235.4	88.4	0.0	3.0
2017	B-	2.88	2.76	84.8	185.8	99.2	24.1	-11.3
2016	B-	3.32	1.94	78.2	424.9	165.6	44.7	3.9
2015	B-	2.36	1.56	77.5	359.8	154.0	51.6	0.0

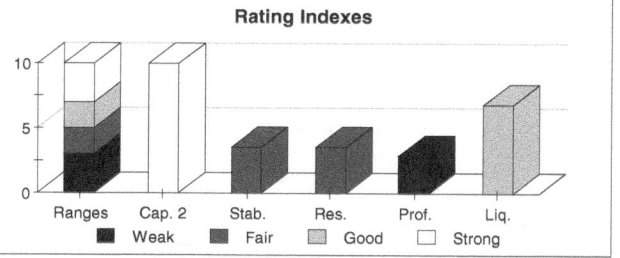

Rating Indexes — Ranges, Cap. 2, Stab., Res., Prof., Liq. — Weak, Fair, Good, Strong

JOHN HANCOCK LIFE & HEALTH INS CO   C   Fair

Major Rating Factors: Good quality investment portfolio (6.0 on a scale of 0 to 10) with minimal exposure to mortgages and minimal holdings in junk bonds. Weak overall results on stability tests (2.8) including weak results on operational trends. Strong capitalization (9.0) based on excellent risk adjusted capital (severe loss scenario). Moreover, capital levels have been consistently high over the last five years.

Other Rating Factors: Excellent profitability (9.2) with operating gains in each of the last five years. Excellent liquidity (9.0).

Principal Business: Group health insurance (74%), individual health insurance (22%), reinsurance (4%), and individual life insurance (1%).

Principal Investments: NonCMO investment grade bonds (60%), mortgages in good standing (7%), CMOs and structured securities (4%), real estate (3%), and misc. investments (17%).

Investments in Affiliates: 1%

Group Affiliation: Manulife Financial Group

Licensed in: All states, the District of Columbia and Puerto Rico

Commenced Business: October 1981

Address: 197 Clarendon Street, Boston, MA 02116-5010

Phone: (617) 572-6000   **Domicile State:** MA   **NAIC Code:** 93610

Data Date	Rating	RACR #1	RACR #2	Total Assets ($mil)	Capital ($mil)	Net Premium ($mil)	Net Income ($mil)
6-20	C	4.31	2.32	17,892.6	1,215.3	341.9	25.3
6-19	B	4.06	2.20	15,208.2	1,072.6	339.4	25.6
2019	B	4.36	2.36	16,068.0	1,108.8	682.1	91.7
2018	B	3.87	2.11	13,819.8	992.8	690.3	144.7
2017	B	3.56	1.95	14,006.8	891.9	686.5	104.6
2016	B	3.12	1.71	11,875.2	723.6	351.9	101.6
2015	B	3.22	1.76	11,150.5	704.6	575.4	40.3

Adverse Trends in Operations

Decrease in premium volume from 2018 to 2019 (1%)
Decrease in asset base during 2018 (1%)
Change in premium mix from 2015 to 2016 (15.2%)
Increase in policy surrenders from 2015 to 2016 (579%)
Decrease in premium volume from 2015 to 2016 (39%)

K S PLAN ADMINISTRATORS LLC   B   Good

Major Rating Factors: Good quality investment portfolio (4.9 on a scale of 0 to 10). Excellent profitability (7.4). Strong capitalization (7.7) based on excellent current risk-adjusted capital (severe loss scenario).

Other Rating Factors: Excellent liquidity (7.0) with sufficient resources (cash flows and marketable investments) to handle a spike in claims.

Principal Business: Medicare (100%)

Mem Phys: 19: 774   18: 776   **19 MLR** 93.3%   / **19 Admin Exp** N/A

Enroll(000): Q2 20: 38   19: 36   18: 34   **Med Exp PMPM:** $965

Principal Investments: Nonaffiliate common stock (54%), cash and equiv (46%)

Provider Compensation ($000): FFS ($206,753), capitation ($194,374), bonus arrang ($3,307)

Total Member Encounters: Phys (667,208), non-phys (12,096)

Group Affiliation: Kelsey-Seybold Medical Group PLLC

Licensed in: TX

Address: 2727 West Holcombe Blvd, Houston, TX 77025

Phone: (713) 442-0757   **Dom State:** TX   **Commenced Bus:** N/A

Data Date	Rating	RACR #1	RACR #2	Total Assets ($mil)	Capital ($mil)	Net Premium ($mil)	Net Income ($mil)
6-20	B	1.94	1.62	128.5	71.6	248.5	3.5
6-19	B+	2.00	1.66	105.7	70.2	215.0	1.0
2019	B+	2.02	1.68	106.4	74.0	433.1	4.6
2018	B+	1.86	1.55	104.3	66.0	375.6	2.2
2017	B+	2.07	1.72	99.9	65.0	345.5	6.5
2016	B+	1.87	1.56	83.5	57.2	334.8	5.9
2015	B+	1.77	1.47	77.2	50.3	320.2	11.5

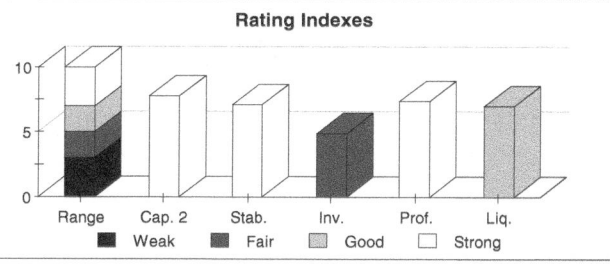

Rating Indexes — Range, Cap. 2, Stab., Inv., Prof., Liq. — Weak, Fair, Good, Strong

KAISER FNDTN HLTH PLAN OF WA | C+ | Fair

Major Rating Factors: Fair overall results on stability tests (4.4 on a scale of 0 to 10). Good liquidity (6.6) with sufficient resources (cash flows and marketable investments) to handle a spike in claims. Weak profitability index (2.2).
Other Rating Factors: Strong capitalization index (8.6) based on excellent current risk-adjusted capital (severe loss scenario). High quality investment portfolio (7.6).
Principal Business: Comp med (57%), Medicare (38%), FEHB (8%)
Mem Phys: 19: 16,828 **18:** 16,395 **19 MLR** 92.4% **/ 19 Admin Exp** N/A
Enroll(000): Q2 20: 436 **19:** 421 **18:** 430 **Med Exp PMPM:** $546
Principal Investments: Long-term bonds (57%), real estate (32%), affiliate common stock (8%), cash and equiv (1%), other (1%)
Provider Compensation ($000): Contr fee ($843,880), FFS ($690,939), capitation ($469,140), bonus arrang ($4,812), other ($770,077)
Total Member Encounters: Phys (4,314,550), non-phys (46,172)
Group Affiliation: Kaiser Foundation Health Plan Inc
Licensed in: WA
Address: 320 Westlake Ave N Suite 100, Seattle,
Phone: (206) 448-5600 **Dom State:** WA **Commenced Bus:** N/A

Data Date	Rating	RACR #1	RACR #2	Total Assets ($mil)	Capital ($mil)	Net Premium ($mil)	Net Income ($mil)
6-20	C+	2.63	2.19	1,663.4	697.6	1,562.6	16.0
6-19	B	3.82	3.18	1,640.2	906.1	1,518.7	132.6
2019	B	3.04	2.53	1,600.4	705.2	3,026.4	5.5
2018	B	3.47	2.89	1,631.0	822.6	2,924.2	-24.5
2017	B+	N/A	N/A	1,537.6	803.6	2,636.5	-45.8
2016	A-	4.69	3.91	1,718.3	970.5	2,447.0	81.1
2015	A-	5.10	4.25	1,692.2	879.3	2,334.4	118.4

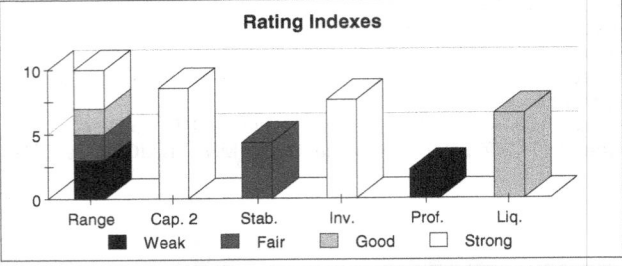

Rating Indexes

KAISER FNDTN HLTH PLAN WA OPTN | C | Fair

Major Rating Factors: Weak profitability index (0.9 on a scale of 0 to 10). Good liquidity (6.3) with sufficient resources (cash flows and marketable investments) to handle a spike in claims. Strong capitalization (7.1) based on excellent current risk-adjusted capital (severe loss scenario).
Other Rating Factors: High quality investment portfolio (9.7).
Principal Business: Comp med (94%), FEHB (6%)
Mem Phys: 19: 49,050 **18:** 46,058 **19 MLR** 88.9% **/ 19 Admin Exp** N/A
Enroll(000): Q2 20: 158 **19:** 162 **18:** 164 **Med Exp PMPM:** $431
Principal Investments: Long-term bonds (75%), cash and equiv (25%)
Provider Compensation ($000): FFS ($833,046), capitation ($854)
Total Member Encounters: Phys (801,032), non-phys (2,214)
Group Affiliation: Kaiser Foundation Health Plan Inc
Licensed in: ID, WA
Address: 601 Union Street Suite 3100, Seattle, WA 98101-1374
Phone: (206) 448-5600 **Dom State:** WA **Commenced Bus:** N/A

Data Date	Rating	RACR #1	RACR #2	Total Assets ($mil)	Capital ($mil)	Net Premium ($mil)	Net Income ($mil)
6-20	C	1.45	1.21	347.1	98.8	453.6	-24.2
6-19	B	2.97	2.47	330.8	141.4	476.1	22.2
2019	B	2.43	2.02	296.7	116.3	945.7	-2.7
2018	B	2.53	2.11	289.9	119.7	935.6	-7.3
2017	B-	1.67	1.39	282.9	125.4	966.2	-5.9
2016	B	2.59	2.16	289.3	131.0	903.9	-7.7
2015	B	3.73	3.11	292.3	142.3	842.1	1.4

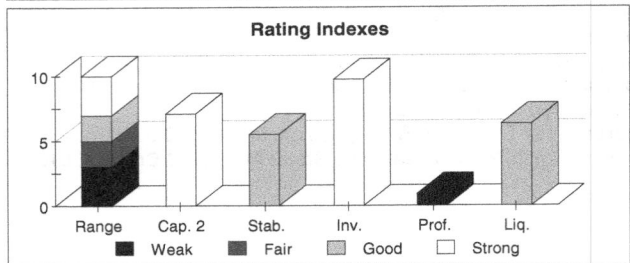

Rating Indexes

KAISER FOUNDATION HEALTH PLAN INC * | A+ | Excellent

Major Rating Factors: Excellent profitability (7.7 on a scale of 0 to 10). Strong capitalization index (10.0) based on excellent current risk-adjusted capital (severe loss scenario). Excellent overall results on stability tests (8.4).
Other Rating Factors: Excellent liquidity (7.3) with ample operational cash flow and liquid investments.
Principal Business: Medicare (25%), Medicaid (3%)
Mem Phys: 19: N/A **18:** N/A **19 MLR** 97.1% **/ 19 Admin Exp** N/A
Enroll(000): Q2 20: 9,303 **19:** 8,944 **18:** 8,944 **Med Exp PMPM:** $724
Principal Investments ($000): Cash and equiv ($9,943,546)
Provider Compensation ($000): None
Total Member Encounters: N/A
Group Affiliation: Kaiser Foundation
Licensed in: CA
Address: 9700 Stockdale Highway, Bakersfield, CA 93311
Phone: (661) 664-5016 **Dom State:** CA **Commenced Bus:** N/A

Data Date	Rating	RACR #1	RACR #2	Total Assets ($mil)	Capital ($mil)	Net Premium ($mil)	Net Income ($mil)
6-20	A+	4.34	3.10	82,017.8	38,683.7	42,708.6	3,392.9
6-19	A+	4.16	3.00	82,153.0	38,254.0	40,401.1	5,203.1
2019	A+	3.93	2.81	79,167.5	35,054.1	79,932.4	7,436.0
2018	A	3.73	2.67	74,754.5	32,235.5	75,176.3	2,503.0
2017	A	3.39	2.44	73,382.8	28,953.4	68,459.4	3,798.0
2016	A	3.86	2.76	64,612.7	27,089.8	60,874.0	3,119.6
2015	A-	3.58	2.57	62,625.8	24,897.0	57,241.2	1,867.9

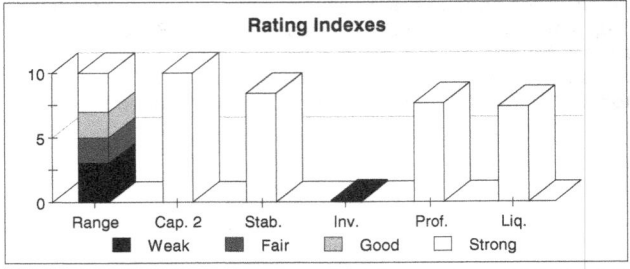

Rating Indexes

KAISER FOUNDATION HP INC HI   C   Fair

Major Rating Factors: Weak profitability index (0.9 on a scale of 0 to 10). Good overall results on stability tests (6.5). Good liquidity (6.8) with sufficient resources (cash flows and marketable investments) to handle a spike in claims.
Other Rating Factors: Strong capitalization index (9.7) based on excellent current risk-adjusted capital (severe loss scenario). High quality investment portfolio (9.7).
Principal Business: Comp med (62%), Medicare (28%), Medicaid (6%), FEHB (5%)
Mem Phys: 19: 600 **18:** 471 **19 MLR** 97.4% **/ 19 Admin Exp** N/A
Enroll(000): Q2 20: 255 **19:** 254 **18:** 252 **Med Exp PMPM:** $527
Principal Investments: Long-term bonds (69%), real estate (28%), cash and equiv (4%)
Provider Compensation ($000): Salary ($943,266), contr fee ($201,170), FFS ($14,082), other ($448,681)
Total Member Encounters: Phys (739,453), non-phys (586,416)
Group Affiliation: Kaiser Foundation Health Plan Inc
Licensed in: HI
Address: 711 Kapiolani Boulevard, Honolulu,
Phone: (808) 432-5955 **Dom State:** HI **Commenced Bus:** N/A

Data Date	Rating	RACR #1	RACR #2	Total Assets ($mil)	Capital ($mil)	Net Premium ($mil)	Net Income ($mil)
6-20	C	3.55	2.96	916.8	248.8	856.5	-26.9
6-19	B	2.47	2.06	571.5	119.7	825.5	-8.3
2019	B	2.64	2.20	763.0	136.4	1,648.4	-120.3
2018	B	2.99	2.49	584.3	144.7	1,582.2	-26.7
2017	C-	2.15	1.79	471.3	137.9	1,470.4	-85.5
2016	C	2.19	1.83	421.6	86.2	1,369.0	-22.8
2015	B-	2.02	1.69	424.5	75.2	1,270.6	-17.4

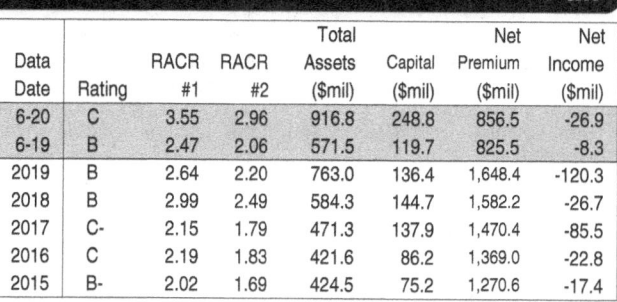

KAISER FOUNDATION HP MID-ATL STATES   C   Fair

Major Rating Factors: Fair profitability index (3.9 on a scale of 0 to 10). Fair capitalization index (2.9) based on good current risk-adjusted capital (moderate loss scenario). Fair overall results on stability tests (3.8).
Other Rating Factors: Good liquidity (6.6) with sufficient resources (cash flows and marketable investments) to handle a spike in claims. High quality investment portfolio (7.1).
Principal Business: Comp med (52%), Medicare (21%), FEHB (18%), Medicaid (7%), other (2%)
Mem Phys: 19: 22,526 **18:** 21,018 **19 MLR** 93.1% **/ 19 Admin Exp** N/A
Enroll(000): Q2 20: 736 **19:** 720 **18:** 749 **Med Exp PMPM:** $488
Principal Investments: Real estate (57%), long-term bonds (38%), cash and equiv (1%), other (4%)
Provider Compensation ($000): Contr fee ($987,223), salary ($794,357), FFS ($124,560), capitation ($13,406), other ($2,285,065)
Total Member Encounters: Phys (2,155,163), non-phys (1,050,158)
Group Affiliation: Kaiser Foundation Health Plan Inc
Licensed in: DC, MD, VA
Address: 2101 East Jefferson Street, Rockville,
Phone: (301) 816-2424 **Dom State:** MD **Commenced Bus:** N/A

Data Date	Rating	RACR #1	RACR #2	Total Assets ($mil)	Capital ($mil)	Net Premium ($mil)	Net Income ($mil)
6-20	C	1.86	1.55	1,938.5	695.6	2,494.7	126.5
6-19	B	1.82	1.52	1,642.9	518.4	2,291.6	77.6
2019	B	1.09	0.91	1,711.0	350.5	4,546.3	69.9
2018	B	1.54	1.28	1,654.8	437.0	4,196.9	23.8
2017	C	0.48	0.40	1,352.8	160.2	3,556.5	-85.0
2016	B	0.97	0.80	1,172.5	198.7	3,264.8	16.8
2015	B	1.10	0.91	1,148.5	209.2	2,981.7	-5.1

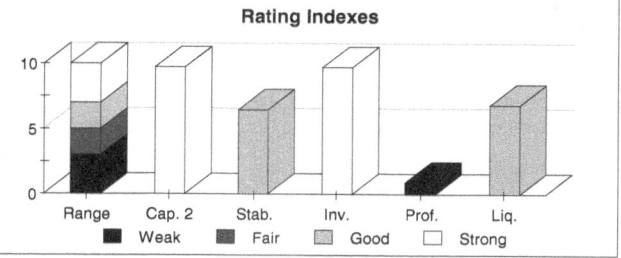

KAISER FOUNDATION HP NORTHWEST   B   Good

Major Rating Factors: Good overall profitability index (5.5 on a scale of 0 to 10). Good liquidity (6.8) with sufficient resources (cash flows and marketable investments) to handle a spike in claims. Fair overall results on stability tests (4.1) in spite of steady enrollment growth, averaging 4% over the past five years.
Other Rating Factors: Strong capitalization index (9.6) based on excellent current risk-adjusted capital (severe loss scenario). High quality investment portfolio (7.8).
Principal Business: Comp med (60%), Medicare (28%), dental (4%), FEHB (3%), other (5%)
Mem Phys: 19: 1,520 **18:** 1,483 **19 MLR** 91.3% **/ 19 Admin Exp** N/A
Enroll(000): Q2 20: 550 **19:** 552 **18:** 541 **Med Exp PMPM:** $594
Principal Investments: Long-term bonds (65%), real estate (34%), cash and equiv (1%)
Provider Compensation ($000): Salary ($1,784,528), contr fee ($585,119), FFS ($134,769), capitation ($6,928), other ($1,420,902)
Total Member Encounters: Phys (2,250,062), non-phys (689,679)
Group Affiliation: Kaiser Foundation Health Plan Inc
Licensed in: OR, WA
Address: 500 NE Multnomah Street Suite, Portland,
Phone: (503) 813-2800 **Dom State:** OR **Commenced Bus:** N/A

Data Date	Rating	RACR #1	RACR #2	Total Assets ($mil)	Capital ($mil)	Net Premium ($mil)	Net Income ($mil)
6-20	B	3.44	2.87	1,223.0	578.4	2,271.3	187.9
6-19	B	4.25	3.54	1,347.3	556.2	2,155.2	84.8
2019	B	2.74	2.28	1,180.0	383.2	4,307.7	113.3
2018	B	3.54	2.95	1,254.5	463.1	4,027.1	-7.0
2017	B-	2.31	1.93	1,192.0	353.2	3,765.2	-1.6
2016	B	4.39	3.66	1,399.4	479.9	3,558.6	40.4
2015	B-	3.99	3.32	1,477.6	419.3	3,357.5	-13.5

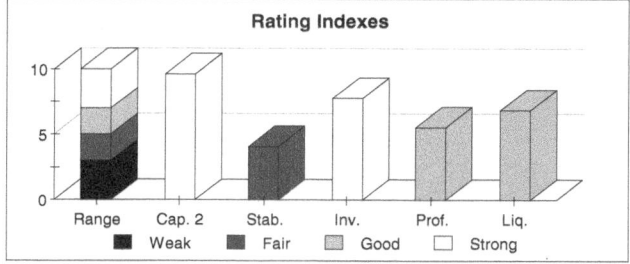

KAISER FOUNDATION HP OF CO   B-   Good

Major Rating Factors: Fair profitability index (4.0 on a scale of 0 to 10). Good overall results on stability tests (5.4). Strong capitalization index (10.0) based on excellent current risk-adjusted capital (severe loss scenario).
Other Rating Factors: High quality investment portfolio (8.6). Excellent liquidity (6.9) with sufficient resources (cash flows and marketable investments) to handle a spike in claims.
Principal Business: Comp med (62%), Medicare (32%), FEHB (5%), other (1%)
Mem Phys: 19: 1,213 **18:** 1,225 **19 MLR** 88.6% **/ 19 Admin Exp** N/A
Enroll(000): Q2 20: 553 **19:** 573 **18:** 589 **Med Exp PMPM:** $510
Principal Investments: Long-term bonds (78%), real estate (21%)
Provider Compensation ($000): Contr fee ($1,297,418), salary ($606,249), FFS ($108,766), capitation ($34,441), other ($1,529,979)
Total Member Encounters: Phys (3,920,769), non-phys (1,779,577)
Group Affiliation: Kaiser Foundation Health Plan Inc
Licensed in: CO
Address: 10350 E DAKOTA AVENUE, DENVER,
Phone: (800) 632-9700 **Dom State:** CO **Commenced Bus:** N/A

Data Date	Rating	RACR #1	RACR #2	Total Assets ($mil)	Capital ($mil)	Net Premium ($mil)	Net Income ($mil)
6-20	B-	5.32	4.44	1,656.8	841.4	2,030.1	242.9
6-19	B	3.51	2.93	1,586.2	569.3	2,056.5	138.9
2019	B	3.94	3.29	1,502.5	588.5	4,032.9	245.2
2018	B	2.66	2.21	1,694.2	433.0	3,855.8	-147.9
2017	C	0.82	0.69	1,300.4	184.6	3,689.2	-49.6
2016	B	2.53	2.10	1,383.0	375.5	3,507.4	1.1
2015	B-	2.82	2.35	1,392.5	393.6	3,285.8	-17.0

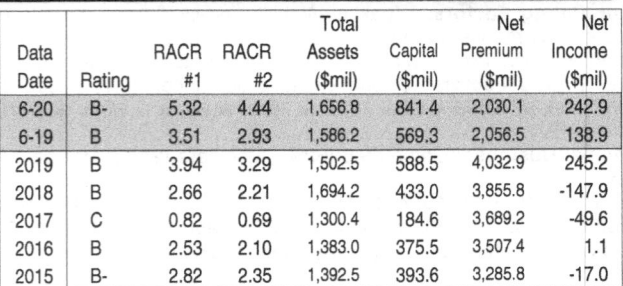

Rating Indexes

KAISER FOUNDATION HP OF GA   C   Fair

Major Rating Factors: Fair capitalization index (2.9 on a scale of 0 to 10) based on good current risk-adjusted capital (moderate loss scenario). Weak profitability index (0.9). Good liquidity (6.5) with sufficient resources (cash flows and marketable investments) to handle a spike in claims.
Other Rating Factors: High quality investment portfolio (8.7). Excellent overall results on stability tests (7.3).
Principal Business: Comp med (70%), Medicare (19%), FEHB (9%), other (2%)
Mem Phys: 19: 859 **18:** 837 **19 MLR** 97.6% **/ 19 Admin Exp** N/A
Enroll(000): Q2 20: 284 **19:** 291 **18:** 337 **Med Exp PMPM:** $531
Principal Investments: Long-term bonds (68%), real estate (30%), cash and equiv (2%)
Provider Compensation ($000): Contr fee ($438,720), FFS ($153,337), other ($1,295,932)
Total Member Encounters: Phys (1,461,897), non-phys (365,330)
Group Affiliation: Kaiser Foundation Health Plan Inc
Licensed in: (No states)
Address: 9 Piedmont Center 3495 Piedmon, Atlanta,
Phone: (404) 364-7000 **Dom State:** GA **Commenced Bus:** N/A

Data Date	Rating	RACR #1	RACR #2	Total Assets ($mil)	Capital ($mil)	Net Premium ($mil)	Net Income ($mil)
6-20	C	1.27	1.06	744.5	235.0	960.7	-55.6
6-19	B	1.59	1.33	704.6	255.6	973.5	-42.1
2019	B	1.34	1.11	729.0	181.4	1,928.7	-61.5
2018	B	1.14	0.95	720.5	182.9	2,065.2	-201.3
2017	C-	0.79	0.65	499.3	123.3	1,659.3	2.2
2016	C-	1.08	0.90	494.4	125.7	1,458.6	-9.1
2015	D	1.12	0.93	487.8	118.5	1,319.7	-30.1

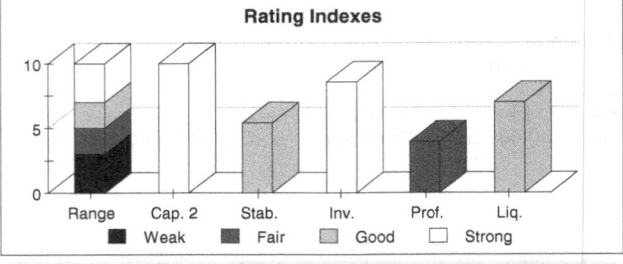

Rating Indexes

KAISER PERMANENTE INS CO *   A   Excellent

Major Rating Factors: Strong capitalization (10.0 on a scale of 0 to 10) based on excellent current risk-adjusted capital (severe loss scenario). High quality investment portfolio (9.9). Excellent liquidity (7.0) with sufficient resources (cash flows and marketable investments) to handle a spike in claims.
Other Rating Factors: Good overall profitability index (6.3).
Principal Business: Comp med (75%), dental (24%).
Mem Phys: 19: 971,502 **18:** 924,558 **19 MLR** 87.1% **/ 19 Admin Exp** N/A
Enroll(000): Q2 20: 232 **19:** 237 **18:** 237 **Med Exp PMPM:** $45
Principal Investments: Long-term bonds (82%), cash and equiv (18%)
Provider Compensation ($000): Contr fee ($88,204), bonus arrang ($15,597), FFS ($13,338), capitation ($4,971), other ($16)
Total Member Encounters: Phys (79,521), non-phys (182,452)
Group Affiliation: Kaiser Foundation Health Plan Inc
Licensed in: CA, CO, DC, GA, HI, KS, MD, MO, OH, OR, SC, VA, WA
Address: 300 Lakeside Drive 13th Floor, Oakland, CA 94612
Phone: (877) 847-7572 **Dom State:** CA **Commenced Bus:** N/A

Data Date	Rating	RACR #1	RACR #2	Total Assets ($mil)	Capital ($mil)	Net Premium ($mil)	Net Income ($mil)
6-20	A	7.52	6.26	220.6	125.1	81.7	2.2
6-19	A-	12.44	10.37	203.1	122.5	71.4	2.3
2019	A	10.42	8.68	206.8	122.3	150.4	1.8
2018	A-	12.17	10.14	181.5	119.8	118.2	2.1
2017	B	10.10	8.41	188.1	118.1	115.5	6.5
2016	B	13.54	11.28	179.2	111.7	123.1	8.4
2015	B	12.65	10.54	174.3	103.7	126.2	7.2

Rating Indexes

KANSAS SUPERIOR SELECT INC — D+ — Weak

Major Rating Factors: Weak profitability index (0.3 on a scale of 0 to 10). Fair capitalization (4.8) based on good current risk-adjusted capital (severe loss scenario). Good liquidity (6.3) with sufficient resources (cash flows and marketable investments) to handle a spike in claims.
Other Rating Factors: High quality investment portfolio (9.9).
Principal Business: Medicare (100%)
Mem Phys: 18: 3,262 **17:** N/A **18 MLR** 83.0% **/ 18 Admin Exp** N/A
Enroll(000): Q3 19: 0 **18:** 0 **17:** N/A **Med Exp PMPM:** $1,586
Principal Investments: Cash and equiv (86%), long-term bonds (14%)
Provider Compensation ($000): Contr fee ($1,460)
Total Member Encounters: Phys (11,846), non-phys (3,035)
Group Affiliation: Kansas Superior Select Inc
Licensed in: KS
Address: 7200 West 13th Ste 9, Wichita, KS 67212
Phone: (620) 251-6700 **Dom State:** KS **Commenced Bus:** N/A

Data Date	Rating	RACR #1	RACR #2	Total Assets ($mil)	Capital ($mil)	Net Premium ($mil)	Net Income ($mil)
9-19	D+	0.90	0.75	2.9	1.2	5.1	-1.1
9-18	N/A	N/A	N/A	2.5	1.6	1.8	-0.5
2018	D+	1.04	0.87	2.9	1.4	3.3	-0.7
2017	N/A	N/A	N/A	1.6	1.4	N/A	-1.0
2016	N/A	N/A	N/A	N/A	N/A	N/A	N/A
2015	N/A	N/A	N/A	N/A	N/A	N/A	N/A
2014	N/A	N/A	N/A	N/A	N/A	N/A	N/A

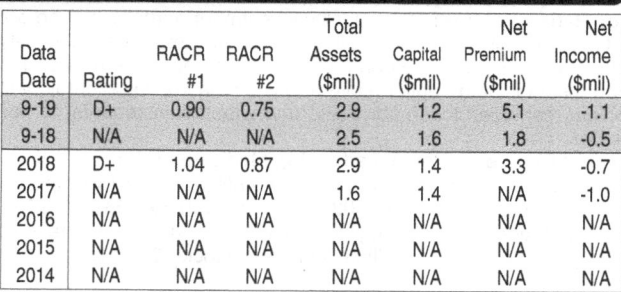

Rating Indexes

KERN HEALTH SYSTEMS * — B+ — Good

Major Rating Factors: Excellent profitability (7.8 on a scale of 0 to 10). Strong capitalization index (9.4) based on excellent current risk-adjusted capital (severe loss scenario). Excellent overall results on stability tests (7.7).
Other Rating Factors: Excellent liquidity (7.6) with ample operational cash flow and liquid investments.
Principal Business: Medicaid (100%)
Mem Phys: 19: N/A **18:** N/A **19 MLR** 133.1% **/ 19 Admin Exp** N/A
Enroll(000): Q2 20: 260 **19:** 245 **18:** 245 **Med Exp PMPM:** $346
Principal Investments ($000): Cash and equiv ($205,469)
Provider Compensation ($000): None
Total Member Encounters: N/A
Group Affiliation: None
Licensed in: CA
Address: 1055 West 7th Street, Los Angeles, CA 90017
Phone: (213) 694-1250 **Dom State:** CA **Commenced Bus:** June 1996

Data Date	Rating	RACR #1	RACR #2	Total Assets ($mil)	Capital ($mil)	Net Premium ($mil)	Net Income ($mil)
6-20	B+	4.46	2.74	699.5	221.7	420.8	7.0
6-19	B+	4.43	2.72	376.4	206.6	407.4	3.8
2019	B+	4.32	2.66	632.1	215.8	767.4	13.1
2018	B	4.39	2.69	388.4	202.7	767.9	11.1
2017	B-	4.80	2.93	341.3	191.6	719.9	19.3
2016	B-	4.85	2.96	349.3	172.3	671.5	61.3
2015	C+	3.41	2.08	267.4	111.0	559.6	33.8

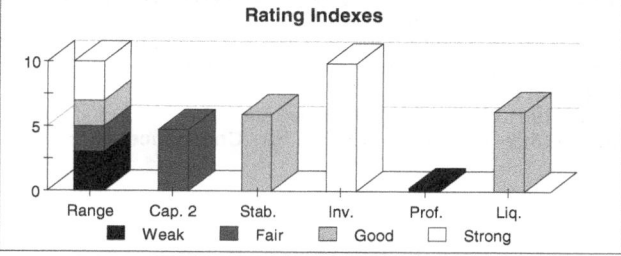

Rating Indexes

KEYSTONE HEALTH PLAN CENTRAL INC — D — Weak

Major Rating Factors: Weak profitability index (1.1 on a scale of 0 to 10). Good overall results on stability tests (5.2). Good liquidity (6.8) with sufficient resources (cash flows and marketable investments) to handle a spike in claims.
Other Rating Factors: Strong capitalization index (7.2) based on excellent current risk-adjusted capital (severe loss scenario). High quality investment portfolio (7.0).
Principal Business: Medicare (81%), comp med (18%)
Mem Phys: 19: 4,898 **18:** 4,705 **19 MLR** 87.6% **/ 19 Admin Exp** N/A
Enroll(000): Q2 20: 31 **19:** 34 **18:** 35 **Med Exp PMPM:** $552
Principal Investments: Long-term bonds (78%), cash and equiv (22%)
Provider Compensation ($000): Contr fee ($206,630), capitation ($17,949), bonus arrang ($1,716)
Total Member Encounters: Phys (585,673), non-phys (130,690)
Group Affiliation: Capital Blue Cross Inc
Licensed in: PA
Address: 2500 Elmerton Avenue, Harrisburg,
Phone: (717) 541-7000 **Dom State:** PA **Commenced Bus:** N/A

Data Date	Rating	RACR #1	RACR #2	Total Assets ($mil)	Capital ($mil)	Net Premium ($mil)	Net Income ($mil)
6-20	D	1.50	1.25	86.7	38.2	120.8	1.1
6-19	C-	2.90	2.41	89.7	41.2	134.6	-2.7
2019	C-	2.62	2.18	82.5	40.0	260.7	-5.6
2018	C-	3.00	2.50	81.1	42.8	250.6	-5.4
2017	C	2.34	1.95	88.4	49.6	229.1	1.6
2016	C+	2.32	1.93	146.1	45.1	307.9	-14.0
2015	C+	4.03	3.35	119.0	55.8	239.0	-11.3

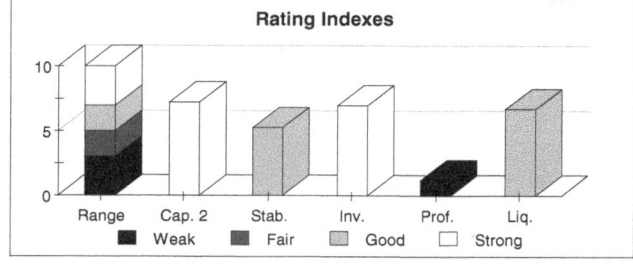

Rating Indexes

KEYSTONE HEALTH PLAN EAST INC * B+ Good

Major Rating Factors: Good quality investment portfolio (5.8 on a scale of 0 to 10). Good overall results on stability tests (6.6). Excellent profitability (8.7).
Other Rating Factors: Strong capitalization index (9.0) based on excellent current risk-adjusted capital (severe loss scenario). Excellent liquidity (6.9) with sufficient resources (cash flows and marketable investments) to handle a spike in claims.
Principal Business: Comp med (61%), Medicare (39%)
Mem Phys: 19: 39,555 18: 36,352 **19 MLR** 78.8% / **19 Admin Exp** N/A
Enroll(000): Q2 20: 385 19: 403 18: 429 **Med Exp PMPM:** $503
Principal Investments: Long-term bonds (65%), nonaffiliate common stock (11%), pref stock (8%), affiliate common stock (6%), cash and equiv (5%), other (4%)
Provider Compensation ($000): Contr fee ($1,461,146), capitation ($948,814), FFS ($40,173), bonus arrang ($28,532)
Total Member Encounters: Phys (5,158,598), non-phys (1,638,305)
Group Affiliation: Independence Health Group Inc
Licensed in: PA
Address: 1901 Market Street, Philadelphia,
Phone: (215) 241-2400 **Dom State:** PA **Commenced Bus:** N/A

Data Date	Rating	RACR #1	RACR #2	Total Assets ($mil)	Capital ($mil)	Net Premium ($mil)	Net Income ($mil)
6-20	B+	2.97	2.47	1,526.3	580.5	1,478.1	55.3
6-19	B	3.71	3.09	1,329.9	582.0	1,578.4	93.0
2019	B+	3.40	2.83	1,308.2	553.3	3,143.3	212.7
2018	B	3.07	2.56	1,203.0	476.7	3,274.5	154.5
2017	B-	2.57	2.14	1,246.5	477.9	3,089.8	131.3
2016	C+	2.64	2.20	1,221.4	397.5	3,072.9	44.3
2015	C	3.26	2.71	1,179.9	465.8	2,959.7	32.9

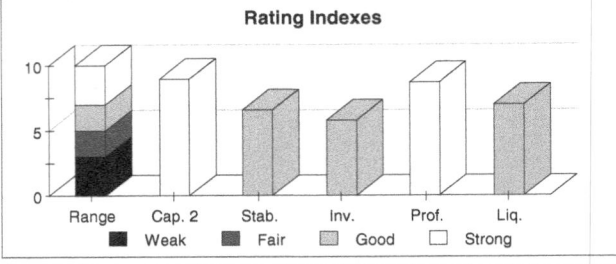

Rating Indexes

LA HEALTH SERVICE & INDEMNITY CO B Good

Major Rating Factors: Good overall profitability index (5.1 on a scale of 0 to 10). Fair quality investment portfolio (3.9). Strong capitalization (10.0) based on excellent current risk-adjusted capital (severe loss scenario).
Other Rating Factors: Excellent liquidity (6.9) with sufficient resources (cash flows and marketable investments) to handle a spike in claims.
Principal Business: Comp med (74%), FEHB (18%), med supp (5%), other (1%)
Mem Phys: 19: 40,466 18: 38,537 **19 MLR** 86.9% / **19 Admin Exp** N/A
Enroll(000): Q2 20: 748 19: 747 18: 728 **Med Exp PMPM:** $235
Principal Investments: Long-term bonds (36%), affiliate common stock (35%), nonaffiliate common stock (21%), cash and equiv (3%), real estate (3%), other (2%)
Provider Compensation ($000): FFS ($1,207,567), contr fee ($827,211), capitation ($3,576), other ($14,047)
Total Member Encounters: Phys (5,247,784), non-phys (3,066,093)
Group Affiliation: None
Licensed in: LA
Address: 5525 Reitz Avenue, Baton Rouge, LA 70809
Phone: (225) 295-3307 **Dom State:** LA **Commenced Bus:** N/A

Data Date	Rating	RACR #1	RACR #2	Total Assets ($mil)	Capital ($mil)	Net Premium ($mil)	Net Income ($mil)
6-20	B	5.46	4.55	2,367.0	1,543.2	1,233.4	101.2
6-19	B	6.69	5.58	2,293.3	1,506.3	1,175.1	79.8
2019	B	5.14	4.28	2,229.2	1,453.8	2,381.0	61.6
2018	B	6.09	5.08	2,094.5	1,371.7	2,402.6	127.5
2017	B	5.81	4.84	1,993.4	1,252.2	2,392.0	95.0
2016	B	5.54	4.62	1,789.8	1,113.1	2,526.0	-4.8
2015	B	5.46	4.55	1,671.2	1,080.1	2,555.3	-50.6

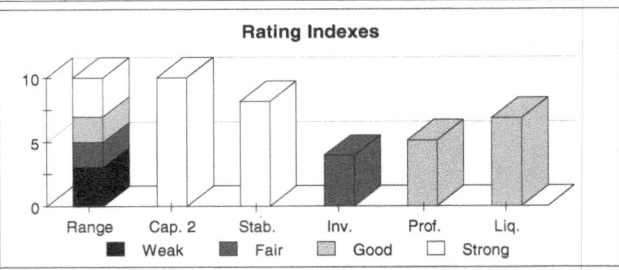

Rating Indexes

LEGAL SERVICE PLANS OF VIRGINIA INC C+ Fair

Major Rating Factors: Poor capitalization (2.9 on a scale of 0 to 10) based on weak current risk-adjusted capital (moderate loss scenario). Excellent profitability (8.0). High quality investment portfolio (9.3).
Other Rating Factors: Excellent liquidity (7.8) with ample operational cash flow and liquid investments.
Principal Business: Other (100%)
Mem Phys: 18: N/A 17: N/A **18 MLR** 31.9% / **18 Admin Exp** N/A
Enroll(000): Q3 19: N/A 18: 38 17: 38 **Med Exp PMPM:** $80
Principal Investments: Long-term bonds (90%), cash and equiv (10%)
Provider Compensation ($000): Capitation ($3,034)
Total Member Encounters: N/A
Group Affiliation: Trident
Licensed in: VA
Address: One Pre-Paid Way, Ada, OK 74820
Phone: (580) 436-1234 **Dom State:** VA **Commenced Bus:** N/A

Data Date	Rating	RACR #1	RACR #2	Total Assets ($mil)	Capital ($mil)	Net Premium ($mil)	Net Income ($mil)
9-19	C+	0.61	0.51	1.2	0.3	7.3	1.6
9-18	B	N/A	N/A	1.9	1.4	7.1	1.8
2018	B	2.16	1.80	1.7	1.2	9.5	2.5
2017	B	N/A	N/A	2.0	1.1	9.3	1.3
2016	B	2.05	1.71	2.4	1.3	9.1	1.1
2015	B	1.72	1.43	2.4	1.1	8.7	0.8
2014	N/A	N/A	N/A	2.4	1.0	8.4	N/A

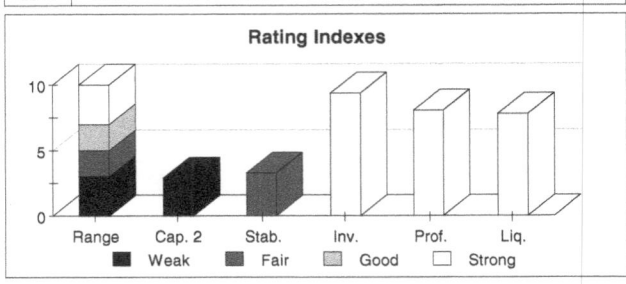

Rating Indexes

LIBERTY ADVANTAGE LLC

D   **Weak**

Major Rating Factors: Weak profitability index (0.9 on a scale of 0 to 10). Good capitalization (6.9) based on excellent current risk-adjusted capital (severe loss scenario). High quality investment portfolio (9.3).
Other Rating Factors: Excellent liquidity (7.0) with sufficient resources (cash flows and marketable investments) to handle a spike in claims.
Principal Business: Medicare (100%)
Mem Phys: 18: 10,722   **17:** N/A   **18 MLR** 87.3%   **/ 18 Admin Exp** N/A
Enroll(000): Q3 19: 1   **18:** 1   **17:** N/A   **Med Exp PMPM:** $1,788
Principal Investments: Cash and equiv (100%)
Provider Compensation ($000): Contr fee ($7,104), capitation ($4,217), bonus arrang ($52)
Total Member Encounters: Phys (9,922), non-phys (28,130)
Group Affiliation: Liberty Healthcare Insurance LLC
Licensed in: NC
Address: 2324 S 41st St, Wilmington, NC 28403
Phone: (804) 396-6412   **Dom State:** NC   **Commenced Bus:** N/A

Data Date	Rating	RACR #1	RACR #2	Total Assets ($mil)	Capital ($mil)	Net Premium ($mil)	Net Income ($mil)
9-19	D	1.24	1.03	7.3	3.2	13.1	-0.5
9-18	N/A	N/A	N/A	4.7	1.5	11.4	-0.7
2018	D	0.82	0.68	4.9	2.2	15.4	-0.5
2017	N/A	N/A	N/A	2.2	2.2	N/A	-0.5
2016	N/A	N/A	N/A	N/A	N/A	N/A	N/A
2015	N/A	N/A	N/A	N/A	N/A	N/A	N/A
2014	N/A	N/A	N/A	N/A	N/A	N/A	N/A

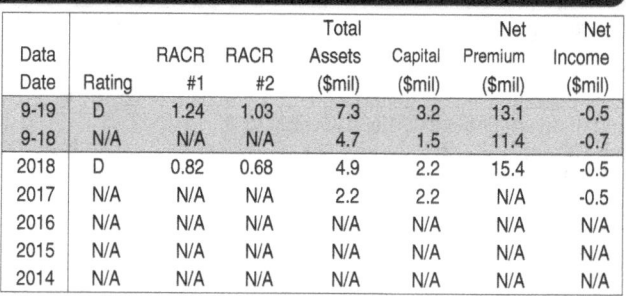

Rating Indexes

LIBERTY UNION LIFE ASR CO

C+   **Fair**

Major Rating Factors: Good overall profitability index (6.7 on a scale of 0 to 10). Good liquidity (6.6) with sufficient resources (cash flows and marketable investments) to handle a spike in claims. Strong capitalization (10.0) based on excellent current risk-adjusted capital (severe loss scenario).
Other Rating Factors: High quality investment portfolio (9.5).
Principal Business: Dental (8%), other (90%)
Mem Phys: 19: N/A   **18:** N/A   **19 MLR** 54.1%   **/ 19 Admin Exp** N/A
Enroll(000): Q2 20: 8   **19:** 9   **18:** 9   **Med Exp PMPM:** $90
Principal Investments: Long-term bonds (88%), cash and equiv (7%), nonaffiliate common stock (5%)
Provider Compensation ($000): Contr fee ($10,025), FFS ($242)
Total Member Encounters: Phys (38,936), non-phys (19,504)
Group Affiliation: None
Licensed in: AL, AZ, DE, GA, IN, IA, MI, MS, MO, MT, NE, NM, NC, ND, OH, WV
Address: 560 Kirts Blvd Ste 125, Troy, MI 48084-4133
Phone: (248) 583-7123   **Dom State:** MI   **Commenced Bus:** N/A

Data Date	Rating	RACR #1	RACR #2	Total Assets ($mil)	Capital ($mil)	Net Premium ($mil)	Net Income ($mil)
6-20	C+	9.97	8.31	14.9	8.5	8.7	0.3
6-19	N/A	N/A	N/A	N/A	N/A	N/A	N/A
2019	C+	9.76	8.13	13.4	8.3	17.4	0.0
2018	C+	9.46	7.88	14.4	8.1	16.4	5.0
2017	C	N/A	N/A	15.8	3.8	18.5	-0.1
2016	C-	3.76	3.13	14.0	4.2	22.2	0.2
2015	C-	3.24	2.70	14.5	4.0	24.8	0.0

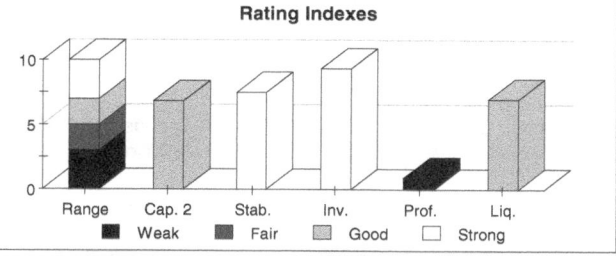

Rating Indexes

LIFE INS CO OF ALABAMA

C+   **Fair**

Major Rating Factors: Fair overall results on stability tests (4.9 on a scale of 0 to 10). Good quality investment portfolio (6.4) despite mixed results such as: no exposure to mortgages and large holdings of BBB rated bonds but no exposure to junk bonds. Good overall profitability (5.5). Return on equity has been low, averaging 2.9%.
Other Rating Factors: Good liquidity (6.6). Strong capitalization (8.8) based on excellent risk adjusted capital (severe loss scenario).
Principal Business: Individual health insurance (71%), individual life insurance (21%), and group health insurance (8%).
Principal Investments: NonCMO investment grade bonds (67%), CMOs and structured securities (19%), policy loans (4%), real estate (3%), and cash (1%).
Investments in Affiliates: None
Group Affiliation: None
Licensed in: AL, AR, FL, GA, KY, LA, MS, NC, OK, SC, TN
Commenced Business: August 1952
Address: 302 Broad Street, Gadsden, AL 35901
Phone: (256) 543-2022   **Domicile State:** AL   **NAIC Code:** 65412

Data Date	Rating	RACR #1	RACR #2	Total Assets ($mil)	Capital ($mil)	Net Premium ($mil)	Net Income ($mil)
6-20	C+	3.37	2.19	128.3	40.0	18.8	0.9
6-19	B	3.75	2.51	123.3	38.3	18.8	-1.3
2019	C+	3.82	2.50	126.8	40.4	37.5	0.1
2018	B	4.03	2.69	123.9	41.4	37.2	-0.3
2017	B	3.52	2.17	124.8	42.5	36.7	2.2
2016	B	3.39	2.03	120.8	40.6	36.0	2.2
2015	A-	3.37	2.10	116.6	38.7	36.3	2.8

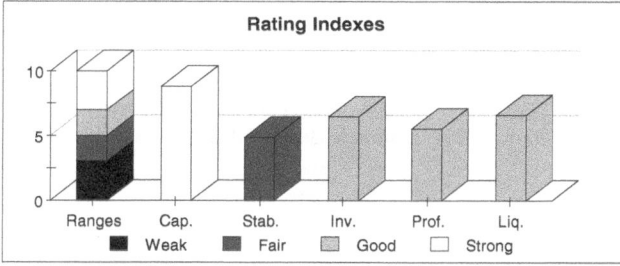

Rating Indexes

LIFE INS CO OF BOSTON & NEW YORK *

A- **Excellent**

Major Rating Factors: Good quality investment portfolio (6.5 on a scale of 0 to 10) despite mixed results such as: no exposure to mortgages and large holdings of BBB rated bonds but small junk bond holdings. Good overall profitability (6.4) despite operating losses during the first six months of 2020. Return on equity has been fair, averaging 6.8%. Good liquidity (6.7).

Other Rating Factors: Excellent overall results on stability tests (7.0) excellent operational trends and good risk diversification. Strong capitalization (8.7) based on excellent risk adjusted capital (severe loss scenario).

Principal Business: Individual life insurance (66%), individual health insurance (17%), and group health insurance (16%).

Principal Investments: NonCMO investment grade bonds (59%), policy loans (20%), CMOs and structured securities (9%), common & preferred stock (5%), and misc. investments (6%).

Investments in Affiliates: None

Group Affiliation: Boston Mutual Group

Licensed in: NY

Commenced Business: March 1990

Address: 4300 Camp Road PO Box 331, Athol Springs, NY 14010

Phone: (212) 684-2000 **Domicile State:** NY **NAIC Code:** 78140

Data Date	Rating	RACR #1	RACR #2	Total Assets ($mil)	Capital ($mil)	Net Premium ($mil)	Net Income ($mil)
6-20	A-	3.67	2.12	175.9	35.4	11.7	-0.7
6-19	A-	3.72	2.20	165.9	33.8	11.5	1.4
2019	A-	3.80	2.20	172.8	35.6	24.3	2.6
2018	A-	3.48	2.14	160.1	32.3	23.5	2.7
2017	A-	3.30	2.36	150.4	30.1	22.6	1.5
2016	A-	3.15	2.49	141.4	28.9	22.0	1.5
2015	A-	2.91	2.40	130.4	26.6	21.5	3.3

Rating Indexes

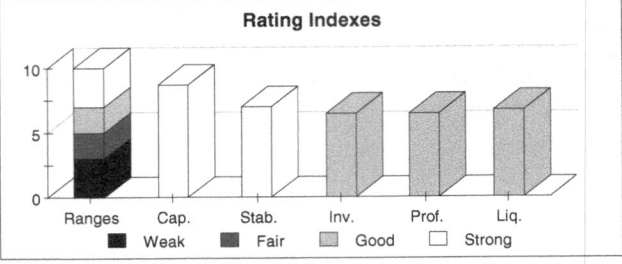

Ranges / Cap. / Stab. / Inv. / Prof. / Liq.
■ Weak ■ Fair ▨ Good □ Strong

LIFE INS CO OF NORTH AMERICA

B **Good**

Major Rating Factors: Good overall results on stability tests (6.0 on a scale of 0 to 10). Stability strengths include good operational trends and excellent risk diversification. Good quality investment portfolio (5.4) despite significant exposure to mortgages . Mortgage default rate has been low. large holdings of BBB rated bonds in addition to small junk bond holdings. Strong capitalization (8.3) based on excellent risk adjusted capital (severe loss scenario).

Other Rating Factors: Excellent profitability (7.9) with operating gains in each of the last five years. Excellent liquidity (7.0).

Principal Business: Group health insurance (59%), group life insurance (37%), and reinsurance (3%).

Principal Investments: NonCMO investment grade bonds (71%), mortgages in good standing (10%), noninv. grade bonds (5%), CMOs and structured securities (2%), and misc. investments (12%).

Investments in Affiliates: 8%

Group Affiliation: CIGNA Corp

Licensed in: All states, the District of Columbia and Puerto Rico

Commenced Business: September 1957

Address: 2 LIBERTY PLC 1601 CHESTNUT ST, PHILADELPHIA, PA 19192-2362

Phone: (215) 761-1000 **Domicile State:** PA **NAIC Code:** 65498

Data Date	Rating	RACR #1	RACR #2	Total Assets ($mil)	Capital ($mil)	Net Premium ($mil)	Net Income ($mil)
6-20	B	2.90	1.89	9,027.0	2,155.9	2,091.4	127.1
6-19	B	2.60	1.68	8,775.6	1,801.3	1,969.8	123.7
2019	B	3.13	2.04	9,469.3	2,303.9	3,931.0	330.3
2018	B	2.62	1.69	8,667.9	1,776.2	3,730.7	299.0
2017	B	2.62	1.69	8,900.7	1,798.2	3,730.5	334.4
2016	B	2.20	1.41	8,604.4	1,477.8	3,751.3	111.9
2015	B	2.34	1.51	8,141.6	1,495.3	3,674.5	236.6

Adverse Trends in Operations

Decrease in capital during 2018 (1%)
Decrease in asset base during 2018 (3%)
Decrease in capital during 2016 (1%)
Increase in policy surrenders from 2015 to 2016 (392%)

LIFE OF THE SOUTH INS CO

C **Fair**

Major Rating Factors: Fair capitalization for the current period (4.4 on a scale of 0 to 10) based on fair risk adjusted capital (moderate loss scenario) reflecting some improvement over results in 2017. Fair quality investment portfolio (4.9). Fair overall results on stability tests (3.7) including weak risk adjusted capital in prior years.

Other Rating Factors: Excellent profitability (7.2) with operating gains in each of the last five years. Excellent liquidity (7.8).

Principal Business: Credit health insurance (46%), credit life insurance (36%), individual health insurance (18%), and reinsurance (1%).

Principal Investments: CMOs and structured securities (39%), nonCMO investment grade bonds (24%), common & preferred stock (18%), and cash (4%).

Investments in Affiliates: 13%

Group Affiliation: Tiptree Inc

Licensed in: All states except CA, NY, WI, PR

Commenced Business: January 1982

Address: 2350 Prince Ave Bldg 1 Ste 4, Athens, GA 30603

Phone: (904) 407-1097 **Domicile State:** GA **NAIC Code:** 97691

Data Date	Rating	RACR #1	RACR #2	Total Assets ($mil)	Capital ($mil)	Net Premium ($mil)	Net Income ($mil)
6-20	C	0.86	0.68	132.5	27.1	28.6	1.5
6-19	C	0.77	0.61	121.1	21.5	34.0	1.6
2019	C	0.75	0.60	131.2	21.7	72.3	0.7
2018	C	0.79	0.63	111.0	22.8	65.2	2.3
2017	C	0.66	0.48	103.0	19.3	62.5	4.6
2016	C	0.71	0.53	103.4	20.4	63.1	1.7
2015	C-	0.90	0.73	91.6	21.7	64.2	2.8

Risk-Adjusted Capital Ratio #1
(Moderate Loss Scenario)

Range / 2015 / 2016 / 2017 / 2018 / 2019 / 6-20
■ Weak ▨ Fair □ Good

LIFEMAP ASR CO

B-   **Good**

Major Rating Factors: Good liquidity (6.8 on a scale of 0 to 10) with sufficient resources to handle a spike in claims. Good overall results on stability tests (5.3). Stability strengths include excellent operational trends and excellent risk diversification. Fair quality investment portfolio (4.9).
Other Rating Factors: Fair profitability (4.6). Strong capitalization (8.1) based on excellent risk adjusted capital (severe loss scenario).
Principal Business: Group health insurance (58%), group life insurance (37%), and individual health insurance (6%).
Principal Investments: CMOs and structured securities (43%), nonCMO investment grade bonds (27%), common & preferred stock (25%), and cash (5%).
Investments in Affiliates: 2%
Group Affiliation: Regence Group
Licensed in: AK, AZ, CA, ID, MT, OR, RI, UT, WA, WY
Commenced Business: July 1966
Address: 100 SW MARKET STREET, PORTLAND, OR 97201
Phone: (503) 225-6069 **Domicile State:** OR **NAIC Code:** 97985

Data Date	Rating	RACR #1	RACR #2	Total Assets ($mil)	Capital ($mil)	Net Premium ($mil)	Net Income ($mil)
6-20	B-	2.38	1.71	104.4	55.8	36.9	1.7
6-19	B-	2.08	1.50	98.6	52.8	38.3	2.6
2019	B-	2.38	1.72	103.6	55.7	76.5	3.9
2018	B-	1.96	1.44	94.2	48.0	80.1	-0.6
2017	B-	1.92	1.40	97.2	47.6	84.3	-0.2
2016	B-	1.50	1.11	84.0	38.4	81.0	-0.3
2015	B-	1.55	1.14	83.1	39.4	76.4	-1.4

Adverse Trends in Operations

Decrease in premium volume from 2018 to 2019 (4%)
Decrease in premium volume from 2017 to 2018 (5%)
Decrease in asset base during 2018 (3%)
Decrease in capital during 2016 (3%)

LIFESECURE INS CO

C-   **Fair**

Major Rating Factors: Fair overall results on stability tests (3.3 on a scale of 0 to 10). Weak profitability (2.9) with investment income below regulatory standards in relation to interest assumptions of reserves. Strong current capitalization (7.8) based on excellent risk adjusted capital (severe loss scenario) reflecting improvement over results in 2015.
Other Rating Factors: High quality investment portfolio (7.1). Excellent liquidity (9.0).
Principal Business: Individual health insurance (64%), reinsurance (29%), individual life insurance (5%), group health insurance (1%), and individual annuities (1%).
Principal Investments: NonCMO investment grade bonds (82%), CMOs and structured securities (17%), and cash (1%).
Investments in Affiliates: None
Group Affiliation: Blue Cross Blue Shield of Michigan
Licensed in: All states except NY, PR
Commenced Business: July 1954
Address: 10559 Citation Drive Suite 300, Brighton, MI 48116
Phone: (810) 220-7700 **Domicile State:** MI **NAIC Code:** 77720

Data Date	Rating	RACR #1	RACR #2	Total Assets ($mil)	Capital ($mil)	Net Premium ($mil)	Net Income ($mil)
6-20	C-	2.45	1.55	494.3	49.6	42.8	1.2
6-19	D	2.31	1.49	440.5	44.3	40.8	-2.7
2019	D+	2.46	1.59	467.1	48.0	82.3	0.8
2018	D	2.47	1.60	416.0	46.9	81.5	0.9
2017	D	2.66	1.75	366.3	46.3	72.5	-3.4
2016	D	2.05	1.33	309.2	32.5	61.9	-0.5
2015	D	1.32	0.85	262.3	18.0	50.4	-10.3

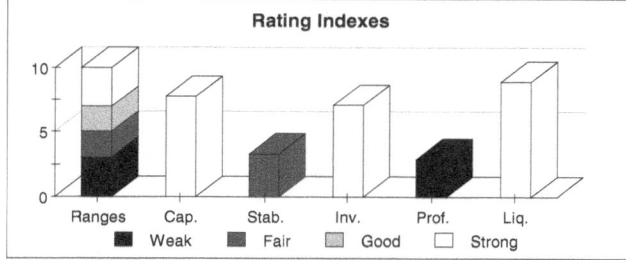

Rating Indexes (Ranges, Cap., Stab., Inv., Prof., Liq.) — Weak, Fair, Good, Strong

LIFEWISE ASR CO *

A   **Excellent**

Major Rating Factors: Excellent overall results on stability tests (7.2 on a scale of 0 to 10). Strengths that enhance stability include excellent operational trends and excellent risk diversification. Strong capitalization (10.0) based on excellent risk adjusted capital (severe loss scenario). Furthermore, this high level of risk adjusted capital has been consistently maintained over the last five years. High quality investment portfolio (8.0).
Other Rating Factors: Excellent profitability (9.3) with operating gains in each of the last five years. Excellent liquidity (7.2).
Principal Business: Group health insurance (100%).
Principal Investments: CMOs and structured securities (45%), nonCMO investment grade bonds (42%), cash (7%), and noninv. grade bonds (1%).
Investments in Affiliates: None
Group Affiliation: PREMERA
Licensed in: AK, CA, ID, IL, OR, WA
Commenced Business: November 1981
Address: 7001 220th Street SW, Mountlake Terrace, WA 98043
Phone: (425) 918-4575 **Domicile State:** WA **NAIC Code:** 94188

Data Date	Rating	RACR #1	RACR #2	Total Assets ($mil)	Capital ($mil)	Net Premium ($mil)	Net Income ($mil)
2019	A	7.47	5.52	249.5	178.2	173.4	24.7
2018	A	7.62	5.63	194.7	153.6	146.3	25.4
2017	A	7.25	5.38	168.2	128.2	130.0	20.4
2016	A	6.77	5.05	142.7	108.1	118.3	11.6
2015	A	6.80	5.11	133.5	96.5	105.7	6.7

Rating Indexes (Ranges, Cap., Stab., Inv., Prof., Liq.) — Weak, Fair, Good, Strong

LIFEWISE HEALTH PLAN OF WASHINGTON

B   **Good**

Major Rating Factors: Good overall profitability index (5.9 on a scale of 0 to 10). Strong capitalization (10.0) based on excellent current risk-adjusted capital (severe loss scenario). High quality investment portfolio (8.2).
Other Rating Factors: Excellent liquidity (7.1) with ample operational cash flow and liquid investments.
Principal Business: Comp med (100%)
Mem Phys: 19: 61,307 **18:** 49,633 **19 MLR** 74.5% **/ 19 Admin Exp** N/A
Enroll(000): Q2 20: 40 **19:** 17 **18:** 21 **Med Exp PMPM:** $400
Principal Investments: Long-term bonds (85%), cash and equiv (15%)
Provider Compensation ($000): Contr fee ($90,184), FFS ($1,831)
Total Member Encounters: Phys (151,335), non-phys (55,285)
Group Affiliation: Premera Blue Cross
Licensed in: WA
Address: 7001 220th St SW, Mountlake Terrace, WA 98043
Phone: (425) 918-4000 **Dom State:** WA **Commenced Bus:** N/A

Data Date	Rating	RACR #1	RACR #2	Total Assets ($mil)	Capital ($mil)	Net Premium ($mil)	Net Income ($mil)
6-20	B	10.13	8.44	166.7	98.6	117.5	5.9
6-19	B-	12.13	10.11	115.9	90.6	63.0	7.7
2019	B-	13.74	11.45	121.9	93.0	121.0	9.8
2018	B-	11.19	9.32	108.3	83.2	139.8	13.2
2017	B	4.23	3.53	115.7	70.0	183.0	-0.7
2016	B	6.84	5.70	121.1	71.2	176.0	-3.1
2015	B+	6.08	5.07	147.6	75.4	243.2	4.9

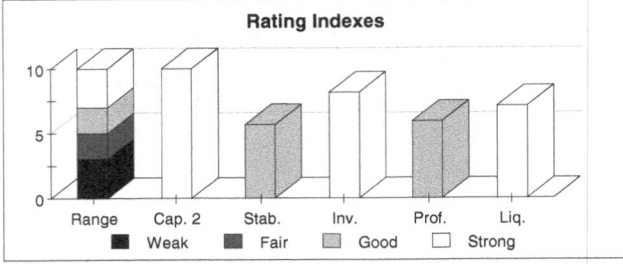

LIFEWORKS ADVANTAGE, LLC

D+   **Weak**

Major Rating Factors: Weak profitability index (0.9 on a scale of 0 to 10). Fair capitalization (3.0) based on weak current risk-adjusted capital (moderate loss scenario). Good liquidity (6.3) with sufficient resources (cash flows and marketable investments) to handle a spike in claims.
Other Rating Factors: High quality investment portfolio (9.9).
Principal Business: Medicare (100%)
Mem Phys: 18: 3,359 **17:** 991 **18 MLR** 86.1% **/ 18 Admin Exp** N/A
Enroll(000): Q3 19: 1 **18:** 1 **17:** 1 **Med Exp PMPM:** $1,781
Principal Investments: Cash and equiv (52%), long-term bonds (48%)
Provider Compensation ($000): Contr fee ($9,499), capitation ($5,223), bonus arrang ($131)
Total Member Encounters: Phys (12,704), non-phys (22,802)
Group Affiliation: MFA LifeWorks LLC
Licensed in: VA
Address: 10900 Nuckols Road STE 110, Glen Allen, VA 23060
Phone: (804) 396-6412 **Dom State:** VA **Commenced Bus:** N/A

Data Date	Rating	RACR #1	RACR #2	Total Assets ($mil)	Capital ($mil)	Net Premium ($mil)	Net Income ($mil)
9-19	D+	0.64	0.53	5.3	2.1	15.2	0.4
9-18	N/A	N/A	N/A	4.0	1.4	13.2	-0.8
2018	U	0.56	0.47	3.9	1.9	17.8	-0.4
2017	N/A	N/A	N/A	3.1	1.5	13.9	-0.3
2016	N/A	N/A	N/A	1.9	1.9	N/A	-0.9
2015	N/A	N/A	N/A	N/A	N/A	N/A	N/A
2014	N/A	N/A	N/A	N/A	N/A	N/A	N/A

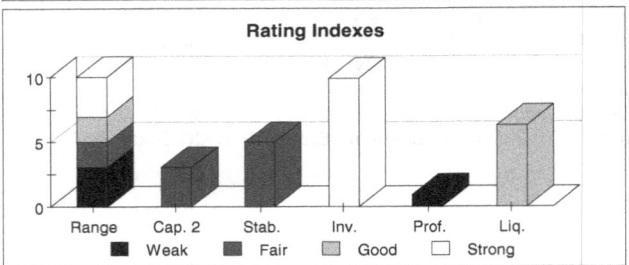

LINCOLN LIFE ASSR CO OF BOSTON

C+   **Fair**

Major Rating Factors: Fair overall results on stability tests (3.2 on a scale of 0 to 10) including negative cash flow from operations for 2019. Good quality investment portfolio (5.9) despite large exposure to mortgages . Mortgage default rate has been low. large holdings of BBB rated bonds in addition to small junk bond holdings. Weak profitability (2.3) with investment income below regulatory standards in relation to interest assumptions of reserves.
Other Rating Factors: Strong capitalization (7.2) based on excellent risk adjusted capital (severe loss scenario). Excellent liquidity (10.0).
Principal Business: Group health insurance (56%), group life insurance (28%), individual life insurance (14%), and individual annuities (2%).
Principal Investments: NonCMO investment grade bonds (65%), mortgages in good standing (27%), CMOs and structured securities (7%), and noninv. grade bonds (1%).
Investments in Affiliates: None
Group Affiliation: Liberty Mutual Group
Licensed in: All states except PR
Commenced Business: January 1964
Address: 175 Berkeley Street, Dover, NH 19087
Phone: (484) 583-1400 **Domicile State:** NH **NAIC Code:** 65315

Data Date	Rating	RACR #1	RACR #2	Total Assets ($mil)	Capital ($mil)	Net Premium ($mil)	Net Income ($mil)
6-20	C+	2.50	1.14	4,396.3	316.8	0.3	18.2
6-19	B-	3.70	1.69	3,969.2	403.1	0.7	28.7
2019	C+	3.41	1.55	4,269.3	394.0	1.2	35.0
2018	B-	4.68	2.16	3,866.3	375.4	-14,181.3	158.5
2017	B	1.96	1.14	19,045.9	1,336.7	2,929.6	50.6
2016	B	1.90	1.11	17,479.3	1,161.0	2,714.5	5.3
2015	B	1.77	1.04	16,054.1	966.4	2,501.1	69.9

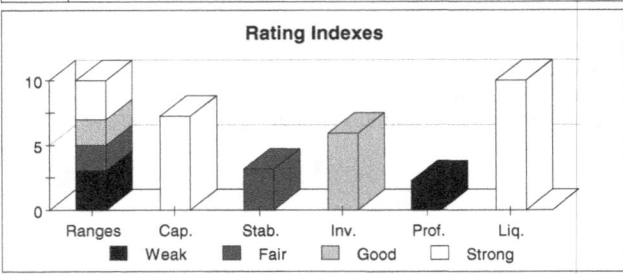

LOCAL INITIATIVE HEALTH AUTH LA   C   Fair

Major Rating Factors: Weak liquidity (0.0 on a scale of 0 to 10) as a spike in claims may stretch capacity. Good overall profitability index (5.8). Good overall results on stability tests (6.0).
Other Rating Factors: Strong capitalization index (8.3) based on excellent current risk-adjusted capital (severe loss scenario).
Principal Business: Medicaid (91%), Medicare (3%)
Mem Phys: 19: N/A **18:** N/A **19 MLR** 93.0% **/ 19 Admin Exp** N/A
Enroll(000): Q2 20: 2,192 **19:** 2,170 **18:** 2,170 **Med Exp PMPM:** $284
Principal Investments ($000): Cash and equiv ($1,899,259)
Provider Compensation ($000): None
Total Member Encounters: N/A
Group Affiliation: None
Licensed in: CA
Address: 750 Medical Center Court Ste 2, Chula Vista, CA 91911
Phone: (619) 421-1659 **Dom State:** CA **Commenced Bus:** April 1997

Data Date	Rating	RACR #1	RACR #2	Total Assets ($mil)	Capital ($mil)	Net Premium ($mil)	Net Income ($mil)
6-20	C	3.22	1.97	4,319.6	1,035.6	4,124.4	-47.7
6-19	C	1.96	1.20	4,412.6	1,060.9	3,991.4	185.0
2019	C	3.38	2.06	4,550.7	1,083.3	8,095.8	207.5
2018	C	1.27	0.78	3,938.1	875.8	7,595.6	180.1
2017	C	0.90	0.55	4,623.3	695.7	8,999.0	150.6
2016	C	0.69	0.42	4,136.1	523.8	7,755.3	30.9
2015	C	1.20	0.73	2,857.7	492.9	6,366.0	272.9

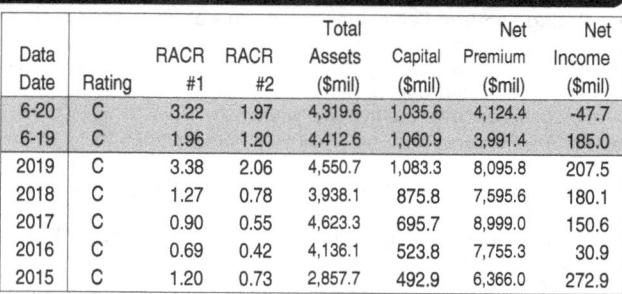

LOUISIANA HEALTHCARE CONNECTIONS INC   E+   Very Weak

Major Rating Factors: Weak profitability index (1.9 on a scale of 0 to 10). Strong capitalization (7.0) based on excellent current risk-adjusted capital (severe loss scenario). High quality investment portfolio (7.9).
Other Rating Factors: Excellent liquidity (7.0) with sufficient resources (cash flows and marketable investments) to handle a spike in claims.
Principal Business: Medicaid (100%)
Mem Phys: 19: 22,316 **18:** 23,375 **19 MLR** 86.9% **/ 19 Admin Exp** N/A
Enroll(000): Q2 20: 476 **19:** 452 **18:** 470 **Med Exp PMPM:** $372
Principal Investments: Cash and equiv (60%), long-term bonds (40%)
Provider Compensation ($000): Contr fee ($906,845), bonus arrang ($717,664), salary ($416,883), capitation ($36,613)
Total Member Encounters: Phys (2,196,537), non-phys (4,035,439)
Group Affiliation: None
Licensed in: LA
Address: 8585 Archives Avenue Suite 31, Baton Rouge, LA 70809
Phone: (314) 725-4477 **Dom State:** LA **Commenced Bus:** N/A

Data Date	Rating	RACR #1	RACR #2	Total Assets ($mil)	Capital ($mil)	Net Premium ($mil)	Net Income ($mil)
6-20	E+	1.32	1.10	559.9	178.4	1,348.7	1.3
6-19	E+	2.59	2.16	558.4	132.0	1,155.4	-6.5
2019	E+	1.46	1.22	536.2	138.3	2,406.6	-6.7
2018	E	2.61	2.17	561.3	133.2	2,279.9	-18.0
2017	E	1.30	1.08	486.0	109.5	2,103.5	-36.0
2016	E	1.40	1.17	451.1	96.5	1,740.3	-22.9
2015	E	1.56	1.30	247.5	88.4	1,188.1	-17.1

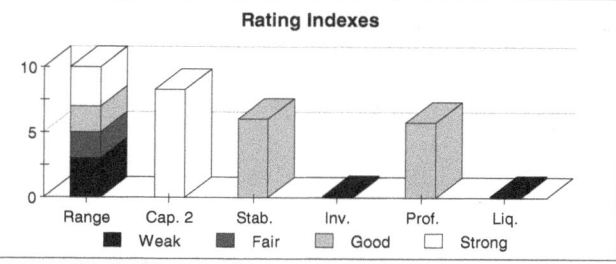

LOYAL AMERICAN LIFE INS CO   B   Good

Major Rating Factors: Good overall results on stability tests (5.6 on a scale of 0 to 10). Stability strengths include excellent operational trends, good risk adjusted capital for prior years and excellent risk diversification. Good quality investment portfolio (6.1) despite mixed results such as: no exposure to mortgages and large holdings of BBB rated bonds but minimal holdings in junk bonds. Good overall profitability (6.8).
Other Rating Factors: Good liquidity (6.6). Strong capitalization (7.2) based on excellent risk adjusted capital (severe loss scenario).
Principal Business: Individual health insurance (75%), reinsurance (21%), individual life insurance (2%), and group health insurance (1%).
Principal Investments: NonCMO investment grade bonds (79%), common & preferred stock (21%), and noninv. grade bonds (2%).
Investments in Affiliates: 21%
Group Affiliation: CIGNA Corp
Licensed in: All states except NY, PR
Commenced Business: July 1955
Address: 1300 East Ninth Street, Cleveland, OH 44114
Phone: (512) 451-2224 **Domicile State:** OH **NAIC Code:** 65722

Data Date	Rating	RACR #1	RACR #2	Total Assets ($mil)	Capital ($mil)	Net Premium ($mil)	Net Income ($mil)
6-20	B	1.30	1.11	395.6	159.5	185.9	18.0
6-19	B-	1.15	0.98	349.9	131.0	184.4	5.5
2019	B-	1.14	0.99	367.9	134.9	371.9	14.0
2018	B-	1.07	0.92	338.7	116.8	345.3	8.5
2017	B-	0.95	0.82	310.6	96.6	311.5	9.1
2016	C+	1.08	0.91	272.9	86.3	281.7	15.6
2015	C+	1.00	0.86	266.7	85.6	278.5	16.5

Adverse Trends in Operations

Increase in policy surrenders from 2018 to 2019 (196%)
Increase in policy surrenders from 2017 to 2018 (494%)
Increase in policy surrenders from 2016 to 2017 (5060%)

LUMICO LIFE INSURANCE CO   C   Fair

Major Rating Factors: Fair overall results on stability tests (4.0 on a scale of 0 to 10) including excessive premium growth. Weak profitability (2.1). Return on equity has been low, averaging -4.8%. Strong capitalization (10.0) based on excellent risk adjusted capital (severe loss scenario). Capital levels have been relatively consistent over the last five years.

Other Rating Factors: High quality investment portfolio (8.1). Excellent liquidity (8.5).

Principal Business: Individual life insurance (69%) and individual health insurance (31%).

Principal Investments: NonCMO investment grade bonds (87%) and CMOs and structured securities (14%).

Investments in Affiliates: None

Group Affiliation: Swiss Re Limited

Licensed in: All states except NY, PR

Commenced Business: May 1966

Address: 5025 N CENTRAL AVE SUITE 546, JEFFERSON CITY, MO 65101

Phone: (877) 794-7773 **Domicile State:** MO **NAIC Code:** 73504

Data Date	Rating	RACR #1	RACR #2	Total Assets ($mil)	Capital ($mil)	Net Premium ($mil)	Net Income ($mil)
6-20	C	10.48	9.43	144.8	96.7	7.5	2.5
6-19	C	7.55	6.79	80.1	54.3	3.8	-10.2
2019	C	10.57	9.51	127.5	97.5	9.5	-12.8
2018	C	6.43	5.79	60.3	46.1	5.5	-0.1
2017	C	6.15	5.53	53.1	42.2	3.6	-1.2
2016	B	6.33	5.70	52.6	43.3	3.8	-4.6
2015	B	6.23	5.60	32.2	30.0	4.4	-0.5

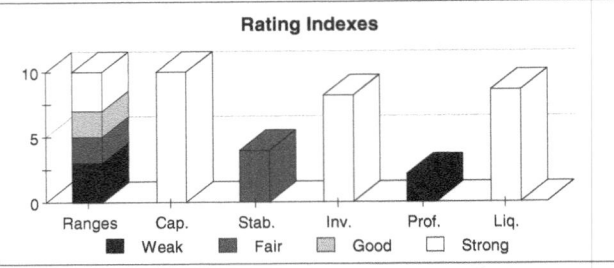

Rating Indexes

MADISON NATIONAL LIFE INS CO INC   C+   Fair

Major Rating Factors: Fair overall results on stability tests (3.5 on a scale of 0 to 10). Good overall profitability (5.5). Return on equity has been good over the last five years, averaging 10.7%. Strong overall capitalization (10.0) based on excellent risk adjusted capital (severe loss scenario). Nevertheless, capital levels have fluctuated during prior years.

Other Rating Factors: High quality investment portfolio (8.6). Excellent liquidity (7.3).

Principal Business: Group health insurance (64%), group life insurance (23%), individual life insurance (7%), individual annuities (6%), and reinsurance (1%).

Principal Investments: NonCMO investment grade bonds (86%), cash (3%), common & preferred stock (1%), and CMOs and structured securities (1%).

Investments in Affiliates: None

Group Affiliation: Geneve Holdings Inc

Licensed in: All states except NY, PR

Commenced Business: March 1962

Address: 1241 John Q Hammons Drive, Madison, WI 53717-1929

Phone: (800) 356-9601 **Domicile State:** WI **NAIC Code:** 65781

Data Date	Rating	RACR #1	RACR #2	Total Assets ($mil)	Capital ($mil)	Net Premium ($mil)	Net Income ($mil)
6-20	C+	4.23	3.08	206.5	83.9	55.5	2.9
6-19	A-	1.49	1.42	343.8	202.5	50.2	8.2
2019	C+	4.32	3.14	201.9	83.3	100.4	16.5
2018	B	1.44	1.37	337.4	196.0	93.9	16.0
2017	B-	1.48	1.41	326.3	179.6	87.9	12.8
2016	C+	1.48	1.41	329.7	179.0	86.9	-1.6
2015	B-	1.95	1.71	256.9	116.7	126.4	20.3

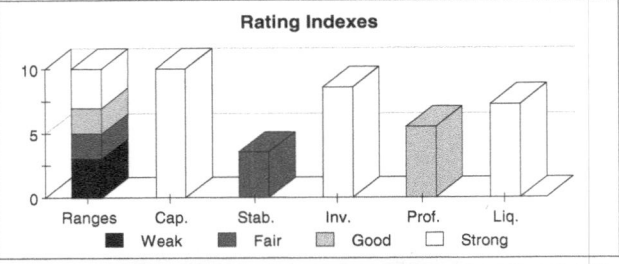

Rating Indexes

MAGELLAN BEHAVIORAL HEALTH OF PA INC   B-   Good

Major Rating Factors: Excellent profitability (7.7 on a scale of 0 to 10). Strong capitalization (6.9) based on excellent current risk-adjusted capital (severe loss scenario). High quality investment portfolio (9.9).

Other Rating Factors: Excellent liquidity (7.0) with ample operational cash flow and liquid investments.

Principal Business: Medicaid (100%)

Mem Phys: 19: 820 **18:** 728 **19 MLR** 90.7% **/ 19 Admin Exp** N/A

Enroll(000): Q2 20: 450 **19:** 458 **18:** 435 **Med Exp PMPM:** $90

Principal Investments: Cash and equiv (100%)

Provider Compensation ($000): Contr fee ($488,101)

Total Member Encounters: Phys (670,491), non-phys (1,564,518)

Group Affiliation: Magellan Health Inc

Licensed in: PA

Address: 105 Terry Drive Suite 103, Newtown, PA 18940

Phone: (215) 504-3907 **Dom State:** PA **Commenced Bus:** N/A

Data Date	Rating	RACR #1	RACR #2	Total Assets ($mil)	Capital ($mil)	Net Premium ($mil)	Net Income ($mil)
6-20	B-	1.29	1.07	120.8	66.8	267.7	-1.0
6-19	C+	1.55	1.29	123.8	68.7	269.1	4.9
2019	B-	1.55	1.29	126.5	67.9	536.3	10.3
2018	C+	1.42	1.19	124.3	63.9	543.4	13.3
2017	B-	1.13	0.94	103.8	53.6	489.0	5.0
2016	C+	1.37	1.14	107.9	50.6	460.3	5.7
2015	B-	1.41	1.18	92.7	44.9	395.2	5.4

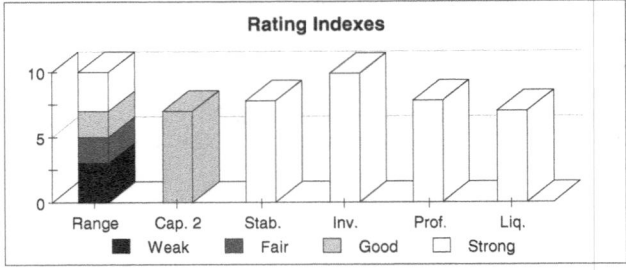

Rating Indexes

MAGELLAN COMPLETE CARE OF ARIZONA — D+ — Weak

Major Rating Factors: Weak profitability index (0.2 on a scale of 0 to 10). Strong capitalization (8.9) based on excellent current risk-adjusted capital (severe loss scenario). High quality investment portfolio (9.9).
Other Rating Factors: Excellent liquidity (8.0) with ample operational cash flow and liquid investments.
Principal Business: Medicaid (100%)
Mem Phys: 18: 4,822 **17:** N/A **18 MLR** 95.1% **/ 18 Admin Exp** N/A
Enroll(000): Q3 19: 16 **18:** 5 **17:** N/A **Med Exp PMPM:** $539
Principal Investments: Cash and equiv (81%), long-term bonds (19%)
Provider Compensation ($000): Contr fee ($1,439)
Total Member Encounters: Phys (78,102), non-phys (37,349)
Group Affiliation: Magellan Health Inc
Licensed in: AZ
Address: 4801 E Washington Street Sui, Phoenix, AZ 85034
Phone: (480) 624-9735 **Dom State:** AZ **Commenced Bus:** N/A

Data Date	Rating	RACR #1	RACR #2	Total Assets ($mil)	Capital ($mil)	Net Premium ($mil)	Net Income ($mil)
9-19	D+	2.89	2.41	26.1	6.2	56.3	-5.8
9-18	N/A	N/A	N/A	N/A	N/A	N/A	N/A
2018	D+	4.42	3.69	17.4	9.8	5.7	-2.3
2017	N/A	N/A	N/A	1.5	1.5	N/A	N/A
2016	N/A	N/A	N/A	1.5	1.5	N/A	N/A
2015	N/A	N/A	N/A	1.5	1.5	N/A	N/A
2014	N/A	N/A	N/A	1.5	1.5	N/A	N/A

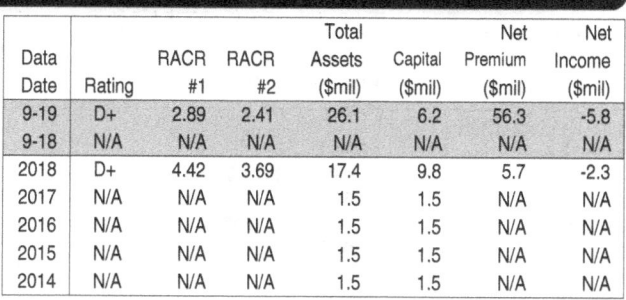

Rating Indexes

MAGELLAN COMPLETE CARE OF LOUISIANA — C+ — Fair

Major Rating Factors: Excellent profitability (7.7 on a scale of 0 to 10). Strong capitalization (9.1) based on excellent current risk-adjusted capital (severe loss scenario). High quality investment portfolio (9.9).
Other Rating Factors: Excellent liquidity (7.1) with ample operational cash flow and liquid investments.
Principal Business: Medicaid (100%)
Mem Phys: 18: 1,385 **17:** N/A **18 MLR** 75.8% **/ 18 Admin Exp** N/A
Enroll(000): Q3 19: 3 **18:** 3 **17:** N/A **Med Exp PMPM:** $1,867
Principal Investments: Long-term bonds (63%), cash and equiv (37%)
Provider Compensation ($000): Contr fee ($2,221)
Total Member Encounters: Phys (186), non-phys (386,302)
Group Affiliation: Magellan Health Inc
Licensed in: LA
Address: 8550 United Plaza Blvd Suite, Baton Rouge, LA 70809
Phone: (314) 387-5044 **Dom State:** LA **Commenced Bus:** N/A

Data Date	Rating	RACR #1	RACR #2	Total Assets ($mil)	Capital ($mil)	Net Premium ($mil)	Net Income ($mil)
9-19	C+	3.00	2.50	24.7	6.2	49.7	2.4
9-18	N/A	N/A	N/A	3.1	3.1	N/A	N/A
2018	D+	1.80	1.50	12.0	3.9	12.4	0.8
2017	N/A	N/A	N/A	3.1	3.1	N/A	N/A
2016	N/A	N/A	N/A	3.1	3.1	N/A	N/A
2015	N/A	N/A	N/A	3.1	3.1	N/A	N/A
2014	N/A	N/A	N/A	3.0	3.0	N/A	N/A

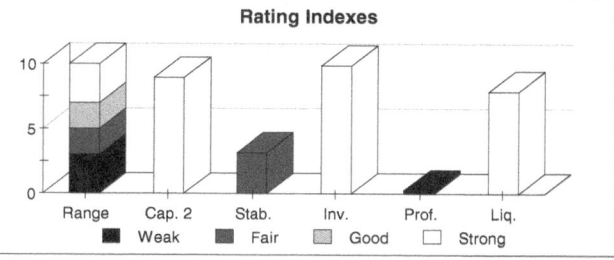

Rating Indexes

MAGELLAN COMPLETE CARE OF VA — D+ — Weak

Major Rating Factors: Weak profitability index (0.9 on a scale of 0 to 10). Good liquidity (6.8) with sufficient resources (cash flows and marketable investments) to handle a spike in claims. Strong capitalization (7.8) based on excellent current risk-adjusted capital (severe loss scenario).
Other Rating Factors: High quality investment portfolio (9.9).
Principal Business: Medicaid (100%)
Mem Phys: 18: 25,065 **17:** 15,805 **18 MLR** 100.8% **/ 18 Admin Exp** N/A
Enroll(000): Q3 19: 83 **18:** 54 **17:** 14 **Med Exp PMPM:** $1,321
Principal Investments: Cash and equiv (87%), long-term bonds (13%)
Provider Compensation ($000): Contr fee ($402,784), capitation ($29,211)
Total Member Encounters: Phys (1,967,142), non-phys (1,651,815)
Group Affiliation: Magellan Health Inc
Licensed in: VA
Address: 8621 Robert Fulton Drive, Columbia, MD 21046
Phone: (314) 387-4269 **Dom State:** VA **Commenced Bus:** N/A

Data Date	Rating	RACR #1	RACR #2	Total Assets ($mil)	Capital ($mil)	Net Premium ($mil)	Net Income ($mil)
9-19	D+	2.02	1.68	221.4	81.7	603.8	-7.3
9-18	N/A	N/A	N/A	124.3	36.8	338.5	-33.6
2018	D+	1.50	1.25	149.9	61.2	473.2	-42.4
2017	N/A	N/A	N/A	45.5	12.9	73.8	-10.1
2016	N/A	N/A	N/A	4.4	4.4	N/A	N/A
2015	N/A	N/A	N/A	N/A	N/A	N/A	N/A
2014	N/A	N/A	N/A	N/A	N/A	N/A	N/A

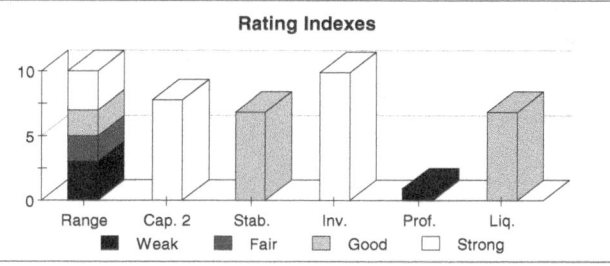

Rating Indexes

MAGELLAN LIFE INS CO

B- **Good**

Major Rating Factors: Excellent profitability (7.7 on a scale of 0 to 10). Strong capitalization (6.9) based on excellent current risk-adjusted capital (severe loss scenario). High quality investment portfolio (9.9).
Other Rating Factors: Excellent liquidity (7.3) with ample operational cash flow and liquid investments.
Principal Business: Other (100%)
Mem Phys: 19: N/A **18:** N/A **19 MLR** 83.5% **/ 19 Admin Exp** N/A
Enroll(000): Q2 20: 642 **19:** 860 **18:** 170 **Med Exp PMPM:** $4
Principal Investments: Cash and equiv (84%), long-term bonds (16%)
Provider Compensation ($000): Other ($32,580)
Total Member Encounters: N/A
Group Affiliation: Magellan Health Inc
Licensed in: AZ, CA, DE, GA, HI, IN, KS, MS, MT, NE, NM, ND, SC, SD, TN, TX, UT, WV, WY
Address: 1209 Orange Street, Wilmington, DE 19801
Phone: (619) 326-9204 **Dom State:** DE **Commenced Bus:** N/A

Data Date	Rating	RACR #1	RACR #2	Total Assets ($mil)	Capital ($mil)	Net Premium ($mil)	Net Income ($mil)
6-20	B-	1.31	1.09	12.0	9.9	18.5	3.2
6-19	B-	7.03	5.86	13.9	10.6	22.4	0.5
2019	B-	1.62	1.35	11.8	9.0	39.6	1.4
2018	B-	6.53	5.44	11.0	10.0	11.7	0.6
2017	B	1.57	1.31	21.8	15.2	58.2	3.8
2016	C-	1.62	1.35	16.2	11.5	61.3	7.1
2015	U	3.05	2.54	13.1	9.1	25.6	3.5

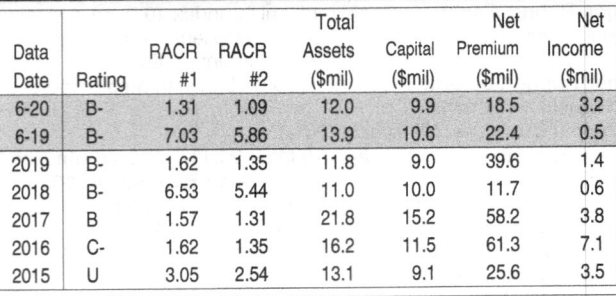

Rating Indexes

MAGNA INS CO

D **Weak**

Major Rating Factors: Weak profitability index (0.9 on a scale of 0 to 10). Poor capitalization (2.4) based on weak current risk-adjusted capital (moderate loss scenario). High quality investment portfolio (9.1).
Other Rating Factors: Excellent liquidity (7.5) with ample operational cash flow and liquid investments.
Principal Business: Other (100%)
Mem Phys: 18: N/A **17:** N/A **18 MLR** 0.8% **/ 18 Admin Exp** N/A
Enroll(000): Q3 19: 0 **18:** 7 **17:** 33 **Med Exp PMPM:** $14
Principal Investments: Long-term bonds (71%), cash and equiv (29%)
Provider Compensation ($000): Other ($61)
Total Member Encounters: N/A
Group Affiliation: Magna Holding Company LLC
Licensed in: AL, AR, FL, IL, IN, KY, LA, MS, MO, SC, TN, TX
Address: 190 CAPITOL STREET SUITE 800, JACKSON, MS 39201-2155
Phone: (985) 206-5113 **Dom State:** MS **Commenced Bus:** N/A

Data Date	Rating	RACR #1	RACR #2	Total Assets ($mil)	Capital ($mil)	Net Premium ($mil)	Net Income ($mil)
9-19	D	0.54	0.45	5.1	2.9	7.7	-0.7
9-18	C-	N/A	N/A	5.1	2.8	9.1	-0.1
2018	U	0.60	0.50	5.7	2.9	12.6	-0.7
2017	C-	N/A	N/A	4.1	2.3	4.4	-0.7
2016	C-	14.53	12.10	2.7	2.4	0.4	0.0
2015	N/A	N/A	N/A	3.0	2.5	2.8	N/A
2014	N/A	N/A	N/A	2.6	2.4	0.9	N/A

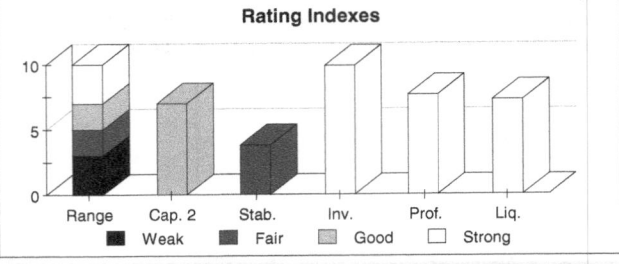

Rating Indexes

MAGNOLIA HEALTH PLAN INC

D+ **Weak**

Major Rating Factors: Weak profitability index (0.9 on a scale of 0 to 10). Good liquidity (6.9) with sufficient resources (cash flows and marketable investments) to handle a spike in claims. Strong capitalization (7.5) based on excellent current risk-adjusted capital (severe loss scenario).
Other Rating Factors: High quality investment portfolio (8.0).
Principal Business: Medicaid (99%)
Mem Phys: 19: 16,274 **18:** 14,527 **19 MLR** 92.7% **/ 19 Admin Exp** N/A
Enroll(000): Q2 20: 197 **19:** 197 **18:** 238 **Med Exp PMPM:** $410
Principal Investments: Cash and equiv (60%), long-term bonds (40%)
Provider Compensation ($000): Contr fee ($1,046,352), capitation ($24,120), salary ($16,473)
Total Member Encounters: Phys (1,066,905), non-phys (2,385,154)
Group Affiliation: None
Licensed in: MS
Address: 111 East Capitol Street Suite, Jackson, MS 39201
Phone: (314) 725-4477 **Dom State:** MS **Commenced Bus:** N/A

Data Date	Rating	RACR #1	RACR #2	Total Assets ($mil)	Capital ($mil)	Net Premium ($mil)	Net Income ($mil)
6-20	D+	1.72	1.43	284.1	164.3	563.2	22.9
6-19	D+	1.21	1.01	209.4	89.2	587.4	-41.6
2019	D+	1.90	1.58	269.4	126.8	1,166.3	-69.8
2018	D+	1.24	1.03	220.3	91.6	1,280.6	-50.1
2017	D	1.25	1.05	261.2	124.2	1,251.3	-39.2
2016	D	1.21	1.01	197.6	85.1	1,248.5	-43.3
2015	D	1.26	1.05	167.0	56.2	879.6	-28.8

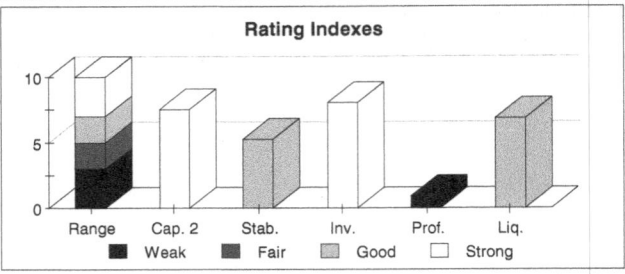

Rating Indexes

MAINE COMMUNITY HEALTH OPTIONS   D+   Weak

Major Rating Factors: Low quality investment portfolio (2.4 on a scale of 0 to 10). Fair profitability index (4.3). Fair capitalization (2.9) based on good current risk-adjusted capital (moderate loss scenario).
Other Rating Factors: Excellent liquidity (7.5) with ample operational cash flow and liquid investments.
Principal Business: Comp med (100%)
Mem Phys: 19: 35,907 **18:** 33,126 **19 MLR** 83.0% **/ 19 Admin Exp** N/A
Enroll(000): Q2 20: 28 **19:** 37 **18:** 50 **Med Exp PMPM:** $429
Principal Investments: Cash and equiv (69%), long-term bonds (31%)
Provider Compensation ($000): FFS ($221,150), bonus arrang ($317)
Total Member Encounters: Phys (178,395), non-phys (85,845)
Group Affiliation: None
Licensed in: ME, NH
Address: 150 MILL STREET SUITE 3, LEWISTON, ME 4240
Phone: (207) 402-3330 **Dom State:** ME **Commenced Bus:** N/A

Data Date	Rating	RACR #1	RACR #2	Total Assets ($mil)	Capital ($mil)	Net Premium ($mil)	Net Income ($mil)
6-20	D+	2.01	1.67	182.1	78.0	91.0	0.6
6-19	N/A	N/A	N/A	N/A	N/A	N/A	N/A
2019	D+	2.19	1.83	182.4	84.2	242.5	25.2
2018	D+	0.82	0.68	170.7	57.3	380.3	25.3
2017	D	N/A	N/A	72.9	33.7	266.2	-6.3
2016	D	0.43	0.36	102.0	38.6	377.8	-14.0
2015	N/A	N/A	N/A	167.6	49.8	287.0	-74.0

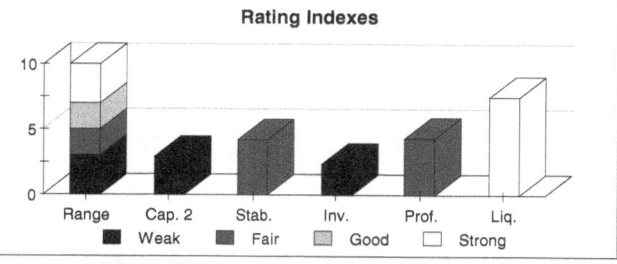

Rating Indexes
Range Cap. 2 Stab. Inv. Prof. Liq.
■ Weak ■ Fair ▨ Good □ Strong

MAMSI L&H INS CO   C   Fair

Major Rating Factors: Low quality investment portfolio (0.3 on a scale of 0 to 10). Excellent profitability (9.1). Strong capitalization (7.9) based on excellent current risk-adjusted capital (severe loss scenario).
Other Rating Factors: Excellent liquidity (7.2) with ample operational cash flow and liquid investments.
Principal Business: Comp med (78%), Medicare (22%)
Mem Phys: 19: 62,697 **18:** 67,359 **19 MLR** 77.9% **/ 19 Admin Exp** N/A
Enroll(000): Q2 20: 25 **19:** 25 **18:** 23 **Med Exp PMPM:** $410
Principal Investments: Cash and equiv (97%), long-term bonds (3%)
Provider Compensation ($000): Contr fee ($98,351), FFS ($15,328), capitation ($586), bonus arrang ($87)
Total Member Encounters: Phys (230,913), non-phys (42,025)
Group Affiliation: None
Licensed in: AL, AR, DC, DE, LA, MD, MO, MT, ND, TX, VA, WV
Address: 800 KING FARM BLVD, ROCKVILLE, MD 20850
Phone: (301) 762-8205 **Dom State:** MD **Commenced Bus:** N/A

Data Date	Rating	RACR #1	RACR #2	Total Assets ($mil)	Capital ($mil)	Net Premium ($mil)	Net Income ($mil)
6-20	C	2.11	1.76	63.4	29.6	80.7	2.7
6-19	C+	3.39	2.82	44.3	23.5	74.5	0.7
2019	C+	3.71	3.09	53.5	30.5	151.8	6.8
2018	C+	3.32	2.77	40.3	23.0	131.4	8.9
2017	C+	N/A	N/A	30.9	14.1	83.0	5.4
2016	C+	2.90	2.42	21.9	8.8	61.6	4.2
2015	C+	5.42	4.52	21.1	11.7	52.6	4.9

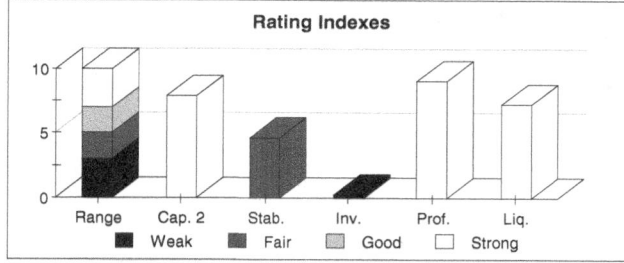

Rating Indexes
Range Cap. 2 Stab. Inv. Prof. Liq.
■ Weak ■ Fair ▨ Good □ Strong

MANHATTAN LIFE INS CO   B   Good

Major Rating Factors: Good overall results on stability tests (5.0 on a scale of 0 to 10) despite fair financial strength of affiliated Manhattan Life Group Inc and excessive premium growth. Other stability subfactors include good operational trends, good risk adjusted capital for prior years and good risk diversification. Good quality investment portfolio (6.1) despite mixed results such as: minimal exposure to mortgages and large holdings of BBB rated bonds but small junk bond holdings. Good overall profitability (5.5) although investment income, in comparison to reserve requirements, is below regulatory standards.
Other Rating Factors: Good liquidity (5.9). Strong capitalization (7.0) based on excellent risk adjusted capital (severe loss scenario).
Principal Business: Individual health insurance (66%), individual annuities (26%), individual life insurance (4%), group health insurance (2%), and reinsurance (2%).
Principal Investments: NonCMO investment grade bonds (65%), CMOs and structured securities (11%), mortgages in good standing (7%), common & preferred stock (5%), and misc. investments (7%).
Investments in Affiliates: 4%
Group Affiliation: Manhattan Life Group Inc
Licensed in: All states, the District of Columbia and Puerto Rico
Commenced Business: August 1850
Address: 225 Community Drive Suite 11, Great Neck, NY 11021
Phone: (713) 529-0045 **Domicile State:** NY **NAIC Code:** 65870

Data Date	Rating	RACR #1	RACR #2	Total Assets ($mil)	Capital ($mil)	Net Premium ($mil)	Net Income ($mil)
6-20	B	1.50	1.03	657.2	65.7	68.9	4.7
6-19	B	1.47	1.03	639.8	63.0	37.5	5.5
2019	B	1.55	1.08	647.3	66.0	93.7	13.0
2018	B	1.39	0.98	633.3	59.0	79.8	12.3
2017	B	1.30	0.94	581.1	54.1	90.1	8.6
2016	B	1.26	0.94	543.1	51.1	125.6	13.9
2015	B	1.18	0.91	484.6	47.1	152.1	11.2

Manhattan Life Group Inc Composite Group Rating: C+ Largest Group Members	Assets ($mil)	Rating
WESTERN UNITED LIFE ASR CO	1225	B-
MANHATTANLIFE ASSR CO OF AM	738	C+
MANHATTAN LIFE INS CO	647	B
FAMILY LIFE INS CO	141	C

MANHATTANLIFE ASSR CO OF AM

C+   Fair

Major Rating Factors: Fair overall results on stability tests (4.7 on a scale of 0 to 10) including fair risk adjusted capital in prior years. Good current capitalization (5.9) based on good risk adjusted capital (severe loss scenario) reflecting some improvement over results in 2016. Good quality investment portfolio (5.2).

Other Rating Factors: Good liquidity (6.5). Excellent profitability (7.3) despite modest operating losses during 2016.

Principal Business: Individual health insurance (57%), group health insurance (19%), reinsurance (14%), individual life insurance (9%), and group life insurance (1%).

Principal Investments: NonCMO investment grade bonds (51%), common & preferred stock (22%), mortgages in good standing (6%), CMOs and structured securities (4%), and misc. investments (8%).

Investments in Affiliates: 22%

Group Affiliation: Manhattan Life Group Inc

Licensed in: All states except NY, PR

Commenced Business: September 1963

Address: 425 W Capitol Ave Ste 1800, Little Rock, AR 72201

Phone: (713) 529-0045   **Domicile State:** AR   **NAIC Code:** 61883

Data Date	Rating	RACR #1	RACR #2	Total Assets ($mil)	Capital ($mil)	Net Premium ($mil)	Net Income ($mil)
6-20	C+	0.98	0.86	750.4	193.4	120.1	16.2
6-19	C	0.89	0.78	720.6	167.5	122.5	6.0
2019	C	0.92	0.82	737.8	179.4	237.7	7.2
2018	C	0.82	0.73	700.5	153.7	251.4	19.3
2017	C	0.62	0.57	390.8	102.4	113.8	4.3
2016	C	0.61	0.55	385.0	95.6	99.9	-1.6
2015	C	0.64	0.59	327.0	92.9	100.0	2.6

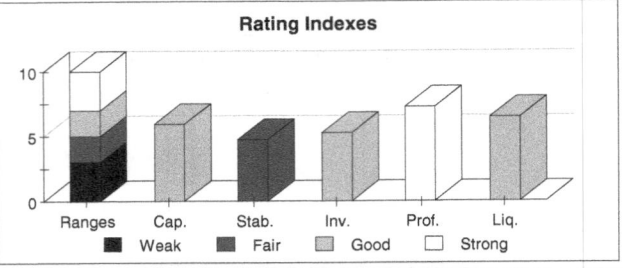

Rating Indexes

MARQUIS ADVANTAGE, INC.

D+   Weak

Major Rating Factors: Fair profitability index (3.7 on a scale of 0 to 10). Fair capitalization (2.9) based on good current risk-adjusted capital (moderate loss scenario). High quality investment portfolio (9.9).

Other Rating Factors: Excellent liquidity (7.4) with ample operational cash flow and liquid investments.

Principal Business: Medicare (100%)

Mem Phys: 18: 4,605   **17:** 1,393   **18 MLR** 82.8%   **/ 18 Admin Exp** N/A

Enroll(000): Q3 19: 0   **18:** 0   **17:** 0   **Med Exp PMPM:** $1,541

Principal Investments: Cash and equiv (100%)

Provider Compensation ($000): Contr fee ($6,630), capitation ($970), bonus arrang ($139)

Total Member Encounters: Phys (3,205), non-phys (12,839)

Group Affiliation: Marquis Companies I Inc

Licensed in: OR

Address: 4560 SE International Way #100, Milwaukee, OR 97222

Phone: (804) 396-6412   **Dom State:** OR   **Commenced Bus:** N/A

Data Date	Rating	RACR #1	RACR #2	Total Assets ($mil)	Capital ($mil)	Net Premium ($mil)	Net Income ($mil)
9-19	D+	1.04	0.86	6.7	3.4	8.8	0.4
9-18	N/A	N/A	N/A	5.4	2.6	6.9	-0.4
2018	U	0.93	0.78	5.2	3.1	9.5	0.0
2017	N/A	N/A	N/A	4.9	3.1	6.7	0.1
2016	N/A	N/A	N/A	3.0	3.0	N/A	-0.7
2015	N/A	N/A	N/A	N/A	N/A	N/A	N/A
2014	N/A	N/A	N/A	N/A	N/A	N/A	N/A

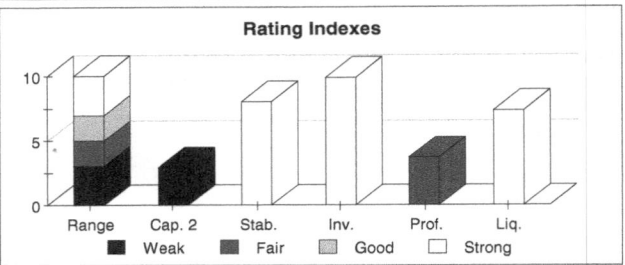

Rating Indexes

MARTINS POINT GENERATIONS ADVANTAGE

B   Good

Major Rating Factors: Fair profitability index (4.7 on a scale of 0 to 10). Strong capitalization (8.1) based on excellent current risk-adjusted capital (severe loss scenario). High quality investment portfolio (7.3).

Other Rating Factors: Excellent liquidity (6.9) with sufficient resources (cash flows and marketable investments) to handle a spike in claims.

Principal Business: Medicare (100%)

Mem Phys: 19: 17,782   **18:** 17,514   **19 MLR** 89.2%   **/ 19 Admin Exp** N/A

Enroll(000): Q2 20: 55   **19:** 51   **18:** 45   **Med Exp PMPM:** $688

Principal Investments: Long-term bonds (43%), cash and equiv (37%), nonaffiliate common stock (20%)

Provider Compensation ($000): Bonus arrang ($403,237), contr fee ($6,288), capitation ($1,362)

Total Member Encounters: Phys (805,109), non-phys (629,265)

Group Affiliation: Martins Point Health Care Inc

Licensed in: ME, NH

Address: 331 VERANDA STREET, PORTLAND, ME 4103

Phone: (207) 774-5801   **Dom State:** ME   **Commenced Bus:** N/A

Data Date	Rating	RACR #1	RACR #2	Total Assets ($mil)	Capital ($mil)	Net Premium ($mil)	Net Income ($mil)
6-20	B	2.25	1.87	168.5	90.7	241.0	34.8
6-19	N/A	N/A	N/A	N/A	N/A	N/A	N/A
2019	B	1.36	1.14	126.2	57.7	456.0	-11.0
2018	B	1.84	1.53	120.7	66.7	401.3	15.7
2017	C	1.60	1.34	99.9	56.9	391.0	11.5
2016	D+	1.28	1.07	88.4	43.3	329.3	-13.2
2015	N/A	N/A	N/A	73.6	36.9	275.1	N/A

Rating Indexes

MATTHEW THORNTON HEALTH PLAN   B   Good

Major Rating Factors: Fair overall results on stability tests (4.5 on a scale of 0 to 10) based on a significant 19% decrease in enrollment during the period, a decline in the number of member physicians during 2020. Excellent profitability (9.3). Strong capitalization index (10.0) based on excellent current risk-adjusted capital (severe loss scenario).
Other Rating Factors: High quality investment portfolio (8.0). Excellent liquidity (6.9) with sufficient resources (cash flows and marketable investments) to handle a spike in claims.
Principal Business: Comp med (93%), Medicare (7%)
Mem Phys: 19: 17,653 **18:** 22,513 **19 MLR** 76.7% **/ 19 Admin Exp** N/A
Enroll(000): Q2 20: 84 **19:** 87 **18:** 107 **Med Exp PMPM:** $404
Principal Investments: Long-term bonds (99%), other (1%)
Provider Compensation ($000): Bonus arrang ($391,176), contr fee ($26,523), FFS ($20,410), capitation ($2,247)
Total Member Encounters: Phys (586,057), non-phys (283,819)
Group Affiliation: Anthem Inc
Licensed in: NH
Address: 1155 ELM STREET, MANCHESTER,
Phone: (603) 541-2000 **Dom State:** NH **Commenced Bus:** N/A

Data Date	Rating	RACR #1	RACR #2	Total Assets ($mil)	Capital ($mil)	Net Premium ($mil)	Net Income ($mil)
6-20	B	4.08	3.40	331.0	173.4	274.8	42.8
6-19	B	4.65	3.87	342.5	166.3	290.2	30.4
2019	B	4.39	3.66	249.1	131.6	569.5	46.4
2018	B	3.84	3.20	288.2	135.5	712.8	80.4
2017	B	2.22	1.85	199.4	95.7	531.3	24.3
2016	B	3.32	2.77	202.4	94.1	508.0	13.3
2015	A-	4.17	3.47	218.8	111.3	514.6	33.9

Rating Indexes

MCLAREN HEALTH PLAN COMMUNITY   B-   Good

Major Rating Factors: Fair quality investment portfolio (3.4 on a scale of 0 to 10). Strong capitalization (7.0) based on excellent current risk-adjusted capital (severe loss scenario). Excellent liquidity (7.1) with ample operational cash flow and liquid investments.
Other Rating Factors: Weak profitability index (2.2).
Principal Business: Comp med (100%)
Mem Phys: 18: 31,182 **17:** 29,199 **18 MLR** 88.5% **/ 18 Admin Exp** N/A
Enroll(000): Q3 19: 20 **18:** 29 **17:** 28 **Med Exp PMPM:** $358
Principal Investments: Cash and equiv (97%), long-term bonds (3%)
Provider Compensation ($000): Contr fee ($116,087), FFS ($5,750), capitation ($978)
Total Member Encounters: Phys (156,637), non-phys (26,796)
Group Affiliation: None
Licensed in: MI
Address: G3245 Beecher Rd, Flint, MI 48532
Phone: (888) 327-0671 **Dom State:** MI **Commenced Bus:** N/A

Data Date	Rating	RACR #1	RACR #2	Total Assets ($mil)	Capital ($mil)	Net Premium ($mil)	Net Income ($mil)
9-19	B-	1.34	1.12	37.4	16.6	84.1	-2.3
9-18	B-	N/A	N/A	41.0	20.3	108.3	5.9
2018	B-	1.49	1.25	40.2	18.9	143.8	4.6
2017	B-	N/A	N/A	35.7	14.6	119.4	-2.2
2016	C+	1.75	1.46	32.3	13.9	61.0	-1.0
2015	N/A	N/A	N/A	3.1	3.0	N/A	N/A
2014	N/A	N/A	N/A	3.0	3.0	N/A	N/A

Rating Indexes

MCLAREN HEALTH PLAN INC   C+   Fair

Major Rating Factors: Good overall results on stability tests (6.2 on a scale of 0 to 10). Low quality investment portfolio (1.5). Excellent profitability (9.1).
Other Rating Factors: Strong capitalization index (8.2) based on excellent current risk-adjusted capital (severe loss scenario). Excellent liquidity (7.1) with ample operational cash flow and liquid investments.
Principal Business: Medicaid (100%)
Mem Phys: 19: 33,779 **18:** 31,182 **19 MLR** 84.5% **/ 19 Admin Exp** N/A
Enroll(000): Q2 20: 220 **19:** 203 **18:** 202 **Med Exp PMPM:** $274
Principal Investments: Cash and equiv (62%), nonaffiliate common stock (29%), affiliate common stock (9%), real estate (1%)
Provider Compensation ($000): Contr fee ($635,150), FFS ($26,766), capitation ($11,245)
Total Member Encounters: Phys (1,581,346), non-phys (331,372)
Group Affiliation: None
Licensed in: MI
Address: G-3245 Beecher Rd, FLINT,
Phone: (810) 733-9723 **Dom State:** MI **Commenced Bus:** N/A

Data Date	Rating	RACR #1	RACR #2	Total Assets ($mil)	Capital ($mil)	Net Premium ($mil)	Net Income ($mil)
6-20	C+	2.33	1.94	324.0	177.6	392.4	29.0
6-19	B-	2.17	1.81	243.4	131.4	384.2	17.0
2019	B-	2.06	1.72	258.2	150.0	785.6	32.5
2018	B	1.90	1.58	227.9	115.9	694.2	15.6
2017	B+	1.30	1.08	200.8	100.6	840.4	22.2
2016	B	1.20	1.00	207.5	83.0	929.6	20.5
2015	B	1.01	0.84	231.5	70.8	902.6	23.4

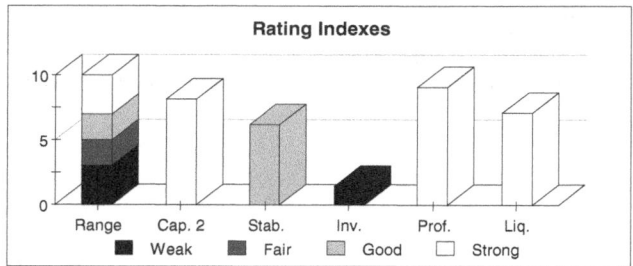

Rating Indexes

MCNA INS CO — B- — Good

Major Rating Factors: Fair liquidity (3.4 on a scale of 0 to 10) as cash resources may not be adequate to cover a spike in claims. Excellent profitability (7.5). Strong capitalization (7.7) based on excellent current risk-adjusted capital (severe loss scenario).
Other Rating Factors: High quality investment portfolio (8.7).
Principal Business: Medicaid (100%)
Mem Phys: 19: 12,018 **18:** 9,641 **19 MLR** 108.0% **/ 19 Admin Exp** N/A
Enroll(000): Q2 20: 4,094 **19:** 3,749 **18:** 3,830 **Med Exp PMPM:** $16
Principal Investments: Long-term bonds (64%), cash and equiv (34%), pref stock (2%)
Provider Compensation ($000): FFS ($755,856)
Total Member Encounters: N/A
Group Affiliation: UnitedHealth Group Incorporated
Licensed in: (No states)
Address: 100 Congress Avenue Suite 1100, Austin, TX 78701
Phone: (800) 494-6262 **Dom State:** TX **Commenced Bus:** N/A

Data Date	Rating	RACR #1	RACR #2	Total Assets ($mil)	Capital ($mil)	Net Premium ($mil)	Net Income ($mil)
6-20	B-	1.93	1.61	358.8	126.3	363.6	48.5
6-19	C	2.05	1.71	213.4	138.7	352.2	11.6
2019	C+	1.96	1.64	201.7	128.3	694.8	24.2
2018	U	1.79	1.49	184.1	121.7	726.5	17.4
2017	N/A	N/A	N/A	175.8	125.1	594.9	17.0
2016	N/A	N/A	N/A	171.9	121.4	551.4	N/A
2015	N/A	N/A	N/A	160.0	111.8	556.6	N/A

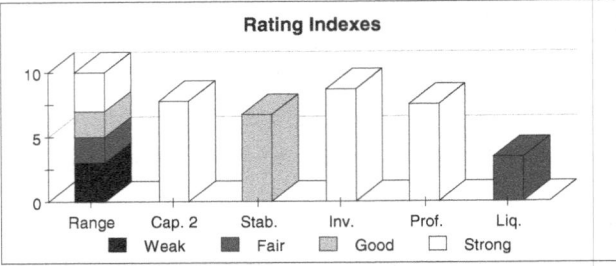

Rating Indexes

MCS ADVANTAGE INC — E+ — Very Weak

Major Rating Factors: Excellent profitability (8.5 on a scale of 0 to 10). Strong capitalization (7.5) based on excellent current risk-adjusted capital (severe loss scenario). High quality investment portfolio (9.9).
Other Rating Factors: Excellent liquidity (7.0) with sufficient resources (cash flows and marketable investments) to handle a spike in claims.
Principal Business: Medicare (100%)
Mem Phys: 19: 11,222 **18:** 11,334 **19 MLR** 83.1% **/ 19 Admin Exp** N/A
Enroll(000): Q2 20: 179 **19:** 168 **18:** 207 **Med Exp PMPM:** $729
Principal Investments: Long-term bonds (63%), cash and equiv (36%), nonaffiliate common stock (1%)
Provider Compensation ($000): Contr fee ($1,129,151), capitation ($317,855)
Total Member Encounters: N/A
Group Affiliation: Medical Card System Inc
Licensed in: PR
Address: Suite 203 255 Ponce de LeÃ³n A, San Juan, PR 917
Phone: (787) 758-2500 **Dom State:** PR **Commenced Bus:** N/A

Data Date	Rating	RACR #1	RACR #2	Total Assets ($mil)	Capital ($mil)	Net Premium ($mil)	Net Income ($mil)
6-20	E+	1.71	1.43	499.5	210.8	1,002.5	14.6
6-19	D	1.76	1.47	431.0	225.8	924.1	21.4
2019	D+	1.53	1.27	416.2	188.6	1,821.2	67.9
2018	D-	1.52	1.27	396.2	205.2	1,926.2	42.6
2017	E+	N/A	N/A	379.7	156.1	1,690.9	51.3
2016	E	0.64	0.53	257.4	82.5	1,763.2	19.5
2015	E	0.47	0.40	287.3	55.7	1,535.4	6.3

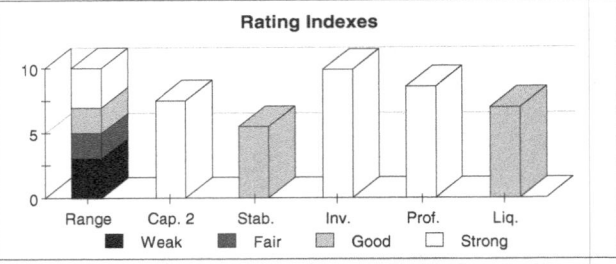

Rating Indexes

MD INDIVIDUAL PRACTICE ASSOC INC — C — Fair

Major Rating Factors: Fair overall results on stability tests (4.3 on a scale of 0 to 10). Low quality investment portfolio (0.3). Excellent profitability (8.8).
Other Rating Factors: Strong capitalization index (10.0) based on excellent current risk-adjusted capital (severe loss scenario). Excellent liquidity (7.2) with ample operational cash flow and liquid investments.
Principal Business: FEHB (100%)
Mem Phys: 19: 55,148 **18:** 55,087 **19 MLR** 86.4% **/ 19 Admin Exp** N/A
Enroll(000): Q2 20: 26 **19:** 31 **18:** 36 **Med Exp PMPM:** $571
Principal Investments: Cash and equiv (98%), long-term bonds (2%)
Provider Compensation ($000): Contr fee ($189,192), FFS ($25,271), capitation ($3,773), bonus arrang ($60)
Total Member Encounters: Phys (369,718), non-phys (30,089)
Group Affiliation: None
Licensed in: DC, MD, VA
Address: 800 KING FARM BLVD, ROCKVILLE,
Phone: (240) 683-5250 **Dom State:** MD **Commenced Bus:** N/A

Data Date	Rating	RACR #1	RACR #2	Total Assets ($mil)	Capital ($mil)	Net Premium ($mil)	Net Income ($mil)
6-20	C	9.12	7.60	89.0	56.1	115.7	14.2
6-19	C	8.90	7.41	71.4	46.8	124.0	10.5
2019	C	11.56	9.64	70.3	44.0	246.8	17.6
2018	C	9.81	8.17	81.7	51.9	281.8	24.8
2017	C	9.10	7.58	84.5	56.4	288.7	30.7
2016	B-	8.30	6.92	72.3	33.1	307.8	17.1
2015	C	5.68	4.74	76.3	32.2	350.0	16.5

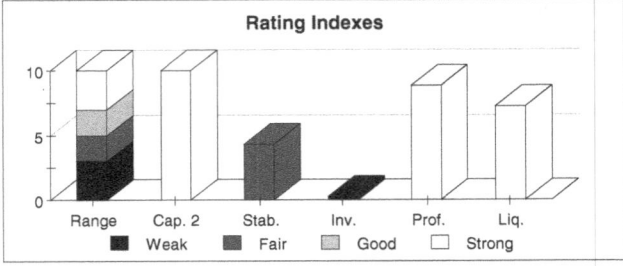

Rating Indexes

MDWISE INC *   B+   Good

Major Rating Factors: Good overall results on stability tests (5.8 on a scale of 0 to 10). Excellent profitability (8.1). Strong capitalization index (7.9) based on excellent current risk-adjusted capital (severe loss scenario).
Other Rating Factors: High quality investment portfolio (9.9). Excellent liquidity (7.2) with ample operational cash flow and liquid investments.
Principal Business: Medicaid (100%)
Mem Phys: 18: 30,035   **17:** 28,242   **18 MLR** 95.1%   / **18 Admin Exp** N/A
Enroll(000): Q3 19: 288   **18:** 302   **17:** 347   **Med Exp PMPM:** $313
Principal Investments: Cash and equiv (69%), long-term bonds (31%)
Provider Compensation ($000): Capitation ($1,202,531)
Total Member Encounters: N/A
Group Affiliation: None
Licensed in: IN
Address: 1200 Madison Avenue Suite 400, Indianapolis,
Phone: (317) 822-7300   **Dom State:** IN   **Commenced Bus:** N/A

Data Date	Rating	RACR #1	RACR #2	Total Assets ($mil)	Capital ($mil)	Net Premium ($mil)	Net Income ($mil)
9-19	B+	2.08	1.73	389.2	130.8	929.4	18.2
9-18	B	N/A	N/A	335.3	91.5	934.5	5.1
2018	B+	1.57	1.31	356.1	100.4	1,264.0	23.9
2017	B	N/A	N/A	379.3	103.0	1,513.4	11.5
2016	B	1.32	1.10	199.6	93.8	1,433.7	28.8
2015	B	1.47	1.23	144.2	69.4	1,033.2	20.3
2014	N/A	N/A	N/A	76.6	39.0	583.8	N/A

Rating Indexes

MEDAMERICA INS CO   C   Fair

Major Rating Factors: Fair overall capitalization (3.9 on a scale of 0 to 10) based on mixed results -- excessive policy leverage mitigated by fair risk adjusted capital (moderate loss scenario). Fair overall results on stability tests (3.8) including weak risk adjusted capital in prior years, negative cash flow from operations for 2019. Good liquidity (6.6).
Other Rating Factors: Low quality investment portfolio (0.8). Weak profitability (1.0).
Principal Business: N/A
Principal Investments: NonCMO investment grade bonds (76%), common & preferred stock (6%), noninv. grade bonds (5%), and CMOs and structured securities (3%).
Investments in Affiliates: 1%
Group Affiliation: Lifetime Healthcare Inc
Licensed in: All states except FL, NY, PR
Commenced Business: August 1966
Address: 651 Holiday Drive Foster Plaza, Pittsburgh, PA 15220-2740
Phone: (585) 238-4464   **Domicile State:** PA   **NAIC Code:** 69515

Data Date	Rating	RACR #1	RACR #2	Total Assets ($mil)	Capital ($mil)	Net Premium ($mil)	Net Income ($mil)
6-20	C	0.86	0.44	1,123.4	29.8	8.8	5.9
6-19	C	0.64	0.36	1,241.6	29.4	29.9	0.6
2019	C	0.98	0.49	1,126.9	28.8	-52.5	-102.8
2018	C	0.85	0.47	1,199.8	31.0	57.3	-134.6
2017	C	0.99	0.54	960.2	31.2	62.2	-8.7
2016	B-	1.14	0.62	939.2	31.7	64.6	-1.2
2015	B	1.23	0.67	890.9	34.4	63.2	-45.8

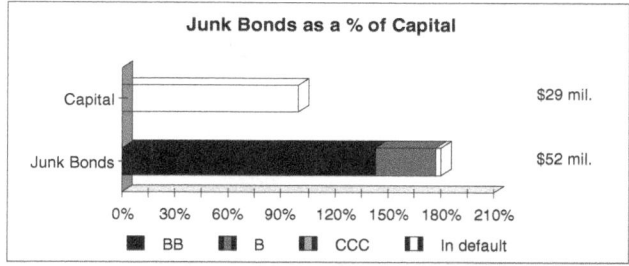

Junk Bonds as a % of Capital

Capital $29 mil.
Junk Bonds $52 mil.

MEDCO CONTAINMENT INS CO OF NY   C   Fair

Major Rating Factors: Weak profitability index (0.9 on a scale of 0 to 10). Strong capitalization (9.0) based on excellent current risk-adjusted capital (severe loss scenario). High quality investment portfolio (9.9).
Other Rating Factors: Excellent liquidity (7.6) with ample operational cash flow and liquid investments.
Principal Business: Other (100%)
Mem Phys: 19: N/A   **18:** N/A   **19 MLR** 78.5%   / **19 Admin Exp** N/A
Enroll(000): Q2 20: 85   **19:** 91   **18:** 97   **Med Exp PMPM:** $90
Principal Investments: Cash and equiv (97%), long-term bonds (3%)
Provider Compensation ($000): FFS ($103,098)
Total Member Encounters: N/A
Group Affiliation: None
Licensed in: NY
Address: 433 River Street Suite 800, Troy, NY 12180
Phone: (800) 322-5455   **Dom State:** NY   **Commenced Bus:** N/A

Data Date	Rating	RACR #1	RACR #2	Total Assets ($mil)	Capital ($mil)	Net Premium ($mil)	Net Income ($mil)
6-20	C	2.93	2.44	84.8	40.9	57.1	-8.2
6-19	C	5.69	4.74	125.1	46.9	72.8	-4.2
2019	C	5.88	4.90	72.5	49.6	127.3	-1.6
2018	C	6.20	5.17	70.0	51.2	138.6	0.8
2017	B-	4.07	3.39	66.1	49.9	129.9	-5.6
2016	B	5.71	4.76	67.4	55.8	123.8	5.2
2015	B-	9.27	7.72	59.4	47.6	102.3	-0.5

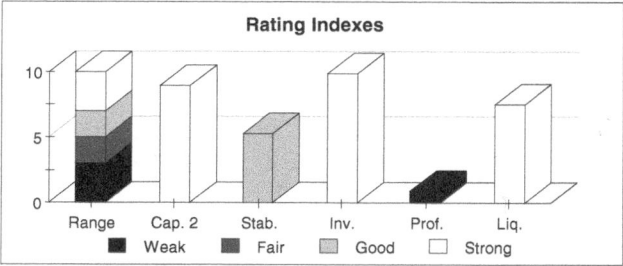

Rating Indexes

MEDCO CONTAINMENT LIFE INS CO   D+   Weak

Major Rating Factors: Low quality investment portfolio (1.0 on a scale of 0 to 10). Fair profitability index (4.6). Strong capitalization (8.4) based on excellent current risk-adjusted capital (severe loss scenario).
Other Rating Factors: Excellent liquidity (8.8) with ample operational cash flow and liquid investments.
Principal Business: Other (100%)
Mem Phys: 19: N/A **18:** N/A **19 MLR** 81.3% **/ 19 Admin Exp** N/A
Enroll(000): Q2 20: 694 **19:** 804 **18:** 815 **Med Exp PMPM:** $76
Principal Investments: Cash and equiv (99%), long-term bonds (1%)
Provider Compensation ($000): FFS ($860,447)
Total Member Encounters: N/A
Group Affiliation: None
Licensed in: All states except NY
Address: 3000 Ericsson Drive Suite #28, Warrendale, PA 15086
Phone: (800) 332-5455 **Dom State:** PA **Commenced Bus:** N/A

Data Date	Rating	RACR #1	RACR #2	Total Assets ($mil)	Capital ($mil)	Net Premium ($mil)	Net Income ($mil)
6-20	D+	2.44	2.03	645.6	248.7	414.6	-17.7
6-19	C	5.28	4.40	794.2	364.7	486.3	-25.6
2019	C	3.57	2.97	981.0	268.3	896.8	21.3
2018	C	5.62	4.69	1,163.6	388.4	896.1	11.6
2017	B-	6.07	5.06	1,292.5	418.4	790.6	22.0
2016	A-	6.54	5.45	1,689.0	462.5	672.2	80.5
2015	B	6.25	5.21	1,391.5	403.5	657.7	28.5

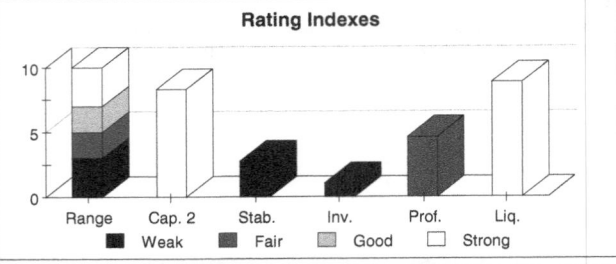

MEDICA COMM HEALTH PLAN   C+   Fair

Major Rating Factors: Fair overall results on stability tests (4.4 on a scale of 0 to 10). Good overall profitability index (5.2). Strong capitalization index (10.0) based on excellent current risk-adjusted capital (severe loss scenario).
Other Rating Factors: High quality investment portfolio (8.6). Excellent liquidity (8.3) with ample operational cash flow and liquid investments.
Principal Business: Comp med (100%)
Mem Phys: 19: 113,371 **18:** 109,221 **19 MLR** 78.2% **/ 19 Admin Exp** N/A
Enroll(000): Q2 20: 10 **19:** 6 **18:** 7 **Med Exp PMPM:** $843
Principal Investments: Long-term bonds (65%), cash and equiv (35%)
Provider Compensation ($000): Contr fee ($38,852), bonus arrang ($26,474)
Total Member Encounters: Phys (55,703), non-phys (8,935)
Group Affiliation: None
Licensed in: MN, WI
Address: 401 CARLSON PARKWAY, MINNETONKA,
Phone: (952) 992-2900 **Dom State:** WI **Commenced Bus:** N/A

Data Date	Rating	RACR #1	RACR #2	Total Assets ($mil)	Capital ($mil)	Net Premium ($mil)	Net Income ($mil)
6-20	C+	16.24	13.54	154.8	119.2	46.7	4.1
6-19	C+	19.29	16.07	139.3	108.7	44.2	17.5
2019	C+	22.13	18.44	136.9	115.1	81.2	23.8
2018	C+	15.66	13.05	144.1	91.3	83.0	18.0
2017	C	N/A	N/A	110.3	72.1	274.7	15.3
2016	C	0.75	0.63	98.2	27.6	221.6	-32.3
2015	B	4.32	3.60	67.8	40.1	66.5	-12.4

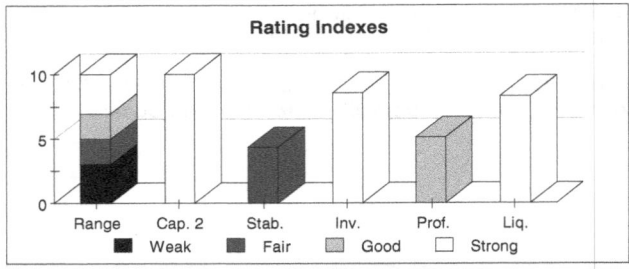

MEDICA HEALTH PLANS   C+   Fair

Major Rating Factors: Fair profitability index (4.6 on a scale of 0 to 10). Fair overall results on stability tests (4.5) based on an excessive 132% enrollment growth during the period. Strong capitalization index (10.0) based on excellent current risk-adjusted capital (severe loss scenario).
Other Rating Factors: High quality investment portfolio (7.1). Excellent liquidity (6.9) with sufficient resources (cash flows and marketable investments) to handle a spike in claims.
Principal Business: Medicaid (68%), Medicare (28%), med supp (4%)
Mem Phys: 19: 113,371 **18:** 109,221 **19 MLR** 90.0% **/ 19 Admin Exp** N/A
Enroll(000): Q2 20: 71 **19:** 69 **18:** 30 **Med Exp PMPM:** $1,167
Principal Investments: Long-term bonds (43%), nonaffiliate common stock (20%), real estate (16%), cash and equiv (14%), other (7%)
Provider Compensation ($000): Contr fee ($698,734), bonus arrang ($239,566), capitation ($1,670), other ($5,257)
Total Member Encounters: Phys (1,963,705), non-phys (1,373,075)
Group Affiliation: None
Licensed in: IA, MN, ND, SD
Address: 401 CARLSON PARKWAY, MINNETONKA,
Phone: (952) 992-2900 **Dom State:** MN **Commenced Bus:** N/A

Data Date	Rating	RACR #1	RACR #2	Total Assets ($mil)	Capital ($mil)	Net Premium ($mil)	Net Income ($mil)
6-20	C+	4.58	3.82	609.2	410.4	565.4	72.8
6-19	C+	6.30	5.25	568.8	328.4	545.9	27.9
2019	C+	5.00	4.16	587.9	346.6	1,089.2	54.9
2018	C+	5.67	4.72	539.7	293.1	732.6	39.6
2017	C	2.81	2.35	482.0	287.9	1,269.9	78.5
2016	C	1.80	1.50	803.3	317.4	2,327.5	-189.9
2015	B+	4.37	3.64	896.8	504.0	1,777.0	45.4

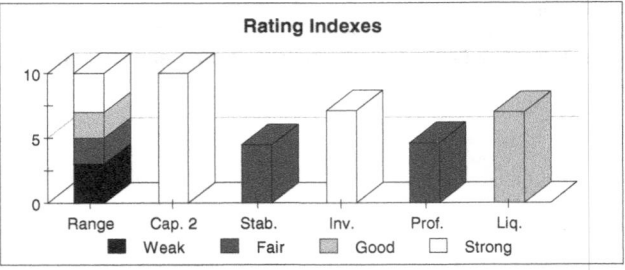

MEDICA HEALTHCARE PLANS INC   B   Good

Major Rating Factors: Good capitalization (6.4 on a scale of 0 to 10) based on good current risk-adjusted capital (severe loss scenario). Good liquidity (6.7) with sufficient resources (cash flows and marketable investments) to handle a spike in claims. Excellent profitability (8.1).
Other Rating Factors: High quality investment portfolio (8.9).
Principal Business: Medicare (100%)
Mem Phys: 19: 46,725   **18:** 42,366   **19 MLR** 88.3%   **/ 19 Admin Exp** N/A
Enroll(000): Q2 20: 44   **19:** 45   **18:** 46   **Med Exp PMPM:** $1,157
Principal Investments: Long-term bonds (91%), cash and equiv (9%)
Provider Compensation ($000): Contr fee ($414,283), capitation ($124,084), FFS ($71,033), bonus arrang ($20,216)
Total Member Encounters: Phys (916,071), non-phys (319,005)
Group Affiliation: None
Licensed in: FL
Address: 9100 SOUTH DADELAND BOULEVARD, MIAMI, FL 33156
Phone: (305) 670-8440   **Dom State:** FL   **Commenced Bus:** N/A

Data Date	Rating	RACR #1	RACR #2	Total Assets ($mil)	Capital ($mil)	Net Premium ($mil)	Net Income ($mil)
6-20	B	1.14	0.95	215.8	65.4	397.9	15.2
6-19	B	1.47	1.22	158.3	48.6	355.9	6.5
2019	B	1.54	1.29	161.0	55.5	704.7	21.4
2018	B	1.33	1.10	154.2	43.3	661.7	13.3
2017	E	0.78	0.65	146.7	37.2	547.9	5.1
2016	E	2.32	1.93	139.6	61.4	533.9	24.9
2015	E-	1.82	1.52	132.9	54.1	523.1	11.6

MEDICA INS CO   B   Good

Major Rating Factors: Good overall profitability index (6.9 on a scale of 0 to 10). Good quality investment portfolio (5.5). Strong capitalization (10.0) based on excellent current risk-adjusted capital (severe loss scenario).
Other Rating Factors: Excellent liquidity (6.9) with sufficient resources (cash flows and marketable investments) to handle a spike in claims.
Principal Business: Comp med (84%), Medicare (13%), other (3%)
Mem Phys: 19: 113,371   **18:** 103,390   **19 MLR** 80.6%   **/ 19 Admin Exp** N/A
Enroll(000): Q2 20: 463   **19:** 455   **18:** 532   **Med Exp PMPM:** $489
Principal Investments: Long-term bonds (69%), cash and equiv (15%), nonaffiliate common stock (14%), pref stock (2%)
Provider Compensation ($000): Contr fee ($1,772,605), bonus arrang ($897,892), other ($99,723)
Total Member Encounters: Phys (4,218,056), non-phys (1,449,600)
Group Affiliation: None
Licensed in: IA, KS, MN, MO, NE, ND, OK, SD, WI
Address: 401 CARLSON PARKWAY, MINNETONKA, MN 55305
Phone: (952) 992-2900   **Dom State:** MN   **Commenced Bus:** N/A

Data Date	Rating	RACR #1	RACR #2	Total Assets ($mil)	Capital ($mil)	Net Premium ($mil)	Net Income ($mil)
6-20	B	7.30	6.09	2,030.6	1,280.0	1,619.2	199.3
6-19	B	5.22	4.35	1,631.6	956.4	1,702.8	247.3
2019	B	6.13	5.11	1,624.7	1,068.9	3,362.1	365.1
2018	B	3.83	3.19	1,397.8	695.2	3,536.4	242.4
2017	B	2.82	2.35	807.5	421.0	2,179.8	53.1
2016	B	2.29	1.91	595.0	277.2	1,967.7	-28.7
2015	A-	3.17	2.64	623.1	313.7	1,790.2	-2.3

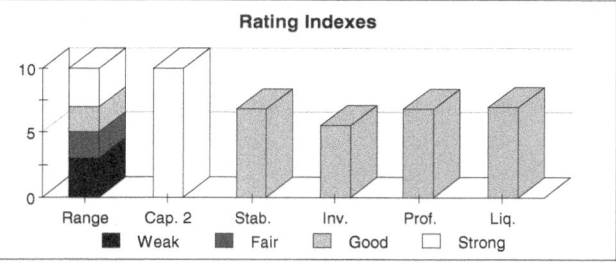

MEDICAL ASSOC CLINIC HEALTH PLAN   B-   Good

Major Rating Factors: Fair profitability index (4.0 on a scale of 0 to 10). Good overall results on stability tests (6.3). Strong capitalization index (7.1) based on excellent current risk-adjusted capital (severe loss scenario).
Other Rating Factors: High quality investment portfolio (7.8). Excellent liquidity (6.9) with sufficient resources (cash flows and marketable investments) to handle a spike in claims.
Principal Business: Comp med (78%), Medicare (22%)
Mem Phys: 18: 4,769   **17:** 390   **18 MLR** 88.4%   **/ 18 Admin Exp** N/A
Enroll(000): Q3 19: 7   **18:** 8   **17:** 7   **Med Exp PMPM:** $248
Principal Investments: Long-term bonds (61%), cash and equiv (31%), nonaffiliate common stock (8%)
Provider Compensation ($000): Capitation ($23,086)
Total Member Encounters: Phys (112,010)
Group Affiliation: Medical Associates Clinic PC
Licensed in: WI
Address: 1605 Associates Drive Suite 10, Dubuque,
Phone: (563) 556-8070   **Dom State:** WI   **Commenced Bus:** N/A

Data Date	Rating	RACR #1	RACR #2	Total Assets ($mil)	Capital ($mil)	Net Premium ($mil)	Net Income ($mil)
9-19	B-	1.44	1.20	4.6	3.4	18.3	0.2
9-18	C+	N/A	N/A	4.5	3.2	19.6	0.3
2018	B-	1.34	1.12	5.4	3.2	26.1	0.3
2017	C+	N/A	N/A	4.2	2.9	25.3	0.1
2016	C+	1.22	1.01	3.2	2.7	25.5	0.1
2015	C+	1.08	0.90	4.0	2.6	25.7	-0.7
2014	N/A	N/A	N/A	4.3	3.4	22.3	N/A

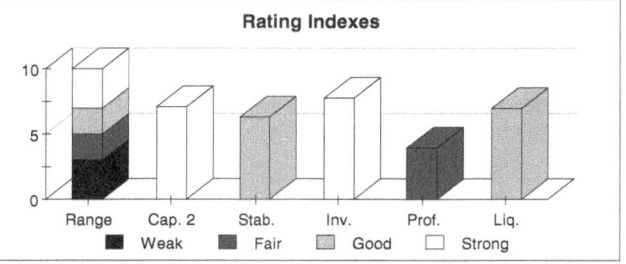

MEDICAL ASSOCIATES HEALTH PLAN INC   B   Good

Major Rating Factors: Good liquidity (6.7 on a scale of 0 to 10) with sufficient resources (cash flows and marketable investments) to handle a spike in claims. Fair profitability index (4.6). Strong capitalization index (8.8) based on excellent current risk-adjusted capital (severe loss scenario).
Other Rating Factors: High quality investment portfolio (7.7). Excellent overall results on stability tests (8.4) based on steady enrollment growth, averaging 2% over the past five years.
Principal Business: Comp med (76%), Medicare (24%)
Mem Phys: 19: 9,080   18: 4,769   **19 MLR** 89.4%   / **19 Admin Exp** N/A
Enroll(000): Q2 20: 26   19: 25   18: 24   **Med Exp PMPM:** $268
Principal Investments: Long-term bonds (69%), cash and equiv (21%), nonaffiliate common stock (10%)
Provider Compensation ($000): Contr fee ($54,736), capitation ($25,150)
Total Member Encounters: Phys (395,865)
Group Affiliation: Medical Associates Clinic PC
Licensed in: IL, IA
Address: 1605 Associates Drive Ste 101, Dubuque,
Phone: (563) 556-8070   **Dom State:** IA   **Commenced Bus:** N/A

Data Date	Rating	RACR #1	RACR #2	Total Assets ($mil)	Capital ($mil)	Net Premium ($mil)	Net Income ($mil)
6-20	B	2.77	2.31	44.2	24.4	50.3	2.9
6-19	B-	2.69	2.24	36.8	22.4	45.2	1.0
2019	B-	2.50	2.08	40.5	21.8	89.9	0.5
2018	B-	2.55	2.12	38.4	21.2	89.1	0.2
2017	B-	2.61	2.18	33.9	20.8	84.8	1.4
2016	B-	2.62	2.18	32.4	19.8	82.5	1.4
2015	B-	2.12	1.77	32.2	18.1	80.3	-1.1

MEDICAL HEALTH INS CORP OF OHIO   C   Fair

Major Rating Factors: Fair quality investment portfolio (3.7 on a scale of 0 to 10). Fair overall results on stability tests (4.9) based on an excessive 67% enrollment growth during the period. Weak profitability index (2.8).
Other Rating Factors: Strong capitalization index (8.2) based on excellent current risk-adjusted capital (severe loss scenario). Excellent liquidity (7.1) with ample operational cash flow and liquid investments.
Principal Business: Comp med (73%), med supp (26%)
Mem Phys: 19: 57,328   18: 53,140   **19 MLR** 81.2%   / **19 Admin Exp** N/A
Enroll(000): Q2 20: 204   19: 214   18: 128   **Med Exp PMPM:** $217
Principal Investments: Cash and equiv (62%), long-term bonds (38%)
Provider Compensation ($000): Contr fee ($476,324), FFS ($2,408), bonus arrang ($1,506), capitation ($598)
Total Member Encounters: Phys (2,190,313), non-phys (1,260,457)
Group Affiliation: None
Licensed in: OH
Address: 2060 East Ninth Street, Cleveland,
Phone: (216) 687-7000   **Dom State:** OH   **Commenced Bus:** N/A

Data Date	Rating	RACR #1	RACR #2	Total Assets ($mil)	Capital ($mil)	Net Premium ($mil)	Net Income ($mil)
6-20	C	2.35	1.96	323.4	104.2	298.9	15.0
6-19	B	4.36	3.63	281.1	105.5	312.9	20.8
2019	B	2.93	2.44	289.7	89.8	621.9	-24.0
2018	B	3.54	2.95	230.9	84.2	497.7	24.4
2017	C+	1.73	1.44	140.5	46.3	305.9	-19.2
2016	B+	3.48	2.90	155.6	66.5	328.2	-18.1
2015	B+	3.99	3.33	123.3	59.6	252.8	-8.4

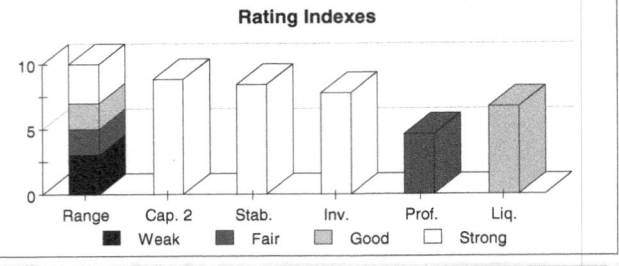

MEDICAL MUTUAL OF OHIO *   A-   Excellent

Major Rating Factors: Excellent profitability (7.5 on a scale of 0 to 10). Strong capitalization (10.0) based on excellent current risk-adjusted capital (severe loss scenario). Excellent liquidity (6.9) with sufficient resources (cash flows and marketable investments) to handle a spike in claims.
Other Rating Factors: Good quality investment portfolio (5.0).
Principal Business: Comp med (77%), Medicare (13%), other (8%)
Mem Phys: 19: 60,311   18: 56,424   **19 MLR** 86.4%   / **19 Admin Exp** N/A
Enroll(000): Q2 20: 1,066   19: 1,080   18: 1,025   **Med Exp PMPM:** $184
Principal Investments: Long-term bonds (51%), cash and equiv (16%), nonaffiliate common stock (13%), affiliate common stock (6%), real estate (2%), other (13%)
Provider Compensation ($000): Contr fee ($2,126,030), FFS ($5,278), bonus arrang ($4,561), capitation ($4,369), other ($173,083)
Total Member Encounters: Phys (4,177,798), non-phys (2,525,353)
Group Affiliation: None
Licensed in: GA, IN, MI, NC, OH, PA, SC, WV, WI
Address: 2060 East Ninth Street, Cleveland, OH 44115-1355
Phone: (216) 687-7000   **Dom State:** OH   **Commenced Bus:** N/A

Data Date	Rating	RACR #1	RACR #2	Total Assets ($mil)	Capital ($mil)	Net Premium ($mil)	Net Income ($mil)
6-20	A-	6.64	5.53	2,702.4	1,900.9	1,450.5	115.5
6-19	A	7.58	6.32	2,559.4	1,921.2	1,364.4	115.7
2019	A-	6.30	5.25	2,541.8	1,802.5	2,745.5	102.8
2018	A	7.08	5.90	2,453.9	1,793.1	2,636.1	128.0
2017	A	7.05	5.88	2,233.7	1,610.5	2,470.3	22.4
2016	A	6.47	5.39	1,991.5	1,395.8	2,368.3	57.9
2015	A-	7.18	5.99	1,853.2	1,352.8	2,146.9	126.7

MEDICO CORP LIFE INS CO   B-   Good

Major Rating Factors: Fair overall results on stability tests (4.9 on a scale of 0 to 10) including fair financial strength of affiliated American Enterprise Mutual Holding. Strong capitalization (8.0) based on excellent risk adjusted capital (severe loss scenario). Moreover, capital levels have been consistently high over the last five years. High quality investment portfolio (7.8).
Other Rating Factors: Excellent profitability (8.2) with operating gains in each of the last five years. Excellent liquidity (7.0).
Principal Business: Individual health insurance (100%).
Principal Investments: NonCMO investment grade bonds (64%), CMOs and structured securities (30%), cash (3%), and noninv. grade bonds (2%).
Investments in Affiliates: None
Group Affiliation: American Enterprise Mutual Holding
Licensed in: All states except CA, CT, MA, NH, NJ, NY, PR
Commenced Business: May 1960
Address: 1010 North 102nd St Ste 201, Des Moines, IA 50309
Phone: (804) 354-7000 **Domicile State:** NE **NAIC Code:** 79987

Data Date	Rating	RACR #1	RACR #2	Total Assets ($mil)	Capital ($mil)	Net Premium ($mil)	Net Income ($mil)
6-20	B-	4.07	3.66	46.4	26.4	0.0	0.2
6-19	B-	3.30	2.97	73.1	25.6	0.0	0.3
2019	B-	3.96	3.57	48.4	25.8	0.0	0.4
2018	B-	3.22	2.89	73.5	25.0	0.0	0.3
2017	A-	3.01	2.71	65.6	22.3	0.0	0.3
2016	B+	3.16	2.85	53.7	21.8	0.0	0.4
2015	B+	4.07	3.66	36.0	21.2	0.0	0.4

American Enterprise Mutual Holding
Composite Group Rating: C
Largest Group Members

Largest Group Members	Assets ($mil)	Rating
GREAT WESTERN INS CO	1370	C-
AMERICAN REPUBLIC INS CO	1135	B-
MEDICO INS CO	53	B-
MEDICO CORP LIFE INS CO	48	B-
AMERICAN REPUBLIC CORP INS CO	15	C

MEDICO INS CO   B-   Good

Major Rating Factors: Good overall profitability (5.2 on a scale of 0 to 10). Return on equity has been fair, averaging 6.2%. Good liquidity (6.8) with sufficient resources to handle a spike in claims. Fair overall results on stability tests (4.9) including fair financial strength of affiliated American Enterprise Mutual Holding.
Other Rating Factors: Strong capitalization (10.0) based on excellent risk adjusted capital (severe loss scenario). High quality investment portfolio (7.7).
Principal Business: Individual health insurance (83%), group health insurance (16%), and individual life insurance (1%).
Principal Investments: NonCMO investment grade bonds (71%), CMOs and structured securities (24%), and cash (3%).
Investments in Affiliates: None
Group Affiliation: American Enterprise Mutual Holding
Licensed in: All states except CT, NJ, NY, PR
Commenced Business: April 1930
Address: 1010 North 102nd St Ste 201, Des Moines, IA 50309
Phone: (800) 228-6080 **Domicile State:** NE **NAIC Code:** 31119

Data Date	Rating	RACR #1	RACR #2	Total Assets ($mil)	Capital ($mil)	Net Premium ($mil)	Net Income ($mil)
6-20	B-	5.07	4.56	57.3	34.6	0.2	0.7
6-19	B-	4.71	4.24	81.8	38.7	0.2	0.6
2019	B-	4.80	4.32	52.7	32.8	0.4	1.3
2018	B-	4.59	4.13	83.7	37.7	0.5	7.1
2017	B	4.28	3.85	81.9	34.8	0.5	1.3
2016	B	4.63	4.16	87.3	38.8	0.6	1.8
2015	B	4.12	3.71	74.3	31.9	0.7	2.1

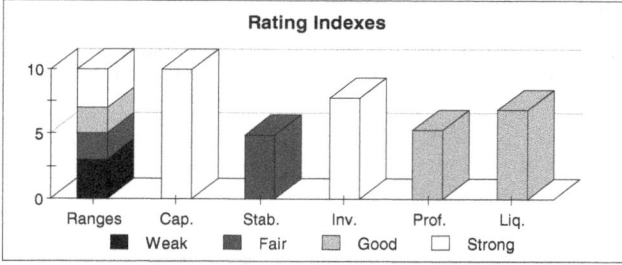

Rating Indexes

Ranges | Cap. | Stab. | Inv. | Prof. | Liq.
■ Weak ■ Fair ▨ Good ☐ Strong

MEDIEXCEL HEALTH PLAN   C-   Fair

Major Rating Factors: Fair overall results on stability tests (3.4 on a scale of 0 to 10) based on an excessive 35% enrollment growth during the period. Poor capitalization index (2.8) based on weak current risk-adjusted capital (moderate loss scenario). Excellent profitability (8.5).
Other Rating Factors: Excellent liquidity (6.9) with sufficient resources (cash flows and marketable investments) to handle a spike in claims.
Principal Business: Managed care (100%)
Mem Phys: 18: N/A **17:** N/A **18 MLR** 72.4% **/ 18 Admin Exp** N/A
Enroll(000): Q3 19: 15 **18:** 13 **17:** 10 **Med Exp PMPM:** $89
Principal Investments ($000): Cash and equiv ($944)
Provider Compensation ($000): None
Total Member Encounters: N/A
Group Affiliation: None
Licensed in: (No states)
Address: 750 Medical Cntr Court Ste 2, Chula Vista, CA 91911-6634
Phone: (855) 633-4392 **Dom State:** CA **Commenced Bus:** N/A

Data Date	Rating	RACR #1	RACR #2	Total Assets ($mil)	Capital ($mil)	Net Premium ($mil)	Net Income ($mil)
9-19	C-	0.74	0.50	4.5	1.6	16.1	0.2
9-18	C-	1.28	0.87	4.4	1.9	13.0	0.6
2018	C-	0.67	0.45	4.4	1.4	17.6	0.1
2017	C-	0.83	0.56	3.8	1.3	12.9	0.1
2016	N/A	N/A	N/A	N/A	N/A	N/A	N/A
2015	N/A	N/A	N/A	N/A	N/A	N/A	N/A
2014	N/A	N/A	N/A	N/A	N/A	N/A	N/A

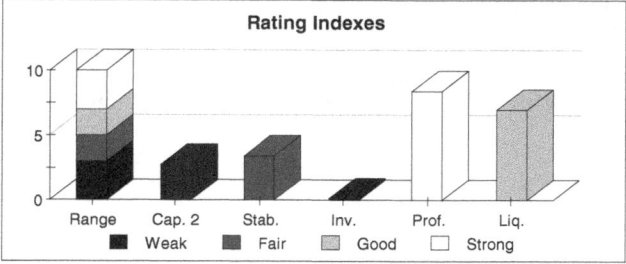

Rating Indexes

Range | Cap. 2 | Stab. | Inv. | Prof. | Liq.
■ Weak ■ Fair ▨ Good ☐ Strong

MEDISUN INC   D   Weak

Major Rating Factors: Weak profitability index (0.9 on a scale of 0 to 10). Fair overall results on stability tests (3.0) based on an inordinate decline in premium revenue in 2019, a steep decline in capital during 2019 and a significant 21% decrease in enrollment during the period. Strong capitalization index (7.0) based on excellent current risk-adjusted capital (severe loss scenario).
Other Rating Factors: High quality investment portfolio (9.5). Excellent liquidity (7.7) with ample operational cash flow and liquid investments.
Principal Business: Medicare (100%)
Mem Phys: 19: 4,311   **18:** 5,830   **19 MLR** 90.1%   **/ 19 Admin Exp** N/A
Enroll(000): Q2 20: 35   **19:** 42   **18:** 53   **Med Exp PMPM:** $789
Principal Investments: Cash and equiv (98%), long-term bonds (2%)
Provider Compensation ($000): Capitation ($376,146), FFS ($35,303)
Total Member Encounters: Phys (888,470), non-phys (230,470)
Group Affiliation: Blue Cross Blue Shield of Arizona In
Licensed in: AZ
Address: 2901 N Central Ave Suite 160, Phoenix,
Phone: (602) 864-4100   **Dom State:** AZ   **Commenced Bus:** N/A

Data Date	Rating	RACR #1	RACR #2	Total Assets ($mil)	Capital ($mil)	Net Premium ($mil)	Net Income ($mil)
6-20	D	1.32	1.10	236.8	47.7	194.1	6.0
6-19	N/A	N/A	N/A	N/A	N/A	N/A	N/A
2019	D+	1.16	0.96	245.3	42.2	451.6	-49.8
2018	B	1.52	1.27	102.0	58.7	562.4	5.3
2017	B-	1.01	0.84	94.5	51.2	658.9	13.0
2016	C+	0.76	0.63	72.4	39.8	590.9	4.3
2015	B-	0.83	0.69	69.3	35.0	467.6	-3.7

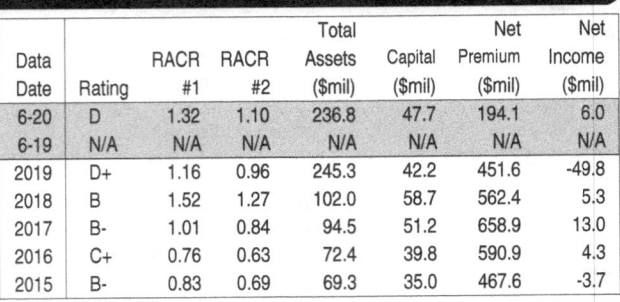

Rating Indexes

MEDSTAR FAMILY CHOICE INC   C   Fair

Major Rating Factors: Fair profitability index (3.1 on a scale of 0 to 10). Strong capitalization (8.1) based on excellent current risk-adjusted capital (severe loss scenario). High quality investment portfolio (9.9).
Other Rating Factors: Excellent liquidity (7.4) with ample operational cash flow and liquid investments.
Principal Business: Medicaid (100%)
Mem Phys: 19: N/A   **18:** N/A   **19 MLR** 88.5%   **/ 19 Admin Exp** N/A
Enroll(000): Q2 20: 94   **19:** 90   **18:** 96   **Med Exp PMPM:** $376
Principal Investments: Cash and equiv (100%)
Provider Compensation ($000): FFS ($271,552), contr fee ($150,733), capitation ($4,943)
Total Member Encounters: N/A
Group Affiliation: MedStar Health Inc
Licensed in: DC, MD
Address: 5233 King Avenue Suite 400, Baltimore, MD 21237
Phone: (410) 933-2200   **Dom State:** MD   **Commenced Bus:** N/A

Data Date	Rating	RACR #1	RACR #2	Total Assets ($mil)	Capital ($mil)	Net Premium ($mil)	Net Income ($mil)
6-20	C	2.26	1.88	207.3	93.7	254.5	15.3
6-19	N/A	N/A	N/A	N/A	N/A	N/A	N/A
2019	C-	1.91	1.59	189.5	80.5	466.4	7.9
2018	C-	1.36	1.13	199.8	72.4	555.0	-11.6
2017	C-	1.10	0.92	230.7	82.8	786.5	-23.1
2016	C-	1.17	0.97	244.5	84.5	749.3	-16.2
2015	N/A	N/A	N/A	219.7	84.2	599.6	N/A

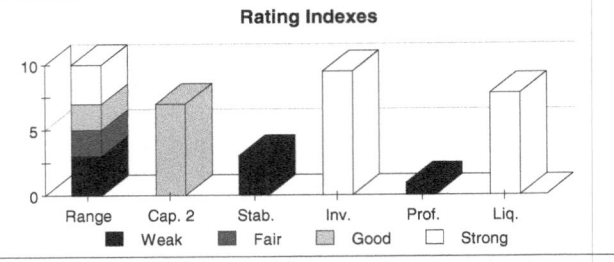

Rating Indexes

MEMBERS HEALTH INS CO   C-   Fair

Major Rating Factors: Weak profitability index (1.0 on a scale of 0 to 10). Strong capitalization (10.0) based on excellent current risk-adjusted capital (severe loss scenario). High quality investment portfolio (9.3).
Other Rating Factors: Excellent liquidity (7.7) with ample operational cash flow and liquid investments.
Principal Business: Med supp (34%), other (66%)
Mem Phys: 19: N/A   **18:** N/A   **19 MLR** 95.1%   **/ 19 Admin Exp** N/A
Enroll(000): Q2 20: 11   **19:** 7   **18:** 8   **Med Exp PMPM:** $113
Principal Investments: Long-term bonds (68%), cash and equiv (17%), nonaffiliate common stock (15%)
Provider Compensation ($000): FFS ($2,646), other ($10,696)
Total Member Encounters: Phys (32,286), non-phys (463,423)
Group Affiliation: None
Licensed in: AL, AZ, AR, CO, GA, ID, IL, IN, KS, KY, MD, MI, MN, MS, MO, MT, NE, NM, ND, OK, OR, PA, SC, SD, TN, TX, UT, WA, WV
Address: 24 West Camelback Road Suite, Phoenix, AZ 85013
Phone: (931) 560-0041   **Dom State:** AZ   **Commenced Bus:** N/A

Data Date	Rating	RACR #1	RACR #2	Total Assets ($mil)	Capital ($mil)	Net Premium ($mil)	Net Income ($mil)
6-20	C-	11.32	9.43	38.1	33.0	8.9	0.8
6-19	C-	14.73	12.28	37.4	31.6	5.0	-1.1
2019	C	13.31	11.10	37.6	32.4	9.4	-1.7
2018	C-	14.87	12.39	37.9	32.2	10.9	-3.7
2017	C-	12.12	10.10	34.4	28.3	6.6	-5.2
2016	C	17.30	14.42	32.8	30.9	2.5	-1.1
2015	C	18.55	15.46	33.4	31.9	2.0	-0.1

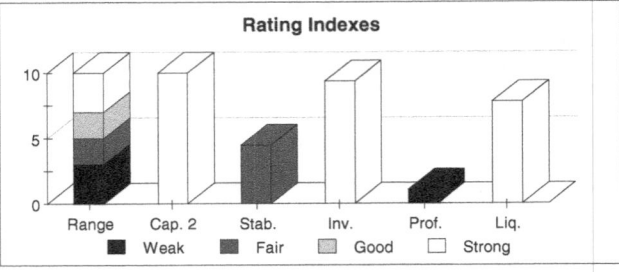

Rating Indexes

MEMORIAL HERMANN HEALTH INS CO   D   Weak

Major Rating Factors: Weak profitability index (0.3 on a scale of 0 to 10). Strong capitalization (7.3) based on excellent current risk-adjusted capital (severe loss scenario). High quality investment portfolio (9.9).
Other Rating Factors: Excellent liquidity (7.5) with ample operational cash flow and liquid investments.
Principal Business: Comp med (96%), Medicare (1%), other (2%)
Mem Phys: 19: 58,717 **18:** 66,924 **19 MLR** 139.8% **/ 19 Admin Exp** N/A
Enroll(000): Q2 20: 2 **19:** 2 **18:** 4 **Med Exp PMPM:** $718
Principal Investments: Cash and equiv (100%)
Provider Compensation ($000): FFS ($17,634)
Total Member Encounters: Phys (8,395), non-phys (12,072)
Group Affiliation: None
Licensed in: TX
Address: 929 Gessner Ste 1500, Houston, TX 77024
Phone: (713) 338-6480 **Dom State:** TX **Commenced Bus:** N/A

Data Date	Rating	RACR #1	RACR #2	Total Assets ($mil)	Capital ($mil)	Net Premium ($mil)	Net Income ($mil)
6-20	D	1.59	1.33	16.4	6.7	5.6	N/A
6-19	C-	2.97	2.48	24.0	17.4	5.8	-2.2
2019	D	1.80	1.50	17.2	6.9	12.4	-11.0
2018	C-	3.12	2.60	27.3	18.1	38.5	3.3
2017	C-	2.06	1.72	38.1	22.6	70.9	-5.1
2016	C-	1.74	1.45	53.3	25.0	92.8	-15.0
2015	C-	1.87	1.55	31.0	16.2	50.2	-9.7

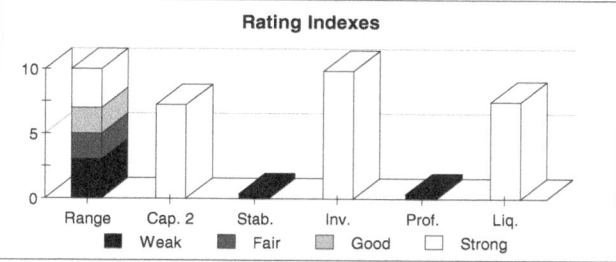

Rating Indexes

MEMORIAL HERMANN HEALTH PLAN INC   C-   Fair

Major Rating Factors: Weak profitability index (1.4 on a scale of 0 to 10). Strong capitalization (7.0) based on excellent current risk-adjusted capital (severe loss scenario). High quality investment portfolio (9.9).
Other Rating Factors: Excellent liquidity (7.4) with ample operational cash flow and liquid investments.
Principal Business: Medicare (53%), comp med (47%)
Mem Phys: 18: 33,005 **17:** 26,125 **18 MLR** 85.4% **/ 18 Admin Exp** N/A
Enroll(000): Q3 19: 7 **18:** 14 **17:** 20 **Med Exp PMPM:** $392
Principal Investments: Cash and equiv (100%)
Provider Compensation ($000): FFS ($70,661)
Total Member Encounters: Phys (74,069), non-phys (77,942)
Group Affiliation: None
Licensed in: TX
Address: 929 Gessner Ste 1500, Houston, TX 77024
Phone: (713) 338-6480 **Dom State:** TX **Commenced Bus:** N/A

Data Date	Rating	RACR #1	RACR #2	Total Assets ($mil)	Capital ($mil)	Net Premium ($mil)	Net Income ($mil)
9-19	C-	1.34	1.11	37.8	13.1	34.1	-3.1
9-18	D+	N/A	N/A	53.3	21.8	60.8	5.1
2018	C-	1.74	1.45	40.5	16.7	78.9	-1.4
2017	D+	N/A	N/A	41.7	16.3	98.4	-7.3
2016	D+	1.10	0.92	26.7	10.5	55.7	-10.9
2015	D+	1.50	1.25	11.9	7.5	18.0	-8.3
2014	N/A	N/A	N/A	7.3	6.5	N/A	N/A

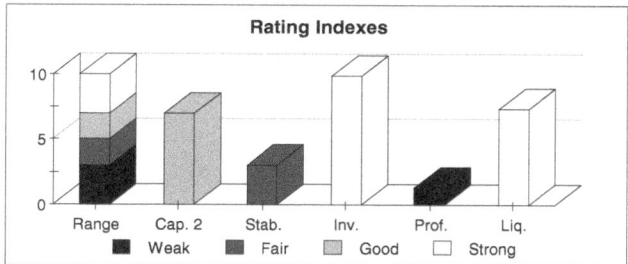

Rating Indexes

MERCYCARE HMO   C   Fair

Major Rating Factors: Fair profitability index (3.4 on a scale of 0 to 10). Fair quality investment portfolio (4.4). Good capitalization (6.8) based on excellent current risk-adjusted capital (severe loss scenario).
Other Rating Factors: Good liquidity (5.8) with sufficient resources (cash flows and marketable investments) to handle a spike in claims.
Principal Business: Comp med (74%), Medicaid (22%), med supp (3%), FEHB (1%)
Mem Phys: 19: 516 **18:** 483 **19 MLR** 92.7% **/ 19 Admin Exp** N/A
Enroll(000): Q2 20: 31 **19:** 29 **18:** 29 **Med Exp PMPM:** $286
Principal Investments: Nonaffiliate common stock (62%), long-term bonds (27%), cash and equiv (10%)
Provider Compensation ($000): Contr fee ($77,060), capitation ($17,837), FFS ($6,085)
Total Member Encounters: N/A
Group Affiliation: None
Licensed in: IL, WI
Address: 580 N Washington, Janesville, WI 53545
Phone: (608) 752-3431 **Dom State:** WI **Commenced Bus:** N/A

Data Date	Rating	RACR #1	RACR #2	Total Assets ($mil)	Capital ($mil)	Net Premium ($mil)	Net Income ($mil)
6-20	C	1.23	1.02	46.4	16.5	62.1	2.6
6-19	C	1.14	0.95	44.1	14.4	N/A	0.1
2019	C	1.07	0.89	41.8	14.1	106.6	3.7
2018	C	0.85	0.71	35.7	10.8	106.8	-2.4
2017	C	1.56	1.30	43.9	17.0	93.0	-1.9
2016	C	1.54	1.29	31.0	15.8	82.0	1.5
2015	C	1.47	1.23	27.3	14.2	79.5	0.0

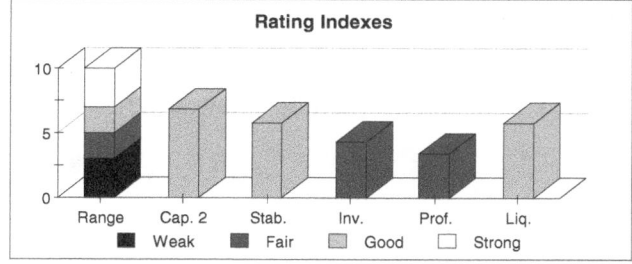

Rating Indexes

MERCYCARE INS CO

D+ **Weak**

Major Rating Factors: Weak profitability index (1.5 on a scale of 0 to 10). Fair quality investment portfolio (3.1). Good liquidity (6.8) with sufficient resources (cash flows and marketable investments) to handle a spike in claims.
Other Rating Factors: Strong capitalization (7.4) based on excellent current risk-adjusted capital (severe loss scenario).
Principal Business: Comp med (100%)
Mem Phys: 19: 516 **18:** 483 **19 MLR** 121.6% **/ 19 Admin Exp** N/A
Enroll(000): Q2 20: 1 **19:** 1 **18:** 1 **Med Exp PMPM:** $57
Principal Investments: Affiliate common stock (87%), long-term bonds (14%)
Provider Compensation ($000): FFS ($234), contr fee ($173), capitation ($46)
Total Member Encounters: N/A
Group Affiliation: None
Licensed in: IL, WI
Address: 580 N Washington, Janesville, WI 53545
Phone: (608) 752-3431 **Dom State:** WI **Commenced Bus:** N/A

Data Date	Rating	RACR #1	RACR #2	Total Assets ($mil)	Capital ($mil)	Net Premium ($mil)	Net Income ($mil)
6-20	D+	1.66	1.39	25.6	22.5	0.4	0.0
6-19	D+	1.64	1.36	15.4	13.8	0.2	-0.2
2019	D+	0.96	0.80	16.2	12.8	0.4	0.0
2018	D+	1.21	1.01	12.3	10.3	0.4	0.3
2017	D+	N/A	N/A	18.8	16.4	0.6	-0.1
2016	D+	1.29	1.08	17.4	15.4	0.6	-1.4
2015	C-	1.33	1.11	16.1	15.2	2.2	-1.0

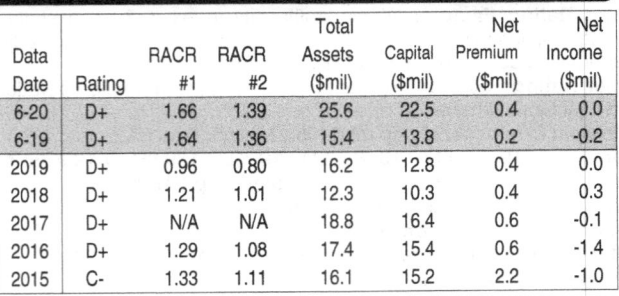

Rating Indexes

MERIDIAN HEALTH PLAN OF ILLINOIS INC

C- **Fair**

Major Rating Factors: Weak profitability index (0.9 on a scale of 0 to 10). Good capitalization (6.4) based on good current risk-adjusted capital (severe loss scenario). Good liquidity (6.9) with sufficient resources (cash flows and marketable investments) to handle a spike in claims.
Other Rating Factors: High quality investment portfolio (9.6).
Principal Business: Medicaid (94%), Medicare (6%)
Mem Phys: 19: 48,746 **18:** 42,324 **19 MLR** 95.0% **/ 19 Admin Exp** N/A
Enroll(000): Q2 20: 785 **19:** 774 **18:** 622 **Med Exp PMPM:** $359
Principal Investments: Cash and equiv (64%), long-term bonds (36%)
Provider Compensation ($000): Contr fee ($2,837,095), FFS ($324,921), capitation ($103,841), bonus arrang ($12,397)
Total Member Encounters: Phys (5,639,426), non-phys (4,419,594)
Group Affiliation: None
Licensed in: IL
Address: 300 S Riverside Plaza Ste 5, Chicago, IL 60604
Phone: (313) 324-3700 **Dom State:** IL **Commenced Bus:** N/A

Data Date	Rating	RACR #1	RACR #2	Total Assets ($mil)	Capital ($mil)	Net Premium ($mil)	Net Income ($mil)
6-20	C-	1.14	0.95	1,119.5	360.6	2,009.3	-88.4
6-19	C	2.02	1.69	845.7	344.9	1,758.1	-47.4
2019	C	1.93	1.61	1,095.3	464.3	3,633.7	-77.0
2018	C	1.02	0.85	685.5	231.8	2,421.4	-179.4
2017	C	0.84	0.70	478.1	128.8	1,436.3	-14.2
2016	B-	0.93	0.78	405.5	96.5	1,125.7	-30.4
2015	B	1.11	0.92	282.6	87.3	1,017.2	7.2

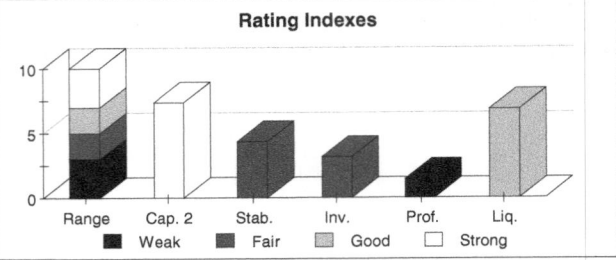

Rating Indexes

MERIDIAN HEALTH PLAN OF MICHIGAN INC

C **Fair**

Major Rating Factors: Fair profitability index (2.9 on a scale of 0 to 10). Good overall results on stability tests (6.8). Good liquidity (6.1) with sufficient resources (cash flows and marketable investments) to handle a spike in claims.
Other Rating Factors: Strong capitalization index (7.5) based on excellent current risk-adjusted capital (severe loss scenario). High quality investment portfolio (9.6).
Principal Business: Medicaid (83%), Medicare (16%), comp med (1%)
Mem Phys: 19: 47,858 **18:** 40,971 **19 MLR** 86.6% **/ 19 Admin Exp** N/A
Enroll(000): Q2 20: 553 **19:** 520 **18:** 519 **Med Exp PMPM:** $279
Principal Investments: Long-term bonds (66%), cash and equiv (34%)
Provider Compensation ($000): Contr fee ($1,476,182), FFS ($190,140), capitation ($44,995), bonus arrang ($11,888)
Total Member Encounters: Phys (6,163,055), non-phys (5,192,294)
Group Affiliation: None
Licensed in: DC, DE, IL, IN, KY, ME, MI, OH
Address: 1 Campus Martius Suite 700, Detroit,
Phone: (313) 324-3700 **Dom State:** MI **Commenced Bus:** N/A

Data Date	Rating	RACR #1	RACR #2	Total Assets ($mil)	Capital ($mil)	Net Premium ($mil)	Net Income ($mil)
6-20	C	1.76	1.47	742.7	292.2	1,126.8	60.6
6-19	C	1.14	0.95	394.8	140.0	966.5	-48.9
2019	C	1.86	1.55	553.5	230.5	2,026.0	-29.2
2018	C	1.07	0.89	423.2	169.9	1,988.4	-88.0
2017	B	1.17	0.97	451.8	186.8	2,201.8	0.5
2016	B+	1.16	0.97	537.4	185.3	2,420.8	3.9
2015	B+	1.09	0.91	477.6	153.4	2,113.2	6.8

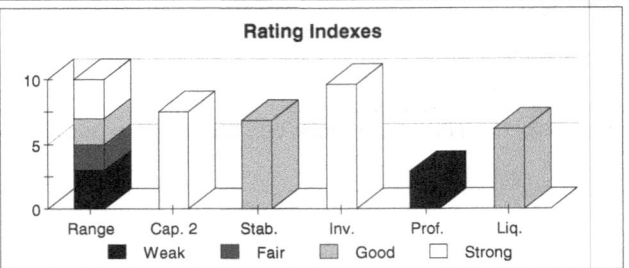

Rating Indexes

MERIT HEALTH INS CO

C+   **Fair**

Major Rating Factors: Good overall profitability index (5.5 on a scale of 0 to 10). Strong capitalization (10.0) based on excellent current risk-adjusted capital (severe loss scenario). High quality investment portfolio (9.9).
Other Rating Factors: Excellent liquidity (8.0) with ample operational cash flow and liquid investments.
Principal Business: Other (100%)
Mem Phys: 18: N/A   **17:** N/A   **18 MLR** 86.5%   / **18 Admin Exp** N/A
Enroll(000): Q3 19: 64   **18:** 88   **17:** 109   **Med Exp PMPM:** $87
Principal Investments: Long-term bonds (66%), cash and equiv (34%)
Provider Compensation ($000): Other ($89,679)
Total Member Encounters: N/A
Group Affiliation: Magellan Health Inc
Licensed in: All states except FL, NV, NJ, PR
Address: 5215 Old Orchard Road Suite 6, Phoenix, AZ 85034
Phone: (224) 935-9809   **Dom State:** IL   **Commenced Bus:** N/A

Data Date	Rating	RACR #1	RACR #2	Total Assets ($mil)	Capital ($mil)	Net Premium ($mil)	Net Income ($mil)
9-19	C+	10.41	8.68	154.8	54.3	46.3	0.2
9-18	C	N/A	N/A	142.0	54.1	80.6	-0.7
2018	C+	9.98	8.31	127.6	53.5	103.7	-1.9
2017	C	N/A	N/A	131.0	51.9	113.3	9.1
2016	C+	5.46	4.55	147.0	58.3	59.8	8.8
2015	B-	3.57	2.98	65.0	47.9	118.5	10.4
2014	N/A	N/A	N/A	67.2	27.0	128.8	N/A

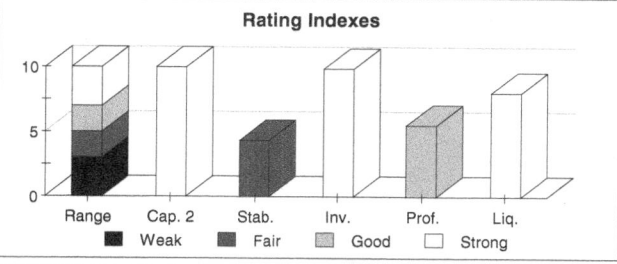

METROPOLITAN LIFE INS CO

B-   **Good**

Major Rating Factors: Good quality investment portfolio (5.4 on a scale of 0 to 10) despite substantial holdings of BBB bonds in addition to junk bond exposure equal to 72% of capital. Exposure to mortgages is significant, but the mortgage default rate has been low. Good overall profitability (6.8). Return on equity has been excellent over the last five years averaging 23.4%. Good liquidity (6.9).
Other Rating Factors: Good overall results on stability tests (5.0) despite excessive premium growth good operational trends, good risk adjusted capital for prior years and excellent risk diversification. Strong capitalization (7.4) based on excellent risk adjusted capital (severe loss scenario).
Principal Business: Group life insurance (32%), group retirement contracts (28%), group health insurance (25%), individual life insurance (10%), and other lines (6%).
Principal Investments: NonCMO investment grade bonds (42%), mortgages in good standing (24%), CMOs and structured securities (16%), noninv. grade bonds (4%), and misc. investments (13%).
Investments in Affiliates: 4%
Group Affiliation: MetLife Inc
Licensed in: All states, the District of Columbia and Puerto Rico
Commenced Business: May 1867
Address: 200 Park Avenue, New York, NY 10166-0188
Phone: (212) 578-9500   **Domicile State:** NY   **NAIC Code:** 65978

Data Date	Rating	RACR #1	RACR #2	Total Assets ($mil)	Capital ($mil)	Net Premium ($mil)	Net Income ($mil)
6-20	B-	2.49	1.28	408,407	13,691.2	14,680.2	1,809.9
6-19	B-	2.09	1.07	388,923	10,618.5	11,413.8	1,729.0
2019	B-	2.20	1.14	389,508	10,914.8	25,210.4	3,859.1
2018	B-	2.14	1.10	378,080	11,098.1	31,708.6	3,656.7
2017	B-	1.17	0.77	396,508	10,384.5	18,256.1	1,982.0
2016	B-	1.33	0.85	396,367	11,194.8	24,891.2	3,444.2
2015	B-	1.43	0.96	390,843	14,485.0	28,388.6	3,703.3

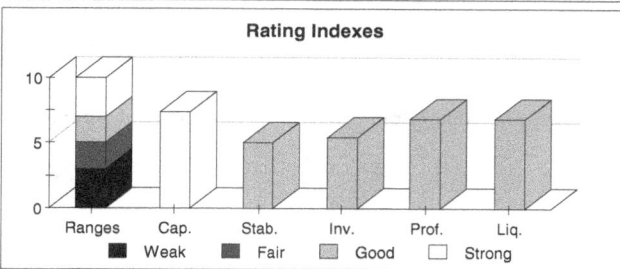

MHS HEALTH WISCONSIN

B   **Good**

Major Rating Factors: Good liquidity (6.9 on a scale of 0 to 10) with sufficient resources (cash flows and marketable investments) to handle a spike in claims. Excellent profitability (9.0). Strong capitalization index (9.4) based on excellent current risk-adjusted capital (severe loss scenario).
Other Rating Factors: High quality investment portfolio (7.7). Excellent overall results on stability tests (7.1).
Principal Business: Medicaid (91%), Medicare (9%)
Mem Phys: 19: 21,405   **18:** 22,918   **19 MLR** 84.5%   / **19 Admin Exp** N/A
Enroll(000): Q2 20: 50   **19:** 42   **18:** 40   **Med Exp PMPM:** $389
Principal Investments: Long-term bonds (90%), cash and equiv (6%), affiliate common stock (2%), other (2%)
Provider Compensation ($000): Contr fee ($142,799), bonus arrang ($37,961), salary ($11,316), capitation ($4,033)
Total Member Encounters: Phys (235,539), non-phys (555,517)
Group Affiliation: None
Licensed in: WI
Address: 10700 W Research Drive Suite 3, Milwaukee,
Phone: (314) 725-4477   **Dom State:** WI   **Commenced Bus:** N/A

Data Date	Rating	RACR #1	RACR #2	Total Assets ($mil)	Capital ($mil)	Net Premium ($mil)	Net Income ($mil)
6-20	B	3.32	2.76	105.9	67.7	128.2	10.8
6-19	B-	4.10	3.42	96.1	48.8	114.8	8.0
2019	B-	4.37	3.64	83.4	56.3	228.9	14.9
2018	B-	4.29	3.57	86.2	51.2	210.3	12.9
2017	C+	N/A	N/A	69.6	50.7	163.3	9.2
2016	C+	4.92	4.10	72.3	51.5	183.6	9.5
2015	C+	4.59	3.83	75.7	46.6	196.8	15.8

MICHIGAN COMPLETE HEALTH INC C- Fair

Major Rating Factors: Weak profitability index (1.1 on a scale of 0 to 10). Low quality investment portfolio (1.6). Strong capitalization (9.6) based on excellent current risk-adjusted capital (severe loss scenario).
Other Rating Factors: Excellent liquidity (7.3) with ample operational cash flow and liquid investments.
Principal Business: Medicare (100%)
Mem Phys: 19: 9,999 **18:** 8,113 **19 MLR** 81.6% / **19 Admin Exp** N/A
Enroll(000): Q2 20: 3 **19:** 3 **18:** 2 **Med Exp PMPM:** $1,903
Principal Investments: Cash and equiv (95%), long-term bonds (5%)
Provider Compensation ($000): Capitation ($21,963), contr fee ($21,906), salary ($3,302)
Total Member Encounters: Phys (78,994), non-phys (203,829)
Group Affiliation: None
Licensed in: MI
Address: 800 Tower Rd Suite 200, Troy, MI 48098
Phone: (314) 725-4477 **Dom State:** MO **Commenced Bus:** N/A

Data Date	Rating	RACR #1	RACR #2	Total Assets ($mil)	Capital ($mil)	Net Premium ($mil)	Net Income ($mil)
6-20	C-	3.47	2.89	36.0	20.5	43.7	2.0
6-19	C	3.65	3.04	21.7	12.6	32.3	-1.6
2019	C	5.38	4.49	30.9	18.2	67.0	1.3
2018	C-	1.91	1.59	11.0	6.5	63.7	-5.0
2017	C-	1.22	1.02	12.0	7.1	54.3	0.6
2016	C-	2.34	1.95	10.6	6.5	46.9	-0.6
2015	C	1.77	1.47	11.3	5.0	60.5	-3.4

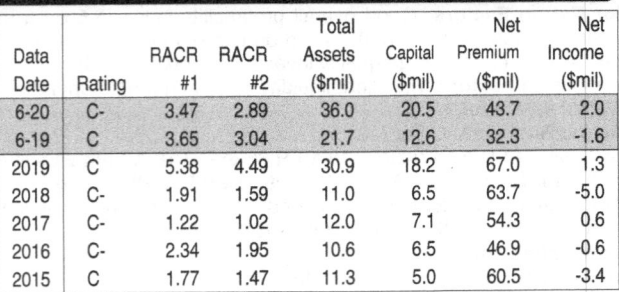

Rating Indexes
Range, Cap. 2, Stab., Inv., Prof., Liq.
Weak Fair Good Strong

MII LIFE INSURANCE INC C- Fair

Major Rating Factors: Weak profitability index (0.4 on a scale of 0 to 10). Low quality investment portfolio (2.3). Strong capitalization (7.1) based on excellent current risk-adjusted capital (severe loss scenario).
Other Rating Factors: Excellent liquidity (7.8) with ample operational cash flow and liquid investments.
Principal Business: Other (63%)
Mem Phys: 19: N/A **18:** N/A **19 MLR** 75.9% / **19 Admin Exp** N/A
Enroll(000): Q2 20: 111 **19:** 92 **18:** 44 **Med Exp PMPM:** $57
Principal Investments: Long-term bonds (96%), cash and equiv (3%), nonaffiliate common stock (1%)
Provider Compensation ($000): Other ($45,262)
Total Member Encounters: N/A
Group Affiliation: Aware Integrated Inc
Licensed in: AL, AR, CA, DC, DE, FL, GA, IN, IA, KS, KY, LA, MD, MI, MN, MT, NE, NJ, NY, NC, ND, OH, OR, PA, SD, TN, UT, WA, WV, WI, WY
Address: 3535 Blue Cross Road, Eagan, MN 55122
Phone: (651) 662-8000 **Dom State:** MN **Commenced Bus:** N/A

Data Date	Rating	RACR #1	RACR #2	Total Assets ($mil)	Capital ($mil)	Net Premium ($mil)	Net Income ($mil)
6-20	C-	1.45	1.21	1,528.1	32.9	35.1	-12.8
6-19	C	2.57	2.14	1,338.1	43.3	18.8	0.7
2019	C	3.90	3.25	1,426.9	52.3	65.7	9.9
2018	C	2.14	1.78	1,196.5	36.0	35.0	0.4
2017	B-	N/A	N/A	985.5	45.0	23.5	2.8
2016	B-	2.91	2.43	813.0	39.9	17.2	9.5
2015	B	2.66	2.21	596.6	27.7	16.2	3.2

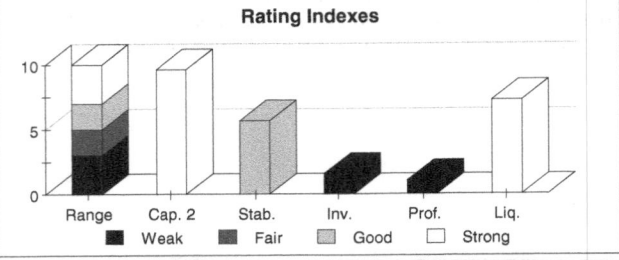

Rating Indexes
Range, Cap. 2, Stab., Inv., Prof., Liq.
Weak Fair Good Strong

MISSOURI CARE INC C Fair

Major Rating Factors: Weak profitability index (0.9 on a scale of 0 to 10). Strong capitalization (7.6) based on excellent current risk-adjusted capital (severe loss scenario). High quality investment portfolio (8.6).
Other Rating Factors: Excellent liquidity (7.0) with sufficient resources (cash flows and marketable investments) to handle a spike in claims.
Principal Business: Medicaid (97%), comp med (3%)
Mem Phys: 19: 41,200 **18:** 36,400 **19 MLR** 89.8% / **19 Admin Exp** N/A
Enroll(000): Q2 20: 246 **19:** 218 **18:** 251 **Med Exp PMPM:** $229
Principal Investments: Cash and equiv (60%), long-term bonds (40%)
Provider Compensation ($000): Contr fee ($512,028), capitation ($112,155), bonus arrang ($11,994)
Total Member Encounters: Phys (794,385), non-phys (505,290)
Group Affiliation: Anthem Inc
Licensed in: MO
Address: 800 Market Street 27th Floor, ST LOUIS, MO 63101
Phone: (813) 206-6200 **Dom State:** MO **Commenced Bus:** N/A

Data Date	Rating	RACR #1	RACR #2	Total Assets ($mil)	Capital ($mil)	Net Premium ($mil)	Net Income ($mil)
6-20	C	1.82	1.52	265.8	96.9	372.8	-47.6
6-19	C	2.75	2.29	211.2	107.7	354.1	10.2
2019	B-	2.40	2.00	201.3	88.0	705.2	-7.0
2018	D+	2.58	2.15	218.6	100.3	767.3	7.8
2017	E	2.05	1.71	207.6	94.1	651.1	15.4
2016	E	2.73	2.27	87.6	42.6	349.5	3.5
2015	E	2.35	1.96	74.1	34.5	308.9	-0.7

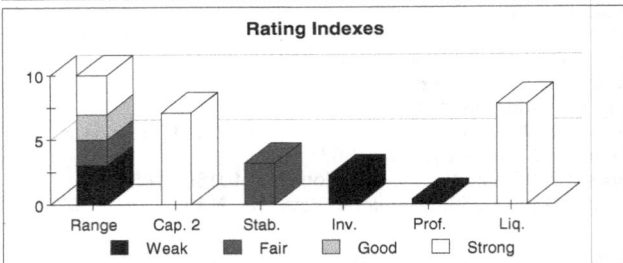

Rating Indexes
Range, Cap. 2, Stab., Inv., Prof., Liq.
Weak Fair Good Strong

MISSOURI CHAMBER FEDN BENEFIT | C | Fair

Major Rating Factors: Weak liquidity (2.8 on a scale of 0 to 10) as a spike in claims may stretch capacity. Excellent profitability (10.0). Strong capitalization (10.0) based on excellent current risk-adjusted capital (severe loss scenario). **Other Rating Factors:** High quality investment portfolio (9.4).
Principal Business: Comp med (100%)
Mem Phys: 18: N/A **17:** N/A **18 MLR** 747.7% **/ 18 Admin Exp** N/A
Enroll(000): Q3 19: 18 **18:** 10 **17:** 1 **Med Exp PMPM:** $217
Principal Investments: Cash and equiv (100%)
Provider Compensation ($000): Contr fee ($9,450), FFS ($6,300)
Total Member Encounters: N/A
Group Affiliation: Missouri Chamber Federation Benefit
Licensed in: MO
Address: 428 East Capitol Avenue #100, Jefferson City, MO 65101
Phone: (573) 634-3511 **Dom State:** MO **Commenced Bus:** N/A

Data Date	Rating	RACR #1	RACR #2	Total Assets ($mil)	Capital ($mil)	Net Premium ($mil)	Net Income ($mil)
9-19	C	5.05	4.21	23.2	2.4	4.6	1.2
9-18	N/A	N/A	N/A	10.0	1.0	1.7	0.5
2018	C-	2.43	2.03	11.9	1.2	2.5	0.6
2017	N/A	N/A	N/A	1.0	0.7	N/A	N/A
2016	N/A	N/A	N/A	N/A	N/A	N/A	N/A
2015	N/A	N/A	N/A	N/A	N/A	N/A	N/A
2014	N/A	N/A	N/A	N/A	N/A	N/A	N/A

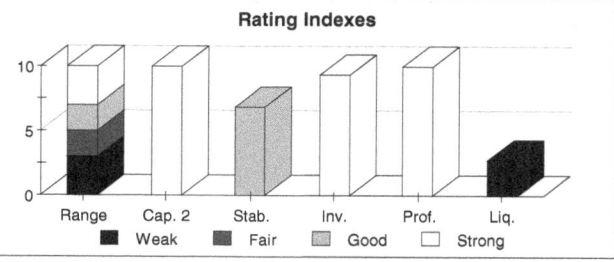

Rating Indexes

MISSOURI MEDICARE SELECT LLC | D+ | Weak

Major Rating Factors: Weak profitability index (0.9 on a scale of 0 to 10). Fair capitalization (4.0) based on fair current risk-adjusted capital (moderate loss scenario). Fair liquidity (4.2) as cash resources may not be adequate to cover a spike in claims. **Other Rating Factors:** High quality investment portfolio (9.9).
Principal Business: Medicare (100%)
Mem Phys: 18: 1,533 **17:** 935 **18 MLR** 104.2% **/ 18 Admin Exp** N/A
Enroll(000): Q3 19: 0 **18:** N/A **17:** 0 **Med Exp PMPM:** N/A
Principal Investments: Long-term bonds (57%), cash and equiv (43%)
Provider Compensation ($000): Contr fee ($2,174), capitation ($435)
Total Member Encounters: Phys (3,591), non-phys (453)
Group Affiliation: American Health Companies Inc
Licensed in: MO
Address: 201 Jordan Road Suite 200, Franklin, TN 37067
Phone: (615) 565-3654 **Dom State:** MO **Commenced Bus:** N/A

Data Date	Rating	RACR #1	RACR #2	Total Assets ($mil)	Capital ($mil)	Net Premium ($mil)	Net Income ($mil)
9-19	D+	0.79	0.65	1.5	1.0	1.3	-0.8
9-18	C-	N/A	N/A	1.6	0.8	2.1	-0.4
2018	D+	0.47	0.40	1.1	0.7	2.0	-0.5
2017	C-	N/A	N/A	1.6	0.8	4.5	-1.0
2016	C-	1.11	0.93	1.7	0.9	4.9	0.2
2015	N/A	N/A	N/A	1.2	1.2	N/A	-0.2
2014	N/A	N/A	N/A	N/A	N/A	N/A	N/A

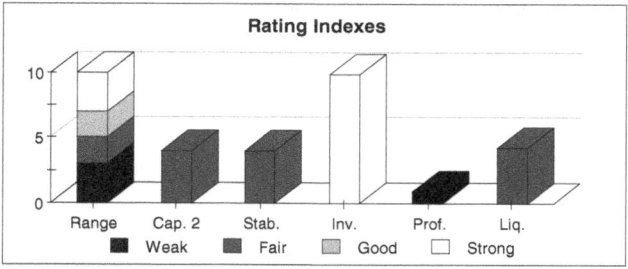

Rating Indexes

MISSOURI VALLEY L&H INS CO | C+ | Fair

Major Rating Factors: Fair profitability index (3.3 on a scale of 0 to 10). Good liquidity (6.6) with sufficient resources (cash flows and marketable investments) to handle a spike in claims. Strong capitalization (7.7) based on excellent current risk-adjusted capital (severe loss scenario). **Other Rating Factors:** High quality investment portfolio (8.5).
Principal Business: Medicare (27%), other (73%)
Mem Phys: 19: 3,817 **18:** 4,041 **19 MLR** 94.9% **/ 19 Admin Exp** N/A
Enroll(000): Q2 20: 8 **19:** 2 **18:** 1 **Med Exp PMPM:** $2,950
Principal Investments: Long-term bonds (96%), cash and equiv (4%)
Provider Compensation ($000): Contr fee ($48,930), FFS ($15,451), capitation ($254)
Total Member Encounters: Phys (17,920), non-phys (8,057)
Group Affiliation: None
Licensed in: KS, MO
Address: 2301 Main Street, Kansas City, MO 64108-2428
Phone: (816) 395-3355 **Dom State:** MO **Commenced Bus:** N/A

Data Date	Rating	RACR #1	RACR #2	Total Assets ($mil)	Capital ($mil)	Net Premium ($mil)	Net Income ($mil)
6-20	C+	1.89	1.58	85.6	50.9	73.0	2.3
6-19	C-	0.96	0.80	42.6	19.6	35.2	-3.9
2019	C	1.54	1.28	63.3	42.3	73.2	-8.6
2018	U	1.27	1.05	33.8	25.6	47.8	5.3
2017	N/A	N/A	N/A	18.1	13.8	26.1	N/A
2016	N/A	N/A	N/A	15.7	10.9	16.0	N/A
2015	N/A	N/A	N/A	16.7	16.1	0.8	N/A

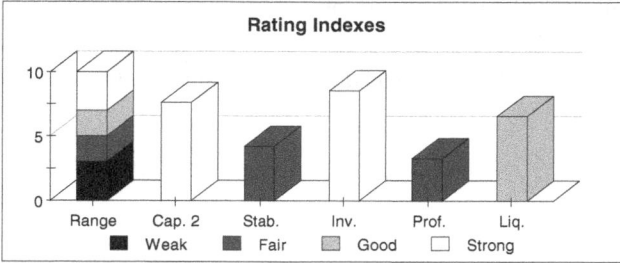

Rating Indexes

MMM FLORIDA INC   D   Weak

Major Rating Factors: Weak profitability index (0.0 on a scale of 0 to 10). Weak liquidity (2.1) as a spike in claims may stretch capacity. Strong capitalization (7.2) based on excellent current risk-adjusted capital (severe loss scenario).
Other Rating Factors: High quality investment portfolio (9.9).
Principal Business: Medicare (100%)
Mem Phys: 19: N/A **18:** N/A **19 MLR** 92.6% **/ 19 Admin Exp** N/A
Enroll(000): Q2 20: 3 **19:** 2 **18:** N/A **Med Exp PMPM:** $1,342
Principal Investments: Cash and equiv (100%)
Provider Compensation ($000): FFS ($13,249), capitation ($6,838), bonus arrang ($379), other ($2,085)
Total Member Encounters: N/A
Group Affiliation: ICH Investments Holdings LP
Licensed in: FL
Address: 5775 Blue Lagoon Drive Suite, Miami, FL 33126
Phone: (844) 212-9858 **Dom State:** FL **Commenced Bus:** N/A

Data Date	Rating	RACR #1	RACR #2	Total Assets ($mil)	Capital ($mil)	Net Premium ($mil)	Net Income ($mil)
6-20	D	1.51	1.26	17.1	11.6	26.4	-4.5
6-19	N/A	N/A	N/A	12.1	4.9	11.8	-4.7
2019	D	1.13	0.94	12.9	6.7	30.4	-11.1
2018	N/A	N/A	N/A	7.1	3.4	N/A	-9.1
2017	N/A	N/A	N/A	13.5	13.1	N/A	-1.8
2016	N/A	N/A	N/A	N/A	N/A	N/A	N/A
2015	N/A	N/A	N/A	N/A	N/A	N/A	N/A

Rating Indexes

MMM HEALTHCARE LLC   E-   Very Weak

Major Rating Factors: Good capitalization (5.5 on a scale of 0 to 10) based on good current risk-adjusted capital (severe loss scenario). Excellent profitability (8.3). High quality investment portfolio (9.9).
Other Rating Factors: Excellent liquidity (6.9) with sufficient resources (cash flows and marketable investments) to handle a spike in claims.
Principal Business: Medicare (100%)
Mem Phys: 19: N/A **18:** N/A **19 MLR** 84.3% **/ 19 Admin Exp** N/A
Enroll(000): Q2 20: 260 **19:** 263 **18:** 215 **Med Exp PMPM:** $756
Principal Investments: Cash and equiv (62%), long-term bonds (38%)
Provider Compensation ($000): FFS ($1,115,519), capitation ($581,565), bonus arrang ($168,346), other ($339,503)
Total Member Encounters: N/A
Group Affiliation: ICH Investments Holdings LP
Licensed in: PR
Address: 350 CHARDON AVE STE 500, SAN JUAN, PR 918
Phone: (787) 622-3000 **Dom State:** PR **Commenced Bus:** N/A

Data Date	Rating	RACR #1	RACR #2	Total Assets ($mil)	Capital ($mil)	Net Premium ($mil)	Net Income ($mil)
6-20	E-	1.01	0.84	689.6	200.5	1,493.6	27.1
6-19	E-	1.15	0.95	528.7	165.5	1,341.7	31.8
2019	E-	0.90	0.75	498.3	176.2	2,696.9	42.2
2018	E-	0.92	0.76	377.2	132.1	2,039.8	24.0
2017	E-	1.14	0.95	395.9	141.9	1,806.3	35.4
2016	E-	1.01	0.85	310.7	117.0	1,593.6	37.3
2015	E-	0.99	0.82	272.5	120.8	1,531.9	11.2

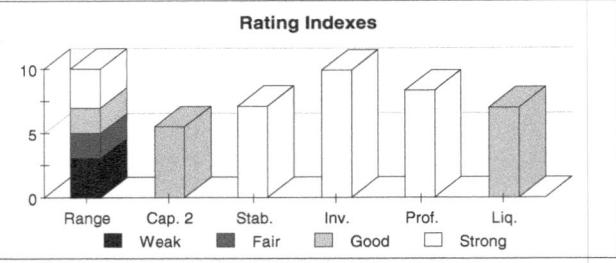

Rating Indexes

MMM MULTI HEALTH LLC   D+   Weak

Major Rating Factors: Weak profitability index (1.8 on a scale of 0 to 10). Poor capitalization (2.0) based on weak current risk-adjusted capital (moderate loss scenario). Good liquidity (5.6) with sufficient resources (cash flows and marketable investments) to handle a spike in claims.
Other Rating Factors: High quality investment portfolio (9.9).
Principal Business: Medicaid (100%)
Mem Phys: 19: N/A **18:** N/A **19 MLR** 91.6% **/ 19 Admin Exp** N/A
Enroll(000): Q2 20: 258 **19:** 257 **18:** 276 **Med Exp PMPM:** $172
Principal Investments: Cash and equiv (60%), long-term bonds (40%)
Provider Compensation ($000): FFS ($301,655), capitation ($82,607), bonus arrang ($20,799), other ($162,986)
Total Member Encounters: N/A
Group Affiliation: ICH Investments Holdings LP
Licensed in: PR
Address: 350 CHARDON AVE STE 350, SAN JUAN, PR 918
Phone: (787) 724-7504 **Dom State:** PR **Commenced Bus:** N/A

Data Date	Rating	RACR #1	RACR #2	Total Assets ($mil)	Capital ($mil)	Net Premium ($mil)	Net Income ($mil)
6-20	D+	0.51	0.42	210.2	41.4	319.4	-4.6
6-19	D	0.98	0.81	134.1	58.0	304.4	4.5
2019	D	0.77	0.64	152.7	49.7	613.8	-6.3
2018	D	0.79	0.66	141.5	50.9	570.7	12.0
2017	D	N/A	N/A	171.7	55.8	541.7	4.2
2016	D	1.10	0.92	63.5	18.8	249.6	-1.3
2015	N/A	N/A	N/A	67.5	15.6	193.4	-2.3

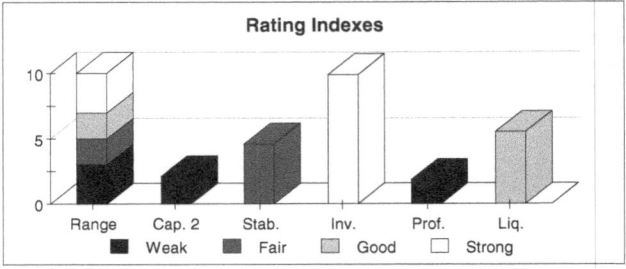

Rating Indexes

MODA HEALTH PLAN INC   E   Very Weak

Major Rating Factors: Weak profitability index (0.9 on a scale of 0 to 10). Good capitalization (6.5) based on good current risk-adjusted capital (severe loss scenario). Good quality investment portfolio (5.7).

Other Rating Factors: Excellent liquidity (6.9) with sufficient resources (cash flows and marketable investments) to handle a spike in claims.

Principal Business: Comp med (68%), Medicare (16%), med supp (15%)

Mem Phys: 19: 36,517 **18:** 33,515 **19 MLR** 95.1% **/ 19 Admin Exp** N/A

Enroll(000): Q2 20: 103 **19:** 97 **18:** 90 **Med Exp PMPM:** $513

Principal Investments: Long-term bonds (43%), affiliate common stock (21%), cash and equiv (20%), nonaffiliate common stock (16%)

Provider Compensation ($000): Contr fee ($338,313), bonus arrang ($238,046), FFS ($17,686), capitation ($4,864)

Total Member Encounters: Phys (113,296), non-phys (86,536)

Group Affiliation: None

Licensed in: AK, CA, ID, OR, TX, WA

Address: 601 SW SECOND AVE, PORTLAND, OR 97204

Phone: (503) 228-6554 **Dom State:** OR **Commenced Bus:** N/A

Data Date	Rating	RACR #1	RACR #2	Total Assets ($mil)	Capital ($mil)	Net Premium ($mil)	Net Income ($mil)
6-20	E	1.15	0.96	334.0	98.2	328.7	-4.8
6-19	E	1.36	1.13	301.3	126.4	340.2	-7.1
2019	E	1.18	0.99	291.1	99.6	640.9	38.9
2018	E	1.43	1.19	317.0	130.8	437.4	-227.1
2017	E	1.04	0.87	251.8	90.2	561.1	44.2
2016	E	0.45	0.38	366.4	77.6	903.9	-12.9
2015	E-	0.42	0.35	558.7	67.0	777.1	-49.5

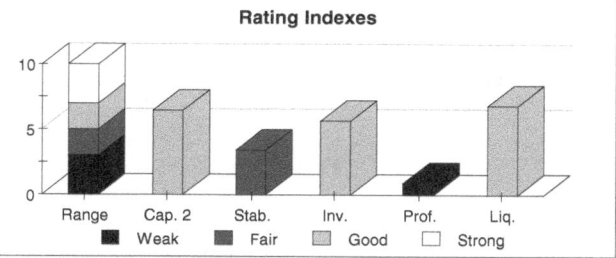

Rating Indexes

MOLINA HEALTHCARE OF CALIFORNIA   C   Fair

Major Rating Factors: Fair overall results on stability tests (3.5 on a scale of 0 to 10). Good overall profitability index (6.8). Strong capitalization index (7.0) based on good current risk-adjusted capital (moderate loss scenario).

Other Rating Factors: Excellent liquidity (7.3) with ample operational cash flow and liquid investments.

Principal Business: Medicaid (72%), Medicare (7%)

Mem Phys: 19: N/A **18:** N/A **19 MLR** 78.6% **/ 19 Admin Exp** N/A

Enroll(000): Q2 20: 585 **19:** 615 **18:** 615 **Med Exp PMPM:** $237

Principal Investments ($000): Cash and equiv ($293,769)

Provider Compensation ($000): None

Total Member Encounters: N/A

Group Affiliation: Molina Healthcare Inc

Licensed in: CA

Address: 200 Oceangate Ste 100, Long Beach, CA 90802

Phone: (800) 562-5442 **Dom State:** CA **Commenced Bus:** April 1989

Data Date	Rating	RACR #1	RACR #2	Total Assets ($mil)	Capital ($mil)	Net Premium ($mil)	Net Income ($mil)
6-20	C	1.16	0.72	758.0	141.4	1,174.4	65.1
6-19	C-	1.36	0.84	763.4	156.0	1,184.0	59.3
2019	C-	1.17	0.73	643.6	143.5	2,334.5	181.1
2018	C-	1.46	0.91	802.7	169.9	2,280.8	85.8
2017	C-	0.94	0.58	878.9	134.7	2,829.7	57.0
2016	C-	1.63	1.01	973.4	208.6	2,470.4	82.3
2015	C-	1.40	0.86	683.8	175.7	2,272.2	65.2

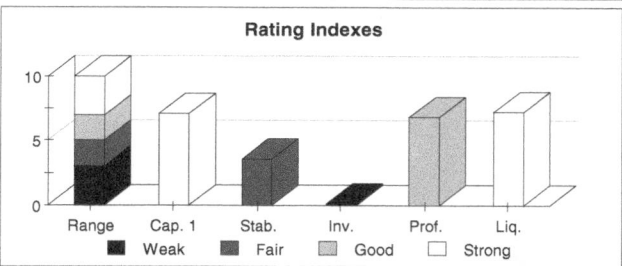

Rating Indexes

MOLINA HEALTHCARE OF FLORIDA INC   D   Weak

Major Rating Factors: Weak profitability index (2.1 on a scale of 0 to 10). Strong capitalization (7.8) based on excellent current risk-adjusted capital (severe loss scenario). High quality investment portfolio (7.6).

Other Rating Factors: Excellent liquidity (7.0) with ample operational cash flow and liquid investments.

Principal Business: Medicaid (56%), comp med (26%), Medicare (4%), other (14%)

Mem Phys: 19: 47,184 **18:** 46,361 **19 MLR** 77.0% **/ 19 Admin Exp** N/A

Enroll(000): Q2 20: 131 **19:** 132 **18:** 313 **Med Exp PMPM:** $312

Principal Investments: Long-term bonds (62%), cash and equiv (38%)

Provider Compensation ($000): Contr fee ($558,215), capitation ($66,341), FFS ($48,540)

Total Member Encounters: Phys (952,692), non-phys (1,619,292)

Group Affiliation: Molina Healthcare Inc

Licensed in: FL

Address: 8300 NW 33rd Street Suite 400, DORAL, FL 33122

Phone: (866) 422-2541 **Dom State:** FL **Commenced Bus:** N/A

Data Date	Rating	RACR #1	RACR #2	Total Assets ($mil)	Capital ($mil)	Net Premium ($mil)	Net Income ($mil)
6-20	D	1.95	1.63	270.3	75.4	326.3	12.8
6-19	C	2.43	2.02	385.8	210.2	398.7	43.5
2019	C	3.58	2.98	256.7	98.3	733.5	53.0
2018	C	3.68	3.07	662.0	334.7	1,845.7	93.8
2017	E	1.11	0.93	1,155.3	233.0	2,578.0	-259.7
2016	E	1.83	1.53	802.9	200.0	1,961.9	-62.0
2015	E	1.94	1.62	632.8	137.0	1,217.3	-38.7

Rating Indexes

MOLINA HEALTHCARE OF ILLINOIS INC　　　　C　　Fair

Major Rating Factors: Fair quality investment portfolio (4.4 on a scale of 0 to 10). Weak profitability index (2.2). Strong capitalization (7.6) based on excellent current risk-adjusted capital (severe loss scenario).
Other Rating Factors: Excellent liquidity (7.0) with ample operational cash flow and liquid investments.
Principal Business: Medicaid (91%), Medicare (9%)
Mem Phys: 19: 30,041 **18:** 26,111 **19 MLR** 77.2% **/ 19 Admin Exp** N/A
Enroll(000): Q2 20: 242 **19:** 224 **18:** 224 **Med Exp PMPM:** $312
Principal Investments: Cash and equiv (99%), long-term bonds (1%)
Provider Compensation ($000): Contr fee ($675,907), FFS ($102,339), capitation ($37,732)
Total Member Encounters: Phys (1,276,342), non-phys (1,893,042)
Group Affiliation: Molina Healthcare Inc
Licensed in: IL
Address: 1520 Kensington Road # 212, OAKBROOK, IL 60523
Phone: (888) 858-2156 **Dom State:** IL **Commenced Bus:** N/A

Data Date	Rating	RACR #1	RACR #2	Total Assets ($mil)	Capital ($mil)	Net Premium ($mil)	Net Income ($mil)
6-20	C	1.80	1.50	332.2	141.7	711.2	25.9
6-19	C	3.23	2.69	268.6	137.0	577.9	24.0
2019	C	2.10	1.75	287.9	116.2	1,076.2	38.6
2018	C	2.69	2.24	242.3	113.7	1,009.0	38.7
2017	E	1.15	0.96	230.9	73.4	752.5	-90.7
2016	E	1.40	1.16	152.2	35.8	796.9	-20.6
2015	N/A	N/A	N/A	125.0	46.4	467.4	-5.9

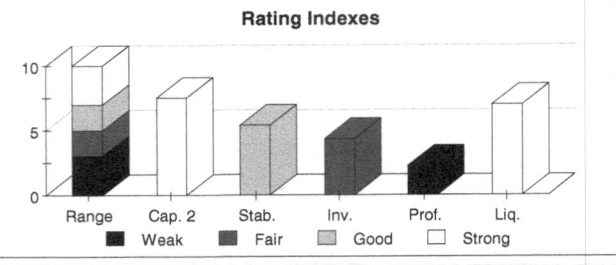

MOLINA HEALTHCARE OF MICHIGAN INC　　　　B　　Good

Major Rating Factors: Fair overall results on stability tests (4.7 on a scale of 0 to 10). Excellent profitability (8.6). Strong capitalization index (8.1) based on excellent current risk-adjusted capital (severe loss scenario).
Other Rating Factors: High quality investment portfolio (9.1). Excellent liquidity (7.0) with ample operational cash flow and liquid investments.
Principal Business: Medicaid (71%), Medicare (27%), comp med (2%)
Mem Phys: 19: 37,806 **18:** 35,274 **19 MLR** 75.5% **/ 19 Admin Exp** N/A
Enroll(000): Q2 20: 377 **19:** 362 **18:** 383 **Med Exp PMPM:** $291
Principal Investments: Cash and equiv (56%), long-term bonds (44%)
Provider Compensation ($000): Contr fee ($1,179,665), FFS ($57,010), capitation ($51,395)
Total Member Encounters: Phys (2,371,762), non-phys (3,536,484)
Group Affiliation: Molina Healthcare Inc
Licensed in: MI
Address: 880 W Long Lake Rd Suite 600, Troy,
Phone: (248) 925-1700 **Dom State:** MI **Commenced Bus:** N/A

Data Date	Rating	RACR #1	RACR #2	Total Assets ($mil)	Capital ($mil)	Net Premium ($mil)	Net Income ($mil)
6-20	B	2.23	1.86	597.3	265.9	891.0	75.3
6-19	B	2.93	2.44	511.8	249.7	852.6	63.5
2019	B	2.38	1.98	470.5	210.3	1,692.5	117.6
2018	B	2.79	2.32	498.5	237.2	1,789.7	97.5
2017	B-	N/A	N/A	422.5	160.3	1,949.3	33.0
2016	B-	2.01	1.68	476.9	172.3	2,104.8	30.9
2015	B-	2.40	2.00	376.0	138.7	1,467.9	53.8

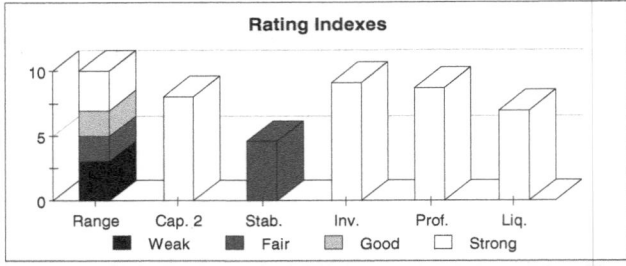

MOLINA HEALTHCARE OF MS INC　　　　D　　Weak

Major Rating Factors: Weak profitability index (0.9 on a scale of 0 to 10). Low quality investment portfolio (0.0). Strong capitalization (10.0) based on excellent current risk-adjusted capital (severe loss scenario).
Other Rating Factors: Excellent liquidity (8.2) with ample operational cash flow and liquid investments.
Principal Business: Medicaid (100%)
Mem Phys: 18: 5,680 **17:** N/A **18 MLR** 84.5% **/ 18 Admin Exp** N/A
Enroll(000): Q3 19: 68 **18:** 26 **17:** N/A **Med Exp PMPM:** $373
Principal Investments: Cash and equiv (99%), long-term bonds (1%)
Provider Compensation ($000): Contr fee ($8,222), FFS ($637), capitation ($406)
Total Member Encounters: Phys (326,808), non-phys (528,376)
Group Affiliation: Molina Healthcare Inc
Licensed in: (No states)
Address: 188 E Capitol St Suite 700, JACKSON, MS 39201
Phone: (844) 826-4333 **Dom State:** MS **Commenced Bus:** N/A

Data Date	Rating	RACR #1	RACR #2	Total Assets ($mil)	Capital ($mil)	Net Premium ($mil)	Net Income ($mil)
9-19	D	9.34	7.78	102.6	31.4	235.0	-17.2
9-18	N/A	N/A	N/A	7.8	6.5	N/A	-2.4
2018	C	10.82	9.02	40.9	28.9	22.8	-3.0
2017	N/A	N/A	N/A	5.0	5.0	N/A	N/A
2016	N/A	N/A	N/A	N/A	N/A	N/A	N/A
2015	N/A	N/A	N/A	N/A	N/A	N/A	N/A
2014	N/A	N/A	N/A	N/A	N/A	N/A	N/A

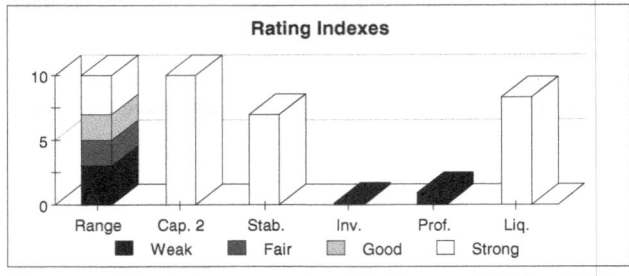

MOLINA HEALTHCARE OF NEW MEXICO | C | Fair

Major Rating Factors: Fair profitability index (4.6 on a scale of 0 to 10). Weak overall results on stability tests (0.0). Strong capitalization index (10.0) based on excellent current risk-adjusted capital (severe loss scenario).
Other Rating Factors: High quality investment portfolio (8.2). Excellent liquidity (7.8) with ample operational cash flow and liquid investments.
Principal Business: Comp med (56%), Medicare (27%), Medicaid (17%)
Mem Phys: 19: 18,236 **18:** 16,939 **19 MLR** 46.7% **/ 19 Admin Exp** N/A
Enroll(000): Q2 20: 23 **19:** 23 **18:** 222 **Med Exp PMPM:** $260
Principal Investments: Cash and equiv (61%), long-term bonds (39%)
Provider Compensation ($000): Contr fee ($161,737), FFS ($14,156), capitation ($2,024)
Total Member Encounters: Phys (109,502), non-phys (199,697)
Group Affiliation: Molina Healthcare Inc
Licensed in: NM
Address: 400 Tijeras Ave NW Suite 200, Albuquerque,
Phone: (505) 348-0410 **Dom State:** NM **Commenced Bus:** N/A

Data Date	Rating	RACR #1	RACR #2	Total Assets ($mil)	Capital ($mil)	Net Premium ($mil)	Net Income ($mil)
6-20	C	4.51	3.76	97.2	35.5	68.0	-0.5
6-19	C	1.40	1.17	208.3	106.2	79.0	27.7
2019	C	7.40	6.17	93.0	34.2	169.5	51.8
2018	C	2.24	1.86	423.6	174.8	1,428.8	14.8
2017	C	1.12	0.94	421.3	118.7	1,414.1	-43.6
2016	C	1.68	1.40	468.3	122.7	1,386.6	-28.5
2015	C	1.61	1.34	409.1	109.7	1,318.0	-1.6

Rating Indexes

MOLINA HEALTHCARE OF OHIO INC | B | Good

Major Rating Factors: Excellent profitability (8.4 on a scale of 0 to 10). Strong capitalization (7.5) based on excellent current risk-adjusted capital (severe loss scenario). High quality investment portfolio (9.3).
Other Rating Factors: Excellent liquidity (6.9) with sufficient resources (cash flows and marketable investments) to handle a spike in claims.
Principal Business: Medicaid (84%), Medicare (12%), comp med (4%)
Mem Phys: 19: 58,475 **18:** 52,032 **19 MLR** 82.0% **/ 19 Admin Exp** N/A
Enroll(000): Q2 20: 328 **19:** 288 **18:** 302 **Med Exp PMPM:** $603
Principal Investments: Long-term bonds (54%), cash and equiv (46%)
Provider Compensation ($000): Contr fee ($1,651,539), capitation ($521,284), FFS ($77,821)
Total Member Encounters: Phys (1,715,170), non-phys (6,439,062)
Group Affiliation: Molina Healthcare Inc
Licensed in: OH
Address: 3000 Corporate Exchange Drive, COLUMBUS, OH 43231
Phone: (888) 562-5442 **Dom State:** OH **Commenced Bus:** N/A

Data Date	Rating	RACR #1	RACR #2	Total Assets ($mil)	Capital ($mil)	Net Premium ($mil)	Net Income ($mil)
6-20	B	1.76	1.46	769.0	306.6	1,606.6	88.1
6-19	B	2.42	2.02	598.2	295.8	1,354.1	69.8
2019	B	2.04	1.70	606.5	266.7	2,727.7	109.2
2018	B	2.28	1.90	609.1	277.9	2,593.0	120.3
2017	B-	1.50	1.25	485.3	229.5	2,398.7	44.7
2016	B-	2.29	1.91	507.2	234.9	2,198.5	45.9
2015	B-	1.92	1.60	440.4	190.7	2,270.8	110.0

Rating Indexes

MOLINA HEALTHCARE OF PUERTO RICO INC | C | Fair

Major Rating Factors: Fair profitability index (4.4 on a scale of 0 to 10). Strong capitalization (7.7) based on excellent current risk-adjusted capital (severe loss scenario). High quality investment portfolio (9.9).
Other Rating Factors: Excellent liquidity (7.0) with sufficient resources (cash flows and marketable investments) to handle a spike in claims.
Principal Business: Medicaid (100%)
Mem Phys: 19: 6,171 **18:** 5,203 **19 MLR** 85.0% **/ 19 Admin Exp** N/A
Enroll(000): Q2 20: 167 **19:** 176 **18:** 252 **Med Exp PMPM:** $174
Principal Investments: Cash and equiv (92%), long-term bonds (8%)
Provider Compensation ($000): Contr fee ($339,085), capitation ($57,891), FFS ($26,032)
Total Member Encounters: N/A
Group Affiliation: Molina Healthcare Inc
Licensed in: PR
Address: 654 Plaza 654 Munoz Rivera Av, SAN JUAN, PR 00918-4123
Phone: (787) 200-3300 **Dom State:** PR **Commenced Bus:** N/A

Data Date	Rating	RACR #1	RACR #2	Total Assets ($mil)	Capital ($mil)	Net Premium ($mil)	Net Income ($mil)
6-20	C	1.92	1.60	174.4	71.7	236.0	4.7
6-19	B	2.83	2.36	194.1	113.0	224.2	7.1
2019	C	2.82	2.35	141.4	67.9	473.5	18.1
2018	C	2.67	2.23	217.5	106.5	710.8	17.5
2017	C-	N/A	N/A	184.4	78.9	731.6	-5.4
2016	C-	1.79	1.49	158.8	66.4	746.3	-9.9
2015	U	1.56	1.30	130.6	49.1	556.6	-5.3

Rating Indexes

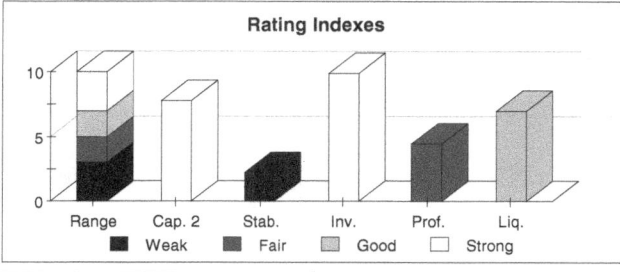

MOLINA HEALTHCARE OF SOUTH CAROLINA   B   Good

Major Rating Factors: Good overall profitability index (5.8 on a scale of 0 to 10). Good quality investment portfolio (6.5). Strong capitalization (7.6) based on excellent current risk-adjusted capital (severe loss scenario).
Other Rating Factors: Excellent liquidity (7.0) with ample operational cash flow and liquid investments.
Principal Business: Medicaid (90%), Medicare (10%)
Mem Phys: 19: 26,529 **18:** 17,007 **19 MLR** 84.7% **/ 19 Admin Exp** N/A
Enroll(000): Q2 20: 146 **19:** 131 **18:** 120 **Med Exp PMPM:** $315
Principal Investments: Cash and equiv (74%), long-term bonds (26%)
Provider Compensation ($000): Contr fee ($454,842), FFS ($24,393), capitation ($6,574)
Total Member Encounters: Phys (707,548), non-phys (925,378)
Group Affiliation: Molina Healthcare Inc
Licensed in: OH, SC
Address: 4105 Faber Place Drive Suite, NORTH CHARLESTON, SC 29405
Phone: (843) 740-1780 **Dom State:** SC **Commenced Bus:** N/A

Data Date	Rating	RACR #1	RACR #2	Total Assets ($mil)	Capital ($mil)	Net Premium ($mil)	Net Income ($mil)
6-20	B	1.87	1.56	212.9	88.6	333.5	11.2
6-19	B	3.15	2.63	172.5	84.6	286.2	9.3
2019	B	2.38	1.99	170.0	75.4	578.8	14.4
2018	C+	2.69	2.24	144.7	70.9	525.2	17.1
2017	C	N/A	N/A	116.3	44.1	463.7	-8.3
2016	C	2.51	2.09	102.3	49.0	411.8	13.4
2015	B-	4.79	3.99	125.5	83.0	369.3	17.3

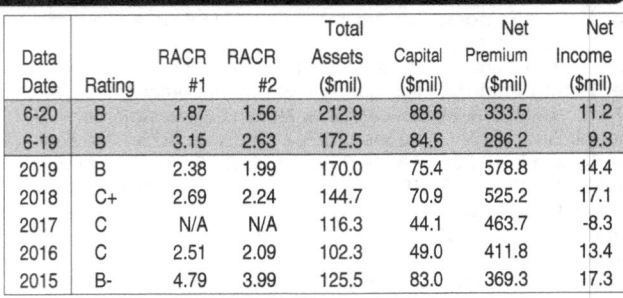

MOLINA HEALTHCARE OF TEXAS INC   B-   Good

Major Rating Factors: Good overall profitability index (6.4 on a scale of 0 to 10). Good liquidity (6.9) with sufficient resources (cash flows and marketable investments) to handle a spike in claims. Strong capitalization (7.1) based on excellent current risk-adjusted capital (severe loss scenario).
Other Rating Factors: High quality investment portfolio (7.0).
Principal Business: Medicaid (70%), comp med (22%), Medicare (8%)
Mem Phys: 19: 75,476 **18:** 69,925 **19 MLR** 81.8% **/ 19 Admin Exp** N/A
Enroll(000): Q2 20: 337 **19:** 324 **18:** 402 **Med Exp PMPM:** $606
Principal Investments: Long-term bonds (72%), cash and equiv (28%)
Provider Compensation ($000): Contr fee ($2,218,988), FFS ($212,246), capitation ($5,715)
Total Member Encounters: Phys (1,687,438), non-phys (8,673,012)
Group Affiliation: Molina Healthcare Inc
Licensed in: TX
Address: 5605 N MacArthur Blvd Suite, IRVING, TX 75038
Phone: (877) 665-4622 **Dom State:** TX **Commenced Bus:** N/A

Data Date	Rating	RACR #1	RACR #2	Total Assets ($mil)	Capital ($mil)	Net Premium ($mil)	Net Income ($mil)
6-20	B-	1.41	1.17	987.0	315.4	1,520.5	19.9
6-19	B	2.12	1.77	1,074.8	373.9	1,538.8	61.7
2019	B-	1.93	1.61	844.6	326.0	3,042.7	99.7
2018	B	2.31	1.93	1,094.2	408.1	3,325.0	187.0
2017	B	1.16	0.97	893.1	250.6	2,864.5	16.8
2016	B-	1.75	1.46	696.6	237.5	2,606.1	82.4
2015	C	1.26	1.05	477.2	148.7	2,056.4	-12.3

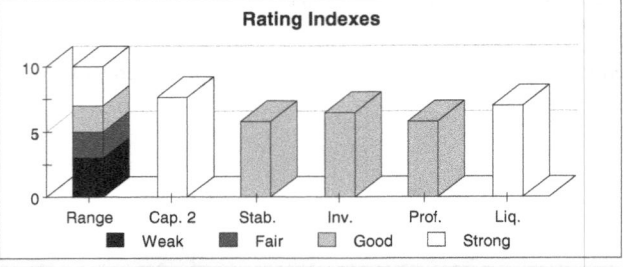

MOLINA HEALTHCARE OF UTAH INC   B   Good

Major Rating Factors: Good quality investment portfolio (6.5 on a scale of 0 to 10). Good overall results on stability tests (6.0). Excellent overall profitability index (7.0).
Other Rating Factors: Strong capitalization index (8.6) based on excellent current risk-adjusted capital (severe loss scenario). Excellent liquidity (7.1) with ample operational cash flow and liquid investments.
Principal Business: Medicaid (58%), Medicare (38%), comp med (3%)
Mem Phys: 19: 25,262 **18:** 19,632 **19 MLR** 77.0% **/ 19 Admin Exp** N/A
Enroll(000): Q2 20: 96 **19:** 78 **18:** 77 **Med Exp PMPM:** $333
Principal Investments: Long-term bonds (53%), cash and equiv (47%)
Provider Compensation ($000): Contr fee ($285,399), FFS ($22,824), capitation ($4,487)
Total Member Encounters: Phys (456,086), non-phys (663,108)
Group Affiliation: Molina Healthcare Inc
Licensed in: UT
Address: 7050 Union Park Center Ste 200, Midvale,
Phone: (801) 858-0400 **Dom State:** UT **Commenced Bus:** N/A

Data Date	Rating	RACR #1	RACR #2	Total Assets ($mil)	Capital ($mil)	Net Premium ($mil)	Net Income ($mil)
6-20	B	2.61	2.18	236.3	83.5	301.1	14.4
6-19	C+	4.33	3.61	178.6	82.5	178.9	12.6
2019	B	3.30	2.75	199.5	69.8	403.5	25.9
2018	C+	3.71	3.09	151.4	70.1	384.1	37.6
2017	C-	1.50	1.25	245.8	70.0	534.9	-2.5
2016	C	1.84	1.53	191.3	50.7	453.9	-19.1
2015	B-	2.58	2.15	122.7	50.8	343.7	0.6

MOLINA HEALTHCARE OF WASHINGTON INC   B   Good

Major Rating Factors: Good overall results on stability tests (6.2 on a scale of 0 to 10). Excellent profitability (8.2). Strong capitalization index (7.5) based on excellent current risk-adjusted capital (severe loss scenario).
Other Rating Factors: High quality investment portfolio (8.0). Excellent liquidity (7.0) with ample operational cash flow and liquid investments.
Principal Business: Medicaid (86%), comp med (9%), Medicare (5%)
Mem Phys: 19: 42,968 **18:** 37,348 **19 MLR** 84.8% **/ 19 Admin Exp** N/A
Enroll(000): Q2 20: 913 **19:** 832 **18:** 781 **Med Exp PMPM:** $237
Principal Investments: Cash and equiv (67%), long-term bonds (33%)
Provider Compensation ($000): Contr fee ($1,468,959), FFS ($637,355), capitation ($196,621), salary ($368)
Total Member Encounters: Phys (4,023,993), non-phys (6,399,153)
Group Affiliation: Molina Healthcare Inc
Licensed in: WA
Address: 21540 - 30th Drive SE   Suite, Bothell,
Phone: (425) 424-1100 **Dom State:** WA **Commenced Bus:** N/A

Data Date	Rating	RACR #1	RACR #2	Total Assets ($mil)	Capital ($mil)	Net Premium ($mil)	Net Income ($mil)
6-20	B	1.78	1.48	957.1	366.9	1,634.3	95.0
6-19	B	1.92	1.60	679.0	280.3	1,348.0	26.8
2019	B	2.02	1.68	945.0	317.3	2,746.5	59.2
2018	B	2.31	1.93	855.1	339.0	2,466.1	53.3
2017	B	1.52	1.27	793.8	304.9	2,657.5	69.5
2016	B	1.78	1.48	685.6	235.9	2,307.8	8.2
2015	B	1.99	1.66	589.8	190.8	1,671.7	-3.4

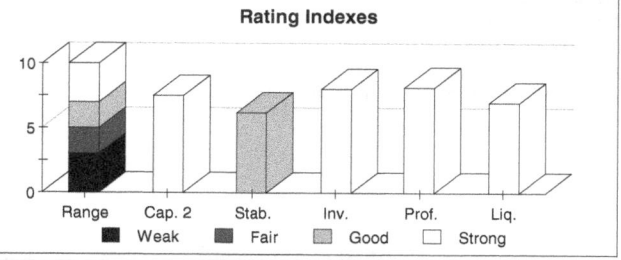

Rating Indexes

MOLINA HEALTHCARE OF WISCONSIN INC   C+   Fair

Major Rating Factors: Good overall profitability index (5.4 on a scale of 0 to 10). Strong capitalization (9.1) based on excellent current risk-adjusted capital (severe loss scenario). High quality investment portfolio (8.1).
Other Rating Factors: Excellent liquidity (7.3) with ample operational cash flow and liquid investments.
Principal Business: Medicaid (59%), comp med (35%), Medicare (6%)
Mem Phys: 19: 21,054 **18:** 20,773 **19 MLR** 72.5% **/ 19 Admin Exp** N/A
Enroll(000): Q2 20: 85 **19:** 64 **18:** 59 **Med Exp PMPM:** $198
Principal Investments: Cash and equiv (97%), long-term bonds (3%)
Provider Compensation ($000): Contr fee ($144,120), FFS ($6,617), capitation ($1,016)
Total Member Encounters: Phys (298,533), non-phys (595,401)
Group Affiliation: Molina Healthcare Inc
Licensed in: WI
Address: 11002 West Park Place, MILWAUKEE, WI 53224-3615
Phone: (888) 999-2404 **Dom State:** WI **Commenced Bus:** N/A

Data Date	Rating	RACR #1	RACR #2	Total Assets ($mil)	Capital ($mil)	Net Premium ($mil)	Net Income ($mil)
6-20	C+	3.01	2.51	95.3	47.8	139.6	10.6
6-19	C	6.05	5.04	69.9	41.6	107.3	10.9
2019	C+	4.05	3.38	63.8	37.9	213.3	21.7
2018	C	4.75	3.96	58.9	30.9	157.4	8.8
2017	E+	1.64	1.37	154.9	68.1	491.3	-12.2
2016	E+	1.86	1.55	141.0	47.2	403.1	-34.2
2015	D	2.04	1.70	69.7	29.9	266.0	4.2

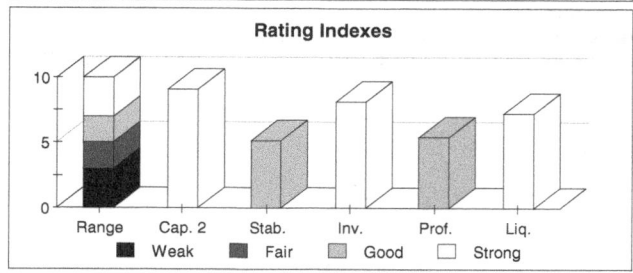

Rating Indexes

MONARCH HEALTH PLAN   E+   Very Weak

Major Rating Factors: Weak liquidity (0.2 on a scale of 0 to 10) as a spike in claims may stretch capacity. Fair overall results on stability tests (3.1). Good capitalization index (5.8) based on good current risk-adjusted capital (severe loss scenario).
Other Rating Factors: Excellent profitability (7.6).
Principal Business: Managed care (100%)
Mem Phys: 19: N/A **18:** N/A **19 MLR** 93.1% **/ 19 Admin Exp** N/A
Enroll(000): Q2 20: 144 **19:** 143 **18:** 143 **Med Exp PMPM:** $396
Principal Investments ($000): Cash and equiv ($146,699)
Provider Compensation ($000): None
Total Member Encounters: N/A
Group Affiliation: None
Licensed in: CA
Address: 11 Technology Drive, Irvine, CA 92618
Phone: (949) 923-3350 **Dom State:** CA **Commenced Bus:** January 2008

Data Date	Rating	RACR #1	RACR #2	Total Assets ($mil)	Capital ($mil)	Net Premium ($mil)	Net Income ($mil)
6-20	E+	1.43	0.87	177.6	88.3	394.1	23.7
6-19	E+	1.23	0.74	185.4	88.4	385.7	12.5
2019	E+	0.88	0.53	155.7	62.8	741.3	16.7
2018	E	0.90	0.54	169.0	73.8	692.1	29.6
2017	E-	0.05	0.03	133.9	44.0	669.4	26.3
2016	E-	N/A	N/A	72.9	17.7	359.8	5.5
2015	E-	N/A	N/A	75.0	12.5	359.9	10.8

Rating Indexes

MONTANA HEALTH COOPERATIVE — D — Weak

Major Rating Factors: Low quality investment portfolio (2.5 on a scale of 0 to 10). Fair profitability index (4.6). Fair capitalization (2.9) based on good current risk-adjusted capital (moderate loss scenario).
Other Rating Factors: Excellent liquidity (6.9) with sufficient resources (cash flows and marketable investments) to handle a spike in claims.
Principal Business: Comp med (100%)
Mem Phys: 19: N/A **18:** N/A **19 MLR** 86.8% **/ 19 Admin Exp** N/A
Enroll(000): Q2 20: 31 **19:** 31 **18:** 45 **Med Exp PMPM:** $469
Principal Investments: Nonaffiliate common stock (44%), cash and equiv (36%), long-term bonds (7%), other (13%)
Provider Compensation ($000): FFS ($98,441), capitation ($48,929), contr fee ($47,275)
Total Member Encounters: N/A
Group Affiliation: None
Licensed in: ID, MT
Address: 810 HIALEAH CT, HELENA, MT 59601
Phone: (406) 447-9510 **Dom State:** MT **Commenced Bus:** N/A

Data Date	Rating	RACR #1	RACR #2	Total Assets ($mil)	Capital ($mil)	Net Premium ($mil)	Net Income ($mil)
6-20	D	1.16	0.96	143.3	75.8	85.4	10.6
6-19	N/A	N/A	N/A	N/A	N/A	N/A	N/A
2019	D	0.94	0.78	145.4	63.4	213.1	15.2
2018	D	0.83	0.69	125.5	41.9	258.0	13.4
2017	D	N/A	N/A	86.0	39.1	156.6	15.1
2016	D	0.62	0.51	51.8	24.0	123.0	-19.7
2015	D+	0.77	0.64	67.2	33.0	135.3	-40.7

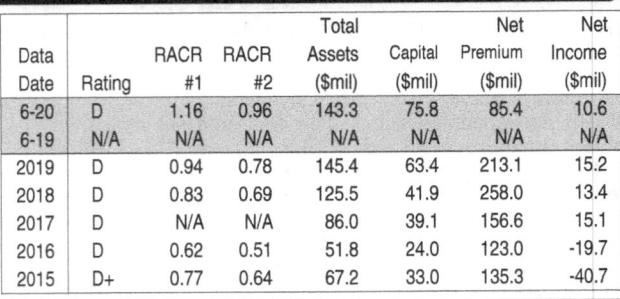

Rating Indexes

MOTIVHEALTH INSURANCE CO — C- — Fair

Major Rating Factors: Weak profitability index (2.8 on a scale of 0 to 10). Strong capitalization (7.5) based on excellent current risk-adjusted capital (severe loss scenario). High quality investment portfolio (9.9).
Other Rating Factors: Excellent liquidity (7.1) with ample operational cash flow and liquid investments.
Principal Business: Comp med (58%), other (42%)
Mem Phys: 18: 15,766 **17:** 27,314 **18 MLR** 82.9% **/ 18 Admin Exp** N/A
Enroll(000): Q3 19: 24 **18:** 18 **17:** 10 **Med Exp PMPM:** $46
Principal Investments: Long-term bonds (54%), cash and equiv (46%)
Provider Compensation ($000): Contr fee ($9,442)
Total Member Encounters: Phys (11,946), non-phys (118,288)
Group Affiliation: None
Licensed in: UT
Address: 10421 S JORDAN GTWY STE 300, SOUTH JORDAN, UT 84095
Phone: (844) 234-4472 **Dom State:** UT **Commenced Bus:** N/A

Data Date	Rating	RACR #1	RACR #2	Total Assets ($mil)	Capital ($mil)	Net Premium ($mil)	Net Income ($mil)
9-19	C-	1.75	1.46	9.8	3.1	9.7	1.2
9-18	D	N/A	N/A	9.4	2.2	7.7	0.6
2018	D	1.19	0.99	7.2	2.0	10.4	0.8
2017	D	N/A	N/A	6.8	1.6	12.0	1.0
2016	D	0.78	0.65	4.6	1.0	4.8	-3.2
2015	N/A	N/A	N/A	2.4	2.2	N/A	-0.9
2014	N/A	N/A	N/A	N/A	N/A	N/A	N/A

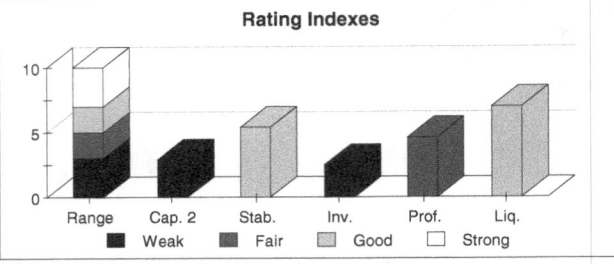

Rating Indexes

MOUNT CARMEL HEALTH INS CO — C+ — Fair

Major Rating Factors: Good liquidity (6.9 on a scale of 0 to 10) with sufficient resources (cash flows and marketable investments) to handle a spike in claims. Weak profitability index (1.9). Strong capitalization (9.3) based on excellent current risk-adjusted capital (severe loss scenario).
Other Rating Factors: High quality investment portfolio (9.6).
Principal Business: Medicare (100%)
Mem Phys: 19: 12,768 **18:** 8,801 **19 MLR** 94.9% **/ 19 Admin Exp** N/A
Enroll(000): Q2 20: 1 **19:** 1 **18:** 1 **Med Exp PMPM:** $903
Principal Investments: Long-term bonds (54%), cash and equiv (46%)
Provider Compensation ($000): Contr fee ($7,047), FFS ($1,098), capitation ($29)
Total Member Encounters: Phys (21,026), non-phys (7,007)
Group Affiliation: None
Licensed in: OH
Address: 6150 EAST BROAD STREET EE320, COLUMBUS, OH 43213
Phone: (614) 546-3211 **Dom State:** OH **Commenced Bus:** N/A

Data Date	Rating	RACR #1	RACR #2	Total Assets ($mil)	Capital ($mil)	Net Premium ($mil)	Net Income ($mil)
6-20	C+	3.20	2.67	7.4	6.0	3.9	0.1
6-19	B-	5.09	4.25	7.1	6.1	4.6	-0.2
2019	B	4.59	3.83	7.0	5.9	8.9	-0.4
2018	B-	5.22	4.35	7.3	6.3	8.7	0.1
2017	D	3.73	3.10	7.7	6.3	8.1	0.0
2016	D	1.40	1.17	9.0	5.4	24.8	-1.3
2015	D	1.67	1.39	6.6	3.6	14.2	-1.1

Rating Indexes

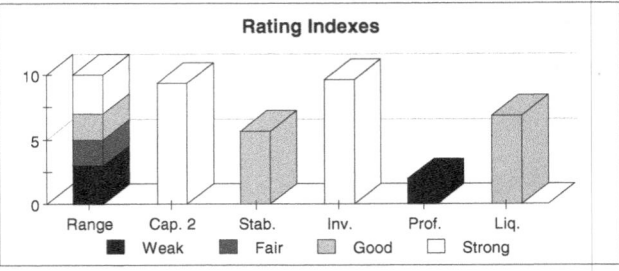

MOUNT CARMEL HEALTH PLAN INC *   B+   Good

Major Rating Factors: Good overall profitability index (5.6 on a scale of 0 to 10). Strong capitalization index (10.0) based on excellent current risk-adjusted capital (severe loss scenario). High quality investment portfolio (9.8).
Other Rating Factors: Excellent overall results on stability tests (7.0). Excellent liquidity (7.4) with ample operational cash flow and liquid investments
Principal Business: Medicare (100%)
Mem Phys: 19: 12,768 **18:** 8,801 **19 MLR** 85.4% **/ 19 Admin Exp** N/A
Enroll(000): Q2 20: 44 **19:** 45 **18:** 49 **Med Exp PMPM:** $866
Principal Investments: Cash and equiv (42%), long-term bonds (39%), nonaffiliate common stock (18%), affiliate common stock (1%)
Provider Compensation ($000): Contr fee ($411,052), FFS ($42,156), bonus arrang ($18,317), capitation ($3,695)
Total Member Encounters: Phys (444,808), non-phys (71,652)
Group Affiliation: None
Licensed in: OH
Address: 6150 East Broad Street EE320, COLUMBUS,
Phone: (614) 546-3211 **Dom State:** OH **Commenced Bus:** N/A

Data Date	Rating	RACR #1	RACR #2	Total Assets ($mil)	Capital ($mil)	Net Premium ($mil)	Net Income ($mil)
6-20	B+	6.42	5.35	407.5	306.1	281.2	19.7
6-19	B	5.39	4.49	359.9	262.7	282.9	16.1
2019	B+	6.06	5.05	368.0	289.9	557.3	44.7
2018	B	4.85	4.05	335.5	238.4	582.5	45.2
2017	B-	3.92	3.26	305.0	200.1	607.2	33.9
2016	C	2.75	2.29	277.9	148.8	566.2	-9.6
2015	C	3.33	2.78	275.3	155.1	509.8	-1.2

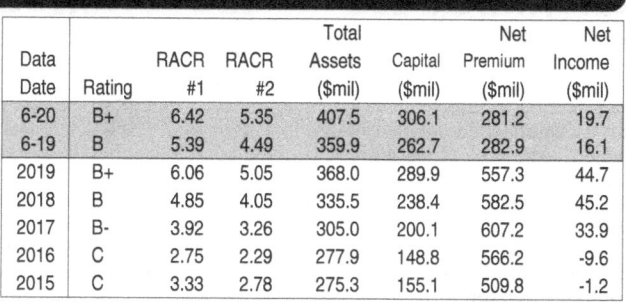

Rating Indexes

MUTUAL OF OMAHA INS CO   C+   Fair

Major Rating Factors: Fair quality investment portfolio (4.7 on a scale of 0 to 10). Fair profitability (4.7). Excellent expense controls. Fair overall results on stability tests (4.8).
Other Rating Factors: Good capitalization (6.0) based on good risk adjusted capital (severe loss scenario). Good liquidity (6.9) with sufficient resources to handle a spike in claims.
Principal Business: Reinsurance (59%), individual health insurance (36%), and group health insurance (5%).
Principal Investments: Common & preferred stock (38%), nonCMO investment grade bonds (38%), CMOs and structured securities (11%), mortgages in good standing (3%), and noninv. grade bonds (1%).
Investments in Affiliates: 38%
Group Affiliation: Mutual Of Omaha Group
Licensed in: All states, the District of Columbia and Puerto Rico
Commenced Business: January 1910
Address: MUTUAL OF OMAHA PLAZA, OMAHA, NE 68175
Phone: (402) 342-7600 **Domicile State:** NE **NAIC Code:** 71412

Data Date	Rating	RACR #1	RACR #2	Total Assets ($mil)	Capital ($mil)	Net Premium ($mil)	Net Income ($mil)
6-20	C+	0.93	0.87	8,980.8	3,494.3	1,830.1	581.9
6-19	B-	0.99	0.92	8,529.2	3,283.5	1,729.5	-59.8
2019	C+	0.88	0.82	9,107.4	3,140.0	3,538.5	-130.6
2018	B-	0.98	0.92	8,084.0	3,172.7	3,282.6	-157.4
2017	B+	1.03	0.96	7,824.4	3,189.6	3,036.5	-7.1
2016	B+	1.07	0.99	7,278.9	3,048.3	2,726.5	103.4
2015	B+	1.02	0.95	6,945.1	2,862.8	2,411.8	11.2

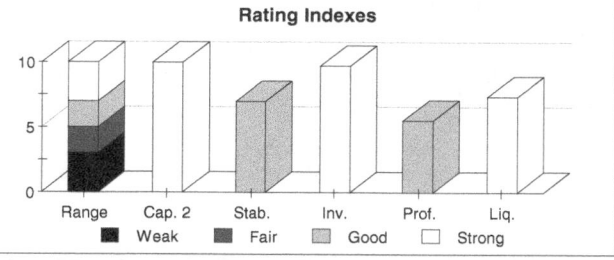

Rating Indexes

MVP HEALTH INS CO   D   Weak

Major Rating Factors: Weak profitability index (1.2 on a scale of 0 to 10). Strong capitalization (8.3) based on excellent current risk-adjusted capital (severe loss scenario). High quality investment portfolio (9.9).
Other Rating Factors: Excellent liquidity (10.0) with ample operational cash flow and liquid investments.
Principal Business: Comp med (100%)
Mem Phys: 19: 49,235 **18:** 50,439 **19 MLR** 90.6% **/ 19 Admin Exp** N/A
Enroll(000): Q2 20: 0 **19:** 0 **18:** 3 **Med Exp PMPM:** $426
Principal Investments: Cash and equiv (96%), long-term bonds (4%)
Provider Compensation ($000): Contr fee ($2,305), FFS ($32)
Total Member Encounters: Phys (2,888), non-phys (2,298)
Group Affiliation: MVP Health Care Inc
Licensed in: NY, VT
Address: 625 State Street, Schenectady, NY 12305
Phone: (518) 370-4793 **Dom State:** NY **Commenced Bus:** N/A

Data Date	Rating	RACR #1	RACR #2	Total Assets ($mil)	Capital ($mil)	Net Premium ($mil)	Net Income ($mil)
6-20	D	2.39	1.99	5.7	5.0	0.0	-0.1
6-19	D-	2.36	1.96	5.2	4.2	0.4	-0.2
2019	D	3.92	3.26	5.8	5.2	0.4	0.2
2018	D-	2.37	1.97	7.3	4.3	19.8	-0.7
2017	E+	N/A	N/A	7.0	3.0	20.9	-1.0
2016	E+	4.98	4.15	31.9	25.0	69.4	10.5
2015	E	2.54	2.12	112.0	64.1	251.3	-9.8

Rating Indexes

MVP HEALTH PLAN INC

B **Good**

Major Rating Factors: Good overall profitability index (5.8 on a scale of 0 to 10). Good quality investment portfolio (6.5). Good overall results on stability tests (6.2).

Other Rating Factors: Strong capitalization index (8.0) based on excellent current risk-adjusted capital (severe loss scenario). Excellent liquidity (6.9) with sufficient resources (cash flows and marketable investments) to handle a spike in claims.

Principal Business: Medicaid (46%), Medicare (28%), comp med (24%), FEHB (2%)

Mem Phys: 19: 46,005 **18:** 47,465 **19 MLR** 91.2% **/ 19 Admin Exp** N/A

Enroll(000): Q2 20: 391 **19:** 374 **18:** 371 **Med Exp PMPM:** $539

Principal Investments: Long-term bonds (51%), cash and equiv (20%), nonaffiliate common stock (7%), other (22%)

Provider Compensation ($000): Contr fee ($2,168,294), capitation ($125,445), FFS ($60,591), bonus arrang ($53,916), other ($52,244)

Total Member Encounters: Phys (6,441,970), non-phys (3,102,110)

Group Affiliation: MVP Health Care Inc

Licensed in: NY, VT

Address: 625 State Street, Schenectady,

Phone: (518) 370-4793 **Dom State:** NY **Commenced Bus:** N/A

Data Date	Rating	RACR #1	RACR #2	Total Assets ($mil)	Capital ($mil)	Net Premium ($mil)	Net Income ($mil)
6-20	B	2.14	1.78	792.4	424.0	1,352.1	28.1
6-19	B	2.08	1.74	765.2	397.0	1,332.0	-2.4
2019	B	2.10	1.75	725.1	404.0	2,672.5	10.8
2018	B	2.12	1.77	736.7	404.7	2,649.0	24.5
2017	B	2.12	1.77	696.1	388.7	2,516.4	43.7
2016	B-	2.30	1.92	736.0	343.5	2,501.8	9.7
2015	B-	3.63	3.02	570.7	389.9	1,560.1	5.8

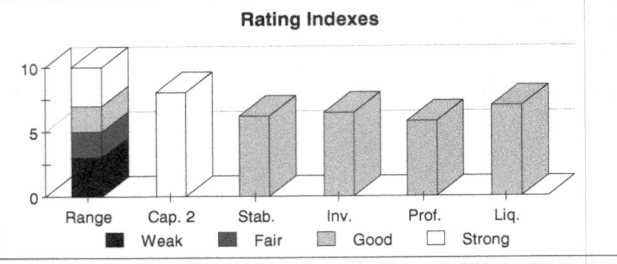

Rating Indexes

MVP HEALTH SERVICES CORP

B- **Good**

Major Rating Factors: Good overall profitability index (5.1 on a scale of 0 to 10). Good capitalization (6.7) based on good current risk-adjusted capital (severe loss scenario). Good liquidity (6.8) with sufficient resources (cash flows and marketable investments) to handle a spike in claims.

Other Rating Factors: High quality investment portfolio (8.7).

Principal Business: Comp med (100%)

Mem Phys: 19: 38,423 **18:** 37,556 **19 MLR** 87.5% **/ 19 Admin Exp** N/A

Enroll(000): Q2 20: 106 **19:** 112 **18:** 130 **Med Exp PMPM:** $444

Principal Investments: Long-term bonds (77%), cash and equiv (13%), nonaffiliate common stock (10%)

Provider Compensation ($000): Contr fee ($559,242), FFS ($14,527), bonus arrang ($8,585), capitation ($3,790), other ($32,188)

Total Member Encounters: Phys (1,410,812), non-phys (479,518)

Group Affiliation: MVP Health Care Inc

Licensed in: NY

Address: 625 State Street, Schenectady, NY 12305

Phone: (518) 370-4793 **Dom State:** NY **Commenced Bus:** N/A

Data Date	Rating	RACR #1	RACR #2	Total Assets ($mil)	Capital ($mil)	Net Premium ($mil)	Net Income ($mil)
6-20	B-	1.19	0.99	204.4	109.7	363.1	17.6
6-19	B-	1.01	0.84	172.0	95.1	361.9	8.8
2019	B	1.07	0.89	186.2	93.2	704.0	6.5
2018	C	0.84	0.70	167.2	85.7	734.1	15.9
2017	C-	0.52	0.44	164.7	70.3	670.6	-20.6
2016	C	0.92	0.77	135.1	69.6	491.4	6.4
2015	C-	0.93	0.78	64.6	28.0	187.6	0.3

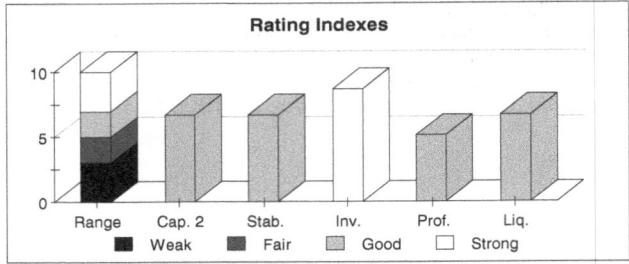

Rating Indexes

MY CHOICE WISCONSIN HEALTH PLAN INC *

B+ **Good**

Major Rating Factors: Good liquidity (6.9 on a scale of 0 to 10) with sufficient resources (cash flows and marketable investments) to handle a spike in claims. Excellent profitability (7.1). Strong capitalization (8.5) based on excellent current risk-adjusted capital (severe loss scenario).

Other Rating Factors: High quality investment portfolio (9.7).

Principal Business: Medicaid (62%), Medicare (38%)

Mem Phys: 19: 20,046 **18:** 19,180 **19 MLR** 87.9% **/ 19 Admin Exp** N/A

Enroll(000): Q2 20: 22 **19:** 5 **18:** 5 **Med Exp PMPM:** $2,283

Principal Investments: Long-term bonds (48%), cash and equiv (47%), nonaffiliate common stock (5%)

Provider Compensation ($000): Contr fee ($118,206), FFS ($27,605)

Total Member Encounters: Phys (202,214), non-phys (5,820,272)

Group Affiliation: My Choice Family Care - Care Wiscons

Licensed in: WI

Address: 1617 Sherman Avenue, Madison, WI 53704

Phone: (608) 240-0020 **Dom State:** WI **Commenced Bus:** N/A

Data Date	Rating	RACR #1	RACR #2	Total Assets ($mil)	Capital ($mil)	Net Premium ($mil)	Net Income ($mil)
6-20	B+	2.56	2.14	74.2	47.1	100.9	6.8
6-19	N/A	N/A	N/A	N/A	N/A	N/A	N/A
2019	B+	1.89	1.57	54.0	35.3	165.7	2.9
2018	B+	2.19	1.83	59.0	36.9	150.3	2.4
2017	B	2.60	2.17	51.8	35.0	129.3	7.1
2016	B	2.11	1.75	43.2	28.4	124.7	6.3
2015	C	1.63	1.36	34.5	21.8	118.8	11.0

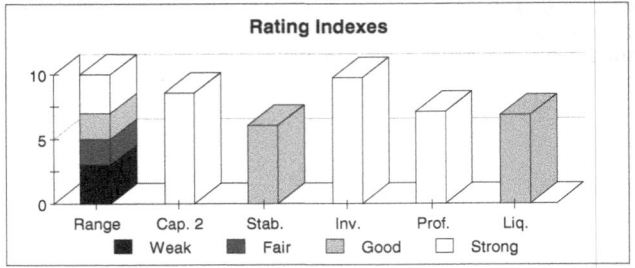

Rating Indexes

NASSAU LIFE INS COMPANY OF TEXAS | D | Weak

Major Rating Factors: Weak overall results on stability tests (1.9 on a scale of 0 to 10) including potential financial drain due to affiliation with Nassau Reinsurance Group Holdings LP. Weak profitability (2.6) with investment income below regulatory standards in relation to interest assumptions of reserves. Fair quality investment portfolio (3.9).
Other Rating Factors: Good liquidity (6.9). Strong capitalization (7.8) based on excellent risk adjusted capital (severe loss scenario).
Principal Business: Individual health insurance (48%), reinsurance (29%), group health insurance (12%), and individual life insurance (11%).
Principal Investments: NonCMO investment grade bonds (51%), CMOs and structured securities (37%), noninv. grade bonds (5%), cash (4%), and policy loans (1%).
Investments in Affiliates: None
Group Affiliation: Nassau Reinsurance Group Holdings LP
Licensed in: All states except NY, PR
Commenced Business: June 1929
Address: 4888 Loop Central Dr Ste 700, Austin, TX 78701
Phone: (407) 547-3800 **Domicile State:** TX **NAIC Code:** 62359

Data Date	Rating	RACR #1	RACR #2	Total Assets ($mil)	Capital ($mil)	Net Premium ($mil)	Net Income ($mil)
6-20	D	3.03	1.51	396.2	48.2	16.0	9.3
6-19	D	2.54	1.35	397.9	38.9	21.8	0.1
2019	D	2.53	1.31	401.8	39.2	40.0	5.7
2018	D	2.62	1.40	390.7	39.6	42.5	5.2
2017	D	2.28	1.26	412.7	35.1	49.1	-4.0
2016	D	2.71	1.71	444.1	55.6	90.0	-11.8
2015	C+	2.75	1.84	394.8	66.6	123.3	34.9

Nassau Reinsurance Group Holdings LP Composite Group Rating: D- Largest Group Members	Assets ($mil)	Rating
NASSAU LIFE INSURANCE CO	11734	D-
PHL VARIABLE INS CO	5931	E-
NASSAU LIFE INS COMPANY OF TEXAS	402	D
NASSAU LIFE ANNUITY CO	276	D+
NASSAU LIFE INS CO OF KS	76	D

NATIONAL FOUNDATION LIFE INS CO * | A | Excellent

Major Rating Factors: Good overall results on stability tests (6.8 on a scale of 0 to 10). Strengths that enhance stability include excellent operational trends and good risk diversification. Strong capitalization (8.7) based on excellent risk adjusted capital (severe loss scenario). Furthermore, this high level of risk adjusted capital has been consistently maintained over the last five years. High quality investment portfolio (8.0).
Other Rating Factors: Excellent profitability (9.3) with operating gains in each of the last five years. Excellent liquidity (7.2).
Principal Business: Individual health insurance (57%), group health insurance (33%), individual life insurance (7%), and reinsurance (2%).
Principal Investments: NonCMO investment grade bonds (42%), CMOs and structured securities (18%), cash (4%), and noninv. grade bonds (1%).
Investments in Affiliates: None
Group Affiliation: Credit Suisse Group
Licensed in: AL, AK, AZ, AR, CA, CO, DC, DE, GA, ID, IN, IA, KS, KY, LA, ME, MS, MO, MT, NE, NV, NM, NC, ND, OH, OK, OR, PA, SC, SD, TN, TX, UT, VA, WA, WY
Commenced Business: November 1983
Address: 300 Burnett Street Suite 200, Fort Worth, TX 76102-2734
Phone: (817) 878-3300 **Domicile State:** TX **NAIC Code:** 98205

Data Date	Rating	RACR #1	RACR #2	Total Assets ($mil)	Capital ($mil)	Net Premium ($mil)	Net Income ($mil)
6-20	A	2.71	2.13	87.8	61.0	55.6	14.2
6-19	B+	1.86	1.44	62.3	40.0	46.3	6.9
2019	B+	2.23	1.74	70.8	46.8	96.2	13.8
2018	B+	1.66	1.28	53.8	33.0	78.6	10.7
2017	B	1.61	1.25	38.9	21.7	53.7	5.4
2016	B	2.10	1.63	33.8	19.9	40.1	5.4
2015	B-	2.08	1.61	29.9	16.5	34.9	6.0

Adverse Trends in Operations
Change in asset mix during 2019 (5%)
Change in asset mix during 2018 (4%)
Change in asset mix during 2016 (4.5%)

NATIONAL GUARDIAN LIFE INS CO | B | Good

Major Rating Factors: Good quality investment portfolio (5.9 on a scale of 0 to 10) despite mixed results such as: minimal exposure to mortgages and large holdings of BBB rated bonds but small junk bond holdings. Good overall profitability (5.4) although investment income, in comparison to reserve requirements, is below regulatory standards. Good liquidity (6.3).
Other Rating Factors: Good overall results on stability tests (5.8) excellent operational trends, good risk adjusted capital for prior years and excellent risk diversification. Strong capitalization (7.1) based on excellent risk adjusted capital (severe loss scenario).
Principal Business: Group health insurance (37%), group life insurance (36%), individual life insurance (19%), reinsurance (4%), and other lines (5%).
Principal Investments: NonCMO investment grade bonds (80%), CMOs and structured securities (6%), common & preferred stock (4%), noninv. grade bonds (2%), and misc. investments (5%).
Investments in Affiliates: 2%
Group Affiliation: NGL Ins Group
Licensed in: All states except NY, PR
Commenced Business: October 1910
Address: 2 East Gilman Street, Madison, WI 53703-1494
Phone: (608) 257-5611 **Domicile State:** WI **NAIC Code:** 66583

Data Date	Rating	RACR #1	RACR #2	Total Assets ($mil)	Capital ($mil)	Net Premium ($mil)	Net Income ($mil)
3-20	B	1.62	1.05	4,372.4	394.1	173.5	1.4
3-19	B-	1.59	1.02	4,139.1	353.4	161.1	6.5
2019	B	1.59	1.03	4,301.6	367.4	659.9	31.2
2018	B-	1.52	0.98	4,080.0	333.2	653.9	30.0
2017	B-	1.53	0.98	3,884.4	322.6	603.4	28.8
2016	B-	1.52	0.95	3,657.9	293.3	553.0	18.1
2015	B-	1.45	0.91	3,422.2	271.1	790.0	-4.5

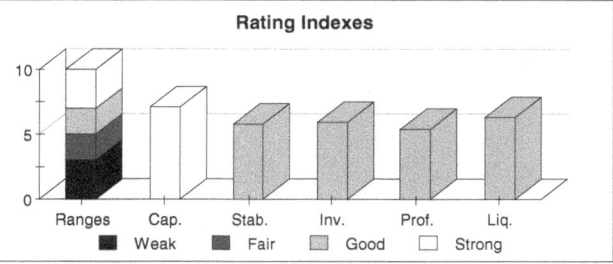

Rating Indexes

Ranges | Cap. | Stab. | Inv. | Prof. | Liq.
■ Weak ▨ Fair ▦ Good ☐ Strong

NATIONAL HEALTH INS CO

C+   Fair

Major Rating Factors: Fair overall results on stability tests (4.1 on a scale of 0 to 10) including negative cash flow from operations for 2019. Good capitalization (6.8) based on good risk adjusted capital (moderate loss scenario). Capital levels have been relatively consistent over the last five years. High quality investment portfolio (8.6).

Other Rating Factors: Excellent profitability (7.0) despite modest operating losses during 2019. Excellent liquidity (7.3).

Principal Business: Group health insurance (86%), individual health insurance (11%), reinsurance (2%), and individual life insurance (1%).

Principal Investments: CMOs and structured securities (49%), nonCMO investment grade bonds (37%), and cash (14%).

Investments in Affiliates: None

Group Affiliation: AmTrust Financial Services Inc

Licensed in: All states except NY, PR

Commenced Business: January 1966

Address: 4455 LBJ Freeway Suite 375, Dallas, TX 75244

Phone: (800) 237-1900 **Domicile State:** TX **NAIC Code:** 82538

Data Date	Rating	RACR #1	RACR #2	Total Assets ($mil)	Capital ($mil)	Net Premium ($mil)	Net Income ($mil)
6-20	C+	2.24	0.93	103.3	32.8	5.9	1.7
6-19	C	1.86	0.78	67.5	20.2	5.0	1.1
2019	C+	2.38	1.00	87.2	31.0	10.3	-0.1
2018	C-	1.99	0.84	59.4	18.9	13.2	1.1
2017	C+	2.08	0.88	50.8	14.6	9.6	3.0
2016	C	3.70	1.64	25.9	12.0	7.6	3.0
2015	C	5.06	2.92	26.0	13.8	1.9	0.9

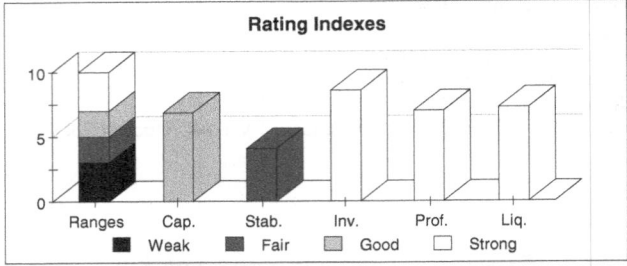

Rating Indexes — Ranges, Cap., Stab., Inv., Prof., Liq. — Weak / Fair / Good / Strong

NATIONAL TEACHERS ASSOCIATES L I C

B-   Good

Major Rating Factors: Good quality investment portfolio (6.3 on a scale of 0 to 10) despite mixed results such as: no exposure to mortgages and substantial holdings of BBB bonds but small junk bond holdings. Fair profitability (3.3) with investment income below regulatory standards in relation to interest assumptions of reserves. Fair overall results on stability tests (4.9).

Other Rating Factors: Strong capitalization (7.3) based on excellent risk adjusted capital (severe loss scenario). Excellent liquidity (8.2).

Principal Business: Individual health insurance (97%) and individual life insurance (3%).

Principal Investments: NonCMO investment grade bonds (48%), CMOs and structured securities (33%), noninv. grade bonds (1%), and cash (1%).

Investments in Affiliates: None

Group Affiliation: Ellard Family Holdings Inc

Licensed in: All states except NY, PR

Commenced Business: July 1938

Address: 4949 Keller Springs Rd, Addison, TX 75001-5910

Phone: (972) 532-2100 **Domicile State:** TX **NAIC Code:** 87963

Data Date	Rating	RACR #1	RACR #2	Total Assets ($mil)	Capital ($mil)	Net Premium ($mil)	Net Income ($mil)
6-20	B-	1.94	1.22	586.9	55.6	65.4	12.1
6-19	B	3.63	2.39	606.8	149.1	65.5	9.0
2019	B-	2.56	1.67	541.0	68.4	130.3	-15.7
2018	B	3.46	2.29	583.6	138.7	130.2	28.9
2017	B	2.89	1.95	544.9	115.9	130.7	20.3
2016	B	2.86	1.94	510.5	102.4	129.2	11.2
2015	B	N/A	N/A	464.1	92.1	123.6	11.1

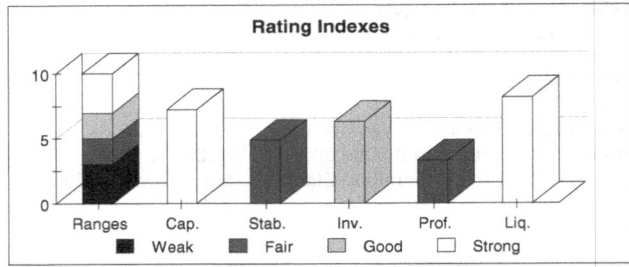

Rating Indexes — Ranges, Cap., Stab., Inv., Prof., Liq. — Weak / Fair / Good / Strong

NEBRASKA TOTAL CARE INC

C   Fair

Major Rating Factors: Weak profitability index (0.9 on a scale of 0 to 10). Weak liquidity (2.6) as a spike in claims may stretch capacity. Strong capitalization (7.8) based on excellent current risk-adjusted capital (severe loss scenario).

Other Rating Factors: High quality investment portfolio (9.0).

Principal Business: Medicaid (100%).

Mem Phys: 18: 21,798 **17:** 13,794 **18 MLR** 94.5% **/ 18 Admin Exp** N/A

Enroll(000): Q3 19: 83 **18:** 83 **17:** 82 **Med Exp PMPM:** $421

Principal Investments: Long-term bonds (71%), cash and equiv (29%)

Provider Compensation ($000): Contr fee ($295,365), bonus arrang ($102,003), salary ($6,518), capitation ($3,309), other ($7,654)

Total Member Encounters: Phys (497,945), non-phys (1,152,791)

Group Affiliation: None

Licensed in: NE

Address: 2525 N 117th Avenue Suite 100, Omaha, NE 68164

Phone: (314) 725-4477 **Dom State:** NE **Commenced Bus:** N/A

Data Date	Rating	RACR #1	RACR #2	Total Assets ($mil)	Capital ($mil)	Net Premium ($mil)	Net Income ($mil)
9-19	C	1.99	1.66	111.8	46.0	341.9	10.8
9-18	N/A	N/A	N/A	107.7	36.2	333.8	-14.9
2018	C-	1.60	1.33	98.2	34.9	444.8	-16.3
2017	N/A	N/A	N/A	112.6	45.7	426.8	-26.8
2016	N/A	N/A	N/A	1.5	1.5	N/A	N/A
2015	N/A	N/A	N/A	N/A	N/A	N/A	N/A
2014	N/A	N/A	N/A	N/A	N/A	N/A	N/A

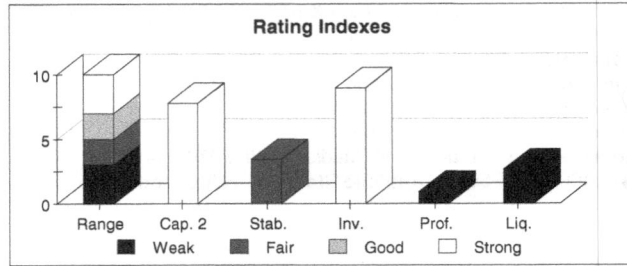

Rating Indexes — Range, Cap. 2, Stab., Inv., Prof., Liq. — Weak / Fair / Good / Strong

NEIGHBORHOOD HEALTH PARTNERSHIP INC | C+ | Fair

Major Rating Factors: Fair capitalization index (3.9 on a scale of 0 to 10) based on fair current risk-adjusted capital (moderate loss scenario). Good overall results on stability tests (5.4). Good liquidity (6.0) with sufficient resources (cash flows and marketable investments) to handle a spike in claims.
Other Rating Factors: Excellent profitability (8.4). High quality investment portfolio (9.0).
Principal Business: Comp med (100%)
Mem Phys: 19: 63,953 **18:** 60,867 **19 MLR** 82.5% **/ 19 Admin Exp** N/A
Enroll(000): Q2 20: 160 **19:** 170 **18:** 159 **Med Exp PMPM:** $342
Principal Investments: Long-term bonds (88%), cash and equiv (12%)
Provider Compensation ($000): Contr fee ($626,228), FFS ($40,386), capitation ($15,690)
Total Member Encounters: N/A
Group Affiliation: None
Licensed in: FL
Address: 7600 CORPORATE CENTER DRIVE, MIRAMAR,
Phone: (800) 825-8792 **Dom State:** FL **Commenced Bus:** N/A

Data Date	Rating	RACR #1	RACR #2	Total Assets ($mil)	Capital ($mil)	Net Premium ($mil)	Net Income ($mil)
6-20	C+	0.77	0.64	268.7	57.2	410.3	26.0
6-19	C	1.24	1.04	197.2	53.7	414.2	23.5
2019	B-	1.25	1.04	216.5	58.3	840.5	37.8
2018	C	0.86	0.72	156.2	37.5	714.4	17.8
2017	B	1.25	1.04	150.6	62.6	622.5	46.0
2016	B	2.11	1.76	149.0	60.2	578.0	41.4
2015	B	1.48	1.24	121.7	39.9	528.5	26.1

NEIGHBORHOOD HEALTH PLAN | D | Weak

Major Rating Factors: Weak profitability index (1.2 on a scale of 0 to 10). Low quality investment portfolio (0.6). Weak overall results on stability tests (1.7) based on a steep decline in capital during 2019.
Other Rating Factors: Good liquidity (6.2) with sufficient resources (cash flows and marketable investments) to handle a spike in claims. Strong capitalization index (8.2) based on excellent current risk-adjusted capital (severe loss scenario).
Principal Business: Comp med (78%), Medicaid (22%)
Mem Phys: 19: 43,924 **18:** 37,912 **19 MLR** 91.9% **/ 19 Admin Exp** N/A
Enroll(000): Q2 20: 121 **19:** 117 **18:** 121 **Med Exp PMPM:** $525
Principal Investments: Nonaffiliate common stock (75%), cash and equiv (4%), other (21%)
Provider Compensation ($000): Contr fee ($457,991), capitation ($222,001), FFS ($4,186), other ($29,193)
Total Member Encounters: Phys (1,143,733), non-phys (633,329)
Group Affiliation: None
Licensed in: MA
Address: 253 Summer St, Somerville,
Phone: (800) 433-5556 **Dom State:** MA **Commenced Bus:** N/A

Data Date	Rating	RACR #1	RACR #2	Total Assets ($mil)	Capital ($mil)	Net Premium ($mil)	Net Income ($mil)
6-20	D	2.28	1.90	285.2	143.2	399.3	-9.8
6-19	D	2.60	2.17	332.9	230.4	406.4	-3.1
2019	D	2.54	2.12	276.6	160.8	792.7	-14.8
2018	D	3.07	2.56	413.0	271.4	1,047.4	0.8
2017	D	2.14	1.78	562.8	337.1	2,422.0	104.5
2016	D	0.99	0.83	531.0	192.4	2,560.0	-130.9
2015	D	1.09	0.91	450.2	186.9	2,163.0	-25.5

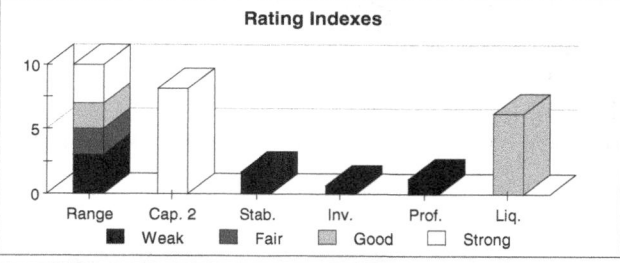

NEIGHBORHOOD HEALTH PLAN OF RI INC | C+ | Fair

Major Rating Factors: Good overall profitability index (5.4 on a scale of 0 to 10). Good capitalization index (5.4) based on good current risk-adjusted capital (severe loss scenario). Good liquidity (6.9) with sufficient resources (cash flows and marketable investments) to handle a spike in claims.
Other Rating Factors: High quality investment portfolio (9.9). Excellent overall results on stability tests (7.2).
Principal Business: Medicaid (91%), comp med (9%)
Mem Phys: 19: 6,706 **18:** 6,740 **19 MLR** 89.8% **/ 19 Admin Exp** N/A
Enroll(000): Q2 20: 197 **19:** 186 **18:** 194 **Med Exp PMPM:** $523
Principal Investments: Long-term bonds (63%), cash and equiv (37%)
Provider Compensation ($000): Contr fee ($1,191,203), capitation ($25,290), bonus arrang ($967)
Total Member Encounters: Phys (6,373,070), non-phys (1,009,846)
Group Affiliation: None
Licensed in: RI
Address: 910 Douglas Pike, Smithfield,
Phone: (401) 459-6000 **Dom State:** RI **Commenced Bus:** N/A

Data Date	Rating	RACR #1	RACR #2	Total Assets ($mil)	Capital ($mil)	Net Premium ($mil)	Net Income ($mil)
6-20	C+	1.00	0.83	353.2	109.7	702.2	8.4
6-19	N/A	N/A	N/A	N/A	N/A	N/A	N/A
2019	C+	0.93	0.77	355.0	101.6	1,345.9	3.7
2018	C+	0.88	0.73	333.9	101.6	1,377.7	6.1
2017	B-	0.85	0.71	382.6	100.3	1,365.9	-1.7
2016	B	1.09	0.91	348.8	102.7	1,121.9	19.7
2015	B-	1.00	0.83	369.5	85.6	1,011.4	28.6

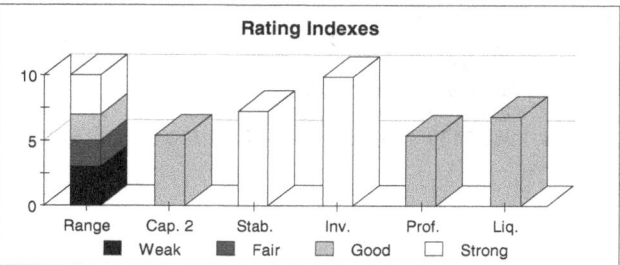

NETWORK HEALTH INS CORP
B   **Good**

Major Rating Factors: Good liquidity (6.7 on a scale of 0 to 10) with sufficient resources (cash flows and marketable investments) to handle a spike in claims. Fair profitability index (4.8). Strong capitalization (7.9) based on excellent current risk-adjusted capital (severe loss scenario).
Other Rating Factors: High quality investment portfolio (9.9).
Principal Business: Medicare (99%), other (1%)
Mem Phys: 19: 16,172 **18:** 14,795 **19 MLR** 84.7% **/ 19 Admin Exp** N/A
Enroll(000): Q2 20: 71 **19:** 72 **18:** 70 **Med Exp PMPM:** $651
Principal Investments: Long-term bonds (90%), cash and equiv (10%)
Provider Compensation ($000): Contr fee ($364,203), FFS ($191,706), capitation ($1,431), bonus arrang ($710)
Total Member Encounters: Phys (410,575), non-phys (178,977)
Group Affiliation: Network Health Inc
Licensed in: WI
Address: 1570 Midway Place, Menasha, WI 54952
Phone: (920) 720-1452 **Dom State:** WI **Commenced Bus:** N/A

Data Date	Rating	RACR #1	RACR #2	Total Assets ($mil)	Capital ($mil)	Net Premium ($mil)	Net Income ($mil)
6-20	B	2.08	1.74	239.6	118.3	287.8	16.3
6-19	C	1.71	1.43	192.6	92.5	337.2	18.3
2019	C+	1.84	1.53	183.5	102.3	653.5	26.9
2018	C	1.38	1.15	161.3	74.6	590.1	-2.3
2017	C	1.17	0.97	172.2	64.5	561.6	-16.6
2016	C	1.65	1.37	185.0	81.5	550.6	-3.3
2015	C	1.65	1.37	176.0	81.7	556.5	-5.7

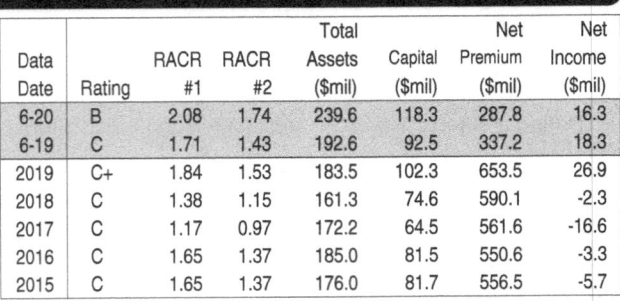

Rating Indexes

NETWORK HEALTH PLAN
B   **Good**

Major Rating Factors: Good overall profitability index (5.4 on a scale of 0 to 10). Good overall results on stability tests (5.5). Good liquidity (6.7) with sufficient resources (cash flows and marketable investments) to handle a spike in claims.
Other Rating Factors: Strong capitalization index (8.1) based on excellent current risk-adjusted capital (severe loss scenario). High quality investment portfolio (9.7).
Principal Business: Comp med (75%), Medicaid (25%)
Mem Phys: 19: 16,172 **18:** 14,795 **19 MLR** 91.7% **/ 19 Admin Exp** N/A
Enroll(000): Q2 20: 81 **19:** 82 **18:** 88 **Med Exp PMPM:** $343
Principal Investments: Long-term bonds (61%), cash and equiv (36%), real estate (2%)
Provider Compensation ($000): Contr fee ($216,891), capitation ($79,860), FFS ($19,265), bonus arrang ($16,364)
Total Member Encounters: Phys (303,173), non-phys (389,622)
Group Affiliation: Network Health Inc
Licensed in: WI
Address: 1570 Midway Place, Menasha,
Phone: (920) 720-1200 **Dom State:** WI **Commenced Bus:** N/A

Data Date	Rating	RACR #1	RACR #2	Total Assets ($mil)	Capital ($mil)	Net Premium ($mil)	Net Income ($mil)
6-20	B	2.20	1.84	138.8	72.0	177.0	16.9
6-19	B	2.32	1.94	115.6	68.5	193.3	12.1
2019	B	1.83	1.53	111.6	54.3	377.5	-4.0
2018	B-	1.97	1.64	106.5	58.3	401.0	10.2
2017	B-	2.28	1.90	92.7	53.0	298.9	11.7
2016	B-	1.52	1.27	102.6	41.4	370.9	0.6
2015	B-	1.60	1.34	103.2	45.3	403.4	6.0

Rating Indexes

NEW ERA LIFE INS CO
C   **Fair**

Major Rating Factors: Fair overall results on stability tests (4.2 on a scale of 0 to 10) including fair risk adjusted capital in prior years. Good current capitalization (5.0) based on good risk adjusted capital (severe loss scenario) reflecting some improvement over results in 2017. Good quality investment portfolio (5.3).
Other Rating Factors: Good liquidity (5.8). Excellent profitability (8.4) despite operating losses during the first three months of 2020.
Principal Business: Individual health insurance (52%), individual annuities (47%), and individual life insurance (2%).
Principal Investments: NonCMO investment grade bonds (45%), mortgages in good standing (28%), common & preferred stock (15%), noninv. grade bonds (6%), and misc. investments (5%).
Investments in Affiliates: 14%
Group Affiliation: New Era Life Group
Licensed in: AL, AZ, AR, CA, CO, DE, FL, GA, IN, KS, KY, LA, MI, MS, MO, MT, NE, NM, NC, ND, OH, OK, PA, SC, SD, TN, TX, UT, WA, WV
Commenced Business: June 1924
Address: 11720 Katy Freeway Suite 1700, Houston, TX 77079
Phone: (281) 368-7159 **Domicile State:** TX **NAIC Code:** 78743

Data Date	Rating	RACR #1	RACR #2	Total Assets ($mil)	Capital ($mil)	Net Premium ($mil)	Net Income ($mil)
3-20	C	0.93	0.75	555.1	98.4	46.9	-0.3
3-19	C	0.99	0.78	546.2	93.8	41.7	0.2
2019	C	0.95	0.78	552.5	100.9	180.0	2.0
2018	C	0.97	0.77	543.1	90.2	152.3	2.8
2017	C	0.94	0.73	538.3	79.3	181.4	3.5
2016	C	0.94	0.72	504.2	75.1	190.3	4.5
2015	C	0.95	0.73	463.5	70.7	111.2	5.1

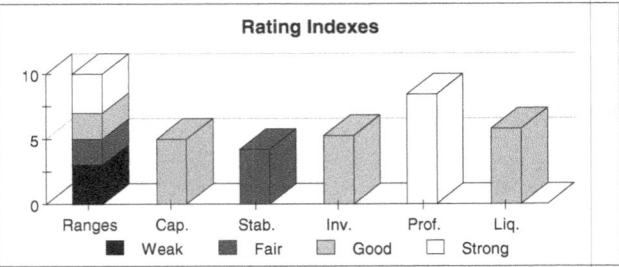

Rating Indexes

NEW MEXICO HEALTH CONNECTIONS

E-   Very Weak

Major Rating Factors: Weak profitability index (0.9 on a scale of 0 to 10). Poor capitalization (0.0) based on weak current risk-adjusted capital (severe loss scenario). Weak liquidity (1.7) as a spike in claims may stretch capacity.
Other Rating Factors: High quality investment portfolio (9.6).
Principal Business: Comp med (100%)
Mem Phys: 19: 10,875 **18:** 10,259 **19 MLR** 446.3% **/ 19 Admin Exp** N/A
Enroll(000): Q2 20: 14 **19:** 17 **18:** 17 **Med Exp PMPM:** $442
Principal Investments: Cash and equiv (60%), long-term bonds (40%)
Provider Compensation ($000): Contr fee ($82,767), FFS ($12,165)
Total Member Encounters: Phys (139,122), non-phys (29,131)
Group Affiliation: None
Licensed in: NM
Address: 6001 Indian School Road NE Sui, Albuquerque, NM 87110
Phone: (866) 668-9002 **Dom State:** NM **Commenced Bus:** N/A

Data Date	Rating	RACR #1	RACR #2	Total Assets ($mil)	Capital ($mil)	Net Premium ($mil)	Net Income ($mil)
6-20	E-	0.22	0.18	28.4	2.3	N/A	-0.1
6-19	N/A	N/A	N/A	N/A	N/A	N/A	N/A
2019	E-	0.18	0.15	25.0	2.0	20.9	0.4
2018	E-	0.06	0.05	45.2	1.5	46.3	6.3
2017	N/A	N/A	N/A	34.2	-4.9	158.6	N/A
2016	E-	0.43	0.36	36.8	10.8	152.5	-17.9
2015	D	1.39	1.16	61.0	31.4	96.2	-23.0

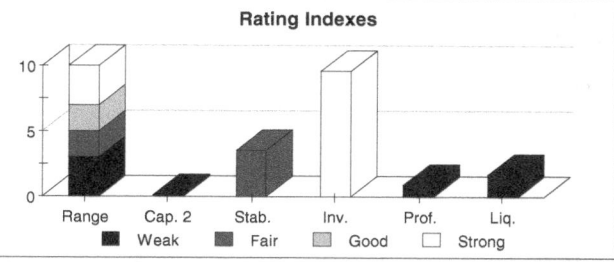

Rating Indexes

Weak Fair Good Strong

NEXTLEVEL HEALTH PARTNERS INC

E-   Very Weak

Major Rating Factors: Weak profitability index (0.9 on a scale of 0 to 10). Poor capitalization (0.0) based on weak current risk-adjusted capital (severe loss scenario). Weak liquidity (0.0) as a spike in claims may stretch capacity.
Other Rating Factors: High quality investment portfolio (9.9).
Principal Business: Medicaid (100%)
Mem Phys: 19: 1,952 **18:** 3,875 **19 MLR** 92.0% **/ 19 Admin Exp** N/A
Enroll(000): Q2 20: 55 **19:** 58 **18:** 48 **Med Exp PMPM:** $421
Principal Investments: Cash and equiv (100%)
Provider Compensation ($000): Contr fee ($226,681)
Total Member Encounters: Phys (369,148), non-phys (129,953)
Group Affiliation: NextLevel Health Innovations Inc
Licensed in: (No states)
Address: 224 S Michigan Ave 7th Floo, Chicago, IL 60604
Phone: (844) 807-9734 **Dom State:** IL **Commenced Bus:** N/A

Data Date	Rating	RACR #1	RACR #2	Total Assets ($mil)	Capital ($mil)	Net Premium ($mil)	Net Income ($mil)
6-20	E-	0.10	0.09	77.9	11.4	172.8	13.9
6-19	N/A	N/A	N/A	N/A	N/A	N/A	N/A
2019	E-	N/A	N/A	53.8	-2.8	269.9	-25.0
2018	C-	0.81	0.68	72.9	22.2	261.5	6.6
2017	N/A	N/A	N/A	N/A	16.8	N/A	N/A
2016	N/A	N/A	N/A	N/A	N/A	N/A	N/A
2015	N/A	N/A	N/A	N/A	N/A	N/A	N/A

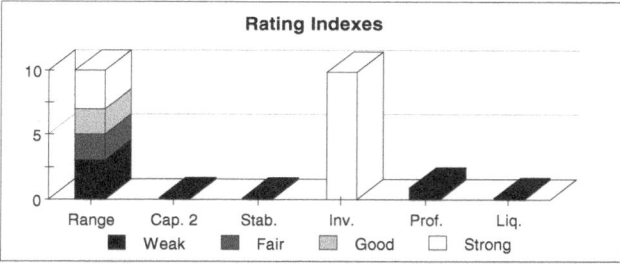

Rating Indexes

Weak Fair Good Strong

NHC ADVANTAGE LLC

C-   Fair

Major Rating Factors: Weak profitability index (0.8 on a scale of 0 to 10). Good liquidity (6.2) with sufficient resources (cash flows and marketable investments) to handle a spike in claims. Strong capitalization (7.5) based on excellent current risk-adjusted capital (severe loss scenario).
Other Rating Factors: High quality investment portfolio (9.9).
Principal Business: Medicare (100%)
Mem Phys: 18: 8,429 **17:** 1,358 **18 MLR** 91.9% **/ 18 Admin Exp** N/A
Enroll(000): Q3 19: 1 **18:** 0 **17:** 0 **Med Exp PMPM:** $1,664
Principal Investments: Long-term bonds (70%), cash and equiv (30%)
Provider Compensation ($000): Contr fee ($1,788), capitation ($669), bonus arrang ($105)
Total Member Encounters: Phys (15,776), non-phys (68,659)
Group Affiliation: None
Licensed in: MO, TN
Address: 39 Sugar Maple Lane, St Charles, MO 63303
Phone: (804) 396-6412 **Dom State:** MO **Commenced Bus:** N/A

Data Date	Rating	RACR #1	RACR #2	Total Assets ($mil)	Capital ($mil)	Net Premium ($mil)	Net Income ($mil)
9-19	C-	1.79	1.49	7.6	1.5	18.8	-0.5
9-18	N/A	N/A	N/A	2.8	1.8	2.0	-0.5
2018	C-	2.10	1.75	2.5	1.8	2.7	-1.0
2017	N/A	N/A	N/A	2.0	1.3	2.6	-0.2
2016	N/A	N/A	N/A	1.6	1.6	N/A	-0.6
2015	N/A	N/A	N/A	N/A	N/A	N/A	N/A
2014	N/A	N/A	N/A	N/A	N/A	N/A	N/A

Rating Indexes

Weak Fair Good Strong

NIPPON LIFE INS CO OF AMERICA *

A-   **Excellent**

Major Rating Factors: Good liquidity (6.6 on a scale of 0 to 10) with sufficient resources to handle a spike in claims. Strong capitalization (9.5) based on excellent risk adjusted capital (severe loss scenario). Furthermore, this high level of risk adjusted capital has been consistently maintained over the last five years. High quality investment portfolio (8.0).

Other Rating Factors: Excellent profitability (7.0) with operating gains in each of the last five years. Excellent overall results on stability tests (7.0) excellent operational trends and excellent risk diversification.

Principal Business: Group health insurance (99%) and group life insurance (1%).

Principal Investments: NonCMO investment grade bonds (72%), CMOs and structured securities (14%), cash (3%), and common & preferred stock (3%).

Investments in Affiliates: None

Group Affiliation: Nippon Life Ins Co Japan

Licensed in: All states except ME, NH, WY, PR

Commenced Business: July 1973

Address: 7115 Vista Drive, West Des Moines, IA 50266

Phone: (212) 682-3000 **Domicile State:** IA **NAIC Code:** 81264

Data Date	Rating	RACR #1	RACR #2	Total Assets ($mil)	Capital ($mil)	Net Premium ($mil)	Net Income ($mil)
6-20	A-	3.40	2.67	246.1	148.5	168.6	5.6
6-19	A-	3.26	2.58	228.5	143.9	179.0	2.6
2019	A-	3.03	2.39	226.5	144.2	360.0	3.5
2018	A-	3.13	2.48	224.1	143.3	350.0	4.5
2017	A-	3.42	2.71	220.7	139.7	311.5	1.5
2016	A-	3.73	2.96	212.3	139.6	285.7	0.5
2015	A-	3.92	3.11	212.6	140.8	277.0	4.6

Rating Indexes

Ranges | Cap. | Stab. | Inv. | Prof. | Liq.
■ Weak ■ Fair ▨ Good □ Strong

NORTHWESTERN LONG TERM CARE INS CO *

B+   **Good**

Major Rating Factors: Good overall results on stability tests (6.8 on a scale of 0 to 10). Stability strengths include excellent operational trends and excellent risk diversification. Good liquidity (6.9) with sufficient resources to handle a spike in claims. Strong capitalization (8.0) based on excellent risk adjusted capital (severe loss scenario).

Other Rating Factors: High quality investment portfolio (8.4). Excellent profitability (7.7) with operating gains in each of the last five years.

Principal Business: Individual health insurance (100%).

Principal Investments: NonCMO investment grade bonds (101%).

Investments in Affiliates: None

Group Affiliation: Northwestern Mutual Group

Licensed in: All states except PR

Commenced Business: October 1953

Address: 720 EAST WISCONSIN AVENUE, MILWAUKEE, WI 53202

Phone: (414) 271-1444 **Domicile State:** WI **NAIC Code:** 69000

Data Date	Rating	RACR #1	RACR #2	Total Assets ($mil)	Capital ($mil)	Net Premium ($mil)	Net Income ($mil)
6-20	B+	10.17	4.10	290.3	176.3	0.0	3.6
6-19	B	9.11	3.68	243.0	145.2	0.0	3.5
2019	B+	10.19	4.12	283.2	173.5	0.0	7.0
2018	B	9.04	3.65	240.4	141.8	0.0	2.9
2017	B	8.03	3.23	200.6	104.1	-0.1	7.5
2016	B	6.46	2.60	172.7	82.2	0.2	2.6
2015	B	6.57	2.65	166.0	79.5	0.3	2.5

Adverse Trends in Operations

Decrease in premium volume from 2016 to 2017 (145%)
Decrease in premium volume from 2015 to 2016 (45%)

OKLAHOMA SUPERIOR SELECT INC

E+   **Very Weak**

Major Rating Factors: Weak profitability index (0.9 on a scale of 0 to 10). Strong capitalization (7.0) based on excellent current risk-adjusted capital (severe loss scenario). High quality investment portfolio (9.9).

Other Rating Factors: Excellent liquidity (6.9) with sufficient resources (cash flows and marketable investments) to handle a spike in claims.

Principal Business: Medicare (100%)

Mem Phys: 19: 2,216 **18:** 1,160 **19 MLR** 78.5% **/ 19 Admin Exp** N/A

Enroll(000): Q2 20: 0 **19:** 0 **18:** 0 **Med Exp PMPM:** $1,784

Principal Investments: Cash and equiv (82%), long-term bonds (18%)

Provider Compensation ($000): Contr fee ($4,207), capitation ($1,605)

Total Member Encounters: Phys (9,757), non-phys (2,888)

Group Affiliation: Mitchell Family Office

Licensed in: OK

Address: 909 S Meridian Avenue Suite 4, Oklahoma City, OK 73108

Phone: (405) 602-5488 **Dom State:** OK **Commenced Bus:** N/A

Data Date	Rating	RACR #1	RACR #2	Total Assets ($mil)	Capital ($mil)	Net Premium ($mil)	Net Income ($mil)
6-20	E+	1.38	1.15	3.6	2.0	4.2	0.0
6-19	E+	1.34	1.12	3.3	1.7	3.5	-0.3
2019	E+	1.44	1.20	3.3	1.9	6.8	-0.2
2018	E+	1.41	1.18	3.6	1.8	5.4	0.1
2017	E+	1.21	1.01	2.8	1.7	4.6	-0.7
2016	E	1.40	1.16	3.7	1.6	4.0	-1.9
2015	E-	0.50	0.42	2.3	0.6	2.9	-3.1

Rating Indexes

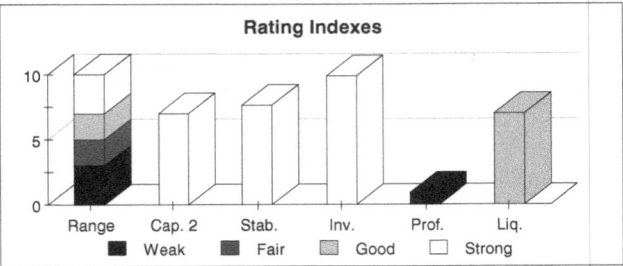

Range | Cap. 2 | Stab. | Inv. | Prof. | Liq.
■ Weak ■ Fair ▨ Good □ Strong

OLD REPUBLIC LIFE INS CO

B-   Good

Major Rating Factors: Good quality investment portfolio (5.2 on a scale of 0 to 10) despite mixed results such as: no exposure to mortgages and substantial holdings of BBB bonds but minimal holdings in junk bonds. Good overall profitability (5.2) although investment income, in comparison to reserve requirements, is below regulatory standards. Fair overall results on stability tests (4.8).

Other Rating Factors: Strong capitalization (10.0) based on excellent risk adjusted capital (severe loss scenario). Excellent liquidity (7.0).

Principal Business: Group health insurance (57%), individual life insurance (24%), and reinsurance (19%).

Principal Investments: NonCMO investment grade bonds (73%), common & preferred stock (18%), policy loans (1%), and noninv. grade bonds (1%).

Investments in Affiliates: None
Group Affiliation: Old Republic Group
Licensed in: All states except NY
Commenced Business: April 1923
Address: 307 NORTH MICHIGAN AVENUE, CHICAGO, IL 60601
Phone: (312) 346-8100 **Domicile State:** IL **NAIC Code:** 67261

Data Date	Rating	RACR #1	RACR #2	Total Assets ($mil)	Capital ($mil)	Net Premium ($mil)	Net Income ($mil)
6-20	B-	4.89	3.02	102.2	41.1	5.0	1.6
6-19	B-	4.10	2.50	106.2	35.4	6.2	-0.5
2019	B-	5.06	3.09	107.8	40.1	13.0	3.7
2018	B-	4.05	2.48	109.0	33.6	14.3	0.8
2017	B-	3.66	2.28	122.7	34.8	18.2	1.7
2016	B-	3.43	2.12	125.0	31.4	19.4	2.3
2015	B-	2.84	1.77	126.9	27.0	18.1	-0.3

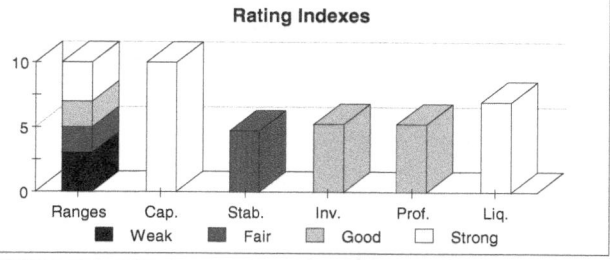

Rating Indexes

(Ranges, Cap., Stab., Inv., Prof., Liq.) — Weak, Fair, Good, Strong

OLD UNITED LIFE INS CO

B   Good

Major Rating Factors: Good overall results on stability tests (5.7 on a scale of 0 to 10) despite negative cash flow from operations for 2019. Other stability subfactors include excellent operational trends and excellent risk diversification. Fair quality investment portfolio (4.6). Strong capitalization (10.0) based on excellent risk adjusted capital (severe loss scenario).

Other Rating Factors: Excellent profitability (8.7) with operating gains in each of the last five years. Excellent liquidity (10.0).

Principal Business: Credit health insurance (51%) and credit life insurance (49%).

Principal Investments: NonCMO investment grade bonds (59%), common & preferred stock (33%), CMOs and structured securities (3%), noninv. grade bonds (1%), and cash (1%).

Investments in Affiliates: None
Group Affiliation: Berkshire Hathaway Inc
Licensed in: All states except ME, NH, NY, PR
Commenced Business: January 1964
Address: 3800 N Central Ave Ste 460, Phoenix, AZ 85012
Phone: (913) 895-0200 **Domicile State:** AZ **NAIC Code:** 76007

Data Date	Rating	RACR #1	RACR #2	Total Assets ($mil)	Capital ($mil)	Net Premium ($mil)	Net Income ($mil)
6-20	B	6.70	4.07	99.7	70.4	3.3	1.9
6-19	B	6.84	4.16	87.0	58.2	2.7	3.3
2019	B	6.39	3.89	95.9	65.1	6.4	4.1
2018	B	6.96	4.21	88.8	52.5	5.6	7.6
2017	B	6.47	4.50	84.7	47.8	6.1	2.9
2016	B	5.88	4.49	81.6	43.9	7.9	1.8
2015	B	5.56	5.01	82.5	42.0	6.2	4.2

Adverse Trends in Operations

Increase in policy surrenders from 2016 to 2017 (120%)
Decrease in premium volume from 2016 to 2017 (22%)
Decrease in asset base during 2016 (1%)
Increase in policy surrenders from 2015 to 2016 (152%)
Change in asset mix during 2016 (5.7%)

OMAHA INS CO

B-   Good

Major Rating Factors: Good current capitalization (6.8 on a scale of 0 to 10) based on good risk adjusted capital (severe loss scenario), although results have slipped from the excellent range during the last year. Good liquidity (5.9) with sufficient resources to handle a spike in claims. Fair overall results on stability tests (4.9) including negative cash flow from operations for 2019.

Other Rating Factors: Weak profitability (2.9) with operating losses during the first six months of 2020. High quality investment portfolio (7.4).

Principal Business: Individual health insurance (100%).

Principal Investments: NonCMO investment grade bonds (47%), CMOs and structured securities (42%), cash (3%), and noninv. grade bonds (2%).

Investments in Affiliates: None
Group Affiliation: Mutual Of Omaha Group
Licensed in: All states except FL, NH, NY, PR
Commenced Business: November 2006
Address: MUTUAL OF OMAHA PLAZA, OMAHA, NE 68175
Phone: (402) 342-7600 **Domicile State:** NE **NAIC Code:** 13100

Data Date	Rating	RACR #1	RACR #2	Total Assets ($mil)	Capital ($mil)	Net Premium ($mil)	Net Income ($mil)
6-20	B-	1.90	0.98	113.4	55.3	38.9	-0.8
6-19	B-	1.64	0.86	93.0	46.3	35.9	-3.9
2019	B-	1.97	1.02	109.5	54.9	73.6	-9.0
2018	B-	1.81	0.95	98.9	49.3	65.5	-6.7
2017	B-	1.84	0.97	98.3	45.2	56.2	-5.3
2016	C+	2.48	1.31	99.2	49.2	44.4	-5.4
2015	C+	3.70	1.97	88.2	54.1	29.3	-5.4

Risk-Adjusted Capital Ratio #2
(Severe Loss Scenario)

(Range, 2015, 2016, 2017, 2018, 2019, 6-20) — Weak, Fair, Good, Strong

ON LOK SENIOR HEALTH SERVICES
B   **Good**

Major Rating Factors: Good overall profitability index (5.8 on a scale of 0 to 10). Good overall results on stability tests (6.4). Strong capitalization index (9.5) based on excellent current risk-adjusted capital (severe loss scenario).
Other Rating Factors: Excellent liquidity (7.2) with ample operational cash flow and liquid investments.
Principal Business: Medicaid (72%), Medicare (27%)
Mem Phys: 19: N/A   **18:** N/A   **19 MLR** 91.0%   **/ 19 Admin Exp** N/A
Enroll(000): Q2 20: 2   **19:** 2   **18:** 2   **Med Exp PMPM:** $8,720
Principal Investments ($000): Cash and equiv ($6,475)
Provider Compensation ($000): None
Total Member Encounters: N/A
Group Affiliation: None
Licensed in: CA
Address: 1333 Bush Street, San Francisco, CA 94109
Phone: (415) 292-8722   **Dom State:** CA   **Commenced Bus:** September 1971

Data Date	Rating	RACR #1	RACR #2	Total Assets ($mil)	Capital ($mil)	Net Premium ($mil)	Net Income ($mil)
6-20	B	3.86	2.81	181.1	142.8	94.4	0.7
6-19	B	4.17	3.03	176.3	137.5	86.6	14.7
2019	B	3.86	2.81	178.8	142.1	174.4	22.3
2018	B	3.72	2.70	160.6	122.9	157.5	-7.0
2017	B	4.10	3.00	167.8	132.9	149.0	21.1
2016	B	3.94	2.85	141.6	106.0	133.2	11.0
2015	B	3.79	2.75	133.7	98.0	115.6	8.5

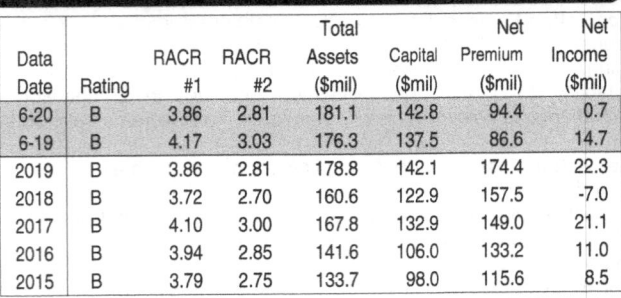

Rating Indexes

OPTIMA HEALTH INS CO
D+   **Weak**

Major Rating Factors: Weak profitability index (0.7 on a scale of 0 to 10). Weak liquidity (0.6) as a spike in claims may stretch capacity. Strong capitalization (7.0) based on excellent current risk-adjusted capital (severe loss scenario).
Other Rating Factors: High quality investment portfolio (9.5).
Principal Business: Comp med (100%)
Mem Phys: 19: 9,591   **18:** 9,222   **19 MLR** 102.5%   **/ 19 Admin Exp** N/A
Enroll(000): Q2 20: 6   **19:** 7   **18:** 7   **Med Exp PMPM:** $510
Principal Investments: Long-term bonds (82%), nonaffiliate common stock (12%), cash and equiv (7%)
Provider Compensation ($000): Contr fee ($37,247), bonus arrang ($848), capitation ($591)
Total Member Encounters: Phys (1,051), non-phys (12,224)
Group Affiliation: None
Licensed in: VA
Address: 4417 Corporation Lane, Virginia Beach, VA 23462
Phone: (757) 552-7401   **Dom State:** VA   **Commenced Bus:** N/A

Data Date	Rating	RACR #1	RACR #2	Total Assets ($mil)	Capital ($mil)	Net Premium ($mil)	Net Income ($mil)
6-20	D+	1.36	1.13	27.2	9.3	19.5	-3.3
6-19	C	2.89	2.41	27.9	13.3	28.3	-1.3
2019	D+	1.23	1.02	22.0	6.1	38.6	-7.8
2018	C	3.06	2.55	30.1	14.3	44.3	0.3
2017	C-	2.24	1.86	27.9	14.6	47.3	-1.8
2016	C	3.15	2.62	28.8	16.1	51.6	-1.5
2015	C	2.75	2.29	28.7	17.4	71.0	-1.5

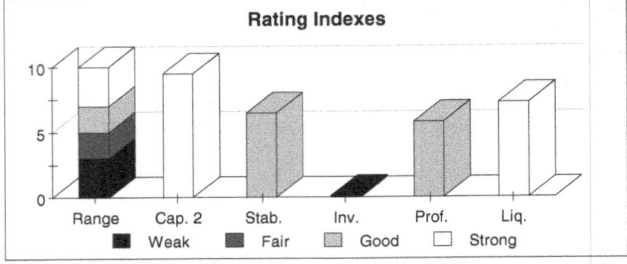

Rating Indexes

OPTIMA HEALTH PLAN
B   **Good**

Major Rating Factors: Good liquidity (6.9 on a scale of 0 to 10) with sufficient resources (cash flows and marketable investments) to handle a spike in claims. Fair profitability index (4.3). Fair overall results on stability tests (4.6) in spite of steady enrollment growth, averaging 6% over the past five years.
Other Rating Factors: Strong capitalization index (7.2) based on excellent current risk-adjusted capital (severe loss scenario). High quality investment portfolio (9.6).
Principal Business: Medicaid (71%), comp med (26%), Medicare (2%)
Mem Phys: 19: 18,667   **18:** 17,219   **19 MLR** 92.6%   **/ 19 Admin Exp** N/A
Enroll(000): Q2 20: 404   **19:** 360   **18:** 347   **Med Exp PMPM:** $529
Principal Investments: Long-term bonds (57%), cash and equiv (33%), nonaffiliate common stock (10%)
Provider Compensation ($000): Contr fee ($2,264,152), capitation ($37,279), bonus arrang ($16,619)
Total Member Encounters: Phys (665,547), non-phys (1,697,033)
Group Affiliation: None
Licensed in: VA
Address: 4417 Corporation Lane, Virginia Beach,
Phone: (757) 552-7401   **Dom State:** VA   **Commenced Bus:** N/A

Data Date	Rating	RACR #1	RACR #2	Total Assets ($mil)	Capital ($mil)	Net Premium ($mil)	Net Income ($mil)
6-20	B	1.54	1.29	803.2	309.3	1,368.3	35.7
6-19	A	1.99	1.66	812.6	351.9	1,201.6	30.9
2019	B+	1.38	1.15	688.6	277.9	2,437.7	-35.0
2018	A	1.76	1.47	791.9	315.6	2,376.0	139.3
2017	A-	2.03	1.69	476.7	244.2	1,502.6	15.7
2016	B+	1.92	1.60	372.9	222.6	1,423.6	9.6
2015	B+	1.96	1.63	352.3	212.4	1,357.3	15.5

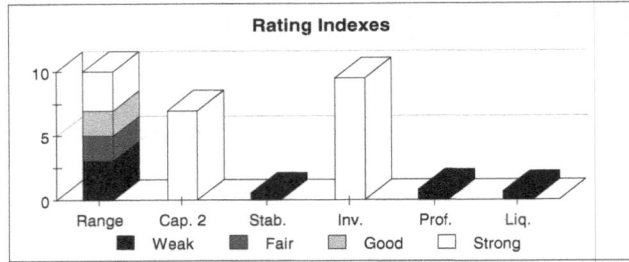

Rating Indexes

OPTIMUM CHOICE INC *   B+   Good

Major Rating Factors: Good overall results on stability tests (5.9 on a scale of 0 to 10). Good liquidity (6.7) with sufficient resources (cash flows and marketable investments) to handle a spike in claims. Excellent profitability (9.1).
Other Rating Factors: Strong capitalization index (8.5) based on excellent current risk-adjusted capital (severe loss scenario). High quality investment portfolio (9.2).
Principal Business: Comp med (97%), Medicare (3%)
Mem Phys: 19: 68,683 **18:** 67,323 **19 MLR** 80.4% **/ 19 Admin Exp** N/A
Enroll(000): Q2 20: 51 **19:** 54 **18:** 59 **Med Exp PMPM:** $325
Principal Investments: Long-term bonds (91%), cash and equiv (9%)
Provider Compensation ($000): Contr fee ($201,501), FFS ($12,788), capitation ($9,385), bonus arrang ($60)
Total Member Encounters: Phys (353,217), non-phys (21,241)
Group Affiliation: None
Licensed in: DC, DE, MD, VA, WV
Address: 800 KING FARM BLVD, ROCKVILLE,
Phone: (240) 632-8109 **Dom State:** MD **Commenced Bus:** N/A

Data Date	Rating	RACR #1	RACR #2	Total Assets ($mil)	Capital ($mil)	Net Premium ($mil)	Net Income ($mil)
6-20	B+	2.53	2.11	119.3	38.6	131.6	0.9
6-19	B	5.97	4.97	119.3	35.7	135.4	2.0
2019	B+	4.54	3.78	101.1	41.5	275.9	8.1
2018	B	5.69	4.75	99.0	33.9	272.3	21.1
2017	B	1.92	1.60	79.0	22.4	221.6	10.8
2016	C+	4.40	3.67	58.2	19.9	182.8	15.4
2015	C	4.71	3.93	60.6	22.8	197.2	15.9

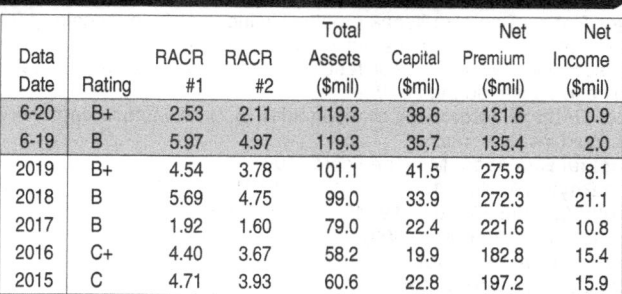

Rating Indexes

OPTIMUM HEALTHCARE INC   B   Good

Major Rating Factors: Good capitalization (6.8 on a scale of 0 to 10) based on excellent current risk-adjusted capital (severe loss scenario). Good liquidity (6.7) with sufficient resources (cash flows and marketable investments) to handle a spike in claims. Excellent profitability (7.8).
Other Rating Factors: High quality investment portfolio (8.1).
Principal Business: Medicare (100%)
Mem Phys: 19: 9,327 **18:** 16,489 **19 MLR** 84.1% **/ 19 Admin Exp** N/A
Enroll(000): Q2 20: 57 **19:** 54 **18:** 60 **Med Exp PMPM:** $928
Principal Investments: Long-term bonds (96%), other (5%)
Provider Compensation ($000): Capitation ($490,362), contr fee ($124,497), FFS ($1,284)
Total Member Encounters: Phys (31,626), non-phys (35,238)
Group Affiliation: Anthem Inc
Licensed in: FL
Address: 5600 MARINER STREET SUITE 227, INDIANAPOLIS, IN 46204
Phone: (813) 506-6000 **Dom State:** FL **Commenced Bus:** N/A

Data Date	Rating	RACR #1	RACR #2	Total Assets ($mil)	Capital ($mil)	Net Premium ($mil)	Net Income ($mil)
6-20	B	1.23	1.02	228.5	59.1	413.3	10.1
6-19	B	2.21	1.84	200.5	66.6	380.5	30.2
2019	B+	2.69	2.24	194.7	82.0	737.2	45.6
2018	B-	1.65	1.38	144.9	49.9	722.1	12.8
2017	E	0.87	0.72	125.6	35.7	611.6	12.0
2016	E-	0.75	0.62	112.5	30.5	529.9	6.7
2015	E-	0.67	0.56	73.7	25.9	415.7	2.6

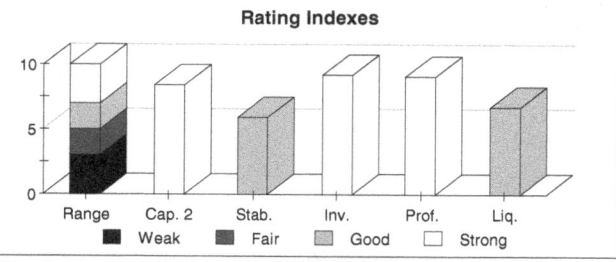

Rating Indexes

OSCAR GARDEN STATE INSURANCE   D   Weak

Major Rating Factors: Weak profitability index (0.4 on a scale of 0 to 10). Low quality investment portfolio (1.6). Strong capitalization (7.0) based on excellent current risk-adjusted capital (severe loss scenario).
Other Rating Factors: Excellent liquidity (7.4) with ample operational cash flow and liquid investments.
Principal Business: Comp med (100%)
Mem Phys: 18: 5,613 **17:** N/A **18 MLR** 152.3% **/ 18 Admin Exp** N/A
Enroll(000): Q3 19: 15 **18:** 11 **17:** N/A **Med Exp PMPM:** $250
Principal Investments: Cash and equiv (100%)
Provider Compensation ($000): FFS ($25,843), capitation ($3)
Total Member Encounters: Phys (14,422), non-phys (4,690)
Group Affiliation: None
Licensed in: NJ
Address: , West Trenton,
Phone: (646) 403-3677 **Dom State:** NJ **Commenced Bus:** N/A

Data Date	Rating	RACR #1	RACR #2	Total Assets ($mil)	Capital ($mil)	Net Premium ($mil)	Net Income ($mil)
9-19	D	1.37	1.14	51.2	6.0	13.1	-1.3
9-18	N/A	N/A	N/A	37.3	5.8	14.7	-5.4
2018	D	2.06	1.72	43.3	8.7	20.9	-9.1
2017	N/A	N/A	N/A	6.3	3.2	N/A	-2.6
2016	N/A	N/A	N/A	N/A	N/A	N/A	N/A
2015	N/A	N/A	N/A	N/A	N/A	N/A	N/A
2014	N/A	N/A	N/A	N/A	N/A	N/A	N/A

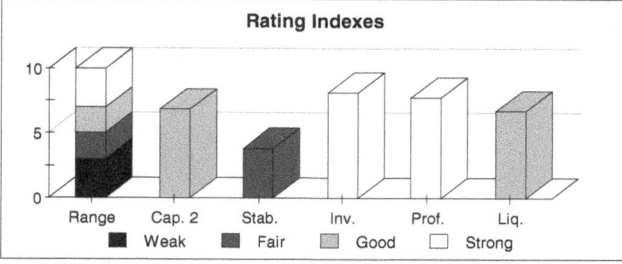

Rating Indexes

OSCAR HEALTH PLAN OF CALIFORNIA

E- Very Weak

Major Rating Factors: Weak profitability index (0.0 on a scale of 0 to 10). Poor capitalization index (0.0) based on weak current risk-adjusted capital (severe loss scenario). Weak overall results on stability tests (0.4) based on a steep decline in capital during 2019.
Other Rating Factors: Excellent liquidity (8.9) with ample operational cash flow and liquid investments.
Principal Business: Managed care (100%)
Mem Phys: 19: N/A **18:** N/A **19 MLR** 101.9% **/ 19 Admin Exp** N/A
Enroll(000): Q2 20: 104 **19:** 40 **18:** 40 **Med Exp PMPM:** $104
Principal Investments ($000): Cash and equiv ($84,046)
Provider Compensation ($000): None
Total Member Encounters: N/A
Group Affiliation: None
Licensed in: CA
Address: 3535 Hayden Avenue Suite 230, Culver City, CA 90232
Phone: (424) 261-4363 **Dom State:** CA **Commenced Bus:** N/A

Data Date	Rating	RACR #1	RACR #2	Total Assets ($mil)	Capital ($mil)	Net Premium ($mil)	Net Income ($mil)
6-20	E-	N/A	N/A	305.2	-107.2	41.5	-4.2
6-19	E-	N/A	N/A	174.4	-72.0	30.2	-7.4
2019	E-	N/A	N/A	221.9	-103.3	49.6	-38.6
2018	E-	N/A	N/A	114.9	-64.7	76.4	-17.5
2017	E-	N/A	N/A	35.0	-47.2	26.3	-20.2
2016	E-	N/A	N/A	16.4	-27.0	9.1	-20.8
2015	N/A	N/A	N/A	N/A	N/A	N/A	N/A

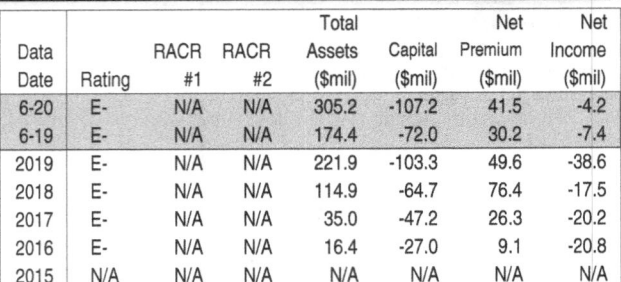

Rating Indexes

OSCAR INS CORP

E- Very Weak

Major Rating Factors: Weak profitability index (0.2 on a scale of 0 to 10). Good liquidity (6.6) with sufficient resources (cash flows and marketable investments) to handle a spike in claims. Strong capitalization (7.7) based on excellent current risk-adjusted capital (severe loss scenario).
Other Rating Factors: High quality investment portfolio (9.9).
Principal Business: Comp med (100%)
Mem Phys: 18: 20,295 **17:** 7,750 **18 MLR** 134.8% **/ 18 Admin Exp** N/A
Enroll(000): Q3 19: 53 **18:** 57 **17:** 43 **Med Exp PMPM:** $351
Principal Investments: Cash and equiv (92%), long-term bonds (8%)
Provider Compensation ($000): FFS ($228,666), capitation ($4,046)
Total Member Encounters: Phys (48,430), non-phys (39,978)
Group Affiliation: None
Licensed in: NY
Address: 75 Varick Street 5th Floor, New York, NY 10013
Phone: (646) 403-3677 **Dom State:** NY **Commenced Bus:** N/A

Data Date	Rating	RACR #1	RACR #2	Total Assets ($mil)	Capital ($mil)	Net Premium ($mil)	Net Income ($mil)
9-19	E-	1.91	1.59	142.6	16.9	116.1	-14.1
9-18	E-	N/A	N/A	251.2	41.3	134.8	1.4
2018	E-	2.59	2.16	187.5	28.0	180.4	-5.2
2017	E-	N/A	N/A	178.2	39.3	126.3	-62.8
2016	E-	1.42	1.18	148.8	45.2	246.3	-123.7
2015	D	1.10	0.92	118.6	21.3	117.4	-92.4
2014	N/A	N/A	N/A	60.0	27.3	56.9	N/A

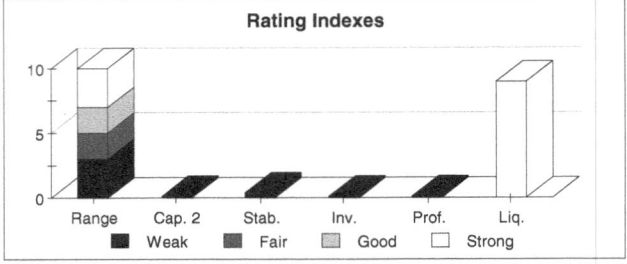

Rating Indexes

OSCAR INS CORP OF NEW JERSEY

D Weak

Major Rating Factors: Weak profitability index (0.9 on a scale of 0 to 10). Strong capitalization (10.0) based on excellent current risk-adjusted capital (severe loss scenario). High quality investment portfolio (9.9).
Other Rating Factors: Excellent liquidity (10.0) with ample operational cash flow and liquid investments.
Principal Business: Comp med (100%)
Mem Phys: 19: N/A **18:** N/A **19 MLR** 13.1% **/ 19 Admin Exp** N/A
Enroll(000): 19: N/A **18:** N/A **Med Exp PMPM:** N/A
Principal Investments: Cash and equiv (100%)
Provider Compensation ($000): FFS ($26)
Total Member Encounters: N/A
Group Affiliation: Mulberry Health Inc.
Licensed in: NJ
Address: 295 Lafayette St, West Trenton,
Phone: (646) 403-3677 **Dom State:** NJ **Commenced Bus:** N/A

Data Date	Rating	RACR #1	RACR #2	Total Assets ($mil)	Capital ($mil)	Net Premium ($mil)	Net Income ($mil)
2019	D	4.52	3.76	7.6	7.5	0.5	2.1
2018	D	3.79	3.15	5.4	5.4	0.3	0.1
2017	D	22.88	19.07	13.1	11.7	1.6	2.4
2016	D	1.09	0.91	70.4	10.2	82.1	-15.0
2015	N/A	N/A	N/A	14.9	4.6	9.0	-12.8

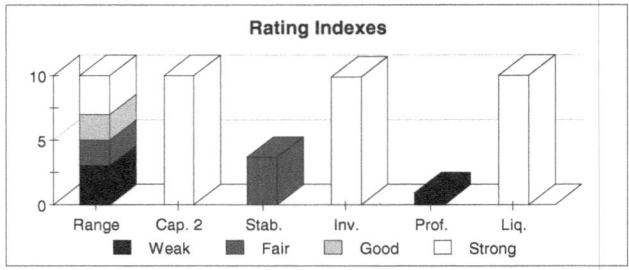

Rating Indexes

OSCAR INSURANCE COMPANY   D-   Weak

Major Rating Factors: Weak profitability index (0.5 on a scale of 0 to 10). Good capitalization (5.1) based on good current risk-adjusted capital (severe loss scenario). High quality investment portfolio (9.2).
Other Rating Factors: Excellent liquidity (7.2) with ample operational cash flow and liquid investments.
Principal Business: Comp med (100%)
Mem Phys: 18: 8,677 **17:** 2,539 **18 MLR** 108.2% **/ 18 Admin Exp** N/A
Enroll(000): Q3 19: 64 **18:** 102 **17:** 28 **Med Exp PMPM:** $298
Principal Investments: Cash and equiv (96%), long-term bonds (4%)
Provider Compensation ($000): FFS ($347,138), capitation ($1,854)
Total Member Encounters: Phys (64,124), non-phys (37,293)
Group Affiliation: None
Licensed in: CO, KS, MI, MO, TN, TX, VA
Address: 1999 Bryan Street Suite 900, Dallas, TX 75201
Phone: (646) 403-3677 **Dom State:** TX **Commenced Bus:** N/A

Data Date	Rating	RACR #1	RACR #2	Total Assets ($mil)	Capital ($mil)	Net Premium ($mil)	Net Income ($mil)
9-19	D-	0.95	0.79	255.4	32.2	81.9	-0.6
9-18	D-	N/A	N/A	291.4	56.0	269.9	1.9
2018	D-	1.72	1.44	301.1	58.4	359.8	-15.9
2017	D-	N/A	N/A	87.7	13.0	75.6	-46.7
2016	D	1.80	1.50	88.1	29.5	88.6	-45.2
2015	N/A	N/A	N/A	17.9	11.6	N/A	-9.1
2014	N/A	N/A	N/A	N/A	N/A	N/A	N/A

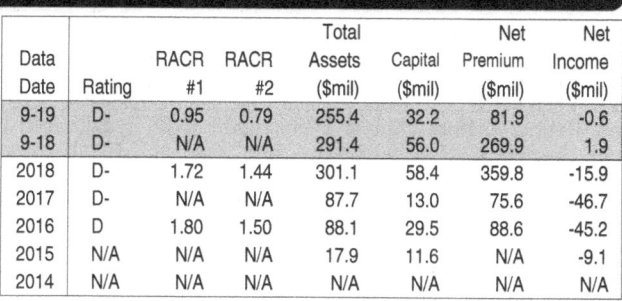

Rating Indexes

Range, Cap. 2, Stab., Inv., Prof., Liq.
Weak / Fair / Good / Strong

OSCAR INSURANCE CORP OF OHIO   D   Weak

Major Rating Factors: Fair profitability index (3.5 on a scale of 0 to 10). Strong capitalization (8.5) based on excellent current risk-adjusted capital (severe loss scenario). High quality investment portfolio (9.9).
Other Rating Factors: Excellent liquidity (7.3) with ample operational cash flow and liquid investments.
Principal Business: Comp med (100%)
Mem Phys: 18: 1,756 **17:** N/A **18 MLR** 86.7% **/ 18 Admin Exp** N/A
Enroll(000): Q3 19: 10 **18:** 10 **17:** N/A **Med Exp PMPM:** $587
Principal Investments: Cash and equiv (97%), long-term bonds (3%)
Provider Compensation ($000): FFS ($65,386), capitation ($160)
Total Member Encounters: Phys (10,654), non-phys (2,667)
Group Affiliation: None
Licensed in: OH
Address: 1300 East 9th St, Cleveland, OH 44114
Phone: (646) 403-3677 **Dom State:** OH **Commenced Bus:** N/A

Data Date	Rating	RACR #1	RACR #2	Total Assets ($mil)	Capital ($mil)	Net Premium ($mil)	Net Income ($mil)
9-19	D	2.60	2.16	43.6	31.5	71.0	10.7
9-18	N/A	N/A	N/A	30.5	16.8	65.3	0.4
2018	D	1.81	1.51	36.8	21.4	86.3	-2.0
2017	N/A	N/A	N/A	7.5	2.5	N/A	-1.4
2016	N/A	N/A	N/A	N/A	N/A	N/A	N/A
2015	N/A	N/A	N/A	N/A	N/A	N/A	N/A
2014	N/A	N/A	N/A	N/A	N/A	N/A	N/A

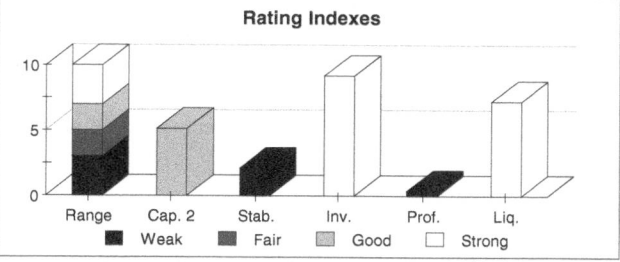

Rating Indexes

Range, Cap. 2, Stab., Inv., Prof., Liq.
Weak / Fair / Good / Strong

OXFORD HEALTH INS INC   B   Good

Major Rating Factors: Good liquidity (6.8 on a scale of 0 to 10) with sufficient resources (cash flows and marketable investments) to handle a spike in claims. Excellent profitability (8.7). Strong capitalization (9.2) based on excellent current risk-adjusted capital (severe loss scenario).
Other Rating Factors: High quality investment portfolio (9.3).
Principal Business: Comp med (97%), Medicare (3%)
Mem Phys: 19: 175,999 **18:** 149,439 **19 MLR** 82.9% **/ 19 Admin Exp** N/A
Enroll(000): Q2 20: 938 **19:** 1,010 **18:** 1,029 **Med Exp PMPM:** $582
Principal Investments: Long-term bonds (90%), cash and equiv (9%), other (2%)
Provider Compensation ($000): Contr fee ($5,198,687), FFS ($1,272,768), capitation ($587,125), bonus arrang ($11,299)
Total Member Encounters: Phys (10,069,811), non-phys (450,119)
Group Affiliation: None
Licensed in: CT, NJ, NY, PA
Address: ONE PENN PLAZA FLOOR 8, NEW YORK, NY 10119
Phone: (203) 447-4500 **Dom State:** NY **Commenced Bus:** N/A

Data Date	Rating	RACR #1	RACR #2	Total Assets ($mil)	Capital ($mil)	Net Premium ($mil)	Net Income ($mil)
6-20	B	3.11	2.59	3,058.9	1,455.2	3,934.9	127.9
6-19	B	3.12	2.60	2,971.4	1,375.8	4,279.7	227.0
2019	B	3.17	2.64	2,920.1	1,484.2	8,535.0	433.0
2018	B	3.03	2.52	2,624.1	1,334.3	8,182.0	410.7
2017	B+	3.55	2.96	2,570.1	1,331.0	7,217.1	365.4
2016	B	3.86	3.21	2,210.8	1,192.6	6,431.1	363.6
2015	B	4.35	3.62	2,195.0	1,257.2	5,819.0	418.5

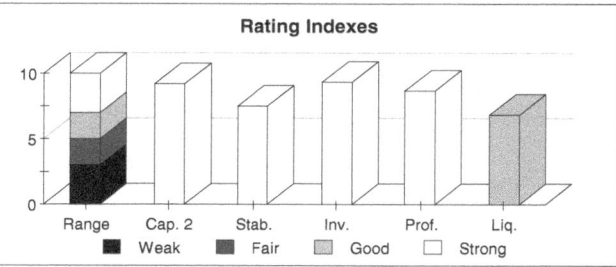

Rating Indexes

Range, Cap. 2, Stab., Inv., Prof., Liq.
Weak / Fair / Good / Strong

OXFORD HEALTH PLANS (CT) INC *

B+ **Good**

Major Rating Factors: Good overall results on stability tests (6.4 on a scale of 0 to 10) despite a decline in the number of member physicians during 2020. Good liquidity (6.8) with sufficient resources (cash flows and marketable investments) to handle a spike in claims. Excellent profitability (10.0)

Other Rating Factors: Strong capitalization index (7.5) based on excellent current risk-adjusted capital (severe loss scenario). High quality investment portfolio (9.9).

Principal Business: Medicare (97%), comp med (3%)

Mem Phys: 19: 50,009 **18:** 58,410 **19 MLR** 81.3% **/ 19 Admin Exp** N/A

Enroll(000): Q2 20: 157 **19:** 156 **18:** 157 **Med Exp PMPM:** $766

Principal Investments: Long-term bonds (98%), cash and equiv (2%)

Provider Compensation ($000): Contr fee ($1,085,962), FFS ($210,084), capitation ($130,254), bonus arrang ($15,790)

Total Member Encounters: Phys (2,941,006), non-phys (989,507)

Group Affiliation: None

Licensed in: CT, NJ

Address: 4 RESEARCH DRIVE, SHELTON,

Phone: (203) 447-4500 **Dom State:** CT **Commenced Bus:** N/A

Data Date	Rating	RACR #1	RACR #2	Total Assets ($mil)	Capital ($mil)	Net Premium ($mil)	Net Income ($mil)
6-20	B+	1.76	1.47	586.6	233.2	890.2	40.7
6-19	B	2.52	2.10	541.5	211.1	889.6	56.8
2019	B+	2.07	1.72	569.6	199.0	1,768.4	90.6
2018	B	2.20	1.84	554.6	183.8	1,661.7	80.9
2017	B-	1.55	1.29	485.6	155.5	1,450.1	78.4
2016	B-	3.61	3.01	220.1	88.7	476.1	8.2
2015	C	3.73	3.11	178.7	79.7	456.1	32.2

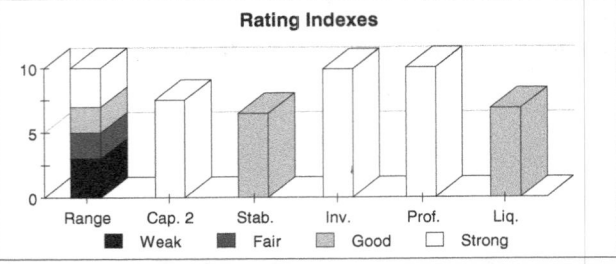

Rating Indexes
Range | Cap. 2 | Stab. | Inv. | Prof. | Liq.
■ Weak ■ Fair ▨ Good ▢ Strong

OXFORD HEALTH PLANS (NJ) INC

B **Good**

Major Rating Factors: Fair overall results on stability tests (4.7 on a scale of 0 to 10) based on a decline in the number of member physicians during 2020. Excellent profitability (9.1). Strong capitalization index (9.3) based on excellent current risk-adjusted capital (severe loss scenario)

Other Rating Factors: High quality investment portfolio (7.1). Excellent liquidity (7.1) with ample operational cash flow and liquid investments.

Principal Business: Medicare (100%)

Mem Phys: 19: 138,682 **18:** 166,357 **19 MLR** 78.7% **/ 19 Admin Exp** N/A

Enroll(000): Q2 20: 52 **19:** 48 **18:** 44 **Med Exp PMPM:** $1,135

Principal Investments: Long-term bonds (67%), cash and equiv (33%)

Provider Compensation ($000): Contr fee ($354,396), capitation ($224,956), FFS ($64,203), bonus arrang ($4,369)

Total Member Encounters: Phys (805,898), non-phys (392,299)

Group Affiliation: None

Licensed in: DE, MO, NJ, OR, PA, RI

Address: 170 WOOD AVENUE FLOOR 3, ISELIN,

Phone: (203) 447-4500 **Dom State:** NJ **Commenced Bus:** N/A

Data Date	Rating	RACR #1	RACR #2	Total Assets ($mil)	Capital ($mil)	Net Premium ($mil)	Net Income ($mil)
6-20	B	3.21	2.67	369.2	170.9	492.2	43.1
6-19	B	7.26	6.05	259.7	160.0	393.9	30.9
2019	B	4.59	3.83	255.8	175.5	806.6	65.1
2018	B	6.71	5.60	269.5	147.2	576.3	40.9
2017	B	4.91	4.09	268.8	146.1	412.7	38.2
2016	B	2.21	1.84	302.8	117.2	1,057.0	48.9
2015	B	2.35	1.96	289.5	121.0	970.1	14.6

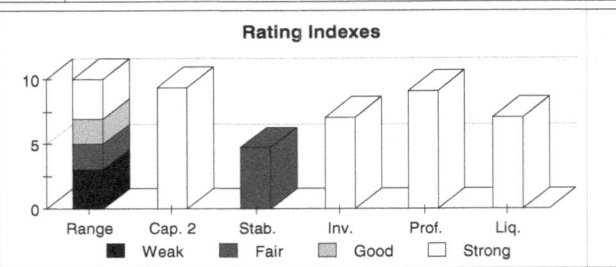

Rating Indexes
Range | Cap. 2 | Stab. | Inv. | Prof. | Liq.
■ Weak ■ Fair ▨ Good ▢ Strong

OXFORD HEALTH PLANS (NY) INC

B **Good**

Major Rating Factors: Fair profitability index (4.6 on a scale of 0 to 10). Fair overall results on stability tests (4.4). Strong capitalization index (10.0) based on excellent current risk-adjusted capital (severe loss scenario).

Other Rating Factors: High quality investment portfolio (9.2). Excellent liquidity (6.9) with sufficient resources (cash flows and marketable investments) to handle a spike in claims.

Principal Business: Medicare (100%)

Mem Phys: 19: 80,953 **18:** 77,487 **19 MLR** 83.3% **/ 19 Admin Exp** N/A

Enroll(000): Q2 20: 55 **19:** 73 **18:** 85 **Med Exp PMPM:** $735

Principal Investments: Long-term bonds (86%), cash and equiv (14%)

Provider Compensation ($000): Contr fee ($564,656), FFS ($84,889), bonus arrang ($8,517), capitation ($4,618)

Total Member Encounters: Phys (1,509,921), non-phys (372,955)

Group Affiliation: None

Licensed in: NY

Address: ONE PENN PLAZA FLOOR 8, NEW YORK,

Phone: (203) 447-4500 **Dom State:** NY **Commenced Bus:** N/A

Data Date	Rating	RACR #1	RACR #2	Total Assets ($mil)	Capital ($mil)	Net Premium ($mil)	Net Income ($mil)
6-20	B	5.14	4.29	487.6	315.8	318.9	40.2
6-19	B	4.93	4.11	448.7	263.4	398.4	22.3
2019	B	6.00	5.00	463.6	275.8	780.5	33.6
2018	B	4.54	3.78	471.6	240.9	871.1	-0.7
2017	B+	3.15	2.62	546.7	267.2	1,105.0	-14.2
2016	B+	3.01	2.51	614.8	282.4	1,707.7	22.4
2015	A	5.32	4.43	821.9	474.7	1,793.4	110.0

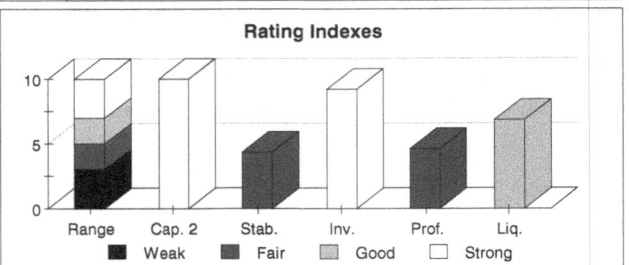

Rating Indexes
Range | Cap. 2 | Stab. | Inv. | Prof. | Liq.
■ Weak ■ Fair ▨ Good ▢ Strong

PA HEALTH & WELLNESS INC　　　　　　　　B-　　　Good

Major Rating Factors: Fair quality investment portfolio (4.0 on a scale of 0 to 10). Excellent profitability (7.5). Strong capitalization (10.0) based on excellent current risk-adjusted capital (severe loss scenario).
Other Rating Factors: Excellent liquidity (7.1) with ample operational cash flow and liquid investments.
Principal Business: Medicaid (99%), Medicare (1%)
Mem Phys: 18: 26,855　**17:** N/A　**18 MLR** 96.1%　**/ 18 Admin Exp** N/A
Enroll(000): Q3 19: 55　**18:** 23　**17:** N/A　**Med Exp PMPM:** $1,739
Principal Investments: Cash and equiv (77%), long-term bonds (23%)
Provider Compensation ($000): Contr fee ($412,112), salary ($14,447), capitation ($972)
Total Member Encounters: Phys (119,241), non-phys (858,125)
Group Affiliation: None
Licensed in: PA
Address: 300 Corporate Center Drive, Camp Hill, PA 17011
Phone: (314) 725-4477　**Dom State:** PA　**Commenced Bus:** N/A

Data Date	Rating	RACR #1	RACR #2	Total Assets ($mil)	Capital ($mil)	Net Premium ($mil)	Net Income ($mil)
9-19	B-	5.42	4.52	359.8	177.4	1,171.3	3.2
9-18	N/A	N/A	N/A	99.8	36.4	354.2	1.2
2018	C-	2.10	1.75	126.3	68.7	483.4	1.5
2017	N/A	N/A	N/A	1.6	1.6	N/A	N/A
2016	N/A	N/A	N/A	1.5	1.5	N/A	N/A
2015	N/A	N/A	N/A	N/A	N/A	N/A	N/A
2014	N/A	N/A	N/A	N/A	N/A	N/A	N/A

Rating Indexes

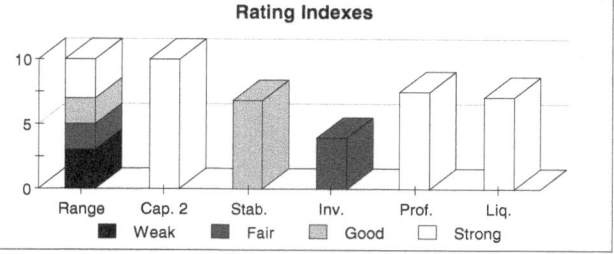

Range　Cap. 2　Stab.　Inv.　Prof.　Liq.
■ Weak　■ Fair　▥ Good　□ Strong

PACIFIC GUARDIAN LIFE INS CO LTD *　　　B+　　　Good

Major Rating Factors: Good overall results on stability tests (6.5 on a scale of 0 to 10). Stability strengths include excellent operational trends and excellent risk diversification. Good quality investment portfolio (6.6) despite large exposure to mortgages . Mortgage default rate has been low. substantial holdings of BBB bonds in addition to minimal holdings in junk bonds. Good liquidity (5.9).
Other Rating Factors: Fair profitability (4.7) with investment income below regulatory standards in relation to interest assumptions of reserves. Strong capitalization (8.0) based on excellent risk adjusted capital (severe loss scenario).
Principal Business: Group health insurance (54%), individual life insurance (36%), and group life insurance (10%).
Principal Investments: Mortgages in good standing (39%), nonCMO investment grade bonds (38%), CMOs and structured securities (14%), policy loans (6%), and misc. investments (3%).
Investments in Affiliates: None
Group Affiliation: Meiji Yasuda Life Ins Co
Licensed in: AK, AZ, CA, CO, HI, ID, IA, LA, MO, MT, NE, NV, NM, OK, OR, SD, TX, UT, WA, WY
Commenced Business: June 1962
Address: 1440 Kapiolani Blvd Ste 1600, Honolulu, HI 96814-3698
Phone: (808) 955-2236　**Domicile State:** HI　**NAIC Code:** 64343

Data Date	Rating	RACR #1	RACR #2	Total Assets ($mil)	Capital ($mil)	Net Premium ($mil)	Net Income ($mil)
6-20	B+	2.82	1.66	579.2	85.1	41.5	0.3
6-19	A-	3.07	1.78	565.8	86.3	44.7	1.1
2019	B+	2.96	1.76	565.5	86.5	77.1	1.4
2018	A-	3.47	2.03	556.9	94.0	77.7	4.8
2017	A-	3.96	2.31	553.9	102.4	74.4	4.0
2016	A-	4.30	2.51	543.1	107.1	74.3	5.2
2015	A-	4.52	2.62	528.4	108.5	70.2	6.7

Adverse Trends in Operations

Decrease in capital during 2019 (8%)
Decrease in capital during 2018 (8%)
Decrease in capital during 2017 (4%)
Decrease in capital during 2016 (1%)

PACIFICARE LIFE & HEALTH INS CO　　　　B-　　　Good

Major Rating Factors: Good overall results on stability tests (5.3 on a scale of 0 to 10) despite fair financial strength of affiliated UnitedHealth Group Inc. Other stability subfactors include excellent operational trends and excellent risk diversification. Strong capitalization (10.0) based on excellent risk adjusted capital (severe loss scenario). High quality investment portfolio (8.2).
Other Rating Factors: Excellent profitability (7.4) with operating gains in each of the last five years. Excellent liquidity (9.8).
Principal Business: Individual health insurance (72%) and group health insurance (28%).
Principal Investments: NonCMO investment grade bonds (75%) and CMOs and structured securities (25%).
Investments in Affiliates: None
Group Affiliation: UnitedHealth Group Inc
Licensed in: All states except NY, PR
Commenced Business: September 1967
Address: 7440 WOODLAND DRIVE, INDIANAPOLIS, IN 46278
Phone: (612) 383-4182　**Domicile State:** IN　**NAIC Code:** 70785

Data Date	Rating	RACR #1	RACR #2	Total Assets ($mil)	Capital ($mil)	Net Premium ($mil)	Net Income ($mil)
6-20	B-	19.29	17.36	193.9	188.7	5.7	2.7
6-19	B	18.87	16.99	188.9	184.1	6.1	1.7
2019	B	19.02	17.12	191.0	186.0	12.0	3.6
2018	B	18.71	16.84	187.5	182.4	12.8	4.3
2017	B	18.62	16.75	187.3	181.5	13.6	3.4
2016	C+	18.52	16.67	189.2	180.8	14.3	3.2
2015	C+	19.90	17.91	205.7	197.4	15.8	4.1

UnitedHealth Group Inc Composite Group Rating: C Largest Group Members	Assets ($mil)	Rating
UNITED HEALTHCARE INS CO	20997	C
SIERRA HEALTH AND LIFE INS CO INC	5301	B
OXFORD HEALTH INS INC	2920	B
UNITED HEALTHCARE OF WISCONSIN INC	2069	B+
UNITED HEALTHCARE INS CO OF NY	1472	B

PACIFICARE LIFE ASR CO
C   **Fair**

Major Rating Factors: Fair profitability index (3.5 on a scale of 0 to 10). Low quality investment portfolio (1.6). Strong capitalization (8.2) based on excellent current risk-adjusted capital (severe loss scenario).
Other Rating Factors: Excellent liquidity (7.5) with ample operational cash flow and liquid investments.
Principal Business: Medicare (100%)
Mem Phys: 19: 313,476 18: 21,168 **19 MLR** 79.7% / **19 Admin Exp** N/A
Enroll(000): Q2 20: 9 **19:** 4 **18:** N/A **Med Exp PMPM:** $639
Principal Investments: Cash and equiv (87%), long-term bonds (13%)
Provider Compensation ($000): Contr fee ($18,331), FFS ($1,830), capitation ($323), bonus arrang ($19)
Total Member Encounters: Phys (56,513), non-phys (18,713)
Group Affiliation: None
Licensed in: AZ, CA, CO, MN, NV, NM, ND, OK, OR, TX, UT, WA
Address: 1675 BROADWAY SUITE 1200, DENVER, CO 80202-0000
Phone: (860) 702-7807 **Dom State:** CO **Commenced Bus:** N/A

Data Date	Rating	RACR #1	RACR #2	Total Assets ($mil)	Capital ($mil)	Net Premium ($mil)	Net Income ($mil)
6-20	C	2.33	1.95	26.1	11.7	42.7	2.1
6-19	U	345.00	287.50	16.4	9.8	13.8	2.7
2019	C+	3.85	3.21	17.9	10.9	29.7	3.8
2018	U	75.03	62.52	6.2	2.1	N/A	-3.1
2017	U	N/A	N/A	5.9	5.0	N/A	0.1
2016	U	21.45	17.87	8.1	7.1	N/A	0.2
2015	N/A	N/A	N/A	8.0	6.9	N/A	0.2

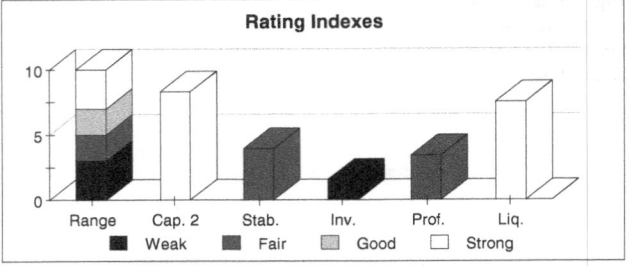

Rating Indexes

PACIFICARE OF COLORADO INC
B   **Good**

Major Rating Factors: Fair overall results on stability tests (4.8 on a scale of 0 to 10). Excellent profitability (8.9). Strong capitalization index (7.8) based on excellent current risk-adjusted capital (severe loss scenario).
Other Rating Factors: High quality investment portfolio (7.9). Excellent liquidity (6.9) with sufficient resources (cash flows and marketable investments) to handle a spike in claims.
Principal Business: Medicare (100%)
Mem Phys: 19: 51,580 18: 46,288 **19 MLR** 83.0% / **19 Admin Exp** N/A
Enroll(000): Q2 20: 341 **19:** 334 **18:** 295 **Med Exp PMPM:** $859
Principal Investments: Long-term bonds (93%), cash and equiv (7%)
Provider Compensation ($000): Capitation ($1,956,025), contr fee ($1,278,141), FFS ($159,963), bonus arrang ($50,817)
Total Member Encounters: Phys (2,533,954), non-phys (609,868)
Group Affiliation: None
Licensed in: AZ, CO, NV
Address: 6465 GREENWOOD PLAZA BLVD SUIT, CENTENNIAL,
Phone: (952) 979-7959 **Dom State:** CO **Commenced Bus:** N/A

Data Date	Rating	RACR #1	RACR #2	Total Assets ($mil)	Capital ($mil)	Net Premium ($mil)	Net Income ($mil)
6-20	B	1.96	1.63	877.0	443.4	2,262.4	95.8
6-19	B	3.57	2.98	790.8	520.0	2,107.3	135.1
2019	B+	2.81	2.34	772.9	502.9	4,143.5	252.7
2018	B	2.66	2.22	664.6	387.2	3,243.6	137.6
2017	B	1.69	1.41	601.9	279.0	2,839.8	97.0
2016	B	1.75	1.46	412.6	182.6	2,469.4	73.4
2015	B	2.78	2.32	209.8	109.3	973.1	43.1

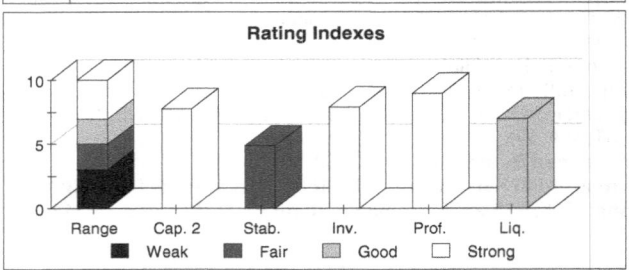

Rating Indexes

PACIFICSOURCE COMMUNITY HEALTH PLANS
B   **Good**

Major Rating Factors: Good overall profitability index (6.2 on a scale of 0 to 10). Good liquidity (6.6) with sufficient resources (cash flows and marketable investments) to handle a spike in claims. Fair quality investment portfolio (3.4).
Other Rating Factors: Strong capitalization (9.3) based on excellent current risk-adjusted capital (severe loss scenario).
Principal Business: Medicare (100%)
Mem Phys: 19: 17,200 18: 20,700 **19 MLR** 85.1% / **19 Admin Exp** N/A
Enroll(000): Q2 20: 36 **19:** 33 **18:** 30 **Med Exp PMPM:** $742
Principal Investments: Affiliate common stock (60%), long-term bonds (31%), nonaffiliate common stock (9%), cash and equiv (1%)
Provider Compensation ($000): Contr fee ($198,814), bonus arrang ($97,497), FFS ($4,877), capitation ($979)
Total Member Encounters: Phys (274,021), non-phys (87,266)
Group Affiliation: None
Licensed in: ID, MT, OR, WA
Address: 2965 NE Conners Ave, Bend, OR 97701
Phone: (541) 385-5315 **Dom State:** OR **Commenced Bus:** N/A

Data Date	Rating	RACR #1	RACR #2	Total Assets ($mil)	Capital ($mil)	Net Premium ($mil)	Net Income ($mil)
6-20	B	3.15	2.63	218.7	169.9	198.7	14.5
6-19	B	3.14	2.62	152.7	100.9	173.2	4.4
2019	B	3.20	2.67	195.5	156.5	343.6	3.6
2018	B	2.64	2.20	127.9	86.4	309.2	-2.4
2017	B-	1.86	1.55	123.4	71.4	357.2	27.0
2016	C	1.92	1.60	123.1	66.4	345.1	5.5
2015	C	1.86	1.55	101.6	59.3	301.1	4.2

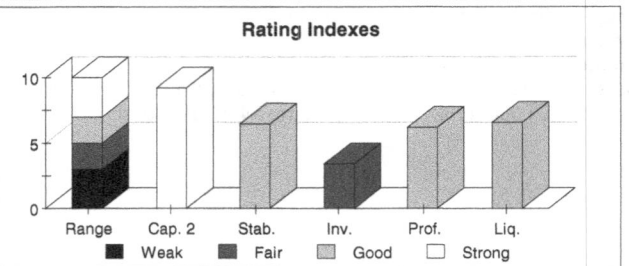

Rating Indexes

PACIFICSOURCE HEALTH PLANS   B-   Good

Major Rating Factors: Fair quality investment portfolio (4.7 on a scale of 0 to 10). Good profitability index (5.0). Good liquidity (6.5) with sufficient resources (cash flows and marketable investments) to handle a spike in claims.
Other Rating Factors: Strong capitalization (8.6) based on excellent current risk-adjusted capital (severe loss scenario).
Principal Business: Comp med (97%), dental (2%), other (1%)
Mem Phys: 19: 49,400 **18:** 51,200 **19 MLR** 87.8% **/ 19 Admin Exp** N/A
Enroll(000): Q2 20: 251 **19:** 249 **18:** 229 **Med Exp PMPM:** $272
Principal Investments: Affiliate common stock (45%), long-term bonds (36%), cash and equiv (11%), nonaffiliate common stock (9%)
Provider Compensation ($000): Contr fee ($485,416), FFS ($259,381), bonus arrang ($41,513), capitation ($434)
Total Member Encounters: Phys (500,406), non-phys (532,973)
Group Affiliation: None
Licensed in: ID, MT, OR, WA
Address: 110 INTERNATIONAL WAY, SPRINGFIELD, OR 97477
Phone: (541) 686-1242 **Dom State:** OR **Commenced Bus:** N/A

Data Date	Rating	RACR #1	RACR #2	Total Assets ($mil)	Capital ($mil)	Net Premium ($mil)	Net Income ($mil)
6-20	B-	2.65	2.20	519.0	349.6	489.1	37.3
6-19	B-	2.44	2.04	376.5	240.3	453.7	12.5
2019	B-	2.27	1.89	447.7	289.9	919.6	24.9
2018	C+	2.09	1.74	319.9	209.0	800.7	13.9
2017	C	1.73	1.44	275.2	165.9	698.9	20.2
2016	C	1.84	1.54	238.1	157.4	547.9	-21.1
2015	C	1.72	1.43	228.9	144.4	564.8	-10.2

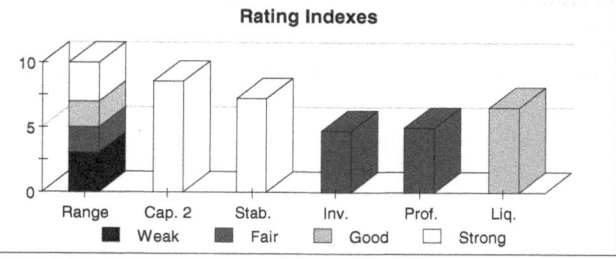

Rating Indexes

Range / Cap. 2 / Stab. / Inv. / Prof. / Liq.
■ Weak ■ Fair ▨ Good □ Strong

PAN-AMERICAN LIFE INS CO   B   Good

Major Rating Factors: Good overall results on stability tests (6.0 on a scale of 0 to 10). Stability strengths include good operational trends and excellent risk diversification. Good quality investment portfolio (5.4) despite mixed results such as: minimal exposure to mortgages and large holdings of BBB rated bonds but small junk bond holdings. Good overall profitability (5.8).
Other Rating Factors: Good liquidity (6.7). Strong capitalization (7.9) based on excellent risk adjusted capital (severe loss scenario).
Principal Business: Group health insurance (55%), reinsurance (32%), individual life insurance (6%), individual health insurance (4%), and group life insurance (3%).
Principal Investments: NonCMO investment grade bonds (50%), CMOs and structured securities (23%), policy loans (5%), common & preferred stock (5%), and misc. investments (14%).
Investments in Affiliates: 2%
Group Affiliation: Pan-American Life
Licensed in: All states except ME, NY, VT
Commenced Business: March 1912
Address: PAN-AMERICAN LIFE CENTER, NEW ORLEANS, LA 70130-6060
Phone: (504) 566-1300 **Domicile State:** LA **NAIC Code:** 67539

Data Date	Rating	RACR #1	RACR #2	Total Assets ($mil)	Capital ($mil)	Net Premium ($mil)	Net Income ($mil)
6-20	B	2.50	1.59	1,279.8	255.8	141.2	7.6
6-19	B	2.28	1.51	1,286.5	252.3	223.8	9.0
2019	B	2.26	1.46	1,276.3	231.6	344.6	5.1
2018	B	2.48	1.61	1,205.2	243.6	217.1	15.5
2017	B	2.41	1.53	1,221.1	234.1	212.9	14.5
2016	B	2.53	1.60	1,260.9	244.6	226.5	21.3
2015	B	2.52	1.62	1,293.7	244.9	237.9	22.0

Adverse Trends in Operations

Decrease in capital during 2019 (5%)
Decrease in asset base during 2018 (1%)
Decrease in capital during 2017 (4%)
Decrease in asset base during 2016 (3%)
Decrease in premium volume from 2015 to 2016 (5%)

PARAMOUNT ADVANTAGE   D   Weak

Major Rating Factors: Fair profitability index (3.1 on a scale of 0 to 10). Good liquidity (5.6) with sufficient resources (cash flows and marketable investments) to handle a spike in claims. Strong capitalization (7.3) based on excellent current risk-adjusted capital (severe loss scenario).
Other Rating Factors: High quality investment portfolio (9.7).
Principal Business: Medicaid (100%)
Mem Phys: 19: 61,879 **18:** 24,310 **19 MLR** 91.7% **/ 19 Admin Exp** N/A
Enroll(000): Q2 20: 213 **19:** 215 **18:** 238 **Med Exp PMPM:** $485
Principal Investments: Long-term bonds (70%), cash and equiv (22%), nonaffiliate common stock (8%)
Provider Compensation ($000): Contr fee ($825,745), FFS ($446,496), capitation ($77,877)
Total Member Encounters: Phys (424,790), non-phys (68,178)
Group Affiliation: ProMedica Health System Inc
Licensed in: OH
Address: 1901 Indian Wood Circle, Maumee, OH 43537
Phone: (419) 887-2500 **Dom State:** OH **Commenced Bus:** N/A

Data Date	Rating	RACR #1	RACR #2	Total Assets ($mil)	Capital ($mil)	Net Premium ($mil)	Net Income ($mil)
6-20	D	1.61	1.34	390.8	205.2	780.9	66.6
6-19	D	0.62	0.51	211.2	56.8	717.7	-85.2
2019	D	1.15	0.96	322.5	142.5	1,493.1	-72.9
2018	B	1.35	1.13	289.6	140.2	1,341.1	-23.5
2017	A-	2.06	1.72	303.4	169.4	1,144.9	27.6
2016	A-	1.81	1.51	290.4	135.3	1,000.4	-12.8
2015	A-	2.13	1.78	269.5	146.2	1,004.2	47.2

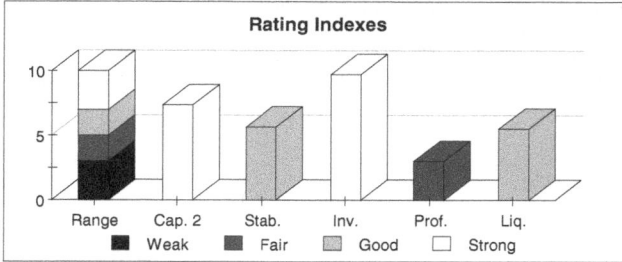

Rating Indexes

Range / Cap. 2 / Stab. / Inv. / Prof. / Liq.
■ Weak ■ Fair ▨ Good □ Strong

PARAMOUNT CARE OF MI INC

D+   **Weak**

Major Rating Factors: Weak overall results on stability tests (0.6 on a scale of 0 to 10) in spite of steady enrollment growth, averaging 5% over the past five years. Excellent profitability (7.8). Strong capitalization index (7.0) based on excellent current risk-adjusted capital (severe loss scenario).
Other Rating Factors: High quality investment portfolio (9.7). Excellent liquidity (7.3) with ample operational cash flow and liquid investments.
Principal Business: Medicare (100%)
Mem Phys: 19: 7,339   **18:** 2,182   **19 MLR** 89.1%   **/ 19 Admin Exp** N/A
Enroll(000): Q2 20: 3   **19:** 2   **18:** 2   **Med Exp PMPM:** $854
Principal Investments: Cash and equiv (100%)
Provider Compensation ($000): Contr fee ($16,409), FFS ($5,156)
Total Member Encounters: Phys (5,267), non-phys (447)
Group Affiliation: ProMedica Health System Inc
Licensed in: MI
Address: 106 Park Place, Dundee,
Phone: (734) 529-7800   **Dom State:** MI   **Commenced Bus:** N/A

Data Date	Rating	RACR #1	RACR #2	Total Assets ($mil)	Capital ($mil)	Net Premium ($mil)	Net Income ($mil)
6-20	D+	1.37	1.14	10.3	6.7	14.3	1.2
6-19	B	4.19	3.49	16.3	13.2	12.0	1.0
2019	C-	1.57	1.31	8.1	5.5	24.3	1.2
2018	B	3.98	3.32	15.3	12.2	22.9	1.5
2017	B	2.88	2.40	15.2	11.2	21.7	2.0
2016	B	4.46	3.72	14.9	11.7	22.3	2.8
2015	B-	3.17	2.64	11.1	8.5	18.7	1.2

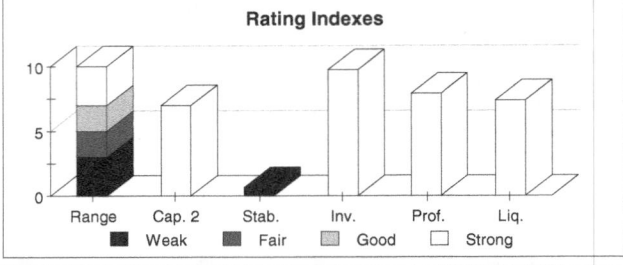

Rating Indexes

PARAMOUNT HEALTH CARE

D   **Weak**

Major Rating Factors: Weak overall results on stability tests (0.4 on a scale of 0 to 10). Fair profitability index (4.0). Good capitalization index (6.8) based on excellent current risk-adjusted capital (severe loss scenario).
Other Rating Factors: High quality investment portfolio (9.9). Excellent liquidity (7.1) with ample operational cash flow and liquid investments.
Principal Business: Medicare (100%)
Mem Phys: 19: 9,884   **18:** 3,081   **19 MLR** 91.9%   **/ 19 Admin Exp** N/A
Enroll(000): Q2 20: 14   **19:** 14   **18:** 14   **Med Exp PMPM:** $977
Principal Investments: Cash and equiv (87%), long-term bonds (13%)
Provider Compensation ($000): Contr fee ($129,194), FFS ($37,757)
Total Member Encounters: Phys (41,038), non-phys (4,168)
Group Affiliation: ProMedica Health System Inc
Licensed in: OH
Address: 1901 Indian Wood Circle, Maumee,
Phone: (419) 887-2500   **Dom State:** OH   **Commenced Bus:** N/A

Data Date	Rating	RACR #1	RACR #2	Total Assets ($mil)	Capital ($mil)	Net Premium ($mil)	Net Income ($mil)
6-20	D	1.22	1.02	72.3	26.0	93.0	8.7
6-19	B	4.09	3.40	97.2	66.4	91.6	3.1
2019	C-	1.35	1.13	54.8	22.9	182.6	0.7
2018	B	3.97	3.31	92.4	62.9	170.9	0.5
2017	C+	4.23	3.52	106.3	70.7	169.9	12.6
2016	C	4.79	3.99	105.3	74.2	176.5	10.4
2015	C	4.10	3.42	91.6	64.5	150.8	-6.5

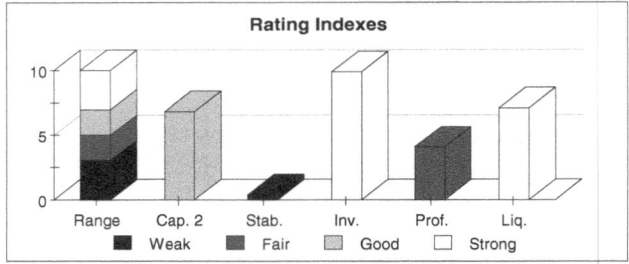

Rating Indexes

PARAMOUNT INS CO (OH)

C-   **Fair**

Major Rating Factors: Excellent profitability (7.6 on a scale of 0 to 10). Strong capitalization (7.1) based on excellent current risk-adjusted capital (severe loss scenario). High quality investment portfolio (9.6).
Other Rating Factors: Excellent liquidity (7.3) with ample operational cash flow and liquid investments.
Principal Business: Comp med (98%), med supp (2%)
Mem Phys: 19: 9,884   **18:** 3,081   **19 MLR** 83.3%   **/ 19 Admin Exp** N/A
Enroll(000): Q2 20: 33   **19:** 30   **18:** 31   **Med Exp PMPM:** $355
Principal Investments: Cash and equiv (70%), long-term bonds (22%), nonaffiliate common stock (7%)
Provider Compensation ($000): FFS ($85,043), contr fee ($41,783)
Total Member Encounters: Phys (30,836), non-phys (3,576)
Group Affiliation: ProMedica Health System Inc
Licensed in: MI, OH
Address: 1901 Indian Wood Circle, Maumee, OH 43537
Phone: (419) 887-2500   **Dom State:** OH   **Commenced Bus:** N/A

Data Date	Rating	RACR #1	RACR #2	Total Assets ($mil)	Capital ($mil)	Net Premium ($mil)	Net Income ($mil)
6-20	C-	1.47	1.22	73.7	27.2	76.0	3.8
6-19	B+	2.80	2.33	84.6	45.9	74.9	2.5
2019	C	1.64	1.36	64.1	24.4	149.6	7.0
2018	A-	2.63	2.19	86.2	41.9	184.1	13.5
2017	A-	1.87	1.56	89.3	35.0	160.9	9.8
2016	B+	2.10	1.75	87.5	30.7	158.0	5.3
2015	B	1.94	1.62	68.8	25.1	146.9	4.6

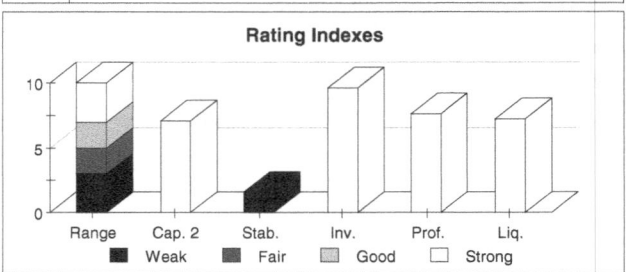

Rating Indexes

PARKLAND COMMUNITY HEALTH PLAN INC   C   Fair

Major Rating Factors: Weak profitability index (2.7 on a scale of 0 to 10). Weak overall results on stability tests (2.6). Good quality investment portfolio (6.1).

Other Rating Factors: Good liquidity (6.0) with sufficient resources (cash flows and marketable investments) to handle a spike in claims. Strong capitalization index (7.8) based on excellent current risk-adjusted capital (severe loss scenario).

Principal Business: Medicaid (91%), comp med (9%)

Mem Phys: 19: 6,932   **18:** 7,258   **19 MLR** 89.2%   **/ 19 Admin Exp** N/A

Enroll(000): Q2 20: 184   **19:** 169   **18:** 183   **Med Exp PMPM:** $237

Principal Investments: Long-term bonds (67%), cash and equiv (33%)

Provider Compensation ($000): Contr fee ($501,147), capitation ($4,857)

Total Member Encounters: Phys (1,377,908), non-phys (488,519)

Group Affiliation: Parkland Community Health Plan Inc

Licensed in: TX

Address: 2777 N Stemmons Freeway Suite, Dallas,

Phone: (214) 266-2100   **Dom State:** TX   **Commenced Bus:** N/A

Data Date	Rating	RACR #1	RACR #2	Total Assets ($mil)	Capital ($mil)	Net Premium ($mil)	Net Income ($mil)
6-20	C	1.99	1.65	154.2	88.8	310.9	27.3
6-19	N/A	N/A	N/A	N/A	N/A	N/A	N/A
2019	C	1.30	1.09	127.8	61.3	569.7	-28.4
2018	B-	1.98	1.65	150.0	89.9	574.7	-5.9
2017	B-	2.43	2.03	144.7	99.6	539.7	17.8
2016	B-	2.45	2.04	144.4	81.6	520.7	3.2
2015	B	2.85	2.38	168.8	98.3	525.7	-13.5

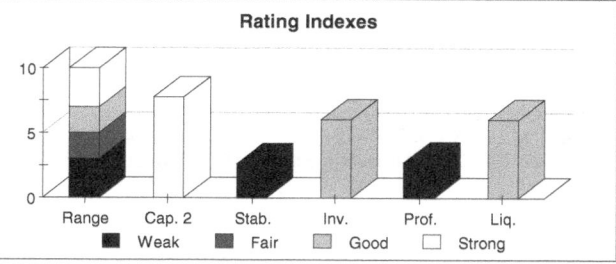

Rating Indexes

PARTNERRE AMERICA INS CO   C+   Fair

Major Rating Factors: Fair liquidity (3.3 on a scale of 0 to 10) as cash resources may not be adequate to cover a spike in claims. Fair overall results on stability tests (3.2) including negative cash flow from operations for 2019.

Other Rating Factors: History of adequate reserve strength (6.3) as reserves have been consistently at an acceptable level. Weak profitability index (2.4) with operating losses during 2017 and 2019. Average return on equity over the last five years has been poor at -0.7%. Strong long-term capitalization index (7.5) based on excellent current risk adjusted capital (severe and moderate loss scenarios), despite some fluctuation in capital levels.

Principal Business: Other accident & health (65%) and other liability (35%).

Principal Investments: Investment grade bonds (108%) and cash (8%).

Investments in Affiliates: None

Group Affiliation: Giovanni Agnelli e C Sapaz

Licensed in: All states, the District of Columbia and Puerto Rico

Commenced Business: August 1919

Address: 1209 ORANGE STREET, Wilmington, DE 19801

Phone: (203) 485-4287   **Domicile State:** DE   **NAIC Code:** 11835

Data Date	Rating	RACR #1	RACR #2	Loss Ratio %	Total Assets ($mil)	Capital ($mil)	Net Premium ($mil)	Net Income ($mil)
6-20	C+	2.40	1.90	N/A	288.6	99.6	14.6	0.9
6-19	C	0.95	0.70	N/A	387.3	98.2	55.7	-10.4
2019	C+	1.29	1.04	74.7	377.0	99.0	85.8	-6.1
2018	C+	0.77	0.57	89.9	380.9	108.3	272.5	0.4
2017	C+	5.89	3.93	126.0	393.0	110.1	38.4	-4.5
2016	C+	10.77	6.63	85.8	370.9	116.0	32.1	0.8
2015	C+	11.97	7.29	90.3	375.8	128.4	32.2	5.6

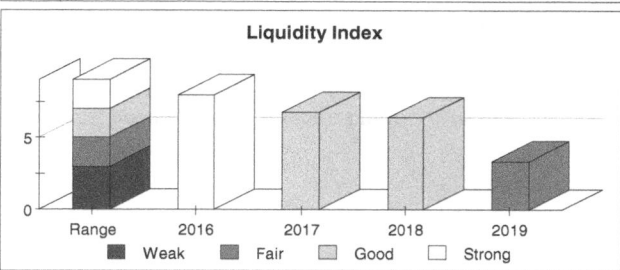

Liquidity Index

PARTNERSHIP HEALTHPLAN OF CALIFORNIA   C   Fair

Major Rating Factors: Weak profitability index (1.9 on a scale of 0 to 10). Good overall results on stability tests (4.9). Strong capitalization index (9.6) based on excellent current risk-adjusted capital (severe loss scenario).

Other Rating Factors: Excellent liquidity (7.1) with ample operational cash flow and liquid investments.

Principal Business: Medicaid (100%)

Mem Phys: 19: N/A   **18:** N/A   **19 MLR** 94.1%   **/ 19 Admin Exp** N/A

Enroll(000): Q2 20: 550   **19:** 551   **18:** 551   **Med Exp PMPM:** $392

Principal Investments ($000): Cash and equiv ($734,554)

Provider Compensation ($000): None

Total Member Encounters: N/A

Group Affiliation: None

Licensed in: CA

Address: 4665 Business Center Drive, Fairfield, CA 94534

Phone: (707) 863-4218   **Dom State:** CA   **Commenced Bus:** November 2005

Data Date	Rating	RACR #1	RACR #2	Total Assets ($mil)	Capital ($mil)	Net Premium ($mil)	Net Income ($mil)
6-20	C	4.67	2.86	1,228.1	576.7	1,484.1	-28.0
6-19	C+	5.27	3.22	1,116.5	604.2	1,417.5	-8.8
2019	C+	4.94	3.03	1,121.9	604.7	2,790.9	-8.5
2018	C+	5.39	3.29	1,082.1	613.0	2,595.1	-144.8
2017	B+	7.59	4.64	1,527.5	772.4	2,491.5	-84.6
2016	A	9.68	5.92	1,717.6	848.1	2,436.1	166.7
2015	A-	8.79	5.36	1,483.2	681.5	2,251.2	267.4

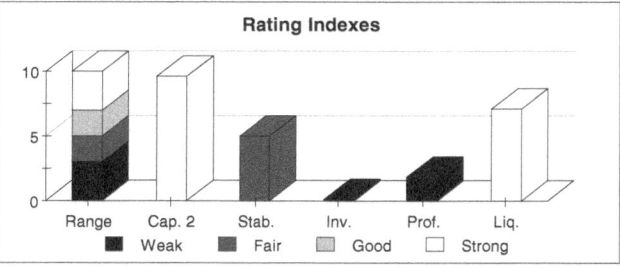

Rating Indexes

PAUL REVERE LIFE INS CO

C+ | Fair

Major Rating Factors: Fair overall results on stability tests (4.8 on a scale of 0 to 10) including fair financial strength of affiliated Unum Group and negative cash flow from operations for 2019. Fair quality investment portfolio (4.1) with large holdings of BBB rated bonds in addition to junk bond exposure equal to 76% of capital. Good overall profitability (6.4).

Other Rating Factors: Strong capitalization (7.0) based on excellent risk adjusted capital (severe loss scenario). Excellent liquidity (7.3).

Principal Business: Individual health insurance (67%), reinsurance (23%), group health insurance (5%), individual life insurance (4%), and group life insurance (1%).

Principal Investments: NonCMO investment grade bonds (87%), noninv. grade bonds (5%), CMOs and structured securities (3%), common & preferred stock (2%), and mortgages in good standing (1%).

Investments in Affiliates: 2%

Group Affiliation: Unum Group

Licensed in: All states except PR

Commenced Business: July 1930

Address: 1 MERCANTILE STREET, WORCESTER, MA 1608

Phone: (423) 294-1011 **Domicile State:** MA **NAIC Code:** 67598

Data Date	Rating	RACR #1	RACR #2	Total Assets ($mil)	Capital ($mil)	Net Premium ($mil)	Net Income ($mil)
6-20	C+	1.60	1.00	3,129.3	194.9	45.4	31.9
6-19	C+	1.66	1.02	3,328.4	206.2	43.5	24.6
2019	C+	1.45	0.90	3,213.5	173.2	90.2	63.8
2018	C+	1.55	0.94	3,410.2	191.1	93.2	70.4
2017	C+	1.40	0.82	3,570.6	177.3	93.8	55.4
2016	C+	1.71	1.01	3,790.4	251.4	95.2	65.6
2015	C+	1.72	1.02	3,977.0	257.7	96.8	63.1

Unum Group
Composite Group Rating: C+
Largest Group Members

	Assets ($mil)	Rating
UNUM LIFE INS CO OF AMERICA	22430	C+
PROVIDENT LIFE ACCIDENT INS CO	7893	C+
FIRST UNUM LIFE INS CO	4069	C+
COLONIAL LIFE ACCIDENT INS CO	3525	C+
PAUL REVERE LIFE INS CO	3214	C+

PEACH STATE HEALTH PLAN INC

B | Good

Major Rating Factors: Excellent profitability (9.1 on a scale of 0 to 10). Strong capitalization (10.0) based on excellent current risk-adjusted capital (severe loss scenario). High quality investment portfolio (8.0).

Other Rating Factors: Excellent liquidity (7.0) with sufficient resources (cash flows and marketable investments) to handle a spike in claims.

Principal Business: Medicaid (98%), Medicare (2%)

Mem Phys: 19: 38,299 **18:** 39,679 **19 MLR** 83.2% **/ 19 Admin Exp** N/A

Enroll(000): Q2 20: 419 **19:** 370 **18:** 369 **Med Exp PMPM:** $209

Principal Investments: Long-term bonds (75%), cash and equiv (20%), affiliate common stock (4%)

Provider Compensation ($000): Contr fee ($824,347), capitation ($74,922), salary ($20,877), bonus arrang ($2,756)

Total Member Encounters: Phys (322,112), non-phys (356,850)

Group Affiliation: None

Licensed in: GA

Address: 1100 Circle 75 Parkway Suite, Atlanta, GA 30339

Phone: (314) 725-4477 **Dom State:** GA **Commenced Bus:** N/A

Data Date	Rating	RACR #1	RACR #2	Total Assets ($mil)	Capital ($mil)	Net Premium ($mil)	Net Income ($mil)
6-20	B	3.62	3.01	441.8	278.6	544.6	18.5
6-19	B-	4.29	3.57	348.2	230.2	548.8	22.5
2019	B-	4.52	3.77	361.8	258.2	1,114.0	49.1
2018	B-	4.33	3.61	357.8	232.3	1,090.1	50.0
2017	C+	N/A	N/A	301.9	201.8	1,133.6	34.2
2016	C+	3.17	2.64	286.7	186.4	1,207.0	69.1
2015	C+	2.77	2.31	314.6	145.6	1,101.6	39.1

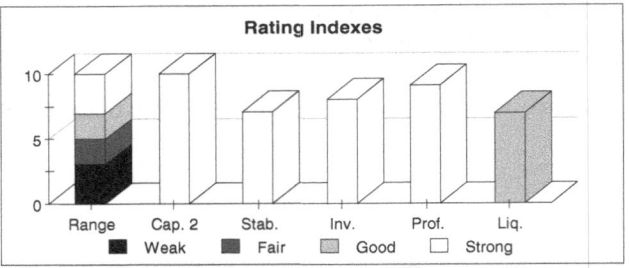

Rating Indexes

PEOPLES HEALTH INC

C | Fair

Major Rating Factors: Low quality investment portfolio (0.2 on a scale of 0 to 10). Excellent profitability (7.8). Strong capitalization (7.0) based on excellent current risk-adjusted capital (severe loss scenario).

Other Rating Factors: Excellent liquidity (7.0) with sufficient resources (cash flows and marketable investments) to handle a spike in claims.

Principal Business: Medicare (100%)

Mem Phys: 18: 5,786 **17:** 5,234 **18 MLR** 85.0% **/ 18 Admin Exp** N/A

Enroll(000): Q3 19: 78 **18:** 64 **17:** 61 **Med Exp PMPM:** $947

Principal Investments: Cash and equiv (99%), long-term bonds (1%)

Provider Compensation ($000): Capitation ($717,115)

Total Member Encounters: Phys (1,537,165), non-phys (81,597)

Group Affiliation: None

Licensed in: LA

Address: 3838 N CAUSEWAY BLVD SUITE, METAIRIE, LA 70002-8306

Phone: (504) 849-4500 **Dom State:** LA **Commenced Bus:** N/A

Data Date	Rating	RACR #1	RACR #2	Total Assets ($mil)	Capital ($mil)	Net Premium ($mil)	Net Income ($mil)
9-19	C	1.36	1.13	78.8	47.9	781.3	3.2
9-18	D	N/A	N/A	93.8	44.5	630.6	1.4
2018	D	0.77	0.64	63.0	44.7	843.7	1.6
2017	D	N/A	N/A	69.3	43.1	768.3	0.8
2016	D	0.73	0.61	65.6	34.9	736.6	1.3
2015	D	0.71	0.59	55.3	33.6	710.4	1.3
2014	N/A	N/A	N/A	52.4	32.3	696.2	N/A

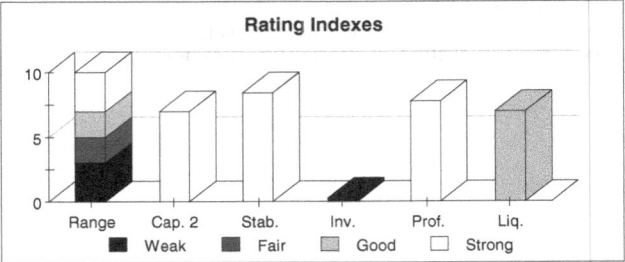

Rating Indexes

PHILADELPHIA AMERICAN LIFE INS CO — B — Good

Major Rating Factors: Good overall results on stability tests (5.8 on a scale of 0 to 10) despite fair financial strength of affiliated New Era Life Group. Other stability subfactors include excellent operational trends, good risk adjusted capital for prior years and good risk diversification. Fair quality investment portfolio (4.8) with large holdings of BBB rated bonds in addition to moderate junk bond exposure. Strong capitalization (7.2) based on excellent risk adjusted capital (severe loss scenario).

Other Rating Factors: Excellent profitability (9.1) with operating gains in each of the last five years. Excellent liquidity (7.0).

Principal Business: Individual health insurance (87%), individual annuities (10%), group health insurance (1%), and individual life insurance (1%).

Principal Investments: NonCMO investment grade bonds (72%), mortgages in good standing (7%), noninv. grade bonds (7%), CMOs and structured securities (7%), and misc. investments (5%).

Investments in Affiliates: None

Group Affiliation: New Era Life Group

Licensed in: All states except NY, RI, PR

Commenced Business: March 1978

Address: 11720 Katy Freeway Suite 1700, Houston, TX 77079

Phone: (281) 368-7159 **Domicile State:** TX **NAIC Code:** 67784

Data Date	Rating	RACR #1	RACR #2	Total Assets ($mil)	Capital ($mil)	Net Premium ($mil)	Net Income ($mil)
6-20	B	1.75	1.12	353.6	66.6	135.3	9.1
6-19	B	1.64	1.12	307.0	51.3	114.5	6.2
2019	B	1.75	1.20	326.1	58.3	239.9	14.8
2018	B	1.56	1.06	303.3	44.3	190.3	8.1
2017	B	1.51	0.97	284.8	35.5	157.2	3.9
2016	B	1.62	1.03	263.3	34.2	141.1	1.4
2015	B	1.46	0.95	235.2	33.9	160.1	1.1

New Era Life Group Composite Group Rating: C+ Largest Group Members	Assets ($mil)	Rating
NEW ERA LIFE INS CO	553	C
PHILADELPHIA AMERICAN LIFE INS CO	326	B
NEW ERA LIFE INS CO OF THE MIDWEST	150	C+
LIFE OF AMERICA INS CO	9	C

PHP INS CO — C- — Fair

Major Rating Factors: Low quality investment portfolio (0.0 on a scale of 0 to 10). Good overall profitability index (5.6). Strong capitalization (10.0) based on excellent current risk-adjusted capital (severe loss scenario).

Other Rating Factors: Excellent liquidity (8.1) with ample operational cash flow and liquid investments.

Principal Business: Comp med (100%)

Mem Phys: 19: 7,226 **18:** 4,381 **19 MLR** 79.9% **/ 19 Admin Exp** N/A

Enroll(000): Q2 20: 3 **19:** 4 **18:** 5 **Med Exp PMPM:** $397

Principal Investments: Cash and equiv (100%)

Provider Compensation ($000): Contr fee ($17,136), FFS ($1,645)

Total Member Encounters: Phys (39,871), non-phys (23,139)

Group Affiliation: None

Licensed in: MI

Address: 1400 EAST MICHIGAN AVENUE, LANSING, MI 48912

Phone: (517) 364-8400 **Dom State:** MI **Commenced Bus:** N/A

Data Date	Rating	RACR #1	RACR #2	Total Assets ($mil)	Capital ($mil)	Net Premium ($mil)	Net Income ($mil)
6-20	C-	4.34	3.62	18.5	15.0	9.4	1.0
6-19	C	3.43	2.86	15.8	13.0	10.5	0.3
2019	C	4.68	3.90	17.1	14.0	21.5	1.2
2018	C	3.26	2.71	17.4	12.9	26.9	0.6
2017	C	2.96	2.47	16.4	12.7	29.7	1.2
2016	C+	3.08	2.57	16.2	11.6	35.7	2.9
2015	C	1.59	1.33	14.0	8.4	42.9	-2.4

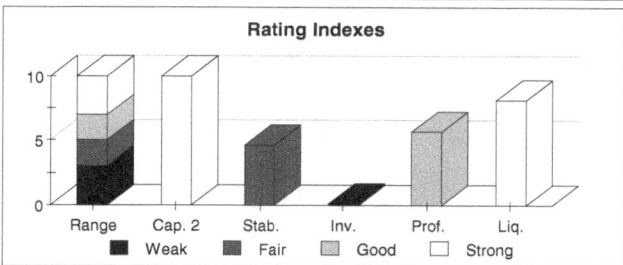

Rating Indexes

PHP INS CO OF IN INC — C+ — Fair

Major Rating Factors: Weak profitability index (2.8 on a scale of 0 to 10). Strong capitalization (10.0) based on excellent current risk-adjusted capital (severe loss scenario). High quality investment portfolio (8.5).

Other Rating Factors: Excellent liquidity (9.0) with ample operational cash flow and liquid investments.

Principal Business: Other (92%)

Mem Phys: 18: N/A **17:** N/A **18 MLR** 85.4% **/ 18 Admin Exp** N/A

Enroll(000): Q3 19: 0 **18:** 0 **17:** 0 **Med Exp PMPM:** $140

Principal Investments: Cash and equiv (52%), long-term bonds (31%), nonaffiliate common stock (17%)

Provider Compensation ($000): Other ($419)

Total Member Encounters: N/A

Group Affiliation: Physicians Health Plan of Northern I

Licensed in: IN

Address: 1700 Magnavox Way Ste 201, Ft Wayne, IN 46804

Phone: (260) 432-6690 **Dom State:** IN **Commenced Bus:** N/A

Data Date	Rating	RACR #1	RACR #2	Total Assets ($mil)	Capital ($mil)	Net Premium ($mil)	Net Income ($mil)
9-19	C+	8.04	6.70	3.6	2.5	0.6	0.1
9-18	U	17.45	14.54	3.0	2.3	0.4	0.0
2018	C+	7.28	6.06	3.0	2.3	0.6	0.0
2017	U	12.84	10.70	2.6	2.3	0.1	-0.1
2016	U	20.54	17.12	2.5	2.4	0.0	0.0
2015	N/A	N/A	N/A	2.4	2.4	0.1	N/A
2014	N/A	N/A	N/A	2.5	2.4	0.8	N/A

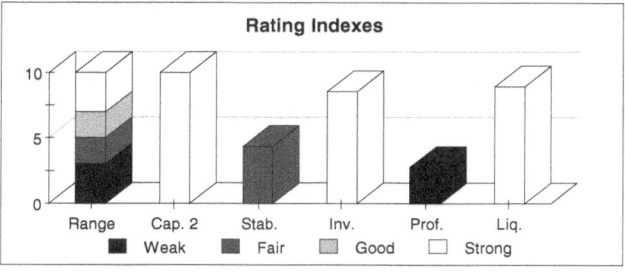

Rating Indexes

PHYSICIANS HEALTH CHOICE OF TEXAS | C | Fair

Major Rating Factors: Fair capitalization (4.2 on a scale of 0 to 10) based on fair current risk-adjusted capital (moderate loss scenario). Weak profitability index (2.5). Low quality investment portfolio (2.0).
Other Rating Factors: Good liquidity (6.9) with sufficient resources (cash flows and marketable investments) to handle a spike in claims.
Principal Business: Medicare (100%)
Mem Phys: 19: 84,567   **18:** 78,116   **19 MLR** 89.0%   **/ 19 Admin Exp** N/A
Enroll(000): Q2 20: 98   **19:** 91   **18:** 77   **Med Exp PMPM:** $1,053
Principal Investments: Cash and equiv (72%), long-term bonds (28%)
Provider Compensation ($000): Capitation ($580,112), contr fee ($428,117), FFS ($73,162), bonus arrang ($5,263)
Total Member Encounters: Phys (2,128,350), non-phys (1,197,138)
Group Affiliation: None
Licensed in: TX
Address: 1311 W PRESIDENT GEORGE BUSH, RICHARDSON, TX 75080
Phone: (952) 936-1300   **Dom State:** TX   **Commenced Bus:** N/A

Data Date	Rating	RACR #1	RACR #2	Total Assets ($mil)	Capital ($mil)	Net Premium ($mil)	Net Income ($mil)
6-20	C	0.81	0.68	188.3	70.9	747.2	-1.5
6-19	C	1.78	1.48	186.7	80.0	630.0	16.3
2019	C	1.36	1.13	207.2	76.7	1,250.0	-0.6
2018	C	1.23	1.03	137.4	54.8	983.0	-6.1
2017	C	N/A	N/A	161.7	50.4	765.2	-6.9
2016	C+	2.32	1.93	64.0	33.5	417.5	-5.5
2015	C+	3.46	2.88	67.7	38.6	372.6	4.4

Rating Indexes

PHYSICIANS HEALTH PLAN OF NO IN * | B+ | Good

Major Rating Factors: Good overall profitability index (6.5 on a scale of 0 to 10). Good quality investment portfolio (6.3). Good liquidity (6.5) with sufficient resources (cash flows and marketable investments) to handle a spike in claims.
Other Rating Factors: Strong capitalization index (9.5) based on excellent current risk-adjusted capital (severe loss scenario). Excellent overall results on stability tests (7.1).
Principal Business: Comp med (100%)
Mem Phys: 19: 21,334   **18:** 16,043   **19 MLR** 88.8%   **/ 19 Admin Exp** N/A
Enroll(000): Q2 20: 35   **19:** 35   **18:** 34   **Med Exp PMPM:** $394
Principal Investments: Long-term bonds (69%), nonaffiliate common stock (19%), cash and equiv (6%), affiliate common stock (3%), real estate (2%)
Provider Compensation ($000): FFS ($136,002), contr fee ($17,876), bonus arrang ($6,499), capitation ($2,350)
Total Member Encounters: Phys (166,803), non-phys (130,162)
Group Affiliation: Physicians Health Plan of Northern I
Licensed in: IN
Address: 8101 West Jefferson Blvd, Fort Wayne,
Phone: (260) 432-6690   **Dom State:** IN   **Commenced Bus:** N/A

Data Date	Rating	RACR #1	RACR #2	Total Assets ($mil)	Capital ($mil)	Net Premium ($mil)	Net Income ($mil)
6-20	B+	3.36	2.80	112.6	73.7	97.6	11.2
6-19	B	3.31	2.76	104.5	66.1	92.8	5.1
2019	B	2.86	2.38	100.8	63.9	185.2	4.2
2018	B	2.85	2.37	94.9	57.9	173.0	7.2
2017	B	3.06	2.55	86.5	56.1	157.1	4.3
2016	B	2.32	1.94	82.3	49.1	180.1	-0.2
2015	B	1.97	1.64	84.6	43.9	192.5	2.7

Rating Indexes

PHYSICIANS HP OF MID-MICHIGAN | C | Fair

Major Rating Factors: Fair profitability index (4.4 on a scale of 0 to 10). Low quality investment portfolio (0.0). Good overall results on stability tests (5.0).
Other Rating Factors: Strong capitalization index (8.0) based on excellent current risk-adjusted capital (severe loss scenario). Excellent liquidity (7.1) with ample operational cash flow and liquid investments.
Principal Business: Comp med (100%)
Mem Phys: 19: 7,801   **18:** 5,143   **19 MLR** 86.9%   **/ 19 Admin Exp** N/A
Enroll(000): Q2 20: 33   **19:** 33   **18:** 34   **Med Exp PMPM:** $381
Principal Investments: Cash and equiv (40%), nonaffiliate common stock (33%), affiliate common stock (20%), real estate (3%), other (4%)
Provider Compensation ($000): Contr fee ($160,404), FFS ($12,467), bonus arrang ($1,249)
Total Member Encounters: Phys (221,815), non-phys (130,101)
Group Affiliation: None
Licensed in: MI
Address: 1400 EAST MICHIGAN AVENUE, LANSING,
Phone: (517) 364-8400   **Dom State:** MI   **Commenced Bus:** N/A

Data Date	Rating	RACR #1	RACR #2	Total Assets ($mil)	Capital ($mil)	Net Premium ($mil)	Net Income ($mil)
6-20	C	2.17	1.81	91.3	56.8	84.6	-1.2
6-19	C	2.57	2.14	100.1	67.2	91.5	0.9
2019	C	2.43	2.02	88.4	61.0	178.7	2.1
2018	C	1.83	1.53	83.1	49.5	199.6	6.0
2017	C	1.96	1.63	83.5	50.3	182.4	9.3
2016	B	2.22	1.85	91.9	62.1	178.6	-1.2
2015	B	2.07	1.72	96.5	60.8	251.8	0.5

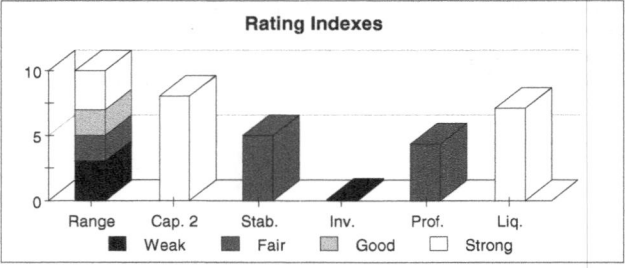

Rating Indexes

PHYSICIANS MUTUAL INS CO *   A+   Excellent

Major Rating Factors: Good quality investment portfolio (5.8 on a scale of 0 to 10) despite mixed results such as: no exposure to mortgages and large holdings of BBB rated bonds but small junk bond holdings. Strong capitalization (9.2) based on excellent risk adjusted capital (severe loss scenario). Furthermore, this high level of risk adjusted capital has been consistently maintained over the last five years. Excellent profitability (8.9) with operating gains in each of the last five years.

Other Rating Factors: Excellent liquidity (7.2). Excellent overall results on stability tests (7.9) excellent operational trends and excellent risk diversification.

Principal Business: Individual health insurance (72%), group health insurance (14%), and reinsurance (14%).

Principal Investments: NonCMO investment grade bonds (47%), CMOs and structured securities (26%), common & preferred stock (18%), noninv. grade bonds (7%), and real estate (1%).

Investments in Affiliates: 7%
Group Affiliation: Physicians Mutual Group
Licensed in: All states except PR
Commenced Business: February 1902
Address: 2600 Dodge Street, Omaha, NE 68131-2671
Phone: (402) 633-1000 **Domicile State:** NE **NAIC Code:** 80578

Data Date	Rating	RACR #1	RACR #2	Total Assets ($mil)	Capital ($mil)	Net Premium ($mil)	Net Income ($mil)
6-20	A+	3.27	2.44	2,506.1	1,058.8	247.7	33.9
6-19	A+	3.51	2.62	2,414.4	1,037.5	242.4	25.9
2019	A+	3.27	2.44	2,480.5	1,037.4	485.8	47.3
2018	A+	3.40	2.56	2,356.3	993.4	463.5	52.1
2017	A+	3.43	2.56	2,291.9	951.2	436.2	39.8
2016	A+	3.41	2.58	2,208.6	919.2	454.5	29.1
2015	A+	3.51	2.65	2,106.2	885.5	454.2	39.6

Rating Indexes

PIEDMONT COMMUNITY HEALTHCARE   D+   Weak

Major Rating Factors: Weak profitability index (0.9 on a scale of 0 to 10). Weak overall results on stability tests (2.4) based on a significant 75% decrease in enrollment during the period. Fair capitalization index (3.0) based on weak current risk-adjusted capital (moderate loss scenario).

Other Rating Factors: Good liquidity (6.9) with sufficient resources (cash flows and marketable investments) to handle a spike in claims. High quality investment portfolio (9.9).

Principal Business: Medicare (75%), comp med (25%)
Mem Phys: 19: 1,671 **18:** 1,302 **19 MLR** 102.6% **/ 19 Admin Exp** N/A
Enroll(000): Q2 20: 2 **19:** 2 **18:** 9 **Med Exp PMPM:** $742
Principal Investments: Cash and equiv (100%)
Provider Compensation ($000): Contr fee ($64,204), FFS ($3,639)
Total Member Encounters: Phys (73,839), non-phys (63,990)
Group Affiliation: Centra Health Inc
Licensed in: VA
Address: 2316 Atherholt Road, Lynchburg,
Phone: (434) 947-4463 **Dom State:** VA **Commenced Bus:** N/A

Data Date	Rating	RACR #1	RACR #2	Total Assets ($mil)	Capital ($mil)	Net Premium ($mil)	Net Income ($mil)
6-20	D+	0.64	0.53	9.8	7.0	5.9	-0.2
6-19	D+	0.94	0.79	24.2	11.1	35.5	-6.1
2019	D+	2.69	2.24	29.4	22.7	57.2	6.8
2018	D+	0.92	0.77	24.8	11.1	77.5	-8.1
2017	D+	0.92	0.77	25.1	12.6	94.4	-6.2
2016	D+	0.88	0.73	24.1	11.5	94.3	-2.5
2015	B-	0.96	0.80	26.7	10.7	84.7	-0.8

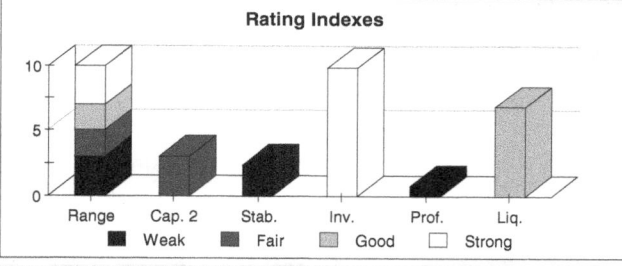

Rating Indexes

PIEDMONT COMMUNITY HEALTHCARE HMO   C   Fair

Major Rating Factors: Weak profitability index (2.8 on a scale of 0 to 10). Good liquidity (6.8) with sufficient resources (cash flows and marketable investments) to handle a spike in claims. Strong capitalization (7.1) based on excellent current risk-adjusted capital (severe loss scenario).

Other Rating Factors: High quality investment portfolio (9.9).
Principal Business: Comp med (100%)
Mem Phys: 18: 1,732 **17:** 1,014 **18 MLR** 85.6% **/ 18 Admin Exp** N/A
Enroll(000): Q3 19: 8 **18:** 20 **17:** 4 **Med Exp PMPM:** $604
Principal Investments: Cash and equiv (100%)
Provider Compensation ($000): Contr fee ($137,794), FFS ($2,661)
Total Member Encounters: Phys (58,158), non-phys (47,388)
Group Affiliation: Centra Health Inc
Licensed in: VA
Address: 2316 Atherholt Road, Lynchburg, VA 24501
Phone: (434) 947-4463 **Dom State:** VA **Commenced Bus:** N/A

Data Date	Rating	RACR #1	RACR #2	Total Assets ($mil)	Capital ($mil)	Net Premium ($mil)	Net Income ($mil)
9-19	C	1.44	1.20	35.4	27.9	54.0	7.6
9-18	C-	N/A	N/A	35.3	18.3	134.3	5.8
2018	C-	0.73	0.61	31.6	14.6	176.2	2.3
2017	C-	N/A	N/A	8.8	3.7	17.7	-1.9
2016	D	1.29	1.08	4.6	3.2	10.7	-1.6
2015	N/A	N/A	N/A	4.6	4.5	N/A	N/A
2014	N/A	N/A	N/A	N/A	N/A	N/A	N/A

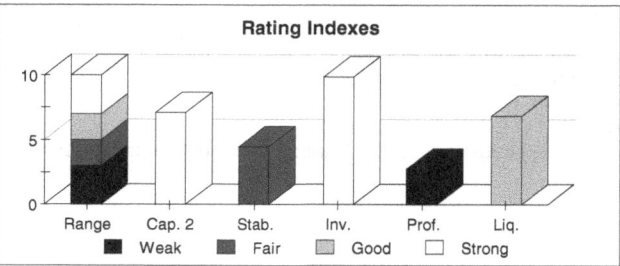

Rating Indexes

PIONEER EDUCATORS HEALTH TRUST

D-   **Weak**

Major Rating Factors: Weak profitability index (1.9 on a scale of 0 to 10). Low quality investment portfolio (0.0). Strong capitalization index (10.0) based on weak current risk-adjusted capital (severe loss scenario).
Other Rating Factors: Excellent liquidity (8.0) with ample operational cash flow and liquid investments.
Principal Business: Comp med (89%), dental (11%)
Mem Phys: 19: N/A **18:** N/A **19 MLR** 104.1% **/ 19 Admin Exp** N/A
Enroll(000): **19:** N/A **18:** 4 **Med Exp PMPM:** N/A
Principal Investments: Cash and equiv (100%)
Provider Compensation ($000): FFS ($3,457)
Total Member Encounters: Phys (6,661), non-phys (5,179)
Group Affiliation: None
Licensed in: OR
Address: 825 NE MULTNOMAH ST SUITE 150, PORTLAND, OR 97232
Phone: (503) 299-3401 **Dom State:** OR **Commenced Bus:** N/A

Data Date	Rating	RACR #1	RACR #2	Total Assets ($mil)	Capital ($mil)	Net Premium ($mil)	Net Income ($mil)
2019	D-	N/A	N/A	2.8	2.7	2.8	0.6
2018	E+	N/A	N/A	3.9	2.1	12.5	N/A
2017	E	N/A	N/A	3.3	0.9	14.7	-0.6
2016	E	0.34	0.28	4.5	1.5	17.4	-0.4
2015	N/A	N/A	N/A	3.3	1.9	21.0	-1.8

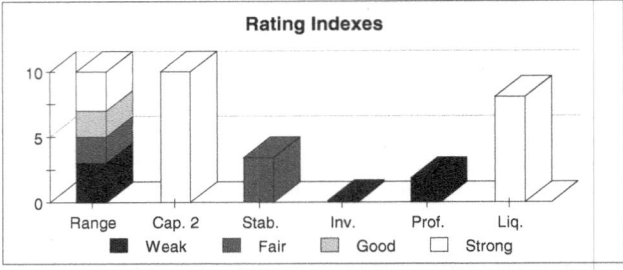

Rating Indexes

PL MEDICO SERV DE SALUD BELLA VISTA

B   **Good**

Major Rating Factors: Good overall profitability index (6.6 on a scale of 0 to 10). Good capitalization index (6.9) based on excellent current risk-adjusted capital (severe loss scenario). Good overall results on stability tests (6.5).
Other Rating Factors: High quality investment portfolio (7.3). Excellent liquidity (7.4) with ample operational cash flow and liquid investments.
Principal Business: Comp med (96%)
Mem Phys: 19: 949 **18:** N/A **19 MLR** 82.0% **/ 19 Admin Exp** N/A
Enroll(000): Q2 20: 19 **19:** 19 **18:** 18 **Med Exp PMPM:** $82
Principal Investments: Cash and equiv (100%)
Provider Compensation ($000): None
Total Member Encounters: N/A
Group Affiliation: Plan Medico Servicios de Salud Bella
Licensed in: (No states)
Address: 770 Avenida Hostos, Mayaguez,
Phone: (787) 833-8070 **Dom State:** PR **Commenced Bus:** N/A

Data Date	Rating	RACR #1	RACR #2	Total Assets ($mil)	Capital ($mil)	Net Premium ($mil)	Net Income ($mil)
6-20	B	1.27	1.06	4.6	2.2	3.9	0.4
6-19	N/A	N/A	N/A	N/A	N/A	N/A	N/A
2019	B-	1.01	0.84	3.8	1.7	7.5	0.4
2018	C	0.85	0.71	3.2	1.3	6.8	0.4
2017	C-	N/A	N/A	2.9	0.9	6.3	0.1
2016	D	0.50	0.42	2.6	0.8	6.1	-0.2
2015	U	0.73	0.61	2.7	1.0	5.6	0.2

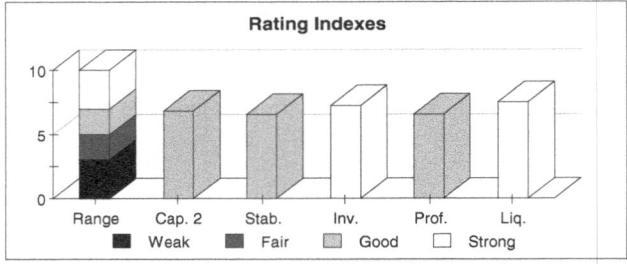

Rating Indexes

PLAN DE SALUD MENONITA

D+   **Weak**

Major Rating Factors: Weak profitability index (0.9 on a scale of 0 to 10). Good capitalization index (5.4) based on good current risk-adjusted capital (severe loss scenario). Good overall results on stability tests (5.0) in spite of healthy premium and capital growth during 2019 but a significant 30% decrease in enrollment during the period.
Other Rating Factors: Good liquidity (6.8) with sufficient resources (cash flows and marketable investments) to handle a spike in claims. High quality investment portfolio (7.2).
Principal Business: Medicaid (86%), comp med (14%)
Mem Phys: 19: N/A **18:** N/A **19 MLR** 92.9% **/ 19 Admin Exp** N/A
Enroll(000): Q2 20: 111 **19:** 105 **18:** 149 **Med Exp PMPM:** $135
Principal Investments: Cash and equiv (64%), long-term bonds (1%), other (35%)
Provider Compensation ($000): FFS ($102,018), capitation ($82,419)
Total Member Encounters: N/A
Group Affiliation: Mennonite General Hospital Inc
Licensed in: PR
Address: P O BOX 44, AIBONITO,
Phone: (787) 625-1380 **Dom State:** PR **Commenced Bus:** N/A

Data Date	Rating	RACR #1	RACR #2	Total Assets ($mil)	Capital ($mil)	Net Premium ($mil)	Net Income ($mil)
6-20	D+	0.98	0.82	49.7	21.2	105.7	-3.3
6-19	N/A	N/A	N/A	N/A	N/A	N/A	N/A
2019	C-	0.65	0.54	42.0	14.2	198.4	-11.6
2018	N/A	N/A	N/A	44.4	4.9	72.3	N/A
2017	C-	N/A	N/A	5.0	3.2	18.7	-0.3
2016	U	0.77	0.64	4.3	2.2	15.4	0.0
2015	N/A	N/A	N/A	5.0	2.7	13.6	0.1

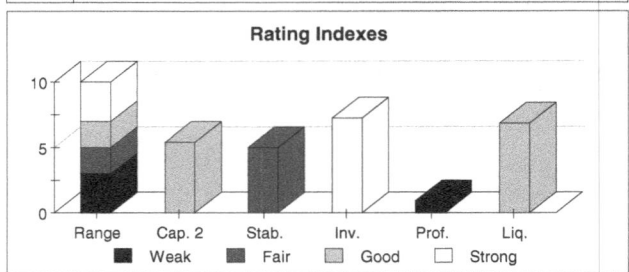

Rating Indexes

PREFERRED CARE PARTNERS INC *

B+ **Good**

Major Rating Factors: Good liquidity (6.5 on a scale of 0 to 10) with sufficient resources (cash flows and marketable investments) to handle a spike in claims. Excellent profitability (8.8). Strong capitalization (7.1) based on excellent current risk-adjusted capital (severe loss scenario).
Other Rating Factors: High quality investment portfolio (8.2).
Principal Business: Medicare (100%)
Mem Phys: 19: 46,725 **18:** 42,617 **19 MLR** 85.6% **/ 19 Admin Exp** N/A
Enroll(000): Q2 20: 212 **19:** 195 **18:** 187 **Med Exp PMPM:** $959
Principal Investments: Long-term bonds (97%), cash and equiv (3%)
Provider Compensation ($000): Contr fee ($1,119,590), capitation ($690,745), FFS ($267,546), bonus arrang ($83,215)
Total Member Encounters: Phys (3,144,026), non-phys (1,123,435)
Group Affiliation: None
Licensed in: FL
Address: 9100 SOUTH DADELAND BOULEVARD, MIAMI, FL 33156
Phone: (305) 670-8438 **Dom State:** FL **Commenced Bus:** N/A

Data Date	Rating	RACR #1	RACR #2	Total Assets ($mil)	Capital ($mil)	Net Premium ($mil)	Net Income ($mil)
6-20	B+	1.43	1.19	706.7	235.6	1,554.3	94.9
6-19	B	1.98	1.65	581.4	208.8	1,306.3	64.4
2019	B+	1.53	1.28	546.0	180.7	2,584.8	97.7
2018	B	1.38	1.15	451.7	139.6	2,261.0	66.6
2017	E	0.76	0.63	411.1	82.0	1,751.8	23.8
2016	E	1.34	1.11	325.0	82.7	1,484.4	13.8
2015	E-	1.76	1.47	169.4	54.9	732.4	24.0

PREFERREDONE COMMUNITY HEALTH PLAN

D+ **Weak**

Major Rating Factors: Weak profitability index (1.5 on a scale of 0 to 10). Fair overall results on stability tests (4.2). Strong capitalization index (9.3) based on excellent current risk-adjusted capital (severe loss scenario).
Other Rating Factors: High quality investment portfolio (8.8). Excellent liquidity (7.1) with ample operational cash flow and liquid investments.
Principal Business: Comp med (100%)
Mem Phys: 19: 47,502 **18:** 43,290 **19 MLR** 78.7% **/ 19 Admin Exp** N/A
Enroll(000): Q2 20: 0 **19:** 0 **18:** 0 **Med Exp PMPM:** $343
Principal Investments: Long-term bonds (87%), cash and equiv (13%)
Provider Compensation ($000): Contr fee ($1,638), FFS ($281), bonus arrang ($99)
Total Member Encounters: N/A
Group Affiliation: None
Licensed in: MN
Address: 6105 Golden Hills Drive, Golden Valley,
Phone: (763) 847-4000 **Dom State:** MN **Commenced Bus:** N/A

Data Date	Rating	RACR #1	RACR #2	Total Assets ($mil)	Capital ($mil)	Net Premium ($mil)	Net Income ($mil)
6-20	D+	3.17	2.64	3.6	3.1	1.2	0.1
6-19	D+	3.65	3.04	3.6	2.9	1.2	0.2
2019	D+	3.88	3.24	3.4	2.9	2.3	0.2
2018	D+	3.41	2.84	3.5	2.7	2.6	-0.3
2017	D	3.29	2.75	3.7	3.0	3.5	-0.5
2016	D	2.26	1.88	5.7	3.5	10.3	0.1
2015	D	0.75	0.63	7.6	3.4	26.1	-0.9

PREFERREDONE INS CO

C **Fair**

Major Rating Factors: Weak profitability index (2.5 on a scale of 0 to 10). Good quality investment portfolio (5.4). Good liquidity (6.1) with sufficient resources (cash flows and marketable investments) to handle a spike in claims.
Other Rating Factors: Strong capitalization (7.1) based on excellent current risk-adjusted capital (severe loss scenario).
Principal Business: Comp med (80%), other (20%)
Mem Phys: 19: 47,502 **18:** 43,290 **19 MLR** 92.7% **/ 19 Admin Exp** N/A
Enroll(000): Q2 20: 153 **19:** 149 **18:** 135 **Med Exp PMPM:** $141
Principal Investments: Long-term bonds (68%), cash and equiv (17%), nonaffiliate common stock (15%)
Provider Compensation ($000): Contr fee ($155,906), FFS ($31,412), bonus arrang ($10,018), other ($48,501)
Total Member Encounters: N/A
Group Affiliation: None
Licensed in: IA, MN, NE, ND, SD, WI
Address: 6105 Golden Hills Drive, Golden Valley, MN 55416-1023
Phone: (763) 847-4000 **Dom State:** MN **Commenced Bus:** N/A

Data Date	Rating	RACR #1	RACR #2	Total Assets ($mil)	Capital ($mil)	Net Premium ($mil)	Net Income ($mil)
6-20	C	1.44	1.20	127.4	58.6	166.7	11.4
6-19	C-	1.11	0.92	98.6	39.2	130.4	-2.2
2019	C-	1.19	0.99	96.0	48.2	269.9	2.9
2018	C-	1.09	0.91	80.9	38.7	230.3	-11.4
2017	C-	1.15	0.96	87.2	44.1	256.0	-2.0
2016	D+	1.40	1.17	78.3	38.9	178.2	-5.8
2015	D+	0.76	0.63	62.9	30.8	153.3	-43.6

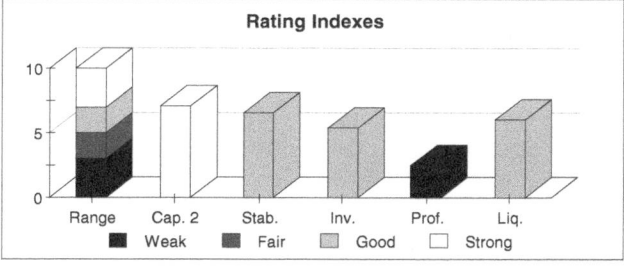

PREMERA BLUE CROSS

B   **Good**

Major Rating Factors: Good overall profitability index (5.7 on a scale of 0 to 10). Good liquidity (6.8) with sufficient resources (cash flows and marketable investments) to handle a spike in claims. Fair quality investment portfolio (4.3).
Other Rating Factors: Strong capitalization (10.0) based on excellent current risk-adjusted capital (severe loss scenario).
Principal Business: Comp med (65%), FEHB (23%), Medicare (8%), med supp (3%), dental (1%)
Mem Phys: 19: 68,037 **18:** 55,256 **19 MLR** 86.8% **/ 19 Admin Exp** N/A
Enroll(000): Q2 20: 732 **19:** 741 **18:** 695 **Med Exp PMPM:** $387
Principal Investments: Long-term bonds (40%), nonaffiliate common stock (23%), affiliate common stock (10%), cash and equiv (4%), real estate (1%), pref stock (1%), other (21%)
Provider Compensation ($000): Contr fee ($3,129,210), FFS ($166,397)
Total Member Encounters: Phys (4,699,460), non-phys (1,614,380)
Group Affiliation: Premera Blue Cross
Licensed in: AK, WA
Address: 7001 220th St SW, Mountlake Terrace, WA 98043
Phone: (425) 918-4000 **Dom State:** WA **Commenced Bus:** N/A

Data Date	Rating	RACR #1	RACR #2	Total Assets ($mil)	Capital ($mil)	Net Premium ($mil)	Net Income ($mil)
6-20	B	5.91	4.93	3,687.2	1,946.5	1,847.7	57.6
6-19	B	8.26	6.88	3,476.4	2,332.8	1,871.0	151.2
2019	B	7.00	5.84	3,602.2	2,314.2	3,925.1	101.9
2018	B	7.77	6.48	3,133.8	2,193.0	3,571.1	400.9
2017	B+	7.04	5.87	2,801.4	1,931.3	3,361.9	115.0
2016	B+	5.17	4.31	2,428.9	1,476.2	3,780.1	45.2
2015	B+	5.27	4.39	2,276.0	1,388.4	3,489.4	12.9

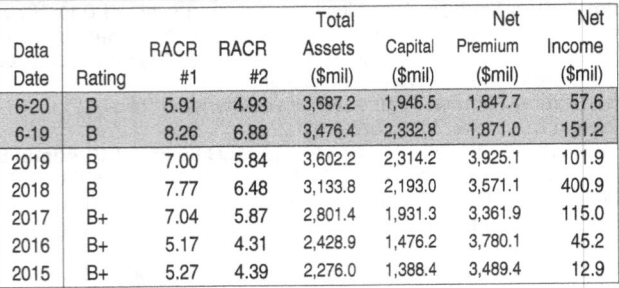

Rating Indexes

PREMIER HEALTH INSURING CORP

E   **Very Weak**

Major Rating Factors: Weak profitability index (0.2 on a scale of 0 to 10). Good quality investment portfolio (6.1). Good liquidity (5.4) with sufficient resources (cash flows and marketable investments) to handle a spike in claims.
Other Rating Factors: Strong capitalization (8.2) based on excellent current risk-adjusted capital (severe loss scenario).
Principal Business: Medicare (100%)
Mem Phys: 18: N/A **17:** 6,508 **18 MLR** 93.1% **/ 18 Admin Exp** N/A
Enroll(000): Q3 19: N/A **18:** N/A **17:** 10 **Med Exp PMPM:** N/A
Principal Investments: Affiliate common stock (58%), cash and equiv (38%), long-term bonds (4%)
Provider Compensation ($000): Contr fee ($24,960), FFS ($2,597), other ($2,303)
Total Member Encounters: Phys (12,972), non-phys (2,747)
Group Affiliation: None
Licensed in: OH
Address: 110 N MAIN ST STE 1200, DAYTON,
Phone: (937) 499-9588 **Dom State:** OH **Commenced Bus:** N/A

Data Date	Rating	RACR #1	RACR #2	Total Assets ($mil)	Capital ($mil)	Net Premium ($mil)	Net Income ($mil)
9-19	E	2.30	1.92	11.0	8.9	-0.4	0.4
9-18	E	N/A	N/A	15.6	11.3	22.7	-3.2
2018	E	2.19	1.82	11.5	8.5	21.7	-5.2
2017	E	N/A	N/A	30.5	15.0	90.5	-12.9
2016	E	1.41	1.18	30.0	15.2	77.0	-21.3
2015	E	1.25	1.04	25.3	14.8	59.5	-14.4
2014	N/A	N/A	N/A	32.8	32.5	N/A	N/A

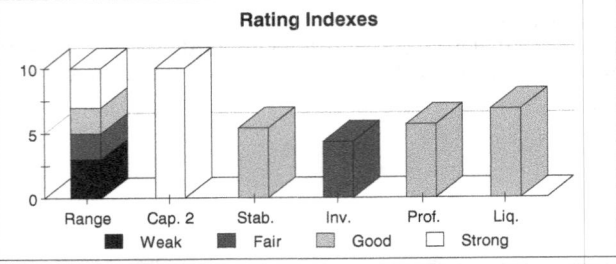

Rating Indexes

PREMIER HEALTH PLAN INC

D-   **Weak**

Major Rating Factors: Weak profitability index (0.0 on a scale of 0 to 10). Strong capitalization (8.6) based on excellent current risk-adjusted capital (severe loss scenario). High quality investment portfolio (9.9).
Other Rating Factors: Excellent liquidity (7.3) with ample operational cash flow and liquid investments.
Principal Business: Comp med (99%)
Mem Phys: 18: 5,468 **17:** 5,147 **18 MLR** 107.4% **/ 18 Admin Exp** N/A
Enroll(000): Q3 19: N/A **18:** 1 **17:** 5 **Med Exp PMPM:** $453
Principal Investments: Cash and equiv (94%), long-term bonds (6%)
Provider Compensation ($000): Contr fee ($6,679), FFS ($329), other ($605)
Total Member Encounters: Phys (3,133), non-phys (995)
Group Affiliation: None
Licensed in: (No states)
Address: 110 N MAIN ST STE 1200, Dayton,
Phone: (937) 499-9588 **Dom State:** OH **Commenced Bus:** N/A

Data Date	Rating	RACR #1	RACR #2	Total Assets ($mil)	Capital ($mil)	Net Premium ($mil)	Net Income ($mil)
9-19	D-	2.61	2.18	6.0	6.0	0.0	0.0
9-18	D-	N/A	N/A	8.7	6.9	2.8	-0.5
2018	D-	2.59	2.15	7.3	5.9	3.9	-1.7
2017	D-	N/A	N/A	14.3	7.6	30.3	-0.9
2016	D-	1.44	1.20	16.9	6.5	20.7	-9.9
2015	E+	2.29	1.91	11.7	5.8	8.2	-3.2
2014	N/A	N/A	N/A	22.7	22.5	N/A	N/A

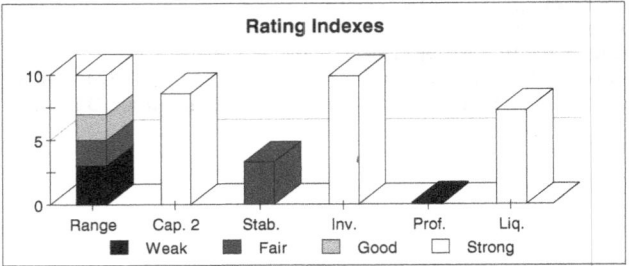

Rating Indexes

PREMIER HEALTH PLAN SERVICES INC

D   **Weak**

Major Rating Factors: Weak profitability index (0.9 on a scale of 0 to 10). Fair overall results on stability tests (4.4) based on fair risk diversification due to the company's size. Strong capitalization index (7.9) based on excellent current risk-adjusted capital (severe loss scenario).
Other Rating Factors: Excellent liquidity (7.3) with ample operational cash flow and liquid investments.
Principal Business: Managed care (100%)
Mem Phys: 19: N/A **18:** N/A **19 MLR** 95.7% **/ 19 Admin Exp** N/A
Enroll(000): Q2 20: 27 **19:** 37 **18:** 37 **Med Exp PMPM:** $211
Principal Investments ($000): Cash and equiv ($38,090)
Provider Compensation ($000): None
Total Member Encounters: N/A
Group Affiliation: Lakewood IPA
Licensed in: CA
Address: 10833 Valley View St Suite 300, Cypress, CA 90630
Phone: (310) 277-9003 **Dom State:** CA **Commenced Bus:** June 2009

Data Date	Rating	RACR #1	RACR #2	Total Assets ($mil)	Capital ($mil)	Net Premium ($mil)	Net Income ($mil)
6-20	D	2.78	1.74	46.3	22.1	42.6	1.0
6-19	D	2.30	1.47	35.4	18.8	47.7	-3.6
2019	D	2.65	1.66	43.7	21.1	93.8	-2.9
2018	D	2.66	1.70	38.8	21.6	87.0	-10.1
2017	D	0.52	0.33	25.2	4.5	89.9	-1.9
2016	C-	0.79	0.49	29.2	6.6	99.6	0.5
2015	U	-262.00	-8.66	27.0	9.2	0.0	1.8

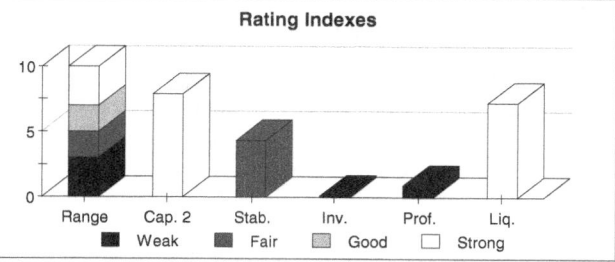

Rating Indexes

PRESBYTERIAN HEALTH PLAN INC

B   **Good**

Major Rating Factors: Good overall results on stability tests (5.2 on a scale of 0 to 10). Good liquidity (6.8) with sufficient resources (cash flows and marketable investments) to handle a spike in claims. Excellent profitability (8.2).
Other Rating Factors: Strong capitalization index (7.2) based on excellent current risk-adjusted capital (severe loss scenario). High quality investment portfolio (9.2).
Principal Business: Medicaid (79%), Medicare (13%), comp med (6%), FEHB (3%)
Mem Phys: 19: 14,754 **18:** 14,729 **19 MLR** 86.2% **/ 19 Admin Exp** N/A
Enroll(000): Q2 20: 463 **19:** 448 **18:** 404 **Med Exp PMPM:** $478
Principal Investments: Long-term bonds (50%), cash and equiv (29%), nonaffiliate common stock (20%).
Provider Compensation ($000): Contr fee ($1,926,313), capitation ($567,180), FFS ($122,964)
Total Member Encounters: Phys (3,055,397), non-phys (2,582,473)
Group Affiliation: None
Licensed in: AZ, NM
Address: 9521 SAN MATEO BLVD NE, ALBUQUERQUE,
Phone: (505) 923-6107 **Dom State:** NM **Commenced Bus:** N/A

Data Date	Rating	RACR #1	RACR #2	Total Assets ($mil)	Capital ($mil)	Net Premium ($mil)	Net Income ($mil)
6-20	B	1.53	1.27	936.5	328.8	1,670.1	77.8
6-19	B	1.66	1.38	678.7	238.2	1,522.4	37.5
2019	B	1.21	1.01	760.9	261.4	3,064.0	60.2
2018	B	1.29	1.07	575.8	182.5	2,149.4	37.6
2017	B	1.89	1.58	488.5	236.3	1,832.5	58.0
2016	B	1.95	1.62	664.9	238.2	1,838.9	31.8
2015	B	1.96	1.63	606.0	209.9	1,658.6	29.8

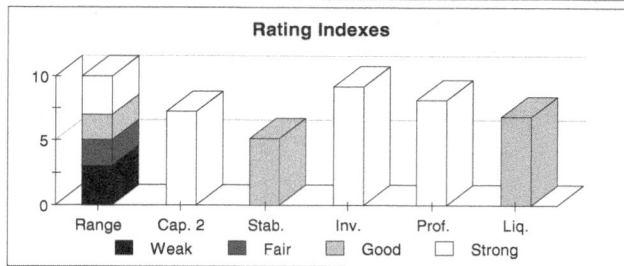

Rating Indexes

PRESBYTERIAN INS CO

C   **Fair**

Major Rating Factors: Weak profitability index (2.4 on a scale of 0 to 10). Good liquidity (5.1) with sufficient resources (cash flows and marketable investments) to handle a spike in claims. Strong capitalization (7.5) based on excellent current risk-adjusted capital (severe loss scenario).
Other Rating Factors: High quality investment portfolio (8.9).
Principal Business: Comp med (57%), Medicare (28%), other (16%)
Mem Phys: 19: 14,754 **18:** 14,729 **19 MLR** 88.3% **/ 19 Admin Exp** N/A
Enroll(000): Q2 20: 46 **19:** 18 **18:** 24 **Med Exp PMPM:** $434
Principal Investments: Long-term bonds (61%), nonaffiliate common stock (31%), cash and equiv (8%)
Provider Compensation ($000): Contr fee ($86,286), FFS ($19,878), capitation ($1,292)
Total Member Encounters: Phys (111,318), non-phys (46,373)
Group Affiliation: None
Licensed in: NM
Address: 9521 SAN MATEO BLVD NE, ALBUQUERQUE, NM 87113
Phone: (505) 923-6107 **Dom State:** NM **Commenced Bus:** N/A

Data Date	Rating	RACR #1	RACR #2	Total Assets ($mil)	Capital ($mil)	Net Premium ($mil)	Net Income ($mil)
6-20	C	1.78	1.48	54.0	38.1	40.6	6.1
6-19	C+	1.81	1.51	48.3	32.4	63.1	2.1
2019	C+	1.65	1.37	45.2	27.7	118.7	-0.6
2018	B-	1.59	1.32	46.6	28.8	136.3	-2.7
2017	B-	N/A	N/A	50.1	30.5	142.9	-7.3
2016	B-	1.22	1.02	46.5	22.8	176.8	-9.1
2015	B	2.19	1.82	53.3	31.6	168.0	1.8

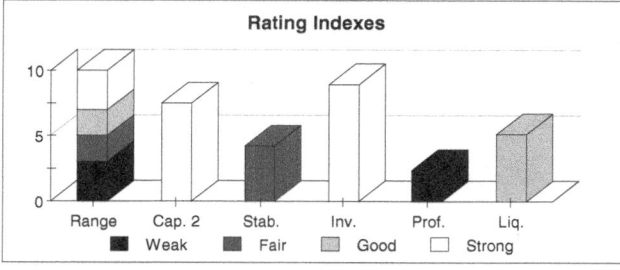

Rating Indexes

PRIMECARE MEDICAL NETWORK INC

B-   Good

Major Rating Factors: Fair overall results on stability tests (4.2 on a scale of 0 to 10) in spite of healthy premium and capital growth during 2019. Rating is significantly influenced by the fair financial results of UnitedHealth Group Inc. Excellent profitability (7.3). Strong capitalization index (7.5) based on excellent current risk-adjusted capital (severe loss scenario).
Other Rating Factors: Excellent liquidity (7.4) with ample operational cash flow and liquid investments.
Principal Business: Managed care (98%)
Mem Phys: 19: N/A **18:** N/A **19 MLR** 81.7% **/ 19 Admin Exp** N/A
Enroll(000): Q2 20: 230 **19:** 209 **18:** 209 **Med Exp PMPM:** $379
Principal Investments ($000): Cash and equiv ($305,885)
Provider Compensation ($000): None
Total Member Encounters: N/A
Group Affiliation: UnitedHealth Group Inc
Licensed in: CA
Address: 3990 Concours Street 5th Floor, Ontario, CA 91764
Phone: (909) 605-8000 **Dom State:** CA **Commenced Bus:** October 1998

Data Date	Rating	RACR #1	RACR #2	Total Assets ($mil)	Capital ($mil)	Net Premium ($mil)	Net Income ($mil)
6-20	B-	2.34	1.44	377.0	121.7	670.5	75.1
6-19	B-	2.87	1.78	335.7	105.0	591.0	43.4
2019	B-	1.60	0.98	311.8	83.5	1,168.9	83.0
2018	B-	1.54	0.95	251.7	56.1	1,005.4	43.1
2017	B	2.47	1.53	236.6	78.6	894.4	35.9
2016	B	1.98	1.23	214.0	62.5	846.4	18.3
2015	B-	1.53	0.95	192.9	44.4	809.8	26.4

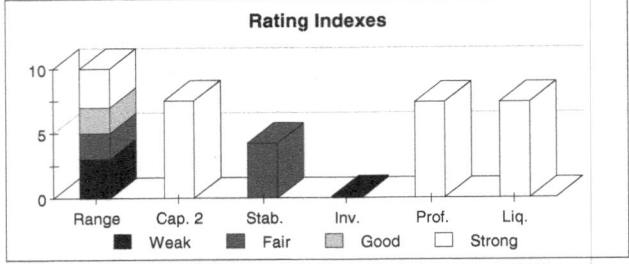

Rating Indexes

PRIORITY HEALTH *

A   Excellent

Major Rating Factors: Excellent profitability (8.5 on a scale of 0 to 10). Strong capitalization index (10.0) based on excellent current risk-adjusted capital (severe loss scenario). High quality investment portfolio (7.7).
Other Rating Factors: Excellent overall results on stability tests (8.1). Excellent liquidity (7.0) with ample operational cash flow and liquid investments
Principal Business: Comp med (52%), Medicare (47%), med supp (1%)
Mem Phys: 19: 21,024 **18:** 19,911 **19 MLR** 87.1% **/ 19 Admin Exp** N/A
Enroll(000): Q2 20: 595 **19:** 544 **18:** 514 **Med Exp PMPM:** $459
Principal Investments: Cash and equiv (34%), long-term bonds (34%), affiliate common stock (22%), nonaffiliate common stock (10%)
Provider Compensation ($000): Contr fee ($1,860,868), bonus arrang ($861,577), FFS ($93,329), capitation ($3,876)
Total Member Encounters: Phys (7,001,849), non-phys (887,873)
Group Affiliation: Spectrum Health System Inc
Licensed in: MI
Address: 1231 East Beltline NE, Grand Rapids,
Phone: (616) 942-0954 **Dom State:** MI **Commenced Bus:** N/A

Data Date	Rating	RACR #1	RACR #2	Total Assets ($mil)	Capital ($mil)	Net Premium ($mil)	Net Income ($mil)
6-20	A	4.20	3.50	1,860.0	1,036.6	1,899.7	47.8
6-19	A	4.05	3.38	1,436.2	913.7	1,702.5	116.8
2019	A	3.58	2.98	1,400.4	878.7	3,405.8	145.6
2018	A	3.21	2.67	1,253.8	759.8	3,180.0	123.8
2017	A	2.61	2.18	1,166.5	669.0	3,015.1	78.7
2016	A-	2.49	2.07	1,000.4	574.5	2,663.2	51.1
2015	A-	2.71	2.26	910.2	529.8	2,187.7	91.1

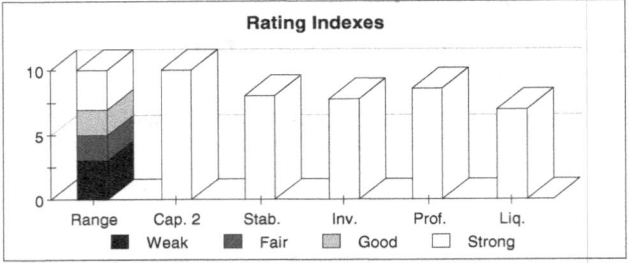

Rating Indexes

PRIORITY HEALTH CHOICE INC *

B+   Good

Major Rating Factors: Good quality investment portfolio (5.5 on a scale of 0 to 10). Excellent profitability (9.3). Strong capitalization (10.0) based on excellent current risk-adjusted capital (severe loss scenario).
Other Rating Factors: Excellent liquidity (7.2) with ample operational cash flow and liquid investments.
Principal Business: Medicaid (99%)
Mem Phys: 19: 9,493 **18:** 8,687 **19 MLR** 73.3% **/ 19 Admin Exp** N/A
Enroll(000): Q2 20: 141 **19:** 126 **18:** 126 **Med Exp PMPM:** $231
Principal Investments: Cash and equiv (58%), nonaffiliate common stock (41%), long-term bonds (1%)
Provider Compensation ($000): Contr fee ($173,425), capitation ($80,408), bonus arrang ($79,407), FFS ($18,570)
Total Member Encounters: Phys (1,387,075), non-phys (298,751)
Group Affiliation: Spectrum Health System Inc
Licensed in: MI
Address: 1231 EAST BELTLINE NE, GRAND RAPIDS, MI 49525-4501
Phone: (616) 942-0954 **Dom State:** MI **Commenced Bus:** N/A

Data Date	Rating	RACR #1	RACR #2	Total Assets ($mil)	Capital ($mil)	Net Premium ($mil)	Net Income ($mil)
6-20	B+	4.16	3.47	254.8	136.1	249.1	18.5
6-19	A-	4.11	3.43	141.9	95.1	203.8	16.9
2019	A-	5.10	4.25	199.8	117.3	471.0	38.1
2018	A-	3.18	2.65	129.3	76.2	396.5	8.7
2017	B+	1.81	1.51	125.1	68.8	517.5	12.8
2016	B+	2.18	1.82	132.3	55.3	484.5	10.5
2015	B+	1.82	1.51	122.8	44.9	452.0	15.2

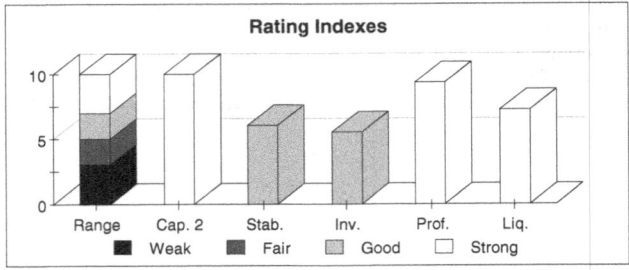

Rating Indexes

PRIORITY HEALTH INS CO   B   Good

Major Rating Factors: Fair quality investment portfolio (3.8 on a scale of 0 to 10). Excellent profitability (8.1). Strong capitalization (8.0) based on excellent current risk-adjusted capital (severe loss scenario).
Other Rating Factors: Excellent liquidity (7.1) with ample operational cash flow and liquid investments.
Principal Business: Comp med (87%), other (13%)
Mem Phys: 19: 21,151 **18:** 20,026 **19 MLR** 77.8% **/ 19 Admin Exp** N/A
Enroll(000): Q2 20: 64 **19:** 69 **18:** 57 **Med Exp PMPM:** $298
Principal Investments: Nonaffiliate common stock (50%), cash and equiv (50%)
Provider Compensation ($000): Contr fee ($124,643), bonus arrang ($48,841), FFS ($43,521)
Total Member Encounters: Phys (461,937), non-phys (30,269)
Group Affiliation: Spectrum Health System Inc
Licensed in: MI
Address: 1231 EAST BELTLINE NE, GRAND RAPIDS, MI 49525-4501
Phone: (616) 942-0954 **Dom State:** MI **Commenced Bus:** N/A

Data Date	Rating	RACR #1	RACR #2	Total Assets ($mil)	Capital ($mil)	Net Premium ($mil)	Net Income ($mil)
6-20	B	2.16	1.80	163.4	70.8	154.7	8.2
6-19	B	3.56	2.97	136.3	62.7	142.6	5.4
2019	B	2.95	2.46	137.3	62.5	293.8	4.3
2018	B	3.01	2.51	119.7	55.6	245.3	4.7
2017	B	1.81	1.51	113.5	53.1	238.5	4.6
2016	B-	2.31	1.93	110.9	47.7	259.2	5.8
2015	B-	2.54	2.11	107.0	44.6	218.7	9.3

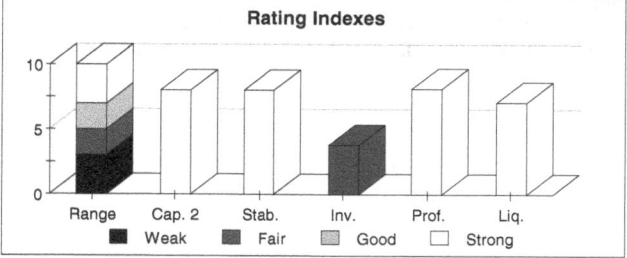

Rating Indexes

Range | Cap. 2 | Stab. | Inv. | Prof. | Liq.
■ Weak ■ Fair ▨ Good ☐ Strong

PROFESSIONAL INS CO   C   Fair

Major Rating Factors: Fair overall results on stability tests (3.6 on a scale of 0 to 10) including potential financial drain due to affiliation with Sun Life Assurance Group. Good quality investment portfolio (6.7) despite mixed results such as: no exposure to mortgages and large holdings of BBB rated bonds but no exposure to junk bonds. Strong capitalization (10.0) based on excellent risk adjusted capital (severe loss scenario).
Other Rating Factors: Excellent profitability (9.0) with operating gains in each of the last five years. Excellent liquidity (7.0).
Principal Business: Individual health insurance (93%) and individual life insurance (7%).
Principal Investments: NonCMO investment grade bonds (80%), CMOs and structured securities (16%), policy loans (2%), and cash (1%).
Investments in Affiliates: None
Group Affiliation: Sun Life Assurance Group
Licensed in: All states except AK, DE, ME, NH, NJ, NY, RI, VT, PR
Commenced Business: September 1937
Address: 350 North St Paul Street, Dallas, TX 75201
Phone: (781) 237-6030 **Domicile State:** TX **NAIC Code:** 68047

Data Date	Rating	RACR #1	RACR #2	Total Assets ($mil)	Capital ($mil)	Net Premium ($mil)	Net Income ($mil)
6-20	C	6.28	5.65	115.2	56.5	7.9	2.5
6-19	C-	5.88	5.29	112.3	52.8	8.7	2.7
2019	C	6.10	5.49	113.7	54.9	17.0	4.8
2018	D+	5.59	5.03	111.2	50.2	19.2	5.1
2017	D	5.02	4.51	109.6	45.0	21.6	4.4
2016	D-	4.68	4.11	110.0	42.0	24.5	4.5
2015	C	4.32	3.34	109.2	38.6	27.7	2.7

Sun Life Assurance Group
Composite Group Rating: D+

Largest Group Members	Assets ($mil)	Rating
SUN LIFE ASR CO OF CANADA	19515	D+
INDEPENDENCE LIFE ANNUITY CO	3529	C
SUN LIFE HEALTH INS CO	965	D
PROFESSIONAL INS CO	114	C

PROMINENCE HEALTHFIRST   D-   Weak

Major Rating Factors: Weak profitability index (0.9 on a scale of 0 to 10). Low quality investment portfolio (0.0). Weak overall results on stability tests (0.6) based on a steep decline in capital during 2019, inconsistent enrollment growth in the past five years due to declines in 2017 and 2018.
Other Rating Factors: Good capitalization index (5.7) based on good current risk-adjusted capital (severe loss scenario). Good liquidity (6.9) with sufficient resources (cash flows and marketable investments) to handle a spike in claims.
Principal Business: Medicare (50%), comp med (50%)
Mem Phys: 19: 8,931 **18:** 5,693 **19 MLR** 82.8% **/ 19 Admin Exp** N/A
Enroll(000): Q2 20: 26 **19:** 21 **18:** 18 **Med Exp PMPM:** $478
Principal Investments: Cash and equiv (61%), nonaffiliate common stock (24%), affiliate common stock (12%), real estate (3%)
Provider Compensation ($000): Contr fee ($109,593), capitation ($8,840)
Total Member Encounters: Phys (223,938), non-phys (60,083)
Group Affiliation: Universal Health Services Inc
Licensed in: NV
Address: 1510 Meadow Wood Lane, Reno,
Phone: (775) 770-9300 **Dom State:** NV **Commenced Bus:** N/A

Data Date	Rating	RACR #1	RACR #2	Total Assets ($mil)	Capital ($mil)	Net Premium ($mil)	Net Income ($mil)
6-20	D-	1.04	0.86	60.4	17.4	93.9	-2.5
6-19	D	4.41	3.68	96.1	58.6	73.3	-2.4
2019	D-	1.61	1.34	59.2	27.0	143.8	-5.8
2018	D	4.77	3.97	95.9	63.3	116.8	-9.7
2017	E	2.29	1.91	99.2	53.0	178.9	-15.4
2016	E	1.41	1.17	91.9	34.3	169.5	-29.7
2015	E	1.22	1.01	55.5	25.8	89.2	-15.8

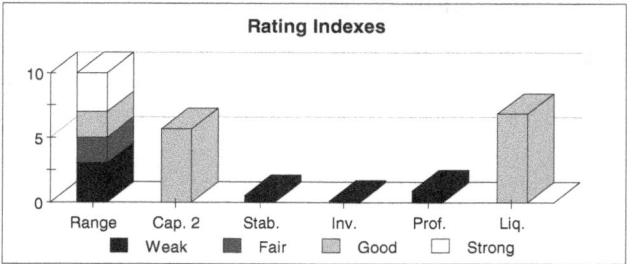

Rating Indexes

Range | Cap. 2 | Stab. | Inv. | Prof. | Liq.
■ Weak ■ Fair ▨ Good ☐ Strong

PROMINENCE HEALTHFIRST OF TEXAS INC   D-   Weak

Major Rating Factors: Weak profitability index (0.9 on a scale of 0 to 10). Low quality investment portfolio (0.0). Strong capitalization (7.6) based on excellent current risk-adjusted capital (severe loss scenario).
Other Rating Factors: Excellent liquidity (7.4) with ample operational cash flow and liquid investments.
Principal Business: Medicare (99%)
Mem Phys: 19: 2,379   **18:** 2,089   **19 MLR** 80.6%   **/ 19 Admin Exp** N/A
Enroll(000): Q2 20: 1   **19:** 1   **18:** 1   **Med Exp PMPM:** $703
Principal Investments: Cash and equiv (100%)
Provider Compensation ($000): Contr fee ($10,029), capitation ($24)
Total Member Encounters: Phys (23,457), non-phys (7,754)
Group Affiliation: Universal Health Services Inc
Licensed in: TX
Address: 1510 Meadow Wood Lane, Reno, NV 89502
Phone: (775) 770-9300   **Dom State:** TX   **Commenced Bus:** N/A

Data Date	Rating	RACR #1	RACR #2	Total Assets ($mil)	Capital ($mil)	Net Premium ($mil)	Net Income ($mil)
6-20	D-	1.80	1.50	7.2	3.1	8.0	-1.7
6-19	D+	16.73	13.94	21.5	19.1	6.4	0.7
2019	D	2.58	2.15	6.7	3.9	12.6	0.0
2018	D+	16.39	13.66	21.6	18.6	12.7	1.7
2017	D+	N/A	N/A	24.3	13.1	39.1	-6.9
2016	D+	1.66	1.38	14.7	6.9	23.2	-6.4
2015	D	9.14	7.61	8.9	7.4	3.6	-2.6

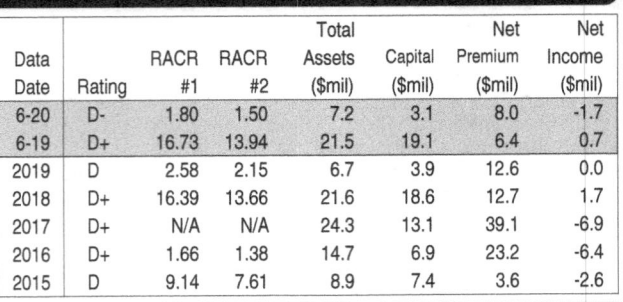

PROMINENCE PREFERRED HEALTH INS CO   D-   Weak

Major Rating Factors: Weak profitability index (0.9 on a scale of 0 to 10). Low quality investment portfolio (1.4). Strong capitalization (7.8) based on excellent current risk-adjusted capital (severe loss scenario).
Other Rating Factors: Excellent liquidity (7.5) with ample operational cash flow and liquid investments.
Principal Business: Comp med (100%)
Mem Phys: 19: 11,985   **18:** 11,081   **19 MLR** 75.5%   **/ 19 Admin Exp** N/A
Enroll(000): Q2 20: 4   **19:** 3   **18:** 2   **Med Exp PMPM:** $322
Principal Investments: Cash and equiv (83%), real estate (17%)
Provider Compensation ($000): Contr fee ($8,693), capitation ($1,635)
Total Member Encounters: Phys (20,071), non-phys (5,115)
Group Affiliation: Universal Health Services Inc
Licensed in: NV
Address: 1510 Meadow Wood Lane, Reno, NV 89502
Phone: (775) 770-9300   **Dom State:** NV   **Commenced Bus:** N/A

Data Date	Rating	RACR #1	RACR #2	Total Assets ($mil)	Capital ($mil)	Net Premium ($mil)	Net Income ($mil)
6-20	D-	1.99	1.66	9.5	4.0	8.2	-1.7
6-19	D-	21.63	18.03	38.8	34.3	6.6	-1.1
2019	D-	2.88	2.40	9.6	5.1	14.5	0.4
2018	D-	22.01	18.34	38.0	34.9	12.5	0.7
2017	E	19.62	16.35	37.5	34.4	14.2	4.0
2016	E	4.88	4.06	37.0	28.7	44.4	-4.7
2015	E	2.80	2.33	40.0	24.3	63.1	-11.4

PROSPECT HEALTH PLAN   E+   Very Weak

Major Rating Factors: Poor capitalization index (2.8 on a scale of 0 to 10) based on weak current risk-adjusted capital (moderate loss scenario). Good overall results on stability tests (5.8) despite fair risk diversification due to the company's size. Excellent profitability (8.4).
Other Rating Factors: Excellent liquidity (7.0) with sufficient resources (cash flows and marketable investments) to handle a spike in claims.
Principal Business: Managed care (104%)
Mem Phys: 19: N/A   **18:** N/A   **19 MLR** 98.1%   **/ 19 Admin Exp** N/A
Enroll(000): Q2 20: 52   **19:** 51   **18:** 51   **Med Exp PMPM:** $436
Principal Investments ($000): Cash and equiv ($5,449)
Provider Compensation ($000): None
Total Member Encounters: N/A
Group Affiliation: PHP Holdings Inc
Licensed in: CA
Address: 10780 Santa Monica Blvd #400, Los Angeles, CA 90025
Phone: (310) 228-3745   **Dom State:** CA   **Commenced Bus:** November 2014

Data Date	Rating	RACR #1	RACR #2	Total Assets ($mil)	Capital ($mil)	Net Premium ($mil)	Net Income ($mil)
6-20	E+	0.50	0.31	31.4	10.7	132.7	1.4
6-19	E+	0.41	0.25	24.3	8.4	135.2	1.8
2019	E+	0.39	0.24	25.7	8.7	257.9	2.7
2018	E+	0.28	0.17	22.4	6.0	243.0	2.1
2017	E+	0.31	0.19	10.3	3.9	133.2	0.9
2016	E	0.31	0.20	21.4	2.6	58.1	0.3
2015	U	2.34	1.42	6.0	2.3	7.1	0.0

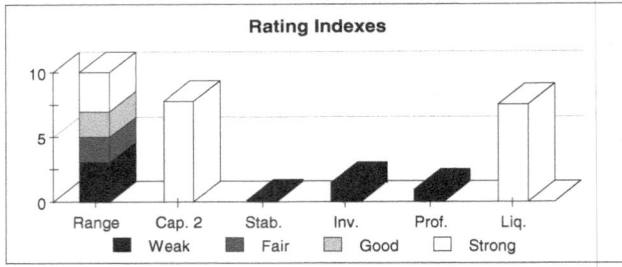

PROVIDENCE HEALTH ASR *

A-   **Excellent**

Major Rating Factors: Strong capitalization (10.0 on a scale of 0 to 10) based on excellent current risk-adjusted capital (severe loss scenario). High quality investment portfolio (9.6). Excellent liquidity (6.9) with sufficient resources (cash flows and marketable investments) to handle a spike in claims.
Other Rating Factors: Good overall profitability index (6.4).
Principal Business: Medicare (77%), Medicaid (23%)
Mem Phys: 19: 17,938   **18:** 18,160   **19 MLR** 92.2%   **/ 19 Admin Exp** N/A
Enroll(000): Q2 20: 111   **19:** 115   **18:** 112   **Med Exp PMPM:** $587
Principal Investments: Long-term bonds (78%), cash and equiv (19%), nonaffiliate common stock (2%), other (1%)
Provider Compensation ($000): Contr fee ($473,584), FFS ($242,823), bonus arrang ($122,951), capitation ($18,534), other ($2,755)
Total Member Encounters: Phys (467,219), non-phys (1,091,060)
Group Affiliation: None
Licensed in: OR, WA
Address: 4400 N E HALSEY BLDG # 2 STE, PORTLAND, OR 97213-1545
Phone: (503) 574-7500   **Dom State:** OR   **Commenced Bus:** N/A

Data Date	Rating	RACR #1	RACR #2	Total Assets ($mil)	Capital ($mil)	Net Premium ($mil)	Net Income ($mil)
6-20	A-	4.18	3.48	586.5	327.9	460.4	36.4
6-19	A-	5.14	4.28	463.7	297.2	441.6	13.7
2019	A-	4.64	3.86	450.3	290.3	868.4	10.5
2018	A-	4.87	4.06	416.7	284.4	824.8	37.1
2017	B	3.96	3.30	394.0	250.0	719.2	37.8
2016	B+	5.18	4.32	376.5	262.4	670.1	24.5
2015	B-	1.91	1.59	40.2	21.3	130.6	4.5

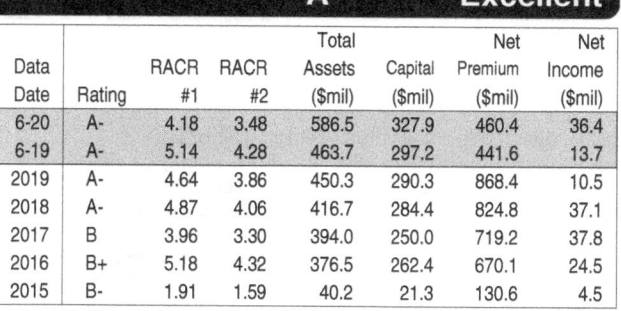

Rating Indexes

PROVIDENCE HEALTH NETWORK

D-   **Weak**

Major Rating Factors: Weak profitability index (0.7 on a scale of 0 to 10). Weak overall results on stability tests (2.9) in spite of healthy premium and capital growth during 2019. Strong capitalization index (7.0) based on good current risk-adjusted capital (moderate loss scenario).
Other Rating Factors: Excellent liquidity (7.0) with sufficient resources (cash flows and marketable investments) to handle a spike in claims.
Principal Business: Managed care (100%)
Mem Phys: 19: N/A   **18:** N/A   **19 MLR** 102.2%   **/ 19 Admin Exp** N/A
Enroll(000): Q2 20: 122   **19:** 54   **18:** 54   **Med Exp PMPM:** $243
Principal Investments ($000): Cash and equiv ($30,864)
Provider Compensation ($000): None
Total Member Encounters: N/A
Group Affiliation: None
Licensed in: CA
Address: 20555 Earl Street, Torrance, CA 90503
Phone: (805) 705-4451   **Dom State:** CA   **Commenced Bus:** November 2013

Data Date	Rating	RACR #1	RACR #2	Total Assets ($mil)	Capital ($mil)	Net Premium ($mil)	Net Income ($mil)
6-20	D-	1.16	0.70	44.5	16.8	103.7	3.1
6-19	E-	0.22	0.13	16.6	1.5	80.5	-3.4
2019	D-	1.07	0.65	32.3	15.4	156.7	-4.6
2018	E-	0.18	0.11	13.6	0.0	135.9	-2.0
2017	E-	0.31	0.19	14.3	2.0	108.7	-2.9
2016	E-	N/A	N/A	11.7	-10.1	89.7	-13.7
2015	E+	0.30	0.18	7.1	1.6	38.6	-2.1

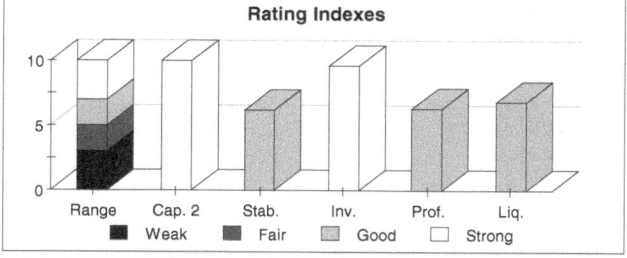

Rating Indexes

PROVIDENCE HEALTH PLAN

B   **Good**

Major Rating Factors: Good quality investment portfolio (6.4 on a scale of 0 to 10). Good liquidity (6.8) with sufficient resources (cash flows and marketable investments) to handle a spike in claims. Fair profitability index (4.7).
Other Rating Factors: Strong capitalization index (10.0) based on excellent current risk-adjusted capital (severe loss scenario). Excellent overall results on stability tests (7.0).
Principal Business: Comp med (100%)
Mem Phys: 19: 17,769   **18:** 16,567   **19 MLR** 87.7%   **/ 19 Admin Exp** N/A
Enroll(000): Q2 20: 187   **19:** 206   **18:** 241   **Med Exp PMPM:** $435
Principal Investments: Long-term bonds (39%), affiliate common stock (37%), nonaffiliate common stock (10%), cash and equiv (7%), real estate (6%), other (1%)
Provider Compensation ($000): Contr fee ($759,467), FFS ($323,326), capitation ($60,199), bonus arrang ($28,374), other ($2,054)
Total Member Encounters: Phys (499,301), non-phys (1,105,100)
Group Affiliation: Providence St Joseph Health
Licensed in: OR, WA
Address: 4400 NE Halsey Bldg # 2 Ste #, PORTLAND,
Phone: (503) 574-7500   **Dom State:** OR   **Commenced Bus:** N/A

Data Date	Rating	RACR #1	RACR #2	Total Assets ($mil)	Capital ($mil)	Net Premium ($mil)	Net Income ($mil)
6-20	B	4.29	3.57	1,064.2	652.0	573.1	13.1
6-19	B	3.96	3.30	949.7	564.2	658.5	38.5
2019	B	4.42	3.69	844.4	603.9	1,278.8	81.7
2018	B	3.87	3.22	863.9	555.5	1,377.6	39.1
2017	B	3.32	2.77	812.4	499.2	1,294.6	16.5
2016	A+	3.65	3.05	750.7	466.2	1,107.6	-28.1
2015	A+	4.31	3.59	799.3	464.6	1,193.2	-63.0

Rating Indexes

PROVIDENT LIFE & ACCIDENT INS CO

C+ **Fair**

Major Rating Factors: Fair quality investment portfolio (4.8 on a scale of 0 to 10) with large holdings of BBB rated bonds in addition to junk bond exposure equal to 62% of capital. Fair overall results on stability tests (4.4). Good overall profitability (6.5). Excellent expense controls. Return on equity has been excellent over the last five years averaging 26.6%.

Other Rating Factors: Good liquidity (6.8). Strong capitalization (7.5) based on excellent risk adjusted capital (severe loss scenario).

Principal Business: Individual health insurance (69%), individual life insurance (30%), and reinsurance (1%).

Principal Investments: NonCMO investment grade bonds (80%), mortgages in good standing (6%), noninv. grade bonds (6%), CMOs and structured securities (3%), and misc. investments (4%).

Investments in Affiliates: None

Group Affiliation: Unum Group

Licensed in: All states except NY

Commenced Business: May 1887

Address: 1 FOUNTAIN SQUARE, CHATTANOOGA, TN 37402-1330

Phone: (423) 294-1011 **Domicile State:** TN **NAIC Code:** 68195

Data Date	Rating	RACR #1	RACR #2	Total Assets ($mil)	Capital ($mil)	Net Premium ($mil)	Net Income ($mil)
6-20	C+	2.65	1.32	7,994.3	660.2	424.7	101.5
6-19	C+	2.59	1.31	7,930.4	647.8	434.9	114.4
2019	C+	2.75	1.38	7,893.4	658.9	763.6	219.4
2018	C+	2.50	1.26	7,994.0	607.3	771.0	204.8
2017	C+	2.44	1.22	8,034.0	605.0	769.3	163.5
2016	C+	2.76	1.38	8,272.6	728.2	840.8	191.7
2015	C+	2.74	1.38	8,325.3	727.5	869.4	178.9

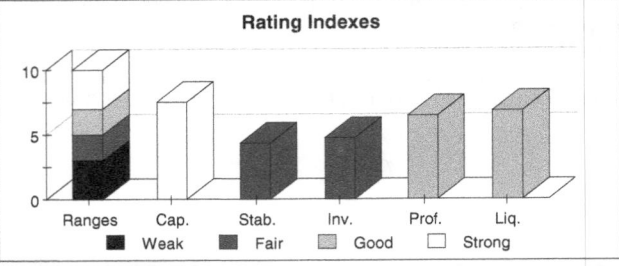

Rating Indexes — Ranges, Cap., Stab., Inv., Prof., Liq. (Weak / Fair / Good / Strong)

PROVIDENT LIFE & CAS INS CO

B- **Good**

Major Rating Factors: Good overall profitability (6.5 on a scale of 0 to 10). Excellent expense controls. Return on equity has been fair, averaging 9.7%. Fair overall results on stability tests (4.9) including fair financial strength of affiliated Unum Group. Fair quality investment portfolio (4.9).

Other Rating Factors: Strong capitalization (9.2) based on excellent risk adjusted capital (severe loss scenario). Excellent liquidity (7.2).

Principal Business: Individual health insurance (94%), reinsurance (3%), group health insurance (2%), and individual life insurance (2%).

Principal Investments: NonCMO investment grade bonds (86%), CMOs and structured securities (5%), noninv. grade bonds (4%), and mortgages in good standing (4%).

Investments in Affiliates: None

Group Affiliation: Unum Group

Licensed in: AK, AR, CO, CT, DC, DE, GA, HI, ID, IL, IA, KY, LA, MA, MS, MO, NE, NH, NJ, NM, NY, NC, ND, OH, OK, PA, RI, SC, SD, TN, VA, WA

Commenced Business: January 1952

Address: 1 FOUNTAIN SQUARE, CHATTANOOGA, TN 37402-1330

Phone: (423) 294-1011 **Domicile State:** TN **NAIC Code:** 68209

Data Date	Rating	RACR #1	RACR #2	Total Assets ($mil)	Capital ($mil)	Net Premium ($mil)	Net Income ($mil)
6-20	B-	4.23	2.46	748.3	133.1	51.1	9.1
6-19	B-	4.18	2.43	740.1	131.5	49.6	-0.1
2019	B-	4.10	2.39	739.3	124.4	99.7	2.1
2018	B-	4.30	2.47	736.0	131.2	94.8	6.1
2017	B-	4.75	2.63	746.7	150.2	92.2	26.0
2016	B-	4.43	2.38	753.2	141.7	90.3	13.7
2015	B-	4.65	2.50	755.8	147.2	87.0	21.3

Unum Group Composite Group Rating: C+ Largest Group Members	Assets ($mil)	Rating
UNUM LIFE INS CO OF AMERICA	22430	C+
PROVIDENT LIFE ACCIDENT INS CO	7893	C+
FIRST UNUM LIFE INS CO	4069	C+
COLONIAL LIFE ACCIDENT INS CO	3525	C+
PAUL REVERE LIFE INS CO	3214	C+

PROVIDER PARTNERS HEALTH PLAN INC

E **Very Weak**

Major Rating Factors: Weak profitability index (0.2 on a scale of 0 to 10). Poor capitalization (2.9) based on weak current risk-adjusted capital (moderate loss scenario). Good liquidity (5.6) with sufficient resources (cash flows and marketable investments) to handle a spike in claims.

Other Rating Factors: High quality investment portfolio (9.9).

Principal Business: Medicare (100%).

Mem Phys: 18: N/A **17:** 2,338 **18 MLR** 66.5% / **18 Admin Exp** N/A

Enroll(000): Q3 19: 1 **18:** 0 **17:** 0 **Med Exp PMPM:** $1,397

Principal Investments: Cash and equiv (76%), long-term bonds (24%)

Provider Compensation ($000): Contr fee ($4,242), capitation ($1,955)

Total Member Encounters: N/A

Group Affiliation: None

Licensed in: IL, MD

Address: 785 ELKRIDGE LANDING ROAD SUI, LINTHICUM HEIGHTS, MD 21090

Phone: (410) 308-2300 **Dom State:** MD **Commenced Bus:** N/A

Data Date	Rating	RACR #1	RACR #2	Total Assets ($mil)	Capital ($mil)	Net Premium ($mil)	Net Income ($mil)
9-19	E	0.61	0.51	4.9	1.5	13.8	-1.9
9-18	E-	N/A	N/A	4.0	2.0	5.6	-2.5
2018	E-	0.68	0.56	3.3	1.7	8.0	-2.1
2017	E-	N/A	N/A	2.4	1.1	6.6	-1.7
2016	E-	0.31	0.26	1.8	0.8	0.7	-1.8
2015	N/A	N/A	N/A	1.8	1.5	N/A	-0.9
2014	N/A	N/A	N/A	N/A	N/A	N/A	N/A

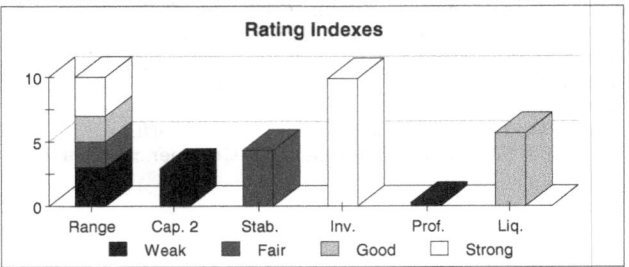

Rating Indexes — Range, Cap. 2, Stab., Inv., Prof., Liq. (Weak / Fair / Good / Strong)

PROVIDER PARTNERS HEALTH PLAN OF PA — E- — Very Weak

Major Rating Factors: Weak profitability index (0.9 on a scale of 0 to 10). Fair capitalization (3.5) based on weak current risk-adjusted capital (moderate loss scenario). Good liquidity (5.2) with sufficient resources (cash flows and marketable investments) to handle a spike in claims.
Other Rating Factors: High quality investment portfolio (9.9).
Principal Business: Medicare (100%)
Mem Phys: 18: N/A **17:** 4,018 **18 MLR** 74.1% **/ 18 Admin Exp** N/A
Enroll(000): Q3 19: 1 **18:** 1 **17:** 0 **Med Exp PMPM:** $1,377
Principal Investments: Cash and equiv (100%)
Provider Compensation ($000): Contr fee ($6,404), capitation ($3,535)
Total Member Encounters: N/A
Group Affiliation: None
Licensed in: PA
Address: 2595 INTERSTATE DR STE 103, HARRISBURG, PA 17110
Phone: (410) 308-2300 **Dom State:** PA **Commenced Bus:** N/A

Data Date	Rating	RACR #1	RACR #2	Total Assets ($mil)	Capital ($mil)	Net Premium ($mil)	Net Income ($mil)
9-19	E-	0.71	0.59	5.0	1.8	12.7	-1.2
9-18	N/A	N/A	N/A	3.7	1.2	9.5	-1.5
2018	U	0.40	0.33	3.4	1.2	12.9	-1.9
2017	N/A	N/A	N/A	3.0	1.4	4.0	-2.4
2016	N/A	N/A	N/A	1.8	1.3	N/A	-1.1
2015	N/A	N/A	N/A	1.7	1.3	N/A	-0.4
2014	N/A	N/A	N/A	1.5	1.5	N/A	N/A

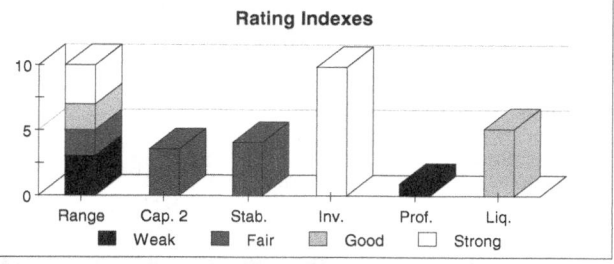

Rating Indexes

PRUITTHEALTH PREMIER INC — D+ — Weak

Major Rating Factors: Weak profitability index (0.9 on a scale of 0 to 10). Poor capitalization (2.4) based on weak current risk-adjusted capital (moderate loss scenario). High quality investment portfolio (9.9).
Other Rating Factors: Excellent liquidity (6.9) with sufficient resources (cash flows and marketable investments) to handle a spike in claims.
Principal Business: Medicare (100%)
Mem Phys: 18: 2,405 **17:** 1,219 **18 MLR** 89.2% **/ 18 Admin Exp** N/A
Enroll(000): Q3 19: 2 **18:** 2 **17:** 0 **Med Exp PMPM:** $1,775
Principal Investments: Cash and equiv (99%), long-term bonds (1%)
Provider Compensation ($000): Contr fee ($19,462), capitation ($12,219), bonus arrang ($264)
Total Member Encounters: Phys (22,983), non-phys (64,825)
Group Affiliation: UNICO Services Inc
Licensed in: GA
Address: 1626 Jeurgens Court, Norcross, GA 30393
Phone: (804) 396-6412 **Dom State:** GA **Commenced Bus:** N/A

Data Date	Rating	RACR #1	RACR #2	Total Assets ($mil)	Capital ($mil)	Net Premium ($mil)	Net Income ($mil)
9-19	D+	0.54	0.45	13.5	3.0	31.9	-1.0
9-18	N/A	N/A	N/A	11.1	3.0	30.6	-0.8
2018	U	0.63	0.53	10.7	3.5	39.9	-0.5
2017	N/A	N/A	N/A	4.2	3.0	8.5	-2.0
2016	N/A	N/A	N/A	4.3	3.1	7.1	N/A
2015	N/A	N/A	N/A	3.2	3.0	N/A	-1.2
2014	N/A	N/A	N/A	N/A	N/A	N/A	N/A

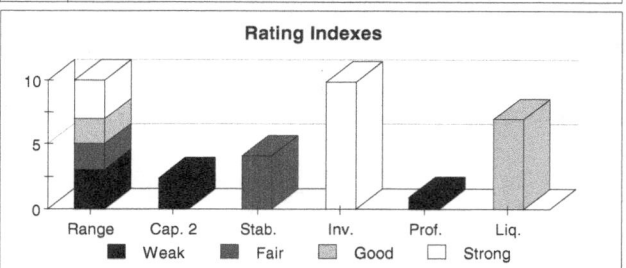

Rating Indexes

PUPIL BENEFITS PLAN INC — C- — Fair

Major Rating Factors: Fair quality investment portfolio (4.7 on a scale of 0 to 10). Excellent profitability (9.8). Strong capitalization (10.0) based on excellent current risk-adjusted capital (severe loss scenario).
Other Rating Factors: Excellent liquidity (8.2) with ample operational cash flow and liquid investments.
Principal Business: Other (100%)
Mem Phys: 19: N/A **18:** N/A **19 MLR** 66.3% **/ 19 Admin Exp** N/A
Enroll(000): Q2 20: 678 **19:** 678 **18:** 622 **Med Exp PMPM:** $0
Principal Investments: Cash and equiv (69%), long-term bonds (23%), nonaffiliate common stock (6%), real estate (1%)
Provider Compensation ($000): FFS ($5,106)
Total Member Encounters: N/A
Group Affiliation: Pupil Benefits Plan Inc
Licensed in: NY
Address: 101 DUTCH MEADOWS LANE, GLENVILLE, NY 12302
Phone: (518) 377-5144 **Dom State:** NY **Commenced Bus:** N/A

Data Date	Rating	RACR #1	RACR #2	Total Assets ($mil)	Capital ($mil)	Net Premium ($mil)	Net Income ($mil)
6-20	C-	7.29	6.07	13.6	10.4	4.2	2.6
6-19	N/A	N/A	N/A	N/A	N/A	N/A	N/A
2019	C-	5.32	4.43	16.7	7.9	8.4	0.5
2018	C-	5.51	4.59	15.3	7.2	8.5	1.5
2017	C-	4.69	3.91	14.5	6.0	8.8	1.1
2016	C-	3.48	2.90	14.3	4.7	9.6	1.6
2015	C-	1.88	1.56	14.3	3.1	9.8	1.2

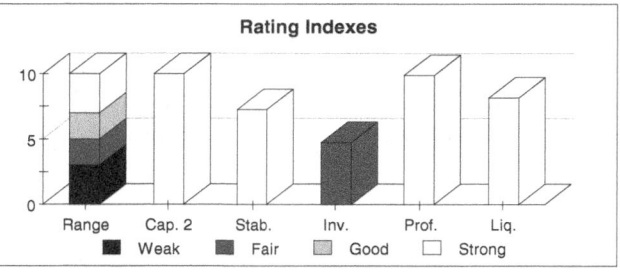

Rating Indexes

QBE INS CORP

B   Good

Major Rating Factors: Good overall long-term capitalization (5.6 on a scale of 0 to 10) based on good current risk adjusted capital (moderate loss scenario). However, capital levels have fluctuated somewhat during past years. History of adequate reserve strength (6.9) as reserves have been consistently at an acceptable level.

Other Rating Factors: Good liquidity (5.3) with sufficient resources (cash flows and marketable investments) to handle a spike in claims. Fair profitability index (3.4) with operating losses during 2017 and the first six months of 2020. Average return on equity over the last five years has been poor at -1.5%. Fair overall results on stability tests (4.1).

Principal Business: Group accident & health (29%), other liability (26%), homeowners multiple peril (11%), aircraft (9%), workers compensation (8%), allied lines (6%), and other lines (11%).

Principal Investments: Investment grade bonds (64%), misc. investments (27%), and non investment grade bonds (9%).

Investments in Affiliates: 8%

Group Affiliation: QBE Ins Group Ltd

Licensed in: All states except PR

Commenced Business: October 1980

Address: 600 N 2ND STE 401, Harrisburg, PA 17101

Phone: (800) 362-5448   **Domicile State:** PA   **NAIC Code:** 39217

Data Date	Rating	RACR #1	RACR #2	Loss Ratio %	Total Assets ($mil)	Capital ($mil)	Net Premium ($mil)	Net Income ($mil)
6-20	B	1.20	0.78	N/A	2,961.3	680.9	550.0	-75.7
6-19	B	1.81	1.21	N/A	2,540.9	756.2	500.0	15.9
2019	B	1.36	0.88	81.5	2,532.4	749.8	1,244.5	-57.5
2018	B	1.87	1.26	67.4	2,182.1	740.7	1,048.9	47.2
2017	B	2.16	1.43	75.6	2,054.3	678.0	890.9	-23.7
2016	B	2.48	1.70	58.8	2,325.0	748.9	846.9	27.7
2015	B-	2.46	1.81	63.9	2,134.5	735.7	597.0	28.8

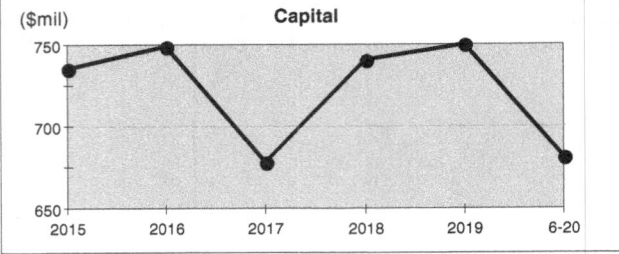

Capital

QCA HEALTH PLAN INC

D   Weak

Major Rating Factors: Weak profitability index (2.4 on a scale of 0 to 10). Weak overall results on stability tests (0.9). Good liquidity (6.8) with sufficient resources (cash flows and marketable investments) to handle a spike in claims.

Other Rating Factors: Strong capitalization index (7.5) based on excellent current risk-adjusted capital (severe loss scenario). High quality investment portfolio (9.0).

Principal Business: Comp med (99%), FEHB (1%)

Mem Phys: 19: 22,143 **18:** 20,660   **19 MLR** 90.6% **/ 19 Admin Exp** N/A

Enroll(000): Q2 20: 59 **19:** 51 **18:** 46   **Med Exp PMPM:** $336

Principal Investments: Cash and equiv (51%), long-term bonds (46%), other (3%)

Provider Compensation ($000): Contr fee ($184,513), FFS ($22,901)

Total Member Encounters: Phys (109,776), non-phys (145,765)

Group Affiliation: None

Licensed in: AR

Address: 12615 Chenal Parkway Suite 300, Little Rock,

Phone: (314) 725-4477 **Dom State:** AR **Commenced Bus:** N/A

Data Date	Rating	RACR #1	RACR #2	Total Assets ($mil)	Capital ($mil)	Net Premium ($mil)	Net Income ($mil)
6-20	D	1.78	1.48	144.0	42.4	130.7	12.0
6-19	D+	1.52	1.27	69.7	14.2	104.7	-8.0
2019	D+	2.19	1.82	97.9	30.8	219.3	-31.3
2018	C	3.81	3.17	112.7	60.0	206.4	16.7
2017	C-	N/A	N/A	75.4	43.6	197.6	11.1
2016	D+	1.46	1.22	75.2	31.9	214.8	-18.3
2015	C-	2.21	1.84	81.3	39.6	205.8	9.3

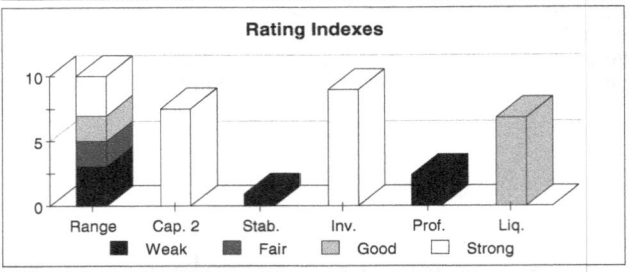

Rating Indexes

Range Cap. 2 Stab. Inv. Prof. Liq.
■ Weak ■ Fair ▨ Good □ Strong

QCC INS CO

B-   Good

Major Rating Factors: Fair quality investment portfolio (3.8 on a scale of 0 to 10). Excellent overall profitability index (6.9). Strong capitalization (9.4) based on excellent current risk-adjusted capital (severe loss scenario).

Other Rating Factors: Excellent liquidity (6.9) with sufficient resources (cash flows and marketable investments) to handle a spike in claims.

Principal Business: Comp med (88%), Medicare (6%), dental (2%), other (3%)

Mem Phys: 19: 66,900 **18:** 62,480   **19 MLR** 75.6% **/ 19 Admin Exp** N/A

Enroll(000): Q2 20: 302 **19:** 302 **18:** 282   **Med Exp PMPM:** $444

Principal Investments: Long-term bonds (63%), nonaffiliate common stock (33%), cash and equiv (2%), other (2%)

Provider Compensation ($000): Contr fee ($1,539,500), FFS ($31,772), capitation ($16,696), bonus arrang ($12,363)

Total Member Encounters: Phys (5,896,431), non-phys (1,014,315)

Group Affiliation: Independence Health Group Inc

Licensed in: AZ, CO, DC, DE, FL, GA, IN, KS, KY, LA, MD, MA, MS, MT, NE, NV, NM, ND, OH, OK, PA, SC, SD, TN, TX, UT, VT, WA, WV

Address: 1901 Market Street, Philadelphia, PA 19103-1480

Phone: (215) 241-2400 **Dom State:** PA **Commenced Bus:** N/A

Data Date	Rating	RACR #1	RACR #2	Total Assets ($mil)	Capital ($mil)	Net Premium ($mil)	Net Income ($mil)
6-20	B-	3.27	2.72	1,499.1	567.1	1,046.0	69.3
6-19	B-	4.88	4.06	1,355.4	642.1	1,035.5	69.8
2019	B-	3.55	2.96	1,249.8	506.5	2,095.6	145.8
2018	B-	4.18	3.48	1,194.9	544.6	2,106.6	193.2
2017	C	2.75	2.29	1,105.6	470.0	2,216.6	83.2
2016	C	2.96	2.46	1,157.6	401.0	2,248.6	-10.6
2015	C	3.13	2.61	1,161.6	408.5	2,246.3	-57.6

Rating Indexes

Range Cap. 2 Stab. Inv. Prof. Liq.
■ Weak ■ Fair ▨ Good □ Strong

QUALCHOICE L&H INS CO
D+   **Weak**

Major Rating Factors: Weak profitability index (2.6 on a scale of 0 to 10). Strong capitalization (8.0) based on excellent current risk-adjusted capital (severe loss scenario). High quality investment portfolio (9.1).
Other Rating Factors: Excellent liquidity (7.1) with ample operational cash flow and liquid investments.
Principal Business: Comp med (95%), med supp (4%)
Mem Phys: 19: 22,143   **18:** 20,660   **19 MLR** 87.0%   **/ 19 Admin Exp** N/A
Enroll(000): Q2 20: 46   **19:** 36   **18:** 28   **Med Exp PMPM:** $316
Principal Investments: Cash and equiv (90%), long-term bonds (10%)
Provider Compensation ($000): Contr fee ($127,354), FFS ($13,783)
Total Member Encounters: Phys (80,700), non-phys (79,779)
Group Affiliation: None
Licensed in: AR, NE
Address: 1 Allied Drive Suite 2520, Little Rock, AR 72202
Phone: (314) 725-4477   **Dom State:** AR   **Commenced Bus:** N/A

Data Date	Rating	RACR #1	RACR #2	Total Assets ($mil)	Capital ($mil)	Net Premium ($mil)	Net Income ($mil)
6-20	D+	2.16	1.80	116.7	34.8	100.8	14.3
6-19	C-	1.09	0.91	40.2	8.9	65.7	-5.5
2019	C	2.33	1.94	71.8	21.7	142.4	-26.2
2018	C	5.51	4.59	74.8	50.9	126.7	23.1
2017	D	1.87	1.56	54.5	27.6	114.3	-2.4
2016	D-	1.97	1.64	51.1	29.9	129.2	-15.5
2015	C	2.57	2.15	44.7	21.3	61.9	-5.1

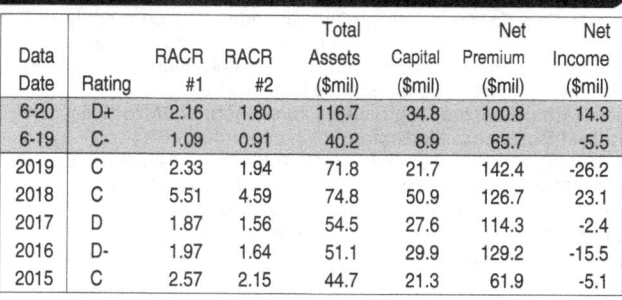

Rating Indexes

QUARTZ HEALTH INS CORP
C-   **Fair**

Major Rating Factors: Fair overall results on stability tests (3.9 on a scale of 0 to 10) based on a significant 97% decrease in enrollment during the period. Weak profitability index (2.3). Low quality investment portfolio (2.0)
Other Rating Factors: Strong capitalization index (7.2) based on excellent current risk-adjusted capital (severe loss scenario). Excellent liquidity (8.7) with ample operational cash flow and liquid investments.
Principal Business: Med supp (76%), comp med (14%), Medicaid (1%)
Mem Phys: 19: 9,454   **18:** 9,567   **19 MLR** 54.6%   **/ 19 Admin Exp** N/A
Enroll(000): Q2 20: 1   **19:** 1   **18:** 35   **Med Exp PMPM:** $144
Principal Investments: Affiliate common stock (94%), cash and equiv (5%), long-term bonds (1%)
Provider Compensation ($000): Capitation ($27,182)
Total Member Encounters: Phys (8,407), non-phys (8,545)
Group Affiliation: University Health Care Inc
Licensed in: IL, WI
Address: 2650 Novation Parkway, Madison,
Phone: (608) 643-2491   **Dom State:** WI   **Commenced Bus:** N/A

Data Date	Rating	RACR #1	RACR #2	Total Assets ($mil)	Capital ($mil)	Net Premium ($mil)	Net Income ($mil)
6-20	C-	1.54	1.28	117.3	115.6	1.6	-0.1
6-19	C-	1.53	1.28	113.9	110.2	2.3	0.6
2019	C-	1.58	1.32	115.2	113.2	4.3	1.2
2018	C-	1.38	1.15	133.1	100.1	193.0	2.8
2017	D+	1.03	0.86	121.8	77.4	240.7	-10.0
2016	D+	0.84	0.70	75.4	33.4	244.1	1.9
2015	D+	0.75	0.62	64.6	29.9	252.0	-9.2

Rating Indexes

QUARTZ HEALTH PLAN CORP
C-   **Fair**

Major Rating Factors: Fair quality investment portfolio (3.6 on a scale of 0 to 10). Weak profitability index (1.2). Good capitalization index (5.7) based on good current risk-adjusted capital (severe loss scenario).
Other Rating Factors: Good overall results on stability tests (5.1). Good liquidity (6.8) with sufficient resources (cash flows and marketable investments) to handle a spike in claims.
Principal Business: Medicare (66%), Medicaid (29%), comp med (4%), med supp (2%)
Mem Phys: 19: 9,454   **18:** 9,567   **19 MLR** 92.5%   **/ 19 Admin Exp** N/A
Enroll(000): Q2 20: 61   **19:** 56   **18:** 47   **Med Exp PMPM:** $340
Principal Investments: Cash and equiv (72%), long-term bonds (18%), affiliate common stock (9%)
Provider Compensation ($000): Capitation ($226,236)
Total Member Encounters: Phys (336,993), non-phys (382,845)
Group Affiliation: Quartz Health Plan Corporation
Licensed in: IA, WI
Address: 1836 South Avenue, La Crosse,
Phone: (608) 643-2491   **Dom State:** WI   **Commenced Bus:** N/A

Data Date	Rating	RACR #1	RACR #2	Total Assets ($mil)	Capital ($mil)	Net Premium ($mil)	Net Income ($mil)
6-20	C-	1.03	0.86	66.1	19.7	132.2	-1.1
6-19	C-	1.94	1.62	55.6	21.1	126.6	0.9
2019	C-	1.40	1.17	54.4	20.6	251.3	0.7
2018	C-	1.54	1.28	45.4	17.0	215.2	-2.1
2017	C-	N/A	N/A	36.2	21.8	269.7	-0.8
2016	C-	1.20	1.00	47.3	20.8	301.4	-5.7
2015	C+	0.65	0.54	38.9	16.1	297.4	-5.0

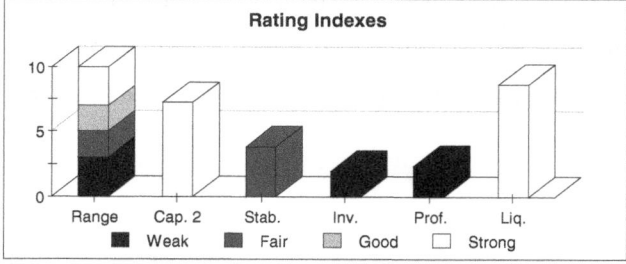

Rating Indexes

QUARTZ HEALTH PLAN MN CORP
C+   **Fair**

Major Rating Factors: Fair profitability index (3.1 on a scale of 0 to 10). Good liquidity (6.9) with sufficient resources (cash flows and marketable investments) to handle a spike in claims. Strong capitalization (7.2) based on excellent current risk-adjusted capital (severe loss scenario).
Other Rating Factors: High quality investment portfolio (9.6).
Principal Business: Medicare (94%), comp med (6%)
Mem Phys: 19: 955 **18:** 847 **19 MLR** 92.7% **/ 19 Admin Exp** N/A
Enroll(000): Q2 20: 3 **19:** 2 **18:** 1 **Med Exp PMPM:** $569
Principal Investments: Cash and equiv (100%)
Provider Compensation ($000): Capitation ($13,931)
Total Member Encounters: Phys (13,926), non-phys (20,819)
Group Affiliation: University Health Care Inc
Licensed in: MN
Address: 226 Second Street North, La Crescent, MN 55947
Phone: (608) 643-2491 **Dom State:** MN **Commenced Bus:** N/A

Data Date	Rating	RACR #1	RACR #2	Total Assets ($mil)	Capital ($mil)	Net Premium ($mil)	Net Income ($mil)
6-20	C+	1.48	1.24	8.9	4.0	10.7	0.2
6-19	C	1.45	1.20	6.0	2.7	7.5	-0.1
2019	C	2.11	1.76	7.2	3.8	15.5	0.1
2018	C	1.45	1.20	4.9	2.7	8.8	-0.2
2017	C	N/A	N/A	2.4	1.9	8.1	-0.1
2016	C	1.20	1.00	2.4	2.1	6.4	0.2
2015	C	1.00	0.83	2.5	1.9	5.3	-0.7

Rating Indexes

QUARTZ HLTH BENEFIT PLANS CORP
C   **Fair**

Major Rating Factors: Fair profitability index (4.2 on a scale of 0 to 10). Fair quality investment portfolio (3.2). Good liquidity (6.8) with sufficient resources (cash flows and marketable investments) to handle a spike in claims.
Other Rating Factors: Strong capitalization index (7.2) based on excellent current risk-adjusted capital (severe loss scenario). Excellent overall results on stability tests (7.0).
Principal Business: Comp med (100%)
Mem Phys: 19: 9,454 **18:** 9,567 **19 MLR** 92.0% **/ 19 Admin Exp** N/A
Enroll(000): Q2 20: 258 **19:** 257 **18:** 237 **Med Exp PMPM:** $426
Principal Investments: Cash and equiv (56%), long-term bonds (32%), nonaffiliate common stock (12%)
Provider Compensation ($000): Capitation ($1,274,462)
Total Member Encounters: Phys (864,336), non-phys (888,747)
Group Affiliation: University Health Care Inc
Licensed in: WI
Address: 840 Carolina Street, Sauk City,
Phone: (608) 643-2491 **Dom State:** WI **Commenced Bus:** N/A

Data Date	Rating	RACR #1	RACR #2	Total Assets ($mil)	Capital ($mil)	Net Premium ($mil)	Net Income ($mil)
6-20	C	1.51	1.26	329.2	107.8	741.6	0.5
6-19	C	1.66	1.38	276.3	102.3	712.4	2.4
2019	C	1.56	1.30	292.0	105.6	1,421.1	7.1
2018	C	1.33	1.11	241.0	82.6	1,276.8	5.8
2017	C	1.18	0.98	170.2	59.7	960.8	0.7
2016	C	1.38	1.15	167.4	61.3	863.5	-8.0
2015	B-	1.23	1.03	148.2	54.1	829.9	-2.7

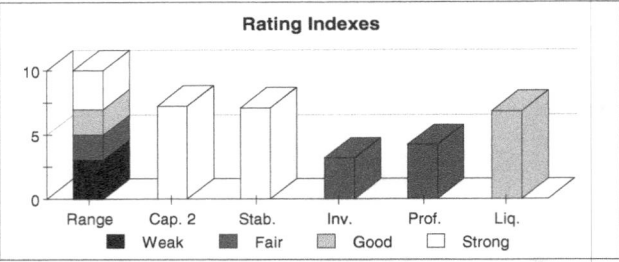

Rating Indexes

REGENCE BL CROSS BL SHIELD OREGON *
A-   **Excellent**

Major Rating Factors: Strong capitalization (10.0 on a scale of 0 to 10) based on excellent current risk-adjusted capital (severe loss scenario). Good overall profitability index (6.7). Good quality investment portfolio (6.4).
Other Rating Factors: Good liquidity (6.8) with sufficient resources (cash flows and marketable investments) to handle a spike in claims.
Principal Business: Comp med (44%), Medicare (32%), FEHB (20%), med supp (1%)
Mem Phys: 19: 31,034 **18:** 27,948 **19 MLR** 86.1% **/ 19 Admin Exp** N/A
Enroll(000): Q2 20: 445 **19:** 420 **18:** 530 **Med Exp PMPM:** $363
Principal Investments: Long-term bonds (67%), nonaffiliate common stock (29%), cash and equiv (1%), affiliate common stock (1%), real estate (1%)
Provider Compensation ($000): Contr fee ($1,480,729), bonus arrang ($203,500), FFS ($89,541), capitation ($293), other ($4,831)
Total Member Encounters: Phys (5,162,620), non-phys (6,945,017)
Group Affiliation: Cambia Health Solutions Inc
Licensed in: OR, WA
Address: 100 SW MARKET STREET, PORTLAND, OR 97201
Phone: (503) 225-5221 **Dom State:** OR **Commenced Bus:** N/A

Data Date	Rating	RACR #1	RACR #2	Total Assets ($mil)	Capital ($mil)	Net Premium ($mil)	Net Income ($mil)
6-20	A-	6.16	5.13	1,622.0	834.8	1,110.5	65.2
6-19	A-	7.47	6.22	1,436.2	857.6	1,052.2	56.7
2019	A-	6.65	5.55	1,462.4	836.6	2,128.5	60.6
2018	A-	6.77	5.65	1,255.6	776.6	1,965.5	62.2
2017	B+	5.65	4.71	1,194.8	730.9	1,913.4	78.8
2016	B+	6.57	5.48	1,092.9	661.0	1,780.8	30.2
2015	B+	5.99	4.99	1,045.8	639.2	1,877.6	25.8

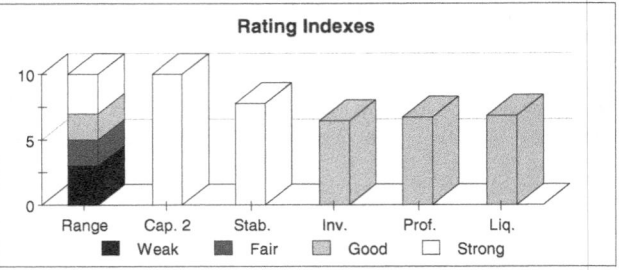

Rating Indexes

REGENCE BLUE CROSS BLUE SHIELD OF UT *   B+   Good

Major Rating Factors: Good overall profitability index (6.4 on a scale of 0 to 10). Good quality investment portfolio (6.5). Strong capitalization (10.0) based on excellent current risk-adjusted capital (severe loss scenario).
Other Rating Factors: Excellent liquidity (6.9) with sufficient resources (cash flows and marketable investments) to handle a spike in claims.
Principal Business: FEHB (45%), comp med (40%), Medicare (9%), med supp (4%)
Mem Phys: 19: 15,954 **18:** 14,688 **19 MLR** 87.6% **/ 19 Admin Exp** N/A
Enroll(000): Q2 20: 232 **19:** 233 **18:** 307 **Med Exp PMPM:** $301
Principal Investments: Long-term bonds (74%), nonaffiliate common stock (16%), cash and equiv (5%), affiliate common stock (5%), real estate (1%)
Provider Compensation ($000): Contr fee ($693,773), FFS ($159,122), bonus arrang ($41,793), capitation ($153), other ($2,354)
Total Member Encounters: Phys (2,894,602), non-phys (2,798,509)
Group Affiliation: Cambia Health Solutions Inc
Licensed in: UT
Address: 2890 EAST COTTONWOOD PARKWAY, SALT LAKE CITY, UT 84121-7035
Phone: (801) 333-2000 **Dom State:** UT **Commenced Bus:** N/A

Data Date	Rating	RACR #1	RACR #2	Total Assets ($mil)	Capital ($mil)	Net Premium ($mil)	Net Income ($mil)
6-20	B+	6.52	5.44	792.1	436.3	515.1	4.2
6-19	B+	9.57	7.98	791.6	455.0	512.3	20.5
2019	B+	8.71	7.26	768.4	459.6	1,059.1	26.3
2018	B+	8.97	7.47	715.9	425.4	1,030.5	77.2
2017	B	5.26	4.38	645.7	353.5	1,036.0	67.5
2016	B-	5.59	4.66	564.0	271.2	1,020.1	8.6
2015	B-	4.97	4.14	529.7	261.8	1,084.9	3.1

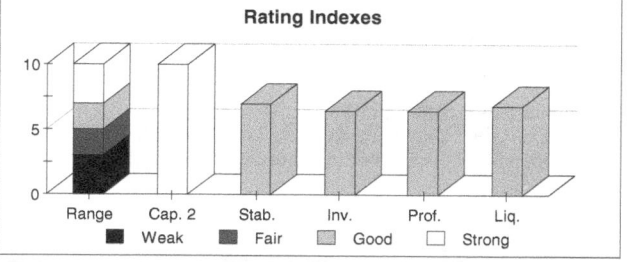
Rating Indexes

REGENCE BLUESHIELD   B   Good

Major Rating Factors: Good overall profitability index (6.0 on a scale of 0 to 10). Good quality investment portfolio (5.3). Good liquidity (6.8) with sufficient resources (cash flows and marketable investments) to handle a spike in claims.
Other Rating Factors: Strong capitalization (10.0) based on excellent current risk-adjusted capital (severe loss scenario).
Principal Business: Comp med (63%), FEHB (17%), Medicare (13%), med supp (6%)
Mem Phys: 19: 40,933 **18:** 38,152 **19 MLR** 81.1% **/ 19 Admin Exp** N/A
Enroll(000): Q2 20: 432 **19:** 438 **18:** 434 **Med Exp PMPM:** $269
Principal Investments: Long-term bonds (56%), nonaffiliate common stock (25%), affiliate common stock (14%), pref stock (2%), real estate (1%), other (5%)
Provider Compensation ($000): Contr fee ($1,144,990), bonus arrang ($134,286), FFS ($91,703), capitation ($343)
Total Member Encounters: Phys (4,672,122), non-phys (5,297,364)
Group Affiliation: Cambia Health Solutions Inc
Licensed in: WA
Address: 1800 NINTH AVENUE, SEATTLE, WA 98101
Phone: (206) 464-3600 **Dom State:** WA **Commenced Bus:** N/A

Data Date	Rating	RACR #1	RACR #2	Total Assets ($mil)	Capital ($mil)	Net Premium ($mil)	Net Income ($mil)
6-20	B	7.77	6.48	1,835.9	1,265.9	835.0	11.1
6-19	B	9.67	8.06	1,748.5	1,287.8	840.6	37.2
2019	B	8.00	6.67	1,759.5	1,304.2	1,715.8	64.1
2018	B	8.98	7.49	1,634.2	1,195.2	1,755.0	75.9
2017	B	7.71	6.42	1,731.0	1,213.9	1,979.6	85.2
2016	B	8.78	7.31	1,652.3	1,150.7	1,673.9	53.7
2015	B	8.18	6.81	1,611.9	1,114.6	1,784.1	11.8

Rating Indexes

REGENCE BLUESHIELD OF IDAHO INC *   B+   Good

Major Rating Factors: Good overall profitability index (6.0 on a scale of 0 to 10). Good quality investment portfolio (6.5). Good liquidity (6.8) with sufficient resources (cash flows and marketable investments) to handle a spike in claims.
Other Rating Factors: Strong capitalization (10.0) based on excellent current risk-adjusted capital (severe loss scenario).
Principal Business: Comp med (68%), Medicare (18%), FEHB (5%), med supp (3%), other (5%)
Mem Phys: 19: 10,971 **18:** 10,004 **19 MLR** 83.1% **/ 19 Admin Exp** N/A
Enroll(000): Q2 20: 162 **19:** 161 **18:** 172 **Med Exp PMPM:** $171
Principal Investments: Long-term bonds (70%), nonaffiliate common stock (17%), real estate (5%), cash and equiv (5%), affiliate common stock (2%)
Provider Compensation ($000): Contr fee ($280,412), bonus arrang ($21,684), FFS ($12,769), capitation ($210), other ($13,438)
Total Member Encounters: Phys (874,100), non-phys (1,176,326)
Group Affiliation: Cambia Health Solutions Inc
Licensed in: ID, WA
Address: 1602 21ST AVENUE, LEWISTON, ID 83501-4061
Phone: (208) 746-2671 **Dom State:** ID **Commenced Bus:** N/A

Data Date	Rating	RACR #1	RACR #2	Total Assets ($mil)	Capital ($mil)	Net Premium ($mil)	Net Income ($mil)
6-20	B+	6.08	5.07	395.1	239.1	191.4	6.2
6-19	B+	8.74	7.28	356.2	230.8	207.2	13.6
2019	B+	8.51	7.09	373.3	245.7	408.2	20.7
2018	B+	8.13	6.77	356.4	214.4	448.2	33.0
2017	B	4.50	3.75	302.4	181.5	467.1	27.4
2016	C+	6.30	5.25	265.4	152.1	418.7	15.6
2015	B-	4.92	4.10	237.7	135.3	433.4	-10.2

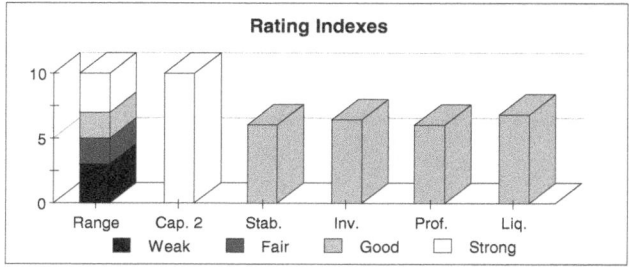
Rating Indexes

RELIANCE STANDARD LIFE INS CO

C+   **Fair**

Major Rating Factors: Fair overall results on stability tests (4.5 on a scale of 0 to 10). Good capitalization (5.4) based on good risk adjusted capital (moderate loss scenario). Moreover, capital levels have been consistent over the last five years. Good liquidity (6.6) with sufficient resources to handle a spike in claims as well as a significant increase in policy surrenders.

Other Rating Factors: Low quality investment portfolio (2.8). Excellent profitability (8.3) with operating gains in each of the last five years.

Principal Business: Individual annuities (48%), group health insurance (30%), group life insurance (16%), group retirement contracts (4%), and reinsurance (1%).

Principal Investments: Mortgages in good standing (30%), CMOs and structured securities (28%), nonCMO investment grade bonds (23%), noninv. grade bonds (8%), and misc. investments (8%).

Investments in Affiliates: 1%

Group Affiliation: Tokio Marine Holdings Inc

Licensed in: All states except NY

Commenced Business: April 1907

Address: 1100 East Woodfield Road, Schaumburg, IL 60173

Phone: (215) 787-4000 **Domicile State:** IL **NAIC Code:** 68381

Data Date	Rating	RACR #1	RACR #2	Total Assets ($mil)	Capital ($mil)	Net Premium ($mil)	Net Income ($mil)
6-20	C+	1.29	0.76	16,728.5	1,580.4	1,215.6	103.8
6-19	C+	2.03	1.07	14,383.3	1,391.4	1,333.9	104.5
2019	C+	1.43	0.85	15,902.9	1,517.1	2,356.0	220.5
2018	C+	1.88	1.01	13,875.0	1,278.3	3,160.5	245.1
2017	B	1.87	1.06	12,172.5	1,152.0	2,202.8	118.3
2016	B	1.91	1.06	10,889.4	1,066.1	1,801.1	166.0
2015	B	1.64	0.89	9,580.8	923.9	1,536.0	124.5

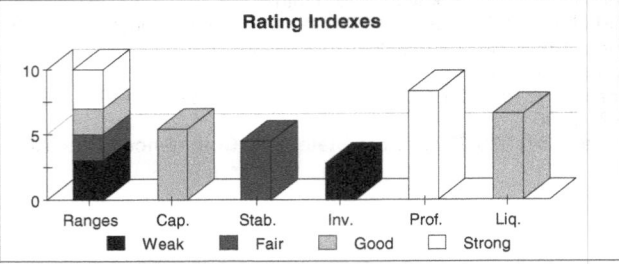

Rating Indexes (Ranges, Cap., Stab., Inv., Prof., Liq.) — Weak / Fair / Good / Strong

RELIASTAR LIFE INS CO

B-   **Good**

Major Rating Factors: Good quality investment portfolio (5.9 on a scale of 0 to 10) despite large holdings of BBB rated bonds in addition to moderate junk bond exposure. Exposure to mortgages is significant, but the mortgage default rate has been low. Good liquidity (5.2) with sufficient resources to handle a spike in claims as well as a significant increase in policy surrenders. Fair profitability (3.7).

Other Rating Factors: Fair overall results on stability tests (3.8) including weak results on operational trends, negative cash flow from operations for 2019 and excessive premium growth. Strong capitalization (7.2) based on excellent risk adjusted capital (severe loss scenario).

Principal Business: Group health insurance (44%), individual life insurance (30%), group life insurance (17%), individual annuities (5%), and other lines (4%).

Principal Investments: NonCMO investment grade bonds (57%), CMOs and structured securities (14%), mortgages in good standing (12%), policy loans (3%), and misc. investments (11%).

Investments in Affiliates: 3%

Group Affiliation: Voya Financial Inc

Licensed in: All states, the District of Columbia and Puerto Rico

Commenced Business: September 1885

Address: 20 WASHINGTON AVENUE SOUTH, MINNEAPOLIS, MN 55401

Phone: (770) 980-5100 **Domicile State:** MN **NAIC Code:** 67105

Data Date	Rating	RACR #1	RACR #2	Total Assets ($mil)	Capital ($mil)	Net Premium ($mil)	Net Income ($mil)
6-20	B-	1.83	1.11	19,407.1	1,551.3	596.9	72.8
6-19	B-	1.74	1.04	19,839.8	1,359.6	462.1	-40.6
2019	B-	1.93	1.16	19,707.3	1,536.3	666.8	35.5
2018	B-	2.05	1.21	20,238.5	1,632.9	1,122.5	100.6
2017	C+	1.98	1.18	19,910.1	1,483.1	633.1	234.3
2016	C+	2.09	1.26	19,828.5	1,662.0	777.1	-506.6
2015	C+	2.03	1.23	19,805.1	1,609.2	740.9	74.2

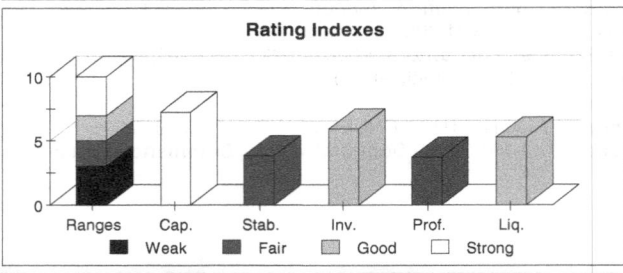

Rating Indexes (Ranges, Cap., Stab., Inv., Prof., Liq.) — Weak / Fair / Good / Strong

RENAISSANCE L&H INS CO OF AMERICA

B   **Good**

Major Rating Factors: Good quality investment portfolio (5.2 on a scale of 0 to 10) despite mixed results such as: no exposure to mortgages and substantial holdings of BBB bonds but minimal holdings in junk bonds. Good overall profitability (6.1). Excellent expense controls. Good overall results on stability tests (5.4) excellent operational trends and good risk diversification.

Other Rating Factors: Strong capitalization (7.3) based on excellent risk adjusted capital (severe loss scenario). Excellent liquidity (7.0).

Principal Business: Individual health insurance (59%), group health insurance (26%), reinsurance (13%), and group life insurance (2%).

Principal Investments: NonCMO investment grade bonds (43%), CMOs and structured securities (28%), and common & preferred stock (22%).

Investments in Affiliates: None

Group Affiliation: Renaissance Health Service Corp

Licensed in: All states except NY, PR

Commenced Business: June 1953

Address: 1209 Orange St, Indianapolis, IN 46202

Phone: (517) 349-6000 **Domicile State:** DE **NAIC Code:** 61700

Data Date	Rating	RACR #1	RACR #2	Total Assets ($mil)	Capital ($mil)	Net Premium ($mil)	Net Income ($mil)
6-20	B	1.65	1.22	101.0	58.6	86.8	12.4
6-19	N/A	N/A	N/A	99.3	65.8	86.6	0.1
2019	C+	1.63	1.21	92.6	56.2	170.5	3.3
2018	N/A	N/A	N/A	95.3	67.8	0.0	3.2
2017	N/A	N/A	N/A	91.9	66.3	0.0	3.7
2016	N/A	N/A	N/A	86.5	65.6	0.0	7.9
2015	N/A	N/A	N/A	79.0	61.4	0.0	9.6

Rating Indexes (Ranges, Cap., Stab., Inv., Prof., Liq.) — Weak / Fair / Good / Strong

RESERVE NATIONAL INS CO

B-   **Good**

Major Rating Factors: Good current capitalization (5.9 on a scale of 0 to 10) based on mixed results -- excessive policy leverage mitigated by excellent risk adjusted capital (severe loss scenario) reflecting improvement over results in 2017. Good liquidity (5.8) with sufficient resources to handle a spike in claims. Fair overall results on stability tests (4.9) including negative cash flow from operations for 2019.

Other Rating Factors: Weak profitability (1.8). High quality investment portfolio (7.5).

Principal Business: Individual health insurance (88%), individual life insurance (7%), reinsurance (3%), and group life insurance (1%).

Principal Investments: NonCMO investment grade bonds (86%), CMOs and structured securities (7%), and noninv. grade bonds (1%).

Investments in Affiliates: None

Group Affiliation: Kemper Corporation

Licensed in: All states except NY, PR

Commenced Business: September 1956

Address: 601 EAST BRITTON ROAD, CHICAGO, IL 60601

Phone: (405) 848-7931 **Domicile State:** OK **NAIC Code:** 68462

Data Date	Rating	RACR #1	RACR #2	Total Assets ($mil)	Capital ($mil)	Net Premium ($mil)	Net Income ($mil)
6-20	B-	1.49	1.14	149.2	45.8	94.0	4.4
6-19	B-	1.07	0.81	140.1	28.2	88.7	-6.7
2019	B-	1.34	1.03	149.9	39.7	177.2	-13.2
2018	B-	1.17	0.89	136.0	30.9	162.6	-9.7
2017	B-	1.03	0.79	121.5	24.8	152.5	-9.3
2016	B+	1.77	1.34	126.9	40.2	143.6	-2.0
2015	A	2.18	1.66	122.8	45.1	132.7	-0.5

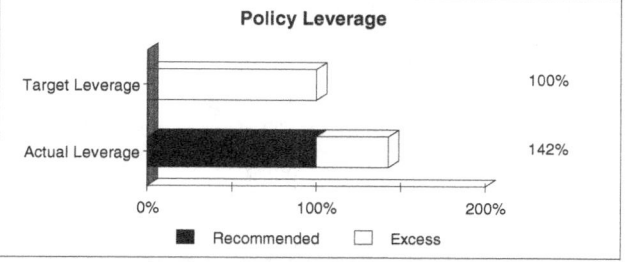

Policy Leverage

Target Leverage — 100%
Actual Leverage — 142%

0%   100%   200%

■ Recommended   □ Excess

RGA REINSURANCE CO

B-   **Good**

Major Rating Factors: Good capitalization (5.9 on a scale of 0 to 10) based on good risk adjusted capital (moderate loss scenario). Capital levels have been relatively consistent over the last five years. Good liquidity (5.9) with sufficient resources to handle a spike in claims as well as a significant increase in policy surrenders. Fair quality investment portfolio (4.2).

Other Rating Factors: Fair overall results on stability tests (4.9). Excellent profitability (7.2) despite modest operating losses during 2015.

Principal Business: Reinsurance (100%).

Principal Investments: NonCMO investment grade bonds (49%), CMOs and structured securities (17%), mortgages in good standing (16%), noninv. grade bonds (7%), and misc. investments (11%).

Investments in Affiliates: 3%

Group Affiliation: Reinsurance Group of America Inc

Licensed in: All states, the District of Columbia and Puerto Rico

Commenced Business: October 1982

Address: 16600 Swingley Ridge Road, Chesterfield, MO 63017-1706

Phone: (636) 736-7000 **Domicile State:** MO **NAIC Code:** 93572

Data Date	Rating	RACR #1	RACR #2	Total Assets ($mil)	Capital ($mil)	Net Premium ($mil)	Net Income ($mil)
3-20	B-	1.60	0.84	41,983.4	2,055.3	693.8	-156.4
3-19	B-	1.80	0.97	36,492.4	2,131.1	725.4	67.2
2019	B-	1.65	0.87	41,587.9	2,150.1	3,377.3	280.4
2018	B-	1.70	0.93	36,983.5	2,078.7	4,488.1	659.9
2017	B-	1.63	0.87	33,356.1	1,584.0	4,286.4	138.4
2016	B-	1.61	0.87	25,432.8	1,521.6	2,636.1	148.6
2015	B-	1.42	0.81	24,593.0	1,503.4	3,364.2	-23.6

Risk-Adjusted Capital Ratio #1
(Moderate Loss Scenario)

Range 2015 2016 2017 2018 2019 3-20

■ Weak   ▦ Fair   □ Good

ROCKY MOUNTAIN HEALTH MAINT ORG

B-   **Good**

Major Rating Factors: Good overall profitability index (5.9 on a scale of 0 to 10). Good overall results on stability tests (6.4). Strong capitalization index (8.5) based on excellent current risk-adjusted capital (severe loss scenario).

Other Rating Factors: Excellent liquidity (7.1) with ample operational cash flow and liquid investments. Low quality investment portfolio (1.8).

Principal Business: Medicaid (64%), comp med (31%), Medicare (2%), other (3%)

Mem Phys: 19: 21,249 **18:** 20,862 **19 MLR** 81.6% **/ 19 Admin Exp** N/A

Enroll(000): Q2 20: 222 **19:** 209 **18:** 223 **Med Exp PMPM:** $141

Principal Investments: Cash and equiv (63%), long-term bonds (31%), real estate (5%), affiliate common stock (1%), other (1%)

Provider Compensation ($000): Contr fee ($193,951), FFS ($101,090), capitation ($65,866)

Total Member Encounters: Phys (1,130,181)

Group Affiliation: None

Licensed in: CO

Address: 2775 Crossroads Blvd, Grand Junction,

Phone: (970) 244-7760 **Dom State:** CO **Commenced Bus:** N/A

Data Date	Rating	RACR #1	RACR #2	Total Assets ($mil)	Capital ($mil)	Net Premium ($mil)	Net Income ($mil)
6-20	B-	2.55	2.13	189.1	87.4	236.6	4.3
6-19	B-	4.04	3.37	149.9	86.2	220.2	11.4
2019	B-	3.57	2.97	158.5	82.3	443.9	9.9
2018	B-	3.51	2.92	161.9	74.2	404.2	21.8
2017	C	1.46	1.22	121.4	50.4	376.0	2.6
2016	C	1.09	0.91	152.3	46.9	449.2	-6.8
2015	C	0.75	0.62	186.5	39.6	481.0	-21.8

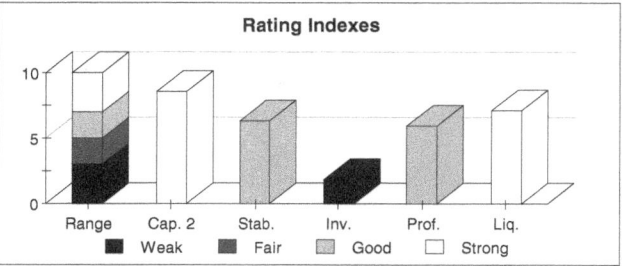

Rating Indexes

Range Cap. 2 Stab. Inv. Prof. Liq.

■ Weak   ▦ Fair   ▨ Good   □ Strong

ROCKY MOUNTAIN HOSPITAL & MEDICAL | B | Good

Major Rating Factors: Good liquidity (6.5 on a scale of 0 to 10) with sufficient resources (cash flows and marketable investments) to handle a spike in claims. Fair quality investment portfolio (3.7). Excellent profitability (8.6).

Other Rating Factors: Strong capitalization (8.6) based on excellent current risk-adjusted capital (severe loss scenario).

Principal Business: Comp med (53%), FEHB (36%), med supp (5%), dental (2%), other (4%)

Mem Phys: 19: 21,787 **18:** 22,058 **19 MLR** 101.4% **/ 19 Admin Exp** N/A

Enroll(000): Q2 20: 673 **19:** 658 **18:** 609 **Med Exp PMPM:** $224

Principal Investments: Affiliate common stock (67%), long-term bonds (48%), other (1%)

Provider Compensation ($000): Bonus arrang ($1,141,351), contr fee ($503,776), FFS ($55,512), capitation ($67), other ($46,677)

Total Member Encounters: Phys (2,217,436), non-phys (1,702,690)

Group Affiliation: Anthem Inc

Licensed in: CO, NV

Address: 700 BROADWAY, DENVER, CO 80273

Phone: (303) 831-2131 **Dom State:** CO **Commenced Bus:** N/A

Data Date	Rating	RACR #1	RACR #2	Total Assets ($mil)	Capital ($mil)	Net Premium ($mil)	Net Income ($mil)
6-20	B	2.63	2.19	1,192.6	620.7	855.7	103.8
6-19	B	3.42	2.85	1,204.8	593.7	869.7	70.0
2019	B	2.52	2.10	1,031.0	501.9	1,733.4	183.6
2018	B	2.61	2.18	964.1	449.8	1,748.7	91.5
2017	B	1.98	1.65	930.1	399.0	1,942.0	71.8
2016	B	2.50	2.09	1,007.6	374.9	2,337.6	87.7
2015	B	3.71	3.09	907.0	387.1	1,907.8	89.7

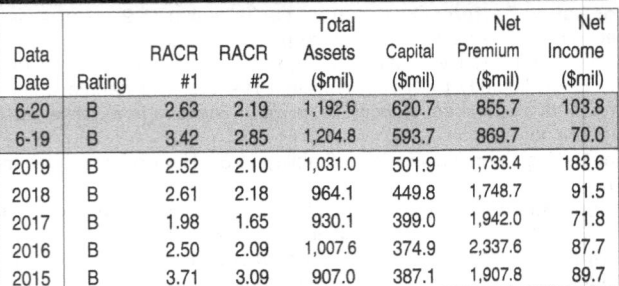

Rating Indexes

RYDER HEALTH PLAN INC | B | Good

Major Rating Factors: Good overall profitability index (5.4 on a scale of 0 to 10). Good overall results on stability tests (5.4). Strong capitalization index (7.8) based on excellent current risk-adjusted capital (severe loss scenario).

Other Rating Factors: High quality investment portfolio (9.8). Excellent liquidity (8.3) with ample operational cash flow and liquid investments.

Principal Business: Comp med (99%)

Mem Phys: 19: N/A **18:** N/A **19 MLR** 71.1% **/ 19 Admin Exp** N/A

Enroll(000): Q2 20: 2 **19:** 2 **18:** 2 **Med Exp PMPM:** $47

Principal Investments: Cash and equiv (84%), long-term bonds (16%)

Provider Compensation ($000): Capitation ($1,237), other ($99)

Total Member Encounters: N/A

Group Affiliation: Ryder Health Plan Inc

Licensed in: PR

Address: 353 FONT MARTELO AVE SUITE 1, HUMACAO,

Phone: (787) 852-0846 **Dom State:** PR **Commenced Bus:** N/A

Data Date	Rating	RACR #1	RACR #2	Total Assets ($mil)	Capital ($mil)	Net Premium ($mil)	Net Income ($mil)
6-20	B	2.02	1.68	1.8	0.8	0.9	0.1
6-19	N/A	N/A	N/A	N/A	N/A	N/A	N/A
2019	B	1.96	1.64	1.7	0.8	1.9	0.1
2018	B	1.41	1.18	1.5	0.6	2.0	0.1
2017	C+	1.64	1.37	1.6	0.7	2.5	0.2
2016	C-	1.24	1.03	1.5	0.5	2.6	0.0
2015	C-	1.28	1.07	1.3	0.5	1.9	-0.2

Rating Indexes

SAMARITAN HEALTH PLANS INC | B- | Good

Major Rating Factors: Good overall profitability index (5.3 on a scale of 0 to 10). Good liquidity (6.8) with sufficient resources (cash flows and marketable investments) to handle a spike in claims. Strong capitalization (6.9) based on excellent current risk-adjusted capital (severe loss scenario).

Other Rating Factors: High quality investment portfolio (9.9).

Principal Business: Medicare (73%), comp med (27%)

Mem Phys: 19: 9,278 **18:** 9,960 **19 MLR** 84.1% **/ 19 Admin Exp** N/A

Enroll(000): Q2 20: 9 **19:** 10 **18:** 11 **Med Exp PMPM:** $679

Principal Investments: Cash and equiv (49%), long-term bonds (44%), nonaffiliate common stock (7%)

Provider Compensation ($000): Contr fee ($81,808)

Total Member Encounters: Phys (119,753), non-phys (68,831)

Group Affiliation: Samaritan Health Services Inc

Licensed in: OR

Address: 3600 NW Samaritan Drive, Corvallis, OR 97330

Phone: (541) 768-5328 **Dom State:** OR **Commenced Bus:** N/A

Data Date	Rating	RACR #1	RACR #2	Total Assets ($mil)	Capital ($mil)	Net Premium ($mil)	Net Income ($mil)
6-20	B-	1.31	1.09	32.7	16.0	51.7	4.7
6-19	N/A	N/A	N/A	N/A	N/A	N/A	N/A
2019	C+	0.94	0.78	24.6	11.8	96.6	0.5
2018	B-	0.90	0.75	25.5	11.5	89.1	-3.1
2017	B	1.39	1.16	30.8	15.3	92.2	5.1
2016	C+	0.94	0.79	20.7	9.5	73.4	2.8
2015	C	0.85	0.71	17.4	8.1	61.1	-0.9

Rating Indexes

SAN FRANCISCO HEALTH AUTHORITY   B-   Good

Major Rating Factors: Good overall results on stability tests (5.1 on a scale of 0 to 10). Strong capitalization index (7.7) based on excellent current risk-adjusted capital (severe loss scenario). Excellent liquidity (8.7) with ample operational cash flow and liquid investments.
Other Rating Factors: Weak profitability index (2.7).
Principal Business: Medicaid (89%)
Mem Phys: 19: N/A **18:** N/A **19 MLR** 95.1% **/ 19 Admin Exp** N/A
Enroll(000): Q1 20: 137 **19:** 141 **18:** 141 **Med Exp PMPM:** $329
Principal Investments ($000): Cash and equiv ($92,589)
Provider Compensation ($000): None
Total Member Encounters: N/A
Group Affiliation: None
Licensed in: (No states)
Address: 50 Beale Street 12th Floor, San Francisco, CA 94105
Phone: (415) 615-4217 **Dom State:** CA **Commenced Bus:** March 1996

Data Date	Rating	RACR #1	RACR #2	Total Assets ($mil)	Capital ($mil)	Net Premium ($mil)	Net Income ($mil)
3-20	B-	2.50	1.57	823.1	103.6	456.7	-5.3
3-19	B-	2.67	1.69	662.6	108.9	140.4	-0.1
2019	B-	2.47	1.56	734.3	103.2	598.3	-5.8
2018	B-	2.66	1.68	624.8	109.0	600.1	-16.9
2017	B	3.01	1.88	632.5	125.8	618.5	12.2
2016	B	2.91	1.83	484.8	112.6	572.8	29.9
2015	B	2.20	1.39	346.1	82.7	545.1	37.8

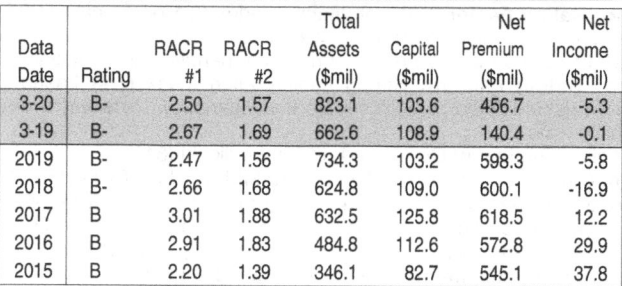

SAN JOAQUIN CNTY HEALTH *   B+   Good

Major Rating Factors: Excellent profitability (7.1 on a scale of 0 to 10). Strong capitalization index (10.0) based on excellent current risk-adjusted capital (severe loss scenario). Excellent overall results on stability tests (7.3).
Other Rating Factors: Excellent liquidity (7.6) with ample operational cash flow and liquid investments.
Principal Business: Medicaid (100%)
Mem Phys: 19: N/A **18:** N/A **19 MLR** 94.4% **/ 19 Admin Exp** N/A
Enroll(000): Q2 20: 348 **19:** 343 **18:** 343 **Med Exp PMPM:** $247
Principal Investments ($000): Cash and equiv ($368,688)
Provider Compensation ($000): None
Total Member Encounters: N/A
Group Affiliation: None
Licensed in: CA
Address: 7751 S Manthey Rd, French Camp, CA 95231-9802
Phone: (888) 936-7526 **Dom State:** CA **Commenced Bus:** N/A

Data Date	Rating	RACR #1	RACR #2	Total Assets ($mil)	Capital ($mil)	Net Premium ($mil)	Net Income ($mil)
6-20	B+	5.42	3.30	880.8	342.1	542.6	-3.9
6-19	B+	5.90	3.59	695.3	359.0	525.3	37.1
2019	B+	5.48	3.33	825.1	346.0	1,088.6	24.1
2018	B+	5.21	3.17	523.8	321.9	1,050.0	31.8
2017	B	3.87	2.35	601.2	290.1	1,036.4	78.1
2016	C+	1.89	1.15	561.1	140.8	920.6	26.7
2015	C+	2.18	1.33	455.2	114.2	729.1	79.9

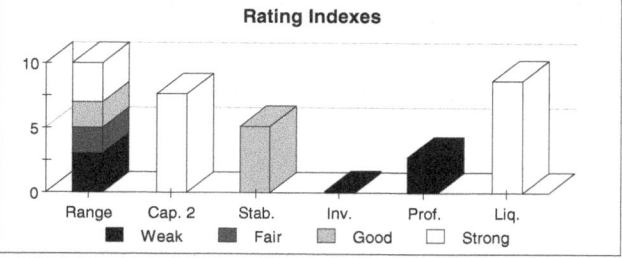

SAN MATEO HEALTH COMMISSION   B   Good

Major Rating Factors: Good overall results on stability tests (5.0 on a scale of 0 to 10). Fair profitability index (3.4). Strong capitalization index (10.0) based on excellent current risk-adjusted capital (severe loss scenario).
Other Rating Factors: Excellent liquidity (7.7) with ample operational cash flow and liquid investments.
Principal Business: Medicaid (75%), Medicare (25%)
Mem Phys: 19: N/A **18:** N/A **19 MLR** 90.0% **/ 19 Admin Exp** N/A
Enroll(000): Q2 20: 114 **19:** 115 **18:** 115 **Med Exp PMPM:** $490
Principal Investments ($000): Cash and equiv ($421,828)
Provider Compensation ($000): None
Total Member Encounters: N/A
Group Affiliation: None
Licensed in: CA
Address: 7751 S Manthey Road, French Camp, CA 95231
Phone: (209) 461-2211 **Dom State:** CA **Commenced Bus:** December 1987

Data Date	Rating	RACR #1	RACR #2	Total Assets ($mil)	Capital ($mil)	Net Premium ($mil)	Net Income ($mil)
6-20	B	6.15	3.78	598.2	329.4	411.2	-18.7
6-19	B	6.53	4.02	624.0	349.0	462.4	9.4
2019	B	6.53	4.02	610.5	348.0	781.2	8.5
2018	B	6.31	3.89	574.4	339.5	770.9	0.3
2017	B+	6.67	4.11	745.3	339.2	906.4	41.8
2016	B+	5.55	3.41	800.6	297.4	792.3	-20.3
2015	A-	6.65	4.08	641.5	317.8	911.0	103.4

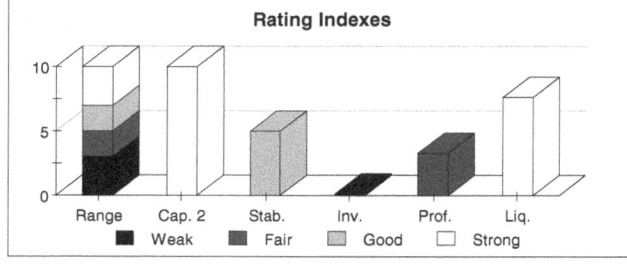

SANFORD HEALTH PLAN

C **Fair**

Major Rating Factors: Fair profitability index (3.1 on a scale of 0 to 10). Good quality investment portfolio (4.9). Good liquidity (6.3) with sufficient resources (cash flows and marketable investments) to handle a spike in claims.
Other Rating Factors: Strong capitalization index (7.4) based on excellent current risk-adjusted capital (severe loss scenario). Excellent overall results on stability tests (7.2).
Principal Business: Comp med (69%), Medicaid (31%)
Mem Phys: 19: 76,949 **18:** 59,836 **19 MLR** 95.1% **/ 19 Admin Exp** N/A
Enroll(000): Q2 20: 153 **19:** 143 **18:** 139 **Med Exp PMPM:** $528
Principal Investments: Long-term bonds (51%), cash and equiv (33%), nonaffiliate common stock (15%), pref stock (1%), other (1%)
Provider Compensation ($000): Contr fee ($884,819)
Total Member Encounters: Phys (602,341), non-phys (691,387)
Group Affiliation: None
Licensed in: IA, ND, SD
Address: 300 Cherapa Place Suite 201, Sioux Falls,
Phone: (605) 328-6868 **Dom State:** SD **Commenced Bus:** N/A

Data Date	Rating	RACR #1	RACR #2	Total Assets ($mil)	Capital ($mil)	Net Premium ($mil)	Net Income ($mil)
6-20	C	1.69	1.41	338.5	156.3	505.6	33.6
6-19	C	1.58	1.32	283.6	139.8	465.4	17.1
2019	C	1.37	1.14	284.8	125.6	946.3	-1.9
2018	C	1.49	1.24	270.8	131.4	908.5	9.7
2017	C	1.43	1.19	268.2	117.7	839.5	11.2
2016	C	0.96	0.80	230.5	86.4	823.7	-8.9
2015	C	0.74	0.62	223.0	55.1	613.2	-73.2

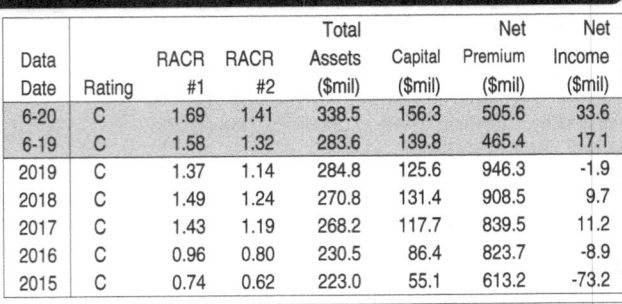

Rating Indexes

SANFORD HEALTH PLAN OF MINNESOTA

D+ **Weak**

Major Rating Factors: Weak profitability index (1.8 on a scale of 0 to 10). Good overall results on stability tests (5.0) based on an excessive 47% enrollment growth during the period. Strong capitalization index (7.6) based on excellent current risk-adjusted capital (severe loss scenario).
Other Rating Factors: High quality investment portfolio (7.5). Excellent liquidity (7.0) with ample operational cash flow and liquid investments.
Principal Business: Comp med (96%), med supp (4%)
Mem Phys: 19: 76,949 **18:** 59,836 **19 MLR** 112.2% **/ 19 Admin Exp** N/A
Enroll(000): Q2 20: 1 **19:** 1 **18:** 1 **Med Exp PMPM:** $436
Principal Investments: Cash and equiv (100%)
Provider Compensation ($000): Contr fee ($5,952)
Total Member Encounters: Phys (3,710), non-phys (4,627)
Group Affiliation: None
Licensed in: MN
Address: 300 Cherapa Place Suite 201, Sioux Falls,
Phone: (605) 328-6868 **Dom State:** MN **Commenced Bus:** N/A

Data Date	Rating	RACR #1	RACR #2	Total Assets ($mil)	Capital ($mil)	Net Premium ($mil)	Net Income ($mil)
6-20	D+	1.87	1.56	4.3	2.6	3.3	0.9
6-19	D+	1.92	1.60	2.9	1.5	2.7	-0.3
2019	D+	1.74	1.45	3.4	1.7	5.7	-1.0
2018	D+	2.35	1.96	3.1	1.8	3.6	-0.9
2017	E+	1.27	1.06	2.3	1.4	1.8	-0.1
2016	E+	1.88	1.57	2.2	1.5	2.4	-0.2
2015	E	2.00	1.67	2.5	1.7	2.6	-0.4

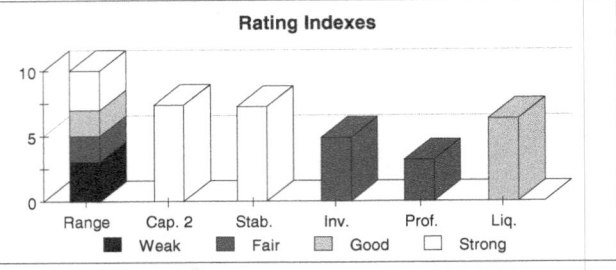

Rating Indexes

SANTA BARBARA SAN LUIS OBISPO REGION

B- **Good**

Major Rating Factors: Fair liquidity (4.4 on a scale of 0 to 10) as cash resources may not be adequate to cover a spike in claims. Good overall profitability index (5.5). Good overall results on stability tests (5.2).
Other Rating Factors: Strong capitalization index (8.7) based on excellent current risk-adjusted capital (severe loss scenario).
Principal Business: Medicaid (100%)
Mem Phys: 19: N/A **18:** N/A **19 MLR** 93.0% **/ 19 Admin Exp** N/A
Enroll(000): Q2 20: 182 **19:** 176 **18:** 176 **Med Exp PMPM:** $415
Principal Investments ($000): Cash and equiv ($230,250)
Provider Compensation ($000): None
Total Member Encounters: N/A
Group Affiliation: None
Licensed in: CA
Address: 801 Gateway Blvd Suite 100, So. San Francisco, CA 94080
Phone: (650) 616-2151 **Dom State:** CA **Commenced Bus:** September 1983

Data Date	Rating	RACR #1	RACR #2	Total Assets ($mil)	Capital ($mil)	Net Premium ($mil)	Net Income ($mil)
6-20	B-	3.74	2.28	521.4	195.8	446.4	-17.1
6-19	B-	3.67	2.24	501.3	216.0	480.9	-11.9
2019	B-	4.06	2.48	558.1	212.8	955.0	-15.0
2018	C	4.19	2.55	394.7	227.9	770.0	9.3
2017	B	4.44	2.68	471.6	218.5	716.3	36.2
2016	C	2.97	1.79	359.9	150.6	658.3	61.2
2015	D-	1.58	0.96	250.1	89.4	597.5	58.9

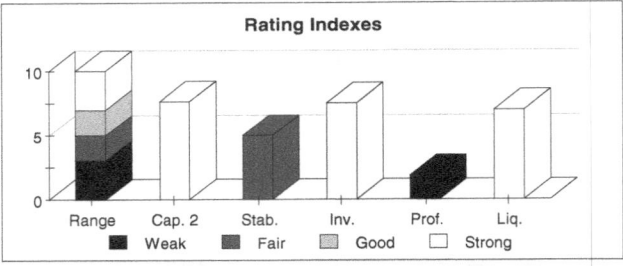

Rating Indexes

SANTA CLARA COUNTY HEALTH AUTHORITY   C   Fair

Major Rating Factors: Good overall results on stability tests (5.8 on a scale of 0 to 10). Excellent profitability (9.7). Strong capitalization index (8.1) based on excellent current risk-adjusted capital (severe loss scenario).
Other Rating Factors: Excellent liquidity (8.1) with ample operational cash flow and liquid investments.
Principal Business: Medicaid (89%), Medicare (11%)
Mem Phys: 19: N/A **18:** N/A **19 MLR** 83.6% **/ 19 Admin Exp** N/A
Enroll(000): Q2 20: 254 **19:** 254 **18:** 254 **Med Exp PMPM:** $326
Principal Investments ($000): Cash and equiv ($301,985)
Provider Compensation ($000): None
Total Member Encounters: N/A
Group Affiliation: None
Licensed in: CA
Address: 4050 Calle Real, Santa Barbara, CA 93110
Phone: (805) 685-9525 **Dom State:** CA **Commenced Bus:** February 1997

Data Date	Rating	RACR #1	RACR #2	Total Assets ($mil)	Capital ($mil)	Net Premium ($mil)	Net Income ($mil)
6-20	C	3.07	1.87	917.0	209.2	554.1	6.0
6-19	C	3.19	1.94	824.6	208.3	697.5	22.2
2019	C	2.98	1.82	913.2	203.2	1,214.7	17.2
2018	C	2.82	1.72	793.2	186.1	1,332.5	12.1
2017	C	2.72	1.65	821.3	173.9	1,524.6	62.8
2016	C	1.67	1.01	576.5	100.3	1,259.2	27.7
2015	C	1.43	0.86	295.9	72.6	959.7	37.4

SANTA CLARA VALLEY   C   Fair

Major Rating Factors: Good overall profitability index (6.9 on a scale of 0 to 10). Good capitalization index (6.8) based on good current risk-adjusted capital (moderate loss scenario). Good overall results on stability tests (6.2).
Other Rating Factors: Good liquidity (6.9) with sufficient resources (cash flows and marketable investments) to handle a spike in claims.
Principal Business: Managed care (99%)
Mem Phys: 19: N/A **18:** N/A **19 MLR** 89.6% **/ 19 Admin Exp** N/A
Enroll(000): Q2 20: 170 **19:** 157 **18:** 157 **Med Exp PMPM:** $270
Principal Investments ($000): Cash and equiv ($156,928)
Provider Compensation ($000): None
Total Member Encounters: N/A
Group Affiliation: None
Licensed in: CA
Address: 2480 North 1st St Suite 200, San Jose, CA 95131
Phone: (408) 885-5606 **Dom State:** CA **Commenced Bus:** September 1985

Data Date	Rating	RACR #1	RACR #2	Total Assets ($mil)	Capital ($mil)	Net Premium ($mil)	Net Income ($mil)
6-20	C	1.00	0.62	285.4	49.1	322.3	4.1
6-19	C-	0.85	0.53	226.0	41.2	280.8	6.1
2019	C	0.90	0.56	247.2	45.0	579.8	9.9
2018	D+	0.71	0.44	203.3	35.1	544.4	5.9
2017	D	0.71	0.44	169.1	29.1	518.2	3.0
2016	D	0.62	0.38	130.8	25.3	514.9	9.8
2015	C	0.78	0.48	96.0	29.4	487.9	8.4

SANTA CRUZ-MONTEREY-MERCED MGD MED   C   Fair

Major Rating Factors: Fair overall results on stability tests (3.9 on a scale of 0 to 10). Weak profitability index (1.1). Good liquidity (6.9) with sufficient resources (cash flows and marketable investments) to handle a spike in claims.
Other Rating Factors: Strong capitalization index (10.0) based on excellent current risk-adjusted capital (severe loss scenario).
Principal Business: Medicaid (100%)
Mem Phys: 19: N/A **18:** N/A **19 MLR** 100.7% **/ 19 Admin Exp** N/A
Enroll(000): Q2 20: 348 **19:** 342 **18:** 342 **Med Exp PMPM:** $1,191
Principal Investments ($000): Cash and equiv ($133,984)
Provider Compensation ($000): None
Total Member Encounters: N/A
Group Affiliation: None
Licensed in: CA
Address: 210 East Hacienda Avenue, Campbell, CA 95008
Phone: (408) 874-1701 **Dom State:** CA **Commenced Bus:** N/A

Data Date	Rating	RACR #1	RACR #2	Total Assets ($mil)	Capital ($mil)	Net Premium ($mil)	Net Income ($mil)
6-20	C	6.85	4.23	733.6	419.0	634.2	-31.8
6-19	C+	7.73	4.80	685.8	475.3	588.6	-44.5
2019	C	7.46	4.61	677.7	450.8	1,221.4	-69.0
2018	B-	8.60	5.34	753.4	519.8	1,145.9	-96.0
2017	B-	11.59	7.13	1,195.0	615.8	1,129.9	23.4
2016	B-	11.77	7.21	1,393.4	592.4	1,075.9	73.1
2015	B-	12.48	7.62	1,097.2	519.2	985.4	118.4

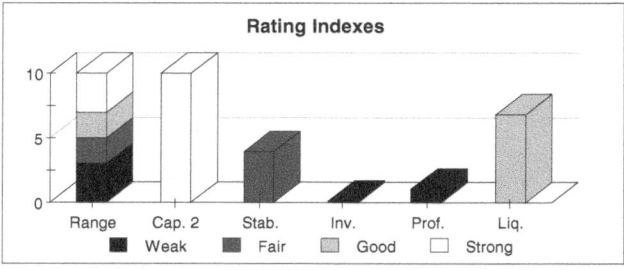

SCAN HEALTH PLAN *

B+   **Good**

Major Rating Factors: Excellent profitability (7.2 on a scale of 0 to 10). Strong capitalization index (8.3) based on excellent current risk-adjusted capital (severe loss scenario). Excellent overall results on stability tests (7.2).
Other Rating Factors: Excellent liquidity (7.2) with ample operational cash flow and liquid investments.
Principal Business: Medicare (98%), Medicaid (2%)
Mem Phys: 19: N/A   **18:** N/A   **19 MLR** 89.7%   **/ 19 Admin Exp** N/A
Enroll(000): Q2 20: 218   **19:** 198   **18:** 198   **Med Exp PMPM:** $1,178
Principal Investments ($000): Cash and equiv ($512,863)
Provider Compensation ($000): None
Total Member Encounters: N/A
Group Affiliation: SCAN Group
Licensed in: CA
Address: 300 Santana Row Suite 300, San Jose, CA 95128
Phone: (650) 404-3798   **Dom State:** CA   **Commenced Bus:** March 1985

Data Date	Rating	RACR #1	RACR #2	Total Assets ($mil)	Capital ($mil)	Net Premium ($mil)	Net Income ($mil)
6-20	B+	3.26	2.02	758.9	484.8	1,728.1	21.6
6-19	B	3.26	2.02	638.1	424.8	1,546.3	9.8
2019	B+	3.15	1.95	691.8	471.0	3,081.3	50.1
2018	B	3.03	1.88	621.9	396.9	2,717.8	32.6
2017	C+	3.06	1.90	563.5	379.0	2,563.2	32.6
2016	C-	2.96	1.84	571.9	332.1	2,251.5	41.2
2015	C	3.10	1.93	569.8	352.2	2,165.1	24.8

Rating Indexes

SCOTT & WHITE HEALTH PLAN

C+   **Fair**

Major Rating Factors: Fair profitability index (4.0 on a scale of 0 to 10). Fair quality investment portfolio (4.2). Good overall results on stability tests (5.0) based on a significant 43% decrease in enrollment during the period.
Other Rating Factors: Good liquidity (6.9) with sufficient resources (cash flows and marketable investments) to handle a spike in claims. Strong capitalization index (7.9) based on excellent current risk-adjusted capital (severe loss scenario).
Principal Business: Medicare (60%), Medicaid (25%), comp med (14%), FEHB (1%)
Mem Phys: 19: 18,000   **18:** 16,648   **19 MLR** 87.1%   **/ 19 Admin Exp** N/A
Enroll(000): Q2 20: 85   **19:** 82   **18:** 142   **Med Exp PMPM:** $502
Principal Investments: Long-term bonds (15%), cash and equiv (13%), nonaffiliate common stock (12%), affiliate common stock (6%), real estate (4%), other (49%)
Provider Compensation ($000): Contr fee ($252,365), capitation ($249,522), FFS ($14,247), bonus arrang ($9,298)
Total Member Encounters: Phys (463,065), non-phys (215,911)
Group Affiliation: None
Licensed in: TX
Address: 1206 WEST CAMPUS DRIVE, TEMPLE,
Phone: (254) 298-3000   **Dom State:** TX   **Commenced Bus:** N/A

Data Date	Rating	RACR #1	RACR #2	Total Assets ($mil)	Capital ($mil)	Net Premium ($mil)	Net Income ($mil)
6-20	C+	2.05	1.71	502.3	303.4	294.1	4.3
6-19	C+	2.94	2.45	404.3	226.9	283.4	1.2
2019	C+	1.89	1.58	453.3	272.7	574.6	20.5
2018	C	2.29	1.91	381.2	213.3	716.1	27.7
2017	C-	0.93	0.77	267.2	99.0	704.9	12.3
2016	C-	0.66	0.55	270.8	97.1	670.1	-59.1
2015	B	1.28	1.07	218.5	83.3	688.9	-12.2

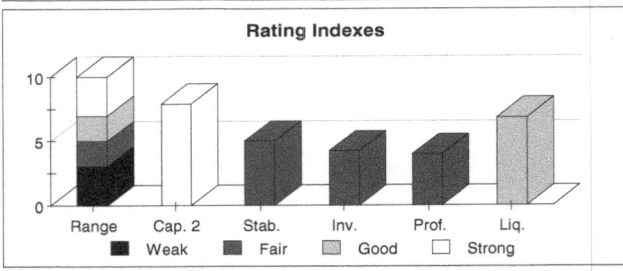

Rating Indexes

SCRIPPS HEALTH PLAN SERVICES INC

C-   **Fair**

Major Rating Factors: Good capitalization index (5.5 on a scale of 0 to 10) based on fair current risk-adjusted capital (moderate loss scenario). Good overall results on stability tests (6.4). Excellent profitability (7.8).
Other Rating Factors: Excellent liquidity (7.0) with sufficient resources (cash flows and marketable investments) to handle a spike in claims.
Principal Business: Managed care (100%)
Mem Phys: 19: N/A   **18:** N/A   **19 MLR** 99.9%   **/ 19 Admin Exp** N/A
Enroll(000): Q2 20: 152   **19:** 144   **18:** 144   **Med Exp PMPM:** $441
Principal Investments ($000): Cash and equiv ($118,680)
Provider Compensation ($000): None
Total Member Encounters: N/A
Group Affiliation: Scripps Health
Licensed in: CA
Address: 3800 Kilroy Airport Way #100, Long Beach, CA 90801-5616
Phone: (562) 989-8320   **Dom State:** CA   **Commenced Bus:** October 1997

Data Date	Rating	RACR #1	RACR #2	Total Assets ($mil)	Capital ($mil)	Net Premium ($mil)	Net Income ($mil)
6-20	C-	0.84	0.51	158.2	43.8	378.7	0.9
6-19	C-	0.88	0.53	138.9	42.2	377.2	2.8
2019	C-	0.82	0.50	124.6	42.9	742.6	2.1
2018	D+	0.82	0.50	115.1	39.4	674.1	2.2
2017	C-	0.78	0.47	119.3	34.7	604.8	3.5
2016	D+	0.77	0.46	90.7	29.1	515.3	2.1
2015	D+	0.64	0.39	85.1	22.3	475.0	0.2

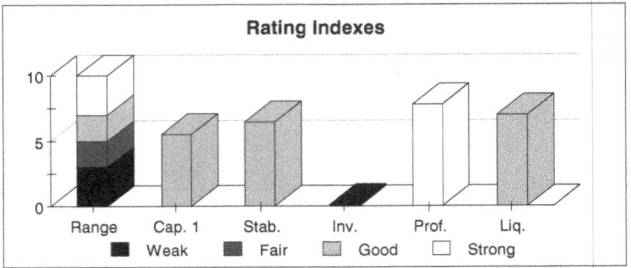

Rating Indexes

SD STATE MEDICAL HOLDING CO   D   Weak

Major Rating Factors: Weak profitability index (2.8 on a scale of 0 to 10). Fair capitalization index (2.9) based on good current risk-adjusted capital (moderate loss scenario). Fair quality investment portfolio (3.1).
Other Rating Factors: Fair overall results on stability tests (3.4) based on an inordinate decline in premium revenue in 2019, a significant 31% decrease in enrollment during the period. Excellent liquidity (7.1) with ample operational cash flow and liquid investments.
Principal Business: Comp med (100%)
Mem Phys: 19: 5,617 **18:** 2,143 **19 MLR** 72.2% **/ 19 Admin Exp** N/A
Enroll(000): Q2 20: 4 **19:** 5 **18:** 7 **Med Exp PMPM:** $353
Principal Investments: Affiliate common stock (36%), cash and equiv (30%), long-term bonds (19%), nonaffiliate common stock (15%)
Provider Compensation ($000): Contr fee ($19,149), FFS ($5,007)
Total Member Encounters: Phys (43,492), non-phys (5,261)
Group Affiliation: None
Licensed in: SD
Address: 2600 W 49th St, Sioux Falls,
Phone: (605) 334-4000 **Dom State:** SD **Commenced Bus:** N/A

Data Date	Rating	RACR #1	RACR #2	Total Assets ($mil)	Capital ($mil)	Net Premium ($mil)	Net Income ($mil)
6-20	D	1.02	0.85	18.3	12.2	10.2	0.9
6-19	N/A	N/A	N/A	N/A	N/A	N/A	N/A
2019	D	0.97	0.81	19.4	11.7	30.8	0.3
2018	D	1.55	1.29	22.9	9.0	36.6	1.4
2017	D	1.10	0.92	26.5	14.8	57.4	6.7
2016	D	0.46	0.39	26.8	9.3	79.2	-4.5
2015	N/A	N/A	N/A	50.3	11.5	107.9	-19.7

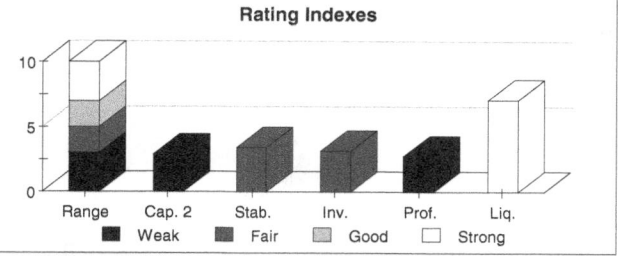

Rating Indexes

SEASIDE HEALTH PLAN   E-   Very Weak

Major Rating Factors: Weak profitability index (0.0 on a scale of 0 to 10). Poor capitalization index (1.2) based on weak current risk-adjusted capital (moderate loss scenario). Weak overall results on stability tests (0.3) based on an inordinate decline in premium revenue in 2019.
Other Rating Factors: Weak liquidity (0.0) as a spike in claims may stretch capacity.
Principal Business: Managed care (100%)
Mem Phys: 19: N/A **18:** N/A **19 MLR** 131.8% **/ 19 Admin Exp** N/A
Enroll(000): Q2 20: 49 **19:** 42 **18:** 42 **Med Exp PMPM:** $92
Principal Investments ($000): Cash and equiv ($3,062)
Provider Compensation ($000): None
Total Member Encounters: N/A
Group Affiliation: None
Licensed in: CA
Address: 10790 Rancho Bernardo Road, San Diego, CA 92127
Phone: (858) 927-5360 **Dom State:** CA **Commenced Bus:** May 2013

Data Date	Rating	RACR #1	RACR #2	Total Assets ($mil)	Capital ($mil)	Net Premium ($mil)	Net Income ($mil)
6-20	E-	0.55	0.35	13.3	7.2	15.1	-8.0
6-19	D-	0.21	0.13	12.2	7.8	21.3	-7.3
2019	E-	N/A	N/A	9.9	2.9	35.3	-19.5
2018	D-	0.26	0.16	12.4	8.1	42.7	-13.3
2017	D-	0.31	0.20	14.0	8.1	40.8	-7.9
2016	D	0.59	0.38	15.1	9.1	31.4	-9.8
2015	D	0.55	0.38	11.2	5.9	21.5	-9.7

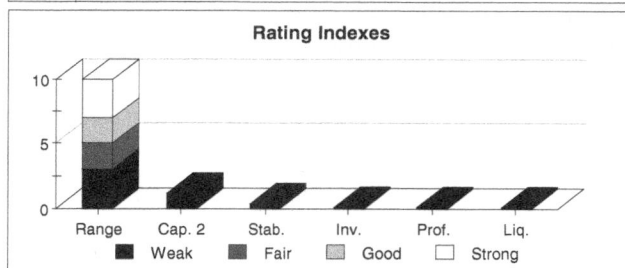

Rating Indexes

SECURITY HEALTH PLAN OF WI INC *   B+   Good

Major Rating Factors: Good overall results on stability tests (5.3 on a scale of 0 to 10). Good liquidity (6.3) with sufficient resources (cash flows and marketable investments) to handle a spike in claims. Excellent profitability (7.3).
Other Rating Factors: Strong capitalization index (9.2) based on excellent current risk-adjusted capital (severe loss scenario). High quality investment portfolio (9.4).
Principal Business: Comp med (48%), Medicare (43%), Medicaid (9%)
Mem Phys: 19: 9,970 **18:** 9,708 **19 MLR** 91.7% **/ 19 Admin Exp** N/A
Enroll(000): Q2 20: 183 **19:** 196 **18:** 205 **Med Exp PMPM:** $507
Principal Investments: Long-term bonds (82%), cash and equiv (13%), real estate (3%), other (2%)
Provider Compensation ($000): Contr fee ($549,741), capitation ($512,945), FFS ($117,726), bonus arrang ($2,557)
Total Member Encounters: N/A
Group Affiliation: Marshfield Clinic Health System Inc
Licensed in: WI
Address: 1515 St Joseph Ave, Marshfield,
Phone: (715) 221-9555 **Dom State:** WI **Commenced Bus:** N/A

Data Date	Rating	RACR #1	RACR #2	Total Assets ($mil)	Capital ($mil)	Net Premium ($mil)	Net Income ($mil)
6-20	B+	3.09	2.57	507.0	281.4	624.3	83.5
6-19	N/A	N/A	N/A	N/A	N/A	N/A	N/A
2019	B+	2.12	1.77	430.4	198.4	1,326.7	47.9
2018	B+	1.69	1.41	395.9	146.6	1,340.1	28.0
2017	B+	1.72	1.43	351.3	172.0	1,222.3	9.8
2016	A-	2.25	1.88	384.0	225.1	1,178.1	11.4
2015	A-	2.06	1.72	350.6	202.4	1,158.3	18.6

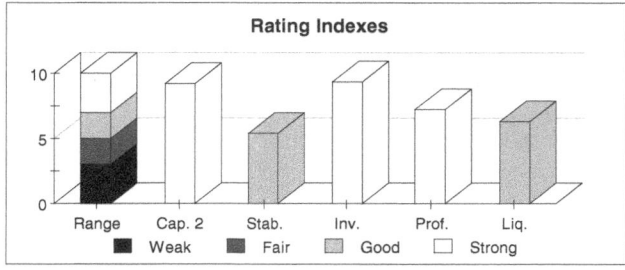

Rating Indexes

SECURITYCARE OF TENNESSEE INC   C   Fair

Major Rating Factors: Weak profitability index (1.7 on a scale of 0 to 10). Strong capitalization (8.5) based on excellent current risk-adjusted capital (severe loss scenario). High quality investment portfolio (9.8).
Other Rating Factors: Excellent liquidity (10.0) with ample operational cash flow and liquid investments.
Principal Business: Medicare (100%)
Mem Phys: 19: N/A   **18:** N/A   **19 MLR** -39.2%   **/ 19 Admin Exp** N/A
Enroll(000): Q2 20: 0   **19:** N/A   **18:** N/A   **Med Exp PMPM:** N/A
Principal Investments: Cash and equiv (87%), long-term bonds (13%)
Provider Compensation ($000): None
Total Member Encounters: N/A
Group Affiliation: BlueCross BlueShield of Tennessee In
Licensed in: TN
Address: 1 Cameron Hill Circle, Chattanooga, TN 37402-0001
Phone: (423) 535-5600   **Dom State:** TN   **Commenced Bus:** N/A

Data Date	Rating	RACR #1	RACR #2	Total Assets ($mil)	Capital ($mil)	Net Premium ($mil)	Net Income ($mil)
6-20	C	2.56	2.14	7.5	7.4	0.3	-0.4
6-19	U	278.90	232.40	8.2	8.1	0.3	0.3
2019	B	4.96	4.13	8.1	7.6	0.2	-0.2
2018	U	271.70	226.40	7.9	7.9	0.0	0.2
2017	B	N/A	N/A	9.1	6.8	27.2	0.8
2016	B	3.01	2.51	9.3	6.8	21.7	-0.6
2015	B	1.93	1.61	6.1	3.7	15.4	-1.3

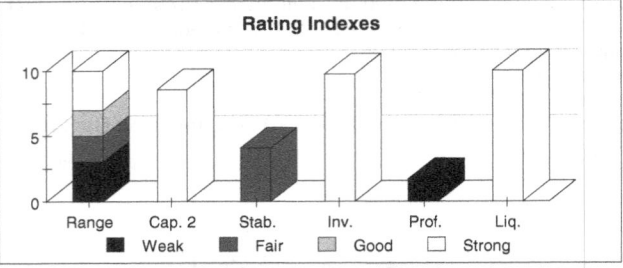

SELECT HEALTH OF SOUTH CAROLINA INC   B   Good

Major Rating Factors: Good overall results on stability tests (6.2 on a scale of 0 to 10). Good liquidity (6.6) with sufficient resources (cash flows and marketable investments) to handle a spike in claims. Fair profitability index (4.5).
Other Rating Factors: Strong capitalization index (7.3) based on excellent current risk-adjusted capital (severe loss scenario). High quality investment portfolio (9.0).
Principal Business: Medicaid (89%), Medicare (11%)
Mem Phys: 19: 24,236   **18:** 22,330   **19 MLR** 91.6%   **/ 19 Admin Exp** N/A
Enroll(000): Q2 20: 358   **19:** 341   **18:** 382   **Med Exp PMPM:** $296
Principal Investments: Long-term bonds (51%), cash and equiv (39%), nonaffiliate common stock (11%)
Provider Compensation ($000): Contr fee ($1,192,706), capitation ($63,054)
Total Member Encounters: Phys (2,585,228), non-phys (1,022,556)
Group Affiliation: Independence Health Group Inc
Licensed in: KY, MS, RI, SC
Address: 4390 Belle Oaks Drive Suite 40, North Charleston,
Phone: (843) 569-1759   **Dom State:** SC   **Commenced Bus:** N/A

Data Date	Rating	RACR #1	RACR #2	Total Assets ($mil)	Capital ($mil)	Net Premium ($mil)	Net Income ($mil)
6-20	B	1.62	1.35	375.1	167.2	704.0	22.2
6-19	B	1.91	1.59	325.8	144.0	714.0	-13.6
2019	B	1.99	1.66	322.7	144.6	1,376.8	-10.1
2018	B	2.01	1.68	336.7	152.6	1,465.7	19.6
2017	B-	1.60	1.33	353.5	166.0	1,364.2	29.9
2016	B-	2.37	1.97	354.0	169.7	1,337.3	46.8
2015	B-	2.12	1.77	271.5	133.3	1,175.8	32.2

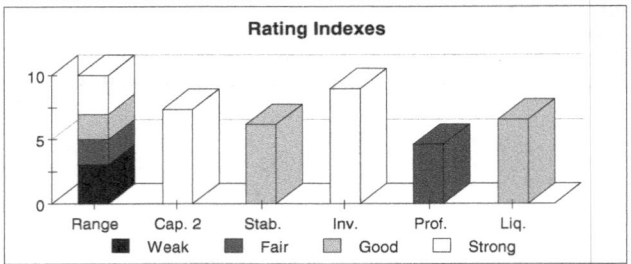

SELECTCARE HEALTH PLANS INC   B   Good

Major Rating Factors: Excellent profitability (7.3 on a scale of 0 to 10). Strong capitalization (8.3) based on excellent current risk-adjusted capital (severe loss scenario). High quality investment portfolio (9.0).
Other Rating Factors: Excellent liquidity (7.1) with ample operational cash flow and liquid investments.
Principal Business: Medicare (100%)
Mem Phys: 19: 14,100   **18:** 8,800   **19 MLR** 82.6%   **/ 19 Admin Exp** N/A
Enroll(000): Q2 20: 2   **19:** 2   **18:** 2   **Med Exp PMPM:** $738
Principal Investments: Long-term bonds (53%), cash and equiv (47%)
Provider Compensation ($000): Contr fee ($15,401), bonus arrang ($603), capitation ($483)
Total Member Encounters: Phys (24,759), non-phys (9,067)
Group Affiliation: None
Licensed in: TX
Address: 4888 Loop Central Dr Ste 700, Houston, TX 77081-2181
Phone: (813) 206-2725   **Dom State:** TX   **Commenced Bus:** N/A

Data Date	Rating	RACR #1	RACR #2	Total Assets ($mil)	Capital ($mil)	Net Premium ($mil)	Net Income ($mil)
6-20	B	2.38	1.98	15.4	9.0	11.2	0.7
6-19	B-	3.75	3.13	13.0	7.6	11.4	0.9
2019	B	4.06	3.38	14.0	8.4	23.2	1.7
2018	C+	3.33	2.78	10.2	6.8	22.8	1.0
2017	C-	1.32	1.10	10.0	5.7	24.3	1.0
2016	C+	3.90	3.25	18.9	14.7	33.7	0.7
2015	C+	3.30	2.75	19.0	14.0	42.7	0.7

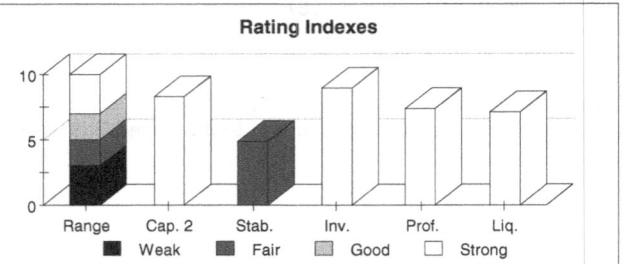

SELECTCARE OF TEXAS INC   C-   Fair

Major Rating Factors: Fair overall results on stability tests (4.3 on a scale of 0 to 10). Good quality investment portfolio (5.8). Good liquidity (6.3) with sufficient resources (cash flows and marketable investments) to handle a spike in claims.
Other Rating Factors: Excellent profitability (8.1). Strong capitalization index (6.9) based on excellent current risk-adjusted capital (severe loss scenario).
Principal Business: Medicare (100%)
Mem Phys: 19: 17,200 **18:** 11,500 **19 MLR** 85.9% **/ 19 Admin Exp** N/A
Enroll(000): Q2 20: 59 **19:** 64 **18:** 65 **Med Exp PMPM:** $1,004
Principal Investments: Long-term bonds (94%), cash and equiv (6%)
Provider Compensation ($000): Capitation ($419,011), contr fee ($265,709), bonus arrang ($30,869)
Total Member Encounters: Phys (614,421), non-phys (246,952)
Group Affiliation: None
Licensed in: TX
Address: 4888 Loop Central Dr Ste 700, Houston,
Phone: (813) 290-6200 **Dom State:** TX **Commenced Bus:** N/A

Data Date	Rating	RACR #1	RACR #2	Total Assets ($mil)	Capital ($mil)	Net Premium ($mil)	Net Income ($mil)
6-20	C-	1.31	1.09	277.2	74.0	461.9	10.7
6-19	B	2.24	1.86	259.7	86.3	474.1	11.0
2019	B	1.75	1.46	229.0	63.8	920.1	34.9
2018	B	1.97	1.64	179.7	75.4	870.9	14.4
2017	B	N/A	N/A	190.0	71.6	842.1	8.2
2016	B	1.27	1.06	160.6	62.6	833.8	10.3
2015	B	1.37	1.14	146.4	61.5	799.0	9.6

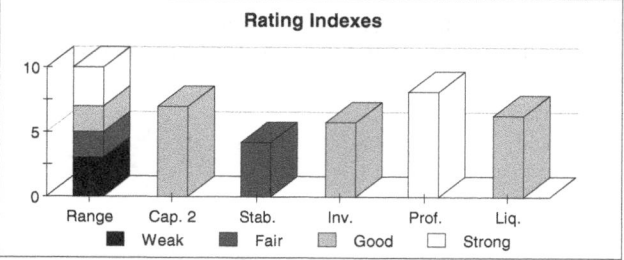

Rating Indexes

SELECTHEALTH BENEFIT ASR CO INC   B   Good

Major Rating Factors: Excellent profitability (8.7 on a scale of 0 to 10). Strong capitalization (8.8) based on excellent current risk-adjusted capital (severe loss scenario). High quality investment portfolio (9.8).
Other Rating Factors: Excellent liquidity (8.3) with ample operational cash flow and liquid investments.
Principal Business: Other (100%)
Mem Phys: 19: N/A **18:** N/A **19 MLR** 16.8% **/ 19 Admin Exp** N/A
Enroll(000): Q2 20: 2 **19:** 0 **18:** 0 **Med Exp PMPM:** $1,665
Principal Investments: Long-term bonds (80%), cash and equiv (20%)
Provider Compensation ($000): FFS ($5,474)
Total Member Encounters: Phys (77), non-phys (47)
Group Affiliation: Intermountain Health Care Inc
Licensed in: ID, UT
Address: 5381Green Street, Murray, UT 84123
Phone: (801) 442-5000 **Dom State:** UT **Commenced Bus:** N/A

Data Date	Rating	RACR #1	RACR #2	Total Assets ($mil)	Capital ($mil)	Net Premium ($mil)	Net Income ($mil)
6-20	B	2.78	2.32	34.1	23.7	20.9	3.5
6-19	B-	3.86	3.21	28.8	19.4	15.8	1.7
2019	B	3.76	3.14	29.3	20.3	35.5	2.6
2018	C+	3.31	2.76	29.2	17.5	31.9	1.3
2017	C	2.11	1.76	29.1	17.1	38.6	1.5
2016	C	3.35	2.79	25.1	16.0	34.4	1.2
2015	B-	2.80	2.33	23.1	15.0	30.7	2.2

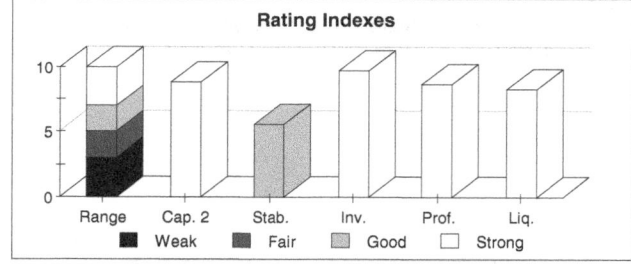

Rating Indexes

SELECTHEALTH INC *   B+   Good

Major Rating Factors: Good overall profitability index (5.4 on a scale of 0 to 10). Good liquidity (6.8) with sufficient resources (cash flows and marketable investments) to handle a spike in claims. Strong capitalization index (10.0) based on excellent current risk-adjusted capital (severe loss scenario).
Other Rating Factors: High quality investment portfolio (7.7). Excellent overall results on stability tests (8.4).
Principal Business: Comp med (76%), Medicare (12%), Medicaid (10%), FEHB (1%)
Mem Phys: 19: 11,888 **18:** 9,342 **19 MLR** 86.7% **/ 19 Admin Exp** N/A
Enroll(000): Q2 20: 767 **19:** 715 **18:** 691 **Med Exp PMPM:** $332
Principal Investments: Long-term bonds (60%), nonaffiliate common stock (26%), cash and equiv (9%), affiliate common stock (2%), other (3%)
Provider Compensation ($000): Bonus arrang ($1,638,083), contr fee ($1,088,277), FFS ($133,551), capitation ($9,833)
Total Member Encounters: Phys (3,639,828), non-phys (1,678,513)
Group Affiliation: Intermountain Health Care Inc
Licensed in: ID, UT
Address: 5381 Green Street, Murray,
Phone: (801) 442-5000 **Dom State:** UT **Commenced Bus:** N/A

Data Date	Rating	RACR #1	RACR #2	Total Assets ($mil)	Capital ($mil)	Net Premium ($mil)	Net Income ($mil)
6-20	B+	3.64	3.03	1,703.8	808.1	1,692.7	50.5
6-19	C+	3.05	2.54	1,383.3	667.1	1,658.5	108.4
2019	B	3.44	2.87	1,374.2	770.0	3,313.0	194.9
2018	C	2.37	1.98	1,123.0	540.0	3,113.3	141.8
2017	C	2.27	1.89	1,090.1	482.3	2,641.9	88.0
2016	C	1.49	1.24	1,085.9	332.0	2,611.6	-136.6
2015	C	1.61	1.35	912.5	298.8	2,029.2	-374.0

Rating Indexes

SENDERO HEALTH PLANS INC　　　　　　　E+　　Very Weak

Major Rating Factors: Weak profitability index (1.9 on a scale of 0 to 10). Fair capitalization (2.9) based on good current risk-adjusted capital (moderate loss scenario). High quality investment portfolio (9.9).
Other Rating Factors: Excellent liquidity (7.6) with ample operational cash flow and liquid investments.
Principal Business: Comp med (100%)
Mem Phys: 19: N/A　**18:** N/A　**19 MLR** 73.9%　**/ 19 Admin Exp** N/A
Enroll(000): Q2 20: 14　**19:** 11　**18:** 23　**Med Exp PMPM:** $398
Principal Investments: Cash and equiv (100%)
Provider Compensation ($000): FFS ($54,112), capitation ($12,982)
Total Member Encounters: Phys (87,261), non-phys (67,043)
Group Affiliation: None
Licensed in: TX
Address: 2028 East Ben White Blvd Ste, Austin, TX 78741
Phone: (512) 978-8454　**Dom State:** TX　**Commenced Bus:** N/A

Data Date	Rating	RACR #1	RACR #2	Total Assets ($mil)	Capital ($mil)	Net Premium ($mil)	Net Income ($mil)
6-20	E+	1.26	1.05	44.4	20.6	51.2	-2.0
6-19	N/A	N/A	N/A	N/A	N/A	N/A	N/A
2019	E+	1.36	1.13	33.8	22.4	83.6	4.8
2018	E	0.47	0.39	56.6	13.1	121.0	-18.9
2017	E-	0.41	0.34	90.4	12.0	145.8	-32.9
2016	E-	0.74	0.62	56.9	11.5	85.1	4.5
2015	E-	0.79	0.66	31.8	11.0	58.6	-4.8

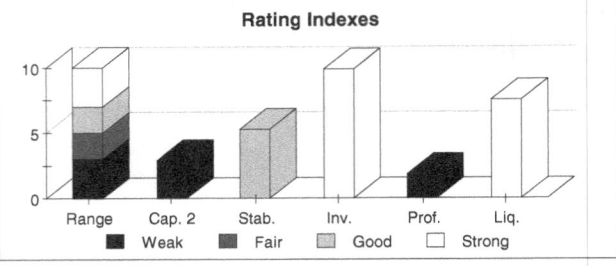

SENIOR WHOLE HEALTH OF NEW YORK INC　　　C+　　Fair

Major Rating Factors: Good overall profitability index (5.6 on a scale of 0 to 10). Strong capitalization (7.4) based on excellent current risk-adjusted capital (severe loss scenario). High quality investment portfolio (9.9).
Other Rating Factors: Excellent liquidity (7.1) with ample operational cash flow and liquid investments.
Principal Business: Medicaid (98%), Medicare (1%), other (1%)
Mem Phys: 19: N/A　**18:** 16,663　**19 MLR** 90.8%　**/ 19 Admin Exp** N/A
Enroll(000): Q2 20: 14　**19:** 15　**18:** 15　**Med Exp PMPM:** $4,222
Principal Investments: Cash and equiv (75%), long-term bonds (25%)
Provider Compensation ($000): Contr fee ($740,630), FFS ($25,596)
Total Member Encounters: N/A
Group Affiliation: Molina Healthcare Inc
Licensed in: NY
Address: 111 Broadway Suite 1505, Brooklyn, NY 11201
Phone: (314) 387-4304　**Dom State:** NY　**Commenced Bus:** N/A

Data Date	Rating	RACR #1	RACR #2	Total Assets ($mil)	Capital ($mil)	Net Premium ($mil)	Net Income ($mil)
6-20	C+	1.65	1.37	257.1	114.1	411.7	44.8
6-19	C-	0.77	0.64	173.7	42.0	402.2	3.7
2019	C	1.21	1.01	207.1	76.0	838.1	30.0
2018	C-	0.57	0.48	176.2	38.4	688.2	-24.6
2017	E	0.82	0.68	153.0	61.4	598.8	7.4
2016	E	0.93	0.78	78.0	26.8	245.7	9.5
2015	E	1.10	0.92	53.6	17.5	133.1	10.6

SEQUOIA HEALTH PLAN INC　　　　　　　E+　　Very Weak

Major Rating Factors: Poor capitalization index (0.0 on a scale of 0 to 10) based on weak current risk-adjusted capital (severe loss scenario). Fair overall results on stability tests (3.6) in spite of healthy premium and capital growth during 2019. Excellent profitability (8.4).
Other Rating Factors: Excellent liquidity (6.9) with sufficient resources (cash flows and marketable investments) to handle a spike in claims.
Principal Business: Managed care (100%)
Mem Phys: 19: N/A　**18:** N/A　**19 MLR** 96.3%　**/ 19 Admin Exp** N/A
Enroll(000): Q2 20: 11　**19:** 8　**18:** 8　**Med Exp PMPM:** $864
Principal Investments ($000): Cash and equiv ($3,241)
Provider Compensation ($000): None
Total Member Encounters: N/A
Group Affiliation: None
Licensed in: (No states)
Address: 3350 S Fairway Ave, Visalia, CA 93277-8109
Phone: (Phone number　**Dom State:** CA　**Commenced Bus:** N/A

Data Date	Rating	RACR #1	RACR #2	Total Assets ($mil)	Capital ($mil)	Net Premium ($mil)	Net Income ($mil)
6-20	E+	0.39	0.24	5.7	3.1	48.0	0.3
6-19	E+	0.38	0.23	3.1	2.6	43.9	0.4
2019	E+	0.36	0.22	3.7	2.9	88.1	0.7
2018	E+	0.32	0.19	2.9	2.2	68.9	0.2
2017	D-	0.56	0.34	2.4	2.0	32.9	0.1
2016	N/A	N/A	N/A	N/A	N/A	N/A	N/A
2015	N/A	N/A	N/A	N/A	N/A	N/A	N/A

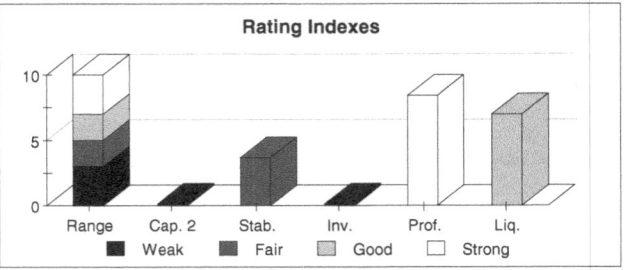

SETON HEALTH PLAN INC   B   Good

Major Rating Factors: Good quality investment portfolio (6.2 on a scale of 0 to 10). Good overall results on stability tests (5.6). Excellent profitability (9.4).
Other Rating Factors: Strong capitalization index (10.0) based on excellent current risk-adjusted capital (severe loss scenario). Excellent liquidity (7.5) with ample operational cash flow and liquid investments.
Principal Business: Medicaid (78%), comp med (22%)
Mem Phys: 19: 5,162 **18:** 5,318 **19 MLR** 156.8% **/ 19 Admin Exp** N/A
Enroll(000): Q2 20: 34 **19:** 31 **18:** 31 **Med Exp PMPM:** $135
Principal Investments: Cash and equiv (61%), nonaffiliate common stock (38%), long-term bonds (1%)
Provider Compensation ($000): Contr fee ($40,245), FFS ($12,737), capitation ($510), other ($2)
Total Member Encounters: Phys (118,587), non-phys (126,157)
Group Affiliation: None
Licensed in: TX
Address: 1345 Philomena Strret, Austin,
Phone: (512) 324-3350 **Dom State:** TX **Commenced Bus:** N/A

Data Date	Rating	RACR #1	RACR #2	Total Assets ($mil)	Capital ($mil)	Net Premium ($mil)	Net Income ($mil)
6-20	B	4.31	3.59	48.9	37.7	16.6	2.9
6-19	B	4.09	3.41	46.7	31.9	15.4	0.5
2019	B	4.09	3.41	47.3	35.3	32.0	3.8
2018	B	3.79	3.16	49.5	29.6	28.9	6.1
2017	B-	3.35	2.79	40.6	25.1	29.1	7.0
2016	C+	1.84	1.53	28.0	17.4	58.3	1.9
2015	C	1.73	1.45	32.6	15.1	53.5	1.5

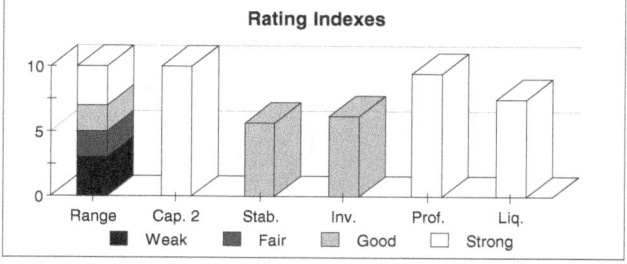

SHA LLC   D   Weak

Major Rating Factors: Weak profitability index (0.9 on a scale of 0 to 10). Good overall results on stability tests (6.2) despite a decline in enrollment during 2019. Good liquidity (6.9) with sufficient resources (cash flows and marketable investments) to handle a spike in claims.
Other Rating Factors: Strong capitalization index (7.4) based on excellent current risk-adjusted capital (severe loss scenario). High quality investment portfolio (9.0).
Principal Business: Comp med (51%), Medicaid (49%)
Mem Phys: 19: 15,389 **18:** 13,065 **19 MLR** 89.4% **/ 19 Admin Exp** N/A
Enroll(000): Q2 20: 120 **19:** 122 **18:** 154 **Med Exp PMPM:** $310
Principal Investments: Cash and equiv (58%), long-term bonds (18%), nonaffiliate common stock (16%), affiliate common stock (5%), real estate (2%)
Provider Compensation ($000): Contr fee ($475,517), FFS ($5,161)
Total Member Encounters: Phys (1,338,683), non-phys (684,983)
Group Affiliation: None
Licensed in: TX
Address: 12940 N Hwy 183, Austin,
Phone: (254) 298-3000 **Dom State:** TX **Commenced Bus:** N/A

Data Date	Rating	RACR #1	RACR #2	Total Assets ($mil)	Capital ($mil)	Net Premium ($mil)	Net Income ($mil)
6-20	D	1.71	1.42	162.7	90.2	240.6	7.7
6-19	D	1.34	1.11	154.8	69.5	273.4	-10.6
2019	D	1.73	1.44	157.9	80.8	535.5	-14.7
2018	E	0.87	0.73	152.8	64.4	584.0	-80.6
2017	E	1.07	0.89	107.2	64.1	563.2	-22.9
2016	E	1.11	0.92	131.5	66.4	614.6	-18.2
2015	E	1.51	1.26	136.3	72.2	510.0	-1.2

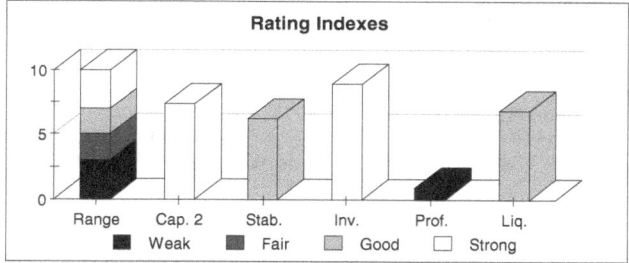

SHARP HEALTH PLAN *   B+   Good

Major Rating Factors: Excellent profitability (8.4 on a scale of 0 to 10). Strong capitalization index (7.3) based on excellent current risk-adjusted capital (severe loss scenario). Excellent overall results on stability tests (7.5).
Other Rating Factors: Excellent liquidity (7.2) with ample operational cash flow and liquid investments.
Principal Business: Medicare (4%)
Mem Phys: 19: N/A **18:** N/A **19 MLR** 87.3% **/ 19 Admin Exp** N/A
Enroll(000): Q2 20: 145 **19:** 143 **18:** 143 **Med Exp PMPM:** $399
Principal Investments ($000): Cash and equiv ($77,423)
Provider Compensation ($000): None
Total Member Encounters: N/A
Group Affiliation: San Diego Hospital Assoc
Licensed in: CA
Address: 2801 Atlantic Avenue, Long Beach, CA 90806
Phone: (714) 377-3215 **Dom State:** CA **Commenced Bus:** November 1992

Data Date	Rating	RACR #1	RACR #2	Total Assets ($mil)	Capital ($mil)	Net Premium ($mil)	Net Income ($mil)
6-20	B+	1.99	1.31	217.8	127.8	416.3	9.4
6-19	B+	1.63	1.07	189.3	98.7	389.7	13.0
2019	B+	1.83	1.21	190.6	118.4	792.2	33.2
2018	B	1.43	0.93	165.8	85.7	744.8	0.0
2017	B	1.51	0.98	135.2	85.5	691.5	15.2
2016	B	1.38	0.89	115.3	70.4	612.1	6.7
2015	B	1.43	0.93	103.4	64.1	498.5	7.9

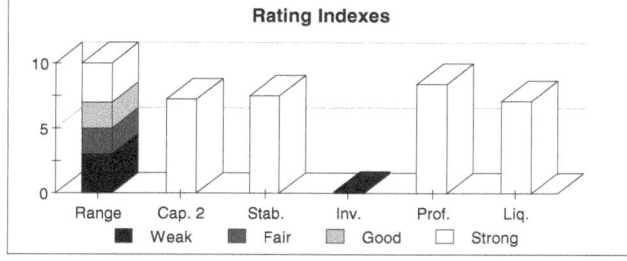

SHELTERPOINT LIFE INS CO *

A   **Excellent**

Major Rating Factors: Good overall results on stability tests (6.9 on a scale of 0 to 10) despite excessive premium growth. Strengths that enhance stability include excellent operational trends and good risk diversification. Strong capitalization (7.4) based on excellent risk adjusted capital (severe loss scenario). Furthermore, this high level of risk adjusted capital has been consistently maintained over the last five years. High quality investment portfolio (7.5).

Other Rating Factors: Excellent profitability (7.1) with operating gains in each of the last five years. Excellent liquidity (7.0).

Principal Business: Group health insurance (98%), reinsurance (2%), and group life insurance (1%).

Principal Investments: NonCMO investment grade bonds (41%), CMOs and structured securities (20%), common & preferred stock (6%), and cash (3%).

Investments in Affiliates: 6%

Group Affiliation: ShelterPoint Group Inc

Licensed in: CA, CO, CT, DC, DE, FL, IL, MD, MA, MI, MN, NJ, NY, NC, PA, RI, SC, TN

Commenced Business: November 1972

Address: 600 NORTHERN BLVD, GREAT NECK, NY 11530

Phone: (516) 829-8100 **Domicile State:** NY **NAIC Code:** 81434

Data Date	Rating	RACR #1	RACR #2	Total Assets ($mil)	Capital ($mil)	Net Premium ($mil)	Net Income ($mil)
6-20	A	1.53	1.28	235.2	64.5	156.4	5.6
6-19	A	2.05	1.72	191.2	72.7	114.5	4.3
2019	A	1.75	1.47	189.4	63.2	213.1	5.4
2018	A	2.08	1.75	156.0	68.4	187.6	8.8
2017	A	2.63	2.23	114.9	61.0	97.2	3.5
2016	A	2.47	2.09	106.5	58.8	91.8	5.5
2015	A	2.38	2.01	107.5	54.9	88.6	5.6

Adverse Trends in Operations

Decrease in capital during 2019 (8%)
Change in asset mix during 2018 (4%)

SHENANDOAH LIFE INS CO

B-   **Good**

Major Rating Factors: Good quality investment portfolio (5.7 on a scale of 0 to 10) despite mixed results such as: minimal exposure to mortgages and large holdings of BBB rated bonds but minimal holdings in junk bonds. Good overall profitability (5.5) despite operating losses during the first six months of 2020. Good liquidity (5.1).

Other Rating Factors: Fair overall results on stability tests (4.6) including negative cash flow from operations for 2019. Strong capitalization (7.1) based on excellent risk adjusted capital (severe loss scenario).

Principal Business: Reinsurance (51%), individual life insurance (34%), and individual health insurance (14%).

Principal Investments: NonCMO investment grade bonds (57%), CMOs and structured securities (29%), policy loans (3%), mortgages in good standing (3%), and misc. investments (6%).

Investments in Affiliates: 1%

Group Affiliation: Reservoir Capital Group LLC

Licensed in: All states except CA, CT, ID, ME, NY, PR

Commenced Business: February 1916

Address: 4415 PHEASANT RIDGE RD STE 300, ROANOKE, VA 24014

Phone: (540) 985-4400 **Domicile State:** VA **NAIC Code:** 68845

Data Date	Rating	RACR #1	RACR #2	Total Assets ($mil)	Capital ($mil)	Net Premium ($mil)	Net Income ($mil)
6-20	B-	1.93	1.07	1,208.4	94.2	219.3	-0.6
6-19	B-	2.82	1.54	972.3	112.0	22.9	3.7
2019	B-	2.39	1.27	1,001.2	99.4	90.7	8.1
2018	B-	2.84	1.55	994.7	108.6	42.8	15.0
2017	B-	2.52	1.37	1,036.4	94.6	40.4	27.4
2016	B-	2.09	1.10	1,077.4	83.7	59.8	14.1
2015	B-	2.11	1.11	1,131.8	87.9	44.8	21.0

Rating Indexes

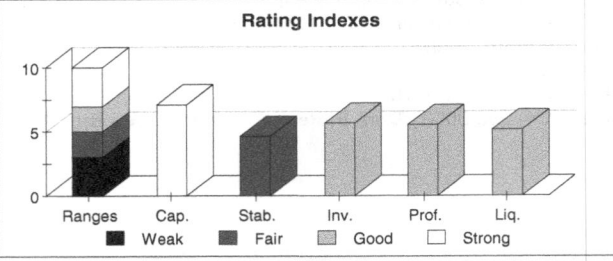

Ranges   Cap.   Stab.   Inv.   Prof.   Liq.
■ Weak   ■ Fair   ▨ Good   □ Strong

SIERRA HEALTH AND LIFE INS CO INC

B   **Good**

Major Rating Factors: Excellent profitability (9.8 on a scale of 0 to 10). Strong capitalization (9.7) based on excellent current risk-adjusted capital (severe loss scenario). High quality investment portfolio (7.6).

Other Rating Factors: Excellent liquidity (7.0) with sufficient resources (cash flows and marketable investments) to handle a spike in claims.

Principal Business: Medicare (98%), comp med (2%)

Mem Phys: 19: 1,427,667 **18:** 1,334,335 **19 MLR** 84.5% **/ 19 Admin Exp** N/A

Enroll(000): Q2 20: 1,445 **19:** 1,509 **18:** 1,394 **Med Exp PMPM:** $884

Principal Investments: Long-term bonds (65%), cash and equiv (35%)

Provider Compensation ($000): Contr fee ($10,985,462), FFS ($3,814,883), capitation ($821,782), bonus arrang ($98,015)

Total Member Encounters: Phys (36,164,086), non-phys (14,182,568)

Group Affiliation: None

Licensed in: All states except PR

Address: 2720 NORTH TENAYA WAY, LAS VEGAS, NV 89128

Phone: (702) 242-7732 **Dom State:** NV **Commenced Bus:** N/A

Data Date	Rating	RACR #1	RACR #2	Total Assets ($mil)	Capital ($mil)	Net Premium ($mil)	Net Income ($mil)
6-20	B	3.51	2.93	6,825.8	3,778.7	9,803.0	1,347.7
6-19	B	2.80	2.34	4,937.0	2,736.5	9,550.0	730.4
2019	B	2.76	2.30	5,301.1	2,956.8	18,882.8	1,124.6
2018	B	2.17	1.81	4,126.5	2,116.5	16,213.6	762.8
2017	B+	1.91	1.60	3,270.0	1,511.8	13,316.8	482.6
2016	B	2.46	2.05	2,396.9	1,177.4	8,918.3	438.3
2015	B	2.03	1.69	1,676.6	779.0	6,732.9	96.0

Rating Indexes

Range   Cap. 2   Stab.   Inv.   Prof.   Liq.
■ Weak   ■ Fair   ▨ Good   □ Strong

SIGNATURE ADVANTAGE LLC   D   Weak

Major Rating Factors: Weak profitability index (0.7 on a scale of 0 to 10). Poor capitalization (1.2) based on weak current risk-adjusted capital (moderate loss scenario). Fair liquidity (4.9) as cash resources may not be adequate to cover a spike in claims.
Other Rating Factors: High quality investment portfolio (9.9).
Principal Business: Medicare (100%)
Mem Phys: 18: 5,714 **17:** 1,054 **18 MLR** 94.3% **/ 18 Admin Exp** N/A
Enroll(000): Q3 19: 0 **18:** 0 **17:** 0 **Med Exp PMPM:** $2,238
Principal Investments: Cash and equiv (84%), long-term bonds (16%)
Provider Compensation ($000): Capitation ($236), other ($4,452)
Total Member Encounters: Phys (12,762), non-phys (3,843)
Group Affiliation: Las Palmas I-SNP LLC
Licensed in: KY
Address: 12201 Bluegrass Parkway, Louisville, KY 40299
Phone: (502) 234-9037 **Dom State:** KY **Commenced Bus:** N/A

Data Date	Rating	RACR #1	RACR #2	Total Assets ($mil)	Capital ($mil)	Net Premium ($mil)	Net Income ($mil)
9-19	D	0.42	0.35	2.2	1.0	5.1	-0.5
9-18	D+	N/A	N/A	2.7	1.0	3.6	-0.2
2018	D+	0.55	0.46	2.5	1.3	4.7	-0.1
2017	D+	N/A	N/A	1.7	-0.3	4.8	-0.5
2016	D+	1.36	1.13	2.2	1.5	4.1	0.1
2015	N/A	N/A	N/A	1.5	1.5	N/A	-1.0
2014	N/A	N/A	N/A	N/A	N/A	N/A	N/A

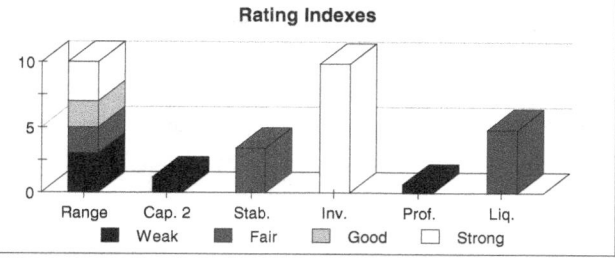

SILVERSCRIPT INS CO   D+   Weak

Major Rating Factors: Low quality investment portfolio (0.0 on a scale of 0 to 10). Excellent profitability (8.2). Strong capitalization (10.0) based on excellent current risk-adjusted capital (severe loss scenario).
Other Rating Factors: Excellent liquidity (7.4) with ample operational cash flow and liquid investments.
Principal Business: Other (100%)
Mem Phys: 19: 68,000 **18:** 68,000 **19 MLR** 100.1% **/ 19 Admin Exp** N/A
Enroll(000): Q2 20: 4,233 **19:** 4,684 **18:** 4,868 **Med Exp PMPM:** $45
Principal Investments: Cash and equiv (99%), long-term bonds (1%)
Provider Compensation ($000): Other ($2,542,975)
Total Member Encounters: N/A
Group Affiliation: None
Licensed in: All states, the District of Columbia and Puerto Rico
Address: 1021 REAMS FLEMING BOULEVARD, FRANKLIN, TN 37064
Phone: (615) 743-6600 **Dom State:** TN **Commenced Bus:** N/A

Data Date	Rating	RACR #1	RACR #2	Total Assets ($mil)	Capital ($mil)	Net Premium ($mil)	Net Income ($mil)
6-20	D+	8.01	6.68	3,694.8	1,053.4	1,387.6	-43.7
6-19	D	6.01	5.01	2,980.2	901.9	1,633.3	-50.5
2019	D	8.56	7.13	2,875.3	1,128.2	2,578.0	109.3
2018	D	6.93	5.78	2,371.8	998.8	2,720.5	28.3
2017	D	8.22	6.85	2,075.4	965.6	2,880.3	214.3
2016	D	6.84	5.70	2,823.6	799.2	2,483.6	206.1
2015	D	7.54	6.29	2,385.7	613.7	2,337.3	38.0

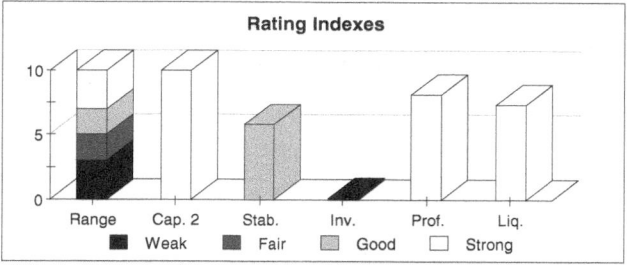

SILVERSUMMIT HEALTHPLAN INC   C   Fair

Major Rating Factors: Weak profitability index (0.9 on a scale of 0 to 10). Strong capitalization (10.0) based on excellent current risk-adjusted capital (severe loss scenario). High quality investment portfolio (9.1).
Other Rating Factors: Excellent liquidity (7.0) with ample operational cash flow and liquid investments.
Principal Business: Medicaid (55%), comp med (45%)
Mem Phys: 18: 5,808 **17:** 9,234 **18 MLR** 84.0% **/ 18 Admin Exp** N/A
Enroll(000): Q3 19: 81 **18:** 76 **17:** 35 **Med Exp PMPM:** $345
Principal Investments: Cash and equiv (62%), long-term bonds (38%)
Provider Compensation ($000): Contr fee ($267,355), salary ($11,491), capitation ($2,917)
Total Member Encounters: Phys (347,098), non-phys (486,604)
Group Affiliation: None
Licensed in: NV
Address: 2500 N Buffalo Drive Suite 2, Las Vegas, NV 89128
Phone: (314) 725-4477 **Dom State:** NV **Commenced Bus:** N/A

Data Date	Rating	RACR #1	RACR #2	Total Assets ($mil)	Capital ($mil)	Net Premium ($mil)	Net Income ($mil)
9-19	C	6.34	5.28	158.0	90.2	349.4	4.9
9-18	N/A	N/A	N/A	124.3	54.6	271.4	-0.8
2018	C-	5.24	4.36	146.4	74.5	372.0	-2.8
2017	N/A	N/A	N/A	27.7	7.7	34.5	-7.6
2016	N/A	N/A	N/A	1.8	0.8	N/A	N/A
2015	N/A	N/A	N/A	N/A	N/A	N/A	N/A
2014	N/A	N/A	N/A	N/A	N/A	N/A	N/A

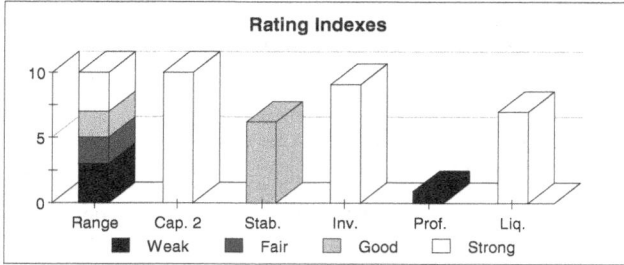

SIMPLY HEALTHCARE PLANS INC   B   Good

Major Rating Factors: Good capitalization (5.0 on a scale of 0 to 10) based on good current risk-adjusted capital (severe loss scenario). Good liquidity (6.5) with sufficient resources (cash flows and marketable investments) to handle a spike in claims. Excellent profitability (7.8).
Other Rating Factors: High quality investment portfolio (8.2).
Principal Business: Medicaid (58%), Medicare (30%), comp med (3%), other (9%)
Mem Phys: 19: 38,319   **18:** 41,161   **19 MLR** 87.7%   **/ 19 Admin Exp** N/A
Enroll(000): Q2 20: 638   **19:** 562   **18:** 582   **Med Exp PMPM:** $415
Principal Investments: Long-term bonds (81%), cash and equiv (11%), other (8%)
Provider Compensation ($000): Bonus arrang ($1,513,506), contr fee ($513,668), FFS ($504,472), capitation ($388,492)
Total Member Encounters: Phys (4,467,677), non-phys (4,397,810)
Group Affiliation: Anthem Inc
Licensed in: FL
Address: 9250 W FLAGLER STREET SUITE 6, MIAMI, FL 33174
Phone: (757) 490-6900   **Dom State:** FL   **Commenced Bus:** N/A

Data Date	Rating	RACR #1	RACR #2	Total Assets ($mil)	Capital ($mil)	Net Premium ($mil)	Net Income ($mil)
6-20	B	0.94	0.78	704.5	226.1	1,806.9	32.7
6-19	B-	1.24	1.03	633.3	218.0	1,624.6	31.1
2019	B	1.50	1.25	642.2	268.1	3,279.1	76.8
2018	B-	1.38	1.15	599.8	245.9	3,171.7	46.6
2017	B+	1.37	1.14	684.8	319.2	3,092.1	115.4
2016	B	1.73	1.44	596.2	214.7	2,965.6	55.6
2015	B-	0.60	0.50	442.4	137.0	2,563.4	21.8

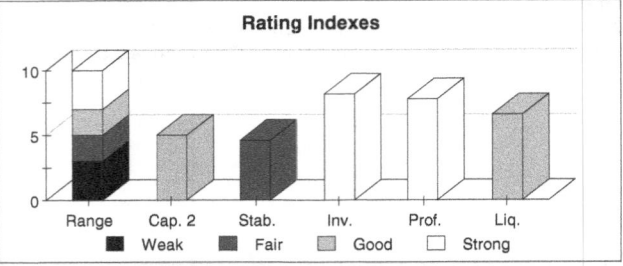

Rating Indexes

SIMPRA ADVANTAGE INC   C   Fair

Major Rating Factors: Fair profitability index (3.9 on a scale of 0 to 10). Good capitalization (6.9) based on excellent current risk-adjusted capital (severe loss scenario). High quality investment portfolio (9.9).
Other Rating Factors: Excellent liquidity (6.9) with sufficient resources (cash flows and marketable investments) to handle a spike in claims.
Principal Business: Medicare (100%)
Mem Phys: 18: 12,650   **17:** N/A   **18 MLR** 88.3%   **/ 18 Admin Exp** N/A
Enroll(000): Q3 19: 3   **18:** 2   **17:** N/A   **Med Exp PMPM:** $1,600
Principal Investments: Cash and equiv (99%), long-term bonds (1%)
Provider Compensation ($000): Contr fee ($28,204)
Total Member Encounters: Phys (38,064), non-phys (160,080)
Group Affiliation: SeniorSelect Partners LLC
Licensed in: AL
Address: 420 North 20th Street Suite 3, Birmingham, AL 35203
Phone: (205) 320-7527   **Dom State:** AL   **Commenced Bus:** N/A

Data Date	Rating	RACR #1	RACR #2	Total Assets ($mil)	Capital ($mil)	Net Premium ($mil)	Net Income ($mil)
9-19	C	1.24	1.04	23.4	8.0	46.6	1.1
9-18	N/A	N/A	N/A	16.5	5.9	29.0	-0.8
2018	D+	1.00	0.84	16.2	6.7	40.7	-0.6
2017	N/A	N/A	N/A	1.4	1.4	N/A	N/A
2016	N/A	N/A	N/A	N/A	N/A	N/A	N/A
2015	N/A	N/A	N/A	N/A	N/A	N/A	N/A
2014	N/A	N/A	N/A	N/A	N/A	N/A	N/A

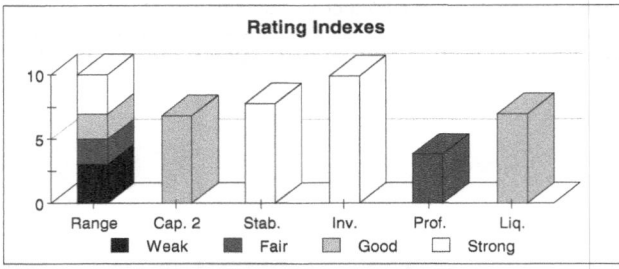

Rating Indexes

SIRIUS AMERICA INS CO   C+   Fair

Major Rating Factors: Fair overall results on stability tests (3.3 on a scale of 0 to 10) including potential drain of affiliation with China Minsheng Investment Co Ltd, excessive premium growth and negative cash flow from operations for 2019. Fair profitability index (3.4) with operating losses during 2017, 2018 and the first six months of 2020. Return on equity has been low, averaging 3.4% over the past five years.
Other Rating Factors: Good long-term capitalization index (6.7) based on good current risk adjusted capital (moderate loss scenario), despite some fluctuation in capital levels. History of adequate reserve strength (5.2) as reserves have been consistently at an acceptable level. Excellent liquidity (7.0) with ample operational cash flow and liquid investments.
Principal Business: Group accident & health (82%), workers compensation (14%), surety (3%), and commercial multiple peril (1%).
Principal Investments: Investment grade bonds (57%), misc. investments (38%), and cash (5%).
Investments in Affiliates: 7%
Group Affiliation: China Minsheng Investment Co Ltd
Licensed in: All states, the District of Columbia and Puerto Rico
Commenced Business: January 1980
Address: 140 BROADWAY - 32ND FLOOR, New York, NY 10005-1123
Phone: (212) 312-2500   **Domicile State:** NY   **NAIC Code:** 38776

Data Date	Rating	RACR #1	RACR #2	Loss Ratio %	Total Assets ($mil)	Capital ($mil)	Net Premium ($mil)	Net Income ($mil)
6-20	C+	1.47	0.92	N/A	1,430.9	519.2	160.6	-15.7
6-19	C	0.89	0.55	N/A	1,252.1	514.5	107.8	-8.8
2019	C+	1.60	1.01	83.9	1,263.1	522.1	257.8	-25.0
2018	B-	0.93	0.57	74.0	1,228.0	522.2	182.0	-9.9
2017	B-	1.60	1.01	107.6	1,337.5	521.8	101.2	-6.4
2016	B-	0.96	0.69	73.8	1,395.1	544.3	217.3	82.7
2015	C+	1.42	0.87	53.7	1,387.6	517.6	283.9	74.7

Rating Indexes

SISTEMAS MEDICOS NACIONALES SA DE CV   B-   Good

Major Rating Factors: Good overall results on stability tests (6.4 on a scale of 0 to 10). Excellent profitability (9.8). Strong capitalization index (8.9) based on excellent current risk-adjusted capital (severe loss scenario).
Other Rating Factors: Excellent liquidity (7.3) with ample operational cash flow and liquid investments.
Principal Business: Managed care (94%), indemnity (6%)
Mem Phys: 19: N/A **18:** N/A **19 MLR** 59.7% **/ 19 Admin Exp** N/A
Enroll(000): Q2 20: 55 **19:** 52 **18:** 52 **Med Exp PMPM:** $105
Principal Investments ($000): Cash and equiv ($12,567)
Provider Compensation ($000): None
Total Member Encounters: N/A
Group Affiliation: None
Licensed in: CA
Address: 8520 Tech Way Suite 200, San Diego, CA 92123-1450
Phone: (858) 499-8240 **Dom State:** CA **Commenced Bus:** January 2000

Data Date	Rating	RACR #1	RACR #2	Total Assets ($mil)	Capital ($mil)	Net Premium ($mil)	Net Income ($mil)
6-20	B-	3.59	2.37	93.3	51.5	55.9	8.5
6-19	B-	3.24	2.15	70.1	39.7	53.1	6.9
2019	B-	2.77	1.82	89.2	42.9	105.4	8.3
2018	B-	2.91	1.93	64.7	34.3	95.5	6.4
2017	C+	2.96	1.97	47.6	28.2	88.0	6.3
2016	C+	3.05	2.02	37.8	22.7	78.6	7.1
2015	C+	2.69	1.79	28.6	17.6	69.1	6.8

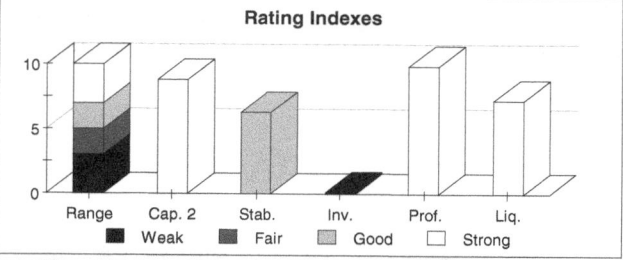

Rating Indexes

SOLIS HEALTH PLANS INC   E+   Very Weak

Major Rating Factors: Weak profitability index (0.0 on a scale of 0 to 10). Poor capitalization (1.9) based on weak current risk-adjusted capital (moderate loss scenario). Weak liquidity (0.0) as a spike in claims may stretch capacity.
Other Rating Factors: High quality investment portfolio (9.8).
Principal Business: Medicare (99%)
Mem Phys: 19: 8,960 **18:** 5,985 **19 MLR** 94.7% **/ 19 Admin Exp** N/A
Enroll(000): Q2 20: 1 **19:** 1 **18:** N/A **Med Exp PMPM:** $1,431
Principal Investments: Cash and equiv (100%)
Provider Compensation ($000): FFS ($5,263), capitation ($2,004), other ($134)
Total Member Encounters: N/A
Group Affiliation: Athena Health Care Holdings LLC
Licensed in: (No states)
Address: 9250 NW 36th Street Suite 400, Doral, FL 33178
Phone: (305) 913-0055 **Dom State:** FL **Commenced Bus:** N/A

Data Date	Rating	RACR #1	RACR #2	Total Assets ($mil)	Capital ($mil)	Net Premium ($mil)	Net Income ($mil)
6-20	E+	0.49	0.41	12.3	4.3	12.6	0.4
6-19	N/A	N/A	N/A	N/A	N/A	N/A	N/A
2019	E+	0.50	0.42	17.0	4.3	11.2	-20.9
2018	N/A	N/A	N/A	12.7	12.1	N/A	-13.0
2017	N/A	N/A	N/A	N/A	N/A	N/A	N/A
2016	N/A	N/A	N/A	N/A	N/A	N/A	N/A
2015	N/A	N/A	N/A	N/A	N/A	N/A	N/A

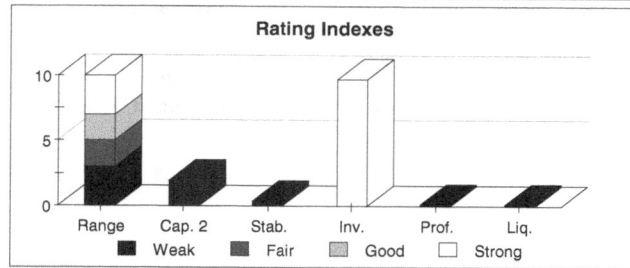

Rating Indexes

SOLSTICE HEALTH INS CO   C+   Fair

Major Rating Factors: Good overall profitability index (6.8 on a scale of 0 to 10). Strong capitalization (8.8) based on excellent current risk-adjusted capital (severe loss scenario). High quality investment portfolio (9.9).
Other Rating Factors: Excellent liquidity (7.4) with ample operational cash flow and liquid investments.
Principal Business: Dental (20%), vision (6%), other (74%)
Mem Phys: 18: 14,341 **17:** 9,532 **18 MLR** 48.6% **/ 18 Admin Exp** N/A
Enroll(000): Q3 19: 110 **18:** 102 **17:** 60 **Med Exp PMPM:** $7
Principal Investments: Cash and equiv (100%)
Provider Compensation ($000): FFS ($2,823)
Total Member Encounters: N/A
Group Affiliation: None
Licensed in: NY
Address: 420 LEXINGTON AVE SUITE 2431, NEW YORK, NY 10170
Phone: (954) 370-1700 **Dom State:** NY **Commenced Bus:** N/A

Data Date	Rating	RACR #1	RACR #2	Total Assets ($mil)	Capital ($mil)	Net Premium ($mil)	Net Income ($mil)
9-19	C+	2.78	2.31	20.5	3.6	15.4	0.6
9-18	C	2.79	2.32	15.6	3.4	12.3	1.4
2018	C+	2.34	1.95	17.2	3.0	16.7	0.9
2017	U	1.37	1.14	5.5	1.7	8.9	0.9
2016	N/A	N/A	N/A	1.4	0.6	2.4	N/A
2015	N/A	N/A	N/A	5.4	2.1	6.4	N/A
2014	N/A	N/A	N/A	1.7	0.6	2.7	N/A

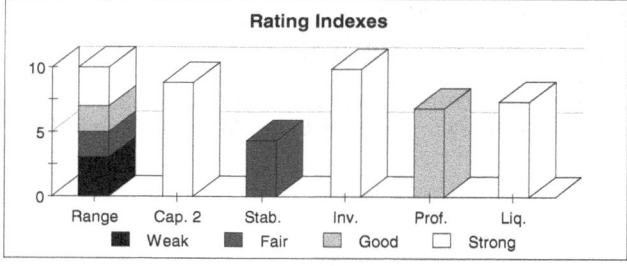

Rating Indexes

SOUNDPATH HEALTH
D   **Weak**

Major Rating Factors: Weak profitability index (0.9 on a scale of 0 to 10). Strong capitalization (10.0) based on excellent current risk-adjusted capital (severe loss scenario). High quality investment portfolio (9.9).
Other Rating Factors: Excellent liquidity (8.5) with ample operational cash flow and liquid investments.
Principal Business: Medicare (100%)
Mem Phys: 19: N/A **18:** 13,540 **19 MLR** ****.*% **/ 19 Admin Exp** N/A
Enroll(000): Q2 20: N/A **19:** N/A **18:** 23 **Med Exp PMPM:** N/A
Principal Investments: Cash and equiv (73%), long-term bonds (27%)
Provider Compensation ($000): Contr fee ($14,029), capitation ($15)
Total Member Encounters: N/A
Group Affiliation: None
Licensed in: WA
Address: 33820 Weyerhaeuser Way S, Federal Way, WA 98001
Phone: (866) 789-7747 **Dom State:** WA **Commenced Bus:** N/A

Data Date	Rating	RACR #1	RACR #2	Total Assets ($mil)	Capital ($mil)	Net Premium ($mil)	Net Income ($mil)
6-20	D	12.16	10.13	45.0	44.0	-0.1	-4.1
6-19	D	2.42	2.02	55.3	50.6	0.5	5.2
2019	D	14.35	11.96	48.6	48.0	0.2	2.1
2018	D-	2.25	1.88	71.5	45.5	188.4	6.1
2017	F	1.50	1.25	66.8	38.5	181.2	-8.8
2016	E	1.55	1.29	55.6	34.8	198.1	-0.9
2015	E	0.38	0.32	50.6	10.6	155.2	-17.3

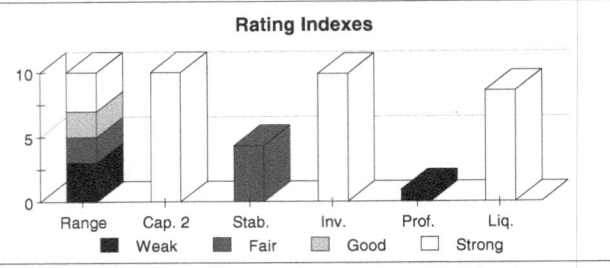

Rating Indexes

SOUTHEASTERN INDIANA HEALTH ORG INC
B-   **Good**

Major Rating Factors: Fair profitability index (4.8 on a scale of 0 to 10). Fair overall results on stability tests (4.6) based on a decline in the number of member physicians during 2020. Strong capitalization index (7.9) based on excellent current risk-adjusted capital (severe loss scenario).
Other Rating Factors: High quality investment portfolio (9.5). Excellent liquidity (7.3) with ample operational cash flow and liquid investments.
Principal Business: Comp med (99%)
Mem Phys: 19: 18,141 **18:** 30,346 **19 MLR** 86.1% **/ 19 Admin Exp** N/A
Enroll(000): Q2 20: 6 **19:** 6 **18:** 6 **Med Exp PMPM:** $427
Principal Investments: Cash and equiv (86%), real estate (14%)
Provider Compensation ($000): Contr fee ($26,698), capitation ($621), FFS ($332)
Total Member Encounters: Phys (26,038), non-phys (12,985)
Group Affiliation: SIHO Holding Inc
Licensed in: IN
Address: 417 WASHINGTON STREET, COLUMBUS,
Phone: (812) 378-7000 **Dom State:** IN **Commenced Bus:** N/A

Data Date	Rating	RACR #1	RACR #2	Total Assets ($mil)	Capital ($mil)	Net Premium ($mil)	Net Income ($mil)
6-20	B-	2.12	1.76	17.8	10.1	18.9	1.0
6-19	N/A	N/A	N/A	N/A	N/A	N/A	N/A
2019	B-	1.90	1.58	15.7	9.2	33.3	1.2
2018	C+	1.72	1.43	13.6	8.9	34.1	0.7
2017	C	1.89	1.57	14.0	9.1	29.9	0.4
2016	C	1.21	1.01	13.0	6.1	33.5	0.6
2015	B	1.75	1.46	16.4	9.1	36.4	-1.6

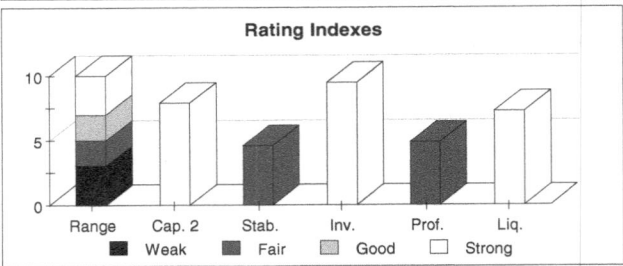

Rating Indexes

SOUTHERN GUARANTY INS CO
C   **Fair**

Major Rating Factors: Fair profitability index (4.0) with operating losses during 2017 and 2018. Return on equity has been fair, averaging 11.2% over the past five years.
Other Rating Factors: Weak overall results on stability tests (2.7) including excessive premium growth. Strong long-term capitalization index (10.0) based on excellent current risk adjusted capital (severe and moderate loss scenarios), despite some fluctuation in capital levels. Excellent liquidity (8.0) with ample operational cash flow and liquid investments.
Principal Business: Other accident & health (100%).
Principal Investments: Misc. investments (47%), investment grade bonds (26%), real estate (14%), and cash (13%).
Investments in Affiliates: None
Group Affiliation: QBE Ins Group Ltd
Licensed in: AL, AZ, AR, FL, GA, IL, IN, IA, KS, KY, LA, MD, MI, MS, NE, NV, NM, NC, OH, OK, OR, PA, SC, TN, TX, UT, WA, WI
Commenced Business: July 1963
Address: 13600 ICOT BLVD BLDG A, Clearwater, FL 33760-3703
Phone: (727) 498-3782 **Domicile State:** WI **NAIC Code:** 19178

Data Date	Rating	RACR #1	RACR #2	Loss Ratio %	Total Assets ($mil)	Capital ($mil)	Net Premium ($mil)	Net Income ($mil)
6-20	C	7.93	4.28	N/A	33.3	30.6	3.1	1.0
6-19	C+	4.53	2.87	N/A	29.2	27.8	1.2	0.1
2019	C+	14.81	8.24	68.8	32.1	30.4	2.7	1.6
2018	B-	4.49	2.69	78.3	26.8	25.7	0.5	-0.7
2017	U	23.76	12.19	0.0	30.3	29.7	0.0	-0.4
2016	C	1.76	1.59	0.0	13.2	4.5	-11.0	2.2
2015	C-	1.47	0.97	63.9	90.3	22.8	30.3	1.7

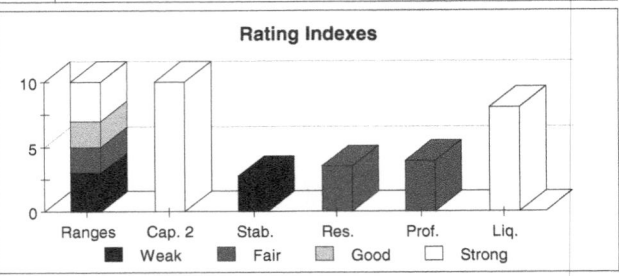

Rating Indexes

SOUTHWEST L&H INS CO   D   Weak

Major Rating Factors: Weak profitability index (0.6 on a scale of 0 to 10). Good liquidity (6.8) with sufficient resources (cash flows and marketable investments) to handle a spike in claims. Strong capitalization (8.3) based on excellent current risk-adjusted capital (severe loss scenario).
Other Rating Factors: High quality investment portfolio (9.9).
Principal Business: Comp med (100%)
Mem Phys: 19: 14,381 **18:** 13,065 **19 MLR** 106.9% **/ 19 Admin Exp** N/A
Enroll(000): Q2 20: 1 **19:** 2 **18:** 2 **Med Exp PMPM:** $431
Principal Investments: Long-term bonds (54%), cash and equiv (27%), nonaffiliate common stock (19%)
Provider Compensation ($000): Contr fee ($8,272), FFS ($17)
Total Member Encounters: Phys (16,231), non-phys (8,685)
Group Affiliation: None
Licensed in: LA, NM, TX
Address: 12940 N Hwy 183, Austin, TX 78750-3203
Phone: (254) 298-3000 **Dom State:** TX **Commenced Bus:** N/A

Data Date	Rating	RACR #1	RACR #2	Total Assets ($mil)	Capital ($mil)	Net Premium ($mil)	Net Income ($mil)
6-20	D	2.42	2.02	8.7	6.6	2.8	1.0
6-19	D	3.79	3.16	9.1	7.4	4.0	-1.2
2019	D	3.03	2.52	8.8	5.7	8.0	-3.2
2018	D	3.76	3.13	10.9	8.4	10.4	-0.7
2017	C-	3.74	3.12	11.4	9.6	8.0	-1.9
2016	C-	3.33	2.77	11.0	7.5	11.1	-2.9
2015	C	1.91	1.59	10.4	5.7	14.6	-5.1

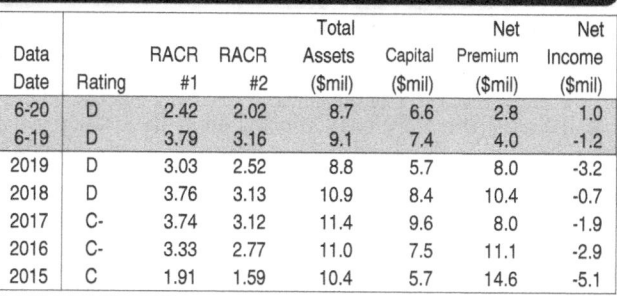

SPARTAN PLAN NY INC   E-   Very Weak

Major Rating Factors: Weak profitability index (0.0 on a scale of 0 to 10). Fair capitalization (3.8) based on fair current risk-adjusted capital (moderate loss scenario). High quality investment portfolio (9.9).
Other Rating Factors: Excellent liquidity (7.5) with ample operational cash flow and liquid investments.
Principal Business: Medicare (100%)
Mem Phys: 18: 7,152 **17:** N/A **18 MLR** 413.3% **/ 18 Admin Exp** N/A
Enroll(000): Q3 19: 0 **18:** 0 **17:** N/A **Med Exp PMPM:** $2,433
Principal Investments: Cash and equiv (100%)
Provider Compensation ($000): Contr fee ($1,240), bonus arrang ($242)
Total Member Encounters: Phys (1,854), non-phys (3,649)
Group Affiliation: Public Sector Pension Investment Boa
Licensed in: NY
Address: 53 Franklin Avenue, Lynbrook, NY 11563
Phone: (804) 396-6412 **Dom State:** NY **Commenced Bus:** N/A

Data Date	Rating	RACR #1	RACR #2	Total Assets ($mil)	Capital ($mil)	Net Premium ($mil)	Net Income ($mil)
9-19	E-	0.75	0.62	2.0	0.5	2.0	-1.5
9-18	N/A	N/A	N/A	2.5	2.3	0.3	-0.5
2018	D	3.05	2.54	2.3	2.1	0.5	-0.7
2017	N/A	N/A	N/A	2.8	2.8	N/A	-0.2
2016	N/A	N/A	N/A	N/A	N/A	N/A	N/A
2015	N/A	N/A	N/A	N/A	N/A	N/A	N/A
2014	N/A	N/A	N/A	N/A	N/A	N/A	N/A

SPARTAN PLAN VA INC   D+   Weak

Major Rating Factors: Weak profitability index (0.2 on a scale of 0 to 10). Fair quality investment portfolio (4.2). Good capitalization (5.0) based on good current risk-adjusted capital (severe loss scenario).
Other Rating Factors: Good liquidity (6.5) with sufficient resources (cash flows and marketable investments) to handle a spike in claims.
Principal Business: Medicare (100%)
Mem Phys: 18: 2,852 **17:** N/A **18 MLR** 358.1% **/ 18 Admin Exp** N/A
Enroll(000): Q3 19: 0 **18:** 0 **17:** N/A **Med Exp PMPM:** $1,787
Principal Investments: Affiliate common stock (70%), cash and equiv (30%)
Provider Compensation ($000): Contr fee ($895), bonus arrang ($244)
Total Member Encounters: Phys (1,524), non-phys (1,724)
Group Affiliation: Public Sector Pension Investment Boa
Licensed in: IL, PA, VA
Address: 7902 Westpark Drive, McLean, VA 22102
Phone: (804) 396-6412 **Dom State:** VA **Commenced Bus:** N/A

Data Date	Rating	RACR #1	RACR #2	Total Assets ($mil)	Capital ($mil)	Net Premium ($mil)	Net Income ($mil)
9-19	D+	0.93	0.77	2.9	2.0	1.5	-0.8
9-18	N/A	N/A	N/A	1.2	1.0	0.3	-0.4
2018	D+	1.65	1.38	3.6	3.4	0.4	-0.6
2017	N/A	N/A	N/A	1.5	1.5	N/A	-0.7
2016	N/A	N/A	N/A	N/A	N/A	N/A	N/A
2015	N/A	N/A	N/A	N/A	N/A	N/A	N/A
2014	N/A	N/A	N/A	N/A	N/A	N/A	N/A

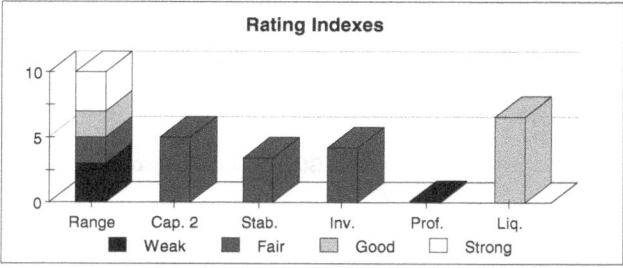

STANDARD INS CO *
B+   **Good**

Major Rating Factors: Good quality investment portfolio (5.1 on a scale of 0 to 10) despite substantial holdings of BBB bonds in addition to moderate junk bond exposure. Exposure to mortgages is large, but the mortgage default rate has been low. Good liquidity (6.5) with sufficient resources to handle a spike in claims as well as a significant increase in policy surrenders. Good overall results on stability tests (6.5) despite excessive premium growth excellent operational trends and excellent risk diversification.
Other Rating Factors: Strong capitalization (7.4) based on excellent risk adjusted capital (severe loss scenario). Excellent profitability (7.5) with operating gains in each of the last five years.
Principal Business: Group retirement contracts (44%), group health insurance (23%), group life insurance (15%), individual annuities (12%), and other lines (6%).
Principal Investments: NonCMO investment grade bonds (46%), mortgages in good standing (39%), CMOs and structured securities (9%), and noninv. grade bonds (3%).
Investments in Affiliates: None
Group Affiliation: Meiji Yasuda Life Ins Company
Licensed in: All states except NY
Commenced Business: April 1906
Address: 1100 SOUTHWEST SIXTH AVENUE, PORTLAND, OR 97204-1093
Phone: (503) 321-7000 **Domicile State:** OR **NAIC Code:** 69019

Data Date	Rating	RACR #1	RACR #2	Total Assets ($mil)	Capital ($mil)	Net Premium ($mil)	Net Income ($mil)
6-20	B+	2.40	1.25	27,265.4	1,497.6	3,266.5	115.0
6-19	B+	2.34	1.22	25,645.4	1,369.9	2,564.5	87.1
2019	B+	2.48	1.29	26,665.4	1,443.7	5,161.6	197.9
2018	B+	2.32	1.21	23,862.6	1,294.0	4,459.1	201.6
2017	B+	2.02	1.06	23,952.0	1,108.4	4,300.3	178.2
2016	B+	2.04	1.06	21,792.1	1,040.4	4,075.8	144.8
2015	B+	2.21	1.16	20,781.6	1,085.0	3,528.4	160.1

Adverse Trends in Operations

Increase in policy surrenders from 2018 to 2019 (26%)
Increase in policy surrenders from 2015 to 2016 (26%)
Decrease in capital during 2016 (4%)

STANDARD LIFE & ACCIDENT INS CO
B   **Good**

Major Rating Factors: Good overall results on stability tests (5.0 on a scale of 0 to 10) despite negative cash flow from operations for 2019. Other stability subfactors include good operational trends and excellent risk diversification. Good overall profitability (6.7). Return on equity has been low, averaging 2.6%. Good liquidity (6.9).
Other Rating Factors: Fair quality investment portfolio (4.9). Strong capitalization (10.0) based on excellent risk adjusted capital (severe loss scenario).
Principal Business: Individual health insurance (40%), group health insurance (31%), reinsurance (20%), individual life insurance (8%), and group life insurance (1%).
Principal Investments: NonCMO investment grade bonds (76%), common & preferred stock (17%), mortgages in good standing (4%), noninv. grade bonds (2%), and misc. investments (2%).
Investments in Affiliates: None
Group Affiliation: American National Group Inc
Licensed in: All states except ME, NH, NJ, NY, PR
Commenced Business: June 1976
Address: ONE MOODY PLAZA, GALVESTON, TX 77550
Phone: (409) 763-4661 **Domicile State:** TX **NAIC Code:** 86355

Data Date	Rating	RACR #1	RACR #2	Total Assets ($mil)	Capital ($mil)	Net Premium ($mil)	Net Income ($mil)
6-20	B	6.72	4.04	482.2	287.3	39.3	4.2
6-19	A-	6.44	4.03	508.6	298.8	43.1	9.5
2019	A-	6.93	4.21	500.4	293.7	81.4	12.4
2018	A-	6.05	3.79	516.9	291.9	107.6	10.9
2017	A-	5.78	3.59	521.6	289.5	98.3	10.7
2016	A-	6.21	3.82	518.8	287.1	95.1	13.6
2015	A-	5.93	3.68	514.5	278.1	105.2	8.6

Adverse Trends in Operations

Decrease in premium volume from 2018 to 2019 (24%)
Decrease in asset base during 2019 (3%)
Decrease in premium volume from 2015 to 2016 (10%)

STANDARD LIFE INS CO OF NY *
A-   **Excellent**

Major Rating Factors: Excellent overall results on stability tests (7.2 on a scale of 0 to 10). Strengths that enhance stability include excellent operational trends and excellent risk diversification. Strong capitalization (10.0) based on excellent risk adjusted capital (severe loss scenario). Furthermore, this high level of risk adjusted capital has been consistently maintained over the last five years. High quality investment portfolio (7.4).
Other Rating Factors: Excellent profitability (7.9) with operating gains in each of the last five years. Excellent liquidity (7.0).
Principal Business: Group health insurance (64%), group life insurance (30%), and individual health insurance (6%).
Principal Investments: NonCMO investment grade bonds (49%), mortgages in good standing (45%), cash (5%), and noninv. grade bonds (1%).
Investments in Affiliates: None
Group Affiliation: Meiji Yasuda Life Ins Company
Licensed in: NY
Commenced Business: January 2001
Address: 360 HAMILTON AVENUE SUITE 210, WHITE PLAINS, NY 10604-2911
Phone: (914) 989-4400 **Domicile State:** NY **NAIC Code:** 89009

Data Date	Rating	RACR #1	RACR #2	Total Assets ($mil)	Capital ($mil)	Net Premium ($mil)	Net Income ($mil)
6-20	A-	5.22	3.49	307.0	117.3	60.6	6.6
6-19	A-	4.91	3.24	303.9	109.0	53.1	13.6
2019	A-	5.71	3.82	305.9	123.2	103.9	23.5
2018	A-	4.56	3.05	303.0	99.0	104.0	1.2
2017	A-	4.90	3.20	292.2	96.2	90.0	11.9
2016	A-	4.25	2.80	286.6	85.9	89.1	3.6
2015	A-	4.14	2.73	282.7	80.9	89.4	6.3

Adverse Trends in Operations

Increase in policy surrenders from 2016 to 2017 (375%)
Increase in policy surrenders from 2015 to 2016 (415%)

STANDARD SECURITY LIFE INS CO OF NY *   B+   Good

Major Rating Factors: Good overall results on stability tests (6.1 on a scale of 0 to 10) despite excessive premium growth. Other stability subfactors include good operational trends and excellent risk diversification. Good overall profitability (5.8). Return on equity has been good over the last five years, averaging 10.2%. Good liquidity (6.9).
Other Rating Factors: Strong capitalization (10.0) based on excellent risk adjusted capital (severe loss scenario). High quality investment portfolio (8.2).
Principal Business: Group health insurance (97%), group life insurance (2%), and individual health insurance (1%).
Principal Investments: NonCMO investment grade bonds (83%), common & preferred stock (1%), cash (1%), and CMOs and structured securities (1%).
Investments in Affiliates: None
Group Affiliation: Geneve Holdings Inc
Licensed in: All states, the District of Columbia and Puerto Rico
Commenced Business: December 1958
Address: 485 Madison Avenue 14th Floor, New York, NY 10022-5872
Phone: (212) 355-4141 **Domicile State:** NY **NAIC Code:** 69078

Data Date	Rating	RACR #1	RACR #2	Total Assets ($mil)	Capital ($mil)	Net Premium ($mil)	Net Income ($mil)
6-20	B+	5.34	4.20	142.7	59.4	70.4	2.4
6-19	B+	7.46	5.75	141.4	73.1	48.3	1.9
2019	B+	6.84	5.30	114.5	57.1	81.2	5.2
2018	B+	6.86	5.24	129.1	70.8	89.0	8.3
2017	B	6.77	5.23	131.5	65.6	80.3	3.6
2016	B+	6.84	5.28	154.9	70.6	84.7	-10.5
2015	A-	3.95	3.20	269.9	125.1	211.0	13.2

Adverse Trends in Operations

Decrease in asset base during 2019 (11%)
Increase in policy surrenders from 2017 to 2018 (1284%)
Decrease in asset base during 2017 (15%)
Decrease in capital during 2016 (44%)
Decrease in premium volume from 2015 to 2016 (60%)

STANFORD HEALTH CARE ADVANTAGE   E-   Very Weak

Major Rating Factors: Weak profitability index (0.7 on a scale of 0 to 10). Weak overall results on stability tests (2.2) in spite of healthy premium and capital growth during 2019. Weak liquidity (0.0) as a spike in claims may stretch capacity.
Other Rating Factors: Fair capitalization index (4.4) based on weak current risk-adjusted capital (moderate loss scenario).
Principal Business: Medicare (100%)
Mem Phys: 19: N/A **18:** N/A **19 MLR** 101.8% **/ 19 Admin Exp** N/A
Enroll(000): Q2 20: 5 **19:** 3 **18:** 3 **Med Exp PMPM:** $1,325
Principal Investments ($000): Cash and equiv ($15,005)
Provider Compensation ($000): None
Total Member Encounters: N/A
Group Affiliation: None
Licensed in: CA
Address: 4365 Executive Drive Suite 500, San Diego, CA 92121
Phone: (858) 658-8662 **Dom State:** CA **Commenced Bus:** August 2013

Data Date	Rating	RACR #1	RACR #2	Total Assets ($mil)	Capital ($mil)	Net Premium ($mil)	Net Income ($mil)
6-20	E-	0.70	0.44	15.0	4.7	25.4	-6.7
6-19	E-	0.74	0.47	21.7	4.1	19.9	-5.1
2019	E-	0.82	0.52	18.0	5.4	43.6	-9.7
2018	E-	0.47	0.30	15.0	2.7	27.5	-14.3
2017	E-	0.95	0.61	9.3	3.5	16.5	-10.7
2016	D	1.82	1.25	5.1	3.0	6.7	-5.7
2015	U	5.31	4.78	3.2	2.6	0.5	-4.2

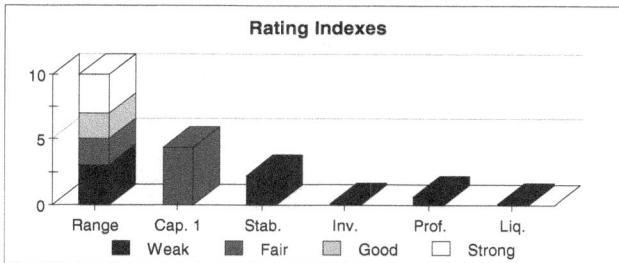

Rating Indexes

STARMOUNT LIFE INS CO   C   Fair

Major Rating Factors: Fair profitability (3.0 on a scale of 0 to 10). Fair overall results on stability tests (3.9) including negative cash flow from operations for 2019. Good current capitalization (5.6) based on mixed results -- excessive policy leverage mitigated by excellent risk adjusted capital (severe loss scenario) reflecting improvement over results in 2017.
Other Rating Factors: Weak liquidity (2.0). High quality investment portfolio (7.4).
Principal Business: N/A
Principal Investments: NonCMO investment grade bonds (82%), cash (11%), real estate (6%), and policy loans (1%).
Investments in Affiliates: None
Group Affiliation: Unum Group
Licensed in: All states except NY, PR
Commenced Business: August 1983
Address: 8485 Goodwood Blvd, PORTLAND, ME 4122
Phone: (225) 926-2888 **Domicile State:** ME **NAIC Code:** 68985

Data Date	Rating	RACR #1	RACR #2	Total Assets ($mil)	Capital ($mil)	Net Premium ($mil)	Net Income ($mil)
6-20	C	2.05	1.60	140.7	75.4	131.8	14.9
6-19	C	1.36	1.05	98.2	49.6	123.4	-1.8
2019	C	1.36	1.06	110.2	49.0	250.6	-14.3
2018	C	1.37	1.08	94.0	45.3	209.9	-9.5
2017	B	1.18	0.92	79.9	37.4	179.7	-2.8
2016	B	1.20	0.94	76.2	32.3	144.3	-0.4
2015	B	N/A	N/A	65.9	28.3	121.0	4.0

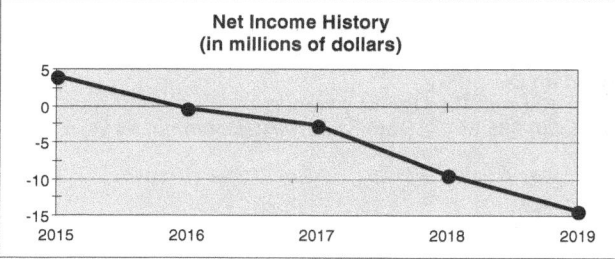

Net Income History
(in millions of dollars)

STEWARD HEALTH CHOICE UTAH INC

E-   Very Weak

Major Rating Factors: Fair profitability index (4.4 on a scale of 0 to 10). Strong capitalization (7.4) based on excellent current risk-adjusted capital (severe loss scenario). High quality investment portfolio (9.9).
Other Rating Factors: Excellent liquidity (7.3) with ample operational cash flow and liquid investments.
Principal Business: Medicaid (97%), Medicare (3%)
Mem Phys: 19: 2,258 **18:** 2,576 **19 MLR** 97.2% **/ 19 Admin Exp** N/A
Enroll(000): Q2 20: 27 **19:** 19 **18:** 19 **Med Exp PMPM:** $292
Principal Investments: Cash and equiv (100%)
Provider Compensation ($000): Contr fee ($62,295), FFS ($3,025)
Total Member Encounters: N/A
Group Affiliation: University of Utah
Licensed in: UT
Address: 406 W South Jordan Parkway Su, South Jordan, UT 84095
Phone: (801) 984-3388 **Dom State:** UT **Commenced Bus:** N/A

Data Date	Rating	RACR #1	RACR #2	Total Assets ($mil)	Capital ($mil)	Net Premium ($mil)	Net Income ($mil)
6-20	E-	1.65	1.37	50.3	15.8	54.9	0.8
6-19	N/A	N/A	N/A	N/A	N/A	N/A	N/A
2019	E-	1.35	1.12	37.5	12.9	67.8	-1.8
2018	E-	2.27	1.90	26.4	14.7	60.3	5.2
2017	E-	1.95	1.62	32.4	13.5	53.5	2.8
2016	E-	1.13	0.94	34.2	10.2	55.6	-1.2
2015	E-	1.30	1.08	20.5	8.4	32.9	0.8

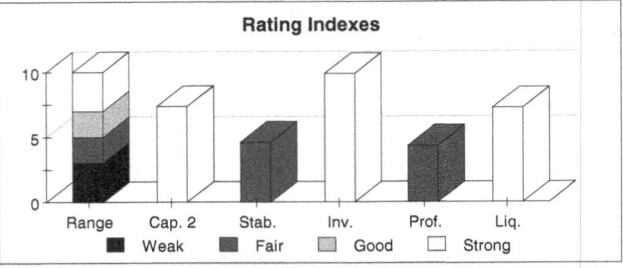

Rating Indexes

SUMMA INS CO

C-   Fair

Major Rating Factors: Weak profitability index (0.9 on a scale of 0 to 10). Strong capitalization (7.3) based on excellent current risk-adjusted capital (severe loss scenario). High quality investment portfolio (9.9).
Other Rating Factors: Excellent liquidity (6.9) with sufficient resources (cash flows and marketable investments) to handle a spike in claims.
Principal Business: Comp med (99%)
Mem Phys: 19: N/A **18:** N/A **19 MLR** 85.1% **/ 19 Admin Exp** N/A
Enroll(000): Q2 20: 18 **19:** 20 **18:** 31 **Med Exp PMPM:** $413
Principal Investments: Long-term bonds (59%), cash and equiv (41%)
Provider Compensation ($000): Contr fee ($113,040), capitation ($337)
Total Member Encounters: Phys (33,589), non-phys (15,240)
Group Affiliation: None
Licensed in: OH
Address: 1200 East Market St Suite 400, Akron, OH 44305
Phone: (330) 996-8410 **Dom State:** OH **Commenced Bus:** N/A

Data Date	Rating	RACR #1	RACR #2	Total Assets ($mil)	Capital ($mil)	Net Premium ($mil)	Net Income ($mil)
6-20	C-	1.59	1.32	45.3	21.9	56.6	-1.7
6-19	C-	1.47	1.22	48.7	25.6	64.1	1.2
2019	C-	1.91	1.59	46.7	24.0	126.0	-0.7
2018	C-	1.36	1.13	50.0	24.0	170.8	-11.9
2017	C-	1.22	1.02	48.3	21.4	170.2	-5.0
2016	C-	1.73	1.44	54.9	28.4	190.6	4.0
2015	C-	1.25	1.04	59.7	24.4	214.9	-7.6

Rating Indexes

SUMMACARE INC

C   Fair

Major Rating Factors: Fair profitability index (3.3 on a scale of 0 to 10). Fair overall results on stability tests (4.6). Good liquidity (6.7) with sufficient resources (cash flows and marketable investments) to handle a spike in claims.
Other Rating Factors: Strong capitalization index (7.2) based on excellent current risk-adjusted capital (severe loss scenario). High quality investment portfolio (9.9).
Principal Business: Medicare (100%)
Mem Phys: 19: N/A **18:** N/A **19 MLR** 85.5% **/ 19 Admin Exp** N/A
Enroll(000): Q2 20: 22 **19:** 23 **18:** 23 **Med Exp PMPM:** $841
Principal Investments: Long-term bonds (53%), affiliate common stock (37%), cash and equiv (10%)
Provider Compensation ($000): Contr fee ($222,037), bonus arrang ($4,784), capitation ($669)
Total Member Encounters: Phys (101,829), non-phys (49,351)
Group Affiliation: None
Licensed in: OH
Address: 10 North Main Street, Akron,
Phone: (330) 996-8410 **Dom State:** OH **Commenced Bus:** N/A

Data Date	Rating	RACR #1	RACR #2	Total Assets ($mil)	Capital ($mil)	Net Premium ($mil)	Net Income ($mil)
6-20	C	1.48	1.24	95.8	49.1	139.6	9.3
6-19	C	1.32	1.10	89.5	43.9	134.6	3.3
2019	C	1.29	1.08	80.9	40.6	269.4	1.2
2018	C	1.19	0.99	78.2	40.0	258.8	-0.3
2017	C	1.09	0.91	75.3	36.4	245.9	-10.9
2016	B-	1.85	1.54	91.4	55.5	252.6	-0.5
2015	B-	1.49	1.24	90.6	51.6	271.4	-5.2

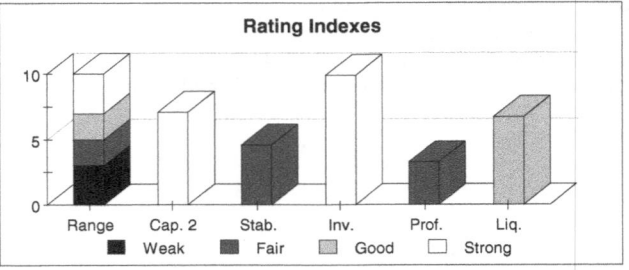

Rating Indexes

SUN LIFE & HEALTH INS CO   D   Weak

Major Rating Factors: Weak profitability (1.1 on a scale of 0 to 10) with investment income below regulatory standards in relation to interest assumptions of reserves. Weak overall results on stability tests (2.2). Good quality investment portfolio (6.9) despite mixed results such as: minimal exposure to mortgages and large holdings of BBB rated bonds but minimal holdings in junk bonds.
Other Rating Factors: Good liquidity (5.8). Strong capitalization (7.6) based on excellent risk adjusted capital (severe loss scenario).
Principal Business: Group health insurance (62%), group life insurance (28%), and reinsurance (10%).
Principal Investments: NonCMO investment grade bonds (72%), CMOs and structured securities (20%), mortgages in good standing (5%), cash (1%), and common & preferred stock (1%).
Investments in Affiliates: None
Group Affiliation: Sun Life Assurance Group
Licensed in: All states, the District of Columbia and Puerto Rico
Commenced Business: January 1975
Address: 201 Townsend Street Ste 900, Lansing, MI 48933
Phone: (781) 237-6030 **Domicile State:** MI **NAIC Code:** 80926

Data Date	Rating	RACR #1	RACR #2	Total Assets ($mil)	Capital ($mil)	Net Premium ($mil)	Net Income ($mil)
6-20	D	2.36	1.39	971.7	113.9	61.6	6.4
6-19	D	2.44	1.45	939.4	109.2	58.9	4.0
2019	D	2.26	1.35	964.9	107.9	120.6	2.7
2018	D	2.34	1.39	930.6	105.4	116.9	7.2
2017	D	2.95	1.74	943.2	129.9	644.6	-68.3
2016	D-	4.36	2.91	485.3	198.5	248.1	-44.8
2015	C	6.46	4.17	447.7	241.5	173.5	17.2

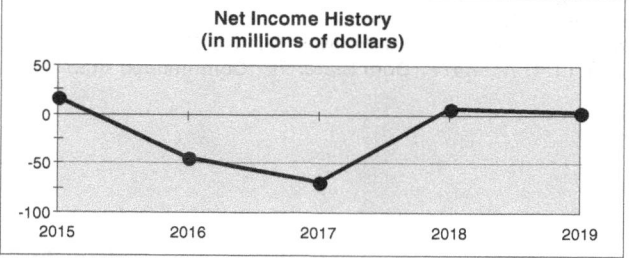

Net Income History
(in millions of dollars)

SUN LIFE ASR CO OF CANADA   D+   Weak

Major Rating Factors: Poor capitalization (2.3 on a scale of 0 to 10) based on weak risk adjusted capital (moderate loss scenario). Low quality investment portfolio (1.9) containing large holdings of BBB rated bonds in addition to moderate junk bond exposure. Exposure to mortgages is significant, but the mortgage default rate has been low. Weak overall results on stability tests (2.3) including weak risk adjusted capital in prior years, negative cash flow from operations for 2019.
Other Rating Factors: Fair profitability (3.4). Good liquidity (5.6).
Principal Business: Group health insurance (63%), group life insurance (14%), individual life insurance (12%), and reinsurance (11%).
Principal Investments: NonCMO investment grade bonds (55%), mortgages in good standing (17%), CMOs and structured securities (15%), real estate (5%), and misc. investments (8%).
Investments in Affiliates: 1%
Group Affiliation: Sun Life Assurance Group
Licensed in: All states except NY
Commenced Business: May 1871
Address: 150 King Street West, Toronto, Ontario, MI 2481
Phone: (781) 237-6030 **Domicile State:** MI **NAIC Code:** 80802

Data Date	Rating	RACR #1	RACR #2	Total Assets ($mil)	Capital ($mil)	Net Premium ($mil)	Net Income ($mil)
6-20	D+	0.66	0.37	20,100.8	887.6	1,086.2	86.8
6-19	D+	0.90	0.53	19,270.0	1,525.0	1,814.5	170.2
2019	D+	0.67	0.38	19,515.5	987.7	2,751.4	156.0
2018	D	0.72	0.42	18,836.1	1,323.9	3,434.0	581.8
2017	D-	0.62	0.35	19,086.1	916.9	1,789.4	259.6
2016	E	0.53	0.32	19,562.8	1,019.0	3,803.2	-535.1
2015	D	1.27	0.74	18,222.4	1,925.8	2,207.2	86.4

Risk-Adjusted Capital Ratio #1
(Moderate Loss Scenario)

SUNFLOWER STATE HEALTH PLAN INC   C   Fair

Major Rating Factors: Fair profitability index (4.0 on a scale of 0 to 10). Fair quality investment portfolio (3.4). Good liquidity (6.9) with sufficient resources (cash flows and marketable investments) to handle a spike in claims.
Other Rating Factors: Strong capitalization (7.1) based on excellent current risk-adjusted capital (severe loss scenario).
Principal Business: Medicaid (87%), comp med (12%)
Mem Phys: 19: 5,994 **18:** 6,095 **19 MLR** 86.2% **/ 19 Admin Exp** N/A
Enroll(000): Q2 20: 169 **19:** 154 **18:** 152 **Med Exp PMPM:** $703
Principal Investments: Cash and equiv (59%), long-term bonds (41%)
Provider Compensation ($000): Contr fee ($1,272,110), capitation ($5,737), bonus arrang ($725)
Total Member Encounters: Phys (805,314), non-phys (3,238,522)
Group Affiliation: None
Licensed in: KS
Address: 8325 Lenexa Drive, Lenexa, KS 66214
Phone: (314) 725-4477 **Dom State:** KS **Commenced Bus:** N/A

Data Date	Rating	RACR #1	RACR #2	Total Assets ($mil)	Capital ($mil)	Net Premium ($mil)	Net Income ($mil)
6-20	C	1.42	1.19	380.0	154.3	838.1	22.8
6-19	C	2.26	1.88	325.7	139.8	759.5	-4.5
2019	C	1.72	1.44	336.4	131.8	1,537.3	-10.1
2018	C	2.32	1.93	284.5	143.8	1,355.5	9.8
2017	C-	N/A	N/A	257.4	134.7	1,114.1	12.1
2016	C-	2.36	1.96	254.0	133.3	1,106.7	9.7
2015	C-	2.21	1.84	265.6	134.8	1,115.0	20.8

Rating Indexes

SUNSHINE HEALTH
C+ **Fair**

Major Rating Factors: Fair profitability index (4.4 on a scale of 0 to 10). Good capitalization (6.8) based on excellent current risk-adjusted capital (severe loss scenario). Good liquidity (6.5) with sufficient resources (cash flows and marketable investments) to handle a spike in claims.
Other Rating Factors: High quality investment portfolio (9.3).
Principal Business: Comp med (51%), Medicaid (48%)
Mem Phys: 19: 39,552 **18:** 35,884 **19 MLR** 93.3% **/ 19 Admin Exp** N/A
Enroll(000): Q2 20: 603 **19:** 590 **18:** 593 **Med Exp PMPM:** $527
Principal Investments: Long-term bonds (65%), cash and equiv (35%)
Provider Compensation ($000): Contr fee ($3,476,127), capitation ($142,698), salary ($103,964), bonus arrang ($92,850)
Total Member Encounters: Phys (3,545,901), non-phys (9,016,281)
Group Affiliation: None
Licensed in: FL
Address: 1301 International Parkway, Sunrise, FL 33323
Phone: (314) 725-4477 **Dom State:** FL **Commenced Bus:** N/A

Data Date	Rating	RACR #1	RACR #2	Total Assets ($mil)	Capital ($mil)	Net Premium ($mil)	Net Income ($mil)
6-20	C+	1.21	1.01	849.2	374.3	1,945.5	13.2
6-19	C-	1.55	1.29	766.2	355.9	2,137.4	12.2
2019	C	1.53	1.27	779.8	363.2	4,111.0	29.6
2018	D+	1.54	1.28	752.5	353.2	3,945.8	-15.5
2017	E	1.35	1.13	735.6	368.5	3,761.9	5.9
2016	E	1.81	1.51	676.5	357.9	3,627.5	23.0
2015	E	1.88	1.57	692.8	330.9	3,125.4	27.1

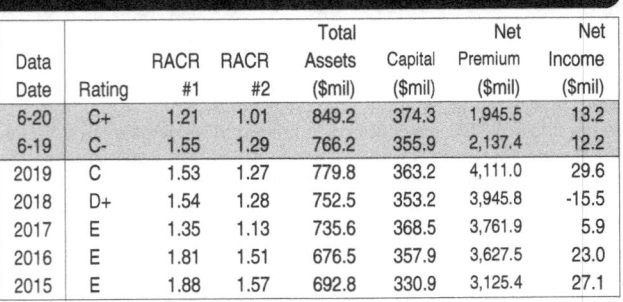

SUNSHINE HEALTH COMMUNITY SOLUTIONS
C- **Fair**

Major Rating Factors: Weak profitability index (0.0 on a scale of 0 to 10). Good liquidity (6.6) with sufficient resources (cash flows and marketable investments) to handle a spike in claims. Strong capitalization (8.3) based on excellent current risk-adjusted capital (severe loss scenario).
Other Rating Factors: High quality investment portfolio (9.9).
Principal Business: Medicare (100%)
Mem Phys: 18: 26,920 **17:** 19,040 **18 MLR** 118.1% **/ 18 Admin Exp** N/A
Enroll(000): Q3 19: 1 **18:** 3 **17:** 0 **Med Exp PMPM:** $842
Principal Investments: Cash and equiv (58%), long-term bonds (42%)
Provider Compensation ($000): Contr fee ($19,037), capitation ($1,028), salary ($551), bonus arrang ($98)
Total Member Encounters: Phys (24,472), non-phys (6,728)
Group Affiliation: None
Licensed in: FL
Address: 1301 International Parkway, Sunrise, FL 33323
Phone: (314) 725-4477 **Dom State:** FL **Commenced Bus:** N/A

Data Date	Rating	RACR #1	RACR #2	Total Assets ($mil)	Capital ($mil)	Net Premium ($mil)	Net Income ($mil)
9-19	C-	2.38	1.98	15.7	6.5	9.1	-1.8
9-18	N/A	N/A	N/A	19.7	11.9	16.0	1.1
2018	C-	2.96	2.47	18.7	8.2	21.7	-2.5
2017	N/A	N/A	N/A	18.0	11.1	1.4	-7.2
2016	N/A	N/A	N/A	19.1	18.3	N/A	-1.6
2015	N/A	N/A	N/A	0.3	-0.1	N/A	N/A
2014	N/A	N/A	N/A	N/A	N/A	N/A	N/A

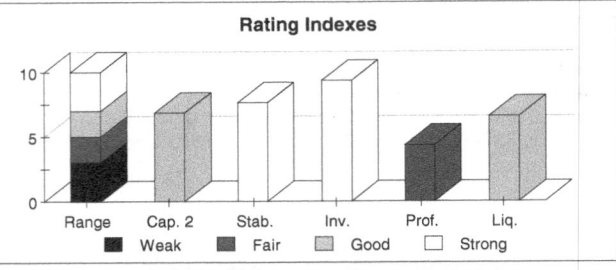

SUPERIOR HEALTHPLAN COMMUNITY SOLUTI
C **Fair**

Major Rating Factors: Weak profitability index (0.8 on a scale of 0 to 10). Strong capitalization (9.8) based on excellent current risk-adjusted capital (severe loss scenario). High quality investment portfolio (9.9).
Other Rating Factors: Excellent liquidity (7.4) with ample operational cash flow and liquid investments.
Principal Business: Medicare (100%)
Mem Phys: 18: 33,870 **17:** 22,932 **18 MLR** 99.6% **/ 18 Admin Exp** N/A
Enroll(000): Q3 19: 2 **18:** 1 **17:** 0 **Med Exp PMPM:** $829
Principal Investments: Cash and equiv (84%), long-term bonds (16%)
Provider Compensation ($000): Contr fee ($7,569), salary ($321), capitation ($7), bonus arrang ($3)
Total Member Encounters: Phys (39,975), non-phys (7,708)
Group Affiliation: None
Licensed in: TX
Address: 5900 E Ben White Blvd, Austin, TX 78704
Phone: (844) 796-6811 **Dom State:** TX **Commenced Bus:** N/A

Data Date	Rating	RACR #1	RACR #2	Total Assets ($mil)	Capital ($mil)	Net Premium ($mil)	Net Income ($mil)
9-19	C	3.57	2.98	10.4	4.9	13.4	0.2
9-18	N/A	N/A	N/A	9.8	6.3	7.4	-0.6
2018	C-	3.49	2.91	10.9	4.8	10.3	-2.1
2017	N/A	N/A	N/A	8.2	6.9	2.8	-0.1
2016	N/A	N/A	N/A	7.7	7.1	N/A	-1.5
2015	N/A	N/A	N/A	N/A	N/A	N/A	N/A
2014	N/A	N/A	N/A	N/A	N/A	N/A	N/A

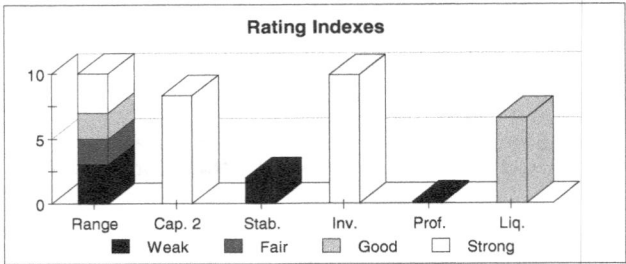

SUPERIOR HEALTHPLAN INC

B-   **Good**

Major Rating Factors: Good quality investment portfolio (6.6 on a scale of 0 to 10). Good liquidity (6.8) with sufficient resources (cash flows and marketable investments) to handle a spike in claims. Excellent profitability (8.5).
Other Rating Factors: Strong capitalization index (7.3) based on excellent current risk-adjusted capital (severe loss scenario). Excellent overall results on stability tests (8.3).
Principal Business: Medicaid (86%), comp med (9%), Medicare (5%)
Mem Phys: 19: 69,118 **18:** 59,918 **19 MLR** 91.9% **/ 19 Admin Exp** N/A
Enroll(000): Q2 20: 565 **19:** 524 **18:** 534 **Med Exp PMPM:** $646
Principal Investments: Long-term bonds (53%), cash and equiv (43%), affiliate common stock (2%), other (2%)
Provider Compensation ($000): Contr fee ($2,316,213), bonus arrang ($1,524,960), salary ($188,094), capitation ($39,332)
Total Member Encounters: Phys (4,036,980), non-phys (13,283,398)
Group Affiliation: None
Licensed in: TX
Address: 2100 South IH 35 Suite 202, Austin,
Phone: (314) 725-4477 **Dom State:** TX **Commenced Bus:** N/A

Data Date	Rating	RACR #1	RACR #2	Total Assets ($mil)	Capital ($mil)	Net Premium ($mil)	Net Income ($mil)
6-20	B-	1.61	1.35	1,040.8	508.5	2,422.3	58.5
6-19	B-	1.87	1.56	866.1	451.6	2,191.2	15.5
2019	B-	1.86	1.55	888.9	472.8	4,448.6	39.6
2018	C+	1.81	1.51	839.7	437.1	4,327.9	63.0
2017	B	1.35	1.12	753.9	369.5	3,957.4	63.8
2016	C+	1.64	1.37	664.3	308.4	3,522.0	52.2
2015	C+	1.68	1.40	620.4	260.9	2,882.1	13.6

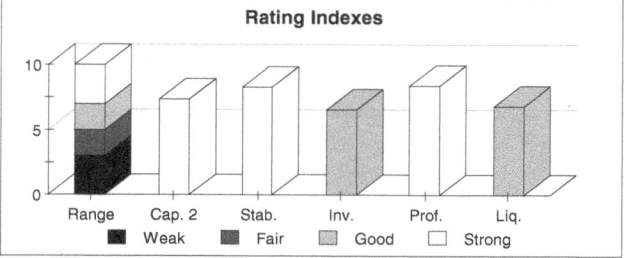

SUPERIOR VISION OF NEW JERSEY INC

C   **Fair**

Major Rating Factors: Good overall profitability index (6.9 on a scale of 0 to 10). Strong capitalization (10.0) based on excellent current risk-adjusted capital (severe loss scenario). High quality investment portfolio (9.9).
Other Rating Factors: Excellent liquidity (8.9) with ample operational cash flow and liquid investments.
Principal Business: Vision (100%)
Mem Phys: 19: 32,229 **18:** N/A **19 MLR** 78.8% **/ 19 Admin Exp** N/A
Enroll(000):   19: 19 **18:** N/A **Med Exp PMPM:** $16
Principal Investments: Cash and equiv (100%)
Provider Compensation ($000): Contr fee ($3,847)
Total Member Encounters: Phys (1,183), non-phys (2,776)
Group Affiliation: Versant Health, Inc.
Licensed in: NJ
Address: 939 Elkridge Landing Rd #200, LINTHICUM,
Phone: (410) 752-0121 **Dom State:** NJ **Commenced Bus:** N/A

Data Date	Rating	RACR #1	RACR #2	Total Assets ($mil)	Capital ($mil)	Net Premium ($mil)	Net Income ($mil)
2019	C	9.68	8.07	5.8	5.0	5.0	0.6
2018	N/A	N/A	N/A	0.1	0.1	N/A	N/A
2017	N/A	N/A	N/A	0.1	0.1	N/A	N/A
2016	N/A	N/A	N/A	0.1	0.1	N/A	N/A
2015	N/A	N/A	N/A	0.1	0.1	N/A	N/A

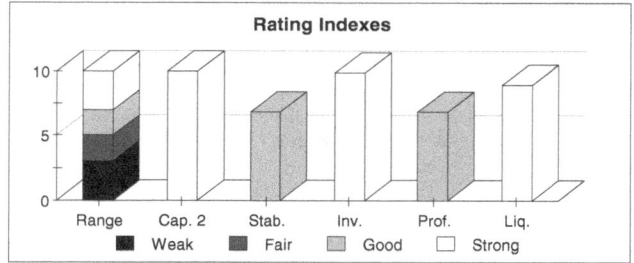

SUTTER HEALTH PLAN

C-   **Fair**

Major Rating Factors: Fair overall results on stability tests (4.0 on a scale of 0 to 10) in spite of healthy premium and capital growth during 2019. Weak profitability index (1.9). Good capitalization index (6.2) based on good current risk-adjusted capital (severe loss scenario).
Other Rating Factors: Excellent liquidity (7.5) with ample operational cash flow and liquid investments.
Principal Business: Managed care (100%)
Mem Phys: 19: N/A **18:** N/A **19 MLR** 83.0% **/ 19 Admin Exp** N/A
Enroll(000): Q2 20: 98 **19:** 84 **18:** 84 **Med Exp PMPM:** $440
Principal Investments ($000): Cash and equiv ($89,997)
Provider Compensation ($000): None
Total Member Encounters: N/A
Group Affiliation: None
Licensed in: CA
Address: 2088 OtayLakesRd #102, Chula Vista, CA 91915
Phone: (619) 407-4082 **Dom State:** CA **Commenced Bus:** April 2013

Data Date	Rating	RACR #1	RACR #2	Total Assets ($mil)	Capital ($mil)	Net Premium ($mil)	Net Income ($mil)
6-20	C-	1.50	0.93	158.2	53.3	283.2	10.4
6-19	D	0.71	0.44	122.6	24.9	248.8	7.4
2019	C-	1.16	0.72	132.5	42.4	517.4	24.4
2018	D	0.48	0.30	95.2	16.9	428.8	-16.1
2017	D	0.92	0.58	98.0	25.2	319.8	-23.9
2016	E+	0.72	0.46	76.2	13.1	188.2	-40.6
2015	E	1.11	0.74	41.4	10.2	77.1	-27.5

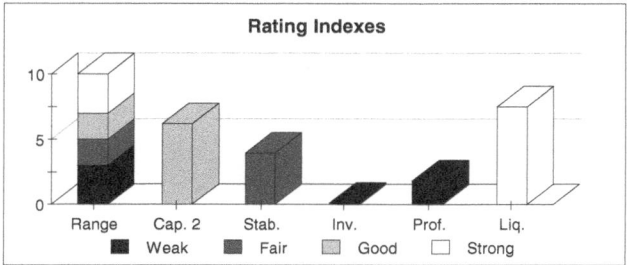

SWBC LIFE INS CO * A- Excellent

Major Rating Factors: Good quality investment portfolio (6.2 on a scale of 0 to 10) with no exposure to mortgages and minimal holdings in junk bonds. Good overall results on stability tests (6.2). Strengths that enhance stability include excellent operational trends and good risk diversification. Strong capitalization (9.7) based on excellent risk adjusted capital (severe loss scenario).

Other Rating Factors: Excellent profitability (8.6) with operating gains in each of the last five years. Excellent liquidity (9.1).

Principal Business: Credit health insurance (45%), credit life insurance (33%), and reinsurance (22%).

Principal Investments: NonCMO investment grade bonds (51%), cash (28%), and common & preferred stock (17%).

Investments in Affiliates: 4%

Group Affiliation: Southwest Business Corp

Licensed in: GA, LA, MI, OK, TN, TX, UT, VA

Commenced Business: December 1980

Address: 9311 San Pedro Ste 600, San Antonio, TX 78216

Phone: (210) 321-7361 **Domicile State:** TX **NAIC Code:** 99538

Data Date	Rating	RACR #1	RACR #2	Total Assets ($mil)	Capital ($mil)	Net Premium ($mil)	Net Income ($mil)
6-20	A-	4.07	2.83	36.1	25.4	8.7	1.4
6-19	A-	3.84	2.68	32.9	23.4	8.2	1.0
2019	A-	3.87	2.69	34.9	24.3	17.3	2.0
2018	A-	3.73	2.61	32.7	23.2	17.7	2.9
2017	B+	3.44	2.34	31.0	21.0	16.2	2.6
2016	B	2.80	1.86	26.1	16.6	15.0	1.4
2015	B	3.36	2.17	23.5	15.3	8.9	0.3

Adverse Trends in Operations

Decrease in premium volume from 2018 to 2019 (3%)
Increase in policy surrenders from 2017 to 2018 (103%)

SWISS RE LIFE & HEALTH AMER INC C+ Fair

Major Rating Factors: Fair overall results on stability tests (3.3 on a scale of 0 to 10) including fair financial strength of affiliated Swiss Reinsurance Group and negative cash flow from operations for 2019, weak results on operational trends. Good quality investment portfolio (6.7) despite mixed results such as: minimal exposure to mortgages and large holdings of BBB rated bonds but small junk bond holdings. Good overall profitability (5.6).

Other Rating Factors: Good liquidity (5.4). Strong capitalization (7.5) based on excellent risk adjusted capital (severe loss scenario).

Principal Business: Reinsurance (100%).

Principal Investments: NonCMO investment grade bonds (70%), CMOs and structured securities (12%), mortgages in good standing (9%), noninv. grade bonds (2%), and common & preferred stock (1%).

Investments in Affiliates: 8%

Group Affiliation: Swiss Reinsurance Group

Licensed in: All states, the District of Columbia and Puerto Rico

Commenced Business: September 1967

Address: 237 EAST HIGH STREET, JEFFERSON CITY, MO 65101

Phone: (877) 794-7773 **Domicile State:** MO **NAIC Code:** 82627

Data Date	Rating	RACR #1	RACR #2	Total Assets ($mil)	Capital ($mil)	Net Premium ($mil)	Net Income ($mil)
6-20	C+	2.07	1.33	13,054.3	1,568.7	166.0	94.1
6-19	C+	1.56	0.99	13,140.2	1,492.4	-233.5	2,074.9
2019	C+	2.01	1.30	12,728.9	1,531.6	596.5	1,497.7
2018	C	2.00	1.28	15,932.4	2,035.8	6,288.5	-1,164.9
2017	C	1.36	0.86	14,134.1	1,157.4	2,548.5	139.9
2016	C	1.57	0.99	14,226.8	1,380.9	2,289.7	-5.8
2015	C	1.83	1.08	12,264.0	1,318.3	2,983.5	85.8

Swiss Reinsurance Group Composite Group Rating: C+ Largest Group Members	Assets ($mil)	Rating
SWISS REINS AMERICA CORP	15842	C
SWISS RE LIFE HEALTH AMER INC	12729	C+
WESTPORT INS CORP	4782	C+
NORTH AMERICAN SPECIALTY INS CO	496	C
NORTH AMERICAN CAPACITY INS CO	223	C

TAKECARE INS CO D- Weak

Major Rating Factors: Weak profitability index (0.9 on a scale of 0 to 10). Poor capitalization (0.1) based on weak current risk-adjusted capital (moderate loss scenario). Weak liquidity (0.0) as a spike in claims may stretch capacity.

Other Rating Factors: Fair quality investment portfolio (4.7).

Principal Business: Comp med (67%), FEHB (29%), other (4%)

Mem Phys: 19: 383 18: 375 **19 MLR** 91.0% **/ 19 Admin Exp** N/A

Enroll(000): Q2 20: 19 **19:** 21 **18:** 28 **Med Exp PMPM:** $254

Principal Investments: Affiliate common stock (56%), cash and equiv (33%), real estate (8%), other (3%)

Provider Compensation ($000): Contr fee ($49,761), capitation ($34,009)

Total Member Encounters: N/A

Group Affiliation: TakeCare Health Systems LLP

Licensed in: (No states)

Address: BALTEJ PAVILION STE 308 415 C, TAMUNING, GU 96913

Phone: (671) 300-7142 **Dom State:** GU **Commenced Bus:** N/A

Data Date	Rating	RACR #1	RACR #2	Total Assets ($mil)	Capital ($mil)	Net Premium ($mil)	Net Income ($mil)
6-20	D-	0.31	0.26	30.8	8.5	37.2	-3.1
6-19	N/A	N/A	N/A	N/A	N/A	N/A	N/A
2019	C-	0.58	0.48	26.5	10.8	91.3	-3.7
2018	C	1.06	0.89	36.4	15.2	90.7	3.1
2017	D+	N/A	N/A	36.2	15.7	98.4	2.2
2016	C	1.06	0.89	32.1	14.0	101.0	-0.7
2015	C+	1.25	1.04	38.5	18.0	106.3	5.0

Rating Indexes

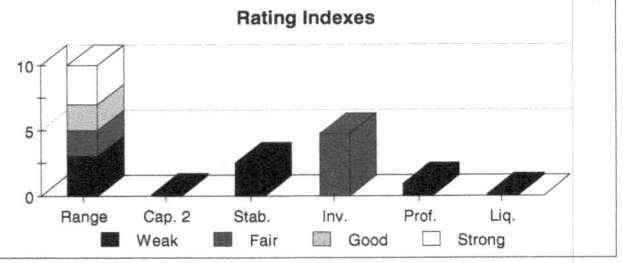

Range, Cap. 2, Stab., Inv., Prof., Liq.
■ Weak ■ Fair ▨ Good □ Strong

TEXAS CHILDRENS HEALTH PLAN INC   C   Fair

Major Rating Factors: Fair profitability index (3.6 on a scale of 0 to 10). Good quality investment portfolio (5.4). Good overall results on stability tests (6.9).
Other Rating Factors: Good liquidity (6.5) with sufficient resources (cash flows and marketable investments) to handle a spike in claims. Strong capitalization index (7.2) based on excellent current risk-adjusted capital (severe loss scenario).
Principal Business: Medicaid (92%), comp med (8%)
Mem Phys: 19: 23,693   **18:** 22,790   **19 MLR** 91.7%   **/ 19 Admin Exp** N/A
Enroll(000): Q2 20: 457   **19:** 418   **18:** 440   **Med Exp PMPM:** $313
Principal Investments: Long-term bonds (54%), cash and equiv (37%), affiliate common stock (9%)
Provider Compensation ($000): Contr fee ($815,749), FFS ($750,029), capitation ($53,280), bonus arrang ($3,507)
Total Member Encounters: Phys (1,910,438), non-phys (1,893,906)
Group Affiliation: Texas Childrens
Licensed in: TX
Address: 6330 West Loop South, Bellaire,
Phone: (832) 828-1020   **Dom State:** TX   **Commenced Bus:** N/A

Data Date	Rating	RACR #1	RACR #2	Total Assets ($mil)	Capital ($mil)	Net Premium ($mil)	Net Income ($mil)
6-20	C	1.51	1.25	424.9	248.9	938.4	89.2
6-19	N/A	N/A	N/A	N/A	N/A	N/A	N/A
2019	D+	0.93	0.78	342.0	160.5	1,757.4	-3.6
2018	D+	0.84	0.70	348.6	141.0	1,677.5	-63.2
2017	D+	0.94	0.78	297.1	138.0	1,562.7	-40.6
2016	B-	1.08	0.90	226.3	104.9	1,067.6	-17.7
2015	B	1.49	1.24	210.4	125.1	958.4	15.7

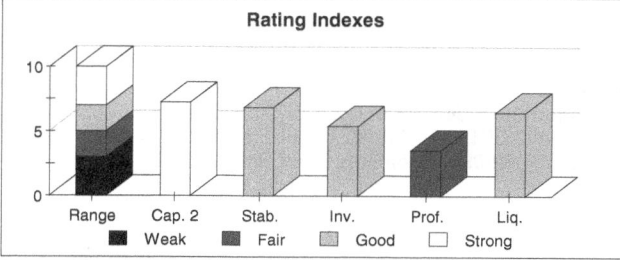

Rating Indexes

TEXAS HLTH + AETNA HLTH INS CO   C   Fair

Major Rating Factors: Weak profitability index (0.9 on a scale of 0 to 10). Strong capitalization (10.0) based on excellent current risk-adjusted capital (severe loss scenario). High quality investment portfolio (8.4).
Other Rating Factors: Excellent liquidity (8.5) with ample operational cash flow and liquid investments.
Principal Business: Comp med (100%)
Mem Phys: 18: 20,738   **17:** 20,281   **18 MLR** 7.3%   **/ 18 Admin Exp** N/A
Enroll(000): Q3 19: 13   **18:** 8   **17:** 4   **Med Exp PMPM:** $285
Principal Investments: Long-term bonds (70%), cash and equiv (16%), affiliate common stock (10%), nonaffiliate common stock (3%)
Provider Compensation ($000): Contr fee ($15,076), FFS ($3,854), bonus arrang ($302)
Total Member Encounters: Phys (118,919), non-phys (131,325)
Group Affiliation: None
Licensed in: TX
Address: 612 E LAMAR BOULEVARD SUITE, ARLINGTON, TX 76011
Phone: (800) 872-3862   **Dom State:** TX   **Commenced Bus:** N/A

Data Date	Rating	RACR #1	RACR #2	Total Assets ($mil)	Capital ($mil)	Net Premium ($mil)	Net Income ($mil)
9-19	C	4.81	4.00	159.4	90.7	183.6	-12.4
9-18	N/A	N/A	N/A	162.1	83.6	208.8	1.8
2018	C	4.30	3.58	164.2	80.7	278.7	-3.7
2017	N/A	N/A	N/A	151.0	46.5	328.1	-3.8
2016	N/A	N/A	N/A	N/A	N/A	N/A	N/A
2015	N/A	N/A	N/A	N/A	N/A	N/A	N/A
2014	N/A	N/A	N/A	N/A	N/A	N/A	N/A

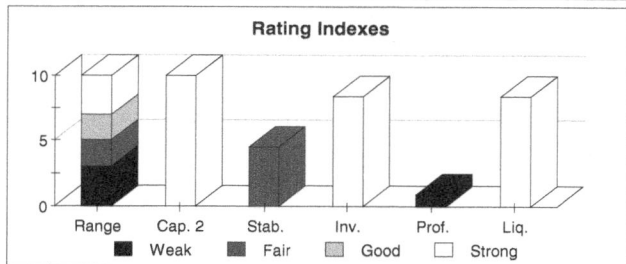

Rating Indexes

TEXAS HLTH + AETNA HLTH PLAN   C   Fair

Major Rating Factors: Weak profitability index (0.9 on a scale of 0 to 10). Strong capitalization (10.0) based on excellent current risk-adjusted capital (severe loss scenario). High quality investment portfolio (8.0).
Other Rating Factors: Excellent liquidity (7.2) with ample operational cash flow and liquid investments.
Principal Business: Comp med (100%)
Mem Phys: 18: 20,313   **17:** 18,309   **18 MLR** 60.8%   **/ 18 Admin Exp** N/A
Enroll(000): Q3 19: 3   **18:** 2   **17:** N/A   **Med Exp PMPM:** $441
Principal Investments: Cash and equiv (60%), long-term bonds (35%), nonaffiliate common stock (6%)
Provider Compensation ($000): Contr fee ($8,196), FFS ($2,591), bonus arrang ($92)
Total Member Encounters: Phys (27,848), non-phys (31,612)
Group Affiliation: None
Licensed in: TX
Address: 612 E LAMAR BOULEVARD SUITE, ARLINGTON, TX 76011
Phone: (800) 872-3862   **Dom State:** TX   **Commenced Bus:** N/A

Data Date	Rating	RACR #1	RACR #2	Total Assets ($mil)	Capital ($mil)	Net Premium ($mil)	Net Income ($mil)
9-19	C	4.16	3.47	16.9	11.3	17.3	1.9
9-18	N/A	N/A	N/A	13.1	4.2	15.8	-2.1
2018	C	3.16	2.63	18.6	8.7	20.9	-3.2
2017	N/A	N/A	N/A	7.5	3.5	14.0	-0.5
2016	N/A	N/A	N/A	N/A	N/A	N/A	N/A
2015	N/A	N/A	N/A	N/A	N/A	N/A	N/A
2014	N/A	N/A	N/A	N/A	N/A	N/A	N/A

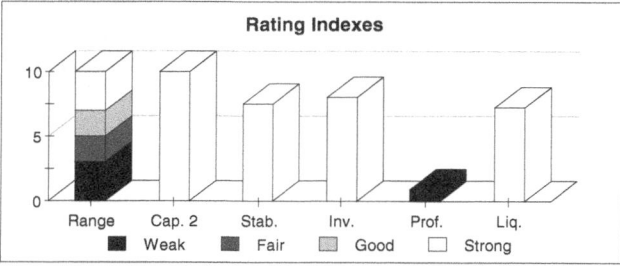

Rating Indexes

THE UNION LABOR LIFE INS CO   B   Good

Major Rating Factors: Good liquidity (6.8 on a scale of 0 to 10) with sufficient resources to handle a spike in claims. Good overall results on stability tests (5.4). Stability strengths include excellent operational trends and excellent risk diversification. Strong capitalization (7.6) based on excellent risk adjusted capital (severe loss scenario). Moreover, capital levels have been consistently high over the last five years.

Other Rating Factors: High quality investment portfolio (7.1). Excellent profitability (8.2) with operating gains in each of the last five years.

Principal Business: Group health insurance (63%), group life insurance (25%), reinsurance (9%), and group retirement contracts (2%).

Principal Investments: NonCMO investment grade bonds (56%), CMOs and structured securities (21%), common & preferred stock (9%), and mortgages in good standing (7%).

Investments in Affiliates: 5%

Group Affiliation: ULLICO Inc

Licensed in: All states except PR

Commenced Business: May 1927

Address: 8403 COLESVILLE ROAD, SILVER SPRING, MD 20910

Phone: (202) 682-0900 **Domicile State:** MD **NAIC Code:** 69744

Data Date	Rating	RACR #1	RACR #2	Total Assets ($mil)	Capital ($mil)	Net Premium ($mil)	Net Income ($mil)
6-20	B	2.14	1.41	4,386.4	134.0	91.3	4.8
6-19	B	2.13	1.38	4,252.6	116.7	80.5	6.0
2019	B	2.18	1.44	4,284.8	129.9	165.5	19.7
2018	B	2.11	1.37	3,892.6	108.7	150.2	13.3
2017	B	2.03	1.31	3,614.2	94.2	138.1	9.3
2016	B-	2.04	1.32	3,354.7	89.2	124.2	10.2
2015	B-	1.52	1.07	3,238.8	79.6	138.3	3.5

Adverse Trends in Operations

Decrease in premium volume from 2015 to 2016 (10%)

THP INS CO   C   Fair

Major Rating Factors: Fair profitability index (4.9 on a scale of 0 to 10). Low quality investment portfolio (1.5). Good liquidity (6.9) with sufficient resources (cash flows and marketable investments) to handle a spike in claims.

Other Rating Factors: Strong capitalization (7.6) based on excellent current risk-adjusted capital (severe loss scenario).

Principal Business: Comp med (47%), Medicare (20%), med supp (17%), other (16%)

Mem Phys: 19: 27,102 **18:** 22,982 **19 MLR** 95.0% **/ 19 Admin Exp** N/A

Enroll(000): Q2 20: 10 **19:** 14 **18:** 21 **Med Exp PMPM:** $497

Principal Investments: Nonaffiliate common stock (78%), cash and equiv (21%)

Provider Compensation ($000): Contr fee ($108,477), capitation ($90)

Total Member Encounters: Phys (307,824), non-phys (79,128)

Group Affiliation: The Health Plan of West Virginia Inc

Licensed in: OH, WV

Address: 1110 Main Street, Wheeling, WV 26003

Phone: (740) 695-3585 **Dom State:** WV **Commenced Bus:** N/A

Data Date	Rating	RACR #1	RACR #2	Total Assets ($mil)	Capital ($mil)	Net Premium ($mil)	Net Income ($mil)
6-20	C	1.86	1.55	69.1	38.6	36.4	7.8
6-19	D+	1.69	1.41	61.8	25.6	59.6	4.5
2019	C-	1.85	1.54	62.0	31.9	108.6	9.6
2018	D+	1.29	1.07	61.0	19.4	112.1	-7.4
2017	D	2.31	1.93	53.1	28.8	92.0	2.5
2016	D	3.00	2.50	43.0	24.1	71.7	2.3
2015	D	3.58	2.99	38.8	24.7	52.8	-1.8

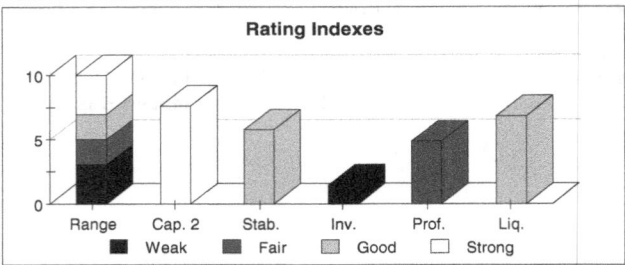

Rating Indexes

TIMBER PRODUCTS MANUFACTURERS TRUST   B   Good

Major Rating Factors: Excellent overall profitability index (6.9 on a scale of 0 to 10). Strong capitalization (9.6) based on excellent current risk-adjusted capital (severe loss scenario). High quality investment portfolio (9.9).

Other Rating Factors: Excellent liquidity (7.1) with ample operational cash flow and liquid investments.

Principal Business: Comp med (96%), dental (4%)

Mem Phys: 19: N/A **18:** N/A **19 MLR** 86.8% **/ 19 Admin Exp** N/A

Enroll(000): Q2 20: 17 **19:** 14 **18:** 12 **Med Exp PMPM:** $219

Principal Investments: Long-term bonds (58%), cash and equiv (42%)

Provider Compensation ($000): Contr fee ($32,923)

Total Member Encounters: Phys (45,136), non-phys (7,610)

Group Affiliation: None

Licensed in: ID, MT, OR, WA, WY

Address: 951 EAST THIRD AVENUE, SPOKANE, WA 99202

Phone: (509) 535-4646 **Dom State:** WA **Commenced Bus:** N/A

Data Date	Rating	RACR #1	RACR #2	Total Assets ($mil)	Capital ($mil)	Net Premium ($mil)	Net Income ($mil)
6-20	B	3.42	2.85	24.1	18.6	23.5	2.6
6-19	N/A	N/A	N/A	N/A	N/A	N/A	N/A
2019	B	2.94	2.45	20.2	15.9	38.9	3.5
2018	C+	2.79	2.33	17.4	14.0	40.7	7.7
2017	D	0.95	0.79	10.7	6.3	47.6	3.4
2016	E+	0.32	0.26	10.0	2.9	57.7	-4.3
2015	C	0.71	0.59	14.2	5.4	54.6	-2.5

Rating Indexes

TOTAL HEALTH CARE INC   C   Fair

Major Rating Factors: Fair overall results on stability tests (3.4 on a scale of 0 to 10) based on a steep decline in capital during 2019. Weak profitability index (2.3). Weak liquidity (1.3) as a spike in claims may stretch capacity.
Other Rating Factors: Good quality investment portfolio (6.6). Strong capitalization index (7.1) based on excellent current risk-adjusted capital (severe loss scenario).
Principal Business: Medicaid (84%)
Mem Phys: 19: 6,101 **18:** 5,751 **19 MLR** 80.4% **/ 19 Admin Exp** N/A
Enroll(000): Q2 20: 54 **19:** 49 **18:** 51 **Med Exp PMPM:** $283
Principal Investments: Cash and equiv (50%), affiliate common stock (49%), long-term bonds (1%)
Provider Compensation ($000): Contr fee ($117,391), capitation ($40,204), FFS ($438), bonus arrang ($281)
Total Member Encounters: Phys (338,564), non-phys (205,784)
Group Affiliation: Spectrum Health System Inc
Licensed in: MI
Address: 3011 W GRAND BLVD SUITE 1600, DETROIT,
Phone: (313) 871-2000 **Dom State:** MI **Commenced Bus:** N/A

Data Date	Rating	RACR #1	RACR #2	Total Assets ($mil)	Capital ($mil)	Net Premium ($mil)	Net Income ($mil)
6-20	C	1.43	1.19	100.9	46.2	94.5	7.1
6-19	C+	1.88	1.57	98.5	56.1	93.2	10.4
2019	C+	1.79	1.49	87.7	38.3	215.1	-5.5
2018	C+	1.70	1.41	85.0	50.4	193.1	6.7
2017	C	1.43	1.19	95.2	47.2	261.2	-15.4
2016	B-	1.48	1.23	83.2	46.5	284.1	-1.8
2015	B-	1.14	0.95	84.2	41.7	322.4	5.9

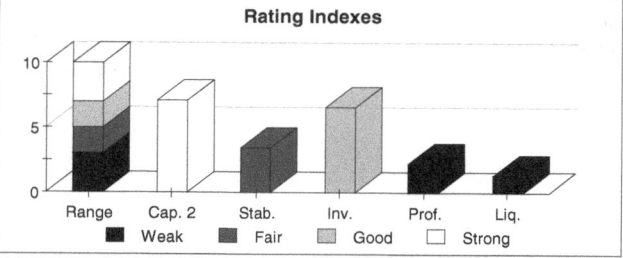

Rating Indexes

TOTAL HEALTH CARE USA INC   B   Good

Major Rating Factors: Excellent profitability (7.4 on a scale of 0 to 10). Strong capitalization (8.3) based on excellent current risk-adjusted capital (severe loss scenario). High quality investment portfolio (9.9).
Other Rating Factors: Excellent liquidity (7.3) with ample operational cash flow and liquid investments.
Principal Business: Comp med (100%)
Mem Phys: 19: 6,533 **18:** 6,201 **19 MLR** 81.1% **/ 19 Admin Exp** N/A
Enroll(000): Q2 20: 37 **19:** 39 **18:** 42 **Med Exp PMPM:** $291
Principal Investments: Cash and equiv (99%), long-term bonds (1%)
Provider Compensation ($000): Contr fee ($125,245), capitation ($7,497), bonus arrang ($405)
Total Member Encounters: Phys (262,090), non-phys (94,858)
Group Affiliation: Spectrum Health System Inc
Licensed in: MI
Address: 3011 W GRAND BLVD SUITE 160, DETROIT, MI 48202
Phone: (313) 871-2000 **Dom State:** MI **Commenced Bus:** N/A

Data Date	Rating	RACR #1	RACR #2	Total Assets ($mil)	Capital ($mil)	Net Premium ($mil)	Net Income ($mil)
6-20	B	2.42	2.02	91.2	37.2	70.3	1.9
6-19	B+	2.59	2.15	93.5	37.5	95.0	5.1
2019	B	3.48	2.90	81.6	35.8	181.2	3.2
2018	B+	2.92	2.43	76.8	42.6	182.2	10.6
2017	B+	3.61	3.01	67.5	45.8	148.0	15.5
2016	B+	2.54	2.12	55.4	29.9	139.3	6.7
2015	B	1.80	1.50	53.5	23.4	154.9	5.5

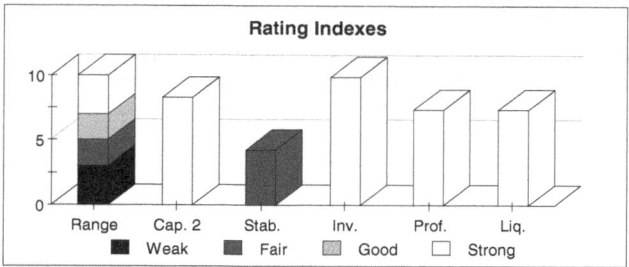

Rating Indexes

TRANS OCEANIC LIFE INS CO *   B+   Good

Major Rating Factors: Good overall profitability (6.9 on a scale of 0 to 10). Excellent expense controls. Return on equity has been fair, averaging 7.3%. Good overall results on stability tests (6.4). Stability strengths include excellent operational trends and good risk diversification. Fair quality investment portfolio (4.5).
Other Rating Factors: Strong capitalization (7.5) based on excellent risk adjusted capital (severe loss scenario). Excellent liquidity (7.6).
Principal Business: Individual health insurance (93%) and individual life insurance (7%).
Principal Investments: NonCMO investment grade bonds (46%), common & preferred stock (21%), CMOs and structured securities (11%), real estate (10%), and cash (6%).
Investments in Affiliates: 4%
Group Affiliation: Trans-Oceanic Group Inc
Licensed in: FL, PR
Commenced Business: December 1959
Address: # 121 ONEILL, SAN JUAN, PR 00918-2404
Phone: (787) 620-2680 **Domicile State:** PR **NAIC Code:** 69523

Data Date	Rating	RACR #1	RACR #2	Total Assets ($mil)	Capital ($mil)	Net Premium ($mil)	Net Income ($mil)
2019	B+	1.97	1.34	77.3	32.4	30.7	2.0
2018	A-	2.54	1.61	74.2	32.8	29.5	1.9
2017	A-	2.59	1.65	72.5	33.3	30.1	1.9
2016	A-	2.54	1.61	70.6	32.8	30.7	1.2
2015	A	3.12	1.95	67.4	35.2	30.4	4.7

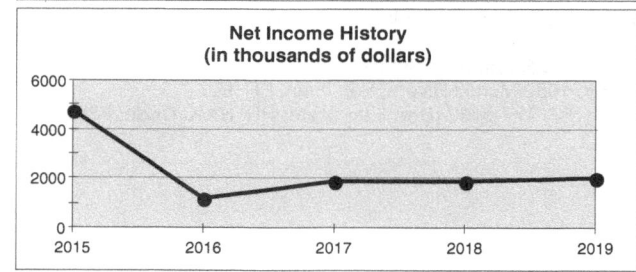

Net Income History
(in thousands of dollars)

TRH HEALTH INS CO | B | Good

Major Rating Factors: Good overall profitability index (5.6 on a scale of 0 to 10). Good liquidity (6.8) with sufficient resources (cash flows and marketable investments) to handle a spike in claims. Strong capitalization (10.0) based on excellent current risk-adjusted capital (severe loss scenario).
Other Rating Factors: High quality investment portfolio (9.4).
Principal Business: Med supp (52%), comp med (48%)
Mem Phys: 19: 663,711 **18:** 710,100 **19 MLR** 80.5% **/ 19 Admin Exp** N/A
Enroll(000): Q2 20: 96 **19:** 99 **18:** 104 **Med Exp PMPM:** $188
Principal Investments: Long-term bonds (77%), cash and equiv (16%), nonaffiliate common stock (7%)
Provider Compensation ($000): FFS ($236,335)
Total Member Encounters: Phys (4,079,819), non-phys (1,208,827)
Group Affiliation: None
Licensed in: TN
Address: 147 Bear Creek Pike, Columbia, TN 38401-2266
Phone: (931) 560-0041 **Dom State:** TN **Commenced Bus:** N/A

Data Date	Rating	RACR #1	RACR #2	Total Assets ($mil)	Capital ($mil)	Net Premium ($mil)	Net Income ($mil)
6-20	B	4.59	3.83	144.2	115.1	136.6	18.5
6-19	C+	3.59	3.00	125.1	91.1	142.7	15.3
2019	B	3.86	3.22	128.3	96.2	282.3	20.8
2018	C	2.61	2.18	104.7	66.7	290.4	19.7
2017	C	1.23	1.02	126.4	62.2	414.9	-11.9
2016	C+	2.41	2.01	127.5	71.1	296.7	-12.3
2015	B-	3.06	2.55	120.7	79.3	287.6	9.8

Rating Indexes

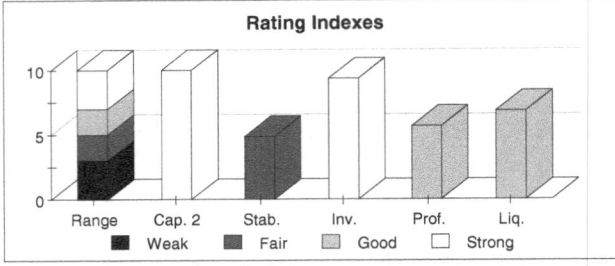

TRILLIUM COMMUNITY HEALTH PLAN INC | C+ | Fair

Major Rating Factors: Good capitalization (6.9 on a scale of 0 to 10) based on excellent current risk-adjusted capital (severe loss scenario). Good liquidity (6.3) with sufficient resources (cash flows and marketable investments) to handle a spike in claims. Weak profitability index (2.3).
Other Rating Factors: High quality investment portfolio (8.3).
Principal Business: Medicaid (93%), Medicare (7%)
Mem Phys: 19: 9,765 **18:** 4,377 **19 MLR** 88.4% **/ 19 Admin Exp** N/A
Enroll(000): Q2 20: 37 **19:** 96 **18:** 94 **Med Exp PMPM:** $438
Principal Investments: Long-term bonds (99%), cash and equiv (1%)
Provider Compensation ($000): Contr fee ($409,573), capitation ($75,310), salary ($12,088), bonus arrang ($7,443)
Total Member Encounters: Phys (543,213), non-phys (1,381,115)
Group Affiliation: None
Licensed in: OR
Address: 555 International Way, Springfield, OR 97477
Phone: (314) 725-4477 **Dom State:** OR **Commenced Bus:** N/A

Data Date	Rating	RACR #1	RACR #2	Total Assets ($mil)	Capital ($mil)	Net Premium ($mil)	Net Income ($mil)
6-20	C+	1.24	1.03	142.6	56.4	122.9	-7.6
6-19	C+	2.26	1.88	155.3	64.1	284.4	8.8
2019	B	2.23	1.86	144.1	64.3	565.7	10.4
2018	C+	2.03	1.70	153.2	57.1	536.1	-13.6
2017	C+	N/A	N/A	156.8	65.5	492.0	7.2
2016	C+	2.49	2.08	174.7	64.5	519.7	5.0
2015	C+	1.61	1.34	154.8	41.3	522.9	14.1

Rating Indexes

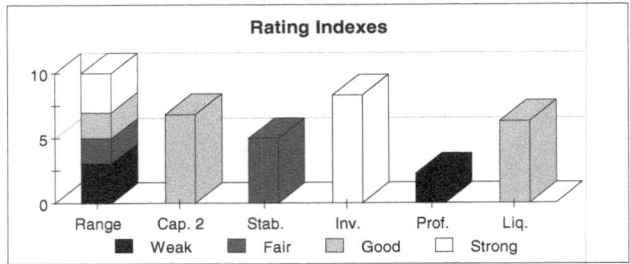

TRIPLE S VIDA INC | B- | Good

Major Rating Factors: Good overall results on stability tests (5.1 on a scale of 0 to 10). Stability strengths include excellent operational trends and good risk diversification. Good overall capitalization (5.1) based on good risk adjusted capital (moderate loss scenario). Nevertheless, capital levels have fluctuated during prior years. Good overall profitability (6.1). Excellent expense controls.
Other Rating Factors: Good liquidity (5.8). Fair quality investment portfolio (4.3).
Principal Business: Individual life insurance (54%), individual health insurance (32%), group life insurance (5%), individual annuities (4%), and other lines (5%).
Principal Investments: NonCMO investment grade bonds (70%), common & preferred stock (12%), CMOs and structured securities (11%), policy loans (2%), and cash (2%).
Investments in Affiliates: 1%
Group Affiliation: Triple-S Management Corp
Licensed in: PR
Commenced Business: September 1964
Address: 1052 Munoz Rivera, San Juan, PR 927
Phone: (787) 777-8432 **Domicile State:** PR **NAIC Code:** 73814

Data Date	Rating	RACR #1	RACR #2	Total Assets ($mil)	Capital ($mil)	Net Premium ($mil)	Net Income ($mil)
9-19	B-	1.08	0.70	696.4	55.4	145.4	0.9
9-18	B-	1.12	0.73	650.2	60.7	136.0	4.8
2018	B-	1.18	0.77	0.0	0.0	0.0	0.0
2017	B-	1.27	0.83	0.0	0.0	0.0	0.0
2016	B-	1.16	0.75	0.0	0.0	0.0	0.0
2015	B-	N/A	N/A	0.0	0.0	0.0	0.0
2014	B-	1.19	0.81	0.0	0.0	0.0	0.0

Adverse Trends in Operations

Decrease in capital during 2018 (10%)

TRIPLE-S ADVANTAGE INC   B   Good

Major Rating Factors: Good overall profitability index (5.2 on a scale of 0 to 10). Good capitalization (6.1) based on good current risk-adjusted capital (severe loss scenario). High quality investment portfolio (9.2).
Other Rating Factors: Excellent liquidity (6.9) with sufficient resources (cash flows and marketable investments) to handle a spike in claims.
Principal Business: Medicare (100%)
Mem Phys: 19: 8,903 **18:** N/A **19 MLR** 79.9% **/ 19 Admin Exp** N/A
Enroll(000): Q2 20: 135 **19:** 128 **18:** 109 **Med Exp PMPM:** $730
Principal Investments: Long-term bonds (79%), nonaffiliate common stock (8%), cash and equiv (7%), other (6%)
Provider Compensation ($000): FFS ($1,035,054), capitation ($115,691)
Total Member Encounters: Phys (2,224,437), non-phys (1,271,145)
Group Affiliation: None
Licensed in: PR
Address: 1441 F D ROOSEVELT AVE, SAN JUAN, PR 920
Phone: (787) 620-1919 **Dom State:** PR **Commenced Bus:** N/A

Data Date	Rating	RACR #1	RACR #2	Total Assets ($mil)	Capital ($mil)	Net Premium ($mil)	Net Income ($mil)
6-20	B	1.09	0.91	427.3	160.2	760.2	14.5
6-19	C+	1.10	0.91	394.7	124.9	698.6	35.3
2019	B	1.48	1.24	415.1	175.0	1,408.2	64.4
2018	C+	0.95	0.79	396.1	112.6	1,130.3	14.8
2017	C	0.64	0.54	273.5	93.1	1,035.6	3.9
2016	C	0.44	0.36	265.8	67.1	1,024.0	-40.2
2015	N/A	N/A	N/A	286.8	87.0	1,097.3	N/A

Rating Indexes

TRIPLE-S SALUD INC   B   Good

Major Rating Factors: Good liquidity (6.5 on a scale of 0 to 10) with sufficient resources (cash flows and marketable investments) to handle a spike in claims. Fair profitability index (2.9). Strong capitalization (7.2) based on excellent current risk-adjusted capital (severe loss scenario).
Other Rating Factors: High quality investment portfolio (7.7).
Principal Business: Medicaid (49%), comp med (39%), FEHB (11%), med supp (1%)
Mem Phys: 19: 14,062 **18:** N/A **19 MLR** 88.7% **/ 19 Admin Exp** N/A
Enroll(000): Q2 20: 817 **19:** 814 **18:** 784 **Med Exp PMPM:** $144
Principal Investments: Long-term bonds (42%), affiliate common stock (22%), nonaffiliate common stock (15%), cash and equiv (9%), other (11%)
Provider Compensation ($000): Contr fee ($1,380,119), capitation ($60,078)
Total Member Encounters: Phys (3,852,507), non-phys (658,693)
Group Affiliation: None
Licensed in: PR
Address: F D Roosevelt Ave 1441, San Juan, PR 920
Phone: (787) 749-4949 **Dom State:** PR **Commenced Bus:** N/A

Data Date	Rating	RACR #1	RACR #2	Total Assets ($mil)	Capital ($mil)	Net Premium ($mil)	Net Income ($mil)
6-20	B	1.55	1.29	884.5	351.0	844.1	-9.6
6-19	B+	2.08	1.74	837.5	367.9	794.5	7.4
2019	B+	2.19	1.83	891.1	437.5	1,581.5	-15.8
2018	B+	2.04	1.70	795.2	362.8	1,565.7	27.7
2017	B	2.11	1.76	761.8	354.6	1,558.0	66.7
2016	B	3.10	2.58	701.1	371.2	1,626.3	38.4
2015	N/A	N/A	N/A	734.6	404.8	1,453.6	N/A

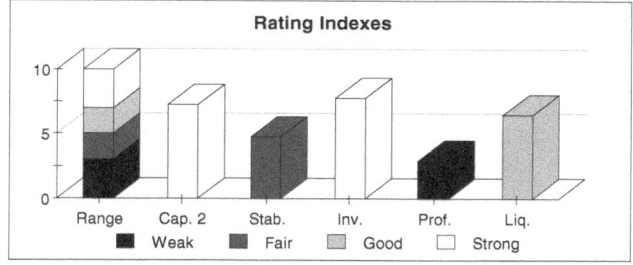

Rating Indexes

TRUE HEALTH NEW MEXICO INC   B   Good

Major Rating Factors: Excellent profitability (7.8 on a scale of 0 to 10). Strong capitalization (7.1) based on excellent current risk-adjusted capital (severe loss scenario). High quality investment portfolio (9.2).
Other Rating Factors: Excellent liquidity (7.7) with ample operational cash flow and liquid investments.
Principal Business: Comp med (100%)
Mem Phys: 18: 10,259 **17:** N/A **18 MLR** 42.2% **/ 18 Admin Exp** N/A
Enroll(000): Q3 19: 16 **18:** 17 **17:** N/A **Med Exp PMPM:** $291
Principal Investments: Cash and equiv (73%), long-term bonds (27%)
Provider Compensation ($000): Contr fee ($48,990), FFS ($10,021)
Total Member Encounters: Phys (106,062), non-phys (25,508)
Group Affiliation: Evolent Health Inc
Licensed in: NM
Address: 2440 Louisiana Blvd NE Suite 6, Albuquerque, NM 87110
Phone: (505) 633-8020 **Dom State:** NM **Commenced Bus:** N/A

Data Date	Rating	RACR #1	RACR #2	Total Assets ($mil)	Capital ($mil)	Net Premium ($mil)	Net Income ($mil)
9-19	B	1.41	1.18	63.9	24.2	135.8	1.2
9-18	N/A	N/A	N/A	48.7	21.2	113.1	0.8
2018	C-	1.30	1.08	65.8	22.3	159.7	1.5
2017	N/A	N/A	N/A	19.6	11.8	9.7	0.1
2016	N/A	N/A	N/A	N/A	N/A	N/A	N/A
2015	N/A	N/A	N/A	N/A	N/A	N/A	N/A
2014	N/A	N/A	N/A	N/A	N/A	N/A	N/A

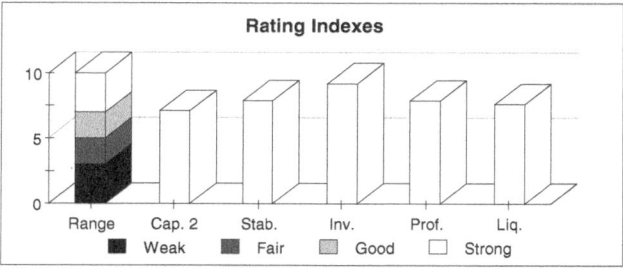

Rating Indexes

TRUSTED HEALTH PLAN INC
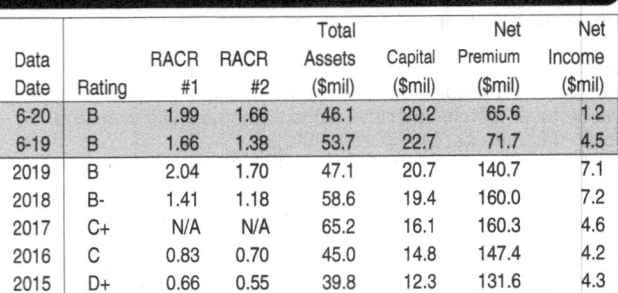
B — **Good**

Major Rating Factors: Good liquidity (6.4 on a scale of 0 to 10) with sufficient resources (cash flows and marketable investments) to handle a spike in claims. Excellent profitability (9.2). Strong capitalization (7.8) based on excellent current risk-adjusted capital (severe loss scenario).
Other Rating Factors: High quality investment portfolio (9.0).
Principal Business: Medicaid (89%), comp med (11%)
Mem Phys: 19: 18,764 **18:** 17,741 **19 MLR** 63.7% **/ 19 Admin Exp** N/A
Enroll(000): Q2 20: 35 **19:** 34 **18:** 34 **Med Exp PMPM:** $219
Principal Investments: Long-term bonds (88%), cash and equiv (12%)
Provider Compensation ($000): Contr fee ($73,437), FFS ($19,408), capitation ($8,310)
Total Member Encounters: Phys (113,771), non-phys (26,614)
Group Affiliation: CareFirst Inc
Licensed in: DC, VA, WV
Address: 1100 New Jersey Avenue SE Suit, WASHINGTON, DC 20003
Phone: (202) 821-1100 **Dom State:** DC **Commenced Bus:** N/A

Data Date	Rating	RACR #1	RACR #2	Total Assets ($mil)	Capital ($mil)	Net Premium ($mil)	Net Income ($mil)
6-20	B	1.99	1.66	46.1	20.2	65.6	1.2
6-19	B	1.66	1.38	53.7	22.7	71.7	4.5
2019	B	2.04	1.70	47.1	20.7	140.7	7.1
2018	B-	1.41	1.18	58.6	19.4	160.0	7.2
2017	C+	N/A	N/A	65.2	16.1	160.3	4.6
2016	C	0.83	0.70	45.0	14.8	147.4	4.2
2015	D+	0.66	0.55	39.8	12.3	131.6	4.3

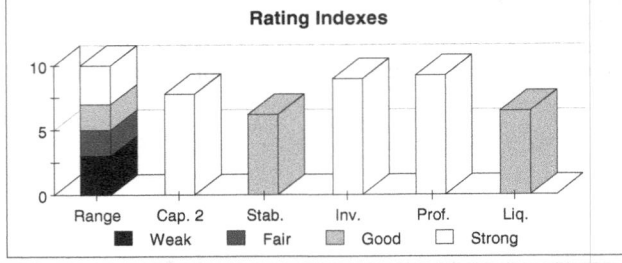

Rating Indexes

Range, Cap. 2, Stab., Inv., Prof., Liq.
■ Weak ■ Fair ▨ Good □ Strong

TRUSTMARK INS CO *
B+ — **Good**

Major Rating Factors: Good overall results on stability tests (6.5 on a scale of 0 to 10). Stability strengths include excellent operational trends and excellent risk diversification. Fair quality investment portfolio (4.8). Fair profitability (4.5). Return on equity has been low, averaging 2.8%.
Other Rating Factors: Strong capitalization (7.7) based on excellent risk adjusted capital (severe loss scenario). Excellent liquidity (7.0).
Principal Business: Group life insurance (51%), group health insurance (28%), individual health insurance (12%), individual life insurance (8%), and reinsurance (1%).
Principal Investments: NonCMO investment grade bonds (38%), CMOs and structured securities (29%), common & preferred stock (10%), mortgages in good standing (7%), and misc. investments (12%).
Investments in Affiliates: None
Group Affiliation: Trustmark Group Inc
Licensed in: All states, the District of Columbia and Puerto Rico
Commenced Business: January 1913
Address: 400 FIELD DRIVE, LAKE FOREST, IL 60045-2581
Phone: (847) 615-1500 **Domicile State:** IL **NAIC Code:** 61425

Data Date	Rating	RACR #1	RACR #2	Total Assets ($mil)	Capital ($mil)	Net Premium ($mil)	Net Income ($mil)
6-20	B+	2.61	1.49	1,752.8	331.7	183.1	20.3
6-19	B+	2.92	1.69	1,648.6	353.8	185.1	7.5
2019	B+	3.02	1.73	1,654.1	330.9	366.2	12.2
2018	B+	3.12	1.80	1,585.5	335.0	366.5	13.8
2017	B+	3.12	1.77	1,548.0	323.8	343.3	22.6
2016	B+	3.12	1.77	1,460.2	294.8	322.0	21.0
2015	B+	3.15	1.77	1,406.8	286.7	293.6	16.3

Adverse Trends in Operations

Decrease in capital during 2019 (1%)

TRUSTMARK LIFE INS CO *
B+ — **Good**

Major Rating Factors: Good overall results on stability tests (6.6 on a scale of 0 to 10). Stability strengths include good operational trends and excellent risk diversification. Strong overall capitalization (10.0) based on excellent risk adjusted capital (severe loss scenario). However, capital levels have fluctuated somewhat during past years. High quality investment portfolio (7.5).
Other Rating Factors: Excellent profitability (7.7) with operating gains in each of the last five years. Excellent liquidity (7.0).
Principal Business: Group health insurance (98%) and group life insurance (2%).
Principal Investments: NonCMO investment grade bonds (68%), CMOs and structured securities (29%), and common & preferred stock (1%).
Investments in Affiliates: None
Group Affiliation: Trustmark Group Inc
Licensed in: All states except PR
Commenced Business: February 1925
Address: 400 FIELD DRIVE, LAKE FOREST, IL 60045-2581
Phone: (847) 615-1500 **Domicile State:** IL **NAIC Code:** 62863

Data Date	Rating	RACR #1	RACR #2	Total Assets ($mil)	Capital ($mil)	Net Premium ($mil)	Net Income ($mil)
6-20	B+	8.10	5.57	296.8	180.9	67.6	9.6
6-19	B+	9.08	6.35	332.6	190.5	63.2	13.1
2019	B+	8.46	5.87	276.7	172.8	119.4	24.1
2018	B+	8.38	5.94	319.9	175.5	124.6	25.7
2017	B+	7.49	4.70	303.0	164.4	112.6	17.4
2016	B+	6.63	4.33	308.6	162.7	137.4	16.7
2015	B+	5.62	3.77	321.3	159.8	163.7	8.4

Adverse Trends in Operations

Decrease in capital during 2019 (2%)
Decrease in asset base during 2019 (14%)
Decrease in premium volume from 2016 to 2017 (18%)
Decrease in asset base during 2017 (2%)
Decrease in premium volume from 2015 to 2016 (16%)

TSG GUARD INC   D+   Weak

Major Rating Factors: Weak profitability index (0.9 on a scale of 0 to 10). Good capitalization (6.8) based on excellent current risk-adjusted capital (severe loss scenario). High quality investment portfolio (9.9).
Other Rating Factors: Excellent liquidity (7.0) with ample operational cash flow and liquid investments.
Principal Business: Medicare (100%)
Mem Phys: 19: 13,160 **18:** 7,500 **19 MLR** 73.9% **/ 19 Admin Exp** N/A
Enroll(000): Q2 20: 0 **19:** 0 **18:** N/A **Med Exp PMPM:** $1,618
Principal Investments: Cash and equiv (71%), long-term bonds (26%), nonaffiliate common stock (3%)
Provider Compensation ($000): Contr fee ($3,614)
Total Member Encounters: Phys (4,726), non-phys (8,233)
Group Affiliation: None
Licensed in: OH
Address: 7171 Keck Park Circle NW, North Canton, OH 44720
Phone: (330) 498-8200 **Dom State:** OH **Commenced Bus:** N/A

Data Date	Rating	RACR #1	RACR #2	Total Assets ($mil)	Capital ($mil)	Net Premium ($mil)	Net Income ($mil)
6-20	D+	1.22	1.01	3.3	1.9	5.5	-0.2
6-19	N/A	N/A	N/A	N/A	N/A	N/A	N/A
2019	D+	1.22	1.02	3.4	1.9	6.7	-0.3
2018	N/A	N/A	N/A	1.7	1.7	N/A	-1.0
2017	N/A	N/A	N/A	N/A	N/A	N/A	N/A
2016	N/A	N/A	N/A	N/A	N/A	N/A	N/A
2015	N/A	N/A	N/A	N/A	N/A	N/A	N/A

TUFTS ASSOCIATED HEALTH MAINT ORG   C   Fair

Major Rating Factors: Fair quality investment portfolio (2.9 on a scale of 0 to 10). Good overall profitability index (6.4). Good overall results on stability tests (5.5).
Other Rating Factors: Good liquidity (6.7) with sufficient resources (cash flows and marketable investments) to handle a spike in claims. Strong capitalization index (9.1) based on excellent current risk-adjusted capital (severe loss scenario).
Principal Business: Medicare (51%), comp med (42%), Medicaid (6%)
Mem Phys: 19: 67,631 **18:** 62,944 **19 MLR** 85.7% **/ 19 Admin Exp** N/A
Enroll(000): Q2 20: 283 **19:** 285 **18:** 289 **Med Exp PMPM:** $674
Principal Investments: Nonaffiliate common stock (38%), long-term bonds (27%), affiliate common stock (17%), real estate (10%), other (8%)
Provider Compensation ($000): Contr fee ($1,030,668), capitation ($824,994), FFS ($239,853), bonus arrang ($234,812)
Total Member Encounters: Phys (1,796,876), non-phys (629,219)
Group Affiliation: Health Plan Holdings Inc
Licensed in: MA, RI
Address: 705 Mount Auburn Street, Watertown,
Phone: (617) 972-9400 **Dom State:** MA **Commenced Bus:** N/A

Data Date	Rating	RACR #1	RACR #2	Total Assets ($mil)	Capital ($mil)	Net Premium ($mil)	Net Income ($mil)
6-20	C	3.03	2.53	1,269.3	666.6	1,372.0	11.4
6-19	C	4.05	3.37	1,174.1	695.4	1,373.4	31.2
2019	C	3.93	3.28	1,170.0	748.3	2,698.4	81.2
2018	C	3.75	3.12	1,085.1	642.5	2,582.0	89.1
2017	C+	3.50	2.92	1,086.8	644.3	2,555.3	85.0
2016	B	2.95	2.45	1,245.3	786.5	2,553.4	-3.2
2015	B	3.12	2.60	1,126.6	745.4	2,519.1	54.6

TUFTS HEALTH FREEDOM INS CO   C-   Fair

Major Rating Factors: Weak profitability index (2.0 on a scale of 0 to 10). Strong capitalization (7.0) based on excellent current risk-adjusted capital (severe loss scenario). High quality investment portfolio (7.1).
Other Rating Factors: Excellent liquidity (7.0) with sufficient resources (cash flows and marketable investments) to handle a spike in claims.
Principal Business: Comp med (100%)
Mem Phys: 19: 67,631 **18:** 62,944 **19 MLR** 88.7% **/ 19 Admin Exp** N/A
Enroll(000): Q2 20: 18 **19:** 20 **18:** 19 **Med Exp PMPM:** $418
Principal Investments: Cash and equiv (50%), long-term bonds (50%)
Provider Compensation ($000): Contr fee ($87,231), FFS ($14,640)
Total Member Encounters: Phys (65,978), non-phys (35,137)
Group Affiliation: UnitedHealth Group Incorporated
Licensed in: NH
Address: 705 Mount Auburn Street, Watertown, MA 2472
Phone: (617) 972-9400 **Dom State:** NH **Commenced Bus:** N/A

Data Date	Rating	RACR #1	RACR #2	Total Assets ($mil)	Capital ($mil)	Net Premium ($mil)	Net Income ($mil)
6-20	C-	1.34	1.12	49.3	18.2	54.9	3.1
6-19	C-	2.62	2.18	48.4	17.1	57.0	-0.4
2019	C-	2.29	1.91	45.8	17.7	114.9	-2.9
2018	C-	2.81	2.35	44.6	18.4	95.5	-1.3
2017	C	N/A	N/A	27.4	10.5	42.9	-2.7
2016	C	8.60	7.17	20.3	13.3	5.3	-2.2
2015	N/A	N/A	N/A	15.7	12.5	N/A	-6.5

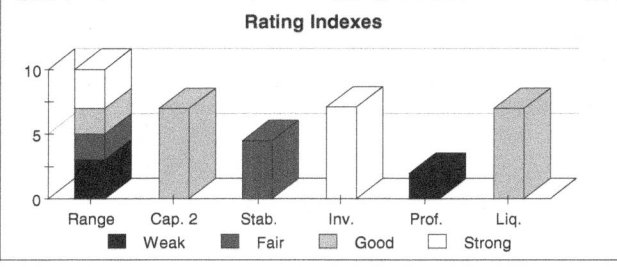

TUFTS HEALTH PUBLIC PLANS INC

C   **Fair**

Major Rating Factors: Fair profitability index (3.4 on a scale of 0 to 10). Low quality investment portfolio (1.6). Good liquidity (6.3) with sufficient resources (cash flows and marketable investments) to handle a spike in claims.
Other Rating Factors: Strong capitalization (7.5) based on excellent current risk-adjusted capital (severe loss scenario).
Principal Business: Medicaid (69%), comp med (31%)
Mem Phys: 19: 40,077   **18:** 33,941   **19 MLR** 91.2%   **/ 19 Admin Exp** N/A
Enroll(000): Q2 20: 486   **19:** 455   **18:** 439   **Med Exp PMPM:** $365
Principal Investments: Nonaffiliate common stock (73%), long-term bonds (25%), cash and equiv (2%)
Provider Compensation ($000): Bonus arrang ($1,059,206), contr fee ($831,414), FFS ($27,471)
Total Member Encounters: Phys (6,119,268), non-phys (1,572,494)
Group Affiliation: Health Plan Holdings Inc
Licensed in: MA, RI
Address: 705 Mount Auburn Street, Watertown, MA 02472-1508
Phone: (617) 972-9400   **Dom State:** MA   **Commenced Bus:** N/A

Data Date	Rating	RACR #1	RACR #2	Total Assets ($mil)	Capital ($mil)	Net Premium ($mil)	Net Income ($mil)
6-20	C	1.74	1.45	871.4	323.7	1,193.5	-26.6
6-19	C	2.69	2.24	842.5	361.0	1,063.7	45.8
2019	C	2.34	1.95	767.7	330.5	2,191.0	7.6
2018	C	2.11	1.76	654.0	278.7	2,151.8	54.0
2017	C	1.59	1.33	581.8	247.3	1,792.5	-6.1
2016	C+	1.98	1.65	529.7	193.5	1,528.3	-9.6
2015	C+	2.39	1.99	490.6	202.2	1,326.7	34.0

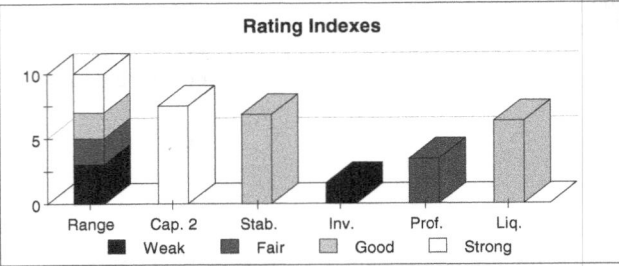

Rating Indexes

TUFTS INS CO

B-   **Good**

Major Rating Factors: Fair profitability index (3.9 on a scale of 0 to 10). Strong capitalization (8.4) based on excellent current risk-adjusted capital (severe loss scenario). High quality investment portfolio (9.9).
Other Rating Factors: Excellent liquidity (7.0) with sufficient resources (cash flows and marketable investments) to handle a spike in claims.
Principal Business: Comp med (78%), med supp (12%), other (11%)
Mem Phys: 19: 67,631   **18:** 62,944   **19 MLR** 82.2%   **/ 19 Admin Exp** N/A
Enroll(000): Q2 20: 64   **19:** 65   **18:** 60   **Med Exp PMPM:** $332
Principal Investments: Long-term bonds (72%), cash and equiv (20%), nonaffiliate common stock (9%)
Provider Compensation ($000): Contr fee ($196,906), FFS ($52,687), other ($9,902)
Total Member Encounters: Phys (334,984), non-phys (147,336)
Group Affiliation: Health Plan Holdings Inc
Licensed in: AZ, CA, CT, DC, FL, GA, IL, IN, ME, MD, MA, MI, NH, NY, NC, OH, PA, RI, TX, VT, VA
Address: 705 Mount Auburn Street, Watertown, MA 02472-1508
Phone: (617) 972-9400   **Dom State:** MA   **Commenced Bus:** N/A

Data Date	Rating	RACR #1	RACR #2	Total Assets ($mil)	Capital ($mil)	Net Premium ($mil)	Net Income ($mil)
6-20	B-	2.48	2.07	137.2	71.8	151.9	-0.2
6-19	C	3.91	3.26	117.7	71.5	154.4	2.4
2019	C+	3.94	3.29	132.0	74.1	312.5	16.0
2018	C	3.88	3.23	113.5	70.8	294.4	9.4
2017	C-	1.79	1.49	98.9	52.6	278.8	-9.7
2016	C-	3.01	2.51	101.6	50.7	258.4	-21.9
2015	D+	3.32	2.77	97.8	53.4	263.1	-5.9

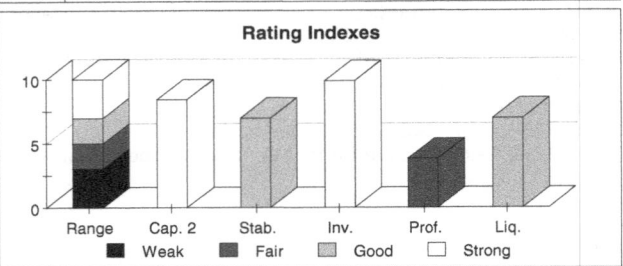

Rating Indexes

U S HEALTH & LIFE INS CO

B   **Good**

Major Rating Factors: Good overall profitability index (5.7 on a scale of 0 to 10). Strong capitalization (7.9) based on excellent current risk-adjusted capital (severe loss scenario). High quality investment portfolio (9.9).
Other Rating Factors: Excellent liquidity (7.8) with ample operational cash flow and liquid investments.
Principal Business: Comp med (45%), other (54%)
Mem Phys: 19: N/A   **18:** N/A   **19 MLR** 76.8%   **/ 19 Admin Exp** N/A
Enroll(000): Q2 20: 5   **19:** 6   **18:** 9   **Med Exp PMPM:** $232
Principal Investments: Cash and equiv (69%), long-term bonds (26%), real estate (5%)
Provider Compensation ($000): Contr fee ($19,464)
Total Member Encounters: Phys (24,554), non-phys (12,726)
Group Affiliation: None
Licensed in: AK, AZ, DC, DE, ID, IL, IN, KS, LA, MI, NE, NM, ND, OH, OR, SC, SD, TN, TX, UT, VA, WI
Address: 8220 Irving Rd, Sterling Heights, MI 48312
Phone: (586) 693-4300   **Dom State:** MI   **Commenced Bus:** N/A

Data Date	Rating	RACR #1	RACR #2	Total Assets ($mil)	Capital ($mil)	Net Premium ($mil)	Net Income ($mil)
6-20	B	2.04	1.70	30.7	16.8	8.2	1.4
6-19	N/A	N/A	N/A	N/A	N/A	N/A	N/A
2019	B	1.89	1.57	28.8	15.4	24.5	1.7
2018	B	4.46	3.71	28.4	13.7	32.7	-0.5
2017	B	2.99	2.49	26.4	14.2	31.8	0.3
2016	B	2.94	2.45	31.2	14.0	33.7	2.6
2015	B	2.60	2.16	29.5	11.3	38.4	3.0

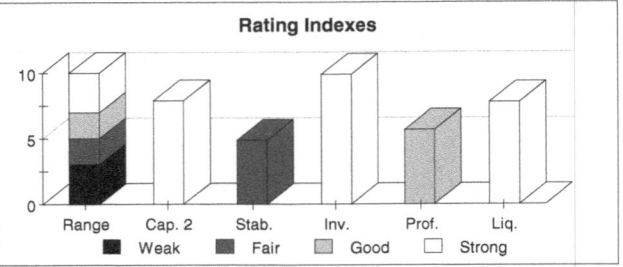

Rating Indexes

UCARE HEALTH INC   C+   Fair

Major Rating Factors: Weak profitability index (1.0 on a scale of 0 to 10). Low quality investment portfolio (0.0). Strong capitalization (10.0) based on excellent current risk-adjusted capital (severe loss scenario).
Other Rating Factors: Excellent liquidity (10.0) with ample operational cash flow and liquid investments.
Principal Business: Comp med (96%), Medicare (4%)
Mem Phys: 18: N/A   **17:** N/A   **18 MLR** 94.9%   **/ 18 Admin Exp** N/A
Enroll(000): Q3 19: 2   **18:** N/A   **17:** N/A   **Med Exp PMPM:** N/A
Principal Investments: Cash and equiv (100%)
Provider Compensation ($000): FFS ($6,367)
Total Member Encounters: Phys (9,562), non-phys (16,040)
Group Affiliation: None
Licensed in: MN, WI
Address: 500 Stinson Boulevard NE, Minneapolis, MN 55413
Phone: (612) 676-6500   **Dom State:** WI   **Commenced Bus:** N/A

Data Date	Rating	RACR #1	RACR #2	Total Assets ($mil)	Capital ($mil)	Net Premium ($mil)	Net Income ($mil)
9-19	C+	15.27	12.72	37.6	34.7	19.0	-0.5
9-18	C+	15.25	12.71	34.7	34.7	4.5	0.1
2018	C+	15.45	12.87	35.3	35.3	6.7	0.7
2017	E	4.58	3.82	19.7	19.6	8.9	5.0
2016	E	6.24	5.20	15.7	14.5	1.6	4.7
2015	E	0.77	0.64	22.9	9.7	55.8	-9.1
2014	N/A	N/A	N/A	23.5	3.6	73.9	N/A

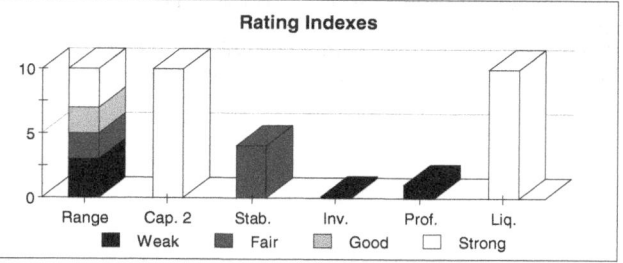

UCARE MINNESOTA   B   Good

Major Rating Factors: Good overall results on stability tests (5.2 on a scale of 0 to 10). Good liquidity (6.1) with sufficient resources (cash flows and marketable investments) to handle a spike in claims. Fair profitability index (4.0).
Other Rating Factors: Strong capitalization index (8.8) based on excellent current risk-adjusted capital (severe loss scenario). High quality investment portfolio (7.2).
Principal Business: Medicaid (66%), Medicare (30%), comp med (4%)
Mem Phys: 19: 40,024   **18:** 38,194   **19 MLR** 94.0%   **/ 19 Admin Exp** N/A
Enroll(000): Q2 20: 485   **19:** 429   **18:** 402   **Med Exp PMPM:** $679
Principal Investments: Long-term bonds (64%), nonaffiliate common stock (17%), cash and equiv (12%), real estate (3%), affiliate common stock (1%), other (3%)
Provider Compensation ($000): Contr fee ($3,285,406), FFS ($171,802), capitation ($6,986)
Total Member Encounters: Phys (2,078,201), non-phys (3,216,844)
Group Affiliation: None
Licensed in: MN
Address: 500 Stinson Boulevard NE, Minneapolis,
Phone: (612) 676-6500   **Dom State:** MN   **Commenced Bus:** N/A

Data Date	Rating	RACR #1	RACR #2	Total Assets ($mil)	Capital ($mil)	Net Premium ($mil)	Net Income ($mil)
6-20	B	2.82	2.35	1,488.0	759.8	1,964.1	109.3
6-19	B	2.97	2.48	1,431.2	703.6	1,835.8	20.6
2019	B	2.39	1.99	1,221.4	659.4	3,709.6	-31.0
2018	B	2.76	2.30	1,340.5	662.8	3,419.1	39.8
2017	B	3.22	2.69	1,251.2	619.4	2,726.2	86.7
2016	B+	4.14	3.45	938.5	516.2	1,686.7	-25.0
2015	A	2.16	1.80	1,233.9	546.4	3,513.9	27.7

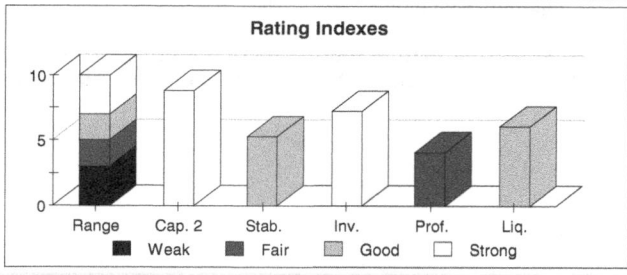

UHC OF CALIFORNIA INC   B   Good

Major Rating Factors: Good capitalization index (6.2 on a scale of 0 to 10) based on good current risk-adjusted capital (severe loss scenario). Good overall results on stability tests (5.7). Rating is significantly influenced by the fair financial results of UnitedHealth Group Inc. Excellent profitability (7.0).
Other Rating Factors: Excellent liquidity (7.0) with sufficient resources (cash flows and marketable investments) to handle a spike in claims.
Principal Business: Medicare (73%)
Mem Phys: 19: N/A   **18:** N/A   **19 MLR** 86.3%   **/ 19 Admin Exp** N/A
Enroll(000): Q2 20: 1   **19:** 829   **18:** 829   **Med Exp PMPM:** $574
Principal Investments ($000): Cash and equiv ($344,508)
Provider Compensation ($000): None
Total Member Encounters: N/A
Group Affiliation: UnitedHealth Group Inc
Licensed in: CA
Address: 1221 Broadway 3rd Floor, Oakland, CA 94612
Phone: (510) 470-0590   **Dom State:** CA   **Commenced Bus:** March 1975

Data Date	Rating	RACR #1	RACR #2	Total Assets ($mil)	Capital ($mil)	Net Premium ($mil)	Net Income ($mil)
6-20	B	1.49	0.93	1,169.8	433.7	3,503.5	93.5
6-19	B-	1.31	0.82	881.0	389.7	3,451.7	137.3
2019	B	1.68	1.05	960.9	482.4	6,750.8	278.1
2018	B-	1.33	0.83	885.7	393.7	6,693.4	211.3
2017	C	0.73	0.45	865.6	238.3	6,605.9	91.2
2016	C+	0.98	0.61	837.4	293.1	6,668.2	114.0
2015	C+	1.18	0.73	778.4	314.4	6,267.3	143.7

ULTIMATE HEALTH PLANS INC

E-   **Very Weak**

Major Rating Factors: Weak profitability index (0.9 on a scale of 0 to 10). Strong capitalization (7.0) based on excellent current risk-adjusted capital (severe loss scenario). High quality investment portfolio (9.9).
Other Rating Factors: Excellent liquidity (6.9) with sufficient resources (cash flows and marketable investments) to handle a spike in claims.
Principal Business: Medicare (100%)
Mem Phys: 19: 1,242 **18:** 935 **19 MLR** 89.1% **/ 19 Admin Exp** N/A
Enroll(000): Q2 20: 7 **19:** 8 **18:** 7 **Med Exp PMPM:** $687
Principal Investments: Cash and equiv (98%), other (2%)
Provider Compensation ($000): FFS ($59,158), capitation ($4,482), contr fee ($2,131)
Total Member Encounters: Phys (255,092), non-phys (11,689)
Group Affiliation: Ultimate Healthcare Holdings LLC
Licensed in: FL
Address: 1244 Mariner Boulevard, Spring Hill, FL 33609
Phone: (352) 835-7151 **Dom State:** FL **Commenced Bus:** N/A

Data Date	Rating	RACR #1	RACR #2	Total Assets ($mil)	Capital ($mil)	Net Premium ($mil)	Net Income ($mil)
6-20	E-	1.33	1.11	30.3	14.0	46.2	7.6
6-19	N/A	N/A	N/A	N/A	N/A	N/A	N/A
2019	E-	0.62	0.52	21.4	6.8	71.8	-6.2
2018	E	0.35	0.29	17.6	3.9	62.2	-8.0
2017	E	N/A	N/A	15.0	6.2	56.5	-1.6
2016	E	0.83	0.69	12.8	6.5	52.0	0.4
2015	E	0.77	0.64	9.9	5.1	39.2	-0.5

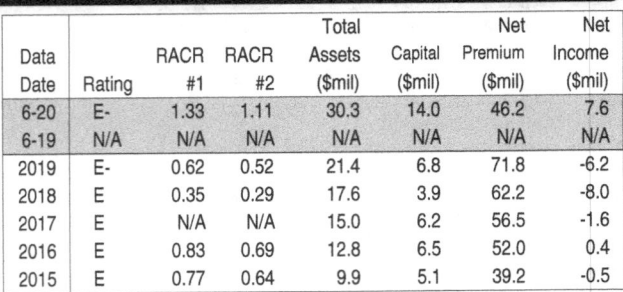

Rating Indexes

UNICARE HEALTH PLAN OF WEST VIRGINIA *

A   **Excellent**

Major Rating Factors: Excellent profitability (8.9 on a scale of 0 to 10). Strong capitalization (8.8) based on excellent current risk-adjusted capital (severe loss scenario). High quality investment portfolio (9.9).
Other Rating Factors: Excellent liquidity (6.9) with sufficient resources (cash flows and marketable investments) to handle a spike in claims.
Principal Business: Medicaid (100%)
Mem Phys: 19: 1,530 **18:** 1,486 **19 MLR** 86.0% **/ 19 Admin Exp** N/A
Enroll(000): Q2 20: 162 **19:** 154 **18:** 137 **Med Exp PMPM:** $241
Principal Investments: Long-term bonds (78%), cash and equiv (22%)
Provider Compensation ($000): Contr fee ($248,560), bonus arrang ($147,169), FFS ($17,865), capitation ($4,005)
Total Member Encounters: Phys (1,039,577), non-phys (1,003,886)
Group Affiliation: Anthem Inc
Licensed in: WV
Address: 200 ASSOCIATION DRIVE SUITE 2, CHARLESTON, WV 25311
Phone: (877) 864-2273 **Dom State:** WV **Commenced Bus:** N/A

Data Date	Rating	RACR #1	RACR #2	Total Assets ($mil)	Capital ($mil)	Net Premium ($mil)	Net Income ($mil)
6-20	A	2.83	2.36	186.1	116.7	291.4	19.2
6-19	B+	3.88	3.23	162.0	97.7	225.2	11.9
2019	A-	3.35	2.80	154.7	96.7	490.0	19.3
2018	B+	3.41	2.84	150.9	85.3	449.0	21.4
2017	A-	1.50	1.25	116.5	71.1	503.0	1.9
2016	B+	2.52	2.10	120.0	71.7	484.5	15.7
2015	A-	3.20	2.67	100.9	58.8	314.7	2.0

Rating Indexes

UNIMERICA INS CO

B-   **Good**

Major Rating Factors: Good overall results on stability tests (5.3 on a scale of 0 to 10) despite fair financial strength of affiliated UnitedHealth Group Inc. Other stability subfactors include good operational trends and excellent risk diversification. Strong overall capitalization (10.0) based on excellent risk adjusted capital (severe loss scenario). However, capital levels have fluctuated somewhat during past years. High quality investment portfolio (8.5).
Other Rating Factors: Excellent profitability (8.4) with operating gains in each of the last five years. Excellent liquidity (7.0).
Principal Business: Group health insurance (96%), group life insurance (2%), and reinsurance (2%).
Principal Investments: NonCMO investment grade bonds (81%) and CMOs and structured securities (19%).
Investments in Affiliates: None
Group Affiliation: UnitedHealth Group Inc
Licensed in: All states except NY, PR
Commenced Business: December 1980
Address: 10701 WEST RESEARCH DRIVE, MILWAUKEE, WI 53226-0649
Phone: (952) 205-3110 **Domicile State:** WI **NAIC Code:** 91529

Data Date	Rating	RACR #1	RACR #2	Total Assets ($mil)	Capital ($mil)	Net Premium ($mil)	Net Income ($mil)
6-20	B-	4.47	3.50	441.8	226.3	205.9	23.3
6-19	B	4.80	3.72	450.2	251.4	199.6	20.6
2019	B	3.88	3.02	396.0	204.8	404.0	47.0
2018	B	4.14	3.24	436.7	230.7	431.8	62.5
2017	B	1.73	1.39	502.5	186.1	874.3	31.4
2016	B	1.43	1.15	476.4	154.7	877.0	21.1
2015	B	1.99	1.59	435.9	167.7	669.4	65.7

UnitedHealth Group Inc Composite Group Rating: C Largest Group Members	Assets ($mil)	Rating
UNITED HEALTHCARE INS CO	20997	C
SIERRA HEALTH AND LIFE INS CO INC	5301	B
OXFORD HEALTH INS INC	2920	B
UNITED HEALTHCARE OF WISCONSIN INC	2069	B+
UNITED HEALTHCARE INS CO OF NY	1472	B

UNION FIDELITY LIFE INS CO   E   Very Weak

Major Rating Factors: Weak profitability (1.5 on a scale of 0 to 10) with operating losses during the first three months of 2020. Return on equity has been low, averaging -47.4%. Weak liquidity (2.6) as a spike in claims or a run on policy withdrawals may stretch capacity. Weak overall results on stability tests (0.3) including weak risk adjusted capital in prior years, negative cash flow from operations for 2019.

Other Rating Factors: Fair quality investment portfolio (3.3). Good capitalization (5.6) based on good risk adjusted capital (moderate loss scenario).

Principal Business: Reinsurance (91%), group health insurance (4%), group life insurance (2%), individual life insurance (1%), and individual health insurance (1%).

Principal Investments: NonCMO investment grade bonds (82%), CMOs and structured securities (8%), mortgages in good standing (5%), and noninv. grade bonds (2%).

Investments in Affiliates: 1%

Group Affiliation: General Electric Corp Group

Licensed in: All states except NY, PR

Commenced Business: February 1926

Address: 7101 College Blvd Ste 1400, Overland Park, KS 66210

Phone: (913) 982-3700 **Domicile State:** KS **NAIC Code:** 62596

Data Date	Rating	RACR #1	RACR #2	Total Assets ($mil)	Capital ($mil)	Net Premium ($mil)	Net Income ($mil)
3-20	E	1.39	0.70	20,412.2	637.6	57.9	-73.4
3-19	E	1.36	0.69	20,654.0	658.3	57.0	-20.9
2019	E	1.57	0.80	20,382.8	728.6	245.0	-32.0
2018	E	1.44	0.73	20,505.2	667.8	253.5	-298.8
2017	E	1.14	0.57	20,435.4	536.6	263.9	-1,210.0
2016	D+	1.53	0.76	19,644.5	765.8	266.4	-65.0
2015	D+	0.89	0.46	19,365.0	428.3	276.3	-60.9

Net Income History (in millions of dollars)

UNION HEALTH SERVICE INC   C   Fair

Major Rating Factors: Fair profitability index (3.2 on a scale of 0 to 10). Good capitalization index (6.2) based on good current risk-adjusted capital (severe loss scenario). Good liquidity (6.9) with sufficient resources (cash flows and marketable investments) to handle a spike in claims.

Other Rating Factors: High quality investment portfolio (8.1). Excellent overall results on stability tests (7.2) based on steady enrollment growth, averaging 2% over the past five years but a decline in the number of member physicians during 2020.

Principal Business: FEHB (6%), Medicare (2%), other (92%)

Mem Phys: 19: 132 **18:** 290 **19 MLR** 100.4% **/ 19 Admin Exp** N/A

Enroll(000): Q2 20: 47 **19:** 48 **18:** 48 **Med Exp PMPM:** $147

Principal Investments: Long-term bonds (41%), cash and equiv (33%), nonaffiliate common stock (26%)

Provider Compensation ($000): FFS ($25,810), contr fee ($2,067), other ($57,026)

Total Member Encounters: Phys (50,297), non-phys (200,761)

Group Affiliation: Union Health Service Inc

Licensed in: IL

Address: 1634 W POLK STREET, CHICAGO,

Phone: (312) 423-4200 **Dom State:** IL **Commenced Bus:** N/A

Data Date	Rating	RACR #1	RACR #2	Total Assets ($mil)	Capital ($mil)	Net Premium ($mil)	Net Income ($mil)
6-20	C	1.10	0.92	30.0	17.9	44.9	2.5
6-19	N/A	N/A	N/A	N/A	N/A	N/A	N/A
2019	C	1.02	0.85	30.5	16.5	84.6	-1.6
2018	C+	0.91	0.76	27.4	14.3	80.8	-0.7
2017	B	1.01	0.85	28.3	14.0	73.5	-0.5
2016	B	1.00	0.83	25.6	14.8	73.7	1.0
2015	B	1.02	0.85	23.7	14.9	70.0	0.5

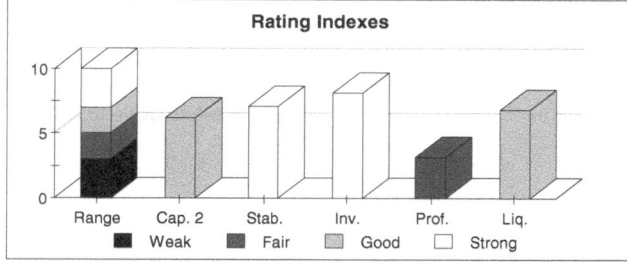

Rating Indexes

Range, Cap. 2, Stab., Inv., Prof., Liq.

Weak   Fair   Good   Strong

UNION MEDICAL CENTER   C-   Fair

Major Rating Factors: Excellent profitability (9.4 on a scale of 0 to 10). Strong capitalization index (10.0) based on weak current risk-adjusted capital (severe loss scenario). High quality investment portfolio (9.9).

Other Rating Factors: Excellent liquidity (7.9) with ample operational cash flow and liquid investments.

Principal Business: Comp med (100%)

Mem Phys: 19: N/A **18:** N/A **19 MLR** 62.1% **/ 19 Admin Exp** N/A

Enroll(000): 19: 7 **18:** 7 **Med Exp PMPM:** N/A

Principal Investments: Cash and equiv (117%)

Provider Compensation ($000): Salary ($3,119), other ($611)

Total Member Encounters: N/A

Group Affiliation: None

Licensed in: IL

Address: 1649 W Adams St, CHICAGO,

Phone: (312) 829-0850 **Dom State:** IL **Commenced Bus:** N/A

Data Date	Rating	RACR #1	RACR #2	Total Assets ($mil)	Capital ($mil)	Net Premium ($mil)	Net Income ($mil)
2019	C-	N/A	N/A	2.6	2.2	6.2	0.1
2018	U	N/A	N/A	2.4	2.0	6.3	0.2
2017	N/A	N/A	N/A	2.2	1.8	6.2	0.4
2016	N/A	N/A	N/A	1.9	1.4	6.1	0.1
2015	N/A	N/A	N/A	1.7	1.3	5.9	0.2

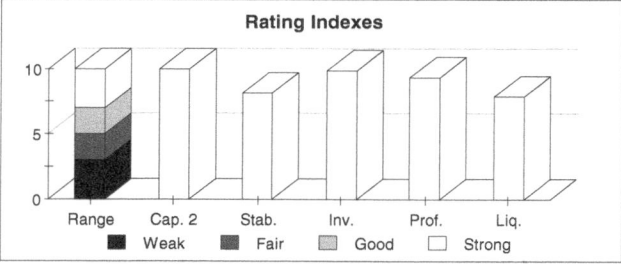

Rating Indexes

Range, Cap. 2, Stab., Inv., Prof., Liq.

Weak   Fair   Good   Strong

UNION SECURITY INS CO | B | Good

Major Rating Factors: Good overall results on stability tests (5.6 on a scale of 0 to 10) despite negative cash flow from operations for 2019. Other stability subfactors include good operational trends and excellent risk diversification. Good quality investment portfolio (5.4) despite mixed results such as: minimal exposure to mortgages and large holdings of BBB rated bonds but small junk bond holdings. Good overall profitability (6.0).

Other Rating Factors: Good liquidity (6.0). Strong capitalization (7.7) based on excellent risk adjusted capital (severe loss scenario).

Principal Business: Group health insurance (50%), individual health insurance (21%), individual life insurance (13%), group life insurance (11%), and other lines (4%).

Principal Investments: NonCMO investment grade bonds (64%), CMOs and structured securities (16%), common & preferred stock (6%), mortgages in good standing (5%), and misc. investments (8%).

Investments in Affiliates: 1%
Group Affiliation: Assurant Inc
Licensed in: All states except NY, PR
Commenced Business: September 1910
Address: 2323 GRAND BOULEVARD, TOPEKA, KS 66614
Phone: (651) 361-4000 **Domicile State:** KS **NAIC Code:** 70408

Data Date	Rating	RACR #1	RACR #2	Total Assets ($mil)	Capital ($mil)	Net Premium ($mil)	Net Income ($mil)
6-20	B	2.87	1.47	2,610.6	125.8	2.1	14.6
6-19	B	2.90	1.50	2,640.0	131.1	1.9	33.7
2019	B	2.81	1.46	2,608.5	123.6	3.9	48.1
2018	B	2.86	1.48	2,448.4	126.3	3.8	90.0
2017	B	2.37	1.23	2,698.7	113.9	4.1	106.2
2016	B	3.14	1.62	2,690.3	158.5	-1,468.9	481.7
2015	B	1.91	1.26	4,711.8	428.4	1,028.4	71.5

Adverse Trends in Operations

Change in premium mix from 2016 to 2017 (22.2%)
Decrease in capital during 2017 (28%)
Decrease in asset base during 2016 (43%)
Decrease in capital during 2016 (63%)
Decrease in premium volume from 2015 to 2016 (243%)

UNION SECURITY LIFE INS CO OF NY | C+ | Fair

Major Rating Factors: Fair overall results on stability tests (3.9 on a scale of 0 to 10). Good overall profitability (5.3). Return on equity has been good over the last five years, averaging 14.0%. Strong overall capitalization (10.0) based on excellent risk adjusted capital (severe loss scenario). Nevertheless, capital levels have fluctuated during prior years.

Other Rating Factors: High quality investment portfolio (8.1). Excellent liquidity (10.0).

Principal Business: Group health insurance (56%), individual health insurance (38%), group life insurance (2%), individual annuities (2%), and other lines (2%).

Principal Investments: NonCMO investment grade bonds (91%), CMOs and structured securities (6%), and cash (1%).

Investments in Affiliates: None
Group Affiliation: Assurant Inc
Licensed in: NY
Commenced Business: April 1974
Address: 212 HIGHBRIDGE STREET SUITE D, NEW YORK, NY 10005
Phone: (315) 637-4232 **Domicile State:** NY **NAIC Code:** 81477

Data Date	Rating	RACR #1	RACR #2	Total Assets ($mil)	Capital ($mil)	Net Premium ($mil)	Net Income ($mil)
6-20	C+	6.06	5.46	54.7	42.5	0.3	0.5
6-19	C+	6.15	5.53	57.2	44.1	0.3	1.8
2019	C+	6.38	5.74	56.6	44.7	0.7	2.5
2018	C+	6.72	6.05	59.9	48.2	0.8	5.0
2017	C+	7.06	6.36	66.7	52.7	1.0	6.3
2016	B-	8.30	7.47	81.0	67.4	-72.0	22.0
2015	B+	4.34	3.91	128.3	39.5	21.6	3.3

Rating Indexes

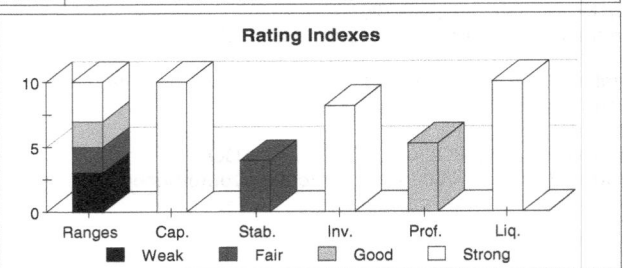

UNITED AMERICAN INS CO | B | Good

Major Rating Factors: Good overall results on stability tests (5.5 on a scale of 0 to 10) despite negative cash flow from operations for 2019. Other stability subfactors include good operational trends, good risk adjusted capital for prior years and excellent risk diversification. Good quality investment portfolio (6.2) despite mixed results such as: no exposure to mortgages and large holdings of BBB rated bonds but small junk bond holdings. Good overall profitability (6.6).

Other Rating Factors: Fair liquidity (4.8). Strong capitalization (7.1) based on excellent risk adjusted capital (severe loss scenario).

Principal Business: Individual health insurance (55%), group health insurance (35%), reinsurance (4%), individual annuities (3%), and individual life insurance (2%).

Principal Investments: NonCMO investment grade bonds (75%), common & preferred stock (10%), noninv. grade bonds (4%), CMOs and structured securities (3%), and policy loans (1%).

Investments in Affiliates: 10%
Group Affiliation: Torchmark Corp
Licensed in: All states except NY, PR
Commenced Business: August 1981
Address: 10306 REGENCY PARKWAY DR, OMAHA, NE 68114
Phone: (972) 529-5085 **Domicile State:** NE **NAIC Code:** 92916

Data Date	Rating	RACR #1	RACR #2	Total Assets ($mil)	Capital ($mil)	Net Premium ($mil)	Net Income ($mil)
6-20	B	1.42	1.08	755.1	171.4	268.2	22.1
6-19	B-	1.51	1.13	721.6	163.8	256.6	5.0
2019	B-	1.25	0.96	707.6	147.8	515.1	5.4
2018	B-	1.52	1.14	743.3	158.3	488.5	30.4
2017	B-	1.56	1.17	766.7	162.0	481.4	88.1
2016	B-	1.07	0.78	1,563.3	157.7	706.0	37.1
2015	B-	1.24	0.90	1,559.7	192.7	815.3	80.1

Adverse Trends in Operations

Decrease in asset base during 2019 (5%)
Decrease in premium volume from 2016 to 2017 (32%)
Decrease in asset base during 2017 (51%)
Decrease in capital during 2016 (18%)
Decrease in premium volume from 2015 to 2016 (13%)

UNITED HEALTHCARE INS CO C Fair

Major Rating Factors: Fair overall results on stability tests (3.4 on a scale of 0 to 10) including fair risk adjusted capital in prior years. Good current capitalization (5.1) based on mixed results -- excessive policy leverage mitigated by good risk adjusted capital (severe loss scenario) reflecting some improvement over results in 2016. Good quality investment portfolio (6.4).

Other Rating Factors: Weak liquidity (1.4). Excellent profitability (9.1) with operating gains in each of the last five years.

Principal Business: Group health insurance (87%), individual health insurance (9%), and reinsurance (4%).

Principal Investments: NonCMO investment grade bonds (48%), CMOs and structured securities (24%), common & preferred stock (20%), noninv. grade bonds (6%), and misc. investments (1%).

Investments in Affiliates: 19%
Group Affiliation: UnitedHealth Group Inc
Licensed in: All states except NY
Commenced Business: April 1972
Address: 185 ASYLUM STREET, HARTFORD, CT 06103-3408
Phone: (877) 832-7734 **Domicile State:** CT **NAIC Code:** 79413

Data Date	Rating	RACR #1	RACR #2	Total Assets ($mil)	Capital ($mil)	Net Premium ($mil)	Net Income ($mil)
6-20	C	1.09	0.92	21,367.3	7,726.7	27,594.1	1,646.2
6-19	C	1.07	0.90	20,357.8	7,509.1	27,856.4	1,307.5
2019	C	1.05	0.89	20,997.1	8,535.5	55,642.1	3,177.4
2018	C	1.05	0.88	20,752.5	8,128.2	54,442.0	3,080.5
2017	C	0.89	0.75	19,617.5	6,355.2	50,538.6	2,599.6
2016	C	0.79	0.67	17,922.6	5,250.4	44,379.2	1,924.6
2015	C	0.89	0.75	15,791.2	5,589.7	41,950.2	1,930.3

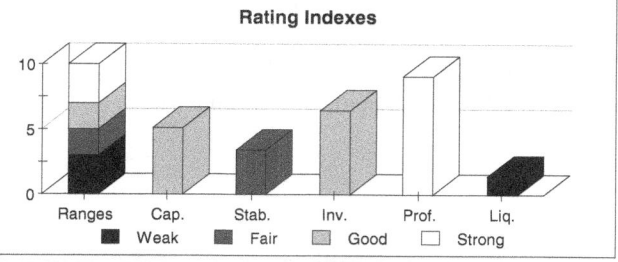

Rating Indexes

Ranges Cap. Stab. Inv. Prof. Liq.
■ Weak ■ Fair ▨ Good □ Strong

UNITED HEALTHCARE INS CO OF IL * A- Excellent

Major Rating Factors: Excellent profitability (9.3 on a scale of 0 to 10). Strong capitalization (7.5) based on excellent current risk-adjusted capital (severe loss scenario). High quality investment portfolio (7.5).

Other Rating Factors: Excellent liquidity (7.0) with ample operational cash flow and liquid investments.

Principal Business: Comp med (100%)
Mem Phys: 19: 110,280 **18:** 54,728 **19 MLR** 82.8% **/ 19 Admin Exp** N/A
Enroll(000): Q2 20: 229 **19:** 210 **18:** 217 **Med Exp PMPM:** $387
Principal Investments: Long-term bonds (57%), cash and equiv (42%), other (1%)
Provider Compensation ($000): Contr fee ($947,523), FFS ($55,448), capitation ($1,330), bonus arrang ($1,108)
Total Member Encounters: Phys (2,491,739), non-phys (88,204)
Group Affiliation: None
Licensed in: CT, IL, MA
Address: 200 EAST RANDOLPH STREET SUIT, CHICAGO, IL 60601
Phone: (312) 424-4460 **Dom State:** IL **Commenced Bus:** N/A

Data Date	Rating	RACR #1	RACR #2	Total Assets ($mil)	Capital ($mil)	Net Premium ($mil)	Net Income ($mil)
6-20	A-	1.74	1.45	453.6	164.1	641.5	20.2
6-19	B+	2.64	2.20	535.9	178.1	573.1	46.5
2019	B+	2.29	1.90	520.0	154.3	1,200.4	63.2
2018	B+	2.41	2.01	361.6	162.5	1,249.1	71.4
2017	B+	1.73	1.44	350.1	153.1	1,211.2	87.8
2016	B	1.95	1.63	302.3	109.9	1,065.1	44.0
2015	B	2.47	2.06	266.0	117.3	939.9	60.5

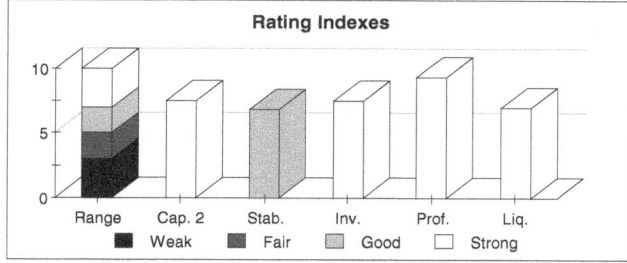

Rating Indexes

Range Cap. 2 Stab. Inv. Prof. Liq.
■ Weak ■ Fair ▨ Good □ Strong

UNITED HEALTHCARE INS CO OF NY B Good

Major Rating Factors: Fair liquidity (4.6 on a scale of 0 to 10) as cash resources may not be adequate to cover a spike in claims. Excellent profitability (8.6). Strong capitalization (10.0) based on excellent current risk-adjusted capital (severe loss scenario).

Other Rating Factors: High quality investment portfolio (9.3).

Principal Business: Medicare (49%), med supp (26%), comp med (15%), dental (2%), other (7%)
Mem Phys: 19: 118,666 **18:** 91,159 **19 MLR** 120.0% **/ 19 Admin Exp** N/A
Enroll(000): Q2 20: 1,435 **19:** 1,429 **18:** 1,400 **Med Exp PMPM:** $156
Principal Investments: Long-term bonds (95%), cash and equiv (5%)
Provider Compensation ($000): Contr fee ($2,023,757), FFS ($547,946), capitation ($39,854), bonus arrang ($19,819), other ($19,613)
Total Member Encounters: Phys (10,598,726), non-phys (1,308,956)
Group Affiliation: None
Licensed in: DC, NY
Address: 2950 EXPRESSWAY DRIVE SOUTH S, ISLANDIA, NY 11749-1412
Phone: (877) 832-7734 **Dom State:** NY **Commenced Bus:** N/A

Data Date	Rating	RACR #1	RACR #2	Total Assets ($mil)	Capital ($mil)	Net Premium ($mil)	Net Income ($mil)
6-20	B	7.53	6.28	1,547.5	730.6	1,264.6	102.3
6-19	B	8.00	6.67	1,389.3	667.1	1,125.1	62.0
2019	B	8.34	6.95	1,472.5	716.6	2,215.9	116.6
2018	B-	7.22	6.01	1,350.4	601.4	2,257.0	102.2
2017	B-	8.28	6.90	1,261.8	506.3	1,774.5	52.2
2016	B-	19.57	16.30	1,228.8	462.9	1,664.4	61.4
2015	B-	36.40	30.33	1,223.3	474.4	1,448.9	48.2

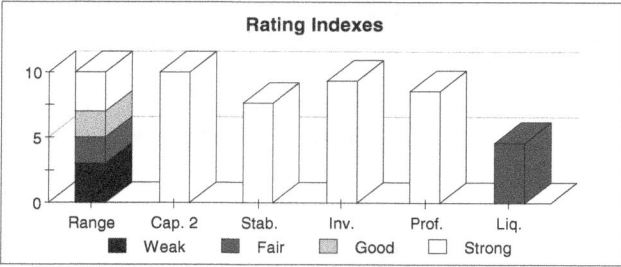

Rating Indexes

Range Cap. 2 Stab. Inv. Prof. Liq.
■ Weak ■ Fair ▨ Good □ Strong

UNITED HEALTHCARE OF ALABAMA INC — D — Weak

Major Rating Factors: Weak overall results on stability tests (0.6 on a scale of 0 to 10). Good overall profitability index (5.7). Good liquidity (6.9) with sufficient resources (cash flows and marketable investments) to handle a spike in claims.
Other Rating Factors: Strong capitalization index (8.5) based on excellent current risk-adjusted capital (severe loss scenario). High quality investment portfolio (8.9).
Principal Business: Medicare (92%), comp med (5%), Medicaid (3%)
Mem Phys: 19: 16,186 **18:** 14,988 **19 MLR** 85.9% **/ 19 Admin Exp** N/A
Enroll(000): Q2 20: 43 **19:** 15 **18:** 11 **Med Exp PMPM:** $785
Principal Investments: Cash and equiv (50%), long-term bonds (50%)
Provider Compensation ($000): Contr fee ($85,590), FFS ($32,583), capitation ($9,785), bonus arrang ($657)
Total Member Encounters: Phys (312,965), non-phys (143,527)
Group Affiliation: None
Licensed in: AL
Address: 33 INVERNESS CENTER PARKWAY, BIRMINGHAM,
Phone: (205) 437-8500 **Dom State:** AL **Commenced Bus:** N/A

Data Date	Rating	RACR #1	RACR #2	Total Assets ($mil)	Capital ($mil)	Net Premium ($mil)	Net Income ($mil)
6-20	D	2.52	2.10	116.8	37.4	276.1	21.4
6-19	C	40.95	34.13	46.7	19.3	73.3	3.2
2019	C	2.11	1.75	48.0	16.0	154.2	-0.2
2018	C	68.18	56.81	78.7	36.0	93.9	2.1
2017	C	125.90	104.90	74.9	38.3	2.8	4.3
2016	B	2.46	2.05	176.2	56.4	559.7	10.2
2015	B	3.66	3.05	142.7	51.2	455.7	20.6

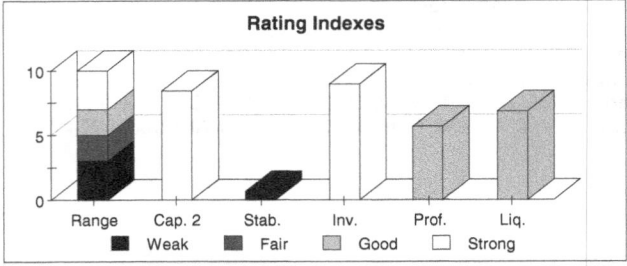

Rating Indexes

UNITED HEALTHCARE OF ARIZONA INC — D+ — Weak

Major Rating Factors: Low quality investment portfolio (0.1 on a scale of 0 to 10). Weak overall results on stability tests (2.6) based on a steep decline in capital during 2019, an inordinate decline in premium revenue in 2019. Excellent profitability (7.5).
Other Rating Factors: Strong capitalization index (7.5) based on excellent current risk-adjusted capital (severe loss scenario). Excellent liquidity (7.3) with ample operational cash flow and liquid investments.
Principal Business: Comp med (100%)
Mem Phys: 19: 30,926 **18:** 28,509 **19 MLR** 86.8% **/ 19 Admin Exp** N/A
Enroll(000): Q2 20: 16 **19:** 16 **18:** 16 **Med Exp PMPM:** $489
Principal Investments: Cash and equiv (98%), long-term bonds (2%)
Provider Compensation ($000): Contr fee ($84,821), FFS ($6,126), capitation ($1,376), bonus arrang ($66)
Total Member Encounters: Phys (188,531), non-phys (8,425)
Group Affiliation: None
Licensed in: AZ
Address: 1 EAST WASHINGTON STREET, PHOENIX,
Phone: (952) 979-6171 **Dom State:** AZ **Commenced Bus:** N/A

Data Date	Rating	RACR #1	RACR #2	Total Assets ($mil)	Capital ($mil)	Net Premium ($mil)	Net Income ($mil)
6-20	D+	1.72	1.44	47.7	17.3	50.1	2.2
6-19	C	3.54	2.95	51.0	17.0	53.9	3.0
2019	C	2.85	2.37	40.3	16.1	106.6	1.5
2018	C	4.83	4.03	49.1	23.8	125.2	9.1
2017	C-	2.76	2.30	53.5	22.5	127.3	6.1
2016	C	4.41	3.67	39.4	17.4	111.4	0.6
2015	C	2.85	2.38	64.9	32.3	256.3	14.0

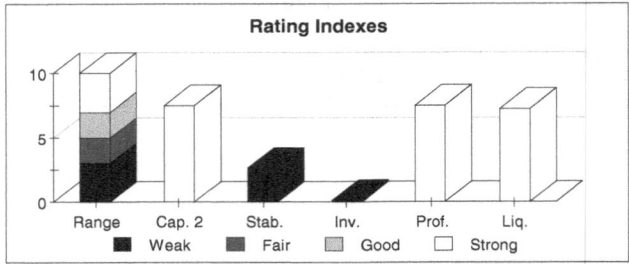

Rating Indexes

UNITED HEALTHCARE OF ARKANSAS INC — B- — Good

Major Rating Factors: Fair overall results on stability tests (4.6 on a scale of 0 to 10) in spite of healthy premium and capital growth during 2019 but an excessive 55% enrollment growth during the period. Excellent profitability (8.0). Strong capitalization index (7.9) based on excellent current risk-adjusted capital (severe loss scenario).
Other Rating Factors: High quality investment portfolio (9.9). Excellent liquidity (7.3) with ample operational cash flow and liquid investments.
Principal Business: Medicare (84%), comp med (16%)
Mem Phys: 19: 11,550 **18:** 10,794 **19 MLR** 80.7% **/ 19 Admin Exp** N/A
Enroll(000): Q2 20: 22 **19:** 14 **18:** 9 **Med Exp PMPM:** $639
Principal Investments: Cash and equiv (99%), long-term bonds (1%)
Provider Compensation ($000): Contr fee ($78,713), FFS ($17,541), capitation ($2,569), bonus arrang ($963)
Total Member Encounters: Phys (247,724), non-phys (86,187)
Group Affiliation: None
Licensed in: AR
Address: 1401 CAPITOL AVE 3RD FLOOR STE, LITTLE ROCK,
Phone: (501) 664-7700 **Dom State:** AR **Commenced Bus:** N/A

Data Date	Rating	RACR #1	RACR #2	Total Assets ($mil)	Capital ($mil)	Net Premium ($mil)	Net Income ($mil)
6-20	B-	2.05	1.71	67.2	28.5	105.1	8.8
6-19	B-	5.11	4.26	40.7	21.2	62.0	2.5
2019	B-	3.07	2.55	47.1	24.8	131.1	6.2
2018	B-	4.55	3.79	28.9	18.8	65.2	4.9
2017	D-	6.14	5.12	21.7	17.0	22.1	4.4
2016	D-	2.49	2.08	43.1	16.7	41.7	-9.7
2015	B	6.74	5.61	10.0	7.1	10.2	0.9

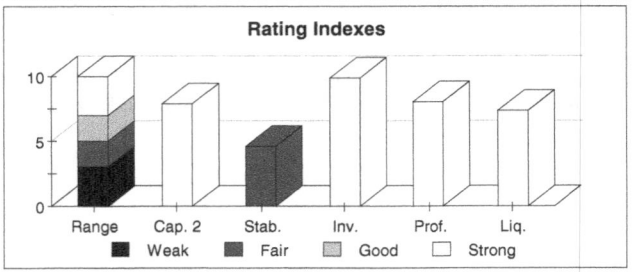

Rating Indexes

UNITED HEALTHCARE OF COLORADO INC
C   Fair

Major Rating Factors: Low quality investment portfolio (0.1 on a scale of 0 to 10). Good overall results on stability tests (6.2). Excellent profitability (8.0).
Other Rating Factors: Strong capitalization index (8.7) based on excellent current risk-adjusted capital (severe loss scenario). Excellent liquidity (7.6) with ample operational cash flow and liquid investments.
Principal Business: Comp med (100%)
Mem Phys: 19: 27,386 **18:** 25,905 **19 MLR** 73.7% **/ 19 Admin Exp** N/A
Enroll(000): Q2 20: 24 **19:** 24 **18:** 24 **Med Exp PMPM:** $257
Principal Investments: Cash and equiv (99%), long-term bonds (1%)
Provider Compensation ($000): Contr fee ($67,263), capitation ($3,954), FFS ($3,301), bonus arrang ($66)
Total Member Encounters: Phys (139,157), non-phys (4,017)
Group Affiliation: None
Licensed in: CO
Address: 6465 SOUTH GREENWOOD PLAZA BLV, CENTENNIAL,
Phone: (952) 936-1300 **Dom State:** CO **Commenced Bus:** N/A

Data Date	Rating	RACR #1	RACR #2	Total Assets ($mil)	Capital ($mil)	Net Premium ($mil)	Net Income ($mil)
6-20	C	2.70	2.25	61.7	24.8	56.1	4.8
6-19	C	3.98	3.32	53.9	19.7	51.4	4.4
2019	C	3.89	3.24	47.5	20.6	99.8	6.5
2018	C	3.15	2.63	43.1	15.4	92.3	4.9
2017	D-	1.46	1.22	35.8	10.9	73.2	0.8
2016	D-	1.74	1.45	31.8	9.8	87.9	0.0
2015	C	3.12	2.60	18.4	5.9	36.4	-0.9

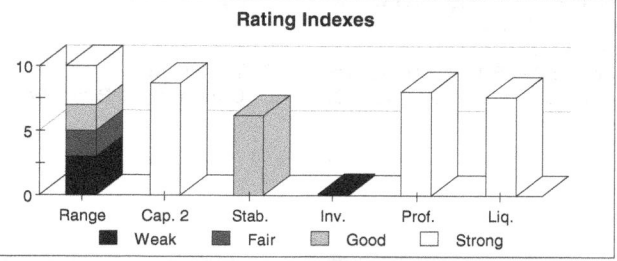

Rating Indexes

UNITED HEALTHCARE OF FLORIDA INC
C+   Fair

Major Rating Factors: Good overall profitability index (5.4 on a scale of 0 to 10). Good capitalization index (5.8) based on good current risk-adjusted capital (severe loss scenario). Good liquidity (6.6) with sufficient resources (cash flows and marketable investments) to handle a spike in claims.
Other Rating Factors: Weak overall results on stability tests (2.7). High quality investment portfolio (8.4).
Principal Business: Medicaid (67%), comp med (33%)
Mem Phys: 19: 69,064 **18:** 62,780 **19 MLR** 87.1% **/ 19 Admin Exp** N/A
Enroll(000): Q2 20: 346 **19:** 350 **18:** 395 **Med Exp PMPM:** $412
Principal Investments: Long-term bonds (79%), cash and equiv (21%)
Provider Compensation ($000): Contr fee ($1,426,799), FFS ($294,580), capitation ($100,695), bonus arrang ($8,143)
Total Member Encounters: Phys (2,856,159), non-phys (1,719,820)
Group Affiliation: None
Licensed in: FL
Address: 495 NORTH KELLER ROAD SUITE 20, MAITLAND,
Phone: (407) 659-6900 **Dom State:** FL **Commenced Bus:** N/A

Data Date	Rating	RACR #1	RACR #2	Total Assets ($mil)	Capital ($mil)	Net Premium ($mil)	Net Income ($mil)
6-20	C+	1.05	0.87	440.3	158.4	962.1	28.8
6-19	C+	1.87	1.56	521.0	254.3	1,030.3	16.0
2019	B-	1.90	1.59	453.5	213.7	2,070.6	39.8
2018	C+	1.72	1.43	534.9	231.1	2,493.0	32.9
2017	D+	1.56	1.30	598.7	269.3	2,454.9	91.2
2016	D+	2.15	1.79	792.7	348.7	3,000.4	84.7
2015	C	1.48	1.23	808.6	274.5	3,248.8	-12.9

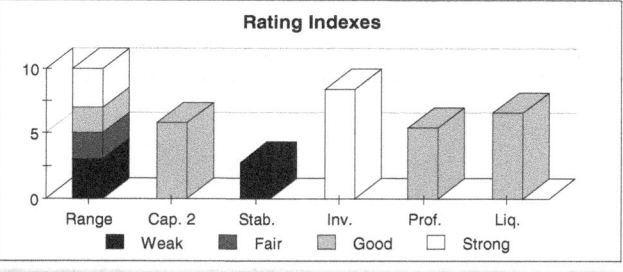

Rating Indexes

UNITED HEALTHCARE OF GEORGIA INC
B   Good

Major Rating Factors: Good overall profitability index (5.9 on a scale of 0 to 10). Good overall results on stability tests (5.0) based on a significant 23% decrease in enrollment during the period. Good liquidity (6.6) with sufficient resources (cash flows and marketable investments) to handle a spike in claims.
Other Rating Factors: Strong capitalization index (7.4) based on excellent current risk-adjusted capital (severe loss scenario). High quality investment portfolio (9.4).
Principal Business: Comp med (56%), Medicare (44%)
Mem Phys: 19: 31,083 **18:** 30,341 **19 MLR** 85.8% **/ 19 Admin Exp** N/A
Enroll(000): Q2 20: 41 **19:** 46 **18:** 60 **Med Exp PMPM:** $473
Principal Investments: Long-term bonds (96%), cash and equiv (4%)
Provider Compensation ($000): Contr fee ($255,960), FFS ($29,860), capitation ($4,952), bonus arrang ($1,080)
Total Member Encounters: Phys (589,169), non-phys (126,187)
Group Affiliation: None
Licensed in: GA
Address: 3720 DAVINCI COURT SUITE 300, NORCROSS,
Phone: (770) 300-3501 **Dom State:** GA **Commenced Bus:** N/A

Data Date	Rating	RACR #1	RACR #2	Total Assets ($mil)	Capital ($mil)	Net Premium ($mil)	Net Income ($mil)
6-20	B	1.68	1.40	105.8	52.9	152.7	14.1
6-19	C+	1.89	1.58	91.4	39.7	171.7	9.7
2019	B	2.30	1.92	91.3	44.2	331.3	12.9
2018	C+	1.54	1.28	95.5	31.5	363.7	-8.3
2017	B	1.64	1.36	89.5	39.1	281.5	14.0
2016	C+	2.54	2.12	105.0	45.2	287.3	21.9
2015	C	2.72	2.27	91.5	28.0	174.0	-35.2

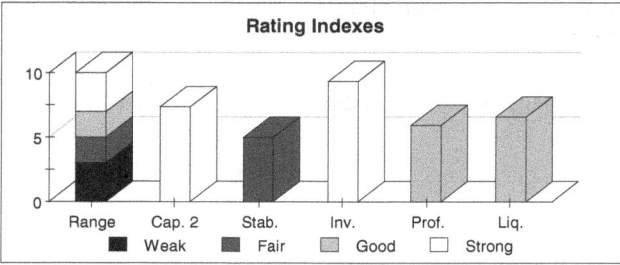

Rating Indexes

UNITED HEALTHCARE OF ILLINOIS INC

B   **Good**

Major Rating Factors: Good liquidity (6.9 on a scale of 0 to 10) with sufficient resources (cash flows and marketable investments) to handle a spike in claims. Excellent profitability (10.0). Strong capitalization index (8.6) based on excellent current risk-adjusted capital (severe loss scenario).
Other Rating Factors: High quality investment portfolio (7.5). Excellent overall results on stability tests (6.9).
Principal Business: Comp med (100%)
Mem Phys: 19: 127,253   18: 54,760   **19 MLR** 79.3%   **/ 19 Admin Exp** N/A
Enroll(000): Q2 20: 32   19: 34   18: 34   **Med Exp PMPM:** $322
Principal Investments: Long-term bonds (88%), cash and equiv (12%)
Provider Compensation ($000): Contr fee ($118,577), FFS ($6,772), capitation ($3,374), bonus arrang ($284)
Total Member Encounters: Phys (298,309), non-phys (9,673)
Group Affiliation: None
Licensed in: IL, IN
Address: 200 EAST RANDOLPH STREET, CHICAGO,
Phone: (312) 803-5900   **Dom State:** IL   **Commenced Bus:** N/A

Data Date	Rating	RACR #1	RACR #2	Total Assets ($mil)	Capital ($mil)	Net Premium ($mil)	Net Income ($mil)
6-20	B	2.63	2.19	70.6	34.3	79.5	5.2
6-19	B	4.67	3.89	70.2	36.2	80.7	8.1
2019	B	3.90	3.25	59.3	29.8	163.2	11.5
2018	B	3.71	3.09	58.8	28.5	178.6	10.1
2017	B-	1.77	1.48	53.2	23.7	173.0	9.3
2016	B-	2.56	2.13	38.5	17.5	135.1	10.2
2015	C	2.89	2.41	32.1	16.0	108.0	7.2

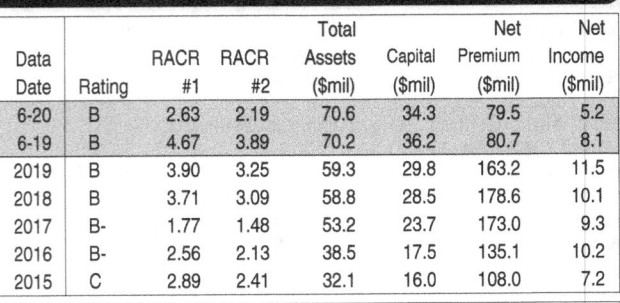

Rating Indexes

UNITED HEALTHCARE OF KENTUCKY LTD

B-   **Good**

Major Rating Factors: Good overall profitability index (5.8 on a scale of 0 to 10). Good overall results on stability tests (5.9). Strong capitalization index (7.5) based on excellent current risk-adjusted capital (severe loss scenario).
Other Rating Factors: Excellent liquidity (7.0) with ample operational cash flow and liquid investments. Low quality investment portfolio (2.5).
Principal Business: Comp med (94%), Medicare (6%)
Mem Phys: 19: 21,379   18: 19,818   **19 MLR** 84.7%   **/ 19 Admin Exp** N/A
Enroll(000): Q2 20: 28   19: 29   18: 33   **Med Exp PMPM:** $394
Principal Investments: Cash and equiv (65%), long-term bonds (35%)
Provider Compensation ($000): Contr fee ($134,290), FFS ($9,052), capitation ($3,196), bonus arrang ($11)
Total Member Encounters: Phys (250,258), non-phys (19,998)
Group Affiliation: None
Licensed in: IN, KY
Address: 230 LEXINGTON GREEN CIRCLE, LEXINGTON,
Phone: (859) 825-6132   **Dom State:** KY   **Commenced Bus:** N/A

Data Date	Rating	RACR #1	RACR #2	Total Assets ($mil)	Capital ($mil)	Net Premium ($mil)	Net Income ($mil)
6-20	B-	1.76	1.47	62.1	31.9	84.4	3.9
6-19	B-	2.50	2.08	47.8	23.4	85.7	5.2
2019	B-	2.75	2.29	56.1	29.2	171.7	2.0
2018	B-	2.04	1.70	44.2	18.9	158.6	4.2
2017	C+	1.28	1.06	33.8	14.4	113.4	4.8
2016	C	1.53	1.28	31.7	9.9	105.1	-2.5
2015	B	2.85	2.38	29.8	14.7	90.1	3.4

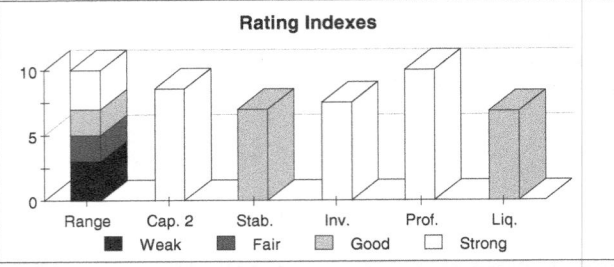

Rating Indexes

UNITED HEALTHCARE OF LOUISIANA INC

B   **Good**

Major Rating Factors: Good liquidity (6.9 on a scale of 0 to 10) with sufficient resources (cash flows and marketable investments) to handle a spike in claims. Fair quality investment portfolio (4.4). Excellent profitability (7.4).
Other Rating Factors: Strong capitalization index (7.3) based on excellent current risk-adjusted capital (severe loss scenario). Excellent overall results on stability tests (7.7).
Principal Business: Medicaid (99%)
Mem Phys: 19: 25,078   18: 23,066   **19 MLR** 85.7%   **/ 19 Admin Exp** N/A
Enroll(000): Q2 20: 454   19: 424   18: 449   **Med Exp PMPM:** $377
Principal Investments: Long-term bonds (57%), cash and equiv (43%)
Provider Compensation ($000): Contr fee ($1,086,626), FFS ($483,584), capitation ($369,724), bonus arrang ($9,997)
Total Member Encounters: Phys (4,336,114), non-phys (2,037,108)
Group Affiliation: None
Licensed in: LA
Address: 3838 N CAUSEWAY BLVD SUITE 260, METAIRIE,
Phone: (504) 849-1603   **Dom State:** LA   **Commenced Bus:** N/A

Data Date	Rating	RACR #1	RACR #2	Total Assets ($mil)	Capital ($mil)	Net Premium ($mil)	Net Income ($mil)
6-20	B	1.60	1.33	607.2	234.2	1,284.5	60.2
6-19	B	1.97	1.64	532.7	201.0	1,153.2	33.8
2019	B	1.72	1.44	627.3	180.6	2,347.4	20.5
2018	B	1.67	1.39	562.2	168.3	2,252.3	-3.6
2017	D	1.44	1.20	550.2	171.7	1,998.6	55.6
2016	D	1.56	1.30	479.2	126.5	1,644.8	43.9
2015	D	1.45	1.21	275.9	84.5	1,069.8	29.5

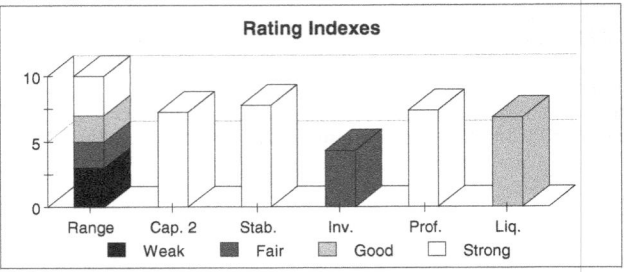

Rating Indexes

UNITED HEALTHCARE OF MID-ATLANTIC   B   Good

Major Rating Factors: Good overall profitability index (6.7 on a scale of 0 to 10). Good overall results on stability tests (5.4). Good liquidity (6.9) with sufficient resources (cash flows and marketable investments) to handle a spike in claims.

Other Rating Factors: Strong capitalization index (7.8) based on excellent current risk-adjusted capital (severe loss scenario). High quality investment portfolio (7.3).

Principal Business: Medicaid (88%), comp med (8%), Medicare (3%)

Mem Phys: 19: 62,910 **18:** 58,540 **19 MLR** 85.4% **/ 19 Admin Exp** N/A

Enroll(000): Q2 20: 333 **19:** 309 **18:** 245 **Med Exp PMPM:** $423

Principal Investments: Long-term bonds (70%), cash and equiv (30%)

Provider Compensation ($000): Contr fee ($1,151,256), FFS ($310,900), capitation ($6,069), bonus arrang ($424)

Total Member Encounters: Phys (2,294,489), non-phys (1,419,212)

Group Affiliation: None

Licensed in: DC, MD, VA

Address: 800 KING FARM BOULEVARD, ROCKVILLE,

Phone: (866) 297-9264 **Dom State:** MD **Commenced Bus:** N/A

Data Date	Rating	RACR #1	RACR #2	Total Assets ($mil)	Capital ($mil)	Net Premium ($mil)	Net Income ($mil)
6-20	B	2.01	1.68	633.4	267.2	1,024.4	74.0
6-19	B-	2.84	2.37	450.9	142.7	874.6	-16.0
2019	B	2.01	1.67	476.1	196.2	1,794.0	38.9
2018	B	3.09	2.58	338.3	155.7	980.8	47.2
2017	B-	1.62	1.35	300.4	104.5	861.5	39.2
2016	B	3.02	2.51	321.2	139.8	896.7	62.4
2015	C+	2.33	1.94	350.5	138.5	894.5	-64.2

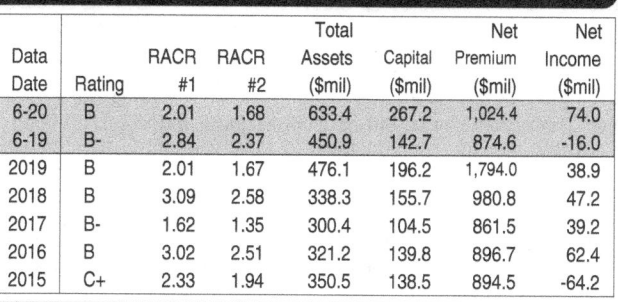

Rating Indexes

UNITED HEALTHCARE OF MISSISSIPPI INC   B   Good

Major Rating Factors: Good overall profitability index (5.6 on a scale of 0 to 10). Good quality investment portfolio (6.0). Good overall results on stability tests (5.5) despite a decline in enrollment during 2019.

Other Rating Factors: Good liquidity (6.9) with sufficient resources (cash flows and marketable investments) to handle a spike in claims. Strong capitalization index (8.2) based on excellent current risk-adjusted capital (severe loss scenario).

Principal Business: Medicaid (89%), comp med (11%)

Mem Phys: 19: 11,753 **18:** 11,220 **19 MLR** 85.3% **/ 19 Admin Exp** N/A

Enroll(000): Q2 20: 209 **19:** 203 **18:** 225 **Med Exp PMPM:** $345

Principal Investments: Long-term bonds (73%), cash and equiv (27%)

Provider Compensation ($000): Contr fee ($614,556), FFS ($242,058), capitation ($3,261), bonus arrang ($366)

Total Member Encounters: Phys (1,943,876), non-phys (1,125,323)

Group Affiliation: None

Licensed in: MS

Address: 795 WOODLANDS PARKWAY SUITE 30, RIDGELAND,

Phone: (504) 849-1603 **Dom State:** MS **Commenced Bus:** N/A

Data Date	Rating	RACR #1	RACR #2	Total Assets ($mil)	Capital ($mil)	Net Premium ($mil)	Net Income ($mil)
6-20	B	2.35	1.96	303.6	198.9	520.9	34.1
6-19	B-	2.43	2.03	262.9	171.6	495.6	4.7
2019	B	2.77	2.31	255.8	168.7	993.4	21.5
2018	C+	2.33	1.95	277.0	164.8	1,144.6	32.6
2017	C	N/A	N/A	286.6	140.6	1,106.6	-30.2
2016	B-	1.33	1.11	223.4	96.8	1,233.0	8.9
2015	B-	1.32	1.10	220.6	66.8	897.1	-14.6

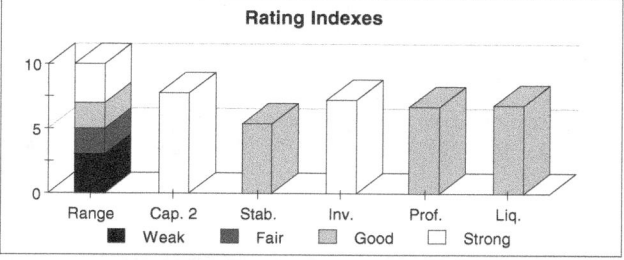

Rating Indexes

UNITED HEALTHCARE OF NC INC   C   Fair

Major Rating Factors: Fair profitability index (3.8 on a scale of 0 to 10). Fair quality investment portfolio (3.7). Fair overall results on stability tests (4.1).

Other Rating Factors: Strong capitalization index (10.0) based on excellent current risk-adjusted capital (severe loss scenario). Excellent liquidity (7.2) with ample operational cash flow and liquid investments.

Principal Business: Comp med (100%)

Mem Phys: 19: 44,209 **18:** 39,218 **19 MLR** 79.8% **/ 19 Admin Exp** N/A

Enroll(000): Q2 20: 78 **19:** 90 **18:** 94 **Med Exp PMPM:** $362

Principal Investments: Long-term bonds (52%), cash and equiv (48%)

Provider Compensation ($000): Contr fee ($379,812), FFS ($27,629), capitation ($6,760), bonus arrang ($1,398)

Total Member Encounters: Phys (847,655), non-phys (25,041)

Group Affiliation: None

Licensed in: NC

Address: 3803 NORTH ELM STREET, GREENSBORO,

Phone: (336) 282-0900 **Dom State:** NC **Commenced Bus:** N/A

Data Date	Rating	RACR #1	RACR #2	Total Assets ($mil)	Capital ($mil)	Net Premium ($mil)	Net Income ($mil)
6-20	C	4.05	3.38	284.3	155.7	186.0	-19.4
6-19	C	5.82	4.85	270.6	166.3	255.6	6.2
2019	C	6.46	5.39	261.1	178.4	505.5	19.3
2018	C	3.00	2.50	180.7	81.8	496.9	-1.2
2017	C+	4.08	3.40	181.3	109.4	397.6	31.6
2016	B	3.24	2.70	403.7	148.4	931.0	26.4
2015	B	2.00	1.67	375.5	126.9	1,280.4	6.5

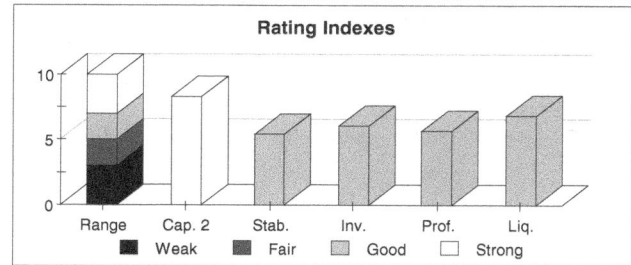

Rating Indexes

UNITED HEALTHCARE OF NEW ENGLAND INC   B   Good

Major Rating Factors: Good overall results on stability tests (5.6 on a scale of 0 to 10) based on steady enrollment growth, averaging 8% over the past five years. Good liquidity (6.6) with sufficient resources (cash flows and marketable investments) to handle a spike in claims. Excellent profitability (8.3).
Other Rating Factors: Strong capitalization index (7.7) based on excellent current risk-adjusted capital (severe loss scenario). High quality investment portfolio (8.6).
Principal Business: Medicare (60%), Medicaid (39%)
Mem Phys: 19: 126,240 **18:** 134,473 **19 MLR** 85.6% **/ 19 Admin Exp** N/A
Enroll(000): Q2 20: 165 **19:** 155 **18:** 154 **Med Exp PMPM:** $589
Principal Investments: Long-term bonds (84%), nonaffiliate common stock (13%), cash and equiv (3%)
Provider Compensation ($000): Contr fee ($767,635), FFS ($215,534), capitation ($102,849), bonus arrang ($7,987)
Total Member Encounters: Phys (2,236,768), non-phys (1,142,401)
Group Affiliation: None
Licensed in: MA, NH, PA, RI, VT
Address: 475 KILVERT STREET SUITE 310, WARWICK,
Phone: (203) 447-4444 **Dom State:** RI **Commenced Bus:** N/A

Data Date	Rating	RACR #1	RACR #2	Total Assets ($mil)	Capital ($mil)	Net Premium ($mil)	Net Income ($mil)
6-20	B	1.88	1.57	409.2	190.4	695.7	29.7
6-19	B	2.53	2.11	322.0	150.6	644.4	21.5
2019	B	2.24	1.87	374.5	163.2	1,305.2	35.1
2018	B	2.25	1.87	331.0	132.6	1,160.8	18.4
2017	B-	1.79	1.49	326.4	113.9	974.5	23.6
2016	B-	2.76	2.30	313.5	119.0	866.6	12.7
2015	B	3.53	2.94	363.9	147.2	768.5	27.5

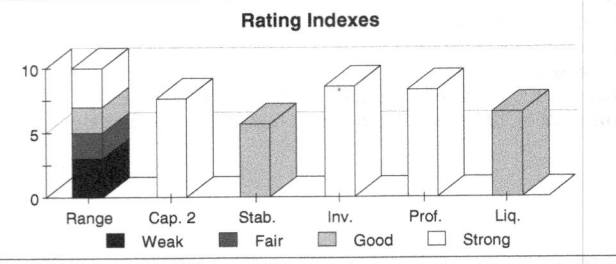

Rating Indexes

UNITED HEALTHCARE OF NY INC   B   Good

Major Rating Factors: Good liquidity (5.7 on a scale of 0 to 10) with sufficient resources (cash flows and marketable investments) to handle a spike in claims. Fair profitability index (3.6). Fair overall results on stability tests (4.7).
Other Rating Factors: Strong capitalization index (7.4) based on excellent current risk-adjusted capital (severe loss scenario). High quality investment portfolio (9.2).
Principal Business: Medicaid (50%), Medicare (38%), comp med (4%), other (8%)
Mem Phys: 19: 115,808 **18:** 97,444 **19 MLR** 89.5% **/ 19 Admin Exp** N/A
Enroll(000): Q2 20: 658 **19:** 696 **18:** 794 **Med Exp PMPM:** $510
Principal Investments: Long-term bonds (92%), cash and equiv (8%)
Provider Compensation ($000): Contr fee ($3,599,486), FFS ($686,956), capitation ($176,285), bonus arrang ($74,703), other ($114,772)
Total Member Encounters: Phys (9,323,813), non-phys (5,351,766)
Group Affiliation: None
Licensed in: NY
Address: 77 WATER STREET 14TH / 15TH FL, NEW YORK,
Phone: (203) 447-4439 **Dom State:** NY **Commenced Bus:** N/A

Data Date	Rating	RACR #1	RACR #2	Total Assets ($mil)	Capital ($mil)	Net Premium ($mil)	Net Income ($mil)
6-20	B	1.66	1.38	1,500.1	593.3	2,448.6	27.7
6-19	B+	1.74	1.45	1,481.4	541.3	2,716.4	-72.2
2019	B+	1.81	1.51	1,322.3	542.8	5,192.5	-71.3
2018	B+	1.96	1.64	1,295.8	613.0	5,344.2	46.6
2017	B+	N/A	N/A	1,195.0	570.8	4,412.6	107.1
2016	B+	2.55	2.12	1,096.2	568.0	3,870.2	115.2
2015	B+	2.77	2.31	846.1	455.9	3,025.2	106.0

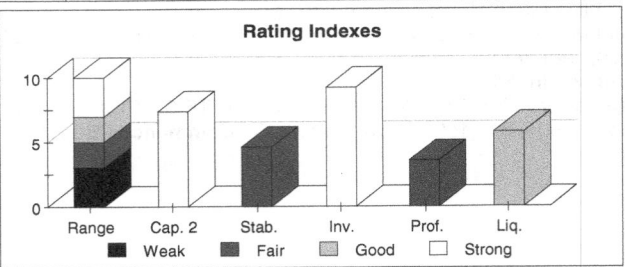

Rating Indexes

UNITED HEALTHCARE OF OHIO INC   C   Fair

Major Rating Factors: Weak overall results on stability tests (1.5 on a scale of 0 to 10) based on a significant 24% decrease in enrollment during the period, a steep decline in capital during 2019. Excellent profitability (7.6). Strong capitalization index (10.0) based on excellent current risk-adjusted capital (severe loss scenario).
Other Rating Factors: High quality investment portfolio (9.9). Excellent liquidity (8.1) with ample operational cash flow and liquid investments.
Principal Business: Comp med (100%)
Mem Phys: 19: 76,405 **18:** 76,285 **19 MLR** 78.1% **/ 19 Admin Exp** N/A
Enroll(000): Q2 20: 7 **19:** 8 **18:** 11 **Med Exp PMPM:** $392
Principal Investments: Cash and equiv (97%), long-term bonds (3%)
Provider Compensation ($000): Contr fee ($39,017), FFS ($2,534), capitation ($822), bonus arrang ($334)
Total Member Encounters: Phys (65,566), non-phys (3,153)
Group Affiliation: None
Licensed in: KY, OH
Address: OH020-3010 9200 WORTHINGTON RO, WESTERVILLE,
Phone: (614) 698-3774 **Dom State:** OH **Commenced Bus:** N/A

Data Date	Rating	RACR #1	RACR #2	Total Assets ($mil)	Capital ($mil)	Net Premium ($mil)	Net Income ($mil)
6-20	C	3.98	3.31	27.8	18.2	20.7	1.1
6-19	C	14.32	11.93	55.5	45.5	29.5	3.9
2019	C	9.74	8.12	36.1	27.2	53.5	5.2
2018	C	14.90	12.42	58.2	47.5	57.7	6.3
2017	D+	17.30	14.42	79.2	69.0	41.6	4.2
2016	C	18.09	15.07	88.6	64.1	81.6	5.4
2015	C	2.43	2.02	177.5	78.5	682.6	37.7

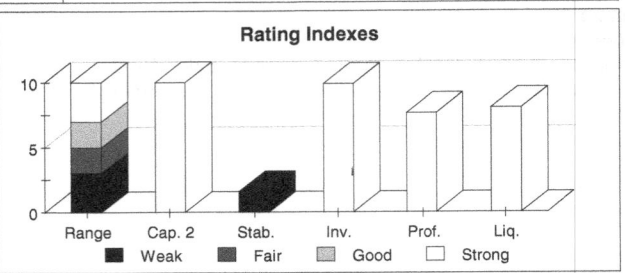

Rating Indexes

UNITED HEALTHCARE OF THE MIDLANDS *   B+   Good

Major Rating Factors: Good liquidity (6.8 on a scale of 0 to 10) with sufficient resources (cash flows and marketable investments) to handle a spike in claims. Excellent profitability (7.5). Strong capitalization index (7.7) based on excellent current risk-adjusted capital (severe loss scenario).
Other Rating Factors: High quality investment portfolio (9.0). Excellent overall results on stability tests (7.2) based on healthy premium and capital growth during 2019.
Principal Business: Medicare (87%), Medicaid (13%)
Mem Phys: 19: 150,418   **18:** 140,626   **19 MLR** 82.9%   **/ 19 Admin Exp** N/A
Enroll(000): Q2 20: 337   **19:** 343   **18:** 325   **Med Exp PMPM:** $729
Principal Investments: Long-term bonds (93%), cash and equiv (7%)
Provider Compensation ($000): Contr fee ($2,247,516), FFS ($404,628), capitation ($199,982), bonus arrang ($53,041)
Total Member Encounters: Phys (6,115,701), non-phys (2,721,347)
Group Affiliation: None
Licensed in: AL, AR, IL, IN, IA, KS, MO, NE
Address: 2717 NORTH 118TH STREET, OMAHA,
Phone: (402) 445-5600   **Dom State:** NE   **Commenced Bus:** N/A

Data Date	Rating	RACR #1	RACR #2	Total Assets ($mil)	Capital ($mil)	Net Premium ($mil)	Net Income ($mil)
6-20	B+	1.93	1.61	1,032.6	476.5	1,793.8	125.4
6-19	B	2.39	1.99	895.4	368.1	1,785.7	99.7
2019	B+	1.83	1.52	835.3	358.4	3,569.9	167.4
2018	B	1.97	1.64	729.7	302.7	3,102.5	124.3
2017	B	1.17	0.98	645.5	193.3	2,542.9	126.3
2016	B	2.21	1.84	207.3	72.2	573.2	-8.4
2015	B+	1.75	1.46	90.9	26.0	286.4	-11.6

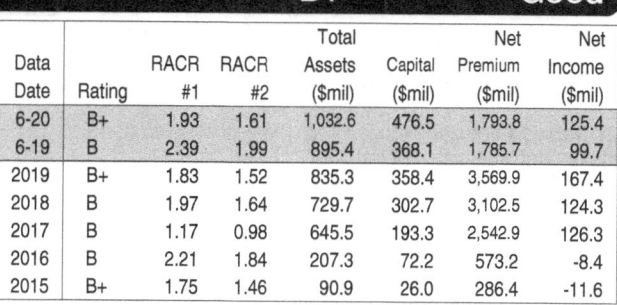

UNITED HEALTHCARE OF THE MIDWEST INC   C   Fair

Major Rating Factors: Fair quality investment portfolio (2.9 on a scale of 0 to 10). Weak liquidity (2.1) as a spike in claims may stretch capacity. Good overall results on stability tests (5.5).
Other Rating Factors: Excellent profitability (9.3). Strong capitalization index (9.0) based on excellent current risk-adjusted capital (severe loss scenario).
Principal Business: Medicaid (57%), Medicare (42%), comp med (2%)
Mem Phys: 19: 134,167   **18:** 126,438   **19 MLR** 162.9%   **/ 19 Admin Exp** N/A
Enroll(000): Q2 20: 369   **19:** 329   **18:** 318   **Med Exp PMPM:** $511
Principal Investments: Cash and equiv (58%), long-term bonds (42%)
Provider Compensation ($000): Contr fee ($1,530,334), capitation ($223,966), FFS ($200,755), bonus arrang ($2,733)
Total Member Encounters: Phys (2,478,332), non-phys (2,299,861)
Group Affiliation: None
Licensed in: IL, KS, MO
Address: 13655 RIVERPORT DRIVE MO050-10, MARYLAND HEIGHTS,
Phone: (314) 592-7000   **Dom State:** MO   **Commenced Bus:** N/A

Data Date	Rating	RACR #1	RACR #2	Total Assets ($mil)	Capital ($mil)	Net Premium ($mil)	Net Income ($mil)
6-20	C	2.92	2.43	589.7	258.0	758.4	56.8
6-19	C+	4.53	3.77	518.5	182.2	597.0	13.4
2019	C+	3.12	2.60	459.6	202.9	1,232.4	32.7
2018	C+	4.72	3.94	451.1	190.3	860.4	40.3
2017	C+	4.70	3.92	422.4	179.2	528.7	5.2
2016	C+	2.82	2.35	490.5	179.6	1,275.7	56.5
2015	C+	2.67	2.22	408.7	144.1	1,025.2	14.0

UNITED HEALTHCARE OF TX INC *   B+   Good

Major Rating Factors: Excellent profitability (8.2 on a scale of 0 to 10). Strong capitalization index (10.0) based on excellent current risk-adjusted capital (severe loss scenario). High quality investment portfolio (9.9).
Other Rating Factors: Excellent overall results on stability tests (7.0) based on healthy premium and capital growth during 2019. Excellent liquidity (7.5) with ample operational cash flow and liquid investments.
Principal Business: Comp med (100%)
Mem Phys: 19: 87,792   **18:** 84,979   **19 MLR** 80.9%   **/ 19 Admin Exp** N/A
Enroll(000): Q2 20: 46   **19:** 42   **18:** 27   **Med Exp PMPM:** $298
Principal Investments: Cash and equiv (100%)
Provider Compensation ($000): Contr fee ($107,727), FFS ($10,267), bonus arrang ($367), capitation ($84)
Total Member Encounters: Phys (221,696), non-phys (7,518)
Group Affiliation: None
Licensed in: TX
Address: 1311 W PRESIDENT GEORGE BUSH H, RICHARDSON,
Phone: (952) 936-1300   **Dom State:** TX   **Commenced Bus:** N/A

Data Date	Rating	RACR #1	RACR #2	Total Assets ($mil)	Capital ($mil)	Net Premium ($mil)	Net Income ($mil)
6-20	B+	7.06	5.88	95.9	44.0	110.6	14.8
6-19	B	13.43	11.19	73.2	28.8	69.8	6.8
2019	B+	8.07	6.72	76.0	30.2	155.5	8.3
2018	B	10.48	8.73	55.2	22.3	122.1	11.4
2017	B	2.44	2.03	47.7	18.7	112.1	12.6
2016	B-	2.18	1.82	30.9	7.7	80.2	5.4
2015	C	2.17	1.81	14.4	5.5	27.9	-1.1

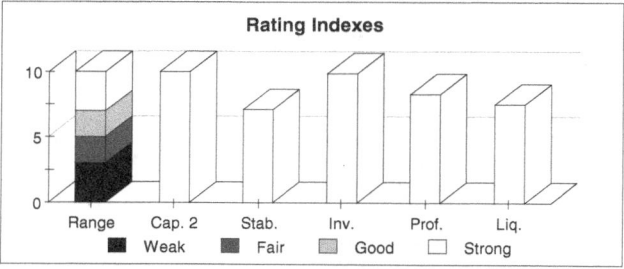

UNITED HEALTHCARE OF UTAH   B   Good

Major Rating Factors: Good capitalization index (6.9 on a scale of 0 to 10) based on excellent current risk-adjusted capital (severe loss scenario). Good liquidity (6.9) with sufficient resources (cash flows and marketable investments) to handle a spike in claims. Excellent profitability (8.1).
Other Rating Factors: High quality investment portfolio (9.0). Excellent overall results on stability tests (6.9).
Principal Business: Medicare (99%), comp med (1%)
Mem Phys: 19: 18,138   **18:** 17,905   **19 MLR** 87.0%   **/ 19 Admin Exp** N/A
Enroll(000): Q2 20: 91   **19:** 81   **18:** 80   **Med Exp PMPM:** $823
Principal Investments: Long-term bonds (94%), cash and equiv (6%)
Provider Compensation ($000): Capitation ($753,609), contr fee ($53,709), FFS ($30,762), bonus arrang ($1,957)
Total Member Encounters: Phys (1,306,880), non-phys (607,474)
Group Affiliation: None
Licensed in: UT
Address: 2525 LAKE PARK BOULEVARD, SALT LAKE CITY,
Phone: (952) 936-1300   **Dom State:** UT   **Commenced Bus:** N/A

Data Date	Rating	RACR #1	RACR #2	Total Assets ($mil)	Capital ($mil)	Net Premium ($mil)	Net Income ($mil)
6-20	B	1.24	1.03	166.8	86.6	531.9	0.1
6-19	B	2.51	2.09	224.1	94.7	457.0	17.3
2019	B	1.84	1.53	146.3	86.5	905.1	16.9
2018	B	2.04	1.70	181.8	78.1	810.8	15.4
2017	B	1.34	1.12	180.2	60.7	668.1	6.0
2016	B	2.68	2.24	121.8	55.0	514.7	3.5
2015	B-	3.55	2.96	110.1	59.9	443.6	31.4

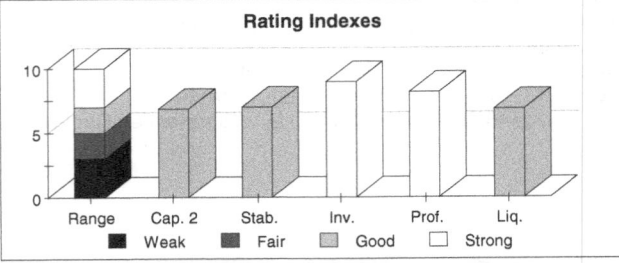

Rating Indexes

UNITED HEALTHCARE OF WISCONSIN INC *   B+   Good

Major Rating Factors: Good liquidity (6.9 on a scale of 0 to 10) with sufficient resources (cash flows and marketable investments) to handle a spike in claims. Excellent profitability (10.0). Strong capitalization index (9.6) based on excellent current risk-adjusted capital (severe loss scenario).
Other Rating Factors: High quality investment portfolio (9.5). Excellent overall results on stability tests (7.4).
Principal Business: Medicare (92%), Medicaid (6%), comp med (2%)
Mem Phys: 19: 257,626   **18:** 240,865   **19 MLR** 80.1%   **/ 19 Admin Exp** N/A
Enroll(000): Q2 20: 839   **19:** 723   **18:** 678   **Med Exp PMPM:** $682
Principal Investments: Long-term bonds (91%), cash and equiv (9%)
Provider Compensation ($000): Contr fee ($4,678,666), FFS ($517,604), capitation ($362,770), bonus arrang ($147,358)
Total Member Encounters: Phys (13,166,077), non-phys (6,042,136)
Group Affiliation: None
Licensed in: AZ, IL, IA, KY, NC, OH, TN, VA, WI
Address: WI030-1000 10701 WEST RESEARCH, WAUWATOSA,
Phone: (414) 443-4000   **Dom State:** WI   **Commenced Bus:** N/A

Data Date	Rating	RACR #1	RACR #2	Total Assets ($mil)	Capital ($mil)	Net Premium ($mil)	Net Income ($mil)
6-20	B+	3.47	2.89	2,701.9	1,253.8	4,324.5	439.1
6-19	B+	3.27	2.73	2,098.0	1,080.2	3,653.4	286.5
2019	B+	2.89	2.41	2,069.4	1,042.3	7,259.1	498.6
2018	B+	2.54	2.11	1,705.5	833.4	6,426.8	383.8
2017	B+	2.44	2.03	1,760.0	665.9	5,491.3	358.4
2016	B	2.26	1.89	1,223.8	452.6	4,484.3	199.9
2015	B	3.76	3.13	489.4	270.3	1,502.6	53.6

Rating Indexes

UNITED OF OMAHA LIFE INS CO   B   Good

Major Rating Factors: Good quality investment portfolio (5.1 on a scale of 0 to 10) despite large holdings of BBB rated bonds in addition to moderate junk bond exposure. Exposure to mortgages is significant, but the mortgage default rate has been low. Good liquidity (5.9) with sufficient resources to handle a spike in claims as well as a significant increase in policy surrenders. Good overall results on stability tests (6.0) despite excessive premium growth good operational trends and excellent risk diversification.
Other Rating Factors: Strong capitalization (7.3) based on excellent risk adjusted capital (severe loss scenario). Excellent profitability (7.4) with operating gains in each of the last five years.
Principal Business: Individual life insurance (33%), individual health insurance (18%), group retirement contracts (17%), group health insurance (15%), and other lines (17%).
Principal Investments: NonCMO investment grade bonds (57%), CMOs and structured securities (20%), mortgages in good standing (13%), noninv. grade bonds (2%), and misc. investments (3%).
Investments in Affiliates: 3%
Group Affiliation: Mutual Of Omaha Group
Licensed in: All states except NY
Commenced Business: November 1926
~~ress:~~ MUTUAL OF OMAHA PLAZA, OMAHA, NE 68175
~~ne:~~ (402) 342-7600   **Domicile State:** NE   **NAIC Code:** 69868

Data Date	Rating	RACR #1	RACR #2	Total Assets ($mil)	Capital ($mil)	Net Premium ($mil)	Net Income ($mil)
6-20	B	2.15	1.21	26,836.2	1,916.2	2,118.1	95.2
6-19	B	2.18	1.23	24,987.6	1,747.9	1,291.8	42.2
2019	B	2.08	1.18	26,246.4	1,761.9	3,717.4	136.2
2018	B	2.06	1.18	23,038.8	1,639.4	3,263.6	55.4
2017	B	2.00	1.14	22,803.2	1,605.7	4,024.6	61.7
2016	B	1.89	1.06	20,698.2	1,429.5	3,692.0	9.0
2015	B	1.90	1.11	19,622.5	1,441.7	3,572.3	153.6

Adverse Trends in Operations

Change in premium mix from 2017 to 2018 (7%)
Decrease in premium volume from 2017 to 2018 (19%)

UNITED WORLD LIFE INS CO *   B+   Good

Major Rating Factors: Good overall results on stability tests (5.4 on a scale of 0 to 10) despite negative cash flow from operations for 2019. Other stability subfactors include good operational trends and excellent risk diversification. Good overall profitability (5.2). Return on equity has been low, averaging 4.4%. Good liquidity (6.4).

Other Rating Factors: Strong capitalization (7.5) based on excellent risk adjusted capital (severe loss scenario). High quality investment portfolio (7.6).

Principal Business: Individual health insurance (100%).

Principal Investments: CMOs and structured securities (47%) and nonCMO investment grade bonds (45%).

Investments in Affiliates: None

Group Affiliation: Mutual Of Omaha Group

Licensed in: All states except CT, NY, PR

Commenced Business: April 1970

Address: MUTUAL OF OMAHA PLAZA, OMAHA, NE 68175

Phone: (402) 342-7600 **Domicile State:** NE **NAIC Code:** 72850

Data Date	Rating	RACR #1	RACR #2	Total Assets ($mil)	Capital ($mil)	Net Premium ($mil)	Net Income ($mil)
6-20	B+	3.25	1.35	141.0	49.7	0.4	1.3
6-19	B+	3.76	1.57	135.7	46.2	0.4	1.1
2019	B+	3.20	1.33	147.3	46.1	1.1	1.4
2018	B+	3.95	1.66	128.5	44.6	1.2	2.8
2017	B+	4.96	2.11	122.8	48.7	1.3	1.9
2016	B+	5.42	2.30	119.8	51.4	1.3	4.8
2015	B+	4.92	2.09	123.7	48.9	1.4	-0.5

Adverse Trends in Operations

Decrease in premium volume from 2018 to 2019 (8%)
Decrease in capital during 2018 (9%)
Decrease in capital during 2017 (5%)
Decrease in asset base during 2016 (3%)
Decrease in premium volume from 2015 to 2016 (5%)

UNITEDHEALTHCARE BENEFITS OF TEXAS   B   Good

Major Rating Factors: Good capitalization index (6.9 on a scale of 0 to 10) based on excellent current risk-adjusted capital (severe loss scenario). Good overall results on stability tests (6.9) based on steady enrollment growth, averaging 6% over the past five years. Good liquidity (6.8) with sufficient resources (cash flows and marketable investments) to handle a spike in claims.

Other Rating Factors: Excellent profitability (7.3). High quality investment portfolio (7.7).

Principal Business: Medicare (100%)

Mem Phys: 19: 97,582 **18:** 90,503 **19 MLR** 88.5% **/ 19 Admin Exp** N/A

Enroll(000): Q2 20: 288 **19:** 258 **18:** 248 **Med Exp PMPM:** $1,182

Principal Investments: Long-term bonds (71%), cash and equiv (28%)

Provider Compensation ($000): Capitation ($3,079,700), contr fee ($474,259), FFS ($51,089), bonus arrang ($31,386)

Total Member Encounters: Phys (3,443,457), non-phys (1,876,800)

Group Affiliation: None

Licensed in: TX

Address: 1311 W PRESIDENT GEORGE BUSH H, RICHARDSON,

Phone: (952) 979-7329 **Dom State:** TX **Commenced Bus:** N/A

Data Date	Rating	RACR #1	RACR #2	Total Assets ($mil)	Capital ($mil)	Net Premium ($mil)	Net Income ($mil)
6-20	B	1.27	1.06	663.6	300.9	2,385.7	-10.0
6-19	B	2.55	2.13	542.5	341.4	2,098.1	53.3
2019	B	1.76	1.47	518.7	312.5	4,108.0	97.7
2018	B	2.19	1.82	504.3	292.5	3,566.8	49.5
2017	B-	1.70	1.42	503.2	257.8	3,115.7	66.8
2016	B	2.28	1.90	403.3	226.9	2,727.3	35.8
2015	B	2.51	2.09	459.2	241.3	2,609.2	84.5

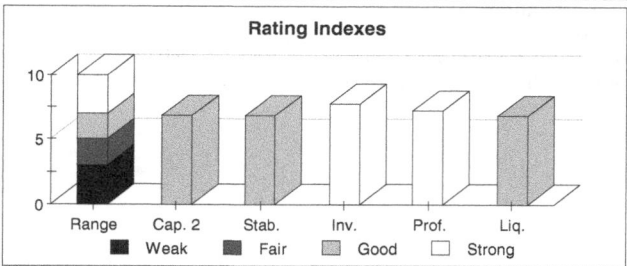

Rating Indexes

UNITEDHEALTHCARE COMMUNITY PLAN INC *   B+   Good

Major Rating Factors: Good overall results on stability tests (5.8 on a scale of 0 to 10). Excellent profitability (8.9). Strong capitalization index (7.9) based on excellent current risk-adjusted capital (severe loss scenario).

Other Rating Factors: High quality investment portfolio (9.4). Excellent liquidity (7.0) with ample operational cash flow and liquid investments.

Principal Business: Medicaid (96%), Medicare (3%)

Mem Phys: 19: 44,788 **18:** 41,468 **19 MLR** 78.6% **/ 19 Admin Exp** N/A

Enroll(000): Q2 20: 270 **19:** 254 **18:** 249 **Med Exp PMPM:** $243

Principal Investments: Cash and equiv (64%), long-term bonds (30%), other (5%)

Provider Compensation ($000): Contr fee ($431,647), FFS ($246,510), capitation ($33,939), bonus arrang ($5,315)

Total Member Encounters: Phys (2,033,896), non-phys (1,133,330)

Group Affiliation: None

Licensed in: MI

Address: 26957 NORTHWESTERN HIGHWAY SUI, SOUTHFIELD,

Phone: (248) 559-5656 **Dom State:** MI **Commenced Bus:** N/A

Data Date	Rating	RACR #1	RACR #2	Total Assets ($mil)	Capital ($mil)	Net Premium ($mil)	Net Income ($mil)
6-20	B+	2.10	1.75	336.3	153.7	476.0	21.7
6-19	B	3.16	2.63	270.5	151.4	466.0	19.5
2019	B+	2.67	2.23	290.3	139.0	941.0	33.5
2018	B	2.75	2.30	260.9	131.3	872.2	25.1
2017	B	1.58	1.32	257.2	124.8	1,064.1	18.5
2016	B	2.38	1.98	289.8	122.2	1,242.1	26.8
2015	B	1.89	1.58	282.9	95.8	1,232.2	44.2

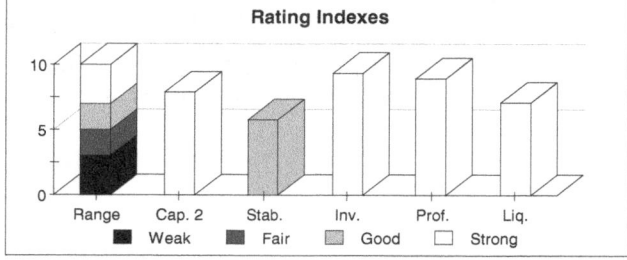

Rating Indexes

UNITEDHEALTHCARE COMMUNITY PLAN TX

B   Good

Major Rating Factors: Good overall profitability index (5.3 on a scale of 0 to 10). Good overall results on stability tests (6.8) based on steady enrollment growth, averaging 3% over the past five years. Good liquidity (6.6) with sufficient resources (cash flows and marketable investments) to handle a spike in claims.

Other Rating Factors: Strong capitalization index (7.0) based on excellent current risk-adjusted capital (severe loss scenario). High quality investment portfolio (9.4).

Principal Business: Medicaid (72%), Medicare (27%)

Mem Phys: 19: 84,567   **18:** 78,116   **19 MLR** 87.6%   **/ 19 Admin Exp** N/A

Enroll(000): Q2 20: 295   **19:** 274   **18:** 270   **Med Exp PMPM:** $749

Principal Investments: Long-term bonds (87%), cash and equiv (13%)

Provider Compensation ($000): Contr fee ($1,918,106), FFS ($525,875), capitation ($31,333), bonus arrang ($4,975)

Total Member Encounters: Phys (3,364,974), non-phys (4,110,900)

Group Affiliation: None

Licensed in: TX

Address: 14141 S W FREEWAY, SUGAR LAND,

Phone: (832) 500-6437   **Dom State:** TX   **Commenced Bus:** N/A

Data Date	Rating	RACR #1	RACR #2	Total Assets ($mil)	Capital ($mil)	Net Premium ($mil)	Net Income ($mil)
6-20	B	1.34	1.11	627.5	304.7	1,512.1	42.0
6-19	B-	1.35	1.12	561.3	217.7	1,384.4	13.8
2019	B	1.58	1.32	603.0	270.4	2,799.5	62.6
2018	B-	1.21	1.01	559.0	194.6	2,567.2	-18.2
2017	B	1.00	0.83	558.6	186.8	2,303.2	-39.7
2016	B+	1.72	1.43	549.9	220.1	2,369.4	33.8
2015	B+	2.25	1.88	571.4	229.7	2,072.5	73.4

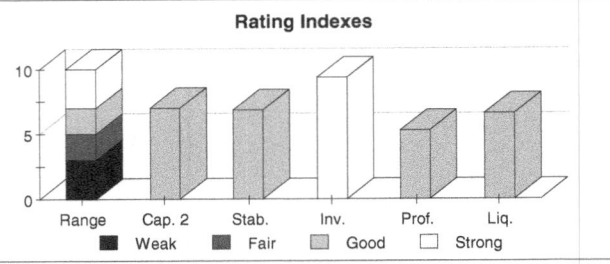

Rating Indexes

UNITEDHEALTHCARE COMMUNITYPLAN OHIO *

B+   Good

Major Rating Factors: Good quality investment portfolio (6.7 on a scale of 0 to 10). Good liquidity (6.9) with sufficient resources (cash flows and marketable investments) to handle a spike in claims. Excellent profitability (8.6).

Other Rating Factors: Strong capitalization (7.8) based on excellent current risk-adjusted capital (severe loss scenario).

Principal Business: Medicaid (100%)

Mem Phys: 19: 75,680   **18:** 64,894   **19 MLR** 86.7%   **/ 19 Admin Exp** N/A

Enroll(000): Q2 20: 347   **19:** 308   **18:** 304   **Med Exp PMPM:** $620

Principal Investments: Long-term bonds (77%), cash and equiv (23%)

Provider Compensation ($000): Contr fee ($1,437,094), FFS ($549,281), capitation ($271,688), bonus arrang ($3,550)

Total Member Encounters: Phys (3,677,616), non-phys (2,337,921)

Group Affiliation: None

Licensed in: OH

Address: 5900 PARKWOOD PLACE, DUBLIN, OH 43016

Phone: (952) 931-4014   **Dom State:** OH   **Commenced Bus:** N/A

Data Date	Rating	RACR #1	RACR #2	Total Assets ($mil)	Capital ($mil)	Net Premium ($mil)	Net Income ($mil)
6-20	B+	2.03	1.69	739.4	393.9	1,567.0	79.4
6-19	B	2.11	1.75	491.1	271.7	1,242.3	-37.0
2019	B+	2.37	1.97	635.0	355.9	2,638.5	42.8
2018	B	2.77	2.31	576.7	362.8	2,510.5	124.7
2017	B	N/A	N/A	494.6	273.1	2,231.8	78.8
2016	B	2.14	1.78	449.4	219.7	2,059.4	22.9
2015	B	2.27	1.89	430.3	226.9	2,145.2	120.5

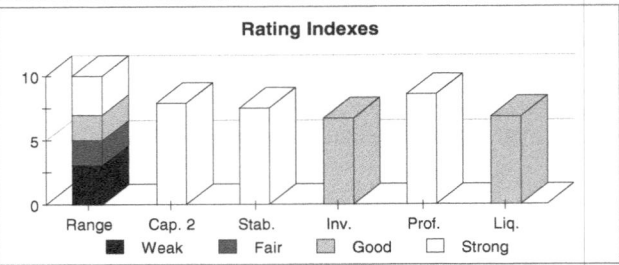

Rating Indexes

UNITEDHEALTHCARE INS CO RIVER VALLEY

B   Good

Major Rating Factors: Good liquidity (6.8 on a scale of 0 to 10) with sufficient resources (cash flows and marketable investments) to handle a spike in claims. Excellent profitability (7.1). Strong capitalization (8.1) based on excellent current risk-adjusted capital (severe loss scenario).

Other Rating Factors: High quality investment portfolio (9.9).

Principal Business: Comp med (56%), Medicare (44%)

Mem Phys: 19: 401,335   **18:** 364,451   **19 MLR** 81.9%   **/ 19 Admin Exp** N/A

Enroll(000): Q2 20: 281   **19:** 249   **18:** 238   **Med Exp PMPM:** $502

Principal Investments: Long-term bonds (83%), cash and equiv (17%)

Provider Compensation ($000): Contr fee ($1,249,830), FFS ($203,726), capitation ($47,962), bonus arrang ($3,683)

Total Member Encounters: Phys (3,124,265), non-phys (799,740)

Group Affiliation: None

Licensed in: AR, GA, IL, IA, KS, KY, LA, MS, MO, NJ, NC, OH, OK, SC, TN, TX, VA

Address: 1 KONE COURT 101 17TH STREET, MOLINE, IL 61265

Phone: (309) 736-4600   **Dom State:** IL   **Commenced Bus:** N/A

Data Date	Rating	RACR #1	RACR #2	Total Assets ($mil)	Capital ($mil)	Net Premium ($mil)	Net Income ($mil)
6-20	B	2.24	1.87	736.8	309.5	1,237.5	126.7
6-19	B	2.51	2.09	469.8	195.9	900.9	57.7
2019	B	1.88	1.56	504.7	192.7	1,848.2	69.5
2018	B	1.85	1.54	395.1	142.5	1,395.6	35.2
2017	B	1.47	1.22	276.3	108.7	974.5	14.2
2016	B	1.97	1.64	261.9	92.1	896.7	0.8
2015	B	2.36	1.97	219.5	93.1	722.6	-12.2

Rating Indexes

UNITEDHEALTHCARE INSURANCE COMPANY O   E+   Very Weak

Major Rating Factors: Fair profitability index (4.6 on a scale of 0 to 10). Strong capitalization (10.0) based on excellent current risk-adjusted capital (severe loss scenario). High quality investment portfolio (9.9).
Other Rating Factors: Excellent liquidity (7.3) with ample operational cash flow and liquid investments.
Principal Business: Medicare (100%)
Mem Phys: 19: 957,713 18: 32,252 **19 MLR** 83.3% / **19 Admin Exp** N/A
Enroll(000): Q2 20: 68 19: 37 18: 740 **Med Exp PMPM:** $1,115
Principal Investments: Cash and equiv (97%), long-term bonds (3%)
Provider Compensation ($000): Capitation ($38,982), bonus arrang ($30,470), contr fee ($17,606)
Total Member Encounters: Phys (753,811), non-phys (392,747)
Group Affiliation: None
Licensed in: All states except NY, PR
Address: 1600 MCCONNOR PARKWAY 2ND FL, SCHAUMBURG, IL 60173
Phone: (224) 231-1451 **Dom State:** IL **Commenced Bus:** N/A

Data Date	Rating	RACR #1	RACR #2	Total Assets ($mil)	Capital ($mil)	Net Premium ($mil)	Net Income ($mil)
6-20	E+	5.04	4.20	362.3	189.1	533.9	82.7
6-19	E+	5.82	4.85	191.1	123.2	199.0	15.7
2019	E+	4.03	3.36	203.1	108.7	479.8	21.3
2018	E+	4.95	4.13	338.0	104.9	541.5	-17.7
2017	E+	N/A	N/A	357.7	67.0	474.2	-54.3
2016	C	4.96	4.13	531.6	59.1	357.9	-38.8
2015	D-	1.23	1.03	228.3	22.6	173.0	-1.8

Rating Indexes

Range, Cap. 2, Stab., Inv., Prof., Liq.
Weak · Fair · Good · Strong

UNITEDHEALTHCARE LIFE INS CO   C   Fair

Major Rating Factors: Fair profitability (3.3 on a scale of 0 to 10). Excellent expense controls. Return on equity has been low, averaging -13.4%. Fair overall results on stability tests (4.3). Good liquidity (6.4) with sufficient resources to handle a spike in claims.
Other Rating Factors: Strong capitalization (8.4) based on excellent risk adjusted capital (severe loss scenario). High quality investment portfolio (8.0).
Principal Business: Group health insurance (97%) and individual health insurance (3%).
Principal Investments: NonCMO investment grade bonds (74%) and CMOs and structured securities (25%).
Investments in Affiliates: None
Group Affiliation: UnitedHealth Group Inc
Licensed in: All states except MA, NY, PR
Commenced Business: December 1982
Address: 3100 AMS BOULEVARD, GREEN BAY, WI 54313
Phone: (800) 232-5432 **Domicile State:** WI **NAIC Code:** 97179

Data Date	Rating	RACR #1	RACR #2	Total Assets ($mil)	Capital ($mil)	Net Premium ($mil)	Net Income ($mil)
2019	C	2.42	1.93	239.3	136.6	0.0	14.3
2018	C	2.76	2.18	241.2	158.9	471.7	15.6
2017	C	2.68	2.12	224.2	142.9	435.6	32.1
2016	C	1.44	1.14	508.1	167.5	960.8	-9.0
2015	C	1.61	1.28	488.4	137.1	700.9	-143.0

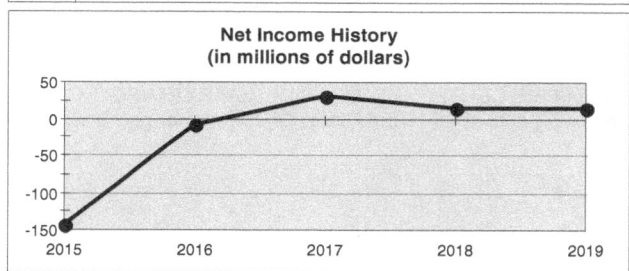

Net Income History
(in millions of dollars)

2015, 2016, 2017, 2018, 2019

UNITEDHEALTHCARE OF NEW MEXICO INC   C   Fair

Major Rating Factors: Excellent profitability (8.2 on a scale of 0 to 10). Strong capitalization (10.0) based on excellent current risk-adjusted capital (severe loss scenario). High quality investment portfolio (8.7).
Other Rating Factors: Excellent liquidity (9.1) with ample operational cash flow and liquid investments.
Principal Business: Medicare (79%), Medicaid (21%)
Mem Phys: 19: 7,382 18: 12,227 **19 MLR** 55.9% / **19 Admin Exp** N/A
Enroll(000): Q2 20: 8 19: 6 18: 2 **Med Exp PMPM:** $516
Principal Investments: Cash and equiv (85%), long-term bonds (15%)
Provider Compensation ($000): Contr fee ($18,298), FFS ($7,866), capitation ($2,014), bonus arrang ($859)
Total Member Encounters: Phys (67,079), non-phys (36,930)
Group Affiliation: None
Licensed in: NM
Address: 8801 HORIZON BOULEVARD N E S, ALBUQUERQUE, NM 87113
Phone: (505) 449-4131 **Dom State:** NM **Commenced Bus:** N/A

Data Date	Rating	RACR #1	RACR #2	Total Assets ($mil)	Capital ($mil)	Net Premium ($mil)	Net Income ($mil)
6-20	C	48.03	40.02	162.9	143.0	34.7	6.7
6-19	C+	7.83	6.53	174.5	126.8	18.9	5.5
2019	C+	64.42	53.68	158.0	135.7	52.0	11.4
2018	C+	9.76	8.13	238.0	161.0	543.6	52.9
2017	E	2.82	2.35	263.8	121.3	790.0	11.0
2016	E	20.02	16.69	355.2	136.0	865.4	34.4
2015	E	9.31	7.75	362.6	126.2	918.9	14.9

Rating Indexes

Range, Cap. 2, Stab., Inv., Prof., Liq.
Weak · Fair · Good · Strong

UNITEDHEALTHCARE OF OKLAHOMA INC   B   Good

Major Rating Factors: Excellent profitability (10.0 on a scale of 0 to 10). Strong capitalization index (8.7) based on excellent current risk-adjusted capital (severe loss scenario). High quality investment portfolio (9.9).
Other Rating Factors: Excellent overall results on stability tests (8.3). Excellent liquidity (7.0) with sufficient resources (cash flows and marketable investments) to handle a spike in claims
Principal Business: Medicare (79%), comp med (21%)
Mem Phys: 19: 15,024 **18:** 14,041 **19 MLR** 80.3% **/ 19 Admin Exp** N/A
Enroll(000): Q2 20: 49 **19:** 50 **18:** 52 **Med Exp PMPM:** $695
Principal Investments: Long-term bonds (73%), cash and equiv (27%)
Provider Compensation ($000): Contr fee ($397,161), FFS ($13,994), capitation ($8,735), bonus arrang ($3,468)
Total Member Encounters: Phys (840,114), non-phys (166,779)
Group Affiliation: None
Licensed in: OK
Address: 7666 E 61ST STREET SUITE 500, TULSA,
Phone: (512) 347-2600 **Dom State:** OK **Commenced Bus:** N/A

Data Date	Rating	RACR #1	RACR #2	Total Assets ($mil)	Capital ($mil)	Net Premium ($mil)	Net Income ($mil)
6-20	B	2.75	2.29	186.8	92.9	261.0	30.2
6-19	B	3.19	2.66	149.6	87.4	270.8	24.7
2019	B	3.42	2.85	146.0	78.8	524.8	41.9
2018	B	2.32	1.93	117.0	62.7	490.1	26.9
2017	B	1.63	1.36	122.3	58.3	425.3	32.9
2016	B	1.91	1.59	106.7	42.9	401.5	6.6
2015	B-	2.21	1.84	106.5	41.2	353.5	2.1

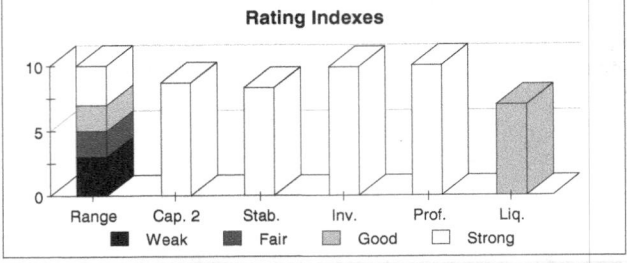

Rating Indexes

UNITEDHEALTHCARE OF OREGON *   B+   Good

Major Rating Factors: Good overall results on stability tests (6.9 on a scale of 0 to 10). Excellent profitability (9.6). Strong capitalization index (8.8) based on excellent current risk-adjusted capital (severe loss scenario).
Other Rating Factors: High quality investment portfolio (8.2). Excellent liquidity (6.9) with sufficient resources (cash flows and marketable investments) to handle a spike in claims.
Principal Business: Medicare (100%)
Mem Phys: 19: 60,664 **18:** 57,039 **19 MLR** 80.4% **/ 19 Admin Exp** N/A
Enroll(000): Q2 20: 176 **19:** 141 **18:** 133 **Med Exp PMPM:** $769
Principal Investments: Long-term bonds (89%), cash and equiv (11%)
Provider Compensation ($000): Contr fee ($1,035,076), capitation ($166,356), FFS ($46,731), bonus arrang ($27,279)
Total Member Encounters: Phys (2,372,200), non-phys (467,643)
Group Affiliation: None
Licensed in: OR, WA
Address: FIVE CENTERPOINTE DRIVE, LAKE OSWEGO,
Phone: (952) 936-1300 **Dom State:** OR **Commenced Bus:** N/A

Data Date	Rating	RACR #1	RACR #2	Total Assets ($mil)	Capital ($mil)	Net Premium ($mil)	Net Income ($mil)
6-20	B+	2.79	2.33	645.9	293.1	1,023.8	91.5
6-19	B+	3.42	2.85	479.3	254.8	798.1	53.5
2019	B+	3.34	2.79	479.1	261.7	1,603.4	102.6
2018	B+	2.73	2.28	402.3	202.4	1,410.5	56.2
2017	B+	1.71	1.43	371.7	149.2	1,233.7	19.9
2016	B	2.22	1.85	260.1	107.4	975.1	4.1
2015	B-	7.21	6.01	126.9	89.1	256.0	8.4

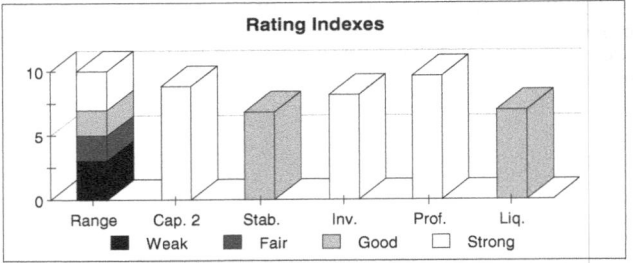

Rating Indexes

UNITEDHEALTHCARE OF PENNSYLVANIA INC   B   Good

Major Rating Factors: Good overall results on stability tests (6.9 on a scale of 0 to 10). Excellent profitability (8.4). Strong capitalization index (10.0) based on excellent current risk-adjusted capital (severe loss scenario).
Other Rating Factors: High quality investment portfolio (7.6). Excellent liquidity (7.0) with ample operational cash flow and liquid investments.
Principal Business: Medicaid (93%), comp med (7%)
Mem Phys: 19: 68,102 **18:** 47,685 **19 MLR** 81.6% **/ 19 Admin Exp** N/A
Enroll(000): Q2 20: 277 **19:** 257 **18:** 258 **Med Exp PMPM:** $316
Principal Investments: Long-term bonds (71%), cash and equiv (29%)
Provider Compensation ($000): Contr fee ($671,806), FFS ($290,970), capitation ($16,765), bonus arrang ($406)
Total Member Encounters: Phys (1,792,096), non-phys (1,000,493)
Group Affiliation: None
Licensed in: PA
Address: 1001 BRINTON ROAD, PITTSBURGH,
Phone: (412) 858-4000 **Dom State:** PA **Commenced Bus:** N/A

Data Date	Rating	RACR #1	RACR #2	Total Assets ($mil)	Capital ($mil)	Net Premium ($mil)	Net Income ($mil)
6-20	B	4.01	3.34	644.4	239.0	649.3	19.4
6-19	B	4.37	3.64	592.7	192.7	597.0	2.8
2019	B	5.02	4.19	455.0	219.2	1,204.3	28.7
2018	B	4.33	3.61	400.6	190.6	1,241.1	45.2
2017	B	3.41	2.84	411.9	199.6	1,239.9	57.4
2016	B	7.66	6.39	525.8	173.0	1,347.1	30.5
2015	B	2.51	2.09	428.2	143.0	1,123.0	8.8

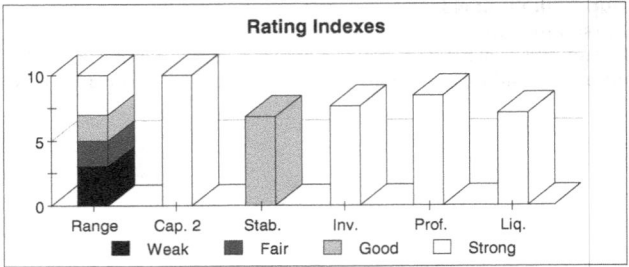

Rating Indexes

UNITEDHEALTHCARE OF WASHINGTON INC | B | Good

Major Rating Factors: Good liquidity (6.9 on a scale of 0 to 10) with sufficient resources (cash flows and marketable investments) to handle a spike in claims. Excellent profitability (7.3). Strong capitalization (8.7) based on excellent current risk-adjusted capital (severe loss scenario).
Other Rating Factors: High quality investment portfolio (9.0).
Principal Business: Medicaid (70%), comp med (30%)
Mem Phys: 19: 47,218 **18:** 41,364 **19 MLR** 84.8% **/ 19 Admin Exp** N/A
Enroll(000): Q2 20: 253 **19:** 231 **18:** 252 **Med Exp PMPM:** $264
Principal Investments: Long-term bonds (71%), cash and equiv (29%)
Provider Compensation ($000): Contr fee ($570,691), capitation ($139,091), FFS ($35,368), bonus arrang ($3,962)
Total Member Encounters: Phys (1,669,395), non-phys (542,062)
Group Affiliation: None
Licensed in: WA
Address: 1111 3RD AVENUE SUITE 1100, SEATTLE, WA 98101
Phone: (952) 936-1300 **Dom State:** WA **Commenced Bus:** N/A

Data Date	Rating	RACR #1	RACR #2	Total Assets ($mil)	Capital ($mil)	Net Premium ($mil)	Net Income ($mil)
6-20	B	2.70	2.25	318.9	168.4	492.3	14.8
6-19	B	3.72	3.10	315.4	185.9	426.3	35.5
2019	B	3.52	2.94	323.3	157.0	864.8	19.3
2018	C+	3.07	2.56	287.2	152.1	923.2	17.2
2017	C	N/A	N/A	358.3	144.1	1,076.8	10.8
2016	C	2.68	2.23	358.1	140.7	1,027.2	16.3
2015	B	3.14	2.62	480.4	222.4	1,428.2	15.0

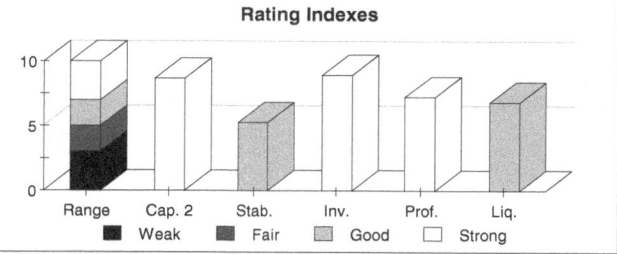

UNITEDHEALTHCARE PLAN RIVER VALLEY | B | Good

Major Rating Factors: Good overall results on stability tests (5.2 on a scale of 0 to 10). Good liquidity (6.9) with sufficient resources (cash flows and marketable investments) to handle a spike in claims. Excellent profitability (7.5).
Other Rating Factors: Strong capitalization index (8.0) based on excellent current risk-adjusted capital (severe loss scenario). High quality investment portfolio (9.1).
Principal Business: Medicaid (73%), Medicare (23%), comp med (3%)
Mem Phys: 19: 134,073 **18:** 135,644 **19 MLR** 84.5% **/ 19 Admin Exp** N/A
Enroll(000): Q2 20: 519 **19:** 509 **18:** 937 **Med Exp PMPM:** $462
Principal Investments: Long-term bonds (84%), cash and equiv (14%), other (1%)
Provider Compensation ($000): Contr fee ($3,787,462), FFS ($336,006), capitation ($110,527), bonus arrang ($22,135)
Total Member Encounters: Phys (7,273,297), non-phys (4,308,745)
Group Affiliation: None
Licensed in: IL, IA, TN, VA
Address: 1300 RIVER DRIVE SUITE 200, MOLINE,
Phone: (309) 736-4600 **Dom State:** IL **Commenced Bus:** N/A

Data Date	Rating	RACR #1	RACR #2	Total Assets ($mil)	Capital ($mil)	Net Premium ($mil)	Net Income ($mil)
6-20	B	2.16	1.80	1,216.8	652.9	1,674.2	139.1
6-19	B	1.34	1.12	1,363.4	449.0	3,059.6	-4.5
2019	B	2.38	1.98	1,110.2	615.9	4,701.0	157.6
2018	B	1.38	1.15	1,274.7	463.0	6,121.5	-30.0
2017	B	1.92	1.60	1,243.6	446.3	4,007.7	66.1
2016	B	2.61	2.17	1,063.1	434.3	3,591.4	126.0
2015	B-	2.79	2.33	1,131.1	423.3	3,404.1	62.5

UNIVERSAL CARE | E | Very Weak

Major Rating Factors: Weak profitability index (0.9 on a scale of 0 to 10). Weak liquidity (1.5) as a spike in claims may stretch capacity. Fair capitalization index (4.1) based on weak current risk-adjusted capital (moderate loss scenario).
Other Rating Factors: Fair overall results on stability tests (3.1).
Principal Business: Medicare (101%)
Mem Phys: 19: N/A **18:** N/A **19 MLR** 87.7% **/ 19 Admin Exp** N/A
Enroll(000): Q2 20: 0 **19:** 36 **18:** 36 **Med Exp PMPM:** $1,141
Principal Investments ($000): Cash and equiv ($33,889)
Provider Compensation ($000): None
Total Member Encounters: N/A
Group Affiliation: None
Licensed in: CA
Address: 5701 Katella Ave MS CA120-0368, Cypress, CA 90630
Phone: (916) 451-1592 **Dom State:** CA **Commenced Bus:** November 1985

Data Date	Rating	RACR #1	RACR #2	Total Assets ($mil)	Capital ($mil)	Net Premium ($mil)	Net Income ($mil)
6-20	E	0.66	0.42	119.8	25.1	305.0	-31.9
6-19	E-	N/A	N/A	132.9	-9.4	244.7	7.8
2019	E-	N/A	N/A	140.9	-19.8	500.2	-2.6
2018	E-	N/A	N/A	97.8	-17.2	327.6	-11.5
2017	E-	N/A	N/A	58.8	-5.6	188.4	-4.8
2016	E-	N/A	N/A	52.9	-4.6	142.0	-1.6
2015	E-	N/A	N/A	30.4	-13.7	95.3	-3.2

UNIVERSITY HEALTH ALLIANCE

B   **Good**

Major Rating Factors: Fair quality investment portfolio (4.2 on a scale of 0 to 10). Excellent profitability (8.5). Strong capitalization (9.3) based on excellent current risk-adjusted capital (severe loss scenario).
Other Rating Factors: Excellent liquidity (7.1) with ample operational cash flow and liquid investments.
Principal Business: Comp med (81%), dental (2%), other (16%)
Mem Phys: 19: 4,025 **18:** 3,900 **19 MLR** 81.0% **/ 19 Admin Exp** N/A
Enroll(000): Q2 20: 59 **19:** 61 **18:** 62 **Med Exp PMPM:** $368
Principal Investments: Nonaffiliate common stock (58%), cash and equiv (37%), long-term bonds (5%)
Provider Compensation ($000): FFS ($195,032), contr fee ($60,423), capitation ($5,796), bonus arrang ($719)
Total Member Encounters: Phys (372,598), non-phys (191,772)
Group Affiliation: None
Licensed in: HI
Address: 700 BISHOP ST SUITE 300, HONOLULU, HI 96813
Phone: (808) 532-2019 **Dom State:** HI **Commenced Bus:** N/A

Data Date	Rating	RACR #1	RACR #2	Total Assets ($mil)	Capital ($mil)	Net Premium ($mil)	Net Income ($mil)
6-20	B	3.21	2.67	200.4	125.4	158.8	10.4
6-19	N/A	N/A	N/A	N/A	N/A	N/A	N/A
2019	B	3.20	2.67	184.3	125.3	333.5	24.6
2018	C+	2.27	1.89	137.8	87.0	327.9	28.7
2017	C+	1.94	1.62	115.9	67.8	287.0	18.6
2016	C+	1.40	1.17	96.5	50.1	272.7	3.6
2015	C+	1.43	1.19	83.6	46.3	240.8	-0.9

Rating Indexes

UNIVERSITY HEALTH CARE INC

D-   **Weak**

Major Rating Factors: Weak profitability index (1.8 on a scale of 0 to 10). Poor capitalization index (0.0) based on weak current risk-adjusted capital (severe loss scenario). Weak overall results on stability tests (0.0).
Other Rating Factors: Weak liquidity (0.0) as a spike in claims may stretch capacity. High quality investment portfolio (9.9).
Principal Business: Medicaid (98%), Medicare (2%)
Mem Phys: 19: 32,388 **18:** 27,234 **19 MLR** 95.0% **/ 19 Admin Exp** N/A
Enroll(000): Q2 20: N/A **19:** 311 **18:** 320 **Med Exp PMPM:** $487
Principal Investments: Cash and equiv (153%), nonaffiliate common stock (2%)
Provider Compensation ($000): Contr fee ($1,470,942), capitation ($339,995), FFS ($45,153)
Total Member Encounters: Phys (2,650,284), non-phys (2,611,524)
Group Affiliation: University of Louisville Physicians
Licensed in: KY
Address: 5100 Commerce Crossings Drive, Louisville,
Phone: (502) 585-7900 **Dom State:** KY **Commenced Bus:** N/A

Data Date	Rating	RACR #1	RACR #2	Total Assets ($mil)	Capital ($mil)	Net Premium ($mil)	Net Income ($mil)
6-20	D-	0.13	0.11	16.2	8.8	0.6	2.5
6-19	N/A	N/A	N/A	N/A	N/A	N/A	N/A
2019	D-	0.10	0.08	13.2	4.2	1,943.3	5.2
2018	D+	0.72	0.60	363.6	69.7	1,945.9	-122.6
2017	B	1.46	1.22	454.4	213.4	1,925.0	17.1
2016	B	1.37	1.15	414.6	196.8	1,747.8	-57.9
2015	B+	1.94	1.62	444.2	249.9	1,653.1	39.1

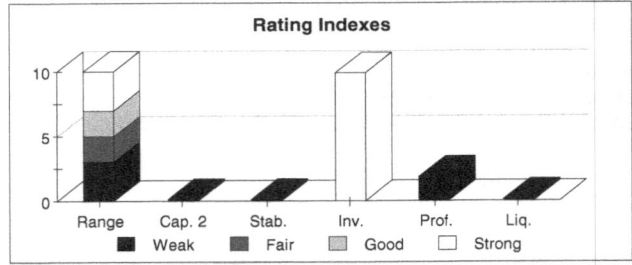

Rating Indexes

UNIVERSITY OF UTAH HEALTH INS PLANS

B-   **Good**

Major Rating Factors: Fair quality investment portfolio (4.8 on a scale of 0 to 10). Good overall profitability index (6.7). Strong capitalization (10.0) based on excellent current risk-adjusted capital (severe loss scenario).
Other Rating Factors: Excellent liquidity (7.6) with ample operational cash flow and liquid investments.
Principal Business: Comp med (100%)
Mem Phys: 18: 37,492 **17:** 16,463 **18 MLR** 74.5% **/ 18 Admin Exp** N/A
Enroll(000): Q3 19: 28 **18:** 30 **17:** 10 **Med Exp PMPM:** $385
Principal Investments: Long-term bonds (50%), cash and equiv (39%), pref stock (10%)
Provider Compensation ($000): Contr fee ($121,012), FFS ($3,904)
Total Member Encounters: Phys (151,451), non-phys (111,461)
Group Affiliation: None
Licensed in: UT
Address: 6053 Fashion Square Drive Sui, Murray, UT 84107
Phone: (801) 587-6480 **Dom State:** UT **Commenced Bus:** N/A

Data Date	Rating	RACR #1	RACR #2	Total Assets ($mil)	Capital ($mil)	Net Premium ($mil)	Net Income ($mil)
9-19	B-	3.64	3.03	119.1	58.0	141.5	13.1
9-18	D+	N/A	N/A	81.5	32.4	122.3	12.1
2018	C	2.69	2.24	110.6	44.1	181.1	24.3
2017	D+	N/A	N/A	35.8	20.5	51.1	1.8
2016	D+	2.22	1.85	17.1	10.6	19.1	-4.2
2015	N/A	N/A	N/A	4.8	3.8	N/A	-1.2
2014	N/A	N/A	N/A	2.0	2.0	N/A	N/A

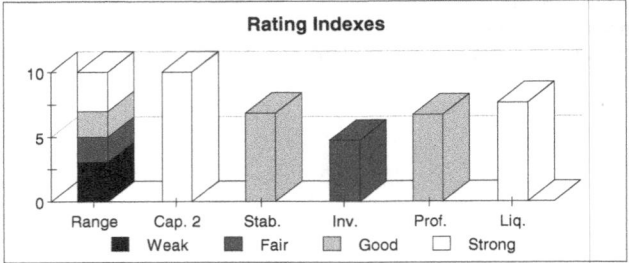

Rating Indexes

UNUM INS CO   C   Fair

Major Rating Factors: Fair overall results on stability tests (3.8 on a scale of 0 to 10). Weak profitability (2.1) with investment income below regulatory standards in relation to interest assumptions of reserves. Strong overall capitalization (10.0) based on excellent risk adjusted capital (severe loss scenario). However, capital levels have fluctuated somewhat during past years.
Other Rating Factors: High quality investment portfolio (7.1). Excellent liquidity (7.0).
Principal Business: Group health insurance (91%) and individual life insurance (9%).
Principal Investments: NonCMO investment grade bonds (80%), CMOs and structured securities (17%), and cash (1%).
Investments in Affiliates: None
Group Affiliation: Unum Group
Licensed in: All states except NY, PR
Commenced Business: February 1966
Address: 2211 CONGRESS STREET, PORTLAND, ME 4122
Phone: (423) 294-1011 **Domicile State:** ME **NAIC Code:** 67601

Data Date	Rating	RACR #1	RACR #2	Total Assets ($mil)	Capital ($mil)	Net Premium ($mil)	Net Income ($mil)
6-20	C	4.91	3.03	75.2	48.1	22.6	1.0
6-19	C	6.87	3.84	65.6	46.6	9.9	0.1
2019	C	6.06	3.55	67.3	47.3	21.5	1.0
2018	C	6.92	4.51	62.8	46.9	4.8	1.2
2017	C	6.93	4.58	60.0	46.1	0.0	1.9
2016	C	6.79	4.45	59.5	45.0	0.0	1.8
2015	C	6.71	4.19	57.0	43.7	0.0	2.5

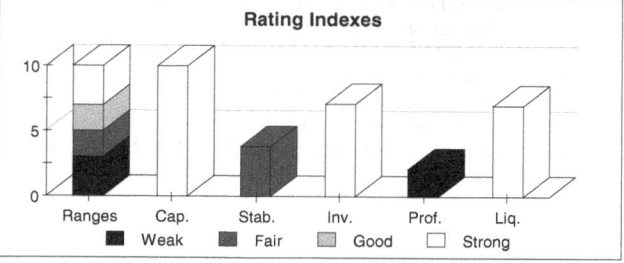

Rating Indexes

UNUM LIFE INS CO OF AMERICA   C+   Fair

Major Rating Factors: Fair quality investment portfolio (3.6 on a scale of 0 to 10) with large holdings of BBB rated bonds in addition to significant exposure to junk bonds. Fair overall results on stability tests (4.8). Strong overall capitalization (7.2) based on excellent risk adjusted capital (severe loss scenario). However, capital levels have fluctuated somewhat during past years.
Other Rating Factors: Excellent profitability (7.3) with operating gains in each of the last five years. Excellent liquidity (7.4).
Principal Business: Group health insurance (63%), group life insurance (30%), individual health insurance (5%), and reinsurance (1%).
Principal Investments: NonCMO investment grade bonds (75%), noninv. grade bonds (11%), mortgages in good standing (6%), and CMOs and structured securities (4%).
Investments in Affiliates: None
Group Affiliation: Unum Group
Licensed in: All states except NY
Commenced Business: September 1966
Address: 2211 CONGRESS STREET, PORTLAND, ME 4122
Phone: (207) 575-2211 **Domicile State:** ME **NAIC Code:** 62235

Data Date	Rating	RACR #1	RACR #2	Total Assets ($mil)	Capital ($mil)	Net Premium ($mil)	Net Income ($mil)
6-20	C+	2.13	1.12	22,729.7	1,715.8	1,819.5	264.6
6-19	C+	2.27	1.20	22,044.6	1,737.2	1,867.8	238.2
2019	C+	2.29	1.22	22,429.8	1,765.8	3,755.0	454.8
2018	C+	2.41	1.28	22,022.4	1,834.2	3,616.2	493.2
2017	C+	2.35	1.24	21,455.0	1,728.0	3,486.2	378.2
2016	C+	2.33	1.23	21,077.8	1,686.5	3,348.0	349.3
2015	C+	2.28	1.22	20,552.3	1,567.3	3,168.1	203.5

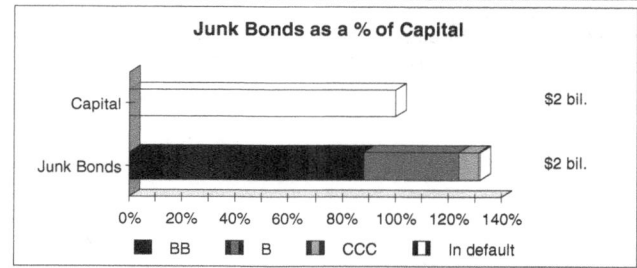

Junk Bonds as a % of Capital

UPMC FOR YOU INC *   B+   Good

Major Rating Factors: Good quality investment portfolio (6.6 on a scale of 0 to 10). Good liquidity (6.9) with sufficient resources (cash flows and marketable investments) to handle a spike in claims. Excellent profitability (7.9).
Other Rating Factors: Strong capitalization (8.0) based on excellent current risk-adjusted capital (severe loss scenario).
Principal Business: Medicaid (88%), Medicare (12%)
Mem Phys: 19: 42,788 **18:** 33,093 **19 MLR** 89.8% **/ 19 Admin Exp** N/A
Enroll(000): Q2 20: 617 **19:** 520 **18:** 491 **Med Exp PMPM:** $670
Principal Investments: Long-term bonds (69%), cash and equiv (5%), other (26%)
Provider Compensation ($000): Contr fee ($3,838,360), capitation ($321,978)
Total Member Encounters: Phys (4,494,132), non-phys (6,643,005)
Group Affiliation: None
Licensed in: PA
Address: 600 Grant Street, Pittsburgh, PA 15219
Phone: (412) 434-1200 **Dom State:** PA **Commenced Bus:** N/A

Data Date	Rating	RACR #1	RACR #2	Total Assets ($mil)	Capital ($mil)	Net Premium ($mil)	Net Income ($mil)
6-20	B+	2.13	1.78	1,528.6	646.1	3,061.9	132.5
6-19	B+	2.03	1.69	1,265.5	445.5	2,327.7	28.9
2019	B+	1.99	1.66	988.4	515.9	4,670.7	56.7
2018	B+	1.89	1.57	810.4	413.9	3,603.0	36.8
2017	B+	2.12	1.77	668.5	425.4	2,650.0	72.7
2016	B+	2.49	2.07	750.6	351.4	2,383.2	105.6
2015	B	1.64	1.37	527.8	247.6	2,061.8	66.4

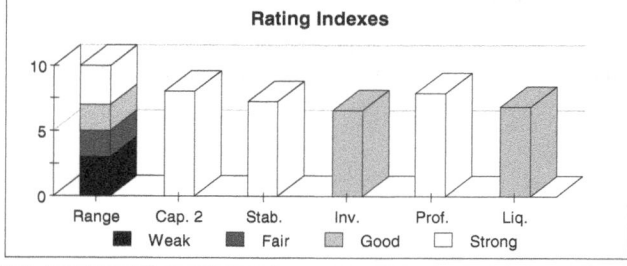

Rating Indexes

UPMC HEALTH BENEFITS INC　　　　　　　　　　　C　　　Fair

Major Rating Factors: Fair long-term capitalization index (3.5 on a scale of 0 to 10) based on fair current risk adjusted capital (severe loss scenario). Fair reserve development (3.7) as the level of reserves has at times been insufficient to cover claims. In 2017, the one year reserve development was 22% deficient.
Other Rating Factors: Weak overall results on stability tests (2.8). Good overall profitability index (5.7) despite operating losses during 2019. Return on equity has been low, averaging 3.5% over the past five years. Good liquidity (5.8) with sufficient resources (cash flows and marketable investments) to handle a spike in claims.
Principal Business: Workers compensation (56%), other accident & health (28%), and group accident & health (16%).
Principal Investments: Investment grade bonds (72%), misc. investments (26%), cash (1%), and non investment grade bonds (1%).
Investments in Affiliates: None
Group Affiliation: UPMC Health System
Licensed in: DE, MD, OH, PA, WV
Commenced Business: February 2000
Address: 600 Grant Street, Pittsburgh, PA 15219
Phone: (412) 434-1200　**Domicile State:** PA　**NAIC Code:** 11018

Data Date	Rating	RACR #1	RACR #2	Loss Ratio %	Total Assets ($mil)	Capital ($mil)	Net Premium ($mil)	Net Income ($mil)
6-20	C	0.81	0.50	N/A	298.2	136.1	96.7	8.1
6-19	C	0.84	0.53	N/A	282.1	131.6	80.3	5.1
2019	C	0.81	0.50	80.9	297.2	129.9	168.2	-2.7
2018	C	0.85	0.53	72.3	274.5	120.0	140.2	11.4
2017	D+	1.01	0.62	81.5	237.5	110.6	117.7	3.4
2016	D+	0.58	0.36	74.5	170.5	56.4	101.0	0.1
2015	D+	0.96	0.59	76.9	147.9	45.3	91.2	1.1

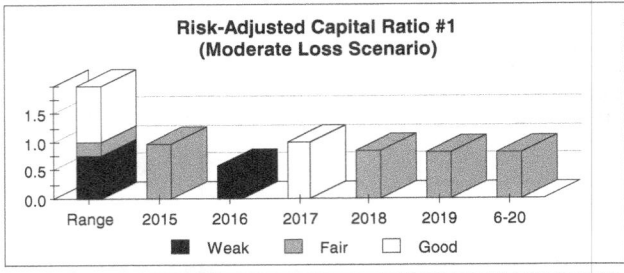

Risk-Adjusted Capital Ratio #1
(Moderate Loss Scenario)

UPMC HEALTH COVERAGE INC　　　　　　　　　　C+　　　Fair

Major Rating Factors: Low quality investment portfolio (1.2 on a scale of 0 to 10). Excellent profitability (9.5). Strong capitalization (10.0) based on excellent current risk-adjusted capital (severe loss scenario).
Other Rating Factors: Excellent liquidity (7.9) with ample operational cash flow and liquid investments.
Principal Business: Comp med (100%)
Mem Phys: 19: 19,160　**18:** 17,047　**19 MLR** 89.2%　**/ 19 Admin Exp** N/A
Enroll(000): Q2 20: 5　**19:** 5　**18:** 5　**Med Exp PMPM:** $419
Principal Investments: Cash and equiv (99%), long-term bonds (1%)
Provider Compensation ($000): Contr fee ($26,773)
Total Member Encounters: Phys (40,410), non-phys (26,757)
Group Affiliation: None
Licensed in: MD, PA
Address: 600 Grant Street, Pittsburgh, PA 15219
Phone: (412) 434-1200　**Dom State:** PA　**Commenced Bus:** N/A

Data Date	Rating	RACR #1	RACR #2	Total Assets ($mil)	Capital ($mil)	Net Premium ($mil)	Net Income ($mil)
6-20	C+	4.05	3.38	25.1	19.8	20.1	3.4
6-19	B-	7.19	5.99	20.5	16.8	15.9	1.0
2019	B-	5.90	4.92	19.7	16.4	30.2	0.6
2018	B-	6.78	5.65	19.1	15.8	27.5	1.0
2017	B	N/A	N/A	17.4	14.9	32.8	3.9
2016	B	5.27	4.39	15.7	10.9	27.7	1.8
2015	B	6.57	5.48	14.7	9.8	27.5	7.7

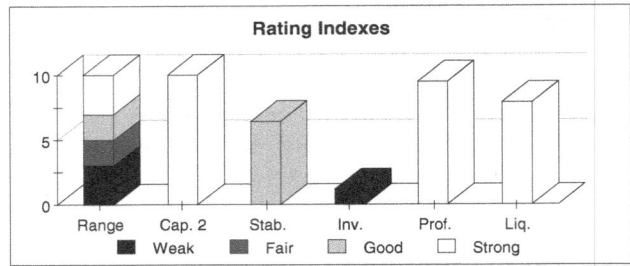

Rating Indexes

UPMC HEALTH NETWORK INC　　　　　　　　　　C+　　　Fair

Major Rating Factors: Fair quality investment portfolio (3.1 on a scale of 0 to 10). Excellent profitability (8.3). Strong capitalization (7.5) based on excellent current risk-adjusted capital (severe loss scenario).
Other Rating Factors: Excellent liquidity (7.6) with ample operational cash flow and liquid investments.
Principal Business: Medicare (100%)
Mem Phys: 19: 42,396　**18:** 32,531　**19 MLR** 86.2%　**/ 19 Admin Exp** N/A
Enroll(000): Q2 20: 9　**19:** 10　**18:** 9　**Med Exp PMPM:** $845
Principal Investments: Cash and equiv (88%), affiliate common stock (3%), other (10%)
Provider Compensation ($000): Contr fee ($98,319)
Total Member Encounters: Phys (148,389), non-phys (152,166)
Group Affiliation: None
Licensed in: PA
Address: 600 Grant Street, Pittsburgh, PA 15219
Phone: (412) 434-1200　**Dom State:** PA　**Commenced Bus:** N/A

Data Date	Rating	RACR #1	RACR #2	Total Assets ($mil)	Capital ($mil)	Net Premium ($mil)	Net Income ($mil)
6-20	C+	1.76	1.47	60.6	48.9	53.9	6.0
6-19	C+	4.19	3.49	50.3	40.3	57.0	5.5
2019	C+	2.42	2.02	52.2	42.9	112.8	7.8
2018	C+	3.32	2.77	43.1	34.9	97.8	7.0
2017	C	1.97	1.64	36.3	28.2	84.3	9.1
2016	C	3.00	2.50	38.1	19.3	82.2	8.5
2015	D+	2.68	2.23	40.9	25.6	92.2	2.6

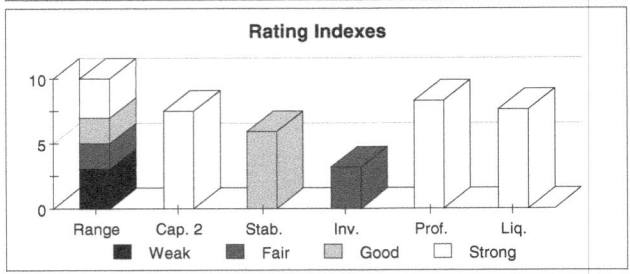

Rating Indexes

UPMC HEALTH OPTIONS INC   B   Good

Major Rating Factors: Good liquidity (6.7 on a scale of 0 to 10) with sufficient resources (cash flows and marketable investments) to handle a spike in claims. Fair profitability index (4.7). Strong capitalization (7.5) based on excellent current risk-adjusted capital (severe loss scenario).
Other Rating Factors: High quality investment portfolio (7.0).
Principal Business: Comp med (100%)
Mem Phys: 19: 37,584   **18:** 28,556   **19 MLR** 90.4%   **/ 19 Admin Exp** N/A
Enroll(000): Q2 20: 435   **19:** 431   **18:** 424   **Med Exp PMPM:** $412
Principal Investments: Long-term bonds (62%), nonaffiliate common stock (22%), cash and equiv (16%)
Provider Compensation ($000): Contr fee ($2,147,103)
Total Member Encounters: Phys (3,401,592), non-phys (2,125,148)
Group Affiliation: None
Licensed in: PA
Address: 600 Grant Street, Pittsburgh, PA 15219
Phone: (412) 434-1200   **Dom State:** PA   **Commenced Bus:** N/A

Data Date	Rating	RACR #1	RACR #2	Total Assets ($mil)	Capital ($mil)	Net Premium ($mil)	Net Income ($mil)
6-20	B	1.73	1.44	638.4	348.6	1,214.6	89.4
6-19	C+	1.99	1.66	529.7	280.8	1,220.6	30.3
2019	C+	1.70	1.41	488.5	263.2	2,387.7	7.1
2018	C+	1.70	1.42	461.8	240.0	2,212.4	19.4
2017	C+	N/A	N/A	461.7	222.0	1,984.7	5.0
2016	C+	1.88	1.57	358.2	191.3	1,551.5	-49.6
2015	C	0.89	0.74	344.0	167.7	1,312.9	-76.3

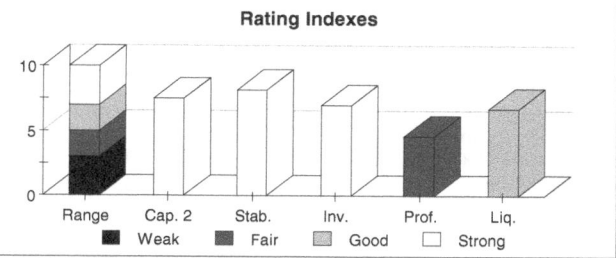

Rating Indexes

UPMC HEALTH PLAN INC   C+   Fair

Major Rating Factors: Good overall results on stability tests (5.7 on a scale of 0 to 10). Low quality investment portfolio (2.7). Excellent profitability (7.7).
Other Rating Factors: Strong capitalization index (8.0) based on excellent current risk-adjusted capital (severe loss scenario). Excellent liquidity (7.0) with sufficient resources (cash flows and marketable investments) to handle a spike in claims.
Principal Business: Medicare (96%), FEHB (4%)
Mem Phys: 19: 44,150   **18:** 34,738   **19 MLR** 87.3%   **/ 19 Admin Exp** N/A
Enroll(000): Q2 20: 160   **19:** 163   **18:** 191   **Med Exp PMPM:** $835
Principal Investments: Long-term bonds (33%), nonaffiliate common stock (25%), other (45%)
Provider Compensation ($000): Contr fee ($1,637,281), capitation ($14)
Total Member Encounters: Phys (2,439,607), non-phys (2,559,356)
Group Affiliation: None
Licensed in: OH, PA, WV
Address: 600 Grant Street, Pittsburgh,
Phone: (412) 434-1200   **Dom State:** PA   **Commenced Bus:** N/A

Data Date	Rating	RACR #1	RACR #2	Total Assets ($mil)	Capital ($mil)	Net Premium ($mil)	Net Income ($mil)
6-20	C+	2.13	1.78	984.5	360.4	921.5	96.1
6-19	C+	1.85	1.54	767.3	207.9	941.9	37.7
2019	C+	2.12	1.76	608.6	277.9	1,859.6	48.0
2018	B-	1.68	1.40	566.6	190.2	1,736.2	52.9
2017	A-	1.67	1.39	551.8	260.5	1,605.0	54.1
2016	B+	1.92	1.60	454.5	211.7	1,490.4	27.1
2015	B	1.21	1.00	350.9	185.8	1,371.4	3.3

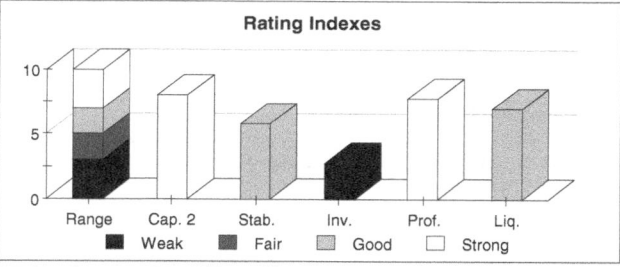

Rating Indexes

UPPER PENINSULA HEALTH PLAN INC   B   Good

Major Rating Factors: Good overall results on stability tests (5.1 on a scale of 0 to 10) based on steady enrollment growth, averaging 1% over the past five years. Fair quality investment portfolio (4.5). Excellent profitability (8.0).
Other Rating Factors: Strong capitalization index (8.2) based on excellent current risk-adjusted capital (severe loss scenario). Excellent liquidity (7.1) with ample operational cash flow and liquid investments.
Principal Business: Medicaid (64%), Medicare (35%)
Mem Phys: 19: 1,943   **18:** 1,731   **19 MLR** 76.0%   **/ 19 Admin Exp** N/A
Enroll(000): Q2 20: 51   **19:** 49   **18:** 49   **Med Exp PMPM:** $370
Principal Investments: Cash and equiv (47%), long-term bonds (41%), real estate (12%)
Provider Compensation ($000): Contr fee ($207,655), FFS ($8,251), bonus arrang ($632)
Total Member Encounters: Phys (321,479), non-phys (287,919)
Group Affiliation: Apollo Global Management Inc
Licensed in: MI
Address: 853 W Washington St, Marquette,
Phone: (906) 225-7500   **Dom State:** MI   **Commenced Bus:** N/A

Data Date	Rating	RACR #1	RACR #2	Total Assets ($mil)	Capital ($mil)	Net Premium ($mil)	Net Income ($mil)
6-20	B	2.27	1.90	111.6	54.0	142.6	6.3
6-19	B+	3.89	3.24	107.1	57.9	126.5	9.5
2019	B+	4.55	3.79	117.1	68.3	286.3	21.1
2018	B+	3.76	3.13	108.2	55.7	254.4	10.9
2017	A	2.16	1.80	94.5	55.2	292.8	12.0
2016	B	1.80	1.50	82.6	44.7	283.6	8.9
2015	B-	1.68	1.40	77.4	36.3	248.1	13.1

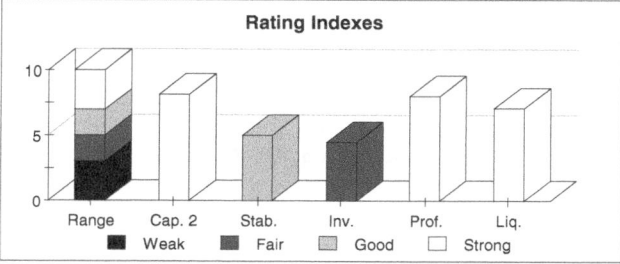

Rating Indexes

US FIRE INS CO   C   Fair

Major Rating Factors: Fair overall results on stability tests (3.7 on a scale of 0 to 10) including potential drain of affiliation with Fairfax Financial. Fair profitability index (3.2) with operating losses during 2017 and the first six months of 2020. Average return on equity over the last five years has been poor at -1.5%.

Other Rating Factors: Good long-term capitalization index (6.6) based on good current risk adjusted capital (moderate loss scenario). Over the last several years, capital levels have remained relatively consistent. Ample reserve history (7.6) that can protect against increases in claims costs. Excellent liquidity (7.0) with ample operational cash flow and liquid investments.

Principal Business: Group accident & health (36%), inland marine (26%), other liability (9%), auto liability (7%), workers compensation (7%), surety (6%), and other lines (9%).

Principal Investments: Investment grade bonds (46%), misc. investments (44%), cash (4%), non investment grade bonds (3%), and real estate (3%).

Investments in Affiliates: 27%

Group Affiliation: Fairfax Financial

Licensed in: All states, the District of Columbia and Puerto Rico

Commenced Business: April 1824

Address: 1209 ORANGE STREET, Wilmington, DE 19801

Phone: (973) 490-6600   **Domicile State:** DE   **NAIC Code:** 21113

Data Date	Rating	RACR #1	RACR #2	Loss Ratio %	Total Assets ($mil)	Capital ($mil)	Net Premium ($mil)	Net Income ($mil)
6-20	C	1.24	0.98	N/A	4,499.8	1,397.1	883.0	-247.7
6-19	C	1.20	0.95	N/A	4,234.0	1,346.2	781.6	64.9
2019	C	1.19	0.93	63.0	4,444.8	1,406.1	1,773.9	41.7
2018	C	1.22	0.99	63.3	4,085.8	1,317.6	1,505.0	80.0
2017	C	1.15	0.94	64.7	4,094.3	1,302.3	1,418.1	-132.0
2016	C	1.35	1.04	63.7	3,949.6	1,218.9	1,370.7	32.3
2015	C	1.45	1.14	64.1	3,736.1	1,178.0	1,262.9	94.5

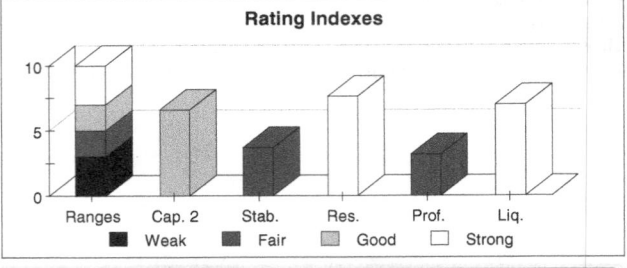

Rating Indexes

USABLE LIFE *   B+   Good

Major Rating Factors: Good overall profitability (6.2 on a scale of 0 to 10). Return on equity has been excellent over the last five years averaging 17.7%. Good liquidity (6.5) with sufficient resources to handle a spike in claims. Good overall results on stability tests (5.7). Stability strengths include good operational trends and excellent risk diversification.

Other Rating Factors: Strong capitalization (8.7) based on excellent risk adjusted capital (severe loss scenario). High quality investment portfolio (7.0).

Principal Business: Reinsurance (50%), group life insurance (23%), group health insurance (20%), individual health insurance (6%), and individual life insurance (1%).

Principal Investments: NonCMO investment grade bonds (74%), CMOs and structured securities (14%), common & preferred stock (7%), cash (2%), and misc. investments (3%).

Investments in Affiliates: None

Group Affiliation: Arkansas Bl Cross Bl Shield Group

Licensed in: All states except NY, PR

Commenced Business: December 1980

Address: 320 W Capitol Suite 700, Little Rock, AR 72201

Phone: (501) 375-7200 **Domicile State:** AR **NAIC Code:** 94358

Data Date	Rating	RACR #1	RACR #2	Total Assets ($mil)	Capital ($mil)	Net Premium ($mil)	Net Income ($mil)
6-20	B+	2.91	2.13	496.4	246.1	235.2	16.4
6-19	A-	2.84	2.11	498.5	259.9	231.8	3.5
2019	B+	2.81	2.07	476.2	230.5	458.5	17.6
2018	A-	2.84	2.13	514.7	273.8	572.6	142.5
2017	A-	2.80	2.10	535.3	278.1	586.1	37.8
2016	B+	2.41	1.80	498.2	241.6	587.8	24.3
2015	B+	2.07	1.52	467.9	215.3	580.2	27.3

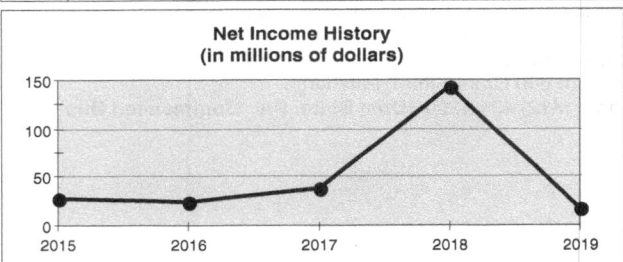

Net Income History (in millions of dollars)

USABLE MUTUAL INS CO *   B+   Good

Major Rating Factors: Good overall profitability index (5.2 on a scale of 0 to 10). Good quality investment portfolio (6.7). Strong capitalization (10.0) based on excellent current risk-adjusted capital (severe loss scenario).

Other Rating Factors: Excellent liquidity (7.0) with sufficient resources (cash flows and marketable investments) to handle a spike in claims.

Principal Business: Comp med (70%), FEHB (12%), med supp (11%), Medicare (5%), other (1%).

Mem Phys: 19: 18,930 **18:** 18,605 **19 MLR** 80.1% **/ 19 Admin Exp** N/A

Enroll(000): Q2 20: 619 **19:** 618 **18:** 619 **Med Exp PMPM:** $258

Principal Investments: Long-term bonds (42%), affiliate common stock (26%), cash and equiv (10%), real estate (4%), nonaffiliate common stock (4%), other (14%)

Provider Compensation ($000): Contr fee ($1,919,392), bonus arrang ($22,450)

Total Member Encounters: Phys (3,033,569), non-phys (2,709,582)

Group Affiliation: None

Licensed in: AR, TX

Address: 601 S Gaines, Little Rock, AR 72201

Phone: (501) 378-2000 **Dom State:** AR **Commenced Bus:** N/A

Data Date	Rating	RACR #1	RACR #2	Total Assets ($mil)	Capital ($mil)	Net Premium ($mil)	Net Income ($mil)
6-20	B+	4.49	3.74	1,921.0	955.9	1,187.0	53.3
6-19	B	5.23	4.36	1,892.5	910.3	1,208.3	53.7
2019	B	4.42	3.68	1,852.1	919.1	2,395.0	84.5
2018	B	4.79	3.99	1,747.3	830.5	2,480.2	-21.3
2017	A	4.71	3.92	1,664.5	866.3	2,523.7	30.7
2016	A+	4.98	4.15	1,623.7	842.8	2,466.7	9.8
2015	A+	5.52	4.60	1,579.9	817.8	2,239.7	4.3

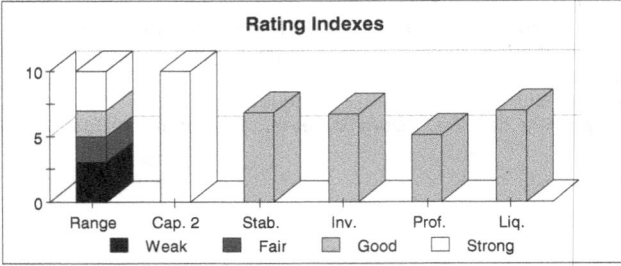

Rating Indexes

UTIC INS CO
B   **Good**

Major Rating Factors: Good overall results on stability tests (5.8 on a scale of 0 to 10). Stability strengths include good operational trends and good risk diversification. Fair quality investment portfolio (4.1). Fair profitability (3.2).
Other Rating Factors: Strong capitalization (8.5) based on excellent risk adjusted capital (severe loss scenario). Excellent liquidity (7.3).
Principal Business: Individual health insurance (60%) and reinsurance (40%).
Principal Investments: NonCMO investment grade bonds (66%), common & preferred stock (19%), cash (3%), CMOs and structured securities (3%), and noninv. grade bonds (1%).
Investments in Affiliates: None
Group Affiliation: Bl Cross & Bl Shield of AL Group
Licensed in: AL, TN
Commenced Business: February 1964
Address: 450 Riverchase Parkway East, Birmingham, AL 35244
Phone: (205) 220-2100 **Domicile State:** AL **NAIC Code:** 81531

Data Date	Rating	RACR #1	RACR #2	Total Assets ($mil)	Capital ($mil)	Net Premium ($mil)	Net Income ($mil)
6-20	B	3.36	2.02	129.7	31.7	7.1	1.7
6-19	B+	2.67	1.64	109.5	25.2	7.7	1.2
2019	B	2.34	1.42	116.3	20.4	16.0	-2.2
2018	B+	2.64	1.66	101.4	22.8	20.0	1.3
2017	B+	2.60	1.66	94.4	22.8	21.0	2.5
2016	B	2.53	1.79	84.5	20.1	22.9	0.7
2015	B	2.63	2.20	74.7	20.1	19.9	9.6

Adverse Trends in Operations

Decrease in capital during 2019 (11%)
Decrease in premium volume from 2018 to 2019 (20%)
Decrease in premium volume from 2017 to 2018 (5%)
Decrease in premium volume from 2016 to 2017 (8%)

UTMB HEALTH PLANS INC
B-   **Good**

Major Rating Factors: Fair overall results on stability tests (4.3 on a scale of 0 to 10) based on a decline in the number of member physicians during 2020. Good overall profitability index (6.5). Strong capitalization index (10.0) based on excellent current risk-adjusted capital (severe loss scenario).
Other Rating Factors: High quality investment portfolio (8.7). Excellent liquidity (10.0) with ample operational cash flow and liquid investments.
Principal Business: Med supp (100%)
Mem Phys: 19: 23 **18:** 26 **19 MLR** 62.3% **/ 19 Admin Exp** N/A
Enroll(000): Q2 20: 0 **19:** 0 **18:** 0 **Med Exp PMPM:** $147
Principal Investments: Cash and equiv (100%)
Provider Compensation ($000): Capitation ($171), FFS ($127)
Total Member Encounters: Phys (351), non-phys (1,289)
Group Affiliation: None
Licensed in: TX
Address: 301 University Blvd Rte 0985, Galveston,
Phone: (409) 766-4000 **Dom State:** TX **Commenced Bus:** N/A

Data Date	Rating	RACR #1	RACR #2	Total Assets ($mil)	Capital ($mil)	Net Premium ($mil)	Net Income ($mil)
6-20	B-	61.72	51.43	6.1	6.0	0.2	0.1
6-19	N/A	N/A	N/A	N/A	N/A	N/A	N/A
2019	B-	61.99	51.66	6.1	6.1	0.5	0.1
2018	B-	55.33	46.11	5.5	5.4	0.6	0.2
2017	B-	N/A	N/A	5.6	5.5	1.2	0.7
2016	B-	49.96	41.63	5.7	5.1	0.7	0.3
2015	B-	51.16	42.63	6.3	5.6	0.7	0.3

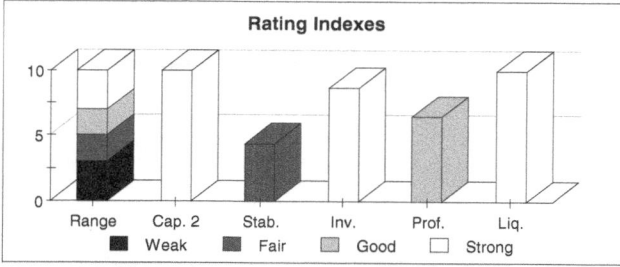

Rating Indexes

VANTAGE HEALTH PLAN INC
C+   **Fair**

Major Rating Factors: Fair quality investment portfolio (4.0 on a scale of 0 to 10). Good overall profitability index (6.3). Good capitalization index (6.9) based on excellent current risk-adjusted capital (severe loss scenario).
Other Rating Factors: Good overall results on stability tests (6.7). Good liquidity (6.8) with sufficient resources (cash flows and marketable investments) to handle a spike in claims.
Principal Business: Medicare (63%), comp med (37%)
Mem Phys: 19: 17,544 **18:** 14,205 **19 MLR** 86.0% **/ 19 Admin Exp** N/A
Enroll(000): Q2 20: 38 **19:** 39 **18:** 43 **Med Exp PMPM:** $695
Principal Investments: Real estate (57%), cash and equiv (16%), other (28%)
Provider Compensation ($000): Contr fee ($312,921), FFS ($26,476), capitation ($2,767)
Total Member Encounters: Phys (566,587), non-phys (98,879)
Group Affiliation: None
Licensed in: LA
Address: 130 DeSiard Street Suite 300, Monroe,
Phone: (318) 361-0900 **Dom State:** LA **Commenced Bus:** N/A

Data Date	Rating	RACR #1	RACR #2	Total Assets ($mil)	Capital ($mil)	Net Premium ($mil)	Net Income ($mil)
6-20	C+	1.23	1.03	109.7	47.3	199.0	8.0
6-19	N/A	N/A	N/A	N/A	N/A	N/A	N/A
2019	C+	2.00	1.67	90.4	46.7	385.8	0.0
2018	D+	0.75	0.62	98.3	37.9	402.9	3.0
2017	C-	0.62	0.52	76.8	24.2	408.0	2.6
2016	C-	0.75	0.63	93.8	28.2	368.6	17.3
2015	C	0.85	0.70	64.1	24.0	270.0	1.2

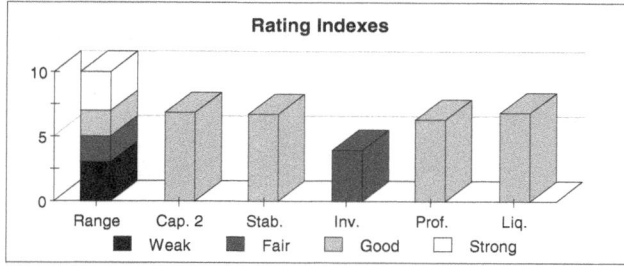

Rating Indexes

VENTURA COUNTY HEALTH CARE PLAN   E+   Very Weak

Major Rating Factors: Fair capitalization index (4.1 on a scale of 0 to 10) based on weak current risk-adjusted capital (moderate loss scenario). Fair overall results on stability tests (3.1). Good overall profitability index (5.2).
Other Rating Factors: Excellent liquidity (7.0) with sufficient resources (cash flows and marketable investments) to handle a spike in claims.
Principal Business: Managed care (100%)
Mem Phys: 19: N/A **18:** N/A **19 MLR** 89.2% **/ 19 Admin Exp** N/A
Enroll(000): Q2 20: 0 **19:** 15 **18:** 15 **Med Exp PMPM:** $397
Principal Investments ($000): Cash and equiv ($8,565)
Provider Compensation ($000): None
Total Member Encounters: N/A
Group Affiliation: None
Licensed in: CA
Address: 5455 Garden Grove Blvd Ste 500, Westminster, CA 92683
Phone: (562) 981-4004 **Dom State:** CA **Commenced Bus:** June 1996

Data Date	Rating	RACR #1	RACR #2	Total Assets ($mil)	Capital ($mil)	Net Premium ($mil)	Net Income ($mil)
6-20	E+	0.66	0.42	17.8	6.5	38.2	0.7
6-19	E	0.48	0.30	17.5	4.8	40.7	0.9
2019	E	0.59	0.37	17.6	5.8	80.4	1.9
2018	E-	0.39	0.25	18.6	3.9	79.9	2.4
2017	E-	0.22	0.14	18.5	1.5	75.1	0.6
2016	E-	0.19	0.12	17.9	1.3	63.5	-5.0
2015	B-	1.31	0.82	17.4	8.7	57.6	-1.6

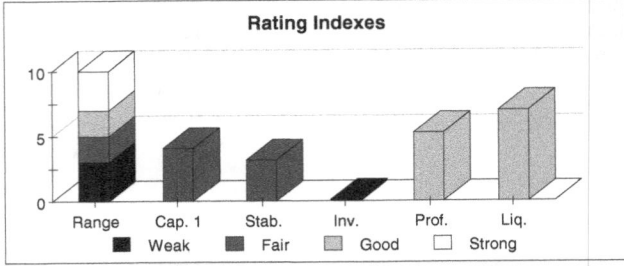

Rating Indexes — Range, Cap. 1, Stab., Inv., Prof., Liq. / Weak, Fair, Good, Strong

VERMONT HEALTH PLAN LLC   C   Fair

Major Rating Factors: Weak profitability index (2.5 on a scale of 0 to 10). Good overall results on stability tests (5.5). Strong capitalization index (10.0) based on excellent current risk-adjusted capital (severe loss scenario).
Other Rating Factors: High quality investment portfolio (8.4). Excellent liquidity (7.3) with ample operational cash flow and liquid investments.
Principal Business: Med supp (54%), comp med (46%)
Mem Phys: 19: 8,421 **18:** 8,200 **19 MLR** 86.4% **/ 19 Admin Exp** N/A
Enroll(000): Q2 20: 11 **19:** 11 **18:** 11 **Med Exp PMPM:** $215
Principal Investments: Long-term bonds (61%), cash and equiv (39%)
Provider Compensation ($000): FFS ($21,111), contr fee ($7,665)
Total Member Encounters: Phys (9,256), non-phys (14,550)
Group Affiliation: None
Licensed in: VT
Address: 445 Industrial Lane, Berlin,
Phone: (802) 223-6131 **Dom State:** VT **Commenced Bus:** N/A

Data Date	Rating	RACR #1	RACR #2	Total Assets ($mil)	Capital ($mil)	Net Premium ($mil)	Net Income ($mil)
6-20	C	6.88	5.74	38.6	32.9	14.6	1.7
6-19	C	7.87	6.56	38.5	30.0	16.7	-1.7
2019	C	7.93	6.61	37.9	31.3	33.3	-0.5
2018	C+	8.30	6.92	38.3	31.8	31.9	-0.7
2017	C+	7.10	5.91	38.5	32.5	28.5	-1.9
2016	B-	9.12	7.60	40.1	34.4	30.6	1.1
2015	B-	5.53	4.61	43.1	33.2	50.9	-0.7

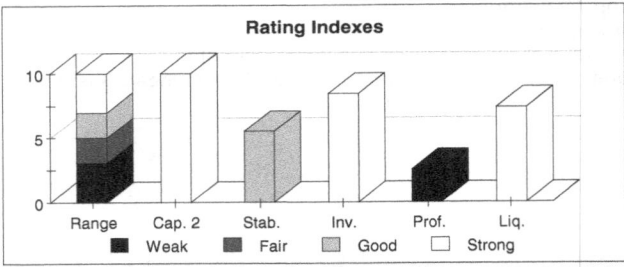

Rating Indexes — Range, Cap. 2, Stab., Inv., Prof., Liq. / Weak, Fair, Good, Strong

VIBRA HEALTH PLAN INC   E-   Very Weak

Major Rating Factors: Weak profitability index (0.3 on a scale of 0 to 10). Weak liquidity (0.0) as a spike in claims may stretch capacity. Strong capitalization (7.8) based on excellent current risk-adjusted capital (severe loss scenario).
Other Rating Factors: High quality investment portfolio (9.9).
Principal Business: Medicare (100%)
Mem Phys: 18: 10,794 **17:** 10,794 **18 MLR** 99.8% **/ 18 Admin Exp** N/A
Enroll(000): Q3 19: 1 **18:** 1 **17:** 1 **Med Exp PMPM:** $804
Principal Investments: Cash and equiv (100%)
Provider Compensation ($000): Contr fee ($12,713)
Total Member Encounters: Phys (14,506), non-phys (2,419)
Group Affiliation: None
Licensed in: PA
Address: 4000 Crums Mill Road Suite 20, Harrisburg, PA 17103
Phone: (717) 510-6200 **Dom State:** PA **Commenced Bus:** N/A

Data Date	Rating	RACR #1	RACR #2	Total Assets ($mil)	Capital ($mil)	Net Premium ($mil)	Net Income ($mil)
9-19	E-	2.00	1.67	7.0	3.4	10.7	-8.2
9-18	N/A	N/A	N/A	7.5	2.5	9.5	-8.1
2018	C-	2.11	1.76	7.8	3.6	12.6	-10.3
2017	N/A	N/A	N/A	8.1	5.4	8.3	-12.3
2016	N/A	N/A	N/A	4.4	3.2	N/A	-8.7
2015	N/A	N/A	N/A	2.6	2.1	N/A	-0.9
2014	N/A	N/A	N/A	N/A	N/A	N/A	N/A

Rating Indexes — Range, Cap. 2, Stab., Inv., Prof., Liq. / Weak, Fair, Good, Strong

VIRGINIA PREMIER HEALTH PLAN INC   C+   Fair

Major Rating Factors: Fair profitability index (4.6 on a scale of 0 to 10). Good overall results on stability tests (5.5) despite a decline in the number of member physicians during 2020. Low quality investment portfolio (1.4).

Other Rating Factors: Strong capitalization index (7.6) based on excellent current risk-adjusted capital (severe loss scenario). Excellent liquidity (6.9) with sufficient resources (cash flows and marketable investments) to handle a spike in claims.

Principal Business: Medicaid (93%), Medicare (7%)

Mem Phys: 19: 24 **18:** 21,840 **19 MLR** 88.6% **/ 19 Admin Exp** N/A

Enroll(000): Q2 20: 274 **19:** 285 **18:** 215 **Med Exp PMPM:** $538

Principal Investments: Cash and equiv (42%), nonaffiliate common stock (28%), long-term bonds (4%), other (26%)

Provider Compensation ($000): Contr fee ($1,649,131), capitation ($118,342)

Total Member Encounters: N/A

Group Affiliation: None

Licensed in: VA

Address: 600 E Broad St Suite 400, Richmond,

Phone: (804) 819-5151 **Dom State:** VA **Commenced Bus:** N/A

Data Date	Rating	RACR #1	RACR #2	Total Assets ($mil)	Capital ($mil)	Net Premium ($mil)	Net Income ($mil)
6-20	C+	1.85	1.54	569.1	294.2	1,045.3	83.8
6-19	N/A	N/A	N/A	N/A	N/A	N/A	N/A
2019	C+	1.03	0.86	465.9	213.6	2,000.0	36.1
2018	C+	0.88	0.74	355.7	161.4	1,462.7	-82.8
2017	B+	N/A	N/A	366.4	206.1	1,206.9	25.8
2016	B+	1.85	1.54	302.8	199.8	1,070.4	30.7
2015	B+	1.51	1.26	281.9	168.3	1,024.6	16.3

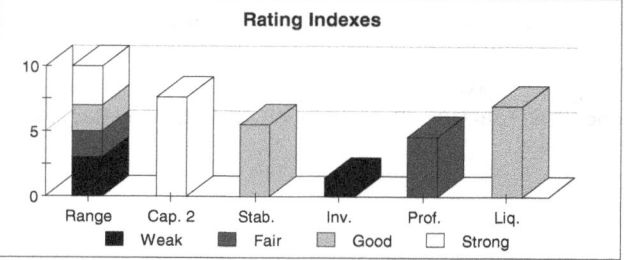

VISTA HEALTH PLAN INC *   B+   Good

Major Rating Factors: Excellent overall profitability index (6.9 on a scale of 0 to 10). Strong capitalization index (8.4) based on excellent current risk-adjusted capital (severe loss scenario). High quality investment portfolio (7.4).

Other Rating Factors: Excellent overall results on stability tests (7.8). Excellent liquidity (7.1) with ample operational cash flow and liquid investments

Principal Business: Medicaid (98%), Medicare (2%)

Mem Phys: 18: 56,902 **17:** 49 **18 MLR** 94.1% **/ 18 Admin Exp** N/A

Enroll(000): Q3 19: 806 **18:** 735 **17:** 713 **Med Exp PMPM:** $531

Principal Investments: Long-term bonds (62%), cash and equiv (38%)

Provider Compensation ($000): Capitation ($4,718,714)

Total Member Encounters: Phys (5,657,661), non-phys (1,577,198)

Group Affiliation: Independence Health Group Inc

Licensed in: PA

Address: 1901 Market Street, Philadelphia,

Phone: (215) 241-2400 **Dom State:** PA **Commenced Bus:** N/A

Data Date	Rating	RACR #1	RACR #2	Total Assets ($mil)	Capital ($mil)	Net Premium ($mil)	Net Income ($mil)
9-19	B+	2.50	2.08	1,350.1	408.1	5,687.2	4.7
9-18	B-	N/A	N/A	1,052.4	306.3	3,758.9	-17.4
2018	B	2.00	1.67	982.8	327.7	5,009.8	3.6
2017	B-	N/A	N/A	880.4	282.7	4,379.1	3.5
2016	B-	2.14	1.78	1,158.0	278.5	4,574.3	3.2
2015	B-	1.75	1.46	453.3	227.9	3,750.6	3.0
2014	N/A	N/A	N/A	546.1	188.0	3,079.1	N/A

VITALITY HEALTH PLAN OF CA INC   E-   Very Weak

Major Rating Factors: Weak profitability index (0.3 on a scale of 0 to 10). Poor capitalization index (0.0) based on weak current risk-adjusted capital (severe loss scenario). Weak overall results on stability tests (1.5) based on poor risk diversification due to the size of the company's affiliate group.

Other Rating Factors: Weak liquidity (0.1) as a spike in claims may stretch capacity.

Principal Business: None

Mem Phys: 19: N/A **18:** N/A **19 MLR** N/A **/ 19 Admin Exp** N/A

Enroll(000): Q2 20: 0 **19:** N/A **18:** N/A **Med Exp PMPM:** N/A

Principal Investments ($000): None

Provider Compensation ($000): None

Total Member Encounters: N/A

Group Affiliation: Vitality Health Plans Inc

Licensed in: (No states)

Address: , , CA 90703-2679

Phone: (866) 333-3530 **Dom State:**   **Commenced Bus:** N/A

Data Date	Rating	RACR #1	RACR #2	Total Assets ($mil)	Capital ($mil)	Net Premium ($mil)	Net Income ($mil)
6-20	E-	N/A	N/A	4.8	-32.4	59.1	-4.3
6-19	N/A	N/A	N/A	N/A	N/A	N/A	N/A
2019	N/A	N/A	N/A	N/A	N/A	N/A	N/A
2018	N/A	N/A	N/A	N/A	N/A	N/A	N/A
2017	N/A	N/A	N/A	N/A	N/A	N/A	N/A
2016	N/A	N/A	N/A	N/A	N/A	N/A	N/A
2015	N/A	N/A	N/A	N/A	N/A	N/A	N/A

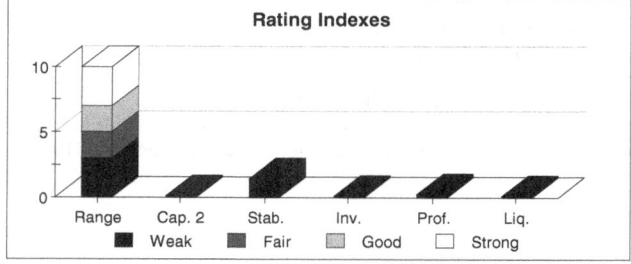

VIVA HEALTH INC *

A-   Excellent

Major Rating Factors: Strong capitalization index (8.4 on a scale of 0 to 10) based on excellent current risk-adjusted capital (severe loss scenario). High quality investment portfolio (9.9). Excellent overall results on stability tests (8.2) despite a decline in the number of member physicians during 2020.
Other Rating Factors: Excellent liquidity (6.9) with sufficient resources (cash flows and marketable investments) to handle a spike in claims. Good overall profitability index (6.3).
Principal Business: Medicare (87%), comp med (13%)
Mem Phys: 19: 15 **18:** 13,618 **19 MLR** 86.6% **/ 19 Admin Exp** N/A
Enroll(000): Q2 20: 73 **19:** 74 **18:** 73 **Med Exp PMPM:** $763
Principal Investments: Long-term bonds (69%), cash and equiv (31%)
Provider Compensation ($000): Contr fee ($512,805), capitation ($159,818), FFS ($15,859)
Total Member Encounters: Phys (1,541,338), non-phys (1,750,333)
Group Affiliation: None
Licensed in: AL
Address: 417 20TH STREET NORTH SUITE 11, BIRMINGHAM,
Phone: (205) 558-7466 **Dom State:** AL **Commenced Bus:** N/A

Data Date	Rating	RACR #1	RACR #2	Total Assets ($mil)	Capital ($mil)	Net Premium ($mil)	Net Income ($mil)
6-20	A-	2.48	2.06	225.3	141.0	417.4	11.3
6-19	N/A	N/A	N/A	N/A	N/A	N/A	N/A
2019	A-	2.28	1.90	214.9	129.5	785.5	10.0
2018	B+	2.36	1.97	207.2	123.2	735.3	12.3
2017	B+	2.31	1.93	208.2	110.9	710.6	13.5
2016	B+	2.23	1.86	181.0	97.2	625.2	10.6
2015	B	1.74	1.45	161.1	83.1	610.4	-3.6

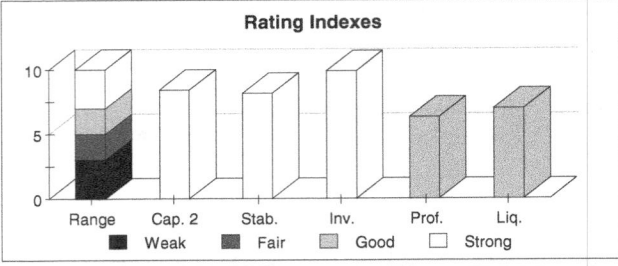

Rating Indexes

Range Cap. 2 Stab. Inv. Prof. Liq.
■ Weak ■ Fair ☐ Good ☐ Strong

VOLUNTEER STATE HEALTH PLAN INC *

A+   Excellent

Major Rating Factors: Strong capitalization index (8.8 on a scale of 0 to 10) based on excellent current risk-adjusted capital (severe loss scenario). Good overall profitability index (6.2). Good quality investment portfolio (6.7).
Other Rating Factors: Good overall results on stability tests (6.4) despite a decline in the number of member physicians during 2020. Good liquidity (6.8) with sufficient resources (cash flows and marketable investments) to handle a spike in claims.
Principal Business: Medicaid (89%), Medicare (11%)
Mem Phys: 19: 30 **18:** 28,338 **19 MLR** 84.5% **/ 19 Admin Exp** N/A
Enroll(000): Q2 20: 552 **19:** 535 **18:** 520 **Med Exp PMPM:** $355
Principal Investments: Long-term bonds (69%), nonaffiliate common stock (19%), cash and equiv (9%), pref stock (2%)
Provider Compensation ($000): Contr fee ($2,232,681), capitation ($43,682), bonus arrang ($567)
Total Member Encounters: Phys (5,678,299), non-phys (493,765)
Group Affiliation: BlueCross BlueShield of Tennessee In
Licensed in: (No states)
Address: 1 Cameron Hill Circle, Chattanooga,
Phone: (423) 535-5600 **Dom State:** TN **Commenced Bus:** N/A

Data Date	Rating	RACR #1	RACR #2	Total Assets ($mil)	Capital ($mil)	Net Premium ($mil)	Net Income ($mil)
6-20	A+	2.78	2.31	987.7	536.9	1,441.7	66.5
6-19	A+	2.99	2.50	876.2	406.6	1,309.0	-18.8
2019	A+	3.10	2.58	903.6	489.8	2,690.3	58.5
2018	A+	3.02	2.52	860.0	410.9	2,576.0	-12.2
2017	A+	2.80	2.34	803.5	479.8	2,484.1	48.3
2016	A+	3.36	2.80	737.6	420.8	2,440.8	109.6
2015	A+	3.00	2.50	805.5	330.8	2,196.7	75.2

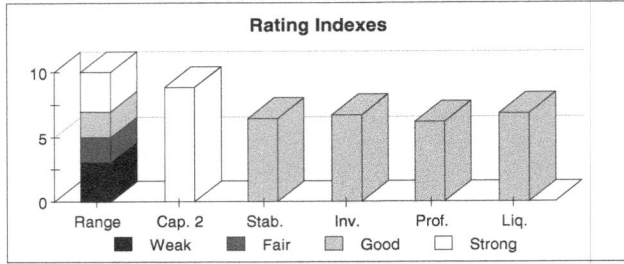

Rating Indexes

Range Cap. 2 Stab. Inv. Prof. Liq.
■ Weak ■ Fair ☐ Good ☐ Strong

WASHINGTON NATIONAL INS CO

D+   Weak

Major Rating Factors: Weak overall results on stability tests (2.7 on a scale of 0 to 10) including potential financial drain due to affiliation with CNO Financial Group Inc. Fair quality investment portfolio (4.8) with large holdings of BBB rated bonds in addition to moderate junk bond exposure. Fair profitability (4.6). Return on equity has been fair, averaging 8.9%.
Other Rating Factors: Good capitalization (5.7) based on good risk adjusted capital (severe loss scenario). Good liquidity (6.6).
Principal Business: Individual health insurance (57%), group health insurance (32%), individual life insurance (7%), reinsurance (3%), and individual annuities (1%).
Principal Investments: NonCMO investment grade bonds (68%), CMOs and structured securities (18%), mortgages in good standing (3%), noninv. grade bonds (2%), and misc. investments (8%).
Investments in Affiliates: 1%
Group Affiliation: CNO Financial Group Inc
Licensed in: All states except NY
Commenced Business: September 1923
Address: 11825 NORTH PENNSYLVANIA STREE, CARMEL, IN 46032
Phone: (317) 817-6100 **Domicile State:** IN **NAIC Code:** 70319

Data Date	Rating	RACR #1	RACR #2	Total Assets ($mil)	Capital ($mil)	Net Premium ($mil)	Net Income ($mil)
6-20	D+	1.42	0.84	5,651.2	334.9	368.0	26.5
6-19	D+	1.53	0.90	5,561.2	360.2	357.5	19.8
2019	D+	1.56	0.93	5,604.2	347.6	717.0	59.5
2018	D+	1.52	0.89	5,466.1	365.8	703.3	61.2
2017	D+	1.71	0.95	5,418.5	373.2	688.9	26.7
2016	D+	2.09	1.09	5,397.6	431.1	663.1	-53.0
2015	D+	1.70	0.93	4,807.8	333.1	649.7	60.9

CNO Financial Group Inc Composite Group Rating: D+ Largest Group Members	Assets ($mil)	Rating
BANKERS LIFE CAS CO	16369	D+
WASHINGTON NATIONAL INS CO	5604	D+
COLONIAL PENN LIFE INS CO	836	D+
BANKERS CONSECO LIFE INS CO	523	D

WEA INS CORP   C   Fair

Major Rating Factors: Fair quality investment portfolio (4.4 on a scale of 0 to 10). Fair overall results on stability tests (3.7) including negative cash flow from operations for 2019. Good liquidity (6.1) with sufficient resources to handle a spike in claims.
Other Rating Factors: Weak profitability (2.8). Excellent expense controls. Strong capitalization (7.3) based on excellent risk adjusted capital (severe loss scenario).
Principal Business: Group health insurance (100%).
Principal Investments: NonCMO investment grade bonds (48%), common & preferred stock (25%), CMOs and structured securities (21%), and cash (3%).
Investments in Affiliates: 1%
Group Affiliation: Wisconsin Education Assn Ins Trust
Licensed in: WI
Commenced Business: July 1985
Address: 45 NOB HILL ROAD, Madison, WI 53713-0000
Phone: (608) 276-4000 **Domicile State:** WI **NAIC Code:** 72273

Data Date	Rating	RACR #1	RACR #2	Total Assets ($mil)	Capital ($mil)	Net Premium ($mil)	Net Income ($mil)
6-20	C	1.64	1.17	746.9	203.0	322.8	36.2
6-19	C	1.70	1.22	706.8	199.8	303.9	2.4
2019	C	1.47	1.05	701.8	170.2	585.2	-31.5
2018	C	1.52	1.10	661.5	170.7	603.8	20.2
2017	C	1.85	1.27	661.0	167.0	466.6	1.4
2016	C	1.57	1.09	644.9	140.9	496.6	1.1
2015	C	1.70	1.20	644.2	160.7	550.6	-34.2

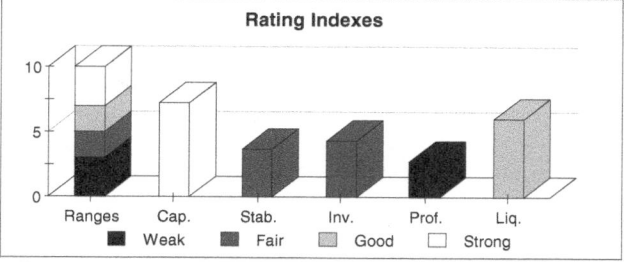

WELLCALL INC   C-   Fair

Major Rating Factors: Fair overall results on stability tests (4.1 on a scale of 0 to 10) in spite of healthy premium and capital growth during 2019. Good overall profitability index (5.8). Strong capitalization index (7.6) based on excellent current risk-adjusted capital (severe loss scenario).
Other Rating Factors: Excellent liquidity (7.5) with ample operational cash flow and liquid investments.
Principal Business: Managed care (100%)
Mem Phys: 19: N/A **18:** N/A **19 MLR** 946.2% **/ 19 Admin Exp** N/A
Enroll(000): Q2 20: 79 **19:** 63 **18:** 63 **Med Exp PMPM:** $14
Principal Investments ($000): Cash and equiv ($1,910)
Provider Compensation ($000): None
Total Member Encounters: N/A
Group Affiliation: None
Licensed in: (No states)
Address: 1004 Industrial Way Ste A, Lodi, CA 95240-3142
Phone: (415) 621-1606 **Dom State:** CA **Commenced Bus:** N/A

Data Date	Rating	RACR #1	RACR #2	Total Assets ($mil)	Capital ($mil)	Net Premium ($mil)	Net Income ($mil)
6-20	C-	2.40	1.56	4.5	3.7	0.6	0.8
6-19	C-	2.38	1.56	4.5	3.1	0.6	0.7
2019	C-	1.87	1.22	4.7	2.9	1.2	1.5
2018	C-	1.74	1.14	3.2	2.3	1.0	1.2
2017	C-	2.35	1.55	3.9	3.1	0.8	0.6
2016	N/A	N/A	N/A	N/A	N/A	N/A	N/A
2015	N/A	N/A	N/A	N/A	N/A	N/A	N/A

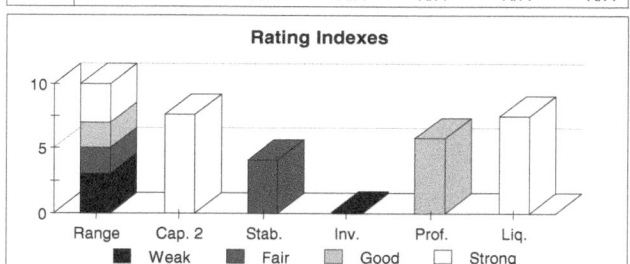

WELLCARE HEALTH INS OF ARIZONA INC   B-   Good

Major Rating Factors: Fair profitability index (3.4 on a scale of 0 to 10). Good quality investment portfolio (5.8). Good liquidity (6.8) with sufficient resources (cash flows and marketable investments) to handle a spike in claims.
Other Rating Factors: Strong capitalization (7.2) based on excellent current risk-adjusted capital (severe loss scenario).
Principal Business: Medicaid (63%), Medicare (37%).
Mem Phys: 19: 22 **18:** 20,300 **19 MLR** 84.2% **/ 19 Admin Exp** N/A
Enroll(000): Q2 20: 66 **19:** 60 **18:** 64 **Med Exp PMPM:** $806
Principal Investments: Long-term bonds (56%), cash and equiv (44%)
Provider Compensation ($000): Contr fee ($545,171), capitation ($56,228), bonus arrang ($9,443)
Total Member Encounters: Phys (355,834), non-phys (371,845)
Group Affiliation: None
Licensed in: AL, AK, AZ, AR, CO, DC, DE, FL, GA, HI, ID, IL, IN, IA, KS, KY, LA, MD, MI, MN, MS, MO, MT, NE, NV, NM, NC, ND, OK, OR, SC, SD, TN, TX, UT, VA, WA, WY
Address: 949 Kamokila Blvd Suite 350, Kapolei, HI 96707
Phone: (813) 206-6200 **Dom State:** AZ **Commenced Bus:** N/A

Data Date	Rating	RACR #1	RACR #2	Total Assets ($mil)	Capital ($mil)	Net Premium ($mil)	Net Income ($mil)
6-20	B-	1.53	1.27	238.1	80.8	407.6	5.4
6-19	C	1.85	1.54	205.1	68.4	358.4	4.5
2019	C	2.17	1.81	208.1	75.7	707.9	-2.0
2018	C	1.76	1.47	201.7	64.6	711.8	-3.8
2017	C	1.30	1.08	206.0	68.9	706.3	12.0
2016	C	2.63	2.19	223.9	97.4	731.0	10.4
2015	C	2.28	1.90	217.6	86.1	739.3	1.0

WELLCARE HEALTH INS OF KENTUCKY INC

C+

Fair

Major Rating Factors: Fair quality investment portfolio (3.8 on a scale of 0 to 10). Good liquidity (6.7) with sufficient resources (cash flows and marketable investments) to handle a spike in claims. Excellent profitability (7.9).
Other Rating Factors: Strong capitalization (7.5) based on excellent current risk-adjusted capital (severe loss scenario).
Principal Business: Medicaid (90%), Medicare (7%), other (3%)
Mem Phys: 19: 54 **18:** 47,400 **19 MLR** 89.8% **/ 19 Admin Exp** N/A
Enroll(000): Q2 20: 821 **19:** 770 **18:** 552 **Med Exp PMPM:** $282
Principal Investments: Long-term bonds (74%), cash and equiv (26%)
Provider Compensation ($000): Contr fee ($2,558,008), capitation ($112,890), bonus arrang ($7,295)
Total Member Encounters: Phys (2,828,756), non-phys (3,349,878)
Group Affiliation: None
Licensed in: All states except FL, ME, MI, NH, NY, NC, TX, VT, PR
Address: 13551 Triton Park Blvd Suite, Louisville, KY 40223
Phone: (813) 206-6200 **Dom State:** KY **Commenced Bus:** N/A

Data Date	Rating	RACR #1	RACR #2	Total Assets ($mil)	Capital ($mil)	Net Premium ($mil)	Net Income ($mil)
6-20	C+	1.77	1.47	1,034.5	328.6	1,762.3	18.5
6-19	B-	2.28	1.90	836.4	330.1	1,503.2	38.3
2019	C+	2.18	1.82	774.8	303.6	2,946.8	94.2
2018	C+	2.48	2.07	811.5	362.9	3,023.4	126.7
2017	B-	1.56	1.30	908.1	313.7	2,815.2	80.2
2016	C	1.97	1.64	682.9	283.2	2,753.4	42.2
2015	C+	2.10	1.75	691.8	301.3	2,763.2	119.0

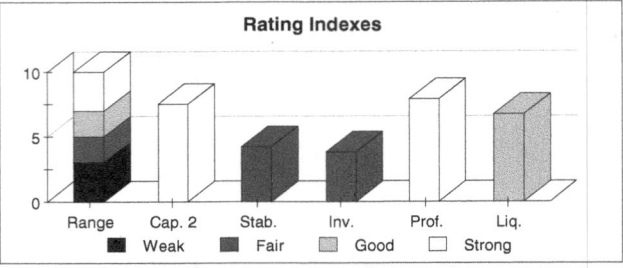

Rating Indexes

WELLCARE HEALTH INS OF NEW YORK INC

C+

Fair

Major Rating Factors: Weak profitability index (2.8 on a scale of 0 to 10). Strong capitalization (10.0) based on excellent current risk-adjusted capital (severe loss scenario). High quality investment portfolio (9.9).
Other Rating Factors: Excellent liquidity (10.0) with ample operational cash flow and liquid investments.
Principal Business: Medicare (100%)
Mem Phys: 18: 3,100 **17:** N/A **18 MLR** 101.5% **/ 18 Admin Exp** N/A
Enroll(000): Q3 19: 0 **18:** 0 **17:** N/A **Med Exp PMPM:** $642
Principal Investments: Cash and equiv (92%), long-term bonds (8%)
Provider Compensation ($000): Contr fee ($460)
Total Member Encounters: Phys (1,293), non-phys (389)
Group Affiliation: WellCare Health Plans Inc
Licensed in: NY
Address: One New York Plaza 15th Floor, New York, NY 10004
Phone: (813) 206-6200 **Dom State:** NY **Commenced Bus:** N/A

Data Date	Rating	RACR #1	RACR #2	Total Assets ($mil)	Capital ($mil)	Net Premium ($mil)	Net Income ($mil)
9-19	C+	4.10	3.42	6.9	6.2	1.1	0.1
9-18	N/A	N/A	N/A	6.2	6.1	0.3	N/A
2018	C-	4.01	3.34	6.1	6.1	0.5	0.0
2017	N/A	N/A	N/A	6.1	6.1	N/A	N/A
2016	N/A	N/A	N/A	6.1	6.1	N/A	N/A
2015	N/A	N/A	N/A	6.1	6.1	N/A	N/A
2014	N/A	N/A	N/A	12.1	12.1	N/A	N/A

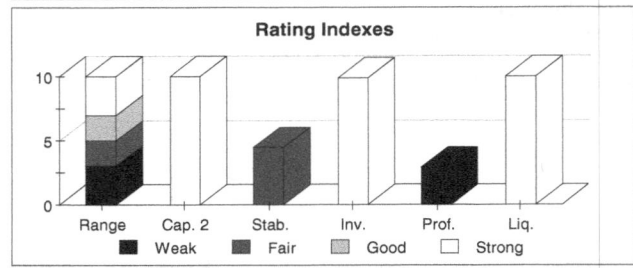

Rating Indexes

WELLCARE HEALTH PLANS OF NEW JERSEY

B

Good

Major Rating Factors: Fair profitability index (4.2 on a scale of 0 to 10). Strong capitalization (7.3) based on excellent current risk-adjusted capital (severe loss scenario). High quality investment portfolio (9.9).
Other Rating Factors: Excellent liquidity (7.0) with sufficient resources (cash flows and marketable investments) to handle a spike in claims.
Principal Business: Medicaid (86%), Medicare (14%)
Mem Phys: 19: 36 **18:** 29,700 **19 MLR** 85.5% **/ 19 Admin Exp** N/A
Enroll(000): Q2 20: 102 **19:** 84 **18:** 76 **Med Exp PMPM:** $769
Principal Investments: Cash and equiv (91%), long-term bonds (9%)
Provider Compensation ($000): Contr fee ($735,680), capitation ($15,137), bonus arrang ($2,025)
Total Member Encounters: Phys (727,700), non-phys (1,004,447)
Group Affiliation: None
Licensed in: NJ
Address: 550 Broad Street Suite 1200, Newark, NJ 7102
Phone: (813) 206-6200 **Dom State:** NJ **Commenced Bus:** N/A

Data Date	Rating	RACR #1	RACR #2	Total Assets ($mil)	Capital ($mil)	Net Premium ($mil)	Net Income ($mil)
6-20	B	1.59	1.33	247.9	102.3	513.3	6.1
6-19	B-	2.45	2.04	194.5	87.5	411.1	4.0
2019	B	2.15	1.79	216.0	95.4	886.3	-2.6
2018	C+	2.33	1.94	184.3	82.5	717.0	4.5
2017	C	1.52	1.27	157.9	69.1	589.4	-2.1
2016	C-	3.34	2.79	159.5	73.1	454.6	10.0
2015	C-	2.46	2.05	140.4	46.5	350.0	1.3

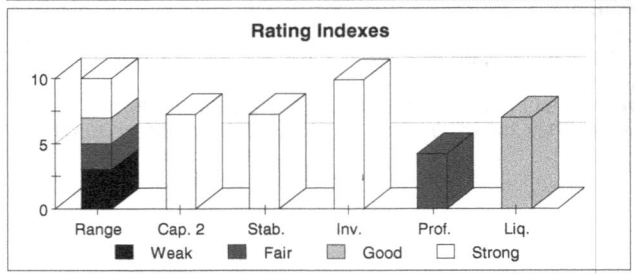

Rating Indexes

WELLCARE OF CONNECTICUT INC　　　C　　Fair

Major Rating Factors: Weak profitability index (2.9 on a scale of 0 to 10). Good overall results on stability tests (5.6) despite a decline in the number of member physicians during 2020. Strong capitalization index (8.5) based on excellent current risk-adjusted capital (severe loss scenario).
Other Rating Factors: High quality investment portfolio (8.9). Excellent liquidity (7.2) with ample operational cash flow and liquid investments.
Principal Business: Medicare (100%)
Mem Phys: 19: 34　**18:** 29,000　**19 MLR** 80.3%　**/ 19 Admin Exp** N/A
Enroll(000): Q2 20: 9　**19:** 10　**18:** 9　**Med Exp PMPM:** $836
Principal Investments: Cash and equiv (87%), long-term bonds (13%)
Provider Compensation ($000): Contr fee ($91,414), capitation ($2,172), bonus arrang ($803)
Total Member Encounters: Phys (124,050), non-phys (75,301)
Group Affiliation: None
Licensed in: CT
Address: 902 Chapel Street, Hamden,
Phone: (813) 206-6200　**Dom State:** CT　**Commenced Bus:** N/A

Data Date	Rating	RACR #1	RACR #2	Total Assets ($mil)	Capital ($mil)	Net Premium ($mil)	Net Income ($mil)
6-20	C	2.51	2.10	52.7	29.0	63.5	1.1
6-19	C	4.06	3.38	48.3	26.8	58.5	1.0
2019	C	4.21	3.51	45.3	28.3	117.4	2.3
2018	C	3.92	3.27	42.1	25.9	99.8	-4.6
2017	C	2.37	1.98	35.7	22.4	86.5	-1.9
2016	C+	4.55	3.79	39.1	24.2	81.2	-3.4
2015	C+	3.07	2.56	45.0	27.5	146.5	6.1

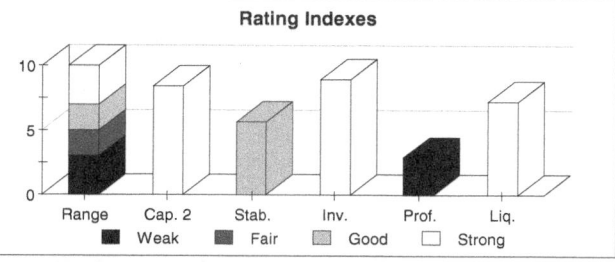

Rating Indexes

WELLCARE OF FLORIDA INC　　　D+　　Weak

Major Rating Factors: Good capitalization index (5.4 on a scale of 0 to 10) based on good current risk-adjusted capital (severe loss scenario). Good quality investment portfolio (5.1). Good liquidity (6.8) with sufficient resources (cash flows and marketable investments) to handle a spike in claims.
Other Rating Factors: Excellent profitability (9.3). Excellent overall results on stability tests (8.1) based on healthy premium and capital growth during 2019 but a decline in the number of member physicians during 2020.
Principal Business: Medicaid (76%), Medicare (22%), comp med (2%)
Mem Phys: 19: 61　**18:** 53,300　**19 MLR** 87.6%　**/ 19 Admin Exp** N/A
Enroll(000): Q2 20: 1,138　**19:** 1,132　**18:** 873　**Med Exp PMPM:** $443
Principal Investments: Long-term bonds (63%), cash and equiv (37%)
Provider Compensation ($000): Contr fee ($5,143,230), capitation ($242,837), bonus arrang ($141,769)
Total Member Encounters: Phys (7,391,523), non-phys (5,664,818)
Group Affiliation: None
Licensed in: FL
Address: 8735 Henderson Road, Tampa,
Phone: (813) 206-6200　**Dom State:** FL　**Commenced Bus:** N/A

Data Date	Rating	RACR #1	RACR #2	Total Assets ($mil)	Capital ($mil)	Net Premium ($mil)	Net Income ($mil)
6-20	D+	0.99	0.83	1,805.3	444.4	3,745.3	107.9
6-19	B	1.92	1.60	1,192.4	343.4	3,228.0	83.6
2019	B	1.00	0.83	1,309.3	340.8	6,745.2	205.1
2018	B-	1.59	1.32	749.1	274.4	3,757.4	138.1
2017	E	0.75	0.62	761.8	182.4	3,835.7	137.5
2016	E	1.02	0.85	688.9	170.8	3,679.1	128.0
2015	E-	1.03	0.86	568.1	167.1	3,554.9	49.6

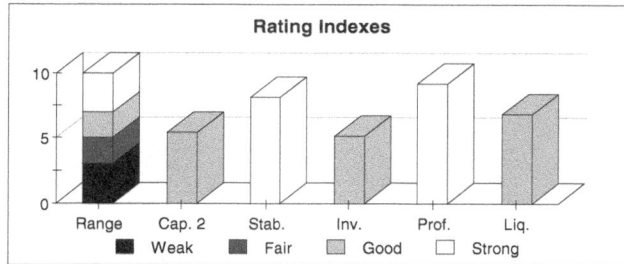

Rating Indexes

WELLCARE OF GEORGIA INC *　　　B+　　Good

Major Rating Factors: Excellent profitability (8.3 on a scale of 0 to 10). Strong capitalization (8.1) based on excellent current risk-adjusted capital (severe loss scenario). High quality investment portfolio (8.6).
Other Rating Factors: Excellent liquidity (7.1) with ample operational cash flow and liquid investments.
Principal Business: Medicaid (65%), Medicare (30%), comp med (5%)
Mem Phys: 19: 55　**18:** 49,600　**19 MLR** 81.2%　**/ 19 Admin Exp** N/A
Enroll(000): Q2 20: 582　**19:** 531　**18:** 544　**Med Exp PMPM:** $261
Principal Investments: Cash and equiv (68%), long-term bonds (32%)
Provider Compensation ($000): Contr fee ($1,585,651), capitation ($127,682), bonus arrang ($19,421)
Total Member Encounters: Phys (2,691,948), non-phys (1,515,960)
Group Affiliation: None
Licensed in: GA
Address: 211 Perimeter Center Parkway, Atlanta, GA 30346
Phone: (813) 206-6200　**Dom State:** GA　**Commenced Bus:** N/A

Data Date	Rating	RACR #1	RACR #2	Total Assets ($mil)	Capital ($mil)	Net Premium ($mil)	Net Income ($mil)
6-20	B+	2.25	1.87	685.5	303.8	1,126.4	76.5
6-19	B	2.57	2.15	580.3	268.1	1,058.2	66.2
2019	B	2.31	1.93	502.1	226.0	2,102.4	105.7
2018	B-	2.04	1.70	494.8	206.7	2,078.6	39.0
2017	B-	1.63	1.36	496.4	222.2	2,100.1	87.2
2016	C	1.96	1.63	493.6	195.2	2,041.1	16.7
2015	C	1.83	1.52	374.6	175.4	1,991.3	1.2

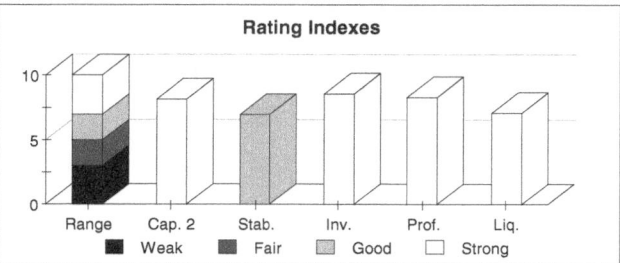

Rating Indexes

WELLCARE OF NEBRASKA INC

B- **Good**

Major Rating Factors: Excellent profitability (8.0 on a scale of 0 to 10). Strong capitalization (10.0) based on excellent current risk-adjusted capital (severe loss scenario). High quality investment portfolio (9.1).
Other Rating Factors: Excellent liquidity (7.2) with ample operational cash flow and liquid investments.
Principal Business: Medicaid (100%)
Mem Phys: 18: 27,000 **17:** 16 **18 MLR** 83.9% **/ 18 Admin Exp** N/A
Enroll(000): Q3 19: 79 **18:** 80 **17:** 80 **Med Exp PMPM:** $298
Principal Investments: Cash and equiv (71%), long-term bonds (29%)
Provider Compensation ($000): Contr fee ($297,916)
Total Member Encounters: Phys (373,586), non-phys (297,171)
Group Affiliation: WellCare Health Plans Inc
Licensed in: NE
Address: 8055 O Street Suite 300, LINCOLN, NE 68510
Phone: (813) 206-6200 **Dom State:** NE **Commenced Bus:** N/A

Data Date	Rating	RACR #1	RACR #2	Total Assets ($mil)	Capital ($mil)	Net Premium ($mil)	Net Income ($mil)
9-19	B-	3.91	3.26	171.2	58.4	262.4	12.3
9-18	N/A	N/A	N/A	177.0	52.8	252.6	9.9
2018	C-	3.35	2.80	168.4	46.8	341.3	14.0
2017	N/A	N/A	N/A	142.5	43.0	348.1	0.8
2016	N/A	N/A	N/A	26.9	26.8	N/A	-0.1
2015	N/A	N/A	N/A	N/A	N/A	N/A	N/A
2014	N/A	N/A	N/A	N/A	N/A	N/A	N/A

WELLCARE OF SOUTH CAROLINA INC

B **Good**

Major Rating Factors: Good overall profitability index (6.1 on a scale of 0 to 10). Strong capitalization (7.9) based on excellent current risk-adjusted capital (severe loss scenario). High quality investment portfolio (7.6).
Other Rating Factors: Excellent liquidity (7.1) with ample operational cash flow and liquid investments.
Principal Business: Medicaid (88%), Medicare (12%)
Mem Phys: 19: 37 **18:** 32,200 **19 MLR** 83.2% **/ 19 Admin Exp** N/A
Enroll(000): Q2 20: 97 **19:** 86 **18:** 79 **Med Exp PMPM:** $278
Principal Investments: Cash and equiv (64%), long-term bonds (36%)
Provider Compensation ($000): Contr fee ($279,315), bonus arrang ($3,628), capitation ($1,429)
Total Member Encounters: Phys (444,360), non-phys (224,544)
Group Affiliation: None
Licensed in: SC
Address: 200 Center Point Circle Suite, Columbia, SC 29210
Phone: (813) 206-6200 **Dom State:** SC **Commenced Bus:** N/A

Data Date	Rating	RACR #1	RACR #2	Total Assets ($mil)	Capital ($mil)	Net Premium ($mil)	Net Income ($mil)
6-20	B	2.08	1.73	141.3	58.9	204.1	-5.3
6-19	B-	3.96	3.30	109.4	64.4	162.5	3.0
2019	B-	3.52	2.93	112.2	63.2	343.2	13.1
2018	B-	3.77	3.14	104.9	61.0	304.2	7.6
2017	B-	2.76	2.30	114.1	66.6	297.1	16.2
2016	C	3.64	3.03	110.1	53.4	277.6	4.9
2015	C	3.85	3.21	78.7	43.2	222.7	12.5

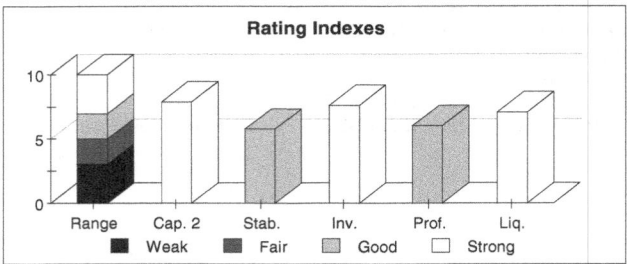

WELLCARE OF TEXAS INC *

A- **Excellent**

Major Rating Factors: Excellent profitability (8.4 on a scale of 0 to 10). Strong capitalization (8.0) based on excellent current risk-adjusted capital (severe loss scenario). High quality investment portfolio (8.6).
Other Rating Factors: Excellent liquidity (7.1) with ample operational cash flow and liquid investments.
Principal Business: Medicare (100%)
Mem Phys: 19: 25 **18:** 24,900 **19 MLR** 79.1% **/ 19 Admin Exp** N/A
Enroll(000): Q2 20: 45 **19:** 43 **18:** 49 **Med Exp PMPM:** $607
Principal Investments: Long-term bonds (55%), cash and equiv (45%)
Provider Compensation ($000): Contr fee ($300,802), capitation ($12,766), bonus arrang ($7,286)
Total Member Encounters: Phys (529,827), non-phys (225,808)
Group Affiliation: None
Licensed in: AZ, TX
Address: 4888 Loop Central Drive Suite, Houston, TX 77081
Phone: (813) 206-6200 **Dom State:** TX **Commenced Bus:** N/A

Data Date	Rating	RACR #1	RACR #2	Total Assets ($mil)	Capital ($mil)	Net Premium ($mil)	Net Income ($mil)
6-20	A-	2.13	1.77	201.1	67.7	223.7	11.8
6-19	B	2.54	2.12	153.0	54.2	215.0	15.5
2019	B	2.88	2.40	152.7	57.6	409.4	30.7
2018	B-	2.78	2.31	132.3	60.0	423.2	11.7
2017	C	1.70	1.41	121.7	58.4	409.7	10.7
2016	C	2.51	2.09	130.1	58.0	387.8	1.1
2015	C	2.57	2.14	105.2	55.4	366.8	2.1

WELLCARE PRESCRIPTION INS INC   D   Weak

Major Rating Factors: Weak liquidity (2.3 on a scale of 0 to 10) as a spike in claims may stretch capacity. Fair profitability index (4.5). Strong capitalization (10.0) based on excellent current risk-adjusted capital (severe loss scenario).
Other Rating Factors: High quality investment portfolio (9.9).
Principal Business: Other (100%)
Mem Phys: 19: N/A **18:** N/A **19 MLR** 193.5% **/ 19 Admin Exp** N/A
Enroll(000): Q2 20: 4,096 **19:** 3,824 **18:** 963 **Med Exp PMPM:** $42
Principal Investments: Cash and equiv (83%), long-term bonds (17%)
Provider Compensation ($000): Contr fee ($1,463,885)
Total Member Encounters: N/A
Group Affiliation: None
Licensed in: All states except AL, AR, CO, CT, MN, MT, RI, PR
Address: 4110 George Road Suite 300, Tampa, FL 33634
Phone: (813) 206-6200 **Dom State:** FL **Commenced Bus:** N/A

Data Date	Rating	RACR #1	RACR #2	Total Assets ($mil)	Capital ($mil)	Net Premium ($mil)	Net Income ($mil)
6-20	D	4.25	3.54	2,713.2	166.4	1,327.3	-66.7
6-19	C	8.11	6.75	1,008.3	184.6	502.3	10.2
2019	C	6.45	5.38	953.5	233.6	966.9	48.1
2018	C	8.41	7.01	1,136.5	191.6	762.4	91.9
2017	E	7.23	6.03	1,491.3	245.2	834.5	38.0
2016	E	10.83	9.02	852.9	209.5	755.6	68.4
2015	E-	6.07	5.06	721.2	141.3	814.8	23.6

Rating Indexes

Range, Cap. 2, Stab., Inv., Prof., Liq.
■ Weak ■ Fair ▨ Good □ Strong

WELLFLEET INS CO   C-   Fair

Major Rating Factors: Fair profitability index (4.1) with operating losses during 2015 and the first six months of 2020. Average return on equity over the last five years has been poor at 0.0%.
Other Rating Factors: Fair overall results on stability tests (3.0) including excessive premium growth. Strong long-term capitalization index (10.0) based on excellent current risk adjusted capital (severe and moderate loss scenarios), despite some fluctuation in capital levels. Excellent liquidity (8.4) with ample operational cash flow and liquid investments.
Principal Business: Group accident & health (93%), other accident & health (5%), and workers compensation (2%).
Principal Investments: Misc. investments (47%), cash (47%), and investment grade bonds (6%).
Investments in Affiliates: None
Group Affiliation: Berkshire-Hathaway
Licensed in: All states except NY, PR
Commenced Business: August 1987
Address: 5814 Reed Road, Fort Wayne, IN 46835-3568
Phone: (260) 485-9622 **Domicile State:** IN **NAIC Code:** 32280

Data Date	Rating	RACR #1	RACR #2	Loss Ratio %	Total Assets ($mil)	Capital ($mil)	Net Premium ($mil)	Net Income ($mil)
6-20	C-	10.36	9.32	N/A	129.2	62.1	0.1	-0.2
6-19	C-	16.94	15.24	N/A	93.8	64.2	0.0	0.6
2019	C-	9.31	8.38	84.1	155.0	64.1	0.2	1.1
2018	C-	13.10	11.79	84.2	104.5	63.3	0.0	0.9
2017	U	131.24	118.10	0.0	65.1	63.7	0.0	0.7
2016	U	41.53	21.05	104.7	67.6	62.6	-55.0	2.2
2015	U	4.87	1.44	N/A	116.1	59.0	0.0	-4.3

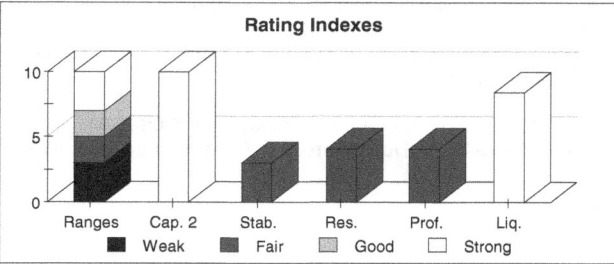

Rating Indexes

Ranges, Cap. 2, Stab., Res., Prof., Liq.
■ Weak ■ Fair ▨ Good □ Strong

WELLFLEET NEW YORK INS CO   C   Fair

Major Rating Factors: Weak overall results on stability tests (2.9 on a scale of 0 to 10) including negative cash flow from operations for 2019. History of adequate reserve strength (6.1) as reserves have been consistently at an acceptable level.
Other Rating Factors: Good overall profitability index (6.5) despite operating losses during the first six months of 2020. Return on equity has been fair, averaging 9.0% over the past five years. Strong long-term capitalization index (8.3) based on excellent current risk adjusted capital (severe and moderate loss scenarios), despite some fluctuation in capital levels. Excellent liquidity (7.8) with ample operational cash flow and liquid investments.
Principal Business: Group accident & health (91%) and workers compensation (9%).
Principal Investments: Cash (72%), misc. investments (20%), and investment grade bonds (8%).
Investments in Affiliates: None
Group Affiliation: Berkshire-Hathaway
Licensed in: All states except PR
Commenced Business: January 1929
Address: Marine Air Terminal LaGuardia, Flushing, NY 11371
Phone: (260) 485-9622 **Domicile State:** NY **NAIC Code:** 20931

Data Date	Rating	RACR #1	RACR #2	Loss Ratio %	Total Assets ($mil)	Capital ($mil)	Net Premium ($mil)	Net Income ($mil)
6-20	C	2.52	1.80	N/A	84.2	28.4	12.0	-0.5
6-19	C	3.24	2.31	N/A	85.1	29.5	10.8	0.6
2019	C	2.73	1.96	84.4	90.3	29.4	23.3	0.2
2018	C	2.97	2.13	86.2	86.8	28.9	22.8	1.3
2017	C	2.17	1.79	78.3	96.2	27.0	14.3	9.0
2016	U	6.97	6.28	111.0	42.2	22.3	-17.5	2.3
2015	U	2.05	1.00	0.0	43.3	20.2	0.0	0.4

Berkshire-Hathaway Composite Group Rating: B- Largest Group Members	Assets ($mil)	Rating
NATIONAL INDEMNITY CO	285940	B-
GOVERNMENT EMPLOYEES INS CO	41582	B
COLUMBIA INS CO	30809	C+
BERKSHIRE HATHAWAY LIFE INS CO OF NE	20830	C+
GENERAL REINS CORP	18422	C+

WELLMARK HEALTH PLAN OF IOWA

B **Good**

Major Rating Factors: Fair quality investment portfolio (4.4 on a scale of 0 to 10). Excellent profitability (8.2). Strong capitalization index (10.0) based on excellent current risk-adjusted capital (severe loss scenario).

Other Rating Factors: Excellent overall results on stability tests (7.9) despite a decline in the number of member physicians during 2020. Excellent liquidity (6.9) with sufficient resources (cash flows and marketable investments) to handle a spike in claims.

Principal Business: Comp med (100%)

Mem Phys: 19: 12 **18:** 10,982 **19 MLR** 74.7% **/ 19 Admin Exp** N/A

Enroll(000): Q2 20: 101 **19:** 98 **18:** 90 **Med Exp PMPM:** $318

Principal Investments: Long-term bonds (62%), nonaffiliate common stock (34%), cash and equiv (1%), other (3%)

Provider Compensation ($000): Bonus arrang ($180,259), contr fee ($164,481), FFS ($24,822), capitation ($1,465)

Total Member Encounters: Phys (428,863), non-phys (324,872)

Group Affiliation: Wellmark Inc

Licensed in: IA

Address: 1331 Grand Avenue, Des Moines,

Phone: (515) 376-4500 **Dom State:** IA **Commenced Bus:** N/A

Data Date	Rating	RACR #1	RACR #2	Total Assets ($mil)	Capital ($mil)	Net Premium ($mil)	Net Income ($mil)
6-20	B	5.55	4.62	433.3	253.6	269.3	42.6
6-19	B	8.48	7.06	356.2	237.9	252.8	46.2
2019	B	6.21	5.17	347.4	209.0	490.6	49.3
2018	B	6.82	5.69	286.1	191.2	419.9	35.1
2017	B	5.63	4.70	283.1	189.6	384.0	28.1
2016	B	7.23	6.03	232.7	153.6	316.0	5.5
2015	B+	6.08	5.07	227.6	148.2	358.7	-9.4

Rating Indexes

WELLMARK INC

B- **Good**

Major Rating Factors: Fair quality investment portfolio (3.6 on a scale of 0 to 10). Good overall profitability index (6.1). Good liquidity (6.9) with sufficient resources (cash flows and marketable investments) to handle a spike in claims.

Other Rating Factors: Strong capitalization (10.0) based on excellent current risk-adjusted capital (severe loss scenario).

Principal Business: Comp med (61%), med supp (16%), FEHB (10%), dental (1%), other (11%)

Mem Phys: 19: 9 **18:** 9,204 **19 MLR** 84.8% **/ 19 Admin Exp** N/A

Enroll(000): Q2 20: 1,197 **19:** 1,213 **18:** 1,224 **Med Exp PMPM:** $147

Principal Investments: Long-term bonds (38%), affiliate common stock (23%), nonaffiliate common stock (21%), cash and equiv (9%), real estate (6%), other (3%)

Provider Compensation ($000): Contr fee ($1,297,428), bonus arrang ($493,832), FFS ($184,246), other ($218,465)

Total Member Encounters: Phys (3,386,423), non-phys (2,265,612)

Group Affiliation: Wellmark Inc

Licensed in: IA, SD

Address: 1331 Grand Avenue, Des Moines, IA 50309-2901

Phone: (515) 376-4500 **Dom State:** IA **Commenced Bus:** N/A

Data Date	Rating	RACR #1	RACR #2	Total Assets ($mil)	Capital ($mil)	Net Premium ($mil)	Net Income ($mil)
6-20	B-	6.84	5.70	3,078.5	1,995.1	1,273.2	80.8
6-19	B-	6.70	5.59	2,754.8	1,816.0	1,288.5	114.3
2019	B-	6.35	5.29	2,762.2	1,853.7	2,560.2	158.7
2018	B-	5.78	4.82	2,438.7	1,567.3	2,625.9	127.5
2017	B-	N/A	N/A	2,423.5	1,524.1	2,646.9	43.1
2016	B-	5.36	4.47	2,129.5	1,330.3	2,656.3	-26.5
2015	B	5.40	4.50	2,043.9	1,322.0	2,535.8	-1.8

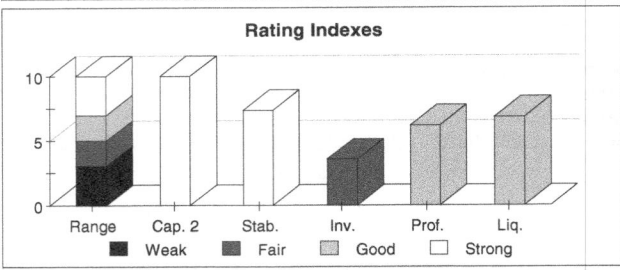

Rating Indexes

WELLMARK OF SOUTH DAKOTA INC

B **Good**

Major Rating Factors: Fair quality investment portfolio (4.2 on a scale of 0 to 10). Excellent profitability (7.1). Strong capitalization (10.0) based on excellent current risk-adjusted capital (severe loss scenario).

Other Rating Factors: Excellent liquidity (7.0) with sufficient resources (cash flows and marketable investments) to handle a spike in claims.

Principal Business: Comp med (69%), FEHB (22%), med supp (8%), other (1%)

Mem Phys: 19: 2 **18:** 2,793 **19 MLR** 82.3% **/ 19 Admin Exp** N/A

Enroll(000): Q2 20: 161 **19:** 163 **18:** 166 **Med Exp PMPM:** $320

Principal Investments: Long-term bonds (63%), nonaffiliate common stock (35%), cash and equiv (2%), real estate (1%)

Provider Compensation ($000): Contr fee ($524,864), FFS ($103,549), bonus arrang ($9,327)

Total Member Encounters: Phys (793,331), non-phys (515,602)

Group Affiliation: Wellmark Inc

Licensed in: SD

Address: 1601 West Madison Street, Sioux Falls, SD 57104-5710

Phone: (605) 373-7200 **Dom State:** SD **Commenced Bus:** N/A

Data Date	Rating	RACR #1	RACR #2	Total Assets ($mil)	Capital ($mil)	Net Premium ($mil)	Net Income ($mil)
6-20	B	5.93	4.94	566.8	339.9	386.5	42.5
6-19	B+	7.68	6.40	532.1	329.1	383.9	43.4
2019	B+	6.90	5.75	507.3	300.7	763.2	53.4
2018	B+	6.61	5.51	472.7	283.1	779.3	48.7
2017	B+	N/A	N/A	476.0	291.1	742.1	41.0
2016	B+	6.17	5.14	414.4	238.6	696.1	4.5
2015	B+	6.02	5.01	407.3	232.7	694.8	27.7

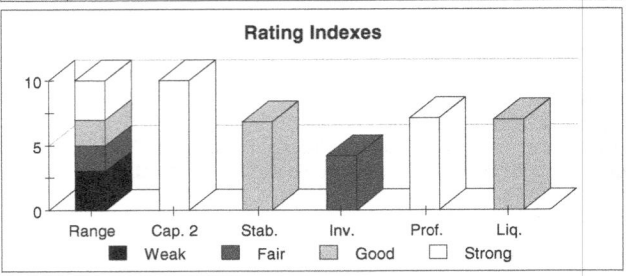

Rating Indexes

WELLMARK VALUE HEALTH PLAN INC   C+   Fair

Major Rating Factors: Excellent profitability (7.7 on a scale of 0 to 10). Strong capitalization (10.0) based on excellent current risk-adjusted capital (severe loss scenario). High quality investment portfolio (9.9).
Other Rating Factors: Excellent liquidity (10.0) with ample operational cash flow and liquid investments.
Principal Business: Comp med (100%)
Mem Phys: 18: 5,490   **17:** 4   **18 MLR** 56.4%   **/ 18 Admin Exp** N/A
Enroll(000): Q3 19: 4   **18:** 1   **17:** 2   **Med Exp PMPM:** $100
Principal Investments: Cash and equiv (100%)
Provider Compensation ($000): FFS ($625), bonus arrang ($618), contr fee ($11), capitation ($8)
Total Member Encounters: Phys (16,165), non-phys (8,015)
Group Affiliation: Wellmark Inc
Licensed in: IA
Address: 1331 Grand Avenue, Des Moines, IA 50309-2901
Phone: (515) 376-4500   **Dom State:** IA   **Commenced Bus:** N/A

Data Date	Rating	RACR #1	RACR #2	Total Assets ($mil)	Capital ($mil)	Net Premium ($mil)	Net Income ($mil)
9-19	C+	11.61	9.67	23.7	15.3	27.2	8.6
9-18	N/A	N/A	N/A	9.0	7.0	1.3	0.6
2018	C+	5.22	4.35	8.6	6.7	1.2	0.2
2017	N/A	N/A	N/A	10.5	6.5	11.2	1.7
2016	N/A	N/A	N/A	5.0	4.8	N/A	-0.2
2015	N/A	N/A	N/A	N/A	N/A	N/A	N/A
2014	N/A	N/A	N/A	N/A	N/A	N/A	N/A

WEST VIRGINIA FAMILY HEALTH PLAN INC   B   Good

Major Rating Factors: Excellent profitability (8.1 on a scale of 0 to 10). Strong capitalization (9.3) based on excellent current risk-adjusted capital (severe loss scenario). High quality investment portfolio (9.9).
Other Rating Factors: Excellent liquidity (7.1) with ample operational cash flow and liquid investments.
Principal Business: Medicaid (100%)
Mem Phys: 19: 9   **18:** 9,803   **19 MLR** 90.6%   **/ 19 Admin Exp** N/A
Enroll(000): Q2 20: N/A   **19:** N/A   **18:** 63   **Med Exp PMPM:** N/A
Principal Investments: Cash and equiv (58%), long-term bonds (42%)
Provider Compensation ($000): Contr fee ($194,628), capitation ($1,284), bonus arrang ($295)
Total Member Encounters: Phys (333,226), non-phys (258,158)
Group Affiliation: None
Licensed in: WV
Address: 614 Market Street, Parkersburg, WV 26101
Phone: (304) 424-7700   **Dom State:** WV   **Commenced Bus:** N/A

Data Date	Rating	RACR #1	RACR #2	Total Assets ($mil)	Capital ($mil)	Net Premium ($mil)	Net Income ($mil)
6-20	B	3.19	2.66	44.1	40.9	0.0	-0.2
6-19	B	2.78	2.31	75.9	40.8	155.0	4.9
2019	B	5.30	4.41	50.0	40.8	181.2	5.6
2018	C	2.51	2.09	79.1	35.9	337.7	1.8
2017	C-	N/A	N/A	67.1	25.0	324.1	18.6
2016	C-	0.28	0.23	60.7	8.3	299.6	4.9
2015	C	1.36	1.14	51.0	4.9	102.6	0.8

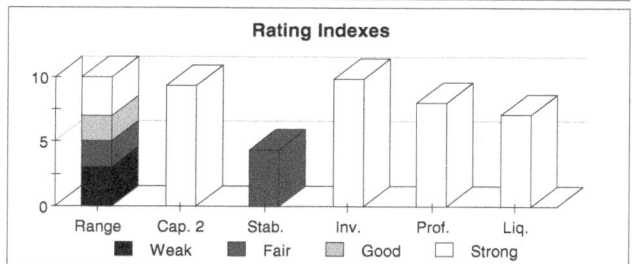

WESTERN GROCERS EMPLOYEE BENEFITS   E-   Very Weak

Major Rating Factors: Weak profitability index (1.9 on a scale of 0 to 10). Weak liquidity (0.0) as a spike in claims may stretch capacity. Strong capitalization index (10.0) based on weak current risk-adjusted capital (severe loss scenario).
Other Rating Factors: High quality investment portfolio (9.6).
Principal Business: Comp med (94%), dental (6%)
Mem Phys: 19: N/A   **18:** N/A   **19 MLR** 108.6%   **/ 19 Admin Exp** N/A
Enroll(000): Q2 20: N/A   **19:** 6   **18:** 7   **Med Exp PMPM:** $313
Principal Investments: Long-term bonds (59%), cash and equiv (41%)
Provider Compensation ($000): FFS ($23,672)
Total Member Encounters: Phys (40,870), non-phys (50,145)
Group Affiliation: None
Licensed in: AK, OR, WA
Address: 12901 SE 97TH AVE #200, CLACKAMAS, OR 97015
Phone: (503) 968-2360   **Dom State:** OR   **Commenced Bus:** N/A

Data Date	Rating	RACR #1	RACR #2	Total Assets ($mil)	Capital ($mil)	Net Premium ($mil)	Net Income ($mil)
6-20	E-	N/A	N/A	2.3	1.5	N/A	0.9
6-19	N/A	N/A	N/A	N/A	N/A	N/A	N/A
2019	E-	N/A	N/A	5.5	0.6	22.9	-2.7
2018	E+	N/A	N/A	6.6	3.3	21.2	-0.2
2017	E	N/A	N/A	7.1	3.5	19.3	0.6
2016	E	-0.77	-0.64	6.0	2.9	16.4	-1.7
2015	N/A	N/A	N/A	7.6	4.6	15.6	-1.3

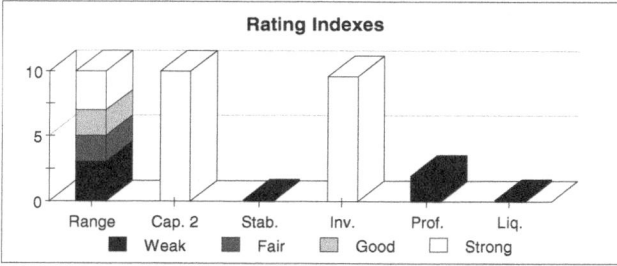

WESTERN HEALTH ADVANTAGE

E   **Very Weak**

Major Rating Factors: Poor capitalization index (0.0 on a scale of 0 to 10) based on weak current risk-adjusted capital (severe loss scenario). Fair overall results on stability tests (3.3) based on a significant 100% decrease in enrollment during the period. Good profitability index (4.9).
Other Rating Factors: Excellent liquidity (6.9) with sufficient resources (cash flows and marketable investments) to handle a spike in claims.
Principal Business: Managed care (100%)
Mem Phys: 19: N/A **18:** N/A **19 MLR** 90.9% **/ 19 Admin Exp** N/A
Enroll(000): Q2 20: 0 **19:** 0 **18:** 126 **Med Exp PMPM:** $734,221,138
Principal Investments ($000): Cash and equiv ($36,459)
Provider Compensation ($000): None
Total Member Encounters: N/A
Group Affiliation: None
Licensed in: CA
Address: 2349 Gateway Oaks Suite 100, Sacramento, CA 95833
Phone: (916) 563-3183 **Dom State:** CA **Commenced Bus:** May 1997

Data Date	Rating	RACR #1	RACR #2	Total Assets ($mil)	Capital ($mil)	Net Premium ($mil)	Net Income ($mil)
6-20	E	0.21	0.13	81.6	12.8	336.6	-0.7
6-19	E	0.24	0.15	72.7	11.4	404.6	1.1
2019	E	0.23	0.14	68.2	13.5	807.7	3.2
2018	E	0.22	0.14	63.0	10.2	760.7	0.0
2017	E	0.19	0.12	60.0	10.3	758.7	4.6
2016	E	0.18	0.11	83.5	8.8	664.4	1.5
2015	E	0.15	0.09	93.9	7.3	594.9	-13.2

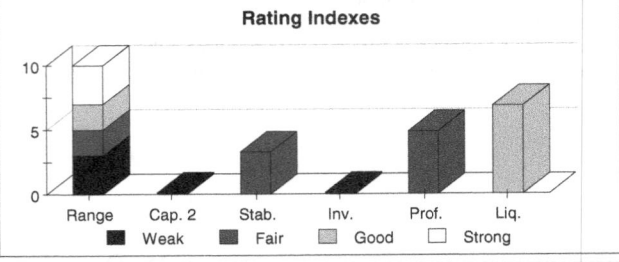

Rating Indexes

WESTPORT INS CORP

C+   **Fair**

Major Rating Factors: Fair profitability index (3.3 on a scale of 0 to 10) with operating losses during 2018. Return on equity has been fair, averaging 5.6% over the past five years. Fair overall results on stability tests (3.8) including negative cash flow from operations for 2019.
Other Rating Factors: Good long-term capitalization index (5.6) based on good current risk adjusted capital (moderate loss scenario), despite some fluctuation in capital levels. History of adequate reserve strength (5.9) as reserves have been consistently at an acceptable level. Good liquidity (6.8) with sufficient resources (cash flows and marketable investments) to handle a spike in claims.
Principal Business: Group accident & health (40%), other liability (17%), allied lines (16%), fire (12%), earthquake (5%), inland marine (4%), and other lines (6%).
Principal Investments: Investment grade bonds (85%) and misc. investments (15%).
Investments in Affiliates: 13%
Group Affiliation: Swiss Reinsurance
Licensed in: All states, the District of Columbia and Puerto Rico
Commenced Business: September 1981
Address: 237 EAST HIGH STREET, Jefferson City, MO 65101-3206
Phone: (816) 235-3700 **Domicile State:** MO **NAIC Code:** 39845

Data Date	Rating	RACR #1	RACR #2	Loss Ratio %	Total Assets ($mil)	Capital ($mil)	Net Premium ($mil)	Net Income ($mil)
6-20	C+	1.96	1.32	N/A	4,585.6	1,566.2	280.0	66.3
6-19	C	1.36	0.83	N/A	5,058.6	1,493.6	362.0	198.9
2019	C+	1.71	1.14	81.3	4,781.9	1,479.0	124.8	170.5
2018	B-	1.31	0.78	74.4	5,450.1	1,634.1	2,292.9	-245.2
2017	B	1.61	1.04	77.1	5,517.6	1,535.5	321.9	93.8
2016	B	1.78	1.23	80.1	4,730.1	1,558.6	287.1	189.7
2015	B-	1.48	1.03	61.5	4,693.0	1,505.3	281.6	177.3

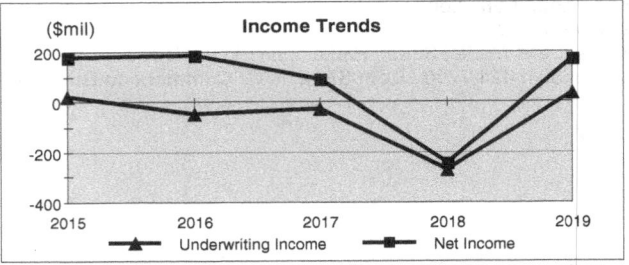

Income Trends

WISCONSIN COLLABORATIVE INSURANCE CO

B-   **Good**

Major Rating Factors: Strong capitalization (10.0 on a scale of 0 to 10) based on excellent current risk-adjusted capital (severe loss scenario). High quality investment portfolio (9.9). Excellent liquidity (7.2) with ample operational cash flow and liquid investments.
Other Rating Factors: Weak profitability index (1.9).
Principal Business: Comp med (100%)
Mem Phys: 18: 8,924 **17:** 8 **18 MLR** 95.3% **/ 18 Admin Exp** N/A
Enroll(000): Q3 19: 12 **18:** 13 **17:** N/A **Med Exp PMPM:** $344
Principal Investments: Cash and equiv (100%)
Provider Compensation ($000): Bonus arrang ($23,434), contr fee ($7,239), FFS ($5,545)
Total Member Encounters: Phys (63,072), non-phys (35,683)
Group Affiliation: None
Licensed in: WI
Address: N17 W24340 RIVERWOOD DRIVE, WAUKESHA, WI 53188
Phone: (262) 523-4020 **Dom State:** WI **Commenced Bus:** N/A

Data Date	Rating	RACR #1	RACR #2	Total Assets ($mil)	Capital ($mil)	Net Premium ($mil)	Net Income ($mil)
9-19	B-	4.36	3.63	32.4	23.5	43.0	7.2
9-18	N/A	N/A	N/A	21.1	13.2	30.4	2.6
2018	B-	3.03	2.52	26.4	16.3	43.7	0.1
2017	N/A	N/A	N/A	18.1	9.3	N/A	-1.9
2016	N/A	N/A	N/A	4.1	3.6	N/A	-6.4
2015	N/A	N/A	N/A	N/A	N/A	N/A	N/A
2014	N/A	N/A	N/A	N/A	N/A	N/A	N/A

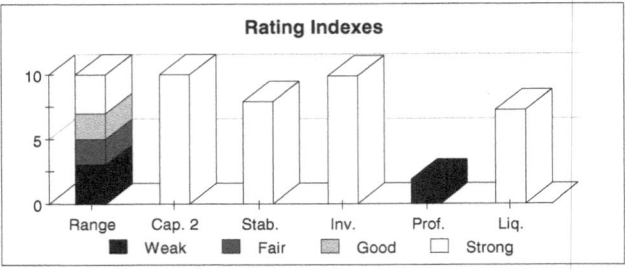

Rating Indexes

WISCONSIN PHYSICIANS SERVICE INS

C   **Fair**

Major Rating Factors: Low quality investment portfolio (2.2 on a scale of 0 to 10). Good overall profitability index (6.2). Strong capitalization (10.0) based on excellent current risk-adjusted capital (severe loss scenario).
Other Rating Factors: Excellent liquidity (6.9) with sufficient resources (cash flows and marketable investments) to handle a spike in claims.
Principal Business: Comp med (45%), med supp (42%), dental (2%), other (11%)
Mem Phys: 19: N/A   **18:** N/A   **19 MLR** 75.1%   **/ 19 Admin Exp** N/A
Enroll(000): Q2 20: 93   **19:** 94   **18:** 102   **Med Exp PMPM:** $228
Principal Investments: Long-term bonds (32%), cash and equiv (19%), affiliate common stock (17%), nonaffiliate common stock (16%), real estate (15%)
Provider Compensation ($000): Contr fee ($186,802), FFS ($59,843), other ($18,655)
Total Member Encounters: Phys (812,405), non-phys (303,913)
Group Affiliation: None
Licensed in: IL, IN, MI, OH, WI
Address: 1717 WEST BROADWAY, MADISON, WI 53713-1895
Phone: (608) 977-5000   **Dom State:** WI   **Commenced Bus:** N/A

Data Date	Rating	RACR #1	RACR #2	Total Assets ($mil)	Capital ($mil)	Net Premium ($mil)	Net Income ($mil)
6-20	C	3.69	3.08	351.0	175.0	173.9	13.4
6-19	C	2.58	2.15	280.7	132.3	174.7	5.3
2019	C	3.59	2.99	329.2	168.5	346.0	21.2
2018	C	2.49	2.08	289.3	127.7	396.0	-1.3
2017	C	N/A	N/A	277.1	122.2	417.1	11.8
2016	C	1.83	1.53	267.8	109.8	435.4	8.8
2015	C-	1.35	1.12	265.5	93.9	547.5	-7.1

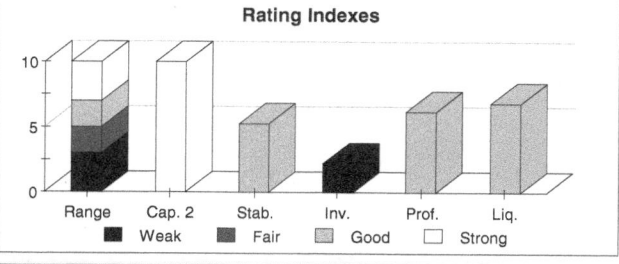

Rating Indexes

WMI MUTUAL INS CO

B   **Good**

Major Rating Factors: Good profitability index (5.0 on a scale of 0 to 10). Good liquidity (6.7) with sufficient resources (cash flows and marketable investments) to handle a spike in claims. Strong capitalization (10.0) based on excellent current risk-adjusted capital (severe loss scenario).
Other Rating Factors: High quality investment portfolio (8.1).
Principal Business: Comp med (93%), dental (3%), med supp (3%)
Mem Phys: 19: N/A   **18:** N/A   **19 MLR** 77.1%   **/ 19 Admin Exp** N/A
Enroll(000): Q2 20: 4   **19:** 5   **18:** 5   **Med Exp PMPM:** $210
Principal Investments: Long-term bonds (66%), nonaffiliate common stock (25%), cash and equiv (6%), affiliate common stock (3%)
Provider Compensation ($000): Other ($13,370)
Total Member Encounters: N/A
Group Affiliation: None
Licensed in: AZ, ID, MT, NV, NM, UT, WA
Address: 4393 S RIVERBOAT RD #380, TAYLORSVILLE, UT 84123
Phone: (801) 263-8000   **Dom State:** UT   **Commenced Bus:** N/A

Data Date	Rating	RACR #1	RACR #2	Total Assets ($mil)	Capital ($mil)	Net Premium ($mil)	Net Income ($mil)
6-20	B	4.32	3.60	16.7	12.4	8.0	0.1
6-19	N/A	N/A	N/A	N/A	N/A	N/A	N/A
2019	B	4.39	3.66	16.9	12.7	16.6	1.5
2018	B-	3.39	2.83	14.8	10.7	18.1	0.7
2017	C	3.85	3.21	14.6	10.3	17.9	1.5
2016	C	2.40	2.00	13.8	8.4	18.0	-1.1
2015	N/A	N/A	N/A	14.7	9.3	18.4	N/A

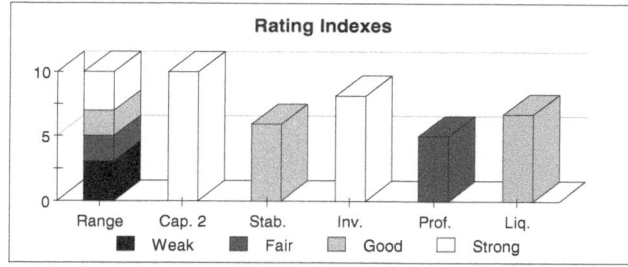

Rating Indexes

WPS HEALTH PLAN INC

C-   **Fair**

Major Rating Factors: Weak profitability index (0.7 on a scale of 0 to 10). Good liquidity (5.3) with sufficient resources (cash flows and marketable investments) to handle a spike in claims. Strong capitalization (7.3) based on excellent current risk-adjusted capital (severe loss scenario).
Other Rating Factors: High quality investment portfolio (9.5).
Principal Business: Comp med (100%)
Mem Phys: 19: 21   **18:** 11,046   **19 MLR** 100.2%   **/ 19 Admin Exp** N/A
Enroll(000): Q2 20: 11   **19:** 12   **18:** 14   **Med Exp PMPM:** $510
Principal Investments: Long-term bonds (102%)
Provider Compensation ($000): Contr fee ($54,764), FFS ($18,581)
Total Member Encounters: Phys (77,066), non-phys (29,420)
Group Affiliation: None
Licensed in: WI
Address: 1400 LOMBARDI AVE SUITE 50, GREEN BAY, WI 54304
Phone: (920) 490-6900   **Dom State:** WI   **Commenced Bus:** N/A

Data Date	Rating	RACR #1	RACR #2	Total Assets ($mil)	Capital ($mil)	Net Premium ($mil)	Net Income ($mil)
6-20	C-	1.63	1.36	28.3	14.6	33.8	-0.9
6-19	C-	1.76	1.46	27.1	12.7	35.6	-2.3
2019	C-	1.90	1.58	24.7	13.0	72.0	-6.5
2018	C-	1.80	1.50	28.4	13.1	89.1	-3.5
2017	C-	1.37	1.14	34.0	16.1	106.0	-6.7
2016	C-	1.40	1.17	50.4	23.1	185.8	-6.0
2015	C-	1.36	1.13	50.2	20.2	150.2	-22.4

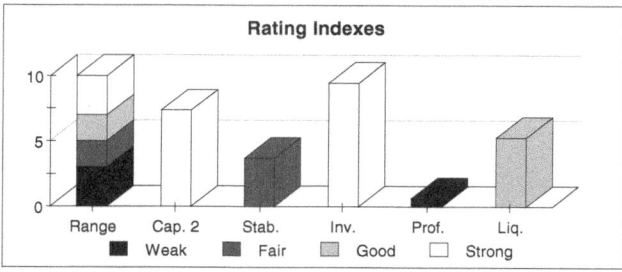

Rating Indexes

WV SENIOR ADVANTAGE INC   C   Fair

Major Rating Factors: Fair profitability index (3.2 on a scale of 0 to 10). Strong capitalization (7.6) based on excellent current risk-adjusted capital (severe loss scenario). High quality investment portfolio (9.9).

Other Rating Factors: Excellent liquidity (7.4) with ample operational cash flow and liquid investments.

Principal Business: Medicare (100%)

Mem Phys: 18: 3,071   **17:** 598   **18 MLR** 84.9%   **/ 18 Admin Exp** N/A

Enroll(000): Q3 19: 1   **18:** 1   **17:** 1   **Med Exp PMPM:** $1,463

Principal Investments: Cash and equiv (100%)

Provider Compensation ($000): Contr fee ($5,560), capitation ($3,193), bonus arrang ($359)

Total Member Encounters: Phys (9,320), non-phys (32,410)

Group Affiliation: Stonerise Senior Advantage Holdings

Licensed in: WV

Address: 700 Chappell Road, Charleston, WV 25303

Phone: (304) 348-2630   **Dom State:** WV   **Commenced Bus:** N/A

Data Date	Rating	RACR #1	RACR #2	Total Assets ($mil)	Capital ($mil)	Net Premium ($mil)	Net Income ($mil)
9-19	C	1.85	1.54	7.0	3.1	11.3	0.6
9-18	N/A	N/A	N/A	5.7	2.4	7.6	0.2
2018	U	1.63	1.35	5.0	2.7	10.3	0.3
2017	N/A	N/A	N/A	4.8	2.2	11.9	-0.5
2016	N/A	N/A	N/A	2.1	2.1	N/A	-1.2
2015	N/A	N/A	N/A	N/A	N/A	N/A	N/A
2014	N/A	N/A	N/A	N/A	N/A	N/A	N/A

Rating Indexes

Range   Cap. 2   Stab.   Inv.   Prof.   Liq.

■ Weak   ■ Fair   ▨ Good   ☐ Strong

Section III

Weiss
Recommended Companies

A compilation of those

U.S. Health Insurers

receiving a Weiss Safety Rating
of A+, A, A-, or B+.

Companies are listed in alphabetical order.

Section III Contents

This section provides contact addresses and phone numbers for all recommended carriers analyzed by Weiss Ratings. It contains all insurers receiving a Safety Rating of A+, A, A-, or B+. If an insurer is not on this list, it should not automatically be assumed that the firm is weak. Indeed, there are many firms that have not achieved a B+ or better rating but are in relatively good condition with adequate resources to cover their risk during an average recession. Not being included in this list should not be construed as a recommendation to cancel policies.

1. **Safety Rating**

    Our rating is measured on a scale from A to F and considers a wide range of factors. Highly-rated companies are, in our opinion, less likely to experience financial difficulties than lower-rated firms. See *About Weiss Safety Ratings* for more information.

2. **Insurance Company Name**

    The legally-registered name, which can sometimes differ from the name that the company uses for advertising. An insurer's name can be very similar to the name of other companies, so make sure you note the exact name before contacting your agent.

3. **Address**

    The address of the main office where you can contact the firm for additional financial data or for the location of local branches and/or registered agents.

4. **Telephone Number**

    The number to call for additional financial data or for the phone numbers of local branches and/or registered agents.

Weiss Safety Ratings are not deemed to be a recommendation concerning the purchase or sale of the securities of any insurance company that is publicly owned

RATING	INSURANCE COMPANY NAME	ADDRESS	CITY	STATE	ZIP	PHONE
B+	MY CHOICE WISCONSIN HEALTH PLAN INC	1617 SHERMAN AVENUE	MADISON	WI	53704	(608) 240-0020
B+	ADVANCE INS CO OF KANSAS	1133 SW TOPEKA BLVD	TOPEKA	KS	66629	(785) 273-9804
B+	AETNA BETTER HLTH OF KY INS CO	9900 CORPORATE CAMPUS DRIVE S	LOUISVILLE	KY	40223	(855) 300-5528
B+	ALLIANZ LIFE INS CO OF NY	1633 BROADWAY, 42ND FLOOR	NEW YORK	NY	10019	(763) 765-2913
A	AMALGAMATED LIFE INS CO	333 WESTCHESTER AVENUE	WHITE PLAINS	NY	10604	(914) 367-5275
A-	AMERICAN FAMILY LIFE ASR CO OF NY	22 CORPORATE WOODS BLVD STE 2	ALBANY	NY	12211	(518) 438-0764
B+	AMERICAN FAMILY MUTL INS CO SI	6000 AMERICAN PARKWAY	MADISON	WI	53783	(608) 242-4100
B+	AMERICAN FIDELITY ASR CO	9000 CAMERON PARKWAY	OKLAHOMA CITY	OK	73114	(405) 523-2000
B+	AMERIGROUP INS CO	3800 BUFFALO SPEEDWAY SUITE 4	HOUSTON	TX	77098	(757) 490-6900
A-	AMERIGROUP NEW JERSEY INC	4425 CORPORATION LANE	VIRGINIA BEACH	VA	23462	(757) 490-6900
A-	AMERIGROUP WASHINGTON INC	705 FIFTH AVENUE SOUTH SUITE	SEATTLE	WA	98104	(757) 490-6900
A-	AMGP GEORGIA MANAGED CARE CO INC	4170 ASHFORD DUNWOODY ROAD	ATLANTA	GA	30319	(678) 587-4840
A-	ANTHEM KENTUCKY MANAGED CARE PLAN	13550 TRITON PARK BLVD	LOUISVILLE	KY	40223	(888) 641-5224
B+	ANTHEM LIFE INS CO	220 VIRGINIA AVENUE	INDIANAPOLIS	IN	46204	(614) 433-8800
B+	ASSURITY LIFE INS CO	2000 Q STREET	LINCOLN	NE	68503	(402) 476-6500
B+	AULTCARE INS CO	2600 SIXTH STREET SW	CANTON	OH	44710	(330) 363-4057
A	BERKLEY LIFE & HEALTH INS CO	11201 DOUGLAS AVE	URBANDALE	IA	50322	(609) 584-6990
B+	BEST LIFE & HEALTH INS CO	AUSTIN	AUSTIN	TX	78752	(949) 253-4080
B+	BLUE CARE NETWORK OF MICHIGAN	20500 CIVIC CENTER DRIVE	SOUTHFIELD	MI	48076	(248) 799-6400
B+	BLUE CROSS & BLUE SHIELD MA HMO BLUE	101 HUNTINGTON AVENUE SUITE 1	BOSTON	MA	2199	(617) 246-5000
A-	BLUE CROSS BLUE SHIELD HEALTHCARE GA	3350 PEACHTREE ROAD, NE	ATLANTA	GA	30326	(404) 842-8000
A-	BLUE CROSS BLUE SHIELD OF ALABAMA	450 RIVERCHASE PARKWAY EAST	BIRMINGHAM	AL	35244	(205) 220-2100
A+	BLUE CROSS BLUE SHIELD OF ARIZONA	2444 W LAS PALMARITAS DRIVE	PHOENIX	AZ	85021	(602) 864-4100
A	BLUE CROSS BLUE SHIELD OF MS, MUTUAL	3545 LAKELAND DRIVE	FLOWOOD	MS	39232	(601) 664-4590
B+	BLUE CROSS BLUE SHIELD OF NC	4705 UNIVERSITY DRIVE BUILDIN	DURHAM	NC	27707	(919) 489-7431
B+	BLUE CROSS COMPLETE OF MICHIGAN	4000 TOWN CENTER SUITE 1300	SOUTHFIELD	MI	48075	(215) 937-8000
A+	BLUE CROSS OF CALIFORNIA	1 WELLPOINT WAY	THOUSAND OAKS	CA	91362	(916) 403-0526
B+	BLUE CROSS OF IDAHO HEALTH SERVICE	3000 E PINE AVE	MERIDIAN	ID	83642	(208) 345-4550
A-	BLUEBONNET LIFE INS CO	3545 LAKELAND DR	FLOWOOD	MS	39232	(601) 664-4218
A-	BLUECROSS BLUESHIELD OF TENNESSEE	1 CAMERON HILL CIRCLE	CHATTANOOGA	TN	37402	(423) 535-5600
B+	BOSTON MUTUAL LIFE INS CO	120 ROYALL STREET	CANTON	MA	02021	(781) 828-7000
A+	CALIFORNIA PHYSICIANS SERVICE	50 BEALE STREET 22ND FLOOR	SAN FRANCISCO	CA	94105	(415) 229-5195
A-	CAPITAL DISTRICT PHYSICIANS HEALTH P	500 PATROON CREEK BOULEVARD	ALBANY	NY	12206	(518) 641-3000
A	CAPITAL HEALTH PLAN INC	2140 CENTERVILLE PLACE	TALLAHASSEE	FL	32308	(850) 383-3333
A+	CHESAPEAKE LIFE INS CO	1833 SOUTH MORGAN ROAD	OKLAHOMA CITY	OK	73128	(817) 255-3100
B+	CHILDRENS COMMUNITY HEALTH PLAN INC	9000 W WISCONSIN AVE	MILWAUKEE	WI	53226	(800) 482-8010
A-	CHRISTIAN FIDELITY LIFE INS CO	1999 BRYAN STREET SUITE 900	DALLAS	TX	75201	(602) 263-6666
A-	CIGNA LIFE INS CO OF NEW YORK	140 EAST 45TH STREET	NEW YORK	NY	10017	(215) 761-1000
A-	CMNTY CARE HLTH PLAN OF NV INC	9133 W RUSSELL ROAD	LAS VEGAS	NV	89148	(757) 490-6900
B+	COMMUNITY CARE BEHAVIORAL HEALTH	339 SIXTH AVENUE SUITE 1300	PITTSBURGH	PA	15222	(412) 454-2120
B+	COMPANION LIFE INS CO	2501 FARAWAY DRIVE	COLUMBIA	SC	29219	(803) 735-1251
B+	COMPANION LIFE INS CO OF CA	731 SANSOME STREET 2ND FLOOR	SAN FRANCISCO	CA	94111	(803) 735-1251
A	COMPCARE HEALTH SERVICES INS CORP	N17 W24340 RIVERWOOD DRIVE	WAUKESHA	WI	53188	(262) 523-4020
A+	COUNTRY LIFE INS CO	1701 N TOWANDA AVENUE	BLOOMINGTON	IL	61701	(309) 821-3000
A-	DEAN HEALTH PLAN INC	1277 DEMING WAY	MADISON	WI	53717	(608) 836-1400
B+	DEARBORN LIFE INS CO	300 EAST RANDOLPH STREET	CHICAGO	IL	60601	(800) 348-4512
B+	DELAWARE AMERICAN LIFE INS CO	1209 ORANGE STREET	WILMINGTON	DE	19801	(302) 594-2000
A	EMI HEALTH	5101 S COMMERCE DR	MURRAY	UT	84107	(801) 262-7476

RATING	INSURANCE COMPANY NAME	ADDRESS	CITY	STATE	ZIP	PHONE
B+	ENTERPRISE LIFE INS CO	300 BURNETT STREET SUITE 200	FORT WORTH	TX	76102	(817) 878-3300
A-	ESSENCE HEALTHCARE INC	13900 RIVERPORT DRIVE	ST LOUIS	MO	63043	(314) 209-2780
B+	FARM BUREAU LIFE INS CO	5400 UNIVERSITY AVENUE	WEST DES MOINES	IA	50266	(515) 225-5400
A-	FARM BUREAU LIFE INS CO OF MISSOURI	701 SOUTH COUNTRY CLUB DRIVE	JEFFERSON CITY	MO	65109	(573) 893-1400
A	FEDERATED LIFE INS CO	121 EAST PARK SQUARE	OWATONNA	MN	55060	(507) 455-5200
A-	FIDELITY SECURITY LIFE INS CO	3130 BROADWAY	KANSAS CITY	MO	64111	(816) 756-1060
B+	FIDELITY SECURITY LIFE INS CO OF NY	162 PROSPECT HILL RD STE 101A	BREWSTER	NY	10509	(800) 821-7303
A-	FIRST RELIANCE STANDARD LIFE INS CO	590 MADISON AVENUE 29TH FLOOR	NEW YORK	NY	10022	(212) 303-8400
A	FLORIDA HEALTH CARE PLAN INC	1340 RIDGEWOOD AVENUE	HOLLY HILL	FL	32117	(386) 676-7100
B+	FREEDOM LIFE INS CO OF AMERICA	300 BURNETT STREET SUITE 200	FORT WORTH	TX	76102	(817) 878-3300
A	GARDEN STATE LIFE INS CO	ONE MOODY PLAZA	GALVESTON	TX	77550	(409) 763-4661
B+	GEISINGER HEALTH PLAN	100 NORTH ACADEMY AVENUE	DANVILLE	PA	17822	(570) 271-8777
B+	GERBER LIFE INS CO	1311 MAMARONECK AVENUE	WHITE PLAINS	NY	10605	(914) 272-4000
B+	GOLDEN SECURITY INS CO	1 CAMERON HILL CIRCLE	CHATTANOOGA	TN	37402	(423) 535-5600
B+	GROUP HOSP & MEDICAL SERVICES INC	840 FIRST STREET NE	WASHINGTON	DC	20065	(410) 581-3000
A	GUARDIAN LIFE INS CO OF AMERICA	10 HUDSON YARDS	NEW YORK	NY	10001	(212) 598-8000
B+	HEALTH CARE SVC CORP A MUT LEG RES	300 EAST RANDOLPH STREET	CHICAGO	IL	60601	(312) 653-6000
A-	HEALTH FIRST COMM PLANS INC	6450 US HIGHWAY 1	ROCKLEDGE	FL	32955	(321) 434-5600
A-	HEALTH OPTIONS INC	4800 DEERWOOD CAMPUS	JACKSONVILLE	FL	32246	(904) 791-6111
B+	HEALTH PLAN OF NEVADA INC	2720 NORTH TENAYA WAY	LAS VEGAS	NV	89128	(702) 242-7732
B+	HEALTHFIRST HEALTH PLAN INC	100 CHURCH STREET	NEW YORK	NY	10007	(212) 801-6000
A	HEALTHNOW NY INC	257 WEST GENESEE STREET	BUFFALO	NY	14202	(716) 887-6900
B+	HEALTHPARTNERS INS CO	8170 33RD AVENUE SOUTH	MINNEAPOLIS	MN	55440	(952) 883-6000
B+	HEALTHSPRING OF FLORIDA INC	8600 NW 41ST STREET SUITE 201	DORAL	FL	33166	(305) 229-7461
B+	HEALTHSUN HEALTH PLANS INC	3250 MARY STREET SUITE 400	COCONUT GROVE	FL	33133	(305) 448-8100
B+	HIGHMARK BCBSD INC	800 DELAWARE AVENUE	WILMINGTON	DE	19801	(302) 421-3000
B+	HMO COLORADO	700 BROADWAY	DENVER	CO	80273	(303) 831-2131
A+	HMO LOUISIANA INC	5525 REITZ AVENUE	BATON ROUGE	LA	70809	(225) 295-3307
A+	HMO PARTNERS INC	320 WEST CAPITOL	LITTLE ROCK	AR	72201	(501) 221-1800
B+	HUMANA BENEFIT PLAN OF ILLINOIS	4501 NORTH STERLING AVE 2ND	PEORIA	IL	61615	(502) 580-1000
A	HUMANA INS CO (WI)	1100 EMPLOYERS BOULEVARD	DEPERE	WI	54115	(920) 336-1100
A-	HUMANA MEDICAL PLAN INC	3501 SOUTHWEST 160TH AVENUE	MIRAMAR	FL	33027	(305) 626-5616
B+	HUMANA WISCONSIN HEALTH	N19W24133 RIVERWOOD DRIVE SUIT	WAUKESHA	WI	53188	(262) 408-4300
B+	ILLINOIS MUTUAL LIFE INS CO	300 SW ADAMS STREET	PEORIA	IL	61634	(309) 674-8255
A-	INDEPENDENT CARE HEALTH PLAN	1555 N RIVERCENTER DRIVE SUI	MILWAUKEE	WI	53212	(414) 223-4847
B+	INDEPENDENT HEALTH ASSOC INC	511 FARBER LAKES DRIVE	BUFFALO	NY	14221	(716) 631-3001
A	INLAND EMPIRE HEALTH PLAN	300 S PARK AVENUE	POMONA	CA	91769	(909) 623-6333
A+	KAISER FOUNDATION HEALTH PLAN INC	9700 STOCKDALE HIGHWAY	BAKERSFIELD	CA	93311	(661) 664-5016
A	KAISER PERMANENTE INS CO	300 LAKESIDE DRIVE 13TH FLOOR	OAKLAND	CA	94612	(877) 847-7572
B+	KERN HEALTH SYSTEMS	1055 WEST 7TH STREET	LOS ANGELES	CA	90017	(213) 694-1250
B+	KEYSTONE HEALTH PLAN EAST INC	1901 MARKET STREET	PHILADELPHIA	PA	19103	(215) 241-2400
A-	LIFE INS CO OF BOSTON & NEW YORK	4300 CAMP ROAD PO BOX 331	ATHOL SPRINGS	NY	14010	(800) 645-2317
A	LIFEWISE ASR CO	7001 220TH STREET SW	MOUNTLAKE TERRACE	WA	98043	(425) 918-4575
B+	MDWISE INC	2955 NORTH MERIDIAN STREET SUI	INDIANAPOLIS	IN	46208	(317) 822-7300
A-	MEDICAL MUTUAL OF OHIO	2060 EAST NINTH STREET	CLEVELAND	OH	44115	(216) 687-7000
B+	MIDLAND NATIONAL LIFE INS CO	8300 MILLS CIVIC PARKWAY	WEST DES MOINES	IA	50266	(515) 440-5500
B+	MOUNT CARMEL HEALTH PLAN INC	6150 EAST BROAD STREET SUITE	COLUMBUS	OH	43213	(614) 546-3211
A-	NATIONAL BENEFIT LIFE INS CO	30-30 47TH AVENUE SUITE 625	LONG ISLAND CITY	NY	11101	(718) 361-3636

RATING	INSURANCE COMPANY NAME	ADDRESS	CITY	STATE	ZIP	PHONE
A	NATIONAL FOUNDATION LIFE INS CO	300 BURNETT STREET SUITE 200	FORT WORTH	TX	76102	(817) 878-3300
B+	NATIONAL INCOME LIFE INS CO	1020 SEVENTH NORTH ST SUITE	LIVERPOOL	NY	13088	(315) 451-8180
A-	NEW YORK LIFE INS CO	51 MADISON AVENUE	NEW YORK	NY	10010	(212) 576-7000
A-	NIAGARA LIFE & HEALTH INS CO	300 INTERNATIONAL DRIVE SUITE	WILLIAMSVILLE	NY	14221	(803) 735-1251
A-	NIPPON LIFE INS CO OF AMERICA	6965 VISTA DRIVE	WEST DES MOINES	IA	50266	(212) 682-3000
B+	NORTH AMERICAN INS CO	575 DONOFRIO DRIVE SUITE 100	MADISON	WI	53719	(877) 667-9368
B+	NORTHWESTERN LONG TERM CARE INS CO	720 EAST WISCONSIN AVENUE	MILWAUKEE	WI	53202	(414) 271-1444
B+	NORTHWESTERN MUTUAL LIFE INS CO	720 EAST WISCONSIN AVENUE	MILWAUKEE	WI	53202	(414) 271-1444
B+	OPTIMUM CHOICE INC	800 KING FARM BOULEVARD	ROCKVILLE	MD	20850	(240) 632-8109
B+	OXFORD HEALTH PLANS (CT) INC	FOUR RESEARCH DRIVE	SHELTON	CT	06484	(203) 447-4500
B+	OXFORD LIFE INS CO	2721 NORTH CENTRAL AVENUE	PHOENIX	AZ	85004	(602) 263-6666
B+	PACIFIC GUARDIAN LIFE INS CO LTD	1440 KAPIOLANI BLVD STE 1600	HONOLULU	HI	96814	(808) 955-2236
B+	PHYSICIANS HEALTH PLAN OF NO IN	1700 MAGNAVOX WAY	FORT WAYNE	IN	46804	(260) 432-6690
A-	PHYSICIANS LIFE INS CO	2600 DODGE STREET	OMAHA	NE	68131	(402) 633-1000
A+	PHYSICIANS MUTUAL INS CO	2600 DODGE STREET	OMAHA	NE	68131	(402) 633-1000
B+	PREFERRED CARE PARTNERS INC	9100 SOUTH DADELAND BOULEVARD	MIAMI	FL	33156	(305) 670-8438
B+	PRINCIPAL LIFE INS CO	711 HIGH STREET	DES MOINES	IA	50392	(515) 247-5111
A	PRIORITY HEALTH	1231 EAST BELTLINE, NE	GRAND RAPIDS	MI	49525	(616) 942-0954
B+	PRIORITY HEALTH CHOICE INC	1231 EAST BELTLINE NE	GRAND RAPIDS	MI	49525	(616) 942-0954
A-	PROVIDENCE HEALTH ASR	4400 N E HALSEY BLDG # 2 STE	PORTLAND	OR	97213	(503) 574-7500
A-	REGENCE BL CROSS BL SHIELD OREGON	100 SW MARKET STREET	PORTLAND	OR	97201	(503) 225-5221
B+	REGENCE BLUE CROSS BLUE SHIELD OF UT	2890 EAST COTTONWOOD PARKWAY	SALT LAKE CITY	UT	84121	(801) 333-2000
B+	REGENCE BLUESHIELD OF IDAHO INC	1602 21ST AVENUE	LEWISTON	ID	83501	(208) 746-2671
B+	SAN JOAQUIN CNTY HEALTH	7751 S MANTHEY RD	FRENCH CAMP	CA	95231	(888) 936-7526
B+	SCAN HEALTH PLAN	300 SANTANA ROW SUITE 300	SAN JOSE	CA	95128	(650) 404-3798
B+	SECURITY HEALTH PLAN OF WI INC	1515 NORTH SAINT JOSEPH AVENUE	MARSHFIELD	WI	54449	(715) 221-9555
B+	SELECTHEALTH INC	5381 GREEN STREET	MURRAY	UT	84123	(801) 442-5000
A	SENTRY LIFE INS CO	1800 NORTH POINT DRIVE	STEVENS POINT	WI	54481	(715) 346-6000
B+	SHARP HEALTH PLAN	2801 ATLANTIC AVENUE	LONG BEACH	CA	90806	(714) 377-3215
A	SHELTERPOINT LIFE INS CO	1225 FRANKLIN AVE STE 475	GARDEN CITY	NY	11530	(516) 829-8100
A	SOUTHERN FARM BUREAU LIFE INS CO	1401 LIVINGSTON LANE	JACKSON	MS	39213	(601) 981-7422
B+	STANDARD INS CO	1100 SOUTHWEST SIXTH AVENUE	PORTLAND	OR	97204	(971) 321-7000
A-	STANDARD LIFE INS CO OF NY	333 WESTCHESTER AVENUE SUITE	WHITE PLAINS	NY	10604	(914) 989-4400
B+	STANDARD SECURITY LIFE INS CO OF NY	485 MADISON AVENUE 14TH FLOOR	NEW YORK	NY	10022	(212) 355-4141
A-	SWBC LIFE INS CO	9311 SAN PEDRO STE 600	SAN ANTONIO	TX	78216	(210) 321-7361
A+	TEACHERS INS & ANNUITY ASN OF AM	730 THIRD AVENUE	NEW YORK	NY	10017	(212) 490-9000
B+	TRANS OCEANIC LIFE INS CO	#121 ONEILL	SAN JUAN	PR	00918	(787) 620-2680
B+	TRUSTMARK INS CO	400 FIELD DRIVE	LAKE FOREST	IL	60045	(847) 615-1500
B+	TRUSTMARK LIFE INS CO	400 FIELD DRIVE	LAKE FOREST	IL	60045	(847) 615-1500
A	UNICARE HEALTH PLAN OF WEST VIRGINIA	200 ASSOCIATION DRIVE SUITE 2	CHARLESTON	WV	25311	(877) 864-2273
B+	UNITED FARM FAMILY LIFE INS CO	225 SOUTH EAST STREET	INDIANAPOLIS	IN	46202	(317) 692-7200
A-	UNITED HEALTHCARE INS CO OF IL	200 EAST RANDOLPH STREET SUIT	CHICAGO	IL	60601	(312) 424-4460
B+	UNITED HEALTHCARE OF THE MIDLANDS	2717 NORTH 118TH STREET	OMAHA	NE	68164	(402) 445-5600
B+	UNITED HEALTHCARE OF TX INC	9800 HEALTH CARE LANE MN006-W5	MINNETONKA	MN	55343	(952) 936-1300
B+	UNITED HEALTHCARE OF WISCONSIN INC	10701 WEST RESEARCH DRIVE	WAUWATOSA	WI	53226	(414) 443-4000
B+	UNITED WORLD LIFE INS CO	3300 MUTUAL OF OMAHA PLAZA	OMAHA	NE	68175	(402) 342-7600
B+	UNITEDHEALTHCARE COMMUNITY PLAN INC	26957 NORTHWESTERN HIGHWAY	SOUTHFIELD	MI	48033	(248) 559-5656
B+	UNITEDHEALTHCARE COMMUNITYPLAN OHIO	5900 PARKWOOD PLACE	DUBLIN	OH	43016	(952) 931-4014

RATING	INSURANCE COMPANY NAME	ADDRESS	CITY	STATE	ZIP	PHONE
B+	UNITEDHEALTHCARE OF OREGON	9800 HEALTH CARE LANE	MINNETONKA	MN	55343	(952) 936-1300
B+	UNIVERSAL LIFE INS CO	CALLE BOLIVIA #33 6TO PISO	SAN JUAN	PR	917	(787) 641-7171
B+	UPMC FOR YOU INC	600 GRANT STREET	PITTSBURGH	PA	15219	(412) 434-1200
A	USAA LIFE INS CO	9800 FREDERICKSBURG RD	SAN ANTONIO	TX	78288	(210) 531-8722
B+	USABLE LIFE	320 W CAPITOL SUITE 700	LITTLE ROCK	AR	72201	(501) 375-7200
B+	USABLE MUTUAL INS CO	601 S GAINES	LITTLE ROCK	AR	72201	(501) 378-2000
B+	VISTA HEALTH PLAN INC	1901 MARKET STREET	PHILADELPHIA	PA	19103	(215) 241-2400
A-	VIVA HEALTH INC	417 20TH STREET, NORTH	BIRMINGHAM	AL	35203	(205) 558-7466
A+	VOLUNTEER STATE HEALTH PLAN INC	ONE CAMERON HILL CIRCLE	CHATTANOOGA	TN	37402	(423) 535-5600
B+	VOYA RETIREMENT INS & ANNUITY CO	ONE ORANGE WAY	WINDSOR	CT	06095	(860) 580-4646
B+	WELLCARE OF GEORGIA INC	211 PERIMETER CENTER PARKWAY	ATLANTA	GA	30346	(813) 206-6200
A-	WELLCARE OF TEXAS INC	4888 LOOP CENTRAL DRIVE SUITE	HOUSTON	TX	77081	(813) 206-6200

Section IV

Weiss
Recommended Companies
by State

A summary analysis of those

U.S. Health Insurers

receiving a Weiss Safety Rating
of A+, A, A-, or B+.

Companies are ranked by Safety Rating
in each state where they are licensed to do business.

Section IV Contents

This section provides a list of the recommended carriers licensed to do business in each state. It contains all insurers receiving a Safety Rating of A+, A, A-, or B+. If an insurer is not on this list, it should not automatically be assumed that the firm is weak. Indeed, there are many firms that have not achieved a B+ or better rating but are in relatively good condition with adequate resources to cover their risk during an average recession. Not being included in this list should not be construed as a recommendation to cancel policies.

Companies are ranked within each state by their Safety Rating, and are listed alphabetically within each rating category. Companies with the same rating should be viewed as having the same relative strength regardless of their ranking in this table.

1. Insurance Company Name	The legally-registered name, which can sometimes differ from the name that the company uses for advertising. An insurer's name can be very similar to the name of other companies which may not be on our Recommended List, so make sure you note the exact name before contacting your agent.
2. Domicile State	The state which has primary regulatory responsibility for the company. It may differ from the location of the company's corporate headquarters. You do not have to be living in the domicile state to purchase insurance from this firm, provided it is licensed to do business in your state.
3. Total Assets	All assets admitted by state insurance regulators in millions of dollars as of the most recent year end. This includes investments and current business assets such as receivables from agents, reinsurers and subscribers.

Weiss Safety Ratings are not deemed to be a recommendation concerning the purchase or sale of the securities of any insurance company that is publicly owned.

Alabama

INSURANCE COMPANY NAME	DOM. STATE	TOTAL ASSETS ($MIL)	INSURANCE COMPANY NAME	DOM. STATE	TOTAL ASSETS ($MIL)
Rating: A+					
CHESAPEAKE LIFE INS CO	OK	253.5			
COUNTRY LIFE INS CO	IL	10,112.1			
PHYSICIANS MUTUAL INS CO	NE	2,506.1			
TEACHERS INS & ANNUITY ASN OF AM	NY	320,701.0			
Rating: A					
AMALGAMATED LIFE INS CO	NY	154.2			
BERKLEY LIFE & HEALTH INS CO	IA	382.0			
FEDERATED LIFE INS CO	MN	2,189.3			
GARDEN STATE LIFE INS CO	TX	147.1			
GUARDIAN LIFE INS CO OF AMERICA	NY	65,189.0			
HUMANA INS CO (WI)	WI	10,594.3			
NATIONAL FOUNDATION LIFE INS CO	TX	87.8			
SENTRY LIFE INS CO	WI	8,165.9			
SOUTHERN FARM BUREAU LIFE INS CO	MS	14,723.1			
USAA LIFE INS CO	TX	26,903.7			
Rating: A-					
BLUE CROSS BLUE SHIELD OF ALABAMA	AL	4,861.0			
BLUEBONNET LIFE INS CO	MS	69.5			
CHRISTIAN FIDELITY LIFE INS CO	TX	58.3			
CIGNA LIFE INS CO OF NEW YORK	NY	449.3			
FIDELITY SECURITY LIFE INS CO	MO	980.9			
NATIONAL BENEFIT LIFE INS CO	NY	595.9			
NEW YORK LIFE INS CO	NY	198,377.0			
NIPPON LIFE INS CO OF AMERICA	IA	246.1			
PHYSICIANS LIFE INS CO	NE	1,730.5			
VIVA HEALTH INC	AL	225.3			
Rating: B+					
AMERICAN FIDELITY ASR CO	OK	6,608.0			
AMERIGROUP INS CO	TX	322.8			
ANTHEM LIFE INS CO	IN	799.2			
ASSURITY LIFE INS CO	NE	2,670.3			
BEST LIFE & HEALTH INS CO	TX	30.1			
BOSTON MUTUAL LIFE INS CO	MA	1,547.3			
COMPANION LIFE INS CO	SC	489.5			
DEARBORN LIFE INS CO	IL	1,657.5			
DELAWARE AMERICAN LIFE INS CO	DE	106.1			
FREEDOM LIFE INS CO OF AMERICA	TX	418.7			
GERBER LIFE INS CO	NY	4,677.1			
HUMANA BENEFIT PLAN OF ILLINOIS	IL	1,104.8			
ILLINOIS MUTUAL LIFE INS CO	IL	1,520.9			
MIDLAND NATIONAL LIFE INS CO	IA	62,252.9			
NORTH AMERICAN INS CO	WI	19.2			
NORTHWESTERN LONG TERM CARE INS CO	WI	290.3			
NORTHWESTERN MUTUAL LIFE INS CO	WI	295,371.0			
OXFORD LIFE INS CO	AZ	2,408.0			
PRINCIPAL LIFE INS CO	IA	208,421.0			
STANDARD INS CO	OR	27,265.4			
STANDARD SECURITY LIFE INS CO OF NY	NY	142.7			
TRUSTMARK INS CO	IL	1,752.8			
TRUSTMARK LIFE INS CO	IL	296.8			
UNITED HEALTHCARE OF THE MIDLANDS	NE	1,032.6			
UNITED WORLD LIFE INS CO	NE	141.0			
USABLE LIFE	AR	496.4			
VOYA RETIREMENT INS & ANNUITY CO	CT	110,637.0			

Alaska

INSURANCE COMPANY NAME	DOM. STATE	TOTAL ASSETS ($MIL)
Rating: A+		
CHESAPEAKE LIFE INS CO	OK	253.5
COUNTRY LIFE INS CO	IL	10,112.1
PHYSICIANS MUTUAL INS CO	NE	2,506.1
TEACHERS INS & ANNUITY ASN OF AM	NY	320,701.0
Rating: A		
AMALGAMATED LIFE INS CO	NY	154.2
BERKLEY LIFE & HEALTH INS CO	IA	382.0
GARDEN STATE LIFE INS CO	TX	147.1
GUARDIAN LIFE INS CO OF AMERICA	NY	65,189.0
HUMANA INS CO (WI)	WI	10,594.3
LIFEWISE ASR CO	WA	249.5
NATIONAL FOUNDATION LIFE INS CO	TX	87.8
SENTRY LIFE INS CO	WI	8,165.9
USAA LIFE INS CO	TX	26,903.7
Rating: A-		
FIDELITY SECURITY LIFE INS CO	MO	980.9
NATIONAL BENEFIT LIFE INS CO	NY	595.9
NEW YORK LIFE INS CO	NY	198,377.0
NIPPON LIFE INS CO OF AMERICA	IA	246.1
PHYSICIANS LIFE INS CO	NE	1,730.5
Rating: B+		
AMERICAN FIDELITY ASR CO	OK	6,608.0
ANTHEM LIFE INS CO	IN	799.2
ASSURITY LIFE INS CO	NE	2,670.3
BEST LIFE & HEALTH INS CO	TX	30.1
BOSTON MUTUAL LIFE INS CO	MA	1,547.3
COMPANION LIFE INS CO	SC	489.5
DEARBORN LIFE INS CO	IL	1,657.5
DELAWARE AMERICAN LIFE INS CO	DE	106.1
GERBER LIFE INS CO	NY	4,677.1
HEALTH CARE SVC CORP A MUT LEG RES	IL	33,429.9
HUMANA BENEFIT PLAN OF ILLINOIS	IL	1,104.8
MIDLAND NATIONAL LIFE INS CO	IA	62,252.9
NORTHWESTERN LONG TERM CARE INS CO	WI	290.3
NORTHWESTERN MUTUAL LIFE INS CO	WI	295,371.0
OXFORD LIFE INS CO	AZ	2,408.0
PACIFIC GUARDIAN LIFE INS CO LTD	HI	579.2
PRINCIPAL LIFE INS CO	IA	208,421.0
STANDARD INS CO	OR	27,265.4
STANDARD SECURITY LIFE INS CO OF NY	NY	142.7
TRUSTMARK INS CO	IL	1,752.8
TRUSTMARK LIFE INS CO	IL	296.8
UNITED WORLD LIFE INS CO	NE	141.0
USABLE LIFE	AR	496.4
VOYA RETIREMENT INS & ANNUITY CO	CT	110,637.0

Arizona

INSURANCE COMPANY NAME	DOM. STATE	TOTAL ASSETS ($MIL)
Rating: A+		
BLUE CROSS BLUE SHIELD OF ARIZONA	AZ	2,830.5
CHESAPEAKE LIFE INS CO	OK	253.5
COUNTRY LIFE INS CO	IL	10,112.1
PHYSICIANS MUTUAL INS CO	NE	2,506.1
TEACHERS INS & ANNUITY ASN OF AM	NY	320,701.0
Rating: A		
AMALGAMATED LIFE INS CO	NY	154.2
BERKLEY LIFE & HEALTH INS CO	IA	382.0
FEDERATED LIFE INS CO	MN	2,189.3
GARDEN STATE LIFE INS CO	TX	147.1
GUARDIAN LIFE INS CO OF AMERICA	NY	65,189.0
HUMANA INS CO (WI)	WI	10,594.3
NATIONAL FOUNDATION LIFE INS CO	TX	87.8
SENTRY LIFE INS CO	WI	8,165.9
USAA LIFE INS CO	TX	26,903.7
Rating: A-		
CHRISTIAN FIDELITY LIFE INS CO	TX	58.3
FIDELITY SECURITY LIFE INS CO	MO	980.9
NATIONAL BENEFIT LIFE INS CO	NY	595.9
NEW YORK LIFE INS CO	NY	198,377.0
NIPPON LIFE INS CO OF AMERICA	IA	246.1
PHYSICIANS LIFE INS CO	NE	1,730.5
WELLCARE OF TEXAS INC	TX	201.1
Rating: B+		
AMERICAN FAMILY MUTL INS CO SI	WI	24,090.2
AMERICAN FIDELITY ASR CO	OK	6,608.0
AMERIGROUP INS CO	TX	322.8
ANTHEM LIFE INS CO	IN	799.2
ASSURITY LIFE INS CO	NE	2,670.3
BEST LIFE & HEALTH INS CO	TX	30.1
BOSTON MUTUAL LIFE INS CO	MA	1,547.3
COMPANION LIFE INS CO	SC	489.5
COMPANION LIFE INS CO OF CA	CA	29.6
DEARBORN LIFE INS CO	IL	1,657.5
DELAWARE AMERICAN LIFE INS CO	DE	106.1
ENTERPRISE LIFE INS CO	TX	148.0
FARM BUREAU LIFE INS CO	IA	9,479.7
FREEDOM LIFE INS CO OF AMERICA	TX	418.7
GERBER LIFE INS CO	NY	4,677.1
HEALTH CARE SVC CORP A MUT LEG RES	IL	33,429.9
HUMANA BENEFIT PLAN OF ILLINOIS	IL	1,104.8
ILLINOIS MUTUAL LIFE INS CO	IL	1,520.9
MIDLAND NATIONAL LIFE INS CO	IA	62,252.9
NORTHWESTERN LONG TERM CARE INS CO	WI	290.3
NORTHWESTERN MUTUAL LIFE INS CO	WI	295,371.0
OXFORD LIFE INS CO	AZ	2,408.0
PACIFIC GUARDIAN LIFE INS CO LTD	HI	579.2
PRINCIPAL LIFE INS CO	IA	208,421.0
STANDARD INS CO	OR	27,265.4
STANDARD SECURITY LIFE INS CO OF NY	NY	142.7
TRUSTMARK INS CO	IL	1,752.8
TRUSTMARK LIFE INS CO	IL	296.8
UNITED FARM FAMILY LIFE INS CO	IN	2,442.0
UNITED HEALTHCARE OF WISCONSIN INC	WI	2,701.9

INSURANCE COMPANY NAME	DOM. STATE	TOTAL ASSETS ($MIL)
UNITED WORLD LIFE INS CO	NE	141.0
USABLE LIFE	AR	496.4
VOYA RETIREMENT INS & ANNUITY CO	CT	110,637.0

Arkansas

INSURANCE COMPANY NAME	DOM. STATE	TOTAL ASSETS ($MIL)
Rating:	**A+**	
CHESAPEAKE LIFE INS CO	OK	253.5
COUNTRY LIFE INS CO	IL	10,112.1
HMO PARTNERS INC	AR	129.5
PHYSICIANS MUTUAL INS CO	NE	2,506.1
TEACHERS INS & ANNUITY ASN OF AM	NY	320,701.0
Rating:	**A**	
AMALGAMATED LIFE INS CO	NY	154.2
BERKLEY LIFE & HEALTH INS CO	IA	382.0
FEDERATED LIFE INS CO	MN	2,189.3
GARDEN STATE LIFE INS CO	TX	147.1
GUARDIAN LIFE INS CO OF AMERICA	NY	65,189.0
HUMANA INS CO (WI)	WI	10,594.3
NATIONAL FOUNDATION LIFE INS CO	TX	87.8
SENTRY LIFE INS CO	WI	8,165.9
SOUTHERN FARM BUREAU LIFE INS CO	MS	14,723.1
USAA LIFE INS CO	TX	26,903.7
Rating:	**A-**	
BLUEBONNET LIFE INS CO	MS	69.5
CHRISTIAN FIDELITY LIFE INS CO	TX	58.3
FIDELITY SECURITY LIFE INS CO	MO	980.9
NATIONAL BENEFIT LIFE INS CO	NY	595.9
NEW YORK LIFE INS CO	NY	198,377.0
NIPPON LIFE INS CO OF AMERICA	IA	246.1
PHYSICIANS LIFE INS CO	NE	1,730.5
Rating:	**B+**	
AMERICAN FIDELITY ASR CO	OK	6,608.0
AMERIGROUP INS CO	TX	322.8
ANTHEM LIFE INS CO	IN	799.2
ASSURITY LIFE INS CO	NE	2,670.3
BEST LIFE & HEALTH INS CO	TX	30.1
BOSTON MUTUAL LIFE INS CO	MA	1,547.3
COMPANION LIFE INS CO	SC	489.5
DEARBORN LIFE INS CO	IL	1,657.5
DELAWARE AMERICAN LIFE INS CO	DE	106.1
ENTERPRISE LIFE INS CO	TX	148.0
FREEDOM LIFE INS CO OF AMERICA	TX	418.7
GERBER LIFE INS CO	NY	4,677.1
GOLDEN SECURITY INS CO	TN	69.3
HEALTH CARE SVC CORP A MUT LEG RES	IL	33,429.9
HUMANA BENEFIT PLAN OF ILLINOIS	IL	1,104.8
ILLINOIS MUTUAL LIFE INS CO	IL	1,520.9
MIDLAND NATIONAL LIFE INS CO	IA	62,252.9
NORTHWESTERN LONG TERM CARE INS CO	WI	290.3
NORTHWESTERN MUTUAL LIFE INS CO	WI	295,371.0
OXFORD LIFE INS CO	AZ	2,408.0
PRINCIPAL LIFE INS CO	IA	208,421.0
STANDARD INS CO	OR	27,265.4
STANDARD SECURITY LIFE INS CO OF NY	NY	142.7
TRUSTMARK INS CO	IL	1,752.8
TRUSTMARK LIFE INS CO	IL	296.8
UNITED HEALTHCARE OF THE MIDLANDS	NE	1,032.6
UNITED WORLD LIFE INS CO	NE	141.0
USABLE LIFE	AR	496.4
USABLE MUTUAL INS CO	AR	1,921.0

INSURANCE COMPANY NAME	DOM. STATE	TOTAL ASSETS ($MIL)
VOYA RETIREMENT INS & ANNUITY CO	CT	110,637.0

California

INSURANCE COMPANY NAME	DOM. STATE	TOTAL ASSETS ($MIL)
Rating: A+		
BLUE CROSS OF CALIFORNIA	CA	7,804.6
CALIFORNIA PHYSICIANS SERVICE	CA	10,417.9
CHESAPEAKE LIFE INS CO	OK	253.5
KAISER FOUNDATION HEALTH PLAN INC	CA	82,017.8
PHYSICIANS MUTUAL INS CO	NE	2,506.1
TEACHERS INS & ANNUITY ASN OF AM	NY	320,701.0
Rating: A		
AMALGAMATED LIFE INS CO	NY	154.2
BERKLEY LIFE & HEALTH INS CO	IA	382.0
FEDERATED LIFE INS CO	MN	2,189.3
GARDEN STATE LIFE INS CO	TX	147.1
GUARDIAN LIFE INS CO OF AMERICA	NY	65,189.0
HUMANA INS CO (WI)	WI	10,594.3
INLAND EMPIRE HEALTH PLAN	CA	1,685.2
KAISER PERMANENTE INS CO	CA	220.6
LIFEWISE ASR CO	WA	249.5
NATIONAL FOUNDATION LIFE INS CO	TX	87.8
SENTRY LIFE INS CO	WI	8,165.9
SHELTERPOINT LIFE INS CO	NY	235.2
USAA LIFE INS CO	TX	26,903.7
Rating: A-		
CAPITAL DISTRICT PHYSICIANS HEALTH P	NY	660.1
FIDELITY SECURITY LIFE INS CO	MO	980.9
NATIONAL BENEFIT LIFE INS CO	NY	595.9
NEW YORK LIFE INS CO	NY	198,377.0
NIPPON LIFE INS CO OF AMERICA	IA	246.1
PHYSICIANS LIFE INS CO	NE	1,730.5
Rating: B+		
AMERICAN FIDELITY ASR CO	OK	6,608.0
ANTHEM LIFE INS CO	IN	799.2
ASSURITY LIFE INS CO	NE	2,670.3
BEST LIFE & HEALTH INS CO	TX	30.1
BOSTON MUTUAL LIFE INS CO	MA	1,547.3
COMPANION LIFE INS CO OF CA	CA	29.6
DEARBORN LIFE INS CO	IL	1,657.5
DELAWARE AMERICAN LIFE INS CO	DE	106.1
GERBER LIFE INS CO	NY	4,677.1
HUMANA BENEFIT PLAN OF ILLINOIS	IL	1,104.8
ILLINOIS MUTUAL LIFE INS CO	IL	1,520.9
KERN HEALTH SYSTEMS	CA	699.5
MIDLAND NATIONAL LIFE INS CO	IA	62,252.9
NORTHWESTERN LONG TERM CARE INS CO	WI	290.3
NORTHWESTERN MUTUAL LIFE INS CO	WI	295,371.0
OXFORD LIFE INS CO	AZ	2,408.0
PACIFIC GUARDIAN LIFE INS CO LTD	HI	579.2
PRINCIPAL LIFE INS CO	IA	208,421.0
SAN JOAQUIN CNTY HEALTH	CA	880.8
SCAN HEALTH PLAN	CA	758.9
SHARP HEALTH PLAN	CA	217.8
STANDARD INS CO	OR	27,265.4
STANDARD SECURITY LIFE INS CO OF NY	NY	142.7
TRUSTMARK INS CO	IL	1,752.8
TRUSTMARK LIFE INS CO	IL	296.8
UNITED FARM FAMILY LIFE INS CO	IN	2,442.0

INSURANCE COMPANY NAME	DOM. STATE	TOTAL ASSETS ($MIL)
UNITED WORLD LIFE INS CO	NE	141.0
USABLE LIFE	AR	496.4
VOYA RETIREMENT INS & ANNUITY CO	CT	110,637.0

Colorado

INSURANCE COMPANY NAME	DOM. STATE	TOTAL ASSETS ($MIL)

INSURANCE COMPANY NAME	DOM. STATE	TOTAL ASSETS ($MIL)
VOYA RETIREMENT INS & ANNUITY CO	CT	110,637.0

Rating: A+

INSURANCE COMPANY NAME	DOM. STATE	TOTAL ASSETS ($MIL)
CHESAPEAKE LIFE INS CO	OK	253.5
COUNTRY LIFE INS CO	IL	10,112.1
PHYSICIANS MUTUAL INS CO	NE	2,506.1
TEACHERS INS & ANNUITY ASN OF AM	NY	320,701.0

Rating: A

INSURANCE COMPANY NAME	DOM. STATE	TOTAL ASSETS ($MIL)
AMALGAMATED LIFE INS CO	NY	154.2
BERKLEY LIFE & HEALTH INS CO	IA	382.0
FEDERATED LIFE INS CO	MN	2,189.3
GARDEN STATE LIFE INS CO	TX	147.1
GUARDIAN LIFE INS CO OF AMERICA	NY	65,189.0
HUMANA INS CO (WI)	WI	10,594.3
KAISER PERMANENTE INS CO	CA	220.6
NATIONAL FOUNDATION LIFE INS CO	TX	87.8
SENTRY LIFE INS CO	WI	8,165.9
SHELTERPOINT LIFE INS CO	NY	235.2
SOUTHERN FARM BUREAU LIFE INS CO	MS	14,723.1
USAA LIFE INS CO	TX	26,903.7

Rating: A-

INSURANCE COMPANY NAME	DOM. STATE	TOTAL ASSETS ($MIL)
CHRISTIAN FIDELITY LIFE INS CO	TX	58.3
FIDELITY SECURITY LIFE INS CO	MO	980.9
NATIONAL BENEFIT LIFE INS CO	NY	595.9
NEW YORK LIFE INS CO	NY	198,377.0
NIPPON LIFE INS CO OF AMERICA	IA	246.1
PHYSICIANS LIFE INS CO	NE	1,730.5

Rating: B+

INSURANCE COMPANY NAME	DOM. STATE	TOTAL ASSETS ($MIL)
AMERICAN FAMILY MUTL INS CO SI	WI	24,090.2
AMERICAN FIDELITY ASR CO	OK	6,608.0
ANTHEM LIFE INS CO	IN	799.2
ASSURITY LIFE INS CO	NE	2,670.3
BEST LIFE & HEALTH INS CO	TX	30.1
BOSTON MUTUAL LIFE INS CO	MA	1,547.3
COMPANION LIFE INS CO	SC	489.5
DEARBORN LIFE INS CO	IL	1,657.5
DELAWARE AMERICAN LIFE INS CO	DE	106.1
FARM BUREAU LIFE INS CO	IA	9,479.7
FREEDOM LIFE INS CO OF AMERICA	TX	418.7
GERBER LIFE INS CO	NY	4,677.1
HEALTH CARE SVC CORP A MUT LEG RES	IL	33,429.9
HMO COLORADO	CO	442.7
HUMANA BENEFIT PLAN OF ILLINOIS	IL	1,104.8
ILLINOIS MUTUAL LIFE INS CO	IL	1,520.9
MIDLAND NATIONAL LIFE INS CO	IA	62,252.9
NORTH AMERICAN INS CO	WI	19.2
NORTHWESTERN LONG TERM CARE INS CO	WI	290.3
NORTHWESTERN MUTUAL LIFE INS CO	WI	295,371.0
OXFORD LIFE INS CO	AZ	2,408.0
PACIFIC GUARDIAN LIFE INS CO LTD	HI	579.2
PRINCIPAL LIFE INS CO	IA	208,421.0
STANDARD INS CO	OR	27,265.4
STANDARD SECURITY LIFE INS CO OF NY	NY	142.7
TRUSTMARK INS CO	IL	1,752.8
TRUSTMARK LIFE INS CO	IL	296.8
UNITED WORLD LIFE INS CO	NE	141.0
USABLE LIFE	AR	496.4

Connecticut

INSURANCE COMPANY NAME	DOM. STATE	TOTAL ASSETS ($MIL)	INSURANCE COMPANY NAME	DOM. STATE	TOTAL ASSETS ($MIL)
Rating: **A+**					
CHESAPEAKE LIFE INS CO	OK	253.5			
COUNTRY LIFE INS CO	IL	10,112.1			
PHYSICIANS MUTUAL INS CO	NE	2,506.1			
TEACHERS INS & ANNUITY ASN OF AM	NY	320,701.0			
Rating: **A**					
AMALGAMATED LIFE INS CO	NY	154.2			
BERKLEY LIFE & HEALTH INS CO	IA	382.0			
FEDERATED LIFE INS CO	MN	2,189.3			
GARDEN STATE LIFE INS CO	TX	147.1			
GUARDIAN LIFE INS CO OF AMERICA	NY	65,189.0			
HUMANA INS CO (WI)	WI	10,594.3			
SENTRY LIFE INS CO	WI	8,165.9			
SHELTERPOINT LIFE INS CO	NY	235.2			
USAA LIFE INS CO	TX	26,903.7			
Rating: **A-**					
AMERICAN FAMILY LIFE ASR CO OF NY	NY	1,043.6			
FIDELITY SECURITY LIFE INS CO	MO	980.9			
NATIONAL BENEFIT LIFE INS CO	NY	595.9			
NEW YORK LIFE INS CO	NY	198,377.0			
NIAGARA LIFE & HEALTH INS CO	NY	17.2			
NIPPON LIFE INS CO OF AMERICA	IA	246.1			
PHYSICIANS LIFE INS CO	NE	1,730.5			
UNITED HEALTHCARE INS CO OF IL	IL	453.6			
Rating: **B+**					
ALLIANZ LIFE INS CO OF NY	NY	3,829.8			
AMERICAN FIDELITY ASR CO	OK	6,608.0			
ANTHEM LIFE INS CO	IN	799.2			
ASSURITY LIFE INS CO	NE	2,670.3			
BOSTON MUTUAL LIFE INS CO	MA	1,547.3			
DEARBORN LIFE INS CO	IL	1,657.5			
DELAWARE AMERICAN LIFE INS CO	DE	106.1			
GERBER LIFE INS CO	NY	4,677.1			
HEALTH CARE SVC CORP A MUT LEG RES	IL	33,429.9			
HUMANA BENEFIT PLAN OF ILLINOIS	IL	1,104.8			
ILLINOIS MUTUAL LIFE INS CO	IL	1,520.9			
MIDLAND NATIONAL LIFE INS CO	IA	62,252.9			
NORTHWESTERN LONG TERM CARE INS CO	WI	290.3			
NORTHWESTERN MUTUAL LIFE INS CO	WI	295,371.0			
OXFORD HEALTH PLANS (CT) INC	CT	586.6			
OXFORD LIFE INS CO	AZ	2,408.0			
PRINCIPAL LIFE INS CO	IA	208,421.0			
STANDARD INS CO	OR	27,265.4			
STANDARD SECURITY LIFE INS CO OF NY	NY	142.7			
TRUSTMARK INS CO	IL	1,752.8			
TRUSTMARK LIFE INS CO	IL	296.8			
USABLE LIFE	AR	496.4			
VOYA RETIREMENT INS & ANNUITY CO	CT	110,637.0			

Delaware

INSURANCE COMPANY NAME	DOM. STATE	TOTAL ASSETS ($MIL)
Rating: A+		
CHESAPEAKE LIFE INS CO	OK	253.5
COUNTRY LIFE INS CO	IL	10,112.1
PHYSICIANS MUTUAL INS CO	NE	2,506.1
TEACHERS INS & ANNUITY ASN OF AM	NY	320,701.0
Rating: A		
AMALGAMATED LIFE INS CO	NY	154.2
BERKLEY LIFE & HEALTH INS CO	IA	382.0
FEDERATED LIFE INS CO	MN	2,189.3
GARDEN STATE LIFE INS CO	TX	147.1
GUARDIAN LIFE INS CO OF AMERICA	NY	65,189.0
HUMANA INS CO (WI)	WI	10,594.3
NATIONAL FOUNDATION LIFE INS CO	TX	87.8
SENTRY LIFE INS CO	WI	8,165.9
SHELTERPOINT LIFE INS CO	NY	235.2
USAA LIFE INS CO	TX	26,903.7
Rating: A-		
FIDELITY SECURITY LIFE INS CO	MO	980.9
FIRST RELIANCE STANDARD LIFE INS CO	NY	237.6
NATIONAL BENEFIT LIFE INS CO	NY	595.9
NEW YORK LIFE INS CO	NY	198,377.0
NIPPON LIFE INS CO OF AMERICA	IA	246.1
PHYSICIANS LIFE INS CO	NE	1,730.5
Rating: B+		
AMERICAN FIDELITY ASR CO	OK	6,608.0
AMERIGROUP INS CO	TX	322.8
ANTHEM LIFE INS CO	IN	799.2
ASSURITY LIFE INS CO	NE	2,670.3
BOSTON MUTUAL LIFE INS CO	MA	1,547.3
COMPANION LIFE INS CO	SC	489.5
DEARBORN LIFE INS CO	IL	1,657.5
DELAWARE AMERICAN LIFE INS CO	DE	106.1
FREEDOM LIFE INS CO OF AMERICA	TX	418.7
GERBER LIFE INS CO	NY	4,677.1
HEALTH CARE SVC CORP A MUT LEG RES	IL	33,429.9
HIGHMARK BCBSD INC	DE	745.7
HUMANA BENEFIT PLAN OF ILLINOIS	IL	1,104.8
HUMANA WISCONSIN HEALTH ORGANIZATION	WI	1,259.4
ILLINOIS MUTUAL LIFE INS CO	IL	1,520.9
MIDLAND NATIONAL LIFE INS CO	IA	62,252.9
NORTHWESTERN LONG TERM CARE INS CO	WI	290.3
NORTHWESTERN MUTUAL LIFE INS CO	WI	295,371.0
OPTIMUM CHOICE INC	MD	119.3
OXFORD LIFE INS CO	AZ	2,408.0
PRINCIPAL LIFE INS CO	IA	208,421.0
STANDARD INS CO	OR	27,265.4
STANDARD SECURITY LIFE INS CO OF NY	NY	142.7
TRUSTMARK INS CO	IL	1,752.8
TRUSTMARK LIFE INS CO	IL	296.8
UNITED WORLD LIFE INS CO	NE	141.0
USABLE LIFE	AR	496.4
VOYA RETIREMENT INS & ANNUITY CO	CT	110,637.0

District of Columbia

INSURANCE COMPANY NAME	DOM. STATE	TOTAL ASSETS ($MIL)
Rating: A+		
CHESAPEAKE LIFE INS CO	OK	253.5
PHYSICIANS MUTUAL INS CO	NE	2,506.1
TEACHERS INS & ANNUITY ASN OF AM	NY	320,701.0
Rating: A		
AMALGAMATED LIFE INS CO	NY	154.2
BERKLEY LIFE & HEALTH INS CO	IA	382.0
GARDEN STATE LIFE INS CO	TX	147.1
GUARDIAN LIFE INS CO OF AMERICA	NY	65,189.0
HUMANA INS CO (WI)	WI	10,594.3
KAISER PERMANENTE INS CO	CA	220.6
NATIONAL FOUNDATION LIFE INS CO	TX	87.8
SENTRY LIFE INS CO	WI	8,165.9
SHELTERPOINT LIFE INS CO	NY	235.2
USAA LIFE INS CO	TX	26,903.7
Rating: A-		
CIGNA LIFE INS CO OF NEW YORK	NY	449.3
FIDELITY SECURITY LIFE INS CO	MO	980.9
FIRST RELIANCE STANDARD LIFE INS CO	NY	237.6
NATIONAL BENEFIT LIFE INS CO	NY	595.9
NEW YORK LIFE INS CO	NY	198,377.0
NIPPON LIFE INS CO OF AMERICA	IA	246.1
PHYSICIANS LIFE INS CO	NE	1,730.5
Rating: B+		
ALLIANZ LIFE INS CO OF NY	NY	3,829.8
AMERICAN FIDELITY ASR CO	OK	6,608.0
ANTHEM LIFE INS CO	IN	799.2
ASSURITY LIFE INS CO	NE	2,670.3
BEST LIFE & HEALTH INS CO	TX	30.1
BOSTON MUTUAL LIFE INS CO	MA	1,547.3
COMPANION LIFE INS CO	SC	489.5
DEARBORN LIFE INS CO	IL	1,657.5
DELAWARE AMERICAN LIFE INS CO	DE	106.1
GERBER LIFE INS CO	NY	4,677.1
GROUP HOSP & MEDICAL SERVICES INC	DC	3,122.9
HEALTH CARE SVC CORP A MUT LEG RES	IL	33,429.9
HUMANA BENEFIT PLAN OF ILLINOIS	IL	1,104.8
MIDLAND NATIONAL LIFE INS CO	IA	62,252.9
NORTH AMERICAN INS CO	WI	19.2
NORTHWESTERN LONG TERM CARE INS CO	WI	290.3
NORTHWESTERN MUTUAL LIFE INS CO	WI	295,371.0
OPTIMUM CHOICE INC	MD	119.3
OXFORD LIFE INS CO	AZ	2,408.0
PRINCIPAL LIFE INS CO	IA	208,421.0
STANDARD INS CO	OR	27,265.4
STANDARD SECURITY LIFE INS CO OF NY	NY	142.7
TRUSTMARK INS CO	IL	1,752.8
TRUSTMARK LIFE INS CO	IL	296.8
UNITED WORLD LIFE INS CO	NE	141.0
USABLE LIFE	AR	496.4
VOYA RETIREMENT INS & ANNUITY CO	CT	110,637.0

Florida

INSURANCE COMPANY NAME	DOM. STATE	TOTAL ASSETS ($MIL)
Rating:	**A+**	
CHESAPEAKE LIFE INS CO	OK	253.5
COUNTRY LIFE INS CO	IL	10,112.1
PHYSICIANS MUTUAL INS CO	NE	2,506.1
TEACHERS INS & ANNUITY ASN OF AM	NY	320,701.0
Rating:	**A**	
AMALGAMATED LIFE INS CO	NY	154.2
BERKLEY LIFE & HEALTH INS CO	IA	382.0
CAPITAL HEALTH PLAN INC	FL	666.5
FEDERATED LIFE INS CO	MN	2,189.3
FLORIDA HEALTH CARE PLAN INC	FL	247.7
GARDEN STATE LIFE INS CO	TX	147.1
GUARDIAN LIFE INS CO OF AMERICA	NY	65,189.0
HUMANA INS CO (WI)	WI	10,594.3
SENTRY LIFE INS CO	WI	8,165.9
SHELTERPOINT LIFE INS CO	NY	235.2
SOUTHERN FARM BUREAU LIFE INS CO	MS	14,723.1
USAA LIFE INS CO	TX	26,903.7
Rating:	**A-**	
CHRISTIAN FIDELITY LIFE INS CO	TX	58.3
FIDELITY SECURITY LIFE INS CO	MO	980.9
HEALTH FIRST COMM PLANS INC	FL	104.0
HEALTH OPTIONS INC	FL	2,831.6
HUMANA MEDICAL PLAN INC	FL	3,307.4
NATIONAL BENEFIT LIFE INS CO	NY	595.9
NEW YORK LIFE INS CO	NY	198,377.0
NIPPON LIFE INS CO OF AMERICA	IA	246.1
PHYSICIANS LIFE INS CO	NE	1,730.5
Rating:	**B+**	
AMERICAN FAMILY MUTL INS CO SI	WI	24,090.2
AMERICAN FIDELITY ASR CO	OK	6,608.0
ANTHEM LIFE INS CO	IN	799.2
ASSURITY LIFE INS CO	NE	2,670.3
BEST LIFE & HEALTH INS CO	TX	30.1
BOSTON MUTUAL LIFE INS CO	MA	1,547.3
COMPANION LIFE INS CO	SC	489.5
DEARBORN LIFE INS CO	IL	1,657.5
DELAWARE AMERICAN LIFE INS CO	DE	106.1
FREEDOM LIFE INS CO OF AMERICA	TX	418.7
GERBER LIFE INS CO	NY	4,677.1
HEALTH CARE SVC CORP A MUT LEG RES	IL	33,429.9
HEALTHSPRING OF FLORIDA INC	FL	184.2
HEALTHSUN HEALTH PLANS INC	FL	299.0
HUMANA BENEFIT PLAN OF ILLINOIS	IL	1,104.8
ILLINOIS MUTUAL LIFE INS CO	IL	1,520.9
MIDLAND NATIONAL LIFE INS CO	IA	62,252.9
NORTHWESTERN LONG TERM CARE INS CO	WI	290.3
NORTHWESTERN MUTUAL LIFE INS CO	WI	295,371.0
OXFORD LIFE INS CO	AZ	2,408.0
PREFERRED CARE PARTNERS INC	FL	706.7
PRINCIPAL LIFE INS CO	IA	208,421.0
STANDARD INS CO	OR	27,265.4
STANDARD SECURITY LIFE INS CO OF NY	NY	142.7
TRANS OCEANIC LIFE INS CO	PR	77.3
TRUSTMARK INS CO	IL	1,752.8

INSURANCE COMPANY NAME	DOM. STATE	TOTAL ASSETS ($MIL)
TRUSTMARK LIFE INS CO	IL	296.8
UNITED WORLD LIFE INS CO	NE	141.0
USABLE LIFE	AR	496.4
VOYA RETIREMENT INS & ANNUITY CO	CT	110,637.0

Georgia

INSURANCE COMPANY NAME	DOM. STATE	TOTAL ASSETS ($MIL)
WELLCARE OF GEORGIA INC	GA	685.5

Rating: A+

INSURANCE COMPANY NAME	DOM. STATE	TOTAL ASSETS ($MIL)
CHESAPEAKE LIFE INS CO	OK	253.5
COUNTRY LIFE INS CO	IL	10,112.1
PHYSICIANS MUTUAL INS CO	NE	2,506.1
TEACHERS INS & ANNUITY ASN OF AM	NY	320,701.0

Rating: A

INSURANCE COMPANY NAME	DOM. STATE	TOTAL ASSETS ($MIL)
AMALGAMATED LIFE INS CO	NY	154.2
BERKLEY LIFE & HEALTH INS CO	IA	382.0
FEDERATED LIFE INS CO	MN	2,189.3
GARDEN STATE LIFE INS CO	TX	147.1
GUARDIAN LIFE INS CO OF AMERICA	NY	65,189.0
HUMANA INS CO (WI)	WI	10,594.3
KAISER PERMANENTE INS CO	CA	220.6
NATIONAL FOUNDATION LIFE INS CO	TX	87.8
SENTRY LIFE INS CO	WI	8,165.9
SOUTHERN FARM BUREAU LIFE INS CO	MS	14,723.1
USAA LIFE INS CO	TX	26,903.7

Rating: A-

INSURANCE COMPANY NAME	DOM. STATE	TOTAL ASSETS ($MIL)
AMGP GEORGIA MANAGED CARE CO INC	GA	401.2
BLUE CROSS BLUE SHIELD HEALTHCARE GA	GA	2,685.2
CHRISTIAN FIDELITY LIFE INS CO	TX	58.3
FIDELITY SECURITY LIFE INS CO	MO	980.9
MEDICAL MUTUAL OF OHIO	OH	2,702.4
NATIONAL BENEFIT LIFE INS CO	NY	595.9
NEW YORK LIFE INS CO	NY	198,377.0
NIPPON LIFE INS CO OF AMERICA	IA	246.1
PHYSICIANS LIFE INS CO	NE	1,730.5
SWBC LIFE INS CO	TX	36.1

Rating: B+

INSURANCE COMPANY NAME	DOM. STATE	TOTAL ASSETS ($MIL)
AMERICAN FAMILY MUTL INS CO SI	WI	24,090.2
AMERICAN FIDELITY ASR CO	OK	6,608.0
ANTHEM LIFE INS CO	IN	799.2
ASSURITY LIFE INS CO	NE	2,670.3
BEST LIFE & HEALTH INS CO	TX	30.1
BOSTON MUTUAL LIFE INS CO	MA	1,547.3
COMPANION LIFE INS CO	SC	489.5
DEARBORN LIFE INS CO	IL	1,657.5
DELAWARE AMERICAN LIFE INS CO	DE	106.1
FREEDOM LIFE INS CO OF AMERICA	TX	418.7
GERBER LIFE INS CO	NY	4,677.1
HEALTH CARE SVC CORP A MUT LEG RES	IL	33,429.9
HUMANA BENEFIT PLAN OF ILLINOIS	IL	1,104.8
ILLINOIS MUTUAL LIFE INS CO	IL	1,520.9
MIDLAND NATIONAL LIFE INS CO	IA	62,252.9
NORTHWESTERN LONG TERM CARE INS CO	WI	290.3
NORTHWESTERN MUTUAL LIFE INS CO	WI	295,371.0
OXFORD LIFE INS CO	AZ	2,408.0
PRINCIPAL LIFE INS CO	IA	208,421.0
STANDARD INS CO	OR	27,265.4
STANDARD SECURITY LIFE INS CO OF NY	NY	142.7
TRUSTMARK INS CO	IL	1,752.8
TRUSTMARK LIFE INS CO	IL	296.8
UNITED WORLD LIFE INS CO	NE	141.0
USABLE LIFE	AR	496.4
VOYA RETIREMENT INS & ANNUITY CO	CT	110,637.0

Hawaii

INSURANCE COMPANY NAME	DOM. STATE	TOTAL ASSETS ($MIL)
Rating: A+		
CHESAPEAKE LIFE INS CO	OK	253.5
PHYSICIANS MUTUAL INS CO	NE	2,506.1
TEACHERS INS & ANNUITY ASN OF AM	NY	320,701.0
Rating: A		
AMALGAMATED LIFE INS CO	NY	154.2
BERKLEY LIFE & HEALTH INS CO	IA	382.0
GARDEN STATE LIFE INS CO	TX	147.1
GUARDIAN LIFE INS CO OF AMERICA	NY	65,189.0
HUMANA INS CO (WI)	WI	10,594.3
KAISER PERMANENTE INS CO	CA	220.6
SENTRY LIFE INS CO	WI	8,165.9
USAA LIFE INS CO	TX	26,903.7
Rating: A-		
FIDELITY SECURITY LIFE INS CO	MO	980.9
NATIONAL BENEFIT LIFE INS CO	NY	595.9
NEW YORK LIFE INS CO	NY	198,377.0
NIPPON LIFE INS CO OF AMERICA	IA	246.1
PHYSICIANS LIFE INS CO	NE	1,730.5
Rating: B+		
AMERICAN FIDELITY ASR CO	OK	6,608.0
ANTHEM LIFE INS CO	IN	799.2
ASSURITY LIFE INS CO	NE	2,670.3
BEST LIFE & HEALTH INS CO	TX	30.1
BOSTON MUTUAL LIFE INS CO	MA	1,547.3
COMPANION LIFE INS CO OF CA	CA	29.6
DEARBORN LIFE INS CO	IL	1,657.5
DELAWARE AMERICAN LIFE INS CO	DE	106.1
GERBER LIFE INS CO	NY	4,677.1
HUMANA BENEFIT PLAN OF ILLINOIS	IL	1,104.8
MIDLAND NATIONAL LIFE INS CO	IA	62,252.9
NORTHWESTERN LONG TERM CARE INS CO	WI	290.3
NORTHWESTERN MUTUAL LIFE INS CO	WI	295,371.0
OXFORD LIFE INS CO	AZ	2,408.0
PACIFIC GUARDIAN LIFE INS CO LTD	HI	579.2
PRINCIPAL LIFE INS CO	IA	208,421.0
STANDARD INS CO	OR	27,265.4
STANDARD SECURITY LIFE INS CO OF NY	NY	142.7
TRUSTMARK INS CO	IL	1,752.8
TRUSTMARK LIFE INS CO	IL	296.8
UNITED WORLD LIFE INS CO	NE	141.0
USABLE LIFE	AR	496.4
VOYA RETIREMENT INS & ANNUITY CO	CT	110,637.0

Idaho

INSURANCE COMPANY NAME	DOM. STATE	TOTAL ASSETS ($MIL)
Rating:	**A+**	
CHESAPEAKE LIFE INS CO	OK	253.5
COUNTRY LIFE INS CO	IL	10,112.1
PHYSICIANS MUTUAL INS CO	NE	2,506.1
TEACHERS INS & ANNUITY ASN OF AM	NY	320,701.0
Rating:	**A**	
AMALGAMATED LIFE INS CO	NY	154.2
BERKLEY LIFE & HEALTH INS CO	IA	382.0
EMI HEALTH	UT	198.8
FEDERATED LIFE INS CO	MN	2,189.3
GARDEN STATE LIFE INS CO	TX	147.1
GUARDIAN LIFE INS CO OF AMERICA	NY	65,189.0
HUMANA INS CO (WI)	WI	10,594.3
LIFEWISE ASR CO	WA	249.5
NATIONAL FOUNDATION LIFE INS CO	TX	87.8
SENTRY LIFE INS CO	WI	8,165.9
USAA LIFE INS CO	TX	26,903.7
Rating:	**A-**	
CHRISTIAN FIDELITY LIFE INS CO	TX	58.3
FIDELITY SECURITY LIFE INS CO	MO	980.9
NATIONAL BENEFIT LIFE INS CO	NY	595.9
NEW YORK LIFE INS CO	NY	198,377.0
NIPPON LIFE INS CO OF AMERICA	IA	246.1
PHYSICIANS LIFE INS CO	NE	1,730.5
Rating:	**B+**	
AMERICAN FAMILY MUTL INS CO SI	WI	24,090.2
AMERICAN FIDELITY ASR CO	OK	6,608.0
ANTHEM LIFE INS CO	IN	799.2
ASSURITY LIFE INS CO	NE	2,670.3
BEST LIFE & HEALTH INS CO	TX	30.1
BLUE CROSS OF IDAHO HEALTH SERVICE	ID	1,144.5
BOSTON MUTUAL LIFE INS CO	MA	1,547.3
COMPANION LIFE INS CO	SC	489.5
DEARBORN LIFE INS CO	IL	1,657.5
DELAWARE AMERICAN LIFE INS CO	DE	106.1
FARM BUREAU LIFE INS CO	IA	9,479.7
GERBER LIFE INS CO	NY	4,677.1
HEALTH CARE SVC CORP A MUT LEG RES	IL	33,429.9
HUMANA BENEFIT PLAN OF ILLINOIS	IL	1,104.8
ILLINOIS MUTUAL LIFE INS CO	IL	1,520.9
MIDLAND NATIONAL LIFE INS CO	IA	62,252.9
NORTHWESTERN LONG TERM CARE INS CO	WI	290.3
NORTHWESTERN MUTUAL LIFE INS CO	WI	295,371.0
OXFORD LIFE INS CO	AZ	2,408.0
PACIFIC GUARDIAN LIFE INS CO LTD	HI	579.2
PRINCIPAL LIFE INS CO	IA	208,421.0
REGENCE BLUESHIELD OF IDAHO INC	ID	395.1
SELECTHEALTH INC	UT	1,703.8
STANDARD INS CO	OR	27,265.4
STANDARD SECURITY LIFE INS CO OF NY	NY	142.7
TRUSTMARK INS CO	IL	1,752.8
TRUSTMARK LIFE INS CO	IL	296.8
UNITED WORLD LIFE INS CO	NE	141.0
USABLE LIFE	AR	496.4
VOYA RETIREMENT INS & ANNUITY CO	CT	110,637.0

Illinois

INSURANCE COMPANY NAME	DOM. STATE	TOTAL ASSETS ($MIL)
Rating:	**A+**	
CHESAPEAKE LIFE INS CO	OK	253.5
COUNTRY LIFE INS CO	IL	10,112.1
PHYSICIANS MUTUAL INS CO	NE	2,506.1
TEACHERS INS & ANNUITY ASN OF AM	NY	320,701.0
Rating:	**A**	
AMALGAMATED LIFE INS CO	NY	154.2
BERKLEY LIFE & HEALTH INS CO	IA	382.0
FEDERATED LIFE INS CO	MN	2,189.3
GARDEN STATE LIFE INS CO	TX	147.1
GUARDIAN LIFE INS CO OF AMERICA	NY	65,189.0
HUMANA INS CO (WI)	WI	10,594.3
LIFEWISE ASR CO	WA	249.5
SENTRY LIFE INS CO	WI	8,165.9
SHELTERPOINT LIFE INS CO	NY	235.2
USAA LIFE INS CO	TX	26,903.7
Rating:	**A-**	
CHRISTIAN FIDELITY LIFE INS CO	TX	58.3
ESSENCE HEALTHCARE INC	MO	260.9
FIDELITY SECURITY LIFE INS CO	MO	980.9
INDEPENDENT CARE HEALTH PLAN	WI	107.2
NATIONAL BENEFIT LIFE INS CO	NY	595.9
NEW YORK LIFE INS CO	NY	198,377.0
NIPPON LIFE INS CO OF AMERICA	IA	246.1
PHYSICIANS LIFE INS CO	NE	1,730.5
UNITED HEALTHCARE INS CO OF IL	IL	453.6
Rating:	**B+**	
ALLIANZ LIFE INS CO OF NY	NY	3,829.8
AMERICAN FAMILY MUTL INS CO SI	WI	24,090.2
AMERICAN FIDELITY ASR CO	OK	6,608.0
ANTHEM LIFE INS CO	IN	799.2
ASSURITY LIFE INS CO	NE	2,670.3
BEST LIFE & HEALTH INS CO	TX	30.1
BOSTON MUTUAL LIFE INS CO	MA	1,547.3
COMPANION LIFE INS CO	SC	489.5
DEARBORN LIFE INS CO	IL	1,657.5
DELAWARE AMERICAN LIFE INS CO	DE	106.1
ENTERPRISE LIFE INS CO	TX	148.0
FREEDOM LIFE INS CO OF AMERICA	TX	418.7
GERBER LIFE INS CO	NY	4,677.1
HEALTH CARE SVC CORP A MUT LEG RES	IL	33,429.9
HUMANA BENEFIT PLAN OF ILLINOIS	IL	1,104.8
ILLINOIS MUTUAL LIFE INS CO	IL	1,520.9
MIDLAND NATIONAL LIFE INS CO	IA	62,252.9
NORTH AMERICAN INS CO	WI	19.2
NORTHWESTERN LONG TERM CARE INS CO	WI	290.3
NORTHWESTERN MUTUAL LIFE INS CO	WI	295,371.0
OXFORD LIFE INS CO	AZ	2,408.0
PRINCIPAL LIFE INS CO	IA	208,421.0
STANDARD INS CO	OR	27,265.4
STANDARD SECURITY LIFE INS CO OF NY	NY	142.7
TRUSTMARK INS CO	IL	1,752.8
TRUSTMARK LIFE INS CO	IL	296.8
UNITED FARM FAMILY LIFE INS CO	IN	2,442.0
UNITED HEALTHCARE OF THE MIDLANDS	NE	1,032.6

INSURANCE COMPANY NAME	DOM. STATE	TOTAL ASSETS ($MIL)
UNITED HEALTHCARE OF WISCONSIN INC	WI	2,701.9
UNITED WORLD LIFE INS CO	NE	141.0
USABLE LIFE	AR	496.4
VOYA RETIREMENT INS & ANNUITY CO	CT	110,637.0

Indiana

INSURANCE COMPANY NAME	DOM. STATE	TOTAL ASSETS ($MIL)
Rating: A+		
CHESAPEAKE LIFE INS CO	OK	253.5
COUNTRY LIFE INS CO	IL	10,112.1
PHYSICIANS MUTUAL INS CO	NE	2,506.1
TEACHERS INS & ANNUITY ASN OF AM	NY	320,701.0
Rating: A		
AMALGAMATED LIFE INS CO	NY	154.2
BERKLEY LIFE & HEALTH INS CO	IA	382.0
FEDERATED LIFE INS CO	MN	2,189.3
GARDEN STATE LIFE INS CO	TX	147.1
GUARDIAN LIFE INS CO OF AMERICA	NY	65,189.0
HUMANA INS CO (WI)	WI	10,594.3
NATIONAL FOUNDATION LIFE INS CO	TX	87.8
SENTRY LIFE INS CO	WI	8,165.9
USAA LIFE INS CO	TX	26,903.7
Rating: A-		
CHRISTIAN FIDELITY LIFE INS CO	TX	58.3
FIDELITY SECURITY LIFE INS CO	MO	980.9
INDEPENDENT CARE HEALTH PLAN	WI	107.2
MEDICAL MUTUAL OF OHIO	OH	2,702.4
NATIONAL BENEFIT LIFE INS CO	NY	595.9
NEW YORK LIFE INS CO	NY	198,377.0
NIPPON LIFE INS CO OF AMERICA	IA	246.1
PHYSICIANS LIFE INS CO	NE	1,730.5
Rating: B+		
AMERICAN FAMILY MUTL INS CO SI	WI	24,090.2
AMERICAN FIDELITY ASR CO	OK	6,608.0
ANTHEM LIFE INS CO	IN	799.2
ASSURITY LIFE INS CO	NE	2,670.3
BEST LIFE & HEALTH INS CO	TX	30.1
BOSTON MUTUAL LIFE INS CO	MA	1,547.3
COMPANION LIFE INS CO	SC	489.5
DEARBORN LIFE INS CO	IL	1,657.5
DELAWARE AMERICAN LIFE INS CO	DE	106.1
FREEDOM LIFE INS CO OF AMERICA	TX	418.7
GERBER LIFE INS CO	NY	4,677.1
HEALTH CARE SVC CORP A MUT LEG RES	IL	33,429.9
HUMANA BENEFIT PLAN OF ILLINOIS	IL	1,104.8
ILLINOIS MUTUAL LIFE INS CO	IL	1,520.9
MDWISE INC	IN	389.2
MIDLAND NATIONAL LIFE INS CO	IA	62,252.9
NORTH AMERICAN INS CO	WI	19.2
NORTHWESTERN LONG TERM CARE INS CO	WI	290.3
NORTHWESTERN MUTUAL LIFE INS CO	WI	295,371.0
OXFORD LIFE INS CO	AZ	2,408.0
PHYSICIANS HEALTH PLAN OF NO IN	IN	112.6
PRINCIPAL LIFE INS CO	IA	208,421.0
STANDARD INS CO	OR	27,265.4
STANDARD SECURITY LIFE INS CO OF NY	NY	142.7
TRUSTMARK INS CO	IL	1,752.8
TRUSTMARK LIFE INS CO	IL	296.8
UNITED FARM FAMILY LIFE INS CO	IN	2,442.0
UNITED HEALTHCARE OF THE MIDLANDS	NE	1,032.6
UNITED WORLD LIFE INS CO	NE	141.0
USABLE LIFE	AR	496.4

INSURANCE COMPANY NAME	DOM. STATE	TOTAL ASSETS ($MIL)
VOYA RETIREMENT INS & ANNUITY CO	CT	110,637.0

Iowa

INSURANCE COMPANY NAME	DOM. STATE	TOTAL ASSETS ($MIL)	INSURANCE COMPANY NAME	DOM. STATE	TOTAL ASSETS ($MIL)
Rating: A+					
CHESAPEAKE LIFE INS CO	OK	253.5			
COUNTRY LIFE INS CO	IL	10,112.1			
PHYSICIANS MUTUAL INS CO	NE	2,506.1			
TEACHERS INS & ANNUITY ASN OF AM	NY	320,701.0			
Rating: A					
AMALGAMATED LIFE INS CO	NY	154.2			
BERKLEY LIFE & HEALTH INS CO	IA	382.0			
FEDERATED LIFE INS CO	MN	2,189.3			
GARDEN STATE LIFE INS CO	TX	147.1			
GUARDIAN LIFE INS CO OF AMERICA	NY	65,189.0			
HUMANA INS CO (WI)	WI	10,594.3			
NATIONAL FOUNDATION LIFE INS CO	TX	87.8			
SENTRY LIFE INS CO	WI	8,165.9			
USAA LIFE INS CO	TX	26,903.7			
Rating: A-					
FIDELITY SECURITY LIFE INS CO	MO	980.9			
NATIONAL BENEFIT LIFE INS CO	NY	595.9			
NEW YORK LIFE INS CO	NY	198,377.0			
NIPPON LIFE INS CO OF AMERICA	IA	246.1			
PHYSICIANS LIFE INS CO	NE	1,730.5			
Rating: B+					
AMERICAN FAMILY MUTL INS CO SI	WI	24,090.2			
AMERICAN FIDELITY ASR CO	OK	6,608.0			
AMERIGROUP INS CO	TX	322.8			
ANTHEM LIFE INS CO	IN	799.2			
ASSURITY LIFE INS CO	NE	2,670.3			
BEST LIFE & HEALTH INS CO	TX	30.1			
BOSTON MUTUAL LIFE INS CO	MA	1,547.3			
COMPANION LIFE INS CO	SC	489.5			
DEARBORN LIFE INS CO	IL	1,657.5			
DELAWARE AMERICAN LIFE INS CO	DE	106.1			
FARM BUREAU LIFE INS CO	IA	9,479.7			
FREEDOM LIFE INS CO OF AMERICA	TX	418.7			
GERBER LIFE INS CO	NY	4,677.1			
HEALTHPARTNERS INS CO	MN	475.5			
HUMANA BENEFIT PLAN OF ILLINOIS	IL	1,104.8			
ILLINOIS MUTUAL LIFE INS CO	IL	1,520.9			
MIDLAND NATIONAL LIFE INS CO	IA	62,252.9			
NORTHWESTERN LONG TERM CARE INS CO	WI	290.3			
NORTHWESTERN MUTUAL LIFE INS CO	WI	295,371.0			
OXFORD LIFE INS CO	AZ	2,408.0			
PACIFIC GUARDIAN LIFE INS CO LTD	HI	579.2			
PRINCIPAL LIFE INS CO	IA	208,421.0			
STANDARD INS CO	OR	27,265.4			
STANDARD SECURITY LIFE INS CO OF NY	NY	142.7			
TRUSTMARK INS CO	IL	1,752.8			
TRUSTMARK LIFE INS CO	IL	296.8			
UNITED FARM FAMILY LIFE INS CO	IN	2,442.0			
UNITED HEALTHCARE OF THE MIDLANDS	NE	1,032.6			
UNITED HEALTHCARE OF WISCONSIN INC	WI	2,701.9			
UNITED WORLD LIFE INS CO	NE	141.0			
USABLE LIFE	AR	496.4			
VOYA RETIREMENT INS & ANNUITY CO	CT	110,637.0			

Kansas

INSURANCE COMPANY NAME	DOM. STATE	TOTAL ASSETS ($MIL)	INSURANCE COMPANY NAME	DOM. STATE	TOTAL ASSETS ($MIL)
Rating:	**A+**				
CHESAPEAKE LIFE INS CO	OK	253.5			
COUNTRY LIFE INS CO	IL	10,112.1			
PHYSICIANS MUTUAL INS CO	NE	2,506.1			
TEACHERS INS & ANNUITY ASN OF AM	NY	320,701.0			
Rating:	**A**				
AMALGAMATED LIFE INS CO	NY	154.2			
BERKLEY LIFE & HEALTH INS CO	IA	382.0			
FEDERATED LIFE INS CO	MN	2,189.3			
GARDEN STATE LIFE INS CO	TX	147.1			
GUARDIAN LIFE INS CO OF AMERICA	NY	65,189.0			
HUMANA INS CO (WI)	WI	10,594.3			
KAISER PERMANENTE INS CO	CA	220.6			
NATIONAL FOUNDATION LIFE INS CO	TX	87.8			
SENTRY LIFE INS CO	WI	8,165.9			
USAA LIFE INS CO	TX	26,903.7			
Rating:	**A-**				
CHRISTIAN FIDELITY LIFE INS CO	TX	58.3			
FIDELITY SECURITY LIFE INS CO	MO	980.9			
NATIONAL BENEFIT LIFE INS CO	NY	595.9			
NEW YORK LIFE INS CO	NY	198,377.0			
NIPPON LIFE INS CO OF AMERICA	IA	246.1			
PHYSICIANS LIFE INS CO	NE	1,730.5			
Rating:	**B+**				
ADVANCE INS CO OF KANSAS	KS	65.6			
AMERICAN FAMILY MUTL INS CO SI	WI	24,090.2			
AMERICAN FIDELITY ASR CO	OK	6,608.0			
ANTHEM LIFE INS CO	IN	799.2			
ASSURITY LIFE INS CO	NE	2,670.3			
BEST LIFE & HEALTH INS CO	TX	30.1			
BOSTON MUTUAL LIFE INS CO	MA	1,547.3			
COMPANION LIFE INS CO	SC	489.5			
DEARBORN LIFE INS CO	IL	1,657.5			
DELAWARE AMERICAN LIFE INS CO	DE	106.1			
ENTERPRISE LIFE INS CO	TX	148.0			
FARM BUREAU LIFE INS CO	IA	9,479.7			
FREEDOM LIFE INS CO OF AMERICA	TX	418.7			
GERBER LIFE INS CO	NY	4,677.1			
HUMANA BENEFIT PLAN OF ILLINOIS	IL	1,104.8			
ILLINOIS MUTUAL LIFE INS CO	IL	1,520.9			
MIDLAND NATIONAL LIFE INS CO	IA	62,252.9			
NORTH AMERICAN INS CO	WI	19.2			
NORTHWESTERN LONG TERM CARE INS CO	WI	290.3			
NORTHWESTERN MUTUAL LIFE INS CO	WI	295,371.0			
OXFORD LIFE INS CO	AZ	2,408.0			
PRINCIPAL LIFE INS CO	IA	208,421.0			
STANDARD INS CO	OR	27,265.4			
STANDARD SECURITY LIFE INS CO OF NY	NY	142.7			
TRUSTMARK INS CO	IL	1,752.8			
TRUSTMARK LIFE INS CO	IL	296.8			
UNITED HEALTHCARE OF THE MIDLANDS	NE	1,032.6			
UNITED WORLD LIFE INS CO	NE	141.0			
USABLE LIFE	AR	496.4			
VOYA RETIREMENT INS & ANNUITY CO	CT	110,637.0			

Kentucky

INSURANCE COMPANY NAME	DOM. STATE	TOTAL ASSETS ($MIL)
Rating: A+		
CHESAPEAKE LIFE INS CO	OK	253.5
COUNTRY LIFE INS CO	IL	10,112.1
PHYSICIANS MUTUAL INS CO	NE	2,506.1
TEACHERS INS & ANNUITY ASN OF AM	NY	320,701.0
Rating: A		
AMALGAMATED LIFE INS CO	NY	154.2
BERKLEY LIFE & HEALTH INS CO	IA	382.0
FEDERATED LIFE INS CO	MN	2,189.3
GARDEN STATE LIFE INS CO	TX	147.1
GUARDIAN LIFE INS CO OF AMERICA	NY	65,189.0
HUMANA INS CO (WI)	WI	10,594.3
NATIONAL FOUNDATION LIFE INS CO	TX	87.8
SENTRY LIFE INS CO	WI	8,165.9
SOUTHERN FARM BUREAU LIFE INS CO	MS	14,723.1
USAA LIFE INS CO	TX	26,903.7
Rating: A-		
ANTHEM KENTUCKY MANAGED CARE PLAN	KY	314.7
CHRISTIAN FIDELITY LIFE INS CO	TX	58.3
FIDELITY SECURITY LIFE INS CO	MO	980.9
HUMANA MEDICAL PLAN INC	FL	3,307.4
NATIONAL BENEFIT LIFE INS CO	NY	595.9
NEW YORK LIFE INS CO	NY	198,377.0
NIPPON LIFE INS CO OF AMERICA	IA	246.1
PHYSICIANS LIFE INS CO	NE	1,730.5
Rating: B+		
AETNA BETTER HLTH OF KY INS CO	KY	536.6
AMERICAN FIDELITY ASR CO	OK	6,608.0
ANTHEM LIFE INS CO	IN	799.2
ASSURITY LIFE INS CO	NE	2,670.3
BEST LIFE & HEALTH INS CO	TX	30.1
BOSTON MUTUAL LIFE INS CO	MA	1,547.3
COMPANION LIFE INS CO	SC	489.5
DEARBORN LIFE INS CO	IL	1,657.5
DELAWARE AMERICAN LIFE INS CO	DE	106.1
FREEDOM LIFE INS CO OF AMERICA	TX	418.7
GERBER LIFE INS CO	NY	4,677.1
HEALTH CARE SVC CORP A MUT LEG RES	IL	33,429.9
HUMANA BENEFIT PLAN OF ILLINOIS	IL	1,104.8
HUMANA WISCONSIN HEALTH ORGANIZATION	WI	1,259.4
ILLINOIS MUTUAL LIFE INS CO	IL	1,520.9
MIDLAND NATIONAL LIFE INS CO	IA	62,252.9
NORTHWESTERN LONG TERM CARE INS CO	WI	290.3
NORTHWESTERN MUTUAL LIFE INS CO	WI	295,371.0
OXFORD LIFE INS CO	AZ	2,408.0
PRINCIPAL LIFE INS CO	IA	208,421.0
STANDARD INS CO	OR	27,265.4
STANDARD SECURITY LIFE INS CO OF NY	NY	142.7
TRUSTMARK INS CO	IL	1,752.8
TRUSTMARK LIFE INS CO	IL	296.8
UNITED HEALTHCARE OF WISCONSIN INC	WI	2,701.9
UNITED WORLD LIFE INS CO	NE	141.0
USABLE LIFE	AR	496.4
VOYA RETIREMENT INS & ANNUITY CO	CT	110,637.0

Louisiana

INSURANCE COMPANY NAME	DOM. STATE	TOTAL ASSETS ($MIL)	INSURANCE COMPANY NAME	DOM. STATE	TOTAL ASSETS ($MIL)
Rating: **A+**					
CHESAPEAKE LIFE INS CO	OK	253.5			
COUNTRY LIFE INS CO	IL	10,112.1			
HMO LOUISIANA INC	LA	862.1			
PHYSICIANS MUTUAL INS CO	NE	2,506.1			
TEACHERS INS & ANNUITY ASN OF AM	NY	320,701.0			
Rating: **A**					
AMALGAMATED LIFE INS CO	NY	154.2			
BERKLEY LIFE & HEALTH INS CO	IA	382.0			
FEDERATED LIFE INS CO	MN	2,189.3			
GARDEN STATE LIFE INS CO	TX	147.1			
GUARDIAN LIFE INS CO OF AMERICA	NY	65,189.0			
HUMANA INS CO (WI)	WI	10,594.3			
NATIONAL FOUNDATION LIFE INS CO	TX	87.8			
SENTRY LIFE INS CO	WI	8,165.9			
SOUTHERN FARM BUREAU LIFE INS CO	MS	14,723.1			
USAA LIFE INS CO	TX	26,903.7			
Rating: **A-**					
BLUEBONNET LIFE INS CO	MS	69.5			
CHRISTIAN FIDELITY LIFE INS CO	TX	58.3			
FIDELITY SECURITY LIFE INS CO	MO	980.9			
NATIONAL BENEFIT LIFE INS CO	NY	595.9			
NEW YORK LIFE INS CO	NY	198,377.0			
NIPPON LIFE INS CO OF AMERICA	IA	246.1			
PHYSICIANS LIFE INS CO	NE	1,730.5			
SWBC LIFE INS CO	TX	36.1			
Rating: **B+**					
AMERICAN FIDELITY ASR CO	OK	6,608.0			
AMERIGROUP INS CO	TX	322.8			
ANTHEM LIFE INS CO	IN	799.2			
ASSURITY LIFE INS CO	NE	2,670.3			
BEST LIFE & HEALTH INS CO	TX	30.1			
BOSTON MUTUAL LIFE INS CO	MA	1,547.3			
COMPANION LIFE INS CO	SC	489.5			
DEARBORN LIFE INS CO	IL	1,657.5			
DELAWARE AMERICAN LIFE INS CO	DE	106.1			
ENTERPRISE LIFE INS CO	TX	148.0			
FREEDOM LIFE INS CO OF AMERICA	TX	418.7			
GERBER LIFE INS CO	NY	4,677.1			
HUMANA BENEFIT PLAN OF ILLINOIS	IL	1,104.8			
ILLINOIS MUTUAL LIFE INS CO	IL	1,520.9			
MIDLAND NATIONAL LIFE INS CO	IA	62,252.9			
NORTH AMERICAN INS CO	WI	19.2			
NORTHWESTERN LONG TERM CARE INS CO	WI	290.3			
NORTHWESTERN MUTUAL LIFE INS CO	WI	295,371.0			
OXFORD LIFE INS CO	AZ	2,408.0			
PACIFIC GUARDIAN LIFE INS CO LTD	HI	579.2			
PRINCIPAL LIFE INS CO	IA	208,421.0			
STANDARD INS CO	OR	27,265.4			
STANDARD SECURITY LIFE INS CO OF NY	NY	142.7			
TRUSTMARK INS CO	IL	1,752.8			
TRUSTMARK LIFE INS CO	IL	296.8			
UNITED WORLD LIFE INS CO	NE	141.0			
USABLE LIFE	AR	496.4			
VOYA RETIREMENT INS & ANNUITY CO	CT	110,637.0			

Maine

INSURANCE COMPANY NAME	DOM. STATE	TOTAL ASSETS ($MIL)	INSURANCE COMPANY NAME	DOM. STATE	TOTAL ASSETS ($MIL)
Rating: A+					
CHESAPEAKE LIFE INS CO	OK	253.5			
COUNTRY LIFE INS CO	IL	10,112.1			
PHYSICIANS MUTUAL INS CO	NE	2,506.1			
TEACHERS INS & ANNUITY ASN OF AM	NY	320,701.0			
Rating: A					
AMALGAMATED LIFE INS CO	NY	154.2			
BERKLEY LIFE & HEALTH INS CO	IA	382.0			
FEDERATED LIFE INS CO	MN	2,189.3			
GARDEN STATE LIFE INS CO	TX	147.1			
GUARDIAN LIFE INS CO OF AMERICA	NY	65,189.0			
HUMANA INS CO (WI)	WI	10,594.3			
NATIONAL FOUNDATION LIFE INS CO	TX	87.8			
SENTRY LIFE INS CO	WI	8,165.9			
USAA LIFE INS CO	TX	26,903.7			
Rating: A-					
FIDELITY SECURITY LIFE INS CO	MO	980.9			
NATIONAL BENEFIT LIFE INS CO	NY	595.9			
NEW YORK LIFE INS CO	NY	198,377.0			
PHYSICIANS LIFE INS CO	NE	1,730.5			
Rating: B+					
AMERICAN FIDELITY ASR CO	OK	6,608.0			
ANTHEM LIFE INS CO	IN	799.2			
ASSURITY LIFE INS CO	NE	2,670.3			
BOSTON MUTUAL LIFE INS CO	MA	1,547.3			
COMPANION LIFE INS CO	SC	489.5			
DEARBORN LIFE INS CO	IL	1,657.5			
DELAWARE AMERICAN LIFE INS CO	DE	106.1			
GERBER LIFE INS CO	NY	4,677.1			
HEALTH CARE SVC CORP A MUT LEG RES	IL	33,429.9			
HUMANA BENEFIT PLAN OF ILLINOIS	IL	1,104.8			
ILLINOIS MUTUAL LIFE INS CO	IL	1,520.9			
MIDLAND NATIONAL LIFE INS CO	IA	62,252.9			
NORTHWESTERN LONG TERM CARE INS CO	WI	290.3			
NORTHWESTERN MUTUAL LIFE INS CO	WI	295,371.0			
OXFORD LIFE INS CO	AZ	2,408.0			
PRINCIPAL LIFE INS CO	IA	208,421.0			
STANDARD INS CO	OR	27,265.4			
STANDARD SECURITY LIFE INS CO OF NY	NY	142.7			
TRUSTMARK INS CO	IL	1,752.8			
TRUSTMARK LIFE INS CO	IL	296.8			
UNITED WORLD LIFE INS CO	NE	141.0			
USABLE LIFE	AR	496.4			
VOYA RETIREMENT INS & ANNUITY CO	CT	110,637.0			

Maryland

INSURANCE COMPANY NAME	DOM. STATE	TOTAL ASSETS ($MIL)
Rating:	**A+**	
CHESAPEAKE LIFE INS CO	OK	253.5
COUNTRY LIFE INS CO	IL	10,112.1
PHYSICIANS MUTUAL INS CO	NE	2,506.1
TEACHERS INS & ANNUITY ASN OF AM	NY	320,701.0
Rating:	**A**	
AMALGAMATED LIFE INS CO	NY	154.2
BERKLEY LIFE & HEALTH INS CO	IA	382.0
FEDERATED LIFE INS CO	MN	2,189.3
GARDEN STATE LIFE INS CO	TX	147.1
GUARDIAN LIFE INS CO OF AMERICA	NY	65,189.0
HUMANA INS CO (WI)	WI	10,594.3
KAISER PERMANENTE INS CO	CA	220.6
SENTRY LIFE INS CO	WI	8,165.9
SHELTERPOINT LIFE INS CO	NY	235.2
USAA LIFE INS CO	TX	26,903.7
Rating:	**A-**	
FIDELITY SECURITY LIFE INS CO	MO	980.9
NATIONAL BENEFIT LIFE INS CO	NY	595.9
NEW YORK LIFE INS CO	NY	198,377.0
NIPPON LIFE INS CO OF AMERICA	IA	246.1
PHYSICIANS LIFE INS CO	NE	1,730.5
Rating:	**B+**	
AMERICAN FIDELITY ASR CO	OK	6,608.0
AMERIGROUP INS CO	TX	322.8
ANTHEM LIFE INS CO	IN	799.2
ASSURITY LIFE INS CO	NE	2,670.3
BEST LIFE & HEALTH INS CO	TX	30.1
BOSTON MUTUAL LIFE INS CO	MA	1,547.3
COMPANION LIFE INS CO	SC	489.5
DEARBORN LIFE INS CO	IL	1,657.5
DELAWARE AMERICAN LIFE INS CO	DE	106.1
FREEDOM LIFE INS CO OF AMERICA	TX	418.7
GERBER LIFE INS CO	NY	4,677.1
GROUP HOSP & MEDICAL SERVICES INC	DC	3,122.9
HEALTH CARE SVC CORP A MUT LEG RES	IL	33,429.9
HUMANA BENEFIT PLAN OF ILLINOIS	IL	1,104.8
ILLINOIS MUTUAL LIFE INS CO	IL	1,520.9
MIDLAND NATIONAL LIFE INS CO	IA	62,252.9
NORTH AMERICAN INS CO	WI	19.2
NORTHWESTERN LONG TERM CARE INS CO	WI	290.3
NORTHWESTERN MUTUAL LIFE INS CO	WI	295,371.0
OPTIMUM CHOICE INC	MD	119.3
OXFORD LIFE INS CO	AZ	2,408.0
PRINCIPAL LIFE INS CO	IA	208,421.0
STANDARD INS CO	OR	27,265.4
STANDARD SECURITY LIFE INS CO OF NY	NY	142.7
TRUSTMARK INS CO	IL	1,752.8
TRUSTMARK LIFE INS CO	IL	296.8
UNITED FARM FAMILY LIFE INS CO	IN	2,442.0
UNITED WORLD LIFE INS CO	NE	141.0
USABLE LIFE	AR	496.4
VOYA RETIREMENT INS & ANNUITY CO	CT	110,637.0

Massachusetts

INSURANCE COMPANY NAME	DOM. STATE	TOTAL ASSETS ($MIL)
Rating: **A+**		
CHESAPEAKE LIFE INS CO	OK	253.5
COUNTRY LIFE INS CO	IL	10,112.1
PHYSICIANS MUTUAL INS CO	NE	2,506.1
TEACHERS INS & ANNUITY ASN OF AM	NY	320,701.0
Rating: **A**		
AMALGAMATED LIFE INS CO	NY	154.2
BERKLEY LIFE & HEALTH INS CO	IA	382.0
FEDERATED LIFE INS CO	MN	2,189.3
GARDEN STATE LIFE INS CO	TX	147.1
GUARDIAN LIFE INS CO OF AMERICA	NY	65,189.0
HUMANA INS CO (WI)	WI	10,594.3
SENTRY LIFE INS CO	WI	8,165.9
SHELTERPOINT LIFE INS CO	NY	235.2
USAA LIFE INS CO	TX	26,903.7
Rating: **A-**		
AMERICAN FAMILY LIFE ASR CO OF NY	NY	1,043.6
FIDELITY SECURITY LIFE INS CO	MO	980.9
NATIONAL BENEFIT LIFE INS CO	NY	595.9
NEW YORK LIFE INS CO	NY	198,377.0
NIPPON LIFE INS CO OF AMERICA	IA	246.1
PHYSICIANS LIFE INS CO	NE	1,730.5
UNITED HEALTHCARE INS CO OF IL	IL	453.6
Rating: **B+**		
AMERICAN FIDELITY ASR CO	OK	6,608.0
ANTHEM LIFE INS CO	IN	799.2
ASSURITY LIFE INS CO	NE	2,670.3
BLUE CROSS & BLUE SHIELD MA HMO BLUE	MA	2,748.4
BOSTON MUTUAL LIFE INS CO	MA	1,547.3
COMPANION LIFE INS CO	SC	489.5
DEARBORN LIFE INS CO	IL	1,657.5
DELAWARE AMERICAN LIFE INS CO	DE	106.1
GERBER LIFE INS CO	NY	4,677.1
HEALTH CARE SVC CORP A MUT LEG RES	IL	33,429.9
HUMANA BENEFIT PLAN OF ILLINOIS	IL	1,104.8
ILLINOIS MUTUAL LIFE INS CO	IL	1,520.9
MIDLAND NATIONAL LIFE INS CO	IA	62,252.9
NORTHWESTERN LONG TERM CARE INS CO	WI	290.3
NORTHWESTERN MUTUAL LIFE INS CO	WI	295,371.0
OXFORD LIFE INS CO	AZ	2,408.0
PRINCIPAL LIFE INS CO	IA	208,421.0
STANDARD INS CO	OR	27,265.4
STANDARD SECURITY LIFE INS CO OF NY	NY	142.7
TRUSTMARK INS CO	IL	1,752.8
TRUSTMARK LIFE INS CO	IL	296.8
UNITED FARM FAMILY LIFE INS CO	IN	2,442.0
UNITED WORLD LIFE INS CO	NE	141.0
USABLE LIFE	AR	496.4
VOYA RETIREMENT INS & ANNUITY CO	CT	110,637.0

Michigan

INSURANCE COMPANY NAME	DOM. STATE	TOTAL ASSETS ($MIL)
Rating: **A+**		
CHESAPEAKE LIFE INS CO	OK	253.5
COUNTRY LIFE INS CO	IL	10,112.1
PHYSICIANS MUTUAL INS CO	NE	2,506.1
TEACHERS INS & ANNUITY ASN OF AM	NY	320,701.0
Rating: **A**		
AMALGAMATED LIFE INS CO	NY	154.2
BERKLEY LIFE & HEALTH INS CO	IA	382.0
FEDERATED LIFE INS CO	MN	2,189.3
GARDEN STATE LIFE INS CO	TX	147.1
GUARDIAN LIFE INS CO OF AMERICA	NY	65,189.0
HUMANA INS CO (WI)	WI	10,594.3
PRIORITY HEALTH	MI	1,860.0
SENTRY LIFE INS CO	WI	8,165.9
SHELTERPOINT LIFE INS CO	NY	235.2
USAA LIFE INS CO	TX	26,903.7
Rating: **A-**		
FIDELITY SECURITY LIFE INS CO	MO	980.9
MEDICAL MUTUAL OF OHIO	OH	2,702.4
NATIONAL BENEFIT LIFE INS CO	NY	595.9
NEW YORK LIFE INS CO	NY	198,377.0
NIPPON LIFE INS CO OF AMERICA	IA	246.1
PHYSICIANS LIFE INS CO	NE	1,730.5
SWBC LIFE INS CO	TX	36.1
Rating: **B+**		
AMERICAN FIDELITY ASR CO	OK	6,608.0
AMERIGROUP INS CO	TX	322.8
ANTHEM LIFE INS CO	IN	799.2
ASSURITY LIFE INS CO	NE	2,670.3
BEST LIFE & HEALTH INS CO	TX	30.1
BLUE CARE NETWORK OF MICHIGAN	MI	2,936.0
BLUE CROSS COMPLETE OF MICHIGAN	MI	355.7
BOSTON MUTUAL LIFE INS CO	MA	1,547.3
COMPANION LIFE INS CO	SC	489.5
DEARBORN LIFE INS CO	IL	1,657.5
DELAWARE AMERICAN LIFE INS CO	DE	106.1
FREEDOM LIFE INS CO OF AMERICA	TX	418.7
GERBER LIFE INS CO	NY	4,677.1
HEALTH CARE SVC CORP A MUT LEG RES	IL	33,429.9
HUMANA BENEFIT PLAN OF ILLINOIS	IL	1,104.8
ILLINOIS MUTUAL LIFE INS CO	IL	1,520.9
MIDLAND NATIONAL LIFE INS CO	IA	62,252.9
NORTH AMERICAN INS CO	WI	19.2
NORTHWESTERN LONG TERM CARE INS CO	WI	290.3
NORTHWESTERN MUTUAL LIFE INS CO	WI	295,371.0
OXFORD LIFE INS CO	AZ	2,408.0
PRINCIPAL LIFE INS CO	IA	208,421.0
PRIORITY HEALTH CHOICE INC	MI	254.8
STANDARD INS CO	OR	27,265.4
STANDARD SECURITY LIFE INS CO OF NY	NY	142.7
TRUSTMARK INS CO	IL	1,752.8
TRUSTMARK LIFE INS CO	IL	296.8
UNITED WORLD LIFE INS CO	NE	141.0
UNITEDHEALTHCARE COMMUNITY PLAN INC	MI	336.3
USABLE LIFE	AR	496.4

INSURANCE COMPANY NAME	DOM. STATE	TOTAL ASSETS ($MIL)
VOYA RETIREMENT INS & ANNUITY CO	CT	110,637.0

Minnesota

INSURANCE COMPANY NAME	DOM. STATE	TOTAL ASSETS ($MIL)	INSURANCE COMPANY NAME	DOM. STATE	TOTAL ASSETS ($MIL)
Rating: A+					
CHESAPEAKE LIFE INS CO	OK	253.5			
COUNTRY LIFE INS CO	IL	10,112.1			
PHYSICIANS MUTUAL INS CO	NE	2,506.1			
TEACHERS INS & ANNUITY ASN OF AM	NY	320,701.0			
Rating: A					
AMALGAMATED LIFE INS CO	NY	154.2			
BERKLEY LIFE & HEALTH INS CO	IA	382.0			
FEDERATED LIFE INS CO	MN	2,189.3			
GARDEN STATE LIFE INS CO	TX	147.1			
GUARDIAN LIFE INS CO OF AMERICA	NY	65,189.0			
HUMANA INS CO (WI)	WI	10,594.3			
SENTRY LIFE INS CO	WI	8,165.9			
SHELTERPOINT LIFE INS CO	NY	235.2			
USAA LIFE INS CO	TX	26,903.7			
Rating: A-					
FIDELITY SECURITY LIFE INS CO	MO	980.9			
NATIONAL BENEFIT LIFE INS CO	NY	595.9			
NEW YORK LIFE INS CO	NY	198,377.0			
NIPPON LIFE INS CO OF AMERICA	IA	246.1			
PHYSICIANS LIFE INS CO	NE	1,730.5			
Rating: B+					
ALLIANZ LIFE INS CO OF NY	NY	3,829.8			
AMERICAN FAMILY MUTL INS CO SI	WI	24,090.2			
AMERICAN FIDELITY ASR CO	OK	6,608.0			
ANTHEM LIFE INS CO	IN	799.2			
ASSURITY LIFE INS CO	NE	2,670.3			
BOSTON MUTUAL LIFE INS CO	MA	1,547.3			
COMPANION LIFE INS CO	SC	489.5			
DEARBORN LIFE INS CO	IL	1,657.5			
DELAWARE AMERICAN LIFE INS CO	DE	106.1			
FARM BUREAU LIFE INS CO	IA	9,479.7			
FREEDOM LIFE INS CO OF AMERICA	TX	418.7			
GERBER LIFE INS CO	NY	4,677.1			
HEALTH CARE SVC CORP A MUT LEG RES	IL	33,429.9			
HEALTHPARTNERS INS CO	MN	475.5			
HUMANA BENEFIT PLAN OF ILLINOIS	IL	1,104.8			
ILLINOIS MUTUAL LIFE INS CO	IL	1,520.9			
MIDLAND NATIONAL LIFE INS CO	IA	62,252.9			
NORTH AMERICAN INS CO	WI	19.2			
NORTHWESTERN LONG TERM CARE INS CO	WI	290.3			
NORTHWESTERN MUTUAL LIFE INS CO	WI	295,371.0			
OXFORD LIFE INS CO	AZ	2,408.0			
PRINCIPAL LIFE INS CO	IA	208,421.0			
STANDARD INS CO	OR	27,265.4			
STANDARD SECURITY LIFE INS CO OF NY	NY	142.7			
TRUSTMARK INS CO	IL	1,752.8			
TRUSTMARK LIFE INS CO	IL	296.8			
UNITED WORLD LIFE INS CO	NE	141.0			
USABLE LIFE	AR	496.4			
VOYA RETIREMENT INS & ANNUITY CO	CT	110,637.0			

Mississippi

INSURANCE COMPANY NAME	DOM. STATE	TOTAL ASSETS ($MIL)	INSURANCE COMPANY NAME	DOM. STATE	TOTAL ASSETS ($MIL)
Rating: A+					
CHESAPEAKE LIFE INS CO	OK	253.5			
COUNTRY LIFE INS CO	IL	10,112.1			
PHYSICIANS MUTUAL INS CO	NE	2,506.1			
TEACHERS INS & ANNUITY ASN OF AM	NY	320,701.0			
Rating: A					
AMALGAMATED LIFE INS CO	NY	154.2			
BERKLEY LIFE & HEALTH INS CO	IA	382.0			
BLUE CROSS BLUE SHIELD OF MS, MUTUAL	MS	1,156.0			
FEDERATED LIFE INS CO	MN	2,189.3			
GARDEN STATE LIFE INS CO	TX	147.1			
GUARDIAN LIFE INS CO OF AMERICA	NY	65,189.0			
HUMANA INS CO (WI)	WI	10,594.3			
NATIONAL FOUNDATION LIFE INS CO	TX	87.8			
SENTRY LIFE INS CO	WI	8,165.9			
SOUTHERN FARM BUREAU LIFE INS CO	MS	14,723.1			
USAA LIFE INS CO	TX	26,903.7			
Rating: A-					
BLUEBONNET LIFE INS CO	MS	69.5			
CHRISTIAN FIDELITY LIFE INS CO	TX	58.3			
FIDELITY SECURITY LIFE INS CO	MO	980.9			
HUMANA MEDICAL PLAN INC	FL	3,307.4			
NATIONAL BENEFIT LIFE INS CO	NY	595.9			
NEW YORK LIFE INS CO	NY	198,377.0			
NIPPON LIFE INS CO OF AMERICA	IA	246.1			
PHYSICIANS LIFE INS CO	NE	1,730.5			
Rating: B+					
AMERICAN FIDELITY ASR CO	OK	6,608.0			
AMERIGROUP INS CO	TX	322.8			
ANTHEM LIFE INS CO	IN	799.2			
ASSURITY LIFE INS CO	NE	2,670.3			
BEST LIFE & HEALTH INS CO	TX	30.1			
BOSTON MUTUAL LIFE INS CO	MA	1,547.3			
COMPANION LIFE INS CO	SC	489.5			
DEARBORN LIFE INS CO	IL	1,657.5			
DELAWARE AMERICAN LIFE INS CO	DE	106.1			
ENTERPRISE LIFE INS CO	TX	148.0			
FIDELITY SECURITY LIFE INS CO OF NY	NY	41.1			
FREEDOM LIFE INS CO OF AMERICA	TX	418.7			
GERBER LIFE INS CO	NY	4,677.1			
GOLDEN SECURITY INS CO	TN	69.3			
HUMANA BENEFIT PLAN OF ILLINOIS	IL	1,104.8			
ILLINOIS MUTUAL LIFE INS CO	IL	1,520.9			
MIDLAND NATIONAL LIFE INS CO	IA	62,252.9			
NORTHWESTERN LONG TERM CARE INS CO	WI	290.3			
NORTHWESTERN MUTUAL LIFE INS CO	WI	295,371.0			
OXFORD LIFE INS CO	AZ	2,408.0			
PRINCIPAL LIFE INS CO	IA	208,421.0			
STANDARD INS CO	OR	27,265.4			
STANDARD SECURITY LIFE INS CO OF NY	NY	142.7			
TRUSTMARK INS CO	IL	1,752.8			
TRUSTMARK LIFE INS CO	IL	296.8			
UNITED WORLD LIFE INS CO	NE	141.0			
USABLE LIFE	AR	496.4			
VOYA RETIREMENT INS & ANNUITY CO	CT	110,637.0			

Missouri

INSURANCE COMPANY NAME	DOM. STATE	TOTAL ASSETS ($MIL)
Rating: A+		
CHESAPEAKE LIFE INS CO	OK	253.5
COUNTRY LIFE INS CO	IL	10,112.1
PHYSICIANS MUTUAL INS CO	NE	2,506.1
TEACHERS INS & ANNUITY ASN OF AM	NY	320,701.0
Rating: A		
AMALGAMATED LIFE INS CO	NY	154.2
BERKLEY LIFE & HEALTH INS CO	IA	382.0
FEDERATED LIFE INS CO	MN	2,189.3
GARDEN STATE LIFE INS CO	TX	147.1
GUARDIAN LIFE INS CO OF AMERICA	NY	65,189.0
HUMANA INS CO (WI)	WI	10,594.3
KAISER PERMANENTE INS CO	CA	220.6
NATIONAL FOUNDATION LIFE INS CO	TX	87.8
SENTRY LIFE INS CO	WI	8,165.9
USAA LIFE INS CO	TX	26,903.7
Rating: A-		
CHRISTIAN FIDELITY LIFE INS CO	TX	58.3
CIGNA LIFE INS CO OF NEW YORK	NY	449.3
ESSENCE HEALTHCARE INC	MO	260.9
FARM BUREAU LIFE INS CO OF MISSOURI	MO	639.5
FIDELITY SECURITY LIFE INS CO	MO	980.9
INDEPENDENT CARE HEALTH PLAN	WI	107.2
NATIONAL BENEFIT LIFE INS CO	NY	595.9
NEW YORK LIFE INS CO	NY	198,377.0
NIPPON LIFE INS CO OF AMERICA	IA	246.1
PHYSICIANS LIFE INS CO	NE	1,730.5
Rating: B+		
ALLIANZ LIFE INS CO OF NY	NY	3,829.8
AMERICAN FAMILY MUTL INS CO SI	WI	24,090.2
AMERICAN FIDELITY ASR CO	OK	6,608.0
ANTHEM LIFE INS CO	IN	799.2
ASSURITY LIFE INS CO	NE	2,670.3
BEST LIFE & HEALTH INS CO	TX	30.1
BOSTON MUTUAL LIFE INS CO	MA	1,547.3
COMPANION LIFE INS CO	SC	489.5
DEARBORN LIFE INS CO	IL	1,657.5
DELAWARE AMERICAN LIFE INS CO	DE	106.1
FREEDOM LIFE INS CO OF AMERICA	TX	418.7
GERBER LIFE INS CO	NY	4,677.1
HEALTH CARE SVC CORP A MUT LEG RES	IL	33,429.9
HUMANA BENEFIT PLAN OF ILLINOIS	IL	1,104.8
ILLINOIS MUTUAL LIFE INS CO	IL	1,520.9
MIDLAND NATIONAL LIFE INS CO	IA	62,252.9
NORTH AMERICAN INS CO	WI	19.2
NORTHWESTERN LONG TERM CARE INS CO	WI	290.3
NORTHWESTERN MUTUAL LIFE INS CO	WI	295,371.0
OXFORD LIFE INS CO	AZ	2,408.0
PACIFIC GUARDIAN LIFE INS CO LTD	HI	579.2
PRINCIPAL LIFE INS CO	IA	208,421.0
STANDARD INS CO	OR	27,265.4
STANDARD SECURITY LIFE INS CO OF NY	NY	142.7
TRUSTMARK INS CO	IL	1,752.8
TRUSTMARK LIFE INS CO	IL	296.8
UNITED HEALTHCARE OF THE MIDLANDS	NE	1,032.6

INSURANCE COMPANY NAME	DOM. STATE	TOTAL ASSETS ($MIL)
UNITED WORLD LIFE INS CO	NE	141.0
USABLE LIFE	AR	496.4
VOYA RETIREMENT INS & ANNUITY CO	CT	110,637.0

Montana

INSURANCE COMPANY NAME	DOM. STATE	TOTAL ASSETS ($MIL)
Rating: A+		
CHESAPEAKE LIFE INS CO	OK	253.5
COUNTRY LIFE INS CO	IL	10,112.1
PHYSICIANS MUTUAL INS CO	NE	2,506.1
TEACHERS INS & ANNUITY ASN OF AM	NY	320,701.0
Rating: A		
AMALGAMATED LIFE INS CO	NY	154.2
BERKLEY LIFE & HEALTH INS CO	IA	382.0
FEDERATED LIFE INS CO	MN	2,189.3
GARDEN STATE LIFE INS CO	TX	147.1
GUARDIAN LIFE INS CO OF AMERICA	NY	65,189.0
HUMANA INS CO (WI)	WI	10,594.3
NATIONAL FOUNDATION LIFE INS CO	TX	87.8
SENTRY LIFE INS CO	WI	8,165.9
USAA LIFE INS CO	TX	26,903.7
Rating: A-		
CHRISTIAN FIDELITY LIFE INS CO	TX	58.3
FIDELITY SECURITY LIFE INS CO	MO	980.9
NATIONAL BENEFIT LIFE INS CO	NY	595.9
NEW YORK LIFE INS CO	NY	198,377.0
NIPPON LIFE INS CO OF AMERICA	IA	246.1
PHYSICIANS LIFE INS CO	NE	1,730.5
Rating: B+		
AMERICAN FAMILY MUTL INS CO SI	WI	24,090.2
AMERICAN FIDELITY ASR CO	OK	6,608.0
ANTHEM LIFE INS CO	IN	799.2
ASSURITY LIFE INS CO	NE	2,670.3
BEST LIFE & HEALTH INS CO	TX	30.1
BOSTON MUTUAL LIFE INS CO	MA	1,547.3
COMPANION LIFE INS CO	SC	489.5
COMPANION LIFE INS CO OF CA	CA	29.6
DEARBORN LIFE INS CO	IL	1,657.5
DELAWARE AMERICAN LIFE INS CO	DE	106.1
FARM BUREAU LIFE INS CO	IA	9,479.7
GERBER LIFE INS CO	NY	4,677.1
HEALTH CARE SVC CORP A MUT LEG RES	IL	33,429.9
HUMANA BENEFIT PLAN OF ILLINOIS	IL	1,104.8
HUMANA WISCONSIN HEALTH ORGANIZATION	WI	1,259.4
ILLINOIS MUTUAL LIFE INS CO	IL	1,520.9
MIDLAND NATIONAL LIFE INS CO	IA	62,252.9
NORTHWESTERN LONG TERM CARE INS CO	WI	290.3
NORTHWESTERN MUTUAL LIFE INS CO	WI	295,371.0
OXFORD LIFE INS CO	AZ	2,408.0
PACIFIC GUARDIAN LIFE INS CO LTD	HI	579.2
PRINCIPAL LIFE INS CO	IA	208,421.0
STANDARD INS CO	OR	27,265.4
STANDARD SECURITY LIFE INS CO OF NY	NY	142.7
TRUSTMARK INS CO	IL	1,752.8
TRUSTMARK LIFE INS CO	IL	296.8
UNITED WORLD LIFE INS CO	NE	141.0
USABLE LIFE	AR	496.4
VOYA RETIREMENT INS & ANNUITY CO	CT	110,637.0

Nebraska

INSURANCE COMPANY NAME	DOM. STATE	TOTAL ASSETS ($MIL)	INSURANCE COMPANY NAME	DOM. STATE	TOTAL ASSETS ($MIL)
Rating: A+					
CHESAPEAKE LIFE INS CO	OK	253.5			
COUNTRY LIFE INS CO	IL	10,112.1			
PHYSICIANS MUTUAL INS CO	NE	2,506.1			
TEACHERS INS & ANNUITY ASN OF AM	NY	320,701.0			
Rating: A					
AMALGAMATED LIFE INS CO	NY	154.2			
BERKLEY LIFE & HEALTH INS CO	IA	382.0			
FEDERATED LIFE INS CO	MN	2,189.3			
GARDEN STATE LIFE INS CO	TX	147.1			
GUARDIAN LIFE INS CO OF AMERICA	NY	65,189.0			
HUMANA INS CO (WI)	WI	10,594.3			
NATIONAL FOUNDATION LIFE INS CO	TX	87.8			
SENTRY LIFE INS CO	WI	8,165.9			
USAA LIFE INS CO	TX	26,903.7			
Rating: A-					
CHRISTIAN FIDELITY LIFE INS CO	TX	58.3			
FIDELITY SECURITY LIFE INS CO	MO	980.9			
NATIONAL BENEFIT LIFE INS CO	NY	595.9			
NEW YORK LIFE INS CO	NY	198,377.0			
NIPPON LIFE INS CO OF AMERICA	IA	246.1			
PHYSICIANS LIFE INS CO	NE	1,730.5			
Rating: B+					
AMERICAN FAMILY MUTL INS CO SI	WI	24,090.2			
AMERICAN FIDELITY ASR CO	OK	6,608.0			
AMERIGROUP INS CO	TX	322.8			
ANTHEM LIFE INS CO	IN	799.2			
ASSURITY LIFE INS CO	NE	2,670.3			
BEST LIFE & HEALTH INS CO	TX	30.1			
BOSTON MUTUAL LIFE INS CO	MA	1,547.3			
COMPANION LIFE INS CO	SC	489.5			
DEARBORN LIFE INS CO	IL	1,657.5			
DELAWARE AMERICAN LIFE INS CO	DE	106.1			
ENTERPRISE LIFE INS CO	TX	148.0			
FARM BUREAU LIFE INS CO	IA	9,479.7			
FREEDOM LIFE INS CO OF AMERICA	TX	418.7			
GERBER LIFE INS CO	NY	4,677.1			
HEALTH CARE SVC CORP A MUT LEG RES	IL	33,429.9			
HEALTHPARTNERS INS CO	MN	475.5			
HUMANA BENEFIT PLAN OF ILLINOIS	IL	1,104.8			
ILLINOIS MUTUAL LIFE INS CO	IL	1,520.9			
MIDLAND NATIONAL LIFE INS CO	IA	62,252.9			
NORTHWESTERN LONG TERM CARE INS CO	WI	290.3			
NORTHWESTERN MUTUAL LIFE INS CO	WI	295,371.0			
OXFORD LIFE INS CO	AZ	2,408.0			
PACIFIC GUARDIAN LIFE INS CO LTD	HI	579.2			
PRINCIPAL LIFE INS CO	IA	208,421.0			
STANDARD INS CO	OR	27,265.4			
STANDARD SECURITY LIFE INS CO OF NY	NY	142.7			
TRUSTMARK INS CO	IL	1,752.8			
TRUSTMARK LIFE INS CO	IL	296.8			
UNITED HEALTHCARE OF THE MIDLANDS	NE	1,032.6			
UNITED WORLD LIFE INS CO	NE	141.0			
USABLE LIFE	AR	496.4			
VOYA RETIREMENT INS & ANNUITY CO	CT	110,637.0			

Nevada

INSURANCE COMPANY NAME	DOM. STATE	TOTAL ASSETS ($MIL)
Rating: A+		
CHESAPEAKE LIFE INS CO	OK	253.5
COUNTRY LIFE INS CO	IL	10,112.1
PHYSICIANS MUTUAL INS CO	NE	2,506.1
TEACHERS INS & ANNUITY ASN OF AM	NY	320,701.0
Rating: A		
AMALGAMATED LIFE INS CO	NY	154.2
BERKLEY LIFE & HEALTH INS CO	IA	382.0
FEDERATED LIFE INS CO	MN	2,189.3
GARDEN STATE LIFE INS CO	TX	147.1
GUARDIAN LIFE INS CO OF AMERICA	NY	65,189.0
HUMANA INS CO (WI)	WI	10,594.3
NATIONAL FOUNDATION LIFE INS CO	TX	87.8
SENTRY LIFE INS CO	WI	8,165.9
USAA LIFE INS CO	TX	26,903.7
Rating: A-		
CHRISTIAN FIDELITY LIFE INS CO	TX	58.3
CMNTY CARE HLTH PLAN OF NV INC	NV	194.3
FIDELITY SECURITY LIFE INS CO	MO	980.9
NATIONAL BENEFIT LIFE INS CO	NY	595.9
NEW YORK LIFE INS CO	NY	198,377.0
NIPPON LIFE INS CO OF AMERICA	IA	246.1
PHYSICIANS LIFE INS CO	NE	1,730.5
Rating: B+		
AMERICAN FAMILY MUTL INS CO SI	WI	24,090.2
AMERICAN FIDELITY ASR CO	OK	6,608.0
ANTHEM LIFE INS CO	IN	799.2
ASSURITY LIFE INS CO	NE	2,670.3
BEST LIFE & HEALTH INS CO	TX	30.1
BOSTON MUTUAL LIFE INS CO	MA	1,547.3
COMPANION LIFE INS CO	SC	489.5
COMPANION LIFE INS CO OF CA	CA	29.6
DEARBORN LIFE INS CO	IL	1,657.5
DELAWARE AMERICAN LIFE INS CO	DE	106.1
FARM BUREAU LIFE INS CO	IA	9,479.7
FREEDOM LIFE INS CO OF AMERICA	TX	418.7
GERBER LIFE INS CO	NY	4,677.1
HEALTH PLAN OF NEVADA INC	NV	754.1
HMO COLORADO	CO	442.7
HUMANA BENEFIT PLAN OF ILLINOIS	IL	1,104.8
ILLINOIS MUTUAL LIFE INS CO	IL	1,520.9
MIDLAND NATIONAL LIFE INS CO	IA	62,252.9
NORTHWESTERN LONG TERM CARE INS CO	WI	290.3
NORTHWESTERN MUTUAL LIFE INS CO	WI	295,371.0
OXFORD LIFE INS CO	AZ	2,408.0
PACIFIC GUARDIAN LIFE INS CO LTD	HI	579.2
PRINCIPAL LIFE INS CO	IA	208,421.0
STANDARD INS CO	OR	27,265.4
STANDARD SECURITY LIFE INS CO OF NY	NY	142.7
TRUSTMARK INS CO	IL	1,752.8
TRUSTMARK LIFE INS CO	IL	296.8
UNITED WORLD LIFE INS CO	NE	141.0
USABLE LIFE	AR	496.4
VOYA RETIREMENT INS & ANNUITY CO	CT	110,637.0

New Hampshire

INSURANCE COMPANY NAME	DOM. STATE	TOTAL ASSETS ($MIL)	INSURANCE COMPANY NAME	DOM. STATE	TOTAL ASSETS ($MIL)
Rating: A+					
CHESAPEAKE LIFE INS CO	OK	253.5			
PHYSICIANS MUTUAL INS CO	NE	2,506.1			
TEACHERS INS & ANNUITY ASN OF AM	NY	320,701.0			
Rating: A					
AMALGAMATED LIFE INS CO	NY	154.2			
BERKLEY LIFE & HEALTH INS CO	IA	382.0			
FEDERATED LIFE INS CO	MN	2,189.3			
GARDEN STATE LIFE INS CO	TX	147.1			
GUARDIAN LIFE INS CO OF AMERICA	NY	65,189.0			
HUMANA INS CO (WI)	WI	10,594.3			
SENTRY LIFE INS CO	WI	8,165.9			
USAA LIFE INS CO	TX	26,903.7			
Rating: A-					
FIDELITY SECURITY LIFE INS CO	MO	980.9			
NATIONAL BENEFIT LIFE INS CO	NY	595.9			
NEW YORK LIFE INS CO	NY	198,377.0			
PHYSICIANS LIFE INS CO	NE	1,730.5			
Rating: B+					
AMERICAN FIDELITY ASR CO	OK	6,608.0			
ANTHEM LIFE INS CO	IN	799.2			
ASSURITY LIFE INS CO	NE	2,670.3			
BOSTON MUTUAL LIFE INS CO	MA	1,547.3			
COMPANION LIFE INS CO	SC	489.5			
DEARBORN LIFE INS CO	IL	1,657.5			
DELAWARE AMERICAN LIFE INS CO	DE	106.1			
GERBER LIFE INS CO	NY	4,677.1			
HUMANA BENEFIT PLAN OF ILLINOIS	IL	1,104.8			
ILLINOIS MUTUAL LIFE INS CO	IL	1,520.9			
MIDLAND NATIONAL LIFE INS CO	IA	62,252.9			
NORTHWESTERN LONG TERM CARE INS CO	WI	290.3			
NORTHWESTERN MUTUAL LIFE INS CO	WI	295,371.0			
OXFORD LIFE INS CO	AZ	2,408.0			
PRINCIPAL LIFE INS CO	IA	208,421.0			
STANDARD INS CO	OR	27,265.4			
STANDARD SECURITY LIFE INS CO OF NY	NY	142.7			
TRUSTMARK INS CO	IL	1,752.8			
TRUSTMARK LIFE INS CO	IL	296.8			
UNITED FARM FAMILY LIFE INS CO	IN	2,442.0			
UNITED WORLD LIFE INS CO	NE	141.0			
USABLE LIFE	AR	496.4			
VOYA RETIREMENT INS & ANNUITY CO	CT	110,637.0			

New Jersey

INSURANCE COMPANY NAME	DOM. STATE	TOTAL ASSETS ($MIL)
Rating: A+		
PHYSICIANS MUTUAL INS CO	NE	2,506.1
TEACHERS INS & ANNUITY ASN OF AM	NY	320,701.0
Rating: A		
AMALGAMATED LIFE INS CO	NY	154.2
BERKLEY LIFE & HEALTH INS CO	IA	382.0
FEDERATED LIFE INS CO	MN	2,189.3
GARDEN STATE LIFE INS CO	TX	147.1
GUARDIAN LIFE INS CO OF AMERICA	NY	65,189.0
HUMANA INS CO (WI)	WI	10,594.3
SENTRY LIFE INS CO	WI	8,165.9
SHELTERPOINT LIFE INS CO	NY	235.2
USAA LIFE INS CO	TX	26,903.7
Rating: A-		
AMERICAN FAMILY LIFE ASR CO OF NY	NY	1,043.6
AMERIGROUP NEW JERSEY INC	NJ	454.1
FIDELITY SECURITY LIFE INS CO	MO	980.9
NATIONAL BENEFIT LIFE INS CO	NY	595.9
NEW YORK LIFE INS CO	NY	198,377.0
NIPPON LIFE INS CO OF AMERICA	IA	246.1
PHYSICIANS LIFE INS CO	NE	1,730.5
Rating: B+		
AMERICAN FIDELITY ASR CO	OK	6,608.0
ANTHEM LIFE INS CO	IN	799.2
ASSURITY LIFE INS CO	NE	2,670.3
BOSTON MUTUAL LIFE INS CO	MA	1,547.3
DEARBORN LIFE INS CO	IL	1,657.5
DELAWARE AMERICAN LIFE INS CO	DE	106.1
GEISINGER HEALTH PLAN	PA	665.0
GERBER LIFE INS CO	NY	4,677.1
HEALTH CARE SVC CORP A MUT LEG RES	IL	33,429.9
HUMANA BENEFIT PLAN OF ILLINOIS	IL	1,104.8
HUMANA WISCONSIN HEALTH ORGANIZATION	WI	1,259.4
ILLINOIS MUTUAL LIFE INS CO	IL	1,520.9
MIDLAND NATIONAL LIFE INS CO	IA	62,252.9
NORTHWESTERN LONG TERM CARE INS CO	WI	290.3
NORTHWESTERN MUTUAL LIFE INS CO	WI	295,371.0
OXFORD HEALTH PLANS (CT) INC	CT	586.6
OXFORD LIFE INS CO	AZ	2,408.0
PRINCIPAL LIFE INS CO	IA	208,421.0
STANDARD INS CO	OR	27,265.4
STANDARD SECURITY LIFE INS CO OF NY	NY	142.7
TRUSTMARK INS CO	IL	1,752.8
TRUSTMARK LIFE INS CO	IL	296.8
UNITED FARM FAMILY LIFE INS CO	IN	2,442.0
UNITED WORLD LIFE INS CO	NE	141.0
USABLE LIFE	AR	496.4
VOYA RETIREMENT INS & ANNUITY CO	CT	110,637.0

New Mexico

INSURANCE COMPANY NAME	DOM. STATE	TOTAL ASSETS ($MIL)
Rating: A+		
CHESAPEAKE LIFE INS CO	OK	253.5
COUNTRY LIFE INS CO	IL	10,112.1
PHYSICIANS MUTUAL INS CO	NE	2,506.1
TEACHERS INS & ANNUITY ASN OF AM	NY	320,701.0
Rating: A		
AMALGAMATED LIFE INS CO	NY	154.2
BERKLEY LIFE & HEALTH INS CO	IA	382.0
FEDERATED LIFE INS CO	MN	2,189.3
GARDEN STATE LIFE INS CO	TX	147.1
GUARDIAN LIFE INS CO OF AMERICA	NY	65,189.0
HUMANA INS CO (WI)	WI	10,594.3
NATIONAL FOUNDATION LIFE INS CO	TX	87.8
SENTRY LIFE INS CO	WI	8,165.9
USAA LIFE INS CO	TX	26,903.7
Rating: A-		
CHRISTIAN FIDELITY LIFE INS CO	TX	58.3
FIDELITY SECURITY LIFE INS CO	MO	980.9
NATIONAL BENEFIT LIFE INS CO	NY	595.9
NEW YORK LIFE INS CO	NY	198,377.0
NIPPON LIFE INS CO OF AMERICA	IA	246.1
PHYSICIANS LIFE INS CO	NE	1,730.5
Rating: B+		
AMERICAN FAMILY MUTL INS CO SI	WI	24,090.2
AMERICAN FIDELITY ASR CO	OK	6,608.0
AMERIGROUP INS CO	TX	322.8
ANTHEM LIFE INS CO	IN	799.2
ASSURITY LIFE INS CO	NE	2,670.3
BEST LIFE & HEALTH INS CO	TX	30.1
BOSTON MUTUAL LIFE INS CO	MA	1,547.3
COMPANION LIFE INS CO	SC	489.5
DEARBORN LIFE INS CO	IL	1,657.5
DELAWARE AMERICAN LIFE INS CO	DE	106.1
ENTERPRISE LIFE INS CO	TX	148.0
FARM BUREAU LIFE INS CO	IA	9,479.7
FREEDOM LIFE INS CO OF AMERICA	TX	418.7
GERBER LIFE INS CO	NY	4,677.1
HEALTH CARE SVC CORP A MUT LEG RES	IL	33,429.9
HUMANA BENEFIT PLAN OF ILLINOIS	IL	1,104.8
ILLINOIS MUTUAL LIFE INS CO	IL	1,520.9
MIDLAND NATIONAL LIFE INS CO	IA	62,252.9
NORTH AMERICAN INS CO	WI	19.2
NORTHWESTERN LONG TERM CARE INS CO	WI	290.3
NORTHWESTERN MUTUAL LIFE INS CO	WI	295,371.0
OXFORD LIFE INS CO	AZ	2,408.0
PACIFIC GUARDIAN LIFE INS CO LTD	HI	579.2
PRINCIPAL LIFE INS CO	IA	208,421.0
STANDARD INS CO	OR	27,265.4
STANDARD SECURITY LIFE INS CO OF NY	NY	142.7
TRUSTMARK INS CO	IL	1,752.8
TRUSTMARK LIFE INS CO	IL	296.8
UNITED WORLD LIFE INS CO	NE	141.0
USABLE LIFE	AR	496.4
VOYA RETIREMENT INS & ANNUITY CO	CT	110,637.0

New York

INSURANCE COMPANY NAME	DOM. STATE	TOTAL ASSETS ($MIL)
Rating: A+		
PHYSICIANS MUTUAL INS CO	NE	2,506.1
TEACHERS INS & ANNUITY ASN OF AM	NY	320,701.0
Rating: A		
AMALGAMATED LIFE INS CO	NY	154.2
BERKLEY LIFE & HEALTH INS CO	IA	382.0
FEDERATED LIFE INS CO	MN	2,189.3
GARDEN STATE LIFE INS CO	TX	147.1
GUARDIAN LIFE INS CO OF AMERICA	NY	65,189.0
HEALTHNOW NY INC	NY	1,348.6
SHELTERPOINT LIFE INS CO	NY	235.2
Rating: A-		
AMERICAN FAMILY LIFE ASR CO OF NY	NY	1,043.6
CAPITAL DISTRICT PHYSICIANS HEALTH P	NY	660.1
CIGNA LIFE INS CO OF NEW YORK	NY	449.3
FIDELITY SECURITY LIFE INS CO	MO	980.9
LIFE INS CO OF BOSTON & NEW YORK	NY	175.9
NATIONAL BENEFIT LIFE INS CO	NY	595.9
NEW YORK LIFE INS CO	NY	198,377.0
NIAGARA LIFE & HEALTH INS CO	NY	17.2
NIPPON LIFE INS CO OF AMERICA	IA	246.1
STANDARD LIFE INS CO OF NY	NY	307.0
Rating: B+		
ALLIANZ LIFE INS CO OF NY	NY	3,829.8
BOSTON MUTUAL LIFE INS CO	MA	1,547.3
DELAWARE AMERICAN LIFE INS CO	DE	106.1
FIDELITY SECURITY LIFE INS CO OF NY	NY	41.1
GERBER LIFE INS CO	NY	4,677.1
HEALTHFIRST HEALTH PLAN INC	NY	961.8
INDEPENDENT HEALTH ASSOC INC	NY	761.8
NATIONAL INCOME LIFE INS CO	NY	319.9
NORTHWESTERN LONG TERM CARE INS CO	WI	290.3
NORTHWESTERN MUTUAL LIFE INS CO	WI	295,371.0
PRINCIPAL LIFE INS CO	IA	208,421.0
STANDARD SECURITY LIFE INS CO OF NY	NY	142.7
TRUSTMARK INS CO	IL	1,752.8
TRUSTMARK LIFE INS CO	IL	296.8
VOYA RETIREMENT INS & ANNUITY CO	CT	110,637.0

North Carolina

INSURANCE COMPANY NAME	DOM. STATE	TOTAL ASSETS ($MIL)
Rating: A+		
CHESAPEAKE LIFE INS CO	OK	253.5
COUNTRY LIFE INS CO	IL	10,112.1
PHYSICIANS MUTUAL INS CO	NE	2,506.1
TEACHERS INS & ANNUITY ASN OF AM	NY	320,701.0
Rating: A		
AMALGAMATED LIFE INS CO	NY	154.2
BERKLEY LIFE & HEALTH INS CO	IA	382.0
FEDERATED LIFE INS CO	MN	2,189.3
GARDEN STATE LIFE INS CO	TX	147.1
GUARDIAN LIFE INS CO OF AMERICA	NY	65,189.0
HUMANA INS CO (WI)	WI	10,594.3
NATIONAL FOUNDATION LIFE INS CO	TX	87.8
SENTRY LIFE INS CO	WI	8,165.9
SHELTERPOINT LIFE INS CO	NY	235.2
SOUTHERN FARM BUREAU LIFE INS CO	MS	14,723.1
USAA LIFE INS CO	TX	26,903.7
Rating: A-		
FIDELITY SECURITY LIFE INS CO	MO	980.9
HUMANA MEDICAL PLAN INC	FL	3,307.4
MEDICAL MUTUAL OF OHIO	OH	2,702.4
NATIONAL BENEFIT LIFE INS CO	NY	595.9
NEW YORK LIFE INS CO	NY	198,377.0
NIPPON LIFE INS CO OF AMERICA	IA	246.1
PHYSICIANS LIFE INS CO	NE	1,730.5
Rating: B+		
AMERICAN FAMILY MUTL INS CO SI	WI	24,090.2
AMERICAN FIDELITY ASR CO	OK	6,608.0
ANTHEM LIFE INS CO	IN	799.2
ASSURITY LIFE INS CO	NE	2,670.3
BEST LIFE & HEALTH INS CO	TX	30.1
BLUE CROSS BLUE SHIELD OF NC	NC	6,502.9
BOSTON MUTUAL LIFE INS CO	MA	1,547.3
COMPANION LIFE INS CO	SC	489.5
DEARBORN LIFE INS CO	IL	1,657.5
DELAWARE AMERICAN LIFE INS CO	DE	106.1
FREEDOM LIFE INS CO OF AMERICA	TX	418.7
GERBER LIFE INS CO	NY	4,677.1
HUMANA BENEFIT PLAN OF ILLINOIS	IL	1,104.8
ILLINOIS MUTUAL LIFE INS CO	IL	1,520.9
MIDLAND NATIONAL LIFE INS CO	IA	62,252.9
NORTHWESTERN LONG TERM CARE INS CO	WI	290.3
NORTHWESTERN MUTUAL LIFE INS CO	WI	295,371.0
OXFORD LIFE INS CO	AZ	2,408.0
PRINCIPAL LIFE INS CO	IA	208,421.0
STANDARD INS CO	OR	27,265.4
STANDARD SECURITY LIFE INS CO OF NY	NY	142.7
TRUSTMARK INS CO	IL	1,752.8
TRUSTMARK LIFE INS CO	IL	296.8
UNITED FARM FAMILY LIFE INS CO	IN	2,442.0
UNITED HEALTHCARE OF WISCONSIN INC	WI	2,701.9
UNITED WORLD LIFE INS CO	NE	141.0
USABLE LIFE	AR	496.4
VOYA RETIREMENT INS & ANNUITY CO	CT	110,637.0

North Dakota

INSURANCE COMPANY NAME	DOM. STATE	TOTAL ASSETS ($MIL)
Rating: A+		
CHESAPEAKE LIFE INS CO	OK	253.5
COUNTRY LIFE INS CO	IL	10,112.1
PHYSICIANS MUTUAL INS CO	NE	2,506.1
TEACHERS INS & ANNUITY ASN OF AM	NY	320,701.0
Rating: A		
AMALGAMATED LIFE INS CO	NY	154.2
BERKLEY LIFE & HEALTH INS CO	IA	382.0
FEDERATED LIFE INS CO	MN	2,189.3
GARDEN STATE LIFE INS CO	TX	147.1
GUARDIAN LIFE INS CO OF AMERICA	NY	65,189.0
HUMANA INS CO (WI)	WI	10,594.3
NATIONAL FOUNDATION LIFE INS CO	TX	87.8
SENTRY LIFE INS CO	WI	8,165.9
USAA LIFE INS CO	TX	26,903.7
Rating: A-		
AMERICAN FAMILY LIFE ASR CO OF NY	NY	1,043.6
CHRISTIAN FIDELITY LIFE INS CO	TX	58.3
FIDELITY SECURITY LIFE INS CO	MO	980.9
NATIONAL BENEFIT LIFE INS CO	NY	595.9
NEW YORK LIFE INS CO	NY	198,377.0
NIPPON LIFE INS CO OF AMERICA	IA	246.1
PHYSICIANS LIFE INS CO	NE	1,730.5
Rating: B+		
ALLIANZ LIFE INS CO OF NY	NY	3,829.8
AMERICAN FAMILY MUTL INS CO SI	WI	24,090.2
AMERICAN FIDELITY ASR CO	OK	6,608.0
AMERIGROUP INS CO	TX	322.8
ANTHEM LIFE INS CO	IN	799.2
ASSURITY LIFE INS CO	NE	2,670.3
BEST LIFE & HEALTH INS CO	TX	30.1
BOSTON MUTUAL LIFE INS CO	MA	1,547.3
COMPANION LIFE INS CO	SC	489.5
DEARBORN LIFE INS CO	IL	1,657.5
DELAWARE AMERICAN LIFE INS CO	DE	106.1
FARM BUREAU LIFE INS CO	IA	9,479.7
GERBER LIFE INS CO	NY	4,677.1
HEALTHPARTNERS INS CO	MN	475.5
HUMANA BENEFIT PLAN OF ILLINOIS	IL	1,104.8
ILLINOIS MUTUAL LIFE INS CO	IL	1,520.9
MIDLAND NATIONAL LIFE INS CO	IA	62,252.9
NORTH AMERICAN INS CO	WI	19.2
NORTHWESTERN LONG TERM CARE INS CO	WI	290.3
NORTHWESTERN MUTUAL LIFE INS CO	WI	295,371.0
OXFORD LIFE INS CO	AZ	2,408.0
PRINCIPAL LIFE INS CO	IA	208,421.0
STANDARD INS CO	OR	27,265.4
STANDARD SECURITY LIFE INS CO OF NY	NY	142.7
TRUSTMARK INS CO	IL	1,752.8
TRUSTMARK LIFE INS CO	IL	296.8
UNITED FARM FAMILY LIFE INS CO	IN	2,442.0
UNITED WORLD LIFE INS CO	NE	141.0
USABLE LIFE	AR	496.4
VOYA RETIREMENT INS & ANNUITY CO	CT	110,637.0

Ohio

INSURANCE COMPANY NAME	DOM. STATE	TOTAL ASSETS ($MIL)
Rating:	**A+**	
CHESAPEAKE LIFE INS CO	OK	253.5
COUNTRY LIFE INS CO	IL	10,112.1
PHYSICIANS MUTUAL INS CO	NE	2,506.1
TEACHERS INS & ANNUITY ASN OF AM	NY	320,701.0
Rating:	**A**	
AMALGAMATED LIFE INS CO	NY	154.2
BERKLEY LIFE & HEALTH INS CO	IA	382.0
FEDERATED LIFE INS CO	MN	2,189.3
GARDEN STATE LIFE INS CO	TX	147.1
GUARDIAN LIFE INS CO OF AMERICA	NY	65,189.0
HUMANA INS CO (WI)	WI	10,594.3
KAISER PERMANENTE INS CO	CA	220.6
NATIONAL FOUNDATION LIFE INS CO	TX	87.8
SENTRY LIFE INS CO	WI	8,165.9
USAA LIFE INS CO	TX	26,903.7
Rating:	**A-**	
CHRISTIAN FIDELITY LIFE INS CO	TX	58.3
FIDELITY SECURITY LIFE INS CO	MO	980.9
MEDICAL MUTUAL OF OHIO	OH	2,702.4
NATIONAL BENEFIT LIFE INS CO	NY	595.9
NEW YORK LIFE INS CO	NY	198,377.0
NIPPON LIFE INS CO OF AMERICA	IA	246.1
PHYSICIANS LIFE INS CO	NE	1,730.5
Rating:	**B+**	
AMERICAN FAMILY MUTL INS CO SI	WI	24,090.2
AMERICAN FIDELITY ASR CO	OK	6,608.0
ANTHEM LIFE INS CO	IN	799.2
ASSURITY LIFE INS CO	NE	2,670.3
AULTCARE INS CO	OH	106.6
BEST LIFE & HEALTH INS CO	TX	30.1
BOSTON MUTUAL LIFE INS CO	MA	1,547.3
COMPANION LIFE INS CO	SC	489.5
DEARBORN LIFE INS CO	IL	1,657.5
DELAWARE AMERICAN LIFE INS CO	DE	106.1
FREEDOM LIFE INS CO OF AMERICA	TX	418.7
GERBER LIFE INS CO	NY	4,677.1
HEALTH CARE SVC CORP A MUT LEG RES	IL	33,429.9
HUMANA BENEFIT PLAN OF ILLINOIS	IL	1,104.8
HUMANA WISCONSIN HEALTH ORGANIZATION	WI	1,259.4
ILLINOIS MUTUAL LIFE INS CO	IL	1,520.9
MIDLAND NATIONAL LIFE INS CO	IA	62,252.9
MOUNT CARMEL HEALTH PLAN INC	OH	407.5
NORTH AMERICAN INS CO	WI	19.2
NORTHWESTERN LONG TERM CARE INS CO	WI	290.3
NORTHWESTERN MUTUAL LIFE INS CO	WI	295,371.0
OXFORD LIFE INS CO	AZ	2,408.0
PRINCIPAL LIFE INS CO	IA	208,421.0
STANDARD INS CO	OR	27,265.4
STANDARD SECURITY LIFE INS CO OF NY	NY	142.7
TRUSTMARK INS CO	IL	1,752.8
TRUSTMARK LIFE INS CO	IL	296.8
UNITED FARM FAMILY LIFE INS CO	IN	2,442.0
UNITED HEALTHCARE OF WISCONSIN INC	WI	2,701.9
UNITED WORLD LIFE INS CO	NE	141.0

INSURANCE COMPANY NAME	DOM. STATE	TOTAL ASSETS ($MIL)
UNITEDHEALTHCARE COMMUNITYPLAN OHIO	OH	739.4
USABLE LIFE	AR	496.4
VOYA RETIREMENT INS & ANNUITY CO	CT	110,637.0

Oklahoma

INSURANCE COMPANY NAME	DOM. STATE	TOTAL ASSETS ($MIL)
Rating: A+		
CHESAPEAKE LIFE INS CO	OK	253.5
COUNTRY LIFE INS CO	IL	10,112.1
PHYSICIANS MUTUAL INS CO	NE	2,506.1
TEACHERS INS & ANNUITY ASN OF AM	NY	320,701.0
Rating: A		
AMALGAMATED LIFE INS CO	NY	154.2
BERKLEY LIFE & HEALTH INS CO	IA	382.0
FEDERATED LIFE INS CO	MN	2,189.3
GARDEN STATE LIFE INS CO	TX	147.1
GUARDIAN LIFE INS CO OF AMERICA	NY	65,189.0
HUMANA INS CO (WI)	WI	10,594.3
NATIONAL FOUNDATION LIFE INS CO	TX	87.8
SENTRY LIFE INS CO	WI	8,165.9
USAA LIFE INS CO	TX	26,903.7
Rating: A-		
CHRISTIAN FIDELITY LIFE INS CO	TX	58.3
FIDELITY SECURITY LIFE INS CO	MO	980.9
NATIONAL BENEFIT LIFE INS CO	NY	595.9
NEW YORK LIFE INS CO	NY	198,377.0
NIPPON LIFE INS CO OF AMERICA	IA	246.1
PHYSICIANS LIFE INS CO	NE	1,730.5
SWBC LIFE INS CO	TX	36.1
Rating: B+		
AMERICAN FIDELITY ASR CO	OK	6,608.0
ANTHEM LIFE INS CO	IN	799.2
ASSURITY LIFE INS CO	NE	2,670.3
BEST LIFE & HEALTH INS CO	TX	30.1
BOSTON MUTUAL LIFE INS CO	MA	1,547.3
COMPANION LIFE INS CO	SC	489.5
DEARBORN LIFE INS CO	IL	1,657.5
DELAWARE AMERICAN LIFE INS CO	DE	106.1
ENTERPRISE LIFE INS CO	TX	148.0
FARM BUREAU LIFE INS CO	IA	9,479.7
FREEDOM LIFE INS CO OF AMERICA	TX	418.7
GERBER LIFE INS CO	NY	4,677.1
HEALTH CARE SVC CORP A MUT LEG RES	IL	33,429.9
HUMANA BENEFIT PLAN OF ILLINOIS	IL	1,104.8
ILLINOIS MUTUAL LIFE INS CO	IL	1,520.9
MIDLAND NATIONAL LIFE INS CO	IA	62,252.9
NORTH AMERICAN INS CO	WI	19.2
NORTHWESTERN LONG TERM CARE INS CO	WI	290.3
NORTHWESTERN MUTUAL LIFE INS CO	WI	295,371.0
OXFORD LIFE INS CO	AZ	2,408.0
PACIFIC GUARDIAN LIFE INS CO LTD	HI	579.2
PRINCIPAL LIFE INS CO	IA	208,421.0
STANDARD INS CO	OR	27,265.4
STANDARD SECURITY LIFE INS CO OF NY	NY	142.7
TRUSTMARK INS CO	IL	1,752.8
TRUSTMARK LIFE INS CO	IL	296.8
UNITED WORLD LIFE INS CO	NE	141.0
USABLE LIFE	AR	496.4
VOYA RETIREMENT INS & ANNUITY CO	CT	110,637.0

Oregon

INSURANCE COMPANY NAME	DOM. STATE	TOTAL ASSETS ($MIL)
Rating: **A+**		
CHESAPEAKE LIFE INS CO	OK	253.5
COUNTRY LIFE INS CO	IL	10,112.1
PHYSICIANS MUTUAL INS CO	NE	2,506.1
TEACHERS INS & ANNUITY ASN OF AM	NY	320,701.0
Rating: **A**		
AMALGAMATED LIFE INS CO	NY	154.2
BERKLEY LIFE & HEALTH INS CO	IA	382.0
FEDERATED LIFE INS CO	MN	2,189.3
GARDEN STATE LIFE INS CO	TX	147.1
GUARDIAN LIFE INS CO OF AMERICA	NY	65,189.0
HUMANA INS CO (WI)	WI	10,594.3
KAISER PERMANENTE INS CO	CA	220.6
LIFEWISE ASR CO	WA	249.5
NATIONAL FOUNDATION LIFE INS CO	TX	87.8
SENTRY LIFE INS CO	WI	8,165.9
USAA LIFE INS CO	TX	26,903.7
Rating: **A-**		
CHRISTIAN FIDELITY LIFE INS CO	TX	58.3
FIDELITY SECURITY LIFE INS CO	MO	980.9
HUMANA MEDICAL PLAN INC	FL	3,307.4
NATIONAL BENEFIT LIFE INS CO	NY	595.9
NEW YORK LIFE INS CO	NY	198,377.0
NIPPON LIFE INS CO OF AMERICA	IA	246.1
PHYSICIANS LIFE INS CO	NE	1,730.5
PROVIDENCE HEALTH ASR	OR	586.5
REGENCE BL CROSS BL SHIELD OREGON	OR	1,622.0
Rating: **B+**		
AMERICAN FAMILY MUTL INS CO SI	WI	24,090.2
AMERICAN FIDELITY ASR CO	OK	6,608.0
AMERIGROUP INS CO	TX	322.8
ANTHEM LIFE INS CO	IN	799.2
ASSURITY LIFE INS CO	NE	2,670.3
BEST LIFE & HEALTH INS CO	TX	30.1
BOSTON MUTUAL LIFE INS CO	MA	1,547.3
COMPANION LIFE INS CO	SC	489.5
DEARBORN LIFE INS CO	IL	1,657.5
DELAWARE AMERICAN LIFE INS CO	DE	106.1
ENTERPRISE LIFE INS CO	TX	148.0
FARM BUREAU LIFE INS CO	IA	9,479.7
FREEDOM LIFE INS CO OF AMERICA	TX	418.7
GERBER LIFE INS CO	NY	4,677.1
HEALTH CARE SVC CORP A MUT LEG RES	IL	33,429.9
HUMANA BENEFIT PLAN OF ILLINOIS	IL	1,104.8
ILLINOIS MUTUAL LIFE INS CO	IL	1,520.9
MIDLAND NATIONAL LIFE INS CO	IA	62,252.9
NORTH AMERICAN INS CO	WI	19.2
NORTHWESTERN LONG TERM CARE INS CO	WI	290.3
NORTHWESTERN MUTUAL LIFE INS CO	WI	295,371.0
OXFORD LIFE INS CO	AZ	2,408.0
PACIFIC GUARDIAN LIFE INS CO LTD	HI	579.2
PRINCIPAL LIFE INS CO	IA	208,421.0
STANDARD INS CO	OR	27,265.4
STANDARD SECURITY LIFE INS CO OF NY	NY	142.7
TRUSTMARK INS CO	IL	1,752.8

INSURANCE COMPANY NAME	DOM. STATE	TOTAL ASSETS ($MIL)
TRUSTMARK LIFE INS CO	IL	296.8
UNITED WORLD LIFE INS CO	NE	141.0
UNITEDHEALTHCARE OF OREGON	OR	645.9
USABLE LIFE	AR	496.4
VOYA RETIREMENT INS & ANNUITY CO	CT	110,637.0

Pennsylvania

INSURANCE COMPANY NAME	DOM. STATE	TOTAL ASSETS ($MIL)
Rating: A+		
CHESAPEAKE LIFE INS CO	OK	253.5
COUNTRY LIFE INS CO	IL	10,112.1
PHYSICIANS MUTUAL INS CO	NE	2,506.1
TEACHERS INS & ANNUITY ASN OF AM	NY	320,701.0
Rating: A		
AMALGAMATED LIFE INS CO	NY	154.2
BERKLEY LIFE & HEALTH INS CO	IA	382.0
FEDERATED LIFE INS CO	MN	2,189.3
GARDEN STATE LIFE INS CO	TX	147.1
GUARDIAN LIFE INS CO OF AMERICA	NY	65,189.0
HUMANA INS CO (WI)	WI	10,594.3
NATIONAL FOUNDATION LIFE INS CO	TX	87.8
SENTRY LIFE INS CO	WI	8,165.9
SHELTERPOINT LIFE INS CO	NY	235.2
USAA LIFE INS CO	TX	26,903.7
Rating: A-		
CIGNA LIFE INS CO OF NEW YORK	NY	449.3
FIDELITY SECURITY LIFE INS CO	MO	980.9
MEDICAL MUTUAL OF OHIO	OH	2,702.4
NATIONAL BENEFIT LIFE INS CO	NY	595.9
NEW YORK LIFE INS CO	NY	198,377.0
NIPPON LIFE INS CO OF AMERICA	IA	246.1
PHYSICIANS LIFE INS CO	NE	1,730.5
Rating: B+		
AMERICAN FIDELITY ASR CO	OK	6,608.0
AMERIGROUP INS CO	TX	322.8
ANTHEM LIFE INS CO	IN	799.2
ASSURITY LIFE INS CO	NE	2,670.3
BEST LIFE & HEALTH INS CO	TX	30.1
BOSTON MUTUAL LIFE INS CO	MA	1,547.3
COMMUNITY CARE BEHAVIORAL HEALTH	PA	611.0
COMPANION LIFE INS CO	SC	489.5
DEARBORN LIFE INS CO	IL	1,657.5
DELAWARE AMERICAN LIFE INS CO	DE	106.1
FREEDOM LIFE INS CO OF AMERICA	TX	418.7
GEISINGER HEALTH PLAN	PA	665.0
GERBER LIFE INS CO	NY	,4,677.1
HEALTH CARE SVC CORP A MUT LEG RES	IL	33,429.9
HUMANA BENEFIT PLAN OF ILLINOIS	IL	1,104.8
ILLINOIS MUTUAL LIFE INS CO	IL	1,520.9
KEYSTONE HEALTH PLAN EAST INC	PA	1,526.3
MIDLAND NATIONAL LIFE INS CO	IA	62,252.9
NORTH AMERICAN INS CO	WI	19.2
NORTHWESTERN LONG TERM CARE INS CO	WI	290.3
NORTHWESTERN MUTUAL LIFE INS CO	WI	295,371.0
OXFORD LIFE INS CO	AZ	2,408.0
PRINCIPAL LIFE INS CO	IA	208,421.0
STANDARD INS CO	OR	27,265.4
STANDARD SECURITY LIFE INS CO OF NY	NY	142.7
TRUSTMARK INS CO	IL	1,752.8
TRUSTMARK LIFE INS CO	IL	296.8
UNITED FARM FAMILY LIFE INS CO	IN	2,442.0
UNITED WORLD LIFE INS CO	NE	141.0
UPMC FOR YOU INC	PA	1,528.6

INSURANCE COMPANY NAME	DOM. STATE	TOTAL ASSETS ($MIL)
USABLE LIFE	AR	496.4
VISTA HEALTH PLAN INC	PA	1,350.1
VOYA RETIREMENT INS & ANNUITY CO	CT	110,637.0

Puerto Rico

INSURANCE COMPANY NAME	DOM. STATE	TOTAL ASSETS ($MIL)	INSURANCE COMPANY NAME	DOM. STATE	TOTAL ASSETS ($MIL)
Rating: **A+**					
TEACHERS INS & ANNUITY ASN OF AM	NY	320,701.0			
Rating: **A**					
HUMANA INS CO (WI)	WI	10,594.3			
Rating: **A-**					
NEW YORK LIFE INS CO	NY	198,377.0			
Rating: **B+**					
AMERICAN FIDELITY ASR CO	OK	6,608.0			
BOSTON MUTUAL LIFE INS CO	MA	1,547.3			
DEARBORN LIFE INS CO	IL	1,657.5			
GERBER LIFE INS CO	NY	4,677.1			
MIDLAND NATIONAL LIFE INS CO	IA	62,252.9			
PRINCIPAL LIFE INS CO	IA	208,421.0			
STANDARD INS CO	OR	27,265.4			
STANDARD SECURITY LIFE INS CO OF NY	NY	142.7			
TRANS OCEANIC LIFE INS CO	PR	77.3			
TRUSTMARK INS CO	IL	1,752.8			
UNIVERSAL LIFE INS CO	PR	1,953.3			
VOYA RETIREMENT INS & ANNUITY CO	CT	110,637.0			

Rhode Island

INSURANCE COMPANY NAME	DOM. STATE	TOTAL ASSETS ($MIL)
Rating: A+		
CHESAPEAKE LIFE INS CO	OK	253.5
COUNTRY LIFE INS CO	IL	10,112.1
PHYSICIANS MUTUAL INS CO	NE	2,506.1
TEACHERS INS & ANNUITY ASN OF AM	NY	320,701.0
Rating: A		
AMALGAMATED LIFE INS CO	NY	154.2
BERKLEY LIFE & HEALTH INS CO	IA	382.0
FEDERATED LIFE INS CO	MN	2,189.3
GARDEN STATE LIFE INS CO	TX	147.1
GUARDIAN LIFE INS CO OF AMERICA	NY	65,189.0
HUMANA INS CO (WI)	WI	10,594.3
SENTRY LIFE INS CO	WI	8,165.9
SHELTERPOINT LIFE INS CO	NY	235.2
USAA LIFE INS CO	TX	26,903.7
Rating: A-		
FIDELITY SECURITY LIFE INS CO	MO	980.9
NATIONAL BENEFIT LIFE INS CO	NY	595.9
NEW YORK LIFE INS CO	NY	198,377.0
NIPPON LIFE INS CO OF AMERICA	IA	246.1
PHYSICIANS LIFE INS CO	NE	1,730.5
Rating: B+		
AMERICAN FIDELITY ASR CO	OK	6,608.0
ASSURITY LIFE INS CO	NE	2,670.3
BOSTON MUTUAL LIFE INS CO	MA	1,547.3
COMPANION LIFE INS CO	SC	489.5
DEARBORN LIFE INS CO	IL	1,657.5
DELAWARE AMERICAN LIFE INS CO	DE	106.1
GERBER LIFE INS CO	NY	4,677.1
HUMANA BENEFIT PLAN OF ILLINOIS	IL	1,104.8
HUMANA WISCONSIN HEALTH ORGANIZATION	WI	1,259.4
ILLINOIS MUTUAL LIFE INS CO	IL	1,520.9
MIDLAND NATIONAL LIFE INS CO	IA	62,252.9
NORTHWESTERN LONG TERM CARE INS CO	WI	290.3
NORTHWESTERN MUTUAL LIFE INS CO	WI	295,371.0
OXFORD LIFE INS CO	AZ	2,408.0
PRINCIPAL LIFE INS CO	IA	208,421.0
STANDARD INS CO	OR	27,265.4
STANDARD SECURITY LIFE INS CO OF NY	NY	142.7
TRUSTMARK INS CO	IL	1,752.8
TRUSTMARK LIFE INS CO	IL	296.8
UNITED WORLD LIFE INS CO	NE	141.0
USABLE LIFE	AR	496.4
VOYA RETIREMENT INS & ANNUITY CO	CT	110,637.0

South Carolina

INSURANCE COMPANY NAME	DOM. STATE	TOTAL ASSETS ($MIL)	INSURANCE COMPANY NAME	DOM. STATE	TOTAL ASSETS ($MIL)
Rating: A+					
CHESAPEAKE LIFE INS CO	OK	253.5			
COUNTRY LIFE INS CO	IL	10,112.1			
PHYSICIANS MUTUAL INS CO	NE	2,506.1			
TEACHERS INS & ANNUITY ASN OF AM	NY	320,701.0			
Rating: A					
AMALGAMATED LIFE INS CO	NY	154.2			
BERKLEY LIFE & HEALTH INS CO	IA	382.0			
FEDERATED LIFE INS CO	MN	2,189.3			
GARDEN STATE LIFE INS CO	TX	147.1			
GUARDIAN LIFE INS CO OF AMERICA	NY	65,189.0			
HUMANA INS CO (WI)	WI	10,594.3			
KAISER PERMANENTE INS CO	CA	220.6			
NATIONAL FOUNDATION LIFE INS CO	TX	87.8			
SENTRY LIFE INS CO	WI	8,165.9			
SHELTERPOINT LIFE INS CO	NY	235.2			
SOUTHERN FARM BUREAU LIFE INS CO	MS	14,723.1			
USAA LIFE INS CO	TX	26,903.7			
Rating: A-					
CHRISTIAN FIDELITY LIFE INS CO	TX	58.3			
FIDELITY SECURITY LIFE INS CO	MO	980.9			
MEDICAL MUTUAL OF OHIO	OH	2,702.4			
NATIONAL BENEFIT LIFE INS CO	NY	595.9			
NEW YORK LIFE INS CO	NY	198,377.0			
NIPPON LIFE INS CO OF AMERICA	IA	246.1			
PHYSICIANS LIFE INS CO	NE	1,730.5			
Rating: B+					
AMERICAN FAMILY MUTL INS CO SI	WI	24,090.2			
AMERICAN FIDELITY ASR CO	OK	6,608.0			
ANTHEM LIFE INS CO	IN	799.2			
ASSURITY LIFE INS CO	NE	2,670.3			
BEST LIFE & HEALTH INS CO	TX	30.1			
BOSTON MUTUAL LIFE INS CO	MA	1,547.3			
COMPANION LIFE INS CO	SC	489.5			
DEARBORN LIFE INS CO	IL	1,657.5			
DELAWARE AMERICAN LIFE INS CO	DE	106.1			
FREEDOM LIFE INS CO OF AMERICA	TX	418.7			
GERBER LIFE INS CO	NY	4,677.1			
HEALTH CARE SVC CORP A MUT LEG RES	IL	33,429.9			
HUMANA BENEFIT PLAN OF ILLINOIS	IL	1,104.8			
ILLINOIS MUTUAL LIFE INS CO	IL	1,520.9			
MIDLAND NATIONAL LIFE INS CO	IA	62,252.9			
NORTH AMERICAN INS CO	WI	19.2			
NORTHWESTERN LONG TERM CARE INS CO	WI	290.3			
NORTHWESTERN MUTUAL LIFE INS CO	WI	295,371.0			
OXFORD LIFE INS CO	AZ	2,408.0			
PRINCIPAL LIFE INS CO	IA	208,421.0			
STANDARD INS CO	OR	27,265.4			
STANDARD SECURITY LIFE INS CO OF NY	NY	142.7			
TRUSTMARK INS CO	IL	1,752.8			
TRUSTMARK LIFE INS CO	IL	296.8			
UNITED WORLD LIFE INS CO	NE	141.0			
USABLE LIFE	AR	496.4			
VOYA RETIREMENT INS & ANNUITY CO	CT	110,637.0			

South Dakota

INSURANCE COMPANY NAME	DOM. STATE	TOTAL ASSETS ($MIL)	INSURANCE COMPANY NAME	DOM. STATE	TOTAL ASSETS ($MIL)
Rating: A+					
CHESAPEAKE LIFE INS CO	OK	253.5			
COUNTRY LIFE INS CO	IL	10,112.1			
PHYSICIANS MUTUAL INS CO	NE	2,506.1			
TEACHERS INS & ANNUITY ASN OF AM	NY	320,701.0			
Rating: A					
AMALGAMATED LIFE INS CO	NY	154.2			
BERKLEY LIFE & HEALTH INS CO	IA	382.0			
FEDERATED LIFE INS CO	MN	2,189.3			
GARDEN STATE LIFE INS CO	TX	147.1			
GUARDIAN LIFE INS CO OF AMERICA	NY	65,189.0			
HUMANA INS CO (WI)	WI	10,594.3			
NATIONAL FOUNDATION LIFE INS CO	TX	87.8			
SENTRY LIFE INS CO	WI	8,165.9			
USAA LIFE INS CO	TX	26,903.7			
Rating: A-					
CHRISTIAN FIDELITY LIFE INS CO	TX	58.3			
FIDELITY SECURITY LIFE INS CO	MO	980.9			
NATIONAL BENEFIT LIFE INS CO	NY	595.9			
NEW YORK LIFE INS CO	NY	198,377.0			
NIPPON LIFE INS CO OF AMERICA	IA	246.1			
PHYSICIANS LIFE INS CO	NE	1,730.5			
Rating: B+					
AMERICAN FAMILY MUTL INS CO SI	WI	24,090.2			
AMERICAN FIDELITY ASR CO	OK	6,608.0			
AMERIGROUP INS CO	TX	322.8			
ANTHEM LIFE INS CO	IN	799.2			
ASSURITY LIFE INS CO	NE	2,670.3			
BEST LIFE & HEALTH INS CO	TX	30.1			
BOSTON MUTUAL LIFE INS CO	MA	1,547.3			
COMPANION LIFE INS CO	SC	489.5			
DEARBORN LIFE INS CO	IL	1,657.5			
DELAWARE AMERICAN LIFE INS CO	DE	106.1			
FARM BUREAU LIFE INS CO	IA	9,479.7			
FREEDOM LIFE INS CO OF AMERICA	TX	418.7			
GERBER LIFE INS CO	NY	4,677.1			
HEALTHPARTNERS INS CO	MN	475.5			
HUMANA BENEFIT PLAN OF ILLINOIS	IL	1,104.8			
ILLINOIS MUTUAL LIFE INS CO	IL	1,520.9			
MIDLAND NATIONAL LIFE INS CO	IA	62,252.9			
NORTHWESTERN LONG TERM CARE INS CO	WI	290.3			
NORTHWESTERN MUTUAL LIFE INS CO	WI	295,371.0			
OXFORD LIFE INS CO	AZ	2,408.0			
PACIFIC GUARDIAN LIFE INS CO LTD	HI	579.2			
PRINCIPAL LIFE INS CO	IA	208,421.0			
STANDARD INS CO	OR	27,265.4			
STANDARD SECURITY LIFE INS CO OF NY	NY	142.7			
TRUSTMARK INS CO	IL	1,752.8			
TRUSTMARK LIFE INS CO	IL	296.8			
UNITED WORLD LIFE INS CO	NE	141.0			
USABLE LIFE	AR	496.4			
VOYA RETIREMENT INS & ANNUITY CO	CT	110,637.0			

Tennessee

INSURANCE COMPANY NAME	DOM. STATE	TOTAL ASSETS ($MIL)	INSURANCE COMPANY NAME	DOM. STATE	TOTAL ASSETS ($MIL)
Rating: A+			USABLE LIFE	AR	496.4
			VOYA RETIREMENT INS & ANNUITY CO	CT	110,637.0
CHESAPEAKE LIFE INS CO	OK	253.5			
COUNTRY LIFE INS CO	IL	10,112.1			
PHYSICIANS MUTUAL INS CO	NE	2,506.1			
TEACHERS INS & ANNUITY ASN OF AM	NY	320,701.0			

Rating: A

INSURANCE COMPANY NAME	DOM. STATE	TOTAL ASSETS ($MIL)
AMALGAMATED LIFE INS CO	NY	154.2
BERKLEY LIFE & HEALTH INS CO	IA	382.0
FEDERATED LIFE INS CO	MN	2,189.3
GARDEN STATE LIFE INS CO	TX	147.1
GUARDIAN LIFE INS CO OF AMERICA	NY	65,189.0
HUMANA INS CO (WI)	WI	10,594.3
NATIONAL FOUNDATION LIFE INS CO	TX	87.8
SENTRY LIFE INS CO	WI	8,165.9
SHELTERPOINT LIFE INS CO	NY	235.2
SOUTHERN FARM BUREAU LIFE INS CO	MS	14,723.1
USAA LIFE INS CO	TX	26,903.7

Rating: A-

INSURANCE COMPANY NAME	DOM. STATE	TOTAL ASSETS ($MIL)
BLUEBONNET LIFE INS CO	MS	69.5
BLUECROSS BLUESHIELD OF TENNESSEE	TN	5,279.4
CHRISTIAN FIDELITY LIFE INS CO	TX	58.3
CIGNA LIFE INS CO OF NEW YORK	NY	449.3
FIDELITY SECURITY LIFE INS CO	MO	980.9
NATIONAL BENEFIT LIFE INS CO	NY	595.9
NEW YORK LIFE INS CO	NY	198,377.0
NIPPON LIFE INS CO OF AMERICA	IA	246.1
PHYSICIANS LIFE INS CO	NE	1,730.5
SWBC LIFE INS CO	TX	36.1

Rating: B+

INSURANCE COMPANY NAME	DOM. STATE	TOTAL ASSETS ($MIL)
AMERICAN FAMILY MUTL INS CO SI	WI	24,090.2
AMERICAN FIDELITY ASR CO	OK	6,608.0
AMERIGROUP INS CO	TX	322.8
ANTHEM LIFE INS CO	IN	799.2
ASSURITY LIFE INS CO	NE	2,670.3
BEST LIFE & HEALTH INS CO	TX	30.1
BOSTON MUTUAL LIFE INS CO	MA	1,547.3
COMPANION LIFE INS CO	SC	489.5
DEARBORN LIFE INS CO	IL	1,657.5
DELAWARE AMERICAN LIFE INS CO	DE	106.1
FREEDOM LIFE INS CO OF AMERICA	TX	418.7
GERBER LIFE INS CO	NY	4,677.1
GOLDEN SECURITY INS CO	TN	69.3
HUMANA BENEFIT PLAN OF ILLINOIS	IL	1,104.8
ILLINOIS MUTUAL LIFE INS CO	IL	1,520.9
MIDLAND NATIONAL LIFE INS CO	IA	62,252.9
NORTHWESTERN LONG TERM CARE INS CO	WI	290.3
NORTHWESTERN MUTUAL LIFE INS CO	WI	295,371.0
OXFORD LIFE INS CO	AZ	2,408.0
PRINCIPAL LIFE INS CO	IA	208,421.0
STANDARD INS CO	OR	27,265.4
STANDARD SECURITY LIFE INS CO OF NY	NY	142.7
TRUSTMARK INS CO	IL	1,752.8
TRUSTMARK LIFE INS CO	IL	296.8
UNITED HEALTHCARE OF WISCONSIN INC	WI	2,701.9
UNITED WORLD LIFE INS CO	NE	141.0

Texas

INSURANCE COMPANY NAME	DOM. STATE	TOTAL ASSETS ($MIL)
Rating: A+		
CHESAPEAKE LIFE INS CO	OK	253.5
COUNTRY LIFE INS CO	IL	10,112.1
PHYSICIANS MUTUAL INS CO	NE	2,506.1
TEACHERS INS & ANNUITY ASN OF AM	NY	320,701.0
Rating: A		
AMALGAMATED LIFE INS CO	NY	154.2
BERKLEY LIFE & HEALTH INS CO	IA	382.0
FEDERATED LIFE INS CO	MN	2,189.3
GARDEN STATE LIFE INS CO	TX	147.1
GUARDIAN LIFE INS CO OF AMERICA	NY	65,189.0
HUMANA INS CO (WI)	WI	10,594.3
NATIONAL FOUNDATION LIFE INS CO	TX	87.8
SENTRY LIFE INS CO	WI	8,165.9
SOUTHERN FARM BUREAU LIFE INS CO	MS	14,723.1
USAA LIFE INS CO	TX	26,903.7
Rating: A-		
CHRISTIAN FIDELITY LIFE INS CO	TX	58.3
ESSENCE HEALTHCARE INC	MO	260.9
FIDELITY SECURITY LIFE INS CO	MO	980.9
NATIONAL BENEFIT LIFE INS CO	NY	595.9
NEW YORK LIFE INS CO	NY	198,377.0
NIPPON LIFE INS CO OF AMERICA	IA	246.1
PHYSICIANS LIFE INS CO	NE	1,730.5
SWBC LIFE INS CO	TX	36.1
WELLCARE OF TEXAS INC	TX	201.1
Rating: B+		
AMERICAN FAMILY MUTL INS CO SI	WI	24,090.2
AMERICAN FIDELITY ASR CO	OK	6,608.0
AMERIGROUP INS CO	TX	322.8
ANTHEM LIFE INS CO	IN	799.2
ASSURITY LIFE INS CO	NE	2,670.3
BEST LIFE & HEALTH INS CO	TX	30.1
BOSTON MUTUAL LIFE INS CO	MA	1,547.3
COMPANION LIFE INS CO	SC	489.5
COMPANION LIFE INS CO OF CA	CA	29.6
DEARBORN LIFE INS CO	IL	1,657.5
DELAWARE AMERICAN LIFE INS CO	DE	106.1
ENTERPRISE LIFE INS CO	TX	148.0
FREEDOM LIFE INS CO OF AMERICA	TX	418.7
GERBER LIFE INS CO	NY	4,677.1
HEALTH CARE SVC CORP A MUT LEG RES	IL	33,429.9
HUMANA BENEFIT PLAN OF ILLINOIS	IL	1,104.8
ILLINOIS MUTUAL LIFE INS CO	IL	1,520.9
MIDLAND NATIONAL LIFE INS CO	IA	62,252.9
NORTH AMERICAN INS CO	WI	19.2
NORTHWESTERN LONG TERM CARE INS CO	WI	290.3
NORTHWESTERN MUTUAL LIFE INS CO	WI	295,371.0
OXFORD LIFE INS CO	AZ	2,408.0
PACIFIC GUARDIAN LIFE INS CO LTD	HI	579.2
PRINCIPAL LIFE INS CO	IA	208,421.0
STANDARD INS CO	OR	27,265.4
STANDARD SECURITY LIFE INS CO OF NY	NY	142.7
TRUSTMARK INS CO	IL	1,752.8
TRUSTMARK LIFE INS CO	IL	296.8

INSURANCE COMPANY NAME	DOM. STATE	TOTAL ASSETS ($MIL)
UNITED HEALTHCARE OF TX INC	TX	95.9
UNITED WORLD LIFE INS CO	NE	141.0
USABLE LIFE	AR	496.4
USABLE MUTUAL INS CO	AR	1,921.0
VOYA RETIREMENT INS & ANNUITY CO	CT	110,637.0

Utah

INSURANCE COMPANY NAME	DOM. STATE	TOTAL ASSETS ($MIL)
Rating: A+		
CHESAPEAKE LIFE INS CO	OK	253.5
COUNTRY LIFE INS CO	IL	10,112.1
PHYSICIANS MUTUAL INS CO	NE	2,506.1
TEACHERS INS & ANNUITY ASN OF AM	NY	320,701.0
Rating: A		
AMALGAMATED LIFE INS CO	NY	154.2
BERKLEY LIFE & HEALTH INS CO	IA	382.0
EMI HEALTH	UT	198.8
FEDERATED LIFE INS CO	MN	2,189.3
GARDEN STATE LIFE INS CO	TX	147.1
GUARDIAN LIFE INS CO OF AMERICA	NY	65,189.0
HUMANA INS CO (WI)	WI	10,594.3
NATIONAL FOUNDATION LIFE INS CO	TX	87.8
SENTRY LIFE INS CO	WI	8,165.9
USAA LIFE INS CO	TX	26,903.7
Rating: A-		
CHRISTIAN FIDELITY LIFE INS CO	TX	58.3
FIDELITY SECURITY LIFE INS CO	MO	980.9
NATIONAL BENEFIT LIFE INS CO	NY	595.9
NEW YORK LIFE INS CO	NY	198,377.0
NIPPON LIFE INS CO OF AMERICA	IA	246.1
PHYSICIANS LIFE INS CO	NE	1,730.5
SWBC LIFE INS CO	TX	36.1
Rating: B+		
AMERICAN FAMILY MUTL INS CO SI	WI	24,090.2
AMERICAN FIDELITY ASR CO	OK	6,608.0
AMERIGROUP INS CO	TX	322.8
ANTHEM LIFE INS CO	IN	799.2
ASSURITY LIFE INS CO	NE	2,670.3
BEST LIFE & HEALTH INS CO	TX	30.1
BOSTON MUTUAL LIFE INS CO	MA	1,547.3
COMPANION LIFE INS CO	SC	489.5
DEARBORN LIFE INS CO	IL	1,657.5
DELAWARE AMERICAN LIFE INS CO	DE	106.1
FARM BUREAU LIFE INS CO	IA	9,479.7
FREEDOM LIFE INS CO OF AMERICA	TX	418.7
GERBER LIFE INS CO	NY	4,677.1
HEALTH CARE SVC CORP A MUT LEG RES	IL	33,429.9
HUMANA BENEFIT PLAN OF ILLINOIS	IL	1,104.8
ILLINOIS MUTUAL LIFE INS CO	IL	1,520.9
MIDLAND NATIONAL LIFE INS CO	IA	62,252.9
NORTHWESTERN LONG TERM CARE INS CO	WI	290.3
NORTHWESTERN MUTUAL LIFE INS CO	WI	295,371.0
OXFORD LIFE INS CO	AZ	2,408.0
PACIFIC GUARDIAN LIFE INS CO LTD	HI	579.2
PRINCIPAL LIFE INS CO	IA	208,421.0
REGENCE BLUE CROSS BLUE SHIELD OF UT	UT	792.1
SELECTHEALTH INC	UT	1,703.8
STANDARD INS CO	OR	27,265.4
STANDARD SECURITY LIFE INS CO OF NY	NY	142.7
TRUSTMARK INS CO	IL	1,752.8
TRUSTMARK LIFE INS CO	IL	296.8
UNITED WORLD LIFE INS CO	NE	141.0
USABLE LIFE	AR	496.4

INSURANCE COMPANY NAME	DOM. STATE	TOTAL ASSETS ($MIL)
VOYA RETIREMENT INS & ANNUITY CO	CT	110,637.0

Vermont

INSURANCE COMPANY NAME	DOM. STATE	TOTAL ASSETS ($MIL)
Rating: A+		
PHYSICIANS MUTUAL INS CO	NE	2,506.1
TEACHERS INS & ANNUITY ASN OF AM	NY	320,701.0
Rating: A		
AMALGAMATED LIFE INS CO	NY	154.2
BERKLEY LIFE & HEALTH INS CO	IA	382.0
FEDERATED LIFE INS CO	MN	2,189.3
GARDEN STATE LIFE INS CO	TX	147.1
GUARDIAN LIFE INS CO OF AMERICA	NY	65,189.0
HUMANA INS CO (WI)	WI	10,594.3
SENTRY LIFE INS CO	WI	8,165.9
USAA LIFE INS CO	TX	26,903.7
Rating: A-		
AMERICAN FAMILY LIFE ASR CO OF NY	NY	1,043.6
FIDELITY SECURITY LIFE INS CO	MO	980.9
NATIONAL BENEFIT LIFE INS CO	NY	595.9
NEW YORK LIFE INS CO	NY	198,377.0
NIPPON LIFE INS CO OF AMERICA	IA	246.1
PHYSICIANS LIFE INS CO	NE	1,730.5
Rating: B+		
AMERICAN FIDELITY ASR CO	OK	6,608.0
ASSURITY LIFE INS CO	NE	2,670.3
BOSTON MUTUAL LIFE INS CO	MA	1,547.3
COMPANION LIFE INS CO	SC	489.5
DEARBORN LIFE INS CO	IL	1,657.5
DELAWARE AMERICAN LIFE INS CO	DE	106.1
GERBER LIFE INS CO	NY	4,677.1
HUMANA BENEFIT PLAN OF ILLINOIS	IL	1,104.8
ILLINOIS MUTUAL LIFE INS CO	IL	1,520.9
MIDLAND NATIONAL LIFE INS CO	IA	62,252.9
NORTHWESTERN LONG TERM CARE INS CO	WI	290.3
NORTHWESTERN MUTUAL LIFE INS CO	WI	295,371.0
PRINCIPAL LIFE INS CO	IA	208,421.0
STANDARD INS CO	OR	27,265.4
STANDARD SECURITY LIFE INS CO OF NY	NY	142.7
TRUSTMARK INS CO	IL	1,752.8
TRUSTMARK LIFE INS CO	IL	296.8
UNITED WORLD LIFE INS CO	NE	141.0
USABLE LIFE	AR	496.4
VOYA RETIREMENT INS & ANNUITY CO	CT	110,637.0

Virginia

INSURANCE COMPANY NAME	DOM. STATE	TOTAL ASSETS ($MIL)
Rating: A+		
CHESAPEAKE LIFE INS CO	OK	253.5
COUNTRY LIFE INS CO	IL	10,112.1
PHYSICIANS MUTUAL INS CO	NE	2,506.1
TEACHERS INS & ANNUITY ASN OF AM	NY	320,701.0
Rating: A		
AMALGAMATED LIFE INS CO	NY	154.2
BERKLEY LIFE & HEALTH INS CO	IA	382.0
FEDERATED LIFE INS CO	MN	2,189.3
GARDEN STATE LIFE INS CO	TX	147.1
GUARDIAN LIFE INS CO OF AMERICA	NY	65,189.0
HUMANA INS CO (WI)	WI	10,594.3
KAISER PERMANENTE INS CO	CA	220.6
NATIONAL FOUNDATION LIFE INS CO	TX	87.8
SENTRY LIFE INS CO	WI	8,165.9
SOUTHERN FARM BUREAU LIFE INS CO	MS	14,723.1
USAA LIFE INS CO	TX	26,903.7
Rating: A-		
CHRISTIAN FIDELITY LIFE INS CO	TX	58.3
FIDELITY SECURITY LIFE INS CO	MO	980.9
HUMANA MEDICAL PLAN INC	FL	3,307.4
NATIONAL BENEFIT LIFE INS CO	NY	595.9
NEW YORK LIFE INS CO	NY	198,377.0
NIPPON LIFE INS CO OF AMERICA	IA	246.1
PHYSICIANS LIFE INS CO	NE	1,730.5
SWBC LIFE INS CO	TX	36.1
Rating: B+		
AMERICAN FAMILY MUTL INS CO SI	WI	24,090.2
AMERICAN FIDELITY ASR CO	OK	6,608.0
ANTHEM LIFE INS CO	IN	799.2
ASSURITY LIFE INS CO	NE	2,670.3
BEST LIFE & HEALTH INS CO	TX	30.1
BOSTON MUTUAL LIFE INS CO	MA	1,547.3
COMPANION LIFE INS CO	SC	489.5
DEARBORN LIFE INS CO	IL	1,657.5
DELAWARE AMERICAN LIFE INS CO	DE	106.1
FREEDOM LIFE INS CO OF AMERICA	TX	418.7
GERBER LIFE INS CO	NY	4,677.1
GROUP HOSP & MEDICAL SERVICES INC	DC	3,122.9
HEALTH CARE SVC CORP A MUT LEG RES	IL	33,429.9
HUMANA BENEFIT PLAN OF ILLINOIS	IL	1,104.8
HUMANA WISCONSIN HEALTH ORGANIZATION	WI	1,259.4
ILLINOIS MUTUAL LIFE INS CO	IL	1,520.9
MIDLAND NATIONAL LIFE INS CO	IA	62,252.9
NORTHWESTERN LONG TERM CARE INS CO	WI	290.3
NORTHWESTERN MUTUAL LIFE INS CO	WI	295,371.0
OPTIMUM CHOICE INC	MD	119.3
OXFORD LIFE INS CO	AZ	2,408.0
PRINCIPAL LIFE INS CO	IA	208,421.0
STANDARD INS CO	OR	27,265.4
STANDARD SECURITY LIFE INS CO OF NY	NY	142.7
TRUSTMARK INS CO	IL	1,752.8
TRUSTMARK LIFE INS CO	IL	296.8
UNITED HEALTHCARE OF WISCONSIN INC	WI	2,701.9
UNITED WORLD LIFE INS CO	NE	141.0

INSURANCE COMPANY NAME	DOM. STATE	TOTAL ASSETS ($MIL)
USABLE LIFE	AR	496.4
VOYA RETIREMENT INS & ANNUITY CO	CT	110,637.0

Washington

INSURANCE COMPANY NAME	DOM. STATE	TOTAL ASSETS ($MIL)
Rating: A+		
CHESAPEAKE LIFE INS CO	OK	253.5
COUNTRY LIFE INS CO	IL	10,112.1
PHYSICIANS MUTUAL INS CO	NE	2,506.1
TEACHERS INS & ANNUITY ASN OF AM	NY	320,701.0
Rating: A		
AMALGAMATED LIFE INS CO	NY	154.2
BERKLEY LIFE & HEALTH INS CO	IA	382.0
FEDERATED LIFE INS CO	MN	2,189.3
GARDEN STATE LIFE INS CO	TX	147.1
GUARDIAN LIFE INS CO OF AMERICA	NY	65,189.0
HUMANA INS CO (WI)	WI	10,594.3
KAISER PERMANENTE INS CO	CA	220.6
LIFEWISE ASR CO	WA	249.5
NATIONAL FOUNDATION LIFE INS CO	TX	87.8
SENTRY LIFE INS CO	WI	8,165.9
USAA LIFE INS CO	TX	26,903.7
Rating: A-		
AMERIGROUP WASHINGTON INC	WA	314.7
CHRISTIAN FIDELITY LIFE INS CO	TX	58.3
ESSENCE HEALTHCARE INC	MO	260.9
FIDELITY SECURITY LIFE INS CO	MO	980.9
NATIONAL BENEFIT LIFE INS CO	NY	595.9
NEW YORK LIFE INS CO	NY	198,377.0
NIPPON LIFE INS CO OF AMERICA	IA	246.1
PHYSICIANS LIFE INS CO	NE	1,730.5
PROVIDENCE HEALTH ASR	OR	586.5
REGENCE BL CROSS BL SHIELD OREGON	OR	1,622.0
Rating: B+		
AMERICAN FAMILY MUTL INS CO SI	WI	24,090.2
AMERICAN FIDELITY ASR CO	OK	6,608.0
AMERIGROUP INS CO	TX	322.8
ANTHEM LIFE INS CO	IN	799.2
ASSURITY LIFE INS CO	NE	2,670.3
BEST LIFE & HEALTH INS CO	TX	30.1
BOSTON MUTUAL LIFE INS CO	MA	1,547.3
COMPANION LIFE INS CO	SC	489.5
DEARBORN LIFE INS CO	IL	1,657.5
DELAWARE AMERICAN LIFE INS CO	DE	106.1
FARM BUREAU LIFE INS CO	IA	9,479.7
FREEDOM LIFE INS CO OF AMERICA	TX	418.7
GERBER LIFE INS CO	NY	4,677.1
HUMANA BENEFIT PLAN OF ILLINOIS	IL	1,104.8
ILLINOIS MUTUAL LIFE INS CO	IL	1,520.9
MIDLAND NATIONAL LIFE INS CO	IA	62,252.9
NORTHWESTERN LONG TERM CARE INS CO	WI	290.3
NORTHWESTERN MUTUAL LIFE INS CO	WI	295,371.0
OXFORD LIFE INS CO	AZ	2,408.0
PACIFIC GUARDIAN LIFE INS CO LTD	HI	579.2
PRINCIPAL LIFE INS CO	IA	208,421.0
REGENCE BLUESHIELD OF IDAHO INC	ID	395.1
STANDARD INS CO	OR	27,265.4
STANDARD SECURITY LIFE INS CO OF NY	NY	142.7
TRUSTMARK INS CO	IL	1,752.8
TRUSTMARK LIFE INS CO	IL	296.8

INSURANCE COMPANY NAME	DOM. STATE	TOTAL ASSETS ($MIL)
UNITED WORLD LIFE INS CO	NE	141.0
UNITEDHEALTHCARE OF OREGON	OR	645.9
USABLE LIFE	AR	496.4
VOYA RETIREMENT INS & ANNUITY CO	CT	110,637.0

West Virginia

INSURANCE COMPANY NAME	DOM. STATE	TOTAL ASSETS ($MIL)
Rating: **A+**		
CHESAPEAKE LIFE INS CO	OK	253.5
COUNTRY LIFE INS CO	IL	10,112.1
PHYSICIANS MUTUAL INS CO	NE	2,506.1
TEACHERS INS & ANNUITY ASN OF AM	NY	320,701.0
Rating: **A**		
AMALGAMATED LIFE INS CO	NY	154.2
BERKLEY LIFE & HEALTH INS CO	IA	382.0
FEDERATED LIFE INS CO	MN	2,189.3
GARDEN STATE LIFE INS CO	TX	147.1
GUARDIAN LIFE INS CO OF AMERICA	NY	65,189.0
HUMANA INS CO (WI)	WI	10,594.3
SENTRY LIFE INS CO	WI	8,165.9
UNICARE HEALTH PLAN OF WEST VIRGINIA	WV	186.1
USAA LIFE INS CO	TX	26,903.7
Rating: **A-**		
CHRISTIAN FIDELITY LIFE INS CO	TX	58.3
FIDELITY SECURITY LIFE INS CO	MO	980.9
MEDICAL MUTUAL OF OHIO	OH	2,702.4
NATIONAL BENEFIT LIFE INS CO	NY	595.9
NEW YORK LIFE INS CO	NY	198,377.0
NIPPON LIFE INS CO OF AMERICA	IA	246.1
PHYSICIANS LIFE INS CO	NE	1,730.5
Rating: **B+**		
AMERICAN FIDELITY ASR CO	OK	6,608.0
AMERIGROUP INS CO	TX	322.8
ANTHEM LIFE INS CO	IN	799.2
ASSURITY LIFE INS CO	NE	2,670.3
BOSTON MUTUAL LIFE INS CO	MA	1,547.3
COMPANION LIFE INS CO	SC	489.5
DEARBORN LIFE INS CO	IL	1,657.5
DELAWARE AMERICAN LIFE INS CO	DE	106.1
FREEDOM LIFE INS CO OF AMERICA	TX	418.7
GERBER LIFE INS CO	NY	4,677.1
HEALTH CARE SVC CORP A MUT LEG RES	IL	33,429.9
HUMANA BENEFIT PLAN OF ILLINOIS	IL	1,104.8
ILLINOIS MUTUAL LIFE INS CO	IL	1,520.9
MIDLAND NATIONAL LIFE INS CO	IA	62,252.9
NORTHWESTERN LONG TERM CARE INS CO	WI	290.3
NORTHWESTERN MUTUAL LIFE INS CO	WI	295,371.0
OPTIMUM CHOICE INC	MD	119.3
OXFORD LIFE INS CO	AZ	2,408.0
PRINCIPAL LIFE INS CO	IA	208,421.0
STANDARD INS CO	OR	27,265.4
STANDARD SECURITY LIFE INS CO OF NY	NY	142.7
TRUSTMARK INS CO	IL	1,752.8
TRUSTMARK LIFE INS CO	IL	296.8
UNITED WORLD LIFE INS CO	NE	141.0
USABLE LIFE	AR	496.4
VOYA RETIREMENT INS & ANNUITY CO	CT	110,637.0

Wisconsin

INSURANCE COMPANY NAME	DOM. STATE	TOTAL ASSETS ($MIL)
Rating: A+		
CHESAPEAKE LIFE INS CO	OK	253.5
COUNTRY LIFE INS CO	IL	10,112.1
PHYSICIANS MUTUAL INS CO	NE	2,506.1
TEACHERS INS & ANNUITY ASN OF AM	NY	320,701.0
Rating: A		
AMALGAMATED LIFE INS CO	NY	154.2
BERKLEY LIFE & HEALTH INS CO	IA	382.0
COMPCARE HEALTH SERVICES INS CORP	WI	535.2
FEDERATED LIFE INS CO	MN	2,189.3
GARDEN STATE LIFE INS CO	TX	147.1
GUARDIAN LIFE INS CO OF AMERICA	NY	65,189.0
HUMANA INS CO (WI)	WI	10,594.3
SENTRY LIFE INS CO	WI	8,165.9
USAA LIFE INS CO	TX	26,903.7
Rating: A-		
DEAN HEALTH PLAN INC	WI	338.6
FIDELITY SECURITY LIFE INS CO	MO	980.9
INDEPENDENT CARE HEALTH PLAN	WI	107.2
MEDICAL MUTUAL OF OHIO	OH	2,702.4
NATIONAL BENEFIT LIFE INS CO	NY	595.9
NEW YORK LIFE INS CO	NY	198,377.0
NIPPON LIFE INS CO OF AMERICA	IA	246.1
PHYSICIANS LIFE INS CO	NE	1,730.5
Rating: B+		
MY CHOICE WISCONSIN HEALTH PLAN INC	WI	74.2
AMERICAN FAMILY MUTL INS CO SI	WI	24,090.2
AMERICAN FIDELITY ASR CO	OK	6,608.0
ANTHEM LIFE INS CO	IN	799.2
ASSURITY LIFE INS CO	NE	2,670.3
BOSTON MUTUAL LIFE INS CO	MA	1,547.3
CHILDRENS COMMUNITY HEALTH PLAN INC	WI	239.7
COMPANION LIFE INS CO	SC	489.5
DEARBORN LIFE INS CO	IL	1,657.5
DELAWARE AMERICAN LIFE INS CO	DE	106.1
ENTERPRISE LIFE INS CO	TX	148.0
FARM BUREAU LIFE INS CO	IA	9,479.7
GERBER LIFE INS CO	NY	4,677.1
HEALTH CARE SVC CORP A MUT LEG RES	IL	33,429.9
HEALTHPARTNERS INS CO	MN	475.5
HUMANA BENEFIT PLAN OF ILLINOIS	IL	1,104.8
HUMANA WISCONSIN HEALTH ORGANIZATION	WI	1,259.4
ILLINOIS MUTUAL LIFE INS CO	IL	1,520.9
MIDLAND NATIONAL LIFE INS CO	IA	62,252.9
NORTH AMERICAN INS CO	WI	19.2
NORTHWESTERN LONG TERM CARE INS CO	WI	290.3
NORTHWESTERN MUTUAL LIFE INS CO	WI	295,371.0
OXFORD LIFE INS CO	AZ	2,408.0
PRINCIPAL LIFE INS CO	IA	208,421.0
SECURITY HEALTH PLAN OF WI INC	WI	507.0
STANDARD INS CO	OR	27,265.4
STANDARD SECURITY LIFE INS CO OF NY	NY	142.7
TRUSTMARK INS CO	IL	1,752.8
TRUSTMARK LIFE INS CO	IL	296.8
UNITED HEALTHCARE OF WISCONSIN INC	WI	2,701.9

INSURANCE COMPANY NAME	DOM. STATE	TOTAL ASSETS ($MIL)
UNITED WORLD LIFE INS CO	NE	141.0
USABLE LIFE	AR	496.4
VOYA RETIREMENT INS & ANNUITY CO	CT	110,637.0

Wyoming

INSURANCE COMPANY NAME	DOM. STATE	TOTAL ASSETS ($MIL)
Rating: **A+**		
CHESAPEAKE LIFE INS CO	OK	253.5
COUNTRY LIFE INS CO	IL	10,112.1
PHYSICIANS MUTUAL INS CO	NE	2,506.1
TEACHERS INS & ANNUITY ASN OF AM	NY	320,701.0
Rating: **A**		
AMALGAMATED LIFE INS CO	NY	154.2
BERKLEY LIFE & HEALTH INS CO	IA	382.0
FEDERATED LIFE INS CO	MN	2,189.3
GARDEN STATE LIFE INS CO	TX	147.1
GUARDIAN LIFE INS CO OF AMERICA	NY	65,189.0
HUMANA INS CO (WI)	WI	10,594.3
NATIONAL FOUNDATION LIFE INS CO	TX	87.8
SENTRY LIFE INS CO	WI	8,165.9
USAA LIFE INS CO	TX	26,903.7
Rating: **A-**		
CHRISTIAN FIDELITY LIFE INS CO	TX	58.3
FIDELITY SECURITY LIFE INS CO	MO	980.9
NATIONAL BENEFIT LIFE INS CO	NY	595.9
NEW YORK LIFE INS CO	NY	198,377.0
PHYSICIANS LIFE INS CO	NE	1,730.5
Rating: **B+**		
AMERICAN FAMILY MUTL INS CO SI	WI	24,090.2
AMERICAN FIDELITY ASR CO	OK	6,608.0
AMERIGROUP INS CO	TX	322.8
ANTHEM LIFE INS CO	IN	799.2
ASSURITY LIFE INS CO	NE	2,670.3
BEST LIFE & HEALTH INS CO	TX	30.1
BOSTON MUTUAL LIFE INS CO	MA	1,547.3
COMPANION LIFE INS CO	SC	489.5
COMPANION LIFE INS CO OF CA	CA	29.6
DEARBORN LIFE INS CO	IL	1,657.5
DELAWARE AMERICAN LIFE INS CO	DE	106.1
FARM BUREAU LIFE INS CO	IA	9,479.7
FREEDOM LIFE INS CO OF AMERICA	TX	418.7
GERBER LIFE INS CO	NY	4,677.1
HUMANA BENEFIT PLAN OF ILLINOIS	IL	1,104.8
ILLINOIS MUTUAL LIFE INS CO	IL	1,520.9
MIDLAND NATIONAL LIFE INS CO	IA	62,252.9
NORTHWESTERN LONG TERM CARE INS CO	WI	290.3
NORTHWESTERN MUTUAL LIFE INS CO	WI	295,371.0
OXFORD LIFE INS CO	AZ	2,408.0
PACIFIC GUARDIAN LIFE INS CO LTD	HI	579.2
PRINCIPAL LIFE INS CO	IA	208,421.0
STANDARD INS CO	OR	27,265.4
STANDARD SECURITY LIFE INS CO OF NY	NY	142.7
TRUSTMARK INS CO	IL	1,752.8
TRUSTMARK LIFE INS CO	IL	296.8
UNITED WORLD LIFE INS CO	NE	141.0
USABLE LIFE	AR	496.4
VOYA RETIREMENT INS & ANNUITY CO	CT	110,637.0

Section V

Long-Term Care Insurers

A list of rated companies providing

Long-Term Care Insurance

Companies are listed in alphabetical order.

Section V Contents

This section provides contact addresses and phone numbers for all companies who sell long-term care insurance. The long-term care insurers in this section are listed in alphabetical order.

1. Safety Rating Our rating is measured on a scale from A to F and considers a wide range of factors. Highly-rated companies are, in our opinion, less likely to experience financial difficulties than lower-rated firms. See *About Weiss Safety Ratings* for more information.

2. Insurance Company Name The legally registered name, which can sometimes differ from the name that the company uses for advertising. An insurer's name can be very similar to the name of other companies, so make sure you note the exact name before contacting your agent.

3. Address The address of the main office where you can contact the firm for additional financial data or for the location of local branches and/or registered agents.

4. Telephone Number The number to call for additional financial data or for the phone numbers of local branches and/or registered agents.

To compare long-term care insurance policies and to walk through the maze of options, prices, and insurers, see the *Long-Term Care Insurance Planner*. It helps narrow down the choices available by addressing questions such as:

- What can you afford to pay for insurance?

- What type of care and living arrangement will suit your needs?

- When will you most likely need to utilize the insurance benefits?

- How much can you afford to pay from your own savings?

- Do you want a tax-qualified or non-qualified policy?

- What kind of insurance agent are you working with?

The planner offers an easy-to-use analysis tool to help identify the policy that best meets your needs. Based on information provided by insurance agents and literature from the provider, it addresses questions such as:

- How safe is the insurer?

- How are the coverage and facility options defined?

- What are the terms of coverage and reimbursement?

- How will the benefits be triggered?

- What other features are included in the policy?

RATING	INSURANCE COMPANY NAME	ADDRESS	CITY	STATE	ZIP	PHONE
B-	AUTO-OWNERS LIFE INS CO	6101 ANACAPRI BOULEVARD	LANSING	MI	48917	(517) 323-1200
D	BANKERS CONSECO LIFE INS CO	350 JERICHO TURNPIKE SUITE 304	JERICHO	NY	11753	(317) 817-6100
D+	BANKERS LIFE & CAS CO	111 EAST WACKER DRIVE STE 2100	CHICAGO	IL	60601	(312) 396-6000
B	BLUE CROSS BLUE SHIELD OF KANSAS INC	1133 SW TOPEKA BOULEVARD	TOPEKA	KS	66629	(785) 291-7000
A+	COUNTRY LIFE INS CO	1701 N TOWANDA AVENUE	BLOOMINGTON	IL	61701	(309) 821-3000
B	FORETHOUGHT LIFE INS CO	10 W MARKET ST STE 2300	INDIANAPOLIS	IN	46204	(317) 223-2700
C	GENWORTH LIFE INS CO	251 LITTLE FALLS DR	WILMINGTON	DE	19808	(804) 662-2400
C	GENWORTH LIFE INS CO OF NEW YORK	600 THIRD AVENUE SUITE 2400	NEW YORK	NY	10016	(212) 895-4137
C	JOHN HANCOCK LIFE & HEALTH INS CO	197 CLARENDON STREET	BOSTON	MA	02116	(617) 572-6000
B-	JOHN HANCOCK LIFE INS CO (USA)	201 TOWNSEND STREET SUITE 900	LANSING	MI	48933	(617) 572-6000
C-	LIFESECURE INS CO	10559 CITATION DRIVE SUITE 300	BRIGHTON	MI	48116	(810) 220-7700
C+	MADISON NATIONAL LIFE INS CO INC	1241 JOHN Q HAMMONS DRIVE	MADISON	WI	53717	(800) 356-9601
B	MASSACHUSETTS MUTUAL LIFE INS CO	1295 STATE STREET	SPRINGFIELD	MA	1111	(413) 788-8411
C	MEDAMERICA INS CO	651 HOLIDAY DRIVE FOSTER PLAZA	PITTSBURGH	PA	15220	(585) 238-4464
D+	MEDAMERICA INS CO OF NEW YORK	165 COURT STREET	ROCHESTER	NY	14647	(585) 238-4464
C+	MUTUAL OF OMAHA INS CO	MUTUAL OF OMAHA PLAZA	OMAHA	NE	68175	(402) 342-7600
A-	NEW YORK LIFE INS CO	51 MADISON AVENUE	NEW YORK	NY	10010	(212) 576-7000
B+	NORTHWESTERN LONG TERM CARE INS CO	720 EAST WISCONSIN AVENUE	MILWAUKEE	WI	53202	(414) 271-1444
B-	RESERVE NATIONAL INS CO	200 EAST RANDOLPH STREET SUIT	CHICAGO	IL	60601	(405) 848-7931
D+	SILAC INSURANCE CO	299 S MAIN ST #1100	SALT LAKE CITY	UT	84111	(801) 579-3400
B	STATE FARM MUTUAL AUTOMOBILE INS CO	ONE STATE FARM PLAZA	BLOOMINGTON	IL	61710	(309) 766-2311
B	TRANSAMERICA FINANCIAL LIFE INS CO	440 MAMARONECK AVENUE	HARRISON	NY	10528	(914) 627-3630
C+	TRANSAMERICA LIFE INS CO	4333 EDGEWOOD RD NE	CEDAR RAPIDS	IA	52499	(319) 355-8511
B	UNITED OF OMAHA LIFE INS CO	3300 MUTUAL OF OMAHA PLAZA	OMAHA	NE	68175	(402) 342-7600
E+	UNITED SECURITY ASR CO OF PA	673 EAST CHERRY LANE	SOUDERTON	PA	18964	(215) 723-3044
C-	WILMINGTON INSURANCE CO	1403 SILVERSIDE ROAD SUITE 3B	WILMINGTON	DE	19810	(302) 655-0800

Section VI

Medicare Supplement Insurance

Section VI Contents

Part I: Answers to Your Questions About Medigap

What Does Medicare Cover?

What are the Gaps in Medicare Coverage?

Medicare Prescription Drug Bill

Medicare, Medicare Advantage, Part D Sponsors, Medigap –
What Does It All Mean?

Part II: Steps to Follow When Selecting a Medigap Policy

How to Switch Medigap Policies

Part III: Medigap Premium Rates

Tables outlining the typical annual premiums charged for Plan A through

Plan N depending on age and gender.

Part IV: Medicare Supplement Insurers

Part I:
Answers to Your Questions About Medigap

The choices you make today about your health coverage – or the coverage of someone you care for – can have a major impact on both your health and your wealth. Since you are over 65, Medicare will provide you with a basic level of coverage, but there are many gaps in Medicare coverage that you will likely need to fill with a Medicare supplement insurance (Medigap) policy if you decide not to join a Medicare Advantage plan. The purpose of this report is to help you make coverage choices based on the most objective and broadest amount of information possible.

First, you want to understand what the federal Medicare program does and does not cover. We provide you with a clear layout starting on the following page.

Second, you will need to decide whether you want to fill the gaps in coverage by joining a Medicare Advantage plan or by combining Medicare supplement insurance with Medicare benefits. In Part 1 of this guide, we explain the differences between the two approaches.

Third, if you decide to use Medigap, your next step is to find out which plan best suits your needs. To help you figure this out, review Part II of this guide.

Fourth, check out the specific benefits for each plan along with the premium rates charged for those plans in Part III.

Finally, once you've found a couple of alternatives you like the best, call the companies to find the authorized agent nearest you. Phone numbers for the companies' main offices are listed in Part IV. If you need additional information on health insurance and related topics, call the agencies listed under Reference Organizations.

What Does Medicare Cover?

Table 1
MEDICARE (PART A): HOSPITAL INSURANCE-COVERED SERVICES FOR 2021

Service	Benefit	Medicare Pays	You Pay
HOSPITAL CARE (IN PATIENT CARE)			
Semi-private rooms, meals, general nursing, and drugs as part of your inpatient treatment, and other hospital services and supplies.	First 60 days	All but $1,484	$1,484
	61st to 90th day	All but $371 a day	$371 a day
	91st to 150th day*	All but $742 a day	$742 a day
Limited to 190 days in a lifetime, inpatient psychiatric care in a freestanding psychiatric hospital.	Beyond 150 days	Nothing	All costs
SKILLED NURSING FACILITY CARE			
You must have been in a hospital for at least 3 days, enter a Medicare-approved facility generally within 30 days after hospital discharge, and meet other program requirements. **	First 20 days	100% of approved amount	Nothing
	Additional 80 days	All but $185.50 a day	Up to $185.50 a day
	Beyond 100 days	Nothing	All costs
HOME HEALTH CARE			
Part-time or intermittent skilled care, home health services, physical and occupational therapy, durable medical equipment and supplies and other services	For as long as you meet Medicare requirements for home health care benefits	100% of approved amount; 80% of approved amount for durable medical equipment	Nothing for services; 20% of approved amount for durable medical equipment
HOSPICE CARE			
Includes drugs for symptom control and pain relief, medical and support services from a Medicare-approved hospice, and other services not otherwise covered by Medicare. Hospice care is usually given in your home.	For as long as doctor certifies need	All but limited costs for outpatient drugs and inpatient respite care	Limited cost sharing for outpatient drugs and inpatient respite care
BLOOD			
When furnished by a hospital or a skilled nursing facility during a covered stay	Unlimited during a benefit period if medically necessary	80% of the Medicare-approved after the first 3 pints per calendar year	***100% of the first 3 pints then 20% of the approved cost of additional pints.

*   60 reserve days may be used only once.
**   Neither Medicare nor Medicare supplement insurance will pay for most nursing home care.
*** To the extent the three pints of blood are paid for or replaced under one part of Medicare during the calendar year, they do not have to be paid for or replaced under the other part.

Table 2
MEDICARE (PART B): PREVENTIVE SERVICES FOR 2021

Service	Benefit	Medicare Pays	You Pay
"WELCOME TO MEDICARE" PHYSICAL EXAM (ONE-TIME)			
	During the first 12 months that you have Part B, you can get a "Welcome to Medicare" preventive visit.	100% if provider accepts assignment.	If health care provider performs additional test or services during the same visit, you may have to pay coinsurance, and Part B deductible may apply
YEARLY "WELLNESS" VISIT			
	This visit is covered once every 12 months. If you've had Part B for longer than 12 months, you can get a yearly "Wellness" visit.	100% if provider accepts assignment.	If health care provider performs additional test or services during the same visit, you may have to pay coinsurance, and Part B deductible may apply
ABDOMINAL AORTIC ANEURYSM SCREENING			
	A one-time screening ultrasound for people at risk. You must get a referral for it as part of your one-time "Welcome to Medicare" preventive visit.	100% if provider accepts assignment	Nothing for services
ALCOHOL MISUSE SCREENING AND COUNSELING			
	Once every 12 months for adults with Medicare (including pregnant women) who use alcohol, but don't meet the medical criteria for alcohol dependency.	100% if provider accepts assignment	Nothing for services
BONE MASS MEASUREMENT (BONE DENSITY)			
	Once every 24 months (more often if medically necessary) for people who have certain medical conditions or meet certain criteria.	100% if provider accepts assignment	Nothing for services
BREAST CANCER SCREENING (MAMMOGRAMS)			
	Once every 12 months for all women with Medicare who are 40 and older. Medicare covers one baseline mammogram for women between 35 - 39.	100% if provider accepts assignment	Nothing for services
CARDIOVASCULAR DISEASE (BEHAVIORAL THERAPY)			
	One visit per year with a primary care doctor in a primary care setting (like a doctor's office) to help lower your risk	100% if provider accepts assignment	Nothing for services
CARDIOVASCULAR DISEASE SCREENINGS			
	Once every 5 years to test your cholesterol, lipid, lipoprotein, and triglyceride levels.	100% if provider accepts assignment	Nothing for services

Table 2
MEDICARE (PART B): PREVENTIVE SERVICES FOR 2021 (cont'd.)

Service	Benefit	Medicare Pays	You Pay
CERVICAL AND VAGINAL CANCER SCREENING			
	Once every 24 months. Every 12 months if you're at high risk for cervical or vaginal cancer or child-bearing age and had an abnormal Pap test in the past 36 months	100% if the doctor or provider accepts assignment	Nothing for services
COLORECTAL CANCER SCREENING			
Multi-target stool DNA test	Once every 3 years if you meet all conditions: between ages 50-85, show no symptoms of colorectal disease, at average risk for developing colorectal cancer	100% if the doctor or other qualified health care provider accepts assignment.	Nothing for services
Screening facal occult blood test	Once every 12 months if you're 50 or older	100% if the doctor or other qualified health care provider accepts assignment.	Nothing for services
Screening flexible sigmoidoscopy	Once every 48 months if you're 50 or older, or 120 months after a previous screening colonoscopy for those not at high risk.	100% if the doctor or other qualified health care provider accepts assignment.	Nothing for services
Screening colonoscopy	Once every 120 months (high risk every 24 months) or 48 months after a previous flexible sigmoidoscopy. There's no minimum age.	100% if the doctor or other qualified health care provider accepts assignment.	If a polyp or other tissue is found and removed during the colonoscopy, you may have to pay 20% of the Medicare-approved amount for the doctor's services and a copayment in a hospital outpatient setting.
Screening barium enema	Once every 48 months if you're 50 or older (high risk every 24 months) when used instead of a sigmoidoscopy or colonoscopy.	80% of the approved amount	You pay 20% for the doctor's services. In a hospital outpatient setting, you also pay the hospital a copayment.
DERPRESSION SCREENING			
	One screening per year. The screening must be done in a primary care setting (like a doctor's office) that can provide follow-up treatment and referrals.	100% if provider accepts assignment	Nothing for services

Table 2
MEDICARE (PART B): PREVENTIVE SERVICES FOR 2021 (cont'd.)

Service	Benefit	Medicare Pays	You Pay
DIABETES SCREENING			
	Covers these screenings if your doctor determines you're at risk for diabetes. Up to 2 diabetes screenings each year.	100% if your doctor or provider accepts assignment	Nothing for services
DIABETES SELF-MANAGEMENT TRAINING			
	Covers diabetes outpatient self-management training to teach you to cope with and manage your diabetes.	80% of the approved amount	20% of the Medicare approved amount, and the Part B deductible applies
FLU SHOTS			
	Covers one flu shot per flu season	100% if the doctor or provider accepts assignment	Nothing for services
GLAUCOMA TESTING			
	Once every 12 months for those at high risk for glaucoma.	80% of approved amount	20% of the approved amount after the yearly Part B deductible. Copayment in a hospital outpatient setting
HEPATITIS B SHOTS			
	Covers these shots for people at medium or high risk for Hepatitis B	100% if the doctor or provider accepts assignment	Nothing for services
HEPATITIS C SCREENING TEST			
	Covers one Hepatitis C screening test if you meet one of these conditions: – Current or past history of illicit injection drug use – Blood transfusion before 1992 – Born between 1945-1965	100% if the doctor or other qualified health care provider accepts assignment	Nothing for services
HIV SCREENING			
	Once per year for people at increased risk for HIV screenings for pregnant women up to 3 times during a pregnancy	100% if the doctor or provider accepts assignment	Nothing for services

Table 2
MEDICARE (PART B): PREVENTIVE SERVICES FOR 2021 (cont'd.)

Service	Benefit	Medicare Pays	You Pay
LUNG CANCER SCREENING			
	Covers a lung cancer screening with Low Dose Computed Tomography (LDCT) once per year	100% if the primary care doctor or other qualified primary care practitioner accepts assignment	Nothing for services
MEDICAL NUTRITION THERAPY SERVICES			
	Covers medical nutrition therapy and certain related services if you have diabetes or kidney disease, or you have had a kidney transplant in the last 36 months	100% if the doctor or provider accepts assignment	Nothing for services
OBESITY SCREENING AND COUNSELING			
	If you have a body mass index (BMI) of 30 or more, Medicare covers face-to-face individual behavioral therapy sessions to help you lose weight.	100% if the primary care doctor or other qualified primary care practitioner accepts assignment	Nothing for services
PNEUMOCOCCAL SHOT			
	Covers pneumococcal shots to help prevent pneumococcal infections (like certain types of pneumonia). Most people only need a shot once in their lifetime.	100% if the doctor or provider accepts assignment	Nothing for services
PROSTATE CANCER SCREENING			
	Prostate Specific Antigen (PSA) and a digital rectal exam once every 12 months for men over 50 (beginning the day after your 50th birthday)	100% for the PSA test	20% of the Medicare-approved amount, and the Part B deductible applies for the digital rectal exam. In a hospital outpatient setting, you also pay the hospital a copayment.

	Table 2		
MEDICARE (PART B): PREVENTIVE SERVICES FOR 2021 (cont'd.)			
Service	**Benefit**	**Medicare Pays**	**You Pay**
SEXUALLY TRANSMITTED INFECTIONS SCREENING AND COUNSELING			
	Covers screenings for Chlamydia, gonorrhea, syphilis, and Hepatitis B. Covered for people who are pregnant and for certain people who are at increased risk for an STI. Once every 12 months or at certain times during a pregnancy. Covers up to 2 individual, 20-30 minute, face-to-face, high-intensity behavioral counseling sessions each year for sexually active adults.	100% if the primary care doctor or other qualified primary care practitioner accepts assignment	Nothing for services
SMOKING AND TOBACCO-USE CESSATION			
	Includes up to 8 face-to-face visits in a 12-month period	100% if the doctor or other qualified health care provider accepts assignment	Nothing for services

Table 3
MEDICARE (PART B): MEDICAL INSURANCE-COVERED SERVICES FOR 2021

Service	Benefit	Medicare Pays	You Pay
AMBULANCE SERVICES			
	Covers ground ambulance transportation when you need to be transported to a hospital, critical access hospital, or skilled nursing facility for medically necessary services, and transportation in any other vehicle could endanger your health	80% of approved amount (after deductible)	20% of the Medicare-approved amount, and the Part B deductible applies
AMBULATORY SURGICAL CENTERS			
	Covers ground ambulance transportation when you need to be transported to a hospital, critical access hospital, or skilled nursing facility for medically necessary services.	100% for certain preventive services	20% of the Medicare approved amount to both the ambulatory surgical center and the doctor who treats you, and Part B deductible applies.
BLOOD			
		100% if the provider gets blood from a blood bank	A copayment for the blood processing and handling services for each unit of blood you get, and the Part B deductible applies. If the provider has to buy blood for you, you must either pay the provider costs for the first 3 units in a calendar year or have the blood donated by you or someone else.

Table 3
MEDICARE (PART B): MEDICAL INSURANCE-COVERED SERVICES FOR 2021

Service	Benefit	Medicare Pays	You Pay
CARDIAC REHABILITATION			
	Cover comprehensive programs that include exercise, education, and counseling for patients who meet certain conditions. Medicare also covers intensive cardiac rehabilitation programs that are typically more rigorous or more intense than regular cardiac rehabilitation programs.	80% of the approved amount.	20% of the Medicare-approved amount if you get the services in a doctor's office. In a hospital outpatient setting, you also pay the hospital a copayment. The Part B deductible applies.
CHEMOTHERAPY			
	Covers chemotherapy in a doctor's office, freestanding clinic, or hospital outpatient setting for people with cancer.	80% of approved amount	A copayment for chemotherapy in a hospital outpatient setting. Chemotherapy given in a doctor's office or freestanding clinic you pay 20% of the Medicare-approved amount, and the Part B deductible applies.
CHIROPRACTIC SERVICES (LIMITED COVERAGE)			
	Covers manipulation of the spine if medically necessary to correct a subluxation (when one or more of the bones of your spine move out of position)	80% of the approved amount	20% of the Medicare-approved amount, and the Part B deductible applies. **Note:** You pay all costs for any other services or tests ordered by a chiropractor (including X-rays and massage therapy)
CLINICAL RESEARCH STUDIES			
	Covers some costs, like office visits and tests, in qualifying clinical research studies.	80% of the approved amount	20% of the Medicare-approved amount, and the Part B deductible may apply

Table 3
MEDICARE (PART B): MEDICAL INSURANCE-COVERED SERVICES FOR 2021

Service	Benefit	Medicare Pays	You Pay
CONCIERGE CARE			
	When a doctor or group of doctors charges you a membership fee before they'll see you or accept you into their practice.	Not Covered	100% of the membership fees for concierge care (also called concierge medicine, retainer-based medicine, boutique medicine, platinum practice, or direct care)
CONTINUOUS POSITIVE AIRWAY PRESSURE (CPAP) THERAPY			
	A 3-month trial of CPAP therapy if you've been diagnosed with obstructive sleep apnea.	80% of the approved amount	20% of the Medicare-approved amount for rental of the machine and purchase of related supplies (like masks and tubing) and the Part B deductible applies.
DEFIBRILLATOR (IMPLANTABLE AUTOMATIC)			
	Covers these devices for some people diagnosed with heart failure.	80% of the approved amount	20% of the Medicare-approved amount, if the surgery takes place in a outpatient setting. The doctor's services. If you get the device as a hospital outpatient, you also pay the hospital a copayment. The Part B deductible applies.

Table 3
MEDICARE (PART B): MEDICAL INSURANCE-COVERED SERVICES FOR 2021

Service	Benefit	Medicare Pays	You Pay
DIABETES SUPPLIES			
	Covers blood sugar testing monitors, test strips, lancet devices and lancets, blood sugar control solutions, and therapeutic shoes (in some cases). Covers insulin if it's medically necessary to use with an external insulin pump.	80% of the approved amount.	20% of the Medicare approved amount, the Part B deductible applies
DOCTOR AND OTHER HEALTH CARE PROVIDER SERVICES			
	Covers medically necessary doctor services (including outpatient services and some doctor services you get when you're a hospital inpatient) and covered preventive services.	80% of the approved amount.	20% of the Medicare approved amount, the Part B deductible applies
DURABLE MEDICAL EQUIPMENT (LIKE WALKERS)			
	Covers items like oxygen equipment and supplies, wheelchairs, walkers, and hospital beds ordered by a doctor or other health care provider enrolled in Medicare for use in the home	80% of the approved amount.	20% of the Medicare approved amount, the Part B deductible applies
EKG OR ECG (ELECTROCARDIOGRAM) SCREENING			
	One time screening EKG/ECG if referred by your doctor or other health care provider as part of your one-time "Welcome to Medicare" preventive visit	80% of the approved amount.	20% of the Medicare approved amount, the Part B deductible applies. An EKG/ECG is also covered as a diagnostic test.

Table 3
MEDICARE (PART B): MEDICAL INSURANCE-COVERED SERVICES FOR 2021

Service	Benefit	Medicare Pays	You Pay
EMERGENCY DEPARTMENT SERVICES			
	When you have an injury, a sudden illness, or an illness that quickly gets much worse	80% of the approved amount.	A specified copayment for the hospital emergency department visit, and you pay 20% of the Medicare-approved amount for the doctor's or other health care provider's services. The Part B deductible applies. Cost may be different if you're admitted.
EYEGLASSES (LIMITED)			
	One pair of eyeglasses with standard frames (or one set of contact lenses) after cataract surgery that implants an intraocular lens.	80% of the approved amount. Medicare will only pay for contact lenses or eye glasses from a supplier enrolled in Medicare	20% of Medicare-approved amount, and the Part B deductible applies.
FEDERALLY-QUALIFIED HEALTH CENTER SERVICES			
	Covers many outpatient primary care and preventive health services.	80% of the approved amount.	No deductible, and generally, you're responsible for paying 20% of your charges or 20% of the Medicare-approved amount.
FOOT EXAMS AND TREATMENT			
	Covers foot exams and treatment if you have diabetes-related nerve damage and/or meet certain conditions	80% of the approved amount.	20% of the Medicare-approved amount, and the Part B deductible applies. In a hospital outpatient setting, you also pay the hospital copayment.
HEARING AND BALANCE EXAMS			
	Covers these exams if your doctor or other health care provider orders them to see if your need medical treatment.	80% of the approved amount.	20% of the Medicare-approved amount, and the Part B deductible applies. In a hospital outpatient setting, you also pay the hospital a copayment.

Table 3
MEDICARE (PART B): MEDICAL INSURANCE-COVERED SERVICES FOR 2021

Service	Benefit	Medicare Pays	You Pay
HOME HEALTH SERVICES			
	Covers medically necessary part-time or intermittent skilled nursing care, and/or physical therapy, speech-language pathology services, and/or services if you have a continuing need for occupation therapy.	100% for health services.	Nothing for services
KIDNEY DIALYSIS SERVICES AND SUPPLIES			
	Covers 3 dialysis treatments per week if you have End-Stage Renal Disease (ESRD). This includes all ESRD-related drugs and biological, laboratory tests, home dialysis training, support services, equipment, and supplies	80% of the approved amount.	20% of approved Medicare-approved amount, and the Part B applies.
KIDNEY DISEASE EDUCATION SERVICES			
	Covers up to 6 sessions of kidney disease education services if you have Stage IV chronic kidney disease, and your doctor or other health care provider refers you for the service.	80% of the approved amount.	20% of approved Medicare-approved amount, and the Part B applies
LABORATORY SERVICES			
	Covers laboratory services including certain blood tests, urinalysis, certain tests on tissue specimens, and some screening tests.	Generally 100% of approved amount	Nothing for services

Table 3
MEDICARE (PART B): MEDICAL INSURANCE-COVERED SERVICES FOR 2021

Service	Benefit	Medicare Pays	You Pay
MENTAL HEALTH CARE (OUTPATIENT)			
	Covers mental health care services to help with conditions like depression or anxiety. Includes services generally provided in an outpatient setting (like a doctor's or other health care provider's office or hospital outpatient department).	100% of lab tests. 80% of the approved amount. **Note:** Inpatient mental health care is covered under Part A	20% of the Medicare-approved amount and the Part B deductible applies for: • Visits to a doctor or other health care provider to diagnose your condition or monitor or change your prescriptions • Outpatient treatment of your condition (like counseling or psychotherapy)
OCCUPATIONAL THERAPY			
	Covers evaluation and treatment to help you perform activities of daily living (like dressing or bathing) when your doctor or other health care provider certifies you need it.	80% of the approved amount.	20% of the Medicare-approved amount and the Part B deductible applies.
OUTPATIENT HOSPITAL SERVICES			
	Covers many diagnostic and treatment services in hospital outpatient departments.	80% of the approved amount.	20% of the Medicare-approved amount and the Part B deductible applies.
OUTPATIENT MEDICAL AND SURGICAL SERVICES AND SUPPLIES			
	Covers approved procedures like X-rays, casts, stitches, or outpatient surgeries.	80% of the approved amount.	20% of the Medicare-approved amount, and the Part B deductible applies. In a hospital outpatient setting, you also pay the hospital a copayment.
PHYSICAL THERAPY			
	Covers evaluation and treatment for injuries and diseases that change your ability to function when your doctor or other health care provider certifies your need for it.	80% of the approved amount.	20% of the Medicare-approved amount, and the Part B deductible applies.

Table 3
MEDICARE (PART B): MEDICAL INSURANCE-COVERED SERVICES FOR 2021

Service	Benefit	Medicare Pays	You Pay
PRESCRIPTION DRUGS (LIMITED)			
	Covers a limited number of drugs like injections you get in a doctor's office, certain oral anti-cancer drugs, drugs used with some types of durable medical equipment (like a nebulizer or external infusion pump), immunosuppressant drugs and under very limited circumstances.	80% of the approved amount.	20% of the Medicare-approved amount, and the Part B deductible applies.
PROSTHETIC/ORTHOTIC ITEMS			
	Covers arm, leg, back, and neck braces; artificial eyes; artificial limbs (and their replacement parts); some types of breast prostheses (after mastectomy); and prosthetic devices needed to replace an internal body part or function.	80% of the approved amount.	20% of the Medicare-approved amount, and the Part B deductible applies.
PULMONARY REHABILITATION			
	Covers a comprehensive pulmonary rehabilitation program if you have moderate to very severe chronic obstructive pulmonary disease (COPD) and have a referral from the doctor treating this chronic respiratory disease.	80% of the approved amount.	20% of the Medicare-approved amount, and the Part B deductible applies. In a hospital outpatient setting, you also pay the hospital a copayment.
RURAL HEALTH CLINIC SERVICES			
	Covers many outpatient primary care and preventive services in rural health clinics.	80% of the approved amount. 100% for most preventive services.	20% of the Medicare-approved amount, and the Part B deductible applies.

Table 3
MEDICARE (PART B): MEDICAL INSURANCE-COVERED SERVICES FOR 2021

Service	Benefit	Medicare Pays	You Pay
SECOND SURGICAL OPINIONS			
	Covers second surgical opinions for surgery that isn't an emergency.	80% of the approved amount.	20% of the Medicare-approved amount, and the Part B deductible applies.
SPEECH-LANGUAGE PATHOLOGY SERVICES			
	Covers evaluation and treatment to regain and strengthen speech and language skills, including cognitive and swallowing skills, when your doctor or other health care provider certifies you need it.	80% of the approved amount.	20% of the Medicare-approved amount, and the Part B deductible applies.
SURGICAL DRESSING SERVICES			
	Covers medically necessary treatment of a surgical or surgically treated wound.	80% of the approved amount.	20% of the Medicare-approved amount for the doctor's or other health care provider's services
TELEHEALTH			
	Covers limited medical or other health services, like office visits and consultations provided using an interactive, two-way telecommunications system (like real-time audio and video) by an eligible provider who isn't at your location.	80% of the approved amount.	20% of the Medicare-approved amount, and the Part B deductible applies.
TESTS (OTHER THAN LAB TEST)			
	Covers X-rays, MRIs, CT scans, ECG/EKGs, and some other diagnostic tests.	80% of the approved amount.	20% of the Medicare-approved amount, and the Part B deductible applies. You also pay the hospital a copayment that may be more than 20% of the Medicare-approved amount, but in most cases this amount can't be more than the Part A hospital stay deductible.

Table 3
MEDICARE (PART B): MEDICAL INSURANCE-COVERED SERVICES FOR 2021

Service	Benefit	Medicare Pays	You Pay
TRANSPLANTS AND IMMUNOSUPPRESSIVE DRUGS			
	Covers doctor services for heart, lung, kidney, pancreas, intestine, and liver transplants under certain conditions and only in a Medicare-certified facility. Covers bone marrow and cornea transplants under certain conditions.	80% of the approved amount.	20% of the Medicare-approved amount for the drugs, and the Part B deductible applies.
TRAVEL (HEALTH CARE NEEDED WHEN TRAVELING OUTSIDE THE U.S.)			
	Generally doesn't cover health care while you're traveling outside the U.S., there are some exceptions, including cases where Medicare may pay for services that you get while on board a ship within the territorial waters adjoining the land areas of the U.S.	80% of the approved amount.	20% of the Medicare-approved amount, and the Part B deductible applies.
URGENTLY NEEDED CARE			
	Covers urgently needed care to treat a sudden illness or injury that isn't a medical emergency.	80% of the approved amount.	20% of the Medicare-approved amount for the doctor's or other health care provider's services and the Part B deductible applies. In a hospital outpatient setting, you also pay the hospital a copayment

In addition to the services listed, Medicare also helps cover the following: ambulance services, artificial eyes, artificial limbs (prosthetic devices and replacement parts), braces (arm, leg, back, and neck), chiropractic services (limited), eyeglasses (one pair of standard frames after cataract surgery with an intraocular lens), hearing and balance exams ordered by your doctor, kidney dialysis and prosthetic/orthodontic devices (including breast prosthesis after mastectomy).

In some cases and under certain conditions, Medicare may also cover these services: a second surgical opinion by a doctor, telemedicine services (in rural areas), and therapeutic shoes for people with diabetes, and transplants (heart, lung, kidney, pancreas, intestine, bone marrow, cornea, and liver).

Table 4
MEDICARE (PART D): PRESCRIPTION DRUG COVERAGE FOR 2021
Coverage is provided by private companies that have been approved by Medicare

Service	Costs	Medicare Provider Pays	You Pay
Medicare approved drug plans will cover generic and brand-name drugs. Most plans will have a formulary, which is a list of drugs covered by the plan. This list must always meet Medicare's requirements, including: - Inclusion of at least two drugs in every drug category. - Access to retail pharmacies. - For drugs not covered, a procedure must be in place to obtain, if medically necessary.	Premium	– – –	On average, $38.80 per month for basic coverage, and $42.70 per month for enhanced coverage
	First $445 in costs	Nothing	Up to $445 (this is the deductible)
	Costs between $445 and $4,130	$2,764	$921.25 (25% for branded companies, 25% for generic)
	Next $2,420 drug costs	Nothing	Until out of pocket spending, including drug company discount total $6,550
	All additional drug costs	All but co-pay	Co-pay $3.70 generic $9.20 all other drugs

Your plan must, at a minimum, offer this standard level of service and cost coverage outlined here, however, some plans may offer more coverage. Premiums will vary depending on any additional coverage provided by the plan.

What are the Gaps in Medicare Coverage?

Medicare has never covered all medical expenses and never will. The gap between what the doctors charge and the government pays is big and getting bigger. In fact, Medicare was never designed to cover chronic conditions or prolonged medical treatments. It was directed toward Americans age 65 or older who need minor or short-term care – little more. Be sure to understand where Medicare falls short. We can't list all the possible gaps, but here are the ones that affect almost everyone (see the tables on the previous pages for more details):

Gap #1: Deductibles

Medicare has two parts: **Part A** *acts as hospital insurance* and **Part B** *acts as medical insurance.* You are responsible for deductibles under both parts. Under Part A, for instance, you would be responsible for the $1,484 deductible for the first 60 days of a hospital stay. Plus, this $1,408 deductible applies each time you re-enter the hospital after a greater than 60-day span between admissions.

Under Part B, Medicare will pick up 80% of approved medical expenses after you pay a $203 deductible.

Gap #2: Co-Payments

You are responsible for a share of the daily costs if your hospital stay lasts more than 60 days. In 2021, you would be responsible for paying a $371 daily "coinsurance" fee if you stay in the hospital longer than 60 days but less than 90 days. Worse yet, Medicare Part A pays nothing after 90 days – unless you take advantage of the 60 "lifetime reserve days." The 60 reserve days can be used only once, and even then, you would still pay $742 daily for those 60 days.

Gap #3: Shortfalls

A national fee schedule established what physicians on Medicare assignment can charge for their services; Medicare will generally pay 80% of that amount. However, not all physicians are on Medicare assignment. Those who are not on assignment may charge more than the approved amount, leaving you responsible for the shortfall.

Gap #4: Nonpayment

The Original Medicare program does not directly provide any coverage whatsoever for certain services and expenses such as prescription drugs, hearing aids, treatment in foreign countries, and much more.

The bottom line: When all is said and done, the federal Medicare program will cover no more than half to three quarters of your medical expenses. That's why private Medicare supplement insurance, or Medigap, makes sense; its goal is to cover a portion of what Medicare doesn't. But in order for Medigap to make sense for you, you need to find the right policy, from the right company, for a reasonable price.

What about Medicare Prescription Drug Coverage?

The Medicare Prescription Drug, Improvement and Modernization (MMA) Act was passed in 2003. This legislation created Medicare Part D: Prescription Drug Coverage effective January 2006. Coverage is only available by private companies that have been approved by Medicare, not through the Medicare program directly. You can obtain coverage by either directly purchasing Part D coverage through a plan sponsor or in combination with enrollment in a Medicare Advantage health plan offering drug coverage. These drug plans are standardized across providers but they are required to offer a minimum level of coverage. Plans may vary in co-pays, premiums, deductibles, and drug coverage and pharmacy networks. (See Table 4 for an outline of the required coverage.)

To assist you in the selection of a health benefit package complete with prescription drug coverage refer to our *Consumer Guide to Medicare Prescription Drug Coverage* that includes:

➢ Information on the Medicare prescription drug benefit.

➢ Help in making a choice about prescription drug coverage.

➢ What to consider once you enroll.

➢ An index of Medicare approved prescription drug plans.

Medicare, Medicare Advantage, Part D Sponsors, Medigap – What Does It All Mean?

The various terms used regarding coverage of health benefits for seniors is downright confusing. Let us take a moment here to review some of the terminology. The health insurance program for seniors managed by the federal government consists of the Original Medicare, Medicare Advantage, and Part D Prescription Drug Sponsors. Tables 1 through 3 on the preceding pages outline your coverage and coverage gaps under the Original Medicare plan. With this plan you seek services from Medicare providers who then receive payment from the government for the costs they incur for your care.

The Medicare Advantage program allows you to join a private health insurance plan that has contracted with Medicare to provide Part A and B coverage. The Medicare Advantage plans in turn receive funds from the government for providing you with benefits. These plans typically provide coverage beyond what Medicare offers, making supplemental policy unnecessary.

Medicare Part D will allow you to get prescription drug benefits in two ways. One option is to enroll with a Prescription Drug Plan sponsor in combination with your Original Medicare benefits. You will receive benefits from and pay a premium to the plan sponsor who then receives funds from the government. The second option is to enroll with a Medicare Advantage plan that is offering prescription drug coverage. Here you will receive all your benefits from the plan and pay only one premium. Refer to Table 4 for an outline of the minimum coverage that a plan sponsor must offer.

Medicare Supplement insurance, or Medigap as it is commonly referred to, is available through private insurers for those enrollees of the Original Medicare plan to fill the coverage 'gaps' in the Part A and B coverage. Basically, Medigap insurance will reimburse you for the out-of-pocket costs you incur that are not covered under Medicare. This insurance is completely optional.

Of course, if you're lucky, and your employer or union is continuing to cover your health benefits when you retire you won't need any of these types of insurance. But you want to stay educated because you never know when your old employer may discontinue retirement benefits.

Now let's take a closer look at the difference between Medicare supplement insurance policies and Medicare Advantage plans.

Medigap

To make comparing policies from one insurer to another easier Congress standardized and simplified Medigap plans. This means that all Medigap insurers offer the same exact policy (though some companies may offer only a few of the plans). If you live in Wisconsin, Massachusetts, or Minnesota there are different types of Medigap plans that are sold in your state but are still standardized across insurers in each state.

Starting in 2020 Plans C and F are to be discontinued and a high deductible version of Plan G will be introduced. Only if you were first eligible for Medicare prior to January 1, 2020 will you be able to enroll in Plans C or F. Plans D and G have the same coverage as Plans C and F respectively, less the Part D deductible that was normally provided at a substantial premium by insurers. Note, not all insures will continue to offer these plans, even to those who are eligible. In Part II we provide you with a table that outlines what each of the plans cover.

You will have to pay a premium, which can vary greatly, depending on the plan you choose and from which company you buy. Coverage is more expansive than through a Medicare Advantage plan but at a higher price. With a Medigap policy you have the freedom to choose your own doctors or specialists, and you will be covered regardless of which clinic or hospital you attend. Medicare Select plans, a type of Medigap policy, are available in some areas which offer the same benefits but require you to use providers within the policy's network, similar to an HMO. These policies should be cheaper than non-Select plans since your choice of providers is restricted. Medigap plans do not cover long-term/custodial care at home or in a nursing home, hearing aids, vision care, private-duty nursing, dental care, or prescription medicine. Even if you decide that you want a Medigap policy you may find that you will not be approved depending on your health, or you may not find an insurer in your area that sells these types of policies. However, once you do purchase a policy, Medigap policies are guaranteed renewable. This means that an insurance company cannot refuse to renew your policy unless you do not pay the premiums, or you made material misrepresentations on your application. You are typically able to obtain coverage each year once you are approved; however, the premium may change.

You are eligible to purchase a Medigap policy when you have enrolled in Medicare Parts A and B. In all states, there is an open enrollment period that lasts for six months and begins on the first day of the month in which you are both age 65 or older and enrolled in Part B. During this open enrollment period, the insurer cannot deny you coverage for any reason including pre-existing conditions. The insurer can, however, charge you a higher premium for the pre-existing condition or other health and lifestyle factors.

Medicare Advantage Plans

Under Medicare Part C, Medicare Advantage plans were introduced to offer seniors choices in coverage, more benefits at minimal cost, and to reduce the burden on the Medicare program. Insurers will often offer benefits not covered by Medicare, such as dental and vision services, at a lower price than a Medigap policy.

Prior to 2006 most offered some type of prescription drug coverage, but it varied from plan to plan. With the Medicare Prescription drug bill that took effect in 2006, health insurers may still offer prescription drug coverage but the benefits must match or exceed the requirements outlined in Medicare Part D (Refer Table). The insurers will then receive funding from the government for providing the benefits. All coverage is included in one premium charge.

With a Medicare Advantage plan you will not have to file any forms for reimbursement. You may or may not have to pay a premium and/or a co-pay for doctor's visits. In most cases you are restricted to the doctors in the plan's network, and you will need a referral before you see a specialist. Several new types of Medicare Advantage plans (PPOs, Special Need plans, Private Fee-for-Service plans, Medicare Medical Savings Account Plans, and Cost plans) have been introduced recently that vary from the current HMO plans offered including, in some cases, expanded options for accessing providers. Make sure to understand how these plans work before signing on.

There may be limited insurers offering a Medicare Advantage plan in your area and your benefits can be discontinued after the contract period (usually one year). At that time you would have to either choose a new insurer/plan or join the Original Medicare Plan.

Part II:
Steps to Follow When Selecting a Medigap Policy

Follow These Steps When Selecting a Medigap Policy

1. **Determine what benefits you need.** Consider the following:

   - **Income.** If you are living on a **fixed income** and are able to afford only the most basic coverage, favor Plan A, the core plan. Among other things, you'll get an extra 30 days hospitalization per year beyond what Medicare pays. It also covers 100% of the Medicare Part B coinsurance for approved medical services, which is usually 20% of the approved amount.

     You may also want to consider plans, K or L, if they are available in your area. These policies help limit out-of-pocket costs for doctor's services and hospital care at a lower premium; however, you will have to pay more of Medicare's coinsurance and deductibles before the policy pays its share of the costs. These policies also do not cover 'excess' charges billed by your physician. Wisconsin, Massachusetts, and Minnesota also offer a core or basic plan to choose from.

   - **Family History.** You or your family's medical history is such that you want to be prepared to pay for nursing care, consider Plan C. Your $185.00 per-day co-payment under Medicare would be covered up to 100 days for skilled nursing facility care.

   - **Foreign Travel.** If you travel overseas extensively, you can get coverage for emergency care in a foreign country with Plan C through G, M and N. In Massachusetts and Minnesota foreign travel coverage can be found in the Supplement 1 and 2 Plans and to the Basic Medigap Coverage, respectively. In Wisconsin, a Foreign Travel rider can be added.

   - **Plan F is the most popular one.** In 2016, 58.6% of enrollees chose this plan. The next popular, Plan G, had 18.2% of the enrollees.

The chart below shows basic information about the different benefits Medigap policies cover.

X = the plan covers 100% of this benefit

% = the plan covers the percentage of this benefit

Medigap Benefits	Medigap Plans									
	A	B	C¹	D	F²	G³	K	L	M	N
Part A coinsurance and hospital costs up to an additional 365 days after Medicare benefits are used up	X	X	X	X	X	X	X	X	X	X
Part B coinsurance or copayment	X	X	X	X	X	X	50%	75%	X	X⁴
Blood (first 3 pints)	X	X	X	X	X	X	50%	75%	X	X
Part A hospice care coinsurance or copayment	X	X	X	X	X	X	50%	75%	X	X
Skilled nursing facility care coinsurance			X	X	X	X	50%	75%	X	X
Part A deductible		X	X	X	X	X	50%	75%	50%	X
Part B deductible			X		X					
Part B excess charges					X	X				
Foreign travel exchange (up to plan limits)			80%	80%	80%	80%			80%	80%
Out-of-pocket limit⁵							$6,220	$3,110		

1. Plan C will be discontinued in 2020. Only if you were first eligible for Medicare prior to January 1, 2020 will you be able to enroll.
2. Plan F also offers a high-deductible option. If you choose this option, this means you must pay for Medicare-covered cost up to the deductible amount of $2,300 in 2020 before your Medigap plan pays anything. In 2020 only if you were first eligible for Medicare prior to January 1, 2020 will you be able to enroll.
3. Plan G will also offer a high deductible option. If you choose this option, this means you must pay for Medicare-covered cost up to the deductible amount of $2,370 in 2021 before your Medigap plan pays anything.
4. Plan N pays 100% of the Part B coinsurance, except for a copayment of up to $20 for some office visits and up to a $50 copayment for emergency room visits that don't result in inpatient admission.
5. After you meet your out-of-pocket yearly limit and your yearly Part B deductible, the Medigap plan pays 100% of covered services for the rest of the calendar year.

In Massachusetts, Minnesota, and Wisconsin medigap policies are standardized in a different way. They consist of a core plan/core plans and additional riders can be selected to provide additional coverage at a cost.

2. Find out which policies are available to you.

- Not all insurers offer all plans in all areas.

- Will you be denied coverage by some insurers due to your health? Find out which ones and eliminate them from your choices.

- Does the insurer deny coverage for pre-existing conditions? If you are past the 6-month window following enrollment in Medicare Part B, companies most often deny you coverage for a specific period of time. However, some companies do not do this so their annual premium may be higher. You need to consider whether or not the higher premium is worth the coverage.

- Are you a member of AARP? If so, you may be able to obtain a policy through its sponsored insurer. Other affinity organizations also offer coverage through a Medigap insurer. Be sure to check with any groups of which you are a member.

- Do you want a Medicare Select plan? If you buy a Medicare Select policy, you are buying one of the 10 standardized Medigap plans A through N. With a Medicare Select plan, however, you must use the network providers to get full insurance benefits (except in an emergency). For this reason, Medicare Select policies generally cost less. If you don't use a Medicare Select hospital for non-emergency services, you will have to pay what a traditional Medicare plan doesn't pay. Medicare will pay its share of the approved charges no matter what hospital you choose.

3. Compare the premiums. Not only will you want to check out the premium you would be charged for different plans, but it is important to understand that there are three ways that insurance companies set the prices for policies. In order to compare the premium charged by two insurers for the same plan you need to make sure you are comparing apples to apples. No matter which type of pricing your Medigap insurer uses, the price of your policy will likely go up each year because of inflation and rising health care costs.

- **Attained-Age Rating.** With this type of policy the premium will rise as you age. For example: if you buy at 65, you pay what the company charges 65-year-old customers. Then at 66, you will pay whatever the company is charging a 66-year-old. The Medigap policy will go up in cost due to age, in addition to the increased cost of medical care.

- **Issue-Age Rating.** With this policy, the insurance company will charge you based on the age you were when you first signed up; you will always pay the same premium that someone that age pays. Unlike attained-age policies, issue-age policies do not go up because you are another year older. For example: if you first buy at 65, you will always pay the premium the company charges 65-year-old customers—no matter what your age. If you first buy at 70, you will always pay the premium the company charges 70-year-old customers. This is not to say that your premium won't go up. It will increase as the insurer raises rates for that particular age.

- **No-Age Rating or Community Rating.** This is the least common way that policies are priced. No matter how old you are, the policy costs the same. With this structure, younger people pay more than what they would pay for other polices and older people may pay less. The premium is the same for all people who buy this plan regardless of age. For example: XYZ Company will charge a 65-year-old $140, a 75-year-old $140 and an 85-year-old $140.

4. You may only be concerned with catastrophic illness. If so, you may not need to buy a Medigap policy at all, especially if you are relatively healthy, live a healthy lifestyle, and currently only incur routine medical expenses that would cost less than the premiums for a Medigap policy. You could purchase a catastrophic or high-deductible health insurance policy that would kick in when your medical bills exceeded a predetermined level, such as $6,550.

The Medigap K and L plans may also be a good choice. They should cost less than other Medigap plans but will provide a cap on out-of-pocket expenses.

5. What is the insurer's safety rating? If you were to experience the double misfortune of becoming seriously ill and having your insurer fail, you may be responsible for much of your unpaid claims, and it would be difficult to find replacement coverage.

We recommend you choose a company with a B+ or higher Weiss Safety Rating if you can. You should also consider an insurer's level of customer service and timeliness in reimbursing claims. Ask friends about their experiences and contact your state's insurance department or counsel for aging to find out if they keep public complaint records. As an industry, Medigap insurers have a good reputation for paying claims.

How to Switch Medigap Policies

If you are currently holding a Medigap policy and become uncomfortable with your company's financial stability, or if you find a cheaper policy at a stronger company, here are some steps to take before switching policies:

Step 1: Determine if your policy was issued prior to January 1, 1992. If it was, and if it was guaranteed renewable, you did not switch to one of the standard plans. This policy should be compared carefully to the newer standardized plans before switching. Remember: once you switch to one of the new standardized plans, you can never switch back to a non-standard plan.

Furthermore, you should know that if you already have a Medigap policy, it is against federal law for a company to sell you another one. When you buy another policy, you must sign a statement indicating that you are replacing your current policy and do not intend to keep both.

Step 2: Before switching policies, compare benefits and premiums. It is important to note that some of the older non-standard policies may provide superior coverage, and your increased age may make comparable coverage more expensive.

Step 3: Determine any impact on pre-existing conditions. Any portion of a pre-existing condition satisfied under the old policy will be credited to the new policy. Example: The old policy specified that it would not cover a pre-existing condition for the first six months. You switch policies after just two months. As a result, you only have four months to wait under the new policy to be covered for your pre-existing condition.
(Exception: If your new policy has a benefit that was not included in your old policy, a new six-month waiting period may be imposed on that particular benefit.)

Step 4: Use the "free-look" provision which allows you 30 days to review a Medigap policy once you've paid the first premium. If, during the first 30 days, you decide you don't want or need the policy you can return it to the company for a full refund.

Step 5: Do not cancel your old policy until your new policy is in force.

Part III:
Medigap Premium Rates

Basic Medigap Coverage
PLAN A

If you stay in the hospital for longer than 60 days, but less than 90 days, Plan A covers Medicare Part A coinsurance amount of $371 per day (in 2021) for each benefit period.

For each Medicare "hospital reserve day" you use, Plan A pays the $742 (in 2021) per day Medicare Part A coinsurance amount. "Hospital reserve days" are 60 nonrenewable hospital days that Medicare provides which can only be used once in a lifetime. After all Medicare hospital benefits are exhausted, Plan A will cover 100% of Medicare Part A eligible hospital expenses.

If the need arises, Plan A covers costs for the first three pints of blood or equivalent quantities of packed red blood cells received each year in connection with Medicare Parts A and B covered services. Once you have met this 3-pint blood deductible under Medicare Part A, it does not have to be met again under Part B.

After your $203 annual Medicare Part B deductible is met Plan A will cover the coinsurance amount for Medicare approved medical services, which is generally 20% of the approved amount.

Plan A now includes coverage of cost sharing for all Part A Medicare-eligible hospice care and respite care expenses.

If you feel that Plan A fits your needs, take a look at the two tables below to find out what price you should expect to be charged for this plan. The tables outline the typical annual premiums charged for Plan A depending on age and gender. These rates are based on our 2020 nationwide collection of insurance premiums.

PLAN A

Female

Age	Average Premium	Lowest Premium	Highest Premium	Median Premium
65	$ 1,707	$ 606	$ 18,018	$ 1,555
70	$ 1,899	$ 763	$ 20,500	$ 1,719
75	$ 2,190	$ 883	$ 22,106	$ 1,976
80	$ 2,439	$ 993	$ 26,008	$ 2,217
85	$ 2,668	$ 1,035	$ 28,332	$ 2,446
90	$ 2,858	$ 1,035	$ 30,073	$ 2,652
95	$ 3,007	$ 1,035	$ 30,073	$ 2,826

Male

Age	Average Premium	Lowest Premium	Highest Premium	Median Premium
65	$ 1,877	$ 656	$ 19,193	$ 1,731
70	$ 2,092	$ 827	$ 21,836	$ 1,909
75	$ 2,415	$ 958	$ 23,547	$ 2,201
80	$ 2,696	$ 1,076	$ 27,911	$ 2,470
85	$ 2,956	$ 1,122	$ 31,579	$ 2,738
90	$ 3,169	$ 1,122	$ 33,519	$ 2,976
95	$ 3,338	$ 1,122	$ 33,519	$ 3,177

Basic Medigap Coverage
PLAN B

If you stay in the hospital for longer than 60 days, but less than 90 days, Plan B covers Medicare Part A coinsurance amount of $371 per day (in 2021) for each benefit period.

For each Medicare "hospital reserve day" you use, Plan B pays the $742 (in 2021) per day Medicare Part A coinsurance amount. "Hospital reserve days" are 60 nonrenewable hospital days that Medicare provides which can only be used once in a lifetime. After all Medicare hospital benefits are exhausted, Plan B will cover 100% of Medicare Part A eligible hospital expenses.

If the need arises, Plan B covers costs for the first three pints of blood or equivalent quantities of packed red blood cells received each year in connection with Medicare Parts A and B covered services. Once you have met this 3-pint blood deductible under Medicare Part A, it does not have to be met again under Part B.

After your $203 annual Medicare Part B deductible is met Plan B will cover the coinsurance amount for Medicare approved medical services, which is generally 20% of the approved amount.

Plan B now includes coverage of cost sharing for all Part A Medicare-eligible hospice care and respite care expenses.

Additional Features

Plan B includes the core Medigap coverage PLUS one extra benefit:
- It will pay for the $1,484 Medicare Part A in-patient hospital deductible (per benefit period in 2021).

If you feel that Plan B fits your needs, take a look at the two tables below to find out what price you should expect to be charged for this plan. The tables outline the typical annual premiums charged for Plan B depending on age and gender. These rates are based on our 2020 nationwide collection of insurance premiums.

PLAN B

Female

Age	Average Premium	Lowest Premium	Highest Premium	Median Premium
65	$ 2,097	$ 975	$ 10,941	$ 1,892
70	$ 2,397	$ 1,041	$ 11,975	$ 2,226
75	$ 2,775	$ 1,115	$ 13,879	$ 2,641
80	$ 3,033	$ 1,323	$ 16,082	$ 2,862
85	$ 3,245	$ 1,686	$ 18,639	$ 3,055
90	$ 3,410	$ 1,686	$ 21,610	$ 3,211
95	$ 3,528	$ 1,686	$ 25,038	$ 3,316

Male

Age	Average Premium	Lowest Premium	Highest Premium	Median Premium
65	$ 2,286	$ 975	$ 12,587	$ 2,068
70	$ 2,611	$ 1,310	$ 13,770	$ 2,410
75	$ 3,029	$ 1,540	$ 15,953	$ 2,848
80	$ 3,320	$ 1,787	$ 18,496	$ 3,143
85	$ 3,560	$ 1,788	$ 21,447	$ 3,365
90	$ 3,745	$ 1,788	$ 28,840	$ 3,529
95	$ 3,878	$ 1,788	$ 28,798	$ 3,667

Basic Medigap Coverage
PLAN C

If you stay in the hospital for longer than 60 days, but less than 90 days, Plan C covers Medicare Part A coinsurance amount of $371 per day (in 2021) for each benefit period.

For each Medicare "hospital reserve day" you use, Plan C pays the $742 (in 2021) per day Medicare Part A coinsurance amount. "Hospital reserve days" are 60 nonrenewable hospital days that Medicare provides you which can only be used once in a lifetime. After all Medicare hospital benefits are exhausted, Plan C will cover 100% of Medicare Part A eligible hospital expenses.

If the need arises, Plan C covers costs for the first three pints of blood or equivalent quantities of packed red blood cells received each year in connection with Medicare Parts A and B covered services. Once you have met this 3-pint blood deductible under Medicare Part A, it does not have to be met again under Part B.

After your $203 annual Medicare Part B deductible is met, Plan C will cover the coinsurance amount of Medicare approved medical services, which is generally 20% of the approved amount

Plan C now includes coverage of cost sharing for all Part A Medicare-eligible hospice care and respite care expenses.

Additional Features

Plan C includes the core Medigap coverage, plus four extra benefits.
- Your $1,484 Medicare Part A in-patient hospital deductible (per benefit period in 2021)
- Your coinsurance amount for skilled nursing facility care for the 21st through the 100th day of your stay (the amount is $185.50 per day in 2021).
- Your Medicare Part B deductible ($203 per calendar year in 2021).
- Any emergency care you may require when you are in a foreign country after a $250 deductible. This benefit pays 80% of the cost of your care for the first 60 days of each trip, up to $50,000 in your lifetime.

Note: The only difference between Plan C and Plan D is the Part B deductible. Compare the prices between the plans before making your choice.

If you feel that Plan C fits your needs, take a look at the two tables below to find out what price you should expect to be charged for this plan. The tables outline the typical annual premiums charged for Plan C depending on age and gender. These rates are based on our 2020 nationwide collection of insurance premiums.

PLAN C

Female

Age	Average Premium	Lowest Premium	Highest Premium	Median Premium
65	$ 2,465	$ 1,114	$ 6,538	$ 2,205
70	$ 2,819	$ 1,374	$ 7,584	$ 2,586
75	$ 3,304	$ 1,629	$ 8,718	$ 3,119
80	$ 3,643	$ 1,923	$ 9,763	$ 3,470
85	$ 3,917	$ 1,962	$ 10,778	$ 3,737
90	$ 4,098	$ 1,962	$ 10,778	$ 3,951
95	$ 4,252	$ 1,962	$ 10,818	$ 4,106

Male

Age	Average Premium	Lowest Premium	Highest Premium	Median Premium
65	$ 2,678	$ 1,142	$ 6,999	$ 2,419
70	$ 3,069	$ 1,524	$ 8,718	$ 2,812
75	$ 3,597	$ 1,848	$ 10,028	$ 3,396
80	$ 3,978	$ 1,962	$ 10,990	$ 3,802
85	$ 4,286	$ 1,962	$ 12,736	$ 4,117
90	$ 4,490	$ 1,962	$ 12,736	$ 4,351
95	$ 4,662	$ 1,962	$ 12,736	$ 4,548

Basic Medigap Coverage
PLAN D

If you stay in the hospital for longer than 60 days, but less than 90 days, Plan D covers Medicare Part A coinsurance amount of $371 per day (in 2021) for each benefit period.

For each Medicare "hospital reserve day" you use, Plan D pays the $742 (in 2021) per day Medicare Part A coinsurance amount. "Hospital reserve days" are 60 nonrenewable hospital days that Medicare provides you which can only be used once in a lifetime. After all Medicare hospital benefits are exhausted, Plan D will cover 100% of Medicare Part A eligible hospital expenses.

If the need arises, Plan D covers costs for the first three pints of blood or equivalent quantities of packed red blood cells received each year in connection with Medicare Parts A and B covered services. Once you have met this 3-pint blood deductible under Medicare Part A, it does not have to be met again under Part B.

After your $203 annual Medicare Part B deductible is met, Plan D will cover the coinsurance amount of Medicare approved medical services, which is generally 20% of the approved amount

Plan D now includes coverage of cost sharing for all Part A Medicare-eligible hospice care and respite care expenses.

Additional Features
Plan D includes the core Medigap coverage, plus three extra benefits.
- Your $1,484 Medicare Part A in-patient hospital deductible (per benefit period in 2021).
- Your coinsurance amount for skilled nursing facility care for the 21st through the 100th day of your stay (the amount is $185.50 per day in 2021).
- Any emergency care you may require when you are in a foreign country after a $250 deductible. This benefit pays 80% of the cost of your care for the first 60 days of each trip, up to $50,000 in your lifetime.

Note: The only difference between Plan D and Plan C is the Part B deductible. Compare the prices between the plans before making your choice.

If you feel that Plan D fits your needs, take a look at the two tables below to find out what price you should expect to be charged for this plan. The tables outline the typical annual premiums charged for Plan D depending on age and gender. These rates are based on our 2020 nationwide collection of insurance premiums.

PLAN D

Female

Age	Average Premium	Lowest Premium	Highest Premium	Median Premium
65	$ 1,988	$ 1,010	$ 7,370	$ 1,836
70	$ 2,353	$ 1,104	$ 8,706	$ 2,190
75	$ 2,776	$ 1,278	$ 10,088	$ 2,632
80	$ 3,146	$ 1,481	$ 11,464	$ 3,031
85	$ 3,427	$ 1,675	$ 12,655	$ 3,329
90	$ 3,636	$ 1,675	$ 12,655	$ 3,532
95	$ 3,817	$ 1,675	$ 12,655	$ 3,712

Male

Age	Average Premium	Lowest Premium	Highest Premium	Median Premium
65	$ 2,204	$ 1,052	$ 7,388	$ 2,016
70	$ 2,624	$ 1,236	$ 8,983	$ 2,426
75	$ 3,108	$ 1,432	$ 10,923	$ 2,946
80	$ 3,532	$ 1,659	$ 12,905	$ 3,395
85	$ 3,854	$ 1,675	$ 14,956	$ 3,737
90	$ 4,091	$ 1,675	$ 14,956	$ 3,985
95	$ 4,296	$ 1,675	$ 14,956	$ 4,171

Basic Medigap Coverage
PLAN F

If you stay in the hospital for longer than 60 days, but less than 90 days, Plan F covers Medicare Part A coinsurance amount of $371 per day (in 2021) for each benefit period.

For each Medicare "hospital reserve day" you use, Plan F pays the $742 (in 2021) per day Medicare Part A coinsurance amount. "Hospital reserve days" are 60 nonrenewable hospital days that Medicare provides you which can only be used once in a lifetime. After all Medicare hospital benefits are exhausted, Plan F will cover 100% of Medicare Part A eligible hospital expenses.

If the need arises, Plan F covers costs for the first three pints of blood or equivalent quantities of packed red blood cells received each year in connection with Medicare Parts A and B covered services. Once you have met this 3-pint blood deductible under Medicare Part A, it does not have to be met again under Part B.

After your $203 annual Medicare Part B deductible is met, Plan F will cover the coinsurance amount of Medicare approved medical services, which is generally 20% of the approved amount. A high deductible option is available, requiring you to pay the first $2,370 of Medicare covered costs before your Medigap policy pays anything.

Plan F now includes coverage of cost sharing for all Part A Medicare-eligible hospice care and respite care expenses.

Additional Features

Plan F includes all of the basic Medigap coverage plus five extra benefits.

- Your $1,484 Medicare Part A in-patient hospital deductible (per benefit period in 2021).
- Your coinsurance amount for skilled nursing facility care for the 21st through the 100th day of your stay (the amount is $185.50 per day in 2021).
- Any emergency care you may require when you are in a foreign country after a $250 deductible. This benefit pays 80% of the cost of your care for the first 60 days of each trip, up to $50,000 in your lifetime.
- Your deductible for Medicare Part B ($203 in 2021).
- 100% of any excess charges under Medicare Part B. This is the difference between the approved amount for Part B services and the actual charges (up to the charge limitations set by either Medicare or state law).

Note: The only difference between Plan F and Plan G is the Part B deductible. Compare the prices between the plans before making your choice.

If you feel that Plan F fits your needs, take a look at the two tables below to find out what price you should expect to be charged for this plan. The tables outline the typical annual premiums charged for Plan F depending on age and gender. These rates are based on our 2020 nationwide collection of insurance premiums.

PLAN F

Female

Age	Average Premium	Lowest Premium	Highest Premium	Median Premium
65	$ 2,292	$ 1,050	$ 14,640	$ 2,094
70	$ 2,559	$ 1,268	$ 16,080	$ 2,387
75	$ 2,994	$ 1,497	$ 18,900	$ 2,822
80	$ 3,378	$ 1,760	$ 22,080	$ 3,183
85	$ 3,745	$ 1,820	$ 25,620	$ 3,531
90	$ 4,051	$ 1,820	$ 27,780	$ 3,843
95	$ 4,311	$ 1,820	$ 31,020	$ 4,117

Male

Age	Average Premium	Lowest Premium	Highest Premium	Median Premium
65	$ 2,516	$ 1,050	$ 16,620	$ 2,311
70	$ 2,812	$ 1,459	$ 18,420	$ 2,606
75	$ 3,294	$ 1,722	$ 21,780	$ 3,078
80	$ 3,725	$ 1,820	$ 25,500	$ 3,495
85	$ 4,141	$ 1,820	$ 29,580	$ 3,917
90	$ 4,483	$ 1,820	$ 32,040	$ 4,278
95	$ 4,775	$ 1,820	$ 35,760	$ 4,595

Basic Medigap Coverage
PLAN F with High Deductible

If you stay in the hospital for longer than 60 days, but less than 90 days, Plan F-High Deductible covers Medicare Part A coinsurance amount of $371 per day (in 2021) for each benefit period.

For each Medicare "hospital reserve day" you use, Plan F-High Deductible pays the $742 (in 2021) per day Medicare Part A coinsurance amount. "Hospital reserve days" are 60 nonrenewable hospital days that Medicare provides you which can only be used once in a lifetime. After all Medicare hospital benefits are exhausted, Plan F – High Deductible will cover 100% of Medicare Part A eligible hospital expenses.

If the need arises, Plan F-High Deductible covers costs for the first three pints of blood or equivalent quantities of packed red blood cells received each year in connection with Medicare Parts A and B covered services. Once you have met this 3-pint blood deductible under Medicare Part A, it does not have to be met again under Part B.

After your $203 annual Medicare Part B deductible is met, Plan F-High Deductible will cover the coinsurance amount of Medicare approved medical services, which is generally 20% of the approved amount.

Plan F High Deductible includes coverage of cost sharing for all Part A Medicare-eligible hospice care and respite care expenses.

Additional Features
Plan F includes all of the basic Medigap coverage plus five extra benefits.
- Your $1,484 Medicare Part A in-patient hospital deductible (per benefit period in 2021).
- Your coinsurance amount for skilled nursing facility care for the 21st through the 100th day of your stay (the amount is $185.50 per day in 2021).
- Any emergency care you may require when you are in a foreign country after a $250 deductible. This benefit pays 80% of the cost of your care for the first 60 days of each trip, up to $50,000 in your lifetime.
- Your deductible for Medicare Part B ($203 in 2021).
- 100% of any excess charges under Medicare Part B. This is the difference between the approved amount for Part B services and the actual charges (up to the charge limitations set by either Medicare or state law).

Important Notice:
You must meet a $2,370 deductible of unpaid Medicare eligible expenses before benefits are paid by this plan.

If you feel that Plan F with High Deductible fits your needs, take a look at the two tables below to find out what price you should expect to be charged for this plan. The tables outline the typical annual premiums charged for Plan F depending on age and gender. These rates are based on our 2020 nationwide collection of insurance premiums.

PLAN F: with High Deductible

Female

Age	Average Premium	Lowest Premium	Highest Premium	Median Premium
65	$ 642	$ 232	$ 2,008	$ 587
70	$ 731	$ 303	$ 2,162	$ 660
75	$ 859	$ 382	$ 2,476	$ 776
80	$ 981	$ 430	$ 2,715	$ 905
85	$ 1,095	$ 430	$ 3,178	$ 1,020
90	$ 1,177	$ 430	$ 3,908	$ 1,125
95	$ 1,240	$ 430	$ 3,908	$ 1,192

Male

Age	Average Premium	Lowest Premium	Highest Premium	Median Premium
65	$ 699	$ 266	$ 2,304	$ 640
70	$ 799	$ 340	$ 2,465	$ 720
75	$ 943	$ 400	$ 2,722	$ 847
80	$ 1,081	$ 463	$ 2,931	$ 989
85	$ 1,211	$ 474	$ 3,416	$ 1,125
90	$ 1,301	$ 474	$ 4,201	$ 1,252
95	$ 1,372	$ 474	$ 4,555	$ 1,330

Basic Medigap Coverage
PLAN G

If you stay in the hospital for longer than 60 days, but less than 90 days, Plan G covers Medicare Part A coinsurance amount of $371 per day (in 2021) for each benefit period.

For each Medicare "hospital reserve day" you use, Plan G pays the $742 (in 2021) per day Medicare Part A coinsurance amount. "Hospital reserve days" are 60 nonrenewable hospital days that Medicare provides you which can only be used once in a lifetime. After all Medicare hospital benefits are exhausted, Plan G will cover 100% of Medicare Part A eligible hospital expenses.

If the need arises, Plan G covers costs for the first three pints of blood or equivalent quantities of packed red blood cells received each year in connection with Medicare Parts A and B covered services. Once you have met this 3-pint blood deductible under Medicare Part A, it does not have to be met again under Part B.

After your $203 annual Medicare Part B deductible is met, Plan G will cover the coinsurance amount of Medicare approved medical services, which is generally 20% of the approved amount.

Plan G now includes coverage of cost sharing for all Part A Medicare-eligible hospice care and respite care

Additional Features
Plan G includes the core Medigap coverage plus four extra benefits.
- Your $1,484 Medicare Part A in-patient hospital deductible (per benefit period in 2021).
- Your coinsurance amount for skilled nursing care for the 21st through the 100th day of your stay (the amount is $185.50 per day in 2021).
- Any emergency care you may require when you are in a foreign country after a $250 deductible. This benefit pays 80% of the cost of your care for the first 60 days of each trip, up to $50,000 in your lifetime.
- 100% of any excess charges under Medicare Part B. Excess charges are the difference between the approved amount for Part B services and the actual charges (up to the charge limitations set by either Medicare or state law).

Note: The only difference between Plan G and Plan F is the Part B deductible.

Compare the prices between the plans before making your choice.

If you feel that Plan G fits your needs, take a look at the two tables below to find out what price you should expect to be charged for this plan. The tables outline the typical annual premiums charged for Plan G depending on age and gender. These rates are based on our 2020 nationwide collection of insurance premiums.

PLAN G

Female

Age	Average Premium	Lowest Premium	Highest Premium	Median Premium
65	$ 1,819	$ 935	$ 9,060	$ 1,631
70	$ 2,025	$ 1,025	$ 10,020	$ 1,825
75	$ 2,401	$ 1,229	$ 11,700	$ 2,178
80	$ 2,712	$ 1,457	$ 13,740	$ 2,471
85	$ 3,027	$ 1,525	$ 15,900	$ 2,802
90	$ 3,298	$ 1,525	$ 17,220	$ 3,116
95	$ 3,521	$ 1,525	$ 19,883	$ 3,371

Male

Age	Average Premium	Lowest Premium	Highest Premium	Median Premium
65	$ 2,003	$ 1,028	$ 10,380	$ 1,802
70	$ 2,233	$ 1,130	$ 11,400	$ 2,016
75	$ 2,648	$ 1,383	$ 13,500	$ 2,402
80	$ 2,997	$ 1,518	$ 15,780	$ 2,745
85	$ 3,351	$ 1,525	$ 18,360	$ 3,134
90	$ 3,655	$ 1,525	$ 19,860	$ 3,493
95	$ 3,908	$ 1,525	$ 22,868	$ 3,774

Basic Medigap Coverage
PLAN G with High Deductible

If you stay in the hospital for longer than 60 days, but less than 90 days, Plan G-High Deductible covers Medicare Part A coinsurance amount of $371 per day (in 2021) for each benefit period.

For each Medicare "hospital reserve day" you use, Plan G-High Deductible pays the $742 (in 2021) per day Medicare Part A coinsurance amount. "Hospital reserve days" are 60 nonrenewable hospital days that Medicare provides you which can only be used once in a lifetime. After all Medicare hospital benefits are exhausted, Plan G will cover 100% of Medicare Part A eligible hospital expenses.

If the need arises, Plan G-High Deductible covers costs for the first three pints of blood or equivalent quantities of packed red blood cells received each year in connection with Medicare Parts A and B covered services. Once you have met this 3-pint blood deductible under
Medicare Part A, it does not have to be met again under Part B.

After your $203 annual Medicare Part B deductible is met, Plan G will cover the coinsurance amount of Medicare approved medical services, which is generally 20% of the approved amount.

Plan G now includes coverage of cost sharing for all Part A Medicare-eligible hospice care and respite care

Additional Features
Plan G includes the core Medigap coverage plus four extra benefits.
- Your $1,484 Medicare Part A in-patient hospital deductible (per benefit period in 2021).
- Your coinsurance amount for skilled nursing care for the 21st through the 100th day of your stay (the amount is $185.50 per day in 2021).
- Any emergency care you may require when you are in a foreign country after a $250 deductible. This benefit pays 80% of the cost of your care for the first 60 days of each trip, up to $50,000 in your lifetime.
- 100% of any excess charges under Medicare Part B. Excess charges are the difference between the approved amount for Part B services and the actual charges (up to the charge limitations set by either Medicare or state law).

Important Notice:
You must meet a $2,370 deductible of unpaid Medicare eligible expenses before benefits are paid by this plan.

If you feel that Plan G with High Deductible fits your needs, take a look at the two tables below to find out what price you should expect to be charged for this plan. The tables outline the typical annual premiums charged for Plan G depending on age and gender. These rates are based on our 2020 nationwide collection of insurance premiums.

PLAN G: with High Deductible

Female

Age	Average Premium	Lowest Premium	Highest Premium	Median Premium
65	$ 574	$ 232	$ 3,414	$ 547
70	$ 654	$ 303	$ 3,720	$ 611
75	$ 772	$ 382	$ 4,311	$ 721
80	$ 888	$ 430	$ 4,998	$ 844
85	$ 999	$ 430	$ 5,800	$ 963
90	$ 1,085	$ 430	$ 6,718	$ 1,076
95	$ 1,151	$ 430	$ 7,786	$ 1,152

Male

Age	Average Premium	Lowest Premium	Highest Premium	Median Premium
65	$ 626	$ 266	$ 3,924	$ 603
70	$ 716	$ 349	$ 4,277	$ 673
75	$ 849	$ 440	$ 4,957	$ 797
80	$ 980	$ 474	$ 5,753	$ 941
85	$ 1,107	$ 474	$ 6,671	$ 1,077
90	$ 1,203	$ 474	$ 7,725	$ 1,198
95	$ 1,276	$ 474	$ 8,956	$ 1,278

Basic Medigap Coverage
PLAN K

If you stay in the hospital for longer than 60 days, but less than 90 days, Plan K covers Medicare Part A coinsurance amount of $371 per day (in 2021) for each benefit period.

For each Medicare "hospital reserve day" you use, Plan K pays the $742 (in 2021) per day Medicare Part A coinsurance amount. "Hospital reserve days" are 60 nonrenewable hospital days that Medicare provides you which can only be used once in a lifetime. After all Medicare hospital benefits are exhausted, Plan K will cover 100% of Medicare Part A eligible hospital expenses up to 365 days.

If the need arises, Plan K covers 50% of the costs for the first three pints of blood or equivalent quantities of packed red blood cells received each year in connection with Medicare Parts A and B covered services. Once you have met this 3-pint blood deductible under Medicare Part A, it does not have to be met again under Part B.

After your $203 annual Medicare Part B deductible is met, Plan K will cover 50% of the coinsurance amount of Medicare approved medical services, which is generally 20% of the approved amount.

Additional Features

Plan K includes four additional benefits.

- 50% of your $1,484 Medicare Part A in-patient hospital deductible (per benefit period in 2021).
- 50% of your coinsurance amount for skilled nursing facility care for the 21st through the 100th day of your stay (the amount is $185.50 per day in 2021).
- 100% coinsurance for medicare-covered preventive medical care. Preventive care would include physical examinations, flu shots, serum cholesterol screening, hearing tests, diabetes screening, and thyroid function tests.
- 50% of hospice cost-sharing for all Part A Medicare covered expenses and respite care.

Note: There is a $6,220 out-of-pocket annual limit. Once you meet the annual limit, the plans pays 100% of the Medicare Part A and Part B co-payments and coinsurance for the rest of the calendar year. "Excess charges" are not covered and do not count toward the out-of-pocket limit.

If you feel that Plan K fits your needs, take a look at the two tables below to find out what price you should expect to be charged for this plan. The tables outline the typical annual premiums charged for Plan K depending on age and gender. These rates are based on our 2020 nationwide collection of insurance premiums.

PLAN K

Female

Age	Average Premium	Lowest Premium	Highest Premium	Median Premium
65	$ 1,028	$ 396	$ 4,488	$ 948
70	$ 1,187	$ 488	$ 4,753	$ 1,145
75	$ 1,345	$ 581	$ 5,508	$ 1,328
80	$ 1,471	$ 618	$ 6,385	$ 1,462
85	$ 1,569	$ 618	$ 7,398	$ 1,561
90	$ 1,637	$ 618	$ 8,582	$ 1,606
95	$ 1,679	$ 618	$ 9,942	$ 1,616

Male

Age	Average Premium	Lowest Premium	Highest Premium	Median Premium
65	$ 1,096	$ 396	$ 5,154	$ 1,021
70	$ 1,273	$ 488	$ 5,460	$ 1,237
75	$ 1,447	$ 581	$ 6,338	$ 1,430
80	$ 1,592	$ 618	$ 7,344	$ 1,575
85	$ 1,707	$ 618	$ 8,507	$ 1,683
90	$ 1,780	$ 618	$ 9,867	$ 1,723
95	$ 1,827	$ 618	$ 11,438	$ 1,753

Basic Medigap Coverage
PLAN L

If you stay in the hospital for longer than 60 days, but less than 90 days, Plan L covers Medicare Part A coinsurance amount of $371 per day (in 2021) for each benefit period.

For each Medicare "hospital reserve day" you use, Plan L pays the $742 (in 2021) per day Medicare Part A coinsurance amount. "Hospital reserve days" are 60 nonrenewable hospital days that Medicare provides you which can only be used once in a lifetime. After all Medicare hospital benefits are exhausted, Plan L will cover 100% of Medicare Part A eligible hospital expenses up to 365 days.

If the need arises, Plan L covers 75% of the costs for the first three pints of blood or equivalent quantities of packed red blood cells received each year in connection with Medicare Parts A and B covered services. Once you have met this 3-pint blood deductible under Medicare Part A, it does not have to be met again under Part B.

After your $203 annual Medicare Part B deductible is met, Plan L will cover 75% of the coinsurance amount of Medicare approved medical services, which is generally 20% of the approved amount.

Additional Features

Plan L includes four additional benefits.

- 75% of your $1,484 Medicare Part A in-patient hospital deductible (per benefit period in 2021).
- 75% of your coinsurance amount for skilled nursing facility care for the 21st through the 100th day of your stay (the amount is $185.50 per day in 2021).
- 100% coinsurance for medicare-covered preventive medical care. Preventive care would include physical examinations, flu shots, serum cholesterol screening, hearing tests, diabetes screening, and thyroid function tests.
- 75% of hospice cost-sharing for all Part A Medicare covered expenses and respite care.

Note: There is a $3,110 out-of-pocket annual limit. Once you meet the annual limit, the plans pays 100% of the Medicare Part A and Part B co-payments and coinsurance for the rest of the calendar year. "Excess charges" are not covered and do not count toward the out-of-pocket limit.

If you feel that Plan L fits your needs, take a look at the two tables below to find out what price you should expect to be charged for this plan. The tables outline the typical annual premiums charged for Plan L depending on age and gender. These rates are based on our 2020 nationwide collection of insurance premiums.

PLAN L

Female

Age	Average Premium	Lowest Premium	Highest Premium	Median Premium
65	$ 1,662	$ 671	$ 5,651	$ 1,568
70	$ 1,909	$ 711	$ 5,984	$ 1,890
75	$ 2,176	$ 825	$ 6,943	$ 2,163
80	$ 2,368	$ 956	$ 8,044	$ 2,326
85	$ 2,512	$ 980	$ 9,.323	$ 2,430
90	$ 2,624	$ 980	$ 10,805	$ 2,435
95	$ 2,693	$ 980	$ 12,526	$ 2,437

Male

Age	Average Premium	Lowest Premium	Highest Premium	Median Premium
65	$ 1,787	$ 747	$ 6,494	$ 1,712
70	$ 2,062	$ 818	$ 6,882	$ 2,056
75	$ 2,350	$ 950	$ 7,983	$ 2,352
80	$ 2,566	$ 980	$ 9,284	$ 2,519
85	$ 2,732	$ 980	$ 10,717	$ 2,635
90	$ 2,883	$ 980	$ 12,430	$ 2,641
95	$ 2,930	$ 980	$ 14,409	$ 2,643

Basic Medigap Coverage
PLAN M

If you stay in the hospital for longer than 60 days, but less than 90 days, Plan M covers the Medicare Part A coinsurance amount, $371 per day (in 2021) for each benefit period.

For each Medicare "hospital reserve day" you use, Plan M pays the Medicare Part A coinsurance amount, $742 (in 2021) per day. "Hospital reserve days" are 60 nonrenewable hospital days that Medicare provides you which can only be used once in a lifetime. After all Medicare hospital benefits are exhausted, Plan M will cover 100% of Medicare Part A eligible hospital expenses.

If the need arises, Plan M covers costs for the first three pints of blood or equivalent quantities of packed red blood cells received each year in connection with Medicare Parts A and B covered services. Once you have met this 3-pint blood deductible under Medicare Part A, it does not have to be met again under Part B.

After your $203 annual Medicare Part B deductible is met, Plan M will cover the coinsurance amount of Medicare approved medical services, which is generally 20% of the approved amount.

Coverage of cost sharing for all Part A Medicare eligible hospice care and respite care expense is included.

Additional Features

Plan M includes the core Medigap coverage, plus three extra benefits.

- 50% of your Medicare Part A in-patient hospital deductible ($1,484 per benefit period in 2021).
- Your coinsurance amount for skilled nursing facility care for the 21st through the 100th day of your stay (the amount is $185.50 per day in 2021).
- Any emergency care you may require when you are in a foreign country after a $250 deductible. This benefit pays 80% of the cost of your care for the first 60 days of each trip, up to $50,000 in your lifetime.

If you feel that Plan M fits your needs, take a look at the two tables below to find out what price you should expect to be charged for this plan. The tables outline the typical annual premiums charged for Plan M depending on age and gender. These rates are based on our 2020 nationwide collection of insurance premiums.

PLAN M

Female

Age	Average Premium	Lowest Premium	Highest Premium	Median Premium
65	$ 1,948	$ 954	$ 7,800	$ 1,892
70	$ 2,213	$ 1,048	$ 8,520	$ 2,266
75	$ 2,752	$ 1,214	$ 10,020	$ 2,718
80	$ 3,175	$ 1,407	$ 11,700	$ 3,154
85	$ 3,540	$ 1,424	$ 13,560	$ 3,471
90	$ 3,858	$ 1,424	$ 14,700	$ 3,639
95	$ 4,067	$ 1,424	$ 16,440	$ 3,755

Male

Age	Average Premium	Lowest Premium	Highest Premium	Median Premium
65	$ 2,143	$ 954	$ 8,760	$ 2,091
70	$ 2,553	$ 1,174	$ 9,720	$ 2,491
75	$ 3,050	$ 1,360	$ 11,520	$ 2,984
80	$ 3,524	$ 1,424	$ 13,500	$ 3,479
85	$ 3,929	$ 1,424	$ 15,660	$ 3,877
90	$ 4,283	$ 1,424	$ 16,920	$ 4,049
95	$ 4,516	$ 1,424	$ 18,900	$ 4,184

Basic Medigap Coverage
PLAN N

If you stay in the hospital for longer than 60 days, but less than 90 days, Plan N covers the Medicare Part A coinsurance amount, $371 per day (in 2021) for each benefit period.

For each Medicare "hospital reserve day" you use, Plan N pays the Medicare Part A coinsurance amount, $742 (in 2021) per day. "Hospital reserve days" are 60 nonrenewable hospital days that Medicare provides you which can only be used once in a lifetime. After all Medicare hospital benefits are exhausted, Plan N will cover 100% of Medicare Part A eligible hospital expenses.

If the need arises, Plan N covers costs for the first three pints of blood or equivalent quantities of packed red blood cells received each year in connection with Medicare Parts A and B covered services. Once you have met this 3-pint blood deductible under Medicare Part A, it does not have to be met again under Part B.

After your $203 annual Medicare Part B deductible is met, Plan N will cover the coinsurance amount of Medicare approved medical services, which is generally 20% of the approved amount.

Coverage of cost sharing for all Part A Medicare eligible hospice care and respite care expense is included.

Additional Features

Plan N includes the core Medigap coverage, plus four extra features and benefits.
- Your Medicare Part A in-patient hospital deductible ($1,484 per benefit period in 2021).
- You will have a co-payment of up to $20 per physician visit or $50 per Emergency Room visit under Part B. The ER co-pay will be waived if admitted.
- Your coinsurance amount for skilled nursing facility care for the 21st through the 100th day of your stay (the amount is $185.50 per day in 2021).
- Any emergency care you may require when you are in a foreign country after a $250 deductible. This benefit pays 80% of the cost of your care for the first 60 days of each trip, up to $50,000 in your lifetime.

If you feel that Plan N fits your needs, take a look at the two tables below to find out what price you should expect to be charged for this plan. The tables outline the typical annual premiums charged for Plan N depending on age and gender. These rates are based on our 2020 nationwide collection of insurance premiums.

PLAN N

Female

Age	Average Premium	Lowest Premium	Highest Premium	Median Premium
65	$ 1,488	$ 750	$ 7,380	$ 1,334
70	$ 1,676	$ 805	$ 7,980	$ 1,529
75	$ 2,002	$ 993	$ 9,420	$ 1,832
80	$ 2,262	$ 1,063	$ 10,980	$ 2,088
85	$ 2,518	$ 1,093	$ 12,780	$ 2,346
90	$ 2,746	$ 1,093	$ 14,110	$ 2,602
95	$ 2,934	$ 1,093	$ 16,354	$ 2,818

Male

Age	Average Premium	Lowest Premium	Highest Premium	Median Premium
65	$ 1,630	$ 750	$ 8,466	$ 1,460
70	$ 1,841	$ 892	$ 9,240	$ 1,670
75	$ 2,200	$ 1,018	$ 10,860	$ 2,003
80	$ 2,491	$ 1,063	$ 12,720	$ 2,294
85	$ 2,781	$ 1,093	$ 14,760	$ 2,600
90	$ 3,037	$ 1,093	$ 16,225	$ 2,903
95	$ 3,251	$ 1,093	$ 18,802	$ 3,143

Part IV:
Index of Medigap Insurers

Following is a reference list of Medicare supplement insurers with their
Weiss Safety Rating, corporate address, phone number,
and the states in which they are licensed to do business.

RATING	INSURANCE COMPANY NAME	ADDRESS	CITY	STATE	ZIP	PHONE
C-	AETNA HEALTH & LIFE INS CO	151 FARMINGTON AVENUE	HARTFORD	CT	6156	(800) 872-3862
B	AETNA LIFE INS CO	151 FARMINGTON AVENUE	HARTFORD	CT	6156	(800) 872-3862
C	AMALGAMATED LIFE & HEALTH INS CO	333 SOUTH ASHLAND AVENUE	CHICAGO	IL	60607	(914) 367-5000
C+	AMERICAN CONTINENTAL INS CO	1021 REAMS FLEMING BOULEVARD	FRANKLIN	TN	37064	(800) 264-4000
B-	AMERICAN NATIONAL LIFE INS CO OF TX	ONE MOODY PLAZA	GALVESTON	TX	77550	(409) 763-4661
C	AMERICAN PROGRESSIVE L&H I C OF NY	ONE NEW YORK PLAZA, 15 FLOOR	NEW YORK	NY	10004	(314) 725-4477
C	AMERICAN REPUBLIC CORP INS CO	601 SIXTH AVE	DES MOINES	IA	50309	(866) 705-9100
B-	AMERICAN REPUBLIC INS CO	601 SIXTH AVENUE	DES MOINES	IA	50309	(800) 247-2190
C+	AMERICAN RETIREMENT LIFE INS CO	1300 EAST NINTH STREET	CLEVELAND	OH	44114	(512) 451-2224
B-	AMERICO FINANCIAL LIFE & ANNUITY INS	PO BOX 139061	DALLAS	TX	75313	(816) 391-2000
C-	ATLANTIC COAST LIFE INS CO	1565 SAM RITTENBERG BOULEVARD	CHARLESTON	SC	29407	(844) 442-3847
D	BANKERS CONSECO LIFE INS CO	350 JERICHO TURNPIKE SUITE 304	JERICHO	NY	11753	(317) 817-6100
C	BANKERS FIDELITY ASR CO	4370 PEACHTREE RD NE	ATLANTA	GA	30319	(800) 241-1439
C-	BANKERS FIDELITY LIFE INS CO	4370 PEACHTREE ROAD NE	ATLANTA	GA	30319	(800) 241-1439
D+	BANKERS LIFE & CAS CO	111 EAST WACKER DRIVE STE 2100	CHICAGO	IL	60601	(312) 396-6000
B	BLUE CROSS BLUE SHIELD OF KANSAS INC	1133 SW TOPEKA BOULEVARD	TOPEKA	KS	66629	(785) 291-7000
B	CENTRAL STATES H & L CO OF OMAHA	1212 NORTH 96TH STREET	OMAHA	NE	68114	(402) 397-1111
A-	CHRISTIAN FIDELITY LIFE INS CO	1999 BRYAN STREET SUITE 900	DALLAS	TX	75201	(602) 263-6666
B	CIGNA HEALTH & LIFE INS CO	900 COTTAGE GROVE ROAD	BLOOMFIELD	CT	6002	(860) 226-6000
B	CIGNA NATIONAL HEALTH INS CO	1300 EAST NINTH STREET	CLEVELAND	OH	44114	(512) 451-2224
D+	COLONIAL PENN LIFE INS CO	399 MARKET STREET	PHILADELPHIA	PA	19181	(215) 928-8000
B	COLUMBIAN MUTUAL LIFE INS CO	4704 VESTAL PKWY E PO BOX 1381	BINGHAMTON	NY	13902	(607) 724-2472
C	COMBINED INS CO OF AMERICA	111 E WACKER DRIVE	CHICAGO	IL	60601	(800) 225-4500
B+	COMPANION LIFE INS CO	2501 FARAWAY DRIVE	COLUMBIA	SC	29219	(803) 735-1251
C+	CONTINENTAL GENERAL INS CO	11001 LAKELINE BLVD STE 120	AUSTIN	TX	78717	(866) 830-0607
C+	CONTINENTAL LIFE INS CO OF BRENTWOOD	1021 REAMS FLEMING BOULEVARD	FRANKLIN	TN	37064	(800) 264-4000
A+	COUNTRY LIFE INS CO	1701 N TOWANDA AVENUE	BLOOMINGTON	IL	61701	(309) 821-3000
B-	CSI LIFE INS CO	1212 NORTH 96TH STREET	OMAHA	NE	68114	(402) 997-8000
B	ERIE FAMILY LIFE INS CO	100 ERIE INSURANCE PLACE	ERIE	PA	16530	(814) 870-2000
C	FAMILY LIFE INS CO	10777 NORTHWEST FREEWAY	HOUSTON	TX	77092	(713) 529-0045
C+	FIRST HEALTH LIFE & HEALTH INS CO	3200 HIGHLAND AVENUE	DOWNERS GROVE	IL	60515	(630) 737-7900
B	FORETHOUGHT LIFE INS CO	10 W MARKET ST STE 2300	INDIANAPOLIS	IN	46204	(317) 223-2700
C-	GENWORTH LIFE & ANNUITY INS CO	6610 WEST BROAD STREET	RICHMOND	VA	23230	(804) 662-2400
C	GENWORTH LIFE INS CO	251 LITTLE FALLS DR	WILMINGTON	DE	19808	(804) 662-2400
B+	GERBER LIFE INS CO	1311 MAMARONECK AVENUE	WHITE PLAINS	NY	10605	(914) 272-4000
C+	GLOBE LIFE & ACCIDENT INS CO	10306 REGENCY PARKWAY DRIVE	OMAHA	NE	68114	(972) 569-3744
B	GLOBE LIFE INSURANCE CO OF NY	301 PLAINFIELD RD STE 150	SYRACUSE	NY	13212	(315) 451-2544
B	GOLDEN RULE INS CO	7440 WOODLAND DRIVE	INDIANAPOLIS	IN	46278	(317) 290-8100
B-	GOVERNMENT PERSONNEL MUTUAL L I C	2211 NE LOOP 410	SAN ANTONIO	TX	78217	(210) 357-2222
B	GPM HEALTH & LIFE INS CO	1124 W RIVERSIDE AVE STE 400	SPOKANE	WA	99201	(210) 357-2222
B-	GREAT AMERICAN LIFE INS CO	301 EAST FOURTH STREET	CINCINNATI	OH	45202	(800) 228-2860
B-	GREAT SOUTHERN LIFE INS CO	PO BOX 139061	DALLAS	TX	75313	(816) 391-2000
B	GUARANTEE TRUST LIFE INS CO	1275 MILWAUKEE AVENUE	GLENVIEW	IL	60025	(847) 699-0600
B-	HARTFORD LIFE & ACCIDENT INS CO	ONE HARTFORD PLAZA	HARTFORD	CT	06155	(860) 547-5000
B+	HEALTH CARE SVC CORP A MUT LEG RES	300 EAST RANDOLPH STREET	CHICAGO	IL	60601	(312) 653-6000
C	HEALTH NET LIFE INS CO	21281 BURBANK BOULEVARD B3	WOODLAND HILLS	CA	91367	(314) 725-4477
C	HEARTLAND NATIONAL LIFE INS CO	401 PENNSYLVANIA PKWY STE 300	INDIANAPOLIS	IN	46280	(816) 478-0120
B-	HUMANA INS CO OF KENTUCKY	500 WEST MAIN STREET	LOUISVILLE	KY	40202	(502) 580-1000
D+	INDIVIDUAL ASR CO LIFE HEALTH & ACC	5500 WESTERN AVE SUITE 200	OKLAHOMA CITY	OK	73118	(405) 285-0838
C+	LIBERTY BANKERS LIFE INS CO	1605 LBJ FREEWAY SUITE 710	DALLAS	TX	75234	(469) 522-4400
B	LIBERTY NATIONAL LIFE INS CO	10306 REGENCY PARKWAY DR	OMAHA	NE	68114	(972) 569-4000
B-	LINCOLN HERITAGE LIFE INS CO	920 S SPRING ST	SPRINGFIELD	IL	62704	(602) 957-1650

RATING	INSURANCE COMPANY NAME	ADDRESS	CITY	STATE	ZIP	PHONE
B	LOYAL AMERICAN LIFE INS CO	1300 EAST NINTH STREET	CLEVELAND	OH	44114	(512) 451-2224
C	LUMICO LIFE INSURANCE CO	237 E HIGH ST	JEFFERSON CITY	MO	65101	(877) 794-7773
B	MANHATTAN LIFE INS CO	225 COMMUNITY DRIVE SUITE 11	GREAT NECK	NY	11021	(713) 529-0045
B	MASSACHUSETTS MUTUAL LIFE INS CO	1295 STATE STREET	SPRINGFIELD	MA	1111	(413) 788-8411
B-	MEDICO CORP LIFE INS CO	601 SIXTH AVE	DES MOINES	IA	50309	(800) 822-9993
B-	MEDICO INS CO	601 Sixth Ave	DES MOINES	IA	50309	(800) 228-6080
C	MEDICO LIFE & HEALTH INS CO	601 6TH AVENUE	DES MOINES	IA	50309	(800) 228-6080
C+	MUTUAL OF OMAHA INS CO	MUTUAL OF OMAHA PLAZA	OMAHA	NE	68175	(402) 342-7600
D	NASSAU LIFE INS CO OF KS	10851 MASTIN BLVD STE 1000	OVERLAND PARK	KS	66210	(407) 547-3336
D	NASSAU LIFE INS COMPANY OF TEXAS	701 BRAZOS STE 1500	AUSTIN	TX	78701	(407) 547-3800
B	NATIONAL GUARDIAN LIFE INS CO	2 EAST GILMAN STREET	MADISON	WI	53703	(608) 257-5611
B-	NATIONWIDE LIFE INS CO	ONE WEST NATIONWIDE BLVD	COLUMBUS	OH	43215	(614) 249-7111
C	NEW ERA LIFE INS CO	11720 KATY FREEWAY SUITE 1700	HOUSTON	TX	77079	(281) 368-7159
C+	NEW ERA LIFE INS CO OF THE MIDWEST	11720 KATY FREEWAY SUITE 1700	HOUSTON	TX	77079	(281) 368-7159
A-	NEW YORK LIFE INS CO	51 MADISON AVENUE	NEW YORK	NY	10010	(212) 576-7000
B+	NORTH AMERICAN INS CO	575 DONOFRIO DRIVE SUITE 100	MADISON	WI	53719	(877) 667-9368
C	OLD SURETY LIFE INS CO	5201 NORTH LINCOL BLVD	OKLAHOMA CITY	OK	73105	(405) 523-2112
B-	OMAHA INS CO	3300 MUTUAL OF OMAHA PLAZA	OMAHA	NE	68175	(402) 342-7600
B	OMAHA SUPPLEMENTAL INS CO	3300 MUTUAL OF OMAHA PLAZA	OMAHA	NE	68175	(402) 342-7600
B+	OXFORD LIFE INS CO	2721 NORTH CENTRAL AVENUE	PHOENIX	AZ	85004	(602) 263-6666
B-	PACIFICARE LIFE & HEALTH INS CO	7440 WOODLAND DRIVE	INDIANAPOLIS	IN	46278	(612) 383-4182
B	PAN-AMERICAN LIFE INS CO	PAN-AMERICAN LIFE CENTER	NEW ORLEANS	LA	70130	(504) 566-1300
B	PEKIN LIFE INS CO	2505 COURT STREET	PEKIN	IL	61558	(309) 346-1161
B	PHILADELPHIA AMERICAN LIFE INS CO	11720 KATY FREEWAY SUITE 1700	HOUSTON	TX	77079	(281) 368-7159
A-	PHYSICIANS LIFE INS CO	2600 DODGE STREET	OMAHA	NE	68131	(402) 633-1000
A+	PHYSICIANS MUTUAL INS CO	2600 DODGE STREET	OMAHA	NE	68131	(402) 633-1000
B+	PRINCIPAL LIFE INS CO	711 HIGH STREET	DES MOINES	IA	50392	(515) 247-5111
B	PROVIDENT AMER LIFE & HEALTH INS CO	1300 EAST NINTH STREET	CLEVELAND	OH	44114	(512) 451-2224
C	PURITAN LIFE INS CO OF AMERICA	8601 N SCHOTTSDALE ROAD, SUITE	SCOTTSDALE	AZ	85253	(888) 474-9519
B	RENAISSANCE L&H INS CO OF AMERICA	225 S EAST STREET SUITE 360	INDIANAPOLIS	IN	46202	(517) 349-6000
B-	RESERVE NATIONAL INS CO	200 EAST RANDOLPH STREET SUIT	CHICAGO	IL	60601	(405) 848-7931
B-	S USA LIFE INS CO INC	8825 NORTH 23RD AVENUE SUITE	PHOENIX	AZ	85021	(212) 356-0300
B-	SBLI USA MUT LIFE INS CO INC	100 WEST 33RD STREET STE 1007	NEW YORK	NY	10001	(212) 356-0300
D	SENTINEL SECURITY LIFE INS CO	1405 WEST 2200 SOUTH	SALT LAKE CITY	UT	84119	(801) 484-8514
B-	SHENANDOAH LIFE INS CO	4415 PHEASANT RIDGE RD STE 300	ROANOKE	VA	24014	(540) 985-4400
D+	SILAC INSURANCE CO	299 S MAIN ST #1100	SALT LAKE CITY	UT	84111	(801) 579-3400
B	STANDARD LIFE & ACCIDENT INS CO	ONE MOODY PLAZA	GALVESTON	TX	77550	(409) 763-4661
D	STANDARD LIFE & CAS INS CO	4525 S WASATCH BLVD, SUITE 150	SALT LAKE CITY	UT	84124	(801) 538-0376
D	STATE MUTUAL INS CO	210 E SECOND AVENUE SUITE 301	ROME	GA	30161	(706) 291-1054
C	STERLING INVESTORS LIFE INS CO	10201 N ILLINOIS ST SUITE 280	CARMEL	IN	46290	(317) 208-2200
B-	STERLING LIFE INS CO	525 W MONROE ST	CHICAGO	IL	60661	(512) 451-2224
D+	STERLING NATL LIFE INS CO	299 S MAIN ST #1100	SALT LAKE CITY	UT	84111	(801) 579-3400
B-	TALCOTT RESOLUTION LIFE INS CO	1 GRIFFIN ROAD N	WINDSOR	CT	06095	(800) 862-6668
B	TRANSAMERICA FINANCIAL LIFE INS CO	440 MAMARONECK AVENUE	HARRISON	NY	10528	(914) 627-3630
C+	TRANSAMERICA LIFE INS CO	4333 EDGEWOOD RD NE	CEDAR RAPIDS	IA	52499	(319) 355-8511
B	UNICARE LIFE & HEALTH INS CO	220 VIRGINIA AVENUE	INDIANAPOLIS	IN	46204	(877) 864-2273
B	UNIFIED LIFE INS CO	CT CORPORATION SYSTEM 1999 BRY	DALLAS	TX	75201	(877) 492-4678
B	UNION SECURITY INS CO	2900 SW WANAMAKER DR STE 400	TOPEKA	KS	66614	(651) 361-4000
B	UNITED AMERICAN INS CO	10306 REGENCY PARKWAY DR	OMAHA	NE	68114	(972) 529-5085
C	UNITED HEALTHCARE INS CO	185 ASYLUM STREET	HARTFORD	CT	06103	(877) 832-7734
B	UNITED HEALTHCARE INS CO OF NY	2950 EXPRESSWAY DRIVE SOUTH S	ISLANDIA	NY	11749	(877) 832-7734
B	UNITED NATIONAL LIFE INS CO OF AM	1275 MILWAUKEE AVENUE	GLENVIEW	IL	60025	(847) 803-5252

RATING	INSURANCE COMPANY NAME	ADDRESS	CITY	STATE	ZIP	PHONE
B	UNITED OF OMAHA LIFE INS CO	3300 MUTUAL OF OMAHA PLAZA	OMAHA	NE	68175	(402) 342-7600
B+	UNITED WORLD LIFE INS CO	3300 MUTUAL OF OMAHA PLAZA	OMAHA	NE	68175	(402) 342-7600
B-	UNIVERSAL FIDELITY LIFE INS CO	13931 QUAIL POINTE DRIVE	OKLAHOMA CITY	OK	73134	(800) 366-8354
A	USAA LIFE INS CO	9800 FREDERICKSBURG RD	SAN ANTONIO	TX	78288	(210) 531-8722
D+	WASHINGTON NATIONAL INS CO	11825 NORTH PENNSYLVANIA STREE	CARMEL	IN	46032	(317) 817-6100
B-	WESTERN UNITED LIFE ASR CO	929 WEST SPRAGUE AVE	SPOKANE	WA	99201	(713) 529-0045

Section VII

Analysis of Medicare Managed Care Complaints

An analysis of complaints filed against

U.S. Medicare Managed Care Plans

Companies are listed in alphabetical order.

Section VII Contents

As discussed in the previous section, no single measure is an end-all indicator of the quality of service provided by a health insurer. However, if you are a Medicare beneficiary, complaint information can give you a preliminary basis for informed shopping – especially for Medicare Managed Care plans. It will answer questions such as: Does the company have a high rate of enrollee complaints against it? Are most complaints upheld or overturned? Are many withdrawn before a decision is rendered?

The complaint information on the following pages will give you an indication of what beneficiaries, like yourself, have experienced with various Medicare insurers. This section is based on "reconsideration" data, reprinted from the Centers for Medicare and Medicaid Services (formerly known as Health Care Financing Administration) for providers with Medicare contracts.

"Reconsiderations" are complaints by members of Medicare Managed Care plans that have reached a federal review. Once they reach that stage, the complaints have already gone through at least two levels of internal appeals. Consequently, they are relatively serious and involve anywhere from several hundred dollars to many thousands of dollars of unpaid medical bills. In this section, all complaints cited are reconsiderations.

Complaints that were settled within the Plan's internal appeal process are not reflected. It is difficult to say what types of complaints these might be, but, in general, they are more likely to pertain to services of a lower dollar value.

We have made no attempt to render an opinion on the data contained in this section. Rather, we are reprinting the information strictly to help provide you with valuable information when shopping for a Medicare plan.

The Drawbacks of Complaint Data

One problem with the data is the time lag due to the lengthy reconsideration process. A company that has a high complaint rate in this section may have already begun to make improvements in its system to handle the types of issues that were raised in the complaints. Therefore, because it takes so long for a complaint to make it through the federal process, the company may appear to have worse service quality than it currently has.

Conversely, numerous companies that have obtained Medicare contracts very recently (within the past year), may show few or no complaints. But this may reflect merely the fact that the complaints filed against these companies have not yet reached the federal level. So before you make a final decision to select a company with a low level of complaints, find out how long it has had its Medicare contract. We estimate that the contract should be in force for about two years before these data reflect the complaints.

If you are interested in a company with a seemingly high complaint level, do take the time to ask the company what improvements, if any, it has made to correct the problems reflected in the complaint data. If a high rate of complaints against it have been upheld at the federal level, it will be far more difficult to explain away.

The plans included here are those from whom reconsiderations were received during 2020 or companies that had members enrolled in a specific Medicare contract as of July of that year. Not included are: 1) updates for later appeals of cases that have been decided and 2) companies whose contracts are so new that they don't have any current enrollment.

The plan name in this table represents one or more contracts with the Centers for Medicare and Medicaid Services (CMS). You may find some plans listed more than once; this is because they have contracts in different CMS-designated regions (see Column 3). If a plan has more than one contract in a particular region, the reconsideration data have been combined so that the company is only listed once for each region.

Three types of Medicare contracts are included here: risk, cost, and Health Care Prepayment Plans (HCPPs). A Medicare risk contract is one in which the CMS pays the plan a capitalization rate equal to a percentage of the average fee-for-service expense, in a given geographic area. A Medicare cost contract is one in which the CMS reimburses the plan for retroactively determined Part A and B costs. And an HCPP contract is similar to a cost contract but only Part B costs are paid by the CMS.

The following **BOLD** headings are the column reference guides for the tables

1. **Insurance Company Name**   The legally-registered name, which sometimes can differ from the name that the plan uses for advertising. If you cannot find the plan you are interested in, or if you have any doubts regarding the precise name, verify the information before looking it up in this Guide. Also, determine the domicile state for confirmation.

2. **Domicile State**   The state which has primary regulatory responsibility for the company. It may differ from the location of the company's corporate headquarters. You do not have to be living in the domicile state to purchase insurance from this firm, provided it is licensed to do business in your state.

   Also use this column to confirm that you have located the correct company. It is possible for two unrelated companies to have the same name if they are domiciled in different states.

3. **Safety Rating**   Our rating is measured on a scale from A to F and considers a wide range of factors. Highly-rated companies are, in our opinion, less likely to experience financial difficulties than lower rated firms. See *About Weiss Safety Ratings* for more information.

4. Region

The CMS region in which the complaint data applies for a particular company. The regions are as follows:

Boston: 1 (Connecticut, Maine, Massachusetts, New Hampshire, Rhode Island, Vermont), **New York: 2** (New Jersey, New York, Puerto Rico, Virgin Islands), **Philadelphia: 3** (Delaware, District of Columbia, Maryland, Pennsylvania, Virginia, West Virginia), **Atlanta: 4** (Alabama, Florida, Georgia, Kentucky, Mississippi, North Carolina, South Carolina, Tennessee), **Chicago: 5** (Illinois, Indiana, Michigan, Minnesota, Ohio, Wisconsin), **Dallas: 6** (Arkansas, Louisiana, Oklahoma, New Mexico, Texas), **Kansas City: 7** (Iowa, Kansas, Missouri, Nebraska), **Denver: 8** (Colorado, Montana, North Dakota, South Dakota, Utah, Wyoming), **San Francisco: 9** (Arizona, California, Guam, Hawaii, Nevada, Samoa), **Seattle: 10** (Alaska, Idaho, Oregon, Washington).

5. Rate

The rate of reconsiderations per 1,000 members and is calculated as the sum of appeals received per year. Divided by the mid-year (July) enrollment, times 1,000.

"N/R" means that there were "no reconsiderations" for that particular plan's contract in that particular region. "N/E" means there was "no enrollment" during 2020. This happens when the complaints reflect prior enrollments in specific contracts, demonstrate the lag time between enrollment, and the complaint being represented in the reconsideration system.

6. Reconsiderations Received 2016

The number of reconsiderations received by the CMS from the health plan for the Medicare contract(s) only. Regardless of the number of complaints upheld or overturned (See columns 8 and 9), if this number is high relative to other Medicare plans, it signals that the plan has trouble satisfying its policyholders.

The health plan may have other business besides treating Medicare beneficiaries but this figure only pertains to enrollees that are served under a Medicare contract.

7. Reconsiderations Not Yet Decided

The number of reconsiderations received during 2020 that have not yet been settled.

8. Reconsiderations Upheld

The number of cases in which the CMS upheld the decision of the Medicare plan. This is the number of times CMS ruled against the policyholder in favor of the plan. If the number is high relative to the total number of reconsiderations received (Column 6), it is a sign that the firm's complaint process is somewhat ironclad and appeals beyond it are often futile. This, however, does not necessarily mean that the plan was not at fault.

9. Reconsiderations Overturned

The number of cases in which the CMS completely overturned the decision of the Medicare Managed Care plan. This is the number of times the CMS ruled in favor of the policyholder. If the number of complaints overturned is high, relative to the total number of reconsiderations received (Column 6), it is a sign that either the plan is falling short in meeting the needs of its policyholders; or, its complaint process is not streamlined enough to carry complaints to the appropriate conclusion.

10. Reconsiderations Withdrawn

The number of reconsiderations that were withdrawn from review.

The Regional CMS office will investigate the case and determine if the enrolee should revert back to fee-for-service (disenroll). If the CMS does not grant disenrollment, the case re-enters the reconsideration process and follows the same course as other complaints.

A high number of disenrollments may indicate that the plan has failed to clearly identify its coverage limitations at the time the policy is sold.

11. Reconsiderations Dismissed

The number of cases in which the CMS Regional Office decided the appeal is not valid or the CMS Regional Office does not have jurisdiction over the appeal.

INSURANCE COMPANY NAME	DOM. STATE	RATING	REGION	RATE	RECONS REC'VD	RECONS NOT YET DECIDED	RECONS UPHELD	RECONS OVER-TURNED	RECONS WITH-DRAWN	RECONS DISMISSED
MY CHOICE WISCONSIN HEALTH PLAN INC	WI	B+	5	3.78	7	0	6	0	0	1
ABSOLUTE TOTAL CARE INC	SC	B	4	5.46	18	0	16	0	0	2
AETNA BETTER HEALTH OF MICHIGAN INC	MI	B	5	4.94	39	0	18	7	0	14
AETNA HEALTH INC (A CT CORP)	CT	B-	8	4.52	71	0	62	4	0	4
AETNA HEALTH INC (A FLORIDA CORP)	FL	B	8	N/E	--	--	--	--	--	--
AETNA HEALTH INC (A GEORGIA CORP)	GA	C	8	9.14	14	0	13	0	0	1
AETNA HEALTH INC (A MAINE CORP)	ME	B	8	2.90	18	0	16	1	0	1
AETNA HEALTH INC (A NEW JERSEY CORP)	NJ	C	8	4.14	184	0	167	5	0	12
AETNA HEALTH INC (A NEW YORK CORP)	NY	D+	8	6.28	67	0	61	2	0	2
AETNA HEALTH INC (A PA CORP)	PA	B	8	4.38	322	0	283	5	1	33
AETNA HEALTH INC (A TEXAS CORP)	TX	C	8	6.63	244	0	231	3	0	10
AETNA HEALTH OF CALIFORNIA INC	CA	B	8	2.51	36	0	30	0	1	5
AETNA HEALTH OF IOWA INC	IA	C	8	2.30	142	0	125	10	0	6
AETNA HEALTH OF UTAH INC	UT	C	8	1.41	9	0	5	2	0	2
AETNA LIFE INS CO	CT	B	8	3.26	3387	0	3099	83	3	190
AIDS HEALTHCARE FOUNDATION MCO OF FL	FL	D-	9	N/E	--	--	--	--	--	--
ALLIANCE HEALTH & LIFE INS CO	MI	C-	5	1.90	7	0	7	0	0	0
ALOHACARE	HI	C	9	N/E	--	--	--	--	--	--
AMERIGROUP COMMUNITY CARE NM	NM	B-	5	3.91	6	0	6	0	0	0
AMERIGROUP NEW JERSEY INC	NJ	A-	5	10.90	106	0	95	2	0	9
AMERIGROUP TENNESSEE INC	TN	B-	5	1.84	22	0	14	2	0	6
AMERIGROUP TEXAS INC	TX	B	5	2.05	84	0	68	3	0	13
AMERIGROUP TEXAS INC	TX	B	6	5.50	75	0	60	7	0	8
AMERIGROUP WASHINGTON INC	WA	A-	5	1.23	2	0	2	0	0	0
AMERIHEALTH HMO INC	PA	C+	3	N/E	--	--	--	--	--	--
AMERIHEALTH MICHIGAN INC	MI	C	5	11.10	37	0	24	8	0	5
ANTHEM BLUE CROSS LIFE & HEALTH INS	CA	B-	5	3.66	32	0	23	1	0	7
ANTHEM HEALTH PLANS INC	CT	B	5	6.85	232	0	210	8	0	14
ANTHEM HEALTH PLANS OF KENTUCKY INC	KY	B-	5	N/E	--	--	--	--	--	--
ANTHEM HEALTH PLANS OF MAINE INC	ME	B	5	15.96	196	0	152	11	0	32
ANTHEM HEALTH PLANS OF NEW HAMPSHIRE	NH	B	5	1.89	38	0	28	1	0	8
ANTHEM HEALTH PLANS OF VIRGINIA	VA	B	5	0.52	21	0	15	2	0	4
ANTHEM INS COMPANIES INC	IN	B-	5	13.03	388	0	313	13	0	61
ARKANSAS SUPERIOR SELECT INC	AR	E	6	1.07	2	0	1	0	0	1
ASPIRE HEALTH PLAN	CA	E-	9	19.32	64	0	56	7	0	1
ASURIS NORTHWEST HEALTH	WA	B	10	2.10	2	0	1	0	0	0
ATRIO HEALTH PLANS INC	OR	D+	10	27.79	114	0	93	14	0	7
AULTCARE INS CO	OH	B+	5	2.19	44	0	43	0	1	0
AVMED INC	FL	B-	4	1.87	54	0	48	2	0	4
BEHEALTHY FLORIDA INC	FL	C-	4	14.45	140	0	123	14	0	3
BLUE CROSS & BLUE SHIELD MA HMO BLUE	MA	B+	1	4.57	136	0	124	7	0	5
BLUE CROSS & BLUE SHIELD OF FLORIDA	FL	B	4	11.03	340	0	230	15	0	93
BLUE CROSS BLUE SHIELD HEALTHCARE GA	GA	A-	5	N/E	--	--	--	--	--	--
BLUE CROSS BLUE SHIELD OF ALABAMA	AL	A-	4	0.84	75	0	67	3	0	4
BLUE CROSS BLUE SHIELD OF MICHIGAN	MI	B-	5	2.31	402	0	249	17	0	133
BLUE CROSS BLUE SHIELD OF MINNESOTA	MN	C	5	0.31	81	0	73	3	0	5
BLUE CROSS BLUE SHIELD OF NC	NC	B+	4	5.20	185	0	146	19	0	19
BLUE CROSS BLUE SHIELD OF RI	RI	B	1	2.23	117	0	100	10	0	6
BLUE CROSS OF CALIFORNIA	CA	A+	5	N/E	--	--	--	--	--	--
BLUE CROSS OF IDAHO HEALTH SERVICE	ID	B+	10	19.73	343	0	284	23	0	26
BLUECROSS BLUESHIELD OF TENNESSEE	TN	A-	4	5.79	712	0	645	27	7	29
BRAVO HEALTH MID-ATLANTIC INC	MD	B	6	6.21	109	0	90	13	0	5

INSURANCE COMPANY NAME	DOM. STATE	RATING	REGION	RATE	RECONS REC'VD	RECONS NOT YET DECIDED	RECONS UPHELD	RECONS OVER-TURNED	RECONS WITH-DRAWN	RECONS DISMISSED
BRAVO HEALTH PENNSYLVANIA INC	PA	B	6	5.22	218	0	195	18	0	4
BUCKEYE COMMUNITY HEALTH PLAN INC	OH	B	5	1.51	19	0	15	1	0	3
BUCKEYE COMMUNITY HEALTH PLAN INC	OH	B	10	1.97	1	0	1	0	0	0
CALIFORNIA PHYSICIANS SERVICE	CA	A+	9	5.16	433	0	356	16	2	55
CAPITAL ADVANTAGE INS CO	PA	C	3	3.91	52	0	47	3	0	2
CAPITAL DISTRICT PHYSICIANS HEALTH P	NY	A-	2	7.30	282	0	252	24	0	3
CAPITAL HEALTH PLAN INC	FL	A	4	1.65	35	0	31	3	0	1
CARE 1ST HEALTH PLAN INC	CA	B	9	6.22	389	0	296	19	0	72
CARE IMPROVEMENT PLUS OF TEXAS INS	TX	B-	9	9.18	1118	0	873	6	0	234
CARE IMPROVEMENT PLUS SOUTH CENTRAL	AR	B	9	27.10	1304	0	1112	9	0	183
CARE IMPROVEMENT PLUS WI INS	WI	B	9	9.41	83	0	73	0	0	10
CARE N CARE INS CO	TX	C	6	11.68	53	0	44	3	0	6
CAREMORE HEALTH PLAN	CA	B	5	3.88	392	0	330	25	1	34
CAREPLUS HEALTH PLANS INC	FL	B	7	2.91	337	0	315	4	0	17
CARESOURCE OHIO INC	OH	B	5	16.28	306	0	137	38	0	130
CARITEN HEALTH PLAN INC	TN	B	7	1.71	189	0	142	8	0	38
CATHOLIC SPECIAL NEEDS PLAN LLC	NY	C	2	0.57	1	0	0	0	0	1
CDPHP UNIVERSAL BENEFITS INC	NY	B-	2	3.97	16	0	13	3	0	0
CHA HMO INC	KY	B-	7	1.39	27	0	22	0	0	5
CHINESE COMMUNITY HEALTH PLAN	CA	E-	9	6.13	30	0	22	4	0	4
CHRISTUS HEALTH PLAN	TX	C-	6	7.43	10	0	5	0	0	5
CIGNA HEALTH & LIFE INS CO	CT	B	6	N/E	--	--	--	--	--	--
CIGNA HEALTHCARE OF ARIZONA INC	AZ	D+	6	4.07	175	0	147	16	0	12
CIGNA HEALTHCARE OF GEORGIA INC	GA	C	6	5.10	121	0	109	6	0	3
CIGNA HEALTHCARE OF NORTH CAROLINA	NC	D	6	3.93	23	0	20	2	0	1
CIGNA HEALTHCARE OF SOUTH CAROLINA	SC	C	6	4.38	24	0	22	2	0	0
CMNTY CARE HLTH PLAN INC (WI)	WI	B	5	2.10	1	0	1	0	0	0
COMMUNITY CARE ALLIANCE OF ILLINOIS	IL	D	5	11.74	61	0	47	9	1	4
COMMUNITY HEALTH GROUP	CA	C-	9	0.51	3	0	3	0	0	0
COMMUNITY HEALTH PLAN OF WASHINGTON	WA	B-	10	4.08	33	0	21	4	0	7
COMMUNITY INS CO	OH	B-	5	3.26	574	0	494	18	0	57
COMMUNITYCARE HMO INC	OK	C+	6	2.14	52	0	44	4	0	4
COMPCARE HEALTH SERVICES INS CORP	WI	A	5	3.01	63	0	57	2	0	4
CONNECTICARE INC	CT	C-	2	6.53	319	0	280	24	1	12
CONSTELLATION HEALTH LLC	PR	U	2	22.03	137	0	8	10	0	119
CONTRA COSTA HEALTH PLAN	CA	B	9	N/E	--	--	--	--	--	--
COVENTRY HEALTH & LIFE INS CO	MO	B-	8	1.59	255	0	235	5	2	12
COVENTRY HEALTH CARE OF ILLINOIS INC	IL	B	8	1.44	34	0	32	0	0	2
COVENTRY HEALTH CARE OF MISSOURI INC	MO	B	8	1.39	117	0	106	3	0	7
COVENTRY HEALTH CARE OF NEBRASKA INC	NE	U	8	1.53	10	0	9	0	0	1
COVENTRY HEALTH CARE OF VIRGINIA INC	VA	B-	8	13.51	11	0	9	1	0	1
COVENTRY HEALTH CARE OF WEST VA INC	WV	B	8	2.89	19	0	18	0	0	1
DEAN HEALTH PLAN INC	WI	A-	5	29.76	238	0	182	29	1	25
DENVER HEALTH MEDICAL PLAN INC	CO	B	8	6.83	31	0	21	2	0	8
EASY CHOICE HEALTH PLAN	CA	C	4	3.67	109	0	97	7	0	4
ELDERPLAN INC	NY	C+	2	7.77	84	0	71	7	0	5
EMPIRE HEALTHCHOICE ASSURANCE INC	NY	B-	5	3.09	9	0	7	0	0	2
EMPIRE HEALTHCHOICE HMO INC	NY	C	5	N/E	--	--	--	--	--	--
ESSENCE HEALTHCARE INC	MO	A-	7	7.16	465	0	399	33	2	28
EXCELLUS HEALTH PLAN INC	NY	B	2	12.54	922	0	820	82	1	12
FALLON COMMUNITY HEALTH PLAN	MA	C+	1	15.19	297	0	248	35	0	12
FIRSTCAROLINACARE INS CO	NC	D	4	0.92	6	0	3	0	0	3

INSURANCE COMPANY NAME	DOM. STATE	RATING	REGION	RATE	RECONS REC'VD	RECONS NOT YET DECIDED	RECONS UPHELD	RECONS OVER-TURNED	RECONS WITH-DRAWN	RECONS DISMISSED
GATEWAY HEALTH PLAN INC	PA	B-	3	5.37	262	0	244	4	0	14
GATEWAY HEALTH PLAN OF OHIO INC	OH	C-	3	12.64	134	0	109	4	0	21
GEISINGER HEALTH PLAN	PA	B+	3	1.94	136	0	127	4	0	2
GEISINGER INDEMNITY INS CO	PA	C	3	1.56	40	0	39	1	0	0
GHS HEALTH MAINTENANCE ORGANIZATION	OK	C	6	29.60	124	0	57	24	0	39
GHS INS CO	OK	E-	6	20.23	96	0	54	8	0	34
GLOBALHEALTH INC	OK	D	6	N/E	--	--	--	--	--	--
GROUP HEALTH INCORPORATED	NY	D+	2	20.83	1	0	0	0	0	1
GROUP HEALTH PLAN INC	MN	E+	5	0.69	42	0	40	2	0	0
HAP EMPOWERED HEALTH PLAN INC	MI	D+	5	1.78	10	0	2	4	0	4
HARMONY HEALTH PLAN INC	IL	C-	4	4.56	388	0	307	3	0	77
HAWAII MEDICAL SERVICE ASSOCIATION	HI	B	9	0.41	15	0	10	3	0	1
HCSC INS SERVICES CO	IL	E-	6	25.21	345	0	165	87	1	87
HEALTH ALLIANCE MEDICAL PLANS	IL	B-	5	15.10	315	0	238	72	0	2
HEALTH ALLIANCE NORTHWEST HEALTH PL	WA	B	5	8.15	61	0	49	12	0	0
HEALTH ALLIANCE PLAN OF MICHIGAN	MI	C-	5	1.86	107	0	94	2	0	9
HEALTH ALLIANCE-MIDWEST INC	IL	C	5	18.04	9	0	9	0	0	0
HEALTH CARE SVC CORP A MUT LEG RES	IL	B+	5	6.25	125	0	80	26	0	16
HEALTH CARE SVC CORP A MUT LEG RES	IL	B+	6	60.88	1218	0	530	288	1	381
HEALTH INSURANCE PLAN OF GREATER NY	NY	D+	2	3.82	447	0	340	22	0	78
HEALTH NET COMMUNITY SOLUTIONS INC	CA	B	9	4.87	64	0	55	5	0	4
HEALTH NET HEALTH PLAN OF OREGON INC	OR	D	10	2.47	91	0	74	3	0	14
HEALTH NET LIFE INS CO	CA	C	10	1.58	74	0	55	7	1	10
HEALTH NET OF ARIZONA INC	AZ	C+	10	5.37	91	0	70	7	0	13
HEALTH NET OF CALIFORNIA INC	CA	B-	10	2.78	339	0	277	34	2	25
HEALTH NEW ENGLAND INC	MA	B	1	7.19	64	0	52	10	1	1
HEALTH OPTIONS INC	FL	A-	4	6.05	291	0	220	13	0	58
HEALTH PARTNERS PLANS INC	PA	B	3	8.06	166	0	137	24	0	3
HEALTH PLAN OF CAREOREGON INC	OR	C	10	5.72	74	0	71	1	0	1
HEALTH PLAN OF NEVADA INC	NV	B+	9	2.40	117	0	108	1	0	8
HEALTHASSURANCE PENNSYLVANIA INC	PA	B-	8	1.75	123	0	103	0	0	19
HEALTHFIRST HEALTH PLAN INC	NY	B+	2	2.79	427	0	346	3	0	74
HEALTHKEEPERS INC	VA	B-	3	N/E	--	--	--	--	--	--
HEALTHNOW NY INC	NY	A	2	2.40	58	0	55	1	1	1
HEALTHPARTNERS	MN	B	5	N/E	--	--	--	--	--	--
HEALTHSPAN INTEGRATED CARE	OH	U	5	5.64	139	0	95	9	0	35
HEALTHSPRING L&H INS CO	TX	B-	6	12.87	483	0	447	17	0	20
HEARTLANDPLAINS HEALTH	NE	U	8	14.52	8	0	6	1	0	1
HIGHMARK CHOICE CO	PA	U	3	3.74	400	0	356	9	0	33
HIGHMARK SENIOR HEALTH CO	PA	U	3	2.84	423	0	368	18	0	32
HM HEALTH INS CO	PA	U	3	3.62	15	0	13	0	0	2
HMO MINNESOTA	MN	B	5	1.04	9	0	9	0	0	0
HMO MISSOURI INC	MO	C	5	3.61	34	0	24	1	0	9
HMO PARTNERS INC	AR	A+	6	1.01	5	0	2	0	0	3
HOMETOWN HEALTH PLAN INC	NV	D	10	11.38	122	0	94	10	0	15
HORIZON HEALTHCARE OF NEW JERSEY INC	NJ	C+	2	1.79	106	0	59	5	0	42
HORIZON INS CO	NJ	C+	2	7.82	179	0	116	2	1	58
HUMANA BENEFIT PLAN OF ILLINOIS	IL	B+	7	3.78	300	0	210	18	0	71
HUMANA EMPLOYERS HEALTH PLAN OF GA	GA	C	7	2.29	112	0	80	7	0	24
HUMANA HEALTH BENEFIT PLAN LA	LA	B	7	2.24	319	0	248	15	1	54
HUMANA HEALTH CO OF NEW YORK INC	NY	C-	7	3.58	69	0	50	1	0	18
HUMANA HEALTH INS CO OF FL INC	FL	C-	7	N/E	--	--	--	--	--	--

INSURANCE COMPANY NAME	DOM. STATE	RATING	REGION	RATE	RECONS REC'VD	RECONS NOT YET DECIDED	RECONS UPHELD	RECONS OVER-TURNED	RECONS WITH-DRAWN	RECONS DISMISSED
HUMANA HEALTH PLAN INC	KY	D	3	N/E	--	--	--	--	--	--
HUMANA HEALTH PLAN INC	KY	D	5	3.00	24	0	9	2	0	13
HUMANA HEALTH PLAN INC	KY	D	7	2.46	804	0	565	47	0	184
HUMANA HEALTH PLAN OF CALIFORNIA INC	CA	U	7	N/E	--	--	--	--	--	--
HUMANA HEALTH PLAN OF OHIO INC	OH	C	7	N/E	--	--	--	--	--	--
HUMANA HEALTH PLANS OF PUERTO RICO	PR	E-	7	0.39	13	0	4	3	0	5
HUMANA INS CO (WI)	WI	A	7	46.94	4710	0	3545	251	10	872
HUMANA INS CO OF NY	NY	B	7	4.67	45	0	25	9	0	11
HUMANA INS CO OF PUERTO RICO INC	PR	C+	7	1.79	2	0	0	0	0	2
HUMANA MEDICAL PLAN INC	FL	A-	7	1.78	832	0	627	44	2	155
HUMANA MEDICAL PLAN OF MICHIGAN INC	MI	B-	7	2.88	23	0	10	3	0	10
HUMANA MEDICAL PLAN OF PENNSYLVANIA	PA	B-	7	N/E	--	--	--	--	--	--
HUMANA MEDICAL PLAN OF UTAH INC	UT	D+	7	2.47	8	0	7	0	0	1
HUMANA REGIONAL HEALTH PLAN INC	AR	C-	7	N/E	--	--	--	--	--	--
HUMANA WISCONSIN HEALTH ORGANIZATION	WI	B+	5	18.05	102	0	81	11	0	9
HUMANA WISCONSIN HEALTH ORGANIZATION	WI	B+	7	1.58	329	0	230	23	0	72
ILLINICARE HEALTH PLAN INC	IL	C	5	1.70	13	0	10	1	0	2
INDEPENDENT CARE HEALTH PLAN	WI	A-	5	13.01	103	0	85	8	0	10
INDEPENDENT HEALTH ASSOC INC	NY	B+	2	17.73	1161	0	1083	34	1	40
INDEPENDENT HEALTH BENEFITS CORP	NY	B	2	14.15	66	0	63	3	0	0
INDIANA UNIVERSITY HEALTH PLANS INC	IN	E-	5	6.03	86	0	75	8	0	1
INS CO OF SCOTT & WHITE	TX	D+	6	21.03	104	0	88	8	0	8
INTERVALLEY HEALTH PLAN	CA	D+	10	1.39	31	0	25	2	0	4
K S PLAN ADMINISTRATORS LLC	TX	B	6	2.32	76	0	72	1	0	3
KAISER FOUNDATION HEALTH PLAN INC	CA	A+	9	1.08	971	0	855	28	3	84
KAISER FOUNDATION HP MID-ATL STATES	MD	C	9	0.90	65	0	52	7	0	5
KAISER FOUNDATION HP NORTHWEST	OR	B	9	1.25	115	0	106	2	0	5
KAISER FOUNDATION HP OF CO	CO	B-	9	1.34	149	0	135	6	1	7
KAISER FOUNDATION HP OF GA	GA	C	9	1.00	29	0	28	1	0	0
KEYSTONE HEALTH PLAN CENTRAL INC	PA	D	3	4.15	66	0	60	4	0	2
KEYSTONE HEALTH PLAN EAST INC	PA	B+	3	8.22	747	0	661	57	2	23
LOCAL INITIATIVE HEALTH AUTH LA	CA	C	9	5.34	84	0	72	5	0	6
MARTINS POINT GENERATIONS LLC	ME	U	1	8.06	170	0	138	20	0	10
MATTHEW THORNTON HEALTH PLAN	NH	B	5	4.26	11	0	9	0	0	2
MCS ADVANTAGE INC	PR	E+	2	1.65	340	0	256	4	0	78
MEDICA HEALTH PLANS	MN	C+	5	0.27	3	0	3	0	0	0
MEDICA HEALTHCARE PLANS INC	FL	B	9	4.30	193	0	154	1	0	38
MEDICAL ASSOC CLINIC HEALTH PLAN	WI	B-	7	N/E	--	--	--	--	--	--
MEDICAL ASSOCIATES HEALTH PLAN INC	IA	B	7	0.09	1	0	1	0	0	0
MEDISUN INC	AZ	D	9	14.68	801	0	556	89	1	152
MEDSTAR FAMILY CHOICE INC	MD	C	3	10.21	60	0	56	2	0	2
MEMORIAL HERMANN HEALTH PLAN INC	TX	C-	6	31.01	95	0	62	13	0	19
MERIDIAN HEALTH PLAN OF ILLINOIS INC	IL	C-	5	56.10	351	0	320	11	0	18
MERIDIAN HEALTH PLAN OF MICHIGAN INC	MI	C	5	22.04	270	0	227	21	0	19
MHS HEALTH WISCONSIN	WI	B	10	7.60	8	0	7	1	0	0
MICHIGAN COMPLETE HEALTH INC	MO	C-	5	13.83	39	0	21	4	1	13
MMM HEALTHCARE LLC	PR	E-	2	1.76	283	0	188	12	0	81
MODA HEALTH PLAN INC	OR	E	10	20.07	115	0	91	9	1	12
MOLINA HEALTHCARE OF CALIFORNIA	CA	C	9	5.80	66	0	41	9	1	14
MOLINA HEALTHCARE OF CALIFORNIA	CA	C	10	6.75	13	0	8	1	1	3
MOLINA HEALTHCARE OF FLORIDA INC	FL	D	10	6.51	17	0	10	1	0	5
MOLINA HEALTHCARE OF ILLINOIS INC	IL	C	5	14.10	53	0	29	14	1	9

INSURANCE COMPANY NAME	DOM. STATE	RATING	REGION	RATE	RECONS REC'VD	RECONS NOT YET DECIDED	RECONS UPHELD	RECONS OVER-TURNED	RECONS WITH-DRAWN	RECONS DISMISSED
MOLINA HEALTHCARE OF MICHIGAN INC	MI	B	5	5.97	66	0	50	7	0	7
MOLINA HEALTHCARE OF MICHIGAN INC	MI	B	10	8.52	99	0	66	9	0	24
MOLINA HEALTHCARE OF NEW MEXICO	NM	C	10	11.94	60	0	42	6	0	11
MOLINA HEALTHCARE OF OHIO INC	OH	B	5	12.51	172	0	116	10	0	43
MOLINA HEALTHCARE OF OHIO INC	OH	B	10	17.67	5	0	5	0	0	0
MOLINA HEALTHCARE OF SOUTH CAROLINA	SC	B	4	7.20	21	0	12	6	0	3
MOLINA HEALTHCARE OF TEXAS INC	TX	B-	6	13.16	164	0	102	25	0	36
MOLINA HEALTHCARE OF TEXAS INC	TX	B-	10	8.79	14	0	10	1	0	3
MOLINA HEALTHCARE OF UTAH INC	UT	B	10	5.68	64	0	38	9	0	17
MOLINA HEALTHCARE OF WASHINGTON INC	WA	B	10	5.75	57	0	42	4	0	10
MOLINA HEALTHCARE OF WISCONSIN INC	WI	C+	10	7.76	8	0	4	2	0	2
MOUNT CARMEL HEALTH INS CO	OH	C+	5	2.54	2	0	2	0	0	0
MOUNT CARMEL HEALTH PLAN INC	OH	B+	5	3.35	165	0	156	4	1	4
MVP HEALTH PLAN INC	NY	B	2	22.40	678	0	589	63	2	16
NETWORK HEALTH INS CORP	WI	B	8	2.32	4	0	3	1	0	0
OKLAHOMA SUPERIOR SELECT INC	OK	E+	6	N/E	--	--	--	--	--	--
ON LOK SENIOR HEALTH SERVICES	CA	B	9	N/E	--	--	--	--	--	--
OPTIMA HEALTH PLAN	VA	B	3	0.68	2	0	2	0	0	0
OXFORD HEALTH PLANS (CT) INC	CT	B+	9	5.93	854	0	714	2	0	137
OXFORD HEALTH PLANS (NJ) INC	NJ	B	9	3.58	148	0	70	1	0	77
OXFORD HEALTH PLANS (NY) INC	NY	B	9	6.05	523	0	432	0	0	89
PACIFICARE OF COLORADO INC	CO	B	9	2.96	8626	0	21	6	0	232
PACIFICSOURCE COMMUNITY HEALTH PLANS	OR	B	10	10.67	161	0	144	7	0	10
PARAMOUNT HEALTH CARE	OH	D	5	1.38	22	0	19	1	0	2
PEACH STATE HEALTH PLAN INC	GA	B	10	4.63	6	0	6	0	0	0
PIEDMONT COMMUNITY HEALTHCARE	VA	D+	3	4.13	21	0	17	2	0	1
PMC MEDICARE CHOICE LLC	PR	U	2	0.95	40	0	35	0	0	5
PREFERRED CARE PARTNERS INC	FL	B+	9	4.18	755	0	573	1	1	177
PREMERA BLUE CROSS	WA	B	10	10.36	224	0	167	6	0	50
PRESBYTERIAN INS CO	NM	C	6	9.94	31	0	22	7	0	1
PRIORITY HEALTH	MI	A	5	11.26	794	0	731	40	1	17
PROMINENCE HEALTHFIRST OF TEXAS INC	TX	D-	9	32.16	137	0	37	22	0	76
PROVIDENCE HEALTH PLAN	OR	B	10	4.77	269	0	231	25	0	13
QCC INS CO	PA	B-	3	7.39	65	0	56	5	0	4
QUALITY HEALTH PLANS OF NEW YORK INC	NY	F	2	3.29	14	0	6	4	0	3
QUARTZ HEALTH PLAN CORP	WI	C-	5	5.10	80	0	65	5	0	6
QUARTZ HEALTH PLAN MN CORP	MN	C+	5	1.22	1	0	1	0	0	0
REGENCE BL CROSS BL SHIELD OREGON	OR	A-	10	6.46	139	0	124	9	0	6
REGENCE BLUE CROSS BLUE SHIELD OF UT	UT	B+	10	2.80	23	0	22	1	0	0
REGENCE BLUESHIELD	WA	B	10	7.72	73	0	68	3	0	2
REGENCE BLUESHIELD OF IDAHO INC	ID	B+	10	5.83	20	0	17	1	0	2
RIVERLINK HEALTH	OH	U	8	13.40	23	0	19	0	0	4
SAMARITAN HEALTH PLANS INC	OR	B-	10	3.53	18	0	13	2	0	3
SAN MATEO HEALTH COMMISSION	CA	B	9	6.99	63	0	45	10	0	8
SCAN HEALTH PLAN	CA	B+	9	87.62	1143	0	1001	76	2	61
SCOTT & WHITE HEALTH PLAN	TX	C+	6	3.58	100	0	74	13	0	13
SECURITY HEALTH PLAN OF WI INC	WI	B+	5	4.16	190	0	171	16	0	2
SECURITYCARE OF TENNESSEE INC	TN	C	4	N/E	--	--	--	--	--	--
SELECT HEALTH OF SOUTH CAROLINA INC	SC	B	4	7.48	38	0	24	2	0	12
SELECTHEALTH INC	UT	B+	8	3.17	129	0	112	4	0	10
SENIOR WHOLE HEALTH OF NEW YORK INC	NY	C+	1	N/E	--	--	--	--	--	--
SENIOR WHOLE HEALTH OF NEW YORK INC	NY	C+	2	N/E	--	--	--	--	--	--

INSURANCE COMPANY NAME	DOM. STATE	RATING	REGION	RATE	RECONS REC'VD	RECONS NOT YET DECIDED	RECONS UPHELD	RECONS OVER-TURNED	RECONS WITH-DRAWN	RECONS DISMISSED
SHARP HEALTH PLAN	CA	B+	9	11.74	24	0	22	2	0	0
SIDNEY HILLMAN HEALTH CENTRE	IL	U	5	N/E	--	--	--	--	--	--
SIERRA HEALTH AND LIFE INS CO INC	NV	B	9	8.61	6119	0	4398	82	7	1618
SIMPLY HEALTHCARE PLANS INC	FL	B	5	13.24	740	0	698	20	0	18
STANFORD HEALTH CARE ADVANTAGE	CA	E-	9	2.08	6	0	6	0	0	0
SUMMACARE INC	OH	C	5	5.62	133	0	128	2	0	3
SUNSHINE HEALTH	FL	C+	10	2.74	6	0	5	0	0	1
SUPERIOR HEALTHPLAN INC	TX	B-	6	2.30	21	0	13	5	0	3
SUPERIOR HEALTHPLAN INC	TX	B-	10	1.76	3	0	2	0	0	1
SUTTER HEALTH PLAN	CA	C-	9	N/E	--	--	--	--	--	--
THP INS CO	WV	C	3	1.09	2	0	2	0	0	0
TRILLIUM COMMUNITY HEALTH PLAN INC	OR	C+	10	1.14	3	0	1	2	0	0
TRIPLE-S ADVANTAGE INC	PR	B	2	0.97	95	0	81	2	0	11
TRIPLE-S SALUD INC	PR	B	2	2.16	30	0	26	2	0	2
TUFTS ASSOCIATED HEALTH MAINT ORG	MA	C	1	8.88	902	0	858	21	0	21
TUFTS HEALTH PUBLIC PLANS INC	MA	C	1	8.28	22	0	14	5	0	3
UCARE MINNESOTA	MN	B	5	3.90	253	0	209	19	0	21
UHC OF CALIFORNIA INC	CA	B	9	2.26	789	0	651	12	0	124
ULTIMATE HEALTH PLANS INC	FL	E-	4	9.00	61	0	54	1	0	5
UNION HEALTH SERVICE INC	IL	C	5	N/E	--	--	--	--	--	--
UNITED HEALTHCARE INS CO	CT	C	9	82.74	6069	0	4887	59	2	1111
UNITED HEALTHCARE OF ALABAMA INC	AL	D	9	4.46	34	0	32	1	0	1
UNITED HEALTHCARE OF GEORGIA INC	GA	B	9	5.51	80	0	62	1	0	17
UNITED HEALTHCARE OF LOUISIANA INC	LA	B	9	104.13	58	0	58	0	0	0
UNITED HEALTHCARE OF NC INC	NC	C	9	N/E	--	--	--	--	--	--
UNITED HEALTHCARE OF NEW ENGLAND INC	RI	B	9	3.01	177	0	152	1	0	24
UNITED HEALTHCARE OF NY INC	NY	B	9	8.14	486	0	242	3	0	240
UNITED HEALTHCARE OF OHIO INC	OH	C	9	N/E	--	--	--	--	--	--
UNITED HEALTHCARE OF THE MIDLANDS	NE	B+	9	3.87	901	0	738	9	0	153
UNITED HEALTHCARE OF THE MIDWEST INC	MO	C	9	2.13	38	0	29	0	0	9
UNITED HEALTHCARE OF UTAH	UT	B	9	1.21	91	0	64	2	0	25
UNITED HEALTHCARE OF WISCONSIN INC	WI	B+	9	3.05	1468	0	1198	13	0	253
UNITEDHEALTHCARE BENEFITS OF TEXAS	TX	B	9	1.95	478	0	380	3	0	90
UNITEDHEALTHCARE COMMUNITY PLAN TX	TX	B	9	9.33	281	0	250	2	0	29
UNITEDHEALTHCARE OF OKLAHOMA INC	OK	B	9	3.01	96	0	71	2	0	23
UNITEDHEALTHCARE OF OREGON	OR	B+	9	1.66	217	0	158	1	0	57
UNITEDHEALTHCARE PLAN RIVER VALLEY	IL	B	9	2.48	143	0	60	1	0	82
UNIVERSAL CARE	CA	E	9	0.89	25	0	21	4	0	0
UPMC FOR YOU INC	PA	B+	3	8.28	215	0	204	6	0	4
UPMC HEALTH PLAN INC	PA	C+	3	8.73	1251	0	1199	18	5	23
UPPER PENINSULA HEALTH PLAN INC	MI	B	5	36.07	117	0	83	31	0	3
USABLE MUTUAL INS CO	AR	B+	6	0.39	6	0	2	1	0	3
VANTAGE HEALTH PLAN INC	LA	C+	6	13.28	246	0	228	3	0	14
VISTA HEALTH PLAN INC	PA	B+	3	9.79	61	0	46	6	0	7
VIVA HEALTH INC	AL	A-	4	4.10	196	0	180	5	2	9
VOLUNTEER STATE HEALTH PLAN INC	TN	A+	4	0.98	15	0	14	0	0	1
WELLCARE HEALTH INS OF ARIZONA INC	AZ	B-	4	18.64	364	0	333	3	0	28
WELLCARE HEALTH PLANS OF NEW JERSEY	NJ	B	4	4.10	22	0	17	1	0	4
WELLCARE OF CONNECTICUT INC	CT	C	4	9.14	78	0	62	12	0	4
WELLCARE OF FLORIDA INC	FL	D+	4	2.68	258	0	222	4	0	30
WELLCARE OF GEORGIA INC	GA	B+	4	4.62	177	0	134	4	0	37
WELLCARE OF OHIO INC	OH	U	4	N/E	--	--	--	--	--	--

VII. Analysis of Medicare Managed Care Complaints

Spring 2021

INSURANCE COMPANY NAME	DOM. STATE	RATING	REGION	RATE	RECONS REC'VD	RECONS NOT YET DECIDED	RECONS UPHELD	RECONS OVER-TURNED	RECONS WITH-DRAWN	RECONS DISMISSED
WELLCARE OF SOUTH CAROLINA INC	SC	B	4	N/E	--	--	--	--	--	--
WELLCARE OF TEXAS INC	TX	A-	4	12.72	176	0	137	4	0	34

Section VIII

Rating Upgrades and Downgrades

A list of all

U.S. Health Insurers

receiving a rating upgrade or downgrade
during the current quarter.

Section VIII Contents

This section identifies those companies receiving a rating change since the previous edition of this publication, whether it is a new rating to this guide, withdrawn rating, rating upgrade, rating downgrade or a, newly rated company. A rating may be withdrawn due to a merger, dissolution, or liquidation. A rating upgrade or downgrade may entail a change from one letter grade to another, or it may mean the addition or deletion of a plus or minus sign within the same letter grade previously assigned to the company. Ratings are normally updated once each quarter of the year. In some instances, however, a company's rating may be downgraded outside of the normal updates due to overriding circumstances.

1. **Insurance Company Name**

   The legally-registered name, which can sometimes differ from the name that the company uses for advertising. An insurer's name can be very similar to that of another, so verify the company's exact name and state of domicile to make sure you are looking at the correct company.

2. **Domicile State**

   The state which has primary regulatory responsibility for the company. It may differ from the location of the company's corporate headquarters. You do not have to be living in the domicile state to purchase insurance from this firm, provided it is licensed to do business in your state.

3. **Total Assets**

   All assets admitted by state insurance regulators in millions of dollars as of the most recent year end. This includes investments and current business assets such as receivables from agents, reinsurers and subscribers.

4. **New or Current Safety Rating**

   The rating assigned to the company as of the date of this Guide's publication. Our rating is measured on a scale from A to F and considers a wide range of factors. Highly-rated companies are, in our opinion, less likely to experience financial difficulties than lower-rated firms. See *About Weiss Safety Ratings* for more information.

5. **Previous Safety Rating**

   The rating assigned to the company prior to its most recent change.

6. **Date of Change**

   The date on which the rating upgrade or downgrade officially occurred. Normally, all rating changes are put into effect on a single day each quarter of the year. In some instances, however, a rating may have been changed outside of this normal update.

Withdrawn Ratings

INSURANCE COMPANY NAME	DOM. STATE	TOTAL ASSETS ($MIL)	RATING	PREVIOUS RATING	DATE
ALLEGIAN INS CO	TX	3.3	U	D	06/18/21
BRIGHT HLTH INS CO OF AL INC	AL	22.4	U	D	06/18/21
CAREMORE HEALTH PLAN OF ARIZONA INC	AZ	52.6	U	B-	06/18/21
CAREMORE HEALTH PLAN OF NEVADA	NV	31.9	U	B-	06/18/21
HARVARD PILGRIM HEALTH CARE INC	MA	1,001.5	U	C	06/18/21
MG INSURANCE CO	AZ	29.9	U	A	06/18/21
RENAISSANCE L&H INS CO OF AMERICA	IN	50.2	U	B-	06/18/21
SETON INSURANCE COMPANY	TX	8.0	U	D+	06/18/21

Rating Upgrades

AMERICAN BENEFIT LIFE INS CO was upgraded to B- from C+ in April 2021 based on a higher stability index., notably the recent upgrade of affiliated company LIBERTY BANKERS LIFE INS CO to C+ from C.

AMERICAN CONTINENTAL INS CO was upgraded to C+ from C in April 2021 based on capitalization index, a greatly improved five-year profitability index and a higher stability index. composite rating for affiliated Aetna Inc Group rose to B from B-.

AMERICHOICE OF NEW JERSEY INC (NJ) was upgraded to B- from C+ in June 2021 based on expansion in the profitability index, an increase in the capitalization index, and development in the stability index.

BANKERS RESERVE LIFE INS CO OF WI (WI) was upgraded to C+ from C in June 2021 based on expansion in the profitability index, development in the stability index, and an increase in the capitalization index.

BAY AREA ACCOUNTABLE CARE (CA) was upgraded to D from D- in June 2021 based on a substantial increase in the capitalization index, development in the stability index, and progress in the liquidity index.

BLUE CROSS BLUE SHIELD OF MA (MA) was upgraded to B- from C+ in June 2021 based on development in the stability index, expansion in the profitability index, and an increase in the capitalization index.

BLUE CROSS BLUE SHIELD OF VERMONT (VT) was upgraded to B- from C+ in June 2021 based on substantial expansion in the profitability index, an increase in the capitalization index, and development in the stability index.

BOSTON MEDICAL CENTER HEALTH PLAN (MA) was upgraded to B- from C in June 2021 based on expansion in the profitability index and an increase in the capitalization index.

BRAVO HEALTH MID-ATLANTIC INC (MD) was upgraded to B from B- in June 2021 based on expansion in the profitability index, an increase in the capitalization index, and development in the stability index.

BRIGHTHOUSE LIFE INSURANCE CO was upgraded to D+ from D in April 2021 based on a higher capitalization index and a greatly improved five-year profitability index.

CARESOURCE OHIO INC (OH) was upgraded to B from B- in June 2021 based on expansion in the profitability index, an increase in the capitalization index, and development in the stability index.

CINCINNATI EQUITABLE LIFE INS CO was upgraded to B from D in April 2021 based on a greatly improved stability index. composite rating for affiliated Cincinnati Equitable Companies Group rose to B from D.

CMNTY CARE HLTH PLAN OF LA INC (LA) was upgraded to B from B- in June 2021 based on substantial development in the stability index, expansion in the profitability index, and an increase in the capitalization index.

COMPANION LIFE INS CO OF CA was upgraded to B+ from B in April 2021 based on an improved capitalization index, a markedly improved five-year profitability index and a higher stability index. enhanced financial strength of affiliates in Blue Cross Blue Shield of SC Group.

COMPCARE HEALTH SERVICES INS CORP (WI) was upgraded to A from A- in June 2021 based on substantial development in the stability index, an increase in the capitalization index, and expansion in the profitability index.

CONNECTICARE INS CO (CT) was upgraded to B- from C+ in June 2021 based on development in the stability index, an increase in the capitalization index, and expansion in the profitability index.

COVENTRY HEALTH CARE OF ILLINOIS INC (IL) was upgraded to B from B- in June 2021 based on an increase in the capitalization index, expansion in the profitability index, and development in the stability index.

DAVITA HEALTHCARE PARTNERS PLAN INC (CA) was upgraded to D from D- in June 2021 based on substantial progress in the liquidity index, a substantial increase in the capitalization index, substantial development in the stability index, and expansion in the profitability index.

Rating Upgrades (Continued)

DENVER HEALTH MEDICAL PLAN INC (CO) was upgraded to B from B- in June 2021 based on expansion in the profitability index, an increase in the capitalization index, and development in the stability index.

DRISCOLL CHILDRENS HEALTH PLAN (TX) was upgraded to C from C- in June 2021 based on substantial expansion in the profitability index and a substantial increase in the capitalization index.

FALLON COMMUNITY HEALTH PLAN (MA) was upgraded to C+ from C in June 2021 based on substantial expansion in the profitability index, progress in the liquidity index, and an increase in the capitalization index.

FLORIDA MHS INC (FL) was upgraded to C- from D+ in June 2021 based on an increase in the capitalization index and development in the stability index.

GLOBALHEALTH INC (OK) was upgraded to D from D- in June 2021 based on a substantial increase in the capitalization index, substantial development in the stability index, and progress in the liquidity index.

GOLDEN SECURITY INS CO (TN) was upgraded to B+ from B in June 2021 based on expansion in the profitability index, an increase in the capitalization index, and development in the stability index.

HARVARD PILGRIM HC OF NEW ENGLAND (MA) was upgraded to B from B- in June 2021 based on development in the stability index, expansion in the profitability index, and an increase in the capitalization index.

HEALTH PLAN OF WV INC (WV) was upgraded to C from C- in June 2021 based on substantial expansion in the profitability index, an increase in the capitalization index, progress in the liquidity index, and development in the stability index.

HEALTHNOW NY INC (NY) was upgraded to A from B+ in June 2021 based on substantial development in the stability index and expansion in the profitability index.

HEALTHSPRING OF FLORIDA INC (FL) was upgraded to B+ from B in June 2021 based on development in the stability index, expansion in the profitability index, and an increase in the capitalization index.

HIGHMARK BCBSD INC (DE) was upgraded to B+ from B in June 2021 based on substantial development in the stability index and expansion in the profitability index.

HIGHMARK INC (PA) was upgraded to B from C+ in June 2021 based on development in the stability index and expansion in the profitability index.

HOMETOWN HEALTH PROVIDERS INS CO (NV) was upgraded to B- from C+ in June 2021 based on development in the stability index, expansion in the profitability index, and an increase in the capitalization index.

HOOSIER MOTOR MUTUAL INS CO (IN) was upgraded to B from C+ in June 2021 based on substantial expansion in the profitability index and development in the stability index.

HPHC INS CO (MA) was upgraded to C from C- in June 2021 based on substantial expansion in the profitability index, development in the stability index, and an increase in the capitalization index.

HUMANA HEALTH BENEFIT PLAN LA (LA) was upgraded to B from B- in June 2021 based on an increase in the capitalization index, development in the stability index, and expansion in the profitability index.

HUMANA INS CO (WI) (WI) was upgraded to A from B+ in June 2021 based on expansion in the profitability index, development in the stability index, and an increase in the capitalization index.

HUMANADENTAL INS CO (WI) was upgraded to C+ from C in June 2021 based on substantial expansion in the profitability index and an increase in the capitalization index.

INDEPENDENT HEALTH ASSOC INC (NY) was upgraded to B+ from B in June 2021 based on substantial development in the stability index and expansion in the profitability index.

INDEPENDENT HEALTH BENEFITS CORP (NY) was upgraded to B from B- in June 2021 based on expansion in the profitability index, an increase in the capitalization index, and development in the stability index.

INNOVATION HEALTH INS CO (VA) was upgraded to C from C- in June 2021 based on substantial expansion in the profitability index.

LIBERTY BANKERS LIFE INS CO was upgraded to C+ from C in April 2021 based on a higher capitalization index and a higher stability index.

LOYAL AMERICAN LIFE INS CO was upgraded to B from B- in April 2021 based on a markedly improved capitalization index and a higher stability index.

MEDICAL ASSOCIATES HEALTH PLAN INC (IA) was upgraded to B from B- in June 2021 based on expansion in the profitability index, development in the stability index, and an increase in the capitalization index.

MEDSTAR FAMILY CHOICE INC (MD) was upgraded to C from C- in June 2021 based on substantial expansion in the profitability index, an increase in the capitalization index, and development in the stability index.

MERIDIAN HEALTH PLAN OF MICHIGAN INC (MI) was upgraded to C from C- in June 2021 based on substantial expansion in the profitability index, development in the stability index, an increase in the capitalization index, and progress in the liquidity index.

MHS HEALTH WISCONSIN (WI) was upgraded to B from B- in June 2021 based on an increase in the capitalization index, expansion in the profitability index, and development in the stability index.

MISSOURI VALLEY L&H INS CO (MO) was upgraded to C+ from C in June 2021 based on expansion in the profitability index and an increase in the capitalization index.

MVP HEALTH SERVICES CORP (NY) was upgraded to B- from C in June 2021 based on a substantial increase in the capitalization index, substantial development in the stability index, and substantial expansion in the profitability index.

NATIONAL FOUNDATION LIFE INS CO was upgraded to A from B+ in April 2021 based on a higher capitalization index and a markedly improved stability index. composite rating for affiliated Credit Suisse Group rose to B+ from B-.

NETWORK HEALTH INS CORP (WI) was upgraded to B from C+ in June 2021 based on expansion in the profitability index, an increase in the capitalization index, and development in the stability index.

PAVONIA LIFE INS CO OF MICHIGAN was upgraded to D+ from D in April 2021 based on a higher capitalization index, an improved investment safety index and a greatly improved stability index. composite rating for affiliated SNA Capital LLC Group rose to C- from D+.

PAVONIA LIFE INS CO OF NEW YORK was upgraded to C- from D+ in April 2021 based on a markedly improved stability index. composite rating for affiliated SNA Capital LLC Group rose to C- from D+, notably the recent upgrade of affiliated company PAVONIA LIFE INS CO OF MICHIGAN to D+ from D.

PEACH STATE HEALTH PLAN INC (GA) was upgraded to B from B- in June 2021 based on expansion in the profitability index and development in the stability index.

PHYSICIANS HEALTH PLAN OF NO IN (IN) was upgraded to B+ from B in June 2021 based on expansion in the profitability index, development in the stability index, and an increase in the capitalization index.

PLATEAU INS CO was upgraded to B from B- in April 2021 based on a higher capitalization index and an improved five-year profitability index.

PREFERREDONE INS CO (MN) was upgraded to C from C- in June 2021 based on substantial expansion in the profitability index, development in the stability index, an increase in the capitalization index, and progress in the liquidity index.

QUARTZ HEALTH PLAN MN CORP (MN) was upgraded to C+ from C in June 2021 based on expansion in the profitability index.

Rating Upgrades (Continued)

RENAISSANCE L&H INS CO OF AMERICA was upgraded to B from C+ in April 2021 based on a higher capitalization index, a higher investment safety index, a higher five-year profitability index and a markedly improved stability index.

RENAISSANCE L&H INS CO OF NY was upgraded to C+ from C in April 2021 based on an improved capitalization index. enhanced financial strength of affiliates in Renaissance Health Service Corporati Group, notably the recent upgrade of affiliated company RENAISSANCE L&H INS CO OF AMERICA to B from C+.

RIVERSOURCE LIFE INS CO was upgraded to B from C+ in April 2021 based on a higher capitalization index, a higher five-year profitability index and a markedly improved stability index.

SAMARITAN HEALTH PLANS INC (OR) was upgraded to B- from C+ in June 2021 based on expansion in the profitability index and an increase in the capitalization index.

SELECTHEALTH INC (UT) was upgraded to B+ from B in June 2021 based on substantial development in the stability index and expansion in the profitability index.

SILVERSCRIPT INS CO (TN) was upgraded to D+ from D in June 2021 based on development in the stability index.

SUNSHINE HEALTH (FL) was upgraded to C+ from C in June 2021 based on development in the stability index, expansion in the profitability index, and an increase in the capitalization index.

TALCOTT RESOLUTION LIFE INS CO was upgraded to B- from C+ in April 2021 based on a higher five-year profitability index and a markedly improved stability index.

TEXAS CHILDRENS HEALTH PLAN INC (TX) was upgraded to C from D+ in June 2021 based on substantial expansion in the profitability index, a substantial increase in the capitalization index, development in the stability index, and progress in the liquidity index.

THP INS CO (WV) was upgraded to C from C- in June 2021 based on expansion in the profitability index, an increase in the capitalization index, and development in the stability index.

TUFTS INS CO (MA) was upgraded to B- from C+ in June 2021 based on development in the stability index, expansion in the profitability index, and an increase in the capitalization index.

UNICARE HEALTH PLAN OF WEST VIRGINIA (WV) was upgraded to A from A- in June 2021 based on an increase in the capitalization index and expansion in the profitability index.

UNICARE LIFE & HEALTH INS CO was upgraded to B from B- in April 2021 based on a markedly improved capitalization index and a higher five-year profitability index. composite rating for affiliated Anthem Inc Group rose to A- from B.

UNITED AMERICAN INS CO was upgraded to B from B- in April 2021 based on a markedly improved capitalization index, a higher five-year profitability index and a higher stability index.

UNITED HEALTHCARE INS CO OF IL (IL) was upgraded to A- from B+ in June 2021 based on expansion in the profitability index, development in the stability index, and an increase in the capitalization index.

UNIVERSAL CARE (CA) was upgraded to E from E- in June 2021 based on a substantial increase in the capitalization index and development in the stability index.

UNIVERSAL FIDELITY LIFE INS CO was upgraded to B- from C+ in April 2021 based on a markedly improved capitalization index, an improved five-year profitability index and an improved stability index.

UPMC HEALTH NETWORK INC (PA) was upgraded to C+ from C in June 2021 based on a substantial increase in the capitalization index and development in the stability index.

Rating Upgrades (Continued)

UPMC HEALTH OPTIONS INC (PA) was upgraded to B from C+ in June 2021 based on substantial expansion in the profitability index and an increase in the capitalization index.

USABLE MUTUAL INS CO (AR) was upgraded to B+ from B in June 2021 based on development in the stability index and expansion in the profitability index.

VENTURA COUNTY HEALTH CARE PLAN (CA) was upgraded to E+ from E in June 2021 based on an increase in the capitalization index, expansion in the profitability index, and development in the stability index.

WELLCARE HEALTH INS OF ARIZONA INC (AZ) was upgraded to B- from C in June 2021 based on expansion in the profitability index, an increase in the capitalization index, and development in the stability index.

WELLCARE OF GEORGIA INC (GA) was upgraded to B+ from B in June 2021 based on substantial development in the stability index, an increase in the capitalization index, and expansion in the profitability index.

WELLCARE OF SOUTH CAROLINA INC (SC) was upgraded to B from B- in June 2021 based on development in the stability index and an increase in the capitalization index.

WELLCARE OF TEXAS INC (TX) was upgraded to A- from B in June 2021 based on expansion in the profitability index, development in the stability index, and an increase in the capitalization index.

Rating Downgrades

BANKERS FIDELITY ASR CO was downgraded to C from C+ in April 2021 due to capitalization index. In addition, the financial strength of affiliates in Atlantic American Corp is declining Group.

CALIFORNIA HEALTH & WELLNESS PLAN (CA) was downgraded to E from D+ in June 2021 based on a substantial drop in the stability index, a substantial decline in the capitalization index, and a diminishment in the profitability index.

CIGNA HEALTHCARE OF FLORIDA INC (FL) was downgraded to C- from C in June 2021 based on a diminishment in the profitability index and a decrease in the capitalization index.

CIGNA HEALTHCARE OF ILLINOIS INC (IL) was downgraded to D from C in June 2021 based on a substantial drop in the stability index and a decrease in the capitalization index.

COMMUNITY HEALTH GROUP (CA) was downgraded to C- from B- in June 2021 based on a substantial decline in the capitalization index, a substantial drop in the stability index, a substantial diminishment in the profitability index, and contraction in the liquidity index.

COMMUNITYCARE L&H INS CO (OK) was downgraded to D from D+ in June 2021 based on a diminishment in the profitability index.

DAKOTA CAPITAL LIFE INS CO was downgraded to E+ from D in April 2021 due to a significant decline in its investment safety index. In addition, the composite rating for affiliated US Alliance Corp Group fell to E+ from D.

EL PASO FIRST HEALTH PLANS INC (TX) was downgraded to B from B+ in June 2021 based on a drop in the stability index, a decrease in the capitalization index, and a diminishment in the profitability index.

EMPLOYERS PROTECTIVE INS CO was downgraded to B- from B in April 2021 due to a declining capitalization index. In addition, the composite rating for affiliated Hawaii Employers Mutual Insurance Co Group fell to C+ from B.

FIRST PENN-PACIFIC LIFE INS CO was downgraded to B- from B in April 2021 due to a significant decline in its capitalization index, a substantially lower five-year profitability index and a significant decline in its stability index.

FLORIDA COMBINED LIFE INS CO INC was downgraded to C from B in April 2021 due to a substantially lower stability index.

FREEDOM HEALTH INC (FL) was downgraded to B from B+ in June 2021 based on a drop in the stability index, a diminishment in the profitability index, and a decrease in the capitalization index.

GATEWAY HEALTH PLAN OF OHIO INC (OH) was downgraded to C- from C in June 2021 based on a decrease in the capitalization index and a drop in the stability index.

GREAT SOUTHERN LIFE INS CO was downgraded to B- from B in April 2021 due to a substantially lower five-year profitability index and a significant decline in its stability index.

HAP EMPOWERED HEALTH PLAN INC (MI) was downgraded to D+ from C- in June 2021 based on a diminishment in the profitability index and a drop in the stability index.

HNE INS CO (MA) was downgraded to B- from B in June 2021 based on a substantial diminishment in the profitability index and a drop in the stability index.

HOPKINS HEALTH ADV INC (MD) was downgraded to E from D in June 2021 based on a substantial decline in the capitalization index, a substantial drop in the stability index, a diminishment in the profitability index, and contraction in the liquidity index.

HUMANA HEALTH CO OF NEW YORK INC (NY) was downgraded to C- from C in June 2021 based on a decrease in the capitalization index.

HUMANA HEALTH PLAN INC was downgraded to D from C- in June 2021 based on the overall strength of the index ratios.

HUMANA MEDICAL PLAN OF UTAH INC (UT) was downgraded to D+ from C- in June 2021 based on a decrease in the capitalization index.

Rating Downgrades (Continued)

KAISER FNDTN HLTH PLAN OF WA (WA) was downgraded to C+ from B- in June 2021 based on a decrease in the capitalization index.

KAISER FNDTN HLTH PLAN WA OPTN (WA) was downgraded to C from C+ in June 2021 based on a diminishment in the profitability index, a drop in the stability index, and a decrease in the capitalization index.

MEDAMERICA INS CO OF FL was downgraded to C from B in April 2021 due to a significant decline in its capitalization index and a substantially lower investment safety index. In addition, the composite rating for affiliated Lifetime Healthcare Inc Group fell to C from C+.

MEDAMERICA INS CO OF NEW YORK was downgraded to D+ from C in April 2021 due to a substantially lower stability index.

MEDCO CONTAINMENT LIFE INS CO (PA) was downgraded to D+ from C- in June 2021 based on a substantial diminishment in the profitability index.

MID-WEST NATIONAL LIFE INS CO OF TN was downgraded to C+ from B in April 2021 due to a substantially lower capitalization index, a significant decline in its five-year profitability index and a substantially lower stability index. In addition, the composite rating for affiliated Blackstone Investor Group fell to C from B-, as exemplified by recent downgrade of affiliates: UNIMERICA INS CO to B- from B. PACIFICARE LIFE & HEALTH INS CO to B- from B.

MII LIFE INSURANCE INC (MN) was downgraded to C- from C in June 2021 based on a substantial diminishment in the profitability index and a drop in the stability index.

MISSOURI CARE INC (MO) was downgraded to C from B- in June 2021 based on a substantial diminishment in the profitability index.

MOLINA HEALTHCARE OF FLORIDA INC (FL) was downgraded to D from D+ in June 2021 based on a decrease in the capitalization index.

MOLINA HEALTHCARE OF TEXAS INS CO was downgraded to C from C+ in April 2021 due to a declining five-year profitability index. In addition, the composite rating for affiliated Molina Healthcare Inc Group fell to C from B-.

NEIGHBORHOOD HEALTH PARTNERSHIP INC (FL) was downgraded to C+ from B- in June 2021 based on a decrease in the capitalization index and a drop in the stability index.

NEW ENGLAND LIFE INS CO was downgraded to D+ from B in April 2021 due to a substantially lower stability index. In addition, the composite rating for affiliated Brighthouse Financial Inc Group fell to D from B.

OHIO STATE LIFE INS CO was downgraded to E+ from C- in April 2021 due to a significant decline in its investment safety index, a declining five-year profitability index and a declining stability index.

PACIFICARE LIFE & HEALTH INS CO was downgraded to B- from B in April 2021 due to a significant decline in its stability index. In addition, the composite rating for affiliated UnitedHealth Group Inc fell to C from B-, per the recent downgrade of affiliated company UNIMERICA INS CO to B- from B.

PARTNERSHIP HEALTHPLAN OF CALIFORNIA (CA) was downgraded to C from C+ in June 2021 based on a diminishment in the profitability index and a drop in the stability index.

SECURITYCARE OF TENNESSEE INC was downgraded to C from C+ in June 2021 based on the overall strength of the index ratios.

TAKECARE INS CO (GU) was downgraded to D- from D in June 2021 based on a diminishment in the profitability index.

TIME INS CO was downgraded to E- from E in April 2021 due to a significant decline in its capitalization index, a substantially lower five-year profitability index and a substantially lower stability index.

TRILLIUM COMMUNITY HEALTH PLAN INC (OR) was downgraded to C+ from B in June 2021 based on a diminishment in the profitability index.

UNIMERICA INS CO was downgraded to B- from B in April 2021 due to a lower stability index. In addition, the composite rating for affiliated UnitedHealth Group Inc fell to C from B-.

Rating Downgrades (Continued)

UNITED HEALTHCARE OF ALABAMA INC (AL) was downgraded to D from D+ in June 2021 based on a diminishment in the profitability index.

UNITED HEALTHCARE OF FLORIDA INC (FL) was downgraded to C+ from B- in June 2021 based on a substantial drop in the stability index and a decrease in the capitalization index.

UPPER PENINSULA HEALTH PLAN INC (MI) was downgraded to B from B+ in June 2021 based on a substantial drop in the stability index, a diminishment in the profitability index, and a decrease in the capitalization index.

Appendix

Risk-Adjusted Capital in Weiss Rating Models

There are three distinct rating models used to generate the ratings in this Guide. The first model is for companies that register with state insurance departments under the official classification of Life and Annuity Insurers. The second model is for companies that register under the official classification of Property and Casualty Insurers. The third is for health insurers that register as Health plans with the state insurance departments.

A key aspect of both models is the risk-adjusted capital calculations. Therefore, these are discussed in greater detail.

Risk-Adjusted Capital for Life and Annuity Insurers in Weiss Rating Model

Among the most important indicators used in the analysis of an individual company are our two risk-adjusted capital ratios, which are useful tools in determining exposure to investment, liquidity and insurance risk in relation to the capital the company has to cover those risks.

The first risk-adjusted capital ratio evaluates the company's ability to withstand a moderate loss scenario. The second ratio evaluates the company's ability to withstand a severe loss scenario.

In order to calculate these risk-adjusted capital ratios, we follow these steps:

1. Capital Resources	First, we add up all of the company's resources which could be used to cover losses. These include capital, surplus, the Asset Valuation Reserve (AVR), and a portion of the provision for future policyholders' dividends, where appropriate. Additional credit may also be given for the use of conservative reserving assumptions and other "hidden capital" when applicable.
2. Target Capital	Next, we determine the company's target capital. This answers the question: Based upon the company's level of risk in both its insurance business and its investment portfolio, how much capital would it need to cover potential losses during a moderate loss scenario? In other words, we determine how much capital we believe this company *should* have.
3. Risk-Adjusted Capital Ratio #1	We compare the results of step 1 with those of step 2. Specifically, we divide the "capital resources" by the "target capital" and express it in terms of a ratio. This ratio is called RACR #1. (See next page for more detail on methodology.)
	If a company has a Risk-Adjusted Capital Ratio of 1.0 or more, it means the company has all of the capital we believe it requires to withstand potential losses which could be inflicted by a moderate loss scenario. If the company has less than 1.0, it does not currently have all of the basic capital resources we think it needs. During times of financial distress, companies often have access to additional capital through contributions from a parent company, current profits or reductions in policyholder dividends. Therefore, an allowance is made in our rating system for firms with somewhat less than 1.0 Risk-Adjusted Capital Ratios.

4. Risk-Adjusted   We repeat steps 2 and 3, but now assuming a severe loss scenario. This
Capital Ratio #2   ratio is called RACR #2.

5. Capitalization   We convert RACR #1 and #2 into an index. It is measured on a scale of
Index   zero to ten, with ten being the best and seven or better considered strong.
                              A company whose capital, surplus and AVR equal its target capital will
                              have a Risk-Adjusted Capital Ratio of 1.0 and a Risk-Adjusted Capital
                              Index of 7.0.

How We Determine Target Capital

The basic procedure for determining target capital is to ask these questions:

1.   What is the breakdown of the company's investment portfolio and types of business?

2.   For each category, what are the potential losses which could be incurred in the loss scenario?

3.   In order to cover those potential losses, how much in capital resources does the company
        need? It stands to reason that more capital is needed as a cushion for losses on high-risk
        investments, such as junk bonds, than would be necessary for low-risk investments, such as
        AAA-rated utility bonds.

        Unfortunately, the same questions we have raised about Wall Street rating systems with
        respect to how they rate insurance companies can be asked about the way they rate bonds.
        However, we do not rate bonds ourselves. Therefore, we must rely upon the bond ratings of
        other rating agencies. This is another reason why we have stricter capital requirements for the
        insurance companies. It accounts for the fact that they may need some extra protection in case
        an AAA-rated bond may not be quite as good as it appears to be.

        Finally, target capital is adjusted for the company's spread of risk in the diversification of its
        investment portfolio, the size and number of the policies it writes and the diversification of its
        business.

Table 1 on the next page shows target capital percentages used in Weiss Risk-Adjusted Capital
Ratios #1 and #2 (RACR #1 and RACR #2).

The percentages shown in the table answer the question: How much should the firm hold in capital
resources for every $100 it has committed to each category? Several of the items in Table 1 are
expressed as ranges. The actual percentages used in the calculation of target capital for an individual
company may vary due to the levels of risks in the operations, investments or policy obligations of
that specific company.

Table 1. Target Capital Percentages

Asset Risk		Weiss Ratings	
		RACR#1 (%)	RACR#2 (%)
Bonds			
	Government guaranteed bonds	0	0
	Class 1	.5-.75	1-1.5
	Class 2	2	5
	Class 3	5	15
	Class 4	10	30
	Class 5	20	60
	Class 6	20	60
Mortgages			
	In good standing	0.5	1
	90 days overdue	1.7-20	3.8-25
	In process of foreclosure	25-33	33-50
Real Estate			
	Class 1	20	50
	Class 2	10	33
Preferred Stock			
	Class 1	3	5
	Class 2	4	6
	Class 3	7	9
	Class 4	12	15
	Class 5	22	29
	Class 6	30	39
	Class 7	3-30	5-39
Common Stock			
	Unaffiliated	25	33
	Affiliated	25-100	33-100
Short-term investment		0.5	1
Premium notes		2	5
Collateral loans		2	5
Separate account equity		25	33
Other invested assets		5	10
Insurance Risk			
Individual life reserves*		.06-.15	.08-.21
Group life reserves*		.05-.12	.06-.16
Individual Health Premiums			
	Class 1	12-20	15-25
	Class 2	9.6	12
	Class 3	6.4	8
	Class 4	12-28	15-35
	Class 5	12-20	15-25
Group Health Premiums			
	Class 1	5.6-12	7-15
	Class 2	20	25
	Class 3	9.6	12
	Class 4	6.4	8
	Class 5	12-20	15-25
Managed care credit		5-40	6-50
Premiums subject to rate guarantees		100-209	120-250
Individual claim reserves		4	5
Group claim reserves		4	5
Reinsurance		0-2	0-5
Interest Rate Risk			
Policy loans		0-2	0-5
Life reserves		1-2	1-3
Individual annuity reserves		1-3	1-5
Group annuity reserves		1-2	1-3
Guaranteed interest contract reserves		1-2	1-3

All numbers are shown for illustrative purposes. Figures actually used in the formula vary annually based on industry experience.
*Based on net amount at risk.

Investment Class

Descriptions

Government guaranteed bonds		Guaranteed bonds issued by U.S. and other governments which receive the top rating of state insurance commissioners.
Bonds	Class 1	Investment grade bonds rated AAA, AA or A by Moody's or Standard & Poor's or deemed AAA - A equivalent by state insurance commissioners.
	Class 2	Investment grade bonds with some speculative elements, rated BBB or equivalent.
	Class 3	Noninvestment grade bonds, rated BB or equivalent.
	Class 4	Noninvestment grade bonds, rated B or equivalent.
	Class 5	Noninvestment grade bonds, rated CCC, CC or C or equivalent.
	Class 6	Noninvestment grade bonds, in or near default.
Mortgages		Mortgages in good standing
		Mortgages 90 days past due
		Mortgages in process of foreclosure
Real Estate	Class 1	Properties acquired in satisfaction of debt.
	Class 2	Company occupied and other investment properties.
Preferred stock	Class 1	Highest quality unaffiliated preferred stock.
	Class 2	High quality unaffiliated preferred stock.
	Class 3	Medium quality unaffiliated preferred stock.
	Class 4	Low quality unaffiliated preferred stock.
	Class 5	Lowest quality unaffiliated preferred stock.
	Class 6	Unaffiliated preferred stock, in or near default.
	Class 7	Affiliated preferred stock.
Common stock		Unaffiliated common stock.
		Affiliated common stock.
Short-term investments		All investments whose maturities at the time of acquisition were one year or less.
Premium Notes		Loans for payment of premiums.
Collateral loans		Loans made to a company or individual where the underlying security is in the form of bonds, stocks, or other marketable securities.
Separate account assets		Investments held in an account segregated from the general assets of the company, generally used to provide variable annuity benefits.
Other invested assets		Any invested assets that do not fit under the main categories above.
Individual life reserves		Funds set aside for payment of life insurance benefits under an individual contract rather than a company or group, underwriting based on individual profile.
Group life reserves		Funds set aside for payment of life insurance benefits under a contract with at least 10 people whereby all members have a common interest and are joined for a reason other than to obtain insurance.
Individual health premiums	Class 1	Usual and customary hospital and medical premiums which include traditional medical reimbursement plans that are subject to annual rate increases based on the company's claims experience.
	Class 2	Medicare supplement, dental, and other limited benefits anticipating rate increases.
	Class 3	Hospital indemnity plans, accidental death and dismemberment policies, and other limited benefits not anticipating rate increases.
	Class 4	Noncancelable disability income.
	Class 5	Guaranteed renewable disability income.

Group health premiums	Class 1	Usual and customary hospital and medical premiums which include traditional medical reimbursement plans that are subject to annual rate increases based on the company's claims experience.
	Class 2	Stop loss and minimum premium where a known claims liability is minimal or nonexistent.
	Class 3	Medicare supplement, dental, and other limited benefits anticipating rate increases.
	Class 4	Hospital indemnity plans, accidental death and dismemberment policies, and other limited benefits not anticipating rate increases.
	Class 5	Disability Income.
Managed care credit		Premiums for HMO and PPO business which carry less risk than traditional indemnity business. Included in this credit are provider compensation arrangements such as salary, capitation and fixed payment per service.
Premiums subject to rate guarantees		Health insurance premiums from policies where the rate paid by the policyholder is guaranteed for a period of time, such as one year, 15 months, 27 months or 37 months.
Individual claim reserves		Accident and health reserves for claims on individual policies.
Group claim reserves		Accident and health reserves for claims on group policies.
Reinsurance		Amounts recoverable on paid and unpaid losses for all reinsurance ceded; unearned premiums on accident and health reinsurance ceded; and funds held with unauthorized reinsurers.
Policy loans		Loans against the cash value of a life insurance policy.
Life reserves		Reserves for life insurance claims net of reinsurance and policy loans.
Individual annuity reserves		Reserves held in order to pay off maturing individual annuities or those surrendered before maturity.
Group annuity reserves		Reserves held in order to pay off maturing group annuities or those surrendered before maturity.
GIC reserves		Reserves held to pay off maturing guaranteed interest contracts.

Table 2. Bond Default Rates - potential losses as a percent of bond portfolio

	(1)	(2)	(3)	(4)	(5) Weiss	(6)	(7)	(8)
Bond Rating	Moody's 15 Yr Rate (%)	Moody's 12 Yr Rate (%)	Worst Year (%)	3 Cum. Recession Years (%)	15 Year Rate (%)	Assumed Loss Rate (%)	Losses as % of Holdings (%)	RACR #2 Rate (%)
Aaa	0.73	0.55	0.08	0.24	0.79	50	0.95	1.00
Aa	1.39	1.04	0.13	0.39	1.43	50	1.09	1.00
A	4.05	2.96	0.35	1.05	4.02	55	2.02	1.00
Baa	7.27	5.29	0.67	2.02	7.31	60	5.15	5.00
Ba	23.93	19.57	2.04	6.11	25.68	65	23.71	15.00
B	43.37	39.30	4.99	14.96	54.26	70	43.57	30.00

Comments On Target Capital Percentages

The factors that are chiefly responsible for the conservative results of our Risk-Adjusted Capital Ratios are the investment risks of bond Classes 2 - 6, mortgages, real estate and affiliate common stock as well as the interest rate risk for annuities and GICs. Comments on the basis of these figures are found below. Additional comments address factors that vary based on particular performance or risk characteristics of the individual company.

Bonds   Target capital percentages for bonds are derived from a model that factors in historical cumulative bond default rates from the last 45 years and the additional loss potential during a prolonged economic decline. **Table 2** shows how this was done for each bond rating classification. A 15-year cumulative default rate is used (column 1), due to the 15-year average maturity at issue of bonds held by life insurance companies. These are historical default rates for 1970-2015 for each bond class, taken from *Annual Default Study.*

To factor in the additional loss potential of a severe three-year-long economic decline, we reduced the base to Moody's 12-year rate (column 2), determined the worst single year experience (column 3), extended that experience over three years (column 4), and added the historical 12-year rate to the 3-year projection to derive Weiss Ratings 15-year default rate (column 5). The next step was to determine the losses that could be expected from these defaults. This would be equivalent to the capital a company should have to cover those losses. Loss rates were assigned for each bond class (column 6), based on the fact that higher-rated issues generally carry less debt and the fact that the debt is also better secured, leading to higher recovery rates upon default. Column 7 shows losses as a percent of holdings for each bond class. Column 8 shows the target capital percentages that are used in RACR #2 (Table 1, RACR #2 column, Bonds – classes 1 to 6).

Regulations limiting junk bond holdings of insurers to a set percent of assets are a tacit acknowledgement that the reserve requirements used by State Insurance Commissioners are inadequate. If the figure adequately represented full loss potential, there would be no need to limit holdings through legislation since an adequate loss reserve would provide sufficient capital to absorb potential losses.

Mortgages

Mortgage default rates for the Risk-Adjusted Capital Ratios are derived from historical studies of mortgage and real estate losses in selected depressed markets. The rate for RACR #2 (Table 1, RACR #2 column, Mortgages – 90 days overdue) will vary between 3.8% and 25%, based on the performance of the company's mortgage portfolio in terms of mortgage loans 90 days or more past due, in process of foreclosure and foreclosed during the previous year.

Real Estate

The 33% rate (Table 1, RACR #2 column, Real Estate - Class 2) used for potential real estate losses in Weiss Ratings ratios is based on historical losses in depressed markets.

Affiliate Common Stock

The target capital rate on affiliate common stock for RACR #2 can vary between 33% and 100% (Table 1, RACR #2 column, Common stock – Affiliate), depending on the financial strength of the affiliate and the prospects for obtaining capital from the affiliate should the need arise.

Insurance Risk

Calculations of target capital for insurance risk vary according to categories. For individual and group life insurance, target capital is a percentage of net amount at risk (total amount of insurance in force less reserves). Individual and group health insurance risk is calculated as a percentage of premium. Categories vary from "usual and customary hospital and medical premiums" where risk is relatively low because losses from one year are recouped by annual rate increases, to "noncancellable disability income" where the risk of loss is greater because disability benefits are paid in future years without the possibility of recovery.

Reinsurance

This factor varies with the quality of the reinsuring companies and the type of reinsurance being used (e.g., co-insurance, modified co-insurance, yearly renewable term, etc.).

Interest Rate Risk On Annuities

The 1 - 5% rate on individual annuities as a percentage of reserves (Table 1, RACR #2 column 3, Individual annuity reserves), and the 1 - 3% rate for group annuities as a percentage of reserves (Table 1, RACR #2 column 3, Group annuity reserves and GICs), are derived from studies of potential losses that can occur when assets and liabilities are not properly matched.

Companies are especially prone to losses in this area for one of two reasons: (1) They promise high interest rates on their annuities and have not locked in corresponding yields on their investments. If interest rates fall, the company will have difficulties earning the promised rate. (2) They lock in high returns on their investments but allow policy surrenders without market value adjustments. If market values decline and surrenders increase, liquidity problems can result in substantial losses.

The target capital figure used for each company is based on the surrender characteristics of its policies, the interest rate used in calculating reserves and the actuarial analyses found in New York Regulation 126 filing, or similar studies where applicable.

Risk-Adjusted Capital for Property and Casualty Insurers

Over 100 companies that are registered with state insurance departments as property and casualty insurers offer health insurance policies. Our ratings on these companies make use of the data in the Property and Casualty Statutory Statements that are required by state insurance departments. These financial statements employ a system of accounting that differs from that used by companies filing Life and Health Statutory Statements. Some of the chief distinguishing features of the Property and Casualty Statutory Accounting include:

- Life and health companies must hold reserves to protect specifically against investment losses. Property and casualty insurers keep no equivalent protection. One of the consequences of the lack of an investment loss reserve is that property and casualty companies, on the average, hold more nonaffiliated common stock than do life insurers. This factor is considered in our evaluation of capital adequacy.

- Policy reserves for life insurers are reduced to reflect investment income to be earned between the time premiums are received by the company, and the time when claims are to be paid. Property and casualty companies generally do not reduce or discount their reserves for the time value of money.

- Underwriting profits and losses for property and casualty insurers are calculated without reference to investment income.

Despite these factors, it is our goal to provide ratings that consumers can easily understand and to make technical differences as transparent to consumers as possible. The final ratings are intended to give the same message about our opinion of insurers financial strength.

As with the life and health companies, there are two risk-adjusted capital ratios, which measure whether the company has enough capital to cover unexpected losses.

However, unlike the life and health companies, the risks related to pricing and claims are more important, while the risks associated with investments are reduced because there is little exposure to risky investments such as junk bonds or mortgages.

Pricing Risk   The risk that premium levels are not sufficient to establish adequate reserves and/or pay claims and related expenses. Individual target capital percentages are used for each line of business based on the riskiness of the line and the company's own experience with underwriting losses and reserve shortfalls. Target capital requirements are reduced to account for the time value of money.

Risky Lines of Business and Catastrophic Losses

These include fire, earthquake, multiple peril (including storm damage), and similar personal and commercial property coverage. Even excluding Hurricane Andrew, the insured losses from natural disasters since 1989 have been far greater than in previous decades. Yet, too many insurance companies are basing their risk calculations on the assumption that losses will return to more normal levels. They are not ready for the possibility that the pattern of increasing disasters might be a real, continuing trend.

Also considered high-risk lines are medical malpractice, general liability, product liability, and other similar liability coverage. Court awards for damages often run into the millions. These settlement amounts can be very difficult to predict. This uncertainty hinders an insurer's ability to accurately assess how much to charge policyholders and how much to set aside to pay claims. Of special concern are large, unexpected liabilities related to environmental damages such as asbestos. Similar risk may lie hidden in coverage for medical equipment and procedures, industrial wastes, carcinogens, and other substances found in products previously viewed as benign. Companies that offer a variety of types of insurance in addition to health coverage can get into financial difficulties due to any of their lines of business. Accordingly, it is essential that the company's whole operation be strong. If the company is overrun with claims from an earthquake of hurricane, its ability to pay health claims will also be affected.

Risk-Adjusted Capital for Health Insurers

As with the other rating systems, the health insurance system includes two risk-adjusted capital ratios to measure a company's ability to withstand unexpected losses during moderate and severe loss scenarios. Health insurers are more likely exposed to risk from pricing and claims than from investments. They have no interest rate risk, in terms of potential policy surrenders, the way life insurance companies do.

Capital resources include the company's net worth adjusted for surplus notes; credit or penalty for overstating or understating reserves; and credit or penalty for the company's ability to spread risk based on overall net worth of the company's affiliate group.

These health plans file yet another type of statutory statement, different from life and health or property and casualty insurers. Weiss Rating System for health insurers addresses the unique business and accounting factors relevant to these firms. Among the many differences are the following:

- Rather than setting up reserves as a liability the way life insurance companies do, health insurer claims reserves are part of net worth.

- Investments are carried at book value, but market value is shown on Schedule B of the statutory statement. Market values are considered in the capitalization and liquidity indexes.

- Health insurers do not hold reserves to protect specifically against investment losses. This factor is considered in our evaluation of capital adequacy.

- Health insurers do not have long-term obligations like life insurance and annuities. Accordingly, reserves are not discounted for the time value of money. Our analysis examines reserve adequacy by comparing one year's reserve estimates with claims and medical expenses actually paid during the subsequent year, without factoring in investment income.

LONG-TERM CARE INSURANCE PLANNER

This planner is designed to help you decide what kind of long-term care insurance is best for you and help you shop for the policy that meets your needs. Many insurers charge a lot more – or less – for very similar policies. So there's a great benefit to shopping around. No policy is exactly alike. However, if you follow these steps, it will be easier to compare policies side by side:

Step 1: Try to determine, ahead of time, what type of care you think you will need from others <u>beyond</u> the assistance your own family members may be able to provide:

	Yes	No
Custodial Care	[ ]	[ ]
Intermediate Care	[ ]	[ ]
Skilled Care	[ ]	[ ]

This isn't easy, because it's often hard to anticipate your future needs, but try your best to decide if you're going to want access to one of the following. <u>Custodial care</u> is provided by someone without medical training who helps you with daily activities. <u>Intermediate care</u> includes occasional nursing and rehabilitative care supervised by skilled medical personnel. <u>Skilled care</u> includes 24-hour care provided by a skilled nurse or therapist.

Step 2: Decide <u>where</u> you would most likely be receiving the care?

	Yes	No
In-Home Care*	[ ]	[ ]
Nursing Home*	[ ]	[ ]
Adult Day Care	[ ]	[ ]
Assisted Living Facility	[ ]	[ ]
Other _____	[ ]	[ ]

*Typically available with all three levels of care – custodial, intermediate, and skilled.

Most people prefer in-home care. However, if you have no family members to help you at home, in-home care could be prohibitively expensive, especially if it requires skilled care. Nursing homes are designed for 24-hour care and are best utilized for short-term stays. Adult day care is an option, but will probably require someone, such as a family member, who can drop you off and pick you up daily. Assisted living facilities are increasingly popular, offering a good balance between independence and assistance. Other types of care could include hospice care (for the terminally ill) or respite care (temporary assistance to help relieve family members).

Step 3: Check out the facilities in the area in which you plan to live, make sure you're comfortable with them, and find out much how they cost:

	Estimated Costs
In-Home Care	_____
Nursing Home	_____
Assisted Living Facility	_____
Adult Day Care	_____
Other	_____

The insurance company is going to pay you a daily benefit that will be applied toward the cost of your care. Most of the costs above that daily benefit will have to come out of your own pocket. Therefore, find a facility that you'd be comfortable with, and then try to get a general idea of how much it would cost. Each facility may offer a different rate schedule for each level of care it provides, so make sure you understand the differences. For care within your home, contact a home care agency and ask them about the going rates for home nurses and therapists. Also consider costs associated with any modifications that may be needed for your home, such as wheelchair accessibility, handicap rails, etc.

Step 4: Try to estimate how much of the long-term care expenses you will be able to pay on your own: $_____ per month.

Your financial planner may be able to give you an estimate of your retirement income available for health care. However, even a good estimate can be off the mark, so make sure your policy covers enough to avoid being financially strapped by long-term care expenses. Later, make sure your agent takes this information into consideration when he works out the terms of your policy. He should limit your out-of-pocket expenses to what you have indicated here.

Step 5: Try to arrive at a reasonable guess regarding when you might start using the benefits.

_____

Again, it's hard to predict. But if you're in reasonably good health and you have a family history of longevity, that's something to consider. If you're already suffering from chronic health problems, you may need the benefits sooner rather than later. If it's more than 10 years from now, you can buy a long-term care policy with an optional inflation protection feature to help protect against the rising cost of health care. This can add significantly to the cost, but you get what you pay for. Typically, the insurance company will add an extra five percent to your daily benefit, compounded annually. Thus, if the policy provides a $100 daily benefit now, it would rise to $163 in 10 years.

Step 6: Determine whether you prefer a "tax-qualified" policy or a "non-qualified" policy:

	Yes	No
Tax-Qualified Policy	[ ]	[ ]
Non-Qualified Policy	[ ]	[ ]

If you buy a tax-qualified policy, you will be able to claim the policy premiums as itemized medical expenses on your tax return. Furthermore, the benefits you receive will not be subject to federal income taxation, up to a dollar cap. If you purchase a non-qualified policy, you will not be able to itemize the premiums. As to the benefits, the IRS has yet to clarify whether or not they will be subject to federal income taxation. Do not assume that a tax-qualified policy will automatically be more beneficial. Reason: Typically, a tax-qualified policy will have stricter guidelines as to when you can access the policy benefits. You also may not be able to take advantage of the tax benefits. You may want to consult with a tax advisor on this subject.

Step 7: Find insurance agents in your area that specialize in long-term care policies:

Agent Name	Phone Number	Specialization in LTC?	Name of insurance company
_____	_____	(Y / N)	_____
_____	_____	(Y / N)	_____
_____	_____	(Y / N)	_____
_____	_____	(Y / N)	_____

Long-term care insurance is very complex. Therefore, make sure you work with an agent who specializes in long-term care policies, and don't limit your choices to someone you know or who is associated with your broker. The agent should be able to help educate you and clarify any questions you have – not only on policies he or she sells, but on others as well. Try to avoid agents that work strictly with one insurance company. Complete the remaining steps with the direct assistance of the agent you choose.

Step 8: Ask your agent for the names of at least three different policies, from different insurers, that you can compare.

	Policy A	Policy B	Policy C
Insurance Company Name	_____	_____	_____
Policy Name/Number	_____	_____	_____

Step 9: Have your agent check the safety rating for each company.

Safety Rating

Policy A: _____
Policy B: _____
Policy C: _____

It may be a long time before you begin to submit claims. Therefore, you will want to make sure your insurance company will still be viable at that time. If you use the Safety Ratings, we recommend you favor companies with a rating of B+ (good) or higher, and we suggest you avoid companies with a rating of D+ (weak) or lower.

Step 10: Favor companies that have more experience with long-term care insurance.

	Years of experience with long-term care	Have they ever raised rates for existing policyholders?
Policy A:	_____	(Y / N)
Policy B:	_____	(Y / N)
Policy C:	_____	(Y / N)

This should not be a deal breaker. But you're better off with a company that has been offering long-term care policies for a while and has never raised rates for existing policyholders. In contrast, companies that are new in long-term care – or have a history of raising rates on existing policies – are more likely to raise your rates in the future.

Step 11: If you're considering buying a policy with your spouse, check how you qualify for a spousal discount.

Policy A: _____
Policy B: _____
Policy C: _____

In some cases, you may need to be married to qualify; in others you don't have to be formally married. Some insurers require that the policies be exactly the same, while others do not.

Step 12: Ask your agent for quotes on the monthly premiums. Make sure the quotes are based on the preferences and needs that you outlined in steps 1-6.

	Single Policy Premium	Combined Policy Premium	% Savings
Policy A:	_____	_____	_____
Policy B:	_____	_____	_____
Policy C:	_____	_____	_____

If you can buy your long-term care policy with a spouse or significant other, make sure you take advantage of spousal discounts, which can save you up to 20% on the combined premium.

Step 13: Find out exactly what each policy covers in addition to the basics that you require:

	Policy A	Policy B	Policy C
Custodial	(Y / N)	(Y / N)	(Y / N)
Intermediate	(Y / N)	(Y / N)	(Y / N)
Skilled	(Y / N)	(Y / N)	(Y / N)

The actual policies that your agent has suggested may differ somewhat from your wish list of benefits, including some that you did not ask for, or excluding others that you wanted. This may help explain some, but not all, of the price differences.

Step 14: Ask your agent to give you a list of the types of facilities that are included and how they are defined. Facilities may include nursing home care, in-home care, adult day care, hospice care, assisted living facilities, and other options.

Policy A

_____
_____
_____

Policy B

_____
_____

Policy C

_____
_____
_____

Step 15: Find out the basic terms of coverage and reimbursement, as follows:

Policy A: How the company calculates elimination period: _____

Facility of Care	Elimination Periods	Benefit Periods	Daily Benefit
In-home care:	_____	_____	_____
Nursing home	_____	_____	_____
Assisted living:	_____	_____	_____
Adult day care:	_____	_____	_____

Policy B: How the company calculates elimination period: _____

Facility of Care	Elimination Periods	Benefit Periods	Daily Benefit
In-home care:	_____	_____	_____
Nursing home	_____	_____	_____
Assisted living:	_____	_____	_____
Adult day care:	_____	_____	_____

Policy C: How the company calculates elimination period: _____

Facility of Care	Elimination Periods	Benefit Periods	Daily Benefit
In-home care:	_____	_____	_____
Nursing home	_____	_____	_____
Assisted living:	_____	_____	_____
Adult day care:	_____	_____	_____

Elimination Period: This is similar to a deductible. It is the amount of time you pay for services out of your own pocket <u>before</u> the insurance policy takes over. Typically, you can select elimination periods of 0, 30, 60, 90, or 180 days, depending on the policy and insurance company. But you must find out exactly how the elimination period is satisfied. Let's say, for example, you need care on days 1, 4 and 10. With some policies, that would be counted as only THREE days toward your elimination period. With other policies, it would be counted as TEN days, which would mean you'd start collecting the benefits much sooner.

Benefit Period (or maximum): Some companies tell you the length of time the policy will be paid; others just tell you the maximum value of benefits to be paid. The benefit period can typically range from 2 to 5 years, and some may even have an unlimited lifetime period.

Daily Benefit: The amount the policy will pay for each day of covered services. Some plans offer a daily benefit reimbursable on a weekly or monthly basis giving you more flexibility. For example, if you selected a daily benefit of $100 reimbursable on a weekly basis you would be reimbursed for up to $700 dollars per week in expenses no matter how much you incurred on any one day.

Step 16: Determine if the policy is "a pool of money" contract.

Pool of money?
Policy A: (Y / N)
Policy B: (Y / N)
Policy C: (Y / N)

Most current policies will actually give you more time to collect the benefits than indicated by the benefit period. For example, in a four-year policy, if you need care on and off, you may not use up all your benefits in that four-year period. So you could continue to collect those unused benefits in subsequent years as well. These are called "pool of money" contracts. (To calculate your pool, just multiple the total numbers of days by the daily benefit.) Other policies will actually end at the end of the four years, no matter what.

Step 17: Check into the requirements needed to activate the policy.

Policy A: _____

_____

Policy B: _____

_____

Policy C: _____

_____

You will need to meet what is referred to as "benefit triggers" before the policy can begin covering expenses and these can vary from policy to policy. Under most policies, you will be qualified for benefits when you meet certain conditions, such as: 1) The inability to perform activities of daily living ("ADLs"), which typically include bathing, dressing, transferring, toileting, eating, continence, and taking medication on your own; and 2) cognitive impairment. Some plans require you to satisfy either condition (1) or (2); some require that you satisfy both conditions. Still others also allow for a third trigger, often referred to as "medical necessity." This means that a doctor determines if you need care due to an injury or sickness. Make sure you find out the precise requirements of each policy.

Step 18: Find out what other features are included (or can be added by a "rider") to the policy.

Your agent should explain any additional features that may be included in the policies you are comparing including the following:

	Policy A	Policy B	Policy C
Waiver of Premium	(Y / N)	(Y / N)	(Y / N)
Nonforfeiture	(Y / N)	(Y / N)	(Y / N)
Restoration of Benefits	(Y / N)	(Y / N)	(Y / N)
Alternate Care Plan	(Y / N)	(Y / N)	(Y / N)
Bed Reservation	(Y / N)	(Y / N)	(Y / N)
Guaranteed Renewable	(Y / N)	(Y / N)	(Y / N)
Inflation Protection	(Y / N)	(Y / N)	(Y / N)

Your agent will explain the details. Just make sure that you actually need these additional benefits, because they can add substantially to your total costs.

Medicare Prescription Drug Planner

This planner is designed to help you compare the annual premium costs of a senior benefit package that includes prescription drug coverage. In conjunction with the worksheet attached, follow the steps for calculating the costs of prescription drug coverage options. Upon completion, you'll be able to compare the annual cost of each option. In addition to the cost, keep other out-of-pocket expenses, benefit coverage, and provider accessibility in mind, and then select the plan best suited to meet your needs.

STEP ONE: Review the cost of your current health care coverage.

Look up your current coverage and find the premium you pay, if any, for the coverage.

Original Medicare – Part A and Part B coverage

Do you receive benefits directly through the Original Medicare program? .... Y / N

If yes, you may be paying the Part B premium (there is no premium for Part A) yourself or perhaps you have an employer plan or a Medicare Supplement insurance policy that pays the premium.

▶ Record the annual amount, if any, you pay: **Part A and B: $**

Transfer this figure to the available lines under the Part A and B column on the worksheet.

Employer Retirement Plan Coverage

Do you receive benefits through an Employer plan? .... Y / N

If yes, the coverage is most likely comprehensive and includes drug coverage.

▶ Record the annual amount, if any, you pay: **Employer Plan: $ _____**

Transfer this figure to the available lines under the Employer Plan column on the worksheet.

Medicare Supplement Insurance Policy ("Medigap")

Do you own a Medigap Plan? .... Y / N

▶ If so, what do you pay in annual premiums?   **Medigap Plan A thru N: $ _____**

Transfer this figure to the available line under the Medigap Plan column on the worksheet.

Medicare Advantage Plan

Medicare Advantage policies are available through private insurers. You pay the insurer a premium and they provide coverage that is at least as good, if not better, than Medicare Part A and B. In turn, they receive reimbursement from the government. You are often restricted to a network of physicians with these plans.

Do you receive your benefits from a Medicare Advantage insurer? .... Y / N

▶ If so, what do you pay in annual premiums, if any? **Medicare Advantage Plan:** $ _____

Transfer this figure to the Annual Cost column in the Medicare Advantage row on the worksheet. 📝

STEP TWO: Find the cost of your preferred Part D Prescription Drug Provider/Plan.

Part D is the new Prescription Drug component of the Medicare program. Under Part D you can obtain some coverage for your medications through a private provider. These plans will provide, at a minimum, the coverage mandated by the government. Otherwise each plan will vary depending on drugs covered, premiums, co-pays and participating pharmacies.

In this step we guide you through what you need to do in order to select a Part D provider. The average cost for Part D plans range from $38.80 to $42.70 per month. However, the range within each state can be significant. Your goal is to find the lowest cost plan that gives you the best price on the prescriptions you use and has convenient participating pharmacies.

Everything you need to do can be done on the Medicare website, however, you will need a computer and internet access. The site is loaded with information, so we recommend that you first spend a few hours browsing the site to learn more. The site and process of selecting a provider can be overwhelming so you may want to have a family member or someone else to work with you through this process.

First: Gather critical information. Make sure to have the following:

- ✓ Medicare Number .... _____
- ✓ Effective Date of Medicare Part A or B coverage .... _____
- ✓ Birth Date .... _____
- ✓ Zip Code .... _____
- ✓ List of prescription drugs you use and their dosages.

Drug	**Dosage**
_____	_____
_____	_____
_____	_____
_____	_____
_____	_____
_____	_____
_____	_____

- ✓ Preferred pharmacies in your area.

Pharmacy Name

_____

_____

_____

Second: Visit www.Medicare.gov.

We can't list all of the website's steps here but to start out Click [*Compare Medicare Prescription Drug Plans*] and then Click [*Find a Medicare Prescription Drug Plan*]. You will then be asked to enter your personal information. The website will walk you through entering your prescription drugs and dosages so that you can get a list of Part D providers in your state that cover your drugs, the pharmacies and the contact information. You may select three plans to compare side by side at one time.

Third: Narrow down your choices.

Don't overburden yourself trying to compare all 40+ plans available in your state. Narrow your list down to the five or seven plans that cover your prescriptions and contract with local pharmacies. The premium cost of a plan for the minimum coverage will run you between $201.60 to $1,122.00 per year in 2021, depending on where you live.

To narrow down your list further look for plans that reduce your out-of-pocket costs by covering the $445 deductible, the 25% co-payments and/or the $2,420 gap in coverage. After that, the government limits your co-payment to $3.70 for generic drugs and $9.20 all other drugs.

Use the lines below to enter the information to help you compare your choices. Enter the annual Premium charged by the plan and then under Deductible, Co-Pay and Gap enter the dollar amount <u>you would be responsible for</u> under each of the plan choices. Add these across to get an estimate of your total estimated costs under each plan.

Provider/Plan Name:	Premium	Annual Deductible (max $445)	Co-Pay Max (max $921.25)	Cost $2,420 Gap	Total Estimate
_____	_____ +	_____ +	_____ +	_____ =	_____
_____	_____ +	_____ +	_____ +	_____ =	_____
_____	_____ +	_____ +	_____ +	_____ =	_____
_____	_____ +	_____ +	_____ +	_____ =	_____
_____	_____ +	_____ +	_____ +	_____ =	_____

If you still need to narrow down your choices, then look for plans that either reduces your co-payment amount to less than $3.70 for generic drugs and $9.20 all other drugs and/or provide other benefits that you find attractive.

<u>**Final Part D Provider Selection**</u>

Provider / Plan Name   <u>Total Cost Estimate</u>

_____ $ _____

Transfer the total cost estimate of your final selection (above) to the available lines under the Part D column on the worksheet.

STEP THREE: Consider a Medicare Advantage Plan.

If you already have a Medicare Advantage plan that you are happy with, you may want to skip this step.

The Medicare Advantage program allows you to join a private plan that participates in the Medicare program. Medicare Advantage providers receive funds from the government for providing you benefits and often provides coverage beyond what Medicare offers.

Most of these plans provide prescription drug coverage at the same level or better than the requirements set by Medicare, either inclusive in their plan or in combination with a Medicare Part D provider. Either way you will only pay one premium to the Medicare Advantage insurer for all the coverage.

If you already belong to a Medicare Advantage plan they will send you information regarding their coverage for prescription drugs. Otherwise you can find information on the medicare.gov website or from the insurers through the mail, local kiosks or by calling their toll-free numbers. To narrow down your choices based on the prescription drug coverage use the following space to compare the different plans. Don't forget to check Weiss Safety Rating to find out if the insurer is in good financial health.

Provider/Plan Name:	Premium	Annual Deductible (max $445)	Co-Pay Max (max $921.25)	Cost $2,420 Gap	Total Estimate
_____	_____ +	_____ +	_____ +	_____ =	_____
_____	_____ +	_____ +	_____ +	_____ =	_____
_____	_____ +	_____ +	_____ +	_____ =	_____
_____	_____ +	_____ +	_____ +	_____ =	_____
_____	_____ +	_____ +	_____ +	_____ =	_____

Final Medicare Advantage Provider Selection

Provider Plan Name   **Total Cost Estimate**

_____ $ _____

Once you have narrowed down your choices you will then want to consider other benefits that the Medicare Advantage plan offers.

When you have made a selection, transfer this figure to the Annual Cost column in the Medicare Advantage row on the worksheet.

STEP FOUR: Find the cost of your preferred Medicare Supplement Insurance ("Medigap") policy.

If you have a Medigap policy you want to keep, then you may want to skip this step.

Medigap policies are available through private insurers. Prior to 2006 there were 10 standardized plans (referred to as A through J) that an insurer could offer. Starting in 2020 Plans C and F are to be discontinued and a high deductible version of Plan G will be introduced. Medigap policies help to pay the expenses not paid under Medicare Part A and B. You cannot get any prescription drug coverage from these plans as a new policyholder after 2005.

The price of Medigap policies <u>can</u> differ dramatically even within the same city. You can learn more about the various Medigap plans available and the premium rates you would be charged based on your age, gender, and zip code by going to our website at http://www.weissmedigap.com. Once you have educated yourself and are leaning towards the purchase of a supplemental policy, you will need to meet with an insurance agent to further refine your selection and purchase a policy.

Make sure to check the financial stability of any insurer by using Weiss Safety Rating.

Once you have selected a Medicare Supplement policy enter the annual cost under the Medigap Plan column on the worksheet. If you need an estimate to enter into the worksheet until an amount can be determined, use $2000 as a placeholder for the annual price.

STEP FIVE: Complete the worksheet.

If you haven't done so already, use the figures from Steps 1 through 4 to fill in the dollar amounts in the relevant parts of the worksheet to determine your total annual cost for every option you want to consider. Re-use the worksheet if you need to make adjustments.

STEP SIX: Narrow down your choices.

The worksheet helps you to narrow down your choices by providing a snapshot, based on cost, of the prescription drug benefit options available to you. Of course, premiums are only one of the components needed to make a final decision. You must also consider other out-of-pocket costs, completeness of coverage, accessibility, and insurer financial strength.

STEP SEVEN: More Information.

Educate yourself. The www.Medicare.gov website, Medicare & You 2021 Handbook, local workshops, and Medicare benefit agents on hand at 1-800-MEDICARE are available to assist in answering your questions. Take advantage of these resources to make sure you fully understand your options.

RECENT INDUSTRY FAILURES
2021

Institution	Headquarters	Industry	Date of Failure	At Date of Failure	
				Total Assets ($Mil)	Safety Rating
Bedivere Insurance Co.	Connecticut	P&C	3/11/2021	309.5	E- (Very Weak)
American Capital Assr Corp.	Florida	P&C	4/14/2021	119.0	C+ (Fair)

2020

Institution	Headquarters	Industry	Date of Failure	At Date of Failure	
				Total Assets ($Mil)	Safety Rating
Senior Health Ins Co of PA	Indiana	L&A	1/29/2020	1,097.00	E- (Very Weak)
Maidstone Ins. Co	New York	P&C	2/13/2020	36.31	E- (Very Weak)
Windhaven National Ins. Co	Florida	P&C	3/05/2020	119.96	C (Fair)
Time Ins. Co	Puerto Rico	L&A	5/18/2020	18.36	C (Fair)
Houston General Ins. Exch	Texas	P&C	8/11/2020	15.12	C- (Fair)
Quality Health Plans of NY Inc.	Florida	Health	9/09/2020	4.82	E- (Very Weak)
ACCC Insurance Co.	Texas	P&C	10/21/2020	191.5	D+ (Weak)

2019

Company Name	Headquarters	Industry	Date of Failure	At Date of Failure	
				Total Assets ($Mil)	Safety Rating
Capson Physicians Ins Co	Texas	P&C	02/11/19	25.3	D (Weak)
Atlantis Health Plan	Florida	Health	02/27/19	3.0	U (Unrated)
Scottish Re US Inc	North Carolina	L&A	03/06/19	1,560.0	E+ (Very Weak)
Integrand ASR Co	Puerto Rico	P&C	03/07/19	94.2	D+ (Weak)
Family Health Network Inc	Illinois	Health	03/08/19	69.4	U (Unrated)
Southland National Ins. Corp	North Carolina	L&A	06/27/19	354.0	D+ (Weak)
Bankers Life Ins. Co	North Carolina	L&A	06/27/19	397.4	C- (Fair)
Colorado Bankers Life Ins. Co	North Carolina	L&A	06/27/19	2,068.0	C (Fair)
Pavonia Life Ins. Co of Michigan	New Jersey	L&A	07/09/19	1080.0	C (Fair)
Physicians Standard Ins. Co	Missouri	P&C	08/19/19	7.8	E+ (Very Weak)
Florida Specialty Ins Co	Florida	P&C	10/01/19	55.4	D- (Weak)
California Ins. Co	Nebraska	P&C	11/04/19	1150.0	B (Good)
Windhaven Ins. Co	Florida	P&C	12/12/19	148.8	D- (Weak)

2018

Company Name	Headquarters	Industry	Date of Failure	Total Assets ($Mil)	Safety Rating
				At Date of Failure	
Healthcare Providers Ins. Exch	Pennsylvania	P&C	01/12/18	32.6	E- (Very Weak)
Access Ins. Co	Texas	P&C	03/13/18	314.1	C (Fair)
Touchstone Health HMO Inc.	New York	Health	04/19/18	12.5	E+ (Very Weak)
Reliamax Surety Co	South Dakota	P&C	06/27/18	63.0	C (Fair)
Paramount Ins. Co	Maryland	P&C	09/13/18	13.2	D- (Weak)
Real Legacy Asr Co Inc	Puerto Rico	P&C	09/28/18	230.4	D+ (Weak)
Geneva Ins. Co	Indiana	P&C	10/02/18	3.7	U (Unrated)
Merced Property & Casualty Co	California	P&C	12/03/18	23.6	C (Fair)
North Carolina Mutual Life Ins. Co	North Carolina	L&A	12/03/18	26.7	E- (Very Weak)

2017

Company Name	Headquarters	Industry	Date of Failure	At Date of Failure	
				Total Assets ($Mil)	Safety Rating
IFA Insurance Co	New Jersey	P&C	03/07/17	8.4	E (Very Weak)
Public Service Ins Co	New York	P&C	03/16/17	278.5	E (Very Weak)
Zoom Health Plan Inc	Oregon	Health	04/26/17	6.	U (Unrated)
Galen Insurance Co	Missouri	P&C	05/31/17	103.0	E- (Very Weak)
Fiduciary Ins. Co of America	New York	P&C	07/25/17	90.7	E- (Very Weak)
Evergreen Health Inc.	Maryland	Health	07/27/17	37.2	E- (Very Weak)
Minuteman Health Inc	Massachusetts	Health	08/02/17	111.7	E- (Very Weak)
Sawgrass Mutual Ins. Co	Florida	P&C	08/22/17	32.3	D+ (Weak)
Guarantee Ins. Co	Florida	P&C	08/28/17	400.4	E+ (Very Weak)
Oceanus Ins. Co A RRG	South Carolina	P&C	09/04/17	52.9	D- (Weak)

2016

Company Name	Headquarters	Industry	Date of Failure	At Date of Failure	
				Total Assets ($Mil)	Safety Rating
Consumers Choice Health Ins Co	South Carolina	Health	01/06/16	92.4	D (Weak)
Moda Health Plan Inc	Oregon	Health	01/28/16	445.5	D+ (Weak)
Family Health Hawaii MBS	Hawaii	Health	04/07/16	5.5	D (Weak)
Health Republic Ins of NY Corp	New York	Health	04/22/16	525.3	D (Weak)
Coordinated Health Mutual Inc	Ohio	Health	5/26/16	94.9	E (Very Weak)
HealthyCT Inc	Connecticut	Health	07/01/16	112.3	D+ (Weak)
Oregons Health Co-Op	Oregon	Health	07/11/16	46.6	D (Weak)
Land of Lincoln Mut Health Ins Co	Illinois	Health	07/14/16	107.8	D+ (Weak)
Excalibur Reins Corp	Pennsylvania	P&C	07/18/16	9.0	U (Unrated)
Castlepoint Florida Ins	Florida	P&C	07/28/16	100.00	D (Weak)
Castlepoint Insurance Co	New York	P&C	07/28/16	178.4	E (Very Weak)
Castlepoint National Ins Co	California	P&C	07/28/16	355.1	C- (Fair)
Hermitage Insurance Co	New York	P&C	07/28/16	167.6	E+ (Very Weak)
Massachusetts Homeland Ins Co	Massachusetts	P&C	07/28/16	8.9	C (Fair)
North East Insurance Co	Maine	P&C	07/28/16	35.9	D (Weak)
York Ins Co of Maine	Maine	P&C	07/28/16	47.0	C (Fair)
Careconcepts Ins Inc A RRG	Montana	P&C	08/08/16	3.8	E+ (Very Weak)
Freelancers Consumer Operated	New Jersey	Health	09/12/16	135.3	D+ (Weak)
Doctors & Surgeons Natl RRG IC	Kentucky	P&C	10/07/16	9.1	E+ (Very Weak)
American Medical & Life Ins Co	New York	L&A	12/28/16	4.4	U (Unrated)

State Insurance Commissioners'
Website and Departmental Phone Numbers

State	Official's Title	Website Address	Phone Number
Alabama	Commissioner	www.aldoi.org	(334) 269-3550
Alaska	Director	www.dced.state.ak.us/insurance/	(907) 465-2515
Arizona	Director	www.id.state.az.us	(800) 325-2548
Arkansas	Commissioner	www.insurance.arkansas.gov	(800) 282-9134
California	Commissioner	www.insurance.ca.gov	(800) 927-4357
Colorado	Commissioner	www.dora.state.co.us/insurance/	(800) 930-3745
Connecticut	Commissioner	www.ct.gov/cid/	(860) 297-3800
Delaware	Commissioner	www.state.de.us/inscom/	(302) 674-7300
Dist. of Columbia	Commissioner	disr.dc.gov/disr/	(202) 727-8000
Florida	Commissioner	www.fldfs.com	(800) 342-2762
Georgia	Commissioner	www.gainsurance.org	(800) 656-2298
Hawaii	Commissioner	www.hawaii.gov/dcca/areas/ins/	(808) 586-2790
Idaho	Director	www.doi.idaho.gov	(800) 721-3272
Illinois	Director	www.idfpr.com/doi/	(217) 782-4515
Indiana	Commissioner	www.ia.org/idoi/	(317) 232-2385
Iowa	Commissioner	www.iid.state.ia.us	(877) 955-1212
Kansas	Commissioner	www.ksinsurance.org	(800) 432-2484
Kentucky	Executive Director	www.doi.ppr.ky.gov/kentucky/	(800) 595-6053
Louisiana	Commissioner	www.ldi.state.la.us	(800) 259-5300
Maine	Superintendent	www.maine.gov/pfr/insurance/	(800) 300-5000
Maryland	Commissioner	www.mdinsurance.state.md.us	(800) 492-6116
Massachusetts	Commissioner	www.mass.gov/doi/	(617) 521-7794
Michigan	Commissioner	www.michigan.gov/cis/	(877) 999-6442
Minnesota	Commissioner	www.commerce.state.mn.us	(651) 296-4026
Mississippi	Commissioner	www.doi.state.ms.us	(800) 562-2957
Missouri	Director	www.insurance.mo.gov/	(800) 726-7390
Montana	Commissioner	www.sao.state.mt.us	(800) 332-6148
Nebraska	Director	www.nebraska.gov	(402) 471-2306
Nevada	Commissioner	doi.state.nv.us	(775) 687-4270
New Hampshire	Commissioner	www.nh.gov/insurance/	(800) 852-3416
New Jersey	Commissioner	www.state.nj.us/dobi/	(800) 446-7467
New Mexico	Superintendent	www.nmprc.state.nm.us/id.htm	(888) 427-5772
New York	Superintendent	www.ins.state.ny.us	(800) 342-3736
North Carolina	Commissioner	www.ncdoi.com	(800) 546-5664
North Dakota	Commissioner	www.nd.gov/ndins/	(800) 247-0560
Ohio	Director	www.ohioinsurance.gov	(800) 686-1526
Oklahoma	Commissioner	www.oid.state.ok.us	(800) 522-0071
Oregon	Insurance Administrator	www.cbs.state.or.us/ins/	(503) 947-7980
Pennsylvania	Commissioner	www.ins.state.pa.us/ins/	(877) 881-6388
Puerto Rico	Commissioner	www.ocs.gobierno.pr	(787) 722-8686
Rhode Island	Superintendent	www.dbr.state.ri.us	(401) 222-2223
South Carolina	Director	www.doi..sc.gov	(800) 768-3467
South Dakota	Director	www.state.sd.us/drr2/reg/insurance/	(605) 773-3563
Tennessee	Commissioner	www.state.tn.us/commerce/insurance/	(800) 342-4029
Texas	Commissioner	www.tdi.state.tx.us	(800) 252-3439
Utah	Commissioner	www.insurance.utah.gov	(800) 439-3805
Vermont	Commissioner	www.bishca.state.vt.us	(802) 828-3301
Virgin Islands	Lieutenant Governor	www.ltg.gov.vi	(340) 774-7166
Virginia	Commissioner	www.scc.virginia.gov/division/boi/	(877) 310-6560
Washington	Commissioner	www.insurance.wa.gov	(800) 562-6900
West Virginia	Commissioner	www.wvinsurance.gov	(304) 558-3386
Wisconsin	Commissioner	oci.wi.gov	(800) 236-8517
Wyoming	Commissioner	insurance.state.wy.us	(800) 438-5768

Glossary

This glossary contains the most important terms used in this publication.

Admitted Assets
The total of all investments and business interests that are acceptable under statutory accounting rules.

Asset/Liability Matching
The designation of particular investments (assets) to particular policy obligations (liabilities) so that investments mature at the appropriate times and with appropriate yields to meet policy obligations as they come due.

Asset Valuation Reserve (AVR)
A liability established under statutory accounting rules whose purpose is to protect the company's surplus from the effects of defaults and market value fluctuation on stocks, bonds, mortgages, and real estate. This replaces the Mandatory Securities Valuation Reserve (MSVR) and is more comprehensive in that it includes a mortgage loss reserve, whereas the MSVR did not.

Average Recession
A recession involving a decline in real GDP which is approximately equivalent to the average of the postwar recessions of 1957-58, 1960, 1970, 1974-75, 1980, 1981-82, 1990-1991, 2001, and 2007-2009. It is assumed, however, that in today's market, the financial losses suffered from a recession of that magnitude would be greater than those experienced in previous decades. (See also "Severe Recession.").

Capital
Strictly speaking, capital refers to funds raised through the sale of common and preferred stock. Mutual companies have capital in the form of retained earnings. In a more general sense, the term capital is commonly used to refer to a company's equity or net worth, that is, the difference between assets and liabilities (i.e., capital and surplus as shown on the balance sheet).

Capital Resources
The sum of various resources which serve as a capital cushion to losses, including capital, surplus, and Asset Valuation Reserve (AVR).

Capitalization Index
An index, expressed on a scale of zero to ten, with seven or higher considered excellent, that measures the adequacy of the company's capital resources to deal with a variety of business and economic scenarios. It combines Risk-Adjusted Capital Ratios #1 and #2 as well as a leverage test that examines pricing risk.

Cash and Demand Deposits	Includes cash on hand and on deposit. A negative figure indicates that the company has more checks outstanding than current funds to cover those checks. This is not an unusual situation for an insurance company.
Collateralized Mortgage Obligation (CMO)	Mortgage-backed bond that splits the payments from mortgage pools into different classes, called tranches. The investor may purchase a bond or tranche that passes through to him or her the principal and interest payments made by the mortgage holders in that specific maturity class (usually two, five, 10, or 20 years). The risk associated with a CMO is in the variation of the payment speed on the mortgage pool which, if different than originally assumed, can cause the total return to vary greatly.
Common and Preferred Stocks	See "Stocks".
Deposit Funds	Accumulated contributions of a group out of which immediate annuities are purchased as the individual members of the group retire.
Direct Premiums Written	Total gross premiums derived from policies issued directly by the company. This figure excludes the impact of reinsurance.
Safety Rating	Weiss Safety Ratings grade insurers on a scale from A (Excellent) to F (Failed). Ratings are based on five major factors: investment safety, policy leverage, capitalization, profitability, and stability of operations.
Five-Year Profitability Index	See "Profitability Index."
Government Securities	Securities issued and/or guaranteed by U.S. and foreign governments which are rated as highest quality (Class 1) by state insurance commissioners. Included in this category are bonds issued by governmental agencies and guaranteed with the full faith and credit of the government. Regardless of the issuing entity, they are viewed as being relatively safer than the other investment categories. See "Investment Grade Bonds" to determine which items are excluded from this category.
Health Claims Reserve	Funds set aside from premiums for the eventual payment of health benefits after the end of the statement year.
Insurance Risk	The risk that the level of claims and related expenses will exceed current premiums plus reserves allocated for their payment.
Interest Rate Risk	The risk that, due to changes in interest rates, investment income will not meet the needs of policy commitments. This risk can be reduced by effective asset/liability matching.

Invested Assets	The total size of the firm's investment portfolio.
Investment Grade Bonds	This covers all investment grade bonds other than those listed in "Government Securities" (above). Specifically, this includes: (1) nonguaranteed obligations of governments, (2) obligations of governments rated as Class 2 by state insurance commissioners, (3) state and municipal bonds, plus (4) investment grade corporate bonds.
Investment Safety Index	Measured on a scale of zero to ten, with ten being the best and seven or better considered strong. Each investment area is rated as to quality and vulnerability during an unfavorable economic environment (updated using quarterly data when available).
Investments in Affiliates	Includes bonds, preferred stocks, and common stocks, as well as other vehicles which many insurance companies use to invest in, and establish a corporate link with affiliated companies.
Life and Annuity Claims Reserve	Funds set aside from premiums for the eventual payment of life and annuity claims.
Liquidity Index	An index, expressed on a scale from zero to ten, with seven or higher considered excellent, which measures the company's ability to raise the necessary cash to meet policyholder obligations. This index includes a stress test which considers the consequences of a spike in claims or a run on policy surrenders. Sometimes a company may appear to have the necessary resources, but may be unable to sell its investments at the prices at which they are valued in the company's financial statements.
Mandatory Security Valuation Reserve (MSVR)	Reserve for investment losses and asset value fluctuation mandated by the state insurance commissioners for companies registered as life and health insurers. As of December 31, 1992, this was replaced by the Asset Valuation Reserve. HMDI companies are not required to establish such a reserve.
Moderate Loss Scenario	An economic decline from current levels approximately equivalent to that of the average postwar recession.
Mortgages in Good Standing	Mortgages which are current in their payments (excludes mortgage-backed securities).
Net Premiums Written	The total dollar volume of premiums retained by the company. This figure is equal to direct premiums written, plus reinsurance assumed less reinsurance ceded.
Noninvestment Grade Bonds	Low-rated issues, commonly known as "junk bonds," which carry a high risk as defined by the state insurance commissioners. These include bond Classes 3 - 6.
Nonperforming Mortgages	Mortgages which are (a) 90 days or more past due or (b) in process of foreclosure.
Other Investments	Items not included in any of the other categories such as contract loans (which include premium notes), receivables for securities, aggregate write-ins and other invested assets.

Other Structured Securities	Nonresidential-mortgage-related and other securitized loan-backed or asset-backed securities. This category also includes CMOs with noninvestment grade ratings.
Policy Leverage	A measure of insurance risk based on the relationship of net premiums to capital resources.
Policy Loans	Loans to policyholders under insurance contracts.
Profitability Index	Measured on a scale of zero to ten, with ten being the best and seven or better considered strong. A composite of five factors: (1) gain or loss on operations, (2) consistency of operating results, (3) impact of operating results on surplus, (4) adequacy of investment income as compared to the needs of policy reserves, and (5) expenses in relation to industry averages. Thus, the overall index is an indicator of the health of a company's current and past operations.
Purchase Money Mortgages	Mortgages written by an insurance company to facilitate the sale of property owned by the company.
Real Estate	Direct real estate investments including property (a) occupied by the company, (b) acquired through foreclosure and (c) purchased as an investment.
Reinsurance Assumed	Insurance risk acquired by taking on partial or full responsibility for claims on policies written by other companies. (See "Reinsurance Ceded.")
Reinsurance Ceded	Insurance risk sold to another company.
Risk-Adjusted Capital	The capital resources that would be needed in a worsening economic environment (same as "Target Capital").
Risk-Adjusted Capital Ratio #1	The capital resources which a company currently has, in relation to the resources that would be needed to deal with a moderate loss scenario. This scenario is based on historical experience during an average recession and adjusted to reflect current conditions and vulnerabilities (updated using quarterly data when available).
Risk-Adjusted Capital Ratio #2	The capital resources which a company currently has, in relation to the resources that would be needed to deal with a severe loss scenario. This scenario is based on historical experience of the postwar period and adjusted to reflect current conditions and the potential impact of a severe recession (updated using quarterly data when available).
Separate Accounts	Funds segregated from the general account and valued at market. Used to fund indexed products, such as variable life and variable annuity products.
Severe Loss Scenario	An economic decline from current levels in which the loss experience of the single worst year of the postwar period is extended for a period of three years. (See also "Moderate Loss Scenario" above.)
Severe Recession	A prolonged economic slowdown in which the single worst year of the postwar period is extended for a period of three years. (See also "Average Recession" above.)

Stability Index

Measured on a scale of zero to ten. This integrates a wide variety of factors that reflects the company's financial stability and diversification of risk.

State of Domicile

Although most insurance companies are licensed to do business in many states, they have only one state of domicile. This is the state that has primary regulatory responsibility for the company. Use the state of domicile to make absolutely sure that you have the correct company. Bear in mind, however, that this need not be the state where the company's main offices are located.

State Guaranty Funds

Funds that are designed to raise cash from existing insurance carriers to cover policy claims of bankrupt insurance companies.

Stocks

Common and preferred equities, including ownership in affiliates.

Surplus

The difference between assets and liabilities, including paid-in contributed surplus, plus the statutory equivalent of "retained earnings" in noninsurance business corporations.

Target Capital

See "Risk-Adjusted Capital."

Total Assets

Total admitted assets, including investments and other business assets. See "Admitted Assets."